Interim Measures in International Commercial Arbitration

Interim Measures in International Commercial Arbitration

A Comparative Review of the Indian Experience

Ajar Rab

Wolters Kluwer

Published by:
Kluwer Law International B.V.
PO Box 316
2400 AH Alphen aan den Rijn
The Netherlands
E-mail: lrs-sales@wolterskluwer.com
Website: www.wolterskluwer.com/en/solutions/kluwerlawinternational

Sold and distributed by:
Wolters Kluwer Legal & Regulatory U.S.
7201 McKinney Circle
Frederick, MD 21704
United States of America
E-mail: customer.service@wolterskluwer.com

ISBN 978-94-035-3735-1

e-Book: ISBN 978-94-035-3755-9
web-PDF: ISBN 978-94-035-3780-1

Dedicated to the arbitrator, teacher, father, and human being I admire most – Prof. Dr Stefan M. Kröll

About the Author

Prof. (Dr) Ajar Rab is a Partner at Rab & Rab Associates LLP, Dehradun, and an arbitrator. With over eleven years of experience, his practice areas include international arbitration, corporate transactions, and commercial litigation. He handles several arbitrations and commercial litigations relating to energy disputes, EPC contracts, and infrastructure disputes, among many others. He has previously worked with ministries, government bodies, and policy institutes. He is also an International Policy Consultant at Lexidale, a policy firm with offices in the US, Israel and the Netherlands.

Dr Rab is a 'Professor of Practice' at the School of Law, University of Petroleum & Energy Studies, Dehradun, an Adjunct Professor at the National University of Juridical Sciences (NUJS), Kolkata, Visiting Professor at the National Law School of India University (NLSIU), Bangalore, and visiting faculty in other law schools of the country. He frequently trains executives and legal teams of multinational corporations, and civil servants, and teaches courses on Negotiation and Drafting of Commercial Documents, Litigation Strategy, and International Commercial Arbitration at various law universities in India. He is a member of several arbitration institutes across the world and on the advisory board of several academic journals.

He has authored books on 'Real Estate (Regulation and Development) Act, 2016' and on Drafting of Contracts. He has published several academic papers in leading national and international journals. His paper 'Defining the Contours of the Public Policy Exception – A New Test for Arbitrability in India' was recently cited by a Full Bench of the Supreme Court of India in *Vidya Drolia and Others v. Durga Trading Corporation 2020 SCC OnLine SC 108.*

Table of Contents

List of Abbreviations

AAA	American Arbitration Association
AIAC	Asian International Arbitration Center
AIHC	All India High Court Cases
AIR	All India Reporter
All ER (Comm)	All England Reports (Commercial Cases)
ALL ER Rep	All England Law Reports, Reprint
ALR	American Law Reports
AP	Andhra Pradesh
APLJ	Andhra Pradesh Law Journal
Arb LR	Arbitration Law Reporter
Arb.	Arbitration
Bom	Bombay & Mumbai.
Bom CR	Bombay Case Reporter
Bom LR	Bombay Law Reporter
Bus LR	Business Law Report
Cal	Calcutta & Kolkata
CCJ	Caribbean Court of Justice
CDDRL	Center on Democracy, Development, and Rule of Law
CEAC	Chinese European Arbitration Center
Ch. D	Chancery Division
CIArb	Chartered Institute of Arbitrators
Cir	Circuit Court (US)
CLT	Cuttack Law Times
Comp Cas	Company Case

Corp.	Corporation
Corpn	Corporation
Costs LR	Costs Law Reports
CPC	Code of Civil Procedure, 1908
CWN	Calcutta Weekly Notes
D.V.I.	District of the Virgin Islands
DB	Division Bench
Del	Delhi
DIAC	New Delhi International Arbitration Centre
DIS	German Arbitration Institute
DLR	Dominion Law Reports
DLT	Delhi Law Times
DRJ	Delhi Reported Journal
E.D. Mo.	Eastern District of Missouri
EGLR	Estates Gazette Law Reports (UK)
EU	European Union
EWCA	England and Wales Court of Appeals
EWHC	High Court of England and Wales
F./F.2d/F.3d	Federal Reporter
F. Supp/F. Supp. 2d	Federal Supplement
GAIL	Gas Authority of India Limited
GAU	Guwahati
Guj	Gujarat
GWB	Gerechtelijk Wetboek (Belgian Judicial Code Provisions)
HC	High Court
HKC	Hong Kong Cases
HKDC	Hong Kong District Court
HKIAC	Hong Kong International Arbitration Centre
HKLRD	Hong Kong Law Reports and Digest
HP	Himachal Pradesh
IAA	Arbitration and Conciliation Act, 1996
IBA	International Bar Association
ICA	Indian Contract Act, 1872
ICADR	The International Centre For Alternative Dispute Resolution
ICC	International Chamber of Commerce
ICC Rules	International Chamber of Commerce Rules

ICCA	International Council for Commercial Arbitration
ICDR	International Centre for Dispute Resolution
ICJ	International Court of Justice
ICSID	International Centre for Settlement of Investment Disputes
ILR	Indian Law Reports
In re	In reference
Ind Cas	Indian Cases
Iran-US C.T.R	Iran US Claims Tribunal Report
J&K	Jammu & Kashmir
Kar	Karnataka
KB	Kings Bench
Ker	Kerala
Lah	Lahore
LCIA	London Court of International Arbitration
Lloyd's Rep	Lloyd's Law Reports
Mad	Madras
Mah LJ	Maharashtra Law Journal
Manu	Manupatra
MCIA	Mumbai Centre for International Arbitration
Mealey's IAR	Mealey's International Arbitration Report
MP	Madhya Pradesh
MPLJ	Madhya Pradesh Law Journal
N.D. Cal.	United States District Court. Northern District of California.
N.E./N.E. 2d	North Eastern Reporter
N.Y./N.Y.2d	New York Reports
N.Y. App. Div.	New York's Appellate Division
N.Y.S.	West's New York Supplement
N.Y.S.2d	West's New York Supplement 2d series
Nag	Nagpur
NHAI	National Highway Authority of India
NLU Delhi	National Law University - Delhi
NPAC	Nani Palkhivala Arbitration Centre
NUJS Law Review	National University of Juridical Sciences Law Review
NYC	New York Convention on the Recognition and Enforcement of Foreign Arbitral Awards 1958
NZLR	New Zealand Law Reports

P&H	Punjab & Haryana
Pat	Patna
PC	Privy Council
PCA	Permanent Court of Arbitration
PCIJ	Permanent Court of International Justice
PRNZ	Procedure Reports of New Zealand
PTC	Patent and Trademark Cases
Qd R	Queensland Reports
RAC	Russian Arbitration Center
Raj	Rajasthan
SASC	South Australian Supreme Court
SC	Supreme Court
SCALE	Supreme Court Almanac
SCC	Supreme Court Cases
SCR	Supreme Court Reporter
SGCA	Singapore Court of Appeal
SGHC	Singapore High Courts
SIAC	Singapore International Arbitration Center
SLR	Singapore Law Report
SLT	Scots Law Times
Suth. W.R.	Sutherland's Weekly Reports
UKHL	United Kingdom House of Lords
UN Doc	United Nation Document
UNCITRAL	United Nations Commission for International Trade Law
VIAC	Vienna International Arbitral Centre
WB	West Bengal
WG	Working Group
WLR	Weekly Law Reports
Y.B.	Year Book
ZPO	Zivilprozessordnung – German Code of Civil Procedure

Foreword

The availability of interim relief is a central element for any form of efficient dispute resolution. It is thus of considerable importance for the success of arbitration in any given jurisdiction. The effective protection of rights often requires immediate action and it is not possible to wait until all arguments have been exchanged in full and a final decision is rendered. Evidence may have to be secured, the status quo may have to be preserved or measures may be necessary to avoid the occurrence of further damages or even irreparable harm. Additionally, it may be necessary to prevent the dissipation of assets making the enforcement of the final decision impossible or to provide securities to ensure the fulfilment of cost awards.

Whenever the parties have submitted the resolution of the main dispute to arbitration, it seems natural that they have also empowered the arbitral tribunal to make the necessary orders for protecting the process and the parties until the final decision is rendered or even thereafter. However, some of the specific characteristics of interim measures, such as their urgency, the need for ex parte proceedings to ensure efficiency or particularities in their enforcement raise issues in relation to arbitration. The arbitral tribunal may not yet be constituted when measures have to be taken, it may lack the required powers – in particular if the measures concern or affect third parties or if efficient enforcement of the measures granted is not guaranteed. In these and other cases, parties may have to turn to the state courts to get effective and efficient interim relief.

The existence of two potential fora for interim relief, state courts, on the one hand, and the arbitral tribunal, on the other hand, raises questions as to their relationship and coordination. Both have their advantages and disadvantages and each jurisdiction has to decide how to balance the often competing interests of the parties and the institutions involved. Solutions adopted do not only reflect the attitude to arbitration in the particular jurisdiction in general but may also be influenced by the efficiency of the state court system.

Dr Rab's book 'Interim Measures in International Commercial Arbitration: A Comparative Review of the Indian Experience', based on his PhD Thesis which I had the pleasure to supervise, provides a comprehensive discussion of the present status of the law on interim relief in arbitration in India with valuable suggestions to possible legal action to remedy the problems encountered.

The Indian legislator, after largely basing its new arbitration law, the Arbitration and Conciliation Act, 1996 (IAA) on the UNCITRAL Model Law, decided in 2015 not to adopt the new UNCITRAL regime for interim relief. Instead, the new provisions on interim relief included in the IAA in Article 17 were based on the English Arbitration Act 1996. This mixture, as well as the particular problems of the Indian judicial system coupled with the amount of jurisprudence, makes the topic selected highly practical and of relevance even beyond the large Indian arbitration market. That is well reflected by the impressive comparative research done by the author contained in the various annexes.

As the title indicates, the book addresses primarily the legal situation in India. The suggestion made by Dr Rab to remedy defects existing in the Indian context makes the book interesting for readers from other jurisdictions who face the same challenges or have a general comparative interest.

Dr Rab's book thus provides an important contribution to the harmonisation and development of the law of arbitration.

Prof. (Dr) Stefan Kröll

Note

This book is a slightly amended and updated version of the thesis submitted by the author in pursuance of the degree of Doctor of Law in February 2021. The thesis was supervised by Prof. Dr Stefan M. Kröll and Prof. Clifford Larsen.

The thesis was accepted after the oral presentation at the Bucerius Law School – Hochschule für Rechtswissenschaft, Hamburg, Germany on 1 December 2021 by the Doctoral Examinations Committee comprising Prof. Dr h.c. mult. Katharina Boele-Woelki, Prof. Dr Stefan M. Kröll, and the Chairperson, Prof. Dr Michael Fehling.

Acknowledgements

This book is the result of many people who chose to believe in me, time and time again. In absolute honesty, I had never imagined that I would apply for a doctorate, let alone finally submit and publish one. Four people are primarily responsible for it. Mr Michael Friedman, who took time out from his busy schedule and humoured me over lunch as I narrated my hopes of practising law and my love for teaching. Ms Magdalena Kaljaj, who would repeatedly assure me that I am capable of pursuing and finishing my doctoral thesis, and most importantly, my second supervisor, Prof. Clifford Larsen. I stand indebted to him for igniting an interest in the field of arbitration, for always lending an ear to my problems and concerns, and for whole-heartedly supporting me when I told him about my inclination to pursue my doctorate. Lastly, Mr Sulabh Rewari, who helped me decide the topic for the thesis and has guided me whenever I have been stuck with concepts.

I will never be able to find the right words to thank my supervisor, Prof. Stefan M. Kröll. Every single day, for two years, after my Master's, I thought of applying to him for being my supervisor. I could never gather the guts. I had little experience in arbitration and a thesis on Indian law would never be of interest to him. After several pushes from Ms Kaljaj, I finally sent him a mail. To this day, I find it hard to believe he agreed and had faith that I could finish my thesis despite having kids and active court practice. The way he has supported, motivated and inspired is hard to describe. One can learn so much from him in a very short conversation. Despite being packed with commitments, he has always been available and always ensured I kept the right focus. To put my gratitude as briefly as I can, if it weren't for Prof. Kröll, I would have been a very different person and a very different lawyer.

The years I have spent putting this together have come at the cost of the time I would have spent with my children and my beloved wife, Naisan. Her unflinching support, tolerance of my mood swings, bearing with my complaints of being exhausted and taking care of the kids is how I have come this far, in life and in this book. I am ever so grateful to my parents, my brother and sister-in-law, and my mother-in-law for having my back, at home, in court and in the office, as I spent days and nights locked in my chamber.

I stand forever indebted to my associates Mr Shubham Joshi, Mr Ankit Singh and Ms Akansha Rathi. If it weren't for their unconditional availability to help me research, handle my court commitments, entertain and discuss hundreds of thoughts that crossed my mind, I probably would have never finished writing my thesis and publishing this book. My sincere thanks to Ms Kirpen Dhaliwal, Mr Parmeet Singh and Mr Rishi Raj Mukherjee for the invaluable research assistance. I also want to thank Prof. V.S. Elizabeth, who has always guided me to be a better human being and resolved so many dilemmas, both personal and professional, including those associated with pursuing a doctorate and publishing this book.

My heartfelt gratitude to Ms Kiran Nasir Gore for believing in me and this book and to Ms Eleanor Taylor for guiding and spearheading the entire process. Last but not least, to the editorial team at Kluwer Law International who has painstakingly reviewed and refined this book.

To everyone, who has been a part of this journey, and had faith in me - *Thank You!*

Introduction

International trade and commerce have benefitted immensely from the transnational dispute mechanism offered by international commercial arbitration. The flexibility to tailor the dispute resolution mechanism keeping in mind commercial realities remains one of the most attractive features of international arbitration. Parties get to pick the arbitrators of their choice, choose the procedure without reliance on the cumbersome domestic law rules, and benefit from the universal recognition and enforcement of awards under the New York Convention (NYC).

The success of arbitration, like any adjudicatory mechanism, depends on its potential to offer holistic redress to the parties. The mechanism needs to comply with the most fundamental notion of fairness and justice. It needs to safeguard fair and equitable treatment of the parties along with ensuring quick and efficient dispute resolution. The mechanism needs to provide ready enforcement of orders failing which parties may lose faith in the process.

A critical element of such a holistic redressal mechanism is the power to grant interim measures during the pendency of the dispute. When the UNCITRAL Model Law on International Commercial Arbitration (Model Law) was introduced in 1985, the drafters did not address the issue of interim measures in international commercial arbitration in detail. Instead, they only chose to confirm two powers concerning interim measures, i.e., (a) that parties may approach the court for interim measures despite agreeing to have their dispute resolved through arbitration (Article 9 of the Model Law); and (b) the power of the arbitral tribunal to grant interim measures in relation to the subject matter of the arbitration (Article 17 of the Model Law).

The reluctance to provide a detailed regime for interim measures stemmed from the concerns of acceptability by nations on the perceived threat of interference with national laws and sovereignty. Thus, there were various lacunae with respect to the power of the courts and arbitral tribunal to grant interim measures in arbitration. There was also a considerable lack of clarity on the issue of interim measures in support of foreign seated arbitrations, the definition of interim measures, and what kind of measures could be issued by courts in support of arbitrations, domestic or otherwise. There was ambiguity on the apparent inconsistency between moving away from court to arbitration and coming back to the courts for enforcement of interim measures.[1] This lack of clarity was compounded as neither the Geneva Convention on the Execution of Foreign Arbitral Awards of 1927 nor the NYC deal with interim measures of protection.

It is in this context that the jurisprudence with respect to interim measures became murky. Domestic procedural laws and rules started being applied[2] to an adjudicatory process which envisaged a departure from court procedures. Such application of domestic procedural law heavily underscored the genesis of arbitration and the objective of the parties to avoid cumbersome court procedural and evidence rules. Such domestic laws were also, at times, obsolete, unclear, or simply unhelpful in the context of international arbitration.[3]

Parties choose arbitration over court procedures to ensure a commercial understanding of their dispute rather than a formalistic application of the law. However, courts paid little attention to this need and continued to apply their understanding of procedural laws to arbitration. Therefore, a Working Group was constituted by the UNCITRAL in 1999 to specifically address the issue of uniformity and harmonisation of interim measures in international commercial arbitration (Working Group).[4]

It was observed that despite the wide acceptance of the Model Law, there were several lacunae concerning the definition of interim measures, the power of the national courts to issue interim measures in support of foreign seated arbitrations, and the collaboration between courts of different jurisdictions on the enforcement of interim measures.[5] The absence of clearly established international standards for interim measures 'may hinder the effective and efficient functioning of international commercial arbitration'.[6] Arbitrators may refrain from issuing interim measures to avoid unnecessary loss or damage to parties or other undesirable consequences.[7]

1. José Maria Abascal, *The Art of Interim Measures*, in Albert Jan van den Berg (ed.), *International Arbitration 2006: Back to Basics?* 755 (2007).
2. Julian David Mathew *Lew*, Commentary on Interim and Conservatory Measures in ICC Arbitration Cases, *11 (1) ICC Ct. Bull. 6-7 (2000).* (providing examples where arbitrators applied domestic law); John Beechey & Gareth Kenny, *How to Control the Impact of Time Running Between the Occurrence of the Damage and Its Full Compensation: Complementary and Alternative Remedies in Interim Relief Proceedings, in Interest, Auxiliary and Alternative Remedies in International Arbitration*, 5 Doss. ICC Ins. W. Bus. L. 21 (2008); Jason Fry, Simon Greenberg & Francesca Mazza, *The Secretariat's Guide to ICC Arbitration*, ICC Publication No. 729, 359 (2012). c.f. Jose F Sanchez, *Applying the Model Law's Standard for Interim Measures in International Arbitration*, 37 (1) J. Int'l Arb. 49 (2020).
3. Sanchez, *supra* n. 2, at 54.
4. Resolution adopted by General Assembly in its Sixty First Session (18 December 2006), G.A. Res. 61/33, pmbl., U.N. Doc. A/RES/61/33, available at: https://research.un.org/en/docs/ga/quick/regular/61 c.f. Dana Renée Bucy, *How to Best Protect Party Rights: The Future of Interim Relief in International Commercial Arbitration under the Amended UNCITRAL Model Law*, 25 (3) Am. Un. Int'l L. R. 579, 582 (2010).
5. Abascal, *supra* n. 1, at 755.
6. Report of the Secretary General for Settlement of Commercial Disputes, in its Thirty Second Report, 2000, A/CN.9/WG.II/WP.108, available at: https://undocs.org/en/A/CN.9/WG.II/WP.108, c.f. Howard M. Holtzmann & Joseph Neuhaus, et al., *UNCITRAL Model Law, Chapter IV.A (Articles 17 – 17J) – as Amended [Interim Measures and Preliminary Orders]*, in *A Guide to the 2006 Amendments to the UNCITRAL Model Law on International Commercial Arbitration: Legislative History and Commentary* 174 (2015).
7. Sanchez, *supra* n. 2, at 54.

Till 2006, no such international standard was codified. Arbitrators had to deduce standards from arbitral awards and scholarly writings.[8] Therefore, it was imperative to clarify when interim measures can be issued, and how the measures ought to be enforced,[9] especially because enforcing an interim measure may be as important as the final award on merits.[10] Thus, the Working Group completely overhauled the regime of interim measures in 2006 with the introduction of Chapter IVA in the Model Law (2006 Model Law Revisions)to facilitate greater enforceability of interim measures of protection.[11] The revisions, based on measures granted by courts, available written commentary, opinions, and statements of participants were considered to be reflective of the current practices in international trade and were intended to significantly enhance the operation of the Model Law.[12] The revisions were considered necessary in light of reports from practitioners and arbitral institutions that requests for interim measures were becoming increasingly frequent and uncertainty under the Model Law and national laws may compromise the effectiveness of arbitration as a tool for dispute resolution.[13]

The 2006 Model Law Revisions comprise specific provisions on the scope of the power of the arbitral tribunal and the court to grant interim measures, the standards to be followed when considering such requests, and the safeguards to be ensured before an interim measure is granted. However, many countries are yet to adopt the 2006 Model Law Revisions despite the same being in existence for over fifteen years now.[14] One such country which has not adopted the 2006 Model Law Revisions is India.[15]

The Indian experience with arbitration has been the subject of heavy criticism and a conservative approach.[16] India deliberately rejected the English approach which did not adopt the Model Law completely and consciously chose to adopt the Model Law.[17] Hence, the IAA was adopted on 16 August 1996, after considering the recommendation of the General Assembly of the United Nations to adopt the Model Law for ensuring '*uniformity of the law of arbitral procedure and the specific needs of the practice of international commercial arbitration*'.[18]

---

8. *Ibid.*
9. See also Report of the Secretary General for Settlement of Commercial Disputes, in its Thirty Second Report, 2000, A/CN.9/WG.II/WP.108, available at: https://undocs.org/en/A/CN.9/WG.II/WP.108, ¶¶ 73, 104.
10. *Ibid.*
11. UNCITRAL Yearbook, A/CN.9/SER.A/2006, Volume XXXVII (2006), at 415.
12. Mahadev Mohan & Eu-Yen Tay, *The New International Arbitration (Amendment) Bill: A Broader Framework for Interim Relief or Just Tune-up*, 22 Sac. L. J. 299, 302 (2010).
13. Holtzmann, *supra* n. 6 at, 165.
14. *See Appendices.*
15. *Curiously, India was neither a part of the Working Group nor an observer during the discussions.* UNCITRAL Yearbook, *supra* n. 11, at 415.
16. Lomesh K Nidumuri, *Critical Analysis of The Arbitration and Conciliation (Amendment) Act, 2015*, (25 May 2016), available at: https://www.mondaq.com/india/arbitration-dispute-resolution/494184/critical-analysis-of-the-arbitration-and-conciliation-amendment-act-2015.
17. Nakul Dewan, *Interim Measures in Arbitration: A Comparative Analysis of Indian and English Arbitration Act,* Int'l Bus. L. J., 687 (2003).
18. *See* Rachel Thomas, *How Closely Linked Are the UNCITRAL Model Law on International Commercial Arbitration and Indian Arbitration Regulations?*, available at: https://viamediatio

Incorporating Article 5 of the Model Law,[19] which provides for non-interference by the courts, Section 5 of the IAA provides explicitly that the court shall not interfere except where it has been provided for under the IAA. This read with Section 19(1) of the IAA which provides that the arbitral tribunal is not bound by the Code of Civil Procedure, 1908 (CPC), or the Indian Evidence Act, 1872 (Evidence Act) leads to a definite conclusion that the philosophy of the IAA was to minimise the supervisory role of courts in the arbitral process[20] and to distance arbitration from the rigours of court procedure.[21]

However, despite this noble goal, arbitration in India has not been a grand success. India has struggled with the Model Law,[22] especially on the issue of interim measures. Though the IAA was adopted to bring arbitration law in India in line with the Model Law, there is extensive court interference in India primarily due to the reliance on domestic procedural laws such as the CPC and the Specific Relief Act, 1963 (Specific Relief Act). The intent clearly outlined in Article 2A of the Model Law to have 'regard' to the 'international origin' of the Model Law, 'the need to promote uniformity in its application' and 'the observance of good faith',[23] have been largely ignored India.

One of the reasons for this failure is the extensive intervention provided under the IAA with respect to the powers of the court, especially in the context of Sections 9 and 17 of the IAA which deal with interim measures. Even the Supreme Court observed that the IAA does not appear to be a well-drafted legislation, especially in the context of interim measures.[24] Therefore, the IAA was amended in 2015 to categorically address the problems ailing arbitration practice with respect to interim measures.[25]

Currently, about 4,14,04,778 cases are pending in India, 85,178 of which are more than thirty years old, and 2,309,417 cases have been pending for more than ten years.[26] In one estimate, it was observed that it would take 466 years to clear the backlog of the Delhi High Court alone.[27] Therefore, arbitration may be the answer to reducing pendency and providing speedy dispute resolution. However, for that to happen, India has to clear the bottlenecks in its arbitration regime and draw a fine line

ncentre.org/readnews/NDY=/How-closely-linked-are-the-UNCITRAL-Model-Law-on-International-Commercial-Arbitration-and-Indian-Arbitration-Regulations.

19. Mohan, *supra* n. 12, at 301.
20. Indian Arbitration Act, 1996: *Statements of Objects and Reasons.*
21. Sarthak Malhotra & Sujoy Sur, *Standards Applicable to Interim Reliefs in India: A Comprehensive Analytical Investigation*, 5 Indian J. Arb. L. 183 (2016).
22. *Bhatia International v. Bulk Trading S.A. and Anr.* (2002) 4 SCC 105; *Venture Global Engineering v. Satyam Computer Services Limited* (2008) 4 SCC 190; *Yograj Infrastructure Ltd. v. Ssangyong Engineering & Construction Co. Ltd* (2012) 12 SCC 359; *Indtel Technical Services Pte. Ltd. v. W.S. Atkins P.L.C.* (2008) 10 SCC 308; *Citation Infowares Ltd. v. Equinox Corpn.* (2009) 7 SCC 220; *Dozco India (P) Ltd. v. Doosan Infracore Co. Ltd.* (2011) 6 SCC 179.
23. UNCITRAL Model Law, Art. 2A; Sanchez, *supra* n. 2, at 50.
24. *Bhatia International v. Bulk Trading S.A. and Anr.* (2002) 4 SCC 105, ¶35.
25. The Arbitration and Conciliation Amendment Act, 2015; Nick Peacock, Donny Surtani & Kritika Venugopal, *The Dispute Resolution and Arbitration Landscape in India*, (May 2017), available at: https://www.herbertsmithfreehills.com/latest-thinking/arbitration-in-india-dispute-resolution-in-the-worlds-largest-democracy.
26. As of 31 January 2022, available at: https://njdg.ecourts.gov.in/njdgnew/index.php.
27. *It Would Take Delhi HC 466 Yrs to Clear Backlog: CJ*, (13 February 2009), available at:http://archive.indianexpress.com/news/it-would-take-delhi-hc-466-yrs-to-clear-backlog-cj/423127/2.

between court assistance and court intervention, especially in the case of interim measures of protection.

Thus, this study aims to examine the topic of interim measures in international commercial arbitration in order to critically examine the fault lines in arbitration in India when it comes to interim measures. To achieve this objective, the present thesis examines the Model Law, arbitration statutes of over eighty international jurisdictions that have adopted the Model Law, international practice, and jurisprudence on interim measures in international commercial arbitration. The provisions of national arbitration statutes have been examined to understand how different countries have adopted the Model Law and the 2006 Model Law Revisions with respect to interim measures. A list of such countries along with their respective provisions is provided in the Appendices to this book. Similarly, the rules of major arbitral institutes have been compared to ascertain the power and scope of interim measures granted to arbitral tribunals under such rules.

After discussing the approach provided under the Model Law and across jurisdictions, the thesis compares the current position of law in India and the problems plaguing the IAA with respect to interim measures. It looks for solutions from other jurisdictions and the Model Law to remove such bottlenecks. The ultimate goal of this thesis is to critically examine the regime on interim measures in international commercial arbitration in India in order to align with the Model Law and foster certainty, reliability, predictability, and transparency.

In order to achieve the above objective, this thesis examines all reported judgments of the Supreme Court and the High Courts from 1993 to 2022 related to or addressing issues concerning interim measures by the courts and by the arbitral tribunals till 31 January 2022.

It should be noted that these decisions are not judgments passed by the court of the first instance or the arbitral tribunal but are reported decisions of the appellate courts which have considered the decisions of the court of the first instance or the arbitral tribunal in appeal. There are practical difficulties in examining the actual law and practice with respect to interim measures due to the lack of published case law owing to confidentiality concerns, especially in international arbitration.

Therefore, the jurisprudence and comparison can only be drawn from reported or published cases which have either resulted in awards or orders which have been challenged before national courts. Cases related to interim measures before courts have been considered in the context of arbitration. Other cases have not been considered unless they have altered or laid down the position of law in general with respect to the jurisprudence on interim measures.

Some of the countries that have adopted the Model Law have not been compared due to non-availability of information, lack of official translations in English, or practical difficulties in accessing authentic information regarding the same.

Topics such as emergency arbitration, third-party funding and enforcement problems under the CPC are not covered in detail as the topics are quite vast and the scope of the present book is restricted to analysing and comparing the jurisprudence on interim measures in India and how they are similar or different when compared to international jurisprudence or to other nations which have adopted the Model Law.

The book is broadly divided into four parts. Part I comprises the power of the courts to grant interim measures in relation to arbitration proceedings. Part II examines the power of the arbitral tribunal to grant interim measures in arbitration. Part III discusses the enforcement of interim measures granted by the court and the arbitral tribunal. Part IV contains the suggestions and drafted amendments to the IAA with respect to interim measures.

Part I Court-Ordered Interim Measures

CHAPTER 1
The Contours of 'Interim Measures'

In any adjudicatory mechanism, interim measures serve as an essential tool and remedy.[28] Often the final relief sought in litigation or arbitration may be insufficient to protect the rights of an aggrieved party as there is a period between which the claim is made, and the relief is finally awarded. The period intervening in the final adjudication may result in crucial evidence decomposing or disappearing. A recalcitrant party may dissipate assets to make enforcement of the award impossible, or it may take steps to delay or derail arbitration proceedings. Thus, an interim measure, in broad terms, is a remedy that seeks to safeguard the rights of parties pending the final adjudication of their dispute. The effect of interim measures is to distribute the risk for the duration of the main action between the parties, shifting it from the party applying for the interim measure to the other party.[29]

Surprisingly, interim measures have been granted by courts in every legal jurisdiction, yet there is no widely accepted definition of 'interim measures'.[30] They represent different concepts depending on jurisdiction and legal culture and hence, can take various forms. In the context of arbitration, such measures become important as arbitral tribunals devoid of the power to grant interim measures deprive tribunals of being a 'one-stop' mechanism for resolving disputes, leading to delay, inefficiency, and costs.

1. DEFINITION OF 'INTERIM MEASURES' IN ARBITRATION

Different scholars define interim measures differently, but by and large such definitions address the aim or purpose of such measures. Most often, a reference is made to the

28. Julian D.M. Lew, Loukas Mistelis & Stefan Kröll, *Comparative International Commercial Arbitration* ¶23-1 (2003).
29. *Ibid.*, at ¶ 23-2.
30. Stephen Bond, *The Nature of Conservatory and Provisional Measures*, in ICC (ed.), *Conservatory and Provisional Measures in International Arbitration* 8 (1993)., c.f. Ali Yesilirmak, *Provisional Measures in International Commercial Arbitration* 4 (2005).

definition given by the European Court of Justice, i.e., interim measures are '*intended to preserve a factual or legal situation so as to safeguard rights*'.[31] An attempt to bring about a consensus on the definition of interim measures was made in the 2006 Model Law Revisions in the context of arbitration. The language of Article 17(2) of the Model Law now describes an interim measure as '*any temporary measure … by which, at any time prior to the issuance of the award by which the dispute is finally decided, the arbitral tribunal orders a party to*'. Though this definition does not define interim measures per se, it nonetheless throws light on the nature of interim measures.

2. NATURE OF 'INTERIM MEASURES'

According to the definition contained in Article 17(2) of the Model Law, interim measures are (a) temporary instead of permanent and final. This aspect is vital as it implies that such measures can be modified, suspended, or terminated at any time. The definition also clarifies that (b) such measures can be issued at any time before the issuance of the award by which the dispute is finally decided, clearly establishing a broad timeline for issuing such measures. It also specifies that an interim measure cannot operate after the award unless such relief is merged with the award. It is pertinent to mention that these characteristics of interim measures are the same in court proceedings and arbitration proceedings.

3. CLASSIFICATION OF 'INTERIM MEASURES'

Currently, measures sought during arbitration proceedings are referred to as provisional, conservatory, protective, or just interim measures. Commonly, these references are used to mean the same thing and are often used interchangeably.[32] However, *Born* distinguishes 'interim' and 'provisional' measures from 'protective' or 'conservatory' measures. The former pertains to decisions made before the final award where the interim measure is granted usually to protect the party during the arbitration proceedings. Such a measure can be altered or eliminated while passing the final award. The latter is designed to protect or conserve particular rights regardless of it being granted in an interim or final award.[33] However, the reference to interim measures as 'protective' and 'conservatory' refers more to the purpose of the interim measures. In contrast, the words 'provisional', 'interim', or 'interlocutory' refer to the time period of the measures.

In the Model Law and the UNCITRAL Arbitration Rules (UNCITRAL Rules), these measures are known as interim measures. In the English version of the ICC Rules, they are known as conservatory or interim measures. Irrespective of their terminology, they are intended to operate as holding orders to protect the status quo and the integrity of

31. *Mario Recihert v. Dresdner Bank*, Case 261/90 [1992] ECR 2149, ¶34, c.f. Ali Yesilirmak, *supra* n. 30, at 4-5; *Van Uden Maritime BV, trading as Van Uden Africa Line v. Kommanditgesellshcaft in Firma Deco-Line* [1998] ECR 7091, 7133, ¶37, c.f. Lew, *supra* n. 28, at ¶ 23-2.
32. Ali Yesilirmak, *supra* n. 30, at 4-5.
33. Gary Born, *International Commercial Arbitration* 2606-2607 (2021).

the proceedings pending the outcome of the arbitral process.[34] Article 9 of the Model Law uses the term interim measures of protection, but Chapter IVA of the Model Law refers to 'interim measures' only.

3.1. Reference to an Intervening Period

However, not too much literature is available that adequately distinguishes these measures. That is probably the reason the different references are used interchangeably. Surprisingly, not enough attention has been paid to the classification of interim measures. The word 'interim' may be read as belonging to or connected to the intervening period of the dispute, i.e., a temporal relationship to the final award. An interim measure, then, is nothing but a reference only to the time period. Any order which does not end the dispute should be an interim measure since the intervening period may be anything that takes place between the arbitral tribunals' formation and the culmination of proceedings.[35] It does not refer to either the nature of the interim order or its form or content. It only refers to the time period within which the same shall remain in force and the time period during which either party can seek interim measures, i.e., during the course or before the final disposal of any proceeding.

3.2. Reference to a Measure of Protection

Therefore, an interim measure of protection should be distinguished from an interim order as an interim measure of protection is needed for a specific limited time until the final protection is granted, i.e., temporary relief reserving a right pending the final relief.[36] On the other hand, an interim order may refer to any procedural order passed during the pendency of proceedings.

The phrase that describes them best is 'interim measures of protection' clearly identifying their nature, period, and objective. The said phrase should be used to identify such measures and help distinguish these measures from procedural orders issued before the passing of the final award.

The use of the phrase 'measures of protection' would also help courts and tribunals identify their true objective. The expression 'interim measure of protection' is wide enough to mean and include all those measures which are ordinarily granted in arbitration proceedings. Thus, the court or tribunal can grant an interim measure which would (a) have the effect of mitigating loss and as a measure for preservation or (b) custody or sale of goods which are the subject matter of dispute, and (c) can take measures designed provisionally to determine and stabilise the relationship of parties in a long term project and preserve their right either before initiation or during pending of arbitral proceedings.[37]

---

34. Nigel Blackby, & Martin Hunter, *Redfern and Hunter on International Arbitration* 313 (2015).
35. Eduardo Z. Jaramillo, *The Relationship Between Interim and Final Award: Res Judicata Concerns*, in A. van den Berg (ed.), *Arbitration Advocacy in Changing Times* 248 (2011).
36. Ali Yesilirmak, *supra* n. 30, at 6.
37. *The Hyderabad Cricket Association v. Visaka Industries Limited* MANU/AP/0744/2011, ¶10.

The importance and need for interim measures of protection have substantially grown due to globalisation and the increased confidence in arbitration. With arbitration proceedings becoming more and more complex and taking longer to finish, the need for interim measures of protection is only logical. Interim measures of protection typically include anti-suit injunctions, security for costs, interim payments, sale, holdings in escrow accounts, injunctive relief, preserving remedies, handing over of property or information, inspection, administration of companies, and orders as to confidentiality.[38] Interim measures can also extend beyond preserving the status quo to require restoring a previous state of affairs or taking new actions.[39] However, the regime of interim measures in arbitration in India has not caught up with international arbitral practice.

38. James E. Castello, *Arbitral Ex Parte Interim Relief: The View In Favour*, 58 (3) Dis. R. J. 66 (2003).
39. Gary Born, *supra* n. 33, at 2606, 2607.

CHAPTER 2

A Brief History of Interim Measures and Arbitration in India

1. ARBITRATION IN INDIA

In recent times, the Government of India has been actively pursuing amendments and changes to the regime of arbitration in India. Such changes aim to make India a pro-arbitration hub.[40] It is rather strange that a country like India has lagged in arbitration despite having a long history and exposure to arbitration.[41]

Before colonisation and exposure to the 'common law' court system and jurisprudence, India had courts established by the kings along with other tribunals as recognised in ancient *smritis* (legal texts and digest).[42] People recognised the authority of the village council, i.e., *Panchayats*, which literally means 'a body of five persons'. The decision issued by the *Panchayat* was considered to be binding.[43] Such decisions became binding not through any enforcement mechanism but because the *Panchayat* commanded great respect and people believed that the decision of the *Panchayat*

40. Justice B.N. Srikrishna, Report of the High-Level Committee to Review the Institutionalization of Arbitration Mechanism in India, (July 2017), available at: http://legalaffairs.gov.in/sites/default/files/Report-HLC.pdf.
41. Law Commission of India, Report No. 76 – Arbitration Act, 1940, (9 November 1978), available at: http://lawcommissionofindia.nic.in/51-100/Report76.pdf.
42. *Dr. P.B. Gajendragadkar, Address to the Fifth International Arbitration Congress Proceedings of the Fifth International Arbitration Congress,* (7-10 January 1975) New Delhi, BI-3 to BI 4, c.f. Law Commission of India, *ibid.*
43. Krishna Sarma, Momota Oinam & Angshuman Kaushik, *Development and Practice of Arbitration in India: Has It Evolved as an Effective Legal Institution*, CDDRL Working Papers, Number 103 (October 2009), http://docplayer.net/51441019-Cddrl-working-papers-development-and-practice-of-arbitration-in-india-has-it-evolved-as-an-effective-legal-institution-number-103-october-2009.html.

reflected the voice of God.[44] This system of adjudication by village councils was later formalised and recognised by the Constitution of India in Part IX, i.e., Articles 243-243O.[45]

Thus, resolving disputes outside the domain of the court system has always been an integral part of Indian culture. In a certain sense, the *Panchayat* would be the equivalent of an arbitral tribunal with a *sarpanch* (head of the five persons) heading the *Panchayat*.[46] Surprisingly, it is not only that the relevance and validity of arbitration were impliedly recognised, but even appeals were provided against the decision of *kulani* (village council), *sareni* (corporations) and *puga* (assemblies).[47]

With the advent of the British and subsequent colonisation, the East India Company began to incorporate arbitration as a procedure for dispute resolution in their rules and regulations. It started with the Bengal Regulations of 1772, 1780, and 1781, which were explicitly designed to encourage arbitration, followed by Lord Cornwallis' regulations of 1787.

It is worthy of note that the Bengal Regulations did not abolish the system of Panchayats, impliedly recognising their value as an alternative dispute resolution mechanism.[48] Over time, various new regulations were passed by the British and the CPC, 1859 permitted references to arbitration without the intervention of the court. Thus, the first Arbitration Act was passed in 1899, which provided for an arbitrator to be appointed in matters on which suits could be filed before the courts. However, the applicability of such Act was restricted to Presidency Towns or other important commercial towns.[49]

Gradually, statutes and regulations started accepting arbitration as an alternative mechanism for dispute resolution. It was only in 1940 that a uniform law of arbitration was enacted throughout India.[50] Until the passing of the Arbitration Act of 1940 (1940 Act), arbitration was restricted to Presidency Towns or other important commercial towns. Given the presence of the British at the time, unsurprisingly, the 1940 Act was almost a verbatim adoption of the English Arbitration Act, 1934.[51]

In the meantime, the Model Law came into the picture on 21 June 1985, which was drastically different from the 1940 Act. Further, the economy had liberalised in 1991 and India was pitching for foreign investment, but foreign investors required a predictable and efficient system to resolve disputes. Difficulties were being faced in

---

44. Saber Habibi Savadkouhi, *International Commercial Arbitration: A Legal Analysis with Special Reference to the Contemporary Issues under Indian Law*, (2014), available at: https://shodhganga.inflibnet.ac.in/bitstream/10603/110130/11/11_chapter%201.pdf.
45. *See* Sumeet Kachwaha, *The Arbitration Law of India: A Critical Analysis*, 1 (2) Asian Int'l Arb. J. 105-126 (2005).
46. Anirudh Wadhwa & Anirudh Krishnan, *Justice RS Bachawat's Law of Arbitration & Conciliation* 1, 2 (2017).
47. Law Commission of India, *supra* n. 41.
48. *Scott v. Avery* (1843-60), All ER Rep 1.
49. *Sheonath v. Ramnath* (1865) 10 MIA 413.
50. Wadhwa, *supra* n. 46, at 32.
51. Law Commission of India, 246th Report of the Commission on Amendment to the Arbitration and Conciliation Act, 1996, available at: http://lawcommissionofindia.nic.in/reports/report246.pdf.

trade and commerce and with respect to arbitration and the recognition and enforcement of awards.[52] Investors needed the right business environment and commitment to the rule of law. Arbitration was a suitable alternative for addressing all their concerns as courtroom litigation was mired in excessive delay and hurdles.[53]

Thus, there was a need to realign arbitration legislation with global economic practices and arbitration practices. Consequently, aiming for a more pro-arbitration regime, India drafted an entirely new legislation based on the Model Law[54] repealing three different statutes, i.e., (1) The Arbitration (Protocol and Convention) Act, 1937; (2) the 1940 Act; and (3) The Foreign Awards (Recognition and Enforcement) Act, 1961. It categorically refused to follow the British who had rejected the Model Law on the recommendations of the Mustill Committee[55] and enacted the IAA.[56] Interestingly, the IAA did not receive requisite legislative sanction and had to be promulgated as an ordinance twice.[57]

The CPC now expressly recognises arbitration as an effective means of alternative dispute resolution under Section 89(1) of the CPC.[58] After such recognition under the CPC, various legislative amendments were made to the arbitration regime in a piecemeal fashion to support arbitration. All such amendments and proposals will be dealt with in the subsequent chapters. A summary of the amendments is provided below to give an overview of the development of the law with respect to interim measures.

1.1. The Arbitration Act of 1940

The power of the court to grant interim measures under the 1940 Act was restricted to instances during the pendency of a suit or when there were some proceedings taking place. Without the same, an application under Section 41(b) of the 1940 Act was not maintainable. Apart from this limited power with respect to interim measures, unfortunately, the 1940 Act had several shortcomings. It failed to adequately address the social and economic requirements of the society at that time.[59] As in the words of Justice D.A. Desai about how proceedings were conducted under the 1940 Act, he

52. *Bharat Aluminum v. Kaiser Aluminum Technical Services Inc.* (2012) 9 SCC 552, ¶35.
53. Law Commission of India, *supra* n. 51.
54. Nakul, *supra* n. 17, at 667.
55. R. Merkin, *The Arbitration Act 1996: An Annotated Guide* 2 (2000).
56. Saber, *supra* n. 44.
57. Law Commission of India, *supra* n. 51.
58. Indian Code of Civil Procedure, 1908, S. 89: *Settlement of disputes outside the Court.– (1) Where it appears to the Court that there exist elements of a settlement which may be acceptable to the parties, the Court shall formulate the terms of settlement and give them to the parties for their observations and after receiving the observations of the parties, the Court may reformulate the terms of a possible settlement and refer the same for:-*
    (a) arbitration;
    (b) conciliation;
    (c) judicial settlement including settlement through Lok Adalat: or
    (d) mediation.
59. Saber, *supra* n. 44.

observed that the proceedings '*made lawyers laugh and legal philosophers weep … Informal forum chosen by the parties for expeditious disposal of their disputes has by the decisions of the Courts been clothed with "legalese" of unforeseeable complexity*'.[60]

1.2. The Arbitration and Conciliation Act of 1996

India adopted the Model Law with the aspiration of consolidating and amending the law relating to domestic arbitration, international commercial arbitration, and enforcement of foreign arbitral awards.[61] One of the lacunae sought to be addressed by the IAA was the delay in the arbitration process.[62] Among other concerns were court intervention in the arbitral process and the enforcement of an arbitral award as if it were the decree of the court.[63]

The Arbitration Act is divided into three parts. Part I titled 'Arbitration' is contained in ten chapters from Sections 2-43 (Part I). Part II titled 'Enforcement of certain Foreign Awards' contains two chapters from Sections 44-60 (Part II). While Chapter I of Part II provides for applicability of the Convention on the Recognition and Enforcement of Foreign Arbitral Awards (NYC), Chapter II deals with the Geneva Convention of 1927 (Geneva Convention). Part III (Sections 61-81) provides for 'Conciliation' and Part IV (Sections 82-86) provides for Supplementary Provisions.[64]

1.3. The Arbitration and Conciliation Amendment Bill 2003

In 2001, as part of its function to review existing law, the Law Commission undertook a review of the IAA and submitted its report with recommendations.[65] Almost all recommendations were accepted and adopted as the Arbitration and Conciliation (Amendment) Bill, 2003 (2003 Bill).[66] The 2003 Bill sought to address, *inter alia,* issues of expediting awards and setting aside applications, obtaining interim measures in-aid of foreign seated arbitrations, and the ability to apply foreign law to two Indian parties.[67] The 2003 Bill contained extensive suggestions for the regime on interim measures and Section 17 of the IAA was suggested to be redrafted along the lines of the Arbitration Act, 1996 of England (English Arbitration Act).

60. *Bharat Aluminum v. Kaiser Aluminum Technical Services Inc.* (2012) 9 SCC 552, ¶33.
61. Preamble to the Indian Arbitration Act, 1996.
62. Law Commission of India, *supra* n. 51.
63. *Ibid.*
64. Government of India, Ministry of Law and Justice – Proposed Amendments to the Arbitration & Conciliation Act, 1996: A Consultation Paper, available at: https://www.legallyindia.com/images/stories/docs/Arbitration-Act-LawMin-ConsultationPaper-on-Arb-Act-April2010-1.pdf.
65. Law Commission of India, Report No. 176th – Arbitration and Conciliation (Amendment) Bill, 2001, (12 September 2001), available at: http://lawcommissionofindia.nic.in/arb.pdf.
66. Government of India, Ministry of Law and Justice – Proposed Amendments to the Arbitration & Conciliation Act, 1996: A Consultation Paper, available at: https://www.legallyindia.com/images/stories/docs/Arbitration-Act-LawMin-ConsultationPaper-on-Arb-Act-April2010-1.pdf.
67. *Ibid.*

1.4. The Saraf Committee

Before the 2003 Bill could be passed, a committee was constituted under Dr B. P. Saraf (Saraf Committee) to make an in-depth study of the implications of the recommendations contained in the 176th report of the Law Commission as there was severe criticism and resistance from all stakeholders on the proposed amendments.[68] Rightly so, the Saraf Committee gave a report which opined that the suggested amendments and provisions of the 2003 Bill provide for excessive intervention by courts and called for establishing an arbitration institution in India which would compete with global standards to popularise institutional arbitration.[69] The Saraf Committee also recommended that the 2003 Bill be withdrawn and a fresh bill be proposed along the lines of the Model Law noting that the suggested amendments would take India back to the era of 'court-structured and court-controlled arbitration'.[70]

It is pertinent to note that the Saraf Committee specifically provided for a revamp of interim measures in consonance with the 2006 Model Law Revisions, including a separate provision for enforcement.

Subsequently, the 2003 Bill was also referred to the Departmental Related Standing Committee on Personnel, Public Grievance, Law and Justice for examination and report. Based on the opinions of eminent advocates and representatives from trade and industry, public sector undertakings and representatives of the Ministry of Law and Justice, it was recommended that the 2003 Bill should be withdrawn.[71]

1.5. The Arbitration and Conciliation (Amendment) Act 2015

Unfortunately, instead of following up on the cold trail of recommendations of the Saraf Committee, the Arbitration and Conciliation (Amendment) Act, 2015 (2015 Amendment) followed the suggestions contained in the 2003 Bill. The entire regime of interim measures in India under Sections 9 and 17 of the IAA was revamped, albeit not in line with the 2006 Model Law Revisions.

1.6. The Arbitration and Conciliation (Amendment) Act 2019

The Arbitration and Conciliation (Amendment) Act 2019 (2019 Amendment) was passed on 9 August 2019, making several changes to promote institutional arbitration in India. Concerning interim measures, the 2019 Amendment only rectifies a blatant error in Section 17(1) of the IAA (power of the tribunal to grant interim measures) by

---

68. Report of Justice Saraf Committee on Arbitration (29 January 2005), at 5.
69. Government of India, Ministry of Law and Justice – Proposed Amendments to the Arbitration & Conciliation Act, 1996: A Consultation Paper, available at: https://www.legallyindia.com/images/stories/docs/Arbitration-Act-LawMin-ConsultationPaper-on-Arb-Act-April2010-1.pdf.
70. *Supra* n. 68.
71. Government of India, Ministry of Law and Justice – Proposed Amendments to the Arbitration & Conciliation Act, 1996: A Consultation Paper, available at: https://www.legallyindia.com/images/stories/docs/Arbitration-Act-LawMin-ConsultationPaper-on-Arb-Act-April2010-1.pdf.

removing the words '*or at any time after the making of the arbitral award but before it is enforced in accordance with section 36*'.

1.7. The Arbitration and Conciliation (Amendment) Act 2021

The most recent (and unnecessary) intervention in the IAA was the Arbitration and Conciliation (Amendment) 2021 which was passed on 10 March 2021. Surprisingly, the amendment was initially passed as an ordinance in November 2020 without any discussion in the public domain. While the amendment contains any express changes relating to the provisions on interim measures of protection, it adds new grounds of 'fraud' and 'corruption' in securing the contract or making the award without any further explanation. Consequently, the enforcement of awards can be unconditionally stayed if such allegations are made at the post-award stage. In effect, the amendment grants an additional ground to the court to stay the execution of an award.

2. THE SPECIFIC RELIEF ACT 1963

Interim measures and their jurisprudence in India cannot be adequately addressed without referring to the Relief Act, which codifies the equitable remedies available under the common law. The Relief Act was enacted in India to define and amend the law relating to certain kinds of specific reliefs.[72]

One such specific relief is that of specific performance which is granted by the court directing the defendant to do what he had agreed by contract to do. The remedy works in contrast with the remedy by way of damages for breach of contract, i.e., pecuniary compensation for failure to carry out the terms of the contract.[73] Thus, the law of specific relief is part of procedural law as it is a form of judicial redress.[74]

The understanding of the Relief Act is crucial for interim measures and the kind of interim relief that can be granted by courts under the IAA as the courts have repeatedly referred to the Relief Act when considering a request for interim measures as Part III of the Relief Act deals with 'Preventive Relief' containing express provisions on the grant of injunctions.[75] Specifically, Section 41(e) of the Relief Act provides that an injunction cannot be granted where a contract cannot be specifically enforced.

It must be noted that earlier the jurisdiction of the court with respect to specific relief was discretionary and had to be exercised on judicial principles such as the balance of convenience, the possibility of irreparable loss, and injury to the plaintiff.[76] Hence, most courts used to deny interim measures of protection if the party requesting

72. *Adhunik Steels Ltd. v. Orissa Manganese and Mineral (P) Ltd* (2007) 7 SCC 125, ¶16.
73. Fredrick Pollock and Dinshaw Fardunji Mulla, *Pollock & Mulla's Indian Contract and Specific Relief Acts* 2453 (2010).
74. *Adhunik Steels Ltd. v. Orissa Manganese and Mineral (P) Ltd* (2007) 7 SCC 125, ¶16.
75. Indian Specific Relief Act, 1963, Chs VII and VIII.
76. *Geep Batteries (India) Pvt. Ltd. v. Gillette India Ltd.* 2005 (120) DLT 387, ¶8; *Techno Construction v. Kunj Vihar Co-operative Group Housing Society* 2005 (81) DRJ 233, ¶9.

the measure could be compensated for the damages.[77] This position has been changed after 2018.

2.1. The 2018 Amendment to Relief Act

The Specific Relief (Amendment) Act, 2018 (Amended Relief Act) was passed by the Parliament on 23 July 2018 to bring substantial changes to the Relief Act. The amendment is based on the recommendations of an 'Expert Committee on the Specific Relief Act, 1963' (Expert Committee). The report of the Expert Committee recommended that the regime of contract law should be brought in line with the Principles of European Contract Law and the UNIDROIT Principles of International Contracts[78] to make specific relief effective and business-friendly for doing business in India.[79]

2.2. Removal of the 'Adequacy Test'

Under the Relief Act, courts were not bound to grant the remedy of specific relief. Instead, they had the discretion to do so. This discretion resulted in specific relief being granted under exceptional circumstances.[80] The changes to Section 14 of the Relief Act are of importance, especially in the context of interim measures and commercial arbitration. Section 14 of the Relief Act used to contain a list of contracts which were not specifically enforceable. Section 14(a) of the Relief Act provided that '*a contract for the non-performance of which compensation in money is an adequate relief*'. This requirement referred to as the 'adequacy test' was criticised by the Expert Committee.[81]

Thus, the legislative intent of the Relief Act was that specific performance could not be granted in cases where monetary compensation is adequate relief. After the amendment, this position of law has been turned on its head.

Section 21(1) of the Relief Act has been amended to now provide for damages, in addition to specific performance. Earlier the same could be claimed 'in addition or substitution of'. Therefore, specific performance will now be the norm and damages will not be adequate compensation.[82] It will be examined how these changes will affect questions about the availability of interim measures.

---

77. Indian Specific Relief Act, 1963, S. 40.
78. Bhavana Sunder, Ashish Kabra & Vyapak Desai, *Contract Enforcement Finally Sees Relief*, (27 July 2018), available at: http://www.nishithdesai.com/information/research-and-articles/nda-hotline/nda-hotline-single-view/article/contract-enforcement-finally-sees-relief-amendments-to-the-specific-relief-act.html?no_cache=1&cHash=8dafbcfeca599325b1443cdbec7acd25.
79. Report of the Expert Committee on Specific Relief Act, 1963, Government of India, (26 May 2016), available at: http://practicalacademic.blogspot.com/2018/05/download-expert-committee-report-on.html.
80. Bhavana Sunder, *supra* n. 78.
81. *Supra* n. 79.
82. *Ibid.*

CHAPTER 3

Court-Ordered Interim Measures Before Arbitration Proceedings

Today, jurisdictions across the globe recognise arbitration as an effective and suitable method of alternative dispute resolution. Most countries are either bringing rapid changes or replacing existing legislations to align with the Model Law. The recent success of Singapore and Hong Kong as pro-arbitration jurisdictions has evoked the interest of governments and businesses alike.[83]

Usually, jurisdictions are considered pro-arbitration due to their ability to keep up with the needs and changes in international arbitration practice. There is a coordinated effort between the government and the judiciary. Courts acknowledge their limited role in supporting the arbitral process while governments ensure policy changes to guarantee maximum enforcement, minimal court intervention, and rare disruption of arbitration proceedings.

However, this harmony between governments and the court has not always been the same. Initially, the judiciary across jurisdictions was extremely reluctant towards arbitration and held it with mistrust. Arbitral jurisdiction was considered to be a threat to State jurisdiction and the high ideals of impartial justice.[84] Hence, the courts, threatened by a competing mechanism, refused to recognise and enforce arbitration agreements and awards. The basis of such reluctance, apart from subconscious jealousy, was the arbitrator's lack of power to coerce compliance with their decisions.[85]

This view softened over time with the enactment of legislative remedies against possible abuses of ousting the jurisdictions of the court through an arbitration agreement.[86] The concept of a court's assistance came somewhere around the 1920s for recognition and enforcement of arbitration agreements. After that, the assistance was extended to the appointment and removal of arbitrators and compelling witnesses to

83. Piyush Prasad, *Arbitration in Singapore and Hong Kong*, 57 Int'l Imm. Pgm. 2, 3 (2017).
84. Ali Yesilirmak, *supra* n. 30, at 64-65.
85. *Ibid.*
86. *Ibid.*, at 35.

attend. Subsequently, the English and American legislatures extended court assistance to grant interim measures in support of arbitration.[87]

1. COURT ASSISTANCE AND INTERVENTION

At first brush, the idea of approaching the court for interim measures appears to be antithetical to the objective of alternative dispute resolution and its basic premise of resolving the dispute out of court. The parties did not want to have their dispute resolved through courts and hence, opted for arbitration. Therefore, the courts should not entertain a request from parties who have voluntarily chosen to avoid the same courts. However, arbitration is a private adjudicatory process that has no enforcement mechanism and therefore requires court intervention.[88] Arbitration cannot exist without the court's support. Thus, there exists an apparent tension between courts and arbitral tribunals.

1.1. Minimal Court Intervention

The real challenge lies in ensuring that courts are mindful of the will of the parties to have their dispute resolved through arbitration but at the same time, recognise the inherent limitations of the arbitral process and support arbitration as and when required. Therefore, a fine line needs to be drawn by the legislature to ensure that an arbitration statute recognises instances where court assistance would be imperative and at the same time, remind the courts not to interfere unnecessarily. This is the broad intent contained in Article 5 of the Model Law, which states that courts should not interfere in arbitral proceedings '*except where so provided in this Law*'.

At the same time, the Model Law recognises the need for a court's support, especially to grant interim measures of protection. It resolves the apparent tension between courts and arbitral tribunals by explicitly stating in Article 9 that requests for an interim measure of protection from a court will not be incompatible with an arbitration agreement.

1.2. The Lack of Uniformity in Arbitration Statutes

Despite attempting to draw this fine line between court assistance and court intervention, the Model Law leaves it to each individual State to incorporate these provisions into their respective national arbitration statute as they see fit. Therefore, national arbitration statutes while adopting the Model Law, have to provide for (a) the power to grant interim measures to support the arbitral process; (b) limit the scope of such power to minimise unnecessary court intervention; (c) specify the standards to be applied recognising the distinct nature of the arbitral process as compared to court

87. *Ibid.*, at 35-36.
88. Zhivko Stalev, *Interim Measures of Protection in the Context of Arbitration*, in Albert Jan van den Berg (ed.), *International Arbitration in a Challenging World* 105 (1994).

litigation when considering requests for interim measures; and (d) to provide adequate safeguards which recognise that interim measures are exceptional in nature[89] and can have drastic consequences on the parties when granted or refused.

2. THE NEED FOR COURT-ORDERED INTERIM MEASURES

When parties agree to have their dispute resolved through arbitration, there exists a period between a party invoking the arbitration clause and the commencement of arbitral proceedings. During this period, several procedural requirements have to be met such as the nomination of the arbitrator or panel of arbitrators, their consent, mutually agreed date, time, and place of hearing, or to comply with a multi-tier dispute resolution clause.[90] A recalcitrant party may use such period to its advantage to dissipate assets or evidence, alter the contractual or commercial *status quo ante*, or take further steps to pre-empt or position itself for the arbitration.[91]

Similarly, once arbitration proceedings have commenced, there might be times when the arbitral tribunal does not have the power to act or is unable to act effectively.[92] For instance, due to the consensual nature of arbitration, an arbitral tribunal cannot pass orders against third parties.[93] Court support may also be required when the appointment of an arbitrator has been challenged, or due to arbitrators being in different jurisdictions, they cannot convene a hearing for interim measures quickly. In such cases, parties cannot be left remediless and be expected to wait for the arbitral tribunal to be constituted. The damage caused during this time may not be repairable through compensation at the time of passing of the award. Hence, courts are required to support arbitration and further its efficacy as a dispute resolution mechanism.

In many cases, court assistance is the only way through which assets can be saved for future arbitration. The losing party may dissipate all assets and leave the winning party with a worthless award.[94] Therefore, it is of utmost importance that such power to grant interim measures in aid of arbitration proceedings is recognised under

89. Jarrod Wong, *The Issuance of Interim Measures in International Disputes: A Proposal Requiring a Reasonable Possibility of Success on the Underlying Merits*, 33 (3), Ga. J. Int'l & Comp. L. 605, 611(2005).
90. *Larson and Toubro Ltd. (ECC Division) v. National Highway Authority of India* 2009 (4) Arb. LR 163 (Mad), ¶27.
91. Report of UNCITRAL Working Group on the work of its thirty Second session, June 2000, A/CN.9/468, available at: https://undocs.org/en/A/CN.9/468, ¶85.; Gary Born, *supra* n. 33, at 2631, 2632.
92. Singapore International Arbitration Act, 1994, S. 12A(6); English Arbitration Act, 1996, S. 44(5).
93. Shivam Jasra, *Power of Courts and Arbitral Tribunals to Issue Interim Measures in India: A Critical Analysis of 2015 Amendment*, (15 December 2019), available at:https://www.latestlaws.com/articles/power-of-courts-and-arbitral-tribunals-to-issue-interim-measures-in-india-a-critical-analysis-of-2015-amendment-by-shivam-jasra/.
94. *Pacific Reinsurance Management Corporation v. Ohio Reinsurance Corporation*, 935 F.2d 1019, 1022-23, (9th Cir. 1991), c.f. Gary Born, *supra* n. 33, at 2616.

arbitration statutes. This power is essential for strengthening and establishing the effectiveness of the arbitration proceedings.[95]

3. THE POWER TO GRANT INTERIM MEASURES

Today, the prevailing view is that court assistance is required before the commencement of arbitration proceedings.[96] The challenge, as previously discussed,[97] is to demarcate the line between when the court should interfere and when it should not.

3.1. Principle of 'Compatibility' and 'Priority'

One way to resolve the tension is to treat the role of the courts as being complementary to arbitration as opposed to considering it to be interference. This view is referred to as the principle of 'compatibility',[98] or the concept of 'co-operation' where the role of the court is only of assistance and control.[99] Under this principle, the courts recognise the need for court support but pay due respect to the will of the parties to have their dispute resolved through arbitration by the arbitral tribunal, which has 'priority' or exclusivity of jurisdiction over the dispute.[100] Therefore, in a certain sense, judicial assistance is not really an interim measure but a court measure taken in aid of the arbitral process.[101]

3.2. Article 9 of the Model Law

The principle of 'compatibility' between arbitration and court assistance is enshrined in Article 9 of the Model Law. However, Article 9 does little, except recognising the possibility of a party to approach the court despite having agreed to have the dispute resolved through arbitration. It does not shed any light on when courts are to interfere

95. *Paragon Steels Pvt. Ltd. v. European Metal Recycling Ltd.* (2006) 4 Arb LR 299, ¶9; *wherein application for injunction prior to constitution of arbitral tribunal in London under ICC Rules was held maintainable under Indian Arbitration Act, 1996, S. 9 read with Art. 23 of the ICC Rules.*
96. Charles N. Brower & W. Micheal Tupman, *Court-Ordered Provisional Measures Under The New York Convention*, 80 Am. J. Int'l. L. 24, 25 (1986); *also recognized under* English Arbitration Act, 1996, S. 44(2)(e); Austrian Code of Civil Procedure (ZPO), S. 585; Belgium Judicial Code, Art. 1698; Brazil Code of Civil Procedure, Art. 806; French Code of Civil Procedure, Arts 1449 & 1506; German Arbitration Act, S. 1033; Hong Kong Arbitration Ordinance (Cap.609), ss 45 & 60; Dutch Code of Civil Procedure, Art. 1022a; Spanish Arbitration Law, Art. 11(3); Swedish Arbitration Act S. 4 ¶ 3; *this is similar to the position in Switzerland see*, Stephen Balthasar, *International Commercial Arbitration: A Handbook* 649 (2016).
97. *See Introduction.*
98. *The doctrine of compatibility provides that a request to a court or judicial authority for an interim measure of protection is not incompatible with an arbitration agreement. It sets forth that 'the negative effect' of an arbitration agreement, which is to exclude court jurisdiction, does not operate with regard to such interim measures, see*, Report of Secretary General on Analytical Commentary on Draft Text of A Model Law on International Commercial Arbitration, in its Eighteenth Session, (1985), UN Doc A/CN.9/264, available at: https://undocs.org/en/A/CN.9/264, ¶1.
99. Ali Yesilirmak, *supra* n. 30, at 85.
100. Gary Born, *supra* n. 33, at 2712.
101. *Vibroflotation A.G. v. Express Builders Co. Ltd.* [1994] 3 H.K. Cas. 263 (H.C.).

and when they are not. It does not provide for any clarity, provision, or criteria with respect to court-ordered interim measures, leaving it to the national arbitration statutes to provide for the same based on the fear that it may be perceived to be interfering with the sovereignty of nations and hence, nations would be reluctant to accept the Model Law. Another reason for this approach was that the Model Law could not interfere in domestic court procedures and conduct of proceedings.[102]

3.2.1. *Silence of the Model Law on the Court's Power*

As will be seen subsequently, these concerns were largely misplaced and led to inconsistent jurisprudence on court-ordered interim measures. The Working Group recognised this lack of proper guidance and the effect of such a lacuna. It noted that there was uncertainty in some states where there were no provisions dealing with the power of the court to issue interim measures and the result was that there was a lack of uniformity in different states on whether, and under what circumstances, interim measures could be obtained from a court of law.[103]

In the absence of guidance in the Model Law and the similarities between interim measures ordered by the court, arbitrators, lawmakers, and academicians usually refer to the law, usage, and practice of interim measures reported in civil or commercial litigation.[104] It was in this context that the Model Law was revised in 2006 with a special focus on interim measures to establish uniformity with respect to court-ordered interim measures to support arbitration.[105]

3.3. Article 17J of the Model Law

An attempt to bring such uniformity and clarity to court-ordered interim measures in arbitration has been made with the introduction of Article 17J of the Model Law. Article 17J of the Model Law provides that '*A court shall have the same power of issuing an interim measure in relation to arbitration proceedings, irrespective of whether their place is in the territory of this State, as it has in relation to proceedings in courts. The court shall exercise such power in accordance with its own procedures in consideration of the specific features of international arbitration.*'

The language used in Article 17J of the Model Law, has, *inter alia*, the following implications:

102. Sundaresh Menon & Elaine Chao, *Reforming the Model Law Provisions on Interim Measures of Protection*, 2 (1) Asian Int'l Arb. J. 1, 3 (2006).
103. Report of UNCITRAL Working Group on the work of its thirty Second session, June 2000, A/CN.9/468, available at: https://undocs.org/en/A/CN.9/468, ¶86.
104. Abascal, *supra* n. 1, at 756-757.
105. Report of UNCITRAL Working Group on the work of its thirty Second session, June 2000, A/CN.9/468, available at: https://undocs.org/en/A/CN.9/468, ¶¶60 & 87.

(a) court jurisdiction to support arbitration is not limited to supporting arbitral tribunals located within the jurisdiction of the court but extends to arbitral tribunals located outside the jurisdiction of the court;
(b) the court shall have the same power to grant interim measures as those applicable in court proceedings. This is especially important as courts would have jurisdiction to grant orders against third parties;
(c) the language also provides the necessary guidance on when, and how, the court is to exercise jurisdiction and grant relief. The phrase 'specific features of international arbitration' though not explicitly defined serves as the overarching scope for courts to keep in mind, while not interfering in the jurisdiction of the courts at the seat or the jurisdiction of the arbitral tribunal directly.

3.3.1. 'Specific Features of International Arbitration'

Although Article 17J of the Model Law does not shed any particular light as to what are the 'specific features of international arbitration' that the court should keep in mind while granting interim measures, the Chairman of the UNCITRAL Jose Maria Abascal Zamora provided an insight into why parties choose international arbitration. These reasons may be understood as the 'specific features of international arbitration' as these features necessitate that the rules or laws governing the arbitration are completely different from the procedural laws governing civil, or commercial disputes before courts. In his words, in international arbitration, the parties fear alien procedural laws and court practices. The whole rationale for choosing international arbitration over the court is the following:[106]

(a) to prevent home-court advantage to either of the parties;
(b) avoid forum shopping and conflicts of jurisdiction;
(c) right to appoint arbitrators;
(d) reliance on the flexibility of the rules agreed in the arbitration in contrast to the rigidity of procedural laws; and
(e) to avoid delays and costs.

Therefore, the 'specific features' refers to:[107]

(a) Recognition of the autonomous nature of arbitration and respect for party autonomy.
(b) Recognition of the intent of parties to provide for minimum intervention by the courts and only to support arbitration.

---

106. Abascal, *supra* n. 1, at 757.
107. Lira Goswami, *Interim Reliefs: The Role of the Courts*, in A. Van den Berg (ed.), *International Arbitration and National Courts: The Never-Ending Story* 114 (2011).

The reference to 'specific features of international arbitration' at its core requires disassociation from the domestic procedures of a country. Parties opt for arbitration to prevent such home-court advantages and minimise the risk of dealing with unfamiliar or alien laws. The courts need to be sufficiently empowered to grant interim measures in support of arbitration proceedings without sourcing such power or relying on domestic procedural legislations. Hence, many jurisdictions provide that the power of the court to grant interim measures shall be the same as that of the tribunal to prevent reliance on domestic law.

For example, Section 9(2) of the New Zealand Arbitration Act states that the court has the same powers as an arbitral tribunal to grant an interim measure for the purposes of proceedings before that court and that the standards applicable to a request for grant of the interim measure would apply subject to all necessary modifications. Similarly, Section 12A(2) of the Singapore International Arbitration Act states that the court shall have the same power as set out in Section 12(1)(c)-(i), i.e., the powers of the arbitral tribunal, except security for costs and discovery of documents and interrogatories.

3.3.2. *Equal Powers of the Court and Arbitral Tribunal*

Thus, in New Zealand, the power of the tribunal and the court to grant interim measures is the same. In Singapore, the tribunals can grant additional interim measures and hence, in a certain sense, the powers of the tribunal are more than those of the court. However, the real intent is to recognise certain powers of the arbitral tribunal explicitly and not in effect, make the tribunal superior to that of the court.

3.3.3. *Superiority of Courts*

On the contrary, Section 45(3) of the Hong Kong Arbitration Ordinance states that the power conferred under the Section can be exercised by the court irrespective of whether or not similar powers may be exercised by an arbitral tribunal. Therefore, while the section refers to the powers of the arbitral tribunal, it does not limit the power of the court to only such measures as may be granted by an arbitral tribunal. Nonetheless, all three jurisdictions ensure that the primary resort to the power to grant interim measures in aid of arbitration is not the domestic procedural law of the court.

3.3.4. *Hybrid Approach*

Georgia has adopted a hybrid approach combining domestic procedural law with an autonomous provision. Article 23(3) of the Law of Georgia on Arbitration provides that its civil procedure code shall apply '*except article 198 (2)(f) and (i), considering the requirement for arbitration proceedings*'.[108] In such cases, while court-ordered interim

108. *See Appendix A.*

measures are not entirely autonomous, the domestic procedures are not applied directly and the courts have to keep the nature of arbitration proceedings in mind.

Article 17J of the Model Law is a step forward in guiding the court on what to consider when dealing with a request for an interim measure in arbitration. While Article 9 of the Model Law recognises the possibility to go to court, Article 17J of the Model Law clarifies that a court needs to be mindful of the differences between arbitration and domestic litigation when exercising the said power. Furthermore, the reference to the 'specific features of international arbitration' brings within its fold the fact that it is the arbitral tribunal that has to adjudicate the matter and hence, the role of the court is only to support the arbitral process and not decide the dispute.

3.4. Power of Courts in India

India has adopted Article 9 of the Model Law in Section 9 of the IAA, in complete contrast to the Model Law. Section 9 of the IAA provides as follows:

> (1) A party may, before or during arbitral proceedings or at any time after the making of the arbitral award but before it is enforced in accordance with section 36, apply to a Court:
> (i) for the appointment of a guardian for a minor or person of unsound mind for the purposes of arbitral proceedings; or
> (ii) or (ii) for an interim measure of protection in respect of any of the following matters, namely:
> (a) the preservation, interim custody or sale of any goods which are the subject-matter of the arbitration agreement;
> (b) securing the amount in dispute in the arbitration;
> (c) the detention, preservation or inspection of any property or thing which is the subject-matter of the dispute in arbitration, or as to which any question may arise therein and authorising for any of the aforesaid purposes any person to enter upon any land or building in the possession of any party, or authorising any samples to be taken or any observation to be made, or experiment to be tried, which may be necessary or expedient for the purpose of obtaining full information or evidence;
> (d) interim injunction or the appointment of a receiver;
> (e) such other interim measure of protection as may appear to the court to be just and convenient, and the court shall have the same power for making orders as it has for the purpose of, and in relation to, any proceedings before it.
> (2) Where, before the commencement of the arbitral proceedings, a Court passes an order for any interim measure of protection under sub-section (1), the arbitral proceedings shall be commenced within a period of ninety days from the date of such order or within such further time as the court may determine.
> (3) Once the arbitral tribunal has been constituted, the court shall not entertain an application under sub-section (1), unless the court finds that circumstances exist which may not render the remedy provided under section 17 efficacious.

3.4.1. *Divergence from the Model Law*

Evidently, the language of Section 9 of the IAA is not identical to Article 9 of the Model Law.[109] Ironically, the language has been borrowed from Section 44 of the English Arbitration Act,[110] despite England not being a nation that has fully adopted the Model Law.[111]

Similar to the English Arbitration Act, Section 9 of the IAA mentions or lists the situations where interim relief can be granted, recognising the power of the court to grant interim measures in aid of arbitration. Therefore, it can be argued that India has provided an autonomous source of power within the IAA for courts to grant interim measures.

However, Section 9 of the IAA does not provide for the scope of the power, standards to be adopted, procedures to be followed, and the enforcement of such orders. Instead, the concluding lines of Section 9(1) of the IAA state that '*the Court shall have the same power for making orders as it has for the purpose of, and in relation to, any proceedings before it*'. These last lines of Section 9 of the IAA are similar to the language contained in Article 17J of the Model Law, except that such power cannot be used irrespective of whether the arbitration proceedings are in India or not.

Therefore, based on the bare perusal of the language of Section 9 of the IAA, one view can be that the same is already in alignment with Article 17J of the Model Law, and it is only that the courts in India do not have the power to grant interim measures in aid of foreign seated arbitrations. However, this view would ignore the most important phrase in Article 17J of the Model Law which is that '*the court shall exercise such power in accordance with its own procedures in consideration of the specific features of international arbitration*'.

3.4.2. *Different Approaches by Courts*

In the absence of such guiding language, courts in India have taken three different approaches while interpreting the power to grant interim measures under Section 9 of the IAA:

(a) the power to grant interim measures is *pari materia* to the CPC and governed by the Relief Act;[112]
(b) the power under Section 9 of the IAA is an independent provision;
(c) a hybrid of the two approaches, i.e., while the CPC applies to proceedings under Section 9 of the IAA, the same cannot be read 'as it is' for the purpose of the arbitration.

---

109. *Sundaram Finance Ltd. v. NEPC India Ltd.* (1999) 2 SCC 479, ¶14.
110. English Arbitration Act, 1996, S. 44.
111. Justin Williams, Hamish Lal & Richard Hornshaw, *Arbitration Procedures and Practice in the UK (England and Wales): Overview*, available at: https://uk.practicallaw.thomsonreuters.com/4-502-1378?transitionType=Default&contextData=(sc.Default)&firstPage=true&bhcp=1.
112. *For, e.g.*, Thailand Arbitration Act, 2002, S. 16, '*The provisions governing provisional measures under the Civil Procedure Code shall apply mutatis mutandis.*'

3.4.3. *Application of The CPC and Specific Relief Act*

The starting point of analysis under Section 9 of the IAA has been that the CPC applies to request for interim measures and the types of measures being listed under Section 9 of the IAA do not make the power to grant interim measures in aid of arbitration proceedings autonomous or independent.

The basis for this view is the reliance on Section 41(b) of the 1940 Act, which envisaged that the provision of the CPC shall be applicable to all proceedings before the court. Under the IAA, Section 9 uses the phrase that '*the court shall have the same power for making orders as it has for the purpose of, and in relation to, any proceedings before it*'. Hence, the courts are guided by the CPC with respect to the proceedings before them. Consequently, the same shall be applied in the context of arbitration as well.[113]

Courts have held that Section 9 of the IAA replaced Section 41 of the 1940 Act and the same is *pari materia* to Order XXXIX of the CPC. Therefore, the power of the court under Section 9 of the IAA is to be exercised with the same activity which tampers the grant of any discretionary relief,[114] as the relief of interim injunction is wholly equitable in nature.[115]

3.4.4. *Application of Section 94 of the CPC*

It has been held time and again that the source of the court's power to grant interim measures is under Section 94 of the CPC,[116] which is contained in Part VI of the CPC (Supplemental Proceedings). Part VI of the CPC applies to a separate proceeding in an original action in which the court, where the action is pending, is called upon to exercise its jurisdiction in the interest of justice.[117] Therefore, Section 94 of the CPC provides that '*in order to prevent the ends of justice from being defeated, the court may, if it is so prescribed, exercise powers for granting interim measures*'. For each power provided under Section 94 of the CPC, there are corresponding Orders and Rules for

113. OP Malhotra & Indu Malhotra, *The Law and Practice of Arbitration and Conciliation* 381 (2006); *See*, Sarthak, *supra* n. 21, at 186.
114. *Reliance Infocom Ltd. v. Bharat Sanchar Nigam Ltd.* 2005 SCC OnLine Del 156.
115. *Gujarat Bottling Ltd. Co. v. Coca Cola Co.* (1995) 5 SCC 545; *Reliance Infocom Ltd. v. Bharat Sanchar Nigam Ltd.* 2005 SCC OnLine Del 156.
116. Indian Code of Civil Procedure, 1908, S. 94: '*Supplemental Proceedings – In order to prevent the ends of justice from being defeated the Court may, if it is so prescribed:*
    (a) issue a warrant to arrest the defendant and bring him before the Court to show cause why he should not give security for his appearance, and if he fails to comply with any order for security commit him to the civil prison;
    (b) direct the defendant to furnish security to produce any property belonging to him and to place the same at the disposal of the Court or order the attachment of any property;
    (c) grant a temporary injunction and in case of disobedience commit the person guilty thereof to the civil prison and order that his property be attached and sold;
    (d) appoint a receiver of any property and enforce the performance of his duties by attaching and selling his property;
    (e) make such *other interlocutory orders as may appear to the Court to be just and convenient.*'
117. *Vareed Jacob v. Sosamma Geevarghese* (2004) 6 SCC 378, ¶66.

exercise of the said power, which provide the standard and the procedure for implementation.

The true import of the phrase '*if it is so prescribed*' under Section 94 of the CPC is that the power to grant a temporary injunction exists under Section 94 of the CPC only *if it is so prescribed* by the CPC,[118] i.e., if there are corresponding rules provided under the CPC for the exercise of such power. The most frequent reference to the power to grant interim measures is made under Order XXXIX Rule 1 and Rule 2 of the CPC to grant an injunction. This reference does not mean that the court has two powers to grant a temporary injunction, i.e., under Section 94(c) of the CPC and under Order XXXIX Rule 1 and Rule 2 of the CPC. It means that the power is contained in Section 94 of the CPC but has to be exercised in accordance with Order XXXIX Rule 1 or 2.

3.4.5. *Types of Interim Measures under the CPC*

The CPC provides for several types of interim orders such as security for costs (Order XXV of the CPC), Commissions (Order XXVI of the CPC), Arrest Before Judgments (Order XXXVIII Rules 1-4 of the CPC), Attachment Before Judgment (Order XXXVIII Rules 5-13 of the CPC), Temporary Injunctions and Interlocutory Order (Order XXXIX of the CPC), and Appointment of Receiver (Order XL of the CPC). For ease of reference, it is necessary to list out the powers under section 94 of the CPC to grant interim measures and the corresponding Sections, Orders and Rules (Table 3.1):

Table 3.1 Interim Measures under the CPC, 1908

Sl. No.	*Powers under Section 94*	*Corresponding Section, Order and Rule under the CPC*
1.	(a) issue a warrant to arrest the defendant and bring him before the court to show cause why he should not give security for his appearance, and if he fails to comply with any order for security commit him to the civil prison;	Order XXXVIII Rules 1-4, Section 136, Section 145, Order XLIII Rule 1(q).
2.	(b) direct the defendant to furnish security to produce any property belonging to him and to place the same at the disposal of the court or order the attachment of any property;	Order XXXVIII Rules 5-12, Order XXXIX Rule 7, Section 136, Section 145, Order XLIII Rule 1(q)
3.	(c) grant a temporary injunction and in case of disobedience commit the person guilty thereof to the civil prison and order that his property be attached and sold;	Order XXXIX Rules 1-5, Order XLIII Rule 1(r)
4.	(d) appoint a receiver of any property and enforce the performance of his duties by attaching and selling his property;	Order XL Rules 1-5. Section 51(d), Order XLIII Rule 1(s)

118. *Jagjit Singh Khanna v. Dr. Rakhal Das Mullick* AIR 1998 Cal 95.

Sl. No.	*Powers under Section 94*	*Corresponding Section, Order and Rule under the CPC*
5.	(e) make such other interlocutory orders as may appear to the court to be just and convenient.	Order XXXIX Rules 6-10

Source: Indian Code of Civil Procedure, 1908.

Alternatively, the court also has the power to grant an injunction under Section 151 of the CPC. In that case, the court does not grant the injunction under any of the powers conferred by the CPC directly, but its inherent power as a court of law to do justice read with other provisions.

3.4.6. Inherent Power of the Court

Section 151 of the CPC dealing with the inherent power of the court is contained in Part XI (Miscellaneous) of the CPC. The title of Section 151 of the CPC states 'Saving of inherent powers of the Court' and the provision states that '*Nothing in this Code shall be deemed to limit or otherwise affect the inherent power of the Court to make such orders as may be necessary for the ends of justice or to prevent abuse of the process of the Court.*' Therefore, the court can invoke Section 151 of the CPC to grant interim measures as well.

However, it is pertinent to note that Section 151 of the CPC is a residuary provision. The phrase '*if it is so prescribed*' in Section 94 of the CPC has been held to mean that Section 94 of the CPC lists the circumstances in which the court can exercise or grant a particular relief. Ordinarily, the court is not supposed to use its inherent power to make necessary order in the interest of justice, but the court has to see whether the circumstances of the case fall under the ambit of the prescribed rules.[119] The power under Section 151 of the CPC can only be applied if there is no express provision pertaining to the circumstances at hand.[120]

A jurisdiction expressly conferred by a statute and an inherent power, subject to just exceptions must be treated differently.[121] Therefore, the import of the words '*if it is so prescribed*' is that ordinarily, the court is not to use its inherent powers, and the Rules under Order XXXIX of the CPC should be adhered to when the circumstances contained therein exist.[122] It is only in cases where the nature of the interim relief is such that it is not covered by the Rules under Order XXXIX, or any other Rule under the CPC,[123] that the court should resort to the inherent powers under Section 151 of the CPC.[124]

119. *Manohar Lal Chopra v. Rai Bahadur Rao Raja Seth Hiralal* AIR 1962 SC 527.
120. *Vareed Jacob v. Sosamma Geevarghese* (2004) 6 SCC 378, ¶8.
121. *Ibid.*, ¶66.
122. *Manohar Lal Chopra v. Rai Bahadur Rao Raja Seth Hiralal* AIR 1962 SC 527.
123. *Vareed Jacob v. Sosamma Geevarghese* (2004) 6 SCC 378; *Bharat Aluminum v. Kaiser Aluminum Technical Services Inc.* (2012) 9 SCC 552.
124. *Manohar Lal Chopra v. Rai Bahadur Rao Raja Seth Hiralal* AIR 1962 SC 527.

3.4.7. Applicability of the CPC and Relief Act to Section 9 of the IAA

In the landmark judgment of *Adhunik Steels Ltd. v. Orissa Manganese and Mineral (P) Ltd.*[125] *(Adhunik)*, the applicant, i.e., *Adhunik Steels*, argued that the power to grant interim measures of protection under Section 9 of the IAA was independent of Section 94 read with Order XXXIX of the CPC and that the power was also not trammelled by the Relief Act. The crux of the argument, and rightly so, was that the power under Section 9 of the IAA is not controlled, or limited by any other law. Hence, it is autonomous.

The opposing arguments were that in the absence of any criteria, or conditions being mentioned for grant of such interim protection, the CPC and the Relief Act cannot be excluded as the court is to exercise the jurisdiction vested in it as a court to adjudge whether any protective measure is called for. Therefore, the court necessarily has to consider the balance of convenience, and whether a triable issue arises, if not, the establishment of a prima facie case and the other well-known restrictions on the grant of interim orders, i.e., as a contract of personal service cannot be enforced and that no injunction can be granted as envisaged by the Sections 14 and 41 of the Relief Act.[126]

Furthermore, it was argued that it is difficult to imagine that the legislature intended to make a provision dehors the accepted principles regarding the grant of interim injunctions while enacting Section 9 of the IAA. Reliance was placed on the concluding lines stated in Section 9 of the IAA to argue that the only rationale for including such language was that the normal rules which govern the courts with respect to the grant of interim orders would govern the power under Section 9 of the IAA. Moreover, whenever a special procedure or special set of rules is not provided but a party is given a right to approach an ordinary court, then the ordinary rules followed by that court shall govern the exercise of the power conferred by such special Act.[127]

The court considered the decision of the House of Lords in *Channel Tunnel Group Ltd. v. Balfour Beatty Construction Ltd.*[128] *(Channel Tunnel)* wherein the English court held that injunction is a form of specific relief, i.e., it is an order of a court requiring a party to do, or not to do, certain specified act for a limited period, or without limit of time.[129] In a claim for breach of contract, the remedy against the defendant is either damages or specific relief, and that specific relief is of two kinds, i.e., a decree of specific performance and an injunction.[130]

The Supreme Court held that since the grant of relief by way of injunction is governed by the provisions of the Relief Act and Section 9 of the IAA entitles a party to approach the court for an interim injunction, the provisions of the said Acts have to be mandatorily considered. It went on to draw an analogy from Section 28 of the IAA and

125. *Adhunik Steels Ltd. v. Orissa Manganese and Mineral (P) Ltd* (2007) 7 SCC 125.
126. *Ibid.*, ¶10.
127. *Ibid.*, ¶11.
128. *Channel Tunnel Group Ltd. v. Balfour Beatty Construction Ltd.* [1993] 2 WLR 262. *The case has been approved by the Supreme Court in Sundaram Finance Ltd. v. NEPC India Ltd.* (1999) 2 SCC 479.
129. *Adhunik Steels Ltd. v. Orissa Manganese and Mineral (P) Ltd* (2007) 7 SCC 125, ¶16.
130. *Ibid.*, ¶16.

held that even the arbitral tribunal is required to decide the dispute in accordance with substantive law for the time being in force in India if it is not international commercial arbitration. Therefore, Section 9 of the IAA cannot be read in a manner to keep out the substantive law related to interim relief.

The court categorically held that Section 9 of the IAA is not totally independent of the well-known principles governing the grant of interim measures.[131] Interestingly, the court did not arrive at any conclusion and left it to the arbitral tribunal to decide whether the interim measure should be granted or not.

3.4.8. The Problems with the CPC and Relief Act

This view is misplaced as the grant of interim measures is not governed by substantive law but by procedural law.[132] The reference to the power of court being the same as that in a suit pertains to the enforcement of the orders passed under Section 9 of the IAA and not to the adjudication of the request for an interim measure. If such an interpretation was to be true, then why would parties choose arbitration in the first place? The idea of applying the same procedural law to arbitration even in the context of interim measures is antithetical to the most fundamental notion and intent of the parties to avoid cumbersome court procedures and strict rules.

The analysis of the court is also flawed as it equates injunctions issued in support of arbitral proceedings with injunctions issued in a civil suit, which are in aid of final relief. Interim measures of protection issued to support arbitration are different and the parties are not looking for any other specific relief. The aim is only to stabilise the relationship of parties and not to permit one party to aggravate the dispute till the formation of the arbitral tribunal or when the arbitral tribunal does not have the power or is unable to act effectively.

The reference to the Relief Act means that the parties should also be seeking the interim relief as final relief and therefore, inevitably should be requesting a permanent injunction. However, that is not true for arbitration. Parties may seek any type of measure ranging from preventing harm to the arbitral process, requesting security for costs, to securing the amount in dispute, or preservation of evidence, apart from injunctions. Hence, parties are not strictly looking for specific relief as envisaged under the Relief Act. More importantly, there is no statement of claim containing the final relief prayed for, at the time of entertaining an application for interim relief under Section 9 of the IAA.

This critique is supported by an earlier view of the court in *Firm Ashok Traders v. Gurmukh Das Saluja,*[133] (*Firm Ashok Traders*) where the Supreme Court examined in great detail the nature and purpose of the IAA. The court rightly reasoned that the relief sought for an application under Section 9 of the IAA is neither a suit nor a right arising out of a contract and the court under Section 9 of the IAA is only formulating

131. *Ibid.*, ¶21.
132. Gary Born, *supra* n. 33, at 2638-2639.
133. *Firm Ashok Traders v. Gurmukh Das Saluja* AIR 2004 SC 1433.

interim measures to protect the right under adjudication before the arbitral tribunal from being frustrated.[134]

Unfortunately, in a subsequent judgment, the court in *Arvind Construction Company Pvt. Ltd. v. Kalinga Mining Corporation,*[135] (*Arvind Construction*) distinguished *Firm Ashok Traders* and took the view that the Supreme Court did not finally answer the question of whether the power under Section 9 of the IAA is independent of the Relief Act and whether the restrictions placed by the Relief Act would be applicable for the purposes of an application under Section 9 of the IAA.

It held that the power under Section 9 of the IAA is conferred on the District Court and no special procedure is prescribed by the IAA for the exercise of such power. Resorting to the line of reasoning adopted in *Adhunik,* the court observed that the court shall have the same powers as it has for the purpose of any proceeding before it. Therefore, prima facie, the general rules that govern court proceedings while granting an interim injunction are attracted while dealing with an application under Section 9 of the IAA.[136]

This view was followed by other courts[137] which held that the substantive law relating to injunctions is contained in Section 94 of the CPC read with Sections 36-42 of the Relief Act and the procedural part is contained in Order XXXIX of the CPC.[138] Unfortunately, the reliance on the CPC and the Relief Act even after its amendment in 2019 has been upheld while deciding an application under Section 9 of the IAA.[139]

3.4.9. *Independent Provision*

In contrast to the above view and toeing the line of *Firm Ashok Traders*, the Madhya Pradesh High Court held that the powers under Section 9 of the IAA are wide and the only criteria to be considered while considering an application under Section 9 of the IAA are (a) the existence of an arbitration agreement; and (b) the necessity of taking interim measures. The court held that once these two criteria are satisfied, the court could issue any direction that is deemed appropriate. The court categorically rejected the view that the provisions of the Relief Act are applicable to an application under Section 9 of the IAA as the court does not decide the merits of the case, or the rights of the parties but only the existence of a valid arbitration clause and the necessity of interim measures.[140]

---

134. *Ibid.*, ¶13.
135. *Arvind Construction Company Pvt. Ltd. v. Kalinga Mining Corporation* (2007) 6 SCC 798.
136. *Ibid.*, ¶15.
137. *Samay Singh v. Hindustan Petroleum Corporation Ltd.* 2012 SCC OnLine All 1253, ¶23.
138. *Ironically, the court also held that the substantive power to grant interim measure is as contained in section 9 of the IAA, but it does not lay down the manner and circumstances for the exercise of interim measures; Samay Singh v. Hindustan Petroleum Corporation Ltd.* 2012 SCC OnLine All 1253, ¶23.
139. *Provident Multi-Trading Pvt. Ltd. v. Maharashtra Maritime Board, Home Department* MANU/MH/1364/2019, ¶¶22, 23.
140. *NEPA Ltd. v. Manoj Kumar Agarwal,* AIR 1999 MP 57. *It should be noted that this view was categorically rejected in Adhunik Steels Ltd. v. Orissa Manganese and Mineral (P) Ltd.* (2007) 7 SCC 125, ¶17.

Similarly, in a well-reasoned decision, a single judge of the Bombay High Court[141] took the view that Section 9 of the IAA was a self-operative provision and the provisions of the CPC were not applicable. By explicitly providing for clauses (i) to (ii) in Section 9 of the IAA, the legislative intent was to make the IAA a self-operative code with respect to arbitration and conciliation. If the intention was to apply the provisions of the CPC to the IAA, then there was no reason for the legislature to specifically enact Section 9 of the IAA for interim measures. All the said powers would have been available in the different orders in the schedule to the CPC.[142]

Referring to the power of preservation and interim custody, the court held that the power under Order XXXIX Rule 7 is also provided in Section 9(ii)(c) of the IAA.[143] The court made similar references to the appointment of a receiver under Section 9(ii)(d) of the IAA and held that the substantive provisions for granting interim relief as provided in the CPC could not, therefore, be read in Section 9 of the IAA. There are independent provisions incorporated in the IAA itself. The exercise of the power under the IAA must be construed bearing in mind the objective of the IAA and the need to dispose of the matter as expeditiously and not hedged in, by the provisions of the CPC.

Therefore, the court held that the powers under Section 9 of the IAA could not be fettered by reading into it the requirements of granting interim relief which are not provided.[144] The powers of the court under Section 9 of the IAA were not limited by the provisions of the CPC. For example, the power under Section 9(ii)(b) of the IAA is very wide and has to be guided by the paramount consideration that the party having adjudicated a claim in its favour, is in a position to get the fruits of such adjudication on executing the award.[145] The CPC was made applicable to all proceedings before the court under Section 41 of the 1940 Act. However, there is no such provision under the IAA.[146] The source of the power to issue interim relief is contained in Section 9 of the IAA and only the procedural rules of the CPC are applicable for implementation.[147]

Distinguishing the view that in the absence of a specific exclusion of the CPC, its provisions will continue to govern matters contained in the IAA,[148] the court rightly noted that it could not be that the CPC would apply, or would have to be read into as it is when used with relation to the IAA.[149] The procedural aspects are provided in the CPC and the IAA is silent about them. Therefore, where the court exercises its substantive power under Section 9 of the IAA, the court only has to examine whether such order deserves to be passed for justice to the cause. The fetters of the CPC are to be excluded when exercising the power under Section 9 of the IAA and the court is

141. *Pushpa P. Mulchandani v. Admiral Radha Krishin Tahilani* 2000 (4) Mh. LJ. 819.
142. *Ibid.*
143. *Delta Constructions Systems Ltd., Hyderabad v. Narmada Cement Company Ltd.* 2002 (2) Arb. LR 47 (Bom).
144. *Distinguishing the view* in *Global Company v. National Fertilizers Ltd.* 1998 SCC OnLine Del 387.
145. *National Shipping Company of Saudi Arabia v. Sentrans Industries Ltd.* AIR 2004 Bom 136.
146. *Ibid.*, ¶¶ 4-5.
147. *The East India Hotels Ltd. v. Jyoti (P) Ltd.* 1996 (38) DRJ (DB); *Delta Constructions Systems Ltd., Hyderabad v. Narmada Cement Company Ltd.* 2002 (2) Arb. LR 47 (Bom).
148. *Indian Telephone Industries v. Siemens Public Communication* (2002) 5 SCC 510.
149. *National Shipping Company of Saudi Arabia v. Sentrans Industries Ltd.* AIR 2004 Bom 136, ¶10.

supposed to be guided only by equitable considerations in the facts and circumstances of each case.[150]

3.4.10. *Hybrid Approach*

A third approach adopted by the courts is that while the CPC applies to proceedings under Section 9 of the IAA, the CPC cannot be read into Section 9 of the IAA as it is.[151] The interest of the party seeking the relief has to be considered and the relief cannot be restricted by the provisions of the CPC.[152] The court can go beyond the CPC if need be to grant interim relief.[153] Thus, the procedural aspects provided under the CPC are a guiding factor for the exercise of power under Section 9 of the IAA but cannot be restricted by its provision.[154]

A balance needs to be struck between the underlying principles which govern the exercise of an analogous power in the CPC and the need to promote the efficacy of arbitration.[155] The court has the power to mould the interim relief based on subjective consideration of the facts and the interim relief sought to secure the ends of justice and also, preserve the sanctity of the arbitral process.[156]

3.5. Adopting Article 17J of the Model Law in India

The second approach of the courts was in complete harmony with the objective of Article 17J of the Model Law. Reading Section 9 of the IAA as an independent provision dehors the CPC would ensure its autonomous application, keeping in mind the specific features of international arbitration. Unfortunately, though correct, the line of cases adopting the second approach is the minority view and the applicability of the CPC and the Relief Act to proceedings under Section 9 of the IAA is now settled law by the decision of the Supreme Court in *Adhunik Steels* and *Arvind Construction*.

Thus, there is a need to amend Section 9 of the IAA and bring it in line with the autonomous intent behind Article 17J of the Model Law. As discussed above, different jurisdictions incorporate Article 17J of the Model Law differently into their domestic legislation. Given the existing jurisprudence on taking a resort to CPC and the Relief Act, the approach adopted by New Zealand would clarify that the power is to be drawn with reference to the power of the arbitral tribunal and not the CPC. Furthermore,

150. *Ibid.*
151. *Contrary view was taken in Om Sakthi Renergies Limited v. Megatech Control Limited* (2006) 2 Arb. LR 186.
152. *C.V. Rao v. Strategic Port Investments KPC Ltd.* 2014 SCC OnLine Del 4441; *Gatx India Pvt. Ltd. v. Arshiya Rail Infrastructure Ltd.* 216 (2015) D.L.T. 20.
153. *National Shipping Company of Saudi Arabia v. Sentrans Industries Ltd.* AIR 2004 Bom 136, ¶25; *Deccan Chronicle Holdings v. L & T Finance* 2013 SCC OnLine Bom 1005.
154. *Neeru Jain v. Jasmine Buildmart Private Ltd.* 2019 SCC OnLine Del 10731, ¶24; *Indian Telephone Industres v. Siemens Public Communication* (2002) 5 SCC 510; *Goel Associates v. Jivan Bima Rashtriya Avas Samiti Ltd.* 2004 3 RAJ 658.
155. *Nimbus Communications Limited v. Board of Control for Cricket in India* 2012 SCC OnLine 287; *Gatx India Pvt. Ltd. v. Arshiya Rail Infrastructure Ltd.* 216 (2015) D.L.T. 20.
156. *Tata Capital Financial Services Ltd. v. Unity Infraprojects Ltd.* 2015 SCC OnLine Bom 3597.

adopting the approach in New Zealand would also incorporate reference to the standards to be adopted by the court when considering an application under Section 9 of the IAA. It would also remove any ambiguities between the power of the court and that of the tribunal.

4. SCOPE OF THE COURT'S POWER

Courts in India are often accused of being extremely slow and intervening at every stage of the arbitral process.[157] By applying the CPC to a request for interim measures under Section 9 of the IAA, courts have imported domestic law standards and effectively held mini-trials before deciding the request for interim measures.[158] They have blurred the lines between court assistance and court intervention, ignoring the 'specific features of international arbitration'. By heavily emulating Section 44(2) of the English Arbitration Act, India has attempted to sail in two boats. Section 9 of the IAA neither adopts the Model Law approach nor adopts the other subsections of Section 44 of the English Arbitration Act, which limit court intervention,[159] leaving a considerable void concerning the exercise of the power.

Some courts have reiterated that the purpose of Section 9 of the IAA is to provide an efficacious, preservatory, interim, conservatory, and emergency relief necessary for protecting a subject matter of arbitrations till the conclusion of proceedings.[160] The aim is to protect the plaintiff against such injury, which is violative of his right and which cannot be adequately compensated in damages that may be recoverable later in the award.[161] Therefore, the order passed under Section 9 of the IAA should be distinguished from all-time or permanent protection.[162]

The power under Section 9 of the IAA should be exercised sparingly and cautiously, keeping in mind that the objective of the IAA is to create an alternative dispute resolution mechanism and interference of the court is not required at every stage.[163] Hence, the court must act with alacrity and only with a view to supporting the arbitration[164] and promoting the efficacy of arbitration as a mechanism for dispute

157. Krishna Sarma, *supra* n. 43.
158. *Discussed in detail under standards for grant of interim measures before arbitration proceedings.*
159. English Arbitration Act, 1996, S. 44(3)-44(7), *have not been adopted.*
160. *Bharat Aluminum v. Kaiser Aluminum Technical Services Inc.* (2012) 9 SCC 552, ¶155.
161. *Gujarat Bottling Ltd. Co. v. Coca Cola Co.* (1995) 5 SCC 545, ¶46; *Country Development and Management Services Pvt. Ltd. v. Brookside Resorts Pvt. Ltd.* 2006 (4) AD 38 (Del).
162. *Firm Ashok Traders v. Gurmukh Das Saluja* AIR 2004 SC 1433, ¶17.
163. *Sanrachna (India) Inc. v. AB Hotels Ltd.* 2006 (128) DLT 694, ¶4.
164. *CREF Finance Ltd. v. Puri Constructions Ltd.* 2000 (55) DRJ 750, ¶15; *Sea Transport Contractors Ltd. v. Indian Farmers Fertilizers Co-operative Ltd.* 2006 (91) DRJ 83, ¶11; *National Shipping Company of Saudi Arabia v. Sentrans Industries Ltd.* AIR 2004 Bom 136; *Reliance Infocom Ltd. v. Bharat Sanchar Nigam Ltd.* 2005 SCC OnLine Del 156, ¶10; *Kumaradas v. Indian Medical Practitioner's Cooperative Pharmacy & Stores Ltd.*, [2007] (4) RAJ 272.

resolution.[165] It must interfere in exceptional circumstances only[166] since the provisions of the IAA were designed to reduce court interference[167] in accordance with the Model Law. However, all courts have not followed this approach and requests for interim measures have been pending for months and years.[168] Courts have reviewed the merits of the dispute before granting interim measures, albeit with caveats that the view of the court should not influence the arbitral tribunal.[169]

4.1. The Need for a Guiding Provision

In order to ensure that the role of the court under Section 9 of the IAA is one of assistance and not of intervention the language contained in Article 17J of the Model Law should be incorporated in Section 9 of the IAA to provide such guidance. Furthermore, since the phrase 'specific features of international arbitration' mentioned in Article 17J of the Model Law is vague and given the propensity of Indian courts to view a request under Section 9 of the IAA like any other request for interim measures under the CPC, it is suggested that it should be clarified that the scope of the power under Section 9 of the IAA is only to support the arbitral process. Such statutory clarification has been made in Mauritius[170] and would serve as a reminder to courts not to review the merits of the case at the time of considering a request for interim measures. It will also reiterate the primary jurisdiction of the arbitral tribunal.

Therefore Section 9 should provide that the power is to be exercised '*to support the arbitral process and in consideration of the specific features of international arbitration*'. However, that alone will not ensure minimal court intervention. Several other concerns which arise from the actual exercise of the power under Section 9 of the IAA need to be addressed.

Under Section 9 of the IAA, interim measures by courts are contemplated at three stages, i.e., (1) before the commencement of arbitration proceedings; (2) during arbitration proceedings; and (3) after passing of the award but before its enforcement. Hence, each of the stages requires discussion. While the exercise of the power of the

165. *Nimbus Communications Limited v. Board of Control for Cricket in India* 2012 SCC OnLine 287, ¶24.
166. *Deepak Mitra v. District Judge* 1999 SCC OnLine All 609, ¶13.
167. *Bhatia International v. Bulk Trading S.A. and Anr.* (2002) 4 SCC 105, ¶29; *Deccan Asian Infrastructure (Mauritius) Inc. v. BPL Communications Ltd.* (2005) (2) Arb LR 450 (Kar), ¶15.
168. *Ramrameshwari Devi v. Nirmala Devi* (2011) 8 SCC 249; *See generally:* Rishab Gupta & Anokan Ghosh, *Choice Between Interim Relief from Indian Courts and Emergency Arbitrator* (10 May 2017), available at:http://arbitrationblog.kluwerarbitration.com/2017/05/10/choice-between-interim-relief-from-indian-courts-and-emergency-arbitrator/; *Excerpts from the International Seminar on Transnational Litigation organised by Nirma University, India: Session 5: The Fine Line Between Court Assistance and Court Intervention in International Commercial Arbitration with speakers for the panel: Vyapak Desai, Tejas Karia, Rajendra Barot, Nirma University, 23-24 March, 2019. The author was a panellist at the seminar for Session 4 and attended Session 5.*
169. *Ramrameshwari Devi v. Nirmala Devi* (2011) 8 SCC 249; Sharad Bansal, *The Standard of Review of Interim Orders of an Arbitral Tribunal Seated in India: A Significant Step Towards Certainty,* (21 November 2018), available at: http://arbitrationblog.kluwerarbitration.com/2018/11/21/the-standard-of-review-of-interim-orders-of-an-arbitral-tribunal-seated-in-india-a-significant-step-towards-certainty/.
170. Mauritius International Arbitration Act, 2008, S. 2(1).

court to grant interim measures before the commencement of arbitration proceedings is discussed in this chapter, the exercise of the power during arbitration proceedings and after passing of the award but before enforcement is dealt with in Chapter 4.

4.2. Before the Commencement of Arbitration Proceedings

Though the phrase '*before or during arbitral proceedings*' in Section 9(1) of the IAA is self-explanatory, the initial approach by the court was that in the presence of an arbitration clause, interim relief could only be sought from the arbitral tribunal. Since no substantial relief such as the appointment of arbitrator or reference to arbitration has been claimed, the prayer for interim relief cannot be entertained.[171]

The general view was that the proceedings should be initiated in a court in relation to arbitration proceedings before an injunction can be granted by the court.[172] An application under Section 9 of the IAA was not maintainable on the ground that no arbitration proceeding was pending.[173] The court confused the requirement of a suit to be pending before granting interim relief without understanding that a suit for temporary relief *simpliciter* was not maintainable unless a permanent relief was prayed for.[174]

These views subsequently changed.[175] Over time, the courts understood the necessity of interim measures before the formation of the arbitral tribunal, i.e., the intervening period when a request for a reference to arbitration is conveyed by a party under Section 21 of the IAA and the actual formation of the arbitral tribunal.[176]

In *Firm Ashok Traders*,[177] the Supreme Court clarified that the word 'before' means *inter alia 'ahead of; in presence or sight of; under the consideration or cognizance of'*, i.e., the party invoking Section 9 of the IAA should be able to satisfy the court that the arbitration proceedings are contemplated or manifestly intended and that they are positively going to commence within a reasonable time. The order passed should fall within the meaning of the expression 'interim measure of protection' and should be distinguished from an all-time or permanent protection.

171. *Ashok Chawla v. Rakesh Gupta* 1996 (2) Arb. LR 255.
172. *Santram & Co. v. State of Rajasthan* (1997) 1 SCC 147. *It is pertinent to note that this view was extracted from Kamaluddin Ansari & Co. v. Union of India* (1983) 4 SCC 417 *and pertains to* Indian Arbitration Act, 1940, S. 41(b).
173. *Anand David Saidanha v. K. Rathnaraj Ballal*, ILR 1997 Kar 3223.
174. *Ramesh Akre v. Mangalabai Prahlad Akre* AIR 2002 Bom 487 (491), ¶21.
175. *Such as Sundaram Finance Ltd. v. NEPC India Ltd.* (1999) 2 SCC 479; *Adhunik Steels Ltd. v. Orissa Manganese and Mineral (P) Ltd* (2007) 7 SCC 125; *Firm Ashok Traders v. Gurmukh Das Saluja* AIR 2004 SC 1433.
176. *National Building Construction Corpn Ltd. v. IRCON International Ltd.* 1998(1) RAJ 540 (Del), ¶12; *Vijay Mohan v. Real Blue International Pvt. Ltd.* 2019 SCC OnLine Mad 16813, ¶60 *where the Court held that there is no embargo or prohibition under the SIAC Rules to approach the Court before constitution of the arbitral tribunal.*
177. *Firm Ashok Traders v. Gurmukh Das Saluja* AIR 2004 SC 1433.

4.3. Prerequisites for Approaching the Court

Even though the power under Section 9 of the IAA is contemplated at every stage of arbitration, it should be noted that the power under Section 9 of the IAA is not unbridled. The power is subject to limitations, i.e., (a) that the power can be exercised by the court to the same extent and in the same manner as it could for the purpose of any proceeding before it; and (b) the power to grant interim measures should not militate against any power which might be vested in an arbitral tribunal.[178] Moreover, the power under Section 9 of the IAA can only be exercised in support of arbitration and not otherwise. Therefore, certain prerequisites have to be satisfied before the power under Section 9 of the IAA can be invoked.

In an ordinary trial or a civil suit, there needs to be a pending proceeding in which an application is usually filed seeking interim relief till the disposal of the suit. An interim measure in this scenario, therefore, operates until the disposal of the suit, either on merit or dismissal of the suit for default, and has no independent existence.[179]

However, the power under Section 9 of the IAA is different as it does not require the existence of a suit or a pending proceeding and the parties are free to approach the court at any time as long as arbitration proceedings are contemplated by the parties.[180] Therefore, the following criteria need to be met before invoking Section 9(1) of the IAA:[181]

(a) there should be a prima facie valid arbitration agreement which is a *sine qua non*;[182]
(b) the party requesting an interim measure should be party to the arbitration agreement;
(c) there should be a dispute which has arisen with respect to the subject matter of the arbitration agreement;[183]
(d) there should be a manifest intention to take recourse to arbitration proceedings;[184]

178. *Vijay Transport v. A.P. State C.S. Corporation Ltd.* AIR 1983 AP 172; *Parmali Wallace Ltd. v. Union of India*, (1983) 2 Arb LR 487 (Del), ¶18, *wherein no interim relief was granted because neither of the parties referred their dispute to the arbitration.*
179. *Ramesh Akre v. Mangalabai Prahlad Akre* AIR 2002 Bom 487 (491), ¶21.
180. *Firm Ashok Traders v. Gurmukh Das Saluja* AIR 2004 SC 1433.
181. *Jammu Forest Company v. State of J&K* AIR 1968 J&K 86; *Ranjit Chandra v. Union of India* AIR 1963 Cal 594, ¶10.
182. *Rajkumar v. Union of India* 2009 (2) Arb. LR 631 (DB), ¶4 *affirmed in Nasir Husain Films Pvt. Ltd. v. Saregama India Pvt. Ltd.* 2007 SCC OnLine Bom 439; *Rickmers Verwaltung Gmbh v. Indian Oil Corporation Ltd.* (1991) 1 SCC 1; *L.C. Sharma v. P.C. Sharma* 2009 (4) Arb. LR 42 (Del); *Jain Housing and Constructions Ltd. v. V. Ramaiah*, 2009 (4) Arb. LR 107 (Mad) (DB); *Orissa Manganese and Minerals Ltd. v. Synergy Ispat Pvt. Ltd.* 2013 (2) Arb. LR 309 (Cal) (DB), ¶16.
183. *Bimal Ghosh v. Kalpana Majumdar* 2008(1) Arb. LR. 68 (Cal) (DB), ¶11; Ali Yesilirmak, *supra* n. 30, at 6.
184. *Rajkumar v. Union of India* 2009 (2) Arb. LR 631 (DB); *Rajiv Vyas v. Johnwin Manavalan* 2009 (3) Arb. LR 397 (Bom).

(e) the subject matter of arbitration comes within the original civil jurisdiction, both pecuniary and territorial; and
(f) the arbitration agreement should be sufficiently stamped.[185]

4.3.1. Prima Facie Valid Arbitration Agreement

The first prerequisite for seeking interim measures from the court is a valid arbitration agreement.[186] Without there being a clear consent to arbitrate the dispute, parties cannot be permitted to invoke a remedy applicable only to a consent-based dispute resolution mechanism. The court has to be fully satisfied that the IAA applies, otherwise it would lead to a reckless exercise of power which would, in turn, lead to an incalculable and unfortunate injustice.[187]

It is pertinent to mention that if a party invokes the jurisdiction of the court under section 9 of the IAA, then it is implicit that it accepts that there is a final and binding arbitration agreement in existence and cannot challenge the same before the arbitral tribunal.[188] Therefore, the court should consider, first, whether there exists an arbitration agreement[189] and second, whether the applicant intends to take the dispute to arbitration. Only after such satisfaction does the court have jurisdiction to grant an interim measure under Section 9 of the IAA.[190] However, the view of the courts has not been consistent on this issue.

Some courts leave the issue of the validity of the arbitration agreement to be determined by the arbitral tribunal,[191] without a trial.[192] All such challenges have to be made before the arbitral tribunal and the remedy of the aggrieved party is only to

185. *Garware-Wall Ropes Ltd. v. Coastal Marine Constructions & Engineering Ltd.* (2019) 9 SCC 209; *SMS Tea Estates (P) Ltd. v. Chandmari Tea Co. (P) Ltd.* (2011) 14 SCC 66; *Dharmaratnakara Rai Bahadur Arcot Narainswamy Mudaliar Chattram & Other Charities and Others v. Bhaskar Raju & Brothers and Ors.* 2020 SCC OnLine SC 183.
186. *Indian Golf Union v. West Bengal Golf Society* 2020 SCC OnLine Cal 381, ¶56; *Oberoi Constructions Pvt. Ltd. v. Worli Shivshahi Co-op. Housing Society* 2008 (1) Arb. LR 106 (Bom), ¶29; *Rajesh Construction Co. Ltd. v. Ravilal Nanji Dedhia* 2009 (1) Arb. LR 583 (Bom) (DB), ¶21; *Ravinder Singh Ahluwalia v. Kuljinder Singh Ahluwalia* 2009 (4) Arb. LR 130 (Bom), ¶35; *Himalayan Heli Adventures Pvt. Ltd. v. Utair India Pvt. Ltd. & Ors.* 2019 SCC OnLine Del 8843, ¶25; *N. Srinivasa v. Kuttukaran Machine Tools Ltd.* 2009 (1) Arb. LR 499 (SC), ¶15.
187. *Oval Investment Pvt. Ltd. v. India bulls Financial Services Ltd.* 2009 (4) Arb. LR 282 (Del) (DB), ¶11.
188. *Sundaram Finance Ltd. v. NEPC India Ltd.* (1999) 2 SCC 479, ¶19; *GE Capital Transportation Financial Services Ltd. v. Amritajit Mitra & Ors.* 2009 (3) Arb. LR 51 (Cal) (DB), ¶24.
189. *In Indian Gold Union v. West Bengal Gold Society* 2020 SCC OnLine Cal 381, ¶55, *the Court held that the doctrine of severability cannot save an arbitration clause in a contract which has been substituted by a new contract.*
190. Wadhwa, *supra* n. 46, at 1, 2.
191. *S. Raminder Singh v. NCT of Delhi* 2003 (66) DRJ 239, ¶12 *wherein the court held that under what circumstances the documents were executed by authorized or unauthorized person or by misrepresentation or fraud cannot be looked at under Section 9 as long as there exists an arbitration agreement. See, Spectrum Estates Pvt. Ltd. v. Charkop Gagan Vihar CHS Ltd.* 2011 (1) Arb. LR 170 (Bom); *National Highways Authority of India v. Bel-acc Joint Venture* 2009 (4) Arb. LR 287 (Del), ¶9.
192. *Dynasty Stockholdings Pvt. Ltd. & Anr. v. Silva Ltd. & Ors.* 2011 (1) Arb. LR 322 (Mad).

challenge the award under Section 34 of the IAA.[193] However, some courts have held that it is imperative to determine that a valid arbitration agreement exists;[194] such a finding would be final and not prima facie on the facts of the case.[195]

It is settled law that a finding given by a court under section 9 of the IAA is not final and binding on the arbitral tribunal, and the principles of res judicata[196] and estoppel do not apply to such circumstances.[197] Moreover, the examination of the validity of an arbitration agreement cannot amount to a full trial.[198] After the 2015 Amendment, such a position is now statutorily affirmed with the use of the phrase '*refer the parties to arbitration unless it finds that prima facie no valid arbitration agreement exists*' in Section 8(1) of the IAA. This view is also recognised under Section 45 of the IAA after the 2019 Amendment with respect to foreign awards. Thus, the scope of an inquiry into the validity of the arbitration agreement can only be on a prima facie basis.[199]

4.3.2. Arbitrability

Adding to the thresholds to be met before invoking the power under Section 9 of the IAA, a Division Bench of the Delhi High Court considered the arbitrability of the dispute while considering the application seeking interim relief. It is observed that simply because there is a dispute between the parties, it cannot mean that the dispute will fall within the subject matter of the arbitration clause.[200] Therefore, an application under Section 9 of the IAA is not maintainable if the reference is beyond the scope of the arbitration agreement.[201] Similarly, some courts have considered the question of arbitrability of intellectual property disputes[202] and arbitrability in view of other statutes providing for a parallel remedy[203] or special statutes, such as the Presidency Small Cause Court Act, 1882.[204]

193. *Union of India v. Amarlal Wadhwani* 2012 (1) Arb. LR 268 (MP), ¶7.
194. *S.B.P. & Co. v. Patel Engineering Ltd.* (2005) 6 SCC 28, ¶18.
195. *Oberoi Constructions Pvt. Ltd. v. Worli Shivshahi Co-op. Housing Society* 2008 (1) Arb. LR 106 (Bom), ¶11.
196. *Bagchand v. Administrator, Municipal Corpn Indore* AIR 2005 MP 159 (165); *Arjun Singh v. Mohinder Kumar* AIR 1964 SC 1993.
197. *Perma Container (UK) Line Ltd. v. Perma Container Line (India) Pvt. Ltd.* 2010 (2) Arb. LR 133 (Bom), ¶39.
198. *Ashok Kumar v. SBI Officers Association (Delhi Circle)* 2013 (3) Arb. LR 246 (Del). *Also see, Vidya Drolia v. Durga Trading Corpn.* (2021) 2 SCC 1.
199. *Lindsay International Private Limited v. Laxmi Niwas Mittal* 2020 SCC OnLine Cal 1658, ¶27.
200. *Ritika Jhanji v. Raghbir Singh Sehgal* 2009 (2) Arb. LR 488 (Del) (DB), ¶6. *It must be pointed out that there was also a contention raised that two parties arrayed as respondents were not signatories to the agreement and hence there was no arbitration agreement between the parties.*
201. *Centre for Development of Telematics v. Ansal Properties and Infrastructure Ltd.* 2009 (1) Arb. LR 457 (Del) (DB), ¶41; *Tata Capital Finances Services Ltd. v. Deccan Chronicle Holdings Ltd. & Anr.* 2013 (2) Arb. LR 181 (Bom).
202. *Qdseatoman Designs (P) Ltd. v. Lifestyle Equities CV* 2017 SCC OnLine Mad 25864, ¶¶ 36, 37, and 55; *Golden Tobacco Limited v. Golden Tobie Private Limited* 2021 SCC OnLine Del 4506.
203. *The court held that the remedy under Section 9 and Section 17 of the IAA is not barred due to parallel proceedings in the context of SARFAESI proceedings. See, Sarthak Builder Pvt. Ltd. v. Orissa Rural Development Corp. Ltd.* 2014 SCC OnLine Ori 75; *HDFC Bank Ltd. v. Satpal Singh*

Considering arbitrability in detail, akin to a determination at trial, at the stage of interim relief amounts to unnecessary court intervention in complete violation of the mandate of Section 5 of the IAA, Article 5 of the Model Law and the objectives of the IAA which seek to minimise court intervention. The court should restrict itself to a 'bird's-eye view' of the matter or prima facie view as provided in Sections 8 and 45 of the IAA, and as long as there is a valid arbitration agreement invoked by a party to the arbitration agreement, the court should proceed to consider the merits of the interim application.[205] This position of law now stands clarified by the judgment in *Vidya Drolia v. Durga Trading Corp.*[206] where the Supreme Court of India has mandated that courts should only take a prima facie view on the issue of arbitrability before proceeding with any relief in arbitration matters.[207]

4.3.3. Signatories to the Arbitration Agreement

Equally essential and connected to the question of the validity of the arbitration agreement is whether the party applying for an interim measure is a signatory to the arbitration agreement. The power under Section 9 of the IAA cannot be exercised by everyone and only parties to the arbitration agreement should be permitted to invoke Section 9 of the IAA. A third party, who is not a signatory to the arbitration agreement, is not entitled to invoke the power under Section 9 of the IAA.[208]

4.3.4. 'Proposed Party'

For instance, Section 44(3) of the English Arbitration Act and the Singapore Arbitration Act[209] permit a 'proposed party to the arbitral proceedings' to seek interim relief in case

Bakshi 2012 SCC OnLine Del 4815; *Pradeep Kumar Gupta v. State of U.P.* AIR 2010 All 3; *Deccan Chronicle Holdings Ltd. v. Union of India* AIR 2014 AP 78; *M.D. Frozen Foods Exports Pvt. Ltd. v. Hero Fincorp Ltd.* AIR 2017 SC 4481. *For a discussion on arbitrability, public policy exception with respect to special statutes; See generally,* Ajar Rab, *Defining the Contours of The Public Policy Exception: A New Test for Arbitrability in India,* 7 (2) Ind. J. Arb. L. 161-180 (2019). *The said paper was relied upon by the Supreme Court of India in Vidya Drolia v. Durga Trading Corpn.* (2021) 2 SCC 1, *while enunciating the principles to be considered by courts while determining whether a dispute is arbitrable.*

204. *ING Vysya Bank Ltd. v. Modern India Ltd.* 2008 (1) Arb. LR 561 (Bom), ¶23; *Relying on Natraj Studios Pvt. Ltd. v. Navrang Studios* (1981) 1 SCC 523; *Carona Ltd. v. Sumangal Holding*, 2007 (4) Bom. CR 265, ¶11; *Siemens Ltd. v. Captech Online Pvt. Ltd.* Arbitration Petition No. 99 of 2004, ¶36; *BNP Paribas Securities India Pvt. Ltd. v. Cable Corporation of India Ltd.* 2012 (3) Arb. LR 55 (Bom), ¶41.
205. *See,* Indian Arbitration Act, 1996, ss 8(1) & 45.
206. *Vidya Drolia v. Durga Trading Corpn.* (2021) 2 SCC 1.
207. *Ibid.*
208. *K.K. Modi Investment and Financial Services Pvt. Ltd. v. Apollo International Inc.* 2009 (2) Arb. LR 499 (Del).
209. Singapore International Arbitration Act, 1994, S. 12A(4); *See, Maldives Airport Co. Ltd. & Anr. v. GMR Male International Airport Pte Ltd,* [2013] SGCA 16.

of urgency,[210] whereas in India, like many other jurisdictions,[211] only a party to the arbitration may apply for interim measures under Section 9 of the IAA.[212]

While at first brush, the phrase 'proposed party' appears to have a much wider scope than 'party,' the practical difference between the two is of little significance. The phrase 'proposed party' only seeks to buttress the distinction between circumstances where arbitration proceedings have already commenced and the request for an interim measure will obviously be of a party to the arbitration proceedings, whereas when arbitration proceedings have not commenced, a 'proposed party' may approach the court for relief.[213] This is adequately addressed under the current Section 9(1) of the IAA with the use of the phrase, '*A party may, before or during arbitral proceedings or at any time after making of the arbitral award but before it is enforced* … .'

Therefore, there should be a contract between the applicant and respondents for referring disputes between them to an arbitrator.[214] The exception to this position is when there are group companies and an agreement is intended to apply to other related companies as well.[215] However, the circumstances when such an extension of the arbitration agreement is permitted are very limited.[216]

In cases of non-signatories being a party to the arbitration agreement, the court should restrict the inquiry to a prima facie view. In order to balance the interests of all parties, the court may direct the party requesting the interim measure to furnish adequate security.[217]

4.3.5. Existence of a Dispute

The next prerequisite for approaching the court under Section 9 of the IAA is the existence of a dispute. Under the CPC, a right to obtain an interim measure is not a cause of action. It cannot stand on its own.[218] There cannot be an action under the law when there is no dispute between the parties. As discussed earlier, some courts had misinterpreted this to mean that no relief could be granted by a court unless arbitration proceedings were pending.[219] This view was primarily based on the provisions of the 1940 Act.

210. *Sundaram Finance Ltd. v. NEPC India Ltd.* (1999) 2 SCC 479, ¶15.
211. New Zealand, Arbitration Act, 1996, S. 9(1) & Sch. I.
212. *Firm Ashok Traders v. Gurmukh Das Saluja* AIR 2004 SC 1433, ¶13.
213. *Sundaram Finance Ltd. v. NEPC India Ltd.* (1999) 2 SCC 479, ¶16.
214. *K.K. Modi Investment and Financial Services Pvt. Ltd. v. Apollo International Inc.* 2009 (2) Arb. LR 499 (Del), ¶6.
215. *Ibid.*; *Mahanagar Telephone Nigam Ltd. v. Canara Bank* 2019 SCC OnLine 995, ¶10.3; *Kumar Bangur v. Purshottam Das Bangur*, 2011 (1) Arb. LR 370 (Cal), ¶11; *Chloro Controls India (P) Ltd. v. Severn Trent Water Purification Inc.* (2013) 1 SCC 641, ¶165.1; *GMR Energy Limited v. Doosan Power Systems India Private Limited & Ors.* 2017 SCC OnLine Del 11625, ¶64; *Hero Wind Energy Private Limited v. Inox Renewables Limited* 2020 SCC OnLine Del 478, ¶45.
216. *GL Asia Mauritius II Cayman Ltd. v. Pinfold Overseas Ltd. & Anr.* 2013 (2) Arb. LR 334 (Bom), ¶7.
217. *See discussion on Security below.*
218. *Bharat Aluminum v. Kaiser Aluminum Technical Services Inc.* (2012) 9 SCC 552, ¶182.
219. *Ranjeet Chandra v. Union of India* AIR 1963 Cal 594, ¶9; *Nagarchand Goenka v. Surendranath Sarkar*, AIR 1946 Pat 70.

However, the predominant view now is that interim measures can be granted before or in anticipation of any reference to arbitration.[220] It is not required that a dispute, i.e., a pending suit or proceeding exists between the parties to invoke the power under Section 9 of the IAA. Such a requirement is not a pre-condition. The mere existence of an arbitration agreement is sufficient to enable a party to come to the court.[221]

4.3.6. *Intention to Arbitrate*

After an analysis of the validity of the arbitration agreement and the existence of a dispute, the grant of interim measure should have been apparent. However, a frequent problem faced by the Indian courts was that parties would apply for an interim measure, have the same granted and then not take steps for the formation of the arbitral tribunal. Therefore, the judiciary was constrained to create a prerequisite that a party who intends to invoke the arbitration clause and seek an interim measure under Section 9 of the IAA should have an intention to arbitrate.

The party seeking the grant of interim measures should demonstrate adequate proof of steps taken or being taken for initiation of the arbitration proceedings without which Section 9 of the IAA cannot be invoked.[222] The simple rationale of the court was that a party who does not intend to invoke an arbitration clause and does not want to proceed with arbitration is not entitled to any order by way of an interim measure under Section 9 of the IAA.[223] In the Singapore (Domestic) Arbitration Act, the court may make an order discontinuing the proceedings if no party has taken any further steps after the passing of the order for two years.[224]

4.3.7. *No Requirement to Serve a Notice of Arbitration*

There has to be a manifest intention on the part of the applicant to take recourse to arbitration proceeding at the time of filing an application under Section 9 of the IAA. However, it is not necessary that a notice invoking the arbitration clause must be issued and the Court has the discretion to grant interim relief.[225] If the notice has been issued,

220. *Gokuldas v. Union of India* AIR 1983 Ker 169, ¶5.
221. *Sundaram Finance Ltd. v. NEPC India Ltd.* (1999) 2 SCC 479, ¶15 *followed in Escorts Finance Ltd. v. Mohd. Hanif D. Khan* 2003 (Suppl.) Arb. LR 93 (Del) (DB), ¶4; *Alpic Finance Ltd. v. Allied Resins & Chemicals Ltd.* 1999 SCC OnLine Cal 532, ¶5.
222. *National Building Construction Corpn Ltd. v. IRCON International Ltd.* 1998(1) RAJ 540 (Del), ¶12; *Parmali Wallis Ltd. v. Union of India* 1998(2) Arb LR 487 (Del); *Tata Finance Ltd. v. Pragati Paribahan*, AIR 2000 Cal 24, ¶13; *Rashtriya Chemicals and Fertilizers Ltd. v. Sanmit International FZE* 2010 (4) Arb. LR (Bom) (DB), ¶17; *CVCIGP II Client Rosehil Ltd. v. Sanjay Jain* 2019 SCC OnLine Del 7522, ¶7; *Anil Constructions v. Vidarbha Irrigation Development Corporation, Amravati* 2000 (Suppl.) Arb. LR 111 Bom, ¶11.
223. *Sanjay Kapur v. Vikram Kapur* 2019 SCC OnLine Del 9303; *Shriram Transport Finance Company v. Juber Sheikh* 2016 SCC OnLine MP 7282, ¶8.
224. Singapore Domestic Arbitration Act, 2001, S. 6(3).
225. *Gallantt Metal Limited v. Smart Timing Steel Limited* 2019 SCC OnLine Guj 3804, ¶73.

it would be sufficient to establish the manifest intention of the applicant.[226] The courts were also constrained to pass conditional orders and impose such terms as the Court thought fit to ensure that the party requesting the interim measure takes effective steps for commencing the arbitral proceedings.[227]

These concerns have now been addressed with the insertion of Section 9(2) of the IAA by the 2015 Amendment. The said provision provides for the mandatory formation of an arbitral tribunal within ninety days of the passing of an order under Section 9(1) of the IAA. It is clarified that the insertion of Section 9(2) of the IAA does not mean that the party does not have to demonstrate the intention to arbitrate. It only means that the court is not bound to impose terms and conditions for taking effective steps for commencing the arbitral proceedings.

4.3.8. Registration and Stamp Duty

Another curious prerequisite added by the courts is the consideration of the arbitration agreement being sufficiently stamped. It is settled law that an arbitration agreement is not required to be registered under the Registration Act, 1908.[228] However, courts have held that an arbitration agreement without payment of sufficient stamp duty is unenforceable.[229]

This view is erroneous. Many courts have disagreed with this view and held that the parties cannot be rendered remediless pending the issue of sufficiency of stamp duty which is also subject to appeal.[230] Moreover, deficiency of stamp duty can always be rectified under the Indian Stamp Act, 1899 by paying a penalty.[231] To render the arbitration agreement invalid on account of insufficient stamp duty violates party autonomy and the will of the parties to have their dispute resolved through arbitration. In a similar view, the Supreme Court[232] had permitted the appointment of an arbitrator even when a document required mandatory registration under the Registration Act,

226. *Sundaram Finance Ltd. v. NEPC India Ltd.* (1999) 2 SCC 479, ¶19.
227. Wadhwa, *supra* n. 46, at 1, 2.
228. *Biswanath Ghosh v. M/s Hijal Kanya Co-operative Housing Society Ltd.* 2017 SCC OnLine Cal 2486, ¶28. *However, a contrary view was taken in Rupsa Valley Engineering Pvt. Ltd. & Anr. v. Sambhu Nath Saha* 2019 SCC OnLine Cal 1305.
229. *SMS Tea Estates Pvt. Ltd.* v. *Chandmari Tea Co. Pvt. Ltd.* (2011) 14 SCC 66; *Garware-Wall Ropes* v. *Coastal Marine Constructions & Engineering Ltd* (2019) 9 SCC 209; *Dharmaratnakara Rai Bahadur Arcot Narainswamy Mudaliar Chattram & Other Charities and Others v. Bhaskar Raju & Brothers and Ors.* 2020 SCC OnLine SC 183.
230. *Coastal Marine Construction and Engineering Limited v. Garware-Wall Ropes Limited* 2018 SCC OnLine Bom 541; *Universal Enterprises, Mumbai v. Deluxe Laboratories Pvt. Ltd. Mumbai* 2016 SCC OnLine Bom 3963, ¶11; *A.R.C. Overseas Pvt. Ltd. v. Bougainvillea Multiplex and Entertainment Centre Pvt. Ltd.* 2008 (2) AWC 1212, ¶¶ 12&13; *Dharampal Satyapal Ltd. v. Dinesh Enamelled Wires Industries (P) Ltd.* 2010 (2) Arb. LR 444 (All), ¶57; *L & T Finance Limited v. Iris Health Services Ltd.* 2019 SCC OnLine Bom 12535, ¶13.
231. The Indian Stamp Act, 1899, S. 40(1)(b).
232. *SMS Tea Estates (P) Ltd. v. Chandmari Tea Co. (P) Ltd.* (2011) 14 SCC 66.

1908.[233] In a recent judgment, the Supreme Court of India has rightly held that an arbitration clause in an unstamped agreement is valid.[234]

Thus, the question of stamp duty is irrelevant for jurisdiction under Section 9 of the IAA as the existence of the arbitration clause is sufficient for invoking the jurisdiction under the said Section. Courts will, in effect, adjudicate issues of stamp duty before considering a request for interim measures. Such review is not contemplated under the Model Law or specifically provided under the IAA. Hence, any such determination violates the principle enshrined in Section 5 of the IAA for minimising court interference in arbitration and mocks the mandate of Article 17J of the Model Law that the court should exercise the power 'in consideration of the specific features of international arbitration'.

4.4. Jurisdiction of Courts

The last prerequisite to be satisfied before a court can grant an interim measure under Section 9 of the IAA is that the court has jurisdiction, both territorial and pecuniary, like it would have in a suit filed before it.[235] The relief under Section 9 of the IAA has to be claimed before a Principal Civil Court of original jurisdiction,[236] i.e., the Court of the District Judge.[237] However, given the vast expanse of India and the existence of several District Courts, High Courts and the Supreme Court, especially with District Courts being divided based on pecuniary and territorial jurisdiction, the determination of the appropriate court is imperative.[238]

Ordinarily, jurisdiction under the CPC is exercised in the following manner:

(a) where the subject matter is situated;[239]
(b) where the immovable property is situated;[240]
(c) where jurisdiction is uncertain, then the court where the suit has been filed, after recording a statement to the effect of uncertainty;[241]
(d) for compensation for wrong to a person or movables, where the defendant resides, carries on business, or personally works for gain;[242]
(e) in all other cases, where the defendant resides, or cause of action arises.[243]

233. *Ibid.*, ¶29. *See also, Agility Logistics Pvt. Ltd. v. Jagannath Parmeshwar Mills Pvt. Ltd.* 2015 SCC OnLine Bom 2308; *Mr. Badal Mittal v. Lakadawala Developers Pvt. Ltd.* 2013 (5) Mh. L.J 185.
234. *N.N. Global Mercantile (P) Ltd. v. Indo Unique Flame Ltd.* (2021) 4 SCC 379, ¶56.
235. *Oberoi Constructions Pvt. Ltd. v. Worli Shivshahi Co-op. Housing Society* 2008 (1) Arb. LR 106 (Bom), ¶11.
236. Indian Arbitration Act, 1996, S. 2(e); *GE Countrywide Consumer Financial Services Ltd. v. Surjit Singh Bhatia & Mr. Jaspal Kaur* 2006 SCC OnLine Del 372.
237. *Fountain Head Developers v. Maria Arcangela Sequeira* AIR 2007 Bom 149.
238. *See* Indian Code of Civil Procedure, 1908, ss 16-20.
239. Indian Code of Civil Procedure, 1908, S. 16.
240. *Ibid.*, S. 17.
241. *Ibid.*, S. 18.
242. *Ibid.*, S. 19.
243. *Ibid.*, S. 20.

The starting point of this analysis is where would the applicant have filed the suit claiming the same relief as claimed under Section 9 of the IAA?[244] The answer would be determined under the CPC (as mentioned above). However, in the context of arbitration proceedings, this question has been mired in controversy even though an application under Section 9 of the IAA is time-sensitive and deciding jurisdiction after evidence is antithetical to the very purpose of seeking urgent interim relief.[245]

The courts have often confused the governing law clause, forum selection clause, and the seat of arbitration while determining the appropriate court for the purposes of jurisdiction. The confusion stems from the applicability of the basic principles of the CPC regarding jurisdiction[246] and the choice of the parties selecting the courts at a particular location for remedy. The debate has been centred around whether the courts would have jurisdiction where the cause of action arose, where the defendant resides, or will the selection of the seat operate as an exclusive jurisdiction clause to oust the jurisdiction of other courts under the CPC?

4.4.1. *'Seat' in Domestic Arbitration*

'Seat' in arbitration refers to the choice of the parties to have the courts of a particular place exercise supervisory jurisdiction over arbitration proceedings.[247] Such a choice is made on several factors, including the supportive role of the courts and the *lex arbitri*, i.e., the arbitration statute that would apply to the arbitration proceedings. Often, parties choose a seat in which neither of the parties is resident or has business. This is done to ensure that neither party can exercise home-turf advantage, in any manner. Therefore, parties usually choose a 'neutral' place as the 'seat'.

4.4.2. *Neutral Seat in Domestic Arbitration*

However, the idea of a 'neutral' seat in domestic arbitration is difficult as the court at the seat is required to have jurisdiction under the principles of the CPC. Parties in India cannot confer jurisdiction on a court but merely choose between courts that would have jurisdiction under the CPC, i.e., the court should have jurisdiction over some part of the property, or the cause of action should have arisen in the court's jurisdiction, or the defendant should reside within the jurisdiction of the court.[248] In international arbitration, the seat can be located in any country the courts of which may not have jurisdiction otherwise and hence, 'neutral' to both parties.[249]

It should be noted that some argue that the idea of 'seat' is irrelevant for domestic arbitrations and it applies only to international arbitrations as parties choose a neutral

244. *J Polychem India Ltd. v. Kotak Mahindra Bank Ltd.* 2009 (2) Arb. LR 186 (Del), ¶8.
245. *Srei Equipment Finance Limited v. Seirra Infraventure Private Ltd.* 2020 SCC OnLine Cal 1790, ¶26.
246. Indian Code of Civil Procedure, 1908, Ss 15-21.
247. *Punj Lloyd v. GVK Power (Goindwal Sahib)* 2017 SCC OnLine Del 7366, ¶27.
248. *Yeshwant Rao Ganpat Rao Vipat v. Dattatraya Ramchandra Rao Vipat* AIR 1940 Nag 191.
249. *Mikuni Corporation v. UCAL Fuel Systems Ltd.* 2008 (1) Arb. LR 503 (Del), ¶15.

venue.[250] This view is misplaced. Agreeing on a place of arbitration is not limited to having a seat at that place but it carries the adjunct that the courts of that place would advise the supervisory jurisdiction insofar as the arbitration proceedings are concerned.[251]

4.4.3. *Choosing a Seat in Domestic Arbitration*

In line with party autonomy, parties in domestic arbitrations might be inclined to choose the courts of a particular city for speed, efficiency, and a pro-arbitration approach, much like in an international arbitration. For instance, the Delhi High Court takes not more than three days to grant ad interim relief from the date of filing.[252] Courts in certain cities may be more pro-arbitration, e.g., courts in Mumbai recognised an emergency award passed in Singapore under Section 9 of the IAA[253] and are more sensitive to commercial realities.[254] Courts in other cities might not have such a liberal view.[255]

A certain city may also be chosen as it may be the primary place of business of one of the parties and hence, parties may opt for 'home-turf' advantage, especially in the vernacular language, or local connections, or easier enforcement of the award. As per the language of Section 2(1)(e) of the IAA, the court should consider the issue of jurisdiction irrespective of arbitration and see if it would otherwise have had jurisdiction to entertain the subject matter as that of the suit.[256] Therefore, the 'seat' cannot be one where the court would otherwise not have jurisdiction.

4.4.4. *Statutorily Fixing the Seat*

In order to prevent this conflict of jurisdiction between different courts having jurisdiction over arbitration proceedings, Section 42 of the IAA fixes jurisdiction, i.e., seat with that court which had first exercised jurisdiction in relation to arbitration proceedings, except for the appointment of an arbitrator.[257] Section 42 of the IAA provides that '*notwithstanding anything contained elsewhere in law, where an application has been made in a court, that court alone shall have jurisdiction over the arbitral*

250. Niranjan Venkatesa & Shantanu Narvane, *Bhatia International Rightly Overruled: The Consequences of Three Errors in BALCO*, 9 SCC J. 26 (2012).
251. *Punj Lloyd v. GVK Power (Goindwal Sahib)* 2017 SCC OnLine Del 7366, ¶27.
252. Rishab Gupta, *supra* n. 168; Ankit Singh, *Seat and Venue: Why Brahmani River Is Good Law?* (3 October 2019), available at: https://indiacorplaw.in/2019/10/seat-venue-brahmani-river-good-law.html.
253. *HSBC PI Holdings (Mauritius) Ltd. v. Avitel Post Studioz Ltd.* 2014 SCC OnLine Bom 102.
254. *Based on the decisions examined, most reported cases under Section 9 and 17 have been decided by the Courts at Mumbai keeping in mind the will of the parties and their commercial needs.*
255. *Raffles Design International India Private Limited v. Educomp Professional Education Limited* 2016 SCC OnLine Del 5521.
256. *GE Countrywide Consumer Financial Services Ltd. v. Surjit Singh Bhatia & Mr. Jaspal Kaur* 2006 SCC OnLine Del 372.
257. *Rodemadan India Ltd. v. International Trade Expo Centre Ltd.* (2006) 11 SCC 651; *Union of India v. S.R. Constructions Company and Another* (2007) 144 DLT 580.

proceedings and all subsequent applications arising out of that agreement and the arbitral proceedings shall be subject to that court only and in no other court'. The purpose of Section 42 of the IAA is to avoid the institution of simultaneous proceedings at two places or in two different courts and to have all matters arising out of a particular arbitration agreement decided by one court.[258]

Despite the existence of Section 42 of the IAA, the courts have grappled with this conundrum of whether the designation of a seat amounts to exclusive jurisdiction of the courts at the seat or not? Which court has jurisdiction if only the venue is mentioned? Or there is no mention of the seat or the venue? In Spain, this question is determined by considering which court will enforce the award. Such court will have jurisdiction for interim measures as well.[259] However, in a large country like India, such a provision too may not adequately solve the problem as the award may be enforced by more than one court.

4.4.5. *Jurisdiction at the Seat*

Many courts, internationally[260] and domestically, take the view that an arbitration agreement as to the seat is analogous to the exclusive jurisdiction clause and any claim for remedy whether interim or final can only be made at the seat of arbitration[261] and no other court.[262] This view has been reiterated by the Supreme Court and other High Courts.[263] It should be noted that the absence of words like 'alone', 'only', 'exclusive', or 'exclusive jurisdiction' is immaterial to determine exclusive jurisdiction.[264]

The rationale for this view is that when there are two or more courts which have jurisdiction under the CPC to try a suit or proceeding, an arbitration agreement between the parties that the disputes between them shall be tried in one of such courts is not contrary to public policy nor does it contravene the provisions of Section 28 of the

258. *N.K.C. Projects (P) Ltd. v. Utility Energytech and Engineers (P) Ltd.* 2009 (2) Arb. LR 634 (Allahabad) (DB), ¶9.
259. Stephen, *supra* n. 96, at 585; Spanish Arbitration Law, Art. 8(3); Spanish Civil Procedure Act, Art. 724.
260. *Sul America Cia Nacional De Seguros S.A. v. Enesa Engenharia S.A.* [2012] EWCA Civ 638.
261. *Harmony Innovation Shipping v. Gupta Coal India Ltd.* (2015) 9 SCC 172; *Dipankar Singh v. Union of India* 2019 SCC OnLine Del 11121, ¶14; *Reliance Infrastructure Ltd. Mumbai v. Roadway Solution (I) Pvt. Ltd.* 2016 SCC OnLine Bom 16 *relying on Swastik Gases Pvt. Ltd. v. Indian Oil Corporation* (2013) 9 SCC 32; *Konkola Copper Mines PLC. v. U & M Mining Zambia Ltd.* (2014) EWHC 2146 (Comm); *Aniket Sa Investments LLC, Mauritius v. Janapriya Engineers Syndicate Pvt. Ltd.* 2021 SCC OnLine Bom 919, ¶15-18.
262. *Indus Mobile Distribution Pvt. Ltd. v. Data Wind Innovations Pvt. Ltd.* (2017) 7 SCC 678; *affirmed in Indian Infoline Finance Ltd. v. Harshad Hirji Thakkar* 2019 SCC OnLine Del 7342, ¶¶15-16; *Emkay Global Financial Services Ltd. v. Girdhar Sondhi* (2018) 9 SCC 49; *L & T Finance Limited v. Manoj Pathak* 2020 SCC OnLine Bom 177, ¶29.
263. *Pacific Greens Infracon Pvt. Ltd. v. Senior Builders Ltd.* 2009 (2) Arb. LR 214 (Del); *Indus Mobile Distribution Pvt. Ltd. v. Data Wind Innovations Pvt. Ltd.* (2017) 7 SCC 678; *N.K.C. Projects (P) Ltd. v. Utility Energytech and Engineers (P) Ltd.* 2009 (2) Arb. LR 634 (Allahabad) (DB), ¶9.
264. *Swastik Gases Pvt. Ltd. v. Indian Oil Corporation* (2013) 9 SCC 32, ¶57 *followed in Green Power International Pvt. Ltd. v. Triveni Engineering and Industries Ltd.* 2016 SCC OnLine Del 3750.

Indian Contract Act, 1872.[265] This does not mean, however, that courts that would otherwise not have jurisdiction under the CPC can be conferred with jurisdiction.[266] The parties can only choose between two courts having jurisdiction. Therefore, once the parties knowingly and voluntarily agreed to a particular jurisdiction, an application under Section 9 of the IAA cannot be filed in violation of such agreement.[267]

Even a conjoint and harmonious reading of the provisions of Section 2(1)(e) of the IAA, Section 9 of the IAA and Section 42 of the IAA leads to the view that the relevant court for an application under Section 9 of the IAA would be the same court which would have jurisdiction during the arbitral proceedings or after making an award.[268] Therefore, if the seat is designated, Section 42 of the IAA would have no application and a determination by the arbitral tribunal as to the seat would amount to an exclusive jurisdiction clause.[269]

Thus, Section 42 of the IAA presupposes that there is more than one competent forum to hear an application under the IAA and to ensure the efficacy of dispute resolution, Section 42 of the IAA mandates that the court which first seized any application under the IAA would be the only court possessing the jurisdiction to hear all the subsequent applications.[270]

Thus, courts at the seat would have exclusive jurisdiction once the seat has been designated by the parties, irrespective of where the cause of action arose or where the respondent resides.[271] If a court exercises jurisdiction based on the cause of action, it will override the clear intent of the parties present in the forum selection clause and the same would ultimately defeat the provision of Section 20(1) of the IAA as well as the agreement of the parties. The only caveat to this exclusive jurisdiction is that the parties cannot designate a seat at a place where a court would not have jurisdiction under the CPC.[272]

---

265. *Aniket Sa Investments LLC, Mauritius v. Janapriya Engineers Syndicate Pvt. Ltd.* 2021 SCC OnLine Bom 919; *A.B.C. Laminart (P) Ltd. v. A.P. Agencies* (1989) 2 SCC 173; *Hakam Singh v. Gammon (India) Ltd.* (1971) 1 SCC 286; *Geo Miller & Co. Ltd. v. United Bank of India* 1997 (2) Arb. LR 50 (Del).
266. *Mikuni Corporation v. UCAL Fuel Systems Ltd.* 2008 (1) Arb. LR 503 (Del).
267. *Balaji Coke Industry Pvt. Ltd. v. Maa Bhagwati Coke (Guj) Pvt. Ltd.* 2009 (3) Arb. LR 460 (SC).
268. *N.K.C. Projects (P) Ltd. v. Utility Energytech and Engineers (P) Ltd.* 2009 (2) Arb. LR 634 (Allahabad) (DB), ¶11.
269. *Antrix Corp. Ltd. v. Devas Multimedia Pvt. Ltd.* 2018 (4) Arb. LR 66 (Del) (DB), ¶54 *affirming the decision in Priya Hiranandani Vandervala v. Niranjan Hiranandani* 2016 SCC OnLine Del 3435, ¶10; *B.E Simoese von Staraburg Niedenthal v. Chattisgarh Investment Ltd.* (2015) 12 SCC 225. *Unfortunately, the court based the view on the erroneous reasoning that there are very few instances where the parties do not designate any seat. Most often parties fail to designate the seat.*
270. *Antrix Corp. Ltd. v. Devas Multimedia Pvt. Ltd.* 2018 (4) Arb. LR 66 (Del) (DB), ¶54. *It should be noted that the Delhi High Court held that in domestic arbitrations, in the absence of an exclusive jurisdiction clause, designation of a seat alone would not confer courts with exclusive jurisdiction. State of West Bengal and Ors. v. Associated Contractors* (2015) 1 SCC 32. *Since, Section 9 Application are to be filed before the Court within the meaning of Section 2(1)(e) of the Arbitration Act, one such application has been made, only that court would have jurisdiction over all subsequent applications by virtue of Section 42 of the Indian Arbitration Act.*
271. *Ion Exchange (India) Ltd. v. Panasonic Electric Works Ltd.* 2014 SCC OnLine Del 973.
272. *Mikuni Corporation v. UCAL Fuel Systems Ltd.* 2008 (1) Arb. LR 503 (Del).

4.4.6. *Jurisdiction Other Than at the Seat*

In complete contrast to the view above, the Supreme Court[273] took the view that reliance has to be placed on the CPC to determine jurisdiction for an application under Section 9 of the IAA and consequently, Section 20 of the CPC would be attracted.[274] Similarly, in another case,[275] the court had reiterated that relief by a court could not be granted and territorial jurisdiction cannot be exercised if the property is not situated within the jurisdiction of the said court.[276]

The court in the landmark judgment of *Bharat Aluminium Co. v. Kaiser Aluminium Technical Services Inc.*[277] (*BALCO*) noted that there are two courts that would have jurisdiction, i.e., the court where the cause of action arose and the court where the arbitration takes place.[278] Following this distinction, courts subsequently took the view that Section 2(1)(e) of the IAA is purely jurisdictional,[279] and hence, the courts at the seat do not have exclusive jurisdiction but have concurrent jurisdiction with the court where the cause of action arises.[280] Taking a step further and following several previous cases,[281] the Delhi High Court[282] had held that only that court would have jurisdiction where the cause of action arose in the sense as it would have arisen if the suit had been filed. This would also avoid any problems of enforcement.

This view is misplaced and contrary to the goal of a pro-arbitration regime. It completely subverts the intention of the parties and the choice to have a particular court exercise supervisory jurisdiction over the arbitration proceedings.[283] This view stems from the lack of understanding of the arbitration process and relies on domestic procedural principles instead of understanding the 'specific features of international arbitration'.

Furthermore, concerns about enforcement in another territorial jurisdiction are largely misplaced as the CPC contains sufficient provisions for the transfer of an order

273. *Jatinder Nath v. Chopra Land Developers Pvt. Ltd.* 2007 (1) Arb. LR 490 (SC).
274. *Ibid.*, ¶16.
275. *Harshad Chiman Lal Modi v. DLF Universal Ltd.* (2005) 7 SCC 791.
276. *A similar view was taken in Trehan Promoters and Builders Pvt. Ltd. v. Welldone Technologies Parks Development Pvt. Ltd.* 2009 (4) Arb LR 46 (Del).
277. *Bharat Aluminum v. Kaiser Aluminum Technical Services Inc.* (2012) 9 SCC 552.
278. *Ibid.*, ¶96.
279. *Konkola Copper Mines v. Stewarts and Lloyds of India Ltd.* 2013 (4) Arb. LR 19 (Bom) (DB), ¶16.
280. *Antrix Corp. Ltd. v. Devas Multimedia Pvt. Ltd.* 2018 (4) Arb. LR 66 (Del) (DB), ¶48, *this case distinguished Indus Mobile Distribution Pvt. Ltd. v. Data Wind Innovations Pvt. Ltd.* (2017) 7 SCC 678 *and placed reliance on Hinduja LeyLand Finance Ltd. v. Debdas Routh* 2017 SCC Online Cal 16379; *Supreme Housing and Hospitality Pvt. Ltd. v. SRS Private Investments Pawai Ltd.* 2017 SCC OnLine Del 7905.
281. *Gulati Construction Company, Jhansi v. Betwa River Board* AIR 1984 Delhi 299; *Interstate Equipment (India) Pvt. Ltd. v. Bharat Aluminium Company Ltd.* 2004 (1) Arb. LR 456 (Del); *Apparel Export Promotion Council v. Prabhati Patni, Proprietor, Comfort Furnishers* 2005 (3) Arb. LR 518 (Del); *GE Countrywide Consumer Financial Services Ltd. v. Surjit Singh Bhatia & Mr. Jaspal Kaur* 2006 SCC OnLine Del 372; *T.D.M. Construction (India) Ltd. v. Capt. P.K. Srivastava* 2010 (4) Arb. LR 552; *IndusInd Bank Ltd. v. Quality Fabricators and Erectors* 2010 (1) Arb. LR 131 (Bom).
282. *Inox Air Products Ltd. v. Rathi Ispat Ltd.* 2006 (4) Arb. LR 40 (Del).
283. *SE Investments Ltd, v. Arch Pharma Labs Ltd.* 2017 SCC OnLine Bom 630, ¶15.

to another jurisdiction.[284] More importantly, an order by a court at the seat may be voluntarily complied with and may not even require enforcement where the property or asset is located. Therefore, such a restrictive view takes away from the speedy disposal of arbitration disputes and opens the door for misuse and guerrilla tactics unless the parties by conduct waive the exclusive jurisdiction clause and do not object to another's court exercising jurisdiction.[285]

4.4.7. *Jurisdiction When the Seat Is 'Indeterminate'*

It has been held that where the seat is unclear, a court under Section 9 of the IAA has to decide the issue of jurisdiction before finally deciding the application under Section 9 of the IAA.[286] It has to satisfy itself that the subject matter of the arbitration comes within the pecuniary and territorial jurisdiction of the court.[287] Once the court finds that it does not have territorial jurisdiction, it is bound to reject the application and cannot record a finding on merits.[288]

One view is that in the absence of any specification of the seat of arbitration, the venue of arbitration should be taken to mean the place of arbitration as envisaged in section 20(1) of the IAA and would confer jurisdiction on the court in whose jurisdiction the arbitration is held.[289] Contrary to this is the view that parties cannot confer jurisdiction at the venue of the arbitration even if there is no specific clause determining the seat[290] since the subject matter of the suit and the subject matter of the arbitration are distinct as held by the Supreme Court in *BALCO*.[291] A third view is that the court should consider the 'closest connection test' for determining the seat.[292]

4.4.8. *Resolving the Question of Jurisdiction*

The confusion over jurisdiction largely stems from the wording of Section 2(1)(e) of the IAA which uses the phrase '*having jurisdiction to decide the questions forming the subject matter of the arbitration if the same had been the subject matter of a suit*'. However, there is little or no confusion.

---

284. Indian Code of Civil Procedure, 1908, Ss 37-42.
285. *AAA Landmark Private Ltd. v. AKME Projects Ltd.* 2018 SCC OnLine Del 7586, *affirmed* in *Bharat Heavy Electricals Limited v. Uttar Pradesh Rajya Vidhyut Utpadan Nigam Limited* 2019 SCC OnLine Del 7156, ¶9.
286. *Prince Marine Transport Services Ltd. v. Minescape Minerals Pvt. Ltd.* 2016 SCC OnLine Bom 2637, ¶15.
287. *Harita Finance Ltd. v. ATB Projects India Ltd.* 2003 (2) Arb. LR 376, ¶10.
288. *Progressive Constructions Ltd. v. Louis Berger Group Inc.* 2012 (3) Arb. LR 357 (AP)(DB), ¶37.
289. *Adesh Enterprises LLP v. Vinod Kumar Goswami* 2017 SCC OnLine Del 7508; *BGS SGS Soma JV v. NHPC Ltd.* 2019 SCC OnLine SC 1585; *Mankastu Impex Private Ltd. v. Airvisual Ltd.* 2020 SCC OnLine SC 301; *Brahmani River Pellets Limited v. Kamachi Industries Ltd.* 2019 SCC OnLine SC 929; *Golden Edge Engineering Private Limited v. Bharat Heavy Electricals Limited* 2020 SCC OnLine Cal 996, ¶21.
290. *Union of India v. Hardy Exploration and Production (India) Inc.* 2018 SCC OnLine SC 1640.
291. *Anil Kumar Phoolchand Sanghvi v. Chandrakant P. Sanghvi* 2016 SCC OnLine Bom 1048, ¶¶ 37, 39.
292. *Enercon (India) Ltd. v. Enercon GmbH* (2014) 5 SCC 1.

Irrespective of arbitration, it is settled law that parties can choose jurisdiction between different courts.[293] The only caveat is that parties cannot confer jurisdiction over a court which would not have jurisdiction otherwise,[294] i.e., there should be some connection with the court either in terms of property, cause of action, or the residence of the defendant. Therefore, given that exclusive jurisdiction clauses are valid under the ICA, there is little room to argue that the designation of the seat will not confer exclusive jurisdiction on courts. Moreover, giving parallel jurisdiction to two courts violates the basic tenets contained in Section 10 of the CPC, runs contrary to party autonomy, and most importantly, creates hurdles for a speedy and efficient arbitration regime.

Further, in domestic arbitrations, where the seat is not determined but the venue is provided for, unless there are compelling reasons to disregard such a choice, the jurisdiction should be exercised by the courts at the venue, subject to such courts having jurisdiction as per the CPC. Most arbitration clauses are not drafted with much thought and are hardly negotiated. Therefore, an intent that parties wanted to differentiate between 'seat' and 'venue' cannot be given much credence. Also, inevitably the procedural law applicable within India would be the same, there is no merit in providing the parties with forum selection options since the rule of *forum conveniens* is expressly excluded by Section 42 of the IAA.[295]

Moreover, courts at the 'venue' being deemed as the 'seat', as long as they have some connection with the matter, would further provide consistency and predictability. The express choice of 'venue' at least demonstrates some intent in favour of the courts of a particular seat and hence, is a better choice than a determination by the court of a place which the parties never intended to go to. Such a determination ought to be made by the arbitral tribunal and not by the court exercising complementary jurisdiction to the arbitral tribunal.

If the court at the venue has jurisdiction under the CPC and there are no compelling reasons to disregard the choice of the parties, such jurisdiction should be exercised by the courts at the 'venue' as the 'seat'. The court at the venue should only determine if it does not have jurisdiction under the CPC. If neither venue nor seat has been chosen by the parties, the courts should exercise jurisdiction as per the rules provided under the CPC. Therefore, if the court at the seat is not located at the place where the property is to be attached, the provision of Section 136 of the CPC would be applicable and the court shall send it to the relevant court within whose territorial jurisdictional limits the person resides or is situated.[296] Alternatively, the court may decline jurisdiction and direct the parties to approach the appropriate court.

---

293. The Indian Contract Act, 1872, S. 28; *New Moga Transport Co. v. United India Insurance Co. Ltd* (2004) 4 SCC 677; *InterGlobe Aviation Ltd. v. N. Satchidanand* (2011) 7 SCC 463; *Sasan Power Ltd. v. North American Coal Corpn. (India) (P) Ltd.* (2016) 10 SCC 813; *Hinduja LeyLand Finance Ltd. v. Debdas Routh* 2017 SCC Online Cal 16379.
294. *Mikuni Corporation v. UCAL Fuel Systems Ltd.* 2008 (1) Arb. LR 503 (Del).
295. *JSW Steel Ltd. v. Jindal Praxair Oxygen Co. Ltd.* (2006) 11 SCC 521, ¶59.
296. *Sundaram Finance Ltd. v. P. Sakthivel* 2018 SCC OnLine Mad 3080.

4.4.9. *Test for Exercising Jurisdiction*

Therefore, the court should consider the following when exercising jurisdiction:

(a) if the 'seat' is mentioned by the parties in the arbitration agreement, the courts at the 'seat' will have exclusive jurisdiction;
(b) if the 'venue' is mentioned by the parties in the arbitration agreement, but not the 'seat,' the 'venue' should be deemed to be the 'seat,' unless the court at the 'venue' does not have jurisdiction under the CPC;[297]
(c) if neither 'seat' nor 'venue' is mentioned in the arbitration agreement, the court should take a prima facie view if it has jurisdiction under the CPC and proceed with the application under Section 9 of the IAA.

4.4.10. *'Seat' in International Arbitration*

The consideration of jurisdiction for international arbitrations should be entirely different. If the court is not the 'seat', it would be granting interim measures in aid of a foreign seated arbitration which is discussed in Chapter 5.

If the 'seat,' or 'venue' is mentioned in the arbitration agreement, such designation should operate as an exclusive jurisdiction clause. However, there may be circumstances in which the parties mention the 'seat', or 'venue' as 'India' and do not mention the city. In such cases, post the 2015 Amendment, the High Court of 'ordinary original civil jurisdiction' will exercise jurisdiction in international commercial arbitration.[298] Therefore, the parties will have to apply to such High Court, which would have jurisdiction under the CPC, i.e., where the property is situated, the cause of action arose, or where the defendant resides. If the party seeking the interim measure applies to the wrong High Court, such court may direct the parties to approach the appropriate High court.

4.4.11. *Principal Civil Court*

Another facet to the issue of jurisdiction is the provision that the District Judge alone could be the Principal Civil Court as provided under Section 2(1)(e) of the IAA and not any other Judge subordinate to him.[299] The 2015 Amendment brought in sweeping changes to the arbitration regime in India. Among many things, it made a conscious distinction between domestic arbitration and international arbitration.

In order to promote international arbitration, the definition of a court under Section 2(1)(e) of the IAA and jurisdiction for such matter was vested in the High Court of each state instead of the principal civil court, i.e., the District Court (as mentioned above). To further speed up litigation and provide for commercial certainty, The

297. *L&T Finance Ltd. v. Manoj Pathak* 2020 SCC OnLine Bom 177, ¶29.
298. Indian Arbitration Act, 1996, S. 2(1) (e)(ii).
299. *Fountain Head Developers v. Maria Arcangela Sequeira* AIR 2007 Bom 149; *Kapil Kumar Katiyal v. Praveen Chandra Bhanjdeo* 2010 (4) Arb. LR 747 (Cal) (DB).

Commercial Courts, Commercial Division and Commercial Appellate Division of High Courts Act, 2015 (Commercial Courts Act), was brought into effect on the same day as the 2015 Amendment was brought into force. Section 10(3) of the Commercial Courts Act now provides that all arbitration matters would now be filed before the Commercial Courts.[300]

Therefore, the court under Section 2(1)(e) of the IAA would now be the Commercial Court of the District (the equivalent of a District Judge). The Commercial Courts Act also mandates the creation of a commercial division in each High Court. Hence, a request for an interim measure will have to be filed before the Commercial Division of the High Court. Curiously, no such commercial division is provided for the Supreme Court.

5. STANDARDS FOR GRANT OF INTERIM MEASURES BEFORE ARBITRATION PROCEEDINGS

Once the requirements to invoke the power under Section 9 of the IAA are satisfied, the next question which requires examination is the standards which the court is supposed to apply when considering an application under Section 9 of the IAA. Should the court apply the standards under the CPC? Or is Section 9 of the IAA an independent provision which requires application of autonomous standards keeping in mind the 'specific features of international arbitration'?

The determination of applicable standards is essential because such determination draws the fine line between court intervention, court interference, and most importantly, the role of the courts in supporting arbitration proceedings. Under German law, a judge is bound to order interim measures of protection once the prescribed pre-conditions are fulfilled by the party requesting the interim measure.[301] In India, however, Section 9 of the IAA does not provide for any standards. Like many other national arbitration statutes, it refers only to the power of the court being similar to the power in a proceeding before the court. Thus, the courts have interpreted Section 9 of the IAA in light of the provisions of the CPC under which the standards of prima facie case (which is a *sine qua non*),[302] the balance of convenience and irreparable harm are applied.[303]

---

300. *And not a High Court Vaidya Industries v. State of Jharkhand* 2019 SCC OnLine Jhar 1790, ¶27.
301. Jan Schäfer, *Chapter IV: Jurisdiction of Arbitral Tribunal, Section 1041: Interim Measures of Protection*, in Patricia Nacimiento & Stefan Michael Kröll, et al. (eds), *Arbitration in Germany: The Model Law in Practice* 232 (2015).
302. *Himcon Projects Pvt. Ltd. v. LMZ Energy (India) Ltd.* 2012 (3) Arb. LR 248 (Chhattisgarh) (DB), ¶13; S.C. Sarkar & P.C. Sarkar, *Sarkar's Code of Civil Procedure* 2516-2517 (2017).
303. *Modi Rubber Limited v. Guardian International Corporation* 2007 SCC OnLine Del 502; *Assam Company India Ltd. v. Union of India* 2012 (3) Arb. LR 168 9 (Del); *Golden Dreams Arcade Pvt. Ltd. v. Shiv Embroidery Manufacturing Co.* 2009 (4) Arb. LR 291 (Bom) (DB); *CPI India Ltd. v. BPTP Ltd.* 2012 (4) Arb. LR. 294; *Buddha Films Pvt. Ltd. v. Prasar Bharti* 2001 (2) Arb. LR 422 (Del)(DB), *followed in The Bihar State Electricity Board v. M/s Usha Beltron Ltd.* 2001 SCC OnLine Jhar 280, ¶14.

5.1. Prima Facie Case

The jurisprudence on interim measures in India is primarily based on injunctions and consequently heaving driven by the Specific Relief Act. Sir John Woodroffe called an injunction a 'severe remedy', not to be granted at first except upon a clear prima facie case and positive averments on equity.[304] His comment defines precisely the nature and purpose of interim measure (even though he referred only to injunctions) and what ought to be the criteria for the grant or refusal of the same.

5.1.1. Meaning of Prima Facie

According to him, to show a prima facie case, the applicant needs to demonstrate the facts which constitute his ground for relief. It is not essential that the applicant establishes his case with the same degree of certainty as the applicant would at the time of a final hearing. The court cannot and should not determine right or wrong at this stage but should only look at all the facts of the case and determine if the applicant would suffer the alleged threatened injury till the rights of the applicant are being investigated.[305] Thus, the phrase 'prima facie case' literally means 'at first sight' and can also be read as 'on first appearance but subject to further evidence, or information'.[306] Most importantly, a prima facie case does not mean that the applicant should demonstrate that the applicant would succeed at trial.[307]

Over time, courts have expanded, modified, and limited this test. Some courts raised the threshold to the test of 'a serious question to be tried',[308] or 'a strong prima facie case',[309] or a probability that the applicant is entitled to relief.[310] Some held that the court would consider the prima facie case after carefully analysing the pleadings and documents on record.[311]

Others have lowered the threshold to the determination by the court whether there is a bona fide contention between the parties or whether there is a fair and

304. John George Woodroffe, *The Law Relating to Injunctions in British India* 100, 102 (1900).
305. Aditya Swarup, *The Prima Facie Standard for Interim Injunctions in India*, 4 NLU Del. St. L. J. 20, 21 (2017).
306. Black's Law Dictionary (2014) 2-3, 1909, c.f. *ibid.* at 21.
307. *Allahabad Bank v. Rana Sheo Ambar Singh* AIR 1976 All 447.
308. *Bishambar Nath Jaithy v. Municipal Commissioner* AIR 1926 Lah 589; *Damodar Valley Corporation v. Haripada Das* AIR 1978 Cal 489; *Shankarlal Debiprasad v. State of Madhya Pradesh* (1978) MPLJ 419; *United Commercial Bank v. Bank of India* AIR 1981 SC 1426.
309. *Uniply Industries v. Unicorn Plywood Ltd.* AIR 2001 SC 2083 (2086); *J T Stratford & Son Ltd. v. Lindley*, [1965] AC 269; *New Delhi Theatres v. Kailash Chand* AIR 1933 Lah 73; *Andhra University v. PNV Raju* (1974) 1 APLJ 158; *Mukesh v. Deo Narayan* AIR 1987 MP 85; *Shiv Kumar Chadha v. Municipal Corporation of Delhi* (1993) 3 SCC 161.
310. *Challender v. Royle*, (1887) 36 Ch. D 425; *Preston v. Luck* (1884) 27 Ch D 497; *Vithal v. Dawoo* AIR 1931 Nag 106; *Colgate Palmolive Ltd. v. Hindustan Unilever Ltd.* (1999) 7 SCC 1; *Dalpat Kumar v. Prahlad Singh* (1992) 1 SCC 719; *Sreedhara Shenoy v. K Thanumalayam* AIR 1952 Ker 90.
311. *Maria Sequeria Fernandez v. Erasmo Jack* (2012) 5 SCC 370.

substantive question regarding the rights of the parties.[312] A determination with respect to the merits of the case would amount to prejudging the case at the stage of interim relief,[313] and it is not necessary to establish chances of success at this stage.[314] Therefore, it essentially means that the application for interim measures under the CPC should not be 'frivolous or vexatious'.[315]

5.1.2. Prejudging the Merits

Despite the embargo on prejudging the merits, on many occasions, the court has examined the merits of each case to determine the lack of probability of complete subversion of the very nature of interim measures.[316] In a particular instance, the court has gone to the extent of admitting that it is difficult to pass an order for a temporary injunction without prejudging a case to an extent.[317] Such a requirement was justified on the grounds that an injunction would have the consequence of disturbing the status quo instead of preserving it. If the applicant cannot demonstrate the probability of success, the interim measure could be tantamount to permitting a frivolous or vexatious relief.[318]

The Supreme Court[319] held that the determination of a prima facie case rests on the analysis of the pleadings and documents on record[320] and that the court must take into consideration the effective and relevant documents before it[321] ultimately resulting in full scrutiny of the merits of the case. To compound the dilemma, unsurprisingly, the Indian jurisprudence on the question of interim measures blindly borrows the jurisprudence of interlocutory injunctions from England. The jurisprudence relies heavily on the English decision passed in *American Cyanamid Co v. Ethicon,*[322] (*American Cyanamid*) which required that the requesting party demonstrate that 'there was a real question to be tried'.

Even though the decision in *American Cyanamid* was diluted in *National Commercial Bank of Jamaica* v. *Olint Corp Ltd.*[323] effectively removing the requirement

312. *Relying on Walker v. Jones* (1865) L.R.I.P.C. 50, 61; *Israil v. Samser Rahman* AIR 1914 Cal 362; *State of Orissa v. Orissa Oil Industries* AIR 1982 Ori 245; *Akesh Kumar Jain v. Harneet Bakshi* 2001 (92) DLT 745; *Firm Ram Kishun Shah v. Jamuna Prasad* AIR 1951 Pat 469; *State of Bihar v. Thakur Manmohan Das* AIR 1964 Pat 367; *Bhagwat Prasad v. Jitendra Narain* 1991(18) ALR 207.
313. Aditya Swarup, *supra* n. 305 at 23.
314. *Damodar Valley Corporation v. Haripada Das* AIR 1978 Cal 489.
315. *Rajesh Kumar v. Manoj Jain* (1998) 47 DRJ 353; *Prasanta Kumar Ganguly v. Ashir Chandra Sen* 2012 SCC Online Cal 10192; *Damodar Valley Corporation v. Haripada Das* AIR 1978 Cal 489; *Supreme General Films v. Durgaprasad* AIR 1984 Bom 131.
316. *Lakshminarasimhiah v. Yalakki Gowda* AIR 1965 Kant 310.
317. Woodroffe, *supra* n. 304, at 102.
318. *Gogineni Gopaya v. Manikonda* AIR 1927 Mad 188.
319. *Maria Sequeira Fernandes v. Erasmo Jack* 2012 5 SCC 370.
320. *Ibid.*
321. *Pradip Post Trust v. M. D. IDCO* 91 (2001) CLT 682 (691).
322. *American Cyanamide Co. v. Ethicon* [1975] AC 396.
323. *National Commercial Bank of Jamaica v. Olint Corp. Ltd* [2009] 1 WLR 1405, 1409: *The court diluted the test to: (a) the prejudice likely to be suffered by the plaintiff if no injunction is granted and the prejudice likely to be suffered by the defendant if the injunction is granted; (b) the*

of showing a 'prima facie case', nonetheless, the Indian courts followed the outline in *American Cyanamid.* However, instead of adopting it completely, the courts chose to interpret the guidelines to mean that the threshold for grant of an interim injunction is the requirement to show that there is a serious question to be tried.[324] It is pertinent to mention that *American Cyanamid* test was followed by the courts in India for a long time but was expressly referred to only in 1994.[325]

Subsequently, in 2000, the Supreme Court in a landmark decision in *Colgate Palmolive (India) Ltd. v. Hindustan Lever*[326] *(Colgate)* held that the guidelines in *American Cyanamid* were too rigid and doubted their practical application. The court held that *American Cyanamid* could not fetter the flexibility and discretion granted to courts in the grant of interim injunctions and the only application of *American Cyanamid* was that the court should not require affidavit evidence at the stage of interim relief. Subsequently, however, courts permitted a view as to the strengths of the parties on credible evidence.[327] The result of these decisions is that the court can prejudge the dispute with respect to the chances of success of each party.[328]

5.1.3. *The Blurred Lines of Prima Facie Case in India*

Thus, the position of law in India rests on a vague discretion and multiple tests to determine the threshold of 'prima facie case' that the applicant needs to cross when seeking interim relief. Some courts still refer to a serious question to be tried,[329] and some refer to the strength of the parties on the face of the material on record.[330] Such a deep inquiry at the stage of interim relief leads to a 'mini-trial'. Even though *American Cyanamid* looked down on the practice of mini-trial,[331] given the pendency of litigation in India, it is evident that the courts have given complete sanction to such mini-trials. In fact, in *Colgate,* the court went to the extent of observing that *American Cyanamid*

---

likelihood of such a prejudice actually occurring; (c) can the prejudice be compensated by an award of damages or a security; (d) the likelihood of either party being able to satisfy the award of damages; (e) the likelihood that the injunction would later turn out to be wrongly granted, i.e., the court's opinion of the relevant strength of the party's case.

324. *Gobind Pritamdas Malkani v. Amarendranath Sircar* [1980] 50 Comp Cas 219 (Cal); *Amal Kumar Mukherjee v. Clarian Advertising Service Ltd.* [1982] 52 Comp Cas 315 (Cal); *Amar Talkies v. Apsara Cinema* 1982 JLJ 812; *Shankarlal Debiprasad v. State of Madhya Pradesh* (1978) MPLJ 419; *Damodar Valley Corporation v. Haripada Das* AIR 1978 Cal 489.
325. *Power Control Appliances v. Sumeet Machines* (1994) 2 SCC 448.
326. *Colgate Palmolive Ltd. v. Hindustan Unilever Ltd.* (1999) 7 SCC 1.
327. *M Gurudas v. Rasaranjan* (2006) 8 SCC 367; *Nestle India v. Mood Hospitality Private Ltd.* 2010, (42) PTC 514 (Del); *Omega SA v. Avanti Kopp Electricals* 2003 (27) PTC 327 (Mad).
328. *SM Dyechem Ltd. v. Cadbury (India) Ltd.* (2000) 5 SCC 573.
329. *United Commercial Bank v. Bank of India* AIR 1981 SC 1426; *Brajendra Nath v. Kashi Bai* AIR 1946 Pat 177; *Nimcha Coal Ltd. v. Srinivas Goenka* (1966) 70 CWN 1108; *Allappuzha Municipality v. TJ Paul* AIR 1995 Ker 36; *Shakuntala Devi v. Manoj Kumar* 1995 (60) DLT 358.
330. *J Krishnamoorthy v. Bangalore Turf Club* (1975) 2 Kant. LJ 428; *Ratna Paul v. Subhash Ranjan Paul* AIR 2001 Gau 133; *Uniply Industries v. Unicorn Plywood Ltd.* AIR 2001 SC 2083 (2086); *Bate Krishna Damini v. Kailash Chand* AIR 1995 SC 453: *Maria Sequeria Fernandez v. Erasmo Jack* (2012) 5 SCC 370; *A. Shanmugam v. Ariya Kshatriya* (2012) 4 SCALE 666.
331. *American Cyanamide Co. v. Ethicon* [1975] AC 396, at 399-400.

was more misunderstood than understood[332] and that the judgment in no way excluded consideration of the strength of the case at an interim stage. Following this line of thought, the Supreme Court, in another case, held that a temporary injunction passed without recording a prima facie satisfaction on the merits can be set aside in appeal.[333]

5.1.4. Mandatory Injunction

An issue tied very closely to the question of a prima facie case is the standard adopted under Indian law with respect to a mandatory injunction. The onus of proof in such cases is higher,[334] and a high degree of prima facie case requires to be shown.[335] This standard governs all orders passed by the courts directing the parties to take any positive step (as opposed to prohibitory orders), such as the creation of an escrow account, continuing performance of the contract, securing the amount in dispute, preservation of evidence, etc.

In 1990, the Supreme Court, in *Dorab Cawasji Warden v. Coomi Sorab Warden,*[336] *(Dorab)* listed the guidelines for issuing mandatory injunctions as:[337]

(a) the plaintiff has a strong case for trial, i.e., it shall be of a higher standard than a prima facie case that is normally required for a prohibitory injunction;
(b) it is necessary to prevent irreparable or serious injury, which normally cannot be compensated in terms of money; and
(c) the balance of convenience is in favour of the one seeking such relief.

Though the court specifically stated that the above guidelines are neither exhaustive nor complete or absolute, there may be exceptional circumstances which would require the sound judicial discretion of the court.[338]

Following this idea of a higher threshold, it must be noted that courts have held that it is not within the jurisdiction of the court to renew the contract between the

---

332. *Colgate Palmolive Ltd. v. Hindustan Unilever Ltd.* (1999) 7 SCC 1.
333. *Sree Jain Swetambar v. Phudan Singh* (1999) 2 SCC 377.
334. Courts in India have adopted the English jurisprudence which held that '*on motion, as contrasted with the trial, the court was far more reluctant to grant a mandatory injunction; in a normal case the courts must, inter alia, feel a high degree of assurance that at the trial it will appear that the injunction was rightly granted; and this was a higher standard than was required for a prohibitory injunction*'. *Shepherd Homes Ltd. v. Sandham* (1970) 3 All ER 402; *affirmed in Dorab Cawasji Warden v. Coomi Sorab Warden* (1990) 2 SCC 117. *Contrary to this, in Evans Marshall & Co Ltd v. Sertola SA* [1973] 1 WLR 349, the Court of Appeal in England held that '*although the failure of a plaintiff to show that he had a reasonable prospect of obtaining a permanent injunction at the trial was a factor which would normally weigh heavily against the grant of an interlocutory injunction, it was not a factor which, as a matter of law, precluded its grant*'.
335. *Consortium of Deepak Cable India Ltd. & Abir Infrastructure v. Teesta Valley Power Transmission Ltd.* 2014 SCC OnLine Del 4504, ¶54.
336. *Dorab Cawasji Warden v. Coomi Sorab Warden* (1990) 2 SCC 117.
337. *Ibid.*, ¶16.
338. *Ibid.*, ¶17.

parties by way of a mandatory injunction.[339] If the contract is terminated, even though large sums of money may have been invested, a mandatory injunction cannot be ordered and the remedy to the applicant is an action for damages.[340]

As noted above, it is well established that a mandatory interim injunction is not a remedy that is easily granted and can only be granted when the circumstances are exceptional.[341] Thus, a mandatory injunction is granted in the rarest cases and only after hearing the parties,[342] i.e., when greater injustice would have resulted in withholding the grant of mandatory injunction, the grant of such injunction is justified.[343]

5.1.5. 'Prima Facie Case' for Grant of Interim Measures in Arbitration

It is evident that the question of 'prima facie case' is far from settled in domestic jurisprudence under the CPC. On top of that, the Supreme Court decisions in *Adhunik* and *Arvind Construction* make the application of standards under the CPC applicable to Section 9 of the IAA where the relief sought may well transcend beyond the traditional understanding of interim measures based on injunctions.

Applying the standards under the CPC creates uncertainty and confusion. Courts venture into full scrutiny and determination of the merits of the dispute while deciding an application under Section 9 of the IAA, which leads to extensive delay and a 'mini-arbitration' at the stage of interim relief itself.

Furthermore, parties cannot predict the thresholds required to be satisfied as the courts carry wide discretion to determine what a 'prima face case' should be. The dangers of clogging the requirement of a prima facie case by a technical rule or a mathematical formula of the chances of success being over or under 50% were rejected and the court held that the discretion to grant an interim measure should be exercised judiciously and fairly, and not arbitrarily or capriciously.[344]

Some courts have diluted this threshold of a 'prima facie case' in the context of applications under Section 9 of the IAA. A prima facie case does not mean a case to succeed but which fairly needs an inquiry and that the court has to take into account, whether the interim measure sought is in aid of the final relief so as to maintain *status quo ante* or to preserve the status of parties.[345]

It does not mean that the court should examine the merits of the case closely and come to the conclusion that an applicant has a case in which the applicant would rightly succeed. That would amount to prejudging a case on merits. All the courts have

339. *Lt. Col. (Retd.) K.S. Ahluwalia v. Indraprastha Gas Ltd.* 2009 (3) Arb. LR 186 (Del).
340. *Cox and Kings India Ltd. v. Indian Railway Catering and Tourism Corp. Ltd.* 2012 (3) Arb. LR. 212 (SC).
341. *Samir Narain Bhojwani v. Aurora Properties and Investments* 2018 SCC OnLine SC 1048, ¶27; *as previously held in Metro Marines v. Bonus Watch Company Pvt. Ltd.* (2004) 7 SCC 478; *Kishore Kumar Khaitan v. Praveen Kumar Singh* (2006) 3 SCC 312; *Purshottam Vishandas Raheja v. Shrichand Vishandas Raheja* (2011) 6 SCC 73.
342. Sarkar, *supra* n. 302, at 2516-2517.
343. *Amit Sinha v. Sumit Mittal* 2011 (1) Arb. LR 332 (Del) (DB), ¶16.
344. *Allahabad Bank v. Rana Sheo Ambar Singh* AIR 1976 All 447.
345. *Deshmukh and Company v. Avinash V. Khandekar* 2005 (3) MhLJ 387.

to see is whether, on the face of it, the applicant applying for interim relief has a case which needs consideration[346] and the balance of convenience is in favour of the applicant.[347]

Thus, the court while considering an application under Section 9 of the IAA does not have jurisdiction to return a finding on the merits of the claim, but it is not disputed that it has the power to examine the existence of a prima facie case on the assertions of the applicant.[348] Essentially, a mere imagination of one party that the other party may sell its properties in order to defeat the claim is not sufficient under Section 9 of the IAA.[349]

However, even while lowering the threshold, the court has gone into the question of whether the measure is in aid of the final relief. Moreover, to what extent is the prima facie case to be proved still remains unclear. Furthermore, this reasoning cannot apply to interim measures in support of the arbitral process where the only consideration is the existence of a valid arbitration agreement and the necessity of the interim measures. There is no statement of claim and final relief being sought. More often than not, the request for an interim measure would be filed soon after sending the notice invoking arbitration under section 21 of the IAA. The notice of arbitration only contains a summary of the rights involved and the relief claimed, without any evidence. Hence, it is unclear what the possibility of success is supposed to be demonstrated at this stage.

The perplexed jurisprudence on the standard of prima facie case is enough by itself to demonstrate why the standard should not be used in the context of arbitration and why the domestic law standards such as the CPC and the Relief Act cannot adequately cater to the 'specific features of international arbitration'.[350] Reliance on the CPC and the Relief Act completely thwart the role of the courts to support arbitration proceedings.

In cases where mandatory injunctions are required, such as preventing harm to the arbitral process, securing the amount in dispute, preservation of evidence, or restoration of the status quo, the requirement of proving a higher threshold than a 'prima facie case' would in effect defeat the role of the court in supporting arbitration. The requirement of a 'strong case for trial' as outlined in *Dorab* can never exist at the stage of an application under Section 9 of the IAA and the court may never be able to 'restore the status quo' as provided under Article 17(2)(a) of the Model Law. Clearly, the current jurisprudence is inadequate to cater to the requirements of a pro-arbitration regime. Interim measures should stem from commercially reasonable actions and should not be tested on the same standards as the prima facie merits of the parties' claim.[351]

---

346. *Eastern Railway v. Lafarge India Pvt. Ltd.* 2018 (1) Arb. LR 417 (Cal) (DB).
347. *Vishal Retail Ltd. v. Kataria Automobiles Ltd.* 2010 (3) Arb. LR 255 (Guj).
348. *D.R. Sondhi v. Hella Kg Hueck & Co.* 2001 SCC OnLine Del 1273; *Naman Broadcasting and Telecommunications Pvt. Ltd. v. North Delhi Municipal Corporation* 2019 SCC OnLine Del 8082.
349. *Morgan Ventures Ltd. v. NEPC India* 2009 SCC OnLine Del 2258; *ECI-Nayak (JV) v. Ircon International Ltd.* 2019 SCC OnLine Delhi 9418.
350. UNCITRAL Model Law, Art. 17J.
351. Gary Born, *supra* n. 33, at 2683-2684.

Therefore, there is an imperative need for autonomous standards to be provided under the IAA for considering an application under Section 9 of the IAA. Such criteria need to delink consideration of 'prima facie' as applied in a suit under the CPC. Instead, the consideration should cater to the unique nature of arbitration and the role of the court being limited to supporting the arbitral process.

5.2. Balance of Convenience

Similarly, in determining the balance of convenience, the court must weigh the mischief likely to be caused to the applicant, if the injunction is not granted and also, compare the prejudice which is likely to be caused to the other party if the injunction is granted.[352] In the context of an application under Section 9 of the IAA, the court should only consider that the harm likely to result if the interim measure is not ordered till the formation of the arbitral tribunal or till the consideration by the arbitral tribunal outweighs the harm that is likely to result to the party against whom the measure is directed if the measure is granted. The question of balance of convenience ought to be considered with due respect to the principle of 'priority' of the jurisdiction of the arbitral tribunal.

5.3. Irreparable Harm

The question of irreparable harm in the context of an application under Section 9 of the IAA is unnecessary.[353] The court should only consider the existence of a valid arbitration agreement and the necessity of the measure. After the amendment to the Relief Act, damages are not an adequate remedy since the specific performance of contracts is now the norm, rather than the exception.[354] The Expert Committee on the Relief Act explicitly agreed in its first meeting that this change in approach would entail injunctive relief becoming the norm and would reduce the debate on the assessment of compensation at the time of judgment or execution of the decree.[355] Therefore, domestic law requirements should not be applied in the context of an application under Section 9 of the IAA.

5.4. Other Considerations

The application of the CPC and Relief Act to requests for interim measures under Section 9 of the IAA also requires equitable considerations since the CPC and all equity which tempers discretionary relief is applicable to an application under Section 9 of the IAA. Thus, the following considerations would also apply to all such applications:

---

352. *Billimoria v. India Inst. of Architects* 2005 (2) Mah LJ 206 (213) (Bom); *Kamla Homes & Lifestyle Pvt. Ltd. v. Pushp Kamal Co-operative Housing Society Ltd.* 2019 SCC OnLine Bom 823, ¶23.
353. *Discussed in detail in Chapter 7.*
354. *Supra* n. 79, ¶11.3.1.
355. *Ibid.*, ¶11.3.1.

(a) conduct of the applicant and the delay in filing the application;[356]
(b) clean hands;[357]
(c) compatibility with Section 41 of the Specific Relief Act;[358]
(d) consideration of public interest and public convenience while determining the question of balance of convenience;[359] and
(e) the interim measure should not amount to a pre-trial decree.[360]

These other considerations have also found their way into the jurisprudence in the arbitration context. Courts have held that a party invoking jurisdiction under Section 9 of the IAA has to show that it was not at fault, i.e., the conduct of the parties[361] was not responsible for bringing about the state of things complained of.[362] Also, the public interest is a criterion while adjudicating an application under Section 9 of the IAA.[363] Therefore, there is an imperative need to provide clear standards for exercising the power under Section 9 of the IAA as those provided under Article 17A along with Article 17J of the Model Law.

5.5. Articles 17A and 17J of the Model Law: A Guide Towards the Right Standard

As discussed previously, in an attempt not to interfere with the sovereignty of nations and their courts, the Model Law left the questions of court-ordered interim measures largely to national arbitration statutes. This led to inconsistency, disharmony, and applicability of domestic court procedures to applications seeking interim measures in support of the arbitral process.[364] It was this error that the 2006 Model Law Revisions tried to address with the introduction of Articles 17A and 17J of the Model Law.

Article 17A of the Model Law introduces the most widely accepted[365] international standards to be adopted while considering a request for interim measures by the arbitral tribunal. Such widely accepted standards fall within the phrase 'specific features of international arbitration'. Hence, such introduction, albeit for consideration by the arbitral tribunals, clearly indicates that the guiding principles set out under

356. *Gujarat Bottling Ltd. Co. v. Coca Cola Co.* (1995) 5 SCC 545; *Radhey Shyam Nigam v. Jyoti Shrivastava* 2001 AIHC 3706 (3713) (MP).
357. *Kasturibai v. Corporation of City of Hubli* AIR 2003 Kant 170 (171); *Transstroy Tirupati Tiruthani Chennai Tollways Private Limited v. Allahabad Bank* 2019 SCC OnLine Del 9080.
358. *Lalwani Ferro Alloys Pvt. Ltd. v. Umi Special Steel Ltd.* 1998 CWN 556 (DB).
359. *Nagar Nigam, Aligarh v. Udai Singh* AIR 2003 All 34 (42); *Samay Singh v. Hindustan Petroleum Corporation Ltd.* 2012 SCC OnLine All 1253, ¶31.
360. *Sarla Jain v. Sangu Gangadhar* 2016 (3) I.C.C. 246 Hyd.
361. *Kishorsinh Ratansinh Jadeja v. Maruti Corporation* (2009) 11 SC 229, ¶12; *Mandali Ranganna v. T Ramachandra* (2008) 11 SCC 1; *Nizams Institute of Medical Sciences v. T Rajendra* 2009 (1) Arb. LR 72 (AP) (DB).
362. *Consortium of Deepak Cable India Ltd. & Abir Infrastructure v. Teesta Valley Power Transmission Ltd.* 2014 SCC OnLine Del 4504, ¶¶40-41.
363. *Ibid.*, ¶61.
364. Menon, *supra* n. 102, at 29.
365. Sarthak, *supra* n. 21, at 202.

Article 17J of the Model Law may be achieved through the incorporation of Article 17A of the Model Law.

The critical difference between litigation in national courts and arbitration is the territorial origin and scope of application of a domestic legislation like the CPC. Procedural laws that govern domestic legislation are tailor-made to solve disputes before domestic courts.[366] This creates a problem for arbitration which aims to promote flexibility and bolster party autonomy to create fair proceedings for everyone.

Applying the CPC creates hurdles to arbitration even within the domestic spheres and considerable barriers to international commercial arbitration as the CPC is modelled on the organisation and legal structure of the judiciary in India. Moreover, the very essence of arbitration rests on the flexibility afforded to parties not to get sucked into cumbersome domestic laws or foreign laws. Application of domestic law standards under the CPC and the Specific Relief Act defeats this advantage of arbitration.

Furthermore, it makes little or no sense to provide different standards to be applied by the courts when considering a request for interim measures in aid of the arbitral process and by the arbitral tribunal during the arbitration proceedings. The arbitral tribunal cannot be expected to apply domestic law standards when considering whether to suspend, modify, or terminate an interim measure granted by the court.

The real reason for falling back on jurisprudence stemming from civil or commercial litigation is the underlying need to enforce orders.[367] Enforcement of orders should not determine standards to be applied to a request for interim measures.[368] Standards should only determine whether the circumstances necessitate the grant of an interim measure. Enforcement concerns would stem from the type of measure that can be granted in such a situation and their compatibility with the domestic law such as the CPC.

It has been suggested that the standards adopted by Indian Courts are in line with those widely accepted international standards contained in Article 17A of the Model Law.[369] While the same may be true on a superficial analysis of some of the precedents, a detailed examination of the precedents suggests otherwise. The rationale and thought process of the courts suggests that they have not adopted such criteria keeping in mind the larger goal of non-interference and support to the arbitral process but have operated on a 'mix-and-match' approach of borrowing from the Model Law, English jurisprudence, the CPC, and the Specific Relief Act. Very few judgments have clearly outlined the subsidiary role of the courts in supporting arbitration and even fewer have done so with a clear understanding of the 'specific features of international arbitration'.

Hence, the standards to be applied by the courts when considering a request for interim measures should be harmonised with Article 17A of the Model Law (with modifications)[370] as has been done in New Zealand.[371] In one of the discussions of the

366. Abascal, *supra* n. 1, at 757.
367. *Ibid.*, at 756-757.
368. Report of UNCITRAL Working Group on the work of its Thirty Second session, June 2000, A/CN.9/468, available at: https://undocs.org/en/A/CN.9/468, ¶66.
369. Sarthak, *supra* n. 21, at 202.
370. *Discussed in detail in Chapter 7.*

Working Group, it was suggested that the Working Group should consider in the future if Articles 9 and 17 should be redrafted 'so as to apply also to interim measures granted by State courts under article 9 and article 17'.[372] Such harmonisation will promote uniformity, certainty, and predictability, uphold party autonomy, and minimise court intervention. It will make a national arbitration statute a 'complete code' with respect to arbitration and facilitate the goal of arbitration being a 'one-stop' solution for adjudication of disputes. It will also further the autonomous application of Article 17J of the Model Law and ultimately honour the intent of the parties not to apply cumbersome domestic procedures for the resolution of their dispute.

The rejection of domestic law standards in favour of those contained in Article 17A for court-ordered interim measures has been affirmed by the High Court of New Zealand after adopting the 2006 Model Law Revisions. The court rejected the applicability of the High Court rules which required a 'strong arguable case' for the purpose of a freezing order. The court noted that in the absence of the use of the word 'strong' in the test laid down in Article 17A(1)(b) of the Model Law which uses the word 'reasonable possibility of success', the court would disregard the test under domestic law and proceed as if there was no difference in the two tests. The court would only apply the test of a reasonable possibility of success.[373]

6. TYPES OF MEASURES

Once the power, scope, and standards applicable to an application under section 9 of the IAA have been determined, the next question which requires examination is the type of measures that the court can order.

Most countries do not specify the type of measures that can be ordered.[374] They simply adopt the language contained in Article 9 of the Model Law. As discussed previously, the Model Law did not address the issue of court-ordered interim measures for the fear that it would interfere with court powers and procedures. Hence, the power and type of court-ordered interim measures are primarily contained in the domestic procedural law of each country. Even Article 17J of the Model Law reiterates that the power to issue an interim measure in relation to arbitration proceedings shall be the same as a court has in relation to proceedings before it.

However, in a certain sense, Article 17(2) of the Model Law specifies the kind of remedies that are required in commercial disputes and arbitration practice. Hence, it is reasonable to argue that the same gives an indication of the kind of remedies that may be required by the court to exercise the power contained in Article 17J 'in consideration of the specific features of international arbitration'.

371. New Zealand, Arbitration Act, 1996, S. 9(2).
372. UNCITRAL Yearbook, *supra* n. 11, at 461.
373. *Safe Kids in Daily Supervision Ltd. v. McNeill* CIV 2010 - 404 - 1696, 14/4/10, ¶31.
374. *See Appendix A.*

6.1. Comparing the Model Law with Section 9 of the IAA

Contrary to Article 17(2) of the Model Law, in India, the types of measures that can be granted by the court are listed under Section 9 of the IAA, which correspond to Section 44 of the English Arbitration Act.[375] Despite borrowing from the English Arbitration Act, an argument can be made that India consciously provided for the types of measures within Section 9 of the IAA to align with those of Article 17(2) of the Model Law. For the ease of reference and comparison only, the type of measures granted in India can be categorised as follows:

(a) Maintain or restore the status quo pending the determination of the dispute:
 - (i) Section 9(1)(ii)(a) of the IAA – the preservation, interim custody, or sale of any goods which are the subject matter of the arbitration agreement.
 - (ii) Section 9(1)(ii)(d) of the IAA – injunction or appointment of receiver.

(b) Take action that would prevent or refrain from taking action that is likely to cause, current, or imminent harm or prejudice to the arbitral process itself:
 - (i) Section 9(1)(ii)(d) of the IAA – injunction or appointment of receiver.
 - (ii) Section 9(1)(ii)(e) of the IAA – such other interim measure of protection as may appear to the court to be just and convenient.

(c) Provide a means of preserving assets out of which a subsequent award may be satisfied:
 - (i) Section 9(1)(ii)(b) of the IAA – securing the amount in dispute in the arbitration.

(d) Preserve evidence that may be relevant and material to the resolution of the dispute:
 - (i) Section 9(1)(ii)(a) of the IAA – the preservation, interim custody, or sale of any goods which are the subject matter of the arbitration agreement.
 - (ii) Section 9(1)(ii)(c) of the IAA – the detention, preservation, or inspection of any property or thing which is the subject-matter of the dispute in arbitration or as to which any question may arise therein, and authorising for any of the aforesaid purposes any person to enter upon any land or building in the possession of any party, or authorising any samples to be taken, or any observation to be made, or experiment to be tried, which may be necessary or expedient for the purpose of obtaining full information or evidence.

375. Indian Arbitration Act, 1996, S. 9(a), i.e., preservation, interim custody or sale of goods, Indian Arbitration Act, 1996, S. 9(c), i.e., the detention, preservation or inspection of any property, and Indian Arbitration Act, 1996, S. 9(d), i.e., interim injunction or appointment of receiver correspond to English Arbitration Act, 1996, S. 44(3), 44(2)(c), and 44(2)(e).

The only two aberrations are the powers contained in Section 9(1)(i) of the IAA and Section 9(1)(ii)(e) of the IAA.[376]

Section 9(1)(i) of the IAA pertains to the power of appointment of a guardian. There is no reported case where the power under this section has been exercised and it is unlikely that the same may be used in commercial arbitration. This provision serves no purpose and should be deleted. The objective of the provision can be adequately fulfilled by taking recourse to the provisions of the CPC for filing pleadings before the court.[377]

The other deviation from the Model Law is contained in Section 9(1)(ii)(e) of the IAA. Subclauses (a) to (d) of Section 9(1)(ii) of the IAA provide for alternatives available to the court in connection with an arbitral proceeding.[378] Subclause (e) of Section 9(1)(ii) of the IAA, being residuary, provides for '*such other interim measures of protection as may appear to the court to be "just and convenient"*',[379] i.e., such other interim measures as are necessary for the protection of the property in dispute by way of granting interim measures,[380] even if they do not pertain to the subject matter of the dispute in arbitration.[381] Presumably, the provision has been borrowed from Section 94(e) of the CPC as all other types of interim measures have been incorporated under Section 9 except the power to arrest.

It should be noted, however, that the categorisation contemplated above has not been made or endorsed by any court. The categorisation is only for understanding the types of interim measures available to the court to support the arbitral process and compare the application of each type of measure under Section 9 to the measures contemplated under Article 17(2) of the Model Law.

6.2. Maintain or Restore Status Quo

The objective of interim measures is to ensure that the assets of the parties are not dissipated or frittered away,[382] i.e., to maintain the status quo[383] and to preserve the

376. Bangladesh Arbitration Act, 2001, S. 7A.
377. Indian Code of Civil Procedure, 1908, Ord. XXXII.
378. *Harbhajan Singh Kaur v. Unimode Finance* (1997) 2 CALLT 414 HC.
379. *Upheld in MEPC India Ltd. v. Sundaram Finance Ltd.* 1998 (2) Arb. LR 446 (Mad), ¶18.
380. *Nagarchand Goenka v. Surendranath Sarkar* AIR 1946 Pat 70. *At one instance, the court directed the parties to file an application under Section 9(1)(ii)(e) to seek a direction that arbitration proceedings should not be commenced without seeking the approval of the National Company Law Disputes Tribunal. Chennai Metro Rail Limited v. Lanco Infratech Limited* 2019 SCC OnLine Mad 936; *P. Muthulakshmi v. District Registrar* 2019 SCC OnLine Mad 839.
381. *Tata Capital Finances Services Ltd. v. Deccan Chronicle Holdings Ltd. & Anr.* 2013 (2) Arb. LR 181 (Bom), ¶41.
382. *Shaw v. Him Neel Breweries* 2006 133 DLT 153, ¶9, *and that such orders do not fall within a moratorium.*
383. *Coastal Projects Ltd. v. Union of India* 2020 SCC OnLine Gau 932; *Guru Madhwa Seva Samithi v. Katti Ananth Acharya* 2003 AIHC 31(33) (Kant); *National Collateral Management Service Limited v. Neha Mukesh Chandra Gupta & Anr.* 2019 SCC Online Bom 9147; *Tanita Sanjauli Parking Private Ltd. v. Municipal Corporation Shimla* 2019 SCC OnLine HP 1133; *Om Prakash Sharma v. State of HP* 2019 SCC OnLine HP 292.

subject matter of the dispute[384] till the formation of the arbitral tribunal or final adjudication of the dispute by the arbitral tribunal. The reference to the status quo should not be taken to mean some identifiable and precisely definable situation that existed or does exist before passing an interim measure. The purpose of the status quo is to identify the holding and temporary nature of an interim measure and is not intended to create a restrictive threshold requirement.[385]

6.2.1. Difference Between Maintaining and Restoring Status Quo

It should be noted that there exists a distinction between maintaining the status quo and restoring the status quo. The former refers to the prevention of aggravation of the dispute, while the latter refers to preventing a party from unjustly benefiting by its wrongful conduct.[386] Instances of maintaining the status quo include the power of the court to order preservation,[387] interim custody, and sale of any goods which are the subject matter of the arbitration agreement or securing the amount in the dispute.[388] Instances of restoring the status quo would include putting a person back in possession of the property or renewing terminated contracts.[389]

Initially, some courts restricted the power under Section 9 of the IAA to the 'subject matter of arbitration' and the preservation of 'property'.[390] Hence, the power to maintain or restore the status quo could only be exercised with respect to the 'subject matter of arbitration'. However, such an interpretation was rejected in light of Section 9(ii)(e) of the IAA.[391]

It is pertinent to mention that most cases relating to the request for interim measures for maintaining the status quo have been for injunctions restraining the opposite party from invoking a bank guarantee and the court has required the party requesting the status quo to demonstrate 'strong prima facie' based on the applicability of the CPC.[392]

6.2.2. Appointment of Receiver

Several applications under Section 9 of the IAA for maintaining the status quo also require that a receiver be appointed till the dispute is pending or till the arbitral tribunal

384. *Central Coalfields Ltd. v. M/s Jugnoo Construction* AIR 2003 NOC 529, ¶7.
385. *Safe Kids in Daily Supervision Ltd. v. McNeill* CIV 2010 - 404 - 1696, 14/4/10, ¶27.
386. *See Chapter 7.*
387. *An applicant who is the owner of the goods lying in the warehouse is entitled to seek preservation of said goods under Indian Arbitration Act, 1996, S. 9. See, Pawan Hans Helicopters Ltd. v. Aes Aerospace Ltd.* 2008 (2) Arb. LR 63 (Del), ¶24.
388. *CREF Finance Ltd. v. Puri Constructions Ltd.* 2000 (55) DRJ 750; *Sanrachna (India) Inc. v. AB Hotels Ltd.* 2006 (128) DLT 694, ¶4.
389. *Discussed in Chapter 7.*
390. *BLB Institute of Financial Markets Ltd. v. Ramakar Jha* 2008 (4) Arb. LR 12 (Del), ¶32.
391. *Ibid.*
392. *Rail Vikas Nigam Ltd. (RVNL) v. Harish Chandra (India) Ltd.* 2013 (3) Arb. LR 499; *SEPCO Electric Power Construction Corporation v. Talwandi Sabo Power Limited* 2016 SCC OnLine P&H 119; *Mulanur Renewable Energy Pvt. Ltd. v. Regen Powertech Pvt. Ltd.* 2018 (3) Arb. LR 201 (Del) (DB), ¶12.

is formed.[393] The criteria to determine the same has to be based on a 'very good prima facie case' and the party requesting the interim measure has to show not only a conflicting claim to the property, but also emergency, damage, or loss demanding immediate action.[394]

The financial crisis of the defendant and the adamant attitude are also relevant considerations for the appointment of a receiver.[395] However, where the effect of the appointment of a receiver is that of depriving a defendant of a de facto position which may cause irreparable loss to the defendant, in such cases, a receiver cannot be appointed.[396] Therefore, a receiver cannot be appointed merely because it is expedient or convenient to do so or because it would not do any harm.[397] A receiver can only be appointed in case no other remedy or means of accomplishing the desired object of the judicial proceeding is available.[398]

6.2.3. Restoration of Contracts

The other facet of the power to grant the status quo is the relief of restoring the status quo. Based on the provision of the CPC and the Specific Relief Act, it is now settled that injunctions under Section 9 of the IAA for restoring contracts in order to maintain the status quo cannot be granted.[399] Therefore, there can be no restoration of the status quo and hence, restoration of a contract that has been terminated is not possible under Section 9 of the IAA. Based on the pattern of the standards adopted by the courts to maintain or restore the status quo, a party praying for interim relief under the said provision will have to demonstrate a standard much higher than just a prima facie case, i.e., usually requiring a 'strong' or 'very strong' prima facie case.

It is unclear how a party would demonstrate such a 'strong prima facie case' without leading evidence and how the court can determine the same without prejudging the merits. Hence, Article 17(2)(a) read with Article 17A(1) of the Model Law are

---

393. *Kamla Homes and Lifestyle Private Limited v. Pushp Kamal Co-operative Housing Society Limited & Ors.* 2019 SCC Online Bom 823; *Vanit Gupta v. Delta Iron & Steel Company P. Ltd.* 2019 SCC Online Bom 3128; *Magma Fincorp Ltd. v. Madhvi Devi* 2019 SCC OnLine Cal 244; *Srei Equipment Finance Limited v. Misa Developers* 2019 SCC Online Cal 1234; *Magma Fincorp Ltd. v. Rahman Ahamad* 2019 SCC Online Cal 2611; *Reliance Commercial Finance Ltd. v. Vista Mining Pvt. Ltd.* 2019 SCC Online Cal 2648; *Tata Capital Financial Services Limited v. Saifuddin Jamirali Shaikh & Anr.* 2019 SCC Online Cal 2674; *Aditya Birla Finance Ltd. v. Mr. Karnet Illias Fernandes* 2015 SCC OnLine Bom 4774.
394. *T. Krishnaswamy Chetty v. C. Thangavelu Chetty* AIR 1955 Mad 430.
395. *The Motor & General Finance Ltd. v. Bravo Hotels Pvt. Ltd.* 2018 (2) Arb. LR 402 (Del).
396. *Shin Satellite Public Co. Ltd. v. Jain Studios Ltd.* 2008 SCC OnLine Del 1127, ¶37; *Rajeshzvar Nath Gupta v. Administrator General* AIR 1989 Delhi 179; *Syed Khuwaja Syed Ahmed v. The Maharashtra Housing and Area Development Authority* AIR 1983 Bom 73; *Ravi Kumar v. Nisha Vadhera* AIR 1995 Delhi 175.
397. *A contrary view was taken in Firm Ashok Traders v. Gurmukh Das Saluja* AIR 2004 SC 1433, ¶15. *It held that the most basic principle governing the discretion of the court in appointing the receiver is whether it is just and convenient to do so.*
398. *Shin Satellite Public Co. Ltd. v. Jain Studios Ltd.* 2008 SCC OnLine Del 1127, ¶37.
399. *Parsoli Works Pvt. Ltd. v. BMW India Pvt. Ltd.* 2018 (2) Arb. LR 50; *Bharat Catering Corporation v. Indian Railway Catering and Tourism Corporation Limited (IRCTC)* 2009 SCC OnLine Del 3418; *DLF Home Developers Limited v. Shipra Estate Ltd.* 2021 SCC OnLine Del 4902, ¶108.

better standards to adopt as they do not require such a high threshold. A party requesting an interim measure under Section 9 of the IAA may be in a better position to satisfy the court of the standards contemplated in the Model Law instead of the high thresholds provided in reference to the CPC.

6.3. Harm to the Arbitral Process

There haven't been many instances where the court has granted interim relief to protect the arbitral process per se.[400] However, courts have granted interim measures to avoid multiplicity of proceedings if a party is appearing before another forum to protect the right under adjudication till the formation of the arbitral tribunal.[401]

In one instance, this residuary clause has been invoked when the seat and the place of arbitration were the same and the immovable properties were located outside the said seat. The court held that the court at the seat will retain jurisdiction and can order attachment of immovable property located outside the jurisdiction of the seat under section 9(1)(ii)(e) of the IAA.[402]

There are also instances where the court directed that in light of the substantial investment and considering the serious allegations of siphoning, the defendant was directed to submit weekly statements of all receipts and payments as well as fortnightly statements of all its bank accounts.[403] Similarly, the Bombay High Court directed a party to vacate the flat in a rent agreement subject to the landlord providing him alternate accommodation till the finality of the arbitration proceeding,[404] or grant of interim compensation where the defendant builder purchased the property and agreed with the tenant to provide accommodation to the tenant but failed to do so for twelve years.[405] In another instance, the Delhi High Court granted an order of refund of the

400. *In a bizarre case, the Principal District Judge, Panaji, Goa allowed an application under Section 9 of the IAA and granted an injunction requested by the applicant. The respondent filed an appeal under Section 37(1)(a) of the IAA and argued that such an injunction could not be granted in the facts and circumstances of the case, especially because of the fact that at the time of formation of contract and finalization of the contract with the State Government, the same person i.e., the Principal Judge had handled the file in the capacity of the Law Secretary and therefore he should not have taken the matter in the judicial side. The Bombay High Court held that once it is found that the judge had already dealt with the file as the Law Secretary, it was not proper on the part of the judge to take up the matter on the judicial side without disclosing this aspect to the parties. Hence, the appeal was allowed, and the order passed by the Principal Judge was set aside. Government of Goa v. Jaisu Shipping Co. Pvt. Ltd.* 2009 (2) Arb. LR 504 (Bom) (DB), ¶13.

401. *Red Carpet Films Ltd. v. Eros International Films Pvt. Ltd.* 2009 (3) Arb. LR 612 (Bom).

402. *Muthoot Vehicles & Asset Finance Ltd. v. Gopalan Kuttanapan* 2009 SCC OnLine Kerala 2087, ¶11.

403. *SRS Private Investment Powai Ltd. v. Supreme Housing and Hospitality Pvt. Ltd.* 2016 SCC OnLine Del 5446, ¶17.

404. *Heritage Lifestyles and Developers Pvt. Ltd. v. Amar-Villa Co-operative Housing Society Ltd.* 2011 SCC OnLine Bom 349.

405. *Chandra Kant Shankar Pradhan v. Verma Investment Incorporation* AIR 1992 Bom 257.

encashed bank guarantees pending disposal of the setting aside application under section 34 of the IAA.[406]

Therefore, instances of courts granting interim measures to prevent harm to the arbitral process have usually been granted under the residuary clause contained in Section 9(1)(ii)(e) of the IAA.[407] This residuary clause is in complete divergence from the Model Law. Even the 2006 Model Law Revisions do not provide for such extensive power.

The language of Section 9(1)(ii)(e) of the IAA is similar to that contained in Section 94(e) of the CPC which has been held to refer to the provision of Order XXXIX Rules 6-10. Therefore, if the provisions of the CPC are applied, the exercise of this power will have to be interpreted with reference to the said provisions of the CPC. However, if an autonomous interpretation of section 9 of the IAA is preferred, then this power has little or no limitations. It can be exercised depending on the facts and circumstances of the case without any safeguards. For example, in a gross misuse of the provision, a single judge of the Delhi High Court interpreted the power under Section 9 of the IAA to include the power to summon a Managing Director of a company when the court had directed for a deposit of security amount.[408]

There is no need for such a provision if the power under Section 9 of the IAA refers to the generic language contained in Article 17(2) of the Model Law. Courts will be able to grant suitable remedies without the need to resort to a residuary clause. Such exercise of power would also be in alignment with the overarching goal of supporting the arbitral process and in consideration of the 'specific features of international arbitration'.

6.4. Preservation of Assets

Article 17(2)(c) of the Model Law provides for '*a means of preserving assets out of which a subsequent award may be satisfied*'. Using slightly different language, Section 9(1)(ii)(b) of the IAA refers to 'securing the amount in dispute'. Hence, sometimes the courts have granted requests for securing the amount in dispute by ordering the defendant to furnish a bank guarantee because of the various media reports that the company was shutting down its wireless business and reeling under debt.[409] At other times, the court has passed (a) attachment orders; (b) orders for interim payments; (c) garnishee orders.

---

406. *Ishvakoo (India) Pvt. Ltd. v. National Projects Construction Corporation Ltd.* 2019 SCC OnLine Del 8137, ¶41.
407. *See Ashok Kumar v. SBI Officers Association (Delhi Circle)* 2013 (3) Arb. LR 246 (Del); *Jaguar Overseas Limited v. Seagull Maritime Agencies Pvt. Ltd.* 2020 SCC OnLine Del 2000, ¶33.
408. *Indo Arya Central Transport Ltd. v. Container Corporation of India Ltd.* 2008 (1) Arb. LR 229 (Del), ¶13.
409. *ATC Telecom Infrastructure Pvt. Ltd. v. Reliance Communications Ltd.* 2018 (1) Arb. LR 156 (Del), ¶28.

6.4.1. *Attachment Orders*

The phrase 'securing the amount in dispute in the arbitration' is wide enough to include the making of an order of conditional attachment of the property of the person from whom the amount is claimed with a view to ensuring that the amount claimed in the arbitration proceeding is secured.[410] As previously discussed, the ingredients of the CPC are not embodied in Section 9 of the IAA and neither the conditions mentioned in the same order can be read into the power under Section 9 of the IAA.[411] However, the exercise of discretion under Section 9 of the IAA has been guided by the provisions of Orders XXXVIII and XXXIX of the CPC.[412]

The party requesting an order for attachment of assets of the opposite party has to establish a reasonably 'strong prima facie case' and prove that the opposite party is acting in a manner to defeat the realisation of a decree that ultimately may be passed.[413] The court has to be satisfied that such order is necessary to secure the amount in dispute and the same cannot be passed mechanically.[414] Under one view, the court has to consider the requirements of Order XXXVIII Rule 5 of the CPC before granting relief,[415] though there is no specific averment in any particular form as contemplated under Order XXXVIII Rule 5 of the CPC.[416]

Therefore, the conditions under Order XXXVIII Rule 5 of the CPC have to be satisfied before interim relief can be granted under Section 9 of the IAA.[417] Recently, the Madras High Court[418] held that the principles contained in Order XXXVIII Rule 5 of the CPC would apply to an application under Section 9 of the IAA, though the same provisions would not apply to arbitration proceedings.[419] It went on to lay down the test for the grant of an order directing furnishing of security as:

(a) the plaintiff has to demonstrate and establish before the court that the property that is sought to be preserved is under imminent danger of being removed from the jurisdiction of the court or is under imminent threat of being liquidated; and

---

410. *Quippo Construction Equipment Ltd. v. Janardan Nirman Private Ltd.* 2019 SCC OnLine Del 10646; *Yenipoya Minerals and Granites Ltd. v. Maharashtra Apex Corporation Ltd.* 2004 (2) Arb. LR 47 (Karnataka) (DB), ¶6.
411. *Ganesh Benzoplast Ltd. v. Sundaram Finance Ltd.* [2002] (3) RAJ 120 (DB).
412. *Nimbus Communications Limited v. Board of Control for Cricket in India* 2012 SCC OnLine 287; *Right Approach Group Ltd. v. Rosoboron Export Ltd.* 2004 (75) DRJ 104.
413. *Himalayan Heli Adventures Pvt. Ltd. v. Utair India Pvt. Ltd. & Ors.* 2019 SCC OnLine Del 8843, ¶25.
414. *Natrip Implementation Society v. IVRCL Ltd.* 2016 SCC OnLine Del 5023, ¶20.
415. *Intertoll ICS Cecons O & M Co. Pvt. Ltd. v. National Highways Authority of India* 2013 SCC OnLine Del 447, ¶32.
416. *Ganesh Benzoplast Ltd. v. Sundaram Finance Ltd.* [2002] (3) RAJ 120 (DB), ¶¶11, 18.
417. *R.R. Constructions v. St. Ann's Co-operative Group Housing Society* 2008 (1) Arb. LR 424 (Del), ¶43.
418. *Shinago Holdings Pvt. Ltd. v. M. Ethiraj* 2018 (1) Arb. LR 226 (Madras) (DB).
419. *Ibid.*, ¶6 (XIII).

(b) such attempts for removal/liquidation of assets and properties are being made with the intention of defeating a possible decree/award.[420]

The other view is that the court does not need to find out whether the defendant is seeking to dispose of the assets or not before securing the amount in dispute.[421] All that the court has to see is that the arbitral award when obtained would result in a paper decree or a decree which cannot be enforced on account of the act of the party in case of a pending arbitral process.[422] This discretion is to be exercised on the material before the court and the applicant has to make out a case that there is a need for an interim measure of protection. However, once the court passes the order, then the order to secure would be enforced as per the procedure laid down in the CPC.

Based on the above, it is uncertain when and under what conditions will a court grant an attachment order to support the arbitral process. The predominant view though leans in favour of applying the principles of Order XXXVIII Rule 5 of the CPC.[423] Such unpredictability and constant reliance on the CPC, in turn, affect the exercise of the power of the court to address the needs of the parties seeking interim measures to preserve assets out of which a subsequent award may be satisfied.

6.4.2. Interim Payment

The difference in language in Article 17(2)(c) of the Model Law and Section 9(1)(ii)(b) of the IAA is self-evident. While the Model Law refers to the preservation of assets for satisfaction of the award, Section 9(1)(ii)(b) of the IAA refers to 'securing the amount'. Therefore, courts in India have directed parties to make interim payments in order to secure the amount in dispute in the arbitration.

An interim payment is the payment of a certain sum of money to the opposite party as an interim measure which may be revised in the final award. To a certain extent, such payments tend to proceed on prejudging the merits of the case as the grant of such a measure would amount to the final order/execution of the award before the award has become executable.[424] In India, such payments have been recognised under Section 9 of the IAA,[425] but not without dissenting views.[426] Thus, a crystallised

420. *Ibid.*, ¶6 (XV).
421. *Delta Constructions Systems Ltd., Hyderabad v. Narmada Cement Company Ltd.* 2002 (2) Arb. LR 47 (Bom).
422. *Ibid.*; *Global Company v. National Fertilizers Ltd.* 1998 SCC OnLine Del 387, ¶10.
423. *Nimbus Communications Limited v. Board of Control for Cricket in India* 2012 SCC OnLine 287; *Right Approach Group Ltd. v. Rosoboron Export Ltd.* 2004 (75) DRJ 104; *Thar Camps Pvt. Ltd. v. Indus River Cruises Pvt. Ltd.* 2021 SCC OnLine Del 3150; *Pinaka Studios Ltd. v. MX Media and Entertainment Pte. Ltd.* 2021 SCC OnLine Del 5033, ¶39.
424. *Himachal Furitistic Communication Ltd. v. Union of India* 2009 (3) Arb. LR 394; *National Highways Authority of India v. Bhubaneswar Expressway Private Ltd.* 2021 SCC OnLine Del 2421, ¶32.
425. *Neeru Jain v. Jasmine Buildmart Private Ltd.* 2019 SCC OnLine Del 10731; *IRB Tumkur Chitradurga Tollway Ltd. v. National Highways Authority of India* 2019 SCC OnLine Del 11335; *Ratnagiri Gas and Power Pvt. Ltd. v. Joint Venture of Whessoe Oil and Gas Ltd.* 2013 (1) Arb. LR 84 (Del) (DB); *Ishwakoo (India) Pvt. Ltd. v. National Projects Construction Corporation Ltd.* 2019 SCC OnLine Del 8137.

amount lying with a party or arrears of rent[427] can be claimed under Section 9 of the IAA as the claim of an ascertained amount should prevail over an unascertained amount.[428]

However, it must be remembered that an order directing payment of money has the effect of strapping the company severely and impairing its commercial operations.[429] Therefore, such orders should be granted only when the court deems it fit in the given facts and circumstances of each case.[430]

When the parties have rival monetary claims alleging violation of contractual terms, no direction of deposit of money can be made under Section 9 of the IAA to protect the alleged interest of any party. It cannot be assumed based on a prima facie case that the arbitrator may pass an arbitral award in favour of one party unless it is established that the other party has started transferring or has already taken steps to transfer its assets for defrauding its creditors or for avoiding payment of the arbitral award that may be passed.[431]

The court has to keep in mind the drastic nature of demanding payment of security to preserve assets for future enforcement of the award. Unless a clear case not only on the merits of the claim is made out but also that denial of such an order would result in grave injustice is shown and further, that the award will not be executed or that the opposite party is engaging in obstructive conduct,[432] the court should decline an order directing the deposit of security.[433]

Thus, courts in India have provided the relief of 'securing the amount in dispute' by examining the merits of the case and determining if the amount can be secured or when both parties have consented.[434] Examining the merits of the case is contrary to the intent of the Model Law which is restricted to preserving assets for satisfaction of the award. The Working Group categorically rejected interim payments as a form of interim measures of protection.[435] Moreover, such determination of merits is contrary to the role of the courts only to support the arbitral process and in effect, amounts to unnecessary intervention.

---

426. *ANS Construction Private Ltd. v. Ramagundmma Fertilizers and Chemicals Ltd.* 2019 SCC OnLine Del 8694, ¶21; *State of Assam v. Barak Vpatyaka D. U. Karamchari Sanstha* (2009) 5 SCC 694.
427. *Uma Sharma v. Miniso Life Style Private Ltd.* 2020 SCC OnLine Del 979, ¶28.
428. *Aditya Birla Retail Ltd. v. Ashapura Developers* 2009 (4) Arb. LR 125 (Bom).
429. *Ajay Singh v. Kal Airways Pvt. Ltd.* 2017 SCC OnLine Del 8934, ¶32.
430. *Steel Authority of India Ltd. v. AMCI PTY Ltd. & Anr* 2011 SCC OnLine Del 3689. *It is pertinent to note that the application under Section 9 was filed after the passing of the award and before enforcement w.r.t. an ICC award.*
431. *Brand Value Communications Ltd. v. Eskay Video Pvt. Ltd.* 2010 (4) Arb. LR 452 (Calcutta) (DB), ¶13.
432. *Delta Constructions Systems Ltd., Hyderabad v. Narmada Cement Company Ltd.* 2002 (2) Arb. LR 47 (Bom).
433. *Ibid.*
434. *Rajiv K. Luthra v. Mohit Saraf* FAO (OS)(COMM) No. 13/2021. *The author was one of the counsels for the appellant in the case.*
435. Report of UNCITRAL Working Group on the work of its Thirty Second session, June 2000, A/CN.9/468, available at: https://undocs.org/en/A/CN.9/468, ¶65.

6.4.3. *Garnishee Orders*

Another method of 'securing the amount in dispute' is the passing of garnishee orders. The word 'garnish' is derived from an old French word 'garnir' which means to warn or to prepare.[436] Essentially, garnishee orders are passed against third parties who owe money to a judgment debtor. The court directs such third parties to pay the decree-holder directly. Such third parties are called 'garnishee' (referred to as 'refere-provision' in France).[437]

Garnishee orders were introduced in the CPC in 1976 in Order XXI Rules 46 A-46 I of the CPC (Execution of Decrees). It is pertinent to highlight that the Saraf Committee had recommended that the power to pass garnishee orders be included explicitly in Section 9 of the IAA.[438] However, the same was never included in the 2015 Amendment or the 2019 Amendment.

Recently, the Bombay High Court rejected the prayer for a garnishee order because an interim order had already been granted by the arbitral tribunal. The applicant had not taken any steps for the execution of the order,[439] there was no privity of contract,[440] and the principles for grant of garnishee order were not satisfied.[441]

However, the court enunciated the principles which would apply to a garnishee order. The court held that to pass any garnishee order, the court has to determine whether the debt is actually due and payable by the garnishee to the judgment debtor. The said order cannot be passed and no deposit can be ordered when the garnishee has not admitted the debt. Hence, such an order is always discretionary and the court should consider the facts and circumstances of each case and whether it will be inequitable to pass such an order. The court has to consider whether the judgment debtor has a present right to recover any debt from the garnishee and what is the nature of such a right. If such a right is a contingent right, then the decree-holder would also stand in the same position as the judgment debtor qua the garnishee.[442]

It may be argued that since the court has all the powers under Section 9 of the IAA as it would have had in a proceeding before it, the power to pass garnishee orders may be drawn from Order XXI Rules 46 A-46 I of the CPC. However, such an argument is erroneous. Order XXI of the CPC can be invoked only during the execution of a decree. Therefore, drawing the power from the said provision for interim measures is not possible as the said provision is applicable only at the stage of execution of a decree where the rights and liabilities of the parties have been crystallised. The interim measure cannot be suspended, modified or terminated, and would amount to a prejudgment on the merits.

The better view is that there is no power to grant garnishee orders under Section 9 of the IAA. Given that the remedy under Section 9 of the IAA can only be invoked

436. Black's Law Dictionary (8th Ed., St. Paul, Minnestoa: West 2004).
437. Stephen, *supra* n. 96, at 269.
438. *Supra* n. 68, at 33.
439. *Jatin Keshruwala v. DAG Creative Media Pvt. Ltd.* 2019 SCC OnLine Bom 1346, ¶16.
440. *Ibid.*, ¶19.
441. *Ibid.*, ¶18.
442. *Ibid.*, ¶17.

when there is a valid arbitration agreement, it logically follows that such power cannot be extended to passing orders against third parties without providing them with an opportunity of being heard. Moreover, the determination of the debt would amount to a prejudgment of the merits of the dispute. Such determination would be contrary to the scope of the power of the courts under Section 9 of the IAA.

6.5. Preservation of Evidence

The courts may also be called upon to aid the arbitral process by issuing orders under Section 9 of the IAA to preserve evidence.[443] The language contained in Section 9(1)(ii)(c) is quite broad. It refers not only to the preservation of evidence but even inspection of property belonging to any party, taking of samples, or trial of experiments which may be necessary or expedient for the purpose of obtaining full information or evidence. Thus, the court can appoint an independent person to measure construction work and obtain evidence,[444] direct a party to furnish details of assets[445] and accounts.[446] In contrast, Article 17(2)(d) of the Model Law refers to the preservation of evidence that may be 'relevant and material to the resolution of the dispute'. Such evidence may be required to be preserved as the same might fade away in a routine or exceptional course of events, or due to the *mala fide* conduct of a particular party.[447]

6.6. Reconciling the List under Section 9 of the IAA with the Model Law

As discussed earlier, this list may imply that the types of measures available under the IAA have been provided keeping in mind the specific features of international arbitration. However, the actual application of Section 9 of the IAA has been with reference to the types of measures under the CPC and the limitations contained in the Specific Relief Act which has anchored interim measures in support of arbitration proceedings in domestic law, rather than the requirements of arbitral practice. Extending the applicability of the CPC and Relief considerably limits the flexibility of the court to grant interim measures and deviates considerably from Article 17(2) of the Model Law. The use of different standards, conditions, and in certain cases, review of the merits, is completely contrary to the role of the court envisaged under Article 17J of the Model Law. Therefore, in practice Section 9 of the IAA deviates considerably from the types of measures contemplated under Article 17(2) of the Model Law and often without any regard to the 'specific features of international arbitration'. Instead, the primary focus has been to comply with the CPC and the Specific Relief Act.

---

443. *AIDS Health Care Foundation-India Cares v. National AIDS Control Organization* 2009 (3) Arb. LR 601 (Del).
444. *Prima Developers v. Lords Co-operative Group Housing Society Ltd.* 2009 (2) Arb. LR 387 (Del).
445. *Samson Maritime Ltd. v. Hardy Exploration* 2016 SCC Online MAD 9122 *affirmed in Antrix Corp. Ltd. v. Devas Multimedia Pvt. Ltd.* 2018 (4) Arb. LR 66 (Del) (DB).
446. *In TIl Limited v. Mazgaon Dock Shipbuilders Ltd.* 2019 SCC Online Bom 8150 *the court appointed a Court Commissioner for mustering of spares.*
447. Ali Yesilirmak, *supra* n. 30, at 11.

The Working Group had also considered incorporating a list of the types of measures instead of Article 17(2) of the Model Law. However, the proposal was rejected as listing the types of measures narrows down the possibility of future applications and the growing complexity of cases.[448] Providing a list of measures restricts the court to provide appropriate remedies at the time of the emergence of new technologies and the commercial needs of the parties. Therefore, it is better to clarify the power of the court rather than provide a list to ensure uniform solutions.[449]

In order to truly give effect to Article 17J and its autonomous intent, the power of the court should relate to that of the tribunal and as discussed in Chapter 7. The power of the tribunal should contain the generic language used in Article 17(2) of the Model Law. However, the existing list of measures should be retained as a clarification of the power of the court to ensure consistency, harmonisation, and reference to existing jurisprudence.[450] In some cases, the list may serve as a useful clarification of the scope of the power. For example, the language contained in Section 9(1)(ii)(c) is broader than that of the Article 17(2)(d) of the Model Law and hence, a court may grant orders to obtain full information and not necessarily 'preserve evidence' only. The list should also be retained to provide a reference to the courts as to the nature of remedies that can be granted under Section 9 of the IAA. Removing the list completely may be interpreted to mean that the court no longer has the power to grant these types of measures.

These changes would prevent the applicability of the CPC and the Specific Relief Act to applications under Section 9 of the IAA, cater to the specific features of international arbitration, and at the same time not limit the kind of remedies available to the court to grant interim measures of protection in support of the arbitral process.

One of the consequences of referring the power of the court to that of the tribunal under Article 17(2) of the Model Law would be that the power of the court to grant interim measures would be extended to granting security for costs under Article 17(2)(c) of the Model Law. However, Section 12A(2) of the Singapore International Arbitration Act categorically provides that the court can grant the measures listed in Section 12(1)(c)-(i) thereby clearly excluding (a) security for costs; and (b) discovery of documents and interrogatories.[451]

An application under Section 9 of the IAA should not be maintainable as an application for security for costs is a procedural matter which falls within the exclusive domain of the tribunal, as discussed in Chapter 7.[452] In line with the mandate of reducing court interference, the power under Section 9 of the IAA can only be used to support arbitral proceedings till the constitution of the tribunal or where the tribunal is constrained to act. It cannot extend to passing orders on procedural matters which are to be determined by the arbitral tribunal. Moreover, the court will not have enough facts, material, and evidence to make such a determination, and if it did proceed to

448. Marinanne Roth, *Interim Measure*, J. Dis. Res., 425 (2012).
449. Menon, *supra* n. 102, at 3; *See Chapter 7*.
450. *See Appendix A*.
451. Andrew Chan & Renita Sophia Crasta, *Interim Measures in Aid of Foreign Arbitration – A Re-Think*, 20 Sac. L. J., 769, 771 (2008).
452. Ronald Wong, *Interim Relief in aid of International Commercial Arbitration, A Critique on the International Arbitration Act*, 24 Sac. L. J. 499, 528 (2019).

grant such orders, it would amount to prejudging the merits. Hence, the reference of the power of the court to the power of the tribunal should explicitly exclude the power to grant security for costs.

7. LIMITATIONS

On the first reading of Section 9 of the IAA, the scope of the power appears to be quite wide and unrestricted. However, various limitations have been imposed by the courts over a period.[453] Most of such limitations have been applied with reference to the Specific Relief Act. Some of the limitations are discussed below.

7.1. Specific Performance

Before the amendment to the Specific Relief Act, a limitation introduced by the courts on the grant of interim measures under Section 9 of the IAA was the consideration of whether the interim measure would amount to the grant of specific performance. If the specific performance of a contract could not be granted, the court cannot issue an order of injunction.[454]

This position now stands changed after the amendment to the Specific Relief Act, which makes specific performance the norm rather than the exception.[455] Now, all contracts would be specifically enforceable under Section 10 of the Specific Relief Act, subject to the exemptions under Section 14 of the Specific Relief Act.

7.2. Contract Is Determinable

Relying on the Specific Relief Act, no interim measure can be granted when the contract is determinable,[456] i.e., it provides for a termination clause[457] or a contract which can be put to an end,[458] e.g., a distributorship agreement cannot be restored as the same is determinable and not enforceable.[459] Hence, an injunction cannot be granted in view of

453. *In one instance, an order restraining a company, its subsidiaries, distributors, stockists etc. from transferring, utilising or causing to utilise a certain technology for the manufacture, sale, assembly of automatic washing machines considered to be a 'wide' injunction and was set aside. L.G. Electronic Inc. v. Onida Savah Ltd.* 1997 (2) Arb. LR 637.
454. *Urmila and Co Pvt. Ltd. v. J M Baxi and Co.* 1986 Del 336 (341).
455. *See*, The Specific Relief Act, 1963, S. 14(c), *prior to the amendment.*
456. *Ibid.*, ss 14 r/w S. 41; *Inter Ads Exhibition Pvt. Ltd. v. Busworld International Cooperative Vennootschap Met Beperkte Anasprakelijkheid* 2020 SCC OnLine Del 351, ¶56; *Naman Broadcasting and Telecommunications Pvt. Ltd. v. North Delhi Municipal Corporation* 2019 SCC OnLine Del 8082, ¶¶ 10, 13.
457. *Her Highness Maharani Shantidevi P. Gaikwad v. Savjibai Haribai Patel* AIR 2001 SC 1462; *Rajasthan Breweries Ltd. v. The Stroh Brewery Company* AIR 2000 Delhi 450; *Spice Digital Ltd. v. Vistaas Digital Media Pvt. Ltd.* 2012 (114) Bom LR 3696.
458. *Turnaround Logistics (P) Ltd. v. Jet Airways (India) Ltd.* (MANU/DE/8741/2006).
459. *Indian Oil Corporation Ltd. v. Amritsar Gas Service* (1991) 1 SCC 533; *E. Venkatakrishna v. Indian Oil Corporation Ltd.* (2000) 7 SCC 764; *Bharat Petroleum Corporation Ltd. v. Khaybar Transport Pvt. Ltd.* 2011 (86) ALR 511; *Aventis Pastur S.A. v. Cadila Pharmaceuticals Ltd.* 2003 (2) Arb. LR 259 (Guj); *Star India Ltd. v. Arup Bohra* 2003 (2) Arb. LR 202. *It is pertinent to*

Section 41(e) of the Specific Relief Act.[460] This view has been reiterated several times.[461] If the contract is in its nature determinable in accordance with Section 14 of the Specific Relief Act, an injunction restraining the termination of an agreement cannot be granted.[462]

Unfortunately, despite the amendment, Section 14(d) of the Specific Relief Act continues to provide that a contract determinable by its nature cannot be specifically enforced.[463] Therefore, there is an inconsistency between the intent of Sections 10 and 14(d) of the Specific Relief Act. In commercial agreements or daily commercial activities, nearly all contracts have a termination clause and hence, by their very nature are determinable. It is unclear what the practical implication of Section 10 of the Specific Relief Act will be. Interim measures on account of contracts being determinable should not be denied as nearly all commercial agreements would fit into this criterion.

Courts have erroneously placed reliance on the Specific Relief Act keeping in view the nature of final relief claimed in a civil suit. In an arbitration proceeding, the interim measures requested from a court in support of arbitration proceedings may or may not have anything to do with the final relief.[464] Therefore, a court whose primary purpose is only to support arbitral proceedings should not be concerned about the contract being determinable and should not rely on the Specific Relief Act to put unnecessary limitations on the power of the court under Section 9 of the IAA.

7.3. Damages Are Adequate Relief

Another fetter imposed by the court for granting interim measures under Section 9 of the IAA is the requirement to demonstrate 'irreparable harm' or that 'compensation is not adequate relief'. If the non-performance of a contract could be compensated in

---

mention that most of these cases applied Amritsar Gas Services despite the said judgment being passed under the Indian Arbitration Act, 1940; Wanderlust Travels Pvt. Ltd. v. Delhi Tourism and Transport Development Corporation Ltd. 2018 (2) Arb. LR 379 (Del).

460. *Samay Singh v. Hindustan Petroleum Corporation Ltd.* 2012 SCC OnLine All 1253, ¶48.
461. *IL&FS Engineering and Construction Co. Ltd. v. Paschimanchal Vidyut Vitran Nigam Ltd.* 2018 (1) Arb. LR 200 (Del); *Crompton Greaves Ltd v. Hyundai Electronics (1998) 76 DLT 733; Pahuja Seeds Pvt. Ltd. v. Takii and Co. Ltd.* 2012 (2) Arb. LR 40 (Del); *KSL and Industries v. National Textile Corp. Ltd.* 2012 (3) Arb. LR 470 (Del); *RPS Educational Society (Regd.) v. Delhi Development Authority* 2009 (4) Arb. LR 39 (Del); *Energo Engineering Projects Ltd. v. Sri Aishwarya Constructions* 2013 (4) Arb. LR 172 (Mad); *Krishav Trade Concern v. Translumina Therapeutics LLP* 2013 (4) Arb. LR 335 (Del).
462. *Aaxis Nano Technologies Pvt. Ltd. v. S::Can Messteshnik GmbH* 2018 (1) Arb. LR 53 (Del), ¶14. *An order restraining termination of contract was granted in* OMP (I) (COMM) 207/2018, c.f. *V.R. Techiche Consultants Private Ltd. v. Indian Highways Management Company Ltd.* 2019 SCC OnLine Del 11284, ¶3; *Inter Ads Exhibition Pvt. Ltd. v. Busworld International Cooperative Vennootschap Met Beperkte Anasprakelijkheid* 2020 SCC OnLine Del 351, ¶40.
463. *See discussion on contract is determinable. See* Ajar Rab, *Comparing Specific Performance under the Specific Relief (Amendment) Act 2018 with the CISG and the UNIDROIT Principles: The Problems of the 'Un-Common Law' in India*, 7 NLS Buss. L. R 71, 90-91.
464. *However, the court in GVK Airport Holdings Limited v. BID Services Division (Mauritius) Ltd.* 2019 SCC Online Del 8978, ¶¶28 and 29, *even after the amendment to the Specific Relief Act, 1963.*

terms of money,[465] specific performance could not be ordered.[466] Hence, the courts have relied on the erstwhile Section 14(a)[467] and (c)[468] of the Specific Relief Act (which deal with instances when specific performance cannot be ordered) and rejected the request for interim measures whenever compensation is adequate relief.

Now, the earlier Section 14(1)(a) of the Specific Relief Act has been deleted which specifically provided that specific performance could not be ordered where compensation in money was an adequate relief. Furthermore, Section 21(1) of the Specific Relief Act has been amended to provide that damages can be claimed in addition to the relief of specific performance, clearly signifying that damages alone cannot be considered to be a sufficient remedy.

The Expert Committee on the Specific Relief Act criticised this 'adequacy test' and recommended that specific performance should be granted in all cases, barring a few.[469] The deletion of Section 14(1)(a) from the Specific Relief Act signifies the legislative intent to make even those contracts specifically enforceable the non-performance of which can be compensated in terms of money.[470]

It has reiterated that applications under Section 9 of the IAA should be examined and adjudicated upon dehors the provisions of the CPC and the Specific Relief Act. However, till such time as this notion is accepted by the courts or suitable amendments are brought to the IAA, the limitations imposed by the courts by relying on the Specific Relief Act should be rejected and interim measures under Section 9 of the IAA should be granted in consideration of the 'specific features of international arbitration'.

7.4. No Stay of Arbitration Proceedings

An appropriate limitation imposed by the courts is that the provisions of Section 9 of the IAA cannot be invoked to stay arbitration proceedings until the decision of civil suits. It has been held that Section 9 cannot be invoked as it is meant to provide interim measures only and even Section 151 of the CPC cannot be used as Section 9 of the IAA does not contemplate civil proceedings. Hence, what cannot be done directly cannot also be done indirectly.[471] Thus, the power under Section 9 of the IAA cannot be exercised for the stay of arbitration proceedings.[472] In this context, there is a detailed discussion on 'Anti-Arbitration Injunctions' in Chapter 6.

---

465. *Also held in Pepsi Foods v. Jai Drinks Pvt. Ltd.* 1996 (36) DRJ 711; *Shivansh Autozone Pvt. Ltd. v. Honda Cars India Ltd.* 2016 SCC OnLine Del 2428; *Interkardio Pvt. Ltd. v. Gyrus Group Plc.* ILR (2007) 2 Del 1137; *ITE Pvt. India Ltd. v. Delhi Tourism & Transport Development Corporation Ltd.* 2016 (3) Arb. LR 469 (Del) (DB).
466. The Specific Relief Act, 1963, S. 14(1)(a), *prior to the amendment.*
467. *Ibid., a contract for the non-performance of which compensation in money is an adequate relief.*
468. *Ibid., a contract which is in its nature determinable.*
469. *Supra* n. 79, ¶11.3.1.
470. *Ibid.*, ¶11.3.1.
471. *Ramesh Kumar Nathmal Chordiya v. Ld. Principle District Judge* AIR 2014 Bom 1.
472. *Bhatia International v. Bulk Trading S.A. and Anr.* (2002) 4 SCC 105, *affirmed in AIDS Health Care Foundation-India Cares v. National AIDS Control Organization* 2009 (3) Arb. LR 601 (Del); *National Highways Authority of India v. Bel-acc Joint Venture* 2009 (4) Arb. LR 287 (Del), ¶9.

7.5. Third Parties

An important consideration while examining the scope and limitations of the power of the court under Section 9 of the IAA is whether the court can grant an interim measure against a third party, i.e., a non-signatory to the arbitration agreement?

The view of the courts on the issue has not been consistent. Some courts have held that an interim order against third parties cannot be granted under Section 9 of the IAA[473] when an interim order affects third-party rights. Interim orders have far-reaching consequences and cannot be passed in the absence of hearing a third party.[474] Some courts have taken the opposite view. Measures against third parties[475] have been granted where the third party was not a stranger to the contract and was an agent.[476]

A third view has been that there is no general principle of maintainability/non-maintainability with respect to the applicability of Section 9 of the IAA qua third parties and it will have to be determined by the court in the facts of each case whether for the purpose of interim measure of protection and order affecting the third party can be made or not.[477]

7.5.1. Measures Having an Effect on Third Parties

Examining the scope of Section 9 of the IAA in this context, the Court in one instance examined each subclause of Section 9 of the IAA. It held that under subclause (1)(i) of Section 9 of the IAA, a guardian to be appointed might not be a party to the arbitration agreement. Similarly, the goods under subclause (1)(ii)(a) of Section 9 of the IAA may be required to be in the custody of or delivered to, or sold to third parties and further orders against such third parties may be required in connection of such sales.

Under subclause (1)(ii)(b) of Section 9 of the IAA, the amount to be secured may be in the form of money payable or properties in the hands of such party and therefore, the scope of Section 9 of the IAA cannot/ought not to be restricted to securing orders against parties to arbitration only.[478] The reference to the phrase '*shall have the same*

473. *Bengal Ambuja Housing Development Ltd. v. Pramila Sanfui* AIR 2015 SC 3729; *Mikuni Corporation v. UCAL Fuel Systems Ltd.* 2008 (1) Arb. LR 503 (Del); *National Highways Authority of India v. China Coal Construction Group Corporation* 2006 (1) Arb. LR 265 (Del); *Manosh Elias Constructions Pvt. Ltd. v. Manuel John* 2018 SCC OnLine Ker 6383, ¶11; *National Agricultural Co-operative Marketing Federation of India Ltd. v. Earthtech Enterprises Ltd.* 2009 SCC OnLine Del 1046; *Arun Kapur v. Vikram Kapur* 2002 (1) Arb. LR 256 (Del).
474. *Kishorsinh Ratansinh Jadeja v. Maruti Corporation* (2009) 11 SC 229.
475. *K Chandrashekharam v. Vijay Bhargavi Chit Fund Pvt. Ltd.* 2000 (1) ALD 761, *attachment before judgment was ordered against the third party*; *Chunilal Kapoorchandji Shah v. Yuvraj Industries Ltd.* 2010 (1) Arb. L.R. 138 (Guj); *Girish Mulchand Mehta and Durga Jaishankar Mehta v. Mahesh S. Mehta* 2010 (1) Bom. C.R. 31; *Dorling Kindersley (India) Pvt. Ltd. v. Sanguine Technical Publishers* 2013 (3) Arb. LR 52 (Del).
476. *CREF Finance Ltd. v. Puri Constructions Ltd.* 2000 (55) DRJ 750.
477. *Value Advisory Services v. ZTE Corporation* 2009 (3) Arb. LR 315 (Del).
478. *The court specifically noted that similar examples can be given with respect to other clauses also. ibid.*, ¶14; *GL Asia Mauritius II Cayman Ltd. v. Pinfold Overseas Ltd. & Anr.* 2013 (2) Arb. LR 334 (Bom), ¶8; *Mahesh S. Mehta v. Harini Co-op Hsg. Society Ltd.* 2009 SCC OnLine Bom 913, ¶11.

power for making orders' leads to the conclusion that orders against third parties can be made under Section 9 of the IAA.[479]

Thus, an interim order affecting a third party which is claiming a right under the party to an agreement can be passed[480] if such third party makes endeavours to frustrate the contract or the outcome of the contractual obligations. Similarly, an order under Section 9 of the IAA may be passed to prevent the abuse that affects a third-party right.[481]

7.5.2. Application for Interim Measures by a Third Party

However, despite being affected by such orders, a third party to an arbitration agreement cannot make an application to be impleaded in a proceeding pending under Section 9 of the IAA.[482] Taking a contrary view, the Jammu and Kashmir High Court[483] held that a person having a vital interest in the subject matter of the arbitration agreement could not be asked to watch the proceedings from the fence. A stranger may be impleaded as a party under Section 9 of the IAA where the court is convinced that the applicant is a proper and necessary party to the proceeding and the applicant's presence is bound to enable the court to arrive at a just and proper conclusion.

The view of the Jammu and Kashmir High Court is extreme. It will further the court's intervention and promote delay tactics by a respondent. However, there is a growing recognition of the fact that there are certain layered transactions which by their very nature hinge upon the interdependence of the obligations of third parties and hence, whether a third party can be added to arbitration proceedings, or not cannot be a categorical and an unambiguous 'no'.[484]

Courts should only be concerned with the parties to the agreement. Even if an order against a party to the arbitration affects a third party, the same should be granted. On the question of whether a third party is a party to the arbitration agreement or not, the court should leave such determination to the arbitral tribunal. Courts should not implead third parties at the interim stage under Section 9 of the IAA. Impleading third parties in the proceedings is against the consensual nature of arbitration and can have disastrous consequences. If a third party is impleaded at the stage of Section 9 of the

---

479. *Value Advisory Services v. ZTE Corporation* 2009 (3) Arb. LR 315 (Del), ¶15. *The court based its reasoning on the CPC and referred to Sections 47, 60, Order XXI Rules 46 and 46 A-F with respect to execution proceedings and orders against third parties. In pre-decretal stage, the court referred to Order XXXVIII Rule 6 to 11 A of the CPC for similar orders. Given that there is no indication whatsoever in the Arbitration Act that the power under Section 9 has to be restricted with respect to third parties, the same should be permissible.*

480. *Girish Mulchand Mehta and Durga Jaishankar Mehta v. Mahesh S. Mehta* 2010 (1) Bom. C.R. 31; *Gatx India Pvt. Ltd. v. Arshiya Rail Infrastructure Ltd.* 216 (2015) D.L.T. 20; *Blue Coast Infrastructure Development Pvt. Ltd. v. Blue Coast Hotels Ltd.* 2020 SCC OnLine Del 1897, ¶27.

481. *Dorling Kindersley (India) Pvt. Ltd. v. Sanguine Technical Publishers* 2013 (3) Arb. LR 52 (Del).

482. *Srei infrastructure Finance Ltd. v. Bhageeratha Engineering Ltd.* 2009 (3) Arb. LR 342 (Gau), ¶¶10-12; *IndusInd Bank Ltd. v. National Highway Authority of India* 2009 SCC OnLine Del 1352, ¶42; *National Highway Authority of India v. M/s Youone Maharia J.V.* 2010 (4) Arb. LR 413 (Del), ¶ 36.

483. *Mohammad Ishaq Bhat v. Tariq Ahmad Sofi* 2010 (3) Arb. LR 107 (J&K), ¶9.

484. *Nirmala Jain v. Jasbir Singh* 2018 SCC OnLine Del 11342, ¶8.

IAA, will the third party then be bound to participate in the arbitration proceedings as well? That too without giving any consent to arbitration?

It is necessary to clarify that even though third parties should not be allowed to be impleaded under Section 9 of the IAA nor be allowed to invoke Section 9 of the IAA, the scope of the power should nonetheless extend to third parties. Therefore, the court is not curtailed in passing orders against third parties or passing such orders that may affect third parties, e.g., against banks, escrow agents.[485] If the power of the court were to be restricted to the parties to arbitration only, it would be unnecessarily curtailed, making the power akin to that of the tribunal, ultimately frustrating the purpose of interim measures.

8. EX PARTE ORDERS

It is a settled position of law in almost all jurisdictions that the court can grant ex parte relief.[486] Interpreting Article 17C of the Model Law with respect to preliminary orders, the High Court of New Zealand affirmed that Article 17C of the Model Law provides the power to the tribunal to grant orders without notice and hence, a court may issue ex parte orders to ensure that the Arbitration Act remains consistent with the Model Law.[487]

In nearly all applications filed under Section 9 of the IAA, the party requesting interim relief will inevitably seek ad interim or ex parte relief, i.e., without hearing the other party on account of urgency.[488] Courts have accepted such requests under Order XXXIX Rule 1 of the CPC which is the repository of the power to grant orders of a '*temporary injunction, with, or without notice, till further orders, or till the disposal of the suit*'.[489]

The distinction between an interim order and an ad interim order is that an 'interim order' remains in force for the whole period of the suit unless varied or vacated under Order XXXIX Rule 4, or set aside in an appeal. An ad interim order, on the other hand, is an order that operates till the next date of hearing or the hearing of the application for an interim measure on merits.[490] Hence, an ex parte order under Section 9 of the IAA is usually granted as an ad interim order.

8.1. Standard for Grant of Ex Parte Orders

The criteria to be used for such orders are provided under Order XXXIX Rules 1 and 3 of the CPC.[491] Under Order XXXIX Rule 3A of the CPC, a court is bound to dispose of an

485. *A and B v. C, D and E* [2020] EWCA CIV 409.
486. Menon, *supra* n. 102, at 12.
487. *Discovery Geo Corporation v. STP Energy Pte Ltd.* [2012] NZHC 3549, ¶37.
488. *I. Sudershan Rao v. Evershine Builders Private Ltd.* 2013(2) Arb. LR 52 (AP) (DB).
489. *A. Venkatasubbiah Naidu v. S. Chellappan* (2000) 7 SCC 695.
490. *Sucheta Dilip Ghate v. Dilip Shantaram Ghate* AIR 2003 Bom 392 (395).
491. *Morgan Stanley Mutual Fund v. Kartick Das* (1994) 4 SCC 225, ¶36, *where the court listed the considerations to be kept in mind before granting* ex parte *interim measures.*; *I. Sudershan Rao v. Evershine Builders Private Ltd.* 2013(2) Arb. LR 52 (AP) (DB); *Ramrameshwari Devi v.*

application for interim measure within thirty days from the date on which an ex parte injunction was granted and if it is unable to do so, it should record its reason for such inability.[492] Therefore, courts have repeatedly taken the view that ex parte injunctions should be granted for a limited period,[493] such as two weeks.[494] They have also held that in case an ex parte order is granted, then an effort should be made to dispose of the application of interim relief as expeditiously as possible and preferably on the very date the defendant appears in court.[495] However, in practice, the same does not happen often. Applications for interim measures take months before they are heard on merits and the ex parte order granted to a party continues till such time.[496] Courts are also unwilling to modify, suspend, or terminate an ex parte order until the final disposal of the arbitration proceeding or the application under Section 9 of the IAA.[497]

Once an order is passed ex parte, the provisions of Order XXXIX Rule 3 of the CPC which provide for service of the order and copy of the application on the opposite party within three days have to be complied with. However, the effect of non-compliance with such a requirement is not certain. Some courts have held that a party cannot be penalised for the same,[498] while others have held that the consequence would be that such a party cannot be allowed to take advantage of such order.[499] Therefore, there is a need to provide for ex parte orders within the IAA itself.

In England[500] and Singapore,[501] the power to grant orders without notice is contained in the respective arbitration statutes. The threshold for the exercise of such power is 'urgency'. Usually, interim measures in support of the arbitral process are to be granted only after hearing both parties. It is only in cases of urgency that the court may grant a measure without notice.

Nirmala Devi (2011) 8 SCC 249. *The court should keep in mind the following when considering a request for an* ex parte *order: (a) The court should be extremely careful and cautious in granting* ex parte ad interim *injunctions, or stay orders; (b) Ordinarily, short notice should be issued to the defendants and orders should be passed only after hearing the parties; (c) If an* ex parte *order is granted, then the application for interim relief should be disposed of on merits expeditiously after hearing both parties, preferably as soon as the defendant appears in court. This should be done on a priority basis, and undue adjournments should be avoided. (d) If a party has obtained* ex parte *relief on the basis of false pleadings or forged documents, such a party should be adequately punished; (e) At the time of grant of* ex parte *measures, the court must record in the order that if the suit is eventually dismissed, the applicant will have to pay full restitution, actual, or realistic costs and mesne profits.*

492. *Tamilselvi v. Pandiyan Educational Board, Tiruppathur and Ors.* 1995 SCC OnLine Mad 483, ¶12; *A. Venkatasubbiah Naidu v. S. Chellappan* (2000) 7 SCC 695, ¶16.
493. *S.K. Kantikar v. Bhiwandi Nizampura Municipal Council* AIR 2000 Bom 453 (DB).
494. *Maria Sequeira Fernandes v. Erasmo Jack* 2012 5 SCC 370.
495. *Ramrameshwari Devi v. Nirmala Devi* (2011) 8 SCC 249.
496. *Excerpts from the International Seminar on Transnational Litigation organised by Nirma University, India: Session 5: The Fine Line Between Court Assistance and Court Intervention in International Commercial Arbitration with speakers for the panel: Vyapak Desai, Tejas Karia, Rajendra Barot, Nirma University, 23-24 March, 2019. The author was a panellist at the seminar for Session 4 and attended Session 5.*
497. *This has been the experience of the author while practising before multiple fora throughout India.*
498. *Vascon Engineers Ltd. v. Sansara Hotels India Pvt. Ltd.* 2009 (4) Arb. LR 141 (Bom), ¶¶21, 23.
499. *Venkatasubbaiah Naidu v. S. Chellappan* 1997 (2) Arb. LR 650 (Del) (DB), ¶¶13, 15A.
500. English Arbitration Act, 1996, S. 44(3).
501. Singapore International Arbitration Act, 1994, S. 12A(4).

Though these provisions work well in countries such as England and Singapore where the application for interim measures is decided expeditiously, in India nearly all requests are filed as 'urgent' and without a guiding test, the courts are most likely to interpret this requirement extremely subjectively. Since interim measures are supposed to be the exception rather than the norm,[502] granting ex parte orders liberally gives one party a strong tactical advantage, especially when courts might be unwilling to modify, suspend, or terminate the measure.

While one solution can be to require mandatory security in the case of a request for ex parte measures, the necessary test for entertaining a request without notice is contained in Article 17B(2) of the Model Law. Though Article 17B refers to preliminary orders to be granted by the arbitral tribunal, the test of '*prior disclosure of the request for the interim measure to the party against whom it is directed risks frustrating the purpose of the measure*' can be extended to Section 9 of the IAA.

In order to completely dissociate the IAA from the CPC and to make the IAA a complete code for interim measures, it is necessary that the provision for ex parte orders should be specifically incorporated in the IAA along with the test provided under Article 17B(2) of the Model Law.[503] Providing such a test would also be in line with the 'specific features of international arbitration' which envisages equal treatment of parties at all stages.[504] Though such a mandate applies to the tribunal, extending such an obligation to courts, would only further the efficacy and trust of the arbitral process, especially when a request for an interim measure is filed before the court during arbitration proceedings. It would also reduce frivolous or vexatious requests for ex parte orders with a sole view to harass the opposite party. Whenever a court deems it fit, it may always request a party to provide security before granting the measure ex parte.

The court should keep the following considerations in mind when dealing with a request for a grant of ex parte measures:[505]

(a) the court should be convinced that the interim measure would only be effective if taken ex parte;
(b) the conditions in Section 17 of the IAA with respect to standards should be satisfied, and the court should consider the harm likely to result from the order being granted or not;
(c) the ex parte measure should only be effective for no more than fifteen days unless the other party would be heard;
(d) the requesting party should inform the court of all relevant material and circumstances to allow the court to assess whether the conditions have been met and remain fulfilled;

502. Lawrence W Newman & Colin Ong, *Interim Measures in International Arbitration* 246 (2014).
503. Bangladesh Arbitration Act, 2001, S. 7A(3), *provides for the same test.*
504. *See generally:* Maxi Scherer, Dharshini Prasad & Dina Prokic, *The Principle of Equal Treatment in International Arbitration*, (3 September 2018), available at:https://papers.ssrn.com/sol3/papers.cfm?abstract_id=3377237.
505. Prof. (Dr) Hans Van Houtt, *Ten Reasons Against a Proposal for Ex Parte Interim Measures of Protection in Arbitration*, 20 (1) Arb. Int'l 85, 86 (2004).

(e) a mandatory deposit of security should be ordered unless the court deems fit otherwise depending on the facts and circumstances of the case.

In order to ensure that these considerations are addressed by the court, specific reference to court-ordered interim measures without notice should be specifically incorporated under the IAA along with the test in Article 17B(2) of the Model Law. Furthermore, in order to prevent abuse, similar to the provision under the CPC, there should be a statutory mandate to inform the other party of any order passed without notice within three days of such order being passed failing which the order should lapse. If the order is passed during arbitration proceedings, then the court should inform the arbitral tribunal of such order as well. This is particularly important as the passing of the order would trigger the provision for the formation of the arbitral tribunal.

9. OBLIGATION TO FORM A TRIBUNAL IN NINETY DAYS

To cater to the problem of interim orders under Section 9 of the IAA being used endlessly, Section 9(2) was introduced in the IAA by the 2015 Amendment. Prior to the 2015 Amendment, while the courts had stipulated an express requirement of demonstrating the intention to arbitrate, there was a considerable lacuna as to what would happen once interim relief was granted to a particular party who took no further steps towards the formation of the arbitral tribunal. Such methods or dilatory tactics made arbitration in India extremely problematic as it did not contain sufficient procedural protections to ensure the efficacy and effectiveness of arbitration as an alternative dispute resolution mechanism.[506]

9.1. Section 9(2) of the IAA

As discussed previously, though the courts had tried to cover this gap by putting terms and conditions in the orders, errant parties would not invoke arbitration after obtaining an order under Section 9 of the IAA. Thus, the 2015 Amendment added subclause 2 to Section 9 of the IAA which prescribes that the arbitral tribunal should be formed within ninety days of an order being passed under Section 9(1) of the IAA. It is relevant to point out that this requirement is not contained in the Model Law but is contained in several other jurisdictions such as Bhutan,[507] Brazil,[508] Thailand,[509] and Sweden.[510]

506. Gary Born, *supra* n. 33, at 2613; *An example of such dilatory tactic is CVCIGP II Client Rosehil Ltd. v. Sanjay Jain* 2019 SCC OnLine Del 7522; *where an interim order was passed in 2012 but the parties did not proceed with arbitration under the LCIA Rules till January 3, 2019 and the LCIA itself withdrew the arbitration proceedings.*
507. Bhutan Alternative Dispute Resolution Act, 2013, S. 40.
508. Brazil Arbitration Act, 2015, Art. 22-A.
509. Thailand Arbitration Act, 2002, S. 16.
510. Stephen, *supra* n. 96, at 614.

Section 9(2) of the IAA provides:

> (2) Where, before the commencement of the arbitral proceedings, a Court passes an order for any interim measure of protection under sub-section (1), the arbitral proceedings shall be commenced within a period of ninety days from the date of such order or within such further time as the Court may determine.

The prescription of a period like ninety days under Section 9(2) of the IAA is to emphasise the intention of the legislature that an applicant under Section 9 of the IAA should be able to demonstrate immediacy and imminence.[511] It also demonstrates that the power under Section 9 of the IAA should be exercised only in support of the arbitral process and that an arbitral tribunal should be formed at the earliest and that a party need not demonstrate its intention to initiate arbitration proceedings. A party against whom an order is passed may proceed against the interim measure granted as per law on the expiry of ninety days.[512]

It is pertinent to note that in Bhutan, the obligation to take steps for the formation of the arbitral tribunal is within fifteen days of the interim order.[513] In Brazil,[514] Thailand,[515] and Sweden,[516] the period is thirty days. Initially, a period of thirty days (as opposed to the current ninety days), was originally proposed in India as well.[517] This would have been in consonance with Order XXXIX Rule 3A of the CPC.

9.2. Commencement of Ninety days

The introduction of Section 9(2) of the IAA is a step forward in strengthening the arbitration regime in India. However, the language used in the said provision creates uncertainty with respect to its effect, making the provision less effective than intended.

The provision requires that arbitral proceedings have to commence within ninety days from the date of the order when the order is passed before the commencement of arbitral proceedings. Under the IAA, the arbitral proceedings commence when the request to refer the dispute is received by the defendant under Section 21 of the IAA.[518] Thus, there exist grave lacunae in this provision. If a notice invoking arbitration has already been served on the opposite party, have arbitral proceedings commenced for the purposes of Section 9(2) of the IAA? Such an interpretation would be extremely illogical. Furthermore, in the absence of any clarity, whether the time of ninety days should commence from the date of the ad interim/ex parte order or from the date the application under Section 9 of the IAA is finally decided by the court?

511. *Archer Power System Pvt. Ltd. v. Kohli Ventures Ltd.* 2018 (2) Arb. LR 301 (Madras) (DB), ¶9.
512. *Mahesh Sharma v. Maskara Tea Estate* 2020 SCC OnLine Gau 4932, ¶10.
513. Bhutan Alternative Dispute Resolution Act, 2013, S. 40.
514. Brazil Arbitration Act, 2015, Art. 22-A.
515. Thailand Arbitration Act, 2002, S. 16.
516. Stephen, *supra* n. 96, at 614.
517. Law Commission of India, Report No. 246 – Amendment to the Arbitration and Conciliation Act, 1996, (5 August 2014), available at: http://lawcommissionofindia.nic.in/reports/report246.pdf.
518. *Sundaram Finance Ltd. v. NEPC India Ltd.* (1999) 2 SCC 479, ¶13.

If the view is that the period of ninety days would commence on the passing of the ad interim order, then, at the expiry of ninety days the fate of the ad interim order is unknown. Will the ad interim measure expire? Will the proceeding under Section 9 of the IAA become infructuous? Who bears the onus of forming the arbitral tribunal and ensuring the proceedings commence within ninety days? Should the court penalise the parties for not commencing arbitral proceedings within ninety days? Should only the party requesting the interim measure be penalised? Or should the order be extended till the final disposal of the application under Section 9 of the IAA?

Courts have attempted to answer the above questions by holding that the reference to 'such order' under Section 9 of the IAA includes an ad interim order and the same cannot be construed as an order passed beyond the powers conferred under the IAA. Therefore, if a court passes any order in the nature of an interim order, conditional order, or in the nature of finally disposing of the application itself, all such orders would fall within Section 9(1) of the IAA.[519]

It is necessary for slow judicial systems like India that there should be an equal obligation on the courts to decide the interim application within thirty days from the date of filing else the time limit provided in Section 9(2) of the IAA can lead to illogical results; where an award had been passed but the application under Section 9 of the IAA was still pending for final adjudication.[520] Interim measures in support of arbitration must be dealt with by the courts with flexibility, dynamism and speed, failing which they lose their purpose.[521]

9.3. Expiry of Ninety Days

Another lacuna in the 2015 Amendment is that it did not address the question of what happens if the arbitral tribunal is not formed within ninety days. For example, in Sweden, if the arbitral proceedings are not initiated within one month, the measure is rescinded immediately.[522] More importantly, what if the opposite party does not allow the formation of the arbitral tribunal, in that case, will it be sufficient that a party files an application for the appointment of an arbitrator?

9.3.1. Automatic Expiry of Interim Measure

The Karnataka High Court took the view that if proceedings are not commenced within ninety days of the order, the order passed under Section 9(1) of the IAA shall

519. *Manosh Elias Constructions Pvt. Ltd. v. Manuel John* 2018 SCC OnLine Ker 6383, ¶7; *Archer Power System Pvt. Ltd. v. Kohli Ventures Ltd.* 2018 (2) Arb. LR 301 (Madras) (DB).

520. *Excerpts from the International Seminar on Transnational Litigation organised by Nirma University, India: Session 5: The Fine Line Between Court Assistance and Court Intervention in International Commercial Arbitration with speakers for the panel: Vyapak Desai, Tejas Karia, Rajendra Barot, Nirma University, 23-24th March, 2019. The author was a panellist at the seminar for Session 4 and attended Session 5.*

521. Luis Enrique Graham, *Interim Measures: Ongoing Regulations and Practices (A View from the UNCITRAL Arbitration Regime)*, in A. van den Berg (ed.), *50 Year of the New York Convention* 562 (2009).

522. Stephen, *supra* n. 96, at 614.

automatically stand vacated on the expiry of the said period. This is not clearly stated, but clearly implied. Any other interpretation would defeat the intention of the parliament in enacting Section 9(2) of the IAA.[523]

In one instance, it was contended that if an arbitral tribunal has not been formed within ninety days from the date of passing of an interim order under Section 9(1) of the IAA, the very constitution of the arbitral tribunal post the ninety days' period is anti-statute and incompetent.[524] However, the court noted that this section does not stop by prescribing a ninety days' limit but contains the phrase 'within such further period as the court may determine' indicating that the ninety days' time limit is stretchable in an appropriate case, where the courts deem it fit. Thus, where the arbitral tribunal is not constituted within ninety days of an interim order, the court is deemed to have exercised its authority under the latter part, i.e., under Section 9(2) of the IAA.[525] The court observed that a contrary view would lead to a violation of Section 43(3) of the IAA by introducing a limitation period and not answering a question as to what will happen to the cause of action after ninety days? Will the party be at liberty to pursue a remedy under the common law?[526]

In another instance, it was explicitly stated by the court in the order itself that the petitioner shall ensure compliance with Section 9(2) of the IAA[527] and the order passed shall remain in operation only for the period of ninety days. The court also noted that the onus of the appointment of the arbitral tribunal could not be cast solely on the petitioner and the interest of the respondent is adequately protected by Section 9(2) of the IAA which provides for an outer time limit for an interim order to operate and within which time the party seeking the interim measure has to ensure the constitution of the arbitral tribunal.[528]

To read the ninety days limit as an automatic expiry may amount to injustice to the party which has been granted the interim measure. If the respondent does not cooperate in the formation of the arbitral tribunal and the time limit of ninety days expires, an automatic expiry will incentivise recalcitrant conduct by the respondent. While it is true that the petitioner can file an application under Section 11 of the IAA for the appointment of the arbitrator, it is unclear what the fate of the interim order under Section 9 of the IAA will be after ninety days even though an application under Section 11 of the IAA would be pending. Since the power of the court under Section 11 of the IAA is not judicial and only administrative,[529] the court will not be able to continue the said interim order. The petitioner will be left remediless despite having secured an

523. *Paton Constructions Pvt. Ltd. v. Lorven Projects Ltd.* 2018 (4) Arb. LR 141 (Karnataka) (DB), ¶4. *A similar view was taken by the High Court of Calcutta. However, on peculiar facts of the respondents having paid large sums of money, SREI Equipment Finance Limited v. Sharma Transport Agency* 2019 SCC Online Cal 2438.
524. *Chaudhary Avdesh Kumar v. Volleyball Federation of India* 2017 SCC Online Mad 19117.
525. *Ibid.*, ¶ 40.
526. *Ibid.*, ¶ 41.
527. *Otik Hotels and Resorts Pvt. Ltd. v. Indian Railway Catering and Tourism Corporation Ltd.* 2017 SCC OnLine Del 10122, ¶36.
528. *Apeejay Surrendra Park Hotel Limited v. Silver Streak Hotels Pvt. Ltd.* 2018 SCC OnLine Del 9554, ¶13.
529. Law Commission of India, *supra* n. 51, (5 August 2014).

interim order in its favour. Therefore, to read the ninety-day limit as an automatic expiry of the interim order may be incorrect.

9.3.2. *Accountability of the Party Requesting the Interim Measure*

The provision should provide who is responsible for taking steps for the formation of the tribunal or commencement of the proceedings. If the party which is granted the interim measure takes steps such as nominating an arbitrator or filing an application for the appointment of an arbitrator before the court, the purpose of the section would stand fulfilled. A party would not be invoking the jurisdiction of the court without the intention to pursue the arbitration proceedings. Hence, there would be no need to have the order extended in such cases as the order would not automatically expire at the end of ninety days. If for some reason, the party can show sufficient grounds on why it could not take steps for the formation of the tribunal, then the court may extend such orders.

It is pertinent to note that an automatic expiry of the order was suggested in the Report of the 176th Law Commission Report. However, such expiry was proposed when the party who has been granted an interim measure does not take steps for the formation of the tribunal. It was suggested that the party must take steps within thirty days (as opposed to the current provision of ninety days) to have an arbitral tribunal appointed under Section 11 of the IAA, otherwise, the interim order will stand vacated unless the time is extended by the Court.

The report also provided that if the party does not take such steps and if the interim order is vacated, the Court may pass such orders as to restitution which may be necessary in the circumstances of the case.[530] However, the suggestions were not incorporated into the 2015 Amendment leading to a lacuna regarding the fate of the orders after the said period of ninety days has elapsed.

The recommendations contained in the report of the Law Commission should be incorporated into the IAA without the provision for restitution. Such a consideration should be left to the arbitral tribunal while awarding costs and damages at the time of passing of the award. The role of the court is only to support the arbitral process and not in effect become an adjudicatory mechanism for offshoots of the arbitral process. Therefore, broadly, the following provisions should be added to Section 9 of the IAA in place of Section 9(2). However, the steps for appointment should refer to the arbitration agreement as well and not just the process of court-appointed arbitrators under Section 11 of the IAA:

> Where a party makes an application under sub-section (1) for the grant of interim measures before the commencement of arbitral proceedings, the Court shall direct the party in whose favour the interim measure is granted, to take effective steps for the appointment of the arbitral tribunal in accordance with the procedure specified

530. Law Commission of India, *supra* n. 65; Government of India, Ministry of Law and Justice – Proposed Amendments to the Arbitration & Conciliation Act, 1996: A Consultation Paper, available at: https://www.legallyindia.com/images/stories/docs/Arbitration-Act-LawMin-ConsultationPaper-on-Arb-Act-April2010-1.pdf.

in section 11 or as agreed by the parties, within a period of thirty days from the date of such direction.

The Court may direct that if the steps are not taken within the period specified above, the interim measure granted shall stand vacated on the expiry of the said period:

Provided that the Court may, on sufficient cause being shown for the delay in taking such steps, extend the said period.

10. THE VALIDITY OF INTERIM MEASURES GRANTED BY THE COURT AFTER FORMATION OF THE TRIBUNAL

Once an order is granted under Section 9 of the IAA, either before the commencement of arbitration proceedings or during the arbitral proceedings, such orders should be valid and binding unless modified, suspended, or terminated by an arbitral tribunal. Such orders also tend to invariably impact the arbitral proceedings.[531] Some countries, such as Bangladesh,[532] Jordan,[533] Saudi Arabia,[534] and UAE[535] permit the amendment of interim measures by the courts. In the Philippines, such modification is permitted only when the tribunal has no power to act or is unable to act effectively.[536] However, since the power under Section 9 is to be invoked only to support the arbitral process and at the same time minimise court intervention, such power is best left to the arbitral tribunal.

In England, the court if it so orders may specifically state that an order shall cease to have effect in whole or in part on the order of the arbitral tribunal or an arbitral institute or person having power to act in relation to the subject matter of the order.[537] Therefore, such orders would be valid and binding until either (a) the tribunal modifies, suspends, or terminates such orders (such a consequence is implied);[538] or (b) the court specifically orders that an order shall cease to have effect once the tribunal has the power to act. In contrast, in Singapore, the orders passed by the court continue to be valid and binding unless an arbitral tribunal, institute, or person having the power to act in relation to the subject matter of the order expressly makes an order otherwise.[539]

The first approach is a preferable one as it reaffirms the principles of priority of jurisdiction of the arbitral tribunal[540] and reiterates the fact that the role of the court is only to support the arbitral process till the time tribunal has a chance to consider the

531. *DLF Ltd. v. Leighton India Contractor Pvt. Ltd.* 2021 SCC OnLine Del 3772; *Kuber Enterprises v. Doosan Power Systems India Pvt. Ltd.* 2021 SCC OnLine Del 5049, ¶37; *Vidya Mandir Classes Limited v. Harsh Tiwary* 2021 SCC OnLine Del 5435, ¶21.
532. Bangladesh Arbitration Act, 2001, S. 7A(5).
533. Jordan Arbitration Law, 2001, Art. 13.
534. Saudi Arabian Arbitration Act, 2012, Art. 22.
535. UAE Arbitration Law, Art. 18.
536. Alternative Dispute Resolution Act, 2004, S. 28A.
537. English Arbitration Act, 1996, S. 44 (6).
538. Kieron O'Callaghan and Jerome Finnis, *Chapter 20: Support and Supervision by the Courts*, in Julian David Mathew Lew & Harris Bor, et al. (eds), *Arbitration in England, with chapters on Scotland and Ireland* 538 (2013).
539. Singapore International Arbitration Act, 1994, S. 12A(7).
540. Ali Yesilirmak, *supra* n. 30, at 93.

measure. However, the first approach works when the courts understand their limited role and recognise the power of the tribunal to modify, suspend, or terminate interim measures granted by the court.

In India, it would be better to adopt the approach contained under the Singapore International Arbitration Act as it would prevent unnecessary controversies over the power of the court versus the power of the tribunal. It would reiterate the limited role of the courts and incentivise adjudication by the arbitral tribunal.

The problem with adopting the second approach, however, is that the courts may read it as a complete ouster of their power to grant interim measures for a specified time or till the tribunal can act. Hence, in the interest of clarity, consistency, and predictability, a hybrid of both approaches should be adopted in India.

Therefore, a specific provision should be made in the IAA, which provides that '*An order passed by the court under Section 9 shall cease to have effect:*

(a) if the court so orders, in whole or in part (as the case may be) on the order of the arbitral tribunal or any other such institution or person having power to act in relation to the subject matter of the order; or
(b) *in whole or in part (as the case may be) if the arbitral tribunal, or any such arbitral or other institution or person having power to act in relation to the subject-matter of the order, makes an order which expressly relates to the whole or part of the order under Section 9.*'

11. SAFEGUARDS

There are no direct safeguards provided under Section 9 of the IAA with respect to interim measures, presumably leaving the same to be interpreted and applied based on the provisions of the CPC, or due to the fact that an order under Section 9 of the IAA is subject to an appeal under Section 37 of the IAA. The safeguards provided in the 2006 Model Law Revisions should be applicable to court-ordered interim measures, with suitable modifications, as discussed below:

11.1. Suspension, Modification, or Termination

The court has the power to discharge, vary, or set aside any order for an injunction on an application made to the court under Order XXXIX Rule 4 of the CPC.[541] Therefore, the first recourse to a party against an interim order is to invoke the provision of Order XXXIX Rule 4 of the CPC.[542] It has been held that an appeal against such orders should only be preferred under extraordinary circumstances such as non-compliance with

541. *Ecogreen Cleantech Pvt. Ltd. v. IIFL Wealth Finance Ltd.* 2019 SCC Online Bom 7161; *Cosmos Co-Operative Bank Ltd. v. Anoushka Medicare & Diagnostics Pvt. Ltd.* 2019 SCC Online Bom 7215; *Vistra Itcl (India) Ltd. v. Lalit Kumar Jain* 2019 SCC OnLine Del 9435.
542. *K. Sirajudheen v. Sreedhar K. Kottaram* 2009 SCC OnLine Ker 6363, ¶8; *Vinod Seth Thr Kunal Seth v. Sudarshan Kumar Bhayana* 2019 SCC OnLine Del 8349; *Giesecke and Deverient MS India Pvt. Ltd. v. Oriental Bank of Commerce* 2019 SCC OnLine Del 8722.

statutory provisions, or rarest of rare circumstances such as the passing of an order which is perverse, biased, or vitiated by lack of jurisdiction.[543] However, most often appeals are filed by parties against such orders as courts are reluctant to set aside their own orders.[544]

The power to suspend, modify, or terminate an interim measure granted by the court should be vested with the arbitral tribunal in light of the suggestions made above. The limited purpose of the power under Section 9 of the IAA is to support the arbitral process until the commencement of arbitration proceedings. Suspension, modification, or termination of interim measures is an issue tied closely to the facts and circumstances of the case which the arbitral tribunal is most well versed with and best suited to consider. Applications for modification would cause delay and further court intervention.

11.2. Security for Interim Measures

The current position of law in India is that security at an interim stage should only be requested in extraordinary circumstances as it would amount to a determination of the possible extent of the claim that is likely to be awarded.[545] There is no provision for requiring an applicant seeking interim measures to deposit any security with respect to the interim measure. This lack of requiring security is often the reason for frivolous applications being filed under Section 9 of the IAA only to obtain necessary leverage and coerce a settlement. Also, given the slow pace of disposal, applications under Section 9 of the IAA remain pending for years after obtaining ad interim relief.[546]

It was in this context that Sections 9(2) and 9(3) of the IAA were introduced. Therefore, there should be an express provision requiring the court to consider security for such measures in line with Article 17E(1) of the Model Law. The express inclusion of this power would serve as a clear deterrent to frivolous requests and also protect the interest of the opposite party without the need to draw the power from the CPC.

11.3. Disclosure

There is no rule mandating the disclosure of facts and circumstances at the time of filing an application under Section 9 of the IAA. Such a requirement can nonetheless be inferred from the words of Order XXXIX Rule 4 of the CPC which provides that '*if in an application for temporary injunction or in any affidavit supporting such application, a*

543. *Innovative Pharma Surgicals v. P.M. Devices (P) Ltd.* 2004 (3) ALD 228 (DB). *Though an appeal under Order XLIII Rule (1)(r) CPC is maintainable against an* ex parte *order but not against the order refusing to exercise power under Order XXXIX Rule 4 of the CPC; Shri Ravindra Kumar Mohanty v. Smt. Sujata Mohapatra* 2015 (11) OLR 714 *relying on A. Venkatasubbiah Naidu v. S. Chellappan* (2000) 7 SCC 695.
544. *Based on the author's experience while practising before the multiple fora in India.*
545. *ANS Construction Private Ltd. v. Ramagundmma Fertilizers and Chemicals Ltd.* 2019 SCC OnLine Del 8694, ¶21.
546. *Ramrameshwari Devi v. Nirmala Devi* (2011) 8 SCC 249.

party has knowingly made a false or misleading statement'. Thus, this provision may be read to mandate a duty of disclosure impliedly.

However, the duty is restricted to not making false or misleading statements.[547] There is no duty to mandatorily disclose all relevant or material facts and circumstances. Therefore, an errant party may well conceal relevant facts but not, in fact, make a false or misleading statement.

11.3.1. Failure to Disclose

Some courts have tried to incorporate such disclosure requirements.[548] In one instance, it was held that a litigant who approaches the court is bound to produce all the documents executed by him/her which are relevant to the litigation. In case a vital document is withheld in order to gain an advantage on the other side, then that would amount to playing fraud on the court as well on the opposite party.[549] Similarly, a person whose case is based on falsehood has no right to approach the court and his case can be summarily thrown out at any stage of the litigation[550] for suppression, concealment of material facts, and the failure to come to court with clean hands.[551]

Some courts have reiterated time and again that both parties appearing before the court have an unfailing duty to disclose correct facts on which the decision is sought. A party seeking an ex parte order has an implied duty that no prejudicial order is secured against a party by misrepresentation or trick.[552]

11.3.2. The Need for Full Disclosure

It should be noted that these cases pertain to a suit and not an interim application under Section 9 of IAA where an applicant may be able to get an unfair advantage and secure an interim measure without the court ever discovering the suppression of material or fraud since the trial would take place before an arbitral tribunal. Unlike the arbitral tribunal, there is no other material such as a statement of claim or defence by which the court can ascertain all facts. Such disclosure is crucial, especially when the court is entertaining an application under Section 9 of the IAA for ex parte relief[553] and also, under Section 9(3) of the IAA when a party contends that the remedy before the arbitral tribunal may not be efficacious.[554] A party suppressing relevant and material facts

547. *Cycle Equipment (P) Ltd. v. Municipal Corporation of Delhi* ILR (1981) 2 Del 639, ¶17.
548. *IREP Credit Capital Pvt. Ltd. v. Tapaswi Mercantile Pvt. Ltd.* 2019 SCC Online Bom 5719, ¶40.
549. *Badami v. Bhali* (2012) 11 SCC 574; *S.P. Chengalvaraya Naidu v. Jagannath* (1994) 1 SCC 1, ¶6.
550. *S.P. Chengalvaraya Naidu v. Jagannath* (1994) 1 SCC 1, ¶5.
551. *Holy Health Educational Society (Regd.) v. Delhi Development Authority* (1999) 80 DLT 207, ¶20; *Allied Medical Ltd. v. Uttar Pradesh Health Systems Strengthening Project* 2019 SCC OnLine Del 7696.
552. *Cycle Equipment (P) Ltd. v. Municipal Corporation of Delhi* ILR (1981) 2 Del 639, ¶17; *Nehru Place Hotels Limited v. Delhi Development Authority* CS NO. 719/2017.
553. *Siporex Trade SA v. Comdel Commodities Ltd.* [1986] 2 Lloyd's Rep. 428, at 437; *Golf Interstate Oil Corp v. ANT Trade, The Giovanna* [1999] 1 Lloyd's Rep. 867.
554. *See Chapter 4.*

should not be entitled to relief and an ex parte order, if granted, should be set aside[555] along with adequate punishment[556] such as for perjury or contempt of court as both parties appearing before the court have an unfailing duty to disclose correct facts on which the decision is sought. The court may even consider an award of damages to compensate the loss suffered by a party arising from such non-disclosure.[557]

In the absence of a specific statutory duty mandating disclosure, each court may apply the requirement subjectively. Therefore, there should be a specific duty enshrined in Section 9 of the IAA providing that a party requesting an interim measure under Section 9 shall disclose all facts and circumstances likely to be relevant to the court's determination whether to grant the interim measure requested.

11.4. Costs and Damages

Under the CPC, the court may grant compensation when an injunction was granted on insufficient grounds. Section 95 of the CPC states that the court may provide compensation when[558] '*(a) it appears to the Court that such arrest, attachment or injunction was applied for on insufficient grounds, or (b) the suit of the plaintiff fails and it appears to the Court that there was no reasonable or probable grounds for instituting the same* …'.

However, Section 95 of the CPC provides for INR 1,000 as the maximum amount payable. This cap was enhanced by the Supreme Court and now the maximum compensation payable is INR 50,000.[559] Such a cap may not adequately restitute the respondent in commercial transactions. Moreover, all costs and damages incurred on account of the interim measures will have to be proved by the respondent. Therefore, the same should be done by the arbitral tribunal at the time of passing the award. Otherwise, the order of costs itself may become subject to appeal.[560]

12. APPEAL

An appeal is maintainable against an order passed under Section 9 of the IAA under Section 37(1)(b) of the IAA[561] within thirty days[562] to the court which would ordinarily hear the first appeal if it were a decree in a civil suit. Since the Principal Civil Court

555. *Uppal Engineering Company (P) Ltd. v. Simmco Birla Ltd.* 2005 (2) Arb. LR 404 (Del); *Swift-Fortune Ltd. v. Magnifica Marine S.A.* [2007] EWHC 1630 (Comm).
556. *Ramrameshwari Devi v. Nirmala Devi* (2011) 8 SCC 249.
557. UNCITRAL Yearbook, *supra* n. 11, at 453.
558. Sarkar, *supra* n. 302, at 603.
559. *Bank of India v. Lekhi Moni Das* AIR 2000 SC 1172.
560. *See Chapter 7.*
561. *An appeal is maintainable even if an order is to maintain* status quo. *See, Hindustan Antibiotics Ltd. v. Hindustan Max GB Ltd.* 2001 (2) Arb. LR 436 (Del) (DB), ¶27; *Sundaram Finance Ltd. v. Radhamma* 2003 (3) Arb. LR 646 (Ker), ¶4. *Courts have even remanded the matter back to the court of the first instance for reconsidering the application under Section 9 of the IAA. PCM Cement Concrete Private Ltd. v. Union of India* 2020 SCC OnLine Gau 879; *Union of India v. Prestressed Udhog Builworth Private Ltd.* 2020 SCC OnLine Gau 141.
562. Bhutan Alternative Dispute Resolution Act, 2013, S. 39, *provides for appeal within 10 days.*

defined under Section 2(1)(e) of the IAA is the court of the District Judge, the appeal usually is filed before the High Court of the State.

12.1. Standard of Review

With respect to the standard to be adopted by the court at the appellate stage, the courts have held that the principles under Section 37(2)(b) of the IAA ought to be the same as in an appeal against an order under Order XXXIX Rules 1 and 2 of the CPC. Unless it is found that the order has been passed by the court contrary to law or the court has exercised its power perversely, with arbitrariness, or is capricious,[563] or the order was passed in ignorance of the settled principles of law, the appeal cannot be allowed.[564] Thus, the court, while entertaining an appeal, does not exercise the power under Section 9 of the IAA[565] but only sits in a review.[566] The court cannot reassess the material and seek to reach a conclusion different from the one reached by the court under Section 9 of the IAA, as long as the conclusion reached by the court under Section 9 of the IAA was reasonably possible on the material.[567]

However, despite this narrow scope, courts often entail a full review on the merits of whether the order of the District Court under Section 9 was correct or not.[568] A grey area under the IAA is what happens to an application under Section 9 of the IAA when an appeal has been preferred against an order passed under Section 9 of the IAA and the arbitral tribunal is formed? As per Section 9(3) of the IAA, the court no longer has jurisdiction to entertain such an application. Therefore, at the appellate stage, the appeal should either become infructuous or the appellate court should direct the parties to seek the suspension, modification, or termination of the interim measure before the arbitral tribunal. However, courts have taken the view that since the court has 'entertained' the application under Section 9 of the IAA as held in *Arcelor Mittal*[569] the

563. *Emaar MGF Land Ltd. v. Kakade British Realities Pvt. Ltd.* 2013 (4) Arb. LR 349 (Del), ¶7; *Green Infra Wind Energy Ltd. v. Regen Power Tech Pvt. Ltd.* 2018 SCC OnLine Del 8273. *However, the Court substituted its own view against an order passed by the arbitral tribunal under Section 17 in Shabnam Dhillon v. Zee Entertainment Entreprises Ltd.* 2019 SCC OnLine Del 8905.
564. *Bakshi Speedways v. Hindustan Petroleum Corporation* 2009 SCC OnLine Del 2476, ¶4; *Shiningkart Ecommerce Private Ltd. v. Jiayun Data Ltd* 2019 SCC OnLine Del 9169.
565. *Chandrakant P. Saanghvi v. Chandrakant P. Saanghvi* 2015 SCC OnLine Bom 6245, ¶83.
566. Indian Code of Civil Procedure, 1908, S. 114: *Subject as aforesaid, any person considering himself aggrieve:*
   (a) *by a decree or order from which an appeal is allowed by this Code, but from which no appeal has been preferred.*
   (b) *by a decree or order from which no appeal is allowed by this Code, or*
   (c) *by a decision on a reference from a Court of Small Causes, may apply for a review of judgment to the Court which passed the decree or made the order, and the Court may ... such order thereon as it thinks fit.*
567. *Mewa Mishri Enterprises Private Limited v. AST Enterprises Inc.* 2021 SCC OnLine Del 3332, ¶7.
568. Sharad Bansal, *supra* n. 169.
569. *Arcelor Mittal Nippon Steel India Ltd. v. Essar Bulk Terminal Ltd.* 2021 SCC OnLine SC, ¶¶95, 107.

bar under Section 9(3) would not apply and the court can decide the appeal against an order passed under Section 9 of the IAA.[570]

12.2. Appeal after Formation of the Arbitral Tribunal

Another problem with the current provision is that an appeal is provided against any order under Section 9 of the IAA. Thus, an order passed under Section 9(3) of the IAA is also appealable. This makes no pragmatic sense and amounts to excessive intervention by courts. When the arbitral tribunal has formed, it would be in the interest of efficiency, speedy justice, and a pro-arbitration regime that the party intending to file an appeal requests for suspension, modification, or vacation of the order before the arbitral tribunal[571] instead of filing an appeal.

An appeal should only be permitted against an order under Section 9(1) of the IAA only and not Section 9(3) of the IAA. Furthermore, the right to file an appeal should be restricted to situations when arbitral proceedings have not commenced, i.e., when the appointment has not been accepted by the sole arbitrator, or by all the arbitrators if there is more than one, or when the tribunal is unable to act effectively.[572]

Thus, an appeal should be permitted when the tribunal may have been formed and proceedings would have commenced but if the arbitrator(s) has been challenged or the tribunal cannot meet for some reason or such similar circumstances which may prejudice the rights of the party filing the appeal. This would pay due regard to the mandate of minimal court intervention under Section 5 of the IAA and at the same time permit parties to fall back on courts in cases of extreme prejudice whenever the arbitral tribunal is unavailable. For example, if an order has been passed under Section 9 of the IAA which is extremely arbitrary or contrary to law and the tribunal is also unable to act effectively, in such cases the right of the respondent to have the order modified, suspended, or terminated ought to be protected. The respondent cannot be left remediless.

Though there is potential for abuse and frivolous appeals being filed alleging the unavailability of the arbitral tribunal, it is incumbent on the courts to ensure that the intent and purpose of this provision is achieved and it does not become a tool for harassment and delay. Therefore, the court should not ordinarily entertain appeal, save in exceptional circumstances which may cause extreme prejudice to the rights of a party. The court can even require security from the appellant.

Also, there should be an express ouster of the appellate jurisdiction when the arbitral proceedings have commenced and the pending appeal should be transferred to the arbitral tribunal for suspension, modification, or termination of the interim measure. If the request for an interim measure was denied by the court of the first instance, then a party may file a fresh application under Section 17(1) of the IAA. This is essential to reduce pendency of appeals in courts once the arbitral tribunal has been constituted and is able to act effectively.

570. *ARSS – SIPS (JV) v. Union of India* 2021 SCC OnLine Chh 3737, ¶15.
571. Ali Yesilirmak, *supra* n. 30, at 107-108.
572. *See Chapter 4.*

12.3. Furnishing Security at the Time of Filing an Appeal

Furthermore, in order to prevent any dilatory tactics by a party and not in effect provide for an automatic stay[573] of the interim measure, a provision similar to Section 36(2) of the IAA may be incorporated to provide that '*the filing of an appeal shall not by itself render the order under Section 9(1) unenforceable unless the court grants an order of stay of the operation of the order, subject to deposit of security or any other condition as the court deems fit, on a separate application made for that purpose*'.

Thus, the mere filing of the appeal would not render the interim measure unenforceable unless the court specifically orders so. This is required to protect the urgency of interim measures and prevent frivolous appeals. Courts may also require security at the time of granting an order of stay of operation of the order to further curtail dilatory tactics.

12.4. Appeal Against an Ad Interim Order

There is also a grey area under the IAA regarding whether an appeal is maintainable against an ad interim order by the court. While one view has been that an appeal under Section 37 of the IAA is only maintainable against a final order and not against an ad interim order,[574] the more accepted view is that since the jurisdiction to order an interim measure is conferred on the court, it is axiomatic that the power, authority, jurisdiction to order an interim measure is also conferred under Section 9 of the IAA. Therefore, an appeal provided under Section 37 of the IAA can be made against an order granting ad interim measure as well[575] as an ad interim order is also an order under Section 9 of the IAA.[576]

573. *Hindustan Construction Company Ltd. v. Union of India*, MANU/SC/1638/2019; Law Commission of India, *supra* n. 517.
574. *Symphony Services Corporation (India) Pvt. Ltd. v. Sudeep Bhattacharjee* 2008 (3) Arb. LR 295.
575. *Bilasraika Sponge Iron Pvt. Ltd. v. Devi Trading Company* 2012 (1) Arb. LR 175 ADBD; *Hari Kumar v. Shriram Transport Finance Co. Ltd. & Anr.* 2018 (3) Arb. LR 90 (Kerala) (DB), ¶16.
576. *M/s Sai Concrete Pavers Pvt. Ltd., Vishakhapatnam v. National Aluminium Company Ltd., Koraput* 2016 SCC OnLine Ori 132, ¶11.

CHAPTER 4

Court-Ordered Interim Measures During and after Arbitration Proceedings

It is now widely accepted that the arbitral tribunal is the best forum to determine the appropriateness of the measures of each case.[577] This is known as the principle of priority.[578] Following the said principle, many institutional rules restrict the right of the parties to seek interim measures from the courts once the arbitral tribunal has been formed[579] as the arbitral tribunal will be familiar with the legal and factual details of the case. The arbitral tribunal will also be best suited to decide the impact of the interim measure on the case and whether they should be granted as arbitrators contain the necessary expertise with respect to the dispute.[580] Also, the arbitral tribunal can distinguish between interim measure applications which have been brought for dilatory, tactical, or offensive purposes rather than in pursuit of a legitimate interest.[581]

Moreover, sometimes it is more efficacious to have an interim order passed by the arbitral tribunal as opposed to a domestic court, e.g., when the order is to be enforced in another jurisdiction.[582] Thus, whenever possible, interim measures should be granted by the arbitral tribunal and not the court. However, there may be situations

577. *According to a study conducted by the AAA there is a widely felt uncertainty as to the availability of interim relief from arbitration tribunals which results in the limited number of requests.* Richard W Naimark & Stephanie E Keer, *Analysis of UNCITRAL Questionnaires on Interim Relief*, 16 (3) Mealey's Int'l Arb. Rep. 23 (2001). *The Canadian decision, Quintette Coal Limited v. Nippon Steel Corporation* [1989] 1 WWR 120, 132, c.f. Lew, *supra* n. 28, at ¶23-14.
578. Ali Yesilirmak, *supra* n. 30, at 93.
579. Article 25.3, 2014 LCIA Rules. *However, it does allow resort to courts in exceptional circumstances. Similarly,* Art. 23.2, 2017 ICC Rules, *which also permits resort to courts only in appropriate circumstances. See Appendix M.*
580. Markus Wirth, *Interim or Preventive Measures in Support of International Arbitration in Switzerland*, 18(1) ASA Bulletin 31, 45 (2000).
581. Lew, *supra* n. 28, at ¶23-14.
582. Abascal, *supra* n. 1, at 758.

when a tribunal lacks the power to grant the relief or though it has the power, cannot do so effectively.[583]

1. NEED FOR INTERIM MEASURES DURING ARBITRATION PROCEEDINGS

As discussed previously, courts retain concurrent jurisdiction even during arbitration proceedings. However, the role becomes extremely limited to assistance and control – a principle referred to as 'subsidiarity' or 'co-operation'.[584] Therefore, once the arbitral proceedings have commenced, the mandate of Article 5 of the Model Law or Section 5 of the IAA applies and the courts are duty-bound not to intervene in the arbitration proceedings except as specifically provided.

However, most often than not, an arbitration takes over one and a half years to complete.[585] During this time, there may arise situations in which it is neither feasible nor convenient to rely on the powers of the arbitral tribunal alone. Therefore, the intervention of the courts is not only advisable but essential.[586] In fact, without the court's intervention, justice may be denied to a party[587] as a tribunal may not provide an adequate remedy and the court's jurisdiction would have been ousted.

Such instances would stem from the shortcomings related to the peculiar nature and operation of arbitration.[588] After the appointment of the arbitral tribunal, especially in international arbitration, the arbitral tribunal often consists of several members of different nationalities and places of residence or practices.[589] Therefore, to convene a hearing on such short notice may be difficult. Although these concerns may be addressed by modern technology, such as video conference, teleconference, emails, the intervention of courts during arbitral proceedings is considered essential to ensure that when the arbitrators cannot perform certain acts, they should be allowed to request the assistance of the court.[590]

An argument against this concurrent jurisdiction of the courts is that it provides for overlapping jurisdiction. It permits costly and duplicative parallel proceedings and judicial interference in the arbitral process. However, given the inherent limitations on the power of the arbitral tribunal, the courts cannot be wholly ousted of jurisdiction.[591]

583. *See generally,* Kieron, *supra* n. 538.
584. *See generally,* Jarrod Wong, *supra* n. 89.
585. WilliamLaurence Craig, William Park & Jan Paulsson, *International Chamber of Commerce Arbitration* 108 (3d ed. 2000).
586. Luis, *supra* n. 521, at 562.
587. *Coppee-Lavalin v. Ken-Ren Chemicals and Fertilizers Ltd.* (1994) 2 All ER 449.
588. Ali Yesilirmak, *supra* n. 30, at 66; *See,* Howard Holtzmann, *A Task for the 21st Century: Creating a New International Court for Resolving Disputes on the Enforceability of Arbitral Awards,* in Martin Hunter & Arthur Marriott, et al. (eds), *The Internationalization of International Arbitration* 109|113 (1995).
589. *ICC First Interim Award 5835 of 1988,* extracts published in 8 (1) ICC Int'l Ct Arb. Bull. 67 (1997), c.f. Ali Yesilirmak, *supra* n. 30, at 74.
590. Ali Yesilirmak, *supra* n. 30, at 39.
591. *A few U.S. decisions have considered (and rejected) claims that an arbitral tribunal may not order provisional relief because a foreign court enjoys the exclusive power to do so. See Warth*

Even after the constitution of the arbitral tribunal, there may be circumstances where the arbitral tribunal is not in a position to grant effective interim relief either because the interim measure has to be enforced immediately, because it is directed against a third party, or because it is beyond the jurisdiction of the arbitral tribunal.[592] Thus, despite the extra delay and expense, the intervention of the courts is an unarguable necessity. That is the reason one of the exceptions to the mandate of Article 5 of the Model Law is the possibility of court-ordered interim measures during arbitration proceedings

2. POWER TO GRANT INTERIM MEASURES DURING ARBITRATION PROCEEDINGS

There is no specific reference in Article 9 or 17J of the Model Law which authorises the court to grant interim measures during arbitration proceedings. Article 9 and 17J of the Model Law refer to the possibility of approaching the court and the court exercising power as it would in relation to proceedings in court, but none of them clarifies the limits or instances when such power would be unavailable.

The power to grant interim measures during arbitration proceedings can be implied from the broad language of Article 17J of the Model Law which provides that the court can issue an interim measure 'in relation to arbitration proceedings'. The interpretation of the said phrase does not need to be restricted to before the commencement of arbitral proceedings. Such a restrictive interpretation would, in fact, be contrary to the overarching mandate to exercise such power in consideration of the 'specific features of international arbitration' as arbitration cannot exist devoid of court support. Moreover, due to the consensual nature of arbitration and the inherent limitations of the arbitral tribunal, court assistance during arbitration proceedings and the power to grant interim measures would fall within one of the specific features of international arbitration. Even the placement of Article 17J within the Model Law relates to powers exercisable during arbitration proceedings. Hence, the power of the court to grant interim measures is envisaged during arbitration proceedings.

2.1. Section 9(3) of the IAA

Even though Section 9 of the IAA always contemplated court assistance during arbitration proceedings, there was an inconsistency between Section 9(1) of the IAA and Section 17(1) of the IAA, which permitted interim measures by the court and the arbitral tribunal. Therefore, courts assumed that the power of the court was parallel or that the courts were superior to an arbitral tribunal and could grant interim measures at all times.[593]

Line, Ltd v. Merinda Marine Co. 778 F.Supp. 158 (S.D.N.Y. 1991); *In re Noble Navigation Corp.* 1984 WL 432 (S.D.N.Y.), c.f. Gary Born, *supra* n. 33, at 2638-2639.

592. Christopher Boog, *The Laws Governing Interim Measures in International Arbitration*, in Franco Ferrari & Stefan Kröll (ed.), *Conflict of Laws in International Arbitration* 445 (2010).

593. Shivam Jasra, *supra* n. 93.

This inconsistency was resolved by the 2015 Amendment to the IAA when it introduced Section 9(3) of the IAA as an exception to Section 5 of the IAA. Section 9(3) of the IAA provides that '*Once the arbitral tribunal has been constituted, the court shall not entertain an application under sub-section (1), unless the court finds that circumstances exist which may not render the remedy provided under Section 17 efficacious.*'

Thus, the provisions of Section 9(1) of the IAA can be invoked during the arbitration proceedings if the court finds that circumstances exist which may render the remedy sought from the arbitral tribunal to be inefficacious. It should be clarified that the power to grant interim measures during arbitration proceedings under Section 9 of the IAA existed even before the 2015 Amendment. Even before the amendment, courts had taken the view that the jurisdiction of the court would not be wholly ousted during arbitration proceedings.[594] There is nothing contained in the wordings of Section 9 of the IAA that precludes the party from seeking interim relief from the court at any stage of the interim relief, even during the arbitration, unless the relief claim is identical to that put forth before the arbitral tribunal.[595]

2.2. Aligning with the Model Law

However, prior to the amendment, the principle of priority of jurisdiction of the arbitral tribunal for granting interim measures was not expressly affirmed in the IAA. The express recognition of the principle of priority of jurisdiction under Section 9(3) of the IAA post the amendment aligns with Article 17J of the Model Law.

Thus, the inclusion of Section 9(3) of the IAA is a welcome step. It imposes an obligation on the court not to entertain an application for interim measures under Section 9 of the IAA when the tribunal has been constituted. At the same time, it recognises the concurrent jurisdiction of the arbitral tribunal and the national courts, which is in consonance with international jurisprudence[596] and the principle of 'court-subsidiarity'.[597]

2.3. International Practice

Similar to the position in France,[598] England,[599] Singapore,[600] and many other countries[601] once the arbitral tribunal is appointed, relief should be sought from the arbitral

594. *Tata Capital Ltd. v. A.R. Industries Pvt. Ltd.* 2009 (3) Arb LR 218 (Bom).
595. *BPTP Ltd. v. CPI India (I) Ltd.* 2015 SCC OnLine Del 10115, ¶102.
596. Article 26(9), 2013 UNCITRAL Rules; Art. 15.2, 2016 MCIA Rules; Art. 37(5), 2017 SCC Rules; Art. 28(2), 2017 ICC Rules; Art. 27.2, 2017 SIAC Rules; Art. 25.3, 2014 LCIA Rules; Art. 31.3, 2007 Dubai Rules; Art. 37(c), AAA Rules; Art. 25.3, 2018 DIS Rules; Art. 33(5), 2018 VIAC Rules; Art. 26(9), 2012 CEAC; Art. 32(3), 2016 KAC; Gary Born, *supra* n. 33, at 3885-3886; *Partial Award in ICC Case No. 6709*, in Jean-Jacques Arnaldez, Yves Derains & Dominique Hascher (eds), *Collection of ICC Arbitral Awards 1991-1995* 435, 437 (1997); Boog, *supra* n. 592, at 445.
597. *As opposed to a* 'free *choice*' *approach where parties are free to apply to the court or the tribunal for interim measures*. For example, Germany, Ronald Wong, *supra* n. 452, at 512.
598. Denis G. Brock & Laura Feldman, *Recent Trends in the Conduct of Arbitrators*, 30(2) J. Int'l Arb. 177, 184 (2013).

tribunal itself. The court will have no jurisdiction in view of Section 9(3) of the IAA,[602] i.e., a court cannot entertain an application under Section 9(1) if the tribunal has been constituted[603] since the tribunal is best suited and contains the necessary expertise with respect to the dispute.[604]

In Brazil, the role of the court is limited to enforcement alone[605] and interim measures can only be granted by the arbitral tribunal after formation.[606] In Hong Kong[607] and the British Virgin Islands,[608] the court may refuse to grant interim relief on the ground that the matter is currently the subject of arbitral proceedings and the court considers that it is more appropriate for the matter to be dealt with by the arbitral tribunal.[609] A similar consideration is provided under Dutch Law, where the court should take into account 'all circumstances' before granting an interim measure during arbitration proceedings.[610]

Under French law, the role of the court is complementary before the formation of the arbitral tribunal on account of urgency and risk[611] and subsidiary after the formation.[612] This maintains the equilibrium between party autonomy and court involvement by leaning in favour of party autonomy.[613] However, in Russia, courts retain the power to grant interim measures, despite the formation of the arbitral tribunal.[614]

2.4. Emergency Arbitration and Jurisdiction of Courts

The incorporation of Section 9(3) of the IAA signifies that priority is given to the arbitral tribunal to provide interim measures and the power of the court is purely supportive of the arbitral process.[615] Therefore, whenever a tribunal has the power to act and a remedy before such tribunal would be available, the jurisdiction of the court would be curtailed.[616] The increasing prevalence of expedited procedures and emergency arbitration in institutional rules provides alternative remedies and hence, in such instances

599. English Arbitration Act, 1996, S. 44(5).
600. Singapore International Arbitration Act, 1994, S. 12A(6).
601. *See Appendix A and L.*
602. *Shriram Transport Finance Company Ltd. v. Babu P.V.* 2018 SCC OnLine Ker 76; *Tufan Chatterjee Systems Pvt. Ltd. v. Vargheese & Ors.* 2018 SCC OnLine Ker 2269.
603. *Tufan Chatterjee v. Rangan Dhar* 2016 SCC OnLine Cal 483, ¶29; *Md. Rashid v. Md. Arif* 2020 SCC OnLine Cal 2382, ¶11.
604. Markus Wirth, *Supra* n. 580, at 44.
605. Brazil Arbitration Act, 2015, Art. 22.
606. Arbitration Act 2013, S. 22(b); Dutch Code of Civil Procedure, Art. 1022c.
607. Hong Kong Arbitration Ordinance (Cap.609), S. 45(4).
608. Arbitration Act 2013, S. 43(4).
609. Hong Kong Arbitration Ordinance (Cap.609), Ss 45(4) & 60(4); Stephen, *supra* n. 96, at 500.
610. Dutch Code of Civil Procedure, Art. 1051(2).
611. Ali Yesilirmak, *supra* n. 30, at 90.
612. *Ibid.*, at 90.
613. *Ibid.*, at 87.
614. *Ibid.*, at 530.
615. *NCC International AB v. Alliance Concrete Singapore Pte Ltd.* [2008] 2 SLR(R) 565, ¶¶ 29, 31.
616. *State of Gujarat v. Amber Builders* (2020) 2 SCC 540, ¶17.

there is no requirement for courts to be involved.[617] If the rules of an arbitral institute provide for the appointment of an emergency arbitrator and such appointment has been made, the courts should refuse jurisdiction under Section 9(3) of the IAA.[618]

3. SCOPE OF THE POWER DURING ARBITRAL PROCEEDINGS

Courts should, however, be extra cautious when dealing with requests for interim measures after the commencement of arbitral proceedings. The legislative intent is clear that the powers of the court under Section 9 of the IAA and specifically under Section 9(3) of the IAA are to be exercised in aid of arbitral proceedings and not to resolve the dispute at hand either directly or indirectly.[619] Otherwise, it will be too easy for a party which is bent upon a policy of non-cooperation to frustrate the arbitral process.[620]

They should consider necessary safeguards before exercising power under Section 9 of the IAA and should reject any oppressive, frivolous, or vexatious applications.[621] They should also consider the possibility of abuse or tactical advantage and should reject applications where no urgency is demonstrated.[622] For example, if the seat of arbitration is India, then a party may apply to the national court for interim measures as the court might be more receptive to such a request forcing a party to settle.[623] Hence, courts should interfere only when it is clear that the rights of the parties would be prejudicially affected and the tribunal is not in a position to provide a suitable remedy, either because it does not have the power, or because it cannot exercise the said power effectively at that time of such request.

3.1. 'Once the Arbitral Tribunal Has Been Constituted'

It should be noted that the words used in Section 9(3) of the IAA are '*once the arbitral tribunal has been constituted*' as opposed to '*before the commencement of arbitral proceedings*' in Section 9(2) of the IAA. The language does not clarify when this constitution is said to be complete. Is it at the time of nomination of the sole arbitrator? At the date of the first hearing? After the challenge to the appointment of the arbitrator has been resolved?

617. Damian Honey & Martina Kelly, *English Court Support for Arbitration: Recent Development*, (February 2018), available at: https://www.hfw.com/English-Court-Support-for-Arbitration-Recent-Developments-February-2018.
618. *Ashwani Minda v. U-Shin Ltd.* 2020 SCC OnLine Del 1648; *Gerald Metals S.A. v. Timis* [2016] EWHC 2327.
619. *Hero Wind Energy Private Limited v. Inox Renewables Limited* 2020 SCC OnLine Del 478, ¶43; *NCC International AB v. Alliance Concrete Singapore Pte Ltd.* [2008] 2 SLR(R) 565, ¶ 30.
620. *Cetelem SA v. Robust Holdings Ltd.* [2005] 1 CLC 821.
621. *Mc Donald's India Pvt Ltd. v. Vikram Bakshi*, MANU/DE/1684/2016.
622. Ali Yesilirmak, *supra* n. 30, at 87.
623. *Ibid.*, at 52.

3.1.1. *Statutory Arbitrations*

It is unclear from the text of Section 9(3) of the IAA whether the bar under this section to approach the court would apply in the case of statutory arbitrations, or in arbitrations where the arbitration agreement provides for a particular person as an arbitrator, or a particular person holding an office, e.g., managing director of a public sector undertaking.

In these circumstances, an arbitral tribunal would ideally be constituted at the moment when the notice of arbitration is first received. Hence, the bar under Section 9(3) of the IAA ought to apply. Therefore, interim measures may be sought only from the arbitral tribunal unless the arbitrator refuses to provide his/her consent to the arbitration, or in other such circumstances where it can be established that the remedy would be inefficacious or practically impossible, e.g., the death of the arbitrator.

3.1.2. *Acceptance of Appointment*

In Germany, interim measures from the arbitral tribunal are permitted only after the 'completion of the appointment process'.[624] In Brazil[625] and the Philippines,[626] arbitral proceedings are deemed to have commenced when the appointment is accepted by the sole arbitrator or by all the arbitrators if there is more than one. The position adopted in Brazil and the Philippines is clearer than that of Germany as 'completion of the appointment process' is also capable of various meanings ranging from consent to disposal of a challenge against an arbitrator.

The better view is that the bar under Section 9(3) of the IAA should not apply unless the arbitral proceedings have commenced, i.e., the arbitrator(s) have given consent to their appointment.[627] If the appointment is challenged, the arbitral tribunal would not be able to act effectively and hence, the courts could, in such circumstances, exercise jurisdiction.

Further, the adoption of such language would remove the inconsistency between the language used in Section 9(2) of the IAA and Section 9(3) of the IAA. Therefore, the language in Section 9(3) should be changed to '*Once the arbitral proceedings have commenced* … ', and to remove any ambiguity, an explanation should be added below this provision which states that '*Arbitral proceedings would be commenced when the appointment is accepted by the sole arbitrator or by all the arbitrators if there is more than one.*'

624. Stephen, *supra* n. 96, at 398.
625. Brazil Arbitration Law, 2015, Art. 19.
626. Alternative Dispute Resolution Act, 2004, S. 28(a).
627. *This view has been affirmed in Hero Wind Energy Private Limited v. Inox Renewables Limited* 2020 SCC OnLine Del 478, ¶32 *after submission of the doctoral thesis of the author.*

3.2. The Ouster of Jurisdiction of the Court

It is pertinent to note that the jurisdiction of the court to grant interim measures does not automatically get barred once the arbitral tribunal is constituted.[628] The restriction in Section 9(3) of the IAA only means that the court would not ordinarily entertain such an application unless circumstances exist which may not render the remedy under Section 17 of the IAA efficacious.[629] Therefore, the court is not entirely denuded of the power to grant interim measures once the arbitral tribunal has been constituted.[630] This partial restriction cannot be considered a denial of justice as effective protection of rights is available through the arbitral tribunal.[631]

3.2.1. Meaning of 'Shall Not Entertain'

There was a debate on what is the meaning of the word 'entertain' under Section 9(3) of the IAA. It was contended that the word 'entertain' means not only the entertainment of an application at the threshold but also the continuation of the application after the tribunal has been constituted. The opposite contention was that the word 'entertain' only referred to the consideration of an application until the time the arbitral tribunal had not been formed. The answer by the judiciary to this debate has been inconsistent.

One view is that Section 9(3) of the IAA does not operate as an ouster clause in so far as the court's power is concerned. Whenever an ouster is intended, it is made clear by the legislature.[632] If it is accepted that the moment the arbitral tribunal is constituted, the court which is seized of an application under Section 9 of the IAA becomes *corum non judice*, then it would lead to a severe vacuum as there is no provision under the IAA for dealing with pending matters. The latter half of the language in Section 9(3) of the IAA provides that the power of the court is not ousted as it retains the power if the remedy under Section 17 of the IAA is not efficacious.[633]

The other view has been that the moment an arbitral tribunal is constituted under Section 9(3) of the IAA, the court losses its jurisdiction to hear an application for interim measures unless the case falls within the exception provided under Section 9(3) of the IAA.[634] The object of introducing Section 9(3) of the IAA was to avoid courts being flooded with Section 9 applications, to decongest the clogged court system and that an arbitral tribunal can grant interim relief in a timely and efficacious manner.[635] Therefore, an order stating the interim order shall operate until the conclusion of the

628. *Tufan Chatterjee v. Rangan Dhar* 2016 SCC OnLine Cal 483, ¶29.
629. *Bishnu Kumar Yadav v. M.L. Soni & Sons* 2016 SCC OnLine Cal 1420, ¶6.
630. *Energo Engineering Projects Ltd. v. TRF Ltd.* 2016 SCC OnLine Del 6560, ¶27.
631. Ali Yesilirmak, *supra* n. 30, at 105.
632. *Benara Bearings & Pistons Ltd. v. Mahle Engine Components India Pvt. Ltd.* 2017 SCC OnLine Del 7226, ¶ 24; *M. Ashraf v. Kasim V.K.* 2018 SCC OnLine Ker 4913, ¶8.
633. *Ibid.*
634. *Chaudhary Avdesh Kumar v. Volleyball Federation of India* 2017 SCC Online Mad 19117, ¶ 42.
635. *Amazon.com NV Investment Holdings LLC v. Future Retail Ltd.* 2021 SCC OnLine SC 557.

arbitral proceedings[636] was wrong and contrary to the intention of the IAA. It was considered to be violative of the provision of Section 9(3) of the IAA and was set aside since the tribunal had been constituted.[637]

3.2.2. *Lack of a Provision for Transfer of Pending Applications*

However, there is no provision as a transitory measure that requires a court to relegate or transfer the pending application to the arbitral tribunal once such arbitral tribunal has been constituted.[638] Hence, once the arbitral proceedings have commenced and the matter is before the tribunal, an application under Section 9 of the IAA read with Section 151 of the CPC is not maintainable as the same issue is not required to be decided by two forums having concurrent jurisdiction simultaneously.[639] Consequently, an ad interim order was discontinued while deciding the application under Section 9 of the IAA because the arbitral tribunal had been formed and there was no necessity to continue the interim order under Section 9 of the IAA.[640]

3.3. Deemed to Be an Application Before the Arbitral Tribunal

A third view has been that an application under Section 9(1) of the IAA is deemed to be an application under Section 17(1) of the IAA once the arbitral tribunal has been constituted.[641] In the alternative, the parties can consent that such application will be deemed to be an application under Section 17(1) of the IAA[642] and interim order can be granted till the disposal of such application by the arbitral tribunal.[643]

This view is the most reasonable and practical one. If an application under Section 9(1) of the IAA is pending and the arbitral tribunal is formed, the court should transfer the application to the arbitral tribunal[644] or such an application should be deemed to be an application under Section 17(1) of the IAA. The court can even grant

636. *V.K. Sood Engineers and Contractors v. Northern Railways* 2017 SCC OnLine Del 9211, ¶19.
637. *Assam Industrial Development Corp. and Ors. v. Assam Paper Mill Pvt. Ltd. and Ors.* 2017 SCCOnline Gau 629.
638. *Benara Bearings & Pistons Ltd. v. Mahle Engine Components India Pvt. Ltd.* 2017 SCC OnLine Del 7226, ¶25.
639. *Johari Forts & Palaces Pvt. Ltd. v. Maharaja Narendra Singh* 2001 SCC OnLine Raj 671, ¶28.
640. *Monojeet Das v. Sujit Roychowdhury* 2017 SCC OnLine Cal 16309, ¶4.
641. *Hiren Vishanji Shah v. Tarachand Hirji Shah* 2019 SCC Online Bom 8158; *Aquatech Systems (Asia) Pvt. Ltd. v. SKS Power Generation (Chhattisgarh) Ltd.* 2016 SCC OnLine Del 2794, ¶7; *TRF Ltd. v. Energo Engineering Projects Ltd.* 2016 SCC OnLine Del 5212; *Virtuous Retail Pte Ltd. v. Mantri Developers Private Ltd.* 2021 SCC OnLine Bom 3206, ¶25.
642. *Goregaon CHSL v. Dr. Seema Mahadev Paryekar* 2019 SCC Online Bom 3274; *Krishna Kumar Balakrishnan v. Saffron Ganesha Entertainment LLP* 2019 SCC Online Bom 7145; *Bharat Mithalal Nagori v. Manik Nivrutti Kodre* 2019 SCC Online Bom 9094; *Akruti Developers & Builders v. Pancard Clubs Ltd.* 2019 SCC Online Bom 9134; *IRB Ahemdabad Vadodara Super Express Tollway Private Ltd. v. National Highways Authority of India 2019 SCC OnLine Del 10577; Sanjay Arora v. Rajan Chadha* 2021 SCC OnLine Del 4619.
643. *TRF Ltd. v. Energo Engineering Projects Ltd.* 2016 SCC OnLine Del 5212; *Dy. Chief Engineer (Construction) Central v. B.N. Agrawal* 2021 SCC OnLine Bom 1533, ¶22.
644. *Godrej Projects Development Ltd. v. Simoco Telecommunications* 2021 SCC OnLine Cal 2577, ¶6: *This case was decided after the submission of the doctoral thesis of the author.*

interim relief, subject to the satisfaction on facts, till the commencement of arbitral proceedings, to prevent any prejudice against the applicant.

It is necessary to clarify that the term 'transfer' should simply mean directing the parties to submit a copy of their application under Section 9 of the IAA before the arbitral tribunal and the same would then be deemed to be an application under Section 17 of the IAA. It does not mean the transfer of the actual physical record of the court to the arbitral tribunal.

Therefore, the Section 9(3) of the IAA should be substituted with the following language '*Once the arbitral proceedings have commenced, the Court shall not entertain an application under sub-section (1), and the Court shall refer the request, or any pending requests under sub-section(1), to the arbitral tribunal, unless the tribunal ….*'

As discussed in the previous chapter, this reference does not mean that the court would have no jurisdiction to pass any interim order until the tribunal decides the request for the interim measure. Following the English approach, a court would be at liberty to grant interim measures till the arbitral tribunal or institution or person having the power to act in relation to the subject matter of the order passes an order. When such an order is passed, the order of the court will cease to have effect.

It has been suggested that the boundaries between court assistance and court interference should be clarified by providing a list of situations when the court can exercise power under Section 9(3) of the IAA.[645] Providing a list would lead to more problems rather than a solution as the courts may then strictly apply the list and that too could cause injustice.

Another view is that a party should first make an application for an interim measure to the arbitral tribunal and then to the courts[646] as directly approaching the court could lead to the impression that a party is trying to circumvent the arbitral tribunal.[647] However, this may frustrate the request for interim measures, especially when the measure is urgent and may have to be sought without notice to the other party. Therefore, a safeguard or limitation on the scope of the power is contained in Section 9(3) of the IAA, i.e., the court shall not exercise power under Section 9(3) of the IAA '*unless the court finds that circumstances exist which may not render the remedy provided under Section 17 efficacious*'.

3.4. Demarcating the Line for Court Intervention

Recently, the Supreme Court of India held that the expression 'entertain' means 'to consider by application of mind to the issues raised'. The process of consideration could continue till the passing of the award. Thus, the court should not apply its mind once the arbitral tribunal has been constituted, even if an application under Section 9(1) was filed before the constitution of the arbitral tribunal unless the remedy under Section 17 is inefficacious. However, if the court has already applied its mind before the

645. Menon, *supra* n. 102, at 23.
646. *Ibid.*; Singapore International Arbitration Act, 1994, S. 12A(5).
647. Jan Schäfer, *supra* n. 301, at 232.

constitution of the arbitral tribunal, the application can be said to have been 'entertained' and hence, the court would not lose its power to grant interim measures.[648] The legislature could not have intended that a court will decline interim relief after hearing the matter only to remit the parties under Section 17 of the IAA.

Therefore, the current position of law is:[649]

(a) The proscription under Section 9(3) applies only before an application under Section 9(1) has been 'entertained'. The bar is to 'entertaining' the application. The expression 'entertained' has to be understood as 'taken up for consideration'. Once the application has been taken up for consideration, such as where arguments are in progress or judgment reserved, Section 9(3) has no application.

(b) Where the bar applies, the Court has to examine whether the Section 17 remedy would be efficacious. There is no absolute prohibition on deciding the Section 9 application, even where the Arbitral Tribunal stands constituted.

(c) Where the Arbitral Tribunal stands constituted, however, the approach of the Court has to be circumspect. Unless there is some impediment in approaching the Arbitral Tribunal under Section 17, or where the remedy under Section 17 is rendered inefficacious for some clear and apparent reason, the prayer for interim relief ought, appropriately, to be relegated to the Arbitral Tribunal.

3.5. Meaning of 'Efficacious'

While it is clear that the courts should not entertain applications for interim measures of protection once the arbitral tribunal has been formed, it is unclear what meaning should be attached to the word 'efficacious'. Ideally, the term 'may not render the remedy provided under Section 17 efficacious' should mean a 'total paralysis of the arbitral tribunal' or its complete lack of power to fulfil its functions depriving the requesting party of a fundamental right of judgment under fair conditions.[650] Since the power under Section 9(3) of the IAA is similar to Section 44 of the English Arbitration Act, the right interpretation[651] would be to exercise such power only when there is urgency and the arbitral tribunal has no power or is unable to act.[652]

In Singapore, it is considered to mean where the tribunal cannot be constituted expediently or where the arbitral tribunal has no jurisdiction to grant the relief sought.[653] In Qatar, the power can be exercised if the arbitral tribunal 'does not have jurisdiction or is incapable to act effectively'.[654] In contrast, Section 7A(4) of the Bangladesh Arbitration Act, 2001 provides that the court is competent to pass an order if the tribunal has no power or the arbitral tribunal '*has failed to pass an order in such*

648. *Arcelor Mittal Nippon Steel India Ltd. v. Essar Bulk Terminal Ltd.* 2021 SCC OnLine SC, ¶95. *This case was decided after submission of the doctoral thesis by the author.*
649. *Cyfuture India Pvt. Ltd. v. Futuretimes Technology India Pvt. Ltd.* 2021 SCC OnLine Del 4464, ¶6.
650. Ali Yesilirmak, *supra* n. 30, at 90.
651. Lira, *supra* n. 107, at 116.
652. *Seele Middle East FZE v. Drake and Skull International SA Co.* [2013] EWHC 4350.
653. *NCC International AB v. Alliance Concrete Singapore Pte Ltd.* [2008] 2 SLR(R) 565.
654. Qatar Arbitration Law, 2017, Art. 9.

matter'.[655] This effectively opens the flood gates for unlimited court intervention as the courts would review the merits and determine whether a tribunal should have passed an order or not.

3.5.1. *Narrow Scope of Power*

The role of the court during arbitral proceedings has to be a narrow one operating only in situations of urgency or where third parties are involved[656] or where there is delay or lack of knowledge of the constitution of the arbitral tribunal.[657] Since a party has an option to choose between the overlapping powers of the court and the arbitral tribunal to grant interim measures, it should first take recourse to the arbitral tribunal. It should not invoke the court's power unless the arbitral tribunal orders prove ineffective[658] or if there is some impediment in approaching the arbitral tribunal like unavailability of the arbitrator due to sickness, travel, etc., or obtaining interim relief expeditiously from the arbitral tribunal.[659]

The jurisdiction under this section should not be exercised on the vague averment that the order passed by an arbitrator would not be an effective one.[660] For example, when the matter is at the stage of evidence and the arbitral tribunal has already granted a balanced interim order after considering the interest of both the parties, an application under Section 9 of the IAA would not be maintainable and it would be best if the parties approach the arbitral tribunal for that purpose.[661] Therefore, the applicant must plead and set out the circumstances why the remedy under Section 17 of the IAA is not efficacious once the arbitral tribunal has been constituted.[662]

However, the term 'efficacious' has not been defined and, therefore, it opens the doors for court interference. It also incentivises errant parties to abuse the provision and approach the court even after the formation of the arbitral tribunal. Compared to this, the phrase '*has no power or is unable for the time being to act effectively*' as used in England[663] and Singapore[664] are better since they provide for a narrower language. Also, they address questions of whether the remedy is 'efficacious' or not, both in terms of power and urgency.

655. Bangladesh Arbitration Act, 2001, S. 7A(4).
656. *NCC International AB v. Alliance Concrete Singapore Pte Ltd.* [2008] 2 SLR(R) 565, ¶33.
657. *NGC Network India Pvt. Ltd. v. Orangefish Entertainment Pvt. Ltd.* 2018 SCC OnLine Del 11350, ¶44.6.
658. Michael J Mustill & Stewart C Boyd, *The Law and Practice of Commercial Arbitration in England* 296 (1989).
659. *Arcelor Mittal Nippon Steel India Ltd. v. Essar Bulk Terminal Ltd.* 2021 SCC OnLine SC, ¶¶68, 96.
660. *Magma Fincorp Ltd. v. A.K. Power Industries Pvt. Ltd.* 2017 SCC OnLine Cal 18783, ¶1.
661. *Ashok Leyland Ltd. v. Delhi Transport Corporation* 2019 SCC OnLine Del 8586, ¶17; *Jatin Keshruwala v. DAG Creative Media Pvt. Ltd.* 2019 SCC OnLine Bom 1346, ¶¶16-20.
662. *Shriram Transport Finance Company v. Binu T.R.* 2016 SCC OnLine Ker 38185, ¶6.
663. English Arbitration Act, 1996, S. 44(5).
664. Singapore International Arbitration Act, 1994, S. 12(A)(6).

The words '*unless the court finds that circumstances exist which may not render the remedy provided under Section 17 efficacious*' in Section 9(3) of the IAA should be substituted with '*unless the tribunal, under Section 17, has no power or is unable for the time being to act effectively*'. This would bring the IAA in line with the test adopted in most pro-arbitration regimes[665] and the courts would be in a position to borrow from established jurisprudence on the subject in these countries. Moreover, the use of such language would provide more guidance to the court with respect to the scope of this power than relying on a vague term such as 'efficacious'.

4. STANDARDS FOR GRANT OF INTERIM MEASURES DURING ARBITRATION PROCEEDINGS

A bare reading of Section 9(1) of the IAA suggests that the power to grant interim measures is available with the courts even during arbitral proceedings. Section 9(3) of the IAA restricts the scope of the power to instances where the remedy available with the arbitral tribunal may not be efficacious. Therefore, the standards to be adopted under Section 9(1) of the IAA and Section 9(3) of the IAA should not be any different,[666] except for the consideration of the circumstances with respect to the remedy not being 'efficacious'.

However, considerations of the term 'efficacious', or 'has no power or is unable for the time being to act effectively' inevitably require a subjective examination of the facts and circumstances. Therefore, a party seeking an interim measure under Section 9(3) of the IAA should first be able to satisfy the court as to why the arbitral tribunal may not be the most appropriate forum[667] for the interim measure. It cannot be that every case now and then or any sundry reason would permit a party to approach the court under Section 9(3) of the Act. The objective behind the provision is not only to reduce the burden on Courts but also to congregate the determination of the issues relating to the subject matter to the arbitral tribunal.[668] Then it should satisfy the requisite standards of a reasonable possibility of success, urgency, and the balance of convenience.[669]

Some authors contend that urgency can also be of different kinds, i.e., (a) extreme, extraordinary, or exceptional; (b) urgency that does not require instant action; or (c) urgency that may arise in the future. Therefore, court intervention should only be permitted in cases of extreme or extraordinary urgency[670] and not otherwise.[671] Instances of such extreme urgency would include whether there is a manifest threat of

665. *See Appendix A and L.*
666. *GVK Airport Holdings Limited v. BID Services Division (Mauritius) Ltd.* 2019 SCC Online Del 8978, ¶14.
667. Sigvard Jarvin, *Aspects of the Arbitral Proceedings*, in ICC (ed.), *The New 1998 ICC Rules of Arbitration*, ICC Publication No. 586 43 (1997).
668. *Manbhupinder Singh Atwal v. Neeraj Kumarpal Shah* 2019 SCC OnLine Guj 6871, ¶5.4.
669. *See Chapter 7.*
670. *See Appendix A and L.* USA, Zambia and Zimbabwe require a party to demonstrate urgency.
671. Ali Yesilirmak, *supra* n. 30, at 97.

imminent harm, i.e., perishable goods or an impending catastrophe where the arbitral tribunal may not be able to interfere in time.[672]

Different authors propose different considerations to determine when the arbitral tribunal may not be the most appropriate forum or when court assistance may be required during arbitration proceedings. Some suggest the criteria of 'prevention of further damages' or circumstances deemed appropriate by any competent judicial authority.[673] Others suggest 'urgent, or binding and enforceable measures',[674] the need for a measure against a third party,[675] or the possibility of securing an effective alternative interim measure from the arbitral tribunal.[676]

ICC practice indicates that instances when a remedy may not be 'efficacious', or when the arbitral tribunal may not 'have the power or is unable to act effectively' are (a) urgency; (b) the lack of power of the arbitral tribunal to grant the measure requested, e.g., against third parties; and (c) the arbitral tribunal is paralysed, or otherwise unable to act, e.g., resignation, death, the challenge of an arbitrator, or any other reason.[677]

A combination of the above should be used and the following criteria may be adopted to determine whether the arbitral tribunal does not have the power or is unable to act effectively to grant an interim measure during arbitral proceedings:

(a) Extreme urgency[678] or delay in hearing before the tribunal.[679]
(b) Need for ex parte relief as the tribunal would not have the power to grant such measures without hearing the other party.[680]

672. *Ibid.*, at 95; *See also*, Berthold Goldman, *Arbitrage Commercial International, Jurisclasseur Droit International*, Fascicule 586-5-2, No. 77 as translated by Schwartz, *Provisional Measures*, in ICC (ed.), *Conservatory Measures* 58 (1991).

673. M. A. Calvo, *The New ICC Rules of Arbitration – Substantial and Procedural Changes*, 14 (4) J Int'l. Arb. 41, 50 (1997).

674. Craig, *supra* n. 585, at 471.

675. Ali Yesilirmak, *supra* n. 30, at 95.

676. *For instance, rather than asking the tribunal to stop the withdrawal of a letter of credit, a party may request from its tribunal to prohibit the other party from withdrawing on the letter.*, c.f., Ali Yesilirmak, *supra* n. 30, at 97.

677. Ali Yesilirmak, *supra* n. 30, at 97.

678. *The Supreme Court of Mauritius categorically considered urgency as a ground for seeking interim relief directly from the court even though the tribunal had been constituted and the court granted the order till the time the party is able to present the new facts before the arbitral tribunal and also ordered that the same would automatically lapse after a particular date. See, Barnwell Enterprises v. ECP Africa FII Investments LLC* (2013) SCJ 327.

679. *'If a given power could possibly be exercised by a tribunal, then it should be, and parties should not be allowed to make unilateral applications to … [a court]. If, however, a given power could be exercised by the tribunal, but not as effectively, in circumstances where, for example, speed is necessary, the … [court] should be able to step in.' See*, Report of Departmental Advisory Committee on the Arbitration Bill and Supplementary Report on the Arbitration Act 1996 Arbitration, ¶216; *Indus Towers Ltd. v. Sistema Shyam Teleservices Ltd.* 2016 SC OnLine Del 3811, ¶49; Rajendra Barot & Sonali Mathur, *Laying Old Ghosts to Rest, or Not? – The 'Section 9' Engima Continues …*, 5 Ind. J. Arb. L. 168, 178 (2016); Paul Michell, *Interim Measures in Canadian Commercial Arbitration*, 32 The Advoc. Q. 413, 433 (2007). *In one case, the lethargy of the arbitrator in the manner and conduct of the arbitration proceedings was considered to be sufficient to hold that the remedy under Section 17 of the IAA is inefficacious. Srei Equipment Finance Ltd. (SEFL) v. Ray Infra Services Pvt. Ltd.* 2016 SCC OnLine Cal 6765, ¶7.

680. Denis, *supra* n. 598, at 183; *Cape Lambert Resources Ltd. v. MCC Australia Sanjin Mining Pty Ltd.* [2013] WASCA 66, ¶128; *Osmond Ireland Farm Business Ltd. v. McFarland* [2010] IEHC

(c) Lack of power of the arbitral tribunal to grant the measure requested,[681] e.g., against third parties,[682] *Anton Piller* orders.[683]
(d) Pending reference to arbitration under Section 8 of the IAA.[684]
(e) The inability of the arbitral tribunal to act, i.e., challenge the appointment of an arbitrator.[685]
(f) The possibility of securing an effective alternative measure from the arbitral tribunal.
(g) Need for urgent enforcement.[686]
(h) Whether the application has been moved as a delay tactic or to gain an advantage over the other party, i.e., the conduct of the applicant.

5. SAFEGUARDS

When considering a request for interim measures during arbitration proceedings, the court should be especially mindful of protecting the rights of the respondent and the mandate of equal treatment of parties in arbitration. The court may require an explanation from a party seeking interim measures as to why no application was filed before the arbitral tribunal or whether the same was refused. It may even direct that the application be filed before the arbitral tribunal instead.[687]

The party making the application for interim measure should be held to the standard of utmost good faith at the time of making an application under Section 9(3) of the IAA.[688] The duty should comprise: (a) full and fair disclosure of all the facts[689]

295; English Arbitration Act, 1996, Ss 44(3) & 44(6); *ENRC Marketing AG v. OJSC 'Magnitorgorsk Metallurgical Kombinat'* [2011] FCA 1371.

681. Denis, *supra* n. 598, at 184-185.
682. Zia Mody & T.T. Arvind, *Redeeming Sisyphus: The Need to Invigorate Interim Relief in International Commercial Arbitration*, in A. Van den Berg (ed.), *International Arbitration and National Courts: The Never-Ending Story* 134 (2001); Annotated Ordinance of Hong Kong Arbitration Ordinance (Cap.609), ¶¶ 60.07-60.09; *Leviathan Shipping Co. Ltd. v. Sky Sailing Overseas Co. Ltd.* [1998] 4 HKC 347; *Hsin Chong Construction (Asia) Ltd. v. Henble Ltd.* [2005] 3 HKC 27; *Prema Birkdale Horticulture (Macau) Ltd. v. Venetian Orient Ltd.* [2009] 5 HKLRD 89, c.f. Denis, *supra* n. 598, at 182; Rajendra Barot, *supra* n. 679, at 178.
683. *Areeb Rolling Mills Pvt. Ltd. v. Nkgsb Co-operative Bank Ltd.* 2013 (2) Arb. LR 14 (Bom).
684. *Section 8(3) of the IAA allows an arbitral reference to be initiated and concluded notwithstanding the pendency of a civil suit. Therefore, the machinery available under the IAA would not remain suspended until the application under Section 8 of the IAA is decided. Sarai Equipment Finance Ltd. v. Paban Poddar* 2018 (1) Arb. LR 428 (Cal) (DB), ¶14.
685. *Energo Engineering Projects Ltd. v. TRF Ltd.* 2016 SCC OnLine Del 6560, ¶30; *In Toyo Tyre Holdings the court of appeals held that it was an error to deny an injunction when the arbitrator was not appointed under the ICC Rules. The court determined that the ICC Rules provides for conservatory and interim measures and a* status quo *order was necessary to 'preserve the meaningfulness of the arbitral process'. See Toyo Tire Holdings of Americas Inc. v. Continental Tire North America, Inc.* 609 F.3d 975, 981-82 (9th Cir. 2010); Alan Redfern, *Arbitration and the Courts: Interim Measures of Protection: Is the Tide about to Turn*, 30 Tex. Int'l L. J. 71, 83 (1995); Benoit Le Bars & Tejas Shiroor, *Provisional Measures in Investment Arbitration: Wading Through the Murky Waters of Enforcement*, 6 (1) Indian J. Arb. L. 24, 31 (2017).
686. Neil Kaplan, *'Hong Kong'* in Paulsson (gen ed), *International Handbook* 56 (1999).
687. *Petroleum Investment v. Kantupan Holdings Co Ltd.* [2002] 1 All E.R. (Comm) 124; Brian Casey and Janet Mills, *Arbitration Law of Canada: Practice and Procedure* 156 (2005).
688. *Brink's MAT Ltd. v. Elcombe* [1988] 3 ALL ER 188.

likely to be relevant for the court's determination of whether the interim measure should be granted or not, and no material facts in the opinion of the party requesting the measure; and (b) the applicant must make proper enquiries before making the application.[690] Furthermore, courts should insist on the deposit of security, unless there are circumstances which require that no security should be requested from the party requesting the measure.

6. INTERIM MEASURES AFTER PASSING OF THE AWARD BUT BEFORE ENFORCEMENT

It is also now settled, both by the language of Section 9(1) of the IAA and by the courts,[691] that a court has the power to order interim measures after passing of the award and before its execution.[692] However, such measures cannot be granted if the sale proceeds or any benefit under the award would go to the award holder during the pendency of an application under Section 34 of the IAA.[693]

6.1. Need for Interim Measures after Passing of the Award

It should be noted that this provision is unique to the Indian subcontinent and in the jurisdictions compared, the only other countries with a similar provision are Bangladesh and Pakistan.[694] The possible reason for having such a provision can be discerned from the phrase '*Where the time for making an application to set aside the arbitral award under Section 34 has expired*' in Section 36 of the IAA (Enforcement of Awards). Therefore, there will exist a period of ninety days[695] between the passing of the award and its enforcement. It is to cater to such a period that the power under Section 9 was presumably extended to a time after the passing of the award but before its enforcement.

689. *Siporex Trade SA v. Comdel Commodities Ltd.* [1986] 2 Lloyd's Rep. 428; *Golf Interstate Oil Corp v. ANT Trade, The Giovanna* [1999] 1 Lloyd's Rep. 867; *R v. Kensington Income Tax Commissioners, Princess Edmond de Polginac* [1917] 1 KB 486.

690. Nael G., *Interim Measures in International Commercial Arbitration: A Commentary on the Report by Luis Enrique Graham, in Albert van* den Berg (ed.), *50 Years of the New York Convention: ICCA International Arbitration Conference* 588 (2009).

691. *I. Sudershan Rao v. Evershine Builders Private Ltd.* 2013(2) Arb. LR 52 (AP) (DB), ¶20 wherein *the court held that a rule in the civil rules requiring an interim application to be filed in the pending application under section 34 of the Arbitration Act was only directory and not mandatory. This view has also been held in Veda Research Laboratories Ltd. v. Survi Projects* 2010 (3) RAJ 363 (Del) and *Chunilal Kapoorchanji Shah v. Yuvraj Industries Ltd.* 2010 (1) Arb. LR. 138 (Guj), ¶15.

692. *Delta Constructions Systems Ltd., Hyderabad v. Narmada Cement Company Ltd.* 2002 (2) Arb. LR 47 (Bom), ¶12; *Kotak Mahindra Prime Ltd. v. Amin Tharani* 2009 SCC OnLine Bom 1181.

693. *City Corp Finance (India) Ltd. v. Manoj Ray & Anr.* 2017 SCC OnLine Cal 10347, ¶34.

694. Bangladesh Arbitration Act, 2001, S. 7(A)(1); Pakistan Arbitration Act, 1940, S. 16; *See Appendix A.*

695. Indian Arbitration Act, 1996, S. 34(3).

6.2. Power of the Court after Passing of the Award

It is unclear as to which party may apply after the termination of the arbitration proceedings and what criteria should the courts adopt while dealing with such applications? Deciding the issue, the Division Bench of the Bombay High Court in *Maharashtra State Electricity Generation Company Ltd. v. Dirk India Ltd.*,[696] *(Dirk India)* held that an application under Section 9 of the IAA has two vital aspects: (i) the immediate and proximate nexus between the request for the interim measure and the subject matter of the dispute in arbitration; and (ii) the order under Section 9 of the IAA to prevent the claim under arbitration from being frustrated. Therefore, what was contemplated was the preservation of assets for enforcement of the final award.

The court examined these two aspects to conclude that the interim measure has to be a step in aid to the fruition of arbitral proceedings. An award only benefits the winning party and it is only this party that can secure interim relief after the award has been passed to ensure the claim is not frustrated.[697] This view was subsequently followed as well.[698] In one instance, the court held that if specific performance has not been granted in an award, an independent application under Section 9 of the IAA is maintainable to restrain a party from disposing of assets while an application for setting aside the award is still pending.[699] In another instance, the Calcutta High Court[700] upheld the order of appointment of a receiver under Section 9 of the IAA to collect all occupational charges and service charges in aid of execution of the award, which had been challenged.[701]

It has been argued that this view completely misses the fact that a party may want to seek an interim measure till the party approaches a court to set aside the award under Section 34 of the IAA, or in the alternative, when the award has been sent back to the arbitral tribunal on some issue for review.[702] This view was partially accepted in

696. *Maharashtra State Electricity Generation Company Ltd. v. Dirk India Ltd.* 2015 SCC OnLine Bom 747. *Affirmed in Felguera Gruas India Pvt. Ltd. v. Tuticorin Coal Terminal Pvt. Ltd.* 2019 SCC OnLine Bom 9851 ¶23.
697. *Ibid.*, ¶12.
698. *Windworld (India) Ltd. v. Enercon GmbH* 2017 SCC OnLine Bom 1147; *Centrient Pharmaceuticals India Pvt. Ltd. v. Hindustan Antibiotics Ltd.* 2019 SCC Online Bom 1614, ¶26; *Magma Fincorp Limited v. Anisur Rahaman Mallick* 2019 SCC Online Cal 2867; *Tata Capital Financial Services Limited v. Goutam Kumar Mohanty* 2019 SCC Online Cal 3193.
699. *I. Sudershan Rao v. Evershine Builders Private Ltd.* 2013(2) Arb. LR 52 (AP) (DB), ¶20. *The court held that a rule in the civil rules requiring an interim application to be filed in the pending application under section 34 of the Arbitration Act was only directory and not mandatory. This view has also been held in Veda Research Laboratories Ltd. v. Survi Projects* 2010 (3) RAJ 363 (Del) and *Chunilal Kapoorchanji Shah v. Yuvraj Industries Ltd.* 2010 (1) Arb. LR. 138 (Guj); *Mahyco Monsanto Biotech (India) Pvt. Ltd. v. Nuziveedu Seeds Ltd.* 2019 SCC OnLine Bom 9852, ¶17.
700. *Efcalon Tie-up Pvt. Ltd. v. Startrack Agency Pvt. Ltd.* 2019 SCC OnLine Cal 248.
701. *Another such instance is Srei Equiment Finance Limited v. Misa Developers* 2019 SCC Online Cal 1234.
702. Kartikey Mahajan, *Making the Case for Post- award Interim Relief for Award: Debtor*, 3(2) Ind. J. Arb. L. 14, 17 (2014).

Organising Committee, Commonwealth Games v. M/s Nussli (Switzerland) Ltd.(Nussli).[703] The Delhi High Court, considering the judgment in *Dirk India,* took a contrary view. In Justice Sanghi's view, in *Dirk India,* the request was for continuing to perform the contract even after termination of the agreement had been held to be valid in the award. Thus, the request for an interim measure was rightly rejected.

In *Nussli,* the request was to keep the bank guarantee alive till the matter under Section 34 of the IAA has been concluded and the same was allowed. It is pertinent to mention that in *Nussli,* the respondent was a foreign corporation with no assets in India. It should be noted that the judgment of the Delhi High Court was specific to its facts and circumstances and in particular the fact that the counterclaim of the applicant had been partially allowed. Granting the right of seeking interim relief to the award debtor would only further litigation and delay the execution of the award.

While the critique of *Dirk India* does hold water from an academic standpoint of the rights of the losing party (since a 'party' as defined under the IAA can file an application under Section 9 of the IAA), it defies the procedural logic of enforcement.

6.3. Practical Considerations after the 2015 Amendment

If the award has not been challenged under Section 34 of the IAA and the limitation period has not expired, the losing party has either of the two options, i.e., (a) to voluntarily comply with the award; or (b) not to comply with it, forcing the winning party to seek execution of the award as a decree. In the first instance, there would be no occasion to seek an interim measure. In the second instance, the losing party will be forced to apply for setting aside the award under Section 34 of the IAA to resist enforcement of the arbitral award.

After the 2015 Amendment, there is no automatic stay of the award when an application is filed under Section 34 of the IAA.[704] In effect, the award may be enforced before the expiry of the limitation period of ninety days contained in Section 34(3) of the IAA. A stay of operation of the award under Section 36(2) of the IAA would be an interim measure till the disposal of the application for setting aside the award. Hence, if the court hearing the application under Section 34 of the IAA does not deem it fit to stay the execution of the award, why should an interim relief be granted under Section 9 of the IAA?[705]

Conversely, if the court does stay the execution of the award, what kind of interim relief will the losing party request? The award can only be set aside. There cannot be a reversal of the outcome of the award and the losing party cannot become the winning party because an application under Section 34 of the IAA is not an appeal.

---

703. *Organising Committee, Commonwealth Games v. M/s Nussli (Switzerland) Ltd.* (2014) 6 SCC 697.

704. *Board of Control for Cricket in India v. Kochi Cricket Pvt. Ltd. (2018) 6 SCC 287; Ardee Infrastructure Pvt. Ltd. v. Ms. Anuradha Bhatia and Ardee Infrastructure Pvt. Ltd. v. Yashpal & Sons* 2017 (2) Arb. LR 163 (Del).

705. *Delta Construction Systems Ltd. v. Narmada Cement Company Ltd.* 2002 (2) Arb. LR 47 (Bom); *SMJ-RK-SD(JV) v. National Highways Authority of India* 2009 SCC OnLine Del 2317.

Moreover, the courts now require a mandatory deposit[706] of 100% of the amount of the award before staying the execution of the award.[707] Therefore, even if the losing party were to succeed in the setting aside application, the deposit would simply be returned. Hence, there would practically be no foreseeable scenario where the losing party should be entitled to interim relief after the award has been passed.

Another concern expressed with this view has been with respect to the right of third parties and whether they can approach the court for an interim measure after an award has been passed which affects the rights of such third parties.[708] However, this concern also seems unfounded as the third party may file objections under Section 47 of the CPC during the execution of the award.[709] Therefore, to give the right of interim relief post the award to a third party would, in effect, open the flood gates of litigation and delay tactics.

6.4. Removal of the Waiting Period

Furthermore, the remedy under Section 9 of the IAA can only be invoked by a 'party' which under Section 2(1)(h) of the IAA means a party to an arbitration agreement. If this line of argument were to be permitted, then the situation would be that a third party cannot file an application under Section 9 of the IAA before the formation of the arbitral tribunal, or during the arbitration proceedings but may file an application subsequently after passing of the award. This could not have been the intention of the legislature, and more importantly, such an interpretation would run contrary to the golden rule of minimal intervention by courts. The losing party may create artificial causes of action in the garb of third parties to resist enforcement or delay the same after an award has been passed. There is no need to extend the applicability of Section 9 to post-award instances. Interim measures are available under the CPC when seeking enforcement of a decree Order XXI of the CPC. Hence, there is no need to resort to Section 9 of the IAA for the same.[710]

The party securing a favourable award should file for its execution at the earliest and hence, the phrase in Section 36 of the IAA requiring a party to wait for ninety days before filing for enforcement of the award should also be deleted. As noted by the 246th Report of the Law Commission, the rationale for the introduction of Section 36(2) of the IAA was that an admission of a petition under Section 34 of the IAA virtually paralyses the process for the winning party/award creditor.[711] Hence, unless the court orders the stay of the operation of the award, the winning party should be permitted to reap the

706. *Board of Trustees for the Port of Kolkata v. ABG Kolkata Container Terminal Private Ltd.* 2019 SCC OnLine Cal 4009.
707. *Manish v. Godawari Marathawada Irrigation Development Corporation* MANU/SCOR/30132/2018.
708. Kartikey Mahajan, *supra* n. 702, at 20.
709. *SRS Investments Bengal Tiger Ltd. and Ors. v. Rahul Todi and Ors.* MANU/WB/1432/2019.
710. *Centrient Pharmaceuticals India Pvt. Ltd. v. Hindustan Antibiotics Ltd.* 2019 SCC Online Bom 1614, ¶¶27-29; *Mehfuza v. Kadir Yakoob Patrawala* 2019 SCC Online Bom 9142, ¶5.
711. Law Commission of India, *supra* n. 517, at 25.

fruits of the award. The mere filing of an application under Section 34 of the IAA should not operate as an automatic stay.

Therefore, such a waiting period serves no purpose after the incorporation of Section 36(2) of the IAA. After the 2015 Amendment, the courts are at liberty to grant or deny a stay of execution proceedings pending under Section 36 of the IAA. Any prejudice being caused to the winning party during the period after the passing of the arbitral award and before execution can be catered to by the court under Order XXI of the CPC as soon as the enforcement application is filed under Section 36(1) of the IAA.[712] Therefore, the better view is that if no stay is granted under Section 36(2) of the IAA, the arbitral award would be enforceable and an application under Section 9 of the IAA would not be maintainable.[713]

Furthermore, if a party is supposed to wait for ninety days before filing for execution, then Section 36(2) of the IAA would become redundant as there will be no execution proceedings pending. Hence, the question of stay of the operation of the arbitral award would never arise. Conversely, if no application under Section 34 of the IAA has been made for setting aside the arbitral award within ninety days, then a question of stay of proceedings would anyway be moot and the executing court is at liberty to grant interim relief in accordance with Order XXI of the CPC. Therefore, the phrase '*or at any time after making of the arbitral award but before it is enforced in accordance with section 36*' should be deleted from Section 9(1) of the IAA.

712. *Peniel Cashew Company v. Ahcom Sarl Galerie Du Grand* 2018 SCC Online Ker 18569, ¶15.
713. *Centrient Pharmaceuticals India Pvt. Ltd. v. Hindustan Antibiotics Ltd.* 2019 SCC Online Bom 1614, ¶¶27-29.

CHAPTER 5

Interim Measures in Aid of Foreign Seated Arbitrations

The power of the courts to grant interim measures in support of the arbitral process is well recognised and consistently upheld by the courts across jurisdictions. As discussed in the last two chapters, courts at the seat can grant interim measures to prevent the dissipation of assets or pass such orders that prevent an arbitral award from being frustrated. The problem, however, arises when the assets are located beyond the seat of arbitration. In such cases, interim measures may be required from the court where the assets are located since an order from the court of the seat may not be immediately enforceable.[714] However, can a court beyond the seat grant interim measures in aid of a foreign seated arbitration?

1. THE NEED TO SUPPORT FOREIGN SEATED ARBITRATIONS

When the party seeking relief wants interim measures of protection in a jurisdiction apart from the seat, any application in court (not being the court at the seat) would prima facie violate the arbitration agreement and the exclusive jurisdiction of the seat. Article 9 of the Model Law resolves such conflict with respect to the right to approach the courts at the seat and beyond the seat by giving extraterritorial application to Article 9.[715] Despite such extraterritorial application, in the absence of such extraterritorial extension of the power to grant interim measures under a national arbitration statute, several domestic procedural law requirements, such as the existence of a suit, would be required for the court to exercise jurisdiction.

Though it may be argued that courts always retain the inherent jurisdiction to provide interim measures, the scope of such a remedy is constrained by the existing

714. Gary Born, *supra* n. 33, at 2715.
715. UNCITRAL Model Law, Arts 1(2) & 9.

jurisprudence of resorting to the inherent jurisdiction only in exceptional circumstances, the requirement of a cause of action and maintainability of the suit.[716] In foreign seated arbitrations, such measures may be required under circumstances which may not necessarily satisfy the threshold of exceptional circumstances.[717]

One of the acclaimed features of international arbitration is its potential to address issues of jurisdiction and territoriality. In the absence of interim measures being granted by courts other than the seat, a party with sufficient assets in a jurisdiction apart from the seat may conveniently dissipate assets, cause irreparable harm (such as the destruction of evidence), or transfer assets to a third party leaving the other party with a paper award. Thus, a party may take certain actions which would effectively decide the disputes between the parties as to the ultimate relief or render the satisfaction of the award impossible.[718]

There may also be situations where certain types of measures would be unavailable or inefficacious as the arbitral tribunal may not be able to grant them.[719] Thus, the courts in a jurisdiction other than the seat may often be required to grant interim measures in support of foreign seated arbitrations in the interests of both convenience and efficiency.[720] If such measures are not granted, the result may be the frustration of arbitral proceedings themselves.[721] Hence, it becomes imperative that the national arbitration legislation authorises its courts explicitly to grant interim measures in aid of foreign seated arbitrations. Such support is required from all countries to make arbitration genuinely efficacious for the parties.

The Government of India considered such implications of not extending the provisions of Section 9 of the IAA to foreign seated arbitrations. It accepted the lacuna in the law that without providing for applicability of Section 9 of the IAA to foreign seated arbitrations, there would be situations where the parties are left remediless.[722] By the time an Indian party moves an application before the competent foreign court or arbitral tribunal, the foreign party would have moved its assets from India.[723] Hence, there is a need to expressly provide the power to grant interim measures in aid of foreign seated arbitrations.

2. THE POWER TO GRANT INTERIM MEASURES IN AID OF FOREIGN SEATED ARBITRATIONS

Till the passing of the 2006 Model Law Revisions, surprisingly, most legal regimes were silent on the issue of interim measures in support of foreign seated arbitrations,[724]

716. *See Chapter 3 and discussion on* Indian Code of Civil Procedure, 1908, S. 151; *Bharat Aluminum v. Kaiser Aluminum Technical Services Inc.* (2012) 9 SCC 552, ¶175.
717. *Bharat Aluminum v. Kaiser Aluminum Technical Services Inc.* (2012) 9 SCC 552, ¶175.
718. Gary Born, *supra* n. 33, at 2734.
719. *Ibid.*, at 2735.
720. Ali Yesilirmak, *supra* n. 30, at 80.
721. *Badat & Co. v. East India Trading Co.* (1964) 4 SCR 19, ¶31.
722. *Marriot International Inc. v. Ansal Hotels Ltd.* 2000 (56) DRJ (Suppl) 235, 443 (DB).
723. Government of India, Ministry of Law and Justice – Proposed Amendments to the Arbitration & Conciliation Act, 1996: A Consultation Paper, available at: https://www.legallyindia.com/images/stories/docs/Arbitration-Act-LawMin-ConsultationPaper-on-Arb-Act-April2010-1.pdf.
724. Ali Yesilirmak, *supra* n. 30, at 81.

probably due to the lack of attention paid to this issue under the Model Law before 2006 or due to the sensitivity of not interfering with national court systems.[725]

There are several policy considerations and implications when courts exercise jurisdiction in support of a foreign seated arbitration. Parties would have no incentive to select a country (India) as the seat of arbitration if they have access to courts in India even though the seat is abroad.[726] Hence, the lack of a provision permitting courts to grant interim measures in aid of foreign seated arbitrations may be to discourage parties from costly litigation abroad and to promote the arbitration industry at the seat.[727] Also, if assets can be beyond the reach of the courts at the seat, it would encourage objectives, such as India being a wealth management centre.[728]

The contrary view, and the more reasonable one, is that given the international character of contemporary litigation and the need to promote mutual assistance between the courts of various countries, it would be a severe disadvantage if courts are not empowered to grant interim measures even though the arbitration takes place outside India.[729] Such a view is also necessary keeping in mind the objective of the government to make India an international arbitration hub.[730] It is also required to strengthen and establish the efficacy and effectiveness of arbitration proceedings[731] in line with the broader purpose of the NYC.[732]

There has been considerable divergence, especially in the US, on whether the NYC permits interim measures in support of foreign seated arbitrations. In a few cases,[733] especially in *McCreary Tyre & Rubber Co. v. Ceat SpA* (*McCreary*),[734] the courts in the US interpreted Article II(3) of the NYC[735] to hold that national courts were forbidden to grant interim measures in connection with an international arbitration.

The view in *McCreary* was misquoted. The court had rightly refused to grant interim measures in connection with a foreign seated arbitration as the party seeking the interim measure was abusing the law and interfering with the parties' arbitration agreement. The facts were also similar in *Carolina Power & Light Co. v. Uranex*

725. Luis, *supra* n. 521, at 559.
726. Badri Srinivasan, *Arbitration and the Supreme Court: A Tale of Discordance Between the Text and Judicial Determination*, 4(4) NUJS L. R., 639, 641 (2011); *Swift-Fortune Ltd. v. Magnificia Marine S.A.* [2006] SGCA 42.
727. Badri, *supra* n. 726, at 641.
728. Lye K. Cheong & Yeo C. Tat, et al., *Interim Measures in Aid of Foreign Arbitrations, Time for the Deus ex Machina?*, 21 Sac L. J. 429, 430, 435 (2009).
729. *Channel Tunnel Group Ltd. v. Balfour Beatty Construction Ltd.* [1993] 2 WLR 262.
730. Government of India, Ministry of Law & Justice, Cabinet approves the Arbitration and Conciliation (Amendment) Bill, 2018, available at: http://pib.nic.in/newsite/PrintRelease.aspx?relid=177128.
731. *Olex Focas Pvt. Ltd. v. Skodaexport Company Ltd.* 2000 (1) Apex Decisions (Delhi) 527, ¶61.
732. Singapore Parliamentary Debates, Official Report (31 October 1994) Vol. 63 at 625-626 (Associate Professor Ho Peng Kee, Parliamentary Secretary to the Minister for Law).
733. *I.T.A.D. Associates, Inc. v. Podar Bros* 636 F.2d 75 (4th Cir. 1981); *Cooper v. Ateliers de la Motobecane, SA* 442 N.E. 2d 1239.
734. *Mc Creary Tire & Rubber Co. v. Ceat SpA* 501 F.2d 1032 (3rd Cir. 1974).
735. NYC, Art. II(3): (*The court of a Contracting State, when seized of an action in a matter in respect of which the parties have made an agreement within the meaning of this article, shall, at the request of one of the parties, refer the parties to arbitration, unless it finds that the said agreement is null and void, inoperative or incapable of being performed*).

(*Carolina*).[736] However, subsequent judgments misapplied the dictum in *McCreary* and *Carolina* to hold that Article II(3) of the NYC forbade the grant of interim measures in support of a foreign seated arbitration.[737]

In subsequent decisions categorically overruling *McCreary*,[738] the New York Appellate Division, though on flawed reasoning,[739] held that the court was empowered to order attachment in aid of arbitration where the party against whom the arbitration is sought is based in a non-signatory country.[740] As a result of the criticism, the New York Civil Practice Law and Rules (*NYCLR*) were amended to remove the requirement of a country to be a signatory for the grant of interim measures in aid of a foreign seated arbitration.[741] It is pertinent to highlight that the amended the NYCLR does not require personal jurisdiction over the defendant, i.e., even if the assets of the defendant are located within the territory of the US, the interim measure can be granted.[742]

2.1. Article 17J of the Model Law

The most notable recognition of the power to grant interim measures in aid of foreign seated arbitrations has come after the 2006 Model Law Revisions with the incorporation of Article 17J of the Model Law. The Model Law explicitly recognises the power to grant interim measures in aid of foreign seated arbitrations and the extraterritorial effect is incorporated in Article 1(2) of the Model Law. Post the 2006 Model Law Revisions, many countries specifically provide for this power in their arbitration

736. *Carolina Power & Light Co. v. Uranex* 451 F.Supp. 1044 (1977).
737. *I.T.A.D. Associates, Inc. v. Podar Bros* 636 F.2d 75 (4th Cir. 1981); *Mc Donnell Douglas Corp. v. Kingdom of Denmark* 607 F.Supp. 1016 (E.D. Mo. 1985); *Siderius, Inc. v. Compania de Acero del Pacifico, SA* 453 F.Supp. 22 (S.D.N.Y. 1978); *Metropolitan World Tanker Corp. v. P.N. Pertambangan Minjakdangas Bumi Nasional* 427 F.Supp. 2 (S.D.N.Y. 1975); *Drexel Burnham Lambert, Inc. v. Ruebsamen* 531 N.Y.S.2d 547; *Shah v. E. Silk Indus. Ltd.* 493 N.Y.S.2d 150 (1985); *Faberge International Inc. v. Di Pino* 491 N.Y.S.2d 345 (1985); *Lafarge Coppee v. Venezolana de Cementos SACA* 31 F.3d 70 (2d Cir. 1994).
738. For lower court decisions adopting the *Uranex* analysis of the NYC, *see Aggarao v. MOL Ship Management Co.* 675 F.3d 355, 376 (4th Cir. 2012); *Karaha Bodas Co. v. Perusahaan Pertambangan Minyak Dan Gas Bumi Negara* 335 F.3d 357, 365 (5th Cir. 2003); *Borden, Inc. v. Meiji Milk Products Co.* 919 F.2d 822, 826 (2d Cir. 1990); *Ledee v. Ceramiche Ragno* 684 F.2d 184 (1st Cir. 1982); *Bahrain Tele Comm. Co. v. Discoverytel Inc.* 476 F.Supp.2d 176, 181 (D. Conn. 2007); *James Associates (USA) Ltd. v. Anhui Machinery & Equipment Import and Export Corporation* 171 F.Supp.2d 1146 (2001); *Signature Marketing Pty. Ltd. v. Slim Print International LLC* 2001 U.S. Dist. LEXIS 21222; *China National Metal Products Import/Export Company v. Apex Digital, Inc.* 155 F.Supp.2d 1174, 1179 (2001).
739. Gary Born, *supra* n. 33, at 2721.
740. *Intermar Overseas, Inc. v. Argocean S.A.* 503 N.Y.S 2nd 736 (1986), at 496.
741. New York Civil Practice Law and Rules, 2012, S. 7502 (c) was amended to include '*whether or not it is subject to the United Nations Convention on the Recognition and Enforcement of Foreign Arbitral Awards*'.
742. *As opposed to Swift-Fortune Ltd. v. Magnificia Marine S.A.* [2006] SGCA 42 and *Front Carriers Ltd v. Atlantic & Orient Shipping Corporation* [2006] SGHC 127, *which require either the defendant or the subject matter being within the jurisdiction of the courts at Singapore.*

statute[743] though there are still many countries which are yet to adopt the same approach.[744]

However, despite the adoption of the 2006 Model Law Revisions, there should be some connection between the country where the interim measures are sought and the seat of the international arbitration before such interim measures are granted in aid of foreign seated arbitrations.[745] Usually, such a connection will be met if the seat is a signatory to the NYC[746] as the NYC is considered to be a constitutional instrument imposing an obligation on the Contracting States to eliminate the barriers of historic national law rules which restrict the efficacy of international arbitration agreements.[747]

To address the issue of the existence of a connection between the seat and the country issuing interim measures, the power is recognised in each jurisdiction differently. Section 2(3) of the English Arbitration Act simply provides for the applicability of Section 43 (securing the attendance of witnesses) and Section 44 (court powers exercisable in support of arbitral proceedings) of the English Arbitration Act even if the seat of arbitration is outside England, or Wales, or Northern Ireland, or no seat has been designated or determined. Similarly, Section 12A of the Singapore Arbitration Act provides that the section pertaining to interim measures by the court shall apply irrespective of whether the place of arbitration is within the territory of Singapore or not.[748] Both countries provide that the court may refuse the interim measure when it considers it considers it inappropriate to do so.

In contrast, Section 45(5)(a) of the Hong Kong Ordinance provides that the power can only be exercised if the arbitration proceedings *'are capable of giving rise to an arbitral award (whether interim or final) which may be enforced in Hong Kong'*. However, in India, the recognition of this power had been mired in conflicting views of the Indian judiciary before the 2015 Amendment.

2.2. The Law Before the 2015 Amendment

2.2.1. The First Steps in Marriot International

The first landmark judgment to address the issue of interim measures in support of foreign seated arbitrations in India was *Marriot International Inc. v. Ansal Hotels Ltd.*[749] (*Marriot*). The division bench of the Delhi High Court heard an appeal against the dismissal of an application under Section 9 of the IAA on the ground of lack of applicability of Part I of the IAA to arbitrations where the place of arbitration is outside

743. *See Appendix A and L*; Austrian Code of Civil Procedure (ZPO), S. 577(2); Belgium Judicial Code, Art. 1698; English Arbitration Act, 1996, S. 2(3)(b); Hong Kong Arbitration Ordinance (Cap.609), S. 12; Dutch Code of Civil Procedure, Art. 1074 a; Singapore International Arbitration Act, 1994, S. 12 A; Spanish Arbitration Law, Art. 1(2).
744. *See Appendix L.*
745. Cheong, *supra* n. 728, at 453.
746. *Ibid.*, at 453.
747. Gary Born, *supra* n. 33, at 2609.
748. Singapore International Arbitration Act, 1994, S. 12A(1)(b).
749. *Marriot International Inc. v. Ansal Hotels Ltd.* 2000 (56) DRJ (Suppl) 235, 443 (DB).

India, i.e., Kuala Lumpur in this case. The single judge had dismissed the application observing that no strong prima facie case was made out, the balance of convenience was not in favour of the applicant, i.e., Marriot International (*Marriot*), and the grant of interim measures might cause irreparable injury to the respondents, i.e., Ansal Hotels (*Ansal*). No observation was made by the Single Judge on the maintainability of the application and the jurisdiction of the court.

In the appeal, one of the arguments advanced was that even if Part I of the IAA did not apply to foreign seated arbitrations, the court had sufficient inherent power to advance a cause of justice as held previously by the Delhi High Court.[750] The court interpreted Section 2(2)[751] of the IAA and Section 2(5)[752] of the IAA harmoniously and held that the definition in Section 2(2) of the IAA is inclusive and does not exclude foreign seated arbitrations. In its view, such an interpretation was supported by the language in Section 2(5) of the IAA which states that Part I of the IAA shall apply to 'all arbitrations'.[753]

The court noted the applicability of the *Channel Tunnel* in which the court had granted interim measures in aid of foreign seated arbitration. The court took the view that since the Supreme Court had affirmed the applicability of *Channel Tunnel*, it can reasonably be assumed that the Supreme Court did not prescribe a contrary view which would lead to ousting the jurisdiction of the Indian courts.[754]

On the contrary, it was contended by *Ansal* that the words 'all arbitrations' mean that Part I of the IAA would apply to all statutory arbitrations, like the Indian Telegraph Act and those under the bye-laws of certain associations, stock exchanges, and different chambers of commerce, i.e., arbitrations being held not only under an agreement between the parties, but also statutory arbitrations. The reference to 'all arbitrations' was to such arbitrations, but only when the place of arbitration is in India. The legislature did not contemplate the phrase to include foreign seated arbitrations.[755]

Reliance was placed on a previous precedent[756] where the Delhi High Court had held that where the parties were not Indian and the arbitration was to be held in

750. *Dominant Offset Private Limited v. Adamovske Strojimy A.S.* 1997 (2) ALR 335, *the Court was interpreting Section 11 which deals with appointment of an arbitrator and held that Part I would apply to all arbitrations and all proceedings thereto.* This judgment was *followed in Olex Focas Pvt. Ltd. v. Skodaexport Company Ltd.* 2000 (1) Apex Decisions (Delhi) 527.

751. Indian Arbitration Act, 1996, S. 2(2): *This Part shall apply where the place of arbitration is in India: [Provided that subject to an agreement to the contrary, the provisions of Indian Arbitration Act, 1996, Ss. 9, 27 and 37(3)(1)(a) shall also apply to international commercial arbitration, even if the place of arbitration is outside India, and an arbitral award made or to be made in such place is enforceable and recognised under the provisions of Part II of this Act.*

752. Indian Arbitration Act, 1996, S. 2(5): *Subject to the provisions of sub-section (4), and save in so far as is otherwise provided by any law for the time being in force or in any agreement in force between India and any other country or countries, this Part shall apply to all arbitrations and to all proceedings relating thereto.*

753. Lira, *supra* n. 107, at 118; *A similar view was taken in Marriot International Inc. v. Ansal Hotels Ltd.* 2000 (56) DRJ (Suppl) 235, 443 (DB).

754. *Olex Focas Pvt. Ltd. v. Skodaexport Company Ltd.* 2000 (1) Apex Decisions (Delhi) 527, ¶63.

755. *Marriot International Inc. v. Ansal Hotels Ltd.* 2000 (56) DRJ (Suppl) 235, 443 (DB).

756. *Kitechnology NV v. Unicorn GmbH Rahn Plastmaschinen* 1998 (47) DRJ 397.

Frankfurt governed by German law, courts in India will have no jurisdiction and Section 9 of the IAA has no applicability in such cases.[757]

The court analysed Article 9 of the Model Law and held that Section 9 of the IAA is like Article 9 of the Model Law. However, since Article 1(2) of the Model Law had been added with modifications (i.e., section 2(2) applies only when the place of arbitration is in India) and Section 9 of the IAA has been omitted from Part II of the IAA, the legislature did not intend Section 9 of the IAA to apply to arbitrations being held under the Geneva Convention and the NYC outside India.[758] Therefore, the division bench of the Delhi High Court held that Part I of the IAA does not apply to arbitrations that take place outside India.[759]

It observed that the lack of clarity in the IAA regarding the applicability of Part I of the IAA to arbitrations outside India may result in hardship and may even leave a party remediless; however, the court is constrained while interpreting statutes. No matter how unreasonable, unjust, or oppressive a particular construction might be, the court is not empowered to go beyond the contemplation of the legislature. Such a question can only be looked into by the legislature and not by the courts.[760]

2.2.2. The Landmark Decision in Bhatia

After *Marriot*, the question of the power of the court to grant interim measures in aid of foreign seated arbitrations was considered thoroughly for the first time by the Supreme Court in *Bhatia International v. Bulk Trading S.A. (Bhatia)*.[761]

The court took due note of the language of Section 2(2) of the IAA to mean that it is to apply when the place of arbitration is in India and that Part II of the IAA applies to foreign awards. However, it disregarded the plain reading of the text and made a purposive interpretation. It held that the legislature had left a lacuna in the IAA. Neither Part I of the IAA nor Part II of the IAA would apply to countries which are neither signatory to the NYC nor the Geneva Convention. It would result in there being no law governing such arbitrations. Moreover, a party will be left completely remediless and will not be able to seek interim measures even though the property and assets are in India.

The court went on to observe that jurisdiction of a court cannot be ousted unless the statutory provision explicitly indicates or even by the inferential conclusion arrives at such an ouster. Contrary to the view in *Marriot*, it held that an interpretation that results in hardship, serious inconvenience, injustice, absurdity, or anomaly should be

757. *A similar view was taken in* East Coast *Shipping Ltd. v. M.J. Scrap Pvt. Ltd.* 1997 SCC OnLine Cal 73. *The special leave petition before the Supreme Court was rejected by holding the reasoning of the High Court*; Lira, *supra* n. 107, at 118.
758. *Marriot International Inc. v. Ansal Hotels Ltd.* 2000 (56) DRJ (Suppl) 235, 443 (DB).
759. *Relying* on the *Channel Tunnel Group Ltd. v. Balfour Beatty Construction Ltd.* [1993] 2 WLR 262.
760. *Marriot International Inc. v. Ansal Hotels Ltd.* 2000 (56) DRJ (Suppl) 235, 443 (DB), at 452.
761. *Bhatia International v. Bulk Trading S.A. and Anr.* (2002) 4 SCC 105,¶14.

rejected in favour of a more just, reasonable, and sensible interpretation.[762] It is only Part II of the IAA which applies to an arbitration in a signatory country. An interpretation rejecting the applicability of Part I of the IAA to arbitrations outside India would result in the position of law which would effectively mean that the IAA makes no provision for international commercial arbitration which takes place in a non-signatory country.[763] Therefore, Part I of the IAA shall apply to all arbitrations, domestic or international unless the parties by express or implied agreement exclude any of its provisions.[764]

2.2.3. *The Aftermath of Bhatia*

The authority of *Bhatia* as good law has been questioned only once[765] and a contrary view has been taken a few times.[766] Some courts have expressly held that Part I of the IAA had no application when the parties had chosen English law as the law governing the arbitration agreement[767] or where the governing law was Indian, but the seat was in Singapore.[768]

In all other instances, the courts have continued to apply *Bhatia* as a binding precedent[769] extending the applicability of Part I of the IAA even if the seat was in London.[770] In cases where the parties have failed to choose a seat,[771] the absence of an

762. *Ibid.*, ¶14. *Relying* on an earlier judgment interpreting the 1940 Act in *Collector of Customs v. Digvijaysihji Spg. & Wvg. Mills Ltd.* AIR 1961 SC 1549 *which held that the 1940 Act does not distinguish international commercial arbitration between a signatory and a non-signatory country.*
763. *Collector of Customs v. Digvijaysihji Spg. & Wvg. Mills Ltd.* AIR 1961 SC 1549, ¶16.
764. *It is pertinent to point out that the Supreme Court did not consider the judgment in Badat & Co. v. East India Trading Co.* (1964) 4 SCR 19, ¶20, *which had held that the IAA could not apply to non-signatory countries.*
765. *Centrotrade Minerals and Metal Inc. v. Hindustan Copper Ltd.* 2006 (3) Arb LR 201 (SC), ¶109, *as per Justice S.B. Sinha.*
766. *Shreejee Traco (I) Pvt. Ltd. v. Paper Line International Inc.* (2003) 9 SCC 79. *In the context of an application under Section 11 for appointment of arbitrator, the Court held that a plain reading of Part I suggests that it would apply only when the seat of arbitration is in India*; *Liverpool and London Steamship Protection and Indemnity Association Ltd. v. Arabian Tankers Co.* 2003 (3) Arb LR 537 (Bom); *Max India v. General Binding Corporation* (2009) 112 DRJ 611; *DGS Realtors Pvt. Ltd. v. Realogy Corporation* MANU/DE/2115/2009; *Dozco India (P) Ltd. v. Doosan Infracore Co. Ltd.* (2011) 6 SCC 179.
767. *Hardy Oil and Gas Ltd. v. Hindustan Oil Exploration Co. Ltd* 2006 (1) Arb LR 61 (Guj), ¶11.3; *Videocon Industries Ltd. v. Union of India* (2011) 6 SCC 161, ¶32.
768. *Yograj Infrastructure Ltd. v. Ssang Yong Engg. & Construction Co. Ltd.* (2011) 9 SCC 735, ¶47-49.
769. *Indtel Technical Services Pte. Ltd. v. W.S. Atkins P.L.C.* (2008) 10 SCC 308; *Aurohill Global Commodities Ltd. v. M.S.T.C. Ltd.* (2007) 7 SCC 120, ¶12; *National Agricultural Co-op. Marketing Federation India Ltd. v. Gains Trading Ltd.* (2007) 5 SCC 692, ¶7.
770. *Aurohill Global Commodities Ltd. v. M.S.T.C. Ltd.* (2007) 7 SCC 120, ¶13; *Paragon Steels Pvt. Ltd. v. European Metal Recycling Ltd.* (2006) 4 Arb LR 299, ¶8.
771. *Citation Infowares Ltd. v. Equinox Corpn.* (2009) 7 SCC 220, ¶34; *Indtel Technical Services Pte. Ltd. v. W.S. Atkins P.L.C.* (2008) 10 SCC 308, ¶37.

explicit exclusion of Part I of the IAA[772] and the mere choosing of foreign law as the governing law would not be sufficient to justify the ouster of Part I of the IAA.[773]

The most disastrous application of *Bhatia* was in *Venture Global Engineering* v. *Satyam Computer Services Ltd.*[774] (*Venture Global*) where the court held that an award passed in a foreign seated arbitration could be set aside in India[775] due to the applicability of Part I to all arbitrations. This view was in complete disregard of the principle of comity, conflict of law rules, and the fundamental principles of arbitration. The court (relying heavily on *Bhatia*) disregarded the position in the United States,[776] the United Kingdom,[777] and a consistent view of the Indian High Courts[778] - all of which held that an award could only be set aside by a competent court of the country in which the foreign award was made.

It should be noted that these cases were criticised for causing uncertainty and delay,[779] and many cases took the exact opposite view[780] to hold that Section 34 of the IAA (under Part I of the IAA) cannot be resorted to when there are special provisions for enforcement of foreign awards in Part II of the IAA.

The most fundamental problem with *Bhatia* was that it restricted party autonomy. Parties could either completely exclude Part I of the IAA or they had to forcefully adopt all of Part I of the IAA, including the right to have the award set aside under Section 34 of the IAA despite the seat of arbitration being outside India.[781] Only parties completely conversant with the jurisprudence and law laid down in *Bhatia* would read between the lines to exclude 'all or some' provisions of Part I of the IAA.[782]

---

772. *In one instance the court examined the commercial arbitration rules and mediation procedures of the American Arbitration Association, especially Rule 48(c), which provides that the parties to an arbitration shall be deemed to have consented that the judgment upon arbitration award may be entered in any federal or state court having jurisdiction. The court interpreted this to mean that the parties have specifically excluded the application of Part I by opting for the said rules. The Court relied upon the case of Drilling A.S. v. Jagson International Ltd.* 2003 (3) Arb. LR 548 (Bom) as was the case in *Max India Ltd. v. General Binding Corporation* 2009 (3) Arb. LR 162 (Del) (DB).
773. K.V Krishnaprasad, *From Bhatia International to Dozco India: A Response to Vidhu Gupta's 'Stretching the Limits of Statutory Interpretation – Critical Review of Bhatia International v. Bulk Trading'*, 6 Nalsar St. L. R. 69, 78 (2011).
774. *Venture Global Engineering v. Satyam Computer Services Ltd.* (2008) 4 SCC 190.
775. *This erroneous view was followed in, Shin Satellite Public Co. Ltd. v. Jain Studios Ltd.* 2008 SCC OnLine Del 1127, ¶32.
776. *International Standard Electric Corprn. v. Bridas Sociedad Anonima Petrolera, Industrial Y Commercial* 745 F Supp 172; *M&C Corpn. v. Erwin Behr GmbH Co.* KG 87 F 3d 844; *Yusuf Ahmed Alghanim v. Toys 'R' US. Inc. Thr. (HK) Ltd.* 126 F 3d 15; *Karaha Bodas Co. v. Perusahaan Pertambangan Minyak Dan Gas Bumi Negara* 335 F.3d 357, 365 (5th Cir. 2003).
777. *C v. D* 2007 EWHC 1541 (Comm).
778. *Naval Gent Maritime Ltd. v. Shivnath Rai Harnarain (I) Ltd.* 2009 SCC OnLine Del 2961, ¶ 9.
779. Rukmini Das & Anisha Keyal, *Judicial Intervention in International Arbitration*, 2 NUJS Law Review 604 (2009); Cylde & Co, *Arbitration Committee Newsletter*, Vol 22 No. 1 (1 June 2017).
780. *Force Shipping Ltd. v. Ashapura Minechem Ltd.* (2003) 4 Mah LJ 329; *Bulk Trading S.A. v. Dalmia Cement (Bharat) Ltd.* 2006 (1) Arb LR 38 (Del); *Inventa Fischer GmBH & Co. v. Polygenta Technologies Ltd.* 2005(2) Arb LR 125 (Bom); *Goldcrest Exports v. Swissgen N.V.* 2005(3) Arb LR 58 (Bom), ¶23.
781. Badri, *supra* n. 726, at 643.
782. *Bhatia International v. Bulk Trading S.A. and Anr.* (2002) 4 SCC 105, ¶26.

Also, the reasoning that neither Part I of the IAA nor Part II of the IAA shall apply to non-signatory arbitrations was unfounded as most countries were signatories to either of the two conventions. Furthermore, the court in *Bhatia* did not take into consideration Article 1(5) of the Model Law[783] which provides that the IAA cannot have an overriding effect if the arbitration is governed by any other enactment. Hence, the phrase 'every arbitration' should have been read as '*every arbitration provided for by any other enactment for the time being in force*'.[784]

While some have justified the law laid down in *Bhatia* on the ground that the interpretation leads to a 'fair and just arbitration procedure'[785] as an alternative interpretation would lead to the lack of any provision applying to foreign seated arbitrations, such a reading of Part I of the IAA was not necessary. The court did not examine the restriction contained in Section 5 of the IAA to apply only to Part I of the IAA.[786] Thus, the judicial restraint would not have applied to Part II of the IAA and in the absence of any specific provisions, the general law, i.e., the CPC would have become applicable.[787]

2.2.4. *Legislative Reforms Post Bhatia*

After the decision in *Bhatia*, the 176th Report of the Law Commission suggested that clause (b) be added to Section 2(2) of the IAA which would provide that Sections 8, 9, 27, 35 and 36 of the IAA shall be available for international arbitrations outside India,[788] harmonising the IAA with Article 1(2) of the Model Law. Similar suggestions were made in a consultation paper floated by the Ministry of Law and Justice and the Saraf Committee.[789] However, none of these suggestions was accepted.

783. UNCITRAL Model Law, Art. 1(5), ('*This Law shall not affect any other law of this State by virtue of which certain disputes may not be submitted to arbitration or may be submitted to arbitration only according to provisions other than those of this Law*').
784. Krishnaprasad, *supra* n. 773, at 74.
785. Vidhu Gupta, *Stretching the Limits of Statutory Interpretation: Critical Review of Bhatia International v. Bulk Trading*, 5 NALSAR St. L. R. 140, 149 (2010).
786. Krishnaprasad, *supra* n. 773, at 75.
787. *Ibid.*; *Such an interpretation was also considered in Channel Tunnel and upheld by the Supreme Court in Sundaram Finance v. NEPC Limited wherein the court upheld the power of the courts in India to grant interim relief for the protection of the parties and prevent undesirable actions by the parties.*
788. Law Commission of India, *supra* n. 65.
789. Referring to the English Arbitration Act, 1996, Ss 2(1) & 2(2), *it was proposed to amend* S. 2(2) of the IAA as '*(2) This part shall apply only where the place of arbitration is in India. Provided that provisions of Sections 9 and 27 shall also apply to international commercial arbitration where the place of arbitration is not in India if an award made in such place is enforceable and recognised under Part II of this Act.*' *See* Government of India, Ministry of Law and Justice – Proposed Amendments to the Arbitration & Conciliation Act, 1996: A Consultation Paper, available at: https://www.legallyindia.com/images/stories/docs/Arbitration-Act-LawMin-ConsultationPaper-on-Arb-Act-April2010-1.pdf.

2.2.5. *Undoing Bhatia: The Landmark Decision in BALCO*

In 2012, in *BALCO*,[790] the court got the chance to reconsider the decision in *Bhatia* and its implication on Sections 9 and 34 of the IAA. It was called upon to answer five questions, the most important being, '*Does Section 2(2) bar the application of Part I of the Arbitration Act, 1996 (Part I for brevity) to arbitrations where the place is outside India?*'[791]

To answer this question, interestingly, one of the arguments made was that the IAA has not adopted or incorporated the provisions of Model Law, but has merely taken into account the Model Law.[792] It was argued that the IAA defers from the Model Law on vital aspects such as the absence of the word 'only' in Section 2(2) of the IAA which corresponds to Article 1(2) of the Model Law.[793] However, the said argument was categorically rejected.[794] The court affirmed that the IAA had been drafted taking into account the Model Law.[795]

The Model Law is meant to be a guide. Referring to the drafting history of the Model Law, the court took the view that the word 'only' was inserted in Article 1(2) of the Model Law to clarify that Sections 8, 9, 35 and 36 of the IAA would have extraterritorial effect if so legislated by the State. The other provisions would be applicable on a strictly territorial basis.[796] The Indian legislature, while adopting the Model Law did not include the exceptions mentioned in Article 1(2) of the IAA while enacting Section 2(2) of the IAA. Hence, the word 'only' would have been superfluous as none of the exceptions was included in Section 2(2) of the IAA. Therefore, the view in *Bhatia* and *Venture Global* is misplaced.[797]

The court interpreted the phrase 'any other enactment' in Section 2(4) of the IAA to mean only an Act made by the Indian Parliament. Thus, the phrase 'every arbitration' in Section 2(4) of the IAA and the phrase 'all arbitrations' in Section 2(5) of the IAA means that Part I of the IAA applies to all arbitration where Part I of the IAA is otherwise applicable.[798]

Relying on the English court's decision in *Sul America*, the court took the view that if the arbitration agreement provides for a seat/place of arbitration outside India, then Part I of the IAA would not apply.[799] There is no provision under Part II of the IAA similar to Section 9 of the IAA and since Section 36 of the IAA refers to domestic arbitration only, the words before the commencement of arbitral proceedings in

790. *Bharat Aluminum v. Kaiser Aluminum Technical Services Inc.* (2012) 9 SCC 552.
791. *Ibid.*, ¶10; *See*, Delphine Constantin, *Indian Case Law Review: Anti-Arbitration Injunctions*, 2015, Int'l Bus. L. J. 409 (2015).
792. *Konkan Railway Corpn. Ltd. v. Rani Construction (P) Ltd.* (2000) 8 SCC 159; *S.B.P. & Co. v. Patel Engineering Ltd.* (2005) 6 SCC 28.
793. *Ibid.*, ¶12.
794. *Bharat Aluminum v. Kaiser Aluminum Technical Services Inc.* (2012) 9 SCC 552, ¶¶43, 45.
795. The Court *affirmed* the position in *Konkan Railway Corpn. Ltd. v. Rani Construction (P) Ltd.* (2000) 8 SCC 159, ¶ 9.
796. *Bharat Aluminum v. Kaiser Aluminum Technical Services Inc.* (2012) 9 SCC 552, ¶68.
797. *Ibid.*, ¶76.
798. *Ibid.*, ¶84.
799. *Relying on Sul America Cia Nacional De Seguros S.A. v. Enesa Engenharia S.A.* [2012] EWCA Civ 638, ¶124.

Section 9 of the IAA can only mean the arbitrations which take place only in India.[800] Extending the applicability of Section 9 of the IAA to arbitration outside India would violate the policy of territoriality declared in Section 2(2) of the IAA.[801]

The court held that a party would have sufficient remedy at the voluntarily chosen seat of arbitration and simply because the remedy may be more onerous from the viewpoint of one party, it cannot be said that the party will be left remediless. Moreover, once a party has chosen a seat outside India, they have also chosen the necessary incident and consequences.[802] Even if the party will be left remediless, the matter has to be redressed by the legislature.[803]

Furthermore, the court considered the procedural aspects of an action in aid of foreign seated arbitration holding that an inter-party suit solely for dissipation of an asset would not be maintainable[804] as the existence of a suit is a *sin qua non* for the maintainability of a civil suit.[805] Thus, resort to the inherent power of the court cannot be made. Any application under Order XXXIX, or XV of the CPC would also require a suit as a prerequisite and the pendency of the arbitration proceeding outside India would not provide a cause of action for a suit where the main prayer is for an injunction.[806] Such a suit would have to be filed with pleadings related to the merits of the case as required by Order I Rule 1 and Rule 2 of the CPC. The filing of such a suit would run afoul of the provisions of Sections 8 and 45 of the IAA.[807]

Such relief can only be granted when a party can satisfy that the future arbitration award will be in its favour and no relief can be granted on such a contingency. An interlocutory relief can only be granted on the pendency of a dispute in which the parties claim a relief which is likely to result in a final decision upon the subject in dispute. The interim injunction itself should be a part of the substantive relief. Hence, any such suit would be barred under Order VII Rule 11 (a) of the CPC as being without a cause of action since the cause of action would be contingent/speculative.[808]

Relying on the decision in *Siskina*,[809] the Supreme Court held that a right to obtain an interim injunction is not a cause of action and cannot stand on its own. It is merely ancillary and incidental to the pre-existing cause of action. It is granted to preserve the status quo pending the ascertainment of the rights of the parties.[810] Therefore, an inter-party suit simply for interim measures pending a foreign seated arbitration would not be maintainable in India.[811]

800. *Bharat Aluminum v. Kaiser Aluminum Technical Services Inc.* (2012) 9 SCC 552, ¶157.
801. *Ibid.*, ¶158.
802. *Ibid.*, ¶163.
803. *Ibid.*, ¶164.
804. *Ibid.*, ¶172.
805. *Ibid.*, ¶173.
806. *Ibid.*, ¶175.
807. *Ibid.*
808. *Ibid.*
809. *Siskina (Cargo Owners) v. Distos Compania Navieria S.A. (The Siskina)* 1979 AC 210.
810. *Bharat Aluminum v. Kaiser Aluminum Technical Services Inc.* (2012) 9 SCC 552, ¶182.
811. *Ibid.*, ¶183.

It is pertinent to mention that legislative amendments were made in English Law after the judgment in *Siskina* in Section 37(1) of the Senior Courts Act, 1981[812] and Section 25 of the Civil Jurisdiction and Judgments Act, 1982.[813] Before these reforms, an English Court could not have entertained a request for interim relief in aid of foreign seated arbitrations.[814]

Section 25 of the Civil Jurisdiction and Judgments Act, 1982 was further extended by the Civil Jurisdiction and Judgments Act, 1982 (Interim Relief) Order, 1997 and this order enables the High court to grant interim relief in relation to '*proceedings that have been or are about to be commenced*' in a foreign State.[815] However, no such corresponding amendments have been made in India with respect to the power of the court. Hence, injunctive relief under the inherent power of the court cannot be granted in India for a foreign seated arbitration as there is no corresponding provision like Section 37(1) of the English Supreme Court Act, 1981 and Section 25 of the Civil Jurisdiction and Judgments Act, 1982 under Indian Law.[816]

Thus, the court overruled *Bhatia* and the subsequent judgments to hold that Part I of the IAA is applicable only when the seat of arbitration is in India and awards passed by foreign seated tribunals can only be subject to Indian jurisdiction if they are sought to be enforced under Part II of the IAA.[817]

This decision was considered to be a landmark decision in upholding the pro-arbitration and less interventionist judicial approach.[818] However, this judgment effectively closed the door for interim measures in support of foreign seated arbitrations. The court categorically held that the court's power to grant interim relief is traceable to Section 94 of the CPC and in exceptional cases to Section 151 of the CPC and this power can only be invoked once there is a substantive suit for final relief. Therefore, the request for an interim measure under the CPC would be impermissible with respect to foreign seated arbitration. The consequence is that there is no existing provision under the CPC or the IAA to deal with an interim measure for foreign seated arbitration. Hence, the Courts in India cannot grant an interim measure in aid of foreign seated arbitration.[819]

---

812. Senior Courts Act, 1981, S. 37.
813. Civil Jurisdiction and Judgments Act, 1982, S. 25.
814. C. Chatterjee and Anna Lefcovitch, *Guidelines for Enforcement of Worldwide Freezing Orders: An Analysis*, 8(3) J. B. Reg. 244, 256 (2007).
815. Civil Jurisdiction and Judgments Act, 1982 (Interim Relief) Order, 1997, S. 2: *The High Court in England and Wales or Northern Ireland shall have power to grant interim relief under section 25(1) of the Civil Jurisdiction and Judgments Act 1982 in relation to proceedings of the following descriptions, namely:*
    (a) proceedings commenced or to be commenced otherwise than in a Brussels or Lugano Contracting State;
    (b) proceedings whose subject-matter is not within the scope of the 1968 Convention as determined by Article 1 thereof.
816. *Bharat Aluminum v. Kaiser Aluminum Technical Services Inc.* (2012) 9 SCC 552, ¶¶189, 191.
817. Indian Arbitration Act, 1996, Part II.
818. Cylde & Co, *supra* 779.
819. *Bharat Aluminum v. Kaiser Aluminum Technical Services Inc.* (2012) 9 SCC 552, ¶¶ 192-193. *Taking a similar view, in 2015, in Union of India v. Reliance Industries Ltd.* (2015) 10 SCC 213,

2.3. The 2015 Amendment

To undo the view in *BALCO*, the 2015 Amendment made substantial changes to the regime of interim measures in India. It added a proviso to account for the applicability of Part I of the IAA to international commercial arbitration, even if the place of arbitration is outside India.[820] The proviso, in effect, overrules the view of the Supreme Court in *BALCO*. After the 2015 Amendment, Section 2(2) of the IAA provides the following:

> (2) This Part shall apply where the place of arbitration is in India.
>
> Provided that subject to an agreement to the contrary, the provisions of sections 9, 27 and clause (a) of sub-section (1) and sub-section (3) of Section 37 shall also apply to international commercial arbitration, even if the place of arbitration is outside India, and an arbitral award made or to be made in such place is enforceable and recognised under the provisions of Part II of this Act.

Thus, the extraterritorial application of Part I of the IAA was extended to international commercial arbitrations as follows:

(a) Section 9 of the IAA – Interim Measures, etc., by a court.
(b) Section 27 of the IAA – Court Assistance in Taking Evidence.
(c) Section 37(1)(a) of the IAA – Appeal against orders passed under Section 8.
(d) Section 37(3) of the IAA – No second appeal from orders, except the right to appeal to the Supreme Court.

It is pertinent to note that the power to grant interim measures in aid of foreign seated arbitrations stems from a combined reading of Section 2(2) of the IAA and Section 9 of the IAA. The amendment to Section 2(2) of the IAA does not independently confer on the court any power to grant interim measure but only refers to the applicability to Section 9 of the IAA in such cases.[821] Affirming such effect, the Bombay High Court recently granted an ex parte injunction in aid of a foreign seated arbitration restraining the respondent from dealing with alienating or creating third party rights in the machinery belonging to the applicant based on the amendment.[822]

However, such a power is only available when: (a) there is no agreement to the contrary by the parties;[823] (b) the arbitration should fall within the definition of international commercial arbitration; and (c) an arbitral award is enforceable and

the court held that Part I of the IAA was excluded by necessary implication if it is found that the seat is outside India, or the law governing the arbitration agreement is any law other than the Indian law.

820. Indian Arbitration Act, 1996, S. 2(5).
821. Mohan, *supra* n. 12, at 312.
822. *Dalian Harui Heavy Industry International Co. Ltd. v. West Quay Multiport Pvt. Ltd.* Commercial Arbitration Petition No. 688/2019 delivered on 8 July 2019; The court also dismissed an application filed before the 2015 Amendment for the reasons that such power was unavailable before the 2015 Amendment; *Norscot Rig Management Pvt. Ltd. v. Essar Oil Field Services Ltd.* 2019 SCC OnLine Bom 9153, ¶8.
823. *Medima LLC v. Balasore Alloys Ltd.* AP/267/2021, ¶15; *Ultra Deep Subsea Pte Ltd. v. Hindustan Oil Exploration Company Ltd.* 2021 SCC OnLine Bom 5481, ¶20.

recognised under Part II of the IAA. Like the position in Hong Kong,[824] it provides a jurisdictional threshold of India being a *lex executionis* and determination of the award being valid before granting interim measures in aid of a foreign seated arbitration.

2.3.1. Issues after the 2015 Amendment

While the amendment is certainly a step in the right direction, many issues still require consideration before the amendment can be successful at achieving its intended objectives. First and foremost, it should be noted that Section 37(1)(a) of the IAA is a typographical error. It is inconceivable how an appeal from an order refusing to refer parties to an arbitration under Section 8 of the IAA would be filed in the context of a foreign seated arbitration.[825] Unfortunately, this error has not been rectified even in the 2019 Amendment.

Second, the extraterritorial applicability does not extend to Section 17 of the IAA. Consequently, Section 17(2) of the IAA, which provides for enforcement of the orders of the arbitral tribunal as orders of the court would not apply to foreign seated arbitrations.

Third, Section 2(2) of the IAA was amended to provide for the applicability of Section 9 of the IAA to foreign seated arbitrations, but the amendment fails to consider the suggestions of the Law Commission Report.[826] The Law Commission had suggested that the words 'only be' be added after the words 'shall apply' and delete the word 'place' and insert the word 'seat' in its place in Section 2(2) of the IAA. This would ensure that the courts in India can only exercise jurisdiction when the 'seat' is in India and not create confusion about the 'place' of arbitration.

However, the 2015 amendment accepted the other suggestion, which was the addition of the proviso as it now appears without the suggested change in Section 2(2) of the IAA. The rationale for this amendment was that the courts in India could exercise the jurisdiction even if the 'seat' is located outside India,[827] though the phrase in Section 2(2) of the IAA continues to use 'place' instead of 'seat'. The phrase 'place' in Section 2(2) of the IAA should be replaced with 'seat' in line with the recommendations of the Law Commission in the interest of clarity and predictability.

Fourth, the amendment to Section 2(2) of the IAA may not adequately provide for situations where the seat is 'indeterminate'.[828] In England, Section 2(3) of the English Arbitration Act was amended to provide for the grant of interim measures even if the seat of the arbitration was abroad, or not designated, or determined.[829] In Singapore, Section 12-A(3) of the Singapore International Act grants power to the court to refuse interim measures if in the opinion of the court '*the fact that the place of arbitration is*

824. Hong Kong Arbitration Ordinance (Cap.609), S. 45(5).
825. Rajendra Barot, *supra* n. 679, at 175.
826. Law Commission of India, *supra* n. 517, at 37.
827. *Ibid.*
828. Sumit Rai, *Proposed Amendments to the Indian Arbitration Act: A Fraction of the Whole?*, 3 (1) J. Int'l Dis. Stmnt. 169, 181 (2012).
829. David St. John Sutton & Judith Gill, et al., *Russell on Arbitration* 447 (2018).

outside Singapore or likely to be outside Singapore when it is designated or determined makes it inappropriate to do so'.

Similar to England, the phrase *'or no seat has been designated or determined'* should be added to the proviso to Section 2(2) of the IAA after the words *'even if the place is outside India'*. Such a provision would address the controversy relating to the conflicting jurisprudence on 'seat' and 'place' of arbitration and at the same time permit courts in India to grant interim measures without undertaking a full trial to first determine the seat of arbitration.[830]

Fifth, the addition of the proviso to Section 2(2) of the IAA is that all the provisions of Section 9 of the IAA apply to foreign seated arbitrations. Therefore, if any measure is granted under Section 9(1) of the IAA before the commencement of arbitration proceedings outside India, the provision of Section 9(2) of the IAA would be triggered and the arbitral tribunal would have to be formed at the seat within ninety days of such order. The courts in India will have no power to mandate the compliance of such a provision. Moreover, such a power is not required when the courts in India grant interim measures in support of foreign seated arbitrations. Therefore, the extraterritorial application of Section 9 of the IAA should be restricted to Sections 9(1) and 9(3) of the IAA only.

Sixth, since Section 9 of the IAA can be invoked even after the award has been passed but not enforced, it is possible to invoke the provisions of Section 9 of the IAA when the award has been passed by the foreign seated tribunal. As discussed in Chapter 3, the possibility of seeking an interim measure after passing the award but before its enforcement should be removed.

Lastly, the proviso to Section 2(2) of the IAA unambiguously leads to only one conclusion that the powers under Sections 9, 27, 37(1)(a) and 37(3) of the IAA can only be exercised if the arbitral award made, or to be made, is one which will be enforceable and recognised in Part II of the IAA, i.e., under the NYC or the Geneva Convention. This implies that at the stage of considering the requests under either of these sections, the courts in India will have to undertake analysis with respect to the enforceability and recognition of the arbitral award in India in accordance with Section 49 of the IAA.

For an award to be enforceable under Section 49 of the IAA, the courts examine the legality, validity, and existence and only upon such satisfaction deem it to be a decree of the court.[831] Moreover, the court cannot directly enforce an award but has to hear the parties with respect to any objections on the ground of public policy.[832] Thus, the satisfaction of the court as contemplated under Section 49 of the IAA means that

830. Ajar Rab & Ankit Singh, *BGS V. NHPC – Implications Beyond the 'Seat' & 'Venue' Debate*, (5 March 2020), available at: http://rsrr.in/2020/03/05/bgs-v-nhpc-implications-beyond-the-seat-venue-debate/; Ankit Singh, *supra* n. 252; Purvi Kaya, *The Seat vs Venue Conundrum in Cases of Unclear Arbitration Clauses: Hardy and Antrix Bad in Law?*, (14 January 2020), available at: https://indiacorplaw.in/2020/01/seat-vs-venue-conundrum-cases-unclear-arbitration-clauses-hardy-antrix-bad-law.html; Vivek Krishnani, *Determination of Supervisory Jurisdiction by the Indian Supreme Court: Venue in the Driver's 'Seat'?*, (14 October 2019), available at: https://indiacorplaw.in/2019/10/determination-supervisory-jurisdiction-indian-supreme-court-venue-drivers-seat.html.

831. *Furest Day Lawson Ltd. v. Jindal Exports Ltd.* (2001) 6 SCC 356, ¶31.

832. Indian Arbitration Act, 1996, S. 48(2).

none of the grounds as mentioned in Section 48(2) of the IAA exist and no objection has been raised resisting enforcement under Section 48(1) of the IAA.[833]

The determination of the enforceability of the award gives cause for judicial intervention and prejudging the enforceability of the award, especially with respect to public policy at an interim stage. It is pertinent to mention that while Article 17I of the Model Law also provides for such judicial review at the time of enforcement of an interim measure, such review is only with respect to the interim measure and not the award itself.[834]

Moreover, the current position appears to be in consonance with the observation of the court in *Bhatia* that there will be no provision applicable for interim measures in support of foreign seated arbitrations if the seat is in a non-signatory country. This position is not in consonance with Article 17J of the Model Law which provides for the grant of interim measure by the court irrespective of the seat.

To cater to all these concerns, the power to grant interim measures in aid of foreign seated arbitrations should be explicitly included in Section 9 of the IAA. The mere extension of the extraterritorial application in Section 2(2) of the IAA is inadequate to address such issues. Further, the limitation contained in the proviso to Section 2(2) of the IAA '*and an arbitral award made or to be made in such place is enforceable and recognised under the provisions of Part II of this Act*' should be deleted. Such a consideration is unlikely to ever come into play in the absence of jurisdiction of the court over the defendant. These amendments would also be in line with Article 17J of the Model Law, which provides for the power of the court to issue interim measures without being limited to certain countries.

2.3.2. *Interim Measures During Foreign Seated Arbitration Proceedings*

Another issue after the 2015 Amendment is that Section 9 of the IAA, *in toto*, has been made applicable to foreign seated arbitrations. Therefore, a party can invoke Section 9(3) of the IAA and secure an interim measure in support of a foreign seated arbitration on the argument that the remedy before the foreign seated tribunal is not 'efficacious' or that the arbitral tribunal has no power or is unable to act effectively.

Though this position seems to align with the jurisprudence in the United States,[835] England,[836] France,[837] and Singapore,[838] it entails an inherent danger of the Indian courts examining the power of the arbitral tribunal under the *lex arbitri* of a foreign country to determine whether the remedy available under the *lex arbitri* is efficacious or not. Such a determination by the court would be violative of the

833. *Furest Day Lawson Ltd. v. Jindal Exports Ltd.* (2001) 6 SCC 356, ¶¶30 &32.
834. UNCITRAL Model Law, Art. 17I(2).
835. Uniform Arbitration Act, 2000, S. 8(b), '*After an arbitrator is appointed and is authorized and able to act- (2) a party to an arbitration proceeding may move the court for a provisional remedy only if the matter is urgent and the arbitrator is not able to act timely or the arbitrator cannot provide an adequate remedy.*'
836. Ohio Code on International Commercial Arbitration, S. 2712.36.
837. French Code of Civil Procedure, Art. 1449(1).
838. Singapore International Arbitration Act, 1994, S. 12A(6).

principles of international law. For this reason, in Brazil, the position of law is that an interim measure in aid of foreign seated arbitration can only be granted in exceptional circumstances after the arbitral tribunal has been constituted.[839]

Furthermore, this extraterritorial application leaves open the possibility of forum shopping by a party. A party may be able to approach an Indian court under Section 9(3) of the IAA demonstrating why the remedy by the arbitral tribunal is not efficacious without approaching the courts at the seat.

One possible solution to the problem could be the approach adopted by the Delhi High Court. In a pre-amendment case, the court held that if a party elected to apply for an interim measure before the arbitral tribunal, such a party may not seek the same relief from a court.[840] A similar line of reasoning may also be extended to an application under Section 9(3) of the IAA after the foreign seated arbitral tribunal has been formed, but that would leave a party remediless.

Therefore, as suggested in Chapter 4, first, the phrase 'efficacious' should be substituted with 'the tribunal has no power or is unable for the time being to act effectively'. This would provide a more precise standard and prevent examination by Indian courts of whether a remedy in a foreign seated arbitration is truly inefficacious.

3. SCOPE OF INTERIM MEASURES IN AID OF FOREIGN SEATED ARBITRATIONS

One of the key concerns while exercising jurisdiction or granting measures in support of foreign seated arbitrations is the question of the extent of judicial intervention that is required. Section 5 of the IAA provides that a judicial authority should not interfere except as provided in the IAA.[841] However, it should be clarified that Section 5 of the IAA only comes into consideration when the seat is in India. Section 5 of the IAA does not have any extraterritorial applicability and cannot be invoked when the seat is outside India. The restraint on court intervention in such cases stems from considerations of the 'specific features of international arbitration' under Article 17J of the Model Law. Such features, as discussed previously, include the respect for party autonomy, the autonomous nature of arbitration, and the role of the courts at the seat.

Given the potential for abuse, the court should be extremely cautious of granting interim measures in support of foreign seated tribunals and the power should be exercised subject to strict safeguards. Courts should be conscious of the choice of the parties with respect to the seat, the priority of the jurisdiction of the arbitral tribunal, and that the role of the court is only to support the foreign arbitral proceedings. Hence, the court should be wary of examining any issue which would be within the domain of the arbitral tribunal or the court at the seat.

839. *See* Judgment of 12 June 2012, *Itarumã Participaçoes SA v. Participaçoes em Complexos Bioenergétios SA – PCBIOS*, Resp. No. 1,297,974-RJ (Brazilian Superior Tribunal de Justica); *Judgment of 19 June 2012, Petroléo Braileiro SA Petrobras v. Tractebel Energia SA, Resp.* No. 1.297.974–RJ 2011/0240991-9.

840. *Sri Krishan v. Anand* 2009 SCC OnLine Del 2472, ¶16.

841. *Bhatia International v. Bulk Trading S.A. and Anr.* (2002) 4 SCC 105, ¶10.

3.1. 'Inappropriate to do so'

In this context, in England[842] and Singapore,[843] the court may refuse to exercise the powers if the court deems it inappropriate to do so. The phrase 'inappropriate' is inspired by the principle of comity, which is usually regarded as a fundamental principle.[844] In contrast, the standards in Hong Kong are governed by Section 45(5) of the Hong Kong Ordinance which provides that the court shall have regard to the fact that the power is: (a) ancillary to arbitration proceedings outside Hong Kong; and (b) for the purpose of facilitating the process of a court, or arbitral tribunal outside Hong Kong that has primary jurisdiction over the arbitration proceedings. Thus, the criteria, despite being a bit vague, guide the way the court may exercise the discretion and grant interim measures in support of foreign seated arbitrations.

It has been suggested that there is no requirement for legislative guidance for the exercise of such power[845] as the court ought to take into account relevant considerations when deciding to grant interim measures in aid of foreign seated arbitrations. This view ignores the mandate of Article 17J of the Model Law. The considerations relevant for the exercise of the power when a country is the seat cannot be the same for considerations in aid of foreign seated arbitrations as the same would disregard the primary jurisdiction of the courts at the seat and the choice of the parties of the *lex arbitri*. It also leads to subjective exercise and inconsistent use of power.

While the possibility of drawing from world jurisprudence is an option available to the courts in India, it would lead to uncertainty, diverging views of different courts, and more importantly, the courts will most likely draw parallels from jurisprudence in England which stands on a very different turf and has very different statutory provisions from those contained in the IAA.

Moreover, the view that there is no need for legislative guidance may not be suitable for a country like India where there are several instances of excessive judicial intervention in arbitration proceedings.[846] Furthermore, given the lack of clarity and understanding in the exercise of powers by the court with respect to interim measures in India and the problem of excessive delay before the courts, the absence of any legislative restraint can further compound the arbitration woes in India.

It would be prudent to have guidelines for the exercise of such a power as that would provide a degree of certainty with respect to the circumstances in which the interim measure requested will be granted or refused.[847] Therefore, it is necessary to add provisions within Section 9 of the IAA like the United Kingdom, Hong Kong, and Singapore, which would apply to the scope of the power of the court to grant interim measures in aid of foreign seated arbitrations.

---

842. English Arbitration Act, 1996, S. 2(3).
843. Singapore International Arbitration Act, 1994, S. 12A(3).
844. Ministry of Law's Responses to Public Feedback Received, c.f. Mohan, *supra* n. 12, at 325.
845. Cheong, *supra* n. 728, at 455.
846. Andrew de Lotbinière McDougall & Dipen Sabharwal, et al., *Mandatory Time Limit for Rendering Awards under Indian Law: How Good Intentions Can Lead to Bad Outcomes*, 5(2) Ind. J. Arb. L. 188 (2017).
847. Cheong, *supra* n. 728, at 455.

The addition of clauses akin to the approach in England and Singapore, which provide for judicial discretion and permit the court to judge whether the grant of relief would be 'inappropriate' in certain cases, would not work in a place like India where the judiciary is prone to intervention and continues to hold a mistrust towards the arbitral process. Taking a cue from Section 45(5)(a) of the Hong Kong Ordinance, a provision should be added to Section 9 of the IAA in relation to foreign seated arbitrations specifying that '*such power is ancillary to the arbitration proceedings outside India and can only be exercised for facilitating the process of a court or arbitral tribunal outside India that has primary jurisdiction over the arbitration proceedings*'.

4. STANDARDS FOR GRANT OF INTERIM MEASURES IN AID OF FOREIGN SEATED ARBITRATIONS

Given the extraterritorial effect of interim measures granted in-aid of foreign seated arbitrations, the courts must apply the appropriate standards while considering such applications as the potential of abuse without proper safeguards is very high.

Born suggests that the standard used in *Channel Tunnel* was directly focused on the appropriateness of granting interim measures in support of foreign seated arbitration.[848] The court in *Channel Tunnel*[849] had considered the following factors while exercising the power to grant interim measures in aid of foreign seated arbitrations (a) seat of arbitration; (b) *lex arbitri;* (c) substantive law; (d) personal jurisdiction over the defendants; (e) whether the interim measure would resolve most of the dispute; and (f) the natural court to consider the dispute.

Similarly, a US Appellate Court[850] had considered (a) the seat of arbitration; (b) the location of the conduct giving rise to the parties' dispute; (c) the location of the evidence and witnesses; (d) the respective interest of the possible judicial forum in issuing relief; and (e) the ease of enforcing the court's order.

It has been suggested that the criteria to be used when exercising jurisdiction should be (a) the existence of a valid arbitration agreement; and (b) whether it is appropriate for the court to be involved in the case.[851] If the court finds in favour of these two issues, the court should then consider necessity and convenience, i.e., whether the court is the most appropriate court or convenient forum to grant the interim measure.[852] Once the court establishes that it is the most convenient forum, the court should apply its own law to grant or deny the request.[853]

After the addition of the proviso to Section 2(2) of the IAA, the power under Section 9 of the IAA will apply to foreign seated arbitrations. However, in the absence of any specific guidance, the said power would be exercised in the same manner by a

848. Gary Born, *supra* n. 33, at 2753.
849. *Channel Tunnel Group Ltd. v. Balfour Beatty Construction Ltd.* [1993] 2 WLR 262.
850. *Karaha Bodas Co. v. Perusahaan Pertambangan Minyak Dan Gas Bumi Negara* 335 F.3d 357, 365 (5th Cir. 2003).
851. Ali Yesilirmak, *supra* n. 30, at 82.
852. *Ibid.*
853. Report of UNCITRAL Working Group on the work of its Thirty Eighth session, 2003, A/CN.9/524, available at: https://undocs.org/en/A/CN.9/524, ¶77.

court as a proceeding under Section 9 of the IAA. Therefore, the courts will apply the standards used in Section 94, Order XXXVIII[854] and Order XXXIX, Section 151 of the CPC read with the Specific Relief Act.

As discussed previously in Chapter 3, applying the domestic procedural law of a court such as the CPC or the Specific Relief Act would violate the mandate of Article 17J of the Model Law, which requires the consideration of the 'specific features of international arbitration'. More importantly, applying domestic law standards defeats the whole intent of parties to avoid foreign courts and procedures.

Therefore, neither a very high threshold nor onerous proof should be required. It should be remembered that the role of the court is one of assistance only. The party should first have to demonstrate: (a) why the arbitral tribunal and the courts at the seat do not have the power or are unable to act effectively; and (b) that all the ingredients required under Article 17A (with necessary modifications[855]) of the Model Law are satisfied, i.e., urgency and balance of convenience.

Taking a cue from the English court's decision and the guidelines issued in *Rasu Maritima SA v. Perusahaan*[856] are of assistance in determining the appropriate criteria to be applied by courts when dealing with requests for grant of interim measures in aid of foreign seated arbitrations. Lord Denning laid down the criteria for granting an injunction as follows:

(a) the claimant must have a good arguable case;
(b) the claimant must make full and frank disclosure of all material matters in his knowledge;
(c) the claimant must state full particulars of his claim, the amount of it and if the request is made ex parte, any points the defendant has made against such a claim;
(d) the claimant must state the grounds for believing there is a risk of dissipation, or transmission of funds out of the jurisdiction by the defendant; and
(e) the claimant must provide an undertaking for damages to be paid to the defendant if the main action against the defendant fails.

These considerations are not at significant variance from the suggested standards to be applied by courts as discussed in Chapter 3.[857] The court in India would consider the reasonable possibility of success without analysing the chances of success under a foreign law. It will then determine the urgency by examining the right of the party requesting the measure which is threatened or is likely to be threatened by the conduct of the respondent. Such analysis would also include why the interim measure requested cannot be granted by the arbitral tribunal or the courts at the seat, if the grant of the interim measure requires an unacceptable degree of supervision in a foreign

854. *Goodwill Non-Woven(P) Limited v. Xcoal Energy & Resources LLC* 2020 SCC OnLine Del 631, ¶55.
855. *As suggested in Chapter 7.*
856. *Rasu Maritima S.A. v. Perusahaan Pertambangan v. Minyak Dan Gas Bumi Negara (Government of the Republic of Indonesia intervening)* [1978] QB 644, at 661.
857. *See discussion on Standards in Chapter 7.*

land[858] or why the party cannot wait for the final outcome of the arbitration proceedings. Similarly, questions of harm would most likely entail the determination of the effect the interim measure would have on the parties, the arbitral tribunal's jurisdiction, and the jurisdiction of the courts at the seat.

4.1. Consideration of Jurisdiction

If the measure is requested ex parte, the court will determine if the purpose of the interim measure will be frustrated if the measure is not granted without notice to the other party. The only criterion to be added to such standards would be the consideration of jurisdiction over the defendant. Such jurisdiction may not necessarily be in personam, but there should be some 'minimum contact' with the Indian court.[859] It is not necessary that the defendant has assets in India for the court to exercise jurisdiction.[860] The consideration of whether the remedy before the arbitral tribunal or under the *lex arbitri* is not efficacious will be considered under the guiding language of 'the power being ancillary to arbitration proceedings outside India and for the purpose of facilitating the process of a court or arbitral tribunal outside India that has primary jurisdiction over the arbitration proceedings'.

5. TYPES OF MEASURES

Once the standards required for the grant of interim measures have been considered by a court, the court then should consider the type of measures that can be granted in aid of a foreign seated arbitration. Is the court empowered to grant all the reliefs enumerated in Section 9 of the IAA? Or should only certain types of interim measures be permitted? How to ensure that an interim measure is granted only to 'support and not to disrupt'[861] existing or contemplated arbitration proceedings?

It should be remembered that interim measures should be sought at the seat. If a party is permitted to seek any and all kinds of measures which are available at the seat, then in effect the courts in India would be usurping the jurisdiction of the seat.[862] Therefore, one option could be to list the type of orders that may be granted. This may

858. *Big Charter Private Limited v. Ezen Aviation Pty. Ltd.* 2020 SCC OnLine Del 1713, ¶63 *relying on the decision of the Court of Appeal of Singapore in Five Ocean Corporation v. Cingler Ship Pte Ltd,* (2015) SGHC 311; *Maldives Airport Co. Ltd. GMR Male International Airport Pte. Ltd,* (2013) SGCA 16; *SSL International plc v. TTK LIG Ltd.* (2011) EWCA Civ 1170. *It should be noted that the Delhi High Court opined that Singapore International Arbitration Act, 1994, S. 12-A, does permit courts at Singapore to grant interim relief in the pre-arbitral stage* ¶64-65.

859. *(India TV) Independent News Service Pvt Limited v. India Broadcast Live LLC ILR (2007) 2 Del 1231*; Banyan Tree Holding (P) Limited v. A. Murali Krishna Reddy *2010 (42) PTC 361 (Del);* Hindustan Cleanenergy Ltd. v. Maif Investments India 2 Pte. Ltd. *2021 SCC OnLine Del 4102,* ¶45-46.

860. *Goodwill Non-Woven(P) Limited v. Xcoal Energy & Resources LLC* 2020 SCC OnLine Del 631, ¶48-49.

861. *Barnwell Enterprises v. ECP Africa FII Investments LLC* (2013) SCJ 327.

862. Similar to Hong Kong Arbitration Ordinance (Cap.609), S. 45(5)(b); Cheong, *supra* n. 728, at 454.

promote certainty and prevent judicial interference under the garb of judicial assistance.[863] Such a list of the type of orders that can be granted in aid of foreign seated arbitrations would prevent a party from seeking a measure which effectively decides the dispute or procures substantive findings which may have a preclusive effect in the arbitral proceedings.[864]

Another alternative would be not to list any measure and grant freedom to courts to determine the type of measure best suited to the facts and circumstances of the case. While determining the measure, the court ought to keep in mind that the scope of the power to grant such measures being 'ancillary' and for 'facilitating the process'. Therefore, there would be a guiding criterion for the court to ensure that the court does not usurp the primary jurisdiction of the seat and the arbitral tribunal. As discussed in Chapter 3, the adoption of the generic language of Article 17(2) of the Model Law with the specific exclusion of the power to order security for costs can address the requirement of flexibility required while granting interim measures in aid of a foreign seated arbitration. It would also cater to certain specific types of measures discussed below.

5.1. *Mareva* Injunctions

Ordinarily, the request for interim measures in support of foreign seated arbitrations is for the issuance of a freezing order or *Mareva* injunction,[865] i.e., a party may want to preserve his opponent's assets located in different jurisdiction so that at the end of the legal proceedings which involve both time and resources, the party may be able to enforce its judgment and his time and expenditure on legal costs does not go in vain.[866] Although the *Mareva* injunction got its name from the *Mareva* case, it must be stated that the order was first made in the case of *Nippon Kaisha* v. *Karageorgis*.[867]

A *Mareva* injunction, thus, prevents the free exercise of rights by a defendant over his assets in order to protect the requesting party's right of seeking enforcement of his judgment and curtailing the risk of dissipation of assets by the defendant to avoid satisfaction of the judgment in favour of such party.[868] Disobedience of such an order amounts to contempt of court and therefore, has been said to be a 'nuclear weapon' of the law.[869]

Mareva injunctions or freezing orders can be of different types, i.e., (a) a general freezing order covering all of the defendant's assets; (b) a maximum sum order covering the defendant's assets only up to a maximum sum of the claimant's claim plus

863. Cheong, *supra* n. 728, at 429.
864. Gary Born, *supra* n. 33, at 2725-2726.
865. *Mareva Companies Naviera S.A. v. International Bulk Carriers S.A.* (1980) 1 All ER 213, *this case was affirmed in India in the case of Venture Global Engineering v. Satyam Computer Services Limited* (2008) 4 SCC 190; Cheong, *supra* n. 728, at 433.
866. Philip Jeyaretnam, *The Granting of Mareva Injunction in Support of Foreign Court Proceedings*, 28 SAc L. J. 503 (2016).
867. *Nippon Yusen Kaisha v. Karageorgis* [1975] 1 W.L.R. 1093.
868. Philip Jeyaretnam, *supra* n. 866, at 504.
869. *Per Sir John Donaldson M.R. in Bank Mellat v. Nikpour*, [1985] FSR 87, at 92. *Nikpour*, [1985] FSR 87, at 92.

interests and costs; or (c) a freezing order which covers only specific assets of the defendant.[870] It is pertinent to note that a freezing order does not create any priority in terms of title or interest in the goods and just prevents the removal of assets or their dissipation.[871]

Whether *Mareva* injunctions can be granted or not so far has not been considered by the Supreme Court. The views of the Bombay High Court[872] and Delhi High Court[873] seem to be at a slight divergence from each other but ultimately lead to the conclusion that the remedy under Order XXXVIII Rule 5 of the CPC is the only source available for grant of a *Mareva* injunction.

Hence, there is no specific source of power available apart from that contained in Order XXXVIII of the CPC which significantly limits the scope and possibility of issuing a *Mareva* injunction. An alternative source is that the power under Section 9 of the IAA is interpreted as an independent provision and an injunction is granted by Section 9(1)(ii)(a) or (c) of the IAA. A third alternative is to take resort to Section 9(1)(ii)(e) of the IAA to order measures which the court considers to be 'just and convenient'.[874]

Adopting the generic language as provided under Article 17(2) of the Model Law along with the express recognition of the powers under Section 9(1)(ii) of the IAA would adequately empower courts to grant *Mareva* injunctions in aid of foreign seated arbitrations. Moreover, a party seeking such injunctions will not be required to invoke the inherent power of the court or other provisions of the CPC. The court, while considering such requests, will be explicitly authorised by the IAA to grant the type of measure most suited to facilitating the arbitral process outside India including a *Mareva* injunction which may not be possible under the current regime.

5.2. Worldwide Freezing Orders

A recent creation of the English Courts is the grant of worldwide freezing orders.[875] The English Courts have also given detailed guidelines on the exercise of discretion with respect to such orders and their enforcement.[876] However, such orders may not be possible in India as there is no power equivalent to Section 37(1) of the Supreme Court Act, 1981 and Section 25 of the Civil Jurisdiction and Judgments Act, 1982 in India and resort to the inherent power of the court is limited to exceptional circumstances.[877] Adopting the broad language of Article 17(2) of the Model Law would permit the courts to grant orders to '*provide a means of preserving assets out of which a subsequent award may be satisfied*'.

870. Benjamin Andoh, *The Freezing Injunction Today*, 31(2) Bus. L. R. 28, 29 (2010).
871. *It does not seek to improve the claimant's position in insolvency, see ibid.*, at 32.
872. *Iridium India Telecom v. Motorola Inc.* 2003 (6) Bom CR 511.
873. *Rite Approach Group Ltd. v. Rosoborn Export* AIR 2007 Del 145.
874. *Nomihold Securities INC v. Mobile Telesystems Finance SA*, [2012] Bus LR 1289 *affirmed in Himachal Sorang Power Pvt. Ltd. v. NCC Infrastructure Holdings Ltd.* 2019 SCC OnLine Del 7575, ¶108.
875. *Eastern European Engineering Ltd. v. Vijay Construction (Proprietary) Ltd.* [2018] EWHC 1539 (Comm).
876. Chatterjee, *supra* n. 814, at 261.
877. *See Chapter 3.*

6. APPROPRIATE COURT

The court with proper jurisdiction before which an application requesting interim measure in aid of foreign seated arbitration may be filed will be the Commercial Division of the High Court of the State in which the defendant resides, or has a place of business, or where the assets are located.[878] In case the commercial division has not been constituted at such High Court, the same will be filed before the High Court of that State.[879]

7. SAFEGUARDS

To prevent the possibility of forum shopping, the requirement of full disclosure of all facts likely to be relevant for the court's determination,[880] as suggested in Chapter 3, would include all applications made before the arbitral tribunal or the court at the seat. Hence, the courts in India will be in a better position to ascertain whether an interim measure is required in aid of a foreign seated arbitration during an arbitration proceeding.

Additionally, the safeguards in such cases are extremely critical to prevent unnecessary court intervention, especially if such measures are sought ex parte. If the court were to grant such measures, as discussed in Chapter 3, the court should consider taking security in connection with the measure.[881] More importantly, courts should specify that the orders are effective only till the next hearing of the matter before the arbitral tribunal and the arbitral tribunal should subsequently maintain, modify, suspend, or terminate such measures.

878. *The court which would exercise original jurisdiction if a suit was to be filed.* Indian Arbitration Act, 1996, S. 2(1)(e).
879. Indian Arbitration Act, 1996, Ss 2(e) r/w The Commercial Courts Act, 2015, S. 10(1).
880. *Swift-Fortune Ltd. v. Magnificia Marine S.A.* [2006] SGCA 42.
881. *Siporex Trade SA v. Comdel Commodities Ltd.* [1986] 2 Lloyd's Rep. 428; *Golf Interstate Oil Corp v. ANT Trade, The Giovanna* [1999] 1 Lloyd's Rep. 867.

CHAPTER 6
Anti-Suit and Anti-Arbitration Injunctions

Very often, before the commencement of arbitration proceedings, one of the parties approaches the court instead of pursuing the agreed-upon method of resolving their dispute through arbitration or approaches the court even though the arbitration proceedings are currently underway. It is in these circumstances that besides the power of the arbitral tribunal to preserve and enforce the arbitration agreement, the supportive role of courts becomes imperative in creating a pro-arbitration regime.[882] However, sometimes a party may approach the court because it alleges that there is no valid arbitration agreement. In such cases, the court is duty-bound to protect the party from vexatious or oppressive arbitration proceedings.

1. ANTI-SUIT INJUNCTIONS

Initially, when a court restrained a party to a suit/proceeding before it from instituting or prosecuting a case in another court including a foreign court, such an injunction was an anti-suit injunction.[883] Such injunctions also included orders that parties withdraw from or suspend the proceedings.[884]

Therefore, a party can request the court to issue an anti-suit injunction to protect or prevent the jurisdiction of the arbitral tribunal,[885] i.e., either to enforce the arbitration agreement by passing an injunction to stay court proceedings in violation of the arbitration agreement or to prevent the parties from invoking the arbitration agreement.[886] An anti-suit injunction may also be required to be issued by a court when

882. Crina Baltag, *Anti – Suit Injunctions and Other Means of Indirect Enforcement of an Arbitration Agreement*, in Stavaros L. Brekoulakis & Julian D.M. Lew, et al. (eds), *The Evolution and Future of International Arbitration* 251 (2016).
883. *Modi Entertainment Network v. W.S.G. Cricket Pte. Ltd.* (2003) 4 SCC 341, ¶¶ 1182-1183.
884. Emmanuel Gaillard, *Anti-Suit Injunctions in International Arbitration* 1 (2005).
885. Julian D M Lew, *Control of Jurisdiction by Injunctions Issued by National Courts*, in Albert Jan van den Berg (ed.), *International Arbitration 2006: Back to Basics?* 188 (2007).
886. *Ibid.*

one party has challenged the arbitral award and the award creditor files for enforcement of the award in another jurisdiction.[887]

Anti-suit injunctions, therefore, can interact with arbitration in four different ways:[888]

(a) A party may ask a court to issue an anti-suit injunction to enforce the arbitration agreement.
(b) A party may ask the court to issue an anti-arbitration injunction preventing an arbitration from going forward.
(c) A party may request the arbitral tribunal to issue an anti-suit injunction (jurisdiction protection).[889]
(d) A party may ask a court to issue an anti-suit injunction to disallow parallel proceedings regarding the enforcement of a foreign arbitral award.

Thus, an anti-suit injunction enforcing the arbitration agreement is a positive step towards supporting arbitration. Its function is to prevent unconscionable conduct[890] which permits the court to foster a pro-arbitration policy to direct the parties to have their dispute resolved through arbitration.[891]

On the other hand, an anti-arbitration injunction relegates parties back to the courts because there is no valid arbitration agreement.[892] Hence, it has a negative effect on arbitration proceedings and serves no protective function[893] for arbitration. Instead, it protects the fundamental right of a party to approach the court if the arbitration agreement falls within the phrase 'void or inoperative or incapable of being performed' as provided under Article II(3) of the NYC.[894] In such instances, the courts can restrain parties from pursuing arbitration proceedings as they would amount to vexatious or oppressive litigation.[895] Such agreements and awards passed under them cannot be enforced under the NYC.[896] An anti-arbitration injunction, thus, is a remedy where a party requests the court or another arbitral tribunal to direct the respondent not to pursue arbitration or not to appear before another arbitral tribunal.[897]

887. *Karaha Bodas Co. v. Perusahaan Pertambangan Minyak Dan Gas Bumi Negara* 335 F.3d 357, 365 (5th Cir. 2003); *Sabah Shipyard (Pakistan) Ltd. (a company incorporated in Pakistan) v. The Islamic Republic of Pakistan (by the Managing Director, Private Power and Infrastructure Board)* [2007] EWHC 2602 (Comm); *O.N.G.C. v. Western Co. of North America* (1987) 1 SCC 496, ¶3.
888. S. I. Strong, *Anti-Suit Injunctions in Judicial and Arbitral Procedures in the United States*, 66 Am. J. C. L. 153, 172, 173 (2018).
889. *See Chapter 9.*
890. *Seismic Shipping Inc., Westerngeco v. Total E and P UK Plc. the Western Regent* (2005) EWHC 460; *affirmed in Videocon Industries Ltd. v. Union of India* (2011) 6 SCC 161.
891. Jennifer L. Groskie, *US Courts and the Anti-Arbitration Injunction*, 28(2) Arb. Int'l, 295, 308-309 (2012).
892. *Ibid.*, at 296.
893. *Ibid.*, at 309.
894. Sharad Bansal & Divyanshu Agarwal, *Are Anti-Arbitration Injunctions A Malaise? An Analysis in the Context of Indian Law*, 31(4) Arb. Int'l, 613, 620 (2015).
895. Strong, *supra* n. 888, at 163.
896. NYC Arts II(3), V(1)(a).
897. *See* Jennifer, *supra* n. 891, at 295; Julian DM Lew, *Does National Court Involvement Undermine the International Arbitration Process?*, 24 (3) Am. Uni. Int'l L. R. 489 (2009); Giulia Carbone,

The primary source of the power for both the injunctions lies in the inherent power of the court to do justice and to prevent vexatious or oppressive litigation abroad.[898] Since both kinds of injunctions are rooted in the exercise of the inherent power of the court, their jurisprudence is very similar, with certain exceptions. Both injunctions are granted in personam against the parties.[899] Therefore, an analogy can be drawn between the two of them.[900] However, in the context of arbitration, both have different effects.

1.1. Power to Grant Anti-Suit Injunctions

Anti-suit injunctions have been issued since the early 1500s.[901] In the context of arbitration, all major common law systems expressly provide for a stay of litigation brought in violation of a valid arbitration agreement. In England, Section 9 of the English Arbitration Act specifically contains such a provision. In contrast, courts in civil law jurisdictions do not merely stay pending litigations but dismiss them entirely.[902] The United States and Brazil have provisions for direct enforcement or specific performance of the arbitration agreement when a party approaches the court in violation of the arbitration agreement.[903]

Interference of the Court of the Seat with International Arbitration, J. Dis. Res. 217 (2012); John Gaffney, *Non-party Autonomy: Displacing the Negative Effect of the Principle of 'Competence-Competence' in England?*, 29 (1) J. Int'l Arb. 107, 114 (2012); Sharad Bansal, *supra* n. 894, at 620.

898. Stephen M. Schwebel, *Anti-Suit Injunctions in International Arbitration: An Overview*, in Emmanuel Gaillard (ed.), *Anti-Suit Injunctions in International Arbitration* 8 (2005).
899. Crina, *supra* n. 882, at 252-253.
900. Lew, *supra* n. 885, at 190.
901. Jonathan R. C. Arkins & David Joseph, *Jurisdiction and Arbitration Agreements and their Enforcement* 308-381 (2005); David W. Raack, *A History of Injunctions in England Before 1700*, 61 (4) Ind. L J. 539 (1986); Marco Stacher, *You Don't Want to Go There: Antisuit Injunctions in International Commercial Arbitration*, 23 (4) ASA Bull. 640 (2005); George Bermann, *The Use of Anti-Suit Injunctions in International Litigation*, 28 Colum. J. Trans'l L., 589 593 (1990); Trevor Hartley, *Comity and the Use of Antisuit Injunctions in International Litigation*, 35 (3) Am. J. Comp. L. (1987).
902. Gary Born, *Interpreting Section 9(1) of the Arbitration Act 1996: Lombard v. GATX*, (24 May 2012), available at: http://arbitrationblog.kluwerarbitration.com/2012/05/24/interpreting-section-91-of-the-arbitration-act-1996-lombard-v-gatx/?doing_wp_cron=1590838778.755359 8880767822265625; *See* Gary Born, *supra* n. 33, at 1115, 116.
903. Federal Arbitration Act, Ss 4 & 206: which provide that the party aggrieved by the failure, neglect, or refusal of another to arbitrate *under an arbitration agreement may petition the court for an order directing such party participate in the arbitration; Brazil Arbitration Act, 2015, Art. 7 providing, among others, that: Where there is an arbitration clause but one of the parties shows resistance as to the commencement of arbitration, the interested party may request the court to summon the other party to appear in court so that the submission agreement may be signed; the judge shall designate a special hearing for this purpose. It is said that Brazil Arbitration Act, 2015, Art. 7 may only be used when the arbitration clause does not contain all the mandatory elements, since such procedure enables the issuance of a submission agreement which directs the parties to arbitration and which would be unnecessary in the presence of a proper arbitration agreement (meaning that the party would have to resort to the courts to confirm the arbitration agreement)*. Joaquim T. de Paiva Muniz & Ana Tereza Palhares Basílio, *Arbitration Law of Brazil: Practice and Procedure* 65 (2006).

Anti-suit injunctions in support of arbitration are premised on the principle that the court has concurrent jurisdiction and has to play an active role in supporting arbitration. However, the power to issue anti-suit injunctions has been recognised in India, mostly under the inherent power of the courts[904] and not under Section 9 of the IAA.

1.2. Anti-Suit Injunctions under the Model Law

The Working Group agreed that the power to grant an anti-suit injunction falls under Article 17(2)(b) of the Model Law.[905] Hence, if the tribunal's power to grant anti-suit injunctions is recognised under Article 17(2)(b) of the Model Law, the power would be available to the courts under Section 9 of the IAA. As discussed in Chapter 3, the power of the court to grant interim measures should be the same as that of the tribunal and with respect to the type of measures that a tribunal can grant.

Such adoption will also be in line with the adoption of Article 17J of the Model Law. Domestic courts may exercise power to issue interim measures indirectly ordering the stay of proceedings before another court in the interest of arbitral proceedings.[906] Such injunctions would be required in consideration of the 'specific features of international arbitration'. When parties agree to have their dispute resolved through arbitration, courts should not entertain applications in breach of such agreements. They should try to give full effect to such agreements and support the arbitral process as this is the intent behind the NYC and the Model Law.[907]

Such adoption is also required to ensure that enforcement of an arbitration agreement is not granted under the inherent power of the court but under Section 9 of the IAA to prevent harm or prejudice to the arbitral process. In Hong Kong, the power to grant such injunctions has been confirmed under the power of the court to maintain or restore the status quo pending the determination of the dispute.[908] Similarly, in Singapore, the power has been recognised under Section 12A of the Singapore International Arbitration Act.[909] Therefore, there is a precedent for courts to exercise the power to grant anti-suit injunctions based on domestic arbitration statutes read with the Model Law instead of taking resort to the inherent power of the court, subject to meeting jurisdictional requirements.

1.3. Jurisdiction to Grant Anti-Suit Injunctions

If the seat theory is applied to anti-suit injunctions, then the seat would be the most appropriate court to grant the anti-suit injunction, subject to the condition that the

904. *Rajshree Sugars & Chemicals Limited v. AXIS Bank Ltd.* 2008 SCC OnLine Mad 746; *Enercon (India) Ltd. v. Enercon GmbH* (2014) 5 SCC 1, ¶45; *Vivek Rai Gupta v. Niyati Gupta* (2012) SCC OnLine Bom 2185, ¶ 6.
905. *See Discussion in Chapter 6.*
906. Berk Demirkol, *Ordering Cessation of Court Proceedings to Protect the Integrity of Arbitration Agreements under the Brussels Regime*, 65 (2) Int'l Comp. Q. 379, 392 (2016).
907. *Sana Hassib Sabbagh v. Wael Said Khoury* [2019] EWCA Civ 1219.
908. *GM1 and GM 2 v. KC* [2019] HKCFI 2793.
909. *R1 International Pte Ltd v. Lonstroff AG* [2014] SCHC 69.

courts at the seat exercise in personam jurisdiction over the defendant. Hence, anti-suit injunctions issued by the courts at the seat in the exercise of the power conferred by Article 17J of the Model Law can only be issued subject to in personam jurisdiction over the defendant. In the absence of such jurisdiction, the order of the court would have to be enforced in the jurisdiction of the defendant and may be barred by comity.[910] Therefore, for the issuance of anti-suit injunctions, it makes sense to apply to the court that exercises in personam jurisdiction over the defendant. Such court may be the court of the seat or may not be the court of the seat.

1.3.1. 'Natural Forum'

English courts apply the test of 'natural forum' when considering a request for the issuance of an anti-suit injunction in support of the arbitration agreement.[911] 'Natural forum' means that between England and the seat, England is the more appropriate forum, i.e., the English forum has sufficient interest in or connection with the matter to justify the indirect interference with the foreign court.[912] In essence, English courts should have some basis for exercising jurisdiction and the injunction issued can effectively be enforced. Such enforcement would most often require in personam jurisdiction over the defendant.

Since the power to issue anti-suit injunctions has been recognised in India mostly under the inherent power of the courts,[913] they have often held that the court at the seat would be the appropriate court to grant anti-suit injunctions since the choice of the seat amounts to an exclusive jurisdiction clause[914] by an agreement of the parties.[915] Therefore, when parties have identified an exclusive jurisdiction, the same is respected[916] unless a different intention is expressed.[917] The courts have also followed the English approach of 'natural forum'. However, the test has been referred to as *forum conveniens,*[918] i.e., the forum with which has a 'real'[919] or 'substantial' connection.[920]

910. *Airbus Industrie GIE v. Patel* [1999] 1 AC 119; In the matter of: *Gujrat Nre Coke Limited & Anr v. Gregarious Estates* 2012 SCC Online Cal 7624.
911. *Sana Hassib Sabbagh v. Wael Said Khoury* [2019] EWCA Civ 1219, ¶102.
912. *Airbus Industrie GIE v. Patel* [1999] 1 AC 119, at 138.
913. *Rajshree Sugars & Chemicals Limited v. AXIS Bank Ltd.* 2008 SCC OnLine Mad 746; *Enercon (India) Ltd. v. Enercon GmbH* (2014) 5 SCC 1, ¶45; *Vivek Rai Gupta v. Niyati Gupta* (2012) SCC OnLine Bom 2185, ¶ 6.
914. *Enercon (India) Ltd. v. Enercon GmbH* (2014) 5 SCC 1, ¶¶127 &145; *Roger Shashoua v. Mukesh Sharma* (2017) 14 SCC 722.
915. *Glaxosmithkline Consumer Healthcare Ltd. v. Heinz India (P) Ltd.* 2009 SCC OnLine Del 9, ¶24; *Board of Control for Cricket in India v. Essel Sports Pvt. Ltd.* 2010 SCC OnLine Del 443, ¶8.
916. *Moser Baer India Ltd. v. Koninklijke Philips Electronics NV. & Ors.* 151(2008) DLT 180, ¶23.
917. David Joseph Q.C, *Jurisdiction and Arbitration Agreements and their Enforcement* 286 (2010).
918. *Modi Entertainment Network v. W.S.G. Cricket Pte. Ltd.* (2003) 4 SCC 341, ¶24; *Padmini Hindupur v. Abhijit S. Belur,* 2015 SCC OnLine Del 7484.
919. *Ibid.*
920. *Board of Control for Cricket in India v. Essel Sports Pvt. Ltd.* 2010 SCC OnLine Del 443, ¶8.

1.3.2. *Habitual Residence*

It is natural that a party will approach a court under Section 9 of the IAA if it has jurisdiction, either by virtue of being the seat or under the CPC. Section 20 of the CPC uses the test of the place where the defendant '*actually and voluntary resides, or carries on business, or personally works for gain*'.[921] In a similar vein, Article 1(4) of the Model Law makes a reference to jurisdiction to determine if an arbitration is international. It states that when a party has more than one place of business, the place of business which has the closest relationship to the arbitration agreement should be considered or if there is no place of business, then the 'habitual residence' of the party should be considered. Under the IAA, the test to determine if arbitration is international or not is based on nationality or an individual being 'habitually resident' in any country other than India.[922]

1.3.3. *Actual and Voluntary Residence*

The phrase 'actually and voluntarily resides' contained in the CPC is in close alignment with Article 1(4) of the Model Law. Also, the phrase can very well mean 'habitual residence'. It should be noted that while a person may 'ordinarily' be resident in more than one jurisdiction, there can be only one habitual residence.[923] Hence, the phrase 'actually and voluntarily resides' signifies the habitual residence of a party and courts in India would exercise jurisdiction under Section 9 whenever the test in Section 20(c) of the CPC is satisfied, i.e., the courts will have in personam jurisdiction in such cases.[924]

Therefore, such injunctions can be sought either (a) when the party against whom the injunction is sought is an Indian party or resident in India;[925] or (b) when the party is a foreign party or resident abroad. The first instance requires no explanation and the courts would have jurisdiction. In the latter, the courts will first have to ascertain the forum's sufficiency of connection or appropriateness.[926] The court has to determine whether it has jurisdiction in personam over the defendant, i.e., an injunction can only be granted if the defendant resides or carries out business within the jurisdiction of the court.[927]

---

921. Indian Code of Civil Procedure, 1908, S. 20(a) and (b).
922. Indian Arbitration Act, 1996, S. 2(1)(f)(i).
923. Rohan Deshpande, *Habitual Residence under the Indian Arbitration Regime*, (11 June 2020), available at: https://indiacorplaw.in/2020/06/habitual-residence-under-the-indian-arbitratio n-regime.html; *Aslam Deshmukh v. ASAP Fluids Pvt. Ltd.* 2019 SCC OnLine Bom 304; *In re Bates (cited as Mother v. Father)* CA 122/89; *Kapur v. Kapur* [1984] FLR 920; *Shah v. Barnet London Borough* [1983] 2 AC 309]; *Nessa v. Chief Adjudicating Officer*, [1999] 4 All ER 677; *Furest Day Lawson Ltd. v. Jindal Exports Ltd.* (2001) 6 SCC 356.
924. *Vivek Rai Gupta v. Niyati Gupta* (2012) SCC OnLine Bom 2185, ¶6.
925. *Boston Scientific International v. Trivitron Healthcare Pvt Ltd.* 2015 SCC Online Mad 7196, ¶32.
926. Tushar Kumar Biswas, *Introduction to Arbitration in India: The Role of the Judiciary* 89 (2013).
927. *As used in the context of anti-suit injunctions, Modi Entertainment Network v. W.S.G. Cricket Pte. Ltd.* (2003) 4 SCC 341, at 1177; *Bharat Aluminum Company Ltd v. Glencore A G* 2010 SCC Online Ch 116, ¶9.

The courts would not ordinarily exercise jurisdiction where the defendant is wholly outside India even if the cause of action has arisen in India,[928] keeping in mind the possibility of non-compliance if the summons is issued outside territorial jurisdiction. There is also the possibility of the foreign party approaching the court of its own country against the courts in India. Such an exercise may embarrass the political branches of the government and even affect bilateral relationships.[929] However, such concerns should not be determinative in granting or refusing anti-suit or anti-arbitration injunctions.[930]

The law laid down in the *Modi Network* case[931] sufficiently clarifies the scope of the power and questions pertaining to the exercise of jurisdiction. Briefly put, it is

928. *Kohinoor Carpet Manufacturers v. Forbes Gokak Ltd.* 2001 SCC OnLine Bom 1076, ¶¶4-5.

929. Bermann, *supra* n. 901, at 604.

930. Tushar, *supra* n. 926, at 89. *The courts in India have often refused to enforce a foreign award or a foreign judgment; Venture Global Engineering v. Satyam Computer Services Ltd.* (2008) 4 SCC 190; *Satya v. Teja Singh* 1975 AIR 105.

931. *Modi Entertainment Network v. W.S.G. Cricket Pte. Ltd.* (2003) 4 SCC 341, ¶24: *From the above discussion the following principles emerge:*

> (1) In exercising discretion to grant an anti-suit injunction the court must be satisfied of the following aspects:
> (a) the defendant, against whom injunction is sought, is amenable to the personal jurisdiction of the court;
> (b) if the injunction is declined, the ends of justice will be defeated and injustice will be perpetuated; and
> (c) the principle of comity - respect for the court in which the commencement or continuance of action/proceeding is sought to be restrained - must be borne in mind.
>
> (2) In a case where more forums than one are available, the court in exercise of its discretion to grant anti-suit injunction will examine as to which is the appropriate forum (forum conveniens) having regard to the convenience of the parties and may grant anti-suit injunction in regard to proceedings which are oppressive or vexatious or in a *forum non conveniens*.
>
> (3) Where jurisdiction of a court is invoked on the basis of jurisdiction clause in a contract, the recitals therein in regard to exclusive or non-exclusive jurisdiction of the court of choice of the parties are not determinative but are relevant factors and when a question arises as to the nature of jurisdiction agreed to between the parties the court has to decide the same on a true interpretation of the contract on the facts and in the circumstances of each case.
>
> (4) A court of natural jurisdiction will not normally grant anti-suit injunction against a defendant before it where parties have agreed to submit to the exclusive jurisdiction of a court including a foreign court, a forum of their choice in regard to the commencement or continuance of proceedings in the court of choice, save in an exceptional case for good and sufficient reasons, with a view to prevent injustice in circumstances such as which permit a contracting party to be relieved of the burden of the contract; or since the date of the contract the circumstances or subsequent events have made it impossible for the party seeking injunction to prosecute the case in the court of choice because the essence of the jurisdiction of the court does not exist or because of a vis major or force majeure and the like.
>
> (5) Where parties have agreed, under a non-exclusive jurisdiction clause, to approach a neutral foreign forum and be governed by the law applicable to it for the resolution of their disputes arising under the contract, ordinarily no anti-suit injunction will be granted in regard to proceedings in such a forum conveniens and favoured forum as it shall be presumed that the parties have thought over their convenience and all other relevant factors before submitting to the non-exclusive jurisdiction of the court of their choice which cannot be treated just as an alternative forum.
>
> (6) A party to the contract containing jurisdiction clause cannot normally be prevented from approaching the court of choice of the parties as it would amount to aiding

aligned with the submission above that the courts should grant anti-suit injunctions only if the courts exercise in personam jurisdiction over the defendant. If parties have agreed on the seat or an exclusive jurisdiction clause, courts should not interfere, except for good and sufficient reasons in exceptional cases. If the seat is in India, an anti-suit injunction would be issued to protect the jurisdiction of the tribunal. If India is not the seat, the measure ought to be issued in aid of a foreign seated arbitration.

1.4. Scope of Anti-Suit Injunctions

The jurisprudence on the issuance of an anti-suit injunction in arbitration requires the court to be constrained by questions of comity[932] and a country being a reciprocating territory.[933] However, anti-suit injunctions to enforce the arbitration agreement should be granted more liberally as parties should be held to their bargain of choosing to have their dispute resolved through arbitration.[934] They cannot be permitted to escape the arbitration agreement.[935] Since such injunctions are granted against the parties and not any court, questions of comity and territoriality may have limited effect in arbitration.

Since anti-suit injunctions in India have been granted under the court's inherent power, resort to such power is circumscribed by considerations of exceptional circumstances. Reading the power within the IAA would remove such fetters and bring it in line with international jurisdictions and an anti-suit injunction may be granted more freely in order to protect the jurisdiction of the arbitral tribunal.

1.5. Standards for Grant of Anti-Suit Injunctions

The standards to be considered for the issuance of anti-suit injunctions enforcing the arbitration agreement ideally stand on a different footing than the standards applicable to interim injunctions generally. The court has to consider the breach of the arbitration agreement, the more appropriate forum, whether the foreign court proceedings are vexatious or oppressive, and whether any injustice will be suffered by the party who

breach of the contract; yet when one of the parties to the jurisdiction clause approaches the court of choice in which exclusive or non-exclusive jurisdiction is created, the proceedings in that court cannot per se be treated as vexatious or oppressive nor can the court be said to be *forum non conveniens*.

(7) The burden of establishing that the forum of choice is a *forum non conveniens* or the proceedings therein are oppressive or vexatious would be on the party so contending to aver and prove the same.

932. Steven R. Swanson, *Antisuit Injunctions in Support of International Arbitration*, 81 (2) Tul. L. R. 395 (2006); Steven R. Swanson, *The Vexatiousness of a Vexation Rule: International Comity and Antisuit Injunctions*, 30 (1) Geo. Wash. J. Int'l L. & Eco. 1 (1996).
933. *Videocon Industries Ltd. v. Union of India* (2011) 6 SCC 161, ¶99.
934. *Himachal Sorang Power Pvt. Ltd. v. NCC Infrastructure Holdings Ltd.* 2019 SCC OnLine Del 7575, ¶84.
935. *Bhushan Steel Ltd. v. Singapore International Arbitration Centre* 2010 SCC OnLine Del 2236; *Sancorp Confectionary Private Limited v. Gumlink A/S* 2012 SCC OnLine Del 5507, ¶11; *Handicrafts & Handlooms Exports Corporation of India Limited v. Ashok Metal Corporation* 2010 SCC OnLine Del 2099.

has brought the court proceedings.[936] However, courts across jurisdictions generally grant anti-suit injunctions where it is established that court proceedings have been brought in breach of the arbitration agreement[937] on the clear and simple ground that the defendant had promised not to bring them.[938]

In India, the test laid down by the Supreme Court for the grant of anti-suit injunctions is the following:[939]

(a) The court exercises personal jurisdiction over a defendant.[940]
(b) Refusal of such an injunction will lead to the ends of justice being defeated and injustice will be perpetuated.[941]
(c) The principle of comity should be kept in mind and due respect should be given to the court in which the action or proceeding is sought to be restrained.

The test is appropriate and in line with other jurisdictions. It is a settled position of law that an anti-suit injunction should be granted if and only if there is an impending risk of conflicting judgments and if and only if the proceeding in the court of foreign jurisdiction would perpetuate injustice.[942]

1.5.1. *Burden of Proof*

When a party approaches a court in breach of the arbitration agreement, permitting such proceedings to continue would amount to aiding the breach.[943] Therefore, a party seeking enforcement of the arbitration agreement and requesting the issuance of an anti-suit injunction should only prove the prima facie existence of a valid arbitration agreement and proceedings before another forum in violation of it. The burden of proof in such cases cannot be high.

Currently, the test used by Indian courts for the grant of anti-suit injunctions is the test based on the CPC, i.e., prima facie case, the balance of convenience, and an irreparable injury.[944] Courts apply this test to ascertain whether there is a valid

936. Sean Hardy, Pinsent Masons MPillay & Raman Kaur, *Anti-suit Injunctions in Favour of Arbitration: A Permanent Fixture in Singapore?*, available at:https://siarb.org.sg/resources/120-articles/283-anti-suit-injunctions-in-favour-of-arbitration-a-permanent-fixture-in-singapore.
937. *Maldives Airport Co. Ltd. & Anr. v. GMR Male International Airport Pte Ltd.* [2013] SGCA 16; *BC Andaman Co. Ltd. v. Xie Ning Yun* [2017] SGHC 64; *Ever Judger Holding Co Ltd. v. Kroman Celik Sanayii Anonim Sirketi* [2015] 2 HKLRD 866; *Aggeliki Charis Cia Maritime SA v. Pagnan Spa* [1995] 1 Lloyd's Rep. 87; *Donoghue v. Armco Inc.*, [2002] 1 All ER 749.
938. *Aggeliki Charis Cia Maritime SA v. Pagnan Spa* [1995] 1 Lloyd's Rep. 87.
939. *Modi Entertainment Network v. W.S.G. Cricket Pte. Ltd.* (2003) 4 SCC 341, ¶24.
940. Atul Setalvad, *Conflict of Laws* 182-183 (2007).
941. *Union of India v. Bakhshi Amrik Singh* 1962 SCC OnLine P&H 85, at 607; *Videocon Industries Ltd. v. Union of India* (2011) 6 SCC 161, ¶58; *PPN Power Generating Company v. PPN (Mauritius) Co.* 2005 (3) Arb. LR 354, ¶50.
942. *Videocon Industries Ltd. v. Union of India* (2011) 6 SCC 161, ¶97.
943. *Modi Entertainment Network v. W.S.G. Cricket Pte. Ltd.* (2003) 4 SCC 341, ¶24.
944. *Union of India v. Videocon Industries Ltd.* 2012 SCC OnLine Del 1368, ¶110.

arbitration agreement, the risk of conflicting judgments by two forums, and the breach of the arbitration agreement.

Similar considerations would apply to an application under Section 9 for the grant of anti-suit injunctions with reference to the power to prevent harm or prejudice to the arbitral process. The court would consider the prima facie validity of the arbitration agreement[945] when considering the reasonable possibility of success. The right that has been threatened or is likely to be threatened will be the right to have the dispute resolved through arbitration. Similarly, the consideration of harm would include the deprivation of the right of the tribunal to adjudicate the dispute and aiding the breach of the arbitration agreement and the harm to be suffered by the party who has brought the court proceedings in breach of the arbitration agreement. Therefore, the standards applicable to court-ordered interim measures under Section 9 of the IAA would equally apply to anti-suit injunctions.

2. ANTI-ARBITRATION INJUNCTIONS

The idea of an anti-arbitration injunction is premised on the consensual nature of the arbitration. Parties can only be compelled to have their dispute resolved through arbitration when there is a valid legal agreement in force at the time.[946] For example, when there is a forgery or fraud[947] with respect to the arbitration agreement or there is any other arbitration agreement with respect to the subject matter raising a real possibility of parallel arbitration proceedings[948] or where the dispute has already been adjudicated or where the parties have been restrained from enforcing their rights in the agreement due to a court order or regulatory proceeding.[949]

However, even in such cases, the court has been reluctant to grant anti-arbitration injunctions as these are mixed questions of law and fact and determining whether the agreements are inoperative or incapable of being performed would amount to putting the cart before the horse.[950] Therefore, such injunctions have been issued,[951] although rarely.[952]

945. Indian Arbitration Act, 1996, S. 8 & 45.
946. Benson Lim & Adriana Uson, *Relooking at Consent in Arbitration*, (12 February 2019), available at: http://arbitrationblog.kluwerarbitration.com/2019/02/12/relooking-at-consent-in-arbitration/?doing_wp_cron = 1591432623.8983840942382812500000#: ~ :text = International%20treaties%20and%20national%20laws,is%20an%20agreement%20to%20arbitrate.
947. *India Household and Healthcare Ltd. v. LG Household and Healthcare Ltd.* (2007) 5 SCC 510, ¶10.
948. *Elektrim SA, S.A. v. Vivendi Universal SAS.A., Vivendi Telecommunication International S.A., Elektrim Telekomunikacja Sp. z.o.o, Carcom Warszawa Sp. z.o.o.* [2007] EWHC 571 (Comm).
949. Sharad Bansal, *supra* n. 894, at 615.
950. *Himachal Sorang Power Pvt. Ltd. v. NCC Infrastructure Holdings Ltd.* 2019 SCC OnLine Del 7575, ¶101.
951. *Societé Générale de Surveillance S.A. (SGS) v. Islamic Republic of Pakistan* 19 Arb. Int'l 182 (2002); *The Hub Power Company Ltd (HUBCO) v. Water and Power Development Authority of Pakistan (WAPDA)* 16 Arb. In'l 439 (2000); Michael Kerr, *Concord and Conflict in International Arbitration* 13 Arb. Int'l 121, 137 (1997); *Saipem S.p.A. v. The People's Republic of Bangladesh*, ICSID Case No. ARB/05/7, Award (30 June 2009), ¶¶167-168; Ronald J. Bettauer, *India and*

2.1. Power to Grant Anti-Arbitration Agreements

The reluctance to issue such injunctions stems from a debate on whether the courts have the power to grant anti-arbitration injunctions and whether such injunctions are compatible with the NYC and the Model Law,[953] given that neither the NYC nor the Model Law contains an express provision regarding anti-arbitration injunctions. *Fouchard* states that injunctions restraining arbitration proceedings should not be granted 'in an ideal world'.[954] It is, however, now true that there may be a situation where an anti-arbitration injunction may be intuitively justifiable[955] because an arbitral process cannot be completely isolated from the rules of international law.[956] Therefore, such injunctions are required to prevent injustice from being caused to a party by frivolous and vexatious arbitration proceedings.

Anti-arbitration injunctions were historically sought by state entities to sabotage arbitral proceedings initiated by foreign entities to force foreign entities to litigate disputes between their own courts.[957] Most often they were sought by developing countries to frustrate the arbitral process by resorting to judicial protectionism of state entities and national companies,[958] especially South-Asian countries.[959] Now such practice has also been recognised in European countries.[960] Anti-arbitration injunctions are premised on the logic that since parties can be compelled to arbitrate by the

International Arbitration: The Dabhol Experience, 41 Geo. Wash. J. Int'l L. & R. 381 (2009); *Union of India v. Dabhol Power Co.* 2002 SCC OnLine Bom 1491.

952. Lew, *supra* n. 885, at 186.
953. Doak Bishop, *Combating Arbitral Terrorism: Anti-Arbitration Injunctions Increasingly Threaten to Frustrate the International Arbitral System*, available at: https://www.kslaw.com/library/pdf/bishop7.pdf; Andre de A Cavalcanti Abbud and Gustavo Santos Kulesza, *Interim Measures and Anti-Arbitration Injunctions in Brazil*, (4 August 2014), available at: http://kluwerarbitrationblog.com/2014/08/04/interim-measures-and-anti-arbitration-injunctions-in-brazil/; Mostafa A Hagras, *The Egyptian Arbitration Law and Anti-Arbitation Injunctions due to Expiry the Time Limit for the Final Award: Case Study*, available at:https://youngicca-blog.com/the-egyptian-arbitration-law-and-anti-arbitration-injunctions-due-to-expiry-the-time-limit-for-the-final-award-case-study/.
954. Philippe Fouchard, *Anti-Suit Injunctions in International Arbitration What Remedies?: – Anti-Suit Injunctions in International Arbitration* 154 (2005).
955. Hakeem Seriki, *Anti-arbitration Injunctions and the English Courts: Judicial Interference or Judicial Protection?*, Int'l Arb. L. R. 43, 44 (2013).
956. Sairam Subramanian, *Anti-arbitration Injunctions and Their Relief Compatibility with the New York Convention and the Indian Law of Arbitration: Future Directions for Indian Law and Policy*, 34 (2) Arb. Int'l. 185, 215 (2017).
957. Blackby, *supra* n. 34, at 457-458.
958. Doak Bishop, *supra n.* 953.
959. *Societé Générale de Surveillance S.A. (SGS) v. Islamic Republic of Pakistan* 19 Arb. Int'l 182 (2002); *The Hub Power Company Ltd (HUBCO) v. Water and Power Development Authority of Pakistan (WAPDA)* 16 Arb. In'l 439 (2000); Kerr, *supra* n. 951; *Saipem S.p.A. v. The People's Republic of Bangladesh*, ICSID Case No. ARB/05/7, Award (30 June 2009), ¶¶167-168; Ronald J. Bettauer, *India and International Arbitration: The Dabhol Experience*, 41 Geo. Wash. J. Int'l L. & R. 381 (2009); *Union of India v. Dabhol Power Co.* 2002 SCC OnLine Bom 1491.
960. Pierre A. Karrer, *Anti-Arbitration Injunctions: Theory and Practice*, in Albert Jan Van den Berg (ed.), International Arbitration 2006: Back to Basics? 229 (2007) *discussing the position in Switzerland; Air (PTY) Ltd. v. International Air Transport Association (IATA)and C. SA, Republic and Canton of Geneva Judiciary*, Court of First Instance, C/1043/2005-15SP, 2 May 2005; *In France the New Code of Civil Procedure bars the court's jurisdiction to determine the*

court, the court can equally restrain the parties from resorting to arbitration though some consider this to be a step too far.[961]

Such injunctions are also justified on the premise that a detailed statutory regime impliedly overrides inherent jurisdiction,[962] and there is a presumption that the statutory regime is drafted in a manner consistent with treaty obligations.[963] For example, Section 32 of the English Arbitration Act specifically provides for the court to issue a declaration with respect to the jurisdiction of the arbitral tribunal.[964]

The opposite view is that such injunctions are threats and breaches to the efficacy, integrity, and in some cases, the very viability of international arbitration.[965] Anti-arbitration injunctions violate conventional principles of customary law, international public policy, and the accepted principles of international arbitration.[966] Hence, tribunals and courts should be prohibited to enjoin.[967] There was even a suggestion for an 'International Pledge to Arbitrate Commercial Disputes' reaffirming the intent to arbitrate on a future date to prevent anti-arbitration injunctions.[968]

Therefore, such injunctions are considered to de facto deprive the tribunal of its right to determine its own jurisdiction.[969] Despite having agreed to an arbitration agreement and agreeing to have the dispute resolved before a neutral forum, the party invoking arbitration finds itself confronted by a jurisdiction that will judge its conduct according to a very different yardstick. Apart from the paranoia of corruption and xenophobia, everything is suddenly in favour of the defendant, such as language, procedure, practical convenience, ability to use one's own lawyers, or the cultural

validity of an arbitration agreement, John Savage, & Emmanuel Gaillard, *Fouchard Gaillard and Goldman on International Commercial Arbitration* 407 (1999); *The information on the COPEL v. UEGA case was provided by Mr Mauricio Gomm Ferreira Dos Santos who reported on this case in a paper prepared for the 4th Annual ICDR/AAA Meeting in Miami, 26-28 March 2006,* c.f. Lew, *supra* n. 885, at 213.

961. Jennifer, *supra* n. 891, at 307.
962. *Etri Fans Ltd. v. NMB (UK) Ltd.* 1987 WL 492164.
963. *Since this lecture was delivered a contrary decision has been reached in another DIFC case International Electromechanical Services Co LLC v. Al Fattan Engineering LLC Claim No: CF 004/2012,* Judgment 14 October 2012. The case is discussed in Clemmie Spalton *DIFC Court Sends Pro-arbitration Message* (23 October 2012), available at: http://www.globalarbitrationreview.com/news/article/30923/difc-courtsends-pro-arbitration-message/. c.f. David A.R. Williams, *Defining the Role of the Court in Modern International Commercial Arbitration,* Asian Int'l Arb. J. 137, 153 (2014).
964. *AES Ust-Kamenogorsk Hydropower Plant LLP v. Ust-Kamenogorsk Hydropower Plant JSC* [2011] EWCA Civ 647; *Vale do Rio Doce Navegacao SA v. Shanghai Bao Steel Ocean Shipping Co Ltd* [2000] EWHC 205 (Comm); *Dallah Real Estate and Tourism Co v. Ministry of Religious Affairs of the Government of Pakistan* [2010] UKSC 46; Andrew Cannon, *An Anti-suit Injunction to Protect a Non-existent Arbitration,* (30 June 2011), available at:http://arbitrationblog.kluwerarbitration.com/2011/06/30/anti-suit-injunction/.
965. Schwebel, *supra* n. 898, at 5.
966. Lew, *supra* n. 885, at 216; Schwebel, *supra* n. 898, at 5.
967. Pierre, *supra* n. 960, at 230.
968. Michael McIlwrath, *Anti-Arbitration: An International Pledge to Arbitrate Commercial Disputes?,* (29 March 2011), available at: http://arbitrationblog.kluwerarbitration.com/2011/03/29/anti-arbitration-an-international-pledge-to-arbitrate-commercial-disputes/?doing_wp_cron=1590838546.9601058959960937500000.
969. Frédéric Bachand, *The UNCITRAL Model Law's Take on Anti-Suit Injunctions,* in Emmanuel Galliard (ed.), *Anti-suit Injunctions in international Arbitration* 88 (2005).

affinities with the judges.[970] Such advantages to one party are precisely what the parties chose to avoid by opting for arbitration instead of litigation before domestic courts.[971] Thus, anti-arbitration injunctions promote battles in State Courts, which the NYC clearly sought to avoid. Such injunctions lead to diverging decisions and the fight between various jurisdictions on recognition and enforcement.[972]

2.2. International Practice

The practice across jurisdictions has not been consistent with respect to anti-arbitration injunctions. In one of the earliest decisions,[973] a US court held that the power to order an anti-arbitration injunction is concomitant with the power to compel arbitration.[974] When the parties have not entered into a valid and binding arbitration agreement, the court has the authority to enjoin the arbitration proceedings.[975] Also, courts generally have the power to issue an injunction to give effect to their interpretation of a contract and hence can grant an injunction declaring that the contract does not provide for a valid arbitration.[976] If arbitration proceedings are not stayed, it will frustrate the goals of arbitration since there would be a delay and increased expense as the parties litigate in both fora.[977]

On the contrary, another US court[978] refused to grant an anti-arbitration injunction noting that it was not supported by the provision of the Federal Arbitration Act and the NYC. It also held that the power to compel the parties to go for arbitration is not synonymous with the power to enjoin arbitration.[979] Furthermore, when a request for an anti-arbitration injunction is made with respect to a foreign seated arbitration, the issuance of anti-arbitration injunction risks interfering with a proceeding that has been brought in another jurisdiction and is subject to another forum's arbitration law.[980]

Despite the divergence of views, a majority of the decisions by the courts in the United States have held that since the courts can compel arbitration, they can restrain

970. Jan Paulson, *Interference by National Courts in Lawrence*, in W. Newman & Richard D. Hill (eds), *The Leading Arbitrators Guide to International Arbitration* 124 (2004).
971. Lew, *supra* n. 885, at 186.
972. Chrysanthi Markaki, *Anti-suit v. Anti-arbitration Injunctions in International Commercial Arbitration: Which One Prevails in European Union, UK and Greece? Choosing the Most 'Proper' One* 14 (2018), available at: https://repository.ihu.edu.gr/xmlui/bitstream/handle/11544/29126/c.markaki_llm_16-02-2018.pdf?sequence = 2.
973. *Satcom International Group PLC v. Orbcomm International Partners. LP*, 49 F Supp 2d 331, 342.
974. *Société Généralé de Surveillance, SA, v. Raytheon European Management and Systems Co* 643 F 2d. 863 (1st Cir 1981), at 868.
975. *In re American Express Financial Advisors Securities Litigation*, 672 F.3d 113, (2d Cir. 2011), at 140.
976. Jennifer, *supra* n. 891, at 308.
977. *This decision was subsequently followed in Glen P Farrel v. Subway International* 2011 WL 1085017; *Firooz Ghassabian v. Fatollah Hematian, No. 08 Civ. 4400 (SAS)* 2008 WL 3982885, at 2; UNCITRAL Yearbook, A/CN.9/SER.A/2002, Volume (XXXIII: 2002).
978. *URS Corporation v. Lebanese Company for the Development and Reconstruction of Beirut Central District SAL* 512 F. Supp. 2d 199 (2007), ¶15.
979. *Affirmed in the case of, Firooz Ghassabian v. Fatollah Hematian, No. 08 Civ. 4400 (SAS)* 2008 WL 3982885, at 2; UNCITRAL Yearbook, A/CN.9/SER.A/2002, Volume (XXXIII: 2002).
980. Jennifer, *supra* n. 891, at 314-315.

arbitration as well when the arbitration agreement is found to be invalid.[981] The divergence is on the legal basis of the exercise of such power, i.e., whether it is procedural[982] or whether it is an inherent power of the court.[983] It is pertinent to note that some statutes such as the Massachusetts State Arbitration Statute and the New York Civil Procedure Law and Rules specifically provide the authority to the court to stay arbitration proceedings in certain circumstances.[984]

In contrast, initially, the courts in the United Kingdom held that injunctions could only be granted in the circumstances specially stipulated in the English Arbitration Act and there is no provision for anti-arbitration injunctions.[985] This view has now changed. The power to grant anti-arbitration injunctions in the United Kingdom is derived from Section 9(4) of the English Arbitration Act and also Section 37 of the Senior Courts Act 1981.[986] The English Courts have also accepted the compatibility of anti-arbitration injunctions with the NYC.[987] A similar view has been adopted by the courts in Australia and New Zealand that such injunctions can be granted when considered appropriate.[988]

In a similar trend, Article 1448 of the French Civil Procedure Code provides that the court will ordinarily decline jurisdiction when the dispute is subject to an arbitration agreement unless the arbitral tribunal has not yet been seized of the dispute and if the arbitration agreement is manifestly void or manifestly not applicable. This is contrary to the earlier practice followed in most civil law countries[989] and French cases, which held that the issuance of an anti-arbitration injunction in France is not permissible[990] and was considered an assault on the integrity of the arbitral process.[991]

981. *Kaepa Inc. v. Achilles Corporation*, 76 F.3d 624, 626 (5th Cir. 1996); Sharad Bansal, *supra* n. 894, at 618; Jennifer, *supra* n. 891, at 297.
982. *Société Géneralé de Surveillance, SA, v. Raytheon European Management and Systems Co* 643 F 2d. 863 (1st Cir 1981), at 868.
983. *Satcom International Group PLC v. Orbcomm International Partners. LP*, 49 F Supp 2d 331.
984. Massachusetts General Laws, 2018, S. 2(b): *Upon application, the superior court may stay an arbitration proceeding commenced or threatened if it finds that there is no agreement to arbitrate. Such an issue, when in substantial and bona fide dispute, shall be forthwith and summarily determined, and if the court finds for the applicant it shall order a stay of arbitration; otherwise the court shall order the parties to proceed to arbitration*; New York Civil Practice Law and Rules, 2012, S. 7503(b) *Application to stay arbitration. Subject to the provisions of subdivision (c), a party who has not participated in the arbitration and who has not made or been served with an application to compel arbitration, may apply to stay arbitration on the ground that a valid agreement was not made or has not been complied with or that the claim sought to be arbitrated is barred by limitation under subdivision (b) of section 7502.*
985. *Elektrim SA, S.A. v. Vivendi Universal SAS.A., Vivendi Telecommunication International S.A., Elektrim Telekomunikacja Sp. z.o.o, Carcom Warszawa Sp. z.o.o.* [2007] EWHC 571 (Comm).
986. *Fiona Trust & Holding Corporation & Others v. Yuri Privalov & Ors.* [2015] EWHC 527 (Comm).
987. *Welex AG v. Rosa Maritime Ltd. (The Epsilon Rosa)* [2003] EWCA Civ 938.
988. Lew, *supra* n. 885, at 199.
989. Jeffrey Waincymer, *International Arbitration the Process of an Arbitration* 664 (2012); *The same is the position in Switzerland.*
990. *Equatorial Guinea v. Fitzpatrick Equatorial Guinea (29 March 2010); S.A Elf Aquitaine and Total v. Mattei, Lai, Kamara and Reiner* (6 January 2010), *c.f.* Alexis Mourre, *French Courts Firmly Reject Anti-Arbitration Injunctions*, (6 May 2010), available at: http://arbitrationblog.kluwerarbitration.com/2010/05/06/french-courts-firmly-reject-anti-arbitration-injunctions/?doing_wp_cron=1591465914.9855411052703857421875.

In Sweden, the power is clearly recognised as a party may request the court to declare a judgment on the jurisdiction of the tribunal before the arbitrators have rendered an award on the issue.[992] There are no provisions, however, under Swiss Law for granting anti-arbitration injunctions[993] and such injunctions are contrary to the Swiss Legal System.[994]

The most notable recognition of the power to grant anti-suit injunctions is recognised in recital 12 of the Recast Brussels 1 Regulation, which provides language similar to the NYC.[995] Recently, an Argentinian Court ordered a company not to initiate investment arbitration before the ICSID.[996] Therefore, there is a growing trend towards the acceptability of anti-arbitration injunctions across jurisdictions.

However, there are strong views that oppose such injunctions as well. Such views are premised on the fundamental mandate under the NYC that the courts should refer the parties to the arbitration and that the principle of *Kompetenz-kompetenz*[997] mandates that jurisdictional validity is the domain of the arbitral tribunal.[998] This view has been affirmed by the ICSID Tribunal in *Sapem v. Bangladesh.*[999] The tribunal observed that anti-arbitration injunctions amount to a violation of the principle embedded in Article II of the NYC and hence are violative of the obligations of the states under the NYC.[1000]

The opposition to anti-arbitration injunctions arises from two apparent conflicts, i.e., (1) the conflict between Article II(3) and Article V(1)(a) of the NYC; and (2) the conflict between Article 16 of the Model Law and Article II(3) of the NYC.

991. Michael Reisman & Heide Iravani, *The Changing Relation of National Courts and International Commercial Arbitration,* 21 Am. R. Int'l Arb. 5, 33 (2010).
992. Lew, *supra* n. 885, at 196.
993. *Ibid.*, at 194.
994. Marco Stacher & Michael Feit, *Chapter 18, Part VII: Parallel Proceedings and Lis Pendens,* in Manuel Arroyo (ed.), *Arbitration in Switzerland: The Practitioner's Guide* 2639 (2018); *Air (PTY) Ltd. v. International Air Transport Association (IATA)and C. SA, Republic and Canton of Geneva Judiciary,* Court of First Instance, C/1043/2005-15SP, 2 May 2005, c.f. Lew, *supra* n. 885, at 885.
995. Crina, *supra* n. 882, at 257.
996. Emmanuel Kaufman, *An Argentine Court Orders a Corporation Not to Initiate Arbitration Before ICSID: Should Investors Be Worried?,* (5 June 2019), available at:http://arbitrationblog.kluwerarbitration.com/2019/06/05/an-argentine-court-orders-a-corporation-not-to-initiate-arbitration-before-icsid-should-investors-be-worried/?doing_wp_cron = 1589866347.6500990390777587890625.
997. *West Tankers Inc v. Allianz Spa* [2009] ECR 1-663, ¶57; *Amtrust Europe Ltd. v. Trust Risk Group SpA* [2015] EWHC 1927 (Comm.); *Dallah Real Estate and Tourism Co v. Ministry of Religious Affairs of the Government of Pakistan* [2010] UKSC 46, ¶¶ 84-85. *Affirmed in Himachal Sorang Power Pvt. Ltd. v. NCC Infrastructure Holdings Ltd.* 2019 SCC OnLine Del 7575, ¶108.
998. Emmanuel Gaillard, *Reflections on the Use of Anti-Suit Injunction in International Arbitration,* in Loukas Mistelis & Julian Lew (eds), *Pervasive Problems in International Arbitration* 203-15 (2006); *see Nicholas Poon, The Use and Abuse of Anti-Arbitration Injunctions: A Way Forward for Singapore,* 25 Sac. L. J. 244 - 95 (2013); Lew, *supra* n. 885, at 185.
999. *Saipem S.p.A. v. The People's Republic of Bangladesh,* ICSID Case No. ARB/05/7, Decision on Jurisdiction and Recommendation on Provisional Measures (21 March 2007).
1000. Jennifer, *supra* n. 891, at 314.

2.3. Conflict Within the New York Convention

One of the reasons for opposing anti-arbitration injunctions is the language of Article II(3) of the NYC which requires a Contracting State to refer parties to arbitration unless it finds the said agreement to be null and void, inoperative, or incapable of being performed. A similar provision is also contained in Article V(1)(a) of the NYC in the post-award stage as a ground for setting aside the award.[1001]

The argument against anti-arbitration injunctions, therefore, is premised on a mandatory reference to arbitration under Article II(3) of the NYC, with the tribunal deciding its jurisdiction. Thus, the only remedy against an invalid arbitration agreement should be an application for setting aside the award. *Born* argues that every contracting state has the right to review the decision passed by an arbitral tribunal under the enforcement mechanism of the NYC and an anti-arbitration injunction would directly conflict with this right. He argues that when agreeing to arbitrate, the parties not only waive their access to judicial remedies but also affirmatively agree to participate in the resolution of the disputes through the arbitral process.[1002]

The contrary view, however, is that without a proper, enforceable, and controlling arbitration agreement, there is no legal obligation to refer disputes to arbitration.[1003] Therefore, when parties have not in fact 'agreed to arbitrate', such waiver of access to judicial remedies cannot be implied. Article II(3) of the NYC refers to the pre-arbitral stage, where the mere presence of an arbitration clause does not operate as an ouster of the court's jurisdiction.[1004] The language contained in Article II(3) of the NYC protects valid and enforceable arbitration agreements but offers more protection to non-existence or enforceable arbitration agreement.[1005] Thus, the national courts will first have to determine whether the arbitration agreement suffers from any of the three legal infirmities and only in the absence of the same can the parties be referred to arbitration.

The mandate and applicability of Article V(1)(a) of the NYC are entirely different. A bare perusal of the above two articles leads to the conclusion that pre-arbitral interference by courts is contemplated under Article II(3) of the NYC when the court has to ascertain a valid request for arbitration.[1006] Subsequently, after a full trial by the arbitral tribunal, if a party has sufficient grounds to show that the arbitral tribunal incorrectly applied the law chosen by the parties, then an application under Article V(1)(a) can be made to set aside the award.[1007] The validity considered at the stage of a setting aside application would clearly mean something more than a prima facie lack

1001. Subramanian, *supra* n. 956 at 188.
1002. Gary Born, *supra* n. 33, at 1093.
1003. Thomas E. Carbonneau, *Toward a New Federal Law on Arbitration* 16 (2014).
1004. Henry Bernard Eder, *The Key Role of State Courts Before the Commencement of Arbitral Proceedings: Referral to Arbitration and Provisional and Conservatory Measures*, 18(1) Asian Dis. R. 16, 19 (2016).
1005. Julian D.M. Lew, *Anti-Suit Injunctions Issued by National Courts to Prevent Arbitration Proceedings*, in Emamuel Gaillard (ed.), *Anti-Suit Injunctions in International Arbitration* 32 (2005).
1006. Paulson, *supra* n. 970, at 114.
1007. *Shin-Etsu Chemical Co Ltd. v. Aksh Optifibre Ltd.* (2005) 7 SCC 234, ¶¶75, 86 and 104.

of consent, or some mixed questions of law and fact which would not have been apparent at the stage of reference under Article II of the NYC.

Therefore, a party approaching a court of law requesting an interim measure to stay the arbitral proceedings would have to satisfy Article II(3) of the NYC to show that the reference to arbitration would cause injustice to the party as it makes no sense to compel a party to litigate before the arbitral tribunal, the jurisdiction of which the party denies, only to have the award ultimately set aside under Article V(1)(a) of the NYC. If the same cannot be demonstrated, then the overarching mandate of Articles 5 and 8(1) of the Model Law will apply and the parties should be referred to arbitration without any interference by the court.[1008]

The international practice with respect to the standard of review of the validity of the arbitration agreement under Article II(3) of the NYC has, however, not been consistent. Some courts in England,[1009] Ireland,[1010] Germany, some Canadian jurisdictions, New Zealand, and Australia have insisted on a full review of the validity of the arbitration agreement,[1011] but not without due criticism.[1012] Other courts like Singapore,[1013] some Canadian jurisdictions, Bermuda, and Hong Kong limit the review to a prima facie standard.[1014]

Even Article II(3) of the NYC refers to this prima facie determination,[1015] i.e., very fundamental errors,[1016] without evidence.[1017] In contrast, Article V(1)(a) of the NYC refers to invalidity after a full trial,[1018] based on misapplication or misinterpretation of law and facts.

1008. *Marnell Corrao Associates Inc v. Se sation Yachts Ltd.* (2000) 15 PRNZ 608, at 61-62; *Zermalt Holdings v. Nu-Life Upholstery Repairs* [1985] 2 EGLR 14, at 15; *Money v. Ven-Lu-Ree Ltd.* [1988] 2 NZLR 414 (CA), at 417; *Manukau City Council v. Fencible Court Howick Ltd.* [1991] 3 NZLR 410 (CA), at 412; *Lord Mustill's remarks in Pupuke Service Station Ltd v. Caltex Oil (NZ) Ltd.* Appeal No. 63/94, 16 November 1995 *reported as an appendix to Gold and Resource Developments (NZ) Ltd v. Doug Hood Ltd* [2000] 3 NZLR, 318 at 1.

1009. *China Export and Credit Insurance Corp v. Emerald Energy Resources Ltd.* [2018] EWHC 1503 (Comm).

1010. *Barnmore Demolition and Civil Engineering Ltd. & Alandale Logistics Ltd., et al., No. 5910P – though this issue was not finally decided. Even though the court noted that the parties could not even demonstrate the prima facie existence of an arbitration agreement.* Gary Born, *Irish High Court on Full Versus Prima Facie Judicial Consideration of Whether an Arbitration Agreement Exists*, (13 December 2010), available at: http://arbitrationblog.kluwerarbitration.com/2010/12/13/irish-high-court-on-full-versus-prima-facie-judicial-consideration-of-whether-an-arbitration-agreement-exists/?doing_wp_cron=1590838569.4271209239959716796875.

1011. *Ibid.*

1012. Duncan Bagshaw, *Stay No More: English Commercial Court Reviews Section 9 Test (Again)*, (10 August 2018), available at: https://www.shlegal.com/insights/stay-no-more-english-commercial-court-reviews-section-9-test-(again); Georgios Martsekis, *Everyone Should Do His Own or Everyone Should Have His Own? An Analysis on the Requirements of Conferral of the Arbitral Tribunal's Jurisdiction*, (30 May 2020), available at: http://arbitrationblog.kluwerarbitration.com/2020/05/30/everyone-should-do-his-own-or-everyone-should-have-his-own-an-analysis-on-the-requirements-of-conferral-of-the-arbitral-tribunals-jurisdiction/?doing_wp_cron=1591467627.8653640747070312500000.

1013. *Tomolugen Holdings Ltd. and Anrs. v. Silica Investors Ltd and Ors.* [2015] SGCA 57.

1014. Gary Born, *supra* n. 1010.

1015. *Shin-Etsu Chemical Co Ltd. v. Aksh Optifibre Ltd.* (2005) 7 SCC 234, ¶97.

1016. *Lesotho Highlands v. Impreglio SpA* [2005] UKHL 43, at 18.

1017. *Shin-Etsu Chemical Co Ltd. v. Aksh Optifibre Ltd.* (2005) 7 SCC 234, ¶79.

1018. *Ibid.*, ¶¶75, 86 and 104.

2.4. The Conflict Between the New York Convention and the Model Law

Another ground for opposing anti-arbitration injunctions is that they violate the principle contained in Article 16(1) of the Model Law, which explicitly empowers the arbitral tribunal to '*rule on its own jurisdiction, including any objections with respect to the existence or validity of the arbitration agreement*'. In fact, the subsequent sentences specifically refer to the power of the tribunal to hold that the contract is null and void. The issuance of anti-arbitration denies the tribunal this right and the courts should, therefore, refer parties to arbitration under Article 8(1) of the Model Law. Article 8(2) of the Model Law provides that arbitral proceedings may nevertheless be commenced or continued and an award may be made while the issue is pending before the court. Therefore, an anti-arbitration injunction directly violates Article 8(2) of the Model Law.

Article 8(1) of the Model Law also provides for a similar limitation as contained in Article II(3) of the NYC. The mandate to refer parties to arbitration is subject to the court not finding the arbitration agreement null and void, inoperative, or incapable of being performed. It is pertinent to note that the *travaux préparatoires* of Article 5 of the Model Law does not take a stand on the proper role of the courts. It merely requires that any instance of court involvement be listed in the Model Law.[1019] Courts remain able to intervene where matters of international commercial arbitration proceedings are not governed by the Model Law[1020] as the Model Law is not a comprehensive code on all matters related to arbitration or judicial intervention in arbitration proceedings.[1021] The mandate of Article 5 applies only to 'matters governed by this law'.[1022] It does not oust the inherent jurisdiction to stay arbitral proceedings[1023] when the arbitration agreement is null and void, inoperative, or incapable of being performed.

Based on the above, the argument that anti-arbitration injunctions violate the principle of *Kompetenz-kompetenz* may be slightly misplaced. The principle of *Kompetenz-kompetenz* is not inflexible and absolute.[1024] It only serves as a measure to protect the derailment of arbitration proceedings before they begin on the mere

1019. Report of Secretary General on Analytical Commentary on Draft Text of A Model Law on International Commercial Arbitration, in its Eighteenth Session, (1985), UN Doc A/CN.9/264, available at: https://undocs.org/en/A/CN.9/264; UNCITRAL Yearbook, A/CN.9/SER.A/1 985, Volume (XVI: 1985).;*Coppee-Lavalin SA/NV Ken-Ren Chemicals and Fertilisers Ltd.* [1995] 1 AC 38 (HL); *Channel Tunnel Group Ltd. v. Balfour Beatty Construction Ltd.* [1993] 2 WLR 262.

1020. David, *supra* n. 963, at 142. *A similar view was taken in China Ocean Shipping Co., Owners of the M/V Fu Ning Hai v. Whistler International Ltd, Charters of the M/V Fu Ning Hai,* [1999] HKCFI 693 by the Hong Kong Court and by the UK Departmental Advisory Committee. Lord Justice Mustill, *A New Arbitration Act for the United Kingdom?: The Response of the Departmental Advisory Committee to the UNCITRAL Model Law*, 6 (1) Arb. Int'l 3, 51 (1990).

1021. *Carter Holt Harvey Ltd v. Genesis Power Ltd.* [2006] 3 NZLR 794 (HC).

1022. Mustill, *supra* n. 1020.

1023. *Carter Holt Harvey Ltd v. Genesis Power Ltd.* [2006] 3 NZLR 794 (HC); *Vale do Rio Doce Navegacao SA v. Shanghai Bao Steel Ocean Shipping Co Ltd.* [2000] EWHC 205 (Comm), at 48; *AES Ust-Kamenogorks Hydropower Plant LLP v. Ust-Kamenogorsk Hydropower Plant JSC* [2011] EWCA Civ 647; *Nomihold Securities INC v. Mobile Telesystems Finance SA* [2012] Bus LR 1289, at 26 *per Andrew Smith J.*

1024. *Dallah Real Estate and Tourism Co v. Ministry of Religious Affairs of the Government of Pakistan* [2010] UKSC 46; Subramanian, *supra* n. 956 at 189.

allegation that the arbitration clauses are unenforceable due to any number of contract law defences.[1025] It nonetheless respects the point that a person who has not agreed to arbitrate cannot have its legal right affected by the decisions of the tribunal.[1026]

The recognition of this principle is contained in Section 72 of the English Arbitration Act. A person can approach the court if he claims that he is not bound by an arbitration agreement. A party cannot, and should not, be forced to appear before an arbitral tribunal when the very existence of the arbitration agreement is in question and the consent to it is challenged.[1027] If the tribunal is in a foreign jurisdiction, then forcing a party to appear before such a tribunal at the cost of time and money[1028] cannot be justified under the mandate of Article 5 and a partial application of Article 8(1) of the Model Law and Article II(3) of the NYC.[1029]

Therefore, a harmonious reading of Article II(3) of the NYC and Article 16(1) of the Model Law suggests that it is the tribunal which should decide questions of existence and validity of the arbitration agreement unless when a reference is made to a court and it is prima facie apparent that the arbitration agreement is null and void, or inoperative, or incapable of being performed.

Reading the two provisions together, there is little room to contend that court interference is not envisaged at the pre-arbitral stage. To argue that questions of existence and validity can only be determined by the tribunal would render the language '*unless it finds that the agreement is null or void, inoperative, or incapable of being performed*' in Article 8(1) of the Model Law and Article II(3) of the NYC redundant.[1030] The thin line for consideration is simply whether a party which has not even validly signed the arbitration agreement should be compelled to appear before the arbitration tribunal vis-à-vis a party which has signed the arbitration agreement but questions the jurisdiction of the tribunal.[1031]

2.5. Harmonising the Model Law and the New York Convention

It should be noted that questions regarding the implementation of Article II(3) of the NYC are left to the contracting states to answer in their legislation and court practice.[1032] Under the Model Law, a provision permitting a party opposing arbitration to have the arbitration agreement declared invalid was deleted.[1033] Also, the mandate of

1025. William W. Park, *The Arbitrator's Jurisdiction to Determine Jurisdiction, I. Introduction: The Limits of Language*, in Albert Jan Van den Berg (ed.), *International Arbitration 2006: Back to Basics?* 58 (2007).
1026. Steven Gee & Lord Bingham, *AntiSuit Injunctions and Arbitration*, in Mads Andenas & Duncan Fairgrieve (eds), *Tom Bingham and the Transformation of the Law: A Liber Amicorum* 642 (2009).
1027. Nadja Erk-Kubat, *Parallel Proceedings in International Arbitration: A Comparative European Perspective* 74-75 (2014).
1028. *CG Holding Pvt Ltd. v. Ramasamy Athappan* 2011 SCC OnLine Mad 1078, ¶94.
1029. *Bharti Televentures Ltd. v. DSS Enterprises Pvt. Ltd* 2005 (2) Arb. LR 561, ¶1.
1030. *Shin-Etsu Chemical Co Ltd. v. Aksh Optifibre Ltd.* (2005) 7 SCC 234, ¶85.
1031. Lew, *supra* n. 885, at 189.
1032. Nadja, *supra* n. 1027, at 102.
1033. *See* Gary Born, *supra* n. 33.

limiting court interference in Article 5 of the Model Law applies only to the seat of arbitration,[1034] whereas Article 8 applies irrespective of the seat of arbitration.[1035] Moreover, the recognition and enforcement of a fraudulent agreement violate the integrity of the court.[1036]

Hence, the reference contemplated under Article 8(1) of the Model Law and Article II(3) of the NYC is one where the party bringing the claim does so before a court of law, despite having agreed to have the dispute resolved through arbitration. Whereas, an anti-arbitration injunction is sought by the defendant, who has received the notice of arbitration and contends that the same is invalid as there is no arbitration agreement, to begin with. The defendant essentially argues that the defence of *exceptio arbitri* is not applicable.[1037]

A reference illustrating this harmony can be easily discerned from Section 9 of the English Arbitration Act which provides for the grant of a stay of legal proceedings brought in violation of the arbitration agreement unless the court is satisfied that the arbitration agreement is null and void, inoperative, or incapable of being performed.[1038] The English Court confirmed that arbitration tribunals, not courts, have jurisdiction to determine the validity of a contract that is subject to an arbitration agreement, even in cases where that contract has been induced by fraud, misrepresentation or bribery.[1039] This obligation applies even if the seat is outside England.[1040]

The mandate under Article 8(1) of the Model Law and Article II(3) of the NYC is, therefore, very different and primarily seeks to uphold the bargain between the parties. In contrast, the request for an anti-arbitration injunction stems from the right of a party to approach the court for any grievance unless the suit is either expressly or impliedly barred.[1041] Thus, the grievances on which a suit is maintainable are, in essence, recognised in Article 8(1) of the Model Law and Article II(3) of the NYC in the context of arbitration.[1042]

2.6. Jurisdiction for Anti-Arbitration Injunctions

If it is accepted that anti-arbitration injunctions are permissible, then the next plausible question is which court shall have the power to grant them? Will it be the court under the *lex arbitri* or can any other court apart from the *lex arbitri* issue such an injunction

1034. Lew, *supra* n. 885, at 198.
1035. UNCITRAL Model Law, Art. 1(2).
1036. Steven Gee, *supra* n. 1026, at 643.
1037. Nadja, *supra* n. 1027, at 72.
1038. UNCITRAL Model Law, Art. 8(1) '*court before which an action is brought in a matter which is subject of an arbitration shall, if a party so requests no later than when submitting his first statement on the substance of the dispute, refer the parties to arbitration unless it finds that the agreement is null and void, inoperative or incapable of being performed. Unlike* UNCITRAL Model Law, Art. 8, Indian Arbitration Act, 1996, S. 9, *does not instruct the court to "refer the parties to arbitration"*'.
1039. *Fiona Trust & Holding Corporation & Others v. Yuri Privalov & Ors.* [2015] EWHC 527 (Comm).
1040. Indian Arbitration Act, 1996, S. 2(2)(a).
1041. Indian Code of Civil Procedure, 1908, S. 9.
1042. Park, *supra* n. 1025, at 57.

as the NYC applies to all signatories apart from the seat? If anti-arbitration agreements are to be permissible under the NYC, then all signatories would be equally empowered to issue them. Or should it be the court at the place where the requesting party resides? Or should it be the courts of the place whose law the parties have chosen to govern their dispute?

2.6.1. Seat Theory

One view is that the most natural forum for the determination of the dispute is the seat of arbitration[1043] as it promotes legal certainty and reduces the possibility of conflict between the arbitration award and the judgment of a national court.[1044] This view is also taken by the courts in the United States[1045] and the United Kingdom[1046] for two reasons (a) because the court of the seat is given priority over-interpreting its own arbitration laws which it best understands; and (b) that all courts would try to protect their domestic litigants in complete violation of the arbitration agreements.[1047]

However, the argument in favour of the courts at the seat ignores the applicability of the proper law of the contract, i.e., the law which will presumably determine the validity of the arbitration agreement and as such the courts at the seat may not be fully qualified or best equipped to deal with the question. Forcing a party to appear before the courts in a foreign seat would have the same effect as forcing a party to contest a foreign litigation at the cost of its time and money[1048] which is the reason why anti-suit injunctions are also issued.

Also, in the absence of a valid arbitration agreement, it is unclear as to how the seat will have jurisdiction over the parties unless the courts at the seat exercise in personam jurisdiction over the parties. Given that parties often choose a neutral place as the seat and neither party has commercial operations or assets in such jurisdictions, the issuance of an injunction by a court over parties which are not subject to its in personam jurisdiction would result in a paper order incapable of enforcement. The other problem with the seat theory is that a party will be forced to submit to adjudication the non-existence of the arbitration agreement under the law of the seat set forth in an arbitration clause which it contends is not binding.[1049] It should also be noted that members of the tribunal are very often foreigners. Hence, courts would not have personal jurisdiction over them, and as a result, the court would have no jurisdiction to pass orders against the tribunal.[1050]

Approaching any court in any jurisdiction, whether it is the court of the place whose governing law is applicable or the seat, or the place of residence of the

1043. Gaffney, *supra* n. 897, at 116.
1044. *Allianz SpA and Generali Assicurazioni Generali v. West Tankers Inc.* (EU:C:2009:69), ¶17; *Alfred C. Toepfer International GgmbH v. Societe Cargill France*, [1997] EWCA Civ 2811.
1045. Strong, *supra* n. 888, at 176.
1046. *Pena Copper Mines Ltd. v. Rio Tinto Co Ltd.*, (1911) 105 LT 846.
1047. Sharad Bansal, *supra* n. 894, at 621.
1048. *Ibid.*
1049. Jennifer, *supra* n. 891, at 318.
1050. *Noy Vallesina Engineering Spa v. Jindal Drugs Ltd.* 2006 (3) Arb. LR 510 (Bom), ¶45.

defendant, may have the same effect for each party, depending on the jurisdiction and nationality of the parties. Therefore, there must be clear criteria for courts to exercise jurisdiction when issuing anti-arbitration injunctions. In the absence of a proper territorial nexus with the court issuing the anti-arbitration injunction, the efficacy of the same may be compromised and such an order may also be violative of the conflict of law rules of the parties' countries.

2.6.2. Habitual Residence

Allowing every nation to issue an anti-arbitration injunction is also not the right view as it will result in forum shopping and will impede arbitration practice. The better view is that the defendant should approach the court where the defendant 'habitually resides'.[1051] Since the mandate of non-interference contained in Article 5 of the Model Law applies only to the country of the seat in accordance with Article 1(2) of the Model Law[1052] and Article 8 of the Model Law applies irrespective of the seat of arbitration, there exists sufficient basis for pre-arbitral court interference for the respondent to an arbitration proceeding to file a request for an anti-arbitration injunction in the country in which the party resides.[1053]

A possible criticism of this view can be that the claimant (in the arbitration proceedings), in most cases, would not be subject to the in personam jurisdiction of the defendant's court. However, it makes little sense to have an anti-arbitration injunction issued by the court at the seat where neither the defendant nor the claimant resides. The benefit of having the anti-arbitration injunction issued by the court of the place where the defendant habitually resides is that the ultimate enforcement of the award would be rendered futile in the defendant's jurisdiction. Therefore, even though the court may not have jurisdiction at the time of the request for issuance of an anti-arbitration injunction, given that such injunction will be sought from a court where the applicant is habitually resident, the likelihood of the award being enforced before the same court is higher. Hence, the court may subsequently acquire jurisdiction and based on such determination, the court should grant an anti-arbitration injunction.[1054]

1051. *See discussion on* Indian Code of Civil Procedure, S. 20, and UNCITRAL Model Law, Art. 1(4) in jurisdiction of Anti-Suit Injunctions; Sigvard Jarvin, *Comment on ICC No. 4862, Partial Award, 1986,* in Sigvard Jarvin, Yves Derains, & Jan-Jacques Arnaldez (eds), *Collection of ICC Awards 1986-1990* 517 (1994). *For example, Himpurna California Energy Ltd v. Republic of Indonesia,* Interim Award of 26 September 1999; *Salini Costruttori S.P.A. v. The Federal Democratic Republic of Ethiopia, Addis Ababa Water and Sewerage Authority* ICC Case No. 10623/AER/ACS, Award of 7 December 2001; Lew, *supra* n. 885, at 190; *The Hub Power Company Ltd (HUBCO) v. Water and Power Development Authority of Pakistan (WAPDA)* 16 Arb. In'l 439 (2000) c.f. Lew, *supra* n. 885.
1052. Lew, *supra* n. 885, at 198.
1053. *In Austria and Germany, the district court where the respondent has its seat, domicile or habitual residence has jurisdiction to grant an interim measure*; Stephen, *supra* n. 96, at 208 & 397.
1054. *Devi Resources Ltd. v. Ambo Exports Ltd.* MANU/WB/0314/2019, ¶64; *Tayabbhai M. Bagasarwalla v. Hind Rubber Industries (P) Ltd.* (1997) 3 SCC 443.

Indirectly, the arbitral tribunal would be constrained to issue an award or exercise jurisdiction when an anti-arbitration injunction has been issued by the possible *lex executionis*. No arbitrator or arbitral tribunal would risk passing an unenforceable award. Even if the enforcement is sought in another jurisdiction, courts in such jurisdiction may be persuaded not to enforce the award based on considerations of comity and respect for the court which granted the anti-arbitration injunction.

2.6.3. Distinguishing Jurisdiction for Anti-Suit and Anti-Arbitration Injunctions

It is pertinent to distinguish anti-suit injunctions from anti-arbitration injunctions with respect to the appropriate court. A party challenging the validity of the arbitration agreement will approach its domestic courts to issue an anti-arbitration injunction under the inherent power of the court. The opposite party has two options, i.e., (a) to resist the request for an anti-arbitration injunction in such domestic court;[1055] or (b) to approach the courts which exercise in personam jurisdiction over the respondent to grant an anti-suit injunction enforcing the arbitration agreement. Practically, both injunctions will be sought from the same court unless the opposite party conducts business or has assets in several jurisdictions.

2.7. The Indian Position

The question of restraining arbitration proceedings under the inherent power of the court first came up in 1918 when the court granted a stay of arbitration proceedings on the allegation of fraud.[1056] Subsequently, in 1970[1057] a prayer was sought against arbitral proceedings in Moscow. The court traced the power to issue such an injunction placing reliance on Sections 34 and 35 of the 1940 Act, which expressly granted the power of stay of arbitral proceedings.[1058] It is pertinent to mention that this case came up before the IAA was enacted, and at that time, the position in the United Kingdom was also that there was no bar on the courts' power to interfere with the arbitral proceedings.[1059] However, this power was rarely exercised.[1060]

1055. *In British India Steam Navigation Co. Ltd. v. Shanmughavilas Cashew Industries* (1990) 3 SCC 481, *the Court held that an appearance by a foreign defendant merely to protest that the Indian court does not have jurisdiction would not constitute submission to the court's jurisdiction;* Cheshire, & Geoffrey Chevalier, *Cheshire & North's Private International Law* (1987).

1056. *Gajanand Maksara v. Shaikh Taleb Jalauddin* [1918] 46 I.C. 173; *affirmed in G.M. Birla & Co. v. Johurmull Premsukh* AIR 1920 Cal 908, ¶2.

1057. *Tractor Export, Moscow v. M/S. Tarapore & Company & Anr.* 1970 SCR (3) 53.

1058. *This decision was followed in Oil and Natural Gas Commission v. Western Company of North America* 1987 (1) SCC 496, *which was also based on the provisions of the 1940 Act.*

1059. *Bremer Vulkan Schiffbau and Maschinenfabrik Respondents v. South India Shipping Corporation Ltd. Appellants* [1981] AC 909, at 959; *Compagnie Européenne de Céréales v. Tradax Export SA* [1986] 2 Lloyd's Rep 301.

1060. *Compagnie Nouvelle France Navigation SA v. Compagnie Navale Afrique du Nord (The Oranie and the Tunisie)* [1966] 1 Lloyd's Rep 477.

2.7.1. *Lack of a Clear Source of Power*

After this decision and after the enactment of the IAA, courts in India have granted anti-arbitration injunctions, sometimes in the garb of public policy,[1061] sometimes without any clear legal basis[1062] and have sometimes refused the same by referring to the bar under Section 5 of the IAA.[1063] In some instances, it has been argued that the power to issue injunctions under Section 9 of the IAA includes the power to issue anti-arbitration injunctions,[1064] which is contrary to the view that arbitration proceedings cannot be stayed under Section 9 of the IAA.[1065]

In another instance, resort was taken to Article 142 of the Constitution of India to do complete justice and hence, an anti-arbitration injunction was granted.[1066] Thus, the courts have been unclear with respect to the source of the power to issue an anti-arbitration injunction. This issuance of injunctions without referring to any specific provision of law in one view amounts to nothing but 'Arbitral Terrorism'.[1067] In a recent decision, the Delhi High Court denied the power to grant an anti-arbitration injunction relying on Section 41(h) of the Specific Relief Act stating the party has 'an equally efficacious remedy' under Section 16 of the IAA as the tribunal can determine the validity of the arbitration agreement.[1068]

Also, there is no provision to Section 9(4) of the English Arbitration Act and even in England, the resort is taken to the inherent power of the court under Section 37 of the Senior Courts Act, 1981. It is relevant to mention that while the inherent power of the courts is expressly contained in England, in India, there is no such power, except the residuary clause under Section 151 of the CPC. The courts have resorted to applying English jurisprudence without acknowledging the fact that there is no section akin to Section 37 of the Senior Courts Act, 1981 in India. What is even more noteworthy is the reluctance of the courts to use the expression anti-arbitration injunctions.[1069]

2.7.2. *Mandatory Reference to Arbitration*

Before examining the said provisions, it is necessary to highlight that a request for an anti-arbitration injunction cannot be made *simpliciter* for an injunction alone but will usually contain a request for a declaration of the arbitration agreement being invalid. Therefore, a suit for declaration along with a prohibitory injunction will ordinarily be filed under Section 9 of the CPC without any reference or overlap of the IAA. It is in the

1061. *World Sport Group (Mauritius) v. MSM Satellite (Singapore)* 2014 11 SCC 639, ¶¶39-40.
1062. *MSM Satellite (Singapore) v. World Sport Group (Mauritius)* 2010 (112) Bom LR 4292; *Bharti Televentures Ltd. v. DSS Enterprises Pvt. Ltd* 2005 (2) Arb. LR 561, ¶27.
1063. *Chatterjee Petrochem Co. v. Haldia Petrochemicals Ltd.* (2014) 14 SCC 574.
1064. *Bharti Televentures Ltd. v. DSS Enterprises Pvt. Ltd* 2005 (2) Arb. LR 561, ¶27.
1065. *Noy Vallesina Engineering Spa v. Jindal Drugs Ltd.* 2006 (3) Arb. LR 510 (Bom), ¶¶ 6, 40 & 41; *Even Bhatia had categorically held at ¶29 that Section 9 of the IAA does not envisage stay of arbitral proceedings.*
1066. *Bina Modi & Ors. v. Lalit Modi & Ors.* MANU/DE/0685/2020.
1067. Doak Bishop, *supra n.* 953.
1068. *Bina Modi & Ors. v. Lalit Modi & Ors.* MANU/DE/0685/2020.
1069. Subramanian, *supra* n. 956 at 216.

written statement or objections to the jurisdiction of the court that the party invoking arbitration would contend that the parties ought to be referred to arbitration under Section 8 or Section 45 of the IAA[1070] unless the court, akin to the civil law approach, rejects the plaint altogether under the CPC in view of the arbitration agreement.[1071] Therefore, there is a statutory basis for exercising the power under Section 8 (domestic arbitration or where India is the seat) and Section 45 (foreign arbitration) of the IAA. It is pertinent to note that Section 8 does not refer to the language contained under Article II(3) of the NYC. Instead, after 2015, it states that '*unless it[court] finds that prima facie no valid arbitration agreement exists*'. Prior to the amendment in 2015, there was no such language that permitted a court to examine the validity of the arbitration agreement.[1072]

Section 45 of the IAA (applicable to foreign seated arbitrations) provides that 'notwithstanding anything contained in Part I' or in the CPC, a judicial authority '*when seized of an action*' shall refer the parties to the arbitration. The reference to any 'action' which is the subject matter of the NYC may well include a suit for restraining foreign arbitrations.[1073] The rationale for this view is the use of the phrase '*unless it finds that the said agreement is null and void, inoperative or incapable of being performed*' in Section 45 of the IAA akin to Article II(3) of the NYC.

2.7.3. Prima Facie Valid

In *Shin-Etsu,*[1074] the court noted that there is significant difficulty in interpreting the provision of Section 45 of the IAA, which envisages pre-reference judicial interference with the arbitral process.[1075] In the absence of a provision like Section 8(3) of the IAA, which provides the commencement and continuing of an arbitration proceeding despite the pendency of a reference before a court, arbitral proceedings should be stayed till the decision of the court on the nature of the agreement. However, such an interpretation would defeat the credo and ethos of the IAA, which is to enable expeditious arbitration without avoidable intervention by courts.[1076]

The court categorically held that a determination as to the agreement being null and void, incapable of being performed or being operative was necessary because of the use of the word 'shall' in Section 45 of the IAA. It only restricted the scope of enquiry to a 'prima facie view'. In its view, a finding at the stage of determination of

1070. *Devi Resources Ltd. v. Ambo Exports Ltd.* MANU/WB/0314/2019.
1071. *Bhushan Steel Ltd. v. Singapore International Arbitration Centre* 2010 SCC OnLine Del 2236; *Sancorp Confectionary Private Limited v. Gumlink A/S* 2012 SCC OnLine Del 5507, ¶11; *Handicrafts & Handlooms Exports Corporation of India Limited v. Ashok Metal Corporation* 2010 SCC OnLine Del 2099.
1072. Prior to the amendment S. 8 provided that '*(1) A judicial authority before which an action is brought in a manner which is the subject of an arbitration agreement shall, if a party so applies not later than when submitting his first statement on the substance of the dispute, refers to the party in arbitration.*'
1073. Sharad Bansal, *supra* n. 894, at 621.
1074. *Shin-Etsu Chemical Co Ltd. v. Aksh Optifibre Ltd.* (2005) 7 SCC 234.
1075. *Ibid.*, ¶68.
1076. *Ibid.*, ¶72.

Section 45 of the IAA would render Section 48(1)(a)(same as Article V(1)(a) of the NYC) otiose.[1077] The other implication would be that a court in India will determine, with full binding effect, a finding on validity following a summary procedure without admitting all the relevant evidence.[1078] Such an interpretation cannot be preferred. Thus, the courts only have to see whether it is 'plainly arguable' that there is an arbitration agreement.[1079] An award, after a full trial by the tribunal, can always be challenged under Section 48(1)(a) of the IAA.[1080]

Taking a similar view, the Delhi High Court[1081] held that if on a cursory consideration of facts, there is a strong preponderant possibility that one of the parties will needlessly and vexatiously be subject to arbitration, and in so doing compelling it to expand avoidable time, effort, and expense, the IAA requires the court to look into the matter and obliviate a futile and facile reference. Such duty of the court is required to be discharged irrespective of whether it is a domestic or foreign arbitration. In fact, this determination is essential in case it is a foreign arbitration.[1082]

It went on to observe that Parts I and II are wholly dissimilar and entirely incomparable. The non-obstante clause in Section 45 of the IAA has to be interpreted with the assistance of the NYC which expects a court to be satisfied that the agreement has not become null and void, inoperative or incapable of being performed before the court can agree to the request of any person to make a reference under Section 48 of the IAA. Since Chapters I and II of Part II are complete codes in themselves, the necessity to locate the powers of interim orders is no longer necessary.[1083] Therefore, the court drew the power to issue an anti-arbitration injunction from the text of Article II(3) and Section 45 of the IAA itself.

It referred to the power of injunctions enjoyed by the civil courts in common law jurisdictions irrespective of their mention in a particular statute.[1084] It reiterated that a party should not be blindly sent to a foreign land until the arbitration agreement was not found to be null and void, inoperative, and incapable of being performed.[1085] The factum of the existence of the arbitration agreement should be decided by the court as a preliminary issue whenever Part II of the IAA is attracted.[1086] Unfortunately, the

1077. *Ibid.*, ¶85.
1078. *Ibid.*, ¶79.
1079. *Ibid.*, ¶97.
1080. *Ibid.*, ¶¶75, 86 and 104.
1081. *Bharti Televentures Ltd. v. DSS Enterprises Pvt. Ltd* 2005 (2) Arb. LR 561, *a Single Judge Bench of Vikramjeet Sen J.*
1082. *Ibid.*, ¶1.
1083. *Ibid.*, ¶14.
1084. *Rylands v. Fletcher* (1868) LR 3 HL 330; *Donoghue v. Stevenson*, [1932] UKHL 100; *Central London Property Trust Ltd v. High Trees House Ltd.* [1947] KB 130 and *Mareva Companies Naviera S.A. v. International Bulk Carriers S.A.* (1980) 1 All ER 213, *Also affirming Channel Tunnel Group Ltd. v. Balfour Beatty Construction Ltd.* [1993] 2 WLR 262. *This view was also affirmed in Marriot International Inc. v. Ansal Hotels Ltd.* 2000 (56) DRJ (Suppl) 235, 443 (DB).
1085. *Relying on Jagson International Ltd. v. Frontier Drilling* (2004) DLT 189. *However, in that case, on facts it was found that the plaintiff was trying to wriggle out the arbitration agreement on frivolous grounds, much like Mc Creary Tire & Rubber Co. v. Ceat SpA* 501 F.2d 1032 (3rd Cir. 1974).
1086. *Relying on Shivnath Rai Har Narain v. Italgranai Spa* SCC OnLine Del 747.

single judge of the Delhi High Court held that while under Section 8 of the IAA only a prima facie finding is required, under Section 45 of the IAA the enquiry should be in greater detail,[1087] only short of deciding contentious issues of facts going to the root of the disputes.[1088] Such a view effectively sanctions holding a 'mini-trial' under Section 45 of the IAA.

It is pertinent to mention that this decision does not take into account the landmark decision in *Shin-Etsu*[1089] and has been passed by a single-judge bench of the High Court, which has limited precedent value.[1090] Nonetheless, other judgments passed at the time subscribed to a similar view that the court is duty-bound[1091] to conduct an enquiry[1092] into the validity of the arbitration[1093] agreement as the scope of Section 45 of the IAA is wider than of Section 8 which provides no discretion to the court.[1094]

Subsequently, in *Petrochem*, the Supreme Court[1095] extended the application of Section 5 of the IAA to a foreign arbitration to hold that a suit filed to seek an anti-arbitration injunction would not be maintainable under the IAA.[1096] Relying on this view in *Board of Trustees*,[1097] the Calcutta High Court held that Section 5 of the IAA would apply to all arbitrations irrespective of whether they are domestic or international,[1098] but added that Section 5 could not curb the power expressly vested under Section 45 of the IAA. Therefore, it kept the doors of an anti-arbitration injunction open as it held that the power to entertain an action by a civil court is an inherent power and need not be traceable to any statute. Furthermore, Section 45 of the IAA does not limit the nature of the power of the civil court but merely lays down the procedure to be followed when a court is seized of an action relating to an arbitration agreement.[1099]

It held that unless the facts and circumstances of a particular case demonstrate that the continuation of a foreign arbitration would cause a demonstrable injustice, the court should not interfere. However, the court can interfere in the interest of comity

1087. *The Madras High Court made an interesting observation that while the right under Section 8 of the IAA is time-bound and not really substance-bound, the exercise of the right to seek arbitration under Section 45 of the IAA is actually substance-bound and not time-bound; Mr. Ramasamy Athappan v. The Secretariat of the International Chamber of Commerce* 2008 SCC OnLine Mad 789, ¶40.
1088. *Bharti Televentures Ltd. v. DSS Enterprises Pvt. Ltd* 2005 (2) Arb. LR 561, ¶18.
1089. *Shin-Etsu Chemical Co Ltd. v. Aksh Optifibre Ltd.* (2005) 7 SCC 234.
1090. Subramanian, *supra* n. 956 at 211.
1091. *CG Holding Pvt Ltd. v. Ramasamy Athappan* 2011 SCC OnLine Mad 1078, ¶¶100 &110.
1092. *Mr. Ramasamy Athappan v. The Secretariat of the International Chamber of Commerce* 2008 SCC OnLine Mad 789, ¶6. *Relying on Shin-Etsu Chemical Co Ltd. v. Aksh Optifibre Ltd.* (2005) 7 SCC 234.
1093. *Chatterjee Petrochem Co. v. Haldia Petrochemicals Ltd.* (2014) 14 SCC 574.
1094. *CG Holding Pvt Ltd. v. Ramasamy Athappan* 2011 SCC OnLine Mad 1078, ¶100.
1095. Applying *Bhatia* and *Venture Global Engineering v. Satyam Computer Services Limited* (2008) 4 SCC 190.
1096. *Chatterjee Petrochem Co. v. Haldia Petrochemicals Ltd.* (2014) 14 SCC 574, ¶35-42.
1097. *Board of Trustees of the Port of Kolkata v. Louis Dreyfus Armatures SAS* MANU/WB/0695/2014.
1098. *Ibid.*, ¶65.
1099. *These observations were made by the High Court of Calcutta (India).*

and avoidance of inconsistent judgment, and an anti-arbitration can be granted until the determination is concluded by an Indian court.[1100]

The power to grant anti-arbitration injunctions was confirmed in *World Sports Group*.[1101] The court referred to Section 9 of the CPC to take the view that such a suit praying for issuance of an anti-arbitration injunction would be maintainable, but every civil court which entertains such a suit has to follow the mandate of Sections 44 and 45 of the IAA.[1102]

The most recent application of this power was in *Sorang Power*,[1103] where the Delhi High Court was called upon to prevent the commencement of a second arbitration proceeding;[1104] the court considered all the prior precedents and rejected the request for an anti-arbitration injunction against the second arbitral tribunal. The court held that the second arbitral tribunal was sufficiently competent and empowered to determine whether the second arbitration proceedings were an abuse of the process of law.[1105] A similar line of reasoning was adopted in *Khaitan Holdings*,[1106] where the Union of India approached the court for an anti-arbitration injunction and Khaitan Holdings approached the tribunal for an anti-suit injunction in an investment arbitration proceeding. The Delhi High Court rejected the request for an anti-arbitration injunction since the tribunal had been formed and under the principle of *Kompetenz-kompetenz*, the tribunal should decide the issue of jurisdiction.[1107]

The precedents clearly recognise the power to issue anti-arbitration injunctions. The only concern is unnecessary pre-reference court intervention.[1108] Therefore, it is necessary to understand the terms 'null and void, inoperative or incapable of being performed' since the power to issue anti-arbitration injunctions is to be exercised in consonance with Section 45 of the IAA.

2.7.4. Null and Void

The words 'null and void' refer to those cases 'where the arbitration agreement is affected by some invalidity, right from the beginning, such as lack of consent due to misrepresentation, fraud,[1109] duress, undue influence,[1110] or waiver or when it

1100. Relying on *Enercon. It must also be noted that the embargo of Section 5 would only be applicable to arbitrations seated in India, especially in view of the 2015 Amendment adding the proviso to Section 2(2) and the landmark judgment of the Supreme Court in BALCO.*
1101. *World Sport Group (Mauritius) v. MSM Satellite (Singapore)* 2014 11 SCC 639.
1102. *Ibid.*, ¶¶23-24.
1103. *Himachal Sorang Power Pvt. Ltd. v. NCC Infrastructure Holdings Ltd.* 2019 SCC OnLine Del 7575.
1104. *Ibid.*, ¶85.
1105. *Ibid.*, ¶125. *The court even added a caveat that the second tribunal should not consider the judgment of the Delhi High Court and should come to an independent conclusion.* ¶129.
1106. *Union of India v. Khaitan Holdings (Mauritius) Ltd & Ors.* 2019 SCC OnLine Del 6755.
1107. *Ibid.*, ¶¶46-54.
1108. Explicitly concluded in Republic of India through *Ministry of Defence v. Augusta Westland International Ltd.* 2019 SCC OnLine Del 6419 and *World Sport Group (Mauritius) v. MSM Satellite (Singapore)* 2014 11 SCC 639.
1109. *Albon v. Naza Motor Trading Sdn Bhd* [2007] EWCA Civ 1124 [2007] EWCA Civ 1124.
1110. Albert Jan Van Den Berg, *The New York Convention, 1958: An Overview*, available at:https://cdn.arbitration-icca.org/s3fs-public/document/media_document/media012125884227980

contravenes the fundamental policies of the forum state.[1111] In the Indian context, there can be two kinds of invalidity, one from the inception and second, where the agreement becomes void on account of something that made it unenforceable after the inception'.[1112]

2.7.5. *Inoperative*

'Inoperative' refers to an arbitration clause where the clause has ceased to have effect, i.e., '*something which is legally valid, may also, at times, lose its life force and become clinically dead or inoperative, either by the acts of parties or on account of extraneous factors*',[1113] e.g., failure of parties to comply with a time limit, pathological clauses,[1114] or where parties have by conduct impliedly revoked the arbitration agreement[1115] by abandonment, waiver, election, estoppel or renunciation,[1116] or there has already been an arbitral award or court decision with res judicata effect.

Recently, it was clarified by the Supreme Court that an arbitration agreement would become inoperative once the parties had reached a compromise. Any dispute arising subsequently cannot be subject to arbitration based on the clause contained in the prior agreement.[1117]

2.7.6. *Incapable of Being Performed*

'Incapable of being performed' refers to more practical aspects of the prospective arbitration agreements, i.e., it signifies, in effect, frustration and the consequent discharge. If, after the making of the contract, the promise becomes incapable of being fulfilled or performed due to unforeseen contingencies, the contract is frustrated,[1118] e.g., if it is impossible to establish a tribunal.[1119]

Thus, the scope of anti-arbitration injunctions is limited by these three phrases. Even when considering the phrases, the court cannot undertake a trial and has to be restricted to a 'prima facie' view.

---

new_york_convention_of_1958_overview.pdf; *Mr. Ramasamy Athappan v. The Secretariat of the International Chamber of Commerce* 2008 SCC OnLine Mad 789, ¶13; *Affirming the decision in Rhone Mediterranee Compagnia francese di assicurazioni e riassicurazioni v. Achille Lauro* 712 F.2d 50, (3d Cir.1983).

1111. *Mr. Ramasamy Athappan v. The Secretariat of the International Chamber of Commerce* 2008 SCC OnLine Mad 789, ¶13.
1112. *Ibid.*, ¶14.
1113. *Ibid.*, ¶31.
1114. *Lovelock Limited v. Exportles* (1968) 1 Lloyd's Rep. 163.
1115. *F.C.I. v. Yadav Engineer & Contractor* (1982) 2 SCC 499, ¶9.
1116. *Mr. Ramasamy Athappan v. The Secretariat of the International Chamber of Commerce* 2008 SCC OnLine Mad 789, ¶44.
1117. *Zenith Drugs and Allied Agencies Pvt. Ltd. v. Nicholas Piramal India Ltd.* 2019 SCC OnLine SC 946, ¶13.
1118. *Mr. Ramasamy Athappan v. The Secretariat of the International Chamber of Commerce* 2008 SCC OnLine Mad 789, ¶22.
1119. *World Sport Group (Mauritius) v. MSM Satellite (Singapore)* 2014 11 SCC 639, ¶ 33.

It is necessary to highlight that the power under Section 45 of the IAA is to direct parties to arbitration when a party has approached the court in breach of an arbitration agreement. It is not empowered to decide the validity of the arbitration agreement by applying a foreign law (the law governing the validity of the arbitration agreement)[1120] at the request of a party who has been served with a notice of arbitration or has been summoned by an arbitral tribunal to appear before it. Such practice of frustrating the arbitration agreement is exactly what Article 5 of the Model Law, Sections 5 and 45 of the IAA seek to prevent. Therefore, as held in *Shin-Etsu,* the power to grant an anti-arbitration injunction should only be invoked on a 'prima facie view'.[1121] Most jurisdictions take this view, leaving the final validity to be examined in the post-award stage. This position is reiterated by the Law Commission Reports,[1122] the 2015 Amendment to Section 8 of the IAA and the 2019 Amendment which now specifically use the words 'unless it prima facie finds'.

2.8. The 2019 Amendment

The 2019 Amendment is a step forward in preventing unnecessary court intervention and it recognises the harmonious construction envisaged under Article II(3) of the NYC and Article 16(1) of the Model Law. This progressive view is yet to be statutorily adopted in most countries.[1123] Therefore, even though there is an apparent conflict between the duty to determine the existence and validity of the arbitration agreement at a pre-arbitral stage and by the arbitral tribunal, the conflict is now rightly resolved by the 2019 Amendment limiting the scope of interference[1124] to a prima facie view[1125] without holding a mini-trial or requiring extensive interpretation or evidence before referring the parties to arbitration. This also ensures that the courts do not interpret and

1120. *Shin-Etsu Chemical Co Ltd. v. Aksh Optifibre Ltd.* (2005) 7 SCC 234 ¶ 81; *GMR Energy Limited v. Doosan Power Systems India Private Limited & Ors.* 2017 SCC OnLine Del 11625, ¶ 35; *NTPC v. Singer Co.* (1992) 3 SCC 551, ¶23.

1121. *CG Holding Pvt Ltd. v. Ramasamy Athappan* 2011 SCC OnLine Mad 1078, ¶101; *ITE India Pvt. Ltd. v. Mukesh Sharma* 2005 SCC OnLine Del 1398, ¶45; *Bhushan Steel Ltd. v. Singapore International Arbitration Centre* 2010 SCC OnLine Del 2236; *Devendra Kumar Gupta v. Realogy Corporation* 2011 SCC OnLine Del 3050, ¶23; *Havels India Ltd. v. Electrium Sales India Ltd* 2013 SCC OnLine Del 1474, ¶¶ 31-33.

1122. Law Commission of India, *supra* n. 517; Justice B.N. Srikrishna, Report of the High-Level Committee to Review the Institutionalization of Arbitration Mechanism in India, (July 2017), available at: http://legalaffairs.gov.in/sites/default/files/Report-HLC.pdf.

1123. *Birse Construction Ltd. v. St David Ltd (No. 1),* [2000] B.L.R. 57; *Ahmad Al -Naimi (T/A Buildmaster Construction Services) v. Islamic Press Agency Incorporated* [2000] 1 Lloyd's Reporter 522; *Shin-Etsu Chemical Co Ltd. v. Aksh Optifibre Ltd.* (2005) 7 SCC 234, *including an analysis of different approaches in various jurisdictions worldwide*).

1124. *Mr. Ramasamy Athappan v. The Secretariat of the International Chamber of Commerce* 2008 SCC OnLine Mad 789, ¶56.

1125. Justice B.N. Srikrishna, Report of the High-Level Committee to Review the Institutionalization of Arbitration Mechanism in India, (July 2017), available at: http://legalaffairs.gov.in/sites/default/files/Report-HLC.pdf; Toby Landau, *Arbitral Lifelines: The Protection of Jurisdiction by Arbitrators,* in A. van den Berg (ed.), *International Arbitration 2006: Back to Basics?* 282, 290-291 (2007).

apply foreign law, i.e., the law governing the dispute and give a finding which they would otherwise not be competent to give.

The 2019 Amendment also pays due homage to the mandate of Article 16(1) of the Model Law and the principle of *Kompetenz-kompetenz* as it gives priority of jurisdiction to the arbitral tribunal to decide questions of existence and validity of the arbitration agreement[1126] and the court is only expected to interfere when the very basis of consent and the arbitration agreement are put to challenge.[1127] It furthers the goal of being a pro-arbitration country and also enables India to fulfil its treaty obligation enshrined in Article II of the NYC.[1128]

2.9. Scope of Anti-Arbitration Injunctions

The basis of issuing anti-arbitration injunctions is the inherent power of the court to prevent injustice and the right of every individual to approach the civil court under Section 9 of the CPC for any grievance. This inherent power cannot be used in every instance and should be used sparingly.

Taking reference from the discussion by the CCJ,[1129] such power must be exercised with caution.[1130] The court must exercise double the caution it usually exercises in restraining foreign proceedings as it is vital to recognise and enforce the agreement of the parties to the mechanism of dispute resolution. The arbitral tribunal should not be subject to the control of domestic courts before it makes an award.[1131]

This view is also similar to the view of the courts in England, which have held that the power should only be exercised in exceptional circumstances and specifically only where it is clear that the arbitration proceedings have been wrongly brought.[1132] Examples of situations where courts should exercise such a power would be where the matters were not arbitrable and involved matters of criminality,[1133] the non-existence of an arbitration agreement,[1134] and the proceedings being oppressive, vexatious, and

1126. *Kvaerner Cementation India Ltd. v. Bajranglal Agarwal* (2001) 6 SC 265, ¶¶ 3-5.

1127. *A comparison can be drawn with the position in Switzerland where courts exercise unfettered power when the seat of arbitration is abroad.* Marco, *supra* n. 994, at 2636.

1128. *See* Grace Gunah Kim, *After the ECJ's West Tankers: The Clash of Civilizations on the Issue of an Anti-suit Injunction*, 12 (2) Car. J. Conflict Res. 573 (2011).

1129. *British Caribbean Bank Limited (Turks & Caicos) v. The Government of Belize* [2013] CCJ 3 (AJ), PCA Case No. 2010-18.

1130. *Ibid.*, at, ¶40.

1131. *Ibid.*, at, ¶¶ 38 & 41. *With respect to investment arbitration, the court held that domestic courts should intervene 'only with extreme hesitation'.*

1132. Lew, *supra* n. 28, at ¶15-25.

1133. *The Hub Power Company Ltd (HUBCO) v. Water and Power Development Authority of Pakistan (WAPDA)* 16 Arb. In'l 439 (2000); *In this case see, e.g.*, Louise Barrington, *Hubco v. WAPDA: Pakistan Top Court Rejects International Arbitration*, 15 Mealey's Int'l Arb. Rep. 7, A1, (2000); Nudrat B. Majeed, *Commentary on the Hubco Judgment*, 16(4) Arb. Int. 431-438 (2000); *Neil Kaplan, Arbitration in Asia – Developments and Crises* 19(2) J. Int'l Arb. 163 (2002).

1134. *Excalibur Ventures LLC v. Texas Keystone Inc.* [2011] EWHC 1624 (Comm); *Albon v. Naza Motor Trading Sdn Bhd* [2007] EWCA Civ 1124; *Republic of Kazaksthan v. Istil Group Inc,*

unconscionable.[1135] Jurisdictional challenges must be dealt with promptly and firmly. If the courts are too willing to entertain frivolous jurisdictional challenges or appear to be too keen to exert a supervisory role, it will encourage parties to stall arbitration proceedings.[1136] An injunction should not be granted simply because the balance of convenience favours the injunction but only when the validity of the arbitration agreement is in question.[1137]

The Indian courts, in consonance with various other jurisdictions,[1138] have adopted a similar view that the jurisdiction to grant an anti-arbitration injunction must be exercised with caution and granted only if the arbitral proceedings are vexatious or oppressive or inequitable or amount to an abuse of the process of law.[1139] The courts cannot be used to indirectly stay orders passed by arbitral tribunals and there is a mandate of 'minimal court intervention'.[1140] They should be permitted only when there is demonstrable injustice or harassment being caused by the arbitration proceedings.[1141] Such injunctions should be used sparingly as they interfere with the jurisdiction of another court[1142] and should only be granted in extreme cases where the refusal may result in palpable and gross injustice in the meanest sense,[1143] such as serious fraud and matters of public importance.[1144] Therefore, the courts themselves have considerably restricted the scope of the power to grant anti-arbitration injunctions.

2.10. Standards for Grant of Anti-Arbitration Injunctions

Currently, there exists a considerable dilemma over what criteria should be adopted by a court when it is called upon to restrain parties from pursuing arbitration? Should the criteria be that of an ordinary injunction? Or are such criteria inapt?[1145] Are the criteria for an anti-suit injunction the same as the criteria for an anti-arbitration injunction? Or should the criteria be something entirely different?

[2007] EWHC 2729 (Comm); *J Jarvis & Sons Ltd v. Blue Circle Dartford Estates Ltd.* [2007] EWHC 1262 (TCC); *Claxton Engineering Services Ltd v. TXM Olaj-Es Gazkutato Kft* [2011] EWHC 345 (Comm).

1135. *Claxton Engineering Services Ltd v. TXM Olaj-Es Gazkutato Kft* [2011] EWHC 345 (Comm), at 327 & 335, *the court estopped the defendant from bringing arbitration proceedings in Hungary in the absence of an arbitration agreement. Republic of Kazaksthan v. Istil Group Inc* [2007] EWHC 2729 (Comm), at 895, *the injunction was granted as the proceedings would be oppressive, vexatious and unconscionable.*
1136. *Tjong Very Sumito v. Antig Investments* [2009] 4 SLR(R), at 28.
1137. *Compagnie Nouvelle France Navigation SA v. Compagnie Navale Afrique du Nord (The Oranie and the Tunisie)* [1966] 1 Lloyd's Rep 477.
1138. *Lin Ming v. Chen Shu Quan* [2012] 2 HKRLD 547, at 53.
1139. *Modi Entertainment Network v. W.S.G. Cricket Pte. Ltd.* (2003) 4 SCC 341, ¶ 24; *Devi Resources Ltd. v. Ambo Exports Ltd.* MANU/WB/0314/2019, ¶55.
1140. *Chennai Metro Rail Limited v. Lanco Infratech Ltd.* 2020 SCC OnLine Mad 26397, ¶42.
1141. *Lafarge India Pvt. Ltd. v. Emami Realty Ltd.* 2016 SCC OnLine Cal 4964, ¶59.
1142. *Modi Entertainment Network v. W.S.G. Cricket Pte. Ltd.* (2003) 4 SCC 341, ¶24.
1143. *Devi Resources Ltd. v. Ambo Exports Ltd.* MANU/WB/0314/2019, ¶55; *M/s Gowri Spinning Mills Ltd. v. Adimoolam* 2001 SCC OnLine Mad 860, ¶11-12; *JSW Steel Ltd. v. JFE Shoji Trade Corporation* 2009 SCC OnLine Bom 2063.
1144. *RRB Energy Ltd. v. Vestas Wind Systems* 2015 SCC OnLine Del 8734, ¶67.
1145. *Oracle America, Inc. v. Myriad Group AG, No. C 10-05604 (SBA)* 2012 WL 146364, at 7.

The position in Hong Kong and Singapore is that the court should determine whether there is a prima facie case that parties were bound by an arbitration clause. If the same is unclear, parties should be referred to arbitration.[1146] Similarly, Section 32 of the English Arbitration Act empowers the court to grant a declaration on the jurisdiction of the arbitral tribunal and it can be invoked when (i) the determination of jurisdiction by the court is likely to produce substantial saving costs; (ii) the application was made without delay; and (iii) there exist good reasons why the matter should be decided by the court.[1147]

In England, it was observed that a different test should apply to anti-arbitration injunctions than that of anti-suit injunctions,[1148] but no definitive test was laid down. Subsequent decisions have followed the test for anti-suit injunctions,[1149] i.e., the test laid down in *Elektrim SA v. Vivendi Universal SA*(*Elektrim*):[1150]

(a) do the proceedings infringe a legal or equitable right of a party?
(b) whether the proceedings are vexatious, oppressive, or unconscionable?

This test, when applied in the context of arbitration, means that (a) that the stay must not cause injustice to the claimant in the arbitration; and (b) the applicant must satisfy the court that the continuation of arbitration would be oppressive or vexatious on him or abuse of the process of the court.[1151]

In India, the test for anti-arbitration injunctions has been the following:[1152]

(a) Is the court of the view that no valid arbitration agreement exists between the parties?
(b) Is the arbitration agreement null and void, inoperative or incapable of being performed?
(c) Whether the continuation of foreign arbitration proceedings might be oppressive or vexatious or unconscionable,[1153] i.e., where the very issue was

1146. *Pacific Crown Engineering Ltd. v. Hyundai Engineering and Construction Co Ltd.* [2003] 3 HKC 659; *Schindler Lifts (Hong Kong) Ltd. v. Sui Chong Construction & Engineering Co. Ltd.* [2014] HKDC 1348, at 27, *This view has also been followed by the Courts in Singapore in Malini Ventura v. Knight Capital Pte Ltd.* [2015] SGHC 225.
1147. Crina, *supra* n. 882, at 264. C.f. *Toyota Tsusho Sugar Trading Ltd. v. Prolat S.R.L.* [2014] EWHC 3649 (Comm).
1148. *Sana Hassib Sabbagh v. Wael Said Khoury* [2019] EWCA Civ 1219; *Elektrim SA, S.A. v. Vivendi Universal SAS.A., Vivendi Telecommunication International S.A., Elektrim Telekomunikacja Sp. z.o.o, Carcom Warszawa Sp. z.o.o.* [2007] EWHC 571 (Comm), at 248.
1149. Hakeem, *supra* n. 955 at 47.
1150. *Elektrim SA, S.A. v. Vivendi Universal SAS.A., Vivendi Telecommunication International S.A., Elektrim Telekomunikacja Sp. z.o.o, Carcom Warszawa Sp. z.o.o.* [2007] EWHC 571 (Comm).
1151. *Industry Chimiche Italia Centrale v. Alexander G. Tsavliris and Sons Maritime Co. (The Choco Star)* [1987] 1 Lloyd's Report 508, CA; *Amir Weissfisch v. Anthony Julius, Rami Weisfisch, Philip Davis* [2006] EWCA CIV 218.
1152. *Board of Trustees of the Port of Kolkata v. Louis Dreyfus Armatures SAS* MANU/WB/0695/2014.
1153. *Consistently followed in Shin-Etsu*, MSM, *Vikram Bakshi v. McDonalds India Pvt. Ltd.* MANU/DE/3483/2014, ¶73; *World Sport Group (Mauritius) v. MSM Satellite (Singapore)* 2014 11 SCC 639.

whether or not the parties had consented to the arbitration or where there was an allegation that the arbitration agreement was a forgery.[1154]

Initially, in *Tarapore*[1155] and *Dabhol Power*,[1156] the court applied the same test to anti-arbitration injunctions as that of anti-suit injunctions, i.e., oppressive and vexatious nature of proceedings.[1157] While determining whether the proceedings are 'oppressive', the Supreme Court of India has considered the test of 'ends of justice' and 'necessity'.[1158]

In the decision of *Vikram Bakshi v. McDonald's India Pvt. Ltd,*[1159] since a similar issue was already pending before another authority, the court granted an anti-arbitration injunction.[1160] This view was severely criticised,[1161] and in appeal,[1162] the division bench disagreed with the view of the Single Judge. The division bench recognised the special nature of anti-arbitration injunctions and applied the test laid down in the English decision of *Excalibur,*[1163] i.e., exceptional cases, which would mean the proceedings would be oppressive and unconscionable or the lack of consent or that the agreement is a forged one.[1164]

It categorically held that the principles which apply to anti-suit injunctions do not apply to anti-arbitration injunctions[1165] and affirming the view in *World Sport Group*[1166] held that unless and until a party seeking an anti-arbitration injunction can demonstrably show that the arbitration agreement is null and void, inoperative or incapable of being performed, no such relief can be granted in the suit or as an interim measure.[1167] Such challenge has to be a serious challenge to the substantive contract or to the agreement, as in the absence of such challenge, it has to be found that the agreement was valid, operative and capable of being performed; the dispute would be

1154. *Excalibur Ventures LLC v. Texas Keystone Inc.* [2011] EWHC 1624 (Comm), ¶48; *Affirmed Himachal Sorang Power Pvt. Ltd. v. NCC Infrastructure Holdings Ltd.* 2019 SCC OnLine Del 7575, ¶110.
1155. *Tractor Export, Moscow v. M/S. Tarapore & Company & Anr.* 1970 SCR (3) 53.
1156. *Union of India v. Dabhol Power Co.* 2002 SCC OnLine Bom 1491.
1157. *PPN Power Generating Company v. PPN (Mauritius) Co.* 2005 (3) Arb. LR 354; *CG Holding Pvt Ltd. v. Ramasamy Athappan* 2011 SCC OnLine Mad 1078, ¶119.
1158. *Oil and Natural Gas Commission v. Western Company of North America* 1987 (1) SCC 496, ¶18.
1159. *Vikram Bakshi v. McDonalds India Pvt. Ltd.* MANU/DE/3483/2014.
1160. *Ibid.*, ¶73.
1161. Ben Giaretta & Akshay Kishore, Ashurst Singapore, *Anti-arbitration Injunctions: Mixed Signals from India,* (1 January 2015), available at:https://www.ashurst.com/en/news-and-insights/legal-updates/anti-arbitration-injunctions-mixed-signals-fromindia/; Mohit Mahla, *Indian Arbitration Cart: Moving Forward or Backward,* (6 June 2015), available at:http://arbitrationblog.kluwerarbitration.com/2015/06/06/indian-arbitration-cart-moving-forward-or-backward/.
1162. *Vikram Bakshi v. McDonald's India Pvt. Ltd.* MANU/DE/3483/2014, ¶42.
1163. *Excalibur Ventures LLC v. Texas Keystone Inc.* [2011] EWHC 1624 (Comm).
1164. *Vikram Bakshi division bench, McDonald's India Pvt Ltd. v. Vikram Bakshi,* MANU/DE/1684/2016, ¶48.
1165. *Vikram Bakshi v. McDonald's India Pvt. Ltd.* MANU/DE/3483/2014, ¶¶11 and 37, *Affirmed* in *Himachal Sorang Power Pvt. Ltd. v. NCC Infrastructure Holdings Ltd.* 2019 SCC OnLine Del 7575, ¶110.
1166. *World Sport Group (Mauritius) v. MSM Satellite (Singapore)* 2014 11 SCC 639.
1167. *McDonald's India Pvt Ltd. v. Vikram Bakshi,* MANU/DE/1684/2016, ¶52.

referred to arbitration.[1168] The above views have been reiterated in the recent decision in *Sorang Power*.[1169]

It has been suggested that the test for anti-arbitration injunctions in India would be first to satisfy the criteria under Order XXXIX Rule 1 or 2 of the CPC, i.e., a prima facie case, balance of convenience, and irreparable harm. After that, the court would take a prima facie view of whether the agreement is null and void, inoperative, or incapable of being performed, the courts would also determine whether the proceedings would be vexatious or oppressive.[1170]

The test laid down under the CPC is not adequate to cater to the unique problem of anti-arbitration injunctions. It should not be considered when determining whether to grant or deny the request for an anti-arbitration injunction. Moreover, considerations of the injunction being 'just and convenient'[1171] should be rejected.

In the case of requests for anti-arbitration injunctions, the criteria should be restricted to:

(a) prima facie determination whether the arbitration agreement is null and void, inoperative or incapable of being performed; and
(b) the arbitration proceedings would be vexatious or oppressive.[1172]

The court requires to determine in personam jurisdiction at the time of considering the request for an anti-arbitration injunction but does not need to have jurisdiction when the suit is filed if it can be demonstrated that the court will most likely acquire jurisdiction subsequently at the time of enforcement of the award.[1173] When deciding whether arbitration proceedings would be vexatious or oppressive, the court should consider the 'totality of the circumstances'[1174] as well as the stage of proceedings and the expectations of the parties to litigate before the tribunal or a particular court.[1175]

1168. *Chloro Controls India (P) Ltd. v. Severn Trent Water Purification Inc.* (2013) 1 SCC 641, ¶85 *citing State of Orissa v. Klockner and Co.* AIR 1996 SC 2140.
1169. *Himachal Sorang Power Pvt. Ltd. v. NCC Infrastructure Holdings Ltd.* 2019 SCC OnLine Del 7575, ¶127.
1170. Sharad Bansal, *supra* n. 894, at 627.
1171. *Nomihold Securities INC v. Mobile Telesystems Finance SA*, [2012] Bus LR 1289. *Affirmed in Himachal Sorang Power Pvt. Ltd. v. NCC Infrastructure Holdings Ltd.* 2019 SCC OnLine Del 7575, ¶108.
1172. *Thota Gurunath Reddy v. Continental Hospitals Pvt. Ltd.* 2017 SCC OnLine Hyd 425, ¶109; *V.O. Tractoroexport, Moscow v. Tarapore and Co. and Anrs.* (1969) 3 SCC 562, ¶25; *Cetelem SA v. Robust Holdings Ltd.* [2005] 1 CLC 821, ¶74; *Amir Weissfisch v. Anthony Julius, Rami Weisfisch, Philip Davis* [2006] EWCA CIV 218, at 431 *This view has been subsequently followed in Claxton Engineering Services Ltd v. TXM Olaj-Es Gazkutato Kft* [2011] EWHC 345 (Comm), at 335; *Republic of Kazaksthan v. Istil Group Inc* [2007] EWHC 2729 (Comm).
1173. *Devi Resources Ltd. v. Ambo Exports Ltd.* MANU/WB/0314/2019, ¶63.
1174. Lew, *supra* n. 885, at 193.
1175. Lew, *supra* n. 28, at ¶15-32.

2.10.1. *Burden of Proof*

While issuing an anti-arbitration injunction, the burden of proof to be demonstrated by the party resisting arbitration should be high. One extreme view is that it should be high, denoting impossibility, or practical impossibility.[1176] The more reasonable view was taken by the CCJ, which approvingly quoted the test in *Elektrim* and added that the burden of proof is on the parties seeking an injunction and such party must discharge that burden to a higher level than that is required to restrain a foreign proceeding which does not involve a contract to litigate in the foreign court.[1177]

A similar burden of proof has already been used by the courts in India.[1178] However, the prerequisite for the grant of an anti-suit and an anti-arbitration injunction in India is that the court should exercise in personam jurisdiction. As mentioned previously, while the test for anti-suit injunctions should require in personam jurisdiction of the issuing court, an anti-arbitration injunction should not.

3. LIMITATIONS

It is clear from the preceding that the power to grant anti-suit and anti-arbitration injunctions has been affirmed, time and again. The exercise of this power, however, has a certain inherent limitation.

3.1. Granted Against Parties

Anti-suit and anti-arbitration injunctions are made in personam. They may be issued against one or both parties to the arbitration, against the tribunal or a particular arbitration or against the arbitral institution.[1179] If issued against the tribunal, such injunctions will in effect, be passed against arbitrators over whom the court has no jurisdiction. To avoid such problems, such injunctions are, therefore, issued against the parties[1180] over whom the court has jurisdiction, minimising the extraterritorial effect. Therefore, anti-arbitration injunctions do not receive the same level of criticism as traditional anti-suit injunctions as they do not directly interfere with the jurisdiction of a sovereign state.[1181]

3.2. Duty to the Parties

Since the court does not have jurisdiction over an arbitral tribunal, the tribunal may ignore the anti-arbitration injunction and comply with its duties to the parties under the

1176. *Klockner Pentaplast GmbH v. Advance Technology* [2011] 4 HKLRD 262, at 19.
1177. *British Caribbean Bank Limited (Turks & Caicos) v. The Government of Belize,* [2013] CCJ 3 (AJ), PCA Case No. 2010-18, ¶39.
1178. *Modi Entertainment Network v. W.S.G. Cricket Pte. Ltd.* (2003) 4 SCC 341; *Himachal Sorang Power Pvt. Ltd. v. NCC Infrastructure Holdings Ltd.* 2019 SCC OnLine Del 7575; *Devi Resources Ltd. v. Ambo Exports Ltd.* MANU/WB/0314/2019.
1179. Julian, *supra* n. 1005, at 33.
1180. Subramanian, *supra* n. 956 at 186.
1181. Lew, *supra* n. 885, at 189.

applicable arbitration rules and law. There is a growing body of jurisprudence that arbitral tribunals may properly disregard international law violations and continue proceedings notwithstanding anti-arbitration injunctions.[1182] In *Salini*,[1183] the tribunal was of the opinion that arbitral tribunals are not bound by the anti-arbitration injunction issued by courts in view of the fulfilment of the tribunal's larger duty to the parties. Similarly, in *Himpurna*,[1184] the tribunal set aside the anti-arbitration injunction and continued the arbitral proceedings holding that the injunction obtained was inconsistent with the obligations of the Indonesian government as a party to the voluntary arbitration agreement.[1185]

However, tribunals should be cautious of such an approach. They should carefully examine the various effects of the injunction on the tribunal or one of its members or the parties.[1186] An award issued despite an anti-arbitration injunction may not be enforceable in the country which issued the injunction. Since an arbitrator must render an enforceable award,[1187] the arbitrator should remember that ignorance of the injunction may render the award unenforceable.[1188]

3.3. Enforcement Concerns

If the court passing the anti-arbitration injunction is not the seat, then it is equally possible that the arbitral tribunal can ignore the injunction.[1189] However, even in such a case, if enforcement were to be sought in the jurisdiction of such a court, it would most likely be violative of its public policy.[1190] On the other hand, when the anti-arbitration injunction is passed by the court at the seat, the opposing party can simply choose not to participate in the arbitration proceedings and later have the award set aside by the same court.[1191]

The binding effect of such injunctions was considered by the Bombay High Court[1192] where it was called upon to decide whether an interim order passed under Section 9 of the IAA staying the arbitration proceedings was binding on the ICC tribunal. The ICC tribunal took the view that the interim order passed by the court

1182. F.A. Mann, *The Consequences of an International Wrong in International and National Law*, 48 British Y.B. Int'l L 46 (1976-1977); *Salini Costruttori S.P.A. v. The Federal Democratic Republic of Ethiopia, Addis Ababa Water and Sewerage Authority* ICC Case No. 10623/AER/ACS, Award of 7 December 2001.
1183. *Salini Costruttori S.P.A. v. The Federal Democratic Republic of Ethiopia, Addis Ababa Water and Sewerage Authority* ICC Case No. 10623/AER/ACS, Award of 7 December 2001.
1184. *Himpurna California Energy Ltd v. Republic of Indonesia*, Interim Award, 26 September 1999.
1185. Jennifer, *supra* n. 891, at 314.
1186. Lew, *supra* n. 885, at 219.
1187. Christopher Boog, *The Lazy Myth of the Arbitral Tribunal's Duty to Render an Enforceable Award*, (28 January 2013), http://arbitrationblog.kluwerarbitration.com/2013/01/28/the-lazy-myth-of-the-arbitral-tribunals-duty-to-render-an-enforceable-award/.
1188. Lew, *supra* n. 885, at 219.
1189. Nadja, *supra* n. 1027, at 105.
1190. Marco, *supra* n. 901, at 643.
1191. *Devi Resources Ltd. v. Ambo Exports Ltd.* MANU/WB/0314/2019; Jennifer, *supra* n. 891, at 316.
1192. *Noy Vallesina Engineering Spa v. Jindal Drugs Ltd.* 2006 (3) Arb. LR 510 (Bom).

under Section 9 of the IAA was not binding on the tribunal and therefore decided to proceed with the arbitration proceedings.

The court observed that a bare perusal of Section 9 does not vest a power in the court to issue any interim directions or orders to the arbitral tribunal, nor does any other provision in the IAA.[1193] The court found that it had no jurisdiction to pass such an interim order and the same was a nullity in the eyes of the law.[1194] It went on to note that Indian statues are ineffective against foreigners outside the territories of India.[1195] Therefore, apart from Section 9 of the IAA not conferring jurisdiction on the court to pass an order against the tribunal under Section 9, the fact that the tribunal was constituted by the ICC, the proceedings were to take place before the International Court in London and two out of the three members of the tribunal were foreigners, who were not in India, the court had no jurisdiction to pass the interim order.[1196] Relying on a previous precedent,[1197] the court held that an order passed by a court having no jurisdiction is a nullity.[1198] The court laid down the correct position that the court could not effectively pass an order against a foreign tribunal due to lack of jurisdiction. This view is in consonance with the decision in ICC No. 5294, where the arbitral tribunal held that Egyptian Courts do not have jurisdiction over either the proceedings or the arbitrator.[1199]

4. SAFEGUARDS

One view is that the safeguards to prevent an unnecessary exercise of this power are built into the general principles of jurisdiction in India. For the issuance of an anti-suit injunction, an Indian court will only exercise jurisdiction if the foreign defendant carries out business in India or the underlying contract was to be wholly or partly performed in India.[1200] It will not ordinarily exercise jurisdiction where the defendant is wholly outside India even if the cause of action has arisen in India.[1201]

1193. *Ibid.*, ¶¶ 6, 40 & 41; Even *Bhatia had categorically held at ¶29 that Section 9 of the IAA does not envisage stay of arbitral proceedings.*
1194. *Ibid.*, ¶43.
1195. *Relying on ¶20 of the Judgment of the Supreme Court in In British India Steam Navigation Co. Ltd. v. Shanmughavilas Cashew Industries* (1990) 3 SCC 481. *Which had affirmed the judgment of the Privy Council in Sirdar Gurdyal Singh v. The Rajah of Faridkot* 1894 A.C. 670. *Which had held that no territorial legislation can give jurisdiction in a personal action which any foreign court should recognise against absent foreigners owing no allegiance or obedience to the country which has passed such legislation. In case, a party submits to the jurisdiction of an Indian court by litigating in India that would amount to submission of jurisdiction. Otherwise, a decree on a defendant which has not submitted himself to the jurisdiction is by international law and absolute nullity.*
1196. *Noy Vallesina Engineering Spa v. Jindal Drugs Ltd.* 2006 (3) Arb. LR 510 (Bom), ¶45.
1197. *Harshad Chimanlal Modi v. DLF Universal Ltd.* (2005) 7 SCC 791.
1198. *Relying on Kiran Singh v. Chaman Paswan* AIR 1954 SC 340. *Once such order is declared to be a nullity, the declaration relates back to the date on which the order was made and it will be deemed that the order never existed in law. Nawabkhan Abbaskhan v. State of Gujarat* (1974) 2 SCC 121, ¶20.
1199. Award of 22 February 1988 in ICC No. 5294, c.f. Lew, *supra* n. 885, at 215.
1200. Atul Setalvad, *Conflict of Laws* 182-183 (2007).
1201. *Kohinoor Carpet Manufacturers v. Forbes Gokak Ltd.* 2001 SCC OnLine Bom 1076.

Similarly, for the issuance of an anti-arbitration injunction, the court interference, if any, can only be done by the court when the court is 'seized of an action', i.e., a request for an anti-arbitration injunction has been filed and the court, after concluding it has jurisdiction, issues notice to the party invoking arbitration. Such jurisdiction may exist at the time of filing of the suit or will arise in the future for the purposes of enforcement.[1202]

Therefore, the consideration of Section 45 of IAA would arise when the party invoking arbitration resists the suit before the court on the ground that there is an arbitration agreement. Hence, the said court would have prima facie jurisdiction[1203] before issuing an anti-arbitration injunction. This position is far more restrictive than the position in the United States. In the United States courts have exercised jurisdiction even if one party is American and the contract was not even performed in the United States.[1204] However, this position provides the necessary safeguard against unwarranted court intervention.

Moreover, with the standards outlined above for the grant of an anti-suit or an anti-arbitration injunction, along with the varying degree of burden of proof, courts are already exercising extreme caution before issuing such injunctions. Therefore, there is no need for additional safeguards. Furthermore, if a party continues to violate an anti-suit injunction, apart from court enforcement, tribunals will always be at liberty to impose additional costs and damages for violating the arbitration agreement.

1202. *Devi Resources Ltd. v. Ambo Exports Ltd.* MANU/WB/0314/2019.

1203. *The decision was passed by 2:1 majority with Sabharwal J. giving his dissent to the effect that Section 45 of the IAA envisages a full trial. Excalibur Ventures LLC v. Texas Keystone Inc.* [2011] EWHC 1624 (Comm), ¶¶59–60.

1204. Jennifer, *supra* n. 891, at 299. *Also See,* Daniel J. Dorward, *The Forum Non Conveniens Doctrine and the Judicial Protection of Multilateral Corporations from Forum Shopping Plaintiffs,* 19(1) Uni. Penn. J. Int'l Eco. L. 141 (1998); Friedrich K. Juenger, *Forum Shopping, Domestic and International,* 63 (3) Tul. L. R. 556 (1989); Cedric Ryngaert, *Jurisdiction in International Law* 12 (2008); *Gray v. American Radiator & Standard Sanitary Corporation* 22 Ill. 2d 432 (1961); *Perkins v. Benguet Consolidated. Mining Co.* 342 U.S. 437, 438, 445 (1952), c.f. Tushar, *supra* n. 926, at 91.

Part II Tribunal-Ordered Interim Measures

CHAPTER 7

Interim Measures by the Arbitral Tribunal

When parties opt for arbitration as the preferred method of dispute resolution, they contemplate a 'one-stop' mechanism.[1205] If parties have to juggle between courts and arbitral tribunals for the resolution of their dispute, the efficiency and efficacy of arbitration stand substantially compromised. Since parties elect to have their dispute resolved through arbitration, it is the arbitral tribunal which should have the power to grant interim measures as well.

As discussed previously, courts must play a supportive and complementary role until the arbitral tribunal is constituted or when the tribunal does not have the power or is unable to act effectively. Apart from these few instances, the entire adjudication, including requests for interim measures, should be before the arbitral tribunal. Parties cannot be relegated back to courtrooms for seeking interim measures and have the merits decided by the arbitral tribunal.

1. THE NEED FOR TRIBUNAL-ORDERED INTERIM MEASURES

As parties voluntarily choose tribunals over tedious court litigation, the need for empowering arbitral tribunals to tailor and grant interim measures of protection to parties becomes vital. Adjudication of the dispute and the passing of the award require time. Despite speedy resolution of the dispute being a hallmark of arbitration, arbitrations tend not to be completed in less than a year in domestic proceedings[1206] and can even take more than twenty-four to thirty-six months in international proceedings.[1207] During the proceedings, there may be several circumstances that

1205. *A. Ayyasamy v. A. Paramasivam* (2016) 10 SCC 386, ¶46; Opinion of Hoffman J, *Fiona Trust & Holding Corporation & Others v. Yuri Privalov & Ors.* [2015] EWHC 527 (Comm).
1206. Justice B.N. Srikrishna, Report of the High-Level Committee to Review the Institutionalization of Arbitration Mechanism in India, (July 2017), available at: http://legalaffairs.gov.in/sites/default/files/Report-HLC.pdf.
1207. Kaj Hober, *Interim Measures by Arbitrators*, in Albert Jan van den Berg (ed.), *International Arbitration 2006: Back to Basics?* 721 (2007).

necessitate interim measures for either of the parties in the dispute. Hence, the request for an interim measure is very frequent.[1208] However, the need for interim measures from an arbitration is premised on several considerations apart from their requirement during the pendency of arbitration proceedings:[1209]

> *Party Autonomy*: Parties choose, by contract, arbitration over litigation before a court. It is only logical that the choice of the parties should be respected. Directing parties to have the dispute resolved on merits by the arbitral tribunal but taking recourse to courts for interim measures makes little sense. It violates both party autonomy and the entire arbitration agreement.[1210]
>
> *Efficiency:* Parties desire a practical, effective dispute resolution mechanism which finally resolves their dispute. Such an objective can only be achieved through interim measures since very often they are central aspects of commercial disputes.[1211] An arbitral tribunal is well equipped to provide quick and efficient relief[1212] and requests before national courts may sometimes require excessive time[1213] and costs.[1214] Therefore, it is more pragmatic and also appreciated by the parties to the dispute to have all disputes resolved in a single proceeding before a neutral arbitral tribunal[1215] and strengthen the efficiency of arbitration as a dispute resolution process.[1216] To send parties back to court would take away one of the critical features of arbitration, which is to have a less disruptive effect on the parties' overall commercial relationship.[1217]

1208. *Twenty-seven out of thirty-two arbitrators claim to have experienced such requests. Twenty out of thirty-two had experienced such requests up to twenty times and seven arbitrators claim to have experienced it beyond twenty, See, ibid.*; Holtzmann, *supra* n. 6 at, 165.
1209. Ali Yesilirmak, *supra* n. 30, at 49-50.
1210. *Ibid.*
1211. Gary Born, *supra* n. 33, at 2611.
1212. *Ibid.*
1213. Nathalie Voser, *Interim Relief in International Arbitration: The Tendency Towards a More Business-Oriented Approach*, 1(2) Dis. Res. Int'l, 171, 173 (2007).
1214. Report of the Secretary General for Settlement of Commercial Disputes, in its Thirty Second Report, 2000, A/CN.9/WG.II/WP.108, available at: https://undocs.org/en/A/CN.9/WG.II/WP.108, ¶104. ('*Reports from practitioners and arbitral institutions indicate that parties are seeking interim measures in an increasing number of cases. This trend and the lack of clear guidance to arbitral tribunals as to the scope of interim measures that may be issued and the conditions for their issuance may hinder the effective and efficient functioning of international commercial arbitration. To the extent arbitral tribunals are uncertain about issuing interim measures of protection and as a result refrain from issuing the necessary measures, this may lead to undesirable consequences, for example, unnecessary loss or damage may happen or a party may avoid enforcement of the award by deliberately making assets inaccessible to the claimant. Such a situation may also prompt parties to seek interim measures from courts instead of the arbitral tribunals in situations where the arbitral tribunal would be well placed to issue an interim measure; this causes unnecessary cost and delay (e.g., because of the need to translate documents into the language of the court and the need to present evidence and arguments to the judge'*).
1215. Gary Born, *supra* n. 33, at 2611.
1216. Pierre A. Karrer, *Interim Measures Issued by Arbitral Tribunals and the Courts: Less Theory, Please*, in Albert Jan van den Berg (ed.), *International Arbitration and National Courts: The Never Ending Story* 97-98 (2001).
1217. Ali Yesilirmak, *supra* n. 30, at 51-52.

Risk of Foreign Law: The power of the tribunal to grant interim measures prevents the risk of parties having to deal with the laws of a foreign country or a foreign court. Such a scenario also involves inconvenience and additional costs to the parties. For example, there may be costs associated with the translation of documents into the official language of the foreign court.[1218] Parties are likely to have considered such inconvenience and costs as a part of their risk allocation and their will ought to be respected.

Familiarity: Arbitrators are more suited to grant or deny requests for interim measures of protection as they are more acquainted with the facts of the case,[1219] the conduct of the parties, and the objective behind the request.[1220]

Risk of Prejudgment: Interim measures require a prima facie view of the merits of the claim. Relying on the courts creates a risk that they will purport to pre-empt or prejudge decisions of the arbitral tribunal on the merits of the parties' dispute.[1221] There would be nothing left for the tribunal to adjudicate. Moreover, it incentivises parties to settle or gain a strategic advantage in the dispute if the final decision on merits will be prejudged.

Expert Adjudication: Given that arbitrators are chosen for their knowledge and expertise in a particular field, they are likely to be better suited to deal with a request for interim measures. Moreover, arbitrators are generally the best judges to determine the most suitable type and form of the interim measure depending on the facts and circumstances of each case given their expertise on the subject of the dispute. They are also most suited to keep in mind the commercial understanding of the parties.

Preserving Confidentiality: The confidentiality of the dispute remains preserved when interim measures are requested and ordered by an arbitral tribunal as opposed to a court of law where the cases, identity of the parties, and other details of the case are open to the public.[1222]

No Appeal: Interim measures of protection ordered by an arbitral tribunal are less costly than judicial measures due to the lack of appeal. However, appeals against interim orders passed by the arbitral tribunal are permitted in India.[1223]

It is relevant to note that more and more disputes are now becoming arbitrable such as intellectual property disputes, blockchain, taxation, and competition law which means that the need for interim measures is much more than ever before.[1224] It

1218. Voser, *supra* n. 1213, at 173.
1219. Christian Hausmaninger, *The ICC Rules for a Pre-arbitral Referee Procedure: A Step Towards Solving the Problem of Provisional Relief in International Commercial Arbitration?*, 7 ICSID L. R. Fgn. Inv. L. J. 81, 85 (1992).
1220. Ali Yesilirmak, *supra* n. 30, at 51-52.
1221. Gary Born, *supra* n. 33, at 2611.
1222. *Temitayo Bello, Why Arbitration Triumphs Litigation* 11 (2019).
1223. Indian Arbitration Act, 1996, S. 37(2)(b).
1224. David E. Wagoner, *Interim Relief in International Arbitration: Enforcement Is a Substantial Problem*, 51(4) Dis. Res. J. 69, 73 (1996).

was the growth of commercial complexities and the need for interim measures, and the recognition of their role in effective dispute resolution that led to the 2006 Model Law Revisions overhauling the existing regime for interim measures.[1225]

There was a demand to develop a system that not only confirms the availability of interim measures to be granted by the arbitral tribunal but also fulfils two complementary purposes, i.e., (a) the need to count on an interim measures regulation system that illustrates the different choices of interim measures available; and (b) the convenience of creating a system which can help in achieving a balance between the needs of the party requesting the interim measure and those of the party affected by such measure.[1226]

This need for tribunal-ordered interim measures, often to avoid courts, protect confidentiality, and maintain neutrality, is also evident from the growing recognition of the concept of emergency arbitration. Many institutional arbitration institutes, including those in India, now provide for the appointment of an emergency arbitrator before the constitution of the arbitral tribunal to provide for urgent interim measures.[1227]

2. THE POWER TO GRANT INTERIM MEASURES

Historically, interim measures were reserved for the exclusive domain of courts and arbitral tribunals were denied the power to order interim measures.[1228] Some countries follow this position even today.[1229] One rationale for this view was that since the arbitral tribunals do not have coercive powers, such measures should be only granted by the courts.[1230] The other reason to keep the power to grant interim measures restricted to the courts was public policy.[1231] Such concerns stemmed mainly from the

1225. Roth, *supra* n. 448, at 425.
1226. Luis, *supra* n. 521, at 540.
1227. David Wilson, *Emergency Arbitrator Rules among Four Major Arbitral Institutions: Both Alike and Different*, available at: https://www.expertguides.com/articles/emergency-arbitrator-rules-among-four-major-arbitral-institutions-both-alike-and-different/aralfynx; Singhania and Partners, *India: Emergency Arbitration In India: Concept and Beginning*, available at: https://www.mondaq.com/advicecentre/content/3958/Emergency-Arbitration-In-India-Concept-And-Beginning.
1228. Blackby, *supra* n. 34, at 314-315; Gary Born, *supra* n. 33, at 2610, 2611; Quebec Code of Civil Procedure, Art. 940.4; China Civil Procedure Law, 1991, Art. 258 & China Arbitration Law, Art. 28; Stephen, *supra* n. 96, at 267-268.
1229. *See Appendix B*; *For example*, Finland, Thailand, Greece; Roth, *supra* n. 448, at 429; The Nigeria Arbitration and Conciliation Act (Repeal and Re-enactment) Bill 2017 *guarantees the power of arbitrators to grant interim measures*, c.f. Sadaff Habib, *2018 In Review: A Tug of War for International Arbitration in Africa*, (17 January 2019), available at: http://arbitrationblog.kluwerarbitration.com/2019/01/17/2018-in-review-a-tug-of-war-for-international-arbitration-in-africa/.
1230. Gary Born, *supra* n. 33, at 2610, 2611.
1231. *Lew,* supra *n. 2, at 24. However, Gary Born disagrees with this view arguing that there is little evidence suggesting public policy considerations, especially because if the tribunal is competent to decide the issue finally, with binding effect, then there possibly cannot be public policy considerations barring a tribunal from deciding the same issue provisionally,* c.f., Gary Born, *supra* n. 33, at 2610, 2611.

mistrust of the arbitral process and the insecurity of the courts to give up their power.[1232]

In India, the power was specifically recognised only under Section 17 of the IAA and the 1940 Act did not contain any provision authorising the arbitral tribunal to grant interim measures during the pendency of arbitration proceedings. Even after the adoption of the IAA, courts still required the arbitral tribunal to determine whether it had jurisdiction to grant an interim measure.[1233]

However, these historical reservations about interim measures being granted by arbitral tribunals were ill-founded and disrupted the efficient resolution of disputes through arbitration. Today, it is accepted worldwide that arbitrators are the natural judges or the first forum for interim measures of protection whenever parties have entered into an arbitration agreement.[1234] The only exceptions to this rule are if arbitral proceedings have not commenced, or the arbitral tribunal does not have the power or is unable to act effectively. In such cases, it is the courts that will provide interim measures.

2.1. Sources of the Power to Grant Interim Measures

There are various views with respect to the source of the power of the arbitral tribunal to grant interim measures. It can be traced to (a) the agreement of the parties;[1235] (b) the power of the arbitral tribunal to regulate its own procedure;[1236] or (c) the arbitral tribunal's inherent power.[1237] There is also a view that the inherent power of the arbitral tribunal to order interim measures of protection is neither by virtue of the arbitration agreement nor statute but due to the status of the arbitral tribunal as a body

1232. Ali Yesilirmak, *supra* n. 30, at 29.
1233. *Army Welfare Housing Organization v. Gautam Construction & Fisheries Ltd.* AIR 1998 SC 3244, ¶23.
1234. Ali Yesilirmak, *supra* n. 30, at 49.
1235. Gabrielle Kaufmann-Kohler & Antonio Rigozzi, *International Arbitration: Law and Practice in Switzerland* 557 (2015); Lew, *supra* n. 28, at ¶23-8; Alan Redfern, *Interim Measures*, in Newman & Hill (eds), *The Leading Arbitrators' Guide to International Arbitration* 367 (2008); Donald Francis Donovan, *The Arbitrator's Power to Issue Procedural and Interim orders*, 10 (1) ICC Dis. Res. Bull. 57 (1999).
1236. Ali Yesilirmak, *supra* n. 30, at 58; Luis, *supra* n. 521, at 540; Eric Schwartz, *The Practices and Experience of the ICC Court in ICC, Conservatory and Provisional Measures in International Arbitration* 58 (1993), *see* Lawrence Collins, *Dicey and Morris on Conflict of Laws* 170 (1993); Lew, *supra* n. 28, at ¶¶23-8 & 23-9; Sigvard Jarvin, *To What Extent Are Procedural Decisions of Arbitrators Subject to Court Review?*, in Albert Jan van den Berg (ed.), *Improving the Efficiency of Arbitration Agreements and Awards: 40 Years of Application of the New York Convention* 367 (1999); Georgios Petrochilos, *Procedural Law in International Arbitration* (2004), ¶¶5- 01- 5-125.
1237. *David Caron, Interim Measures of Protection: Theory and Practice in Light of the Israel-United States Claims Tribunal*, 46 Rabel J. Comp. Int'l Pvt. L. 465 (1986); Alan Scott Rau, *Provisional Relief in Arbitration: How Things Stand in the United States*, 22 J. Int'l Arb. 7 (2005); Craig, *supra* n. 585, at 460; Donovan, *supra* n. 1235, at 60; Anne Hermann, *Drawing a Contrast: Interim Measure of Protection in International Arbitral Proceedings: The United States v. Germany*, 9 Vind. J. Int'l Arb. 49, 53 (2005); Alexis Mourre, *Judicial Penalties and Specific Performance in International Arbitration*, in De Ly & Levy (eds), *Interest, Auxiliary and Alternative Remedies in International Arbitration* 53 (2008).

for the resolution of disputes.[1238] Another view is that the power to grant interim measures stems from the law of the seat,[1239] i.e., a matter of procedure and therefore, governed primarily by the *lex arbitri.*[1240]

Boog states that an arbitral tribunal should first look at the agreement of the parties and the mandatory rules of law in the *lex arbitri* which prevent it from taking any interim relief decisions.[1241] In his opinion, the implied power theory is unnecessary as most developed jurisdictions accept the arbitral tribunal's authority to grant interim relief.[1242] *Born* asserts that the arbitral tribunal should consider itself competent to order interim measures even when the seat of arbitration would not permit the same. He rests his justifications on the principle of *Kompetenz-kompetenz* and draws support from the agreement of the parties. In his view, jurisdictions other than the seat would be able to enforce such orders.[1243]

It may be added that despite the debate on the source of the power to grant interim measures, all provisions permitting the arbitral tribunal to grant interim measures do little more than empower the arbitral tribunal.[1244] Notwithstanding the different views, the common consensus is that unless the power to grant interim measures is expressly excluded, the arbitral tribunal can order interim measures.[1245]

2.1.1. Article 17 of the Model Law

This view was enshrined in Article 17 of the Model Law before the 2006 Model Law Revisions. The scope of it, however, was curtailed by the phrase '*in respect of the subject matter of the dispute*'. After the 2006 Model Law revisions, the power to grant interim measures continues to be expressly recognised under Article 17(1) of the Model Law, albeit without the use of any limitations, i.e., '*Unless otherwise agreed by the parties, the arbitral tribunal may, at the request of a party, grant interim measures*'. The language of the said provision has been adopted verbatim in the domestic legislation by

1238. David D. Caron, *Interim Measures of Protection: Theory and Practice in Light of the Iran United States Claims Tribunal*, 46 Rabel J. Comp. Int'l Pvt. L. 476 (1986); Michael F. Hoellering, *Interim Measures and Arbitration: The Situation in the United States*, 46(2) Arb. J. 22 (1991); Michael F. Hoellering, *Interim Relief in Aid of International Commercial Arbitration*, 1 Wisc. Int'l L. J. 2 (1984); Sigvard Jarvin, *Choosing the Place of Arbitration: Where Do We Stand?*, 16 Int'l Bus. L. 417, 422 (1988); Schwartz, *supra* n. 1236, at 58; Donovan, *supra* n. 1235, at 66; Alan Scott, *supra* n. 1237; *Charles Construction Company v. Derderian* 586 N.E.2d 992 (Mass. 1992) (*accepting that an arbitrator has inherent and implied authority to grant a security for claim*); *Konkar Maritime Enter., SA v. Compagnie Belge d'Affretement* 668 F. Supp. 267 (S.D.N.Y. 1987); *Southern Seas Navigation Ltd v. Petroleos Mexicanos of Mexico City* 606 F.Supp. 692 (S.D.N. Y. 1985); *Island Creek Coal Sales Co. v. Gainsville* 729 F2d 1046 (6th Cir. 1984); *Sperry International Trade, Inc. v. Israel* 689 F2d. 301 (2d Cir. 1982).
1239. Boog, *supra* n. 592, at 412.
1240. Lew, *supra* n. 28, at ¶23-29.
1241. Boog, *supra* n. 592, at 413.
1242. *Ibid.*
1243. Gary Born, *supra* n. 33, at 2642.
1244. Abascal, *supra* n. 1, at 754.
1245. Gary Born, *supra* n. 33, at 2613.

most countries that have adopted the 2006 Model Law Revisions.[1246] Therefore, national arbitration statutes of countries that have adopted the Model Law and the revisions expressly provide for such power.

It is also pertinent to note that the power to grant interim measures was also recognised by various arbitral institutes well before the 2006 Model Law Revisions.[1247] Even today, most arbitration institutes recognised the power to grant '*any interim measures it [tribunal] deems appropriate*'.[1248] Therefore, the debate on the source of the power with respect to the availability of interim measures by the tribunal is not as significant today. It is now moot that an arbitral tribunal has the power to grant interim measures.

Nonetheless, the source of such power is essential to determine the types of interim measures that can be granted by the arbitral tribunal and their enforcement. A conclusive determination regarding the source of the power is also necessary to understand the procedural challenges that may arise either at the stage of enforcement of the interim measures or on the grounds of 'excess of jurisdiction' as a challenge to the final award.[1249]

The power to grant interim relief is governed by the *lex arbitri*, especially in nations that have adopted the Model Law. Even those countries that have not adopted the Model Law, their arbitration statutes recognise such power.[1250] In the rare absence of express recognition of such power, the arbitral tribunal is at liberty to set its own rules of procedure[1251] and grant interim relief, subject to a contrary agreement of the parties. Therefore, the source of the power is most often the *lex arbitri* and it is this law that determines the scope of the power to grant interim measures.

2.2. Power to Grant Interim Measures in India

In India, the power to grant interim measures is contained in Section 17(1) of the IAA which provides:

1246. New Zealand, Arbitration Act, 1996, S. 17A & Sch. 1; Mauritius International Arbitration Act, 2008, S. 21(1); Brunei International Arbitration Order, 2009 S. 15(1)(J); International Arbitration Act, 1974, S. 17(1) & Sch. 2; NSW Commercial Arbitration Act, 2010, S. 17 (1), and the equivalent provision in the other domestic Acts; Hong Kong Arbitration Ordinance (Cap.609), S. 17; Florida, International Commercial Arbitration Law, S. 684.0028; Belgium Judicial Code, Art. 1691, (*the article refers to 'interim or conservatory measures [the tribunal] deems necessary', with the exception of attachment orders*).
1247. Article 31(1), 1999 SCC Rules, which provided for specific performance as an interim measure; Art. 25.1, 1998 LCIA Rules; Rule 24, 2007 SIAC Rules; Art. 26(1), 1976 UNCITRAL Rules; Section 20.1, 1998 DIS Rules.
1248. Article 26(1), UNCITRAL Rules, 2013; Art. 15.1, 2018 DIAC Rules; Art. 15.1, 2016 MCIA, 2016; Rule 33, NPAC; Rule 13(1), 1996 ICADR Rules; Art. 27.1, 2017 SIAC Rules; Art. 37(1), 2017 SCC Rules; Art. 28(1), 2017 ICC Rules; Art. 25.1, 2014 LCIA Rules, even list out the type of measure that can be granted; Art. 31.1, 2007 Dubai Rules; Rule 37(a), AAA Rules; Art. 25.1, 2018 DIS Rules; Art. 33.1, 2018 VIAC Rules; Rule 8, 2018 AIAC Rules; Art. 26(1), 2012 CEAC Rules; Art. 46(1), 2019 RAC Rules; Art. 32(1), 2016 KAC.
1249. NYC, Art. V.
1250. English Arbitration Act, 1996, S. 38.
1251. UNCITRAL Model Law, Art. 19.

> Section 17 – (1) *A party may, during the arbitral proceedings, apply to the arbitral tribunal:*
> (i) for the appointment of a guardian for a minor or person of unsound mind for the purposes of arbitral proceedings; or
> (ii) for an interim measure of protection in respect of any of the following matters, namely:
> (a) the preservation, interim custody or sale of any goods which are the subject-matter of the arbitration agreement;
> (b) securing the amount in dispute in the arbitration;
> (c) the detention, preservation or inspection of any property or thing which is the subject-matter of the dispute in arbitration, or as to which any question may arise therein and authorising for any of the aforesaid purposes any person to enter upon any land or building in the possession of any party, or authorising any samples to be taken, or any observation to be made, or experiment to be tried, which may be necessary or expedient for the purpose of obtaining full information or evidence;
> (d) interim injunction or the appointment of a receiver;
> (e) such other interim measure of protection as may appear to the arbitral tribunal to be just and convenient,
>
> and the arbitral tribunal shall have the same power for making orders, as the Court has for the purpose of, and in relation to, any proceedings before it.

Therefore, Section 17(1) of the IAA empowers the arbitral tribunal to grant interim measures and also provides the scope of the power with reference to the nature of remedies that can be provided by an arbitral tribunal.

3. SCOPE OF THE POWER

The scope of the power of the tribunal to grant interim measures is considered to be quite broad,[1252] especially if one takes the view that the power stems from the power of the tribunal to regulate its own procedure or its inherent power. Hence, Article 17 of the Model Law was originally drafted in very broad terms.[1253] However, the vast discretion afforded to tribunals led to inconsistent application.[1254] After the 2006 Model Law Revisions, the scope is expressly contained in Article 17(2) of the Model Law to promote consistency and harmonisation across jurisdictions.

3.1. Article 17(2) of the Model Law

Initially, the Working Group considered that the issue of the power of arbitral tribunals to order interim measures should be dealt with by preparing a non-legislative text such as guidelines or practice notes which would comprise issues such as types of interim

1252. Gary Born, *supra* n. 33, at 2612-2613.
1253. Report of UNCITRAL Working Group on the work of its Sixth session, 1983, A/CN.9/245, available at: https://undocs.org/en/A/CN.9/245, ¶71; *See, e.g.*, Alan Redfern & Martin Hunter, *Law and Practice of International Commercial Arbitration* 341 (2004).
1254. Luis, *supra* n. 521, at 541.

measures, discretion for ordering such measures, guidelines on the exercise of such discretion, and circumstances in which interim orders may be passed.[1255] However, this approach was abandoned and the revised articles of the 2006 Model Law Revisions were adopted.[1256]

Article 17(2) of the 2006 Model Law defines an interim measure as:

> an interim measure is any temporary measure, whether in the form of an award or in another form, by which, at any time prior to the issuance of the award by which the dispute is finally decided, the arbitral tribunal orders a party to:
>
> (a) Maintain or restore the status quo pending determination of the dispute;
> (b) Take action that would prevent, or refrain from taking action that is likely to cause, current or imminent harm or prejudice to the arbitral process itself;
> (c) Provide a means of preserving assets out of which a subsequent award may be satisfied; or
> (d) Preserve evidence that may be relevant and material to the resolution of the dispute.

It should be noted that the Working Group was conscious of the fact that Article 17(2) of the Model Law is purposive in its approach.[1257] The intention was very clear. The provisions were supposed to be exhaustive yet generic.[1258] The scope was deliberately kept vast and the items listed in Article 17(2) of the Model Law do not exhaustively contain the circumstances or list of the types of interim measures that can be issued by the arbitral tribunal.

It is pertinent to highlight that the entire debate on interim measures was not based on actual cases or hard data but mostly on anecdotes, rules, or case laws. Even the request for information by the secretariat received very poor feedback.[1259] Thus, the 2006 Model Law Revisions were conceptualised more as an illustrative formulation. The idea was to provide the terms and circumstances for the grant of interim measures, and a definition of interim measures but with the specific goal of not limiting the power of the arbitral tribunal.[1260] Such intent is evident from the phrase '*or prejudice to the arbitral process itself*'.[1261]

1255. Report of UNCITRAL Working Group on the work of its Thirty Second session, June 2000, A/CN.9/468, available at: https://undocs.org/en/A/CN.9/468, ¶81.
1256. Tomas Kennedy-Grant, *Interim Measures under the UNCITRAL Model Law on International Commercial Arbitration: The Impact of the 2006 Amendments*, 10 (1) Asian Int'l Arb. J. 17, 21 (2014).
1257. Report of UNCITRAL Working Group on the work of its Thirty Seventh session, 2002, A/CN.9/23, available at: https://undocs.org/en/A/CN.9/523, ¶¶38.
1258. Luis, *supra* n. 521, at 545, 565.
1259. Abascal, *supra* n. 1, at 756.
1260. Menon, *supra* n. 102, at 6.
1261. UNCITRAL Model Law, Art. 17(2)(b). In Qatar, this phrase has been adopted in a modified manner, Qatar Arbitration Law, 2017, Art. 17(1)(b), provides for '*adopting a measure to prevent the occurrence of current or imminent damage or that would prejudice the Arbitration process itself, or to prevent the adoption of procedures that may possibly result in such damage or prejudice*'.

3.1.1. *Types of Powers*

The power to grant interim measures, therefore, refers to three different kinds of powers, i.e., investigatory, preservatory (status quo), and conservatory (of the award) to be rendered[1262] and can be divided into three broad categories, i.e.:[1263]

(a) preservation of evidence (Article 17(2)(d) of the Model Law) – measures to preserve evidence and prevent it from deterioration;
(b) measures related to the conduct of proceedings & relation between the parties (Article 17(2)(a) & (b) of the Model Law) – measures ordering parties to do or not to do something with an aim to protect a legal right; and
(c) measures aimed to facilitate the enforcement of an award (Article 17(2)(c) of the Model Law) – measures to prevent dissipation of assets or secure the amount in dispute.

3.2. Section 17 of the IAA

Till 2015, the power of the arbitral tribunal to grant interim measures was identical to erstwhile Article 17 of the Model Law.[1264] Hence, the restrictive interpretation of the phrase 'subject matter of the dispute' in Article 17 of the Model Law before the 2006 Model Law Revisions was extended to Section 17(1) of the IAA.

3.2.1. *'Subject Matter of the Dispute'*

Article 17 of the Model Law as originally adopted in 1985 referred to interim measures with respect to the subject matter of the dispute. A narrow view had been taken by some scholars and tribunals[1265] that interim measures of protection can only be granted in relation to the 'subject matter of the dispute,' i.e., tangible property and not otherwise. This was a misconstruction as the reference to 'subject matter of the dispute' was meant to be an illustration of the nature of interim measures within an arbitration proceeding and the text was never intended to restrict the use of interim measures to a tangible subject matter of the dispute.[1266]

Hence, this language was deleted in 2006 to make it more generic and in order to recognise the expansive power of the arbitral tribunal to grant interim measures.[1267] Interestingly, the word 'necessary' was also dropped in the 2006 Model Law but the

1262. Lew, *supra* n. 28, at 595.
1263. Ali Yesilirmak, *supra* n. 30, at 11.
1264. Indian Arbitration Act, 1996, S. 17(1); '*unless otherwise agreed by the parties, the arbitral tribunal may, at the request of the party, order a party to take any interim measure of protection as the tribunal may consider necessary in respect of the subject-matter of the dispute*'.
1265. Luis, *supra* n. 521, at 541.
1266. Note by the Secretariat in UNCITRAL Working Group II (Arbitration) of its Thirty Sixth session, 2002, A/CN.9/WG.II/WP.119, available at: https://undocs.org/en/A/CN.9/WG.II/WP.119, at 12. c.f. Luis, *supra* n. 521, at 542.
1267. UNCITRAL Model Law, Art. 17(1); Gary Born, *supra* n. 33, at 2612-2613.

words 'unless otherwise agreed' were retained as the only exception to the authority of the arbitral tribunal to grant interim measures.

It is relevant to note that Austria and Liechtenstein[1268] have retained the phrase even after the 2006 Model Law Revisions in a slightly different manner. Section 593 of the Austrian CPC grants the power to the tribunal to '*order against the other party such interim or protective measures it deems necessary in respect of the subject-matter in dispute if the enforcement of the claim would be otherwise frustrated or significantly impeded, or there was a risk of irreparable harm*'.

Unsurprisingly, the Indian courts preferred the restrictive interpretation while examining the meaning of the phrase 'subject matter of the dispute' in the context of Section 17(1) of the IAA.[1269] Courts made a comparison with Section 9 of the IAA wherein Section 9(ii)(a) and (c) of IAA which use the phrase 'subject matter of the dispute' and Section 9(ii)(b) of IAA which uses the phrase 'amount in dispute'. The court took the view that since the legislature in the same provision uses two different phrases, it intended to distinguish between the two.[1270]

Therefore, the reference to the subject matter of dispute in Section 9(ii)(a) of the IAA would refer to 'goods' in respect of which there could be an order of 'preservation' and 'interim custody'. The same words in Section 9(ii)(c) of the IAA referred to 'any property or thing' in respect of which there can be an order of 'detention, preservation or inspection of'. It is only when the claim is monetary that Section 9(ii)(b) for securing the amount in dispute would become applicable. On an illogical analogy, the court held that the word 'subject matter of the dispute' in Section 17 of the IAA should be understood as a reference to a tangible subject matter of dispute different from 'amount in dispute'.[1271]

3.3. 2015 Amendment

Post the 2015 Amendment, the phrase 'subject matter of dispute' has now been removed under the revised Section 17(1) of the IAA. This makes the scope of Section 17(1) of IAA abundantly clear and in consonance with the 2006 Model Law Revisions that the arbitral tribunal is not restrained in granting interim measures beyond the 'subject matter of the dispute'. The only reference to the phrase has been retained in Section 17(1)(ii)(a) of IAA which provides for an interim measure of protection in respect of the preservation, interim custody, or sale of any goods which are the subject matter of the arbitration agreement.

1268. Liechtenstein Code of Civil Procedure, S. 610(1).
1269. *Gail India Limited v. Lal Kishan Agarwal Industries Ltd.* (2008) 8 SCC 16, ¶¶14-15; *Intertoll ICS Cecons O & M Co. Pvt. Ltd. v. National Highways Authority of India* 2013 SCC OnLine Del 447, ¶18; *Shin Satellite Public Co. Ltd. v. Jain Studios Ltd.* 2008 SCC OnLine Del 1127, ¶36.
1270. *Intertoll ICS Cecons O & M Co. Pvt. Ltd. v. National Highways Authority of India* 2013 SCC OnLine Del 447, ¶19.
1271. *Ibid.*

3.3.1. Bar on the Exclusion of the Power

Another important change brought in Section 17(1) of the IAA with the 2015 Amendment is the removal of the phrase '*Unless otherwise agreed by the parties*'. Though the language of Section 17(1) of the IAA has been made similar to that of Singapore,[1272] the removal of the phrase has taken away the autonomy of the parties. One of the key features of arbitration is the flexibility granted to the parties to tailor their dispute resolution process and to choose whether or not the arbitral tribunal should have the power to order interim measures. Section 17 of the IAA now reads '*A party may* ....' Thus, the opt-out mechanism envisaged by the Model Law is no longer available and India has moved away from the 'free choice model'.[1273] Earlier, the power under Section 17(1) of the IAA could be exercised when (a) there was not an exclusion by mutual agreement between the parties; and (b) the interim measure of protection had a nexus with the subject matter of the dispute.[1274]

This deletion implies that whenever Part I of the Arbitration Act is applicable, the parties, even by express agreement, cannot oust the jurisdiction of the arbitral tribunal of its power to grant interim measures. This is contrary to most contemporary arbitration regimes.[1275] The omission of the phrase does not appear to be deliberate but is fatal to the concept of party autonomy.[1276] While it is true that such exclusion is more often than not never contained in arbitration agreements, taking away the complete autonomy of the parties to choose a single forum[1277] for interim measures, such as the court, takes away the flexibility of the arbitral process.

3.3.2. Application to Be Made by a Party

Section 17 of the IAA specifically uses the words '*a party may, during the arbitral proceedings*'. Therefore, consistent with international jurisprudence and Article 17(1) of the Model Law, it is only a party to the arbitration which can apply to the arbitral tribunal for interim measures.[1278] Similarly, the arbitral tribunal cannot permit a third party who is not a party to the arbitration agreement to be part of the arbitration proceedings or grant interim relief to the said party.[1279] In Jordan, however, the tribunal has the power to grant interim measures on its own initiative.[1280]

1272. Singapore International Arbitration Act, 1994, S. 12A; Singapore Domestic Arbitration Act, 2001, Ss 12(2) & 12(3), *which do not provide for exclusion of the power to grant interim measures to the tribunal.*
1273. Rajendra Barot, *supra* n. 679, at 177.
1274. *Asian Electronic Ltd., Thane v. MP State Electricity Board & Ors.* 2007 SCC OnLine MP 179, ¶14.
1275. Boog, *supra* n. 592, at 418; Gary Born, *supra* n. 33, at 2636.
1276. According to the *travaux préparatoires*, the provision should neither '*be read as precluding such exclusion agreements, [nor] be read as positively giving effect to such exclusion*'. Resolution adopted on the report of the third committee (18 November 1995), U.N. Doc A/RES/40/17, available at: https://undocs.org/en/A/RES/40/17.
1277. Gary Born, *supra* n. 33, at 2636.
1278. Abascal, *supra* n. 1, at 758.
1279. *National Highways Authority of India v. You one Maharia J.V. and Ors.* 2010 (4) Arb. LR 413, ¶¶24-25.
1280. Jordan Arbitration Law, 2001, Art. 23.

3.4. Scope of the Power of the Tribunal Vis-à-Vis the Court

Given that the text of Section 9 of the IAA was borrowed from the English Arbitration Act and Section 17 of the IAA was drafted along the lines of the Model Law before the 2015 Amendment, the scope of the power to grant interim measures under Section 17(1) of the IAA was considerably restricted by the inconsistent and often an erroneous interpretation of the provision by the Indian courts. Though the adoption of Article 17 of the erstwhile Model Law ought to have signified a more welcoming approach to the issue of interim measures by the judiciary in India, the reverse was true.

3.4.1. The Misplaced Superiority of Courts

In a landmark judgment in *Army Welfare Housing Organisation v. Gautam Construction & Fisheries Ltd.*,[1281] (*Army Welfare*) a three-judge bench of the Supreme Court observed that the arbitrator had not determined the question as to whether he had jurisdiction to pass an interim order or not,[1282] in effect sealing the fate of arbitral tribunals and the power to grant interim measures during arbitration proceedings.

In the court's view, an arbitrator cannot issue any direction which would go beyond the reference of the arbitration agreement as the power of the tribunal to grant interim measures is a limited one.[1283] The court's reasoning was that an award passed under the IAA is not required to be made by a rule of the court. Additionally, the interim order passed under Section 17(1) of the IAA must relate to the protection of the subject matter of the dispute and can only be directed to the parties in the arbitration proceedings. It cannot be directed against third parties.

Moreover, the arbitral tribunal has no power to enforce its own order and no provision has been made for the judicial enforcement of the same.[1284] Also, an interim order passed under Section 17 of the IAA can only continue till the end of arbitration proceedings and if no mention is made or directions are given in the award, such interim order shall come to an end at the conclusion of the arbitration proceedings.[1285]

In another instance, the scope of powers of the arbitral tribunal under Section 17 of IAA was considered at length in *Intertoll ICS Cecons O&M Co. Pvt. Ltd. v. National Highways Authority of India*[1286] *(Intertoll)*. In the instant case by two separate orders, the arbitral tribunal directed the appellant to furnish security of an amount equivalent to the counterclaims filed by the respondent. The court (in appeal) examined the language of Section 17 of the IAA and emphasised the words 'take' and 'protection' to understand the legislative intent behind the words 'subject matter of the dispute' and held that the provision envisaged some tangible property and not an indeterminate

1281. *Army Welfare Housing Organization v. Gautam Construction & Fisheries Ltd.* AIR 1998 SC 3244.
1282. *Ibid.*, ¶23.
1283. *Ibid.*, ¶57.
1284. *Ibid.*, ¶58.
1285. *Suresh Shah v. M/s Tata Consultancy Services Ltd. & Anr.* 2017 SCC OnLine Del 8559, ¶14.
1286. *Intertoll ICS Cecons O & M Co. Pvt. Ltd. v. National Highways Authority of India* 2013 SCC OnLine Del 447, ¶¶18-20.

monetary claim. Relying on earlier precedents,[1287] the court held that the powers of the tribunal under Section 17 of the IAA are not as wide as that of the court under Section 9 of the IAA and the principle underlying Section 9 of the IAA would *ipso facto* not apply to Section 17 of the IAA.[1288] Hence, the scope of the power of the arbitral tribunal was limited, as compared to that of the court under Section 9 of the IAA.

This bias in favour of courts was the prevailing view among the courts in India. It was justified on the ground that the power under Sections 9 and 17 of the IAA are independent[1289] and while there may be some overlap between the two provisions, the power under Section 9 of the IAA is much wider as it extends to the period pre and post the award, during arbitration proceedings,[1290] as well as with regard to the subject matter and nature of the order.[1291] Section 17(1) of the IAA neither confers any power on the arbitral tribunal to enforce its orders nor provides for judicial enforcement of any such order,[1292] and it is for this reason that Section 9 of the IAA gives the court power to pass interim orders during the arbitration proceedings.[1293]

The other justification for this view was that orders passed under Section 17 of the IAA are appealable under Section 37(2)(b) of the IAA and hence always subject to orders of a court in an appeal.[1294] Therefore, it was considered that the court being higher in the hierarchy and being a judicial forum would have primacy over overlapping orders.[1295] These views granting supremacy to the courts had been reaffirmed[1296] in several precedents.[1297]

Fortunately, some courts went against the tide and rejected such narrow interpretation of the scope of powers of the arbitral tribunal. In *Baker Hughes Singapore Pte*

1287. *National Highways Authority of India v. China Coal Construction Group Corporation* 2006 (1) Arb. LR 265 (Del), ¶14 and *Shin Satellite Public Co. Ltd. v. Jain Studios Ltd.* 2008 SCC OnLine Del 1127, ¶36.
1288. *Intertoll ICS Cecons O & M Co. Pvt. Ltd. v. National Highways Authority of India* 2013 SCC OnLine Del 447, ¶18.
1289. *Atul Limited v. Prakash Industries Ltd.* 2003 (2) Arb. LR 489 (Del), ¶2; *SPA Agencies (India) Pvt. Ltd. v. Harish Rawtani* 2010 (2) Arb. LR 221 (AP) (DB), ¶14.
1290. *National Highways Authority of India v. China Coal Construction Group Corporation* 2006 (1) Arb. LR 265 (Del), ¶41; *affirmed in Chunilal Kapoorchanji Shah v. Yuvraj Industries Ltd.* 2010 (1) Arb. LR. 138 (Guj), ¶14; *Ashok Leyland Finance Ltd. v. Sanatan Transport Co. Pvt. Ltd.* 2005 (2) Arb. LR 220 (Bom) (DB), ¶¶7-8.
1291. *National Highways Authority of India v. China Coal Construction Group Corporation* 2006 (1) Arb. LR 265 (Del), ¶14; *Krishna Motor Finance (P) Ltd. v. Iltush Ahammed* 2011 SCC OnLine Cal 1367, ¶6.
1292. *BPL Ltd. v. Morgan Securities and Credit Pvt. Ltd. & Ors.* 2008 (1) Arb. LR 325 (Del), ¶10.
1293. *Sundaram Finance Ltd. v. NEPC India Ltd.* (1999) 2 SCC 479, ¶¶11, 13.
1294. *National Highways Authority of India v. China Coal Construction Group Corporation* 2006 (1) Arb. LR 265 (Del), ¶14.
1295. *Ibid.*, ¶14.
1296. *Shin Satellite Public Co. Ltd. v. Jain Studios Ltd.* 2008 SCC OnLine Del 1127, ¶31.
1297. *Adhunik Steels Limited v. Orissa Manganese and Minerals (P). Ltd.* (2007) 7 SCC 125, ¶5; *Escorts Finance Ltd. v. Mohd. Hanif D. Khan* 2003 (Suppl.) Arb. LR 93 (Del) (DB), ¶4; *Atul Limited v. Prakash Industries Ltd.* 2003 (2) Arb. LR 489 (Del), ¶2; *National Highways Authority of India v. China Coal Construction Group Corporation* 2006 (1) Arb. LR 265 (Del), ¶14; *Modi Rubber Limited v. Guardian International Corporation* 2007 SCC OnLine Del 502, ¶286; *Harita Finance Ltd. v. ATB Projects India Ltd.* 2003 (2) Arb. LR 376, ¶9.

v. *Shiv-vani Oil and Gas Exploration Services Ltd.*[1298] *(Baker Hughes)*, the court held that an application under Section 17 of the IAA could not be put at any disadvantageous position vis-à-vis an application under Section 9 of the IAA and the arbitral tribunal has the power to order the appellant to furnish security to secure the final claim if a prima facie case is made out.[1299]

It must be pointed out that these judgments were passed before the 2015 Amendment and while Section 17(1) of the IAA was a verbatim adoption of Article 17 of the Model Law (as drafted prior to the 2006 Model Law Revisions), Section 9 of the IAA was in complete variance with a list of measures that may be ordered by the court in support of arbitration proceedings. Thus, before the 2015 Amendment, it was necessary for the party applying for interim measures before the arbitral tribunal to show that a specific interim order covered by the express provisions of Section 9 of the IAA was also covered by the limited language of Section 17 of the IAA. This led to many difficulties and parties were forced to apply the interim measures to a court under Section 9 of the IAA even after an arbitral tribunal had been constituted.[1300]

3.4.2. Recognising Equal Powers of the Tribunal

In order to remove such difficulties, Section 17(1) of the IAA is now very similar in content to Section 9 of the IAA as it now enumerates the powers under Section 17 of the IAA.[1301] Thus, after the 2015 Amendment, the powers of the arbitral tribunal are similar to those of the court under the English Arbitration Act.[1302] Further, the provision specifically uses the phrase '*the tribunal shall have the same power for making orders, as the court has, for the purpose of, and in relation to, any proceedings before it*'.[1303] The legislative intent to bring the powers of the arbitral tribunal at par with courts post the amendment is now judicially supported in India.[1304] Even the principle of priority of jurisdiction of the arbitral tribunal has been affirmed by reference to Section 9(3) of the IAA[1305] with a caveat that the arbitral tribunal itself is not a court.[1306]

However, a clear distinction has been drawn between an arbitral tribunal having powers such as that of a court for making orders and the arbitral tribunal being the court itself.[1307] Even the broad language of Section 17(1)(ii)(e) of the IAA only means

1298. *Baker Hughes Singapore Pte v. Shiv-vani Oil and Gas Exploration Services Ltd.* 2014 SCC OnLine Bom 1663.
1299. *Ibid.*, ¶59. *It should be noted that at the time of passing this judgment there was a specific power under Section 17(2) to order security.*
1300. *Shakti International Pvt. Ltd. v. Excel Metal Processors Pvt. Ltd.* 2018 (4) Arb. LR 17 (Bom), ¶54.
1301. *Ibid.*, ¶55.
1302. English Arbitration Act, 1996, S. 44.
1303. Indian Arbitration Act, 1996, S. 17(1)(ii).
1304. *Shakti International Pvt. Ltd. v. Excel Metal Processors Pvt. Ltd.* 2018 (4) Arb. LR 17 (Bom), ¶44.
1305. *Ibid.*, ¶¶56-58.
1306. *Ibid.*, ¶61.
1307. *Ibid.*

that it is for the making of such interim orders that the arbitral tribunals' power is treated as the same as that of the court. The arbitral tribunal will not be able to do everything that a court of law could do, such as appoint its employees or officers to function as a receiver.[1308]

To be meaningful on a practical level, the powers afforded to the arbitrators need to be particularly broad. It should not be too onerous to seek interim measures where fairness demands such measures.[1309] The success of arbitration as a dispute resolution process depends on its ability to function fairly and effectively. To achieve such fairness and effectiveness, the arbitral tribunal must have powers to safeguard the rights of the parties and its own remedial authority during the pendency of the arbitration proceeding.[1310]

For the sake of certainty, it is required that statutory provisions expressly empower arbitrators to issue interim measures, provide the minimum conditions or criteria to be satisfied for grant of such measures, address the issue of ex parte measures, and most importantly, provide for enforcement measures.[1311] However, categorically listing down each type of order that may be passed amounts to over-regulation and a grave impediment to the flexibility required in the arbitral process. Therefore, by providing a list of the types of measures under Section 17(1) of the IAA, the scope of the power to grant interim measures has been unnecessarily restricted.

The other problem that arises with defining the scope of the power is that the Indian regime on interim measures deviates considerably from the Model Law despite the objective of the IAA to align with the Model Law. When efforts are being made to bring the regime in line with the international jurisprudence, such deviations thwart consistency and harmonisation with other jurisdictions. The courts ultimately apply domestic procedural rigours to an application for interim measures and arbitrators are constrained to toe the same line for ensuring enforceability and surviving challenges in appellate courts, especially when the power of the court is considered to be far superior to the powers available to the tribunal.[1312]

The better view with respect to the scope of power of the arbitral tribunal, especially post the 2015 Amendment is that Section 17 of the IAA should properly be interpreted as extending to the preservation of contractual rights or of the equilibrium between the parties.[1313]

The list provided under Section 17(1) of the IAA is inadequate as it leaves open various other kinds of measures such as security for costs, the discovery of documents and interrogatories, giving of evidence by affidavit,[1314] and other measures which have

1308. *Ibid.*, ¶63.
1309. Waincymer, *supra* n. 989, at 620.
1310. Gary Born, *supra* n. 33, at 2604.
1311. Abascal, *supra* n. 1, at 752.
1312. Paul F. Kirgis, *Judicial Review and the Limits of Arbitral Authority: Lessons from the Law of Contract*, 81 St. Johns L R. 99, 101 (2007).
1313. Gary Born, *supra* n. 33, at 2683.
1314. Singapore International Arbitration Act, 1994, S. 12(1); Art. 17(3), Commercial Arbitration Act, (Australian Capital Territory); Brunei International Arbitration Order, 2009 S. 17(6); Canada Commercial Arbitration Act, S. 17(3); Myanmar Arbitration Law, 2016, S. 19(1).

been adopted by countries that have adopted the 2006 Model Law Revisions.[1315] Moreover, it substantially narrows the range of measures that can be adopted by an arbitral tribunal. Instead, adopting the broad wordings contained in Article 17(2) of the Model Law would broaden the scope of the powers of the tribunal and make them consistent with the Model Law.

It would also result in uniformity and the progressive and pro-arbitration jurisprudence from around the world can then be comfortably applied to the question of interim measures in India as opposed to the current practice of 'cherry-picking' provisions and words from the Model Law. Concerns about providing expansive powers to the arbitral tribunal can be addressed with the adoption of clear standards and safeguards for the exercise of such power.

4. STANDARDS FOR GRANT OF INTERIM MEASURES

One of the major drawbacks of the Model Law before 2006 was that it did not guide tribunals on the exercise of power under Article 17 of the Model Law. Such determination was left to the arbitral tribunals and rules. It was thought that it would be best to not provide criteria in order to ensure flexibility which is essential to commercial arbitration as there was a broad range of possible scenarios that the arbitrator and the parties could face when requesting an interim measure.[1316]

Therefore, most domestic legislation and arbitration rules provide for the power of the arbitral tribunal to grant interim measures. However, they provide little guidance with respect to the circumstances in which provisional measures should be granted and instead used generic language and terms such as 'deems necessary' or 'appropriate'. They offer no guidance on the standards to be adopted but more or less confirm the arbitral tribunals' broad authority to grant relief[1317] and leave the same to the arbitral tribunal and the applicable law.[1318]

The absence of clear standards created room for a debate on which law should govern such standards. While it is true that the power of the arbitral tribunal to grant interim measures stems from the law of the seat, it is up for debate whether (a) the standards adopted by domestic courts at the seat should also be applied by the arbitral tribunal, which has been the case in India so far; or (b) is it clear that an arbitral tribunal is neither bound by procedural rules before state courts nor by case law on interim measures at the seat of arbitration?[1319] This area of law has received little attention in India, even though such standards can materially affect the outcome of the request for interim measures.

1315. *See Appendix B.*
1316. Luis, *supra* n. 521, at 542.
1317. Gary Born, *supra* n. 33, at 2649.
1318. *Ibid.*, at 2625.
1319. Voser, *supra* n. 1213, at 176.

4.1. The Necessity of Express Standards

As a result of the vague language, arbitral tribunals applied domestic procedural laws of the seat to a request for interim measures since the power, more often than not, stemmed from the domestic legislation at the seat, i.e., *lex arbitri*. In doing so, the arbitral tribunals effectively relegated the parties back to courtroom procedures and domestic law requirements, completely subverting the intention to have the dispute resolved through a mechanism alternative to a court. It should be noted that an application of domestic procedures was not wholly uncalled for in the absence of unified or commonly accepted transnational standards.

Nonetheless, by applying domestic procedural standards, such as the CPC and the Specific Relief Act, the arbitral tribunals went against the very purpose of arbitration, i.e., to do away with the cumbersome court procedures and fetters in favour of understanding the commercial objectives of the parties. Therefore, the need for a harmonised criterion is imperative, primarily when the arbitral tribunal consists of non-legal arbitrators. In such a case, the arbitral tribunal often lacks the proficiency to cater to requests for interim measures.[1320]

The determination of standards is also vital for consistency and predictability, irrespective of the seat or location of arbitration.[1321] Such determination is critical given that interim measures can be abused as an offensive weapon to exert pressure on the other side.[1322] But the question is which law should govern such standards?

4.2. Applicable Law

There is considerable debate on which law should govern the standards to be adopted by an arbitral tribunal while assessing a request for interim measures. The analysis of which law to apply can have implications on the equal treatment of parties and may result in providing leverage to one party outside the legal proceedings. On the one hand, *Born* suggests three principle choices with respect to the applicable law,[1323] i.e., (a) the law of the arbitral seat;[1324] (b) the law governing the parties underlying the contract;[1325] (c) international standards.[1326]

1320. Ali Yesilirmak, *supra* n. 30, at 74.
1321. Richard, *supra* n. 577, at 23.
1322. Lew, *supra* n. 28, at ¶ 23-31.
1323. Gary Born, *supra* n. 33, at 2644-2645.
1324. *Interim Award in ICC Case No. 8879, 11(1) ICC Ct. Bull. 84, 89 (2000); Interim Award in ICC Case No. 8786, 11(1) ICC Ct. Bull. 81 (2000); Interim Award in ICC Case No. 7544, 11(1) ICC Ct. Bull. 56 (2000); Award in Summary Arbitral Proceedings in NAI Case No. 2212 of 28 July 1999; Interim Award in NAI Case No. 1694 of 12 December 1996.*
1325. *Interim Award in ICC Case No. 8879, 11(1) ICC Ct. Bull. 84 (2000); Award in Summary Arbitral Proceedings in NAI Case No. 2212 of 28 July 1999.*
1326. *Partial Award in ICC Case No. 8113*, 11(1) ICC Ct. Bull. 65 (2000); *Decision of Geneva Chamber of Commerce of 25 September 1997*; *Interim Award in ICC Case No. 8894*, 11(1) ICC Ct. Bull. 94 (2000).

On the other hand, *Boog* asserts that the standards should follow a cascade of (a) mandatory provisions of law;[1327] (b) the law chosen by the parties; (c) international arbitration standards; (d) in exceptional cases, the *lex causae* to the extent that it specifies standards for granting interim relief.[1328]

Some authors observe that arbitrators might be inclined to import criteria into arbitration that are applied by the national courts of their jurisdiction.[1329] Others suggest that the arbitral tribunals have full discretion to determine the standards to be applied and the law to be used.[1330] Hence, a closer examination of these suggestions is as follows.

4.2.1. The Law of the Seat

The default rule for determining the standards to be applied can be the law of the seat[1331] since it is more sensible to adopt national courts standards for interim relief as it would lead to easier enforcement by the court. This view is erroneous because, in international arbitration, the choice of law governing the arbitral tribunal's power to order provisional measures is the law of the seat. However, the choice of law providing the standards for grant of such measures is distinguishable.[1332]

In *Born's* view, since an arbitral tribunal is not a national court, the standard for the exercise of powers should not be co-terminus with national courts and should be defined by sui generis sources of law.[1333] He asserts that, in fact, Article 17A of the Model Law is a clear indication that the standards should not be based on the law of the seat as they would reflect the standards of the courts at the law of the seat.[1334]

Moreover, such a view militates against Article 17J of the Model Law as domestic law procedures and jurisprudence do not account for the 'specific features of arbitration'. As discussed previously, applying the domestic law standards applicable at the seat is violative of the autonomy of the parties and the intention to have their dispute resolved through arbitration.[1335]

1327. *Boog notes that mandatory provisions of law pertaining to the standards or prerequisites for granting interim relief rarely exists and it is conceivable that such standards are contained in lex arbitri or the law applicable to the merits of the dispute and the tribunals must respect either.*
1328. Swiss Civil Code, 1907 Art. 28c(1); *provides that 'where a person can substantiate that he [or she] has been injured by an illegal act or that he [or she] must fear such an act will injure him [or her] and that from this injury a disadvantage will arise which cannot be easily compensated, he [or she] can apply for precautionary measures'*; c.f. Federal Act against Unfair Competition 1986, Art. 14.
1329. Laurent Levy & Filip De Ly, *Interests, Auxiliary and Alternative Remedies in International Arbitration* 109 (2008).
1330. Voser, *supra* n. 1213, at 176; Frank-Bernd Weigand & Antje Baumann, *Practitioner's Handbook on International Commercial Arbitration* (2009), ¶12.119.
1331. Ali Yesilirmak, *supra* n. 30, at 17; Roth, *supra* n. 448, at 428.
1332. Gary Born, *supra* n. 33, at 2644-2645.
1333. *Ibid.*, at 2646.
1334. *Ibid.*, at 2647.
1335. *See Chapter 3.*

One of the acclaimed advantages of arbitration is the freedom of the parties to have their dispute adjudicated by experts or arbitrators who have sufficient knowledge and a special skill set about the subject matter of the dispute. Such subject matter may require very different standards than those contemplated by courts or court procedures. For example, the advent of blockchain and smart contracts is one such area where courts and arbitral tribunals may not be able to provide adequate relief if they continue to apply the standards adopted for traditional interim relief in domestic courts.

The trouble with linking the standards for grant of interim measures with domestic court's standards is that there is no direct logical connection to the law of the seat, except for setting aside applications and enforcement concerns. The dispute over the preservation or sale of disputed goods between a party in the United States and a French party governed by English Law cannot possibly be resolved differently in England, France, the United States, or anywhere else depending on the seat.[1336]

Furthermore, if the parties agree on the 2010 UNCITRAL Arbitration Rules, they agree to the criteria contained in Article 26(3) of the Rules and not the domestic law standards. *Boog* asserts that the arbitral tribunals are not bound by the rules applicable to national courts at the seat of arbitration or elsewhere and interim relief provided by the arbitral tribunal should not be determined by national civil procedure rules and the same should not be binding on the arbitral tribunal.[1337]

4.2.2. Law Governing the Contract

Lew suggests that arbitrators can either use the rules available under the law applicable to the arbitration or settle the issue without making any reference to the applicable law.[1338] The law applicable to the substance of the dispute may provide for certain specific measures and reference to the same would harmonise the interim measures with the final award on merits.[1339] In a similar vein, *Boog* argues that a determination of prima facie case or possibility of success on merits can only be made based on the *lex causae*. In case such a law is not determined, then general principles of international commercial laws should be adopted.[1340]

Therefore, the standards ought to arise from the law governing the merits of the dispute as determining the possibility of success on merits based on any other law would be contrary to the arbitration agreement and the award passed would be open to challenge. However, this view may also not be appropriate as the standard of the possibility of success should not mean anything more than an assessment of whether the claim is frivolous or vexatious as there is a legal question to be tried.[1341] Moreover,

1336. Gary Born, *supra* n. 33, at 2646.
1337. Boog, *supra* n. 592, at 430.
1338. *Lew,* supra *n. 2, at 26.*
1339. Jean Francois Poudret & Sebastien Besson, *Comparative Law of International Arbitration* (2007), ¶ 633.
1340. Boog, *supra* n. 592, at 431.
1341. Mihir Naniwadekar, *On 'Prima Facie' cases and 'Originality': Part I,* (8 November 2008), available at:https://spicyip.com/2008/11/on-prima-facie-cases-and-originality.html.

applying the law applicable to the merits of the dispute to procedural questions may not be appropriate as that may also result in the award being challenged or the law governing the merits may not have clear standards either.

4.2.3. International Standards

One view is that arbitral case law and arbitration rules can help establish the standards.[1342] In *Born's* view, international sources should govern the law applicable to the standards of granting interim measures in international arbitration[1343] as it would lead to the application of a single uniform standard irrespective of the seat and would take into account the international arbitral procedures rather than court procedures. This would encourage consistent results and disregard the choice of law questions.[1344] Furthermore, it would be in line with other procedural issues such as disclosure, taking of evidence, conflict of interest, etc., which are usually governed by international standards such as the IBA Guidelines, etc.

It has also been suggested that in the absence of any clarity with respect to the standards, principles of the procedural law may be adopted,[1345] or the past experiences of arbitrators,[1346] or a comparative law approach.[1347] *Ali* suggests that an arbitral tribunal should take guidance from case laws, comparative analysis of rules, and scholarly opinions.[1348]

It must be emphasised that when it comes to interim measures of protection, precedent is scanty and each arbitral case is and should be considered individually.[1349] Also, one of the problems with applying international standards is the availability of the arbitral tribunal's orders given that most arbitrations are confidential.

Even so, consistency and uniformity have emerged worldwide and this will only grow with the adoption of the 2006 Model Law Revisions. Internationally, five

1342. Ali Yesilirmak, *supra* n. 30, at 162.
1343. Gary Born, *supra* n. 33, at 2646.
1344. *Ibid.*, at 2647.
1345. Bernardo M. Cremades, *The Need for Conservatory and Preliminary Measures*, 27 (5) Int'l Bus. L. 226, 228 (1999); Ali Yesilirmak, *Interim and Conservatory Measures in ICC Arbitral Practice*, 11 (1) ICC Int'l Ct. Arb. Bull. 34 (2000); NAI Interim Award 1694 of 1996, extracts published in XXIII YCA 97 112 (1998); *See, e.g.*, Art. 16, ICC Arbitration Rules 1955; Art. 15, Draft Uniform Law on Inter American Arbitration, Inter American Juridical Yearbook 219 (1955 1957) (Pan American Union, Washington, D.C. 1958); Mauro Rubino-Sammartano, *International Arbitration Law and Practice* 650 (2001); M. I. M. Aboul-Enein, *Issuing Interim Relief Measures in International Arbitration in the Arab States*, 3(1) J. W. Inv. 79 (2002).
1346. Caron, *supra* n. 1238, at 472.
1347. *See also* Art. 17 of the Joint American Law Institute/UNIDROIT Working Group on Principles and Rules of Transnational Civil Procedure, UNIDROIT 2002, Study LXXVI Doc 7 (May 2002). *See* Markus Wirth, *Supra* n. 580, at 37-38.
1348. Ali Yesilirmak, *supra* n. 30, at 231.
1349. *Lew*, supra *n. 2, at* 23, 26; Julian D Lew, *The Case for the Publication of Arbitration Award*, in Jan C. Schultz & Albert J. van den Berg (eds), *The Art of Interim Measures* 223-232 (1982); Horacio A. Grigera-Naon, *Latin America: Overcoming Traditional Hostility Towards Arbitration, in International Commercial Arbitration: Recent Developments* 5 (1988); Craig, *supra* n. 585, at 641; Lew, *supra* n. 28, at ¶¶ 1-44, 2-31, 2-43 and 2-46; R. A. Schutze, *The Precedential Effect of Arbitration Decisions*, 11(3) J. Int'l Arb. 69 (1994).

standards have been recognised for the grant of interim measures. They are as follows:[1350]

(a) Prima facie jurisdiction
(b) Prima facie case
(c) Urgency[1351]
(d) Imminent danger of serious prejudice[1352]
(e) Proportionality.

Therefore, the determination of the applicable law to the question of interim measures is no longer necessary after the introduction of Article 17A of the Model Law.

4.3. Article 17A of the Model Law

The standards provided in Article 17A have been formulated based on similar considerations, as referred above. However, *Born* criticises Article 17A of the 2006 Model Law as unwise and unnecessary because international standards are better formulated to cater to the circumstances of each case and it threatens the ongoing formation of international standards. The more constructive approach to reading Article 17A of the Model Law is to interpret the same in light of international standards and authority and not to restrict them for purely nationalistic standards of courts.[1353]

Born notes that even though the 2006 Model Law provides the standards in Article 17A, however, no arbitration statute incorporates the same.[1354] The absence, or clear rejection, of incorporation of these standards into national legislation is suggestive of the fact that another law might apply to such standards distinct from the law of the seat.[1355] This position is no longer valid. Of the countries that have adopted the 2006 Model Law Revisions, most have adopted Article 17A of the Model Law into their domestic legislation.[1356]

1350. UNCITRAL Rules on Interim measures, ¶¶39, 45, 68, 69 and 77, c.f. Francisco Gonsalez De Cossio, *Interim Measure in Arbitration: Towards a Better Injury Standard,* in Albert Jan Van den Berg (ed.), *Legitimacy: Myths, Realities, Challenges* 269 (2015); Ali Yesilirmak, *supra* n. 30, at 172.
1351. *Costa Rica v. Nicargua,* Request for the indication of Provisional Measure I.C.J, (8 March 2011), ¶¶63-64.
1352. KP Berger states that '*to preserve the legitimate rights of the requesting party, the measures must be "necessary". This requirement is satisfied if the delay in the adjudication of the main claim caused by the arbitral proceeding would lead to a "substantial" (but not necessarily "irreparable" as known in common law doctrine) prejudice for the requesting party*'; K.P. Berger, *International Economic Arbitration,* 9 St. Trans. Eco. L. 336 (1993).
1353. Gary Born, *supra* n. 33, at 2647, 2648.
1354. *Ibid.*, at 2646.
1355. *Ibid.*, at 2646, 2647.
1356. *See Appendix C.* Florida, British Virgin Island, Turkmenistan, South Africa, Slovenia, Rwanda, Philippines, Republic of Korea, New Zealand, Mongolia, Mexico, Mauritius, Lithuania, Jamaica, Ireland, Georgia, Fiji, Costa Rica, Macao, Hong Kong, Hungary, Prince Edward Island, British Columbia, Brunei Darussalam, Bhutan, Belgium, Bahrain, Western Australia, Victoria, Tasmania, South Australia, Queensland, Northern Territory, New South Wales, Australian Capital Territory, Australia.

The international standards are not at great variance from those contained in Article 17A of the Model Law.[1357] Arbitrators often apply or at least consult Article 17A of the Model Law while considering a request for interim measures.[1358] Article 17A(1) of the Model Law (a) contains the same requirements of prima facie jurisdiction, prima facie case, imminent danger or serious prejudice urgency and proportionality. The objection of *Born* with respect to the insertion of Article 17A of the Model Law inevitably leads to the same conclusion, i.e., the applicable international standards used by arbitral tribunals. Therefore, the adoption of Article 17A of the Model Law follows earlier arbitration practice[1359] and is, in fact, the assimilation of international standards.

Boog also states that although the 2006 Model Law does not represent a unified standard of or consensus with regard to international arbitration law, it nevertheless reflects a position of international arbitration that is widely supported among the UNCITRAL Member States. Article 17A of the Model Law aims at reflecting uniform international arbitration practice regarding the prerequisites for ordering an interim relief. National Arbitration Rules drafted based on the Model Law may well serve as a foundation for determining the standards for ordering interim measures.[1360] Thus, Article 17A of the Model Law was introduced to provide the standards to be used by arbitral tribunals when deciding requests for interim measures. The idea was to ensure flexibility and guidance for both the parties and the arbitral tribunal.[1361]

Interestingly, in contrast to the said view, the High Court of New Zealand, after adopting the 2006 Model Law Revisions, observed that the arbitral tribunal should exercise considerable caution before going beyond the criteria set out in Article 17A of the Model Law and the arbitral tribunal should hesitate while considering 'overall justice'.[1362]

4.3.1. *Limitations of Article 17A of the Model Law*

Born takes the view that the difference in standards to be adopted while preserving the status quo or ordering performance of a contract vis-à-vis other provisional measures such as preservation of evidence, enforcement of confidentiality obligations, and security for costs would require different standards than provided in Article 17A of the Model Law.[1363] The same standards as applicable to measures under Article 17(2)(a), (b), (c) of the Model Law cannot be applied to Article 17(2)(d) of the Model Law.[1364]

1357. *This view was also affirmed by the High Court of Hamilton, New Zealand, in Solid Energy New Zealand Ltd. v. HWE Mining Pty Ltd. High Court, Hamilton* CIV 2010 - 419-904, 5/8/10.
1358. Sanchez, *supra* n. 2, at 55.
1359. Blackby, *supra* n. 34, at 315; Karrer, *supra* n. 1216, at 104; Award in ICC Arbitration case no. *8113 of October 1995*, 11(1) ICC CIArb. Bull. 67 (2000); Award in *ICC Arbitration case no. 8786 of September 1996*, 11(1) ICC CIArb. Bull. 83 (2000).
1360. Boog, *supra* n. 592, at 429.
1361. Luis, *supra* n. 521, at 542.
1362. *Safe Kids in Daily Supervision Ltd. v. McNeill* CIV 2010 - 404 - 1696, 14/4/10, ¶36.
1363. Gary Born, *supra* n. 33, at 2650.
1364. *Ibid.*, at 2655.

It is pertinent to note that orders for the preservation of evidence or inspection of properties are often granted by arbitral tribunals.[1365] However, in *Born's* view, such orders do not fall under the category of provisional relief as they are mere directions regarding disclosure and evidentiary matters as part of the tribunal's fact-finding process.[1366] Due to the nature of the measure, the arbitral tribunal may assess whether the property in question is actually relevant to the case in dispute.[1367]

It is also pertinent to note that preservation of evidence or the sampling of goods does not require success on merits, a prima facie case or balance of convenience but instead only requires the need for the evidence. Thus, such criteria should ordinarily be whether the evidence in question is relevant to the dispute and properly or potentially subject to disclosure under the parties' arbitration agreement and any applicable procedural rules.[1368]

In a case where a request was made for safeguarding evidence which could allegedly be destroyed but there was no evidence of shredding or imminent danger, the arbitral tribunal resorted to an 'analysis of interest in play'. The arbitral tribunal rejected the request and held that the request would place an unfair burden on the government because of its excessive breadth and no urgency has been proved.[1369] Similarly, in a construction dispute of a bridge deck which had collapsed, an order was sought to direct the contractor to preserve as evidence sections of the demolished bridge for inspection by the arbitral tribunal and the said measure was granted.[1370]

In France, the test is of the application being 'well-founded'.[1371] In Lithuania, the test for preservation of evidence is that '*1) The evidence requested to be preserved may be significant to the case; 2) There is a real threat that upon failure to undertake the interim measures the evidence requested to be preserved will be destroyed or damaged by the other party thus making them unusable during the arbitral examination*'.[1372]

This is a much clearer standard. However, with the use of the phrase 'relevant and material to the resolution of the dispute' in Article 17(2)(d) of the Model Law, such a standard is subsumed in the determination of the need for the evidence.

During the deliberations of the Working Group, some delegates questioned whether higher standards applicable to the attachment of assets or lower standards with respect to preservations of evidence should be applied by arbitral tribunals in the

1365. *Partial Award in ICC Case No. 10040,* in 11(1) ICC Ct. Bull. 115, 116 (2000);*10040*; *Lew,* supra *n. 2, at* 29; *Interim Award in ICC Case No. 8879,* 11(1) ICC Ct. Bull. 84, 89 (2000); *United Tech. International v. Islamic Republic of Iran,* Decision No. DEC 53-114-3 of 10 December 1986, 13 Iran-US C.T.R. 254, ¶16 (1986); *Behring International Inc. v. Islamic Republic of Iran,* Interim and Interlocutory *Award in IUSCT Case No. ITM/ITL 52-382-3 of 21 June 1985,* 8 Iran-US C.T.R. 238 (1985).
1366. Gary Born, *supra* n. 33, at 2683.
1367. Waincymer, *supra* n. 989, at 634.
1368. Gary Born, *supra* n. 33, at 2683.
1369. *Rail Road Development Corporation v. Republic of Guatemala,* Decision on Provisional Measures in ICSID Case No. ARB/07/23 of 15 October 2008.
1370. Bunni, *supra* n. 690, at 595.
1371. French Code of Civil Procedure, Art. 1469.
1372. Lithuania Arbitration Act, 2012, Art. 20(4).

same manner as by the domestic courts.[1373] It is for this reason that Article 17A(2) of the Model Law differentiates between different measures and the standards applicable to them and ultimately leaves it to the discretion of the arbitral tribunal to determine the 'appropriate' application of the standards contained in Article 17A(1)(a) and (b).

Since the relevance of the evidence to the resolution of the dispute and whether the evidence is material has been provided for under Article 17(2)(d), the tribunal can then assess harm or 'interests in play'. Hence, the discretion granted to the arbitral tribunal to apply the standards contained in Article 17A(1)(a) and (b) as the tribunal considers appropriate is the right approach to determining standards to be applied for requests under Article 17(2)(d) of the Model Law.

4.4. Reasonable Possibility of Success

One of the standards adopted in Article 17A(1)(b) of the Model Law is the reasonable possibility of success on the merits of the claim without the determination affecting the discretion of the arbitral tribunal in making any subsequent determination. This determination has traditionally been known as the test of the 'prima facie case'. The distinction, evident from the deliberate use of broad language under Article 17A(1)(b) of the Model Law, suggests a deviation from court jurisprudence of prima facie case, strong prima facie case, or other such higher standards required to obtain interim measures.

The broad language in Article 17A(1)(b) of the Model Law now expressly recognises that the claimant has to demonstrate a likelihood of success on the merits or as per the wording of the UNCITRAL Draft '*a reasonable possibility that the requesting party will succeed on the merits*'.[1374]

Under the traditional notion of a prima facie case, the arbitral tribunal was not prevented from a broader appreciation of the respective arguments of the parties on the merits.[1375] However, many tribunals and commentators refused to consider the standard of prima facie cases[1376] as it potentially conflicts with the duty of the arbitral tribunal not to prejudge the merits,[1377] especially where the disputes are complicated and involve large sums of money.[1378] *Hober* asserts that identification of the possibility

1373. Report of UNCITRAL Working Group on the work of its Fortieth session, 2004, A/CN.9/547, available at: https://undocs.org/en/A/CN.9/547, ¶¶ 89-91.
1374. Marc Blessing, *State Arbitrations: Predictably Unpredictable Solutions?* 22 (6) J. of Int'l Arb. 435, 460 (2005).
1375. Partial Award in Unidentified ICC Case discussed in Schwartz, *supra* n. 1236, at 60.
1376. *Interim Award in ICC Case No. 8894*, 11(1) ICC Ct. Bull. 94 (2000); *Partial Award in ICC Case No. 3896*, 110 J.D.I. (Clunet) 914 (1983); *Biwater Gauff (Tanzania) Ltd v. Tanzania, Procedural Order No. 1 in ICSID Case No. ARB/05/22 of 31 March 2006*, ¶95; *Tanzania Electricity Supply Co. v. Independent Power Tanzania Ltd, Decision on the Respondent's Request for Provisional Measures in ICSID Case No. ARB/98/8 of 20 December 1999*, ¶6; Lew, *supra* n. 28, at ¶ 23-62; John G. Merrills, *Interim Measures of Protection in the Recent Jurisprudence of the International Court of Justice*, 44 Int'l Comp. L. Q. 90, 114 (1995).
1377. Gary Born, *supra* n. 33, at 2662.
1378. Bunni, *supra* n. 690, at 591.

of success still requires a party to establish a prima facie case.[1379] In contrast, *Abascal* argues that it is impossible to articulate a standard in terms of the merits that is 'anything but a practical or common-sense assessment of the possibility of success'.[1380]

4.4.1. Prejudgment of Merits

In Lithuania, deviating from the Model Law, the standard used is '*his claims are likely to be founded*'.[1381] Here, the language is broader and wide bringing within its ambit any claim 'likely to be founded' as opposed to demonstrating the 'reasonable possibility of success'. Conversely, in Hungary, the language states '*the requesting party will succeed on the merits of the claim*'. This would clearly amount to prejudgment despite the following language providing that the determination shall not affect the discretion of the tribunal for future determinations.[1382]

The requirement of not prejudging the merits connotes that measures granted should not cover what is requested in the main proceedings.[1383] However, it is unclear as to what it means when it is said that an 'arbitral tribunal must refrain from prejudging the merits of the claims'.[1384] The objection against this standard is that, unlike court proceedings where the judge hearing the application for an interim measure will frequently be different from the one adjudicating the merits, in arbitration, it will be the same tribunal dealing with both the issues.[1385] It is particularly difficult to employ the powers of the arbitral tribunal in a manner that would be beyond the prejudgment debate unless the urgent relief is being granted by an emergency arbitrator who will not be hearing the merits of the dispute as part of the tribunal.[1386] The difficulty is that one cannot know at the outset which party is likely to succeed and hence the fairness and efficiency ramifications are not known at the stage of interim measures. In that sense, prejudgment on the merits without having had the fullest opportunity to present the respective cases is unfair.[1387]

1379. Hober, *supra* n. 1207, at 735.
1380. Abascal, *supra* n. 1, at 764.
1381. Lithuania Arbitration Act, 2012, Art. 20(3)(1); *See Appendix C.*
1382. Hungary Arbitration Law, S. 19.
1383. Lew, *supra* n. 28, at ¶23-64.
1384. *Lew,* supra *n. 2, at 27.*
1385. Lew, *supra* n. 28, at ¶23-62.
1386. Elizabeth Kantor, *Emergency Arbitration of Construction Disputes – Choose Wisely or End up Spoilt for Choice*, (15 February 2017), available at:http://arbitrationblog.kluwerarbitration.com/2017/02/15/emergency-arbitration-construction-disputes-choose-wisely-end-spoilt-choice/.
1387. Waincymer, *supra* n. 989, at 621; *Gary B Born* argues that, *ideally, it should mean (a) that the tribunal is not precluded from ultimately deciding the arbitration in any particular manner after the parties have presented their cases, i.e., the grant of interim measure should not alter the final decision in favour of or against one of the parties; (b) that the decision on interim measures should have no res judicata or similar preclusive effect with regard to the decision on merits; (c) that the tribunal does not prejudge the outcome of the arbitration or close its mind to one party's submission or deny one party an opportunity of being heard; and (d) that the same relief that is sought as final relief may ordinarily be issued as an interim measure subject to a revision in the award*; Gary Born, *supra* n. 33, at 2660.

Nonetheless, the issue of the possibility of success can be resolved without determining questions of applicable law, if the standard is kept to a bare minimum, i.e., a party whose case is clearly without merit should not be granted a request for interim measures.[1388] Hence, the consideration of 'reasonable possibility of success' should mean nothing more than a practical or common-sense assessment of the possibility of success, i.e., the claim is not frivolous or vexatious since arbitrators or court at the early stages of arbitration proceedings would not have enough knowledge about the case. The consideration should be limited to a simple assessment that a claim is not at the very threshold dismissible,[1389] e.g., a claim based on vague pleadings.[1390]

4.4.2. Material Demonstrating Prima Facie Case

It is also unclear from the language of Article 17A(1)(b) of the Model Law as to how such 'possibility of success' should be demonstrated by a party seeking the interim measure.[1391] Though the word 'reasonable' is used, the generic term is capable of vastly subjective interpretations. Therefore, the obligation that the arbitral tribunal should not prejudge the merits operates more as a duty of the arbitral tribunal and the court rather than a standard that needs to be proved or satisfied by a claimant requesting a grant of an interim measure. *Bunni* states that the applicant must demonstrate at least three things to the court or tribunal,[1392] i.e., (a) more than bare allegations or assertions; (b) some form of a statement of the grounds upon which the application is relying in support of its application; and (c) affidavits or even oral testimony bearing in mind the serious consequences of such an application.

Therefore, the claimant should demonstrate a good arguable case, i.e., it should sufficiently demonstrate that the claim is not frivolous, vexatious, or without any basis.[1393] It means that the tribunal should not require extensive material on record or require the claimant to demonstrate or argue the entire matter only to ascertain whether the claimant has a '*reasonable possibility of success*'.

In a study, 85% of the participating arbitrators agreed that they require a possibility to succeed on the merits as a fundamental prerequisite for the grant of interim measures. Interestingly, in their view, the possibility should not be 'more than likely', i.e., over 50% but just a mere possibility to succeed.[1394] The applicant must show that its rights are plausible. A reasonable possibility of success can also be based

1388. David D. Caron & Lee M. Caplan, *The UNCITRAL Arbitration Rules: A Commentary* 523 (2013).
1389. Abascal, *supra* n. 1, at 764.
1390. *ECI- Nayak (JV) v. Ircon International Ltd. & Anr.* 2019 SCC OnLine Del 9418.
1391. Menon, *supra* n. 102, at 8 & 9.
1392. Bunni, *supra* n. 690, at 591.
1393. Caron, *supra* n. 1238, at 491; Caron argues that '*It certainly is appropriate that when a case manifestly lack merit, necessarily costly and disruptive interim measures to protect such dubious rights should not be granted. A tribunal must determine prima facie not only whether it is possesses jurisdiction but also whether the question present by the case is frivolous.*'
1394. Hober, *supra* n. 1207, at 735; Sanchez, *supra* n. 2, at 52.

only on inferences.[1395] Therefore, the common consensus is that 'reasonable possibility of success' means nothing more than the request not being frivolous or vexatious. The arbitral tribunal is not required at the stage of interim measures to determine whether there has actually been a breach.[1396] It should only determine whether there is a real possibility of breach or prejudice to the legal rights of the claimant and only take a 'bird's-eye view'.[1397]

Unfortunately, in India, courts have referred to domestic notions of 'prima facie case' and scrutinised interim orders passed by arbitral tribunals on such touchstones. As discussed previously,[1398] the test of prima facie case in India is also not clear and the test is applied with varying degrees of probability. Moreover, courts in certain instances have even insisted on 'mini-trials' to determine such questions.[1399] To prescribe the same standards for tribunals robs arbitration of its advantage of being a dispute resolution mechanism geared towards the commercial understanding of parties. It also thwarts the will of the parties to avoid cumbersome court procedures and precedents. Therefore, the arbitral tribunal should keep in mind the reasonability of commercial decisions and whether a reasonable man operating in that area of commerce would be prejudiced by the facts and circumstances and whether that would ordinarily involve a violation of its legal rights.

The arbitral tribunal should consider (a) that the applicant has demonstrated sufficiently that a right has been infringed or threatened by the defendant and the claim is not frivolous or vexatious; and (b) that the relief sought (objectively) is urgently necessary to protect the right before the full decision on the merits of the case.[1400] Thus, ideally, the standard to be adopted under Section 17 of the IAA should be that 'the case on merits of the requesting party is not vexatious or frivolous'[1401] instead of the test of 'reasonable possibility of success on merits' as envisaged by Article 17A(1)(b) of the Model Law.

1395. *Safe Kids in Daily Supervision Ltd. v. McNeill* CIV 2010 – 404 – 1696, 14/4/10; Sanchez, *supra* n. 2, at 52.
1396. *Oil Platforms (Iran v. U.S.A.), Judgment of 12 December 1996*, [1996] I.C.J. Rep. 803, 856-57 (Higgins, J.) (*Mavrommatis Palestine Concessions*, PCIJ Series A, No. 2 (P.C.I.J. 1924); *Emilio Agustín Maffezini v. The Kingdom of Spain, Procedural Order No. 2 in ICSID Case No. ARB/97/7 of 28 October 1999*, ¶21; *Sergei Paushok, CJSC Golden East Company and CJSC Vostokneftegaz Company v. The Government of Mongolia, Ad HocOrder on Interim Measures of 2 September 2008*, ¶55; *Maffezini v. Spain, Procedural Order No. 2 in ICSID Case No. ARB/97/7 of 28 October 1999*, ¶21; *Decision on Provisional Measures in ICSID Case No. ARB/98/2 of 25 September 2001*, ¶8; *Bosnia and Herzegovina v. Wgoslavia (Serbia And Montenegro)*, [1993] I.C.J. Rep. 325, *Application on the Convention on the Punishment of the Crime of Genocide, Order on Provisional Measures of 13 September 1993*, [1993] I.C.J. Rep. 325, ¶24 (I.C.J.).
1397. Luis, *supra* n. 521, at 550.
1398. *See Chapter 3.*
1399. Mihir, *supra* n. 1341.
1400. Donald Francis Donovan, *The Scope and Enforceability of Provisional Measures in International Commercial Arbitration: A Survey of Jurisdictions, the Work of UNCITRAL and Proposals for Moving Forward*, in Albert Jan Van den Berg (ed.), *International Commercial Arbitration: Important Contemporary Questions* 86 (2009).
1401. Caron, *supra* n. 1238, at 491.

However, the determination of the claim being vexatious or frivolous may result in accusations of prejudging on merits by the tribunal and challenges to arbitrators for bias which is why arbitral tribunals are reluctant to openly voice their consideration of this factor when considering a request for an interim measure.[1402] Thus, from a practical point of view, the language of 'reasonable possibility that the requesting party will succeed on the merits of the claim' contained in Article 17A(1)(a) of the Model Law is preferable. However, when tribunals consider such requirements, the assessment should be primarily that the claims made are not, on their face, frivolous[1403] or vexatious.[1404]

4.5. Urgency

Next, the tribunal should consider whether the relief sought is necessary immediately or in a very short span of time before the dispute is finally decided. This consideration refers to the presence of an imminent danger of prejudice to the right of the party requesting the interim measure.[1405] It must be noted that 'urgency' has two components: (a) the danger should be imminent; and (b) such danger should be prejudicial to the right of the requesting party.

In *ICC Case No. 10596*, the tribunal defined the requirement of urgency as '*the fact that a party's potential losses are likely to increase with the mere passing of time and that it would be unreasonable to expect a party to wait for the final award suffices*'.[1406] Hence, the test of urgency subsumes within it the possibility of prejudice against rights and in a certain sense, the 'possibility of success' as well.

However, the test of urgency is complicated. The requesting party must show that there is an actual risk that a party may do something that would cause damage before the issue is decided by the arbitral tribunal. The damage may be to the arbitral proceeding, to the resolution of the dispute, or may place the enforceability of the award at risk. Therefore, it is unclear how 'urgency' would apply in different circumstances. This test assumes greater importance when applied in the context of ex parte measures. The arbitral tribunal must determine whether the prior disclosure of the request for an interim measure to the opposite party would, in effect, frustrate the purpose of the measure. Hence, in a sense, it is not the test of the urgency but the test of the possibility of frustration which would apply when considering urgency.[1407]

1402. *Ibid.*
1403. Wong, *supra* n. 89, at 619; *Sergei Paushok Cjsc Golden East Company Cjsc Vostokneftegaz Company v. The Government of Mongolia, Ad HocOrder on Interim Measures of 2 September 2008*, ¶55; *Víctor Pey Casado, Président Allende Fondation v. République du Chili, Decision on Provisional Measures in ICSID Case No. ARB/98/2 of 25 September 2001*, ¶8.
1404. Donovan, *supra* n. 1400, at 128.
1405. Ali Yesilirmak, *supra* n. 30, at 174-175.
1406. Schwartz, *supra* n. 1236, at 60, c.f. Ali Yesilirmak, *supra* n. 30, at 179.
1407. Abascal, *supra* n. 1, at 763.

In Lithuania, the test is that '*failure to take these measures may render enforcement of the arbitral award considerably more difficult or impossible*'.[1408] Article 46(2) of the RAC Rules 2019[1409] provides that interim measures shall be introduced if the failure to introduce them may obstruct or frustrate the performance of the award as well as for the purpose of preventing significant harm to any of the parties.

It is pertinent to note that Article 17A of the 2006 Model Law omits the requirement of urgency as a standard while determining the grant of interim measures, even though most arbitrators require urgency as an essential requirement for the grant of interim measures.[1410] One view is that the concept of urgency is implicit in the requirement of serious injury.[1411] The more accepted view is that the degree of urgency which is required may be satisfied where a party can prove that there is a need to obtain the requested measure at a certain point before the issuance of an award.[1412] Thus, the concept of urgency is not as strict as in national courts and interim measures have often been granted when urgency was not fully established or even alleged.[1413]

In one instance, where the parties were still in negotiation and there was no threat to the status quo, the court held that there was no urgency and the request for an interim measure was premature.[1414] There is also a precedent to suggest a higher degree of imminence, i.e., whether the threatened harm will occur within a time frame that makes it reasonable in the circumstances to delay ordering relief until closer to the threatened event.[1415]

The more logical view is that a measure is urgent where action prejudicial to the rights of the other party is likely to be taken before a final decision is taken.[1416] Such determination would include any action of the claimant which is prejudicially affecting any right of the respondent, including the possibility of recovering a costs award.

1408. Lithuania Arbitration Act, 2012, Art. 20(3)(2). *The same is the standard in Russia* i.e., Arbitrazh Procedural Code of Russian Federation, 2002, Art. 91.

1409. Article 46(2), 2019 RAC Rules*: Interim measures shall be introduced if the failure to introduce them may obstruct or frustrate performance of the award, as well as for the purpose of preventing significant harm to any of the Parties.*

1410. Hober, *supra* n. 1207, at 736.

1411. Gary Born, *supra* n. 33, at 2658-2659.

1412. *Biwater Gauff (Tanzania) Ltd v. Tanzania, Procedural Order No. 1 in ICSID Case No. ARB/05/22 of 31 March 2006,* ¶16; *Quiborax S.A., Non Metallic Minerals S.A. and Allan Fosk Kaplún v. Plurinational State of Bolivia, Decision on Provisional Measures in ICSID Case No. ARB/06/2 of 26 February 2010,* ¶150; *Tokios Tokelés v. Ukraine, Procedural Order No. 3 in ICSID Case No. ARB/02/18 of 18 January 2005,* ¶8; *Chevron Corporation and Texaco Petroleum Corporation v. The Republic of Ecuador, Second Interim Award on Interim Measures in PCA Case No. 2009-23 of 16 February 2012,* ¶2; Stuart Abercrombie & Mark David Davis, *The UNCITRAL Arbitration Rules in Practice: The Experience of the Iran-United States Claims Tribunal* 133, 139 (1992); Shabtie Rosenne, *Provisional Measures in International Law* 135 (2005).

1413. Georg Von Segesser & C. Kurth, *Interim Measures*, in Gabrielle Kaufmann-Kohler & B. Stucki (eds) *International Arbitration In Switzerland – A Handbook For Practitioners* 71 (2004).

1414. *Emerald Buildcon Pvt. Ltd. v. New Millienium India Property Developers Pvt. Ltd. & Ors.* 2019 SCC OnLine Bom 873, ¶3.

1415. *Avco Corporation v. Iran Aircraft Industries, Order in IUSCT Case No. 261 of 27 January 1984,* Reprinted in Caron, *supra* n. 1388, at 548.

1416. *Tokios Tokelés v. Ukraine, Procedural Order No. 3 in ICSID Case No. ARB/02/18 of 18 January 2005,* ¶8.

Since most arbitrators require a party to demonstrate urgency and interim measures are required because a party cannot wait till the final adjudication, the phrase '*that a right has been infringed or is threatened to be infringed by the party against whom the measure is requested*' may be added to specifically incorporate the standard of urgency within the IAA. Though it may be argued that providing for such language may make the standards inconsistent with the Model Law, the same may not be true. Even though the consideration of urgency is not expressly provided under Article 17A of the Model Law, such a requirement is considered to be implied,[1417] and international practice suggests that arbitrators require parties to demonstrate urgency[1418] as a *sine qua non.*[1419] Furthermore, the standards enshrined in Article 17A of the Model Law are only suggestive and were meant as guidance.[1420] Hence, the express language would only recognise internationally accepted practice and not in effect deviate from the Model Law.

4.6. Balance of Convenience

Article 17A(1)(a) of the Model Law uses the phrase '*such harm substantially outweighs the harm that is likely to result to the party against whom the measure is directed if the measure is granted*'. In effect, the consideration is that of prejudice to the rights of one party over the other.

It is necessary to point out that when considering the balance of convenience or balance of harm as a standard, the word 'substantial' would make no difference as the tribunal would have to consider the harm that might be caused by not ordering the interim relief requested and whether the measure requested outweighs the harm that may be done to the party against whom such measure is requesting.[1421]

One view has been that the determination of the balance of convenience should only mean consideration of the pros and cons of the measure and the impact on the parties. If the measure provokes less convenience than the injury it avoids, it is in the best interest of both parties to secure it.[1422] The consideration should always entail an analysis of whether the interim measure may be out of proportion to the advantage of the requesting party.[1423]

One test is whether '*Interim measures are economic and proportional to the goal to be achieved by such measures.*'[1424] Article 46(3) of RAC Rules 2019 provides that the interim measure shall correspond to the value of the claim.[1425] Such references, however, considerably restrict the scope of the standard and may exclude genuine

1417. Hober, *supra* n. 1207, at 736.
1418. *Costa Rica v. Nicargua*, Request for the indication of Provisional Measure I.C.J, (8 March 2011), ¶¶63-64.
1419. Hober, *supra* n. 1207, at 736.
1420. Luis, *supra* n. 521, at 542.
1421. Abascal, *supra* n. 1, at 765.
1422. Francisco, *supra* n. 1350, at 275.
1423. Ali Yesilirmak, *supra* n. 30, at 182, c.f. Lew, *supra* n. 28, at ¶23-65.
1424. Lithuania Arbitration Act, 2012, Art. 20(3)(3).
1425. Article 46(3), 2019 RAC Rules: *Interim measures shall correspond to the value of the claim.*

cases which may not necessarily fall within the ambit of 'economic and proportional' or correspond to the value of the claim.

In India, tribunals have applied these considerations drawing from the notion of balance of convenience under Order XXXIX Rule 1 of the CPC and the Specific Relief Act.[1426] References to 'balance of convenience' should be adopted in line with Article 17A(1)(a) of the Model Law and tribunals should consider the harm likely to result if the measure not ordered outweighs the harm that is likely to result to the party against whom the measure is directed if the measure is granted. Even though the word 'substantial' makes no difference, as suggested earlier, the same may be retained to ensure consistency with the Model Law. The consideration of 'substantial' harm will always be dependent on the facts and circumstances of the case, and the arbitral tribunal can always determine the relative proportionality.

Coupled with the language proposed earlier with respect to '*reasonable possibility of success*', the test would cater to the claims not being vexatious or false, the urgent requirement of there being prejudice or likely prejudice to the legal rights of the party seeking the measure and contemplation of harm resulting to both parties if the measure is granted or denied.

4.7. Harm Not Adequately Reparable by Damages

Article 17A(1)(a) of the Model Law uses the phrase '*harm not adequately reparable by an award of damages*' which, though appears to be similar to the notion of 'irreparable harm' under the CPC, is slightly different in practice. There is plenty of precedent from across jurisdictions which understands 'irreparable harm' as the harm that cannot be compensated by damages.[1427] The difference in degree between the use of the phrase 'adequately' and 'irreparable or cannot be compensated' is self-evident.

'Irreparable' harm was understood by the Working Group to include loss of priceless or unique work of art, a business becoming insolvent, loss of essential evidence, loss of an essential business opportunity such as the conclusion of a large contract, harm to the reputation of the business as a result of trademark infringement.[1428] However, such an interpretation was considered to be in conflict with the

1426. *Intertoll ICS Cecons O & M Co. Pvt. Ltd. v. National Highways Authority of India* 2013 SCC OnLine Del 447, ¶10.

1427. *Millicom International Operations B.V. and Sentel GSM SA v. The Republic of Senegal, decision on the Application for Provisional Measures in ICSID Case No. ARB/08/20 of 24 August 2009,* ¶46; *Occidental Petroleum Corporation and Occidental Exploration and Production Company v. The Republic of Ecuador, decision on Provisional Measures in ICSID Case No. ARB/06/11 of 17 August 2007,* ¶ 59; *Tethyan Copper Company Pty Limited v. The Islamic Republic of Pakistan, decision on Claimant's Request for Provisional Measures in ICSID Case No. ARB/12/1 of 13 December 2012,* ¶138; *Tokios Tokelés v. Ukraine, Procedural Order No. 3 in ICSID Case No. ARB/02/18 of 18 January 2005,* ¶8; *Plama Consortium Limited v. Republic of Bulgaria in ICSID Case No. ARB/03/24, order of 6 September 2005,* ¶46.

1428. Report of UNCITRAL Working Group on the work of its Fortieth session, 2004, A/CN.9/547, available at: https://undocs.org/en/A/CN.9/547, ¶86.

current arbitral practice, which would consider circumstances where it would be 'comparatively complicated' to compensate harm with an award of damages.[1429]

Therefore, the language 'harm not adequately reparable by damages' was adopted as it provided a threshold lower than that of 'irreparable harm' and also granted discretion to the arbitral tribunal to determine the level of harm necessary.[1430] *Born* distinguishes between 'irreparable harm' and 'serious' or 'substantial harm,'[1431] though the same is of little consequence. In theory, it is possible to rectify nearly all commercial losses by an award of damages and hence, irreparable harm would never arise.[1432]

However, there is a view which states that irreparable harm must be understood in the economic and not literal sense.[1433] There is a trend in international arbitration which equates irreparable harm with substantial prejudice recognising complex commercial realities where compensation for actual loss suffered might not be possible.[1434] Even in the economic sense, most commercial disputes would be compensable by an award of damages except for reputation.

ICC Tribunals have sometimes considered a financial loss to constitute irreparable harm.[1435] Some tribunals have held that the concept of 'irreparable prejudice' in international law is broader than the Anglo-American law concept of 'irreparable injury' and does not necessarily require showing that injury complained is not remediable by an award of damages, i.e., when there is no certain pecuniary standard for the measure of damages.[1436]

In *ICC Case No. 10596* of 2000, the arbitral tribunal understood 'irreparable harm' as 'significant harm'. It held that '*monetary loss is not irreparable harm ... Although, strictly speaking, this view may be correct, the arbitral tribunal considers that it would be unreasonable to refuse the relief sought on those grounds ... it would be foolish for the tribunal to wait for a foreseeable, or at least plausibly foreseeable, loss to occur, to then provide for its compensation in the form of damages (assuming that B is entitled to such*

1429. *Ibid.*, ¶88.
1430. *Ibid.*, ¶89.
1431. *Irreparable means where the actions of a party are capable of causing or threatening irreparable prejudice to the rights invoked. Serious or substantial harm means harm without requiring that the injury be 'irreparable' in a literal sense.* Gary Born, *supra* n. 33, at 2652-2653.
1432. *Ibid.*
1433. Lew, *supra* n. 28, at ¶23-65.
1434. *Ibid.*
1435. Schwartz, *supra* n. 1236, at 60. c.f., *ibid.*, at 181.
1436. *Interlocutory Award in ICC Case No. 10596*; *Interim Award in ICC Case No. 8786*, 11(1) ICC Ct. Bull. 81, 83 (2000); *Behring International, Inc. v. Islamic Republic of Iran, interim and Interlocutory Award in IUSCT Case No. ITM/ITL 52382-3 of 21 June 1985*, 8 Iran–US CTR 238(1985) (*concept of irreparable prejudice in international law is broader than Anglo-American law concept of irreparable injury and does not necessarily require showing that 'injury complained of is not remediable by an award of damages (i.e., where there is no certain pecuniary standard for the measure of damages ...)*'; Caron, *supra* n. 1388, at 552. (*2010 UNCITRAL Rules adopted 'harm not adequately reparable by an award of damages' due to concerns that 'irreparable harm might present too high a threshold'*); Lew, *supra* n. 28, at ¶23-65; Schwartz, *supra* n. 1236, at 60; Douglas Laycock, *Death of the Irreparable Injury Rule*, 103 Har. L. Rev. 687 (1990).

damages, which is not the issue here), rather than prevent the loss from occurring in the first place … '.[1437]

Ali re-examined various decisions and concluded that the standard used most frequently in assessing interim measures is '*threat of grave or irreparable damage to the counter-party in the arbitration proceedings*'.[1438] In a seminal Irish case,[1439] the Court held that irreparable should mean that it may not be possible to compensate the applicant fairly or properly by way of damages.[1440] Similarly, an ICSID tribunal considered the question of irreparable harm and adopted a two-fold consideration, i.e., (a) actions which should be restrained because their effects, though capable of financial compensation, are such that compensation cannot fully remedy the damage suffered; and (b) actions which may well prove to have infringed a right and caused harm, but in respect to which it will be sufficient to award damages without taking provisional measures.[1441]

Therefore, the true consideration of this standard by the arbitral tribunal should be that the arbitrators have an obligation to try to find an equitable and commercially practicable procedural solution to prevent irreparable and unnecessary injuries to parties.[1442] Harm not reparable by an award of damages should be understood in the economic sense and not a literal sense. The arbitral tribunal must take into account that it may not always be possible to compensate for actual losses suffered or sullied business reputation through damages.[1443] Also, the arbitral tribunals should construe the risk of financial loss or the possibility of lack of enforcement of the final award[1444] to be included in this definition.[1445]

There are instances where tribunals would grant interim measures simply to minimise the commercial damage and would direct parties to undertake specified actions such as to continue the licence or supply of products irrespective of the demonstration of irreparable or serious harm. These measures are usually granted as they overall reduce the damages in the arbitration. Therefore, the grant of these measures is not only prudent but required for efficient and effective dispute resolutions through arbitration. The standards adopted in this instance would not meet the requirement of irreparable or serious harm.[1446]

1437. Jean-Jacques Arnaldez, Yves derains & Dominique Hascher, *Collection of Arbitral Awards 2001-2007/Recueil des sentences arbitrales de la CCI 2001-2007* 321 (2009), c.f. Francisco, *supra* n. 1350, at 262.
1438. *Ali Yesilirmak, Interim and Conservatory Measures in ICC Arbitral Practice 1999-2008*, 22 ICC Bull. S. Supp. 9 (2011).
1439. *Campus Oil Ltd. v. Ministry for Industry and Energy (No. 2)* [1983] 3 ALL ER 188 at 193.
1440. Bunni, *supra* n. 690, at 589.
1441. *Cemex Caracas Investments B.V. and Cemex Caracas II Investments B.V. Bolivarian Republic of Venezuela Decision on Provisional Measures in ICSID Case No. ARB/08/15 of 3 March 2010*, ¶40.
1442. Craig, *supra* n. 585, at 462.
1443. Lew, *supra* n. 28, at ¶23-65.
1444. *See* Born, *supra* n. 7, at 2471. *See also,* Chartered Institute of Arbitrators, International Arbitrators Practice Guideline, Applications for Interim Measures 7, www.ciarb.org/media/4194/guideline-4-applications-forinterim-measures-2015.pdf, C.f. Sanchez, *supra* n. 2, at 65.
1445. Schwartz, *supra* n. 1236, at 45.
1446. Gary Born, *supra* n. 33, at 2654.

In fact, Article 17A(1)(a) of the Model Law adopted 'harm not adequately reparable by an award of damages' due to the concern that 'irreparable harm might present too high a threshold'.[1447] However, how one identifies irreparable harm is usually determined in part by one's view of remedies generally. For a legal system that believes damages are adequate compensation, there is less likelihood that harm would be seen as irreparable; however, systems that support specific performance might see damages as inadequate and would be more inclined towards interim measures that preserve the status quo.[1448]

It is necessary to reiterate in this context that India has now moved from the common law remedy of damages to specific performance as being the primary remedy for breach of contracts. Therefore, the reference to the traditional notion of irreparable harm no longer exists. All harm, in a certain sense, would now be 'irreparable,' requiring specific performance.[1449]

The standard adopted under Article 17A of the Model Law 'harm not adequately reparable by an award of damages' is a more reasonable standard and applied in the Indian context, it ensures that the reliance on the Specific Relief Act's threshold of 'irreparable harm' is not required. Moreover, such an open standard does not account for the conduct of a party which can lead to prejudice to the jurisdiction of the arbitral tribunal or frustrate the final award.[1450]

However, the Expert Committee on the Specific Relief Act noted that a party might not be able to prove all losses suffered and even if claimed, may not be awarded by the tribunal.[1451] In its view, the test of 'irreparable harm' does not permit the grant of an injunction for every contract and is the first 'hurdle' to be met by a party.[1452] The Committee also observed, based on a study,[1453] that the test led to courts granting injunctions based on inferences, rather than facts, without giving reasons while deciding 'inadequacy'. Also, injunctions were granted for the protection of monetary interests as well. Therefore, the Committee recommended removing the 'inadequacy' of compensation test to promote the consistent application of standards.[1454]

It is pertinent to note that some legal systems do not contain the demonstration of damages not being an adequate remedy.[1455] Similarly, the Principles of European Contract Law and the UNIDROIT Principles also do not provide for such consideration.[1456] Even in England, the test has been relaxed to a certain extent,[1457] and some

1447. Caron, *supra* n. 1388, at 552.
1448. Waincymer, *supra* n. 989, at 626.
1449. The Specific Relief Act, 1963, Ss 10 r/w 41.
1450. Gary Born, *supra* n. 33, at 2656.
1451. *Supra* n. 79, ¶11.3.1.
1452. *Ibid.*, ¶11.3.12.
1453. Nilima Bhadbhade, *Specific Performance of Contracts: The Tests of Inadequacy and Effective Enforcement* (2014), c.f. *ibid.*, at 51.
1454. *Ibid.*, ¶11.5.4.
1455. Denmark, France, Germany, Louisiana (USA), Quebec (Canada), Spain c.f. *ibid.*
1456. *Ibid.*, ¶11.3.1.
1457. *Evans Marshall & Co Ltd v. Sertola SA* [1973] 1 WLR 349, c.f., *ibid.*, ¶11.4.1.

argue that the test is dead.[1458] Academic writing in India[1459] and internationally also leans in favour of the removal of the consideration of the 'adequacy test'.[1460]

Moreover, an aspect usually ignored in the test for irreparable harm is that computation of damages happens much later. Therefore, what kind of damage is to be proved at the stage of interim relief is unclear, especially in long and complex transactions spanning over several years. Determining irreparable harm may not be possible in such cases. Inadequacy of damages being sufficient remedy or the lack of it must be proved[1461] by the person requesting the interim measure and the demonstration of the same is dependent on the individual perception of the adjudicator.[1462]

Furthermore, the problem with this standard is that the injury of less import that does not satisfy this threshold will always be forced upon one of the parties.[1463] One view is to consider harm as 'serious harm' and it should only mean whether the risk of grave harm is sufficiently substantial to justify any burden that provisional measure would impose on the respondents.[1464] However, this view caters more to the balance of convenience requirement than to the question of irreparable harm itself. Hence, the more efficient tool is the test of the balance of convenience without taking resort to the question of irreparable harm.[1465]

Thus, arbitral tribunals should consider the grant of interim measures without examining questions of irreparable harm or 'harm not adequately reparable by an award of damages'. Such a consideration is subsumed in the test of 'balance of convenience' or to apply a proportionality test.[1466] Even the Working Group had noted that the element of harm in Article 17A should be interpreted 'in a flexible manner, keeping in mind the balancing degree of harm suffered by' both parties.[1467] Whenever a party is required to show immediate and compelling need, in its analysis of compelling need, the arbitral tribunal is required to ascertain whether the measure requested affects the rights of the party and whether such party may be able to recover losses or damages at the time of execution of the award.

Therefore, the reference to '*harm not adequately reparable by an award of damages is likely to result if the measure is not ordered*' should be removed when

1458. Arnaldez, *supra* n. 1436, at 687.
1459. *Nilima Bhadbhade, Exceptional Nature of Specific Performance*, https:jjwww.academia.eduj3091909j ExceptionaLNature_oCSpeclfic_Performance_in_the_IndianJaw; *Nilima, supra* n. 1453, c.f. *Supra* n. 79, ¶11.4.1.
1460. Nilima, *supra* n. 1453, *ibid.*, ¶11.4.1.
1461. *Brij Ballabh Das v. Mahabir Prasad* AIR 1924 All 529; *Hari Krishna Agarwala v. K C Gupta* AIR 1949 All 440, c.f. *Supra* n. 79, ¶11.3.1.
1462. *Ibid.*, ¶11.5.3.
1463. Francisco, *supra* n. 1350, at 275; *A similar standard has been in the 2010 UNCITRAL Rules.*
1464. Gary Born, *supra* n. 33, at 2655, *Born asserts that instead of adopting the standard of 'irreparable' or 'serious harm' the more pragmatic view is that tribunals should ascertain the likelihood of harm, degree and character of the harm, the balance of hardships and other factors.*
1465. Francisco, *supra* n. 1350, at 275.
1466. Christopher Boog, *Interim Measures in International Arbitration*, in Manuel Arroyo (ed.), *Arbitration in Switzerland: The Practitioner's Guide* 1359-1360 (2013).
1467. UNCITRAL Yearbook, *supra* n. 11, at 452.

adopting Article 17(1)(a) of the Model Law under the IAA, especially after six the 2018 Amendment to the Specific Relief Act.

4.8. Criteria in India

While international jurisprudence pertaining to interim measures has grown and many overlapping questions concerning the power of the tribunal, the scope of such power and the criteria to be adopted by tribunals have been addressed in the 2006 Model Law Revisions, the courts in India continue to confuse two extremely relevant and similar concepts, i.e., (a) the law governing the arbitral tribunal's power; and (b) the law governing the standards applicable to the exercise of such a power.[1468] Inevitably, the tribunals comprising Indian arbitrators have applied the domestic law concepts of the CPC and the Specific Relief Act to arbitrations despite the clear wordings of Section 19(1) of the IAA not to be bound by the CPC, presumably to prevent the orders being set aside in appeal.

The courts in India have reiterated time and again that an interim injunction can only be granted when the applicant has been able to establish (a) a prima facie case; (b) a balance of convenience in its favour; and (c) the applicant will suffer irreparable injury.[1469] The courts have held that though an arbitrator is required to follow the principles of natural justice and fair play, the practice and principles of the CPC[1470] and the Evidence Act are also relevant for taking any decision by any judicial body/authority. An arbitrator is also bound to follow these principles unless otherwise agreed by the parties.[1471]

Therefore, while providing relief under Sections 9(1) and 17(1) of the IAA, courts and tribunals in India have adopted varying standards, primarily relying on the provisions of the CPC and the Specific Relief Act. Though there have been more liberal interpretations post the 2015 Amendment, such as those viewing the power under Section 17(1) of the IAA to be akin to proceedings under Order XXXIX of the CPC but with a wider discretion than what is available to a court under Order XXXIX of the CPC,[1472] the standard under the provision of the CPC has been one of default application. It is important to note that while the result may have been correct in some cases in taking a resort to the provisions of the CPC, the reasoning completely ignores the relevance and purpose of the arbitral process and limits the type of measures available to domestic courts.

A possible line of argument may well be that the standard to grant interim measures is provided under Section 17(1)(ii)(e) of the IAA as the arbitral tribunal may order such other interim measures as may appear to the tribunal to be 'just and

1468. Gary Born, *supra* n. 33, at 2638-2639.
1469. *Ajay Mohan and Ors. v. H.N. Rai and Ors.* (2008) 2 SCC 517, ¶21.
1470. *Yusufkhan v. Prajita Developers Pvt. Ltd.* 2019 SCC Online Bom 505, ¶23.
1471. *Jayant Industrial Packaging Ltd. v. Saraswat Co-operative Bank Ltd.* 2011 SCC OnLine Bom 393, ¶29, *it should be noted that this decision was passed before the 2015 Amendment and now the phrase 'unless otherwise agreed by the parties' has no value.*
1472. *N. Syamala Devi v. E. Raghava Rao & Ors.* 2018 (1) Arb LR 214 (Mad), ¶26.

convenient', a standard akin to 'appropriate', as used in institutional arbitral rules.[1473] Therefore, even if the standard provided under the CPC is not met, the tribunal is free to adopt any other standard. However, the subclause is residuary and it is only after exhausting the applicability of the preceding subclauses that the tribunal resorts to this subclause.

Furthermore, a literal interpretation of the language indicates that the language was to cater to 'such other interim measure of protection', i.e., any other type of measure as opposed to providing a universal standard to assess the request for an interim measure. Also, leaving room for inconsistent interpretations at the hands of subjective tribunals takes away from the goal of harmonisation and consistency, which is the need of the hour for Indian arbitration law.

One solution to prevent the reliance on the CPC and the Specific Relief Act is to adopt a provision which is similar to Article 17A of the Model Law (with modifications, as discussed above). This would not be contrary to the current regime either. An order passed by the court or tribunal dehors of the provisions of the CPC may well be enforceable as both Sections 9 and 17 of the IAA contain that such orders shall be treated as those passed by a court. Hence, there is no reason to continue adopting the standards provided in the CPC while passing interim orders under the IAA. Therefore, misplaced concerns about public policy and mandatory law need not be raised.

Reliance on such domestic procedures is also contrary to the purpose of seeking interim relief from the arbitral tribunal. The courts may not be in a position to appreciate the dispute and may not be able to fit the required relief in pre-determined procedural law standards governing the courts, i.e., prima facie case, the balance of convenience and irreparable injury.

4.8.1. Harmonising the Powers under Sections 9 and 17 of the IAA

Thus, as discussed in Chapter 3, the power to grant court-ordered measures and the type of measures that can be granted should be harmonised with those of the arbitral tribunal. Similarly, the standards for the exercise of powers under Sections 9 and 17 of the IAA should also be harmonised to ensure consistency and prevent reliance on domestic law standards. Thus, the standards must be provided specifically in the IAA in order to fulfil the following objectives:

(a) Such orders would comply with the mandate of Article 17J of the Model Law and would be in line with the 'specific features of international arbitration'.
(b) They would align with the international jurisprudence and standards adopted by international arbitral tribunals.
(c) They can cater to new technologies, issues, and peculiar facts and circumstances of each case, devoid of existing jurisprudence and precedence on similar subjects.

1473. *See Appendix M.*

(d) The appellate court will also have guidance while examining orders passed by the court or tribunal and would not consider them to be perverse or contrary to law if they have not adopted the standards provided in the CPC.[1474]

Such a revamp and express provision of standards in the IAA along the lines of the 2006 Model Law were proposed to be added by the Saraf Committee.[1475] The Saraf Committee had suggested that the only standard required to be satisfied should be that harm not adequately reparable by damages will result if the measure is not granted.[1476] However, the same is yet to be done. Instead, courts and tribunals in India have been resorting to the standards provided in the CPC even though India has adopted the Model Law.

Almost all jurisdictions which have adopted the 2006 Model Law with respect to interim measures have incorporated Article 17A(1) and (2) with minor changes with wording as provided in Appendix C, except for Belgium.[1477] It is suggested that India should adopt a similar approach and harmonise the regime on interim measures with the 2006 Model Law Revisions.

Therefore, the following criteria should be adopted in Section 17 of the IAA:

The party requesting an interim measure must satisfy the arbitral tribunal that:

(i) there is a reasonable possibility that the requesting party will succeed on the merits of the claim;

(ii) a right has been infringed, or is threatened to be infringed, by the party against whom the measure is requested; and

(iii) *the harm likely to result if the measure is not ordered substantially outweighs the harm that is likely to result to the party against whom the measure is directed if the measure is granted.*

Such standards may also be applied by emergency arbitrators as they cater to the requirement of urgency and comparative damage without prejudgment on merits. Furthermore, such standards are broad enough to apply to all types of measures that may be granted by a tribunal and will not be restricted to measures aimed at the resolution of the dispute only.

For the purposes of preservation of evidence, the criteria should be the same as that provided under Article 17A(2) of the Model Law. Such standard grants the discretion to the tribunal to apply the above standards as 'appropriate' after considering the question of relevance and whether the evidence sought to be preserved is material to the resolution of the dispute.

5. TYPES OF MEASURES

Once it is determined that the arbitral tribunal has the power to order interim relief and what standards are to be adopted, the next question is related to the types of measures

1474. *The author argues that the provision for appeal against orders passed under Indian Arbitration Act, 1996, S. 17, should be deleted.*
1475. *Supra* n. 68.
1476. *Ibid.*
1477. Tomas, *supra* n. 1256, at 29.

that may be ordered and which law determines those permissible types of measures.[1478]

The original Article 17 of the Model Law was deliberately formulated in general terms as it was believed that specifying the list of measures would curtail the power of the arbitral tribunal.[1479] Therefore, most countries adopted the broad language of Article 17 of the Model Law. While some provided a list of the measures that can be granted, others provided a list of measures that could not.[1480]

It is pertinent to note that listing the types of measures narrows down the possibility of future applications with international trade continuing to generate new kinds of remedies according to the needs of the parties and the increasing complexity of the cases.[1481] Hence, the UNCITRAL Working Group concluded that the clarification of the powers of the tribunal, instead of a list, would lead to uniform solutions and procedures for arbitral tribunals[1482] as various kinds of measures may be granted by an arbitral tribunal. These may be aimed:[1483]

(a) at facilitating the conduct of arbitral proceedings, i.e., inspection of documents, goods or property, orders for preservation of evidence or orders to maintain the confidentiality of the proceedings, anti-suit injunctions, inspections, the appointment of an expert;
(b) at avoiding loss or damage or maintaining status quo, i.e., orders to continue the performance, a prohibitory injunction restraining a party from doing something, safeguard property or goods or even to minimise damage or the loss of a right, prevent the invoking of a bank guarantee, prohibitory injunctions for making press releases, disclosing confidential material, using intellectual property, relocating assets or evidence;
(c) at facilitating the enforcement of the award, i.e., attachment of assets, freezing orders, order to deposit money or goods with an escrow or providing security for costs.

Therefore, various types of reliefs may be granted by the arbitral tribunal or may be required in each case. The type of relief that may be granted would ultimately depend on the law applicable to the type of measures that can be granted.

5.1. Applicable Law

In the absence of the types of measures being listed in domestic arbitration statutes, i.e., the *lex arbitri*, the arbitral tribunal is at liberty to use any type of interim measures

1478. Boog, *supra* n. 592, at 431.
1479. Report of UNCITRAL Working Group on the work of its Sixth session, 1983, A/CN.9/245, available at: https://undocs.org/en/A/CN.9/245, ¶71. *See, e.g.*, Redfern, *supra* n. 1253, at 341.
1480. *See* Appendices; *see* Menon, *supra* n. 102, at 3-5.
1481. Roth, *supra* n. 448, at 425.
1482. *See* Menon, *supra* n. 102, at 3-5.
1483. *Ibid.*

available under the law applicable to the substance of the dispute, the law of the seat, law of the forum where enforcement will be sought,[1484] subject to mandatory law.[1485]

In Switzerland, the same has to be determined by procedural rules applicable to the arbitration proceedings.[1486] Some authors contend that it should be by the law governing the merits,[1487] and some suggest that the two approaches should be combined.[1488] Some suggest that the law of the jurisdiction where the enforcement is to be sought should be the relevant law[1489] and some state that the arbitral tribunal is free to order any measure that it may deem necessary and appropriate.[1490] On the one hand, *Ali* takes the view that the arbitral tribunal can grant any measure available under any of the laws.[1491] *Boog*, on the other hand, suggests a cascade.[1492] He suggests that by agreeing to certain arbitration rules containing general provisions, the parties agree to vest in the arbitral tribunal a wide discretion to determine the type and content of the interim measure without limiting it to a particular law or set of rules.[1493]

If the parties' agreement or the set of arbitration rules contain no indication as to the types of interim measures which can be ordered, *Boog* asserts that the arbitral tribunal is obliged to refer to international arbitration standards.[1494] Others assert that the type of interim measures that are appropriate in international commercial arbitration is determined according to the specific facts of each dispute and the arbitrator's subjective perception of the risks involved.[1495] Therefore, there are different views with respect to the issue of applicable law governing the types of measures that may be granted by an arbitral tribunal.

5.2. Article 17(2) of the Model Law

These debates are now less relevant after the introduction of Article 17(2) of the Model Law. The express recognition of the broad powers of the arbitral tribunal without limiting the exact type of measures that may be granted impliedly caters to all differing views, without a determination of the law applicable. The broad language in Article 17(2) of the Model Law is adequate to cater to emerging technologies and complex cases as it provides flexibility to the arbitral tribunals to grant tailor-made interim

1484. Ali Yesilirmak, *supra* n. 30, at 204-205.
1485. Lew, supra *n. 2, at 29.*
1486. Markus Wirth, *Supra* n. 580, at 32.
1487. Boog, *supra* n. 592, at 432.
1488. *Ibid.*
1489. Markus Wirth, *Supra* n. 580, at 33.
1490. Von Segesser, *supra* n. 1413, at 71.
1491. Ali Yesilirmak, *supra* n. 30, at 204-205.
1492. *(a) mandatory provisions of law; (b) the parties' agreement; (c) international arbitration standards; (d) lex arbitri; (e) law governing the merits of the dispute; (f) the provisions of national law on civil procedure at the seat are irrelevant; (g) the law at the place of enforcement. But the same should be used with caution because the parties very often comply with the orders voluntarily. Also, the place may not be fixed in the case of movable assets.* Boog, *supra* n. 592, at 441.
1493. *Ibid.*, at 437.
1494. *Ibid.*, at 438.
1495. Lew, *supra* n. 28, at ¶23-30.

measures. Hence, similar language should be adopted in Section 17 of the IAA, clarifying the powers exercisable by the arbitral tribunal with respect to interim measures.

5.3. The Indian Position

Before the 2015 Amendment, India had adopted the broad language of Article 17 of the Model Law without reference to any specific type of measures. The 2003 Bill had proposed to amend Section 17 of the IAA by adding some more powers to the list of powers that can be exercised by the arbitral tribunal, as contained in the English Arbitration Act.[1496] The Saraf Committee had, however, suggested that Section 17 of the IAA should be redrafted along the lines of the Model Law and not the English Arbitration Act.[1497] Unfortunately, the 2015 Amendment followed the philosophy of the 2003 Bill and brought the power of the arbitral tribunal in consonance with the English Arbitration Act rather than the Model Law.

As mentioned earlier, after the 2015 Amendment, Section 17(1) of the IAA, similar to Section 9(1) of the IAA, now provides a list of measures that may be ordered by the arbitral tribunal. It should be noted that the types of measures being listed under Section 17(1) of the IAA were to bring the power of the arbitral tribunal at par with that of the court under Section 9 of the IAA and not to align the power with the Model Law.

As discussed in Chapter 3, the list should be incorporated after the adoption of the generic language of Article 17(2) of the Model Law clarifying the type of measures available. The problems with only providing a list without adopting the provisions of Article 17(2) of the Model Law are discussed below.

5.4. Maintain or Restore Status Quo

Measures under this subclause comprise a party asserting a prima facie claim that the party will suffer serious harm as a consequence of the steps threatened by the respondent to alter the existing status quo.[1498] These requests are the most frequent and common ones in international arbitration.[1499] For example, a party may be prohibited from taking steps such as terminating an agreement, disclosing trade secrets, invoking a bank guarantee or using disputed goods.[1500] It may also be the case

---

1496. Law Commission of India, *supra* n. 65. Government of India, Ministry of Law and Justice – Proposed Amendments to the Arbitration & Conciliation Act, 1996: A Consultation Paper, available at: https://www.legallyindia.com/images/stories/docs/Arbitration-Act-LawMin-ConsultationPaper-on-Arb-Act-April2010-1.pdf.
1497. Law Commission of India, *supra* n. 65.
1498. Gary Born, *supra* n. 33, at 2654.
1499. *Twenty-six out of forty-five arbitrators listed this with a 10%-100% relative frequency*. Hober, *supra* n. 1207, at 733.
1500. International arbitral tribunals have not infrequently issued or accepted the availability of such orders. *See, e.g., Interim Award in ICC Case No. 9324*, 11(1) ICC Ct. Bull. 103 (2000); *Lew,* supra *n. 2, at 29*; *Final Award in ICC Case No. 7895*, 11(1) ICC Ct. Bull. 64 (2000).; *Plama Consortium Ltd v. Republic of Bulgaria, Order in ICSID Case No. ARB/03/24 of 6 September 2005*, ¶38; *Tanzania Electric Supply Company Limited v. Independent Power Tanzania*

that the arbitral tribunal directs the parties not to take steps that would alter the contractual status quo.[1501] These measures aim to avoid or prevent modification of the state of facts or law of the subject matter of the dispute which could render more difficult or impossible later performances.[1502]

5.4.1. Meaning of 'Status Quo'

Sometimes a party may also seek restoration of a *status quo ante* which is now explicitly provided under Article 17(2)(a) of the Model Law and Article 26(2)(a) of the UNCITRAL Rules. However, not much attention has been paid to what the term 'status quo' means. Does it mean 'the last peaceable state between the parties which preceded the present controversy'[1503] or does it mean status quo at the time the relief is granted or requested, or when the arbitration is commenced,[1504] or when the dispute arises?[1505]

Born suggests that the term should simply be interpreted to mean that the arbitral tribunal should consider the relative injury that is likely to be suffered by both parties and adopt the ordinary standards for grant of interim measures.[1506] There is no universally recognised and applied legal concept of the term status quo. In international arbitration, there can be several scenarios and the term status quo would mean very different things in each of them. In some cases, interim relief would mean preserving the existing state of affairs while in others, it could mean the modification of the status quo.

For example, in the case of perishable goods, the interim relief would be to modify the status quo and sell the goods in order to preserve their value. In other cases, such as the termination of the licence agreement for breach of contract by the licensee causing loss of market share of the products sold under the licence, the licensor would be forced to engage a third party to sell the products in order to prevent the loss of market share. In this case, it is unclear as to what ought to be the order of status quo when the defendant requests the tribunal to prohibit the licensor from contracting with the third party.[1507]

Sometimes a status quo order can even mean a mandatory injunction where the arbitral tribunal orders parties to deposit money or assets or shares with an escrow or

---

Limited, Decision on the Respondent's Request for Provisional Measures in ICSID Case No. ARB/98/8 of 20 December 1999, ¶¶5(iv).

1501. Gary Born, *supra* n. 33, at 2668-2669.

1502. *Extract from A Procedural Order in ICC Arbitration No. 12 (1989)*, 12 ASA Bull. 142, 144 (1994); *See also* UNCITRAL Model Law, Art. 17(2)(a); Award in Unidentified ICC Case, discussed in Schwartz, *supra* n. 1236, at 61; *The Islamic Republic of Iran v. The United States of America Decision No. DEC 116-A15(IV) & A24-FT of 18 May 1993*, 29 Iran–US CTR 214 (1993); *Component Builders, Inc. v. Islamic Repub. of Iran, Order in IUSCT Case No. 395 of 10 January 1985*; Committee on International Civil and Commercial Litigation, *Principles on Provisional and Protective Measures in International Litigation*, reprinted in ILA, *Report of the Sixty-Seventh Conference, Helsinki* 202, ¶1 (1996).

1503. *Susanville Indian Rancheria v. Leavitt*, 2007 WL 662197 at 7.

1504. *Order in ICC Case No. 7388*.

1505. *Award in ICC Case No. 6503*, 122 J.D.I. (Clunet) 1022 (1995).

1506. Gary Born, *supra* n. 33, at 2671.

1507. Abascal, *supra* n. 1, at 761.

receiver. Similarly, arbitrators commonly order parties not to suspend partial payments or provide guarantees with a letter of credit or pass other similar directions.[1508] Therefore, not only is the period when the status quo should be considered essential but also, what does a status quo order mean in the facts and circumstances of a particular case?

5.4.2. Maintaining Status Quo

The considerations in the case of maintaining the status quo are different from the restoration of the status quo. Maintaining the status quo would refer to orders that prevent the aggravation of the dispute.[1509] In such circumstances, the risk of serious harm is not required, but the only consideration should be the commercial desirability of stopping unilateral actions by the parties from improving their respective positions in the dispute.[1510] Hence, the relevant period for consideration should be the time at which the request for grant of interim measure is received. Given that the arbitral tribunal is precluded from prejudging the merits, it should, after considering the balance of convenience, maintain the status quo at the time of the request as it would prevent further harm and the harm already suffered would most likely be considered at the time of award of damages.[1511] In any case, the harm already suffered, even though it may have been irreparable, is something that cannot be undone but only made whole through restitution by way of damages.

Examples of such orders range from applications for the preservation of assets or goods that might be required for non-evidentiary purposes simply to mitigate losses during the pendency of the arbitration proceeding, grant of *Mareva* injunctions,[1512]

1508. *Ibid.*
1509. *Order in ICC Case No. 7388; Tokios Tokelés v. Ukraine, in ICSID Case No. ARB/02/18 of 1 July 2003, ¶2; Amco Asia Corporation v. Republic of Indonesia, Request for Provisional Measures in ICSID Case No. ARB/81/1 of 9 December 1983;* Christoph H. Schreuer et al., *The ICSID Convention: A Commentary Article 47* (2009) ¶139. *Other ICSID authorities are to the same effect; Churchill Mining plc v. Republic of Indonesia, Procedural Order No. 3 on Provisional Measures in ICSID Case No. ARB/12/14 of 4 March 2013, ¶46; Quiborax S.A., Non Metallic Minerals S.A. and Allan Fosk Kaplún v. Plurinational State of Bolivia, Decision on Provisional Measures in ICSID Case No. ARB/06/2 of 26 February 2010, ¶117; Burlington Resource Inc. v. Republic of Ecuador, Procedural Order No. 1 in ICSID Case No. ARB/08/5 of 29 June 2009, ¶60; City Oriente Limited v. Republic of Ecuador and Empresa Estatal Petróleos del Ecuador (Petroecuador) [I], Decision on Provisional Measures in ICSID Case No. ARB/06/21 of 19 November 2007, ¶57; Tanzania Electric Supply Company Limited v. Independent Power Tanzania Limited, Decision on the Respondent's Request for Provisional Measures in ICSID Case No. ARB/98/8 of 20 December 1999, ¶12; ICSID Regulations and Rules, Notes, ICSID/4/Rev. 1, 104 (May 1975); Partial Award in ICC Case No. 3896, 110 J.D.I. (Clunet) 914, 918 (1983); Partial Award in ICC Case No. 3892,* in Sigvard Jarvin & Yves Derains (eds), *Collection of ICC Arbitral Awards 1974-1985* 161, 164 (1990).
1510. Schwartz, *supra* n. 1236, at 61; *Award in ICC Case No. 3896,* 110 J.D.I. (Clunet) 914 (1983).
1511. *Guru Madhwa Seva Samithi v. Katti Ananth Acharya* 2003 AIHC 31(33) (Kant).
1512. *Indian Oil Corporation Ltd. v. Iranian Offshore Engineering and Construction Company* 2009 SCC OnLine Del 2898, ¶¶10 & 11.

mandatory injunctions, prohibitory injunctions,[1513] the appointment of a private receiver,[1514] or injunctions in several other situations.[1515]

5.4.3. Restoring Status Quo

Restoring status quo, however, may cause serious prejudice to the respondent, especially if the claim fails on merits. Considerations of restoring status quo would include instances where the right of one party has been so seriously prejudiced that it would be unfair and unjust to permit the respondent to take advantage of its own wrong, e.g., forceful dispossession of a tenant without following the due process of law or illegal termination of a contract or suspension of supply services. However, the arbitral tribunal cannot rewrite a contract and grant a mandatory injunction as the grant of a mandatory injunction to continue with the contract would, in effect, be a final relief.[1516]

In India, while courts and tribunals have readily granted orders to maintain status quo,[1517] orders permitting the restoration of status quo have been rare. The prevalent position of law is that such orders should not be permitted except in extraordinary circumstances.[1518] This is based on the application of the provisions of the CPC and the Specific Relief Act, and the application of this standard by the tribunal has been upheld by the courts as well.[1519] Applying these standards, the relief of restoration of status quo may not be available in India and such orders, even if passed by the tribunal, may not be enforced by the courts.

A similar view was expressed by the Saraf Committee. It had suggested that the restoration of the status quo has far-reaching consequences and this power should be exercised in appropriate cases only by the courts.[1520] However, such a view is uncalled

---

1513. *Tuticorin Coal Terminal Pvt. Ltd. v. Gelguera Gruas India Pvt. Ltd.* 2018 SCC OnLine Bom 1268, ¶18. *The tribunal directed the parties to maintain* status quo *and restrained a party from utilizing the amounts, if any, collected under bank guarantees issued in favour of such party. The order was set aside in appeal on the ground that the bank guarantee was unconditional.*
1514. *Prabhat Steel Traders Pvt. Ltd. v. Excel Metal Processors Pvt. Ltd.* 2018 SCC OnLine Bom 2347, ¶ 40, *the only limitation on the power is while an arbitral tribunal cannot appoint a receiver of the court, but it can very well appoint a private receiver; Anil Pravinbhai Patel v. Pradeep Sardarilal Jain and Ors.* 2017 SCC OnLine Bom 8073, ¶3.
1515. *The transfer of goods from one place to another, the sale of goods or prohibition to sell goods, creating of an escrow account, preserving the* status quo *or anti-suit injunctions in* Ali Yesilirmak, *supra* n. 30, at 208-209.
1516. *Gujarat Chemical Port Terminal Co. Ltd. v. Indian Oil Corporation of India* 2016 SCC Online Bom 2605, ¶¶ 111-112.
1517. *See Chapter 3.*
1518. *Parsoli Works Pvt. Ltd. v. BMW India Pvt. Ltd.* 2018 (2) Arb. LR 50; *Samir Narain Bhojwani v. Aurora Properties and Investments* 2018 SCC OnLine SC 1048, ¶27; *as previously held in Metro Marines v. Bonus Watch Company Pvt. Ltd.* (2004) 7 SCC 478; *Kishore Kumar Khaitan v. Praveen Kumar Singh* (2006) 3 SCC 312; *Purshottam Vishandas Raheja v. Shrichand Vishandas Raheja* (2011) 6 SCC 73.
1519. *Kopastin Holdings Ltd. v. Uday Bahadaur & Anr.* 2018 SCC OnLine Del 10541, ¶¶13 &15.
1520. Government of India, Ministry of Law and Justice – Proposed Amendments to the Arbitration & Conciliation Act, 1996: A Consultation Paper, available at: https://www.legallyindia.com/images/stories/docs/Arbitration-Act-LawMin-ConsultationPaper-on-Arb-Act-April2010-1.pdf.

for. It is reminiscent of the mistrust of the arbitral process and the arbitrators. Therefore, it is necessary to expressly recognise the power to restore the status quo under Section 17 of the IAA.

Furthermore, the adoption of Article 17(2) of the Model Law would liberate the powers of the arbitral tribunal from restrictive interpretations based on the CPC and the Specific Relief Act and bolster arbitral efficacy. It will permit interim measures to be tailored to commercially viable and necessary reliefs, rather than be curtailed by cumbersome domestic law prerequisites.

5.5. Preventing Harm to the Arbitral Process

Measures under this subclause would include instances where the respondent's action appears to be designed to make the ultimate enforcement of an award more difficult.[1521] Arbitral tribunals are likely to consider the conduct of the respondents who have taken steps which may be designed to frustrate the arbitral tribunal's jurisdiction and remedial authority such as disposing of the subject matter of arbitration or altering the circumstances that the award becomes meaningless.[1522]

Requests to prevent harm to the arbitral process are similar to court-ordered anti-suit injunctions.[1523] The phrase 'or prejudice to the arbitral process itself' in Article 17(2)(b) of the Model Law recognises the power of the arbitral tribunal to grant an interim order to prevent obstruction or delay to the arbitral process.

In complete deviance from the Model Law, Section 17(1)(ii)(e) of the IAA provides residual powers to the arbitral tribunal to order '*such other interim measure of protection as may appear to be just and convenient*'. Thus, it may be argued that the arbitral tribunal has wide powers to fashion appropriate interim relief, including passing a mandatory injunction under Section 17(1)(ii)(e) of the IAA to prevent harm to the arbitral process.[1524] However, the relief should be in consonance with the arbitration dispute. If the relief sought at the interim stage is beyond the scope of the relief sought in the arbitration, the same is 'not essential to protect the integrity of that process'.[1525] Naturally, the power under Section 17(1)(ii)(e) of the IAA is not unbridled. Without any specific language in Section 17 of the IAA supporting such an interpretation, the exercise of such power will remain discretionary. Hence, Section 17(1)(ii)(e) should be removed. The flexibility contained in this provision can be addressed by the use of the generic language in Article 17(2) of the Model Law.

1521. Gary Born, *supra* n. 33, at 2654.
1522. *Islamic Republic of Iran v. U.S.A., Decision Nos DEC 116-A15(IV) & A24-FT of 18 May 1993, 29 Iran–US CTR 214 (1993 Interim Award in IUSCT Case No. ITM 34-222-1 of 17 February 1984,* 5 Iran–US CTR 152, 154 (1985); *E-Systems, Inc. v. The Government of the Islamic Republic of Iran, Bank Melli Iran, Interim Award in IUSCT Case No. 13-388-FT of 4 February 1983,* 2 Iran–US CTR 51, 57 (1983); *Plama Consortium Ltd v. Republic of Bulgaria, Order in ICSID Case No. ARB/03/24 of 6 September 2005,* ¶38.
1523. *See Chapter 9.*
1524. *NTPC Ltd. v. Jindal ITF Ltd. & Anr.* 2017 SCC OnLine Del 11219, ¶20.
1525. *After adopting the 2006 Model Law Revisions in Discovery Geo Corporation v. STP Energy Pte Ltd.* [2012] NZHC 3549, ¶44-47.

5.6. Preservation of Assets

Article 17(2)(c) of the Model Law recognises the power of the tribunal to provide for means of preserving assets out of which a subsequent award may be satisfied and arbitral tribunals and courts have ordered such securities.[1526] The provision was understood to require a legal guarantee or security.[1527] Under Section 17, the phrase 'securing the amount in dispute' is used as opposed to the language in Article 17(2)(c) of the Model Law. This has been understood to mean that the tribunal can (a) pass attachment orders; (b) pass orders for interim payments; or (c) require security for payment.

5.6.1. Attachment Orders

In India, attachment orders by the tribunal have been recognised.[1528] The arbitral tribunal can attach a property even though it is not the subject matter of the arbitral proceedings.[1529] It should be noted, however, that, unlike in India, in some jurisdictions, the tribunal has no power to pass attachment orders.[1530]

5.6.2. Interim Payments

To preserve assets, the arbitral tribunal may direct interim payments to preserve assets. The need for such interim payments can be ascertained from an English case,[1531] where a freezing order was granted by the arbitral tribunal for all assets of the respondent in England, but the respondent nonetheless dissipated all assets. Since a freezing order

1526. *Final Award in ICC Case No. 9154*, 11(1) ICC Bull. 98 (2000) (requiring deposit of disputed funds into escrow account); *Interim Awards in ICC Case No. 8670*, 11(1) ICC Ct. Bull. 77 (2000); *Final Award in ICC Case No. 7536*, 11(1) ICC Ct. Bull. 52 (2000), c.f. Lew, *supra* n. 2, at 29 (requiring deposit of specified amount into escrow); *Interim Award in NAI Case No. 1694 of 12 December 1996*, e.g., *On Time Staffing, LLC v. National Union Fire Ins. Co.* 2011 U.S. Dist. LEXIS 50689 (S.D.N.Y.); *Certain Underwriters at Lloyd's, London v. Argonaut Ins. Co.* 264 F.Supp. 2d 926 (N.D. Cal. 2003); *Konkar Maritime Enter., SA v. Compagnie Belge d'Affretement* 668 F.Supp. 267, 271 (S.D.N.Y. 1987); *Compania Chilena De Navegacion Interoceanica, SA v. Norton, Lilly & Co.* 652 F.Supp. 1512, 1516 (S.D.N.Y. 1987); *Sperry International Trade, Inc. v. Israel* 689 F2d. 301 (2d Cir. 1982); *Swift Industries Inc. v. Botany Industry, Inc.* 466 F.2d 1125 (3d Circuit 1972).

1527. Report of UNCITRAL Working Group on the work of its Thirty Ninth session, 2003, A/CN.9/545, available at: https://undocs.org/en/A/CN.9/545, ¶26.

1528. *Reliance Communications Ltd. v. Ericsson India Pvt. Ltd. & Ors.* 2018 SCC OnLine Bom 550, ¶¶30, 31, 36. *The court also observed that the tribunal had taken due cognisance of the fact that proceedings under Insolvency and Bankruptcy Code had been initiated against the party but the same had not been admitted by the National Company Law Tribunal and hence if the interim application and the interim measure was not granted, irretrievable injury would be caused.*

1529. *Sundaram Finance Ltd. v. P. Sathivel* 2018 SCC OnLine Mad 3080, ¶14.

1530. Belgium Judicial Code, Art. 1691; French Code of Civil Procedure, Arts 1449, 1468, 1506; *this is also the position in Switzerland*, Stephen, *supra* n. 96, at 650; *See Chapter 3 and Appendix B.*

1531. *Kastner v. Jason & Sherman v. Kastner* [2004] EWHC 592 (Ch).

creates no charge, lien or other security interest in the assets, an interim payment in such a case would have been a more effective interim measure.[1532]

Therefore, an interim payment is *'an outright payment to the plaintiff, which may be subsequently revised on the final judgement'*.[1533] Under Dutch Law, it is known as *kort geding* and it has no historical equivalent in England[1534] or Switzerland.[1535] The position in Germany is that such measures prejudge the outcome of the main proceedings and hence, cannot be granted, barring one exception, *Leistungsverfügung*, i.e., where it is acknowledged that any other measure would be unreasonable, a creditor can receive interim payment subject to fulfilment of strict requirements.[1536] Hence, interim payments are a controversial measure as they depend primarily on the prejudgment on merits of the dispute by granting what amounts to a partial or final amount for virtually indisputable sums due.[1537]

It should be noted that the power to require interim payment has been recognised by tribunals.[1538] For the criteria, one arbitral tribunal made reference to Article 809(2) of the French New CPC which provides that where the existence of the obligation cannot be seriously denied, the court may order an interim payment on account.[1539] If there is any serious challenge to the right, the arbitral tribunal should tread carefully so as not to prejudge the merits and should seek security for damages before granting the measure.[1540]

In India, interim payments have been recognised as interim measures.[1541] However, the same remain controversial and there have been cases where courts have refused to grant such a measure as would amount to final relief.[1542] Therefore, it is unclear if such measures will be recognised by Indian courts at the time of enforcement. The Working Group was clear that such payments do not fall within the category

1532. Van Vechten Veeder, *The Need for Cross-border Enforcement of Interim Measures Ordered by a State Court in Support of the International Arbitral Process*, in Albert Jan Van den Berg (ed.), *New Horizons in International Commercial Arbitration and Beyond* 255 (2005).

1533. *Provisional payment enables a party survive or contributes to such survival by preserving the party's cash flow*, Lew, *supra* n. 28, at ¶23-55.

1534. Though the power can be read into English Arbitration Act, 1996, S. 39; Veeder, *supra* n. 1532, at 254.

1535. *Ibid.*, at 247.

1536. *Such as the applicant cannot wait for the final outcome and needs the payment so urgently that it would suffer disproportionately high, possibly irreparable damage*; *Ibid.*, at 249.

1537. Gary Born, *supra* n. 33, at 2683.

1538. Ali Yesilirmak, *supra* n. 30, at 218-219.

1539. *Ibid.*

1540. *Ibid.*

1541. *Mudhit Gupta v. Sussane Khan* 2020 SCC OnLine Bom 192, ¶60; *Shiningkart Ecommerce Private Ltd. v. Jiayun Data Ltd* 2019 SCC OnLine Del 9169, ¶40; *Federal Agency for State Property Management of the Russian Federation (Rosemushestvo) v. Saraf Agencies Pvt. Ltd.* 2018 SCC OnLine Cal 3450, ¶15; *Aditya Birla Retail Ltd. v. Ashapura Developers* 2009 (4) Arb. LR 125 (Bom); *Ratnagiri Gas and Power Pvt. Ltd. v. Joint Venture of Whessoe Oil and Gas Ltd.* 2013 (1) Arb. LR 84 (Del) (DB); *Jatin Keshruwala v. DAG Creative Media Pvt. Ltd.* 2019 SCC OnLine Bom 1346.

1542. *State of Assam v. Barak Vpatyaka D. U. Karamchari Sanstha* (2009) 5 SCC 694; *Himachal Furitistic Communication Ltd. v. Union of India* 2009 (3) Arb. LR 394.

of interim measures of protection.[1543] After the adoption of Article 17(2) of the Model Law, the power to 'secure the amount' will have to be read harmoniously. Hence, the exercise of the power will be clarified to prevent prejudgment of merits and passing of orders for interim payments.

5.6.3. *Security for Payment*

Another method used to 'secure the dispute in arbitration' is to require a party to secure the underlying claims in arbitration. A 'security for payment' is a kind of advance payment designed to guarantee the payment and the enforcement of the award.[1544] These requests are designed to ensure that a party's substantive claim, although well-founded, is not rendered useless because of the deterioration in the financial condition of its counterparty or by deliberate diversions of assets, i.e., the payment is aimed to restore an obligation or a right before the final adjudication, provided the said obligation or right is not directly under challenge in the dispute.[1545]

Frequently, the arbitral tribunals now receive an application for security requesting to secure the counterparties underlying claims or an application for security for costs.[1546] It is necessary to clarify that a request for security for payment is different from a request for security for costs.

5.6.4. *Difference Between Security for Payment and Security for Costs*

Distinct from the idea of securing the amount in dispute is security for costs where the arbitral tribunal orders one party or both parties to post security to cover the likely amounts that would be awarded to the counterparty in the event that it prevails in the arbitration and is entitled to recover its cost.[1547]

Requests to secure the amount in dispute are distinct from interim measures of protection to the limited extent that the criteria for determination rest solely on the allocation of risks of the delay of arbitral proceedings. Essentially, the arbitral tribunal has to determine who should bear the risk (and the financial cost of mitigating such a risk) that a party will be unable to satisfy the financial obligations of the final award.[1548]

1543. Report of UNCITRAL Working Group on the work of its Thirty Second session, June 2000, A/CN.9/468, available at: https://undocs.org/en/A/CN.9/468, ¶85.
1544. Ali Yesilirmak, *supra* n. 30, at 213.
1545. *Ibid.*, at 218.
1546. *See Chapter 8.*
1547. *See generally*, Laurence Craig, William W. Park, & Jan Paulsson, *Annotated Guide to the 1998 ICC Arbitration Rules* 138 (1998); Yves Derains & Eric Schwartz, *A Guide to the ICC Rules of Arbitration* 296-297 (2005); Peter Fitzpatrick, *Security for Costs under the Arbitration Act, 1996*, Int'l Arb. L. R. 139 (1998); Locknie Hsu, *Orders for Security for Costs and International Arbitration in Singapore*, Int'l Arb. L. R. 111 (2000); Noah Rubins, *In God We Trust, All others Pay Cash: Security for Costs in International Commercial Arbitration*, 11 Am. R. Int'l Arb. 306 (2000); *Gary Soo*, Securing Costs in Hong Kong Arbitration, Int'l Arb. L. R. 25 (2000).
1548. Gary Born, *supra* n. 33, at 2677-2678.

The party requesting the interim measure needs to demonstrate that the likelihood of the award being rendered futile is quite high[1549] and there is urgency.[1550] The applicant must show a real risk that the payee may not be able to repay and that the risk should be more than nominal. It will not be enough to simply express the concern about the payee's ability to pay but a high degree of likelihood that the payee will not be able to repay if for determination goes in favour of the party seeking interim relief.[1551] Therefore, as long as there are reasonable grounds to believe that the financial condition of a party is inadequate or will deteriorate during the course of the arbitral proceedings, putting the final award at risk of non-enforcement, an arbitral tribunal can order securing the amount in dispute.[1552]

It should, however, be kept in mind that there should be a change in circumstances or re-allocation of risks since the execution of the contract.[1553] If the risk allocation remains the same, as and when the contract was executed, the request for security should be rejected. Similarly, when there is evidence that a party is dissipating assets or encumbering them, then as long as the other criteria of prima facie case, jurisdiction, and the balance of convenience are met, the tribunal can secure the amount in dispute.[1554] In Kenya, the power to order security in respect of any claim or any amount in dispute is provided in the arbitration statute itself.[1555]

The power of the tribunal to order security for payment was recognised in India[1556] under Section 17(2) of the IAA (as it stood prior to the 2015 Amendment) only in a handful of cases. Post the 2015 Amendment, the power is recognised under Section 17(1)(ii)(b) of the IAA but will be governed by Order XXXVIII Rule 5 of the CPC.[1557] However, the predominant view is that such payments cannot be ordered at an interim stage[1558] and the scope of Section 17 of the IAA is limited to directing interim measures

1549. Ali Yesilirmak, *supra* n. 30, at 213.
1550. *ICC case 8786* c.f. Ali Yesilirmak, *supra* n. 30, at 214.
1551. *Manchester Securities Ltd. v. Body Corporate* 172108, [2013] NZHC 177, ¶ 61.
1552. Gary Born, *supra* n. 33, at 2677-2678.
1553. Ali Yesilirmak, *supra* n. 30, at 214.
1554. Gary Born, *supra* n. 33, at 2677-2678.
1555. Kenya Arbitration Act. S. 18(1)(b).
1556. *Baker Hughes Singapore Pte v. Shiv-vani Oil and Gas Exploration Services Ltd.* 2014 SCC OnLine Bom 1663, ¶59; *Unitech Wireless (Tamil Nadu) Pvt. Ltd. v. Viom Networks Ltd.* 2012 SCC OnLine Del 6334, ¶2; *Reliance Communication Ltd. v. Bharti Infratel Ltd.* 2018 SCC OnLine Del 6564, ¶23; *See also, Ratna infrastructure Projects Pvt. Ltd. v. Meja Urja Nigam Pvt. Ltd. (MUNPL).* 2017 SCC Online Del 6384.
1557. *Lanco Infratech v. Hindustan Construction Company Ltd.* 2016 SCC OnLine Del 5365, ¶¶14-35; *Nimbus Communications Limited v. Board of Control for Cricket in India* 2012 SCC OnLine 287, ¶¶17, 22-24, & 27 *affirmed in Yusufkhan v. Prajita Developers Pvt. Ltd.* 2019 SCC Online Bom 505, ¶22; *Steel Authority of India Ltd. v. AMCI PTY Ltd. & Anr* 2011 SCC OnLine Del 3689, ¶45.
1558. *Intertoll ICS Cecons O & M Co. Pvt. Ltd. v. National Highways Authority of India* 2013 SCC OnLine Del 447, ¶43; *Jabed Sheikh v. Tahir Mallick* AIR 1941 Calcutta 639; *Iron and Hardware (India) Co. v. Firm Shamlal and Bros* AIR 1954 Bom 423; *S Milkha Singh v. N.K. Gopala Krishna Mudaliar* AIR 1956 Punjab 174, ¶¶11, 18-19; *BPL Ltd. v. Morgan Securities and Credit Pvt. Ltd. & Ors.* 2008 (1) Arb. LR 325 (Del).

and a mandatory direction to direct payment of money pending adjudication of a dispute is rarely granted.[1559]

Examining the criteria for grant of such a measure in the form of security, the courts in India take the view that such a direction at an interlocutory stage would indeed be an extraordinary measure and has to be preceded by a determination of the possible extent of the claim that is likely to be awarded. It can only be granted when a party is able to establish a strong prima facie case on the merits as well as a case of extreme hardship or an injury.[1560] The purpose cannot be to convert an unsecured debt into a secured debt.[1561] The power of the arbitral tribunal cannot extend to directing the payment of security in the form of a bank guarantee in relation to a speculative claim of damages.[1562] A claim for unliquidated damages does not give rise to a debt until the liability is adjudicated and damages are assessed by an adjudicating authority.[1563]

Contrary to the Indian position, the High Court of New Zealand[1564] justified the 'pay now argue later' regime by holding that it may sometimes be appropriate to grant the request for interim relief when it can be proved that any interim payment may become final because there is no hope of recovery.[1565]

This view is appropriate to the extent that the power is specifically enshrined in Section 17(1)(ii)(b) of the IAA but the provisions of Order XXXVIII Rule 5 of the CPC should not restrict the said power[1566] as the said provision requires a very high threshold to be satisfied.[1567] Adopting the generic language of Article 17(2) of the Model Law would ensure that security is only required to 'provide means' for the satisfaction of the award. It will serve as guiding criteria or objective to be achieved when exercising the power to secure the amount in dispute.

5.7. Preservation of Evidence

Evidence is crucial for the determination of substantial issues and may need to be preserved. It is now undisputed that the arbitral tribunals can order interim measures

---

1559. *Supreme Infrastructure India Ltd. v. Central Public Works Department* 2017 SCC OnLine Del 8228, ¶14.
1560. *Ibid.*, ¶14.
1561. *Mahaguj Colleries Ltd. v. Adani Enterprises Ltd.* 2019 SCC Online Bom 329, ¶ 21.
1562. *Intertoll ICS Cecons O & M Co. Pvt. Ltd. v. National Highways Authority of India* 2013 SCC OnLine Del 447, ¶20.
1563. *Union of India v. Raman Iron Foundry* (1974) 2 SCC 231, ¶11; *Yusufkhan v. Prajita Developers Pvt. Ltd.* 2019 SCC Online Bom 505, ¶33, *distinguishing the case of Baker Hughes where the amount sort to be secured was under an undisputed invoice coupled with serious financial strife of the respondent.*
1564. *Manchester Securities Ltd. v. Body Corporate* 172108, [2013] NZHC 177.
1565. *Ibid.*, ¶60.
1566. *Shabnam Dhillon v. Zee Entertainment Entreprises Ltd.* 2019 SCC OnLine Del 8905, ¶ 38; *National Shipping Company of Saudi Arabia v. Sentrans Industries Ltd.* AIR 2004 Bom 136: *where Justice R.N. Lodha held that Section 9(ii)(b) cannot be restricted by importing the provisions of Order XXXVIII Rule 5 since as a principle of law, Section 9 is a special provision and the only consideration should be that the claimant who obtains an award in its favour is not deprived of the fruits of the adjudication.*
1567. *Raman Tech and Process Engineering v. Solanki Traders* (2008) 2 SCC 302, ¶5; *followed in BMW India Pvt. Ltd. v. Libra Automotives Pvt. Ltd. & Ors.* 2019 SCC OnLine Del 9079, ¶32.

to preserve evidence under most laws and rules.[1568] The power to preserve evidence also entails the power to inspect the property. Post the 2015 Amendment, such power to order the inspection of the property has now been specifically recognised[1569] and includes intangible property as well.[1570]

However, it is relevant to note that it is not the job of the arbitral tribunal to collect evidence on behalf of a party and the other party cannot be directed to bear expenses for collecting evidence if the expenditure involved is huge.[1571] Such expenditure cannot be the cost of arbitration proceedings.[1572]

5.7.1. Anton Piller Injunctions

Anton Piller orders are injunctions granted for discovery, a search of the defendant's premises, and seizing of documents or items to be produced as evidence.[1573] In India, the court has recognised the power of the arbitral tribunal to order inspection but not discovery.[1574] The court held that there is a difference between mere inspection and discovery.

The power under Section 17(1)(ii)(c) of the IAA cannot be the source of power to order discovery and such power can only be found in Section 19 of the IAA of the Act which provides that where no procedure is agreed upon by the parties, the tribunal can devise an appropriate procedure in consonance with known principles of law. Referring to Section 19(4) of the IAA and Section 27 of the IAA, the court held that the power to order disclosure and discovery is implicit but cannot be exercised under Section 17 of the IAA. It based its conclusion on the fact there is no provision for filing an appeal against an order passed under Section 27 of the IAA.[1575]

Thus, *Anton Piller* injunctions can only be granted by the court and not by the arbitral tribunal[1576] and the arbitral tribunal has no power to order inspection and interrogation under Section 17 of the IAA.[1577] Adopting Article 17(2) of the Model Law will clarify that role of interim measures is limited to the preservation of evidence. Some countries have adopted the power of discovery specifically while adopting the

1568. Waincymer, *supra* n. 989, at 620.
1569. *Raymond Limited v. Akshaypat Singhania* 2019 SCC Online Bom 227, ¶22.
1570. *Union of India v. Reliance Industries Ltd. & Ors.* 2018 SCC OnLine Del 13018, ¶62.
1571. *Sometimes in perseveration and collection of evidence, the issue of costs of preserving evidence may arise, e.g., in a construction dispute, the request for determining the amount and quality of work performed was made along with the request to stop work until such determination is made. The arbitral tribunal denied the request as the costs of stopping the construction would be too high, and the party requesting interim relief could resort to other means. See* Abascal, *supra* n. 1, at 763.
1572. *Indian Oil Corporation Ltd. v. Iranian Offshore Engineering and Construction Company* 2009 SCC OnLine Del 2898, ¶5.
1573. Kern Alexander, *The Mareva Injunction and Anton Piller Order: The Nuclear Weapons of English Commercial Litigation*, 11(3) Flo. J. Int'l L. 487, 489 (1997).
1574. *Union of India v. Reliance Industries Ltd. & Ors.* 2018 SCC OnLine Del 13018, ¶65.
1575. *Therefore, the legislative policy appears to be that a remedy of appeal ought not to be provided against an order directing discovery of documents, Union of India v. Reliance Industries Ltd. & Ors.* 2018 SCC OnLine Del 13018, ¶¶67-75.
1576. Benoit, *supra* n. 685, at 31.
1577. *Areeb Rolling Mills Pvt. Ltd. v. Nkgsb Co-operative Bank Ltd.* 2013 (2) Arb. LR 14 (Bom).

2006 Model Law Revisions.[1578] However, in a country like India, the same may not be advisable as there may be a gross misuse of the provision.

6. LIMITATIONS ON THE SCOPE OF POWER UNDER SECTION 17

Despite the noble intent of the 2015 Amendment to grant wide powers to the arbitral tribunal, similar to that of a court under Section 9(1) of the IAA, there exist several limitations to the wide scope of power granted to the arbitral tribunal. It must be clarified that not all the limitations pertain exclusively to India, but in fact, most of them arise out of the inherent nature of the arbitral process.

6.1. Determination of Jurisdiction

One pertinent question that hitherto has been unanswered in Indian jurisprudence is whether an arbitral tribunal should determine jurisdiction prior to the grant of an interim measure. Any interim measure to be granted by the arbitral tribunal requires the arbitral tribunal to be already constituted.[1579] While it has been held that the arbitral tribunal has the power to order interim measures before ruling on its jurisdiction, the arbitral tribunal will not exercise such power unless there is a prima facie basis for jurisdiction.[1580]

6.1.1. Meaning of 'Prima Facie Jurisdiction'

The next question is, what does it mean to have a prima facie basis for jurisdiction? Most often than not, it means that the arbitral tribunal is satisfied that there is at least a prima facie showing that it has jurisdiction over a substantive claim pending before it.[1581] Interestingly, some arbitral tribunals have rejected the issue of addressing the

1578. *See Appendix B.*
1579. William Park, W. Michael Reisman & Laurence Craig et al., *International Commercial Arbitration Cases and Materials and Notes on the Resolution of International Business Disputes* 754 (1997); Ben H. Sheppard Jr. & John M. Townsend, *Holding the Fort Until the Arbitrators Are Appointed: The New ICDR International Emergency Rule*, Dis. Res. J. 75 (2006); Patricia Shaughnessy, *Pre-arbitral Urgent Relief: The New SCC Emergency Arbitrator Rules*, 27 J. Int'l Arb. 337 (2010).
1580. Berger, *supra* n. 1352, at 335; Lew, *supra* n. 28, at ¶23-68; Stephen Bond, *supra* n. 30, at 18; Pyoung-Keun Kang, *The Relationship Between International Arbitration and National Courts with Specific Reference to Provisional Measures* 181-182 (1996); *Perenco Ecuador Ltd v. Republic of Ecuador, Decision on Provisional Measures in ICSID Case No. ARB/08/6 of 8 May 2009*, ¶39; *See also, Quiborax SA v. Plurinational State of Bolivia, Decision on Provisional Measures in ICSID Case No. ARB/06/2 of 26 February 2010*, ¶108.
1581. *Bendone-Derossi International v. Iran, Interim Award in IUSCT Case No. ITM 40-375-1 of 7 June 1984*, 6 Iran–US CTR 130, 131-33 (1984); *Tadjer-Cohen Assocs. v. Islamic Republic of Iran, Award in IUSCT Case No. ITM 50-12118-3 of 11 November 1985, 9 Iran-US C.T.R. 302, 304-05 (1985).*

question of jurisdiction while determining interim measures.[1582] This may not be the most pragmatic view.

Arbitrators must establish or at least decide jurisdiction to avoid the embarrassing situation of having granted interim relief only to decide that the arbitral tribunal does not have jurisdiction subsequently. *Waincymer* asserts that the ability to succeed on the merits makes jurisdictional merit an essential part of the analysis. If the arbitral tribunal is ready to make a jurisdictional determination, it should be ready to make a concurrent determination of the interim measure application. If the arbitral tribunal decides that it lacks jurisdiction, then any provisional measure previously ordered will cease to have any logical effect.[1583] However, a decision on jurisdiction may delay the decision on interim measures effectively frustrating the requests. Therefore, the prima facie threshold should mean just as it did in the Iran-US Claims Tribunal, that it appeared the tribunal had jurisdiction.[1584]

The better view is that while deciding the request for an interim measure, the arbitral tribunal issues a statement justifying why the arbitral tribunal deems that it has prima facie jurisdiction or why it appears that the arbitral tribunal has jurisdiction.[1585] In case there is a doubt about whether the arbitral tribunal has jurisdiction or not, the benefit of the doubt should always be given to the arbitral tribunal[1586] as the tribunal has an inherent right to rule on its own jurisdiction.[1587]

6.2. Passing of Interim Measures Against Third Parties

Another glaring limitation on the power of the arbitral tribunal to grant interim measures is that the Model Law does not empower the arbitral tribunal to take interim measures against third parties not subject to the arbitration agreement as there is a potentially adverse impact on the third parties.[1588] It should be clarified that the jurisdiction can be extended to agents, officers, employees, servants, attorneys, and those controlled by the parties or their officers.[1589] Moreover, it is pertinent to note that on several occasions, the interim measure of protection passed by an arbitral tribunal would inevitably reflect on the rights of third parties.[1590]

1582. Ibrahim F.I. Shihata & Antonio R. Parra, *The Experience of the International Centre for Settlement of Investment Disputes*, 14 (2) ICSID Rev. Inv. L. J. 299, 326 (1999); *Biwater Gauff (Tanzania) Ltd v. United Republic of Tanzania, Procedural Order No. 1 in ICSID Case No. ARB/05/22 of 31 March 2006*, ¶70; *Tokios Tokelés v. Ukraine, Procedural Order No. 1 in ICSID Case No. ARB/02/18 of 1 July 2003*, ¶6.

1583. Waincymer, *supra* n. 989, at 632.

1584. Abascal, *supra* n. 1, at 759.

1585. *Ibid.*, at 756-760.

1586. Ali Yesilirmak, *supra* n. 30, at 176.

1587. UNCITRAL Model Law, Art. 16.

1588. Waincymer, *supra* n. 989, at 624.

1589. *In Order of 1999 in AAA Case No. [1]*, the tribunal expressly extended its order to the above persons (unpublished) c.f. Ali Yesilirmak, *supra* n. 30, at 70.

1590. French Code of Civil Procedure, Arts 149 &1506; Karrer, *supra* n. 1216, at 105.

In France, it is possible to summon third parties for producing documents or an item of evidence before the tribunal, though such orders are not enforceable.[1591] In Turkey, there is a specific prohibition on the grant of interim measures that bind third parties.[1592]

Similarly, in India, if the order is passed against a party to take steps which affect a third party, the same is permissible.[1593] The High Court of Bombay upheld an order passed by an arbitral tribunal without first deciding whether third parties ought to be made parties to the arbitration proceedings or not.[1594] The same court, in another case,[1595] refused to recognise an order permitting the disclosure of documents and information of third parties.

After the 2015 Amendment, an argument can be made that since the power of the court under Section 9(1) of the IAA and the power of the tribunal under Section 17(1) of the IAA has been made *pari materia*, the tribunal can also grant orders against third parties. The intent of the legislature was to grant wider powers to the tribunal, including passing orders against third parties. If such an interpretation is not favoured, the purpose and intent of the 2015 Amendment will stand defeated, which was unequivocally to empower the arbitral tribunal equally with the same power as a court. The rationale was that if the same is not done, parties would not be discouraged from approaching the court.[1596]

This argument can also be sustained on the logic that while arbitration is a private mechanism, the powers of the tribunal are governed by statute, especially after the 2015 Amendment, taking away the autonomy of the parties to exclude the powers of the arbitral tribunal to order interim measures. A further argument can be made that since Section 17(2) of the IAA gives the same sanctity to the orders passed by the arbitral tribunal as if they were passed by the court, there exists sufficient basis for the arbitral tribunal to order interim measures against the third parties.

Contrary to this line of argument, the other interpretation can be based on the privity of contract and the sovereignty of courts among others. If the intent had been to vest the same powers to the arbitral tribunal, then there would have been no reason to take assistance from the court in taking evidence, issuing summons to witnesses or production of documents under Section 27 of the IAA.[1597]

In consonance with international jurisprudence,[1598] the tribunal cannot pass orders against third parties, despite the 2015 Amendment, due to the consensual nature

1591. *And are subject to appeal within 15 days*, French Code of Civil Procedure, Art. 1468.
1592. Turkey Arbitration Law, 2001, Art. 6.
1593. Gary Born, *supra* n. 33, at 2625; However, a contrary view was taken in *State Bank of India v. Ericsson India Private Ltd.* (2018) SCC Online SC 497. The court held that since the rights of a financial creditor were affected by the order of the tribunal, the order cannot be sustained.
1594. *Shailendra Bhadauria and Ors. v. Matrix Partners India Investment and Ors.* 2019 SCC OnLine Bom 1, ¶61.
1595. *Wind World (India) Ltd. and Ors. v. Enercon GmbH and Ors.* (2016) SCC OnLine Bom 1404, ¶¶67-68.
1596. Rajendra Barot, *supra* n. 679, at 179.
1597. *Ibid.*
1598. David St. john Sutton et al., *Russel on Arbitration* 6-131-6-132 (2007): *the tribunal does not have jurisdiction over the third party even though the third party may hold money or properties in dispute and the tribunal thus is less able to secure compliance by parties to the arbitration.*

of arbitration.[1599] Such an interpretation would open the flood gates of dragging third parties without their consent to a process that is essentially an agreement between two parties. Furthermore, such an interpretation may raise serious doubts about the mandate of equal treatment of parties and will also open the award to challenges. Therefore, parties should approach the courts under Section 9(3) of the IAA for orders against third parties. However, this does not mean that arbitral tribunals should not pass an order against the parties to the arbitration that may affect third parties.

6.3. Undertakings

A tribunal may deny the request for an interim measure of protection if the opposite party is willing to provide an undertaking or a declaration in good faith that it will not violate the rights of the requesting party.[1600] Many times, arbitrators are willing to accept a declaration or undertaking from the party against whom the measure is sought that it does not intend to infringe the right in question and hence, does not grant the interim relief in the first place.[1601] It is necessary to clarify that this is not a limitation on the power of the tribunal, but the same is considered to be a practical restraint on the need to grant an interim measure.

6.4. Observations of the Court under Section 9 of the IAA

One of the critical questions, especially after the insertion of Section 9(3) of the IAA is whether the observations of the court would be binding on the arbitral tribunal under Section 17 of the IAA?

In one instance, the court impliedly made it clear that the observations of the court under Section 9 of the IAA would not be binding on the arbitral tribunal and should not prejudice the tribunal as well.[1602] This view has been consistently followed[1603] and the courts have directed the parties to approach the tribunal in light of the enlarged and amplified scope of Section 17 of the IAA, categorically noting that the order of the court will not preclude the parties from seeking such a relief from the arbitral tribunal.[1604]

1599. *Value Advisory Services v. ZTE Corporation* 2009 (3) Arb. LR 315 (Del), ¶71; *Gatx India Pvt. Ltd. v. Arshiya Rail Infrastructure Limited* 216 (2015) D.L.T. 20; *Blue Coast Infrastructure Development Pvt. Ltd. v. Blue Coast Hotels Ltd.* 2020 SCC OnLine Del 1897, ¶27.
1600. *ICC Interim Award 7692 of 1995*, extracts published in 11(1) ICC Ct Int'l Arb 62-63 where the respondent '*undertook not to use any of that technology during the course of arbitration*' c.f. Ali Yesilirmak, *supra* n. 30, at 189-190.
1601. Hober, *supra* n. 1207, at 737.
1602. *M/s Rohit Ferro Tech Ltd. v. Thermax Ltd.* 2016 SCC OnLine Cal 10841, ¶12; *Otik Hotels and Resorts Pvt. Ltd. v. Indian Railway Catering and Tourism Corporation Ltd.* 2017 SCC OnLine Del 10122, ¶¶ 33-35.
1603. *Gammon India Ltd. v. The State of West Bengal and Ors.* 2017 SCC OnLine Cal 2767, ¶4; *Tahnee Heights Co-Op. Housing Society v. Silver Arch Co-op Housing Society Ltd.* 2016 SCC OnLine Bom 2301, ¶¶ 4 & 5.
1604. *Shinago Holdings Pvt. Ltd. v. M. Ethiraj* 201 Arb. LR 226 (Madras) (DB), ¶6 (XXi).

6.4.1. *Modification or Termination Interim Measures Granted by Court*

Courts have expressly provided that the arbitral tribunal may confirm or modify the interim order,[1605] clearly recognising that the arbitral tribunal is not bound by the observations of the court under Section 9(1) of the IAA. Courts have even directed that an application under Section 9(1) of the IAA, shall be deemed to be an application under Section 17(1) of the IAA and the arbitrator should decide the same within twelve weeks.[1606]

Some international arbitral tribunals have concluded that a decision by the national court would be binding and a tribunal cannot modify such measures as tribunals do not have the competence to do so.[1607] In India as well, there are some courts which have taken a similar view.[1608]

Such a view is erroneous as interim orders granted by courts cannot be regarded as an *estoppel* or res judicata for the arbitral tribunal.[1609] Furthermore, it would be contrary to the mandate of minimal court intervention if the parties are expected to apply for such suspension, modification, or termination from the court under Order XXXIX Rule 4 of the CPC even though the tribunal has been constituted.[1610]

Ultimately arbitrators should have the final word and be allowed to overrule, release, or vary interim measures ordered by courts[1611] since it is the tribunal which has the jurisdiction to decide the dispute on merits.[1612] Also, courts apply their own procedural law rather than applying international standards. Hence, an arbitral tribunal should not be bound by court decisions with respect to interim measures as it would violate party autonomy and the intention of the parties to arbitrate.

More importantly, the role of the court is to be supportive of the arbitral process and not to resolve the dispute.[1613] Therefore, once the arbitral process has commenced, there is no justification for the view that the order of the court would be binding on the tribunal. However, tribunals should consider the order of the court with respect to the

1605. *However, the tribunal refused to vacate the order and did not decide the application filed by the NHAI for vacating the order passed by the court under* Indian Arbitration Act, 1996, S. 9.
1606. *Malad Bharat Co-operative Housing Society Ltd. v. Pankaj Parikh* 2018 SCC OnLine Bom 3986, ¶d; *Kanta Bhalla & Ors. v. M/s Supreme Constructions and Developers Pvt. Ltd.* 2018 SCC OnLine Bom 4001, ¶d. *In this case, the direction to the arbitrator was to decide the application within six weeks*; *Mukesh Makandas Mehta & Anr. v. Kamlesh Vrajlal Shah & Ors.* 2018 SCC OnLine Bom 8565, ¶iv; *L& T Housing Finance Ltd. v. Balaji Infrastructure and Ors.* 2018 SCC OnLine Bom 8569, ¶2.
1607. *Partial Award in ICC Case No. 4998*, 113 J.D.I. (Clunet) 1139 (1986); *Award in Unidentified ICC Case*, discussed in Schwartz, *supra* n. 1236, at 57; *See also Order No. 5 Regarding Claimant's Request for Interim Relief in ICC Case of 2 April 2002*, 21 ASA Bull. 810, 816 (2003); *Partial Award in ICC Case No. 4126*, Derains, *supra* n. 1509, at 513-514; Caron, *supra* n. 1388, at 529-530; Markus Wirth, *Supra* n. 580, at 43.
1608. *Tuticorin Coal Terminal Private Limited v. Gelguera Gruas India Private Ltd.* 2018 SCC OnLine Bom 1268, ¶22; *Radio Restaurant v. Jabbir Gulam Rasool Jamal & Anr.* 2011 SCC OnLine Bom 1246, ¶¶6, 8.
1609. *Perma Container (UK) Line Ltd. v. Perma Container Line (India) Pvt. Ltd. and Ors. 2009 SCC OnLine Bom 1391*, ¶42.
1610. *See discussion on: Suspension, Modification & Termination under Safeguards.*
1611. Lew, *supra* n. 28, at ¶23-130.
1612. Paul, *supra* n. 679, at 435.
1613. Gary Born, *supra* n. 33, at 2691.

conduct of the parties.[1614] A second attempt to seek a similar relief before the tribunal should not be permitted.[1615]

6.5. Interim Specific Performance

Tribunals also order what is otherwise known as 'specific performance', i.e., requiring a party to perform a specified act according to a pre-existing contractual or other legal obligation.[1616] Article 31(1)(a) of the SCC Rules, 1999 expressly recognised such orders as part of interim measures.[1617] *Bond* describes such measures as 'interim specific performance of the contract'.[1618]

Such an interim measure is vital to the arbitral process and has been granted several times by international tribunals.[1619] Therefore, the arbitrator has the power to grant relief, such as directing the party to hand over the keys to the opposite party for equitable purposes. Even if a party does not seek the relief of specific performance, the same cannot come in the way of the arbitrator to grant such a relief.[1620] However, the issuance of such orders in India has been fettered by the provision of the Specific Relief Act. The prevailing view is that a tribunal cannot order specific performance of an agreement[1621] as being contrary to the provisions of Sections 14 and 41(e) of the Specific Relief Act.[1622]

It should be noted that this view is prior to the 2018 Amendment to the Specific Relief Act and the new provisions of the Specific Relief Act have not been analysed in this context yet. After the 2018 Amendment to the Specific Relief Act, the tribunal may be able to order specific performance and substituted performance.

1614. *Cogent Ventures (India) Ltd. v. Shree Ram Infrastructures Ltd. & Anr.* 2008 (4) Arb. LR 61, ¶ 22.

1615. *See* discussion under 10.1.

1616. Gary Born, *supra* n. 33, at 2674-2675.

1617. *Unless the parties have agreed otherwise, the Arbitral Tribunal may, during the course of the proceedings and at the request of a party, order a specific performance by the opposing party for the purpose of securing the claim which is to be tried by the Arbitral Tribunal. The Arbitral Tribunal may order the requesting party to provide reasonable security for damage which may be inflicted on the opposing party as a result of the specific performance in question.*

1618. Stephen Bond, *supra* n. 30, at 11.

1619. E Schwartz, *supra* n. 1236, at 61-62; *Decision in Arbitration No. 22 of 1972*, 12 ASA Bulletin 152 (1994); *Perenco Ecuador Ltd v. Republic of Ecuador, Decision on Provisional Measures in ICSID Case No. ARB/08/6 of 8 May 2009*, ¶79(4), (ordering '*provisional measures restraining the Respondents from unilaterally amending, rescinding, terminating, or repudiating the Participation Contracts or engaging in any other conduct which may directly or indirectly affect or alter the legal situation under the Participation Contracts*').

1620. *Sameer Narain Bhojwani v. Bombay Slum Redevelopment Corporation Ltd.* 2016 SCC OnLine Bom 15502, ¶32.

1621. *Tulsi Castings and Machining & Ors. v. India Venture Trust & Ors.* 2014 SCC OnLine Bom 1283, ¶16.

1622. *Mosarbaer Entertainment Ltd. v. Goldmines Telefilms Pvt. Ltd.* 2013 (2) Arb. LR 448 (Bom), ¶¶16-18.

6.6. Finding on the Merits

Most often the interim measures requested are closely connected to the final relief sought in arbitration proceedings. However, there may be instances where the business-oriented aspect of a dispute or commercial relationship of the parties may require a tribunal to grant relief which does not necessarily correspond to the main relief.[1623] The challenge before every tribunal is to determine whether granting the request for interim relief may finally dispose of the matter.

This challenge has to be considered against the risk of the potential damage that may occur if the measure is denied.[1624] No final finding can be arrived at on the rights of the parties during an application under Section 17(1) of the IAA[1625] and the arbitral tribunal cannot draw any final conclusions while dealing with interim measures.[1626] Therefore, questions such as the factum of possession are something that can only be proved after evidence is led by both the parties and cannot be decided by the arbitrator under Section 17(1) of the IAA.[1627]

However, where circumstances demand, arbitral tribunals like courts cannot avoid taking a decision on merits simply because it will result in trying the matter twice or for the reason that it would mirror what would be substantially the final relief claimed. If there was no uncertainty with respect to the legal right of the party claiming interim relief, an injunction should be granted.[1628]

It should be noted that the Working Group specifically concluded that no strict link exists between the final decision on the merits and the justification of the measure granted.[1629] Therefore, as discussed previously,[1630] tribunals should be concerned more about the commercial viability and need for the interim measures requested by the parties. In the event that it substantially mirrors the final relief, the arbitral tribunal is at liberty to order appropriate security with respect to the measure.

6.7. Considerations of Lack of Enforcement

Arbitrators are generally cautious of granting interim measures that would not be capable of enforcement.[1631] In fact, in a survey, a majority of arbitrators said that they

1623. Voser, *supra* n. 1213, at 182.
1624. Abascal, *supra* n. 1, at 751.
1625. *Chandar Mohan Lall v. DLF Commercial Developers Ltd.* 2013 (3) Arb. LR 365 (Del), ¶24; *Bombay Slum Redevelopment Corporation Ltd. v. Samir Narain Bhojwani* 2019 SCC Online Bom 1853, ¶191.
1626. *Nirmal Infrastructure Pvt. Ltd. v. Anant Developers Pvt. Ltd.* 2015 SCC OnLine Bom 5852, ¶56.
1627. *United Media Works Pvt. Ltd. v. Spartan Advertising and Films India Pvt. Ltd.* 2016 SCC OnLine Bom 6455, ¶6.
1628. *National Highways Authority of India v. VIL Rohtak Jind Highway Pvt. Ltd.* 2019 SCC OnLine Del 6545, ¶74.
1629. Luis, *supra* n. 521, at 557.
1630. *See* prima facie *case.*
1631. *Final Award in ICC Case No. 7589,* 11(1) ICC Ct. Bull. 60 (2000); *Final Award in ICC Case No. 7210,* 11(1) ICC Ct. Bull. 49 (2000), c.f. Ali Yesilirmak, *supra* n. 30, at 186.

would usually deny a request for the interim measure if it is unlikely that the measure is incapable of being carried out.[1632]

While arbitrators have a duty to render enforceable awards,[1633] it is unclear if the same duty can be attributed to interim measures. However, given the fact that the orders may be complied with voluntarily, the arbitral tribunal should not hesitate to order interim measures that may be incapable of enforcement. The arbitral tribunal may adopt other coercive measures or pass alternative orders,[1634] or the default may also produce consequences of a breach of contract.[1635] Therefore, tribunals should grant interim measures irrespective of the possibility of their enforcement.

6.8. No Stay of Arbitration Proceedings

A plain reading of Section 17(1) of the IAA clearly shows that the interim measures provided under Section 17(1) relate to the protection of the property or the amount in dispute in the arbitration proceeding and not to the arbitration proceeding in itself. There is no provision in the IAA which provides for the stay of arbitration proceedings upon its commencement.[1636]

7. PROCEDURE

While the power, scope, and criteria of the power of the arbitral tribunal have been determined, it is unclear as to what procedure needs to be followed while granting interim measures. The following procedural questions, even though they have received little attention in the past, deserve to be addressed:

(a) can interim relief be granted ex parte or only after notice to the parties?
(b) whether an oral hearing is required or are written submissions enough?
(c) what is the extent of evidence required?
(d) whether the decision on interim relief can be delegated to the chairperson of the tribunal?[1637]

The answer, according to *Boog*, based on a general consensus, is that such procedural questions should be answered by reference to the curial law, i.e., the relevant procedural provisions of the *lex arbitri*, the set of arbitration rules chosen by the parties, and the procedural rules set by the arbitral tribunal. While the procedural rules set by the arbitral tribunal may be the right point of reference, reference to curial law inevitably would result in the adoption of procedural rules and evidence statutes

1632. Hober, *supra* n. 1207, at 736-737.
1633. Martin Platte, *An Arbitrator's Duty to Render Enforceable Awards*, 20 (3) J. of Int'l Arb. 312 (2003).
1634. *See Chapter 10.*
1635. Abascal, *supra* n. 1, at 766.
1636. *Shree Tirupati Udyog v. Indraprastha Gas Ltd.* 2018 SCC OnLine Del 7718, ¶7.
1637. *See* Boog, *supra* n. 592, at 409 – 419.

(like the CPC and Evidence Act in India). Therefore, the tribunal should determine its own procedure.

7.1. Procedure to Be Followed by an Arbitral Tribunal

Though in principle, that should be the ideal case, a request for an interim measure may be made at the very commencement of arbitration proceedings, even before jurisdiction has been determined. At such a point, it may be challenging to rely on rules set by the tribunal, since there will not be any such rules. Hence, the following should be applied autonomously, irrespective of curial law, i.e.:

(a) A party must request the relief.
(b) There must be a prima facie jurisdiction over the parties.[1638]
(c) Prima facie case should be shown by an affidavit and supporting documents,[1639] wherever possible.
(d) The tribunal must always ensure that fairness between the parties is maintained.
(e) The parties should disclose all facts and circumstances likely to be relevant for the tribunal's determination of whether the interim measure should be granted.

7.2. Burden of Proof

The above considerations should always be adhered to and the tribunal should not set a very high threshold for the material to be placed on record. Whenever the tribunal is concerned about the measure being sought as an offensive tactic or abuse of the process of law, the tribunal should order appropriate security.

When considering the material to be placed on record at the stage of interim measures, the tribunal may look to the criteria provided under Rule 39(1) of the ICSID Arbitration Rules. The said describes the elements that are required to be contained in an application,[1640] i.e., (a) the rights to be preserved should be specified; (b) the measures required; and (c) the circumstances that necessitate such measures. Thus, the tribunal should make a summary assessment of the facts and rights of the parties.[1641] Of course, the tribunal may request further information depending on the facts of the case.

1638. Ali Yesilirmak, *supra* n. 30, at 175.
1639. *Ibid.*, at 173.
1640. *Ibid.*, at 168.
1641. Karrer, *supra* n. 1216, at 109.

8. EX PARTE INTERIM MEASURES

Closely connected to the question of procedural fairness is the topic of the grant of ex parte interim measures by the arbitral tribunal. This topic also assumes significance in the context of emergency arbitration as one party would urgently require interim measures. This question was first considered by the Working Group in its 34th Session in May-June 2001[1642] and by the 39th Session of the Working Group, it was expressed that parties never requested ex parte interim measures.[1643] Thus, there was considerable debate about the inclusion of ex parte measures in the 2006 Model Law Revisions and several concerns were raised as to whether ex parte measures would be eligible for court enforcement.

8.1. The Need for Ex Parte Interim Measures

As per one view, since ex parte measures by courts are permitted without the concerns of equality and full opportunity, the addition of ex parte measures to the text of the Model Law would meet the needs of arbitration practice.[1644] It was argued that denying an ex parte relief may lead to depriving a party of its right of a full opportunity of hearing because the actions of the opposite party may finally dispose of the object of the dispute or cause irreparable damage before the tribunal can render the award.[1645]

It is also possible at times that a party may not be seeking the enforcement of the measure as a primary objective, but it can, as a matter of strategy, use the knowledge that the respondent may not comply to its advantage by making sure the arbitral tribunal draws adverse inferences from this conduct.[1646] Hence, some justified the requirement of ex parte measures for promoting arbitration and its effectiveness.[1647] However, instances of ex parte measures being granted are extremely rare.[1648]

8.2. Concerns with Ex Parte Interim Measures

One of the concerns with the ex parte interim measures is that where the secrecy is crucial, enforceability would not be possible[1649] as there are problems with confidentiality in going to a court.[1650] For example, in Germany, the arbitral tribunal can grant ex parte interim measures which can be enforced with the leave of the court.[1651] Moreover, an ex parte process can provide an opportunity for inappropriate submis

1642. Tomas, *supra* n. 1256, at 25.
1643. Report of UNCITRAL Working Group on the work of its Thirty Ninth session, 2003, A/CN.9/545, available at: https://undocs.org/en/A/CN.9/545, ¶52.
1644. Report of UNCITRAL Working Group on the work of its Thirty Sixth session, 2002, A/CN.9/508, available at: https://undocs.org/en/A/CN.9/508, ¶77.
1645. Abascal, *supra* n. 1, at 751-752.
1646. Luis, *supra* n. 521, at 565.
1647. *Ibid.*, at 545-546.
1648. Ali Yesilirmak, *supra* n. 30, at 221-222.
1649. Menon, *supra* n. 102, at 18.
1650. Castello, *supra* n. 38, at 66.
1651. Jan Schäfer, *supra* n. 301, at 227.

sions that cannot be readily be challenged on an imminent basis and the tribunal will be forced to consider merits on an ex parte basis with the submissions of only one party.[1652] Hence, ex parte measures ought to be reserved for the national courts only as each party should have equal access to the arbitral tribunal and a complete opportunity of hearing and presenting its case in line with Article 18 of the Model Law. This is a fundamental requirement.[1653]

There were also concerns within the Working Group regarding ex parte measures being used for dilatory and unfair practices, along with the possibility of having a damaging effect on third parties.[1654] *Hans van Houtte* argues that it was inappropriate to utilise the Model Law for ex parte measures, which could in turn impact its utility. Such measures are ineffective and hence, would rarely be needed. They are incompatible with the consensual nature of arbitration and sufficient respect for the right to a defence. They cannot be enforced and would only lead to prejudiced arbitrators and irreversible commercial effects. Furthermore, there would be problems in full disclosure and tribunal control and they could impact arbitrator liability or immunity.[1655]

Bunni further adds that a court is better able to control such an application, ensure proper safeguards and sanction abuse. Furthermore, it is best to be available on short notice.[1656] More importantly, such orders could not meet the requirements under the NYC of procedural fairness as per Article V(1)(b).[1657] *Derains* makes the point that enforcement of an ex parte order would require an ex parte order from the court as well.[1658]

1652. Yves Derains, *The View Against Arbitral Ex Parte Interim Relief: Confirmation that the Best May Be the Enemy of the Good*, 58 (3) Dis. Res. J. 62 (2003).
1653. Waincymer, *supra* n. 989, at 628.
1654. Tomas, *supra* n. 1256, at 25; Commonwealth of Australia, International Arbitration Amendment Bill 2009, available at: http://classic.austlii.edu.au/au/legis/cth/bill_em/iaab2010366/memo_2.html 1256, at 25:

> *72 (...) Articles 17B and 17C of the Model Law establish a regime for preliminary orders. These are the equivalent of ex parte orders made by a court in circumstances where there is a perceived risk that a party will attempt to frustrate interim measures. While this proposal received some support from stakeholders, it was extremely controversial when considered by UNCITRAL and was opposed by key stakeholders in Australia during the Review.*
>
> *73. The primary objection to the provisions allowing for preliminary measures [sic] is that such measures are inconsistent with the consensual underpinning of arbitration. Accordingly, Item 14 amends the Act to provide that, despite Art. 17B of the Model Law, preliminary orders are not available under the Act or the Model Law.* Explanatory Memorandum to the International Arbitration Amendment Bill 2009 (Cth) at 11, ¶¶74-75; Revised Explanatory Memorandum to the International Arbitration Amendment Bill 2010 (Cth), at 11, ¶¶72-73.

1655. Hans Van, *supra* n. 505, at 85, 94 (2004).
1656. Bunni, *supra* n. 690, at 604-605.
1657. Waincymer, *supra* n. 989, at 629.
1658. Yves Derains, *supra* n. 1652, at 62.

8.3. Preliminary Orders under Articles 17B and 17C of the Model Law

The 2006 Model Law now provides for preliminary orders which are essentially ex parte orders. The incorporation of Article 17B of the Model Law and Article 17C of the Model Law remains controversial.[1659] Some commentators have questioned the wisdom and practicality of such measures[1660] and only a few jurisdictions have adopted the revised Model Law provisions for ex parte relief.[1661]

The inclusion of ex parte orders or preliminary orders in Article 17C of the Model Law was considered necessary because it was thought that preliminary orders coming directly from the arbitral tribunal would carry more authority and discourage parties from not complying with the order due to the adverse view that the tribunal may take subsequently.[1662] The regime is thus based on the moral authority of the tribunal to ensure compliance and the fact that the party should retain confidence in the impartiality of the arbitral tribunal.

It should be noted that Australia categorically rejected the provisions on ex parte measures provided under Articles 17B and 17C of the Model Law.[1663] Similarly, Austria[1664] does not provide ex parte measures by the tribunal.

8.4. Suitability for India

The criticisms[1665] are justified as no real purpose is served by the provisions and instead the grant of ex parte relief by the tribunal would violate the duty to treat all parties equally. In case of severe urgency, there is sufficient protection provided under Section 9 of the IAA as the court can grant interim measures when the tribunal does not have the power to do so.

The problem with enforcement of ex parte measures is also that they would be subject to mandatory law.[1666] Hence, it is more prudent to file ex parte requests with the court under Section 9(3) of the IAA as the same would comply with mandatory law

1659. Hans Van, *supra* n. 505, at 88.
1660. Castello, *supra* n. 38, at 60-61: Yves Derains, *supra* n. 1652, at 63: Yves Derains, *Arbitral Ex Parte Interim Relief: The View Against*, 58-OCT Dis. Res. J. 62-63 (2003); Hans Van, *supra* n. 505, at 86.
1661. *See Appendix D & E*; Report of UNCITRAL Working Group on the work of its Thirty Sixth Session, 2002, A/CN.9/508, available at: https://undocs.org/en/A/CN.9/508, ¶77; Report of UNCITRAL Working Group on the work of its Thirty Fourth session, 2001, A/CN.9/487, available at: https://undocs.org/en/A/CN.9/487; Report of UNCITRAL Working Group on the work of its Thirty Seventh session, 2002, A/CN.9/523, available at: https://undocs.org/en/A/CN.9/523, ¶¶16-27.
1662. Menon, *supra* n. 102, at 17.
1663. Leon Chung, Elizabeth Macknay & Elizabeth Poulos, *Arbitration Procedures and Practice in Australia: Overview*, available at: https://uk.practicallaw.thomsonreuters.com/1-618-2164?transitionType=Default&contextData=(sc.Default)&firstPage=true&bhcp=1.
1664. Australian Code of Civil Procedure S. 593(1) '*after hearing the other party*'.
1665. Gary Born, *supra* n. 33, at 2696.
1666. *Currently the orders.*

and would also carry along with it the easier process of enforcement, sanction abuse, and also provide proper safeguards.[1667]

One of the possible circumstances in which the relief from the court might be ineffective is when the territorial jurisdiction of the court serves as a hindrance for ex parte measures. In the event the subject matter of the dispute is located outside the seat, obtaining an ex parte measure from that court would make little sense as the same would have to be enforced in another jurisdiction by approaching a court.[1668] In these circumstances, ironically, it may be inefficacious to approach the court for the interim measure as opposed to the arbitral tribunal whose orders might be complied with voluntarily.

However, given that the preliminary orders under Articles 17B and 17C of the Model Law are not enforceable by a court, the chances of voluntary compliance will always remain equal. Moreover, with many countries adopting Article 17J in their arbitration statute, courts would be able to grant interim measures in aid of foreign seated arbitrations. Therefore, the efficacy of the orders of the tribunal versus the court would be at par, especially if they are granted by the court where the enforcement of the award will be sought subsequently. Hence, it is argued that the adoption of the regime on preliminary orders is unnecessary. Instead, the court under Section 9(3) of the IAA should consider taking mandatory security from the party requesting the measure when an interim measure is requested ex parte from the court as there is no one to speak for the party against whom the ex parte order is requested.[1669]

Therefore, instead of adopting an ex parte regime for the arbitral tribunal only on the ground that it might be inefficacious to obtain orders from the court, it is more prudent and efficacious to permit ex parte interim measures to be granted by courts of law during arbitration proceedings and be enforced in most cases. It should be noted that the Saraf Committee had also expressed a similar view. The Committee believed there is a strong possibility of abuse of such power with the arbitral tribunal and a request for ex parte interim measures of protection should be made only to a Court under Section 9 of the IAA.[1670]

9. APPEAL

Most arbitration regimes and the Model Law do not provide for an appeal against an order granting or refusing to grant interim measures by the arbitral tribunal. Uniquely so, India offers the provision of appeal against both, an order under Section 9 of the IAA passed by a court and against Section 17 of the IAA passed by the tribunal.[1671]

1667. Bunni, *supra* n. 690, at 605.
1668. Luis, *supra* n. 521, at 564.
1669. *Ibid.*, at 552.
1670. Government of India, Ministry of Law and Justice – Proposed Amendments to the Arbitration & Conciliation Act, 1996: A Consultation Paper, available at: https://www.legallyindia.com/images/stories/docs/Arbitration-Act-LawMin-ConsultationPaper-on-Arb-Act-April2010-1.pdf.
1671. *Even though Bangladesh Arbitration Act, 2001 is similar to the IAA, it provides no appeal against the orders of the arbitral tribunal. See* Bangladesh Arbitration Act, 2001, S. 21(1).

9.1. Jurisdiction of High Courts under Article 227 of the Constitution of India

To make matters worse, courts have held that even a third party can file an appeal under Section 37 of the IAA[1672] and it has been held that the High Court will have jurisdiction under Article 227 of the Constitution of India[1673] over the arbitral tribunal under the IAA[1674] which means the High Court will have administrative jurisdiction over the tribunal and the jurisdiction of the High Courts can be invoked for the excess of jurisdiction and delay in proceedings.

The small saving grace has been the narrow scope of the exercise of such power by requiring courts to be extremely circumspect while interfering in arbitration proceedings.[1675] Interference can be made when an order passed by an arbitral tribunal is so perverse that it is patently lacking in inherent jurisdiction and such perversity must stare in the face. The court has also permitted the exercise of jurisdiction under Article 227 of the Constitution of India in 'exceptional rarity' or on demonstration of 'bad faith'.[1676] However, such caveats are vague and open the doors for excessive court intervention in arbitration proceedings.

9.2. Limitation Period for Appeal

A grave lacuna in the IAA is that the provision of appeal under Section 37(1)(b) of the IAA grants the party against whom the interim measure is passed thirty days to challenge the said order. Thus, until the expiry of the period, a court will not ordinarily enforce the measure and neither will a party have any incentive to voluntarily comply with the same. This, in effect, completely nullifies the urgency of the interim measure and the need for enforcement. Moreover, a review of the satisfaction of the conditions under Section 17 of the IAA in effect amounts to double litigation over interim measures and runs afoul of the mandate of Section 5 of the IAA and also the objective of a speedy resolution.

9.3. Standard for Review

Furthermore, there is no guidance in the IAA with respect to the standard of review to be used by the appellate courts when examining interim orders passed by the arbitral

---

1672. *As the power under S. 17 is identical to the power under S. 9 post the 2015 Amendment and if a third party is permitted to be part of the proceedings under Section 9, then the party can also file an appeal under S. 37. Prabhat Steel Traders Pvt. Ltd. v. Excel Metal Processors Pvt. Ltd.* 2018 SCC OnLine Bom 2347, ¶50.
1673. *This article states that every High Court shall have superintendence over all Courts and Tribunal within the territory having the jurisdiction except the court established by the armed forces.*
1674. *M/s M. L. Gupta & Associates v. H.P. Housing and Urban Development Authority and Ors.* 2011 SCC OnLine HP 3746, ¶22.
1675. *Deep Industries Ltd. v. Oil and Natural Gas Corporation Ltd.* (2020) 15 SCC 706, ¶16-17; *Future Retail Ltd. v. Amazon.com NV Investment Holdings LLC* 2022 SCC OnLine Del 13, ¶24.
1676. *Surender Kumar Singhal v. Arun Kumar Bhalotia* 2021 SCC OnLine Del 3708, ¶25.

tribunal. The courts have two options (a) to use the criteria provided in Section 34 of the IAA for setting aside the award, or (b) to treat the proceeding as an appeal under the CPC and assess the legality of the order on merits.[1677]

Some courts have taken the view that the scope of interference by the court under Section 37(2) of the IAA is limited and unless the order passed by the arbitral tribunal is perverse or unsustainable in law, the court should not interfere.[1678] Similarly, if the view of the tribunal is a plausible view[1679] or not one which transcends the bounds of reasonableness,[1680] courts should refrain from review.[1681]

Other courts have resorted to a full-blown enquiry[1682] or treated proceedings as a regular appeal under the CPC[1683] or applied mandatory law and set aside an interim order as it violates the fundamental policy of Indian law.[1684]

Therefore, due to the lack of guidance as to the standard of review at the appellate stage, the courts will invariably review the necessity of the interim measure in its entirety. Furthermore, as a tactical advantage, a party may deliberately apply for interim relief before the arbitral tribunal knowing fully well that the same will be rejected and subsequently appeal against the said rejection with a deliberate view to delay and obstruct the proceedings. The courts have even cautioned against such practice where appeals are filed routinely even when there is no irreparable prejudice to a party. The only reason for appeal is that a finding of the appellate court has the potential to effect, to some extent, the future course of arbitral proceedings as well as the final award that may be passed, even if the court enters the usual cautionary caveat that the findings are intended only to dispose of the appeal against the order passed under Section 17 of the IAA.[1685]

Arbitration is meant to be a 'one-stop' mechanism.[1686] The typical remedies of appeal are generally absent from arbitral orders.[1687] The whole rationale for not passing interim measures as awards was to create a regime where challenge procedures were

---

1677. Sharad Bansal, *supra* n. 169.

1678. *IRCON International Ltd. v. Simplex Projects Ltd.* 2016 SCC OnLine Del 4661, ¶38; *Green Infra Wind Energy Ltd. v. Regen Power Tech Pvt. Ltd.* 2018 SCC OnLine Del 8273, ¶16.

1679. *NHAI v. BSC-RBM-Partil Joint Venture* 2018 SCC Online Del 8780 *followed in Artha Vruddhi Securities Ltd. v. Mahavir Prasad Gujjar* (Arbitration Petition No. 547 of 2018 decided on 25 January 2019). *Both these decisions affirmed in Raymond Limited v. Akshaypat Singhania* 2019 SCC Online Bom 227, ¶26.

1680. *Shabnam Dhillon v. Zee Entertainment Enterprises Ltd.* 2019 SCC OnLine Del 8905, ¶ 41.

1681. *H.P. State Road and Other Infrastructure Development Corporation Limited Ltd. v. C & C Construction Ltd.* 2019 SCC Online HP 1884, ¶23; *Metro Buildtech Pvt. Ltd. v. Standard Charted Bank* 2012 (2) ARB. LR 391, ¶12.

1682. *Sanjay Gambhir v. BDR Builders and Developers Pvt. Ltd* 2016 SCC OnLine Del 5366; *Intertoll ICS Cecons O & M Co. Pvt. Ltd. v. National Highways Authority of India* 2013 SCC OnLine Del 447; *NTPC Ltd. v. Jindal ITF Ltd. & Anr.* 2017 SCC OnLine Del 11219, ¶20.

1683. *J.R.S. Crusher and Ors. v. A. Jayakanthan and Ors.* MANU/TN/7894/2019.

1684. *NHAI v. Gwalior-Jhansi Expressway Ltd.* (2018) 8 SCC 243, ¶27.

1685. *Sanjay Arora v. Rajan Chadha* 2021 SCC OnLine Del 4619, ¶92, *affirming the view in NHAI v. Bhubaneswar Expressways Pvt. Ltd.* 2021 SCC OnLine Del 2421 *and DLF Ltd. v. Leighton India Contractor Pvt. Ltd.* 2021 SCC OnLine Del 3772.

1686. *A. Ayyasamy v. A. Paramasivam* (2016) 10 SCC 386, ¶46; Opinion of Hoffman J, *Fiona Trust & Holding Corporation & Others v. Yuri Privalov & Ors.* [2015] EWHC 527 (Comm).

1687. Ali Yesilirmak, *supra* n. 30, at 75.

limited.[1688] The reliance on the CPC at the stage of appeal is antithetical to the foundation of arbitration jurisprudence as the arbitral tribunal has no *lex fori* and in cases of international commercial arbitration, it would give an Indian party home turf advantage at the appellate stage.

The provision of appeal was incorporated under the IAA due to the mistrust of the arbitral process and the ability of arbitrators to provide justice. However, arbitration as a method of dispute resolution has gained considerable trust and integrity, and arbitrators have gained more than sixty-five years of arbitration practice.[1689] Hence, the mistrust is highly misplaced now.[1690] By providing a right of appeal and review based on domestic procedures such as the CPC and the Specific Relief Act, the intention of the parties is completely bulldozed. The right of appeal ought to be removed from the IAA in order to deliver speedier justice, prevent misuse, and make India pro-arbitration.

Hence, removal of the provision for appeal under Section 37(1)(b) of the IAA would further arbitral efficiency, uphold the mandate of minimal court intervention and priority of jurisdiction of the tribunal. Such removal will reaffirm the faith in arbitration as a process and in arbitrators as adjudicators. Moreover, such removal will ensure that the IAA is a complete code in itself with respect to interim measures and there is no need to refer to provisions of the CPC or the Specific Relief Act.

An anticipated concern with such a drastic suggestion will obviously be the lack of safeguards for the party against whom such measure is granted. However, such concerns are misplaced as such removal should be done only after the safeguards provided under Articles 17D-17G of the Model Law have been incorporated in the IAA. The grounds for challenge are well contained in Article 17I of the Model Law and hence, any procedural irregularity can be brought before the court as a ground for refusing enforcement.

Though it may be argued that the argument above does not cater to the scenario where the interim measure requested is refused, such an argument may not be entirely correct. No tribunal would risk denying an interim measure only to create a ground for a challenge at the stage of enforcement of the award. Therefore, since arbitrators have to render an enforceable award, the tribunal ought to be trusted with the decision denying the request for interim measures. Alternatively, if the tribunal denies the request for interim measures, it should expedite the arbitration proceedings.[1691]

10. SAFEGUARDS

As discussed previously, interim measures can be used as offensive weapons to exert on to the opponent or gain a tactical advantage by causing delay or obstructing the

1688. *Ibid.*
1689. *Ibid.*, at 41-42.
1690. Melissa Magliana, *Chapter 3, Part II: Commentary on the Swiss Rules, Article 26 [Interim Measures of Protection]*, in Manuel Arroyo (ed.), *Arbitration in Switzerland: The Practitioner's Guide* 712 (2018).
1691. Ali Yesilirmak, *supra* n. 30, at 233.

proceedings.[1692] Therefore, providing sufficient safeguards[1693] against such misuse is imperative and the characteristics of each type of interim measure should be considered when considering the safeguards necessary.

After the 2006 Model Law Revisions, Article 17D-17E of the Model Law provides various safeguards to prevent abuse and safeguard the interest of the party against whom the interim measure may be ordered:

(a) The tribunal may modify, suspend or terminate an interim measure granted on the application by any party or on its own initiative in exceptional circumstances.[1694]
(b) The tribunal may require the party requesting the interim measure to provide security.[1695]
(c) The party which made the request for interim measures has to promptly disclose any material change in circumstances on the basis of which the measure was requested or granted.[1696]
(d) The tribunal can order costs and damages for damage caused by the interim measure or protection in the event that the tribunal determines that the interim measure ought not to have been granted.[1697]

Unfortunately, even after the 2015 Amendment, which came almost a decade after the 2006 Model Law Revisions, the IAA does not provide for any such safeguards. Even Section 17(2) of the IAA, which granted the tribunal to require a party to provide security in connection with an interim measure, has also been deleted by the 2015 Amendment.

10.1. 'Regime for Costs' under Section 31-A of the IAA

The only change with respect to the introduction of safeguards is the insertion of Section 31-A of the IAA which authorises the court or the arbitral tribunal to determine costs payable by one party to another, the amount of such costs and when such costs are to be paid. Therefore, an arbitral tribunal in India has the power to order costs in connection with an interim measure under Section 31-A of the IAA, especially under Section 31-A(4)(e) of the IAA which provides for costs relating to particular steps taken in the proceedings. Similarly, Section 31-A(4) (f) of the IAA provides for costs relating

1692. *Ibid.*, at 15.
1693. *Ibid.*, at 254.
1694. UNCITRAL Model Law, Art. 17D; Report of UNCITRAL Working Group on the work of its Thirty Ninth session, 2003, A/CN.9/545, available at: https://undocs.org/en/A/CN.9/545, ¶¶ 37-41.
1695. UNCITRAL Model Law, Art. 17E; Report of UNCITRAL Working Group on the work of its Thirty Seventh session, 2002, A/CN.9/23, available at: https://undocs.org/en/A/CN.9/523, ¶48.
1696. UNCITRAL Model Law, Art. 17F.
1697. *Ibid.*, Art. 17G.

only to a distinct part of the proceedings. Hence, Section 31-A of the IAA may account for the power to order costs as envisaged in Article 17G of the Model Law.

However, in the absence of provisions similar to Articles 17D, 17E, and 17F of the Model Law and the deletion of the right to appeal, safeguards similar to those contained in the Model Law must be adopted in the IAA.

10.2. Suspension, Modification and Termination of Measures

An interim order by its very nature is 'temporary' or in the 'interim'. It has no res judicata effect unless issued as an award. The power to suspend, modify or terminate an interim measure granted by a tribunal stems from the nature of interim orders and the inherent power of the tribunal and was recognised even before the 2006 Model Law Revisions.[1698] Therefore, the original text of the Model Law did not provide for a modification regime or the power to the arbitral tribunal to modify an interim measure presumably because such a provision would have been superfluous under the principle of *Kompetenz-kompetenz.*[1699] In Greece, arbitrators still do not have the power to amend revoked interim measures.[1700]

However, it was thought best to confirm the said power explicitly by the introduction of Article 17D which now specifically provides that the arbitral tribunal may modify, suspend or terminate an interim measure, either upon application in exceptional circumstances or upon prior notice to the parties, on the arbitral tribunal's own initiative.[1701] The exceptional circumstances contemplated by the Working Group were 'where the measure or [order] appeared to have been granted on an erroneous or fraudulent basis'.[1702]

10.2.1. Modification of Interim Awards

Under Article 17(2) of the Model Law, an interim measure may be in the form of an award or any other form. It should be noted that if the interim measure is issued as an award, the circumstances for revocation, suspension or modification become extremely limited. A tribunal would then have to pass a declaratory award holding the earlier decision as void. Such instances are rare, and most often than not, interim orders are not passed as awards. More importantly, the mere passing of the orders as awards does not determine their enforceability. It is usually the *lex fori* and its

1698. *Cases Nos. A-4 and A-15, Order (18 January 1984), reprinted in 5 Iran-US CTR 112-114*, c.f. Ali Yesilirmak, *supra* n. 30, at 201.
1699. Pratyush Panjwan & Harshad Pathak, *Assimilating the Negative Effect of Kompetenz-Kompetenz in India: Need to Revisit the Question of Judicial Intervention?* 2 (2), Ind. J. Arb. L. 7-8 (2014).
1700. Greece Code of Civil Procedure, Art. 889(1).
1701. Article 25(6), 2013 UNCITRAL Rules; Art. 26(5), 2012 CEAC Rules; Art. 25.1, 2018 DIS Rules and Art. 33(1), 2018 VIAC Rules *recognises the power to amend, suspend or revoke any interim measure on the application of a party but not on the tribunals own initiative.*
1702. Report of UNCITRAL Working Group on the work of its Thirty Ninth session, 2003, A/CN.9/545, available at: https://undocs.org/en/A/CN.9/545, ¶38.

mandatory law that determines whether an interim order would be considered an award or not.[1703]

Despite the problems of revocation of an award in *Behring International v. Iranian Air Force*,[1704] the tribunal issued an award for security for costs and retained jurisdiction to 'revise or supplement' its decision.[1705] In another instance, an ICC tribunal provided that an interim measure passed by an award shall stay in force for a particular period unless the final award was passed before the expiry of the said period.[1706] The revisions to the 2004 Swiss Rules even provide for the exercise of such power without prior notice to parties in exceptional circumstances.[1707]

India has not expressly adopted Article 17D of the 2006 Model Law and therefore an argument can be made that the tribunal does not have the power to modify interim measures as the legislative intent is clear from the absence of the adoption of Article 17D of the 2006 Model Law. However, such an argument is not feasible given that the 2015 Amendment has hardly adopted the 2006 Model Law Amendments and therefore the presumption of legislative intent one way or the another cannot stem from the reference to the 2015 Amendment.

In an appeal challenging the recall of the interim order granted by the arbitrator, the court held that the arbitrator, without providing the reasons for such review, modification, and recall, in effect rewrote the order and the exercised powers which are akin to that of an appellate court and hence such an order was unsustainable in law.[1708]

This view, however, is an aberration. Courts now consistently recognise the power of the tribunal to suspend, modify, revoke or terminate interim orders,[1709] though arbitrators at times deem it inappropriate to vary/modify an order passed by the Court.[1710] The power is also recognised under Article 15.2 of the DIAC Rules, 2018. As discussed earlier, the said power has been recognised in the case of interim orders passed under Section 9(1) of the IAA. It is only logical that if the tribunal has the power to modify, suspend or revoke the order of the court under Section 9(1) and 9(3) of the IAA, it naturally has the power for its own orders, especially after the 2015 Amendment. In Brazil, after the tribunal has formed, only the tribunal has jurisdiction to maintain, modify or revoke an interim measure granted by the court.[1711]

Another method of interpreting this power would be to take resort to Order XXXIX Rule 4 of the CPC which provides that an order for an injunction may be

1703. *See Chapter 10.*

1704. *Behring International Inc. v. Islamic Republic of Iran, Interim and Interlocutory Award in IUSCT Case No. ITM/ITL 52-382-3* of 21 June 1985, 8 Iran-US C.T.R. 238 (1985).

1705. Ali Yesilirmak, *supra* n. 30, at 203.

1706. *Interim Conservatory Award 10021 of 1999 (unpublished)* c.f. Ali Yesilirmak, *supra* n. 30, at 203.

1707. Article 261, 2004 Swiss Rules; Melissa, *supra* n. 1690, at 712.

1708. *Delhi Development Authority v. Naveen Kumar* 2017 SCC OnLine Del 10240, ¶¶10-12.

1709. *National Highways Authority of India v. VIL Rohtak Jind Highway Pvt. Ltd.* 2019 SCC OnLine Del 6545, ¶74; *Aryana Hospitality Management Services Pvt. Ltd. v. K.M. Dhondiyal & Anr.* 2017 SCC OnLine Del 7645, ¶29; *Monojeet Das v. Sujit Roy Chowdhury & Anr.* 2017 SCC OnLine Cal 16309, ¶5. *A similar observation was made in United Media Works Pvt. Ltd. v. Spartan Advertising and Films India Pvt. Ltd.* 2016 SCC OnLine Bom 6455, ¶7.

1710. *Dinesh Chandrakant Mirani v. Hemlata Chandrakant Mirani* 2019 SCC OnLine Bom, 4860 ¶4.

1711. Brazil Arbitration Act, 2015, Art. 22-B LA.

discharged, varied or set aside by the court on an application made by any party dissatisfied with such order. Though the preceding provision can be relied on to incorporate the safeguards under Article 17D of the Model Law, there are two major differences between Order XXXIX Rule 4 of the CPC and Article 17D of the Model Law.

First and foremost, the court cannot resort to this remedy without an application being made by any party, and second, the mandate in the second proviso is that an order shall not be discharged varied or set aside except on changed circumstances or satisfaction of the court with respect to the undue hardship. This, in effect, makes the threshold higher than Article 17D of the Model Law.

Furthermore, the danger of resorting to this provision is that it only talks about the power of the court and does not say anything with respect to the power of the arbitral tribunal. Order XXXIX Rule 4 of the CPC can only be resorted to in case the interim order is granted under Order XXXIX Rule 1 or Order XXXIX Rule 2 of the CPC. However, as submitted earlier, relying on the provisions of the CPC and the Specific Relief Act with respect to interim measures creates more problems for arbitration than it seeks to resolve.[1712]

Therefore, it would be prudent to specifically empower the arbitral tribunal to modify, suspend or terminate an interim order in consonance with Article 17D of the Model Law for orders passed by the court as well as the tribunal. This would ensure that the procedure adopted by the arbitral tribunal with respect to interim measures does not suffer from the shadow or cloud of the CPC and is truly autonomous. It should be noted that the Saraf Committee had specifically incorporated this power into the redrafted Section 17 of the IAA, but the same was never incorporated into the IAA.[1713]

Till such a power is not incorporated into the IAA, the better view is that the tribunal under Section 17 of the IAA has the power to modify, suspend and terminate interim measures granted earlier, both under the principle of *Kompetenz-kompetenz* and as the tribunal has the same powers for making orders as the court after the 2015 Amendment. Since the courts have the power to modify such measures, it is logical that the tribunal is also vested with the same powers.

10.3. Security for Interim Measures

Article 17E of the Model Law empowers the tribunal to require a party to provide appropriate security in connection with the interim measure requested. The phrase 'security in connection with' is intended to be broad, encompassing within it not only the direct cost of imposing the measure but also consequential damages resulting from the measure.[1714]

Before the 2006 Model Law Revisions[1715] and even today, most arbitral institutes and countries recognise the power of the tribunal to order security with respect to

1712. *See discussion on Standards under Chapter 3 and Chapter 4.*
1713. *Supra* n. 68.
1714. Holtzmann, *supra* n. 6 at, 178.
1715. Article 31(1), 1999 SCC Rules; Art. 26(1), 1976 UNCITRAL Rules; Section 20.1, 1998 DIS Rules.

interim measures.[1716] Some countries use different terms such as guarantee for enforcement,[1717] and indemnity.[1718] It is pertinent to mention that in the draft of the Working Group, it was suggested that the phrase 'any other party' to provide security should be added to account for multi-party arbitrations and to accommodate situations where a party provided counter security. However, the language was not included in the final version.[1719]

Security is very commonly requested from the party requesting interim relief,[1720] and in the event that a party fails to provide said security, the request is usually denied.[1721] However, security is not requested when the applicant has been deprived of the assets by the conduct of the respondent.[1722]

In cases where a status quo is requested by one party, security for damages is a must. Such security is an undertaking to indemnify the opposite party in the event the measure is found to be unjustified at a later stage.[1723] In several instances, arbitral tribunals have requested security in the form of a guarantee for the interim payment,[1724] and costs and potential damages.[1725]

The tribunal should keep in mind the financial capacity of the party requesting the interim measure[1726] and what effect such a request will have on the party's daily operations and ability to continue the litigation. Also, the tribunal should always be mindful of the equities of the case and the circumstances in which the measure is being requested.

Contrary to an application for security for costs, where the financial situation of the opposite party may be relevant, such a consideration is irrelevant for the determination of whether a security is appropriate.[1727] The key criteria should be whether the interim measure requested will cause damage to the opposite party.[1728]

It should be noted that there is no time prescribed under Article 17E of the Model Law at which the security has to be posted. Thus, security may be a condition

---

1716. Article 26(6), 2013 UNCITRAL Rules; Art. 15.1, 2016 MCIA Rules; Art. 27.1, 2017 SIAC Rules; Art. 37(2), 2017 SCC Rules; Art. 28(1), 2017 ICC Rules; Art. 25.2, 2014 LCIA Rules; Art. 31.1, 2007 Dubai Rules; Art. 37(b), AAA Rules; Art. 25.1, 2018 DIS Rules; Art. 33.1, 2018 VIAC Rules; Art. 26(6), 2012 CEAC Rules; Art. 28(2), 2016 KAC Rules.
1717. Bulgarian Arbitration Law, 1998, Art. 21; Oman Arbitration Law, 1997, Art. 24(1).
1718. Norway Arbitration Act, 2004, S. 19.
1719. Report of UNCITRAL Working Group on the work of its Thirty Seventh session, 2002, A/CN.9/523, available at: https://undocs.org/en/A/CN.9/523, ¶48.
1720. Holtzmann, *supra* n. 6 at, 174.
1721. Hober, *supra* n. 1207, at 737.
1722. Report of UNCITRAL Working Group on the work of its Thirty Sixth session, 2002, A/CN.9/508, available at: https://undocs.org/en/A/CN.9/508, ¶60; Report of UNCITRAL Working Group on the work of its Forty Second session, 2005, A/CN.9/573, available at: https://undocs.org/en/A/CN.9/573, ¶63; Report of UNCITRAL Working Group on the work of its Forty First session, 2004, A/CN.9/569, available at: https://undocs.org/en/A/CN.9/569, ¶36.
1723. Ali Yesilirmak, *supra* n. 30, at 187-188.
1724. *ICC Case 7544*, c.f. Ali Yesilirmak, *supra* n. 30, at 189.
1725. Berger, *supra* n. 1352, at 342.
1726. Ali Yesilirmak, *supra* n. 30, at 189.
1727. Bernhard Berger & Franz Kellerhals, *International and Domestic Arbitration in Switzerland* (2015), ¶1294; Melissa, *supra* n. 1690, at 714.
1728. *Ibid.*

precedent or a condition subsequent to the grant of an interim measure.[1729] In Norway, Section 19 of Arbitration Act, 2004 provides that '*the arbitral tribunal may order, by way of a condition for effecting and implementing the measure, whoever has requested such measure to provide, within a specified time limit, security respecting any consequences thereof*'. The power to request security is to be exercised for 'effecting and implementing the measure' as opposed to protecting the rights of the opposite party against a frivolous application. Moreover, the tribunal is to specify the time within which such security is to be granted, making it a condition precedent.

In *Baker Hughes*,[1730] the court made specific reference to Section 17(2) (prior to the 2015 Amendment)[1731] and upheld the power to take security. The power to order security has also been recognised in the form of an injunction in India.[1732] Interestingly, Section 17(2) of the IAA, which specifically enabled the court to order appropriate security by a party requesting the interim measure has been deleted by the 2015 Amendment.

Therefore, an argument can be made that the legislative intent was that the tribunal should no longer have the power to require security before the grant of an interim measure. Such an interpretation would, however, be a stretch. The 2015 Amendment was aimed at bringing the powers of the tribunal at par with that of the courts and mirroring the English Arbitration Act. The deletion of a specific power to take security cannot be justified on the same grounds. It appears that the same was deleted inadvertently as there is no discussion in the public record about the deletion of the same.

This deletion is contrary to Article 17E(1) of the 2006 Model Law and contrary to the principle of equal treatment of parties enshrined in Article 18 of the Model Law. It is widely known that interim measures can often be abused as an offensive weapon to exert pressure on the other side.[1733] A party against whom the interim measure will be granted shall suffer on account of an interim measure that should not have been granted in the first place. Furthermore, the provision serves as a deterrent for frivolous applications (which are quite frequent in India) as well as protects the rights of the opposite party to recover damages later.

It is pertinent to reiterate that a request for security is completely separate and distinct from an application for security for costs,[1734] and security for payment.[1735] Therefore, this provision, in essence, pertains to security for damages caused due to an interim measure and should be specifically incorporated in the IAA. Such adoption will also give legislative support to order for security passed by emergency arbitrators as well. Moreover, wherever the potential for abuse is higher, there should be a

1729. Holtzmann, *supra* n. 6 at, 175.
1730. *Baker Hughes Singapore Pte v. Shiv-vani Oil and Gas Exploration Services Ltd.* 2014 SCC OnLine Bom 1663.
1731. *Ibid.*, ¶22; *The Court also relied on K.G Rathishkumar v. NPR Finance Limited* 2012 SCC Online Kerala 29908.
1732. *SPA Agencies (India) Pvt. Ltd. v. Harish Rawtani* 2010 (2) Arb. LR 221 (AP) (DB).
1733. Lew, *supra* n. 28, at ¶23-4.
1734. *See Chapter 8.*
1735. *See Chapter 7.*

mandatory deposit of security, as discussed previously. Tribunals may even consider taking security before modifying, suspending or terminating an interim measure.

10.4. Disclosure

Article 17F of the Model Law provides for prompt disclosure of any material change in the circumstances on the basis of which the interim measure was granted.[1736] The French and Dutch versions of the Belgian Code refer to the prompt notification to the sole arbitrator or the chairman of the tribunal. However, the same is considered to be an editorial oversight.[1737] It also mandates full disclosure of all circumstances when requesting an ex parte interim measure.[1738] Therefore, it can be argued that full disclosure is not required when requesting an interim measure after notice to the opposite party.

10.4.1. Disclosure of 'Material Change' or 'All Circumstances Likely to Be Relevant'

This creates a vacuum of who determines what ought to be disclosed. Practically, it will be the party requesting the measure who will determine what ought to be disclosed and what not be disclosed. The tribunal can only find out subsequently whether something material was deliberately withheld and compensate for the same through costs and damages as provided under Article 17G of the Model Law.

The differentiation between disclosure of 'all circumstances likely to be relevant' with respect to ex parte measures and disclosure only for materially changed circumstances when requesting an interim measure after notice to the opposite party makes little sense, especially in India where several frivolous applications are filed to gain a strategic advantage.

Since there is no guidance on the term 'material change,' and whether such any 'change' is to be in the opinion of the applicant, respondent or tribunal, it is better to require full disclosure with respect to all facts and circumstances related to the interim measure, subject to privilege and confidentiality concerns. Though it can be argued that on notice, the opposite party will present the complete picture and not just present the version of the party requesting the measure, or maybe an order for security with respect to the interim measure at the stage of the application would prevent such abuse. It would be in the interest of fairness that full disclosure related to the facts and circumstances related to the interim measure is mandated at all times, subject to confidentiality concerns. Such disclosure will further transparency and reduce the arbitrator's liability and enhance immunity.

1736. Article 26(7), 2013 UNCITRAL Rules and Art. 26(7), 2012 CEAC Rule.
1737. Niuscha Bassiri, *Commentary on Part VI of the Belgian Judicial Code, Chapter IV: Article 1696*, in Niuscha Bassiri & Maarten Draye (eds), *Arbitration in Belgium* 245 (2016).
1738. UNCITRAL Model Law, Art. 17F(2).

10.4.2. *Duty of 'Full Disclosure'*

This duty of full disclosure has been judicially recognised by the Supreme Court which has taken the view that a litigant who approaches the court is bound to produce all documents relevant to the litigation and withholding a vital document would amount to plain fraud on the court.[1739] In the event that the party requesting the measure has knowledge of certain facts, which are unknown to the opposite party, full disclosure will serve as a proper safeguard than an indemnity for costs and damages after the termination of the measure which would not have been granted in the first place if full disclosure was mandated.

Thus, the term 'material' should be substituted with 'likely to be relevant' as provided in Article 17F(2) since the term is broader[1740] and would entail a more objective, reasonable person standard of what 'is likely to be relevant', rather than a unilateral view of the applicant of the term 'material'.

Such mandatory disclosure of 'all circumstances likely to be relevant' would also help emergency arbitrators get a broader view of the circumstances. Moreover, such disclosure would help a tribunal assess more easily whether the claim is frivolous or not and consequently protect the rights of the party against whom the interim measure is requested. It will also bring on record the conduct of the party requesting the measure and assist the court in determining whether any security is to be ordered before granting the measure requested.

There is no provision either under the CPC or the Act relating to disclosures such as those provided under Article 17F of the Model Law. Also, given that there is no provision for security as well, effectively there is no protection for the respondent against a party misusing the request for interim measures.

In such a case, the second proviso to Order XXXIX Rule 4 of the CPC would trigger mandating that the order should not be modified, suspended, or terminated. Though an implied duty of disclosure can be implied from the words of the proviso, such a duty will also be only limited to false and misleading statements and would not apply to the active concealment of all facts and circumstances.[1741]

Therefore, it is necessary that a legal duty mandating full disclosure be incorporated under Section 17 of the IAA at the time of applying for the grant of an interim measure. The said duty shall also continue throughout the life of the interim order and any material change in circumstances ought to be disclosed by the party who sought the interim measure. A consequence of non-disclosure would result in suspension or termination of the interim measure or an award for damages, or both for the loss arising

---

1739. *S.P. Chengalvaraya Naidu v. Jagannath* (1994) 1 SCC 1, ¶6; *Badami v. Bhali* (2012) 11 SCC 574, ¶31; *Holy Health Educational Society (Regd.) v. Delhi Development Authority* (1999) 80 DLT 207, ¶20 affirmed in *Allied Medical Ltd. v. Uttar Pradesh Health Systems Strengthening Project* 2019 SCC OnLine Del 7696.

1740. Holtzmann, *supra* n. 6 at, 176.

1741. *See 'Disclosure' under Chapter 3.*

due to such non-disclosure.[1742] A party may also be punished for perjury or contempt.[1743]

10.5. Costs and Damages

The introduction of Article 17G after the 2006 Model Law Revisions clearly establishes the regime for costs and damages.[1744] It mandates that a party requesting an interim measure or applying for a preliminary order shall be liable for any costs and damages caused by the measure. Some countries[1745] and rules of arbitral institutes expressly recognise the power of the tribunal to order costs and damages. Some include expenses and reasonable attorney fees,[1746] some refer to any expense, loss or damage,[1747] and others refer only to damages.[1748] The revisions to the 2012 Swiss Rules now include a provision for compensation of damages for unjustified interim measures of preliminary orders.[1749] Thus, damages arising out of an order of the arbitral tribunal may be sought from the tribunal itself, i.e., costs such as attorney's fees, costs of implementation of the measure, direct or indirect consequential damages, among other things.[1750]

The rationale behind such measure can be determined from the intention of the Working Group. Such measure was meant to create a strict regime establishing a clear and unquestionable liability on the party requesting interim measures in the event the tribunal subsequent to the grant of an interim order, concludes that the measure should not have been granted.[1751] It is unclear what this means.

Does it mean that the party ultimately losing on the merits would be liable or is it a case where subsequent evidence shows that a different outcome of an application on the relevant criteria should have been determined or is it limited to cases where subsequent evidence shows that the applicant improperly obtained the measure by reason of misleading information and submissions?[1752] It is relevant to highlight that the Working Group noted that the final decision on merits is not an essential element in determining whether the interim measure was justified or not.[1753]

Therefore, there are still concerns as to the causation when considering costs and damages, levels of proof, and scenarios where there are multiple causes. More importantly, causation under such a procedural test would not necessarily mirror

1742. UNCITRAL Yearbook, *supra* n. 11, at 453.
1743. Report of UNCITRAL Working Group on the work of its Thirty Ninth session, 2003, A/CN.9/545, available at: https://undocs.org/en/A/CN.9/545, ¶90. *See Alka Chandewar v. Shamshul Ishrar Khan* (2017) 16 SCC 119.
1744. Article 26(8), 2013 UNCITRAL Rules and Art. 26(8), 2012 CEAC Rules.
1745. *See Appendix I.*
1746. Alternative Dispute Resolution Act, 2004, S. 28(7).
1747. Sri Lanka Arbitration Act, 1995, S. 13(1).
1748. Article 1182, The Arbitration Act, (Poland); Swedish Arbitration Act, S. 25.
1749. Article 26(4), 2012 Swiss Rules, Melissa, *supra* n. 1690, at 714.
1750. Report of UNCITRAL Working Group on the work of its Thirty Ninth session, 2003, A/CN.9/545, available at: https://undocs.org/en/A/CN.9/545, ¶¶ 60, 63-64.
1751. Luis, *supra* n. 521, at 553.
1752. Waincymer, *supra* n. 989, at 639.
1753. Note by the Secretariat in UNCITRAL Working Group of its Fortieth session, 2004, A/CN.9/WG. II/WP.127, available at: https://undocs.org/en/A/CN.9/WG.II/WP.127, ¶ 27.

causation of damages provisions under substantive contract law.[1754] Hence, how is the tribunal supposed to infer causation? Should liability be restricted to negligently or fraudulently, or should it even extend to the error of the tribunal?[1755]

10.5.1. Causation for Costs and Damages

This controversy can be curtailed to a certain extent. Article 17G of the Model Law sets forth a direct cause and effect scheme by providing 'for any costs and damages caused by the measure or order to any party'.[1756] Such determination should also include costs and damages for orders granted by an emergency arbitrator if it is determined that they should not have been granted.

It should be noted that the phrase 'any party' should be limited to the parties to the arbitration and not third parties, though they may well suffer damages. If the phrase were to include third parties, it would open the doors for unnecessary litigation and also run contrary to the concept of the consensual nature of arbitration. Moreover, while the tribunal would not be empowered to pass an order against third parties, it would compensate them for costs and damages. This cannot be a viable interpretation.

The grant of costs or damages should relate to full disclosure requirements. Therefore, causation concerns are slightly misplaced if full disclosure at all times is mandated under Article 17G of the Model Law. Furthermore, an order for costs and damages should be passed as an award for effective enforcement.[1757]

In India, there is no provision directly pertaining to costs and damages related to an interim measure. The newly introduced Section 31-A of the IAA, which is analogous to Section 44 of the English Civil Procedure Rules, 1998, can be resorted to for such a power. Section 31-A(1)(a) provides that the court or tribunal shall have the discretion to determine whether costs are payable by one party to another. It also does away with the erstwhile Section 31(8) of the IAA.[1758]

Taking note of the delay tactics by filing frivolous claims, the Supreme Court in *Salem Advocate Bar Association v. Union of India* had observed the following '*judicial notice can be taken of the fact that many unscrupulous parties take advantage of the fact that either the costs are not awarded or nominal costs are awarded on the unsuccessful party*'.[1759] Therefore, this section implements the judgment in spirit and form and allocates cost in a manner which reflects the party's relative success and failure in the arbitration.[1760]

1754. Waincymer, *supra* n. 989, at 640.
1755. Report of UNCITRAL Working Group on the work of its Thirty Ninth session, 2003, A/CN.9/545, available at: https://undocs.org/en/A/CN.9/545, ¶¶ 66.
1756. Note by the Secretariat in UNCITRAL Working Group of its Forty Third session, 2005, A/CN.9/WG.II/WP.138, available at: https://undocs.org/en/A/CN.9/WG.II/WP.138, ¶ 128.
1757. Report of UNCITRAL Working Group on the work of its Forty Third session, 2005, A/CN.9/589, available at: https://undocs.org/en/A/CN.9/589, ¶48.
1758. Indian Arbitration Act, 1996, S. 31(8).
1759. *Salem Advocate Bar Assn. (II) v. Union of India* (2005) 6 SCC 344, ¶34.
1760. Wadhwa, *supra* n. 46, at 1749.

It should be noted that the power does not include awarding damages and is restricted only to costs. This provision was recommended by the Law Commission as an insertion to Section 6, i.e. administrative assistance.[1761] However, the same has been incorporated under Section 31, i.e., Form and Contents of Arbitral Award. It is a welcome step to the extent that it brings Indian jurisprudence in line with international jurisprudence by following the 'costs follow the event' principle. This will disincentivise frivolous litigation and *mala fide* or inequitable conduct.[1762] However, it should be specified that this section provides for costs in general and does not pertain specifically to costs and damages in respect of interim measures of protection.

Moreover, it pertains to costs to be awarded at the time of passing of the award. It does not address the issue of costs and damages as envisaged under Article 17G of the Model Law, which it should or in the alternative, a separate clause along the lines of Article 17G ought to be incorporated into Section 17 of the IAA.

10.5.2. Test for Determining Costs and Damages

When considering the issue of costs and damages, the tribunal should consider whether (a) there was indeed a real urgency; (b) the request was filed with the objective of delaying or obstructing the arbitration proceedings; and (c) the claims of the party requesting the measure were ultimately rejected.[1763]

A relevant question tied to this concept is also whether the tribunal can grant costs and damages for interim measures granted by the courts. Since Article 31-A(1) authorises, both the courts and the tribunal to order costs, it can be argued that the tribunal cannot order costs for interim measures granted by the court.

The better view is that damages arising out of an order of the court may also be sought from the tribunal as the role of the court is only support to arbitration proceedings. Moreover, the interim measures would relate to the subject matter of the dispute and obtaining damages from the tribunal will ensure that all remedies are adjudicated before a single forum.[1764] To relegate parties back to the court for damages, especially if the measure is terminated by the tribunal, would run afoul of the mandate of minimal court intervention enshrined in Section 5 of the IAA and Article 5 of the Model Law.

1761. Justice B.N. Srikrishna, Report of the High-Level Committee to Review the Institutionalization of Arbitration Mechanism in India, (July 2017), available at: http://legalaffairs.gov.in/sites/default/files/Report-HLC.pdf.
1762. Wadhwa, *supra* n. 46, at 1748-1750.
1763. Schwartz, *supra* n. 1236, at 53.
1764. Ali Yesilirmak, *supra* n. 30, at 98. *Only a handful of national laws make reference to the appropriate forum in which to seek damages. In these countries, such as France and Germany, arbitrators are solely empowered to deal with the issue of compensation. In other countries, for example, Canada, China, Italy, and the U.S.* (*see, e.g., Warth Line, Ltd v. Merinda Marine Co.* 778 F.Supp. 158 (S.D.N.Y. 1991), *confirming an arbitral decision on damages arising from foreign court proceedings*), *both judicial authorities and arbitrators seem to be generally empowered to deal with that issue.* In Norway and Scotland, *parties are able to make an agreement to refer any issue on damages to arbitrators. It seems that an arbitration clause covering all disputes connected to the underlying relationship is wide enough to permit any claim on damages arising from unjustified interim remedies relating to such relationship.*

CHAPTER 8

Security for Costs

The 2006 Model Law Revisions, with the use of the generic language in Article 17(2) enhanced the scope of the type of interim measures that could be granted by the arbitral tribunal. The language contained in Article 17(2)(c) of the Model Law is of particularly wide import. It provides for '*a means of preserving assets out of which a subsequent award may be satisfied*'. Such language would include situations comprising an apprehension that the financial health of the claimant is such that even if the respondent were to win, the respondent would not be able to recover even the costs of arbitration. In such situations, the respondent may apply security for costs (*caution judicatum solvi*) requiring the claimant to furnish security for such an eventuality.

1. MEANING OF 'SECURITY FOR COSTS'

In this context, security for costs application may be defined as an application for money, assets, bond, or guarantee which a party provides to the court or arbitral tribunal for costs if that party loses.[1765] It is meant to secure the winning party from receiving any costs which might be awarded in a future award.[1766]

2. NEED FOR AN ORDER OF SECURITY FOR COSTS

It is no longer a secret that arbitrations have become extremely expensive.[1767] Costs of an arbitration run into millions of dollars, averaging a massive USD 97,000 per

1765. *Black's Law Dictionary* 1387 (2004), *c.f.* Ali Yesilirmak, *supra* n. 30, at 214.
1766. Christopher Boog, *Chapter 18, Part III: Interim Measures in International Arbitration*, in Manuel Arroyo (ed.), *Arbitration in Switzerland: The Practitioner's Guide* 2550 (2018).
1767. *Union of India v. Singh Builder Syndicate* (2009) 4 SCC 523, *the Supreme Court had commented on how arbitration matters are conducted in India and are usually the five-star culture and only those with deep pockets can afford the luxury of getting their disputes resolved through arbitration.*

arbitration proceeding as per the last LCIA Report.[1768] While the claimant has the liberty or the choice to determine whether or not to incur this cost, the respondent, having agreed to a valid arbitration agreement, does not have such a choice. The respondent wants to be assured that if it wins, and is awarded costs, the respondent will be paid out of a security or a fund taken in advance.[1769] Thus, an application for security for costs is made and an order is granted with the view to ensure equal treatment[1770] or to re-establish a level playing field in the proceedings.[1771] Such imposition of costs is like incidental damages[1772] and is not levied as a punishment on the losing party. The aim is to compensate the successful party for the expenses which it has borne when it has been forced to litigate without cause.[1773]

However, many scholars view such applications as just an undesirable call to attention in some cases.[1774] If a party has agreed to arbitration, then why should it be permitted to impose a condition on the bringing of a claim by the other party? Most arbitral laws and rules typically have express provisions dealing with advances on fees and costs of the arbitration.[1775] Even in India, under Section 38(1) of the IAA, the tribunal can demand an advance on the costs. Once such fees and costs have been paid in advance, an application for security for costs is unnecessary.[1776] Thus, the practice of ordering security for costs is generally disfavoured in international arbitration,[1777] and there are very few cases where arbitrators have ordered security for costs primarily due to a strong view[1778] that such orders may not be appropriate in arbitration.[1779]

Despite such views, the concept of security for costs is a potentially valuable interim measure[1780] and is gaining more and more acceptance, especially after the arrival of third-party funding.[1781] In the case of third-party funding, the extent of recovery of costs is analogous to damages as the respondent will often have no separate claim for damages and cost recovery is the only outcome they are looking for. This

1768. *The London Court of International Arbitration, Facts and Figures, Costs and Duration: 2013-2016*, available at: http://www.lcia.org/media/download.aspx?MediaId=596.
1769. Blackby, *supra* n. 34, at 317.
1770. Nakul, *supra* n. 17, at 687.
1771. Micha Bühler & Marco Stacher, *Chapter 18, Part IV: Costs in International Arbitration*, in Manuel Arroyo (ed.), *Arbitration in Switzerland: The Practitioner's Guide* 2583 (2018).
1772. *Manindra Chandra Nandi v. Aswini Kumar Acharjya* ILR (1921) 48 Cal 427, at 440-441.
1773. *Vinod Seth v. Devinder Bajaj* (2010) 8 SCC 1, ¶45.
1774. Lew, *supra* n. 28, at 601-602; William Laurence Craig, William Park & John Paulson, *International Chamber of Commerce Arbitration* 468-469 (1998). *In an ICC arbitration, the tribunal awarded extra costs in the final award as the respondent had added costs to the proceedings by bringing an unfounded request for security for costs.* Case 10 in ICC Commission Report, *Decisions on Costs in International Arbitration*, Issue 2 29 (Offprint from ICC Dispute Resolution Bull. 2015).
1775. Lew, *supra* n. 28, at ¶23-53.
1776. Micha Bühler, *supra* n. 1771, at 2573; Waincymer, *supra* n. 989, at 636.
1777. Lew, *supra* n. 28, at 601-602.
1778. *RSM Production Corp. v. Santa Lucia, Decision on Saint Lucia's Request for Security for Costs in ICSID Case No. ARB/12/10 of 13 August 2014*, ¶86.
1779. Lew, *supra* n. 28, at ¶23-54.
1780. Alan Redfern & Sam O'Leary, *Why It Is Time for International Arbitration to Embrace Security for Costs*, 32(3) Arb. Int'l 397, 412-413 (2016).
1781. *Jonas von Goeler, Third-Party Funding in International Arbitration and its Impact on Procedure* 338 (2016).

would arise where the claiming party is impecunious and is being funded by a related entity who will benefit if the claim succeeds but be beyond exposure if they are lost[1782] - an 'arbitral hit and run'.[1783]

After the 2015 Amendment, India now impliedly follows the principle of 'costs follow the event' under Section 31-A(2) of the IAA. In the event that a respondent is successful at defending the claim, the costs will have to be borne by the claimant.[1784] An express provision for security for costs is, therefore, more critical now than ever before. In the absence of a specific power in favour of the tribunal to order security for costs, a respondent may have no recourse to secure its cost award in the event the claimant is impecunious.

3. POWER TO ORDER SECURITY FOR COSTS

The concept of security for costs has been recognised by courts for centuries.[1785] It is a common form of interim relief in England and other Commonwealth jurisdictions.[1786] In India, the power has been recognised under Order XXV[1787] of the CPC as well as the inherent power of the court.[1788]

However, in the context of arbitration, the power to order security for costs is contained only in some institutional arbitration rules,[1789] and national laws.[1790] Earlier, tribunals[1791] and courts[1792] required the power to order security for costs in the

1782. *Coppee-Lavalin SA/NV Ken-Ren Chemicals and Fertilisers Ltd.* [1995] 1 AC 38 (HL); *Channel Tunnel Group Ltd. v. Balfour Beatty Construction Ltd.* [1993] 2 WLR 262 at 72.

1783. *Where claimant's arbitration fees and expenses are being covered by a related entity or individual who stands to gain if the claimant wins but would not be liable to meet any award of costs that might be made if it lost.*; Nadia Darwazeh & Adrien Leleu, *Disclosure and Security for Costs or How to Address Imbalances Created by Third-Party Funding*, 33 (2) J. Int'l Arb. 146 (2016).

1784. Indian Arbitration Act, 1996, S. 31A(2)(a).

1785. Bernhard Berger, *Arbitration Practice: Security for Costs: Trends and Developments in Swiss Arbitral Case Law*, 28 (1) ASA Bulletin 7 (2010).

1786. Gary Born, *supra* n. 33, at 2679. *See Appendix B.*

1787. *'1. When security for costs may be required from plaintiff – c (1) At any stage of a suit, the Court may, either of its own motion or on the application of any defendant, order the plaintiff, for reasons to be recorded, to give within the time fixed by it security for the payment of all costs incurred and likely to be incurred by any defendant.'*

1788. *Hari Nath Singh v. Ram Kumar Bagchi* 1913 SCC OnLine Cal 209; *S. Ramaswami Pillai v. Krishnamal* (1934) 155 Ind Cas 317; *Hira v. Monghibai* A 1938 B 510; *Vali v. Sunday Times* A 1932 SS 33 CONTRA; *Suraj v. Sant* A 1941 A 219; *Bhairabendra Narain Deb v. Udai Narain Deb* (1923) 79 Ind Cas 298; *Mahadev Jiew v. Dr. B.B. Sen* 1951 SCC OnLine Cal 182, ¶23.

1789. Rules 29 (e), MCIA Rules; Rule 27 (K), 2016 SIAC Rules; Art. 25.2, 2014 LCIA Arbitration Rules; Art. 24, 2018 HKIAC Rules; Art. 33, 2018 VIAC Rules.

1790. *See Appendix B*; English Arbitration Act, 1996, S. 38(3); Hong Kong Arbitration Ordinance (Cap.609), S. 56(1)(a); Ireland Arbitration Act, 2010, S. 19; Singapore International Arbitration Act, 1994, S. 12(1). *However, it should be noted that device of security for cost is unfamiliar to many legal systems*. Craig, *supra* n. 1547, at 139.

1791. *ZCC Arbitration dated 12.11.1991*; *Katherine Lynch, Security for Costs in Domestic and International Arbitration in England and Hong Kong*, 12 (2) J. Int'l Arb. 17, 22-23 (1995).

1792. Indian Arbitration Act, 1940, S. 12(6), *the High Court shall have ... ; the same power of making orders in respect of ... Security for Costs [in arbitration cases] ... as it has for the purpose of ... an action or matter in the High Court: Provided that nothing in this subsection shall be taken*

arbitration agreement. In the absence of an express agreement between the parties, the tribunal had no power to order security for costs.[1793] This view changed considerably over the years.[1794]

3.1. Applicable Law

One of the contentious issues in this context was the question of applicable law concerning an application for security for costs. Should an order be granted only if the law governing the dispute permits it? Or should the power be contained in the *lex arbitri or lex fori?* The Queen Mary Task Force Report states that applications for security for costs will be decided under the standards of the applicable national law applied by courts or tribunals[1795] within the mandatory rules of the *lex fori* and *lex arbitri.*[1796]

Therefore, over time, the power to order security for costs could be traced to (a) a specific provision in national arbitration statutes (*lex arbitri*); (b) a specific provision in the arbitration agreement; (c) a subset of the broad interim powers of the tribunal; or (d) the inherent power or general discretion of the tribunal.[1797]

Most countries do not contain an express provision under the *lex arbitri* recognising the power of the tribunal to grant an order for security for costs except for a few jurisdictions.[1798] Ordinarily, the agreement of the parties also does not explicitly provide for such a power. Therefore, the general view is that the power to grant security for costs is usually considered to be part of the power to grant interim measures.[1799]

In Switzerland and France,[1800] it is now a well-established practice that an application for security for cost is an interim measure granted by an arbitral tribunal.[1801] The confirmation of this power to order security for costs may also be implied from the fact it has come up several times in arbitration,[1802] including investor-state

to prejudice any power which may be vested in an arbitrator [by the parties] of making orders … .; Rubins, *supra* n. 1547, at 323.

1793. *ZCC Arbitration dated 12.11.1991*; Lynch, *supra* n. 1791, at 19.

1794. Bernhard, *supra* n. 1785, at 10; Ali Yesilirmak, *supra* n. 30, at 216; Gary Born, *supra* n. 33, at 2679-2680.

1795. Report of the ICCA-Queen Mary Task Force on Third-Party Funding in International Arbitration, (April 2018) No. 4, available at: https://www.arbitration-icca.org/media/10/40280243154551/icca_reports_4_tpf_final_for_print_5_april.pdf, at 172. Goeler, *supra* n. 1781, at 334.

1796. Lew, *supra* n. 28, at ¶23-34 & 23-53.

1797. Micha Bühler, *supra* n. 1771, at 2584; Waincymer, *supra* n. 989, at 646.

1798. Singapore International Arbitration Act, 1994, S. 12(1)(a); Singapore Domestic Arbitration Act, 2001, S. 28(2)(a); Ireland Arbitration Act, 2010, S. 19; Hong Kong Arbitration Ordinance (Cap.609), S. 40; Jamaican Arbitration Act, 2017, S. 25; International Arbitration Act, 1974, S. 23 (K); Commercial Arbitration Act, 2011, S. 17 E; Brunei International Arbitration Order, 2009 S. 20; Fiji International Arbitration Act, 2017, S. 28; *See Appendix.*

1799. Bernhard, *supra* n. 1785, at 10; Ali Yesilirmak, *supra* n. 30, at 216; Gary Born, *supra* n. 33, at 2678.

1800. Weixia Gu, *Security for Costs in International Commercial Arbitration*, 22 (3) J. Int'l Arb. 175, 179 (2005).

1801. Bernhard, *supra* n. 1785, at 10.

1802. *Ibid.*, at 7.

arbitration[1803] and yet there are no reported cases where a state court has set aside or refused to enforce an arbitral award on the ground that the tribunal has ordered security for costs.[1804]

3.2. 'Means of Preserving Assets' under the Model Law

After the 2006 Model Law Revisions, it is now conclusive that the broad interim measure powers contained in Article 17 of the Model Law were intended to encompass security for costs through the words *'a means of preserving assets out of which a subsequent award may be satisfied'* in Article 17(2)(c).[1805]

The Working Group discussions were clear that an application for security for costs was also envisaged under Article 17(2)(c).[1806] Such orders are based on a well-founded concern that a party would be financially unable to satisfy an eventual award. In such cases, the opposite party would have no recourse to protect itself against the risk of its expenditure of time, money and effort being wasted.[1807]

3.2.1. Distinguishing Article 17(2)(C) and Article 17E of the Model Law

There is also a view that an application for security for costs may also come within the ambit of Article 17E of the Model Law if security is being requested in connection with another form of an interim measure.[1808] However, a request for security under Article 17E should not be confused with security for costs. Security under Article 17E may be ordered with a two-fold objective, i.e., (a) that the interim measure being requested is not frivolous or an abuse of the process of law and (b) it provides an effective safeguard should it later transpire that the interim measure was unjustified. An application for security for costs, on the other hand, pertains to the creation of a fund out of which a subsequent award on costs may be satisfied.

3.3. Source of the Power in India

Unlike other jurisdictions, despite a complete overhaul of the regime on interim measures in the 2015 Amendment, there is no express power granted to a tribunal to order security for costs. As discussed earlier,[1809] the type of measures listed in Section 17(1) of the IAA is not broad enough to include an order for security for costs. The variance between the language *'means of preserving assets out of which a subsequent*

1803. *See Generally:* Eduardo Zuleta Jaramillo, *Chapter 40: Security for Costs: Authority of the Tribunal and Third-Party Funding*, in Meg Kinnear & Geraldine R. Fischer, et al. (eds), *Building International Investment Law: The First 50 Years of ICSID* (2015).
1804. Goeler, *supra* n. 1781, at 335.
1805. Report of UNCITRAL Working Group on the work of its Forty Seventh Session, 2007, A/CN.9/641, available at: https://undocs.org/en/A/CN.9/641, ¶48.
1806. *Ibid.*
1807. *On Time Staffing, LLC v. National Union Fire Ins. Co.* 2011 U.S. Dist. LEXIS 50689 (S.D.N.Y.).
1808. Waincymer, *supra* n. 989, at 642.
1809. *See Chapter 8.*

award may be satisfied' in Article 17(2)(c) of the Model Law and '*securing the amount in dispute in the arbitration*' in Section 17(1)(ii)(b) of the IAA makes it *ex facie* evident that there is no power to order security for costs. The words 'amount in dispute' is extremely narrow and cannot be interpreted to include 'costs' within its ambit.

Even if such a broad interpretation were to be accorded if a party is impecunious, the primary question is how will it furnish security for such large sums? Moreover, what will be the consequence of not doing so? The Delhi High Court observed that there is no provision in the IAA which states that on failure by a party to comply with an order of additional security under Section 17 of the IAA, the claim would be rejected. Then, what would be the purpose of passing such an order at all?[1810]

Though it can be argued that the court impliedly affirmed the power to order security for costs and only rejected the concept on concerns of enforceability under the IAA, it should be noted this case was decided before the 2015 Amendment when Section 17(2) expressly provided for security for granting interim measures. It is this security that was considered by the court and not security for costs specifically. Also, the court did not consider Section 38(1) of the IAA, which pertains to 'advance for the costs'.

After the 2015 Amendment, the cost regime under the IAA underwent several changes. The 2015 Amendment introduced Section 31-A of the IAA, i.e., a regime for costs. It provides an extensive description of the meaning of the term 'costs'[1811] and provides details on what the court should consider while determining the costs[1812] and which party shall be liable for the same.[1813]

Therefore, one view is that Section 38(1) of the IAA[1814] can be resorted to as a source for the power of the tribunal to grant security for costs under the broad regime for costs.[1815] Since the language of the provision states that '*as an advance for the costs referred to in sub-section (8) of section 31, which it expects will be incurred in respect of the claim submitted to it*', a possible interpretation could be that costs related to a claim may be granted by the tribunal as the costs shall be fixed by the tribunal under Section 31-A of the IAA.

Further, the second proviso to Section 38(2) of the IAA[1816] empowers the tribunal to suspend or terminate arbitral proceedings in respect of a claim or counterclaim, if the costs are not paid. Similarly, Section 31-A(4)(a) of the IAA refers to 'a proportion of another party's costs' and clause (b) refers to 'a stated amount in respect of another party's costs'. Therefore, a combined reading of the provisions leads to an implied recognition of the power to order security for costs.

The other view can be that the power under Section 38(1) of the IAA has to be read with 38(3) of the IAA which provides for the rendering of accounts for the amount

1810. *Intertoll ICS Cecons O & M Co. Pvt. Ltd. v. National Highways Authority of India* 2013 SCC OnLine Del 447, ¶42.
1811. Indian Arbitration Act, 1996, S. 31-A(1) explanation.
1812. *Ibid.*, S. 31-A(3).
1813. *Ibid.*, S. 31-A(4).
1814. *Ibid.*, S. 38(1).
1815. Madhur Baya, available at: https://globalarbitrationreview.com/jurisdiction/1005746/india.
1816. Indian Arbitration Act, 1996, S. 38(2).

received by the tribunal and return of any unexpected balance to the party or parties. Therefore, what is contemplated under Section 38(1) of the IAA is the 'advance on costs' paid to the arbitral tribunal for meeting administrative expenses but not for the respondent's costs.[1817] This view is also affirmed by the Report of the Law Commission which recommended incorporating the same under the administrative section.[1818] Also, the term 'costs,' pre and post the amendment does not refer to actual costs but only 'reasonable costs'.[1819] Hence, Section 38(1) cannot be the source for the power to grant security for costs as it would not relate to a costs award.

There is also an inconsistency between Section 31(8) of the IAA[1820] and Section 38(1) of the IAA. Section 38(1) of the IAA refers to the unamended Section 31(8) of the IAA where the tribunal had the discretion to order costs and there was no general rule as contained in Section 31-A(2)(a) of the IAA. A conjoint reading of Sections 31-A(1)(a) and 31-A(3)(b) of the IAA suggests that the costs contemplated under Section 31-A of the IAA[1821] are those which can only be determined once the award has been passed and it is determined who the unsuccessful party in the proceedings is. It is then that the tribunal has to consider whether costs are payable or not. Therefore, a security for cost application under Section 38 read with Section 31-A of the IAA would not be maintainable since it would amount to a prejudgment of the merits.

A third view can be to apply the principles of CPC under Order XXV Rule 1 read with Section 151 of the CPC to order security for costs. If this view is preferred and the power to grant security for costs is traced to the CPC, then the mandate of the proviso has to be considered. The proviso has been held to be mandatory in the case of foreign plaintiffs,[1822] and security for costs has been ordered if the plaintiff is a foreign company with no registered office in India and no immovable property or other assets in India.[1823] Reliance on this provision will lead to discrimination against foreign parties if the seat is in India.[1824] The illogical position would thus be that in all international commercial arbitrations seated in India, security for costs would be mandatory.[1825]

Alternatively, tribunals may refer to Order XXV of the CPC along with inherent jurisdiction under Section 151 of the CPC. However, the resort to such an interpretation was rejected by the Supreme Court of India. The court held that Section 151 of the CPC is intended to apply in cases where the CPC does not cover any particular aspect and

1817. Paul, *supra* n. 679, at 427.
1818. Law Commission of India, *supra* n. 517.
1819. Indian Arbitration Act, 1996, S. 31-A(1), Explanation.
1820. *Ibid.*, S. 31(8): which provided that '*Unless otherwise agreed by the parties* – (a) *the costs of an arbitration shall be fixed by the arbitral tribunal.*'
1821. Indian Arbitration Act, 1996, S. 31-A.
1822. *S. Sundaram Pillai v. V.R. Pattabiraman* (1985) 1 SCC 591, ¶63; *Salem Advocate Bar Assn. (II) v. Union of India* (2005) 6 SCC 344; *Vinod Seth v. Devinder Bajaj* (2010) 8 SCC 1.
1823. *Alpha Oil International v. M.T Chem Lilyo* 2014 SCC Online Bom 4838, ¶21; *Fal Shipping Co. Ltd. v. M.T.A Layyah* 2014 SCC Online Bom 1061, ¶17.
1824. CIArb's International Arbitration Practice Guidelines on Applications for Security for Costs 2015, Art. 3.
1825. Paul, *supra* n. 679, at 427.

in the interests of justice requires an exercise of power to cover a particular situation.[1826] In the presence of specific provisions of the CPC relating to costs,[1827] security to costs[1828] and damages,[1829] the court cannot invoke inherent jurisdiction under Section 151 for the ends of justice.[1830] Therefore, the exercise of the power under Section 151 read with Order XXV of the CPC would amount to exercising power not specifically listed under Section 17(1) of the IAA and will also result in the application of the CPC in complete violation of the mandate of Section 19(1) of the IAA.

A more viable interpretation can be that the tribunal may infer such power under Section 17(1)(ii)(e) of the IAA under the words *'such other interim measure of protection as may appear to the tribunal to be just and convenient'*, with or without Order XXV Rule 1. Given the various alternative interpretations, different standards may be applied leading to very different results. Hence, the existence of the power should not be left at the interpretation and discretion of the tribunal. India should adopt the broad language contained in Article 17(2)(c) of the Model Law with the specific provision for security for costs as has been done in various other jurisdictions[1831] in the interest of consistency, uniformity and the larger goal of being a pro-arbitration jurisdiction. Such express inclusion was also proposed under the 2003 Bill but has not been incorporated to date.[1832]

4. SCOPE OF THE POWER

If India were to recognise the tribunal's power to order security for costs in the IAA, even then the scope of the power ought to be confined to 'exceptional circumstances'.[1833] The power should not be one of unfettered and unqualified discretion.[1834] It should be used only when it is shown that it is necessary for the reasonable protection of the respondent.[1835] It should not be exercised if it limits a party's

1826. *Vinod Seth v. Devinder Bajaj* (2010) 8 SCC 1, ¶28 as consistently held in a line of cases such as *Padam Sen v. State of UP* AIR 1961 SC 218, ¶¶ 8-9; *Manohar Lal Chopra v. Rai Bahadur Rao Raja Seth Hiralal* AIR 1962 SC 527, ¶21; *Ram Chand and Sons Sugar Mills (P) Ltd. v. Kanhayalal Bhargava* AIR 1966 SC 1899; *Nain Singh v. Koonwarjee* (1970) 1 SCC 732, ¶4.
1827. Indian Code of Civil Procedure, 1908, Ss 35-A & 35-B.
1828. *Ibid.*, Ord. XXV.
1829. *Ibid.*, S. 95.
1830. *Vinod Seth v. Devinder Bajaj* (2010) 8 SCC 1, ¶ 33.
1831. Singapore International Arbitration Act, 1994, S. 12(1)(a); Singapore Domestic Arbitration Act, 2001, S. 28(2)(a); Ireland Arbitration Act, 2010, S. 19; Hong Kong Arbitration Ordinance (Cap.609), S. 40; Jamaican Arbitration Act, 2017, S. 25; International Arbitration Act, 1974, S. 23(K); Commercial Arbitration Act, 2011, S. 17 E; Brunei International Arbitration Order, 2009 S. 20; Fiji International Arbitration Act, 2017, S. 28; *See Appendix B.*
1832. Government of India, Ministry of Law and Justice – Proposed Amendments to the Arbitration & Conciliation Act, 1996: A Consultation Paper, available at: https://www.legallyindia.com /images/stories/docs/Arbitration-Act-LawMin-ConsultationPaper-on-Arb-Act-April2010-1. pdf.
1833. Alastair Henderson, *Security for Costs in Arbitration in Singapore*, 7(1) Asian Int'l Arb. J. 54, 66 (2011).
1834. *Calico P. A. Ld. v. Jeevanram*, 40 CWN 511, 513 .c.f. Sarkar, *supra* n. 302, at 2202.
1835. Sarkar, *supra* n. 302, at 2202.

ability to present its case[1836] or effectively prevent the claimant from pursuing its claim.[1837]

A contracting party typically bears the risk of having a dispute and the risk of the counterparty going out of business. The risk of one party going out of business is always present at the time of entering into a contract. Therefore, unless the circumstances changed materially and unforeseeably since the execution,[1838] an application for security for costs is not justified.[1839] Similarly, if the financial position of the claimant is poor due to the very actions of the defendants, then a request for security for costs should be denied.[1840]

Even when such a measure is granted, an order for security for costs must only require security for payment of costs incurred or likely to be incurred. It cannot extend to an undertaking to pay damages to the respondent in the event the claim is unsuccessful as damages cannot be assessed or quantified on a threatened breach while the arbitration is still pending.[1841] Therefore, the standards to be adopted when considering an application for security become crucial.

5. STANDARDS

It has been suggested that an interim measure for security for costs demands its own mechanism and requirements because it is very different from an ordinary interim measure.[1842] Questions of prima facie case and irreparable harm are not the focus while considering such applications.[1843] *Born* states that the focus is more on (a) the financial state of the party from whom the security is requested; (b) the extent of third-party funding; and (c) difficulties in enforcing a final award.[1844]

For example, Article 33(6) of the VIAC Rules 2018 provides that the respondent must show that the recoverability of a potential claim for costs is, with a sufficient degree of probability, at risk. Similarly, interpreting Order XXV of the CPC, an Indian court has held that the court should be '*satisfied that there is no resource to recover the cost incurred or likely to be incurred by the defendant*'.[1845]

However, *Bunni* suggests that the standards used for ordinary interim measures may not be completely irrelevant as the tribunal must apply equitable principles.[1846]

1836. Waincymer, *supra* n. 989, at 645.
1837. *Aquila Design (GRP Products) Ltd. v. Cornhill Insurance plc* 1987 WL 492061, at 365.
1838. CIArb's International Arbitration Practice Guidelines on Applications for Security for Costs 2015, Art. 3.
1839. *ICC Case 7047, Final Award (1996)* XXI Yearbook of Commercial Arbitration 79, 1994.
1840. *Peppered & Co. Ltd. v. Bogoff* [1962] (IR) 180; *SEE Company Ltd. v. Public Lightening Services Ltd.* [1987] ILRM 255.
1841. *The court had expressed this view in the context of Order XXV of the CPC and not in an arbitration proceeding, but the same is equally valid in the context of arbitration, see Vinod Seth v. Devinder Bajaj* (2010) 8 SCC 1, ¶ 26.
1842. Waincymer, *supra* n. 989, at 647.
1843. ICCA-Queen Mary Task Force, *supra* n. 1795, at 171.
1844. Gary Born, *supra* n. 33, at 2680.
1845. *New Machine Co. Ltd. v. SB Air Controls Pvt. Ltd.* 2009 SCC OnLine Del 335 *decision dated 13 February 2009 in* I.A. No. 6532 of 2006 in CS (OS) No. 493 of 2006, ¶11.
1846. Bunni, *supra* n. 690, at 599.

The question of '*reasonable possibility of success*' is altered to the existence of a potential, a future claim for reimbursement of costs worthy of protection, i.e., that the applicant has a good title to a claim for reimbursement in case the award is in its favour.[1847] Even if the claimant has a bona fide chance of success, the consideration relevant to determining the application for security for costs would be whether the claimant would be impecunious at the time of the award for costs, if the respondent succeeds in the arbitration proceedings.[1848] Essentially, the possibility is looked at in reverse. The less likely the chances of success of the claim, the higher the need for protection of the potential costs award in favour of the respondent.[1849] Likewise, the question of 'harm' is modified to immediate danger of being deprived of the claim for costs, i.e., a reasonable degree of certainty that the applicant would suffer irreparable harm if the application were to be rejected.[1850]

National arbitration statutes that now provide the power of the tribunal to grant security for costs, however, do not lay down any standard[1851] probably because the ordinary standards applicable to interim measures are intended to apply to such applications as well. England and Singapore have adopted a slightly different solution.[1852] Instead of laying down any clear standard, it specifically mentions that the power should not be exercised only by virtue of nationality or residence of a party.

In *Parkinson and Co. v. Triplan Ltd.*,[1853] the England and Wales Court of Appeal laid down the criteria in connection with security for costs, i.e., (a) is the claimant's claim bona fide and not a sham?; (b) does the claimant have a reasonably good prospect of success?; (c) is there an admission by the respondents on the pleadings or elsewhere that the liability of the respondents exists?; (d) is the application for security for costs being used oppressively to try and stifle a genuine claim?; (e) is the claimant's pure financial circumstances or the result of the conduct by the respondent, such as a delay in payment or a delay in doing its own part of the contractual agreement?

It should be noted that this case was decided before the enactment of the English Arbitration Act, 1996 and the standards discussed were in the context of the power of the court to grant security for costs. The power has now expressly been vested with the tribunal in Section 38(3) of the English Arbitration Act. Despite that, the standards discussed above serve as useful guidance in the context of commercial arbitration.

A similar criterion is provided in the Guidelines issued by the CIArb, which provide the following test:[1854]

1847. Bernhard, *supra* n. 1785, at 10-11.
1848. *Aquila Design (GRP Products) Ltd. v. Cornhill Insurance plc* 1987 WL 492061.
1849. Waincymer, *supra* n. 989, at 647.
1850. Bernhard, *supra* n. 1785, at 11.
1851. English Arbitration Act, 1996, S. 38(3); Hong Kong Arbitration Ordinance (Cap.609), S. 2GB(1)(a); Singapore International Arbitration Act, 1994, S. 12(1).
1852. Otto Sandrock, *The Cautio Judicatum Solvi in Arbitration Proceedings or The Duty of an Alien Claimant to Provide Security for the Costs of the Defendant*, 14(2) J. Int'l Arb. 22 (1997); *Bestfort Developments LLP v. Ras Al Khaimah Investment Authority*, [2016] EWCA Civ 1099.
1853. *Parkinson and Co. v. Triplan Ltd.* [1973] 1 Queen's Bench 609, 626.
1854. CIArb's International Arbitration Practice Guidelines on Applications for Security for Costs 2015, Art. 1(2).

(a) the prospects of success of the claim(s) and defence(s);[1855]
(b) the ability of the claimant to satisfy an adverse costs award and the availability of assets for enforcement of an adverse costs award;[1856]
(c) whether it is fair in all of the circumstances to require one party to provide security for the other party's costs.[1857]

An alternative standard is suggested by *Bunni* and *Goeler*[1858] from an ICC Arbitration:[1859]

> It would be appropriate for the tribunal to exercise its discretion to make an order for security for costs:
> i) If the respondent, which has requested that such an order be addressed to the claimants, can show:
>   a. That the factual situation at the present time is substantially different from that which existed at the time the parties entered into their arbitration convention, and
>   b. That the present situation is of such a nature as to render it highly unfair to require it to conduct an arbitration proceeding without the benefit of such security.
> ii) Unless the claimants, which oppose the making of an order for security for costs, can show
>   a. That the making of such order for security for costs would in effect deny their right or access to arbitration for reasons not attributable to them, and
>   b. That, after having weighed the parties respective interest considering both the subject matter of the dispute and circumstances giving rise to the requests for an order for security for costs, the making of such order would appear to be highly unfair to claimants.

This test used in the ICC arbitration takes a balanced approach and safeguards the interest of both parties. Further, the considerations under (i) above or under the CIArb guidelines are not vastly different from the standards suggested under Chapter 7. The test 'reasonable possibility of success' would entail a possibility of success of the defence of the respondent or that the applicant has a good title to a claim for reimbursement in case the award is in its favour.[1860] The phrase '*is threatened to be infringed by the party against whom the measure is requested*', read with the incorporation of Article 17(2)(c) of the Model Law, would lead to the conclusion that '*assets out of which a subsequent award may be satisfied*' are threatened and hence, deserve protection.

Similarly, the considerations under clause (ii) are considerations very similar to the '*the harm likely to result if the measure is not ordered substantially outweighs the harm that is likely to result to the party against whom the measure is directed if the measure is granted*'. Such an assessment will inevitably comprise considerations of

1855. *Ibid.*, Art. 2.
1856. *Ibid.*, Art. 3.
1857. *Ibid.*, Art. 4.
1858. Goeler, *supra* n. 1781, at 335.
1859. Bunni, *supra* n. 690, at 600-601.
1860. Bernhard, *supra* n. 1785, at 10-11.

enforceability of the award, commercial standing of the parties at the time of the contract, the current financial state of the party from whom the security is requested, and the extent of third-party funding.[1861]

Waincymer summarises six factors referred to in the CIArb Guidelines:[1862] (a) reachable assets of the claimant in the jurisdiction; (b) the application being used as a weapon to block a legitimate claim; (c) the conduct of the applicant in contributing to the claimant's lack of means; (d) the timing of the application; (e) appropriateness of the security determination for the specific nature of arbitration; and (f) equitable concerns in light of all circumstances that should be considered when deciding an application for security for costs. The modifications proposed to Article 17A of the Model Law in Chapter 7 would apply to these factors or considerations as suggested by the CIArb Guidelines in the following manner:

(a) Reasonable Possibility of Success:
  (i) Jurisdiction of the tribunal.
  (ii) Relative Merits of the Case.
(b) A Right is Threatened To Be Infringed:
  (i) Financial Circumstances.
  (ii) Third-Party Funding.
  (iii) Nationality or Residence.
  (iv) Enforceability.
  (v) Time.
(c) Harm:
  (i) Balancing of Interests.
  (ii) Conduct of the Parties.

5.1. Reasonable Possibility of Success

While determining the reasonable possibility of success on merits of the claim, the tribunal is required to first decide its jurisdiction. A request for security for costs is usually made at the beginning of the arbitration proceedings, even before there is a ruling on a jurisdiction by the tribunal.[1863] Even though the tribunal may grant security for costs pending a ruling on jurisdiction,[1864] the more pragmatic view is that the tribunal should determine at least prima facie jurisdiction.[1865] Once the same is determined, the tribunal should consider whether it is sufficiently authorised to order

1861. Commentary on Art. 1(1), CIArb's International Arbitration Practice Guidelines on Applications for Security for Costs 2015. *This makes reference to the Guideline for Interim Measures issued by the institute and provides that the same shall be equally applicable to an application for security for costs.*
1862. CIArb's International Arbitration Practice Guidelines on Applications for Security for Costs 2015.
1863. Commentary on Art. 1.a.(1), *Ibid.*
1864. Bernhard, *supra* n. 1785, at 15.
1865. Commentary on Art. 2, paragraph 1, CIArb's Guidelines for Interim Measures; *ICC Case 12361 (2003)*, (2011) ICC Bull., Special Supplement: Interim, Conservatory and Emergency Measures in ICC Arbitration, 22, at 61.

security for costs in light of the arbitration agreement, arbitration rules and *lex arbitri*.[1866]

After that, the tribunal should determine whether the defence of the respondent is a reasonable one. The arbitral tribunal should not prejudge or predetermine the merits of the case but should take a preliminary view of the relative merits of the case,[1867] i.e., whether there is a prima facie claim made in good faith and a prima facie defence made in good faith.[1868] Therefore, the determination should be restricted to a prima facie view of the defence and not the entire merits of the case. If the defence is one which may (and not certainly) be one where there exists 'a reasonable possibility of success', the tribunal should consider other circumstances as well. If not, it should reject the application for security for costs.

Hence, the reasoning that the traditional standards applied in case of interim measures should not be extended to an application for security for costs,[1869] as it would result in a summary judgment by prejudging the merits[1870] may not be entirely correct. If the tribunal takes only a prima facie view of the defence raised by the respondent or the simple determination that there is a reasonable possibility of the impecuniosity of the claimant. *Waincymer* suggests that to prevent prejudgment of the merits, the applications should be dealt with by a discrete person.[1871] The same may not be feasible as it would raise costs, lead to a delegation of the power of the tribunal, and a possible challenge to the award.

5.2. A Right Is Threatened to Be Infringed

The critical consideration in an application for security for costs is the financial health or financial circumstances of the claimant. Article 3 of the CIArb Guidelines requires consideration of the availability of funds with the claimant to pay the costs awarded, the availability of assets and the possibility of effective enforcement against them.[1872]

The consideration while determining the financial position of the claimant should be whether the financial condition is materially different,[1873] or there is a fundamental change of situation[1874] from the inception of the relationship of the parties,[1875]

1866. Commentary on Art. 1.a. (2), CIArb's International Arbitration Practice Guidelines on Applications for Security for Costs 2015; Commentary on Art. 1, paragraph 3 of the CIArb's Guidelines for Interim Measures.
1867. CIArb's International Arbitration Practice Guidelines on Applications for Security for Costs 2015, Art. 2.
1868. Commentary on Art. 2.a., CIArb's International Arbitration Practice Guidelines on Applications for Security for Costs 2015.
1869. Gary Born, *supra* n. 33, at 2679.
1870. Waincymer, *supra* n. 989, at 649; *In ICC Case No. 6632 the tribunal denied a request for security for costs because it would have led to prejudging of the merits*. Ali Yesilirmak, *supra* n. 30, at 184.
1871. Waincymer, *supra* n. 989, at 650.
1872. CIArb's International Arbitration Practice Guidelines on Applications for Security for Costs 2015, Art. 3.1.
1873. Alastair, *supra* n. 1833, at 72-75.
1874. *Ibid.*
1875. Commentary on Art. 3.b., CIArb's International Arbitration Practice Guidelines on Applications for Security for Costs 2015.

i.e., the applicant must show that the possibility of the claimant honouring a potential costs award has substantially and commercially deteriorated since the conclusion of the agreement and that such deterioration was not commercially foreseeable.[1876]

While considering such facts, the tribunal should first determine why has there been a material change. If the financial health has been affected in a manner that is not commercially unusual[1877] or if it was an accepted consequence of doing business with the party,[1878] then security for costs should not be ordered. If a party's lack of funds is because the respondent to the application for security for costs (the claimant in the arbitration proceedings) has deliberately organised its affairs in such a way as to hide its assets or has been given wrong information about them or has taken any steps to frustrate a future costs award, then the tribunal ought to consider it.[1879]

Often the consideration of the financial circumstances of a party can involve a complex analysis of a company's actual position and also involve contests about highly confidential material and any degree of arbitrariness in making the order would entail immediate damage to the parties subject to it.[1880] The difficulty is that the key data relating to the financial position of the claimant is with the claimant itself and not with the respondent seeking security. Thus, the respondent has to rely on commentary and rumour in the financial press. Further, the respondent has to engage in projections over the likely time period of the arbitration.[1881]

Tribunals have to be cautious while considering the financial circumstances. The threshold of financial distress or impecuniosity of a party should be higher than just a 'reasonable probability', especially when such determination is being made on the basis of projections. An arbitral tribunal should preferably use the standard of 'most likely' instead. Thus, if it is 'most likely' that a costs award will not be satisfied, a tribunal should order security for costs, subject to other considerations and overall circumstances of the case.

Such a consideration would fall within the broad language of '*that a right has been infringed or is threatened to be infringed by the party against whom the measure is requested*'. The phrase 'most likely' is similar to 'is threatened'. Hence, if the satisfaction of a costs award 'is threatened,' an application for security for costs should be allowed. Such determination would also permit the assessment of third-party funding of arbitrations (discussed below).

1876. Weixia, *supra* n. 1800, at 187, 189.
1877. *In Switzerland, the request for security for costs has been turned down even when the opposite party has applied for voluntary liquidation. The tribunal was of the view that voluntary liquidation is a normal commercial risk. CISG Arbitration dated 25 September 1997; ICC Arbitration dated 19 December 2003*; *Even where assets were sufficient despite bankruptcy. Ad-Hoc Arbitration dated 27 November 2002*. In contrast, when the bankruptcy was not voluntary, security for costs was ordered. *Ad-Hoc Arbitration dated 21 December 1998* c.f. *B* Bernhard, *supra* n. 1785, at 9; Waincymer, *supra* n. 989, at 650.
1878. Commentary on Art. 3.b, CIArb's International Arbitration Practice Guidelines on Applications for Security for Costs 2015.
1879. Commentary on Art. 3.c, *Ibid.*
1880. Waincymer, *supra* n. 989, at 650.
1881. *Ibid.*

The consideration of a right being infringed or is threatened to be infringed would also address examination of the facts with respect to the nationality of parties, the possibility of enforcement and the urgency of the measure. While the nationality[1882] or residence of parties should be irrelevant as it would lead to discrimination of foreign parties,[1883] a degree of connection to the seat might still be relevant[1884] in considering enforceability.[1885]

It is relevant to ascertain the possibility of enforcement of a costs award,[1886] especially if it would be more difficult or uncertain than would normally be expected.[1887] The tribunal has to balance the fact the respondent knew the location of the assets and the possibility of enforcement at the time of entering into the contract versus new circumstances such as deliberate moving of assets to a location or exchange control rules.[1888] Therefore, the tribunal has to consider whether the lack of possibility of enforcement would, in effect threaten the infringement of the right to have a costs award executed. However, concerns related to the public policy of the place of the *lex fori* should not be given too much importance since the tribunal can take resort to other measures such as suspension or termination of the proceedings if an order for security for costs is not complied with.[1889]

Further, to determine whether the right is infringed, or is threatened to be infringed, the tribunal would consider the time at which such application is made. An application for security for costs should be made as soon as the risk or facts giving rise to the application are known or ought to have been known.[1890] A failure to make a request for security at the earliest opportunity can be considered a waiver of the right,[1891] or the tribunal may order security for future costs only.[1892]

1882. Jean Kalicki, *Security for Costs in International Arbitration,* 1 Trans. Dis. Mgmt 5 (2006); Micha Bühler, *supra* n. 1771, at 2585; English Arbitration Act, 1996, S. 38(3) and Singapore International Arbitration Act, 1994, S. 12(4).
1883. CIArb's International Arbitration Practice Guidelines on Applications for Security for Costs 2015, Art. 3.
1884. *Coppee-Lavalin SA/NV Ken-Ren Chemicals and Fertilisers Ltd.* [1995] 1 AC 38 (HL), ¶68; *Bank Mellat v. Hellinki Techniki SA* [1983] 3 All ER 428.
1885. Commentary on Art. 3.g., CIArb's International Arbitration Practice Guidelines on Applications for Security for Costs 2015; Waincymer, *supra* n. 989, at 650.
1886. *Coppee-Lavalin SA/NV Ken-Ren Chemicals and Fertilisers Ltd.* [1995] 1 AC 38 (HL), '*In principle, the fact that a party is domiciled outside the arbitral seat, or has its assets abroad, should not be grounds for denying security. That is because of the generally liberal international regime for recognition and enforcement of foreign arbitral awards. However, if a party is domiciled or has its assets in a state that is not a party to the New York Convention (or a similar international agreement), then the case for security for costs relief is materially enhanced.*'
1887. Commentary on Art. 3.g., CIArb's International Arbitration Practice Guidelines on Applications for Security for Costs 2015.
1888. Waincymer, *supra* n. 989, at 651.
1889. Micha Bühler, *supra* n. 1771, at 2578; Melissa, *supra* n. 1690, at 709.
1890. Commentary on Art. 4.c., CIArb's International Arbitration Practice Guidelines on Applications for Security for Costs 2015.
1891. Waincymer, *supra* n. 989, at 651.
1892. Commentary on Art. 4.d. of the CIArb's International Arbitration Practice Guidelines on Applications for Security for Costs 2015.

5.3. Harm

After establishing jurisdiction, another consideration should be meeting the *ex-ante* expectation of the parties and the relative harm to the parties.[1893] The tribunal must strive to match procedure and substance with what the parties intended. It should also ensure equal treatment of the parties[1894] and that both parties are given a fair opportunity to present their case.[1895] The tribunal ought to balance the right of a party to pursue its claim against the right of an opposing party to recover the costs of a defence that defeats the claim,[1896] i.e., a party should not be barred from bringing a claim in arbitration simply because it may not have the fund to pay an adverse costs award.[1897]

Very often the party seeking security for costs is at least in part responsible for the counterparty's financial condition.[1898] In such cases, an order for security for costs would amount to adding insult to injury and should be denied.[1899] If a party has deliberately dissipated assets or assigned its rights with a view to defeat the enforcement of the award, then security should be ordered.[1900] An ordinary act of change of residence or routine business decision should not, however, be considered an act of bad faith.[1901] Another similar factor relevant for consideration is the attitude of the claimant to pay the costs voluntarily.[1902]

The tribunal should keep in mind the oppressive nature of an order for security for costs. A party may use it as a weapon to stave off consideration of the dispute. Therefore, the tribunal should consider whether the respondent is acting in good faith, including in paying its contribution to advances.[1903] Since it is difficult to determine the intent of the respondent at the time of making the application,[1904] the tribunal should consider the conduct, both before and during the course of the proceedings and all of the surrounding circumstances to determine whether it would be fair to require security.[1905]

1893. Weixia, *supra* n. 1800, at 171; *See* Indian Arbitration Act, 1996, S. 18, and UNCITRAL Model Law, Art. 18.
1894. UNCITRAL Model Law, Art. 18.
1895. Commentary on Art. 1.a. (3), CIArb's International Arbitration Practice Guidelines on Applications for Security for Costs 2015.
1896. William Kirtley & Koralie Wietrzykowski, *Should an Arbitral Tribunal Order Security for Costs When an Impecunious Claimant Is Relying upon Third-Party Funding*, 30(1) J. Int'l Arb. 17, 22 (2013).
1897. A. Bucher & P. Tschanz, *International Arbitration in Switzerland* (1988), ¶161, c.f. Gary Born, *supra* n. 33, at 2680; Waincymer, *supra* n. 989, at 647.
1898. *Suncare Constructions Australia Pty Ltd. v. Gainspace Mackay Pty Ltd.* [2016] QSC 67; *Ibid.*
1899. Micha Bühler, *supra* n. 1771, at 2583.
1900. *Higher Regional Court of Düsseldorf, Judgment of 18 February 2015, VI-U (Kart) 3/14, U (Kart) 3/14.*; Bernhard, *supra* n. 1785, at 13.
1901. *Ibid.*, 13-15.
1902. Waincymer, *supra* n. 989, at 650.
1903. Commentary on Art. 4.e., CIArb's International Arbitration Practice Guidelines on Applications for Security for Costs 2015; Waincymer, *supra* n. 989, at 651.
1904. Waincymer, *supra* n. 989, at 651.
1905. '*(a) conduct before, as well as during, the proceedings and in particular the extent to which the parties followed the relevant pre-action protocol;(b) whether it was reasonable for a party to raise, pursue or contest a particular allegation or issue; (c) the manner in which a party has*

A caveat in considering the conduct of the parties is that even where it can be shown that the respondent's behaviour was the cause of the financial condition of the claimant, that very behaviour may be the substance of the dispute as to whether it was valid contractual behaviour or otherwise and may lead to prejudging the merits.[1906] Thus, the tribunal should consider the overall circumstances before deciding on an application for security for costs. The respondent should not derive any advantage from its own wrongdoing. In such cases, greater injustice would be caused to the claimant if security for costs is ordered against the injustice to the respondent if the same is not.[1907]

6. THIRD-PARTY FUNDING

A more difficult issue pertaining to the assessment of potential infringement of the right to recover costs and relative harm is when the claimant has obtained third-party funding.[1908] Essentially, where its legal costs are paid in whole or part by a professional funder who will usually be repaid only in the event of success.

One view is that since a party appears to lack assets to satisfy a final costs award but is pursuing claims in an arbitration with the funding of a third party, it is per se impecunious.[1909] The need for and reliance on third-party funding amounts to a fundamental change[1910] from the inception of the relationship of the parties and could not have been anticipated from the beginning.[1911] Therefore, a strong prima facie case for the security for costs exists[1912] and the mere presence of the third-party funder

pursued or defended his case or a particular allegation or issue; and (d) whether a claimant who has succeeded in his claim, in whole or in part, exaggerated his claim.' Referring to the English Civil Procedure Rules which have received judicial recognition in India in Vinod Seth v. Devinder Bajaj (2010) 8 SCC 1, *albeit with appropriate modifications. Shin Satellite Public Co. Ltd. v. Jain Studios Ltd.* 2008 SCC OnLine Del 1127, ¶50; *RSM Production Corp. v. Santa Lucia, Decision on Saint Lucia's Request for Security for Costs in ICSID Case No. ARB/12/10 of 13 August 2014,* ¶86, *where the claimant was a repeat offender who had failed to pay arbitration costs in the past*; Commentary on Art. 4.a., CIArb's International Arbitration Practice Guidelines on Applications for Security for Costs 2015.

1906. Commentary on Art. 4.b., CIArb's International Arbitration Practice Guidelines on Applications for Security for Costs 2015; Waincymer, *supra* n. 989, at 651.

1907. Bunni, *supra* n. 690, at 600.

1908. *Many countries have recognised third-party funding arrangements, i.e., Australia, the United Kingdom (U.K.), about three-quarters of the United States (U.S.), Canada, New Zealand, the Netherlands, Germany, South Africa, Hong Kong (in international arbitration only, not domestic litigation), and Singapore (in international arbitration only, not domestic litigation)*; *See* Lisa Bench Nieuwveld & Victoria Shannon Sahani, *Third-Party Funding in International Arbitration* (2017).

1909. ICCA-Queen Mary Task Force, *supra* n. 1795, at 174.

1910. *X v. Y and Z, (ICC Case) Procedural Order (3 August 2012)* at 171, published in Philippe Pinsolle, *Third Party Funding and Security for Costs*, Cahiers de L'Arbitrage 399, 416 (2013), c.f. Arne Fuchs & Lisa Richman, *Chapter II: The Arbitration Agreement and Arbitrability, Third-Party Funding in International Arbitration: A Comparative Analysis*, in Christian Klausegger & Peter Klein, et al. (eds), *Austrian Yearbook on International Arbitration* 76 (2020).

1911. Waincymer, *supra* n. 989, at 650.

1912. *Swiss Entity v. Dutch Entity* HKZ Case No. 415, Award, 20 November 2001, 20 ASA Bulletin 467–71 (2002) c.f. Nadia, *supra* n. 1783, at 150; *RSM Production Corp. v. Santa Lucia, Decision on Saint Lucia's Request for Security for Costs in ICSID Case No. ARB/12/10 of 13 August 2014,* ¶86.

should require the posting of security since the third-party funder is not a party to the arbitration.[1913] Moreover, the funder would have contemplated the possibility of bearing the costs.[1914]

While some tribunals and courts have agreed with this view,[1915] others have not.[1916] The danger in accepting this view is that the non-funded party may routinely use this assumption to submit applications for security for costs to delay and deliberately increase the costs of the resolution of meritorious claims. Hence, the mere possibility that someone is financing the arbitration is not sufficient for security to be ordered.[1917]

Article 3(2)c) of the CIArb Guidelines provides that the tribunal ought to take into account the beneficiary of the claim, i.e., whether the claimant is a nominal claimant pursuing a claim for the benefit of another party, who does have funds,[1918] and who has a commercial interest in the outcome of the arbitration. Additional factors should include an assignment of arbitral rights,[1919] accepted business risk, who actually controls the proceedings, and whether the person or entity who stands to benefit if the claimant wins seeks to escape the liability and avoid paying any adverse costs.

Effectively, if a party has become manifestly insolvent and is relying on funds from third parties, then the right to have access to arbitral justice can only be granted when such third parties are also ready and willing to secure the costs of the opposite party.[1920] However, such a view is very simplistic and does not adequately address concerns of lack of jurisdiction over third parties. Hence, the standards to be applied in the context of an application for security for costs when the claimant is being funded by a third party become crucial.

6.1. Standards to Apply When There Is Third-Party Funding

The accepted position, even in the Indian context,[1921] is that the mere use of third-party funding should not be taken to suggest material deterioration of the claimant's finances[1922] and the situation of the funded party should be considered as a whole[1923]

1913. Kirtley, *supra* n. 1896, at 28; Blackby, *supra* n. 34, at 317.
1914. *Arkin v. Borchard Lines* [2005] EWCA Civ 655, ¶45.
1915. *Guaracachi America, Inc. and Rurelec plc v. Plurinational State of Bolivia*, Procedural Order No. 14, PCA Case No. 2011-17, 11 March 2013; ZCC Case No. 415, dated 20 November 2001 c.f. Bernhard, *supra* n. 1785, at 9.
1916. *Strazdins v. ANZ Banking Group Ltd.* [2017] SASC 33; *RSM Production Corp. v. Santa Lucia, Decision on Saint Lucia's Request for Security for Costs in ICSID Case No. ARB/12/10 of 13 August 2014*, ¶86.
1917. *Intertoll ICS Cecons O & M Co. Pvt. Ltd. v. National Highways Authority of India* 2013 SCC OnLine Del 447, ¶39; Sarkar, *supra* n. 302, at 2203.
1918. *Progas Energy Ltd. v. The Islamic Republic of Pakistan* [2018] 1 Costs LR 137, 171.
1919. Waincymer, *supra* n. 989, at 644.
1920. *X S.A.R.L., Lebanon (Claimant) v. Y A.G., Germany, Case Report, ICC Case, Procedural Order No. 3 of 4 July 2008*, 28(1) ASA Bull. (2010), 37-45, c.f. Bernhard, *supra* n. 1785, at 12.
1921. *Intertoll ICS Cecons O & M Co. Pvt. Ltd. v. National Highways Authority of India* 2013 SCC OnLine Del 447, ¶39.
1922. ICCA-Queen Mary Task Force, *supra* n. 1795, at 341.
1923. Goeler, *supra* n. 1781, at 342.

irrespective of any funding arrangement on the basis of *inter alia* impecuniousness.[1924] The ICCA-Queen Mary Task Force on Third-Party Funding in International Arbitration laid down the following criteria for consideration of Third-Party Funding in connection with an application for security for costs:[1925]

(a) The application for security for costs should be determined on the basis of the applicable test without consideration of third-party funding.
(b) The terms of any funding arrangement may be relevant if relied upon to establish that the opposite party can meet any adverse costs award.[1926]

The Task Force recommended the use of a 'broader fairness' test[1927] and whether the funder has undertaken to finance any adverse costs.[1928] There should be a connection between the funding and costs sought to be recovered.[1929] However, such a connection can only be determined if the funding arrangement is disclosed to the tribunal.

The view that an application for security for costs should be considered without consideration of third-party funding makes the standards proposed in Chapter 7 equally applicable to an application for security for costs. Even, if such funding were to be present, the tribunal can take recourse to the generic language of whether the right of the respondent to realise the costs award is threatened and consider the harm likely to result if the application for security for costs is granted or not based on the funder's agreement with respect to costs.

6.2. Disclosure of Third-Party Funding Arrangements

It should be noted that there is no obligation on the funded party to disclose facts related to the funded agreements *sua sponte*. Though a request for disclosure of the identity of the funder may be maintainable. The party requesting disclosure must reasonably specify the funding agreement, substantiate which terms of the agreements

1924. ICCA-Queen Mary Task Force, *supra* n. 1795, at 183; *A similar view was taken in Intertoll ICS Cecons O & M Co. Pvt. Ltd. v. National Highways Authority of India* 2013 SCC OnLine Del 447, ¶39.
1925. ICCA-Queen Mary Task Force, *supra* n. 1795, at 171.
1926. *Ibid.*, at 145.
1927. *Ibid.*, at 174.
1928. *Ibid.*, at 176.
1929. *In re RBS Rights Issue Litigation*, [2017] EWHC 1217 (Ch). The court laid down the following test: '*(i) it is succinctly clear that the funder is to be treated as having in effect become a real party motivated to participate by its commercial interest in the litigation, since commercial litigation funding carried out as a business for profit is likely to be viewed differently from a pure funder acting altruistically to enable access to justice and what it perceives to be a worthwhile case to be adjudicated; (ii) there is a real and not a fanciful risk that a costs award in the defendant's favour will not be satisfied; (iii) there is a sufficient link between the funding and the costs for which recovery is sought; (iv) the risk of liability for costs has sufficiently been brought home, either by express warning, or by reference to what a person in that position should be taken to appreciate as to the inherent risk; and (v) there are other factors, including delay in the making of the application for security or likely adverse effects, such as to tip the overall balance against making an order.*' ¶¶19-31, ¶¶33-36, ¶¶40-45, ¶¶145-146, ¶148.

will be relevant and material to its request and also overcome potential privilege defences.[1930]

The scope of such an investigation should stem from the claimant apparently neither possessing significant internal funds nor having an ongoing business but arbitrating as if it was perfectly solvent.[1931] Thus, the party requesting security for costs should make out a prima facie case of impecuniousness of the claimant[1932] and only subsequently should be allowed the opportunity to present the additional evidence of funding.

Even in such cases, the extent of disclosure should be limited. If the funder has agreed to pay the costs, then the funding arrangement, in limited parts,[1933] can be shown to the tribunal as evidence that no security is required.[1934] The disclosure should always be need-based and non-relevant and confidential parts should be withheld or redacted,[1935] or issues of confidentiality related to third-party funding may also be decided at an early-stage procedural conference.[1936] If the arrangement does not provide for the funding of an award of costs, then the tribunal may order security for costs.[1937]

6.3. Jurisdiction of the Arbitral Tribunal over the Third-Party Funder

It should be noted that the disclosure can be mandated only on the parties to the arbitration. The jurisdiction of the tribunal over a third-party funder still continues to be a grey area. In the absence of jurisdiction over a third-party funder, the respondent will neither be able to claim costs from the impecunious claimant nor from the funder.[1938] The tribunal cannot exercise jurisdiction over third parties[1939] due to the consensual nature of arbitration and the fact that the tribunal derives its authority from the arbitration agreement.[1940] Though such jurisdiction may be extended on the ground of contract law such as (a) incorporation by reference; (b) assumption; (c) agency; (d)

1930. Goeler, *supra* n. 1781, at 340; *A similar view was taken by the court in Reeves v. Sprecher* [2007] EWHC 3226 (CH) *that the court cannot order disclosure of the funding party without an application.*
1931. Goeler, *supra* n. 1781, at 340.
1932. *Abraham v. Thompson* [1997] 4 All ER 362, at 1388-1389.
1933. *The funded party, its counsel or even the funder can provide the tribunal with the witness statement or affidavit stating its identity and whether its arrangement provides for funding of the costs award.*
1934. ICCA-Queen Mary Task Force, *supra* n. 1795, at 183; *Even the termination rights will be an important criteria;* Goeler, *supra* n. 1781, at 340; *Abu-Ghazaleh v. Chaul*, 36 So. 3d 691 (Fla. Dist. Ct. App. 2009) at 694, *The Code of Conduct for Litigation Funders ¶10.1 (2014) requires the funding agreement to 'state whether (and if so to what extent)' the funder is liable to the funded party 'to meet any liability for adverse costs'.*
1935. *In re the Matter of Hellas Telecommunications (Luxembourg)* [2017] EWHC 3465 (CH); Goeler, *supra* n. 1781, at 340.
1936. Aren Goldsmith &Lorenzo Melchionda, *Everything You Ever Wanted to Know (but Were Afraid to Ask) Part Two,* Int'l Bus. L. J. 227 (2012).
1937. Arne Fuchs, *supra* n. 1910; ICCA-Queen Mary Task Force, *supra* n. 1795, at 183.
1938. Rubins, *supra* n. 1547, at 361; Kirtley, *supra* n. 1896, at 29-30.
1939. ICCA-Queen Mary Task Force, *supra* n. 1795, at 10.
1940. Commentary on Art. 3, paragraph 1, CIArb's Guidelines for Interim Measures.

veil-piercing/alter ego; and (e) estoppel,[1941] or some involvement in the performance of the contract.[1942] Jurisdiction by the tribunal may also be exercised if the funder submits to the voluntary jurisdiction of the tribunal[1943] or if the award has an effect on third parties.[1944]

It has been suggested that in India, the question of jurisdiction over third parties might be less significant since an order of the tribunal the order may be enforced under Section 17(2) of the IAA as an order of the court and a court will have jurisdiction over a third party funder. The parties may apply under Section 9 of the IAA for an order for security for costs in case of third-party funding.[1945] This cannot be a valid interpretation. It is a known and accepted principle of law that 'what cannot be done directly, cannot also be done indirectly'.[1946] Jurisdiction over third parties cannot be extended through courts as it would violate their rights and such an order would be enforced without giving the third party an opportunity for a hearing. As discussed in Chapter 3, Section 9 of the IAA can be invoked only to support the arbitral process and not otherwise.

6.4. Third-Party Funding in India

Courts in India have not yet taken a clear stand when it comes to third-party funding. While the earlier decisions of the Privy Council considered it as gambling (void on account of public policy)[1947] or *champerty*,[1948] this view changed and courts held that there was nothing illegal about such arrangements[1949] as long as third-party funding

1941. Dmytro Galagan & Patricia Živković, *If They Finance Your Claim, Will They Pay Me If I Win: Implications of Third-Party Funding on Adverse Costs Awards in International Arbitration*, Euro. Sci. J. 6 (2015), https://papers.ssrn.com/sol3/papers.cfm?abstract_id=2604048.
1942. As Pinsolle *pointed out, '[e]ven in France, where we are very generous and flexible about the involvement of third parties in arbitrations, the party must have some involvement in the contract itself – not the dispute that arises, but the performance of the contract – to become a party to the case'*
1943. Dmytro, *supra* n. 1941, at 7.
1944. Gary Born, *supra* n. 33, at 4122; Stavros L. Brekoulakis & Jonas von Goeler, *Chapter I: The Arbitration Agreement and Arbitrability, It's all about the Money: The Impact of Third-Party Funding on Costs Awards and Security for Costs in International Arbitration*, in Christian Klausegger & Peter Klein, et al. (eds), *Austrian Yearbook on International Arbitration* (2017) ¶¶9.12-9.14.
1945. Badri Srinivasan, *Scope of Jurisdiction to Award Interim Measures vis-à-vis Third Parties (Part VIII)*, (15 November 2010), available at: http://practicalacademic.blogspot.com/2010/11/scope-of-jurisdiction-to-award-interim_15.html; Badri, *supra* n. 726, at 641.
1946. *Manmohan Sharma v. State of Rajasthan* (2014) 5 SCC 782, ¶18.
1947. *Tara Soonduree Chowdhrain v. The Court of Wards* 20 W.R.446; *Mulla Jeffarji Tyeb Ali Saib v. Yacali Kadar Bi* 7 Madras H.C. Rep. 128.
1948. *Ram Gholam Sing v. Keerut Sing* 4 Sud. Dew. Adaw. Rep. 12; *Brijnerain Singh v. Teknerain Singh* 6 Select Rep. 131; *Musstt. Zuhooroonnissa Khanum v. Russick Lal Mitter* 6 Select Pep. 298; *Andrews v. Maharajah Sreesh Chunder Raee S.D.A.* 1849, 340.
1949. *Rattan Chand Hira Chand v. Askar Nawaz Jung* (1991) 3 SCC 67, ¶12; *In re, 'G' Senior Advocate* AIR 1954 SC 557, ¶11; *Ram Coomar Coondoo v. Chunder Canto Mookerjee* 1876 SCC OnLine PC 19 4 IA 23; *Kishen Lal Bhoonick v. Pearee Soondree* S.D.A. 1852, 394; *Panchcouree Mahtoon v. Kalee Churn* 9 Suth. W.R. 490; *Amirtamayi Dasi v. Grose* MANU/WB/0420/1869, ¶10; *Chedambara Chetty v. Renga Krishna Muttu Vira Puchaiya Naicker* Law Rep. 1 Ind. Ap. 242, 264.

was not extortionate, unconscionable or inequitable.[1950] Recently, the courts have impliedly confirmed the acceptance of third-party funding in India, as long as the lawyers are not funding the litigation.[1951] This view has now been accepted in the context of arbitration as well.[1952]

Even legislative amendments by States have either incorporated a specific power under Order XXV to implead and demand security from third persons[1953] since the financer would effectively step in the shoes of the plaintiff[1954] or require security when there are elements of champerty or maintenance.[1955] Therefore, the argument that financing of litigation is contrary to public policy would be of little significance since there is a clear legislative intent to recognise such arrangements. Moreover, the implied acceptance from the judiciary also recognises the possibility of third-party funding.

However, various issues need to be addressed in the context of arbitration and security for costs before third-party funding can be effective in India. First, there is no jurisdiction over a third-party funder in the absence of privity of contract. Therefore, the tribunal cannot pass orders against the third-party funder. Even the party to the arbitration proceeding may not be in a position to compel the funder to do anything.

Second, though Section 17(1) of the IAA does not use restrictive language referring to a 'party' only, such as that contained in Germany and England,[1956] the language used under Section 31-A of the IAA restricts the costs regime to a 'party' only. Therefore, without any legislative amendment, the tribunal cannot hold a third-party funder liable for costs, unless an approach of inherent jurisdiction is adopted or the reference is made to the amended Order XXV of the CPC (as adopted by some States) providing for jurisdiction over third party funder. Even if such an extended interpretation were to be adopted, it is unclear if that would stand the challenge to the award on the grounds of excessive jurisdiction, albeit not being contrary to public policy.

Third, with the adoption of the IBA Guidelines on Conflict of Interest in Schedule 5 and 7 of the IAA, questions of independence and impartiality will have to be addressed, and fourth, after the 2019 Amendment, issues of confidentiality[1957] will have to be overcome.

1950. *Pannalal Gendalal v. Thansing Appaji* 1948 SCC OnLine MP 56, ¶8.
1951. *'In India, funding of litigation by advocates is not explicitly prohibited, but a conjoint reading of Rule 18 (fomenting litigation), Rule 20 (contingency fees), Rule 21 (share or interest in an actionable claim) and Rule 22 (participating in bids in execution, etc.) would strongly suggest that advocates in India cannot fund litigation on behalf of their clients. There appears to be no restriction on third parties (non-lawyers) funding the litigation and getting repaid after the outcome of the litigation.' Bar Council of India v. A.K. Balaji* (2018) 5 SCC 379, ¶38.
1952. *Jayaswal Ashoka Infrastructure (P) Ltd. v. Pansare Lawad Sallagar* 2019 SCC OnLine Bom 578, ¶13.
1953. Economic Law Practice, *Arbitration in India: Curated View*, (2019), available at: https://elplaw.in/wp-content/uploads/2019/05/Arbitration-in-India-curated-views.pdf, at 56.
1954. Bombay High Court Notification P 0102/77, vide Maharashtra Gazette, 4ka, at 420, (15 September 1983); Indian Code of Civil Procedure, 1908, Ord. XXV, R. 3.
1955. Indian Code of Civil Procedure, Ord. XXV.
1956. German Arbitration Act, S. 1057(2), *the tribunal shall 'decide on the amount to be borne by each party'*; Pursuant to English Arbitration Act, 1996, S. 61(1), the tribunal *'may make an award allocating the costs of the arbitration as between the parties'* c.f. Dmytro, *supra* n. 1941, at 6.
1957. Indian Arbitration Act, 1996, S. 42A.

One view can be to permit third-party funding in India as it might reduce frivolous claims. Since third-party funders undertake extensive due diligence of a claim,[1958] a party may not be willing to pursue the claim if, after the diligence, the third-party funder refuses to fund the claim. Another view can be that such an approach may further add litigation between the funder and the funded party, giving rise to multiple litigations and adding to the burden of the courts.

A better approach would be to allow third-party funding only in the context of arbitration, as has been done in Hong Kong[1959] and Singapore.[1960] This is a more pragmatic view and was also recommended by the Sri Krishna Committee Report.[1961] Unless necessary legislative amendments are incorporated in the CPC recognising funding arrangements, it is better to allow third-party funding in the context of arbitration proceedings. It would permit genuine claimants to seek funding and legal course and also limit frivolous arbitration proceedings.

7. TYPE OF MEASURES

If the tribunal decides to grant the request for security for costs, ideally, the tribunal should invite parties to agree on the form of security, which best suits their needs.[1962] Usually, this will take the form of cash or bank guarantee,[1963] or letter of credit,[1964] payment into an escrow account or some lien over the property,[1965] parent company guarantee, bonds, insurance coverage, assignment of a financial instrument, deposit with an independent stakeholder (such as an arbitration institution), or a joint account controlled by the parties' lawyers or a provision with similar liquidity.[1966] It is suggested that the tribunal should not play any role in the handling of security.[1967]

If a guarantee is required, the time and amount for providing security must be stated.[1968] The Task Force noted that a bank guarantee is typically costly and not the most cost-efficient way of providing security for costs. Instead, it is preferable to require evidence of 'a creditworthy third party' or order payment into an escrow account.[1969]

1958. *Lisa, supra* n. 1908, at 193.
1959. Hong Kong Arbitration Ordinance (Cap.609), Part 10 A.
1960. Singapore Civil Law Act, Ss 5A-5B.
1961. Justice B.N. Srikrishna, Report of the High-Level Committee to Review the Institutionalization of Arbitration Mechanism in India, (July 2017), available at: http://legalaffairs.gov.in/sites/default/files/Report-HLC.pdf.
1962. CIArb's International Arbitration Practice Guidelines on Applications for Security for Costs 2015, Art. 5.2.
1963. Alastair, *supra* n. 1833, at 75.
1964. Bernhard, *supra* n. 1785, at 15.
1965. Waincymer, *supra* n. 989, at 652.
1966. Bernhard, *supra* n. 1785, at 15.
1967. Commentary on Art. 5.a, CIArb's International Arbitration Practice Guidelines on Applications for Security for Costs 2015.
1968. Alastair, *supra* n. 1833, at 75.
1969. ICCA-Queen Mary Task Force, *supra* n. 1795, at 183.

The tribunal should also take care that the amount is not excessive or too nominal.[1970] The security should correspond as closely as possible to the security needs of the responding party and minimise as much as possible any oppression of the claiming party.[1971] Therefore, it may be appropriate to consider security in stages and not in a lump sum.[1972]

The determination of the type of measure should also include the costs incurred to date and reasonably expected to be incurred.[1973] Legal costs already paid prior to filing the request for security for costs, should be generally excluded.[1974] The tribunal should determine the amount to be provided taking into account whether the security demanded is realistic and proportionate to the nature and complexity of the dispute, including whether the legal fees claimed are reasonable in terms of both rates and number of hours.[1975]

The issue of security for costs is best left to the arbitral tribunal[1976] and should be recorded in a reasoned procedural order.[1977] Adopting Article 17(2) of the Model Law would provide sufficient flexibility to the tribunal to order any of the measures discussed above. It is pertinent to note that an order for security for costs is a procedural order without any final and binding effect. Therefore, the order is capable of being modified, suspended or revoked in accordance with Article 17D of the Model Law[1978] and should ideally not be issued as an award since the tribunal has the power to suspend or terminate proceedings if the order is not complied with. Moreover, with the adoption of Article 17H of the Model Law, the order would be binding, irrespective of being issued as an award.

8. BURDEN OF PROOF

A request for disclosure of the financial status of the claimant will most likely be denied. Hence, the party seeking security should have some meaningful evidence before requesting security for costs.[1979] The tribunal will require a solid evidentiary basis before granting an order for security for costs,[1980] i.e., annual accounts, statutory

1970. Commentary on Art. 5.b., CIArb's International Arbitration Practice Guidelines on Applications for Security for Costs 2015.
1971. Rubins, *supra* n. 1547, at 320.
1972. Commentary on Art. 5.c., CIArb's International Arbitration Practice Guidelines on Applications for Security for Costs 2015; Neil Kaplan QC, *Interim Measures A Practical Experience*, in Albert Jan van den Berg (ed.), *International Arbitration 2006: Back to Basics?* 772 (2007).
1973. Commentary on Art. 5.c., CIArb's International Arbitration Practice Guidelines on Applications for Security for Costs 2015.
1974. Micha Bühler, *supra* n. 1771, at 2585.
1975. Commentary on Art. 5.a., CIArb's International Arbitration Practice Guidelines on Applications for Security for Costs 2015.
1976. Ali Yesilirmak, *supra* n. 30, at 86.
1977. CIArb's International Arbitration Practice Guidelines on Applications for Security for Costs 2015, Art. 5.
1978. Bernhard, *supra* n. 1785, at 11-12; Micha Bühler, *supra* n. 1771, at 2586.
1979. Waincymer, *supra* n. 989, at 653.
1980. Goeler, *supra* n. 1781, at 339.

returns, or other unpublished past and present financial reports of the claimant.[1981] Thus, the burden of proof is always on the respondent claiming security for costs[1982] and the standard of proof may range between the probability or balance of probabilities.[1983]

However, in the absence of complete information and financial records of the claimant, it is unclear how the respondent is expected to discharge this burden. Whether the respondent should only demonstrate the probability, or will the tribunal require convincing evidence that on a balance of probabilities, there will be non-payment?[1984]

Some argue that the burden should be higher in arbitration given that security discretions should not interfere with the parties' prior agreement to arbitrate.[1985] The better view is to consider the financial circumstances at the time of the dispute and the reasonable expectations of the parties at the time of entering into the arbitration agreement. If the condition of the claimant is significantly worse than the reasonable expectations of the parties at the outset[1986] and it is 'most likely' that a costs award will not be satisfied, security should be ordered.

9. RELEASE OF SECURITY

The tribunal should address the release of the security for costs in its final award,[1987] and the amount of security should be set-off against any amount payable by that party under the award to avoid double payment of costs or the same should be released.[1988]

10. SAFEGUARDS

As discussed in Chapter 7, the safeguards provided after the 2006 Model Law Revisions may be considered for an application for security for costs, depending on the facts and circumstances of each case. The most appropriate safeguard should be the mandatory disclosure of the circumstances likely to be relevant for the tribunal's determination for grant of security for costs. Such disclosure should also include the conduct of the respondent in causing the impecuniosity of the claimant if any. If the respondent does not disclose such facts, then the tribunal can terminate the measure subsequently for suppression of information.

1981. *Ibid.*
1982. Bunni, *supra* n. 690, at 599.
1983. Waincymer, *supra* n. 989, at 653-654.
1984. Weixia, *supra* n. 1800, at 193.
1985. Lew, Mistelis and Kröll support such an approach without elaborating on exactly what those standards should be in Lew, *supra* n. 28, at 601.
1986. Waincymer, *supra* n. 989, at 654.
1987. Bernhard, *supra* n. 1785, at 15.
1988. *Ibid.*

CHAPTER 9
Anti-Suit Injunctions by the Arbitral Tribunal

The 2006 Model Law Revisions have added the much-required clarity on the nature and type of measures that can be granted by a tribunal. Article 17(2)(b) of the Model Law unequivocally grants arbitral tribunals the power to pass necessary interim measures that may prevent 'prejudice to the arbitral process'. However, it is still unclear if such power includes the power of the tribunal to grant anti-suit injunctions to prevent such prejudice to the arbitral process.

As discussed in Chapter 6, the power to grant anti-suit injunctions stems from the inherent power of the court to prevent injustice. However, the consensual nature of arbitration may not grant such vast powers to an arbitral tribunal as such injunctions would be indirectly issued against courts. Nonetheless, it is usually implied, one way or another, that anti-suit injunctions can be identified as a category of interim measures.[1989]

It is necessary to clarify that the term 'anti-suit' used in this chapter is in the context of an arbitral tribunal issuing an injunction restraining a party from invoking the jurisdiction of a court or arbitral tribunal, as opposed to anti-suit injunctions issued by a court (discussed in Chapter 6) to prevent proceedings brought in violation of the arbitration agreement[1990] or where one party seeks enforcement of the arbitration agreement and the other party approaches another court to enjoin the first proceeding.[1991]

1989. Markus Wirth, *Supra* n. 580, at 37.
1990. Crina, *supra* n. 882, at 252-253.
1991. *Modi Entertainment Network v. W.S.G. Cricket Pte. Ltd.* (2003) 4 SCC 341, ¶6; Swanson, *supra* n. 932, at 397; *Michael Hwang discussing the Supreme Court of Singapore in BC Andaman Co. Ltd. v. Xie Ning Yun* [2017] SGHC 64, ¶108.

1. THE NEED FOR ANTI-SUIT INJUNCTIONS

The requirement of an anti-suit injunction arises when the same issues between the same parties are currently being adjudicated by the tribunal,[1992] and one party approaches a court in breach of such proceedings. In such instances, the tribunal is required to prevent the wasted cost of multiple proceedings,[1993] potential conflicting determinations,[1994] aggravation of the dispute and the cross injunctions between the courts and tribunals.[1995] Permitting parallel proceedings undermines the very purposes of arbitration such as neutrality, confidentiality,[1996] and speedy and efficient resolution of disputes. Such parallel proceedings create delays, inefficiencies, and uncertainties, and it is for these reasons that an anti-suit injunction by the arbitral tribunal is required to put a stop to such parallel proceedings.[1997]

1.1. Protection from Contempt of Court

An arbitral tribunal may also be required to issue such injunctions to prevent one party from being forced to engage with the national courts and comply with its outcome to avoid contempt.[1998] In such cases, any orders by the tribunal would be of little consequence,[1999] unless parties are prevented from approaching the courts. In the Indian case of *Dabhol Power*,[2000] a request was made to the arbitral tribunal to prevent the possible adverse impact of order in each country. However, such an application was refused by the tribunal. The effect was litigation in courts in India. Therefore, such injunctions are required to preserve the tribunal's jurisdiction[2001] because a party initiating litigation before a national court usually does so in bad faith or to harass the other party.[2002]

1.2. Protection from Hostile Courts

There may be instances when parties may deploy several tactics to sway the focus of the dispute from arbitration to the court of their nationality. It becomes problematic

1992. *Margaret L. Moses, The Principles and Practice of International Commercial Arbitration* 92 (2008).
1993. *Doleman & Sons v. Ossett Corporation* [1912] 3 KB 256 (EWCA), (England), *referred to as 'inextricable difficulties'*.
1994. *Lin Ming v. Chen Shu Quan* [2012] 2 HKRLD 547.
1995. Gary Born, *supra* n. 33, at 1135; Rahim Moloo, *Arbitrators Granting Antisuit Orders: When Should They and on What Authority?*, 26(5) J. Int'l Arb., 675, 695 (2009); Olga Vishnevskaya, *Anti-Suit Injunctions from Arbitral Tribunals in International Commercial Arbitration: A Necessary Evil?*, 32 (2) J. Int'l Arb., 173, 182 (2015).
1996. Toby Landau, *supra* n. 1125, at 294.
1997. Margaret Moses, *Barring the Courthouse Door? Anti-Suit Injunctions in International Arbitration*, (14 November 2011), available at: http://arbitrationblog.kluwerarbitration.com/2011/11/14/barring-the-courthouse-door-anti-suit-injunctions-in-international-arbitration/.
1998. Toby Landau, *supra* n. 1125, at 293.
1999. *Ibid.*, at 287.
2000. *Union of India v. Dabhol Power Co.* 2002 SCC OnLine Bom 1491.
2001. Gary Born, *supra* n. 33, at 2685-2686.
2002. Margaret, *supra* n. 1992, at 95.

because national courts may be considered unfamiliar, inexperienced, unreliable, inefficient, partial, amenable to pressure or simply hostile. Hence, arbitration is the most preferred mechanism to actively avoid courts. If a party despite voluntarily consenting to an arbitration agreement still pursues a claim before a court, it makes little sense to make the other party appear before a court and challenge its jurisdiction. Instead, it would be far more convenient and pragmatic to prevent this futile exercise if an anti-suit injunction were to be granted by an arbitral tribunal.[2003]

1.3. Inadequacy of Monetary Compensation for Parallel Proceedings

Waincymer suggests that a party seeking an anti-suit injunction from the tribunal should consider alternatives such as an application for monetary compensation in relation to any parallel proceedings instituted by the other party in breach of the arbitration agreement. A party should seek an anti-suit injunction only where the alternative action will frustrate the arbitration process directly.[2004]

However, damages for breach of the arbitration agreement would not be an adequate remedy.[2005] The exact measure of damage due to violation of confidentiality, disclosure of the sensitive document, local pressure, and politics in the court process is never quantifiable.[2006] Moreover, an award for damages may never, in fact, be enforced, especially if the court where enforcement is sought has issued an anti-arbitration injunction. Also, compensation does nothing to prevent the party from pursuing parallel proceedings directly.[2007] Thus, the arbitral tribunal may be the only available source of help, especially where courts are not inclined to grant anti-suit injunctions in favour of arbitration.[2008]

There is an increasing number of cases where such measures are absolutely vital. Hence, anti-suit injunctions constitute 'lifelines' without which the arbitral process may be defeated, especially when there is a cross-border transaction or the intent of the parties is to choose international arbitration motivated by the desire to avoid inexperienced, unreliable, unpredictable, and hostile local courts.[2009] Therefore, in such circumstances, anti-suit injunctions become more important and not granting such injunctions at the appropriate time may render the entire arbitral process futile.

2003. Toby Landau, *supra* n. 1125, at 288.
2004. Waincymer, *supra* n. 989, at 661.
2005. Crina, *supra* n. 882, at 253-255; *Turner v. Grovit and others* [2001] UKHL 65, at 27; Paul Friedland & Kate Brown, *A Claim for Monetary Relief for Breach of Agreement to Arbitrate as a Supplement or Substitute to an Anti-suit Injunction*, in Albert Jan van den Berg (ed.), *International Arbitration 2006: Back to Basics?* 274 (2007).
2006. Poudret, *supra* n. 1339, ¶625; *Lew*, supra *n. 2, at 24*; *Interim Award in ICC Case No. 8894*, 11(1) ICC Ct. Bull. 94 (2000); *Final Award in ICC Case No. 7589*, 11(1) ICC Ct. Bull. 60 (2000); *Final Award in ICC Case No. 7210*, 11(1) ICC Ct. Bull. 49 (2000), *Decision of Geneva Chamber of Commerce of 25 September 1997.*
2007. Rahim, *supra* n. 1955, at 700.
2008. *Ibid.*, at 675-676.
2009. Toby Landau, *supra* n. 1125, at 293.

2. POWER TO ISSUE ANTI-SUIT INJUNCTIONS

There is no consistent view on the power of the tribunal to grant anti-suit injunctions, primarily due to the difference between common law and civil law systems.[2010] The remedy of anti-suit is uniquely a common law remedy. It is not available in civil law jurisdictions,[2011] though it is said that some civil law jurisdictions recognise equivalent remedies.[2012]

Anti-suit injunctions were the creations of the English Courts and have been in existence for centuries,[2013] but the exercise of such a power by the courts was limited. It was considered that such injunctions are inappropriate for judges since they interfere with the jurisdiction of another court.[2014] Therefore, when the grant of anti-suit injunctions was considered inappropriate for judges, it would be even more inappropriate for arbitrators to grant anti-suit injunctions as a private tribunal stands at a lesser pedestal than a national court.[2015]

Thus, the general view among both common and civil law lawyers is that an anti-suit injunction should not be granted by the tribunal as it does not form part of the arbitrator's authority, mandate, or proper function to interfere in a national court process. Moreover, such an injunction is unlikely to be ever recognised or enforced by a court,[2016] especially in view of comity.[2017]

2.1. Concerns of Comity

Landau argues that these concerns are misplaced as national courts are bound by a formal system of international comity and must conduct themselves within sovereign limits with respect to the courts of other sovereign nations. They are subject to doctrines of allocation of jurisdiction such as *forum non conveniens* and *lis alibi pendens*, etc. However, arbitration is a creature of consent free of all such constraints, and in the absence of these considerations, the criticisms levied against anti-suit injunctions do not have much force. There are many factors relevant in international arbitration that strongly favour the availability of such injunctions but have little or no significance for national courts.[2018]

In contrast, *Waincymer* states that comity entails one adjudicator deferring to another rather than one making demands of the other.[2019] Other scholars consider comity as irrelevant to an arbitral tribunal.[2020] *Born* suggests that an anti-suit injunction

2010. *Ibid.*, at 284.
2011. *Germany does not recognize the power to grant anti-suit injunctions, see* Stephen, *supra* n. 96, at 397 & 428; Rahim, *supra* n. 1955, at 679.
2012. Waincymer, *supra* n. 989, at 655.
2013. Bermann, *supra* n. 901, at 593-594, c.f., Marco, *supra* n. 901, at 642.
2014. Trevor Hartley, *supra* n. 901, at 506.
2015. Toby Landau, *supra* n. 1125, at 286.
2016. *Ibid.*, at 286.
2017. *Ibid.*, at 285 & 287.
2018. *Ibid.*, at 287.
2019. Waincymer, *supra* n. 989, at 657.
2020. Rahim, *supra* n. 1955, at 698-699; Toby Landau, *supra* n. 1125, at 287.

is addressed to the parties and not to the forum where the other proceeding was instituted.[2021] Therefore, such injunctions are not against the court of a foreign jurisdiction[2022] or violative of comity.

Though the policy objections to the power of the tribunal to grant anti-suit injunctions continue, several authors, trace the power to (a) the inherent jurisdiction of the arbitral tribunal;[2023] (b) the national law of the seat;[2024] (c) procedural rules;[2025] or (d) the arbitration agreement itself.[2026]

2.2. Inherent Power

There is a view that the tribunal possesses inherent jurisdiction to pass anti-suit injunctions as they are necessary to ensure the orderly and enforceable disposal of disputes over which the tribunal has jurisdiction.[2027] It is within the confines of the power of the tribunal to direct the parties not to act in any way that could jeopardise the prima facie jurisdiction of the tribunal.[2028] This view is also supported by the proposition under international law that the grant of interim measure of protection has been categorised as a 'general principle of law' within the meaning of Article 38(1)(c) of the Statute of the International Court of Justice.[2029]

2.3. Law of the Seat

Levy holds the view that since the type of measures that can be granted in an arbitration proceeding are governed by the *lex arbitri*, the arbitral tribunal can grant anti-suit injunctions if such power is recognised under the law of the seat.[2030]

2.4. Procedural Rules

Moloo states that the broad and generic language contained in institutional rules permits the grant of anti-suit injunctions as a provisional measure. Most rules leave it

---

2021. *D. Caron, L. Caplan & M. Pellonpää, The UNCITRAL Arbitration Rules: A Commentary* 540-43 (2006); Gary Born, *supra* n. 33, at 2692-2693;Toby Landau, *supra* n. 1125, at 289.
2022. *Videocon Industries Ltd. v. Union of India* (2011) 6 SCC 161, ¶97.
2023. Emmanuel Gaillard, *Anti-Suit Injunctions Issued by Arbitrators,* in Albert Jan van den Berg (ed.), *International Arbitration 2006: Back to Basics?* 242 & 251 (2007); Rahim, *supra* n. 1955, at 678-679.
2024. Laurent Lévy, *Anti-Suit Injunctions Issued by Arbitrators,* in Emmanuel Gaillard (ed.), *Anti-Suit Injunctions in International Arbitration* 121 (2005).
2025. Rahim, *supra* n. 1955, at 683-684.
2026. *Ibid.*, at 676.
2027. *Nuclear Tests (Australia v. France), Judgment, I.C.J. Reports 1974, 259-260 (ICJ)*; *Case concerning the Northern Cameroons (Cameroons v. UK) (Preliminary Objection)* I.C.J. Reports 1963, 103 (ICJ)*; Anglo Iranian Oil Company Case (*UK v. Iran*)* I.C.J. Reports 1951, 93 (ICJ); *Electricity Company of Sofia and Bulgaria (Belg. v. Bulg.)* 1939 P.C.I.J. (ser. A/B) No. 79 (Order of Dec. 05) 199 (PCIJ); L. Collins, *Essays in International Litigation and the Conflict of Laws* 169-170 (1994); Mann, *supra* n. 1182 c.f. Toby Landau, *supra* n. 1125, at 292.
2028. Gaillard, *supra* n. 998, at 212.
2029. Toby Landau, *supra* n. 1125, at 292.
2030. Lévy, *supra* n. 2024, at 121.

to the arbitral tribunal to determine what type of interim measure may be granted. For example, the language '*order any interim or conservatory measure it deems appropriate*' contained in the ICC Rules[2031] would allow the grant of such injunctions.[2032]

2.5. Enforcing the Arbitration Agreement

Another view is that the tribunal under the principle of *Kompetenz-kompetenz* is empowered to rule on its own jurisdiction. Once jurisdiction has already been decided by the arbitral tribunal, it makes more sense to restrain a party from pursuing a claim before a national court as the national court may completely undermine the tribunal and may possibly review the jurisdiction of the tribunal.[2033]

In sharp contrast, *Waincymer* asserts that an anti-suit injunction is a permanent denial of an alternative forums jurisdiction and hence cannot be categorised as an interim measure.[2034] Merely listing the advantages of anti-suit injunctions cannot be a basis for the supposed power to issue them.[2035] More importantly, parties cannot be denied the fundamental right of access to courts,[2036] and an anti-suit injunction necessarily requires that the arbitral tribunal affirms its own jurisdiction to the exclusion of courts or competing forums.[2037]

However, these objections ignore the premise that when parties enter into an arbitration agreement, they knowingly waive their resort to domestic courts and then the only issue to be determined is the validity and existence of the agreement.[2038] An anti-suit injunction does not make the arbitral tribunal superior to the court but only seeks to uphold the parties' contract to have the dispute resolved by arbitration.[2039] Therefore, an anti-suit injunction is, in its true sense, only a mechanism to enforce the expectation of parties.[2040]

2.6. International Practice

There have been very few instances where such injunctions have been issued by the arbitral tribunal.[2041] Most requests for anti-suit injunctions have been found in disputes related to construction contracts.[2042] The High Court of England and Wales recognised

2031. Article 28(1), 2017 ICC Rules.
2032. Rahim, *supra* n. 1955, at 683-684.
2033. Toby Landau, *supra* n. 1125, at 290.
2034. Waincymer, *supra* n. 989, at 656.
2035. *Ibid.*, at 655-656.
2036. Gaillard, *supra* n. 2023, at 241; Paul, *supra* n. 2005, at 269.
2037. Lévy, *supra* n. 2024, at 117.
2038. Toby Landau, *supra* n. 1125, at 291.
2039. *Ever Judger Holding Co Ltd. v. Kroman Celik Sanayii Anonim Sirketi* [2015] 2 HKLRD 866; *AES Ust-Kamenogorsk Hydropower Plant LLP v. Ust-Kamenogorsk Hydropower Plant JSC* [2011] EWCA Civ 647.
2040. Toby Landau, *supra* n. 1125, at 288; Rahim, *supra* n. 1955, at 694.
2041. Flavia Foz Mange, *Anti-Suit Injunctions in International Arbitration: Protecting the Procedure or Pushing the Settlement*, 4(2) Dis. Res. Int'l L. 195-196 (2010).
2042. Bunni, *supra* n. 690, at 585.

a tribunal award ordering the claimant to stop bringing claims in relation to an arbitration.[2043] There have also been a few instances by arbitral tribunals seated in Switzerland which have ordered anti-suit injunctions.[2044] Similarly, ICC Tribunals have occasionally ordered parties to refrain from raising a claim before the foreign court[2045] and even awarded damages for failure to obey the order.[2046]

Thus, despite the differing views on the source of the power and the appropriateness of anti-suit injunctions in arbitration, there is a growing trend in favour of such injunctions being issued by tribunals.[2047] Though there exists doubt whether national courts would recognise such orders preventing from exercising jurisdictions, their recognition and enforcement will depend on each court's acceptance of the same and the mandatory law requirements.[2048]

2.7. 'Prejudice to the Arbitral Process': Model Law

Earlier, the Model Law was silent on the power of the tribunal to grant anti-suit injunctions. Therefore, the lack of power of the tribunal to grant such injunctions was premised on the hesitation that interim measures may only be issued with respect to the 'subject matter' of the dispute. In Germany, such injunctions continue to be excluded since the interim measure has to be linked to the subject matter in dispute.[2049]

However, anti-suit injunctions serve to protect the arbitral process[2050] and hence may not be related to the 'subject matter' at all. After the 2006 Model Law Revisions, the power to issue anti-suit injunctions can now be traced explicitly to Article 17(2) (b) of the Model Law as it empowers the tribunal to take any action that would prevent harm or cause prejudice to the arbitration process itself.[2051] Even the Working Group intended that Article 17(2)(b) would include an anti-suit injunction.[2052] Therefore, the debate surrounding the power of tribunals to grant such injunctions is less significant after the introduction of Article 17(2) (b) of the Model Law, especially if Article 17(2)(b) of the Model Law is incorporated into the national arbitration statute. In such cases, the power to grant such injunctions would then be contained in the *lex arbitri.*

2.7.1. Enforcement under Article 17H of the Model Law

Moreover, if the *lex arbitri* incorporates the 2006 Model Law Revisions, concerns on the lack of enforceability of such injunctions by domestic courts can also be considered

2043. *Republic of Ecuador v. Occidental Exploration & Production* [2006] EWHC 345 (Comm.).
2044. *Interim Award in ICC Case No. 8887*, ICC Arb. Bull. 2000; *ICC Interim Award of 14 May 2001.*
2045. Yves Derains and Eric Schwartz, *A Guide to the ICC Rules of Arbitration* 108-109 (2005).
2046. *ICC Case No. 8887* in 11 (1) ICC Ct. Bull. 91 (2000).
2047. S. I. Strong, *Anti-Arbitration Injunctions in Cases Involving Investor-State Arbitration: British Caribbean Bank Ltd. v. the Government of Belize*, 15 J. W. Inv. Tr. 324 (2014).
2048. Chukwudi Paschal Ojiegbe, *From West Tankers to Gazprom: Anti-Suit Injunctions, Arbitral Anti-Suit Orders and the Brussels I Recast*, 11(2) J. P. Int'l L. 267, 286 (2015).
2049. Toby Landau, *supra* n. 1125, at 282.
2050. Jan Schäfer, *supra* n. 301, at 232.
2051. Milica Arsic, *Anti-Suit Injunctions in International Arbitration*, Har. J. L. So. St. S. East Europe 19 (2016).
2052. *Ruhrkohle Handel Inter GmbH et al. v. Fednav Ltd. et al.* (1992) 144 N.R. 70.

resolved to a certain extent as orders passed by an arbitral tribunal would be binding and enforceable under Article 17H of the Model Law as such orders '*shall be recognised as binding and, unless otherwise provided by the arbitral tribunal, enforced upon application*'.

Courts may refuse recognition and enforcement only under Article 17I of the Model Law, most likely, for being against public policy. The likelihood will be higher if the court has issued an anti-arbitration injunction against the same parties for the same arbitration proceeding. Therefore, such injunctions would benefit tremendously from a pro-enforcement language contained in Article 17H(1) of the Model Law. Most countries would encourage the enforcement of orders of the arbitral tribunal to be pro-arbitration.

2.8. Power in India

There exists no provision under Section 17(1) of the IAA which explicitly empowers an arbitral tribunal to grant an anti-suit injunction. In one view, such a power may be traced to Section 17(1)(ii)(e) under the residual clause of 'just and convenient'. Since the issuance of such injunctions in aid of arbitration has been recognised,[2053] it may be argued that the tribunals do contain the power to grant anti-suit injunctions.

Another source to trace such a power could be the view of the Supreme Court in the landmark judgment of *BALCO* that the power of the tribunal to determine its jurisdiction includes the power to protect the same and issue all such orders as may be required.[2054] However, it is unlikely courts would recognise such injunctions, given the current view of courts being superior to arbitral tribunals.[2055]

As discussed in Chapter 7, India should adopt the broad language contained in Article 17(2) of the Model Law. The adoption of such language would in effect recognise the power of tribunals to grant an anti-suit injunction in India. Similarly, the adoption of Article 17H of the Model Law would mitigate the problem of recognition and enforcement of such injunctions as well.[2056]

3. SCOPE OF ANTI-SUIT INJUNCTIONS ISSUED BY ARBITRAL TRIBUNALS

Anti-suit injunctions may be granted more freely in support of arbitration.[2057] Fetters on the power of the tribunal to grant such injunctions lies in the tendency to consider

2053. *Bhupinder Singh Machre v. Vivek Varma* 2013 SCC OnLine Del 1761, ¶35.
2054. *Bharat Aluminum v. Kaiser Aluminum Technical Services Inc.* (2012) 9 SCC 552; K.R. Avinash, *A Comparative Analysis of the Law Relating to the Anti-Arbitration Injunction*, Bharti L. R. 181 (2014).
2055. *See Chapter 6. The author did not come across any reported case in the Indian context where the court has granted or denied enforcement of an anti-suit injunction issued by an arbitral tribunal.*
2056. *Discussed in Chapter 9.*
2057. *Aggeliki Charis Cia Maritime SA v. Pagnan Spa* [1995] 1 Lloyd's Rep. 87; *West Tankers Inc v. RAS Riunione Adriatica di Sicurta SpA* [2005] EWHC 454 (Comm); *Through Transport Mutual Insurance Association (Eurasia) Ltd v. New India Assurance Co Ltd.* [2004] EWCA Civ 1598.

and analyse anti-suit injunctions through the prism of national courts procedures and practice and impose similar constraints as there are on the powers of a judge.[2058]

When granted by a court, anti-suit and anti-arbitration injunctions require jurisdiction in personam over the respondent.[2059] When granted by a tribunal, such questions are not required to be addressed as such injunctions are granted only against one of the parties to the arbitration. The only consideration should be that the standards required for the grant of such injunctions should be clearly met. Hence, such standards should be clear and consistent.

4. STANDARDS TO GRANT AN ANTI-SUIT INJUNCTION BY THE ARBITRAL TRIBUNAL

When a tribunal is faced with a request for the grant of an anti-suit injunction, it is unclear if the tribunal should adopt the standard test for interim relief as enshrined in Article 17A of the Model Law? Should the standard be different, if so, what should such standard be?

One view is that if the resort is taken to the power of the tribunal to grant anti-suit injunctions as interim measures, then the criteria applied to ordinary interim measures would become applicable and the question then would be whether irreparable harm is required.[2060] In *ICC Case No. 8307*, the risk of conflicting decisions and the parties being forced to incur additional expenses was considered irreparable harm,[2061] and an anti-suit injunction was granted. In another case, an anti-suit injunction was granted as the loss of the right to be free of litigation in another forum was considered to be irreparable.[2062]

The other view is that the traditional standards for classic interim relief should be considered in a less restrictive manner in the case of an anti-suit injunction.[2063] A third view is that while determining whether or not to grant anti-suit injunctions, it is pertinent to consider the exercise of the power itself and the alternative of damages for breach of the arbitration agreement.[2064]

Several scholars discuss the considerations to keep in mind while granting an anti-suit injunction. *Waincymer* lists out the following considerations for the grant of an anti-suit injunction by a tribunal:[2065]

(a) Why is the relevant party seeking jurisdiction before an alternative forum?
(b) The likelihood that the party will comply with an order either immediately or because of some enforceability power.

2058. Toby Landau, *supra* n. 1125, at 283.
2059. Lew, *supra* n. 885, at 188.
2060. Waincymer, *supra* n. 989, at 659.
2061. *Interim Award of 14 May 2001 in ICC Case No. 8307.*
2062. *Moloo's discussion of Boeing Co. v. Islamic Republic of Iran in Rahim, supra* n. 1955, at 689.
2063. Olga, *supra* n. 1995, at 193-194.
2064. Waincymer, *supra* n. 989, at 658.
2065. *Ibid.*, at 658-659; Chetan Phull, *U.S. Anti-Suit Injunctions in Support of International Arbitration: Five Questions American Courts Ask*, 31 (1) J. Int'l Arb. 21, 31 (2011).

(c) The possibility that the other forum will respect the order or conversely the possibility that it might engage in retaliatory injunctive action.
(d) The extent to which the application to the other forum aims to directly hamper the arbitral proceedings.
(e) The adverse commercial impact on the party seeking the anti-suit order.

Further *Levy* states that the tribunal should consider the urgency, irreparable harm, and the necessity to facilitate the enforcement of the upcoming award. He adds that anti-suit injunctions should only be granted when one of the parties has committed fraud or otherwise engaged in abusive behaviour in order to revoke the arbitration agreement.[2066]

Gaillard suggests that the standard should be whether the anti-suit injunction is necessary, or urgent, or if a party would suffer irreparable harm, and whether the order would be effective or not.[2067] In Hong Kong, the test is whether Hong Kong is the appropriate forum and whether the foreign suit is brought in bad faith.[2068]

Moloo, on the other hand, suggests that once an arbitration agreement is found to be existing between the parties, an anti-suit injunction should be granted in all circumstances as parties should be held to their bargain. In his view, it is within the jurisdiction of the tribunal to remedy a breach of the arbitration agreement in the same way as a tribunal can remedy any other breach of contract.[2069] This approach is criticised as it treats an anti-suit injunction as a form of negative specific performance of an obligation as opposed to the form of an interim measure. An anti-suit injunction is not a truly specific performance of the arbitration agreement but an order not to do anything that is contrary to it. It does not answer the conceptual challenge of the right of one adjudicator to make negative jurisdictional rulings where they are not empowered as adjudicators.[2070]

Moloo's view soundly resonates with the rationale for an anti-suit injunction. However, given the effect such injunctions can have on parties and also on jurisdictions of the court, an arbitral tribunal needs to consider the following:[2071]

(1) It might be difficult to obtain a stay of proceedings in the foreign forum.
(2) Submission to jurisdiction may be inferred by the foreign court.
(3) The party requesting an anti-suit injunction is sceptical of its ability to obtain a stay of proceedings from the court.
(4) A party is reluctant to incur the expense and inconvenience of approaching a foreign court.
(5) The matter is urgent.

2066. Lévy, *supra* n. 2024, at 126.
2067. Gaillard, *supra* n. 2023, at 264-265.
2068. Stephen, *supra* n. 96, at 428.
2069. Rahim, *supra* n. 1955, at 685-687.
2070. Waincymer, *supra* n. 989, at 660.
2071. Andrew Bell, *Forum Shopping and Venue in Transnational Litigation* 172 (2003) *as cited in* Daniel Tan, *Anti-Suit Injunctions and the Vexing Problem of Comity*, 45 (3) Vir. J. of Int'l L. 287 (2005); Tushar, *supra* n. 926, at 86-87.

Adding to these considerations, such injunctions should be granted once the tribunal has determined its jurisdiction, even if the determination is that of a tribunal's prima facie jurisdiction.[2072] Thus, a tribunal can pass an anti-suit injunction when a decision on jurisdiction is pending.[2073]

The standards proposed under Chapter 7 and the adoption of Article 17A of the Model Law (with modifications) adequately cater to the different views discussed above. Most likely, parties would approach the court at the beginning of the arbitration and the tribunal would determine its jurisdiction and the validity of the arbitration agreement, even if such determination is prima facie. Assessment of the reasonable possibility of success would include considerations of jurisdiction and validity of the arbitration agreement. The party requesting the measure would then demonstrate urgency concerning the threat to the right of the party to have the dispute resolved through arbitration, the right of the tribunal to adjudicate the dispute and its right to prevent harm or prejudice to the arbitral process. Considerations of harm would include the potential harm likely to be suffered due to parallel or multiple proceedings.

Therefore, different standards are not required for the issuance of anti-suit injunctions by the tribunal. The standards contained in Article 17A of the Model Law(with modifications) when applied in a less restrictive manner, address most views which consider the urgency and comparative harm as the standards to be met when granting a request for an anti-suit injunction by the tribunal.

5. TYPES OF MEASURES

Lord Hobhouse[2074] had noted that the term 'anti-suit injunction' is problematic since it gives the impression that such injunctions are addressed to and intended to bind another court. His view is correct, especially in the context of arbitration. The tribunal is neither considering nor determining the jurisdiction of the court. It is rather protecting its own jurisdiction.

'Anti-suit' relief may include (a) an order restraining a party from enforcing the judgment or annulling an award; (b) an application for an anti-suit injunction; (c) commencement of proceedings with an arbitration; (d) making a disclosure application in a foreign forum; or (e) pursuing a third party by way of indemnity or contribution.[2075] Hence, an anti-suit relief may not necessarily fall in the traditional category of an anti-suit injunction as it sometimes takes various forms which are not necessarily 'anti-suit'.

The problem with using the phrase 'anti-suit' injunction in the context of arbitration is that it unnecessarily imports the jurisprudence and thinking of national

2072. Gaillard, *supra* n. 2023, at 265-266.
2073. *Chevron Corporation and Texaco Petroleum Corporation v. The Republic of Ecuador, Second Interim Award on Interim Measures in PCA Case No. 2009-23 of 16 February 2012,* ¶2; *Sergei Paushok Cjsc Golden East Company Cjsc Vostokneftegaz Company v. The Government of Mongolia, Ad HocOrder on Interim Measures of 2 September 2008,* ¶55.
2074. *Turner v. Grovit* [2002] 1 W.L.R. 107, 117, ¶23.
2075. Toby Landau, *supra* n. 1125, at 289.

courts and restricts the scope to an actual injunction restraining a party from commencing or continuing proceedings elsewhere. There is no reason why the power of arbitrators should be circumscribed in such a manner. If the aim is to protect the arbitral process and the expectations of the parties, then the tribunal may order any number of measures such as those described below, which may not fall within the traditional understanding of 'an anti-suit injunction':[2076]

(a) The tribunal may impose notification or reporting requirements upon a party with a view that the parties and the tribunal are fully informed with respect to each step taken before a different forum.
(b) The tribunal may direct the party violating the arbitration agreement to provide information such as a letter or request from the arbitral tribunal.
(c) The tribunal may also direct a party to raise particular points before the other forum.
(d) A tribunal may impose conditions on each step such as requiring an application or securing the prior consent of the tribunal before a party takes any step before another forum.
(e) A tribunal may also impose a recommendation or declaration against a party as opposed to a strict order.
(f) A tribunal may also impose cost penalties on a party.
(g) A tribunal may even impose orders for a limited period of time such as the determination of the jurisdiction by the arbitral tribunal.

Landau suggests that the term such as 'jurisdiction protection' measure may help to clarify the scope of these measures and help in insulating these measures from the jurisprudence applicable to anti-suit injunctions.[2077]

The term 'jurisdiction protection' is more appropriate as it echoes the power to prevent prejudice to the arbitral process itself. Therefore, a tribunal may pass any appropriate order and not necessarily an 'anti-suit injunction' to protect its jurisdiction or the process. As discussed in Chapters 3 and 6, the adoption of the generic language of Article 17(2) of the Model Law along with the clarification of the power to order types of measures currently listed under Section 17(1) of the IAA would provide sufficient flexibility and statutory basis for tribunals to order such measures that may be required to protect the jurisdiction of the tribunal.

6. FORM: AWARD OR ORDER

One key question that requires determination is whether an anti-suit injunction should be made as an award or an order. One view is to grant an anti-suit injunction in the form of an award to minimise concerns of enforceability.[2078] *Waincymer* argues that

2076. *Ibid.*, at 289.
2077. *Ibid.*, at 290.
2078. Arsic, *supra* n. 2051, at 25.

where a tribunal had made a jurisdictional determination that the arbitration agreement is exclusive and there is no possible recourse to an alternative forum, then the decision should be rendered as an award to ensure maximum enforceability.[2079] This is to ensure that in case an anti-suit injunction is not complied with, it must be enforced in the jurisdiction in which the competing court or arbitration proceedings are instituted.[2080]

If the view of the above authors is accepted, then an anti-suit injunction should be enforceable as an award, as it has a preclusive effect[2081] on the issue of jurisdiction. If the tribunal declines jurisdiction, the award is final, if the tribunal admits jurisdiction it should be an interim award.[2082]

In India, under Section 36(1) of the IAA, an award shall be enforced in the same manner as if it were a decree of the court. Until now, anti-suit injunctions have been justified as being directed against the parties and not against a court of law. However, if the injunctions were to be enforced as awards and subsequently as a decree of the court, the bigger question is: can an order of a tribunal directing the proceedings to be stayed before a court of law be enforceable as a decree?

In such a scenario, the conflict of laws rule will apply and it would be subject to such rules that the award may be enforceable or set aside on the grounds of public policy. Even if the conflict of law rules are not applied and the issue is considered from a solely domestic point of view, it is more than likely that such an award would be set aside under Section 34(2)(b)(ii) as being in conflict with the public policy of India as tribunals cannot be superior to the court.[2083] Therefore, while this view attributing finality to interim orders may sound tempting, it brings with it a new set of problems with respect to enforcement.

The determination of the form of the measure may no longer be required if Article 17H of the Model Law is adopted. Article 17H(1) states that an interim measure 'shall be recognised binding'. Hence, if a jurisdiction protection measure is granted by the arbitral tribunal under Article 17(2)(b) of the Model Law, the same would be binding and enforceable under Article 17H(1) of the Model Law on the parties, subject to exceptions under Article 17I of the Model Law.[2084] Moreover, non-compliance with such orders will be considered to be wilful disobedience by a party rather than a decree of the court, which requires execution. Hence, the injunction would continue to have an in personam effect even at the stage of enforcement. It would, thus, not be barred by comity as it would not determine and deny the jurisdiction of a court.

2079. Waincymer, *supra* n. 989, at 661.
2080. Paul, *supra* n. 2005, at 269.
2081. Eduardo, *supra* n. 35, at 231.
2082. Poudret, *supra* n. 1339, ¶644.
2083. *Intertoll ICS Cecons O & M Co. Pvt. Ltd. v. National Highways Authority of India* 2013 SCC OnLine Del 447.
2084. *Discussed in Chapter 10.*

7. SAFEGUARDS

As argued above, since the power of the tribunal to grant jurisdiction protection measures now stems from Article 17(2)(b) of the Model Law, the safeguards suggested under Chapter 7 may equally apply, especially the requirement of mandatory disclosure of facts and circumstances likely to be relevant for the arbitral tribunal's determination whether or not to grant the measure.

PART III Enforcement of Interim Measures

CHAPTER 10

Enforcement of Interim Measures

Private parties such as arbitrators are not empowered to enforce their own decisions because they are not judges or enforcement officers of the country. If arbitrators were to be empowered with coercive powers of enforcement, it would lead to a state of anarchy.[2085] For the longest time until the early twentieth century, there were no legal sanctions for non-compliance with arbitrators' decisions under most national laws.[2086] A provision of interim protection of rights was removed from the ICC Arbitration Rules of 1927 due to enforcement concerns and reincorporated in 1931.[2087]

Initially, the UNCITRAL, when drafting the Model Law, had an impression that providing for an enforcement mechanism was not possible as national procedural regimes would lead to public policy concerns.[2088] It was eventually left out over concerns of encroaching upon the jurisdiction of the courts in each country and the acceptability of the Model Law.[2089] Right from the very beginning, there were concerns about there being provisions for satisfactory enforcement of interim orders passed by arbitral tribunals, what the scope of the powers ought to be, and what procedure should be followed by the arbitral tribunals while issuing interim orders.[2090] The Working Group also noted that the regime on enforcement of interim measures was not satisfactorily developed in most countries.[2091] Therefore, enforcement of interim measures has been a challenge.

The UNCITRAL Working Group decided that one of the priority items should include the enforceability of interim measures[2092] as enforceability is key to the success

2085. Ali Yesilirmak, *supra* n. 30, at 70-71.
2086. *Ibid.*, at 34.
2087. *Ibid.*, at 27.
2088. Menon, *supra* n. 102, at 2.
2089. *Ibid.*, at 2.
2090. *Ibid.*, at 2-3.
2091. *Ibid.*, at 2-3.
2092. Records of General Assembly in its Fifty Fifth Session (UN Doc A/55/17), ¶393.

of arbitration as a method of settling commercial disputes.[2093] It was in this context that the issue of enforceability was delinked from the issue of the power of the arbitral tribunal (as originally contained only in Article 17 of the Model Law) to issue interim measures.[2094]

1. THE NEED FOR ENFORCEMENT OF INTERIM MEASURES

It is undisputed that interim measures may just be as relevant as the final relief and hence, their efficacy and enforceability are crucial.[2095] The efficacy of arbitration as a dispute resolution process and a 'one-stop' solution will be severely compromised if interim measures granted by the tribunal are merely paper tigers. However, it is unclear how a private body created by the consent of parties can exercise the sovereign right of enforcement against a party.[2096] Should national arbitration statutes provide for such power? Can a contractual agreement such as an arbitration agreement confer such sweeping power on the arbitral tribunal? Would that not be against public policy as it would permit parties to circumvent national laws completely and, in a certain sense, undermine the authority of the national courts and national laws?

1.1. Voluntary Compliance

The short answer to these questions is that it is inherent in the constitution of the arbitral tribunal that an arbitral tribunal cannot directly enforce its orders and can only do the same with the help of courts. However, many authors take the view that interim measures are invariably complied with voluntarily[2097] and most arbitrators have never experienced the need for enforcement through courts.[2098] Croatia,[2099] Egypt,[2100] Jordan,[2101] Macedonia,[2102] Switzerland,[2103] and Uruguay[2104] statutorily recognise such voluntary compliance.[2105] Section 42(4) of the English Arbitration Act also permits a part to voluntarily comply with an order within a reasonable time or such time as is mentioned in the order of the tribunal.

A 2012 Queen Mary University and White & Case International Arbitration Survey indicated that interim orders issued by the arbitral tribunals are voluntarily complied with by the parties. About 62% of the compliance is due to potential

2093. Report of UNCITRAL Working Group on the work of its Thirty Second session, June 2000, A/CN.9/468, available at: https://undocs.org/en/A/CN.9/468, ¶60.
2094. *Ibid.*, ¶60.
2095. Luis, *supra* n. 521, at 565.
2096. *Pradeep K.N. v. The Station House Officers* 2017 (1) Arb. LR 57, ¶¶15 and 18.
2097. Lew, *supra* n. 28, at ¶23-83; Abascal, *supra* n. 1, at 753.
2098. Hober, *supra* n. 1207, at 739.
2099. Croatian Law on Arbitration, Art. 16.
2100. Egyptian Arbitration Law, 1994, Art. 24(2).
2101. Jordan Arbitration Law, 2001, Art. 23(b).
2102. Macedonia Arbitration Law, Art. 17.
2103. Switzerland Arbitration Law, 1987, Art. 183(2).
2104. Uruguay Arbitration Law, Art. 17(2).
2105. Croatian Law on Arbitration, Art. 16(2); Macedonia Arbitration Law, Art. 17.

sanctions and reputational impact of non-compliance.[2106] It is said that almost every arbitration counsel knows that the arbitral tribunal would consider non-compliance as an act of bad faith in terms of procedural conduct.[2107] *Born* suggests that the line between direct coercive measures of enforcement and other actions by arbitral tribunals is less clear than assumed. If an arbitral tribunal orders a party to deliver property or funds to it for safekeeping during arbitral proceedings and the party complies with such an order, then the arbitral tribunal exercises power which is very close to a direct enforcement authority.[2108]

This view misconstrues coercive authority with voluntary compliance. Simply because one party voluntarily complies with the order of the arbitral tribunal, it does not mean that the arbitral tribunal has coerced the party into compliance or has the power to enforce its orders. Coercion implies the threat of penal consequences, not just moral authority.

1.2. Concerns with Adverse Inferences

Moreover, many times there may not be any voluntary compliance.[2109] Parties often sideline the moral authority of the arbitral tribunal to gain a tactical advantage.[2110] It is also unclear as to what kind of negative or adverse inferences are to be drawn by an arbitral tribunal for not complying with an order for the collection of evidence or the appointment of a receiver unless a party specifically hinders the implementation of such orders. In the Queen Mary survey, it was empirically found that arbitrators are reluctant to draw adverse inferences as such inferences may become a ground for challenging the award.[2111]

Moreover, in emergency arbitration, the arbitrator(s) passing the final award are going to be different from the emergency arbitrator. No moral authority of the tribunal can be derived in such cases. The chances of voluntary compliance at the threat of adverse inferences may be limited unless such inferences affect the determinations of costs and damages. Hence, enforcement of interim measures cannot rest solely on the moral authority of the arbitral tribunal.

2106. Martin Valasek & Jenna Anne de Jong, *Enforceability of Interim Measures and Emergency Arbitrator Decisions*, (5 July 2018), available at: https://www.lexology.com/library/detail.aspx?g=15f02d64-cc66-445c-9b0c-65f9440c0c4a; Alessandro Villani & Manuela Caccialanza, *Interim Relief Through Emergency Arbitration: An Upcoming Goal or Still an Illusion?*, (14 July 2017), available at: http://arbitrationblog.kluwerarbitration.com/2017/07/14/interim-relief-emergency-arbitration-upcoming-goal-still-illusion/; Michelle Grando, *The Coming of Age of Interim Relief in International Arbitration: A Report from the 28th Annual ITA Workshop*, (20 July 2016), available at: http://arbitrationblog.kluwerarbitration.com/2016/07/20/the-coming-of-age-of-interim-relief-in international-arbitration-a-report-from-the-28th-annual-ita-workshop/.

2107. Luis, *supra* n. 521, at 565.

2108. Gary Born, *supra* n. 33, at 2628.

2109. Ali Yesilirmak, *supra* n. 30, at 239.

2110. *Ibid.*

2111. Queen Mary University of London and White and Case, 2012 International Arbitration Survey: Current and Preferred Practices in the Arbitral Process, available at: http://www.arbitration.qmul.ac.uk/media/arbitration/docs/2012_International_Arbitration_Survey.pdf, at 21.

Furthermore, in 95% of the cases in the Netherlands and 75% in France, parties initiate arbitration with a view that the interim measure will be the final measure. They do not commence proceedings on merits.[2112] Hence, there may not be any occasion for adverse inferences. Instead, robust enforcement mechanisms are required to ensure interim measures are complied with on account of urgency.

An arbitral tribunal is usually located in a neutral venue or a neutral seat. There is a strong likelihood that neither party would have assets within the jurisdiction of the seat for enforcement of the interim order. Thus, there is an imperative need for uniform provisions empowering tribunals to issue orders that are enforceable beyond the seat of arbitration.

Recently, many institutions' rules have incorporated provisions providing for interim relief and emergency arbitrations.[2113] However, the enforcement of interim measures granted by an emergency arbitrator remains subject to debate.[2114] At the stage of enforcement, courts need to weigh the ability to support the process of arbitration meaningfully and at the same time give due respect to the arbitral process and the power of the arbitral tribunal to grant interim relief.[2115] Moreover, many measures such as the ICC Pre Arbitral Reference Rules and other similar efforts have largely failed to provide any satisfactory non-judicial mechanism for enforcing interim measures in arbitration.[2116]

It is emphasised that the need for enforceability is not the same for all interim measures.[2117] Interim measures which require absolute enforcement are related to preventing harm to the arbitral process and for securing the award, i.e., where the failure to comply will result in severe and irreparable consequences.[2118] Interim measures related to evidence may not require enforcement at all or rarely require to be enforced.[2119]

2. POWER OF ENFORCEMENT OF INTERIM MEASURES

The power of enforcement of interim measures has been controversial. Though there is general agreement on the need for enforcement of interim measures granted by arbitral tribunals, the divergence of opinion is primarily on which approach is most suitable to achieve this goal.

2112. Veeder, *supra* n. 1532, at 247.
2113. Victoria Clark & Nadia Hubbuck, *The emergency arbitrator is officially a teenager,* (15 April 2020), available at http://arbitrationblog.practicallaw.com/the-emergency-arbitrator-is-officially-a-teenager.
2114. Martin, *supra* n. 2106; Alessandro, *supra* n. 2106; Michelle, *supra* n. 2106.
2115. Ava Boroso, *Overview of U.S. Court Treatment of Interim Measures in Support of International Arbitration*, Y. Arb. R. 58 (2018).
2116. Gary Born, *supra* n. 33, at 2631.
2117. Report of the Secretary General for Settlement of Commercial Disputes, in its Thirty Second Session, 2000, A/CN.9/WG.II/WP.108, available at: https://undocs.org/en/A/CN.9/WG.II/WP.108, ¶78.
2118. *Ibid.*
2119. Hober, *supra* n. 1207, at 740.

There are three key approaches to the enforcement of interim measures, i.e., (a) national laws to assist enforcement of interim measures; (b) enforcing interim measures as awards; or (c) development of international rules to enforce interim measures.[2120] The first approach requires national laws to recognise interim measures as orders capable of enforcement. Once recognised, they are to be enforced as if they were orders of the court. This requires fewer formalities and can be completed in a much faster time scale. It does not require scrutiny by arbitral institutions which are required for awards.[2121]

The second approach is to make the direction as an award in the hope that it aids enforceability, but it should be remembered that awards cannot be easily reversed.[2122] *Waincymer* argues that it is best to combine both the approaches and make a provisional order and then incorporate the details of the measure in an interim and reasoned award.[2123]

The third approach is one of an international instrument providing for harmonisation and enforcing orders passed by arbitral tribunals outside the jurisdiction of national courts. The only exception being public policy or mandatory law.[2124]

Before the 2006 Model Law Revisions, there was no provision for enforcement of interim orders passed by the arbitral tribunal under the Model Law and the enforcement was left to the adopting state which would be free to provide court assistance in this regard.[2125] In England, under Section 42 of the English Arbitration Act, an English court may order a defaulting party to comply with a 'pre-emptory order'[2126] granted by an arbitral tribunal with the sanctions of contempt of court. However, this can only be done with the leave of the arbitral tribunal. The court has to be satisfied that the applicant has '*exhausted any available arbitral process in respect of failure to comply with the tribunal's order*'[2127] and has had time to comply with the order.[2128] A slightly similar approach is adopted in Brazil. Parties have to request the arbitral tribunal for coercive measures which will grant or deny the request. Once granted, the courts usually enforce the measure.[2129]

In Germany, Bangladesh,[2130] and Singapore, the court may permit the execution of the arbitral tribunal's order at the request of a party.[2131] In Germany, enforcement is allowed through the court but only after satisfying the court on the validity of the

2120. Lew, *supra* n. 28, at 609-614.
2121. Article 28(1), 2012 ICC Rules, *See also, Lew,* supra *n. 2, at* 28, c.f. Waincymer, *supra* n. 989, at 636.
2122. Lew, *supra* n. 28, at 607; c.f. Waincymer, *supra* n. 989, at 637.
2123. *Interim Award in ICC Case No. 8879*, 11 (1) *ICC International Court of Arbitration Bulletin* 88 (2000), c.f. Waincymer, *supra* n. 989, at 637-638.
2124. Lew, *supra* n. 28, at ¶23-96.
2125. Explanatory Note by the UNCITRAL Secretariat on the 1985 Model Law on International Commercial Arbitration as amended in 2006 (20 September 2007), available at: https://www.uncitral.org/pdf/english/texts/arbitration/ml-arb/MLARB-explanatoryNote20-9-07.pdf.
2126. *Passed by an arbitral tribunal under* English Arbitration Act, 1996, S. 41(5).
2127. English Arbitration Act, 1996, S. 42(3).
2128. *Ibid.*, S. 42(4).
2129. Stephen, *supra* n. 96, at 259-260.
2130. Bangladesh Arbitration Act, 2001, S. 21(4).
2131. Hober, *supra* n. 1207, at 725.

agreement and that the measures are not of a disproportionate character.[2132] The order may even be recast, if necessary, for enforcement[2133] and a party may even request the court to cancel or amend a decision on enforcement.[2134]

In Switzerland, enforcement is possible only through the assistance of the court and it is only the tribunal that may apply for enforcement, not the parties.[2135] Contrary to this position, in France[2136] and the Netherlands,[2137] an arbitral tribunal may declare interim awards provisionally enforceable. Interestingly, in Sweden and Norway,[2138] interim measures ordered by the arbitral tribunal are not enforceable and cannot be made enforceable by a court.[2139] In Qatar, the party has to seek written permission from the arbitral tribunal, whereas in Singapore and Sri Lanka[2140] the leave of the court is required[2141] for enforcement of the interim measure.[2142] It should be highlighted that Article 33(1) of the VIAC Rules 2018 provides that the party shall comply with the orders of the arbitral tribunal irrespective of whether they are enforceable before national courts.

Therefore, most jurisdictions recognise the enforcement of orders passed by the arbitral tribunal under the first approach, i.e., with assistance from the courts. The power of enforcement *sans* court intervention, however, is needed on account of the urgency of enforcement. Relying solely on court enforcement involves procedural hurdles of jurisdiction, date of listing, notice to the respondent, and review of the interim measures passed by the arbitral tribunal. Therefore, orders of an arbitral tribunal without the threat of sanctions and compliance mechanisms may be reduced to paper decrees or orders, resulting in undermining the efficacy of the arbitral process. The lack of such power also takes away from the concept of arbitration being a one-stop dispute resolution mechanism.

It should be clarified that it is not being argued that the enforcement should only be done by arbitral tribunals and not by courts. Instead, the better position ought to be that the arbitral tribunal should be empowered to enforce its orders through other measures as well apart from court enforcement. Such measures may be sufficient to protect the right of the parties on an interim basis.[2143]

2132. *K.P. Berger, The New German Arbitration Law in International Perspective* 11 (The Hague 2000).
2133. Austrian Code of Civil Procedure (ZPO), S. 1041(2).
2134. *Ibid.*, S. 1041(3).
2135. Donovan, *supra* n. 1400, at 129.
2136. French Code of Civil Procedure, Art. 1479.
2137. Dutch Code of Civil Procedure, Art. 1051; In the Netherlands, interim orders passed by the tribunal are not enforceable through Dutch Courts but under Dutch Code of Civil Procedure, Art. 1051, *the parties may agree to empower the arbitral tribunal or its Chairman to render an award for provisional relief in summary proceedings*; *see*, Hober, *supra* n. 1207, at 724.
2138. Mikal Brondmo & Jhonny Johansen, et al., *Norway: International Arbitration 2019*, (8 August 2019), available at: https://practiceguides.chambers.com/practice-guides/international-arbitration-2019/norway.
2139. Stephen, *supra* n. 96, at 259.
2140. Sri Lanka Arbitration Act, 1995, S. 13(2).
2141. Singapore International Arbitration Act, 1994, S. 12(6).
2142. Qatar Arbitration Law, 2017, A. 17(3).
2143. *Pacific Reinsurance Management Corporation v. Ohio Reinsurance Corporation*, 935 F.2d 1019, 1022-23, (9th Cir. 1991), *the Ninth Circuit further held that '[g]iven the potential importance of*

Currently, enforcement of the orders of the arbitral tribunal is done in one of the following ways:[2144]

(a) Direct enforcement of interim measures ordered by the arbitral tribunal.[2145]
(b) Seeking assistance from courts in the enforcement of interim measures.[2146]
(c) Recasting tribunal orders to fit the national legal system.[2147]
(d) Unilateral order by the court of its own.[2148]

2.1. Article 17H of the Model Law

The newly introduced Article 17H of the Model Law provides for recognition and enforcement of interim measures. It states that *'an interim measure issued by an arbitral tribunal shall be recognised as binding and, unless otherwise provided by the arbitral tribunal, enforced upon application to the competent court, irrespective of the country in which it was issued, subject to the provisions of article 17 I'*.

The language of the clause has the following implications:

(a) The interim measure is mandatorily binding in every nation that has adopted the Article unless otherwise provided by the tribunal (except Korea).[2149]
(b) The measure shall be enforced upon application to the court.

temporary equitable awards [on provisional relief] in making the arbitration proceedings meaningful, court enforcement of them, when appropriate, is not an "undue intrusion upon the arbitral process", but essential to preserve the integrity of that process', c.f. Ali Yesilirmak, *supra* n. 30, at 239.

2144. Ali Yesilirmak, *supra* n. 30, at 247, c.f. Ronald Wong, *supra* n. 452, at 508.

2145. Ecuador's Mediation and Arbitration Law 1997, Art. 9, c.f. Ronald Wong, *supra* n. 452, at 508. *The author could not cross-check from an official translation of the law in English. Article 9 provides that when the arbitration agreement stipulates, the arbitrators may take assistance of public, judicial, police and administrative officials without having resort to any ordinary judge. When the agreement does not provide so, enforcement can be requested through a court.*

2146. Austrian Code of Civil Procedure (ZPO), S. 593; Brazil Arbitration Law, 2015, Art. 22-B. *It should be noted that the court should ensure that the confidentiality agreed by the parties is maintained during enforcement*; Brazil Arbitration Law, 2015, Art. 22-C; Austrian Code of Civil Procedure (ZPO), S. 1041(2); Bolivia Arbitration Law, Art. 36; English Arbitration Act, 1996, S. 42; Hong Kong Arbitration Ordinance (Cap.609), S. 2GG; Singapore International Arbitration Act, 1994, S. 12(6); Switzerland Arbitration Law, 1987, Art. 183(2).

2147. Austrian Code of Civil Procedure (ZPO), S. 1041(2).

2148. New Zealand, Arbitration Act, 1996, S. 9(3); North Carolina International Commercial Arbitration Act, S. 1-567(39).

2149. Korean Arbitration Act, Art. 18-7 *which has adopted the 2006 Model Revision which provides that 'the party who wishes to obtain recognition of an interim measure issued by an arbitral tribunal may file a petition with a court to seek a decision to approve the measure, and the party who intends to seek compulsory execution on the basis of the interim measure may file a petition with a court to seek a decision that authorizes the execution'*; it should be noted that the phrase 'unless otherwise provided by the tribunal' was sought to be deleted as being unnecessary but was retained as the proposal failed to receive support, UNCITRAL Official Records of the General Assembly, 61st, Supplement No. 17 (A/61/17), ¶129, c.f. Peter Binder, *International Commercial Arbitration and Mediation in UNCITRAL Model Law Jurisdictions* 317-318 (2019).

(c) It is immaterial whether the measure has been issued by a tribunal seated in the country where the enforcement is sought.[2150]
(d) The court where enforcement is sought can only refuse enforcement under Article 17I.

For the first time, interim measures ordered by tribunals have been equated with court-ordered interim measures.[2151] It is pertinent to note that this provision was drafted to ensure consistency with Article 35(1) of the Model Law and proposals to streamline the wording were rejected.[2152]

2.1.1. *'Unless Otherwise Provided by the Tribunal'*

The phrase '*unless otherwise provided by the tribunal*' refers to the middle ground[2153] between the views that no approval of the tribunal is required before enforcement[2154] and enforcement through courts is not required in every case and hence, the approval of the tribunal is necessary.[2155] Therefore, the phrase is supposed to grant the freedom to the arbitral tribunal to pass recommendations which may not be necessarily binding.

2.1.2. *Irrelevance of the Form of the Interim Measure*

The most far-reaching effect of Article 17H(1) is that it dissociates enforceability from concerns of the form of the measure, i.e., order or award. Similar to Russia,[2156] it further explicitly makes all interim orders binding on the parties unless otherwise provided by the tribunal, which implicitly recognises the tribunal's power to impose costs and damages for non-compliance.[2157]

2.1.3. *No Direct Enforcement*

Article 17H(1) also lays down the procedure for enforcement of interim measures, i.e., on an application to a court, clearly rejecting the approach of direct enforcement. This approach alleviates concerns of subversion of sovereign rights of enforcement and pays due homage to the coercive powers of the courts.

2150. *The article has been added to UNCITRAL Model Law, Art. 1(2) to not be restricted by questions of territoriality.*
2151. Binder, *supra* n. 2149, at 318.
2152. Report of UNCITRAL Working Group on the work of its Forty Third session, 2005, A/CN.9/589, available at: https://undocs.org/en/A/CN.9/589, ¶76.
2153. Binder, *supra* n. 2149, at 318.
2154. *UNCITRAL Official Records of the General Assembly*, 61st, Supplement No. 17 (A/61/17), ¶25, c.f. Binder, *supra* n. 2149, at 318.
2155. *Ibid.*, ¶26, c.f. *Ibid.*
2156. Russian Federal Law on International Commercial Arbitration, Art. 17(1), which provides '*the orders and other procedural acts of the arbitral tribunal on taking of interim measures are binding on the parties.*'
2157. *Discussed at 7.2 Costs and Damages (below).*

2.1.4. *Extraterritorial Enforcement*

One of the most notable implications of this provision is the recognition and enforcement of interim measures, irrespective of where the seat of arbitration is located. Since arbitrators usually grant interim measures in neutral places where parties do not have assets, this provision is particularly important.[2158] Giving effect to the non-territorial scope of Article 17H, this article has also been added to Article 1(2) to apply irrespective of the question of territoriality. Therefore, interim measures will be binding and enforced by courts, irrespective of the seat of arbitration, subject only to Article 17I.

2.1.5. *Limited Grounds for Non-recognition of Interim Measure*

Lastly, Article 17H(1) provides that enforcement can be refused 'only' under Article 17I of the Model Law clearly limiting the scope of the courts to refuse enforcement. It should be noted that Article 17I does not provide setting aside the interim measure but only a refusal to enforce.[2159] In contrast, the provision of appeal under Section 17 of the IAA effectively provides for setting aside the interim measure.

2.1.6. *Duty of Disclosure*

Article 17H(2) of the Model Law adds the necessary safeguards at the stage of enforcement, apart from the procedural ones contained in Article 17I. It creates an obligation on the party seeking enforcement under Article 17H(1) of the Model Law to inform the court of any termination, suspension or modification of the interim measure[2160] within a broad timeframe, i.e., the time when the party is seeking enforcement as well as the time after which enforcement has already been obtained. This ensures that the court's assistance is not abused but used only for the efficiency of the arbitration proceedings.[2161] It should be noted that the duty to inform the court of any termination, suspension, or modification is not governed by Article 17F and would be governed by national law.[2162] Thus, a violation of Article 17H(2) would not be a violation of the tribunal but of the court.

2.1.7. *Provision of Security*

In addition to the safeguard of disclosure, the court can also require security if the tribunal has not made any such determination, especially when the measure is going to

2158. *Marianne Roth, UNCITRAL Model Law on International Commercial Arbitration*, in Frank-Bernd Weigand (ed.), *Practitioner's Handbook On International Commercial Arbitration* (2010), ¶14.337, c.f. Roth, *supra* n. 448, at 434.
2159. Holtzmann, *supra* n. 6 at, 179-181.
2160. Report of UNCITRAL Working Group on the work of its Forty Second session, 2005, A/CN.9/573, available at: https://undocs.org/en/A/CN.9/573, ¶27.
2161. Niuscha, *supra* n. 1737, at 245.
2162. Binder, *supra* n. 2149, at 318.

affect third parties.[2163] The test for such a determination is *'if it[court] considers it proper'*. However, the term 'proper' in Article 17H(3) of the Model Law has not been defined. During the discussions of the Working Group, it was suggested that one such instance would be where the jurisdiction of the tribunal has been challenged.[2164]

Another concern is that Article 17(3) of the Model Law is also silent on what is 'necessary' when considering the effect on third parties. One view is that the court will consider if security is warranted. If yes, in which form and what amount, after balancing the interest of all parties against each other. It will determine whether the respondent's or third party's interests are unreasonably harmed in the event of enforcement.[2165]

In the absence of clear guiding criteria, the courts may undertake a review of the decision to grant interim measures. The order to provide security may render the interim measure ineffective if the party seeking enforcement does not have the means to provide such security. In such circumstances, one of the reasons why the tribunal did not order security may also be due to the financial health of the applicant. Therefore, the court should not be guided by the same principles as that of the tribunal while considering the question of security but should only consider a 'manifest' or 'blatant' harm to third parties. It should be determined from the order whether the determination of such harm was considered by the tribunal at all or have circumstances changed since the passing of the order which necessitates the requirement of security. Arbitrators should clarify why no security is being ordered for limiting the scope of judicial review at the time of enforcement of its order.

2.2. Article 17I of the Model Law

The 2006 Model Law Revisions add Article 17I to the regime on interim measures which provides for grounds when the recognition and enforcement of an interim measure may be refused by the court. It contains the 'only' grounds for refusing recognition and enforcement of interim measures which are generally based on the misuse of basic rules of a fair trial. The same operates as a ceiling or a maximum under which a national law could decide to adopt a system more favourable to recognition and enforcement.[2166] Thus, a country can deviate from the said Article and provide for a more favourable system. The grounds for refusing enforcement are divided into two categories.

2163. Report of UNCITRAL Working Group on the work of its Forty Second session, 2005, A/CN.9/573, available at: https://undocs.org/en/A/CN.9/573, ¶27.

2164. Report of the Secretary General for Settlement of Commercial Disputes, in its Thirty Fifth Session, 2000, A/CN.9/WG.II/WP.110, available at: https://undocs.org/en/A/CN.9/WG.II/WP.110, ¶68.

2165. Niuscha, *supra* n. 1737, at 245.

2166. Jean-Paul Beraudo, *Recognition and Enforcement of Interim Measures of Protection Ordered by Arbitral Tribunals*, 22(3) J. of Int'l Arb. 250 (2005); ('*The conditions set forth in this Article are intended to limit the number of circumstances in which the court may refuse to enforce an interim measure of protection. It would not be contrary to the level of harmonization sought to be achieved by these model law provisions if a State were to adopt fewer circumstances in which enforcement may be refused.*').

2.2.1. *Refusal at the Request of a Party*

(1) At the request of a party, i.e.:
  (a) Incapacity of the party or invalidity of the arbitration agreement.
  (b) Failure to provide proper notice of appointment of an arbitrator, or of arbitral proceedings, or the party was unable to present its case.
  (c) Lack of jurisdiction of the tribunal.
  (d) Illegal composition of the arbitral tribunal.
  (e) Failure to provide security in connection with the measure (Article 17(H)(2)).
  (f) Termination or suspension of the measure by the tribunal, a national court at the arbitral seat or national court which issued the interim measure (Article 17(H)(3).

2.2.2. *Cognisance by the Court of Its Own Accord*

(2) When the court considers the same of its own accord, i.e.:
  (a) Incompatibility with the court's powers.
  (b) The subject matter not being 'arbitrable'.
  (c) The public policy of the State.

Therefore, enforcement of an interim measure ordered by the tribunal, irrespective of the seat, will be enforced but for any of the grounds listed above. There is a close alignment between Article 17I and Article 36 of the Model Law[2167] but the provisions of Article 36(1)(a)(i) to (iv) should be applied with caution and may not be applied on a one-to-one basis.[2168]

2.2.3. *No Setting Aside of Interim Measure*

It is reiterated that Article 17I does not provide for setting aside the interim measure but only the refusal to recognise and enforce the same. The only recourse for a party against an interim order would be to apply to the arbitral tribunal itself for suspension, modification or termination of the order. However, Austria has a provision to set aside the interim measure[2169] apart from a provision to refuse enforcement.[2170]

2167. Report of UNCITRAL Working Group on the work of its Thirty Eighth session, 2003, A/CN.9/574, available at: https://undocs.org/en/A/CN.9/524, ¶¶35-36, 42, 58; Report of UNCITRAL Working Group on the work of its Forty Second session, 2005, A/CN.9/573, available at: https://undocs.org/en/A/CN.9/573, ¶73; Binder, *supra* n. 2149, at 321.
2168. Binder, *supra* n. 2149, at 322.
2169. Austrian Code of Civil Procedure (ZPO), S. 593(6).
2170. *Ibid.*, S. 593(4).

2.2.4. *Concerns with Article 17I of the Model Law*

One fundamental problem with Article 17I of the Model Law is that instead of requiring the court to ensure that the interim order complies with Article 17 or Chapter IVA of the Model Law, it instead focuses on Article 36 which provides for situations when the award has been passed on merits.[2171] An interim order is usually a procedural order given during the pendency of the proceedings. Therefore, the test ought to have been in compliance with the necessary safeguards or conditions mentioned in Article 17 or Chapter IV A as that would have provided an incentive for compliance with the conditions and safeguards.[2172] The same was rejected on the ground that it would introduce ambiguity and that the courts may undertake a de novo review on merits.[2173]

However, tribunals are bound to be influenced by the view of the courts in case a measure is refused because of any of the grounds mentioned in Article 36(1)(a)(i) to (iv), especially if the court is the same where an application for setting aside of the award will be brought. If the tribunal does not have jurisdiction, if the arbitration agreement is invalid, or if there is a problem with the composition of the tribunal, then such problems would exist throughout arbitration[2174] and have to be addressed at the stage of setting aside or enforcement of the award. Such issues cannot be considered only for the purpose of interim measures alone. Therefore, in Turkey, the request for enforcement may be decided by a substitute court.[2175]

All procedural challenges contained in Article 36(1)(a)(i)-(iv) were deliberately kept for the final stages of challenge and to permit a review of the same, albeit limited to interim measures, does in practical terms reduce the confidence of tribunals and more importantly, provide for a view of the court of the dispute with respect to the jurisdiction of the tribunal. Such an intention is contrary to the approach of reducing court interference. In Qatar, the only ground for refusing enforcement is if the measure violates public policy.[2176] However, the Working Group rejected this approach as the threshold would be too low and there can be different approaches to public policy.[2177]

Surprisingly, the discussions by the Working Group on the grounds for refusal of recognition and enforcement of interim measures do not sufficiently clarify why the grounds under Article 36 should be considered at the stage of enforcement, except that alignment with the said provision sufficiently addresses the issues of notice, jurisdiction, and opportunity to present the case.[2178] The current reference to Article 36 was justified on the ground that subclause (2) would guard against the risk of any

2171. Report of UNCITRAL Working Group on the work of its Thirty Eighth session, 2003, A/CN.9/574, available at: https://undocs.org/en/A/CN.9/524, ¶57.
2172. Menon, *supra* n. 102, at 25-26.
2173. Report of UNCITRAL Working Group on the work of its Thirty Ninth session, 2003, A/CN.9/545, available at: https://undocs.org/en/A/CN.9/545, ¶¶ 99.
2174. *Ibid.*, ¶ 105.
2175. Turkey Arbitration Law, 2001, Art. 6.
2176. Qatar Arbitration Law, 2017, Art. 17(3).
2177. *See generally:* Report of UNCITRAL Working Group on the work of its Thirty Ninth session, 2003, A/CN.9/545, available at: https://undocs.org/en/A/CN.9/545.
2178. *Ibid.*, ¶27.

determination made by the court on any of the grounds for recognition and enforcement of the interim measure only.[2179]

The second ground for refusal is non-compliance with an order of security. Though many calls were made to delete this ground, the Working Group considered it to be an essential safeguard for the party against whom the measure was directed.[2180]

The third ground for refusal is linked to the duty of disclosure in Article 17H(2) of the Model Law to inform the court if the interim measure has been suspended or terminated by either (1) the arbitral tribunal; (2) the court at the seat of arbitration; or (3) under the law of which that interim measure was granted.

There still exists doubt over the phrase '*or under the law of which that interim measure was granted*'. It is unclear whether the same refers to procedural law or substantive law.[2181] Also, it is unclear how an interim measure would be suspended or terminated by the court at the seat without a provision of an appeal. The only scenario could possibly be where an application for enforcement is brought under Article 17H and the measure is refused.

Even in such a circumstance, Article 17I does not provide for setting aside the interim measure. Hence, it is inconceivable under which circumstance would an interim measure be suspended or terminated by a court at the seat without a provision for setting aside the interim measure, except in a jurisdiction like India which permits an appeal against the order of the tribunal.

2.2.5. Burden of Proof

Further, there is little clarity on who should bear the burden of proof.[2182] The Working Group had considered it best to leave this issue for domestic legislation.[2183] Logically, the party seeking enforcement will approach the competent court for enforcement. In an application for setting aside the award, it is usually the party resisting the enforcement of the award that approaches the court and bears the burden to prove why the award should be set aside.

The approach to the question of burden of proof under Article 36(1)(a) of the Model Law is different from Article 17I(1)(a) with respect to (a) whether there is a substantial question relating to a ground for refusal; and (b) whether the refusal was

2179. *Ibid.*,¶ 105.
2180. Report of UNCITRAL Working Group on the work of its Forty Second session, 2005, A/CN.9/573, available at: https://undocs.org/en/A/CN.9/573, ¶75.
2181. *Ibid.*, ¶78.
2182. Menon, *supra* n. 102, at 23-24; Report of UNCITRAL Working Group on the work of its Thirty Eighth session, 2003, A/CN.9/574, available at: https://undocs.org/en/A/CN.9/524, ¶¶32 -36, 42, 60-61; Report of UNCITRAL Working Group on the work of its Thirty Eighth session, 2003, A/CN.9/524, available at: https://undocs.org/en/A/CN.9/468, ¶77. Report of UNCITRAL Working Group on the work of its Thirty Ninth session, 2003, A/CN.9/545, available at: https://undocs.org/en/A/CN.9/545, 23-24; Report of UNCITRAL Working Group on the work of its Thirty Eighth session, 2003, A/CN.9/524, available at: https://undocs.org/en/A/CN.9 /468, ¶¶32-36, 42, 60-61.
2183. Report of UNCITRAL Working Group on the work of its Forty Second session, 2005, A/CN.9/573, available at: https://undocs.org/en/A/CN.9/573, ¶27.

warranted.[2184] Under Article 17I, the party seeking enforcement does not bear any burden of proof since the orders of the tribunal are binding unless the grounds mentioned under Article 17I are satisfied. Therefore, even though the party seeking enforcement would approach the court, a reverse onus of proof would apply, i.e., the party resisting enforcement would bear the burden of proof.

2.2.6. Standard of Proof

The burden of proof or more accurately the standard of proof required should have been addressed[2185] and the standard, as widely agreed within the Working Group, should have been a prima facie standard given the urgent need for enforcement.[2186] This is imperative for two reasons (1) that the party resisting enforcement has to show only why the enforcement should not be granted as opposed to a higher a standard for setting aside the award; and (2) without a proper standard there is a danger of review of the substance of the measure.

One view can be that such a standard is implicitly contained in Article 17I(2) of the Model Law. Since the court where enforcement is sought cannot review the substance of the measure, the only other standard of burden proof can be a 'prima facie' standard. It is necessary to highlight that the power under Article 17(2) is to determine questions of recognition and enforcement of interim measures only.[2187] Any concerns about the standard being unclear can always be addressed by providing for the same when adopting the same into domestic legislation.

2.2.7. Reformulating the Interim Order

Article 17I(1)(b)(i) provides that to the extent the interim measure is incompatible with the powers of the court, then akin to the provision in Germany,[2188] Austria,[2189] and Liechtenstein,[2190] the court has the power to reformulate the interim measure to the extent necessary to adapt it to its own power or procedures for enforcement without modifying its substance.

In Germany, the court is entitled to review the order to confirm whether it is in consonance with the public policy,[2191] the requirement for interim relief, and to ensure that the interim measure does not pre-empt the decision on merits.[2192] However, in

2184. *Ibid.*, ¶73.
2185. Holtzmann, *supra* n. 6 at, 178.
2186. Report of UNCITRAL Working Group on the work of its Thirty Eighth session, 2003, A/CN.9/524, available at: https://undocs.org/en/A/CN.9/468, ¶61.
2187. *UNCITRAL Official Records of the General Assembly*, 61st, Supplement No. 17 (A/61/17), ¶135, c.f. Binder, *supra* n. 2149, at 323.
2188. German Arbitration Act, S. 1041(2).
2189. Austrian Code of Civil Procedure (ZPO), S. 593(3).
2190. Liechtenstein, Code of Civil Procedure, S. 610(3).
2191. Jan Schäfer, *supra* n. 301, at 234-236.
2192. Stephen, *supra* n. 96, at 398.

case the court has to deal with the issues of arbitrability, public policy, and compatibility with the court's power of enforcement, Article 17I(b)(i) of the Model Law leaves it open for these issues to be dealt with by the courts' own procedure. The only caveat is that the court should modify the interim measure only 'to the extent necessary' and in doing so should not review the merits. Hence, the court would reformulate the measure under its own procedural law to achieve the intended result of the interim measure.

2.3. Acceptability of Articles 17H and 17I of the Model Law

Most jurisdictions that have adopted the 2006 Model Law Revisions have adopted Articles 17H[2193] and 17I[2194] of the Model Law, though some countries have modified the provisions to a certain extent.[2195] For example, Hong Kong has substituted Article 17H with its own version which states that '*an order or direction ... by an arbitral tribunal is enforceable in the same manner as an order or direction of the court that has the same effect, but only with the leave of the Court*' and has provided that Article 17(I) shall not have effect. Brunei and Slovenia[2196] have also incorporated similar provisions[2197] In Singapore, experts have weighed in against the adoption of Articles 17H and 17I of the Model Law.[2198]

A slightly different approach has been taken by Section 593(4) of the Austrian CPC[2199] which provides the circumstances as to when the enforcement of interim measures must be denied. Interestingly, Austria distinguishes between interim measures granted by a tribunal seated in Austria and a foreign seated arbitral tribunal. For measures passed by tribunals seated in Austria, the enforcement of interim measures ordered by an Austrian tribunal must be denied for any ground which would also give a reason for the annulment of an arbitral award, i.e., the grounds listed in Section 611(2), Section 617(6) and (7), and Section 618 ACCP.[2200]

Where the measures are granted by foreign seated arbitral tribunals, interim measures will not be enforced for any of the grounds applicable for refusing the recognition and enforcement of foreign arbitral awards, in particular those grounds enumerated by Article V of the NYC. Besides, interim measures will not be enforced if the enforcement of the measure would be incompatible with a previously requested or issued measure of an Austrian court or with a previously issued measure of a foreign court that is recognised in Austria.[2201]

2193. Belgium Judicial Code, Art. 1696.
2194. Belgium Judicial Code, Art. 1697.
2195. Tomas, *supra* n. 1256, at 27.
2196. *K Puharic, Developments in Slovenian Arbitration Law,* 16 Croatian Arb. Yb 244 (2009).
2197. Brunei International Arbitration Order, 2009 S. 15(6); *See Appendix B.*
2198. *International Arbitration (Amendment) Bill: Ministry of Law's Response to Public Feedback Received,*: https://www.mlaw.gov.sg/files/linkclick1e3a.pdf.
2199. The position is the same in Liechtenstein Code of Civil Procedure, S. 610.
2200. Austrian Code of Civil Procedure (ZPO), Ss 611(2), 617(6), 617(7) & 618.
2201. Stephen, *supra* n. 96, at 316.

2.4. The Indian Position

Before the 2015 Amendment, in India, there was no express recognition of taking assistance of the court for enforcement of the interim measures granted by the arbitral tribunal and such orders were not enforceable.[2202] The predominant view, as expressed by a three-judge bench of the Supreme Court was that an arbitral tribunal is not a court of law and the orders passed by them are not judicial orders.[2203] Section 17 of the IAA did not contain any provision by which the arbitral tribunal can enforce its own orders nor did it provide for judicial enforcement of the orders of the tribunal.[2204] Thus, the purpose of Section 17 of the IAA was severely compromised before the 2015 Amendment[2205] and parties tried an alternative approach to seek enforcement.

In *Sri Krishan v. Anand*,[2206] the Delhi High Court was called upon to answer the question of whether an application under Section 9 of the IAA for enforcement of an order granted by the tribunal is maintainable. The application was filed pleading that the order of the tribunal is toothless and unenforceable. It was contended that the IAA was a complete code in itself, but it does not provide for enforcement of an order passed under Section 17 of the IAA. Furthermore, a petition for contempt of court cannot be filed as the same is maintainable only if a judgment/order/direction or writ or other processes of a court has been wilfully disobeyed as an arbitral tribunal is not a court. Interestingly, it was also contended that the provision of Order XXXIX Rule 2A of the CPC applies to a breach of an order passed under Order XXXIX Rules 1 & 2 only and has no applicability to an order passed under Section 17 of the IAA.[2207]

However, the respondent argued that the order under Section 17 of the IAA would be merged under the final award and then it will be enforceable.[2208] The court relying on the entire gamut of cases on Section 9 of the IAA and its applicability to third parties took the view that the powers under Sections 9 and 17 are distinct.[2209] The court held that permitting an application under Section 9 for enforcement of an order under Section 17 would render the said section otiose and redundant and open the flood gates of court petitions under Section 9.

The legislative intent of Section 17 of the IAA is to make the tribunal an adequate forum not only for the adjudication of disputes but also for interim measures. Therefore, it would serve no purpose to first approach the tribunal under Section 17

2202. *Managing Director, Army Welfare Housing Organization v. Sumangal Services (P) Ltd.* AIR 2004 SC 1344; *India Bulls Financial Services Ltd v. Jubilee Plots and Housing Pvt Ltd.* (2009) SCC OnLine Mad 1078; *Sundaram Finance Ltd. v. NEPC India Ltd.* 1999 (2) SCC 479.
2203. *Managing Director, Army Welfare Housing Organization v. Sumangal Services (P) Ltd.* AIR 2004 SC 1344, ¶43.
2204. *Ibid.*, ¶58.
2205. D. Gracious Timothy, *Recognition and Enforcement of Interim Measures under the Indian Arbitration Amendment Act of 2015*, available at: https://papers.ssrn.com/sol3/papers.cfm?abstract_id = 3045678.
2206. *Sri Krishan v. Anand* 2009 SCC OnLine Del 2472, *followed in India Bulls Financial Services Ltd v. Jubilee Plots and Housing Pvt Ltd.* (2009) SCC OnLine Mad 1078; *Affirmed* in *Alka Chandewar v. Shamshul Ishrar Khan* (2017) 16 SCC 119, ¶7.
2207. *Sri Krishan v. Anand* 2009 SCC OnLine Del 2472, ¶ 3.
2208. *Ibid.*, ¶5.
2209. *Ibid.*, ¶7.

when the same relief can be ordered by the court directly under Section 9. Permitting such an application would mean that the court and the tribunal will be vexed with the same issue at the expense and cost of the parties.[2210]

Thus, the Law Commission of India recommended that Section 17 of the IAA should be amended to give teeth to the orders of the arbitral tribunal and make the same statutorily enforceable in the same manner as the orders of the court.[2211]

2.5. 2015 Amendment

Based on the recommendation of the Law Commission,[2212] the 2015 Amendment substituted Section 17(2) of the IAA.[2213] It now provides that '*Subject to any orders passed in an appeal under section 37, any order issued by the arbitral tribunal under this section shall be deemed to be an order of the Court for all purposes and shall be enforceable under the Code of Civil Procedure, 1908 (5 of 1908), in the same manner as if it were an order of the Court*'.

India has not adopted the approach of direct enforcement of the orders of the tribunal like Ecuador. In Ecuador, arbitrators can take support from the public, judicial, police, and administrative officials to execute interim measures if provided in the arbitration agreement. Thus, tribunals can grant and enforce every measure that they consider appropriate except for imprisonment.[2214]

India has also rejected seeking executory assistance where the leave of the court is required before enforcement.[2215] Now, an order of the tribunal is as binding as that of a court the moment it is passed by the tribunal.[2216] After the 2015 Amendment, an interim order issued by the arbitral tribunal is to be construed as an order of the court for all purposes. Therefore, when a court receives an interim order from the tribunal, it should treat it as if it is one from another court[2217] without any review at the stage of enforcement[2218] unless it is set aside in appeal.[2219]

For enforcement, a civil court may arrest a party or attach a property. It has to take resort to Section 94 of the CPC and not the procedure contemplated for the execution of decrees.[2220] If the court at the seat is not located at the place where the property is to be attached, the provision of Section 136 of the CPC would be applicable

2210. *Ibid.*, ¶9.
2211. Law Commission of India, *supra* n. 517.
2212. *Ibid.*
2213. Indian Arbitration Act, 1996, S. 17(2), *prior to substitution: 'the arbitral tribunal may require a party to provide appropriate security in connection with a measure ordered under sub- section (1)'*.
2214. Ecuador's Mediation and Arbitration Law 1997, Art. 9, c.f. Ronald Wong, *supra* n. 452, at 508.
2215. Bolivia Arbitration Law, Art. 36; English Arbitration Act, 1996, S. 42; Hong Kong Arbitration Ordinance (Cap.609), S. 2 GG; Singapore International Arbitration Act, 1994, S. 12(6).
2216. Zia Mody, *supra* n. 682, at 133.
2217. *Sundaram Finance Ltd. v. P. Sakthivel* 2018 SCC OnLine Mad 3080, ¶¶16 &18.
2218. Mohan, *supra* n. 12, at 334.
2219. Indian Arbitration Act, 1996, S. 37(2) (b).
2220. *Pradeep K.N. v. The Station House Officers* 2017 (1) Arb. LR 57, ¶11.

and the court shall send it to the relevant court within whose territorial jurisdictional limits the person resides or is situated.[2221]

The Calcutta High Court has adopted the view that the power of the tribunal under Section 17 of IAA was always of the widest amplitude. The tribunal all along had the same powers as that of the court under Section 9 of the IAA. Therefore, the 2015 amendment in Section 17(2) of the IAA is only clarificatory and has been made only by way of abundant caution.[2222] It is worthy to note that the High Court issued a direction to all courts to enforce the orders of the tribunal as orders of the court. The court directed other courts to take note of the legislative amendment in 2015 along with the judgment in *Alka Chandewar*[2223] (where the court can even invoke jurisdiction under the Contempt Act for enforcement of the orders of the tribunal) to give effect to the orders passed by the arbitral tribunal.[2224]

It can be said that Section 17(2) of the IAA is more pro-arbitration than many other statutes of the world.[2225] In fact, it is similar to the approach in Ecuador which provides for direct enforcement and some authors have even expressed a view that the 2015 Amendment is in tune with the 2006 Model Law Revisions.[2226] However, a fundamental difference between the two is that Section 37(1)(b) of the IAA provides for an appeal against the orders of the tribunal, whereas the approach in Ecuador is without any safeguards. Moreover, tribunals have no power of enforcement in India directly and the direct enforcement referred to above means that once the arbitral tribunal passes an order, it is deemed to be an order of the court. No review is contemplated before enforcement of such orders except in appeal.

Interpreting Section 17(2) of the IAA, the Kerala High Court has held that the tribunal has no power to enforce its own order and conferring the power of the civil court to the tribunal for passing an interim order does not mean that the tribunal is conferred with the power of enforcement. Enforcement implies the exercise of a sovereign and state function. The tribunal by its constitution or creation inherently lacks the power to deal with any sovereign function or public law as the authority of the tribunal is founded in a contract and the power is regulated by the statute.[2227] This is clear from the provision of Section 27 of the IAA, which requires the tribunal to apply to the court for assistance in taking evidence.[2228] The arbitral tribunal by its very nature of composition cannot exercise any such power vested with a court which discharges

2221. *Sundaram Finance Ltd. v. P. Sakthivel* 2018 SCC OnLine Mad 3080, ¶20.
2222. *Tufan Chatterjee v. Rangan Dhar* 2016 SCC OnLine Cal 483, ¶39.
2223. *Alka Chandewar v. Shamshul Ishrar Khan* (2017) 16 SCC 119, ¶9.
2224. *Sundaram Finance Ltd. v. P. Sakthivel* 2018 SCC OnLine Mad 3080, ¶24.
2225. Bolivia Arbitration Law, Art. 36; California Code of Civil Procedure, S. 1297(92); Egyptian Arbitration Law, 1994, Art. 24; Guatemalan Arbitration Law, Art. 22(2); English Arbitration Act, 1996, Ss 42(3), 42(4) & 42(5); Singapore International Arbitration Act, 1994, S. 12(5); Sri Lanka Arbitration Act, 1995, S. 13; Zimbabwe Arbitration Act, 1996, Art. 17(3); Venezuela Arbitration Law, Art. 28; Tunisian Arbitration Code, Art. 62; Hong Kong Arbitration Ordinance (Cap.609), S. 2GG; Greece Arbitration Law, Art. 17(2); Peru Arbitration Law, Art. 81(2).
2226. Sarthak, *supra* n. 21, at 195.
2227. *Pradeep K.N. v. The Station House Officers* 2017 (1) Arb. LR 57, ¶13.
2228. *Ibid.*, ¶16.

a sovereign function as enforcement signifies that there must be a force to put the order in motion to ensure that the party bound by the order complies such order.[2229]

Unfortunately, the 2015 Amendment is not in consonance with the 2006 Model Law Revisions and blindly borrows from the English jurisprudence which has not entirely adopted the Model Law. A grave lacuna in the IAA is that the provision of appeal under Section 37(1)(b) of the IAA grants the party against whom the interim measure is passed thirty days to challenge the said order. Thus, until the expiry of the period, a court will not ordinarily enforce the measure. This, in effect, completely nullifies the urgency of the interim measure and the need for enforcement.

Moreover, there is no guidance on what is the standard of judicial review at the stage of enforcement. The only safeguard is an appeal against the order of the tribunal. One view is that after the order is confirmed by an appellate court, the order is one that is passed by a court and not by the tribunal per se. Hence, no further judicial review is necessary at the stage of enforcement. The other view can be that Section 17(2) of the IAA does not provide for the grounds, standards, or limits of enforcement.[2230] The judicial review by the appellate court under Section 37(1)(b) of the IAA, without proper guiding criteria, is nothing but a review of the merits of the order of the tribunal. Instead, a better approach may be to adopt the 2006 Model Law for enforcement of interim measures.

2.5.1. Enforcement of Orders Passed by an Emergency Arbitrator

One of the problems with the 2015 Amendment is that there is no provision for recognising orders passed by emergency arbitrators as they do not fall within the definition of 'arbitral tribunal'. Hence, recourse to Section 17(2) of the IAA for enforcement of orders passed by an emergency arbitrator was not available. In order to remedy this glaring lacuna, courts implicitly recognised orders passed by emergency arbitrators through fresh applications under Section 9 of the IAA.[2231] However, there was no express recognition of orders passed by emergency arbitrators as an order under Section 17(2) of the IAA. Such orders were enforced as orders passed by a court under Section 9 of the IAA.

It was only recently that the Delhi High Court expressly held that Section 2(1)(d) of the IAA was wide enough to include an emergency arbitrator.[2232] Unfortunately, this judgment was stayed by an order of the Division Bench of the Delhi High Court.[2233] Finally, the Supreme Court of India struck down the order of the Division Bench and

2229. *Ibid.*, ¶20.
2230. Ronald Wong, *supra* n. 452, at 529.
2231. *Raffles Design International India Private Limited v. Educomp Professional Education Limited* 2016 SCC OnLine Del 5521; *Ashwani Minda v. U-Shin Ltd.* 2020 SCC OnLine Del 1648.
2232. *Amazon.com NV Investment Holdings LLC v. Future Coupons Pvt. Ltd.* 2021 SCC OnLine Del 1279, ¶133.
2233. *Future Coupons Pvt. Ltd. v. Amazon.com NV Investment Holdings LLC* 2021 SCC OnLine Del 4101.

held that '*in so far as Section 17(1) is concerned, the "arbitral tribunal" would, when institutional rules apply, include an Emergency Arbitrator*'.[2234]

The Supreme Court affirming and recognising an emergency arbitrator to be included within the meaning of Section 2(1)(d) of the IAA is certainly a huge leap forward for arbitration jurisprudence in India. However, it should be noted that the seat of arbitration in this case was Delhi and hence, it was easier to apply to Section 17 of the IAA. There continues to be ambiguity on the question of enforcement of orders passed by an emergency arbitrator in a foreign seated arbitration.[2235] The right way forward would be to amend the definition of 'arbitral tribunal' under Section 2(1)(d) of the IAA to expressly include an emergency arbitrator as was suggested by the Srikrishna Committee Report.[2236] This express inclusion will provide maximum recognition and enforcement of interim orders passed by emergency arbitrators.

2.5.2. Interim Order or Interim Award

After the introduction of Section 17(2) of the IAA, interim measures are enforceable as those of the courts, though tribunals are not prevented from granting interim measures as awards. Therefore, both approaches of enforcement are available in India for enforcement of interim measures granted by an arbitral tribunal, i.e., passing the interim measure as an award or taking assistance of the court for enforcement of orders passed by the arbitral tribunal.

3. PASSING THE INTERIM MEASURE AS AN AWARD

The most controversial aspect of interim measures has been the form in which the measure should be granted. Usually, the first issue to be settled is to obtain the enforcing court's authorisation, i.e., whether the interim measure is an award or order.[2237] The Model Law or the rules of various arbitration institutions or international conventions do not prescribe a form in which the temporary measure may be

2234. *Amazon.com NV Investment Holdings LLC v. Future Retail Ltd.* 2021 SCC OnLine SC 557, ¶44-45.

2235. Akash Srivastava, *Emergency Arbitration and India: A Long Overdue Friendship*, 10 (1) Ind. J. Arb. L. 98-112 (2021).

2236. *1. Clause (c) of sub-section (1) of section 2 of the ACA may be amended to add the words 'an emergency award' after the words 'an interim award'.*
2. Clause (d) of sub-section (1) of section 2 of the ACA may be amended to add the words 'and, in the case of an arbitration conducted under the rules of an institution providing for appointment of an emergency arbitrator, includes such emergency arbitrator;' after the words 'panel of arbitrators'.
3. An emergency award may be defined as 'an award made by an emergency arbitrator'; Justice B.N. Srikrishna, Report of the High-Level Committee to Review the Institutionalization of Arbitration Mechanism in India, (July 2017), available at: http://legalaffairs.gov.in/sites/default/files/Report-HLC.pdf.

2237. Beraudo, *supra* n. 2166, at 249.

issued.[2238] The most common language used in the context of interim measures is '*whether in the form of an award or in another form*'.[2239] Most arbitration institutions permit interim orders to be made in the form of an award or any other form.[2240] However, there is no clarity on what form and content an interim order should contain.

The form of the order is of considerable significance since it affects the enforceability of the interim measure. The heart of the controversy is that the NYC has no express guidelines on how to identify an arbitral award. The general understanding is that if the award puts an end to all the disputes and terminates the duty of the arbitrators, it will be a global award,[2241] but if it decides only part of the dispute in a final manner, it will be a partial award.[2242]

It is pertinent to note that some jurisdictions and arbitral institutions[2243] use the word 'partial award' as opposed to an interim award. However, there is no difference between the two as both refer to a piecemeal award dealing with certain claims and accord finality to such claims.[2244] *Waincymer* is of the view that the notion of an interim award is ambiguous and not an ideal expression to use in articulating whether there is an entitlement to interim measure or not. In his view, if the intent is to have the partial award being final as to that part as all awards are required to be, then it is inappropriate to use the phrase 'partial award' for interim measures.[2245]

Usually, orders issued during arbitration proceedings are technical and procedural and are rendered without any formality.[2246] They are nonetheless binding on the parties. The only requirement is that the order has to be in writing and reasoned, but how extensive should such reasoning be? Therefore, in the context of interim measures of protection, while it is true that interim orders are in one sense 'binding' on the parties to the arbitration agreement, the finality of such orders is doubtful. An interim order may be rescinded, suspended, varied, or reopened by the tribunal which pronounced it. It is not 'final' and binding on the parties.[2247] They do not operate as res judicata.

2238. Eduardo, *supra* n. 35, at 233-234.
2239. UNCITRAL Model Law, Art. 17(2).
2240. *Ibid.*; Art. 23(1), ICC Arbitration Rules; Art. 21(2), ICDR Rules; Art. 26(2), 2004 Swiss Rules; Art. 26(2), UNCITRAL Arbitration Rules.
2241. Emmanuel Gaillard and John Savage, *Fouchard Gaillard Goldman on International Commercial Arbitration* 741 (1999).
2242. Eduardo, *supra* n. 35, at 248.
2243. International Chamber of Commerce (ICC).
2244. Gary Born, *supra* n. 33, at 2660.
2245. Waincymer, *supra* n. 989, at 625.
2246. Lew, *supra* n. 28, at ¶24-5; Rolf Trittmann, *When Should Arbitrators Issue Interim or Partial Awards and or Procedural Orders?*, 20(3) J. Int'l Arb. 255, 261 (2003).
2247. *Resort Condominiums International Inc. v. Ray Bolwell*, [1995] 1 Qd R 406; Richard Garnett & Michael Pryles, *Enforcement of Foreign Awards in Australia and New Zealand*, in Luke Notage & Richard Garnett (eds), *International Arbitration in Australia* 62, 67-69, 73-74 (2010); Malcolm Holmes and Chester Brown, *The International Arbitration Act 1974: A Commentary* 62-63 (2011).

3.1. 'Finality' of Issues

Even the 'finality' of the order is subject to debate in that whether finality refers to the end of arbitral proceedings or to the determination of only a particular issue with finality.[2248] The word 'final award' is usually referred to as one that has achieved a sufficient degree of finality in the arbitral seat or is no longer subject to appeal or annulment at the seat.[2249] The broad idea is that the litigious issue, which is the subject matter of arbitration, should be finally decided.[2250] Therefore, the element of finality is the biggest challenge to the enforcement of interim measures under the NYC. This problem is compounded in the case of emergency arbitration as the orders from the tribunal, devoid of finality, are not enforceable under the NYC.[2251]

Arbitration statutes across the world have also not adopted a consistent approach. The Brunei Arbitration Act expressly excludes orders or directions made under Section 15 (including interim measures) from the meaning of the word award.[2252] On the contrary, Article 480 of the French New CPC provides that '*the judgment which decides in its operative part the whole or the part of the main issue, or one which rules upon the procedural plea, a plea seeking a plea of non-admissibility or any other interlocutory application, will, from the time of its pronouncement become res judicata with regard to the dispute which it determines*'. This view was reflected by the first civil law court of the Federal Tribunal.[2253] Therefore, decisions that do not qualify as an award will not be enforced by the French Court.[2254] Similarly, an interim measure in the Netherlands is considered to be an award, unless the tribunal determines otherwise.[2255] Hence, interim measures are always enforceable as an award by the Dutch courts.[2256]

In Spain, as there are no special form requirements, the provisions for setting aside and enforcement of awards apply irrespective of the form of the tribunal's decision on interim measures.[2257] Thus, the Spanish Arbitration Law (Law 60/2003)[2258] and even the Peruvian Arbitration Law of 2008[2259] authorises the arbitrators to define through awards what would be considered as final, not only the issues related to the merits but also jurisdiction and the grant of interim measures.

2248. *See* Eduardo, *supra* n. 35, at 243-245.
2249. Gary Born, *supra* n. 33, at 2606-2607; Eduardo, *supra* n. 35, at 245-246.
2250. *Oberlandesgericht Frankfurt Schieds VZ 278 (May 10, 2007) (Frankfurt)* c.f. Eduardo, *supra* n. 35, at 246.
2251. Article 29(3), ICC Rules *provides that the tribunal is not bound by the decision of the emergency arbitrator and 'may modify, terminate or annul the order or any modification thereto made by the emergency arbitrator'.*
2252. Brunei International Arbitration Order, 2009 S. 2.
2253. *Decision of 13 April 2009, Club Atlético de Madrid SAD v. Sport Lisboa Benfica – Futebol SAD and Fédération Internationale de Football Association (FIFA).*
2254. Stephen, *supra* n. 96, at 370.
2255. Dutch Code of Civil Procedure, Art. 1043b(5).
2256. *Ibid.*, Art. 1062(1).
2257. Spanish Arbitration Law, Art. 23(2).
2258. *Ibid.*, Art. 37(1).
2259. Peru Arbitration Law, Art. 54 *and it is identical to* Spanish Arbitration Law, Art. 37(1).

Many authors[2260] argue that interim measures should be enforceable as they finally dispose of a request for relief pending the conclusion of the arbitration.[2261] However, since such orders are subject to modification, suspension, or termination, it is still doubtful whether they attain the finality required for enforcement. Article 17I provides that an interim order may be refused for enforcement if the tribunal has terminated or suspended the measure. Therefore, the result is that such orders are enforceable unless suspended or terminated. This also is the intent under Article 17H of the Model Law. Moreover, an interim order is passed at an interlocutory stage, without a full hearing of the facts of the issues so the 'finality' of it may be limited.

Although echoing the same view in favour of enforceability, *Graham's* view is that the NYC should not be interpreted as a formalistic crossword, but the intention and purpose of the convention should be looked at.[2262] An interim measure of protection issued as an award will lead to arbitration being a more effective method of dispute resolution as an award will receive greater enforcement.[2263] However, to say that they are enforceable under the NYC is a stretch aimed at taking a purposive interpretation of the NYC without much textual support for the same.[2264]

Finality ought to arise from no expectation of a further decision. Given that interim orders are subject to modification, suspension, and termination, it cannot be said that they finally decide on the requests for the interim measure as the same can be changed later. To enforce an interim order as an award only to subsequently indemnify the respondent makes little sense. Even if the tribunal would have taken security for costs, the damage may be far more than the costs provided and hence, it is more practical not to have interim orders enforced as awards. Therefore, courts, across jurisdictions, however, have not adopted such a liberal view.

The Colombian Supreme Court has ruled that an award on jurisdiction does not resolve the merits of the dispute and hence, cannot be recognised under the NYC.[2265] Similarly, in England and Wales, a measure can only be enforced which settles some issues of the dispute definitively.[2266] Interim orders of courts including an anti-suit injunction are not enforceable in Russia as they are not final decisions.[2267] The

2260. Van Vechten Veeder, *Provisional and Conservatory Measures*, paper presented at the 'New York Convention Day' in New York on 10 June 1998 to celebrate the 40th anniversary of the Convention, published by the United Nations in Enforcing Arbitration Awards under the New York Convention: Experience and Prospects, 1999, at 22; Tijana Kojovic, *Court Enforcement of Arbitral Decisions on Provisional Relief-How is it Provisional?*, 18(5) J. Int'l Arb. 526 (2001); Stalev, *supra* n. 88, at 113; *Mika Savola, Interim Measures and Emergency Arbitrators Proceedings*, 23 Croatian Arbitration Yearbook 86 (2016); Stalev, *supra* n. 88, at 113.

2261. Gary Born, *supra* n. 33, at 2702-2703.

2262. Luis, *supra* n. 521, at 563.

2263. Ali Yesilirmak, *supra* n. 30, at 194-195.

2264. Marike Paulsson, *Chapter 2: The New York Convention as an Instrument*, available at: https://www.arbitration-icca.org/media/9/87217006027030/paulsson_chapter_2.pdf at 51.

2265. *Merck & Co. Inc., et al. v. Tecnoquímicas SA, ICCA Yearbook Commercial Arbitration* XXVI (2001); *Empresa Colombiana de Vías Férreas (Ferrovías) v. Drummond Ltd., Yearbook* XXIX (2004), 643-656, c.f. Luis, *supra* n. 521, at 563-564.

2266. Beraudo, *supra* n. 2166, at 249.

2267. Stephen, *supra* n. 96, at 531.

prevailing opinion, thus, is that the NYC applies to awards that settle a dispute or some issues of the dispute definitively.[2268]

3.2. 'Separate and Independent Claim'

In the United States, some courts have taken the view that if an interim order finally disposes of certain issues, the orders can be enforced as awards.[2269] A District Court held that an interim award to be considered final under the NYC should satisfy two requirements.[2270] First, it should conclusively dispose of a separate independent claim, and second, the party seeking enforcement must be able to identify an immediate need for relief.[2271] It must be noted that this requirement of the separate independent claim is only necessary but not by itself sufficient for confirmation of an interim award.[2272] In Ukraine, an order of an emergency arbitrator issued as an award was recognised as enforceable by the court of the first instance.[2273]

Though the view of the US courts appears to be more liberal, all cases where interim orders have been enforced as awards were peculiar to their facts and circumstances. The possibility of such measures being modified, suspended, or terminated was limited. Hence, their precedent value establishing the US position of law may not be completely accurate.

Also, the reasoning adopted by the US courts skips the fact that an interim measure should be in aid of the final relief and not otherwise. If a separate independent claim is established, but the same is unrelated to the final relief, should the interim measure be granted in the first place? Though the issue may have been resolved with finality, the interim measure may not always dispose of a 'separate and independent' claim. Interestingly, the Swiss Federal Tribunal has, and rightly so, termed the practice as 'dangerous'.[2274]

It should also be noted that parties who are concerned with the enforcement of the interim measures can specifically provide for the form they are to be issued within the arbitration agreement itself. In the absence of such a specification, the arbitrators have complete discretion to decide the form.[2275] The same should be enforceable under

---

2268. Beraudo, *supra* n. 2166, at 249.

2269. *Island Creek Coal Sales Co. v. Gainsville* 729 F2d 1046 (6th Cir. 1984); *Publicis Commun v. True North Coummuns* Inc. 206 F. 3d 725 (7th Cir. 2000*), 729; CE International Resources Holdings LLC v. S.A. Minerals Ltd.* Partnership 2012 US Dist. Lexis 176158.

2270. *Pacific Reinsurance Management Corporation v. Ohio Reinsurance Corporation*, 935 F.2d 1019, 1022-23, (9th Cir. 1991).

2271. *Hall Steel Co., v. Metalloyd Ltd.* 492 F.Supp.2d 715, at 719-720.

2272. *Island Creek Coal Sales Co. v. Gainsville* 729 F2d 1046 (6th Cir. 1984) at 1049-1050, the US Court of Appeal for the Sixth Circuit *'an interim award that finally disposes of all the claims that were submitted to arbitration'*.

2273. The decision was set aside in appeal on the ground of public policy. *See*, Yaroslav Petrov, *JKX vs. Ukraine: An Update on the Enforcement of Emergency Arbitrator's Award*, (12 August 2016), available at: http://arbitrationblog.kluwerarbitration.com/2016/08/12/jkx-vs-ukraine-an-update-on-the-enforcement-of-emergency-arbitrators-award/.

2274. *See judgment of April 13, 2010, X v. Y, DFT 136 III 200.*

2275. *Piero Bernardini, The Italian Law on Arbitration – Text and Notes* 27 (1998); Berger, *supra* n. 1352, at 343; *Lew,* supra *n. 2, at 28* arguing that *'where the request is made for a specific form,*

the NYC. The Uniform Arbitration Act of 2000 adopted by many states in the United States of America provides for enforcement of interim awards.[2276] However, requests made to the tribunal for issuing the interim measure as an award have not always been conceded to.[2277]

3.3. Considerations to Determine the Appropriate Form

Yesilirmak suggests that the tribunal could use the following criteria when determining which form the measure should be issued in:[2278]

(a) Potential savings of time costs for the parties.
(b) Effective and efficient conduct of the arbitration.
(c) Enforceability of the award.
(d) The agreement of the parties.
(e) An analysis of the pros and cons of either form.

3.4. Article 17H of the Model Law: Enforceability Irrespective of Form

In view of Article 17H of the 2006 Model Law, the considerations mentioned above may not be required. The only considerations to be kept in mind are (a) the agreement of the parties; and (b) the mandatory law of the place where the enforcement is going to be sought.[2279] It is necessary to clarify that arbitrators should grant interim measures irrespective of whether the measure will be enforceable or not. The consideration of the mandatory law of the *lex fori* should only be to the extent of the form and nature of the measures' compatibility with the requirements of the *lex fori*. If the *lex fori* will not consider the measure as an award, there is little sense in passing the interim measures as an award. However, if the measure is to be enforced in several jurisdictions, such a consideration is not required.

Also, the finality of the measure by the arbitral tribunal is moot as the *lex executionis* or *lex fori* will use its own criteria, whether under its own arbitration statute or mandatory law to determine whether a particular measure is in the form of an order or award. From a practical point of view, the enforcement of an interim measure will always be subject to the law applied by the court where the enforcement is sought.

---

then the tribunal should not use any discretion. In order to avoid refusal of its request, a party may request both order and award as alternative forms.' See, e.g., ICC Final Award No. 9154 of 1998, extracts published in 11(1) ICC Int'l Ct Arb Bull. 98 103 (2000). *Rather than refusal of its request, if it is made for a specific form, a party may prefer to have interim protection measure in any other form. That is confirmed with the fact that '[f]requently, parties are anxious to have the tribunal's order, whatever its form'.*

2276. David W. Rivkin & Donald F. Donovan, *Arbitration World: Jurisdictional Comparisons, United States, Evidence Gathering* 395, 396 & 404 (2006), c.f., Hober, *supra* n. 1207, at 725.
2277. *ICC Final Award 5804 of 1989; ICC Final Award 7489 of 1993; ICC Case No. 5887*, c.f. Ali Yesilirmak, *supra* n. 30, at 195-196.
2278. Ali Yesilirmak, *supra* n. 30, at 197.
2279. Harshad Pathak & Anirudh Gandhi, *Anti-Arbitration Injunction and Investment Treaty Arbitration – A Tale of Two (Indian) Cities*, 202 ICA Arb. Q. 12-20 (2019).

In this context, Article 17H of the Model Law provides that an interim measure shall be recognised as binding and shall be enforced upon application to the competent court, irrespective of the country in which it was issued, subject to the provisions of Article 17I of the Model Law. This language clearly envisages a regime distinct from the enforcement under the NYC. Hence, concerns over enforcement of anti-suit injunctions issued by an arbitral tribunal are also addressed.[2280] Moreover, Article 17H of the Model Law recognises the power of the court to enforce interim measures as orders of the court without the reliance or the need to term them as awards and resort to the NYC for enforcement. Such a sui generis enforcement mechanism has been adopted by various arbitration statutes.[2281]

Thus, Article 17H of the Model Law is a better standard for enforcement as it mandates enforcement subject to the provisions of Article 17I, which also comprise issues of public policy or *lois de police*. After the adoption of Article 17H of the Model Law, such jurisdictions that have adopted the 2006 Model Law Revisions do not require the interim measure to be in the form of an award.[2282]

After the introduction of these two provisions, the discussion on finality assumes lesser significance as the enforcement of the interim measure is not going to be sought as an award but the same shall be enforceable in its own right. Articles 17H and 17I of the Model Law do not define the form of interim measures whereas Article 36 of the Model Law refers to an 'arbitral award'. Hence, recognition and enforcement are not dependent on the form of the measure,[2283] i.e., an award or an order. The challenge will still be governed by Article 17I and not Article 36.[2284]

This is a welcome change. While it does not decide the controversy of finality one way or another, it fulfils the objective of effective interim relief. In a certain sense, it serves as an international instrument harmonising the enforcement regime for interim measures.[2285] It must be clarified though, that this provision may not adequately address the issue of enforcement of orders passed by an emergency arbitrator as Article 17H of the Model Law uses the language of 'arbitral tribunal,'[2286] unless the definition of an 'arbitral tribunal' includes an emergency arbitrator.

Countries such as Singapore and Hong Kong now include an emergency arbitrator within the definition of an 'arbitral tribunal'[2287] and 'arbitration proceedings'[2288] respectively. In England, such orders are recognised by courts.[2289] In such countries,

2280. *See Chapter 10.*

2281. Christopher Huntley, *The Scope of Article 17: Interim Measures under the UNCITRAL Model Law*, 9 Vind. J. Int'l Com. L. Arb. 69 (2005).

2282. Melissa, *supra* n. 1690, at 712-713.

2283. Holtzmann, *supra* n. 6 at, 177.

2284. *Ibid.*, at 177-183.

2285. Lew, *supra* n. 28, at 614.

2286. *Paata Simsive, Indirect Enforceability of Emergency Arbitrator's Orders*, (15 April 2015), available at: http://arbitrationblog.kluwerarbitration.com/2015/04/15/indirect-enforceability-of-emergency-arbitrators-orders/.

2287. Singapore International Arbitration Act, 1994, S. 2(1).

2288. Hong Kong Arbitration Ordinance (Cap.609), S. 98F.

2289. Justice B.N. Srikrishna, Report of the High-Level Committee to Review the Institutionalization of Arbitration Mechanism in India, (July 2017), available at: http://legalaffairs.gov.in/sites/default/files/Report-HLC.pdf.

the orders passed by an emergency arbitrator may be enforceable under Article 17H of the Model Law. As discussed previously, in India, the definition of the arbitral tribunal should be amended to include an emergency arbitrator to ensure maximum enforceability of interim measures, including those passed by an emergency arbitrator.

3.5. Order or Award: The Indian Position

In India, Section 31(6) of the IAA empowers the tribunal to make an interim award. Section 2(1)(c) of the Arbitration Act defines an 'arbitral award' to include an interim award. However, the definition does not throw any light on what constitutes an interim award and how the same is different from the final arbitral award. Since the arbitral tribunal becomes *functus officio* once the claim is finally decided by the tribunal, an interim award would ordinarily mean an award which is neither a procedural order nor the final award.[2290] Therefore, an interim award must be the final determination of a claim, part of a claim, or a counterclaim by the tribunal.[2291]

The language of Section 31(6) refers to a two-fold test for the determination of an interim award, i.e., (1) the award may be made 'at any time during the arbitral proceedings'; and (2) 'on any matter with respect to which it [tribunal] may make a final award'. Therefore, the first test envisages the continuity of arbitral proceedings as opposed to the culmination of the same.

The second test draws a distinction between procedural matters and matters with respect to which a final award is contemplated. Thus, an interim award is one which must result in the tribunal being rendered *functus officio* for a claim, right, or subject matter,[2292] i.e., an award results in the final determination of the rights of the parties.[2293]

The essence of the distinction lies in the language and form of the order. Where the tribunal directs a party to pay money, the same would be a specific direction to pay a determined sum of money and hence, capable of enforcement based on a combined reading of Section 31(6) and Section 2(1)(c) of the IAA. Any order directing payment of an ascertained sum of money by one party to the other would be a prima facie determination of the *lis* between the parties and hence, would be an interim award and not an interim order under Section 17.[2294] For instance, imposing a condition relating to security would amount to such an order.[2295] On the contrary, mere determination of liability in law to pay an amount requires further adjudication to determine the exact sum and damages.[2296] Therefore, it cannot be termed an interim award.[2297]

2290. *Harinarayan G. Bajaj v. Sharedeal Financial Consultants Pvt. Ltd.* 2002 SCC OnLine Bom 1186, ¶5.
2291. Wadhwa, *supra* n. 46, at 57.
2292. *Ibid.*
2293. *Satwant Singh Sodhi v. State of Punjab* AIR 1999 SC 2040, ¶6.
2294. *Asian Electronic Ltd., Thane v. MP State Electricity Board & Ors.* 2007 SCC OnLine MP 179.
2295. *Ibid.*, ¶¶ 18-19.
2296. *Manganese Ore (India) Ltd. v. Ram Bahadur Thakur Ltd.* 2006 (Suppl) Arb LR 315, 323.
2297. *Commissioner, Kolhapur Municipal Corporation v. Fairdeal Constructions* (2008) 1 Arb LR 312, 316, ¶18.

The test to determine an interim award is how a reasonable recipient would have viewed the tribunal's decision. The determination is one which rests on the substance of the order and not the form,[2298] even though an order may have been passed as an award or the description given by the tribunal states that it is an award.[2299] If a final determination of a particular issue or claim or a substantive right of one party or the other is done by the arbitral tribunal, then the same would be an interim award.[2300] It would then bind the arbitral tribunal in respect of the matter it decides.[2301] Therefore, Section 31(6) of the IAA is clear that only matters qua which the reference is made and part thereof is decided can be said to be an interim award. No other order passed by the arbitrator can be said to be an interim award.[2302]

Based on the foregoing, it is evident that Section 17 of the IAA is intended to support arbitration proceedings and does not contemplate the acceptance or denial of any right 'with respect to which the tribunal may make a final award'.[2303]

This distinction between an 'interim award' and 'interim order' is pertinent since the enforcement mechanism under the CPC is different for both. If the interim measure is passed as an 'award,' it would become a 'decree' under the CPC, whereas an 'order,' would remain an 'order of the court'.

3.5.1. 'Decree' and 'Order'

Section 2(1)(c) of the IAA defines an 'arbitral award' to include an interim award without any further explanation as to what constitutes an award. However, the language used in Section 9 and Section 17 of the IAA specifically uses the word 'order' and does not make any reference to the word 'decree' or 'award'. The word order, therefore, has to be interpreted with reference to Section 2(14) of the CPC, which defines an 'order' as the following:

> '(14) "order" means the formal expression of any decision of a Civil Court which is not a decree;'
>
> A bare reading of the same throws no light on what an 'order' is, except that it is not a 'decree'. A decree, on the other hand, has been defined in section 2(2) of the CPC as the following:
>
> '(2) "decree" means the formal expression of an adjudication which, so far as regards the Court expressing it, conclusively determines the rights of the parties with regard to all or any of the matters in controversy in the suit and may be either preliminary or final ....'

The words 'formal expression of an adjudication' do not cover interim or interlocutory orders.[2304] An interlocutory order is an order by way of aid to the proper

2298. *Michael Wilson v. EMMoTT* (2009) (2008) EWHC 2684 (Comm), ¶58.
2299. *Jain Studios Limited v. Maitry Exports Pvt. Ltd.* 2007 SCC OnLine Del 1898, ¶18.
2300. *Deepak Mitra v. District Judge* 1999 SCC OnLine All 609, ¶10.
2301. *Union of India v. Surendarnath Kanungo* (2005) 2 Arb LR 106, 115.
2302. *Liberty Shoes Limited v. Harish Kumar Gupta* 2006 (4) Arb. LR 225(P&H), ¶13.
2303. *Subhash Chander Chachra v. Ashwani Kumar Chachra* (2007) 137 DLT 401 (Del), ¶31.
2304. *Baliram v. Manohar* A 1943 N 204. c.f. Sarkar, *supra* n. 302, at 16.

adjudication of the claims and disputes arising in the suit itself, e.g., orders by way of receiver, injunction, issuing of a commission for examination of witnesses, discovery, or inspection and such orders do not finally dispose of any dispute or claim in the suit itself.[2305]

Furthermore, this definition excludes any adjudication from which an appeal lies as an appeal from an order. Therefore, the essential elements of a decree are (a) a formal expression of an adjudication; (b) adjudication on the rights of the parties with regard to all or any of the matters in controversy; (c) conclusive determination of rights; and (d) adjudication must be in a suit.[2306]

Applying these definitions in the context of arbitration, an interim order is appealable under Section 37(1)(b) of the IAA for interim measures requested under Sections 9 and 37(2)(b) of the IAA for interim measures requested under Section 17 of the IAA. This means that an appeal under Section 37 against any interim measure shall be an 'Appeal from an Order' as contemplated under Section 2(2)(a) of the CPC and hence, would not be a decree.

It also logically follows that such an order may not be one that conclusively determines the rights of the parties with respect to any and all matters in controversy. Hence, even if an interim measure is passed as an award, it may not be enforced as a 'decree' as it would not meet the requirements of Section 2(2) of the CPC.

Interim awards can only be deemed to be a decree for the purposes of execution[2307] since Section 36(1) of the IAA creates the fiction that awards will be enforced in the same manner 'as it was a decree of the court'. Therefore, the distinction between an 'interim award' and 'interim order' is of great significance as it has the following consequences:

(a) An award is enforced under the provisions of Order XXI of the CPC, whereas interim orders are enforced under Section 94 of the CPC.
(b) It determines the appellate rights available to a party and limits the matters which would form a part of the final award. An order passed by the arbitral tribunal under Section 17 can be challenged under Section 37(2)(b) of the Arbitration Act whereas an interim award cannot be challenged by way of an appeal but can only be set aside under Section 34 of the IAA.[2308]
(c) An interim award is subject to payment of stamp duty under Article 12 of Schedule I to the Indian Stamp Act, 1899 and inadmissible as evidence if not duly stamped.[2309] On the contrary, an interim order is not subject to payment of any stamp duty.[2310]

2305. *German D Republic v. Dynamic & C* A 1972 B 27 c.f. Sarkar, *supra* n. 302, at 20.
2306. *R. Rathinavel Chettiar v. V. Sivaraman* (1999) 4 SCC 89, ¶10; *Rachakonda Venkat Rao v. R. Satya Bai* AIR 2003 SCC 332.
2307. *Lakhamraju Sujatha v. Yuvaraj Finance Pvt. Ltd.* 2009 SCC OnLine AP 718, ¶11.
2308. *The IAA permits an appeal against the order setting aside or refusing to set aside an award,* Indian Arbitration Act, 1996, S. 37(2)(b).
2309. Law Commission of India, Report No. 194 – Verification of Stamp Duties and Registration of Arbitral Awards, (7 June 2005) available at: https://lawcommissionofindia.nic.in/reports/report194.pdf; Indian Registration Act, 1908, S. 17(1)(b) read with S. 35; *An award needs to*

(d) Depending on the arbitral institute, the nomenclature and substance would determine the applicability of various other provisions in the rules of the arbitral institute, e.g., under the ICC rules, interim relief by an emergency arbitrator or an arbitral tribunal is by means of an order and hence not subject to 'scrutiny' as in the case of an award passed under the said rules.[2311] On the contrary, orders passed under various other arbitral rules may be either orders or awards.[2312]

(e) An interim award will operate as res judicata.[2313] It would, however, matter little if the court of enforcement is one of limited jurisdiction, i.e., it is not competent to try the subsequent action or the action in which the issue has been raised subsequently.[2314] Therefore, the tribunal may not be bound by the decision even if such an order is treated to be an interim award by the court since the tribunal would be competent to try the subsequent action or the action in which the issue has been raised.

A situation that may arise if the interim measure is issued as an award is that it would be subject to challenge under Section 34 of the IAA. If the court were to stay the effect and operation of the award under Section 36(2) of the IAA, then will the tribunal await the final adjudication of the application under Section 34 of the Act or proceed with the arbitration proceedings? Also, what happens if the interim measure is not stayed, but the matter is admitted for hearing under Section 34?

Moreover, if the measure is issued as an award, then modification or revocation of the measure becomes extremely difficult.[2315] Therefore, the debate in India surrounding whether interim measures are awards or orders is largely settled that they are not awards and cannot be enforced as such. They are neither final nor decide the rights and liabilities of the parties finally. This view is in consonance with the UNCITRAL Secretariat Report of 1999.[2316]

---

be registered and stamped if it affects immovable property as held in M. Chelamayya v. M. Venkataratnam AIR 1972 SC 1121, ¶13.

2310. *Rikhabdas v. Vallabhdas* AIR 1962 SC 551; *M/s Wilson & Co. Pvt. Ltd. v. K.S. Loka Vinayagam* AIR 1992 Madras 100 (*in a case decided under the Arbitration and Conciliation 1940 Act*).

2311. Article 29(2), ICC Rules of Arbitration.

2312. *See, Appendix M.*

2313. *Waste Management, Inc. v. Mexico (ICSID Case No. ARB(AF)/00/3-IIC 269), Decision on Mexico's Preliminary Objection Concerning the Previous Proceedings of 26 June 2002,* ¶39; *Petrobart Ltd. v. Kyrgyzstan, Award on SCC Case No. 126/2003-IIC 184 (29 March 2005),* ¶ 294 and *Industria Nacional de Alimentos SA and Indalsa Perú v. Peru (ICSID Case No. ARB/03/4-IIC 300), Decision on Annulment of 13 August 2007,* ¶¶64-65; Eduardo, *supra* n. 35, at 241.

2314. *See,* Indian Code of Civil Procedure, 1908, S. 11, explanation VIII. *The same principles analogous thereto should apply in arbitration proceedings, Himachal Sorang Power Pvt. Ltd. v. NCC Infrastructure Holdings Ltd.* 2019 SCC OnLine Del 7575, ¶74.

2315. Caron, *supra* n. 1238, at 513-514.

2316. UNCITRAL Yearbook, A/CN.9/SER.A/1999, Volume XXX (1999), at 395, 410.

The only recourse to an aggrieved party for enforcement of an interim measure is, therefore, under (a) Section 94 of the CPC; (b) the inherent power of the Court under Section 151 of the CPC; or (c) the Contempt Act.[2317]

4. COURT ASSISTANCE FOR ENFORCEMENT OF INTERIM MEASURES

It is clear from the foregoing that if an interim measure is passed as an award, then the provisions of Order XXI of the CPC on the execution of decrees would get triggered.[2318] If the interim measure is not passed as an award, then it would only amount to an 'order',[2319] and its enforcement has to be done under Section 94 of the CPC[2320] read with Order XXXIX Rule 2A, whether the order has been granted under Order XXXIX Rule 1 or 2 or not.[2321] However, it is necessary to clarify that Order XXXIX Rule 1 or 2 pertains only to injunctions[2322] and not to any other form of interim measure that the tribunal may grant. The language of Order XXXIX Rule 2A of the CPC clarifies that the said provision only applies '*in case of disobedience of any injunction granted or other order made under Rule 1 or 2 or breach of any of the terms on which the injunction was granted or the order made*'.

4.1. Section 94 of the CPC

As discussed in Chapter 3, interim measures granted under the CPC are granted under Section 94 of the CPC read with the corresponding Order and Rules under the CPC. Section 94 provides that:

> In order to prevent the ends of justice from being, defeated the Court may, if it is so prescribed:
>
> (a) issue a warrant to arrest the defendant and bring him before the Court to show cause why he should not give security for his appearance, and if he fails to comply with any Order for security commit him to the civil prison;
> (b) direct the defendant to furnish security to produce any property belonging to him and to place the same at the disposal of the Court or Order the attachment of any property;
> (c) grant a temporary injunction and in case of disobedience commit the person guilty thereof to the civil prison and Order that his property be attached and sold;

2317. Ajar Rab, *Arbitration & Conciliation Amendment Act, 2015 – Enforcing Interim Orders, Where Is the Relief?*, 4 NLU Del. St. L. J. 89, 96 (2017).
2318. Indian Arbitration Act, 1996, S. 36(1); *Thummu Koti Nagaiah v. Duddempudi Sambayya* 1962 SCC OnLine AP 107, ¶11.
2319. Indian Code of Civil Procedure, 1908, S. 2(14).
2320. *Pradeep K.N. v. The Station House Officers* 2017 (1) Arb. LR 57, ¶11.
2321. *Rattu v. Mala* 1968 SCC OnLine Raj 3, ¶6; *Hiralal Hargovindas v. Popatlal Sankalchand Patel* 1967 SCC OnLine Guj 46, ¶18; *S. Adaikkala Thevan v. Imperial Bank* 1925 SCC OnLine Mad 466, ¶¶2-3; *Sitaram v. Lachminarain* 1945 SCC OnLine Pat 328, at 611-612; *Thummu Koti Nagaiah v. Duddempudi Sambayya* 1962 SCC OnLine AP 107, ¶12.
2322. Ajar Rab, *supra* n. 2317, at 96.

(d) appoint a receiver of any property and enforce the performance of his duties by attaching and selling his property;
(e) make such other interlocutory Orders as may appear to the Court to be just and convenient.

Therefore, the implication of Section 17(2) of the CPC is that the court will enforce the interim measure granted by the arbitral tribunal under Section 94 and as per the procedure laid down in the corresponding Orders and Rules. However, courts have not enforced the orders per se. Primarily, the view is that the enforcement referred to in Section 17(2) is on account of the disobedience of the interim order.[2323] Therefore, courts have enforced interim measures granted by an arbitral tribunal under Section 94 read with Order XXXIX Rule 2A of the CPC.

4.1.1. Procedure for Enforcement

Once an order is granted under Section 9(1) or 17(1) of the IAA and the respondent fails to comply with the said order, the applicant has to file a fresh case under Section 94 read with Order XXXIX Rule 2A of the CPC under the civil rules applicable to the appropriate court[2324] for wilful disobedience. The court will proceed to issue notices to the respondent to file objections against the said application. Once the response is received, the court will then pass an appropriate order under Rule 2A.[2325] Therefore, enforcement of measures in India could take several months.[2326]

Though there have been instances when the court has ordered police assistance to enforce interim measures granted by the court in a suit, the same approach has not been extended to orders passed arbitral tribunals.[2327] It should be noted that the mechanism for enforcement under Section 94 of the CPC provides for several modes for enforcement of orders depending on the nature of the relief granted. Hence, to confine the power of enforcement to disobedience only may not be correct.

4.1.2. Practical Difficulties in Enforcement of Orders

Currently, the enforcement mechanism works on the principle of deterrence alone but does not, in fact, enforce the order. For attachment of property, Order XXXVIII Rule 7 provides that the attachment shall take place in the same manner as in the execution of the decree. The court can even send a commissioner to attach properties of a party.[2328] Therefore, the better view would be to use the power under Section 94 to implement

2323. *Pradeep K.N. v. The Station House Officers* 2017 (1) Arb. LR 57, ¶¶9-11.
2324. The case is usually registered as a separate Miscellaneous Civil Case.
2325. *In an application for wilful disobedience of the order passed under the Indian Arbitration Act, 1996, S. 9, the respondent took appearance and complied with the order before any order could be passed by the court. See Gannewala v. Mukund Halwasiya* 2019 SCC OnLine All 872.
2326. Zia Mody, *supra* n. 682, at 132.
2327. *Sh. Yousuf and Ors v. Shaik Madhar Saheb* MANU/AP/1188/2002.
2328. *Sundaram Finance Ltd. v. P. Sakthivel* 2018 SCC OnLine Mad 3080, ¶21.

orders using the court machinery instead of resorting to penalising a party for disobedience.[2329]

Restricting the enforcement mechanism to disobedience provides no effective remedy to the applicant seeking enforcement. More importantly, the logic of bringing a fresh proceeding and requiring notice to be served defeats the whole purpose of the interim measure sought to be enforced and ignores urgency. Therefore, the idea that interim measures should be enforceable at the time they are granted is completely vitiated.[2330]

Furthermore, the CPC is silent on the actual enforcement of the order under Rule 2A. Unlike, corresponding pro formas for all other rules, there is no pro forma for complying with the order under Rule 2A. It is unclear whether the Court Commissioner will proceed to arrest the respondent, whether the attachment has to be done under the provisions of Order XXXVIII of the CPC or whether the arrest shall be carried out as provided in consonance with the provisions of the Code of Criminal Procedure. Therefore, the court and the parties have no choice but to resort to Section 151 for enforcement, making enforcement mostly discretionary.[2331]

Additionally, fetters have been placed by the courts to the effect that the power under Order XXXIX Rule 2A should be used sparingly[2332] since the allegation of wilful disobedience is in the nature of criminal liability. It has to be proved that there was not only mere 'disobedience' but that such disobedience was 'wilful' and 'conscious'.[2333] Therefore, it should be statutorily clarified that the interim measures granted by an arbitral tribunal should be enforced under Section 94 of the CPC in the interest of clarity and to actually enforce the measure, rather than penalise for non-compliance.

4.2. Contempt Jurisdiction

Extending the enforcement regime on the threat of penalty, an alternative is to invoke the contempt jurisdiction of the court read in light of Section 27(5) of the IAA.[2334] Earlier, orders of the tribunal could not be enforced as orders of the court since a tribunal was not a court and hence, resort to contempt jurisdiction was barred. Even the Evidence Act did not recognise an arbitrator as a court.[2335] In line with this jurisprudence, courts repeatedly held that there was no power of enforcement of interim measures granted by the tribunal.[2336]

2329. *Rayapati Audemma v. Pothineni Narasimham* AIR 1971 AP 53.
2330. Ronald Wong, *supra* n. 452, at 503.
2331. Ajar Rab, *supra* n. 2317, at 98.
2332. *Sitaram v. Ganesh Das* 1973 SCC OnLine All 296, ¶¶2-3.
2333. *Future Coupons Private Limited v. Amazon.com NV Investment Holdings* LLC 2022 SCC OnLine SC 126, ¶45. *For a discussion on the meaning of the word 'wilful', see Ram Kishan v. Tarun Bajaj* (2014) 16 SCC 204, ¶12.
2334. *Pradeep K.N. v. The Station House Officers* 2017 (1) Arb. LR 57, ¶¶8-9.
2335. The Evidence Act, 1872, S. 3.
2336. *Managing Director, Army Welfare Housing Organization v. Sumangal Services (P) Ltd.* AIR 2004 SC 1344, ¶58; *India Bulls Financial Services Ltd v. Jubilee Plots and Housing Pvt Ltd.* (2009) SCC OnLine Mad 1078; *Sundaram Finance Ltd v. NEPC India Ltd.* 1999 (2) SCC 479.

Before the 2015 Amendment, the Delhi High Court interpreted Section 27(5) and took the view that the said provision provides a remedy for a breach as the words 'making any other default' or 'guilty of any contempt to the arbitral tribunal during the conduct of any proceedings' were sufficient to provide for enforcement. The arbitral tribunal would make such a representation to the court after being satisfied that the party/person is in default or in contempt and once such representation is received, a court would be competent to deal with such party either under the provisions of the Contempt of Courts Act or under the provision of Order XXXIX Rule 2A of CPC.[2337]

However, it is unclear how, before the 2015 Amendment, the court would have deemed the order of the tribunal to be an order under Order XXXIX Rule 1 or 2 of the CPC. Hence, the statutory basis and legal validity of such an interpretation are doubtful. The court would enforce an order under Order XXXIX Rule 2A, without there being an order passed under Order XXXIX Rule 1 or 2.

The court justified this view by relying on the legislative intent to resolve the dispute between parties expeditiously. The Learned Single Judge Rajiv Sahai Endlaw J. noted that there was no other judgment of any court supporting his view. However, he supported his view by replying to two other cases[2338] and placing reliance on a judgment of the Bombay High Court[2339] which had held that the power of contempt of arbitral tribunal had been conferred explicitly under Section 27(5) in a significant departure from the 1940 Act. The Bombay High Court had, however, warned that such power must be wielded with extreme caution, circumspection, and in view of the judicial restraint provided for under the IAA.

He then noted that the title or heading could not limit or narrow the otherwise wide amplitude of subsection (5) of Section 27 of the IAA.[2340] To limit the applicability of this section with respect to the appearance of witnesses before the arbitral tribunal only would render the words 'any other default' and 'guilty of any contempt' otiose. He further relied on Section 37(2)(b) to state that an order of the arbitral tribunal is appealable, which discloses the legislative intent of the same being in the exercise of the judicial function.[2341]

More importantly, Endlaw J. referred to the 2006 Model Law Revisions qua the powers of the arbitrators to grant interim measures and the provision for an application to the court for enforcement of the said orders. He was of the opinion that the IAA contained the provision for enforcement in Section 27(5) way before the 2006 Model Law. It is pertinent to highlight that though Section 27(5) of the IAA provides for contempt of orders of the arbitral tribunal,[2342] it does not grant the power to the

2337. *Sri Krishan v. Anand* 2009 SCC OnLine Del 2472, ¶11.

2338. *Maharashtra State Electricity Board v. Datar Switchgear Ltd.* 2002 SCC OnLine Bom 983; *Saurashtra Chemicals Ltd. v. Hon'ble Justice K. Ramamoorthy Retd.* (2005) SCC OnLine Guj 578.

2339. *Anuptech Equipments Pvt. Ltd. v. Ganpati Co-operative Housing Society Ltd.* AIR 1999 Bombay 219.

2340. *Managing Director, Army Welfare Housing Organization v. Sumangal Services (P) Ltd.* AIR 2004 SC 1344 and *Sundaram Finance Ltd v. NEPC India Ltd.* 1999 (2) SCC 479.

2341. *Sri Krishan v. Anand* 2009 SCC OnLine Del 2472, ¶14.

2342. Indian Arbitration Act, 1996, S. 27(5): provides that '*persons failing to attend in accordance with such process, or making any other fault, or refusing to give their evidence, or guilty of any*

tribunal to punish the defaulting party but only provides for seeking the assistance of the court. Therefore, the party seeking enforcement would apply to the tribunal under Section 27(5) of the IAA and once the tribunal is satisfied, the tribunal would apply to the court for assistance.[2343] In effect, he envisioned a *double exequatur* of the order before enforcement.

After this judgment, the Supreme Court[2344] held that merely because an order or decree is executable, it would not take away the contempt jurisdiction of the court. If it is proved that the violation of the order or decree is such that it would warrant punishment under the Contempt Act on the ground that the contempt substantially interferes or tends to substantially interfere with the due course of justice, then the court would exercise contempt jurisdiction.

This view was affirmed by the division bench of the Supreme Court[2345] which held a party in contempt of court under the Contempt Act for disobeying the order of the arbitral tribunal. Subsequently, this view was confirmed by the Supreme Court in *Alka Chandewar v. Shamshul Ishrar Khan.*[2346] In this case, the arbitral tribunal had passed an injunction under Section 17 of the IAA directing the respondent not to dispose of assets without the leave of the arbitral tribunal. However, the respondent violated the said order and the sole arbitrator referred the contempt of the order to the High Court to pass necessary orders under Section 27(5) of the IAA. The High Court took the view that Section 27(5) of the IAA does not empower the tribunal to make a representation to the court for contempt if the orders, including the interim orders passed by the arbitrators except in respect of taking evidence, are violated by the party.[2347]

The Supreme Court rejected the view of the High Court and took the view that Section 27(5) provides for the guilt of 'any' contempt during the conduct of arbitral proceedings. The court resorted to the marginal note as an internal aid to interpretation. It held that the entire objective of providing that a party may approach the tribunal instead of the court for interim relief would be defeated if interim orders passed by the tribunals are toothless. It is to give teeth to such orders that an express provision has been made in Section 27(5) of the Arbitration Act.[2348] The court relying on *Srikrishan* went on to hold that a party can elect between a court and a tribunal for pursuing interim measures.[2349] If the orders under Section 17 were not enforceable, Section 17 would be rendered a dead letter.[2350]

---

contempt to the arbitral tribunal during the conduct of arbitral proceedings, shall be subject to the like disadvantages, penalties and punishments by order of the Court on the representation of the arbitral tribunal as they would incur for the like offences is suits tried before the Court'.

2343. *Sri Krishan v. Anand* 2009 SCC OnLine Del 2472, ¶¶9-10.

2344. *Rama Narang v. Ramesh Narang* (2006) 11 SCC 114, ¶24.

2345. *Maruti Udyog Ltd. v. Mahender C. Mehta* (2007) 13 SCC 220, ¶¶35-38. *However, it is pertinent to mention that the contempt jurisdiction was invoked on the basis of an undertaking given by the parties to the Supreme Court that they would furnish the security and comply with the orders of the arbitrator.*

2346. *Alka Chandewar v. Shamshul Ishrar Khan* (2017) 16 SCC 119, *affirmed* at ¶7.

2347. *Ibid.*, ¶29.

2348. *Ibid.*, ¶6.

2349. *Ibid.*

2350. *Ibid.*, ¶7.

Interestingly, the court briefly addressed Section 17(2) of the IAA as amended by the 2015 Amendment and referring to the 246th Report of the Law Commission held that the 2015 Amendment intended to curtail the cumbersome procedure of having to apply to the High Court for contempt of its orders. The court observed that Section 17(2) of the IAA was enacted to provide a 'complete solution' to the problem.[2351] Therefore, the court set aside the view of the High Court and accepted the view that the contempt jurisdiction can be invoked under Section 27(5) of the Arbitration Act for not complying with the orders passed by the arbitral tribunals under Section 17 of the Act without any need first to approach the tribunal.

4.3. Limits of Contempt Jurisdiction

It should be noted that the Supreme Court has time and again reiterated that contempt jurisdiction cannot be invoked to be used in abundance or misused. It cannot be invoked for the execution of decree or implementation of an order where an alternative remedy in law exists. Hence, the resort to contempt jurisdiction under Section 10 of the Contempt Act is unwarranted since there is a provision for enforcement contained in Order XXXIX Rule 2A of the CPC.[2352] Discretion is given to the court to be exercised for the maintenance of the court's dignity and majesty of the law. Furthermore, an aggrieved party has no right to insist that the court should exercise jurisdiction as the contempt is between the contemnor and the court.[2353]

The Supreme Court laid down the test of whether the default is wilful, i.e., where there is contumacy on the part of the defendant or a wilful attempt to disregard the order of the court. The rule should be used as a last resort. The court also referred to the power of arrest under Section 51 read with Order XXI Rule 37 that there must be some element of bad faith beyond mere indifference to pay, some deliberate or recusant disposition in the past or alternatively current means to pay a decree or substantial part of it.

What needs to be established is not the mere omission to pay but the attitude of refusal, verging on dishonest disowning of the obligation under the decree.[2354] The Bombay High Court held that the court under Section 9 has the power in exceptional cases to impose sanctions against a recalcitrant party such as by the grant of the stay of the arbitration proceedings to secure compliance with an interim order for the furnishing of security, but that power has to be exercised with caution and circumspection. A mere default in payment cannot justify the exercise of such power and an element of bad faith or contumacious conduct is required.[2355]

Therefore, the enforcement of interim measures through the threat of contempt jurisdiction is largely discretionary. Moreover, often, the breach/default is not obvious

2351. *Ibid.*, ¶9.
2352. *Nitinkumar Pramodbhai Pandya v. Spenta Colour Lab Pvt. Ltd.* 1994 SCC OnLine Guj 122, ¶5; *Gajjan Singh v. Tersam Lal* 2001 SCC OnLine P&H 626, ¶¶10-11.
2353. *R. N. Dey v. Bhagyabati Pramanik* (2000) 4 SCC 400, ¶7.
2354. *Jolly Geroge Varghese v. Bank of Cochin* (1980) 2 SCC 360, ¶11.
2355. *Maharashtra State Electricity Board v. Datar Switchgear Ltd.* 2002 SCC OnLine Bom 983, ¶61; *Sri Sai Krishna Constructions v. Glove Infracom* 2019 SCC Online Bom 1406.

and the averment of one party on such breach/default may require adjudication. The approach of enforcement, without any adjudication of whether contempt has even been committed by the respondent, can be violative of the principle of equal treatment of the parties and plainly against the principles of natural justice.

The view in *Srikrishna* was a better view, where a tribunal would first determine if contempt had been committed and then the tribunal would refer the violation to the court. This view would also reduce court interference in reviewing whether a contempt has been committed and the cumbersome process of a fresh adjudication, including the service of summons. However, this is not to say that such a position should be adopted. The safeguard of review can be undertaken under Article 17I, as discussed previously.

Even though the decision in *Alka Chandewar* settles the issue of whether it is necessary to first seek the approval of the court before resorting to enforcement, the resort to direct enforcement comes with its own problems. It does little to address the needs of the party that has an interim measure order in its favour. Therefore, while the threat of contempt definitely gives more teeth to the enforcement regime, it does little to address the situation of the aggrieved.[2356]

As a parallel, reference may be made to Order XXI Rule 36(5) which provides that in addition to attachment and civil prison, if a decree for specific performance or injunction has not been obeyed, '*the Court may, in lieu of or in addition to all or any of the processes aforesaid, direct that the act required to be done may be done as far as practicable by the decree-holder or some other person appointed by the Court, at the cost of the judgement-debtor, and upon the act being done, the expenses incurred may be ascertained in such manner as the Court may direct and may be recovered as if they included in the decree*'. The explanation to the said provisions provides that 'the act required to be done' covers prohibitory as well as mandatory injunctions. Thus, the provision permits substituted performance of decrees and actually enforces the decree rather than attaching the assets of a party or putting the party in jail.

5. INCORPORATING ARTICLES 17H AND 17I IN INDIA

It is clear from the above that despite an overhaul in 2015 with respect to the enforcement of interim measures, there continues to be a lack of clarity on how enforcement will actually take place. It is necessary to determine the provision for enforcement of the interim measure since it would consequently trigger the provisions of appeal, review or revision under the CPC.[2357]

Moreover, after the judgment in *Alka Chandewar*, an interim order may be enforced by the court of competent jurisdiction under Order XXXIX Rule 2A of the CPC as an order of the court and by the High Court under contempt jurisdiction (since courts below the High Court and Supreme Court cannot exercise contempt jurisdiction).[2358] The lower courts can only punish disobedience. It is unclear as to how the High Court will exercise jurisdiction within procedural rules where the District Court will be the

2356. Sarkar, *supra* n. 302, at 2063.
2357. Ajar Rab, *supra* n. 2317, at 93.
2358. The Contempt of Courts Act, 1971, S. 10.

court of the first instance and will exercise jurisdiction under Order XXXIX Rule 2A of the CPC. Also, parties would prefer to approach the High Courts in contempt jurisdiction as opposed to the District Court. This, however, would run afoul of the jurisdiction contained under Section 42 of the IAA, especially if the parties had approached the District Court under Section 9 of the IAA.

This interpretation also leaves the question of enforcement of orders passed by foreign seated arbitral tribunals open. After the 2015 Amendment, Section 27(5) of the IAA is applicable, even if the place of arbitration is outside India. Hence, an argument can be made that enforcement of interim measures granted by foreign seated tribunals could, thus, be enforced by invoking the contempt jurisdiction. However, such contempt will neither be of a court nor tribunal seated in India. Hence, the practical applicability of such an approach is doubtful.

The better course of action would be to expressly adopt Articles 17H and 17I of the Model Law. India should adopt Article 17H of the Model Law and delete provisions for an appeal as it amounts to setting aside the interim measure. Such an effect is contrary to the intent of Article 17H of the Model Law and amounts to review on merits which is violative of the mandate of minimal court intervention.

The current approach contained in Section 17(2) of the IAA equates tribunal-ordered interim measures with those ordered by the courts. However, it contains no safeguards as it mandates no duty on the party seeking enforcement to inform the court of any suspension, modification or termination of the interim measure, leaving open the room for abuse. Therefore, India should adopt a provision similar to Article 17H(2) of the Model Law mandating the party seeking enforcement to promptly inform the court of the change in the interim measure. This would further add efficiency to the arbitration proceedings and ensure a speedy resolution.

Given the tendency of excessive court intervention and delay in enforcement of awards[2359] and the likelihood of courts undertaking an extensive judicial review of the grounds mentioned under Article 36 of the Model Law,[2360] the word prima facie should be added to Article 17I(1) when the same is incorporated under the IAA. Also, the clarification in Article 17(2) should not be removed to ensure the scope of review at the stage of recognition and enforcement is limited to an interim measure only. The same should be retained to ensure courts are not prejudiced by such determinations when considering the application for setting aside the award subsequently as the determination would have been restricted to recognition and enforcement of the interim measure.

Furthermore, as observed by the Law Commission, there is considerable delay in the enforcement of awards and applications are pending for about six to twelve months even when the enforcement is uncontested. It takes about two years for contested

2359. *Centrotrade Minerals and Metal Inc. v. Hindustan Copper Ltd.* 2006 (3) Arb LR 201 (SC). *An award was finally enforced after nineteen years;* Shaneen Parikh & Shalaka Patil, *The Centrotrade Enforcement Saga Ends on a High Note*, (20 August 2020), available at: https://corporate.cyrilamarchandblogs.com/2020/08/the-centrotrade-enforcement-saga-ends-on-a-high-note/.

2360. Law Commission of India, *supra* n. 517; Justice B. N. Srikrishna, Report of the High-Level Committee to Review the Institutionalisation of Arbitration Mechanism in India, (30 July 2017), available at: http://legalaffairs.gov.in/sites/default/files/Report-HLC.pdf.

applications and about three years for enforcement of a foreign arbitral award.[2361] For this reason, Section 34(6) was included in the IAA which sets an outer limit of one year for the disposal of an application of setting aside the award under Section 34. Despite the recommendation of the Sri Krishna Committee, the same time limit was not extended to foreign arbitral awards under Section 48. Clearly, the requirement of a timeline is necessary for a country like India, where the courts are already overburdened with pending matters and the chance of delay in enforcement of interim measures is extremely high.[2362] If such delay is not prevented, the interim measure will lose its efficacy and urgency. Hence, a timeline of fifteen days should be provided for the disposal of an application seeking enforcement of the interim measure.

Such modifications to Articles 17H and 17I of the Model Law would prevent arbitrary enforcement and also lay down clear guidelines for the courts to refuse enforcement. Furthermore, such adoption would cater to the enforcement of interim orders issued by foreign seated tribunals as well as emergency arbitrators.

However, the above concerns would continue with respect to the actual enforcement of interim measures even after the adoption of Articles 17H and 17I. The enforcement would still fall within the scope of Order XXXIX Rule 2A of the CPC. The problems of conflict between the High Court and the District Court with respect to contempt jurisdiction would continue. In international commercial arbitrations, it is the High Court which will exercise jurisdiction for enforcement of interim measures and hence capable of exercising contempt jurisdiction as well. In domestic arbitrations, it would be the District Court which will exercise jurisdiction and would not have the power of contempt. Ideally, amendments to the CPC and the Contempt Act would have been the most suitable remedy to cure the ills of enforcement. However, the same are beyond the scope of the present book.

Nonetheless, for the sake of clarity, while adopting Article 17H of the Model Law, it should be statutorily clarified that the enforcement of an interim measure granted by the tribunal shall be enforced under Section 94 of the CPC. It is crucial to identify a legal basis for enforcement as an order of the court.[2363] It is on a legal basis that the court may recast the measure for enforcement. Thus, the reference to Section 94 of the CPC will reduce the ambiguity with respect to the enforcement regime. Since Section 94 provides for different kinds of methods to be used depending on the nature of the interim relief granted, a court will follow the procedure provided in the corresponding Orders and Rules to enforce the interim measure granted. This would reduce conflicts of the interim measures being incompatible with the powers of the court.

2361. Simon Greenberg, Christopher Kee and et. al., *International Commercial Arbitration: An Asia-Pacific Perspective* 446 (2011); Justice B. N. Srikrishna, Report of the High-Level Committee to Review the Institutionalisation of Arbitration Mechanism in India, (30 July 2017), 68, available at: http://legalaffairs.gov.in/sites/default/files/Report-HLC.pdf.

2362. Zia Mody, *supra* n. 682, at 132.

2363. Ronald Wong, *supra* n. 452, at 509, 510. *In Germany, the court had to find a basis to translate Mareva injunction into the German Legal System*; Jan Schaefer, *New English, German and Hong Kong Law Compared*, 2.2 Elec. J. Comp. L. (1998), available at:https://www.ejcl.org//22/art22-2.html; Austrian Code of Civil Procedure (ZPO), S. 890.

Even if the arbitral tribunal were to grant an interim measure which would not fall within the powers provided under Section 94 (a)-(d), the court would be sufficiently empowered to '*make such other interlocutory orders as may appear to the Court to be just and convenient*' under the residuary provision contained in Section 94(e) of the CPC to ensure compatibility with the CPC. Therefore, an explicit reference to Section 94 would make interim measures enforceable as orders passed by the court under Section 94 of the CPC.

An added advantage of this approach would be that it will also clarify to the courts that it is only for the purposes of enforcement that the court has to take resort to the CPC and not for the purposes of the power, scope or standards with respect to interim measures in arbitration. Furthermore, the explicit reference to Section 94 would grant flexibility to the court to enforce the order depending on the nature of the relief granted by the arbitral tribunal. It would prevent the enforcement mechanism from being driven only by the threat of disobedience or contempt.

Currently, the resort to Order XXXIX Rule 2A of the CPC creates an inconsistency as the provision pertains only to injunctions. As discussed previously, tribunals may grant various other orders which may not be injunctions per se. Hence, the traditional jurisprudence of such provision being resorted to with extreme caution may not necessarily be extended to the enforcement of interim measures under the IAA.

Furthermore, the entire process of enforcement is made futile by the provision of appeal against the orders passed under Order XXXIX Rule 2A.[2364] Therefore, once Article 17I is incorporated in the IAA, there should be a specific ouster of the provision of appeal against orders passed under Section 94 of the CPC when enforcement is being carried out under Section 17 of the IAA.

An express provision referring to enforceability would also align the Indian regime with Article 17H of the Model Law, which requires a party to seek recognition and enforcement of an interim measure. The current jurisprudence requires a party to prove disobedience or contempt of the tribunal's order. Only after the court is satisfied with such disobedience or contempt does the court resort to the attachment of property or detention in civil prison. The benefit of an explicit reference to Section 94 would prevent the requirement to prove disobedience or contempt. Currently, the party has to first convince the arbitral tribunal to grant the interim measure and then convince the court that the same has been disobeyed. Adopting Article 17H would do away with this requirement and a party would only have to demonstrate why it should be granted an interim measure.

An order passed by the tribunal would be recognised as binding, subject to Article 17I, and would be enforced by the court by passing an appropriate order under the CPC. Hence, it would be in harmony with the enforcement regime envisaged under Article 17H of the Model Law which states that the order of the arbitral tribunal 'shall' be 'binding' and 'enforced upon application'. This approach would also cater to the enforcement of orders passed by foreign seated tribunals. The court would enforce such orders depending on the nature of relief under the CPC. It would also have the

2364. Indian Code of Civil Procedure, 1908, Ord. XLIII, R 1 (r).

leeway to suitably reformulate the interim measure by resorting to Section 94(e) of the CPC.

More importantly, resort to the contempt jurisdiction of the High Court or the provision of disobedience should be restricted for extreme cases and should not be the default enforcement mechanism under any regime. Using the maximum power available to a court for enforcement under ordinary circumstances risks the sanctity and respect of courts. A default by a party even subsequent to exercise of contempt jurisdiction may leave the courts with little or no choice for any further recourse.

6. ENFORCEMENT OF INTERIM MEASURES BY THE ARBITRAL TRIBUNAL

In light of this discussion, it is clear that the Indian regime should clarify the provisions of enforcement and adopt Article 17H and Article 17I of the Model Law. However, several limitations within the CPC hinder the actual enforcement of interim measures in India but are not being discussed as they are beyond the scope of the present book. Therefore, several other alternatives of enforcement through the tribunal may be considered. It is imperative to afford a higher degree of independence to the arbitral tribunal, which is necessary to maintain the integrity of the process of arbitration.[2365] Such measures and their suitability in the Indian context are considered below:

6.1. Substituted Performance

The tribunal may order the execution of performance measures by substitution or setting specific deadlines for compliance and issuing reminders.[2366] This would lead to actual enforcement of the order, instead of just the threat of punishment by a court. The applicant would receive effective protection of its interests. Currently, enforcement is sought on the threat of attachment of properties or imprisonment of the respondent, which effectively does little in addressing the relief sought by the applicant. If a recalcitrant respondent is willing to suffer attachment or imprisonment, the applicant has no remedy to prevent the actual prejudice to its rights or legal position.

Empowering the tribunal to order the execution of performance by substitution or setting specific deadlines would lead to more holistic redressal, without the need to turn to court enforcement per se. It is pertinent to note that such an alternative was considered by the Working Group. It was discussed that a tribunal might order a financial guarantee as a counterpart of the enforcement, but the same was not incorporated.[2367]

Countries such as Croatia,[2368] Egypt,[2369] Jordan,[2370] Macedonia,[2371] Switzerland,[2372] and Uruguay[2373] permit enforcement of orders through court assistance only

2365. Sarthak, *supra* n. 21, at 195.
2366. Boog, *supra* n. 1766, at 2559.
2367. Beraudo, *supra* n. 2166, at 250-251.
2368. Croatia Law on Arbitration, Art. 16.
2369. Egyptian Arbitration Law, 1994, Art. 24(2).

after a party fails to comply with it voluntarily. Therefore, a party which requested the interim measure can be given liberty to either approach the arbitral tribunal to permit substituted performance or approach the court for enforcement of the order when a reasonable time has expired, or a party has not complied with the order of the tribunal within the time provided in such order.

In India, reference may be made to Order XXI Rule 36(5) of the CPC which provides that in addition to attachment and civil prison, if a decree for specific performance or injunction has not been obeyed, '*the Court may, in lieu of or in addition to all or any of the processes aforesaid, direct that the act required to be done may be done as far as practicable by the decree-holder or some other person appointed by the Court …* '. The explanation to the said provisions provides that 'the act required to be done' covers prohibitory as well as mandatory injunctions. Thus, a similar provision can be considered to be incorporated under the IAA. Furthermore, with the express recognition of substituted performance under Section 20 of the Specific Relief Act, such relief will not be contrary to domestic law.

Therefore, a party who has been granted an interim measure may file an application for substituted performance, in lieu of the enforcement of the order by the court. Any costs and damages arising from such substituted performance should be borne by the party against whom the measure was granted. The power of the tribunal to grant substituted performance should be included in the IAA to grant more teeth to the enforcement regime without relying solely on court assistance. Therefore, a provision may be added to the list of measures clarifying the power of the tribunal which provides that '*upon request by the party in whose favour an order was passed under sub-section (1), direct the party making the request to do the act required to be done under the order, as far as practicable, if the party against whom the order was passed fails to comply with the order voluntarily within a reasonable time, or such time as provided in the order*'.

6.2. Costs and Damages

An arbitral tribunal may hold a defaulting party liable for costs and damages arising out of or related to the act of non-compliance with the order of the tribunal.[2374] Such non-compliance with the order of the arbitral tribunal can be considered to be a breach of the arbitration agreement and can be compensated by way of damages at the time of passing the award.[2375] The power to impose such costs and damages is based on a

2370. Jordan Arbitration Law, 2001, Art. 23(b).
2371. Macedonia Arbitration Law, Art. 17.
2372. Switzerland Arbitration Law, 1987, Art. 183(2).
2373. Uruguay Arbitration Law, Art. 17(2).
2374. English Arbitration Act, 1996, S. 41(d); *Boog, supra* n. 1766, at 2559; Stalev, *supra* n. 88, at 110.
2375. *ICC Case No. 8887* in 11 (1) ICC Ct. Bull. 91 (2000).

broad interpretation of the arbitration agreement, a breach of contract due to a breach of the dispute resolution clause.[2376]

Also, such a power can be traced to the inherent power of the tribunal to order interim measures of protection[2377] and parties, usually, comply with interim orders due to a negative costs award being granted on account of non-cooperative behaviour.[2378] Such power is also recognised under Article 9(7) of the IBA Rules on Taking of Evidence where the tribunal is empowered to impose costs if a party has not acted in good faith in taking of evidence.[2379]

The important consideration for the tribunal would be the allocation of costs to sanction a party for failure. This may, in essence, amount to a hidden private sanction, unless the costs can be directly attributed to the interim measures and can be linked to the failure to comply.[2380] Therefore, the scope of costs would extend to the expenses made due to non-compliance.[2381] In *Mine v. Guinea*,[2382] the tribunal ordered that the claimant should pay a portion of Guinea's cost and legal fees which were incurred in defending a parallel proceeding initiated by the claimant even though the tribunal had ordered Guinea to withdraw the litigation in national courts.[2383] The tribunal imposed a cost for non-compliance with the anti-arbitration injunction. Similarly, the tribunal-ordered costs for the failure of compliance in *AGIP v. Congo*.[2384] Therefore, the power to impose costs for non-compliance is well recognised.

Such a view has been accepted by the Delhi High Court recently. The court held that if a party does not cooperate in the expeditious disposal of arbitration proceedings, the arbitral tribunal is not powerless and can impose costs in the exercise of its power under a second proviso to Section 24 of the IAA.[2385]

It has also been suggested that arbitrators can award damages for non-compliance with the interim orders.[2386] However, the power to impose damages for non-compliance is not as clearly defined. In common law countries, damages for the breach of the arbitration agreement have been awarded and mostly represented the

2376. D. Alan Redfern, *supra* n. 685, at 81; Karrer, *supra* n. 1216, at 103; *J. Flex in* West *Tankers* Inc *v. RAS Riunione Adriatica di Sicurta* SpA [2005] EWHC 454 (Comm), *upheld in appeal; CMA CGM SA v. Hyundai Mipo Dockyard Co Ltd.* [2008] EWHC 2791, ¶46, c.f. Crina, *supra* n. 882, at 253.
2377. Ali Yesilirmak, *supra* n. 30, at 243-244.
2378. Niuscha, *supra* n. 1737, at 243.
2379. *If the Arbitral Tribunal determines that a Party has failed to conduct itself in good faith in the taking of evidence, the Arbitral Tribunal may, in addition to any other measures available under these Rules, take such failure into account in its assignment of the costs of the arbitration, including costs arising out of or in connection with the taking of evidence.*
2380. Melissa, *supra* n. 1690, at 711.
2381. Karrer, *supra* n. 1216, at 103.
2382. *Maritime International Nominees Establishment v. The Republic of Guinea, ICSID Case No. ARB 84/4, Order for Interim Measures (December 4, 1985)* 4 ICSID Rep. 77 (1997).
2383. *Ibid.*
2384. *AGIP S.p.A. v. People's Republic of the Congo, ICSID Case No. ARB/77/1, Award* (30 November 1979) Award, 1 ICISD Rep. 306 (1993).
2385. *Rail Vikas Nigam Ltd. v. Railone-Tarmat-Durga (JV)* 2018 SCC OnLine Del 6655, ¶18.
2386. Stalev, *supra* n. 88, at 110; Karrer, *supra* n. 1216, at 103; *Caline Mouawad and Elizabeth Silbert, A Guide to Interim Measure in Investor-State Arbitration,* 29 (3) Arb. Int'l 423 (2013).

cost of the parallel proceedings.[2387] In Germany, the language used in Section 1041(4) of the ZPO suggests that damages may be awarded as a party is obliged to 'compensate the party for damage resulting from the enforcement' of a measure which was 'unjustified from the outset'. Similarly, Norway provides for 'indemnifying other parties for the loss suffered as a result of the measure',[2388] and in Poland, the phrase used is 'is liable for damages caused thereby'.[2389]

Even in common law countries, it should be noted that damages for non-compliance can only be ordered if the non-compliance of the interim relief aggravated the harm and not otherwise.[2390] Such harm will have to be demonstrated by a party as well. Therefore, damages may be awarded to the party who suffers a loss due to wilful contempt of the orders.[2391] Such damages should be limited to the damage suffered due to non-compliance and cannot amount to punitive damages. The imposition of damages, especially punitive damages, will be subject to mandatory law requirements. Another problem with awarding damages is that such a measure may not adequately address the enforceability concerns of measures that are intended to prevent imminent harm or preserve a right which is currently being threatened.[2392]

After the 2006 Model Law Revisions, the power to order costs and damages by the tribunal is formally recognised under Article 17G of the Model Law. Though the exercise of such a power is circumscribed to circumstances where the tribunal concludes that such measures should not have been granted in the first place, Article 17G, nonetheless, recognises the power to award costs and damages.

Since the power is, in essence, used to penalise the applicant who has obtained the interim measure when the same should not have been granted, there is little room to argue against such a levy of costs and damages for non-enforcement, which too, would be akin to making the respondent liable for recalcitrant conduct. Furthermore, Article 17H(1) of the Model Law mandates that all interim orders shall be binding on the parties, implicitly accepting the view that non-compliance amounts to a breach of binding obligations under the arbitration agreement. Hence, damages may be a remedy for redressing the breach.

In India, one author, commenting on the regime before the 2015 Amendment, states that the arbitral tribunal has no power of enforcement under Section 17 of the IAA and failure to comply with the orders can only have one consequence, i.e., the arbitral tribunal can take into account in its final decision, particularly in the assessment of damages.[2393]

Therefore, the power to grant costs and damages for non-compliance or disobedience of the orders of the arbitral tribunal should be expressly contained in the IAA.

2387. *Mantovani v. Caprelli SpA* [1980] Lloyds Rep 375; *Paramedics Electromedicina Comercial Ltd v. GE Medical Systems Information Technologies, Inc* F.3d 645 (2d Cir.2004).

2388. Norway Arbitration Act, 2004, S. 19.

2389. Article 1182, Civil Procedure Code (Norway); *The phrase used in* Qatar Arbitration Law, 2017, Arts 17(3) & 17(4) is '*pay costs and compensation*'; *The phrase used in* Sri Lanka Arbitration Act, 1995, S. 13(1), is '*security for any expense, loss of damage*'.

2390. Benoit, *supra* n. 685, at 36.

2391. Steven Gee, *supra* n. 1026, at 638.

2392. Donovan, *supra* n. 1400, at 126.

2393. Sumeet Kachwaha, *supra* n. 45.

This would ensure that the non-compliance or disobedience is decided by the arbitral tribunal itself. It would also prevent challenges at the time of enforcement about 'excess of jurisdiction' when awarding costs and damages for non-compliance.

Since costs and damages will always be considered at the time of passing of the final award, any other procedural transgressions by the tribunal will be subject to judicial scrutiny before enforcement. Therefore, any concern with respect to a tribunal imposing damages for non-compliance without any safeguard of procedural challenges on account of 'excess of jurisdiction' or 'proper opportunity to present its case' will suitably be addressed when a party applies to set aside the award. Even if the tribunal were to pass the costs and damages as an interim award, enforcement would again be subject to the right of a party to have the award set aside on account of procedural violations.

6.3. Striking off Pleadings

Another measure that the tribunal can take is of striking off the pleadings of the non-compliant party. A similar power is contained in Section 41(a) of the English Arbitration Act which permits a tribunal to issue a preliminary order directing a party that in the event of a default, a party shall not be entitled to rely upon any allegation or material which was the subject matter of the order. It is pertinent to note that the scope is restricted by the phrase 'subject matter of the order' and does not extend to all pleadings. Section 41(c) of the English Arbitration Act authorises a tribunal to proceed to an award on the basis of such materials as have been properly provided to it.

In India, such power to strike out the defence of a party under summary proceedings is recognised under Order XV. Two states[2394] have added provisions for striking off the defence of the party if the entire rent along with interest due is not deposited on or before the first date of hearing in a tenancy suit. Thus, there is a statutory basis for such power and the same would not be in violation of public policy.

This power should, however, be used extremely cautiously. An order striking out pleadings cannot be passed as a matter of course, merely because a party is in breach of a condition imposed by the court. Such power should be exercised for adequate reasons, where the default is wilful and the conduct of defaulting party results in substantial or serious prejudice against the other party.[2395] A suit is not likely to be thrown out, or a defence struck without adequate reasons.[2396]

However, in the context of arbitration, the power may violate the overarching principle of equal treatment of parties and decide the dispute after giving the full opportunity to each party to present its case.[2397] Such a measure may suffice as a

2394. Indian Code of Civil Procedure, 1908, Ord. XV R. 5 (State Amendment of Punjab and Haryana, and Uttar Pradesh, India).

2395. *Ashapura Minechem Ltd. v. Pacific Basin IHX (UK) Ltd.* 2013 SCC OnLine Bom 141, ¶16.

2396. *Babbar Sewing Machine Co. v. Trilok Nath Mahajan* (1978) 4 SCC 188; Indian Code of Civil Procedure, 1908, Ord. VII, R. 11 & 12.

2397. UNCITRAL Model Law, Art. 18.

ground for setting aside the award passed.[2398] Therefore, such a measure may cause more problems than it seeks to resolve.

6.4. Penalties

Penalties remain a controversial topic with respect to the power of the tribunal to impose the same for non-compliance with its orders. One view is that the tribunal lacks the power to enforce its measure and cannot impose penalties for non-compliance.[2399] Some authors take the view that unless specifically agreed by parties or unless such a power can be derived from the applicable law,[2400] or mandatory law, penalties cannot be ordered.[2401]

Some suggest that the tribunal has powers of enforcement as it can order financial penalties of a contractual nature which will compel a party to comply with the orders of the tribunal.[2402] A moderate view is that tribunals do not have the power to impose monetary sanctions for non-compliance but can direct payment of all unnecessary costs generated by other proceedings.[2403] In French, Dutch and Belgian Laws penalties can be awarded[2404] for non-compliance with the orders of the tribunal. Under common law jurisdictions, such penalties may be violative of public policy.[2405]

Providing for such a power in the IAA or national arbitration statutes may not adequately address the issue of enforcement. Much like costs and damages, such penalties would not address the issues of urgency. Moreover, the scope and ceiling of such penalties may have to be provided, failing which they might give rise to challenges to the award on the grounds of an excess of jurisdiction or violation of public policy. Such scope would also have to define the proportion of penalty imposed on the damage caused by non-compliance. Therefore, if the purpose of such penalties is to deter recalcitrant parties through monetary sanctions, such a purpose is better served through the imposition of costs and damages rather than the imposition of penalties, even if the same are permitted under the *lex arbitri* or mandatory law of the *lex fori.*

2398. NYC Art. V(1)(b).
2399. Lew, *supra* n. 28, at ¶23-31; Waincymer, *supra* n. 989, at 624.
2400. Melissa, *supra* n. 1690, at 710-711.
2401. Ali Yesilirmak, *supra* n. 30, at 212.
2402. E.A Schwartz, *The Practice & Experience of ICC Courts: in Conservatory & Provisional Measures in International Arbitration, ICC International Court of Arbitration* 45, 49 (1993).
2403. Mange, *supra* n. 2041, at 207.
2404. Georg von Segesser & Christopher Boog, *Chapter 6: Interim Measures*, in Elliott Geisinger & Nathalie Voser (eds), *International Arbitration in Switzerland: A Handbook for Practitioners* 119 (2013); French Code of Civil Procedure Arts 1468 & 1506; Dutch Code of Civil Procedure, Art. 1056.
2405. H Collins, *The Law of Contract* (2003); Gregory Klass, *Contract Law in the United States* (2012); Ajar Rab, *Contract Law and Specific Relief: The 'Un-common' Indian Law*, (25 November 2019), available at: https://ijiel.in/blog/f/contract-law-and-specific-relief-the-%E2%80%98un-common%E2%80%99-indian-law?blogcategory=International+Commercial+Law.

6.5. Adverse Inferences

Very often, it is suggested that the real source of power available with an arbitral tribunal is the power to draw adverse inferences against a non-compliant party.[2406] According to *Redfern and Hunter*, it would take a brave (or even foolish) party to choose to deliberately ignore interim measures ordered by the tribunal as the tribunal will judge the merits of its disputes.[2407] However, as rightly asserted by *Born*, non-compliant parties often give several reasons such as local laws, changed circumstances, acts of third parties etc. for non-compliance.

Adverse inferences would not seem appropriate except in cases where there is no other logical reason for failure to comply.[2408] Therefore, the tribunal may not be able to draw such inferences, in the presence of proper justification. Moreover, there may be instances where the benefit of non-compliance far outweighs the threat of an adverse inference.[2409] In a 2012 Queen Mary survey, it was empirically found that arbitrators are reluctant to draw adverse inferences as such inferences may become a ground for challenging the award.[2410]

The power to draw such inference is statutorily contained in Section 41(b) of the English Arbitration Act. However, the exercise of such a power may violate the obligation of equal treatment of the parties under Article 18 of the Model Law since the tribunal should decide the dispute between the parties on the law and evidence before it.[2411] Therefore, such a power can only be exercised when non-compliance has a direct causal link[2412] with the outcome of the merits, such as non-production of evidence.[2413]

It is unclear though why arbitrators should continue to act in good faith and uphold their duties of equal treatment if the party deliberately violates the order of the tribunal. The grant of interim measures is based on equitable principles under common law and hence, if a party has breached its obligations, there can be no equity in its favour. Also, adverse inferences may be exercised in cases of appreciation of evidence or parties are aware that arbitrators will subconsciously remember the acts of defiance.[2414]

Therefore, if a party was to disobey an anti-suit injunction by the tribunal, the tribunal may negatively influence the result of the final award, but a party may take the risk if it has good reason to believe that the award will not be enforced.[2415] Therefore, adverse inferences are not by themselves sufficient for securing compliance and enforcement of interim measures. However, violations of orders may influence the

2406. Schwartz *supra*, n. 2402, at 49. *Lew*, supra *n. 2, at 24; E.A Schwartz, The Practice & Experience of ICC Courts: in Conservatory & Provisional Measures in International Arbitration*, ICC International Court of Arbitration 49 (1993).
2407. Redfern, *supra* n. 1253, at 338.
2408. Waincymer, *supra* n. 989, at 624.
2409. Gary Born, *supra* n. 33, at 2628.
2410. Queen Marry, *supra* n. 2111.
2411. Karrer, *supra* n. 1216, at 101, 103.
2412. Boog, *supra* n. 1766, at 2559.
2413. Melissa, *supra* n. 1690, at 711.
2414. *Ibid.*
2415. Mange, *supra* n. 2041, at 207.

determination of costs and damages, even when a party does not comply with the order of an emergency arbitrator.

6.6. Suspension or Termination of proceedings

A tribunal may even order suspension or termination of the arbitration proceedings. This power has been recognised only when the parties fail to comply with an order for security for costs,[2416] especially after an ultimate grace period.[2417] Thus, security for costs differs from other interim measures awarded by the tribunal as it is self-enforcing and no aid from the court is required.[2418] The arbitral tribunal should consider what powers it has for enforcement in case of non-compliance under the applicable national law or arbitration rules[2419] and only then suspend or terminate the proceedings.

Under the English Arbitration Act, if the order is not complied with, the tribunal may dismiss the claim if the security is not provided after a pre-emptory order providing a date for compliance.[2420] However, the same would not amount to res judicata.[2421]

The power to suspend or terminate proceedings is specifically recognised under the IAA in the proviso to Section 38(2) of the IAA. If a claimant is not willing to furnish necessary security for costs, there is little justification in continuing presumably frivolous or vexatious proceedings against the respondent. Also, enforcing the said measure through an order of the court will serve no purpose if the non-compliant party is not in a position to furnish security in the first place. This does not mean, however, that the tribunal has the power to terminate the proceedings for all non-compliances as it would violate the duty of equal treatment and fair hearing.

7. ENFORCEMENT OF INTERIM MEASURES PASSED BY FOREIGN SEATED TRIBUNALS

Before the 2015 Amendment, the Law Commission had succinctly identified the problem that a party would have no recourse under the IAA to enforce interim measures passed by a foreign seated tribunal. It may either enforce an interim order through a civil suit or under contempt proceedings.[2422] For enforcement of an interim order through a civil suit, the party in whose favour the order has been granted will file a suit to enforce the interim order as a foreign judgment under Section 44A of the

2416. Article 25.2, 2014 LCIA Rules; Art. 33(7), 2018 VIAC Rules; c.f. Melissa, *supra* n. 1690, at 709; Other measures may include stay of proceedings or other such procedural orders as the tribunal consider appropriate, *see* Commentary on Art. 5.¶3(e), CIArb's International Arbitration Practice Guidelines, Applications for Security for Costs.
2417. Micha Bühler, *supra* n. 1771, at 2586.
2418. Paul, *supra* n. 679, at 426.
2419. Commentary on Art. 5.¶3 (e), CIArb International Arbitration Practice Guidelines, Applications for Security for Costs.
2420. *Ibid.*. English Arbitration Act, 1996, S. 41(5)(6).
2421. Waincymer, *supra* n. 989, at 653.
2422. *Marriot International Inc. v. Ansal Hotels Ltd.* 2000 (56) DRJ (Suppl) 235, 443 (DB); *Bharat Aluminum v. Kaiser Aluminum Technical Services Inc.* (2012) 9 SCC 552.

CPC.[2423] However, an interim order would not be conclusive as required under Section 13 of CPC. It would fall within the exception under Section 13(b) of the CPC, which states that a foreign judgment shall not be conclusive when it has not been given on the merits of the case. Hence, an interim measure obtained from a court, or an arbitral tribunal outside India would not be enforceable as it would not fall within the definition of a 'foreign judgment'.[2424] Furthermore, such an order would also not fall within the definition of 'Judgment,'[2425] or 'Decree'[2426] under the CPC. Since only decrees or judgments are executable under Section 44A of CPC, such an option would provide no effective relief to the party.

An alternative recourse would be that if a party obtains an interim order from a foreign court or an arbitral tribunal, it can seek enforcement of such order in the jurisdiction of the seat under contempt proceedings and get such an order enforced under Section 44A of the CPC. Hence, the lacuna was cured by the amendment in 2015 to account for foreign seated arbitrations.

Nonetheless, the position of law before the 2015 Amendment and post the amendment remains the same. Interim orders or directions passed by a foreign seated tribunal would not be enforceable in India.[2427] Even though Section 2(2) was amended by the 2015 Amendment to provide for the applicability of Sections 9 and 27 to foreign seated tribunals, since Section 17(2) of the IAA was not made territory neutral, interim measures issued by an arbitral tribunal seated outside India will not be enforceable. The only recourse can be to (a) apply to the Court under Section 9 of the Arbitration Act for similar relief;[2428] or (b) invoke contempt jurisdiction under Section 27(5) of the IAA; or (c) invoke the inherent power of the court,[2429] subject to procedural rules being satisfied. Usually, when state courts are faced with decisions of foreign courts, the enforcement depends on the existence of a treaty and the duty to enforce, or in common law countries on the principle of the most convenient forum.[2430]

In arbitration, however, the Model Law provides for recognition of an interim measure under Article 17H(1) and states that the same shall be binding. It further provides that an interim measure issued by the tribunals shall be enforced upon application to the competent court, irrespective of the country in which it was issued subject to provisions of Article 17I which provide for the grounds for refusing recognition or enforcement.

Article 1696(1) of the Belgian Judicial Code (adopting Article 17H of the Model Law) provides for enforcement of arbitration measures issued by foreign seated tribunals. It specifically provides that the measure shall be recognised as binding and enforced by the Court of First Instance, irrespective of the country in which it was

2423. *HSBC PI Holdings (Mauritius) Ltd. v. Avitel Post Studioz Ltd.* 2014 SCC OnLine Bom 102.
2424. Indian Code of Civil Procedure, 1908, S. 2(6).
2425. *Ibid.*, S. 2(9).
2426. *Ibid.*, S. 2(2).
2427. *Badat & Co. v. East India Trading Co.* (1964) 4 SCR 19, ¶30.
2428. *Raffles Design International India Private Limited v. Educomp Professional Education Limited* 2016 SCC OnLine Del 5521, ¶105.
2429. Nakul, *supra* n. 17, at 669.
2430. Christer Söderlund, *Lis Pendens, Res Judicata and the Issue of Parallel Judicial Proceedings*, 22 (4), J. Int'l Arb. 301, 303 (2005), c.f., Eduardo Z, *supra* n. 35, at 236.

issued.[2431] Therefore, if a party is ordinarily residing in Belgium or has assets in Belgium, a measure can be enforced,[2432] and enforcement may be refused on grounds similar to those laid down in Article 17I of the Model Law.[2433]

In Germany, courts can grant leave for the enforcement of an interim measure or protection passed by a foreign arbitral tribunal and the party requesting the enforcement does not need to show that the opposite party has failed or refused to comply with the order.[2434] It should be noted that an application for leave of enforcement can only be made after paying a separate court fee.[2435]

Australia, Switzerland, and Hong Kong permit enforcement if interim measures are issued by foreign seated tribunals.[2436] The United States is probably the most pro-enforcement regime when it comes to the enforcement of interim measures.[2437] However, enforcement in Hong Kong is possible only when the relief granted would give rise to an award (interim or final) enforceable in Hong Kong.[2438] The scope of this support to foreign seated arbitration orders is limited by the language that the court only exercises its power to support the foreign arbitral tribunal which retains primary jurisdiction over the matter.[2439] Sometimes the court may also require the approval of the tribunal before enforcement.[2440]

The IAA does not contain any express provision *pari materia* to Article 17H of the Model Law for enforcement of interim orders granted by an arbitral tribunal outside India and Section 17 is not applicable in respect of foreign seated arbitration. The only two methods for enforcing the same would be either (a) to file a suit[2441] or (b) reapplying for the interim measure under Section 9 of the IAA.

An interim order issued by a foreign seated tribunal should not be confused with an interim award rendered by a foreign seated tribunal and its recognition and enforcement under Part II of the Arbitration Act.[2442] In one instance, interim relief was granted by an emergency arbitrator in Singapore for freezing the bank account of the opposite party. The order was converted into a Singapore court decree. The petitioner subsequently applied to the courts in India, under Section 9 on the strength of the court decree and the said order was enforced in India.[2443] It must be noted, however, that this

2431. Belgium Judicial Code, Art. 1696; Niuscha, *supra* n. 1737, at 239.
2432. Niuscha, *supra* n. 1737, at 244.
2433. Belgium Judicial Code, Art. 1697 as revised with effect from 01 September, 2013.
2434. Jan Schäfer, *supra* n. 301, at 234.
2435. *Ibid.*, at 236.
2436. Ali Yesilirmak, *supra* n. 30, at 259.
2437. *In re Application of Mesa Power Group, LLC* 878 F.Supp.2d 1296, 1303 (S.D. Fla. 2012); *In re Consorcio Ecuatoriano de Telecomunicaciones S.A. v. JAS Forwarding (USA), Inc.*, 685 F.3d 987, (11th Cir. 2012).
2438. Hong Kong Arbitration Ordinance (Cap.609), S. 60(6); *Prema Birkdale Horticulture (Macau) Ltd. v. Venetian Orient Ltd.* [2009] 5 HKLRD 89, ¶6.
2439. Hong Kong Arbitration Ordinance (Cap.609), S. 60(6).
2440. *Vibroflotation A.G. v. Express Builders Co. Ltd.* [1994] 3 H.K. Cas. 263 (H.C.), ¶20; Kenya Arbitration Act. S. 18(2).
2441. *Raffles Design International India Private Limited v. Educomp Professional Education Limited* 2016 SCC OnLine Del 5521, ¶104.
2442. *Avitel Post Studioz Ltd. v. HSBC PI Holdings (Mauritius) Ltd.* 2014 SCC OnLine Bom 929; *Thyssen Stahlunion GmbH v. Steel Authority of India Ltd.* (1999) 9 SCC 334, 371.
2443. *Ibid.*

was not a case of direct enforcement of a measure passed by a foreign seated tribunal but the enforcement of an order under Section 9 as a domestic order of the court. This approach has been followed subsequently as well.[2444]

The Delhi High Court held that recourse to Section 9 is not available for enforcing orders of the tribunal, but that does not mean that the court cannot independently apply its mind and grant interim relief in cases it is warranted.[2445] The court went on to observe that under Article 17I(2) of the 2006 Model Law, the court enforcing an interim order passed by an arbitral tribunal in prescribed form undertakes a review of the substance of the interim measure. To that extent, a court while examining a similar relief under Section 9 of the Act would be unfettered by the findings or the view of the arbitral tribunal.[2446] However, a person guilty of not following the orders passed by a foreign seated arbitral tribunal cannot be proceeded against for contempt under Section 27(5) of the Act.[2447]

Thus, interim orders should be enforced, subject to Article 17I of the Model Law. As discussed previously, India should adopt Articles 17H and 17I as this would also permit recognition and enforcement of orders of foreign seated tribunals as well as emergency arbitrators, irrespective of the seat.[2448]

2444. *Ashwani Minda v. U-Shin Ltd.* 2020 SCC OnLine Del 1648; *Matthew Gearing, Sheila Ahuja & Arun Mal, Ashwani Minda v. U-Shin The Delhi High Court's recent observations on emergency arbitrator relief and the availability of court-ordered interim measures* (27 May 2020), (Allen & Overy).

2445. *Raffles Design International India Private Limited v. Educomp Professional Education Limited* 2016 SCC OnLine Del 5521, ¶105.

2446. *Ibid.*, ¶106.

2447. *Ibid.*, ¶107.

2448. Chiann Bao, *International Arbitration in Asia on the Rise: Cause & Effect*, 4(1) Arb. Br. 31, 38 (2014).

PART IV The Way Forward

Conclusion

Arbitration in India is not a recent phenomenon and has been in existence much before the formal judicial system was introduced by the British. Several legislative changes have been made to bring India at par with the current trends in international practice and improve the arbitration regime in the country. The most notable legislative intent in this direction is contained in the IAA which consciously incorporates the Model Law to minimise court intervention and remove the bottlenecks hindering arbitration practice in India.

One such bottleneck has been the regime on interim measures of protection where courts have continued to mistrust the arbitral process and in the absence of appropriate guiding criteria within the IAA, have applied domestic procedural laws such as the CPC and the Specific Relief Act. Apart from constant judicial intervention, several provisions such as those of appeal, the inconsistent language between the provisions pertaining to interim measures, and the lack of adequate safeguards have pushed India towards a regressive arbitration jurisdiction instead of promoting it as an arbitration hub. Though the legislature has tried to fix the loopholes in the IAA and attempted to address judicial precedents which negatively impacted the practice of international arbitration, the piecemeal patch fixes have in fact created more confusion.

The most regrettable consequence of these patchy fixes is that the regime on interim measures of protection in international commercial arbitration in India has fallen out of sync with the Model Law and instead aligned itself with the English Arbitration Act. This thesis has attempted to find a holistic redressal to such issues while ensuring that the IAA is in line with the Model Law, based on a comparison with other Model Law jurisdictions and the current international practice in arbitration. Therefore, based on the observations made in the preceding chapters, it is suggested that India should amend the existing provisions in the IAA with those suggested below.

Suggested Provisions

Section 2. Definitions: (1)(d) 'arbitral tribunal' means a sole arbitrator or a panel of arbitrators and, in the case of an arbitration conducted under the rules of an institution providing for appointment of an emergency arbitrator, includes such emergency arbitrator;
Scope: (2) This part shall apply where the seat of arbitration is in India.
Provided that, subject to an agreement to the contrary, the provision of Sections 9(1), 9(4), 27, 17A, 17B, 37(1)(b) shall also apply to international commercial arbitration, even if the seat of arbitration is outside India, or no seat has been designated or determined.

Section 9. Interim Measures, etc., by Court:

(1) A party may, before or during arbitral proceedings, apply to a Court for issuing an interim measure of protection in relation to arbitral proceedings and the Court shall have the same powers to issue an interim measure of protection as contained in Sections 17(2) and 17(3)(a)-(d), irrespective of whether the seat of those proceedings is in India, as the Court has for the purpose of, and in relation to, any proceedings before it.
(2) In exercising the power under subsection (1) in relation to arbitral proceedings which have been or are to be commenced outside India, the court must have regard to the fact that the power is ancillary to the arbitration proceeding outside India and for the purposes of facilitating the process of a court or arbitral tribunals outside India that has primary jurisdiction over the arbitral proceedings.
(3) The court must exercise the powers referred to in this Section in accordance with Section 17(4) and Section 17(6) to support the arbitral process, and in consideration of the 'specific features of international arbitration,' and finally dispose of the application under subsection (1) within thirty days of the date of filing of such application:

(3) (a) Where a party makes an application under subsection (1) for the grant of interim measures of protection before the commencement of arbitration, the Court shall direct the party in whose favour the interim measure of protection is granted, to take effective steps for the appointment of the arbitral tribunal in accordance with the procedure specified in Section 11, or as agreed by the parties, within a period of thirty days from the date of such direction.

(b) The Court may direct that if the steps are not taken within the period specified in subsection (a) above, the interim measure of protection granted shall stand vacated on the expiry of the said period:

> *Provided that* the Court may, on sufficient cause being shown for the delay in taking such steps, extend the said period.

(4) Once the arbitral proceedings have commenced, the Court shall not entertain an application under sub-section (1), and the Court shall refer the request, or any pending requests under subsection (1), to the arbitral tribunal, unless the arbitral tribunal has no power, or is unable for the time being to act effectively.

Explanation – Arbitration proceedings shall be deemed to be commenced when the appointment is accepted by the sole arbitrator or by all the arbitrators if there is more than one.

(5) The Court may pass any order under subsection (1) or (4) of this Section, without notice to the other party, where the court considers that prior disclosure of the request for the interim measure of protection to the party against whom it is directed risks frustrating the purpose of the measure.

(6) Any order passed by the Court under subsection (5) of this Section, without notice to the other party, shall be communicated to the other party and arbitral tribunal, as applicable, within three days of such order being passed, failing which such order shall automatically lapse.

(7) The party requesting the interim measure of protection under subsections (1) and (4) shall disclose all facts and circumstances likely to be relevant to the court's determination whether to grant the interim measure of protection requested.

(8) An order passed by the court under Section 9 shall cease to have effect:

(a) if the court so orders, in whole or in part (as the case may be) on the order of the arbitral tribunal or any other such institution or person having the power to act in relation to the subject matter of the order; or

(b) in whole or in part (as the case may be) if the arbitral tribunal, or any such arbitral or other institution or person having the power to act in relation to the subject matter of the order, makes an order which expressly relates to the whole or part of the order under Section 9.

Section 17. Interim measures of protection ordered by the arbitral tribunal:

(1) Unless otherwise agreed by the parties, the arbitral tribunal may, at the request of a party, grant interim measures of protection.
(2) An interim measure of protection is any temporary measure, whether in the form of an award or in another form, by which, at any time prior to the issuance of the award by which the dispute is finally decided, the arbitral tribunal orders a party to:
 (a) maintain or restore the status quo pending determination of the dispute; or
 (b) take action that would prevent, or refrain from taking action that is likely to cause, current or imminent harm or prejudice to the arbitral process itself; or
 (c) provide a means of preserving assets out of which a subsequent award may be satisfied; or
 (d) preserve evidence that may be relevant and material to the resolution of the dispute.
(3) An interim measure of protection referred to in subsection (2) above shall include, but not be limited to, any of the following interim measures of protection, namely:
 (a) the preservation, interim custody or sale of any goods which are the subject matter of the arbitration agreement;
 (b) securing the amount in dispute in the arbitration;
 (c) the detention, preservation or inspection of any property or thing which is the subject matter of the dispute in arbitration, or as to which any question may arise therein and authorising for any of the aforesaid purposes any person to enter upon any land or building in the possession of any party or authorising any samples to be taken or any observation to be made, or experiment to be tried, which may be necessary or expedient for the purpose of obtaining full information or evidence;
 (d) interim injunction or the appointment of a receiver;
 (e) security for costs;
 (f) upon request by the party in whose favour an order was passed under subsection (1), (2) or this subsection, direct the party making the request to do the act required to be done under the order, as far as practicable, if the party against whom the order was passed fails to comply with the order voluntarily within a reasonable time, or such time as provided in the order. (6) order costs and damages for the act done in subclause (f), in addition to costs and damages for non-compliance or disobedience of orders passed under subsection (1).
(4) (a) The party requesting an interim measure of protection under Section 17(2)(a), (b) or (c) or Section 17(3)(a)(b) or (d) must satisfy the arbitral tribunal that:

(iv) there is a reasonable possibility that the requesting party will succeed on the merits of the claim;
(v) a right has been infringed, or is threatened to be infringed, by the party against whom the measure is requested; and
(vi) the harm likely to result if the measure is not ordered, substantially outweighs the harm that is likely to result to the party against whom the measure is directed if the measure is granted.

(b) The determination on the possibility referred to in subsection (3)(a)(ii) above does not affect the discretion of the arbitral tribunal in making any subsequent determination.
(c) With regard to a request for an interim measure of protection under Section 17(2)(d) or 17(3)(c), the requirements in subsection 4(a) shall apply only to the extent the arbitral tribunal considers appropriate.

(5) The arbitral tribunal may modify, suspend or terminate an interim measure of protection passed by the tribunal under this Section, on the application of any party or, in exceptional circumstances and on prior notice to the parties, on the arbitral tribunal's own initiative.
(6) The arbitral tribunal may require the party requesting an interim measure of protection to provide appropriate security in connection with the measure.
(7) The party requesting the interim measure of protection under this Section shall disclose all facts and circumstances likely to be relevant to the court's determination whether to grant the interim measure of protection requested and shall promptly disclose any material change in the circumstances on the basis of which the measure was requested or granted.
(8) The arbitral tribunal may, at any time in the arbitral proceedings, order the party who requested the interim measure of protection to pay costs and damages caused by the measure or order to any party if the arbitral tribunal later determines that, in the circumstances, the measure or the order requested should not have been granted.

Section 17A. Recognition and enforcement of interim measures of protection:

(1) An interim measure of protection granted by an arbitral tribunal shall be recognised as binding and unless otherwise provided by the arbitral tribunal, enforced, within fifteen days, upon application to Court under Section 94 of the CPC, 1908, irrespective of the country in which it was issued, subject to the provisions of Section 17B.
(2) The party who is seeking, or has obtained recognition or enforcement of an interim measure of protection, shall promptly inform the court of any termination, suspension, or modification of the interim measure of protection.
(3) The Court may, if it considers it appropriate, order the applicant to provide appropriate security if:

(a) The arbitral tribunal has not already made a decision with respect to the provision of security.
(b) The decision with respect to the provision of security is necessary to protect the rights of third parties.

Section 17B. Grounds for refusing recognition or enforcement:

(1) Recognition or enforcement of an interim measure of protection may be refused only:
  (a) At the request of the respondent if the Court is prima facie satisfied that:
    (i) The refusal is warranted on the grounds set out in Section 34(2)(a) or 48(1)(a)-(d).
    (ii) The arbitral tribunal's decision with respect to the provision of security in connection with the interim measure of protection granted by it has not been complied with.
    (iii) The interim measure of protection has been suspended or terminated by the arbitral tribunal or, if so empowered, by the Court of the country which is the seat of arbitration.
  (b) If the Court finds that:
    (i) The interim measure of protection is incompatible with the powers conferred on the Court unless the Court decides to reformulate the interim measure of protection to the extent necessary to adapt it to its own powers and procedures for the purposes of enforcing that interim measure of protection and without modifying its substance.
    (ii) Any of the grounds set out in Section 34(2)(b) or 48(2) apply to the recognition and enforcement of the interim measure of protection.
(2) Any determination made by the court on any ground in subsection (1) shall be effective only for the purposes of the application to recognise and enforce the interim measure of protection.
(3) The court shall not, in making the determination with respect to the recognition or enforcement sought, undertake a review of the substance of the interim measure of protection.
(4) No appeal shall lie to any court under any order passed under this Section or subsection (1) of Section 17A.

Section 36. Enforcement:

(1) Subject to the provisions of subsection (2), an award shall be enforced in accordance with the provisions of the CPC, 1908, in the same manner as if it were a decree of the Court.
(2) Where an application to set aside the arbitral award has been filed in the Court under Section 34, the filing of such an application shall not by itself render that award unenforceable, unless the Court grants an order of stay of the

operation of the said arbitral award in accordance with the provisions of subsection (3), on a separate application made for that purpose.

(3) Upon the filing of an application under subsection (2) for a stay of the operation of the arbitral award, the Court may, subject to such conditions as it may deem fit, grant the operation of such award for reasons to be recorded in writing.

Provided that the Court shall, while considering the application for grant of stay in the case of an arbitral award for payment of money, have due regard to the provisions for grant of stay of a money decree under the provisions of the CPC, 1908.

37. Appealable orders:

(1) An appeal shall lie from the following orders (and from no others) to the Court authorised by law to hear appeals from original decrees of the Court passing the order, namely:
  (a) refusing to refer the parties to arbitration under Section 8;
  (b) Subject to the commencement of arbitral proceedings, granting or refusing to grant any measure under Section 9, or if the arbitral proceedings have commenced, when the tribunal is unable to act effectively:
    (ba) Notwithstanding anything contained herein, an appeal filed under subsection (1)(b) shall not render the interim measure granted under Section 9 of the Act unenforceable, unless the Court grants an order of stay of the operation of such interim measure, subject to such conditions as it deems fit, for reasons to be recorded in writing.
    (bb) Any appeal pending on the commencement of arbitral proceedings shall be transferred to the arbitral tribunal and shall be deemed to be an application before the arbitral tribunal under Section 17(5) of the Act and shall be decided by the arbitral tribunal only.
  (c) setting aside or refusing to set aside an arbitral award under Section 34.

(2) Appeal shall also lie to a court from an order of the arbitral tribunal accepting the plea referred to in subsection (*2*) or subsection (*3*) of Section 16.

(3) No second appeal shall lie from any order passed in appeal under this section, but nothing in this section shall affect or take away any right to appeal to the Supreme Court.

Appendices

Appendix A (Article 9)

Sr. No.	Country	Provision
1.	Australia - International Arbitration Act 1974[1]	Same as UNCITRAL Model Law 2006 Section 16 Model Law to have force of law (1) Subject to this Part, the Model Law has the force of law in Australia. (2) In the Model Law: Arbitration agreement has the meaning given in Option 1 of Article 7 of the Model Law. State means Australia (including the external Territories) and any foreign country. This State means Australia (including the external Territories). Model Law under Part V, Schedule 2 of the Arbitration Act, 1974
2.	Australian Capital Territory – Commercial Arbitration Act, 2017 A2017-7[2]	Same as Article 9 of UNCITRAL Model Law 2006 Article 9
3.	Austria - Austrian Arbitration Act, 2013[3]	Same as Article 9 of UNCITRAL Model Law 2006 Section 585
4.	Bahrain - Bahrain Arbitration Law No. 9/2015[4]	Same as UNCITRAL Model Law 2006 Article 1 Taking into account the provisions of international conventions in force in the Kingdom of Bahrain

1. https://www.legislation.gov.au/Details/C2011C00342.
2. http://classic.austlii.edu.au/au/legis/act/consol_act/caa2017219/s9.html.
3. https://www.viac.eu/images/law/ZPO_Schiedsrecht_2014_en_im_VIAC_Layout.pdf
4. https://pernetmartial.eu/sites/default/files/lois/Bahrain-Loi-d-arbitrage-arbitration-act-ley-de-a rbitraje.pdf

Sr. No.	Country	Provision
		1. The provisions of the "UNCITRAL" Model Law on International Commercial Arbitration Act attached to this law shall apply to all arbitration whatever the nature of the legal relationship of the dispute herewith, if this arbitration takes place in the Kingdom of Bahrain or abroad and that two parties agreed to comply with the provisions of the attached law. 2. The provisions of the attached law shall apply to all arbitration which begins after its entry into force even if based on an arbitration agreement concluded before the entry into force of this law.
5.	Bangladesh - The Arbitration Act, 2001[5]	Section 7A Powers of court and High Court Division to make interim orders:- (1) Notwithstanding anything contained in section 7 unless the parties agree otherwise, upon prayer of either parties, before or during continuance of the proceedings or until enforcement of the award under section 44 or 45 in the case of international commercial arbitration the High Court Division and in the case of other arbitrations the court may pass order in the following matters: (a) To appoint guardian for minor or insane to conduct on his/her behalf arbitral proceedings. (b) To take into interim custody of or sale of or other protective measures in respect of goods or property included in the arbitration agreement. (c) To restrain any party to transfer certain property or pass injunction on transfer of such property which is intended to create impediment on the way of enforcement of award. (d) To empower any person to seize, preserve, inspect, to take photograph, collect specimen, examine, to take evidence of any goods or property included in arbitration agreement and for that purpose to enter into the land or building in possession of any party. (e) To issue ad interim injunction; (f) To appoint receiver; and (g) To take any other interim protective measures which may appear reasonable or appropriate to the court or the High Court Division. (2) The similar powers of the court or the High Court Division as are available in relation to any other legal proceedings shall be available to the court or the High Court Division as the case may be, while passing orders under sub section (1). (3) Before passing order upon application received under sub-section (1) the court or the High Court Division shall serve notice upon the other party: Provided that f the court or the High Court Division is satisfied that in the event the order is not passed instantaneously, the purpose of making interim measures shall be frustrated, there shall be no necessity of serving such notice.

5. http://www.mccibd.org/images/uploadimg/act_and_policy/corporate_governance/The-Arbitration-Act-2001.pdf

Sr. No.	Country	Provision
		(4) If the court or the High Court Division is satisfied that Arbitration Tribunal has no power to initiate proceedings in any matter under sub-section (1) or the Arbitration Tribunal has failed to pass order in such matter, the Court or the High Court Division as the case may be, shall be competent to pass order under this section. (5) The Court or the High Court Division f considers appropriate shall be competent to cancel, alter or amend the order passed under this section. (6) Where any Arbitration Tribunal or any institution or person empowered in any matters relating to orders passed under sub-section (1) passed any order in such matters, the order passed by the court or High Court Division as the case may be, in the same matter, shall be entirely or the relevant part thereof inoperative.
6.	Belgium - Belgian Judicial Code Provisions[6]	Art. 1683 It is not incompatible with an arbitration agreement for a request to be made to a court for an interim or conservatory measure before or during arbitral proceedings and for a court to grant such measure, nor shall any such request imply a waiver of the arbitration agreement.
7.	Bhutan - Alternative Dispute Resolution Act of Bhutan 2013[7]	Section 38 Interim measure by Court It is not incompatible with an arbitration agreement for a party to request, before or during arbitral proceedings, from a court an interim measure of protection and for a court to grant such measure. Section 39 If a party is aggrieved by an order issued under section 38 of this Act, he or she may appeal to the higher court within ten working days of the receipt of order. Section 40 If the court grants interim measures under section 38 of this Act before the commencement of arbitration, it shall direct the party to take effective steps for the appointment of the arbitral tribunal in accordance with the procedure specified in Chapter IV, within a period of fifteen working days from the date of such direction.
8.	British Columbia - International Commercial Arbitration Act [RSBC 1996] Chapter 233[8]	Section 9 It is not incompatible with an arbitration agreement for a party to request from a court, before or during arbitral proceedings, an interim measure of protection and for a court to grant that measure.

6. http://www.arbiter.com.sg/pdf/laws/Belgian%20Judicial%20Code%20Provisions%20(2013).pdf
7. https://www.nationalcouncil.bt/assets/uploads/docs/acts/2014/Alternative_Dispute_Resolution_Act_of_Bhutan_2013_eng10th.pdf
8. http://www.bclaws.ca/civix/document/id/complete/statreg/96233_01

Sr. No.	Country	Provision
9.	British Virgin Islands - Virgin Islands Arbitration Act, 2013[9]	UNCITRAL Model Law to have effect in the Virgin Islands. Section 4. The provisions of the UNCITRAL Model Law have the force of law in the Virgin Islands, subject to the modifications and supplements expressly provided in this Act. Same as Article 9 of UNCITRAL Model Law 2006 Section 19. Application of article 9 of the UNCITRAL Model Law
10.	Bulgaria - Law on International Commercial Arbitration State Gazette (SG) No. 60 of 05.08.1988[10]	Art. 9. Each of the parties to an arbitration agreement may request from a court to order a provisional remedy of the claim or perpetuation of the evidence before or during the arbitration proceedings.
11.	Cambodia - The Commercial Arbitration Law of the Kingdom of Cambodia 2006[11]	Same as Article 9 of UNCITRAL Model Law 2006 Article 9
12.	Canada - Commercial Arbitration Act R.S.C., 1985, c. 17 (2nd Supp.)[12]	Schedule 1- Commercial Arbitration Code Adopted UNCITRAL Model Law 1985 Article 9
13.	Connecticut - Chapter 909 Arbitration Proceedings[13]	Sec. 52-407hh. Provisional remedies. (a) Before an arbitrator is appointed and is authorized and able to act, the court, upon motion of a party to an arbitration proceeding and for good cause shown, may enter an order for provisional remedies to protect the effectiveness of the arbitration proceeding to the same extent and under the same conditions as if the controversy were the subject of a civil action.
14.	Croatia - Law on Arbitration Official Gazette no. 88/2001[14]	Article 44 Interim court measures of protection of claims A party to arbitral proceedings may apply to the court to grant interim measures for protection of a claim. It is not incompatible with an arbitration agreement for a party to request from a court, before or during arbitral proceedings, an interim measure for protection of a claim and for a court to grant such a measure.

9. http://www.bviiac.org/Portals/0/Files/Arbitration%20Documents/ArbitrationAct2013.pdf
10. http://www.newyorkconvention.org/11165/web/files/document/1/6/16200.pdf
11. https://www.cambodiaip.gov.kh/DocResources/372a361b-7a97-44b3-9810-79e5e6ea85f4_c786a043-b88d-4f64-9429-60a330efdc5f-en.pdf
12. https://laws-lois.justice.gc.ca/eng/acts/C-34.6/index.html
13. https://www.cga.ct.gov/current/pub/chap_909.htm
14. http://www.vsrh.hr/CustomPages/Static/HRV/Files/Legislation__Law-Arbitration-RC.pdf

Sr. No.	Country	Provision
15.	Cyprus - The International Commercial Arbitration Law, 1987[15]	Same as Article 9 of UNCITRAL Model Law 2006 Section 9 Interim measures by Court
16.	Denmark - Danish Arbitration Act 2005[16]	Section 9 The courts may, at the request of a party, grant an order for an interim measure of protection or for enforcement even if the parties have agreed to submit the dispute to arbitration.
17.	Egypt - Law No. 27/1994 Promulgating the Law Concerning Arbitration in Civil and Commercial Matters[17]	Article 14 Upon request of either party to the arbitration, the court referred to in Article 9 may order the taking of an interim or conservatory measure, whether before the commencement of the arbitral proceedings or during said proceedings.
18.	Florida –Chapter 684 – International Commercial Arbitration, Title XXXIX Commercial Relations, 2020 Florida Statutes[18]	Same as Article 9 of the UNCITRAL Model Law 2006 Article 684.001Arbitration Agreement and Interim Measures by a Court
19.	Fiji - International Arbitration Act 2017 (Act No. 44 of 2017)[19]	Same as Article 9 of UNCITRAL Model Law 2006 Section 14
20.	France – Book IV – Arbitration of the Code of Civil procedure Decree no. 2011-48[20]	Article 1449 The existence of an arbitration agreement, insofar as the arbitral tribunal has not yet been constituted, shall not preclude a party from applying to a court for measures relating to the taking of evidence or provisional or conservatory measures.
21.	Georgia - Chapter 9 Arbitration, Title 9 Civil Practice, Georgia Code 2019[21]	Section 9-9-30 Before or during arbitral proceedings, a party may request from a court an interim measure of protection, and a court may grant such measure, and such request shall not be deemed to be incompatible with an arbitration agreement.

15. https://www.uv.es/medarb/observatorio/leyes-arbitraje/europa-resto/chipre-international-commercial-arbitration-law.pdf
16. https://voldgiftsinstituttet.dk/wp-content/uploads/2015/01/danish_arbitration_act_2005.pdf
17. https://www.wipo.int/edocs/lexdocs/laws/en/eg/eg020en.pdf
18. https://www.flsenate.gov/Laws/Statutes/2020/684.001
19. https://www.fiji.gov.fj/getattachment/d9502667-6491-4592-85b2-eff97f245fed/Act-44---International-Arbitration-Act.aspx
20. http://www.iaiparis.com/pdf/FRENCH_LAW_ON_INTERNATIONAL_ARBITRATION.pdf

Sr. No.	Country	Provision
22.	Germany – Tenth Book of the Code of Civil Procedure, Arbitration Procedure[22]	Section 1033 Arbitration agreement and interim measures by court It is not incompatible with an arbitration agreement for a court to grant, before or during arbitral proceedings, an interim measure of protection relating to the subject-matter of the arbitration upon request of a party.
23.	Greece – Code of Civil Procedure, Book VII, Book VIII[23]	Article 889 1. The arbitrators may not order, amend, or revoke interim measures of protection. 2. If the competent court has ordered interim measures of protection and a time period has been fixed for the filing of an action or a situation has arisen calling for the application of paragraph 5 of article 715 and paragraph 5 of article 729, the applicant shall be bound to initiate within the prescribed time period the arbitral proceedings. The provisions of paragraph 2 of article 693, paragraph 5, item 2 of article 715 and paragraph 5, item 2 of article 729 shall also be applied in such a case.
24.	Hong Kong - Cap. 609 Arbitration Ordinance[24]	Same as Article 9 of UNCITRAL Model Law Section 21- Article 9 of UNCITRAL Model Law (Arbitration agreement and interim measures by court)
25.	Hungary - Act LX of 2017 on Arbitration[25]	Section 10 Compatibility of the arbitration agreement with the measures of the court and the notary The party's request made prior to the commencement of the arbitral proceedings for the issuance of an order of payment, or submitted to a Hungarian court prior to or during the arbitral proceedings for a preliminary taking of evidence (Chapter XXIV of Pp.), for a provisional measure (Chapter VIII of Pp.), for a security measure [Chapter X of Act LIII of 1994 on judicial enforcement (hereinafter "Vht.")], for the insertion of an enforcement clause into a document [sections 23/B (1) a) and 23/C of Vht.], or for the provision of a security [section 6:523 of Act V of 2013 on the Civil Code (hereinafter "Ptk.")], as well as his request submitted to any foreign court for a similar measure and the measure of the court granting such request shall not be deemed incompatible with the arbitration agreement.

21. http://ga.elaws.us/law/section9-9-30
22. https://sccinstitute.com/media/29988/german-arbitration-act.pdf
23. https://www.uv.es/medarb/observatorio/leyes-arbitraje/europa-resto/grecia-ccp-domestic-arbitration.pdf
24. https://www.elegislation.gov.hk/hk/cap609
25. https://www.ilo.org/dyn/natlex/docs/ELECTRONIC/106843/131257/F-266585574/J2017T0060P_20180102_FIN.pdf

Sr. No.	Country	Provision
26.	Ireland - Arbitration Act 2010 Number 1 of 2010[26]	Section 6 – Adoption of Model Law Subject to this Act, the Model Law shall have the force of law in the State and shall apply to arbitrations under arbitration agreements concerning— (a) international commercial arbitrations, or (b) arbitrations which are not international commercial arbitrations. Same as Article 9 of the UNCITRAL Model Law 2006 Article 9 under Schedule 1 - TEXT OF UNCITRAL MODEL LAW ON INTERNATIONAL COMMERCIAL ARBITRATION
27.	Jamaica - The Arbitration Act, 2017 (Act 13 of 2017)[27]	Same as Article 9 of UNCITRAL Model Law Section 12
28.	Japan - Arbitration Law (Law No.138 of 2003)[28]	Article 15 Arbitration Agreement and Interim Measures by Court It is not incompatible with an arbitration agreement for a party to request, before or during arbitral proceedings, from a court an interim measure of protection and for a court to grant such measure in respect of any civil dispute which is the subject of the arbitration agreement.
29.	Jordan - Law No. 31 of 2001 (Jordan) Arbitration Law[29]	Article 13 It is not incompatible with an arbitration agreement for a party to request, before or during arbitral proceedings, from a "Judge of Summary Matters" that a provisional or conservatory measure be taken in accordance with the "Law of Civil Procedures" and such measure may be withdrawn in the same manner.
30.	Kenya - Chapter 49 Arbitration Act (The Arbitration Act, 1995)[30]	Section 7 Interim measures by court (1) It is not incompatible with an arbitration agreement for a party to request from the High Court, before or during arbitral proceedings, an interim measure of protection and for the High Court to grant that measure. (2) Where a party applies to the High Court for an injunction or other interim order and the arbitral tribunal has already ruled on any matter relevant to the application, the High Court shall treat the ruling or any finding of fact made in the course of the ruling as conclusive for the purposes of the application.
31.	Liechtenstein - Liechtenstein Arbitration Law (Code of Civil Procedure)[31]	Section 602 Arbitration Agreement and Interim Measures by Court It is not incompatible with an arbitration agreement for a party to request, before or during arbitral proceedings, from a court an interim or protective measure and for a court to grant such a measure.

26. http://www.irishstatutebook.ie/eli/2010/act/1/enacted/en/pdf
27. http://extwprlegs1.fao.org/docs/pdf/jam172060.pdf
28. https://japan.kantei.go.jp/policy/sihou/arbitrationlaw.pdf
29. https://www.ilo.org/dyn/natlex/docs/ELECTRONIC/63091/95325/F1864661120/JOR63091.pdf
30. https://ncia.or.ke/wp-content/uploads/2021/02/ArbitrationAct4of1995_2.pdf

Sr. No.	Country	Provision
32.	Lithuania - The Republic of Lithuania Law on Commercial Arbitration, 2012[32]	Article 27 Taking of Interim Measures and Preservation of Evidence by a Court Order (1) A party shall be entitled to request Vilnius Regional Court to take interim measures or require to preserve evidence before the commencement of arbitral proceedings or the constitution of an arbitral tribunal. At the request of the party, the Court may apply interim measures or require to preserve evidence also after the constitution of the arbitral tribunal. Accordingly, the other party shall have the right, according to the procedure established by the Code of Civil Procedure, to apply for the security for compensation for losses likely to result from taking of interim measures or preservation of evidence. (2) A refusal of the Court to take interim measures or preserve evidence shall not preclude a party, during arbitral proceedings, from requesting an arbitral tribunal to apply interim measures or preserve evidence.
33.	Louisiana - RS 9 Title 9. Civil Code-Ancillaries[33]	Same as Article 9 of UNCITRAL Model Law 2006 §4249. Arbitration agreement and interim measures by court
34.	Macedonia - Law on International Commercial Arbitration of the Republic of Macedonia[34]	Same as Article 9 of UNCITRAL Model Law 2006 Article 9
35.	Malaysia - Arbitration Act 2005, Act 646[35]	Section 11 Arbitration agreement and interim measures by High Court (1) A party may, before or during arbitral proceedings, apply to a High Court for any interim measure and the High Court may make the following orders for: (a) security for costs; (b) discovery of documents and interrogatories; (c) giving of evidence by affidavit; (d) appointment of a receiver; (e) securing the amount in dispute; (f) the preservation, interim custody or sale of any property which is the subject-matter of the dispute; (g) ensuring that any award which may be made in the arbitral proceedings is not rendered ineffectual by the dissipation of assets by a party; and (h) an interim injunction or any other interim measure.

31. https://www.newyorkconvention.org/11165/web/files/document/2/1/21372.pdf
32. https://e-seimas.lrs.lt/portal/legalAct/lt/TAD/35954312dcb311e6be918a531b2126ab?jfwid=-wd7z7zum0
33. http://legis.la.gov/legis/Law.aspx?d=408447
34. https://www.international-arbitration-attorney.com/wp-content/uploads/2013/07/Macedonia-Arbitration-Law.pdf
35. http://www.newyorkconvention.org/11165/web/files/document/1/6/16298.pdf

Sr. No.	Country	Provision
		(2) Where a party applies to the High Court for any interim measure and an arbitral tribunal has already ruled on any matter which is relevant to the application, the High Court shall treat any findings of fact made in the course of such ruling by the arbitral tribunal as conclusive for the purposes of the application. (3) This section shall also apply in respect of an international arbitration, where the seat of arbitration is not in Malaysia.
36.	Maldives - Act No: 10/2013, Arbitration Act[36]	No equivalent provision as Article 9 of the UNCITRAL Model Law 2006
37.	Malta - CAP. 387 Arbitration Act[37]	CAP. 387 Arbitration Act has adopted Article 9 of the UNCITRAL Model Law 1985 in its FIRST SCHEDULE
38.	Mauritius - The International Arbitration Act, 2008 (Act 37 of 2008)[38]	Section 2 Compatibility of interim measures (1) It is not incompatible with an arbitration agreement for a party to request, before or during arbitral proceedings, from the Supreme Court or a Court in a foreign state an interim measure of protection in support of arbitration and for the Court to grant such a measure. (2) An application to the Supreme Court under subsection (1) shall be made and determined in accordance with section 23.
39.	Montenegro - Decree on the Promulgation of the Law on Arbitration, 2015[39]	Same as Article 9 of UNCITRAL Model Law 2006 Article 11
40.	Myanmar - Arbitration Law The Pyidaungsu Hluttaw Law No. 5/2016[40]	Section 11 Power of the Court to intervene in Arbitration (a) Unless otherwise agreed by the parties, if a party requests the court, the court shall have power to make decision as its own jurisdiction for: (1) taking evidence; (2) the preservation any evidence; (3) pass an order related to the property in disputes in arbitration or any property which is related to the subject-matter of the dispute; (4) inspection, taking photo for evidence, preservation and seizure of the property which is related to the dispute; (5) samples to be taken from, or any observation to be made of or experiment conducted upon, any property which is or forms part of the subject-matter of the dispute; (6) allow to enter in the premises owned by or under the control of the parties to disputes for the purpose of above mentions matters; (7) sale of any property which is the subject-matter of the dispute; (8) an interim injunction or appointment of a receiver;

36. https://miac.gov.mv/media/documents/Arbitration%20Act.pdf
37. http://justiceservices.gov.mt/DownloadDocument.aspx?app=lom&itemid=8854&l=1
38. https://www.wipo.int/edocs/lexdocs/laws/en/mu/mu020en.pdf
39. https://www.privrednakomora.me/sites/pkcg.org/files/multimedia/main_pages/files/2012/09/final_eng_zakon_o_arbitrazi_final_0.pdf

Sr. No.	Country	Provision
		(b) If the interim measure is needed urgently in arbitration, the court may pass an order relating to preservation of evidence and related properties upon the application of a party as require. (c) If the interim measure is not needed urgently, upon the application of a party in arbitration, the court shall deal such matter after delivering a notice to the other parties and arbitral tribunal and with the approval of the arbitration tribunal or with the written consent of the other party. (d) The court shall only deal with the matters which the authorized person of the parties or arbitral tribunal or arbitral institution or other institution has no authority to do or not able to handle effectively. (e) An order made by the court shall cease to have effect in whole or in part if the arbitral tribunal makes an order which expressly relates to the order under subsection (a).
41.	New South Wales - Commercial Arbitration Act 2010 No 61[41]	Same as Article 9 of UNCITRAL Model Law 2006 Section 9
42.	New Zealand - The Arbitration Act, 1996 No 99[42]	Schedule I - Rules applying to arbitration agreement Article 9 Arbitration agreement and interim measures by court (1) It is not incompatible with an arbitration agreement for a party to request, before or during arbitral proceedings, from a court an interim measure and for a court to grant such measure. (2) For the purposes of paragraph (1), the High Court or the District Court has the same powers as an arbitral tribunal to grant an interim measure under article 17A for the purposes of proceedings before that court, and that article and article 17B apply accordingly subject to all necessary modifications. (3) Where a party applies to a court for an interim injunction or other interim order and an arbitral tribunal has already ruled on any matter relevant to the application, the court shall treat the ruling or any finding of fact made in the course of the ruling as conclusive for the purposes of the application.
43.	Nigeria - Arbitration and Conciliation Act, Chapter 19 Laws of the Federation of Nigeria 1990[43]	First Schedule Arbitration Rules Article 26 Interim Measures of Protection (3) A request for interim measures addressed by any party to court shall not be deemed incompatible with the agreement to arbitrate, or as a waiver of the agreement.

40. http://www.newyorkconvention.org/11165/web/files/document/2/1/21098.pdf
41. https://legislation.nsw.gov.au/view/html/inforce/current/act-2010-061#sec.9
42. http://www.legislation.govt.nz/act/public/1996/0099/latest/whole.html#DLM403277
43. http://www.shiac.org/upload_files/file/2016/20160222134959_3710.pdf

Sr. No.	Country	Provision
44.	Northern Territory of Australia - Commercial Arbitration (National Uniform Legislation) Act 2011[44]	Same as Article 9 of UNCITRAL Model Law 2006 Section 9
45.	Norway - Act of 14 May 2004 No. 25 relating to Arbitration (The Arbitration Act)[45]	Section 8 Provisional security The courts may determine application of provisional security pursuant to Chapters 14 and 15 of the Enforcement Act even if a dispute is subject to arbitration.
46.	Oman - The Omani Law of Arbitration in Civil and Commercial Disputes – Royal Decree 47/97[46]	Article 14 The Court, referred to in Article 9 of this Law, on the basis of a request made by one of the parties to the arbitration, may issue such order, to take temporary or precautionary measures either before commencement of the arbitration proceedings or during the course of its progress.
47.	Ontario - International Commercial Arbitration Act, 2017, S.O. 2017, c. 2, Sched. 5[47]	Section 5 Application of Model Law (1) Subject to this Act, the Model Law on International Commercial Arbitration, adopted by the United Nations Commission on International Trade Law on 21 June 1985, as amended by the United Nations Commission on International Trade Law on 7 July 2006, set out in Schedule 2, has force of law in Ontario. Same (2) With respect to article 7 of the Model Law, option I applies in Ontario; option II does not. Same (3) The Model Law applies to international commercial arbitration agreements and awards made in international commercial arbitrations, whether made before or after the coming into force of this Act. Schedule 2 Article 9
48.	Oregon – Oregon International Commercial Arbitration and Conciliation Act[48]	36.470 Interim judicial relief; factors considered by court; determination of arbitral tribunal's jurisdiction. (1) It is not incompatible with an arbitration agreement for a party to request from a court, before or during arbitral proceedings, an interim measure of protection or for the court to grant such a measure.

44. https://legislation.nt.gov.au/api/sitecore/Act/PDF?id=11692
45. https://www.chamber.no/wp-content/uploads/2014/02/Norwegian_Arbitration_Act.pdf
46. http://www.newyorkconvention.org/11165/web/files/document/2/1/21103.pdf
47. https://laws-lois.justice.gc.ca/PDF/C-34.6.pdf
48. https://www.oregonlegislature.gov/bills_laws/ors/ors036.html

Sr. No.	Country	Provision
		(2) Any party to an arbitration governed by ORS 36.450 to 36.558 may request from the circuit court the enforcement of an order of an arbitral tribunal granting an interim measure of protection pursuant to ORS 36.486. Enforcement shall be granted pursuant to the law applicable to the granting of the type of interim relief requested. (3) Measures which the circuit court may grant in connection with a pending arbitration include, but are not limited to: (a) An order of attachment issued to assure that the award to which the applicant may be entitled is not rendered ineffectual by the dissipation of party assets. (b) A preliminary injunction granted in order to protect trade secrets or to conserve goods which are the subject matter of the arbitral dispute. (4) In considering a request for interim relief, the court, subject to subsection (5) of this section, shall give preclusive effect to any and all findings of fact of the arbitral tribunal, including the probable validity of the claim which is the subject of the award for interim relief that the arbitral tribunal has previously granted in the proceeding in question, provided that such interim award is consistent with public policy. (5) Where the arbitral tribunal has not ruled on an objection to its jurisdiction, the court shall not grant preclusive effect to the tribunal's findings until the court has made an independent finding as to the jurisdiction of the arbitral tribunal. If the court rules that the arbitral tribunal did not have jurisdiction, the application for interim measures of relief shall be denied. Such a ruling by the court that the arbitral tribunal lacks jurisdiction is not binding on the arbitral tribunal or subsequent judicial proceedings.
49.	Pakistan - The Arbitration Act, 1940 Act No. X of 1940[49]	Section 16 Power of Court to pass interim orders. (1) Notwithstanding anything contained in section 17, at anytime after the filing of the award, whether notice of the filing has been served or not, upon being satisfied by affidavit or otherwise that a party has taken or is about to take steps to defeat, delay or obstruct the execution of any decree that may be passed upon the award, or that speedy execution of the award is just and necessary, the Court may pass such interim orders as it deems necessary. (2) Any person against whom such interim orders have been passed may show cause against such orders, and the Court, after hearing the parties, may pass such further orders as it deems necessary and just. Second Schedule - Power of Court 1. The preservation, interim custody or sale of any goods which are subject matter of the reference. 2. Securing the amount in difference in the reference.

49. https://www.wipo.int/edocs/lexdocs/laws/en/pk/pk066en.pdf

Sr. No.	Country	Provision
		3. The detention, preservation or inspection of any property or thing which is the subject of the reference or as to which any question may arise therein and authorizing for any of the aforesaid purposes any person to enter upon or into any land or building in the possession or any party to the reference, or authorizing any samples to be taken or any observation to be made, or experiment to be tried, which may be necessary or expedient for the purpose of obtaining full information or evidence. 4. Interim injunctions or the appointment of a receiver. 5. The appointment of a guardian for a minor or person of unsound mind for the purposes of arbitration proceedings.
50.	Philippines - Alternative Dispute Resolution Act of 2004 Republic Act No. 9285[50]	Section. 28. Grant of Interim Measure of Protection. - (a) It is not incompatible with an arbitration agreement for a party to request, before constitution of the tribunal, from a Court an interim measure of protection and for the Court to grant such measure. After constitution of the arbitral tribunal and during arbitral proceedings, a request for an interim measure of protection or modification thereof, may be made with the arbitral tribunal or to the extent that the arbitral tribunal has no power to act or is unable to act effectively, the request may be made with the Court. The arbitral tribunal is deemed constituted when the sole arbitrator or the third arbitrator who has been nominated, has accepted the nomination and written communication of said nomination and acceptance has been received by theparty making request... (b) The following rules on interim or provisional relief shall be observed: (1) Any party may request that provision relief be granted against the adverse party: (2) Such relief may be granted: (i) to prevent irreparable loss or injury: (ii) to provide security for the performance of any obligation; (iii) to produce or preserve any evidence; or (iv) to compel any other appropriate act or omission.
51.	Poland - Polish Act of 17 November 1964 - Code of Civil Procedure, Part Five Arbitration[51]	Article 1166 1. Submission of a dispute for resolution by arbitration does not exclude the possibility of granting interim measures of protection by the court in respect of claims pursued before the arbitral tribunal. 2. Paragraph 1 also applies when the place of arbitration is outside the borders of the Republic of Poland or has not been determined.

50. http://www.newyorkconvention.org/11165/web/files/document/2/1/21107.pdf
51. https://www.uv.es/medarb/observatorio/leyes-arbitraje/europa-resto/polonia-ccp-arbitration.pdf

Sr. No.	Country	Provision
52.	Qatar - Law No. 2 of 2017 Promulgating the Civil and Commercial Arbitration Law-The Law of Arbitration in Civil and Commercial Matters[52]	Article (9) In situations where the Arbitral Tribunal, or any other person to whom the Parties have granted certain authority, does not have jurisdiction, or is incapable to act effectively at the time, the Competent Judge, on the application of one of the Parties, may order interim or precautionary measures, including the measures stipulated in Article 17(1) of this Law, either before the commencement of or during the arbitral proceedings. The said application shall not be deemed a waiver by the Party of its right to uphold the Arbitration Agreement.
53.	Queensland - Commercial Arbitration Act 2013 No. 8[53]	Same as Article 9 of UNCITRAL Model Law 2006 Section 9
54.	Republic of Costa Rica - Costa Rican Law for International Arbitration Law Number: 8937[54]	Same as Article 9 of UNCITRAL Model Law 2006 Article 9
55.	Republic of Korea – Arbitration Act[55]	Article 10 Arbitration Agreement and Interim Measures by Court A party to arbitration agreement may request, before the commencement of or during arbitral proceedings, from a court an interim measure of protection and for a court to grant such measure.
56.	Russia - Russian Federation Law on International Commercial Arbitration[56]	Same as Article 9 of UNCITRAL Model Law 2006 Article 9
57.	Rwanda – Law on arbitration and conciliation in commercial matters, N° 005/2008[57]	Article 11 Arbitration agreement and interim measures of the court One of the parties to arbitration may request the court, before or during arbitral proceedings, for an interim measure and of which the court may grant. Such a measure shall not be contrary to arbitration agreement.

52. https://www.qicdrc.gov.qa/sites/default/files/inline-files/law_no._02_2017_promulgating_the_civil_and_commercial_arbitration_law.pdf
53. https://www.legislation.qld.gov.au/view/pdf/inforce/2013-05-17/act-2013-008
54. https://arbitratlaw.com/wp-content/uploads/2017/01/Costa-Rican-Intl-Arbitration-Law.pdf
55. https://elaw.klri.re.kr/eng_service/lawView.do?hseq=38889&lang=ENG
56. http://www.newyorkconvention.org/11165/web/files/document/2/2/22335.pdf
57. http://www.newyorkconvention.org/11165/web/files/document/2/1/21110.pdf

Sr. No.	Country	Provision
58.	Saudi Arabia - Law of Arbitration Royal Decree No. M/34[58]	Article 22 1. The competent court may, upon the request of either party, order provisional or precautionary measures prior to commencing arbitration proceedings, or upon request by the arbitration tribunal during arbitration proceedings. Said measures may be revoked in the same way, unless otherwise agreed by the two parties to arbitration. 2. The competent court may, upon request by the arbitration tribunal, issue an order of judicial delegation. 3. The arbitration tribunal may, as it deems fit, seek the assistance of the competent agency in the arbitration proceedings, such as calling a witness or an expert, ordering the submission of a document or a copy thereof, reviewing said document, or any other proceeding, without prejudice to the right of the arbitration tribunal to conduct said proceeding independently.
59.	Serbia - Law on Arbitration No. 46/2006[59]	Article 15 Interim Measures Each party may, before or during arbitral proceedings, request from a court interim measure, and the court may grant such measures. Paragraph 1 of this Article shall also apply when the arbitration agreement concerns an arbitration in another State.
60.	Singapore - Arbitration Act (Chapter 10) (Domestic Arbitration Law)[60]	Section 6 Stay of Legal Proceedings (1) Where any party to an arbitration agreement institutes any proceedings in any court against any other party to the agreement in respect of any matter which is the subject of the agreement, any party to the agreement may, at any time after appearance and before delivering any pleading or taking any other step in the proceedings, apply to that court to stay the proceedings so far as the proceedings relate to that matter. (2) The court to which an application has been made in accordance with subsection (1) may, if the court is satisfied that — (a) there is no sufficient reason why the matter should not be referred in accordance with the arbitration agreement; and (b) the applicant was, at the time when the proceedings were commenced, and still remains, ready and willing to do all things necessary to the proper conduct of the arbitration, make an order, upon such terms as the court thinks fit, staying the proceedings so far as the proceedings relate to that matter. (3) Where a court makes an order under subsection (2), the court may, for the purpose of preserving the rights of parties, make such interim or supplementary orders as the court thinks fit in relation to any property which is or forms part of the subject of the dispute to which the order under that subsection relates.

58. https://www.wipo.int/edocs/lexdocs/laws/en/sa/sa057en.pdf
59. https://www.wipo.int/edocs/lexdocs/laws/en/rs/rs028en.pdf
60. https://sso.agc.gov.sg/Act/AA2001

Sr. No.	Country	Provision
		(4) Where no party to the proceedings has taken any further step in the proceedings for a period of not less than 2 years after an order staying the proceedings has been made, the court may, on its own motion, make an order discontinuing the proceedings without prejudice to the right of any of the parties to apply for the discontinued proceedings to be reinstated. (5) For the purposes of this section, a reference to a party includes a reference to any person claiming through or under such party.
61.	Singapore - International Arbitration Act (Chapter 143A) (International Arbitration Law)[61]	Section 3 Model Law to have force of law (1) Subject to this Act, the Model Law, with the exception of Chapter VIII thereof, shall have the force of law in Singapore. (2) In the Model Law — "State" means Singapore and any country other than Singapore; "this State" means Singapore. Same as Article 9 of UNCITRAL Model Law 2006
62.	Slovakia - [Slovak] Act No. 244/2002 of 3 April 2002 on Arbitration[62]	Section 2 Arbitral Proceedings and Court Proceedings (1) If a dispute under Section 1(1) is already being dealt with in court proceedings, the parties to such proceedings may agree, in or out of court, to have the dispute resolved in arbitration. Such agreement must contain an arbitration agreement under Section 3. Such agreement, once delivered to the court, shall constitute both a withdrawal of the application and the consent of the respondent with the withdrawal for the purposes of special regulations. (2) It is not incompatible with the arbitral proceedings if, before commencement of arbitral proceedings, or after the commencement but before the appointment of an arbitrator (arbitrators), a party requests from a court an interim measure and for a court to grant such a measure. It is further not incompatible with the arbitral proceedings if a party requests from a court an interim measure against a third party which is not a party to the arbitration agreement. (3) The provisions of Subsection (2) and Section 27 shall be applied also in cases where the place of arbitration has not yet been determined or is outside the territory of the Slovak Republic.
63.	Slovenia - Law on Arbitration of Slovenia[63]	Article 12 Arbitration Agreement and Interim Measures by Court It is not incompatible with an arbitration agreement for a court to grant, at the request of a party, before or during arbitral proceedings an interim measure of protection relating to the subject matter of the arbitration. This applies also in the case of arbitral proceedings abroad.

61. https://sso.agc.gov.sg/act/iaa1994
62. https://www.international-arbitration-attorney.com/wp-content/uploads/2013/07/Slovakia-Arbitration-Law-1.pdf
63. http://www.sloarbitration.eu/Portals/0/Arbitrazno-pravo/Law%20on%20Arbitration%20of%20Slovenia.pdf

Sr. No.	Country	Provision
64.	South Africa - The Arbitration Act, 1965[64]	Section 21 (1) For the purposes of and in relation to a reference under an arbitration agreement, the court shall have the same power of making orders in respect of- (a) security for costs; (b) discovery of documents and interrogatories; (c) the examination of any witness before a commissioner in the Republic or in the territory or abroad and the issue of a commission or a request for such examination; (d) the giving of evidence by affidavit; (e) the inspection or the interim custody or the preservation or the sale of goods or property; (f) an interim interdict or similar relief; (g) securing the amount in dispute in the reference; (h) substituted service of notices required by this Act or of summonses; and (i) the appointment of a receiver, as it has for the purposes of and in relation to any action or matter in that court. (2) The provisions of sub-section (1) shall not be construed so as to derogate from any power which may be vested in an arbitration tribunal of making orders with reference to any of the matters referred to in the said sub-section. (3) Notwithstanding anything to the contrary in the arbitration agreement, the court may at any time, on the application of any party to the reference, order that the umpire shall enter upon the reference in lieu of the arbitrators in all respects as if he were a sole arbitrator.
65.	South Australia - South Australia Commercial Arbitration Act 2011[65]	Same as Article 9 of UNCITRAL Model Law 2006 Section 9
66.	Spain - Act 60/2003 of 23 December on Arbitration[66]	Article 11 Arbitration agreement and substantive claim before court 3. The arbitration agreement will not prevent a party, prior to or during the arbitral proceedings, from applying to a court for interim measures, or the court from granting such measures.
67.	Sri Lanka - Arbitration Act. No. 11 of 1995[67]	No equivalent provision as Article 9 of the UNCITRAL Model Law 2006

64. https://www.gov.za/sites/default/files/gcis_document/201505/act-42-1965.pdf
65. https://www.legislation.sa.gov.au/LZ/C/A/COMMERCIAL%20ARBITRATION%20ACT%202011/CURRENT/2011.32.UN.PDF
66. https://www.mjusticia.gob.es/cs/Satellite/Portal/1292426982249?blobheader=application%2Fpdf&blobheadername1=Content-Disposition&blobheadervalue1=attachment%3B+filename%3DAct_on_arbitration_%28Ley_60_2003__de_arbitraje%29.PDF
67. http://www.slnarbcentre.com/pdf/ARBITRATION-ACT.pdf

Sr. No.	Country	Provision
68.	Sweden - The Swedish Arbitration Act (SFS 1999:116)[68]	Section 4 A court may not, over an objection of a party, rule on an issue which, pursuant to an arbitration agreement, shall be decided by arbitrators. A party must invoke an arbitration agreement on the first occasion that a party pleads his case on the merits in the court. The invocation of an arbitration agreement raised on a later occasion shall have no effect unless the party had a legal excuse and invoked such as soon as the excuse ceased to exist. The invocation of an arbitration agreement shall be considered notwithstanding that the party who invoked the agreement has allowed an issue which is covered by the arbitration agreement to be determined by the Debt Enforcement Authority in a case concerning expedited collection procedures. During the pendency of a dispute before arbitrators or prior thereto, a court may, irrespective of the arbitration agreement, issue such decisions in respect of security measures as the court has jurisdiction to issue.
69.	Switzerland - Private International Law Act 1987, Chapter 12: International Arbitration[69]	No equivalent provision as Article 9 of the UNCITRAL Model Law 2006.
70.	Tasmania - Commercial Arbitration Act, 2011, Act 13 of 2011[70]	Same as Article 9 of UNCITRAL Model Law 2006 Section 9
71.	Texas – Chapter 172. Arbitration and Conciliation of International Commercial Disputes, Civil Practice and Remedies Code[71]	Sec. 172.175. INTERIM ORDERS. (a) A party to an arbitration agreement may request an interim measure of protection from a district court before or during an arbitration. (b) A party to an arbitration may request from the court enforcement of an order of an arbitration tribunal granting an interim measure of protection under Section 172.083. The court shall grant enforcement as provided by the law applicable to the type of interim relief requested.

68. https://sccinstitute.com/media/37089/the-swedish-arbitration-act.pdf
69. https://www.swissarbitration.org/wp-content/uploads/2021/05/20210129-Chapter-12-PILA_Translation_English.pdf
70. https://www.legislation.tas.gov.au/view/html/inforce/current/act-2011-013
71. https://statutes.capitol.texas.gov/Docs/CP/htm/CP.172.htm

Sr. No.	Country	Provision
		(c) In connection with a pending arbitration, the court may take appropriate action, including: (1) ordering an attachment issued to assure that the award to which the applicant may be entitled is not rendered ineffectual by the dissipation of party assets; or (2) granting a preliminary injunction to protect a trade secret or to conserve goods that are the subject matter of the dispute. (d) In considering a request for interim relief, the court shall give preclusive effect to a finding of fact of the arbitration tribunal in the arbitration, including a finding of fact relating to the probable validity of the claim that is the subject of the order for interim relief that the tribunal has granted, if the interim order is consistent with public policy. (e) If the arbitration tribunal has not ruled on an objection to its jurisdiction, the court may not grant preclusive effect to the tribunal's finding until the court makes an independent finding as to the jurisdiction of the tribunal. If the court rules that the tribunal did not have jurisdiction under applicable law, the court shall deny the application for interim measures of relief.
72.	Thailand - Arbitration Act B.E. 2545[72]	Section 16 A party to an arbitration agreement may file a motion requesting the competent court to issue an order imposing provisional measures to protect his interest before or during the arbitral proceedings. If the court views that had such proceedings been conducted in court, the court would have been able to issue such order, the court may proceed as requested. The provisions governing provisional measures under the Civil Procedure Code shall apply mutatis mutandis. Where the court issues an order at the party's request pursuant to paragraph one, if the party filing the motion fails to carry out the arbitral proceedings within thirty days from the date of the court's order or within the period prescribed by the court, that order shall be deemed cancelled upon the expiration of such period of time.
73.	Tunisia - Law n° 93-42 issued on April 26, related to the promulgation of the Arbitration Code[73]	Article 54 It shall not be incompatible with an arbitration agreement that a party requests from a court, prior to or during arbitral proceedings, a conservatory measure of protection. The court can grant such a measure.

72. https://tai.coj.go.th/th/file/get/file/20190328ecac5333356ffad0331bd601151db9f4142557.pdf
73. https://arbitrationlaw.com/sites/default/files/free_pdfs/Tunisia%20Arbitration%20Code.pdf

Sr. No.	Country	Provision
74.	Turkey - Turkish International Arbitration Law, Law no. 4686, 2001[74]	Article 6 Interim measures of protection and interim attachments It is not incompatible with an arbitration agreement for a party to request, before or during arbitral proceedings, from a court an interim measure of protection or an interim attachment and for a court to grant such measure or attachment. Unless otherwise agreed by the parties, the arbitral tribunal may, at the request of a party, order an interim measure of protection or an interim attachment during arbitral proceedings. The arbitral tribunal may require any party to provide appropriate security in connection with such measure or attachment. The arbitral tribunal shall not grant interim measures or interim attachments [a] that are required to be enforced through execution offices or to be executed through other official authorities or [b] that bind third parties. If a party does not comply with the interim measure or attachment, the other party may request the assistance of the competent court for taking an interim measure of protection or an interim attachment. The competent court, if necessary, may hear [the case in question] through a substitute court. The parties' right to make a request [for interim measures of protection or interim attachments to a court] in accordance with the Code of Civil Procedure and the Code of Execution is reserved. Any decision of a court, with respect to interim measures of protection or interim attachments, that is given upon a request of a party prior to commencement of arbitration or during arbitral proceedings, shall automatically cease to have effect where the decision of the arbitral tribunal becomes enforceable or where the arbitral tribunal denies [to hear] the case in its decision.
75.	Uganda - Chapter 4 The Arbitration and Conciliation Act[75]	Article 6 Interim measures by court (1) A party to an arbitration agreement may apply to the court, before or during arbitral proceedings, for an interim measure of protection, and the court may grant that measure. (2) Where a party applies to the court for an injunction or other interim order and the arbitral tribunal has already ruled on any matter relevant to the application, the court shall treat the ruling or any finding of fact made in the course of the ruling as conclusive for the purposes of the application.
76.	Ukraine - The Law of Ukraine on International Commercial Arbitration[76]	Same as Article 9 of UNCITRAL Model Law 2006 Article 9

74. http://www.camera-arbitrale.it/Documenti/tial_turkey.pdf
75. https://ulii.org/akn/ug/act/2000/7/eng@2008-06-27
76. http://arbitrations.ru/userfiles/file/Law/Arbitration%20acts/ukraininan%20law%20on%20arbitration.pdf

Sr. No.	Country	Provision
77.	United Arab Emirates - Federal Law No. (6) of 2018 on Arbitration[77]	Article (18) General Jurisdiction to Consider Arbitral Measures 1. The Competent Court shall have jurisdiction to consider arbitration issues referred hereunder in accordance with the procedural laws of the State. The Competent Court shall exercise exclusive jurisdiction until the conclusion of all arbitral proceedings. 2. The chief justice of the Court may, at the request of a party, or at the request of the Arbitral Tribunal, order such interim or conservatory measures as he may consider necessary to be taken in respect of existing or potential arbitral proceedings, whether before the commencement or the arbitral proceedings or during their course. 3. Taking the measures referred to in the preceding section of this article shall not stay the arbitral proceedings and shall not amount to a waiver of the Arbitration Agreement. 4. If the chief justice of the Court issues an order under section 2 of this article, the order shall only cease to have effect in whole or in part by a decision issued by the chief justice of the Court.
78.	Uruguay - Law 19,636 Approve Rules for International Commercial Arbitration[78]	Article 9 (Arbitration agreement and adoption of provisional measures by the court) .- It shall not be inconsistent with an arbitration agreement that a party, either prior to or during the arbitration proceedings, requests a provisional injunction from a court or that the court grant such measures.
79.	Venezuela - Venezuelan Commercial Arbitration Act[79]	No equivalent provision as Article 9 of the UNCITRAL Model Law 2006
80.	Victoria - Commercial Arbitration Act 2011 No. 50 of 2011[80]	Same as Article 9 of UNCITRAL Model Law 2006 Section 9
81.	Western Australia - Commercial Arbitration Act 2012, 023 of 2012[81]	Same as Article 9 of UNCITRAL Model Law 2006 Section 9

77. https://www.tamimi.com/crm-media-uploader/fileupload/server/php/files/UAE%20Arbitration%20Law%20-%20Federal%20Law%20No%20%206%20of%202018.pdf
78. http://www.impo.com.uy/bases/leyes-originales/19636-2018
79. https://arbitrationlaw.com/sites/default/files/free_pdfs/Venezula%20Commercial%20Arbitration%20Act.pdf
80. http://arbitration.site/wp-content/uploads/2019/06/CAA-Vic-.pdf
81. https://www.legislation.wa.gov.au/legislation/prod/filestore.nsf/FileURL/mrdoc_25084.pdf/$FILE/Commercial%20Arbitration%20Act%202012%20-%20%5B00-b0-06%5D.pdf?OpenElement

Sr. No.	Country	Provision
82.	Zambia - The Arbitration Act, 2000 No. 19 of 2000[82]	Section 11 Arbitration agreement and interim measures by court (1) A party may, before or during arbitral proceedings, request from a court an interim measure of protection and, subject to subsections (2), (3) and (4), the court may grant such measure. (2) Upon a request in terms of subsection (1), the court may grant: (a) an order for the preservation, interim custody, sale or inspection of any goods which are the subject matter of the dispute; (b) an order securing the amount in dispute or the costs and expenses of the arbitral proceedings; (c) an interim injunction or other interim order; or (d) any other order to ensure that an award which may be made in the arbitral proceedings is not rendered ineffectual. (3) Where the court intends to grant an order or an injunction requested under subsection (2), and an arbitral tribunal has already ruled or made a finding of fact on a matter relevant to the request, the court shall treat the ruling or finding made in the course of the arbitral proceedings as conclusive for the purpose of the request. (4) The court shall not grant an order or injunction under this section unless— (a) the arbitral tribunal has not yet been appointed and the matter is urgent; (b) the arbitral tribunal is not competent to grant the order or injunction; or (c) the urgency of the matter makes it impracticable to seek such order or injunction from the arbitral tribunal; and the court shall not grant any order or injunction where the arbitral tribunal, being competent to grant the order or injunction, has already determined an application therefor.
83.	Zimbabwe - Chapter 7:15 Arbitration Act[83]	SCHEDULE (Section 2) Article 9 Arbitration agreement and interim measures by court (1) It is not incompatible with an arbitration agreement for a party to request, before or during arbitral proceedings, from the High Court an interim measure of protection and, subject to paragraphs (2) and (3) of this article, for the High Court to grant such measure. (2) Upon a request in terms of paragraph (1) of this article, the High Court may grant— (a) an order for the preservation, interim custody or sale of any goods which are the subject-matter of the dispute; or (b) an order securing the amount in dispute or the costs of the arbitral proceedings; or (c) an interdict or other interim order; or (d) any other order to ensure that any award which may be made in the arbitral proceedings is not rendered ineffectual.

82. http://www.newyorkconvention.org/11165/web/files/document/2/1/21396.pdf
83. https://zimlii.org/akn/zw/act/1996/6/eng@2016-12-31

Sr. No.	Country	Provision
		(3) The High Court shall not grant an order or interdict in terms of paragraph (1) of this article unless— (a) the arbitral tribunal has not yet been appointed and the matter is urgent; or (b) the arbitral tribunal is not competent to grant the order or interdict; or (c) the urgency of the matter makes it impracticable to seek such order or interdict from the arbitral tribunal; and the High Court shall not grant any such order or interdict where the arbitral tribunal, being competent to grant the order or interdict, has determined an application therefor. (4) The decision of the High Court upon any request made in terms of paragraph (1) of this article shall not be subject to appeal.

Appendix B (Article 17)

Sr. No.	Country	Provision
1.	Australia - International Arbitration Act 1974[84]	Same as UNCITRAL Model Law 2006 Sec 16 Model Law to have force of law (1) Subject to this Part, the Model Law has the force of law in Australia. (2) In the Model Law: Arbitration agreement has the meaning given in Option 1 of Article 7 of the Model Law. State means Australia (including the external Territories) and any foreign country. This State means Australia (including the external Territories). Model Law under Part V, Schedule 2 of the Arbitration Act, 1974
2.	Australian Capital Territory – Commercial Arbitration Act, 2017 A2017-7[85]	Section 17 Power of arbitral tribunal to order interim measures (Model Law art 17) (1) Unless otherwise agreed by the parties, the arbitral tribunal may, at the request of a party, grant interim measures. (2) An interim measure is any temporary measure, whether in the form of an award or in another form, by which, at any time prior to the issuance of the award by which the dispute is finally decided, the arbitral tribunal orders a party to— (a) maintain or restore the status quo pending determination of the dispute; or (b) take action that would prevent, or refrain from taking action that is likely to cause, current or imminent harm or prejudice to the arbitral process itself; or (c) provide a means of preserving assets out of which a subsequent award may be satisfied; or

84. https://www.legislation.gov.au/Details/C2011C00342
85. http://classic.austlii.edu.au/au/legis/act/consol_act/caa2017219/s17.html

Sr. No.	Country	Provision
		(d) preserve evidence that may be relevant and material to the resolution of the dispute. (3) Without limiting subsection (2), the arbitral tribunal may make orders with respect to any of the following: (a) security for costs; (b) discovery of documents and interrogatories; (c) giving of evidence by affidavit; (d) the inspection of any property which is or forms part of the subject-matter of the dispute; (e) the taking of photographs of any property which is or forms part of the subject-matter of the dispute; (f) samples to be taken from, or any observation to be made of or experiment conducted on, any property which is or forms part of the subject-matter of the dispute; (g) dividing, recording and strictly enforcing the time allocated for a hearing between the parties (a stop clock arbitration). Note Subsections (1) and (2) are substantially the same as the Model Law, art 17. There is no equivalent s (3) in the Model Law.
3.	Austria - Austrian Arbitration Act, 2013[86]	Section 593 - Ordering of Interim or Protective Measures (1) Unless otherwise agreed by the parties, the arbitral tribunal may, upon request of a party and after hearing the other party, order against the other party such interim or protective measures it deems necessary in respect of the subject-matter in dispute if the enforcement of the claim were otherwise frustrated or significantly impeded, or there were a risk of irreparable harm. The arbitral tribunal may request any party to provide appropriate security inconnection with such measure. (2) Measures referred to in paragraph (1) shall be in writing; a signed exemplar of the order shall be served upon each party. In arbitral proceedings with more than one arbitrator the signature of the chairman or, if he is prevented from signing, the signature of another arbitrator shall suffice, provided that the chairman or another arbitrator records on the order the reason for any omitted signature. Section 606 paragraphs (2), (3), (5) and (6) shall apply accordingly.
4.	Bahrain - Bahrain Arbitration Law No. 9/2015[87]	Same as UNCITRAL Model Law 2006 Article 1 Taking into account the provisions of international conventions in force in the Kingdom of Bahrain 1. The provisions of the "UNCITRAL" Model Law on International Commercial Arbitration Act attached to this law shall apply to all arbitration whatever the nature of the legal relationship of the dispute herewith, if this arbitration takes place in the Kingdom of Bahrain or abroad and that two parties agreed to comply with the provisions of the attached law.

86. https://www.viac.eu/images/law/ZPO_Schiedsrecht_2014_en_im_VIAC_Layout.pdf
87. https://pernetmartial.eu/sites/default/files/lois/Bahrain-Loi-d-arbitrage-arbitration-act-ley-de-arbitraje.pdf

Sr. No.	Country	Provision
		2. The provisions of the attached law shall apply to all arbitration which begins after its entry into force even if based on an arbitrationagreement concluded before the entry into force of this law.
5.	Bangladesh - The Arbitration Act, 2001[88]	Section 21 - Powers of the arbitration tribunal to make interim orders.- (1) Unless otherwise agreed by the parties, the arbitral tribunal may, at the request of a party, order a party to take any interim measure of protection as the arbitral tribunal may consider necessary in respect of the subject matter of the dispute, and no appeal shall lie against this order.
6.	Belgium - Belgian Judicial Code Provisions[89]	Art. 1691 Without prejudice to the powers accorded to the courts and tribunals by virtue of article 1683, and unless otherwise agreed by the parties, the arbitral tribunal may order any interim or conservatory measures it deems necessary. However, the arbitral tribunal may not authorise attachment orders.
7.	Bhutan - Alternative Dispute Resolution Act of Bhutan 2013[90]	Section 114 Arbitral tribunal to order interim measures At any time before the settlement of dispute or final arbitral award is rendered, the arbitral tribunal may grant an interim measure that may order a party to: (1) Maintain or restore the status quo pending determination of the dispute; (2) Take action that would prevent, or refrain from taking action that is likely to cause, current or imminent harm or prejudice to the arbitral process itself; (3) Provide a means of preserving assets out of which a subsequent award may be satisfied; or (4) Preserve evidence that may be relevant and material to the resolution of the dispute.
8.	British Columbia - International Commercial Arbitration Act [RSBC 1996] Chapter 233[91]	Section 17 Power of arbitral tribunal to order interim measures (1) Unless otherwise agreed by the parties and subject to section 17.01, the arbitral tribunal may, at the request of a party, grant an interim measure. (2) In this Act, "interim measure" means any temporary measure, whether in the form of an arbitral award or in another form, by which, at any time before the issuance of the arbitral award by which the dispute is finally decided, the arbitral tribunal orders a party to (a) maintain or restore the status quo pending determination of the dispute, (b) take action that would prevent, or refrain from taking action that is likely to cause, current or imminent harm or prejudice to the arbitral process itself,

88. http://www.mccibd.org/images/uploadimg/act_and_policy/corporate_governance/The-Arbitration-Act-2001.pdf
89. http://www.arbiter.com.sg/pdf/laws/Belgian%20Judicial%20Code%20Provisions%20(2013).pdf
90. https://www.nationalcouncil.bt/assets/uploads/docs/acts/2014/Alternative_Dispute_Resolution_Act_of_Bhutan_2013_eng10th.pdf

Sr. No.	Country	Provision
		(c) provide a means of preserving assets out of which a subsequent arbitral award may be satisfied, (d) preserve evidence that may be relevant and material to the resolution of the dispute, or (e) provide appropriate security for costs in connection with arbitral proceedings.
9.	British Virgin Islands - Virgin Islands Arbitration Act, 2013[92]	UNCITRAL Model Law to have effect in the Virgin Islands. Section 4. The provisions of the UNCITRAL Model Law have the force of law in the Virgin Islands, subject to the modifications and supplements expressly provided in this Act. Section 33. Application of article 17 of the UNCITRAL Model Law (1) Article 17 of the UNCITRAL Model Law, the text of which is reproduced below, has effect: "Article 17. Power of arbitral tribunal to order interim measures (1) Unless otherwise agreed by the parties, the arbitral tribunal may, at the request of a party, grant interim measures. (2) An interim measure is any temporary measure, whether in the form of an award or in another form, by which, at any time prior to the issuance of the award by which the dispute is finally decided, the arbitral tribunal orders a party to: (a) Maintain or restore the status quo pending determination of the dispute; (b) Take action that would prevent, or refrain from taking action that is likely to cause, current or imminent harm or prejudice to the arbitral process itself; (c) Provide a means of preserving assets out of which a subsequent award may be satisfied; or (d) Preserve evidence that may be relevant and material to the resolution of the dispute.". (2) An interim measure referred to in article 17 of the UNCITRAL Model Law, as provided in subsection (1), is to be construed as including an injunction but not including an order under section 54. (3) Where an arbitral tribunal has granted an interim measure, the tribunal may, on the application of any party, make an award to the same effect as the interim measure.
10.	Bulgaria - Law on International Commercial Arbitration State Gazette (SG) No. 60 of 05.08.1988[93]	Art. 21. Unless otherwise agreed on by the parties, the Arbitral Tribunal may on a request of one of them order the other party to tale appropriate measure for securing the rights of the petitioner. If such measures are admitted the Arbitral Tribunal may determine a guaranty which the petitioner shall produce.

91. http://www.bclaws.ca/civix/document/id/complete/statreg/96233_01
92. http://www.bviiac.org/Portals/0/Files/Arbitration%20Documents/ArbitrationAct2013.pdf
93. http://www.newyorkconvention.org/11165/web/files/document/1/6/16200.pdf

Sr. No.	Country	Provision
11.	Cambodia - The Commercial Arbitration Law of the Kingdom of Cambodia 2006[94]	Article 25: Power of Arbitral Panel to Order Interim Measures Unless otherwise agreed by the parties, the arbitral panel may, at the request of a party, order any party to take such interim measure of protection as the arbitral panel may consider necessary in respect of the subject matter of the dispute.
12.	Canada - Commercial Arbitration Act R.S.C., 1985, c. 17 (2nd Supp.)[95]	Schedule 1- Commercial Arbitration Code Adopted UNCITRAL Model Law 1985 Article 17 - Power of Arbitral Tribunal to Order Interim Measures Unless otherwise agreed by the parties, the arbitral tribunal may, at the request of a party, order any party to take such interim measure of protection as the arbitral tribunal may consider necessary in respect of the subject-matter of the dispute.
13.	Connecticut - Chapter 909 Arbitration Proceedings[96]	Sec. 52-407hh. Provisional remedies. (b) After an arbitrator is appointed and is authorized and able to act: (1) The arbitrator may issue such orders for provisional remedies, including interim awards, as the arbitrator finds necessary to protect the effectiveness of the arbitration proceeding and to promote the fair and expeditious resolution of the controversy, to the same extent and under the same conditions as if the controversy were the subject of a civil action; and (2) A party to an arbitration proceeding may move the court for a provisional remedy only if the matter is urgent and the arbitrator is not able to act timely or the arbitrator cannot provide an adequate remedy. (c) A party does not waive a right of arbitration by making a motion under subsection (a) or (b) of this section.
14.	Croatia - Law on Arbitration Official Gazette no. 88/2001[97]	Article 16 Interim measures in arbitral proceedings (1) Unless otherwise agreed by the parties, the arbitral tribunal may, at the request of a party, order any party to take such interim measures of protection as the arbitral tribunal may consider necessary in respect of the subject-matter of the dispute. The arbitral tribunal may require any party to provide appropriate security in connection with such measure. (2) If a party to which interim measures relate does not agree to undertake them voluntarily, the party that made the motion for such measures may request their enforcement before the competent court

94. https://www.cambodiaip.gov.kh/DocResources/372a361b-7a97-44b3-9810-79e5e6ea85f4_c786a043-b88d-4f64-9429-60a330efdc5f-en.pdf
95. https://laws-lois.justice.gc.ca/eng/acts/C-34.6/index.html
96. https://www.cga.ct.gov/current/pub/chap_909.htm
97. http://www.vsrh.hr/CustomPages/Static/HRV/Files/Legislation__Law-Arbitration-RC.pdf

Sr. No.	Country	Provision
15.	Cyprus – The International Commercial Arbitration Law, 1987[98]	Section 17 - Power of arbitral tribunal to order interim measures. Unless otherwise agreed by the parties, the arbitral tribunal may, at the request of a party, order any party to take such interim measure of protection as the arbitral tribunal may consider necessary in respect of the subject matter of the dispute.
16.	Denmark – Danish Arbitration Act 2005[99]	Section 17. The arbitral tribunal may, at the request of a party, order any party to take such interim measure of protection as the arbitral tribunal may consider necessary in respect of the subject-matter of the dispute.
17.	Egypt - Law No. 27/1994 Promulgating the Law Concerning Arbitration in Civil and Commercial Matters[100]	Article 24 1. Both parties to the arbitration may agree to confer upon the arbitral tribunal the power to order, upon request of either party, interim or conservatory measures considered necessary in respect of the subject matter of the dispute and to require any party to provide appropriate security to cover the costs of the ordered measure.
18.	Florida Chapter 684 – International Commercial Arbitration, Title XXXIX Commercial Relations, 2020 Florida Statutes[101]	Same as Article 17 of the UNCITRAL Model Law 2006 Article 684.0018 Power of arbitral tribunal to order interim measures.
19.	Fiji – International Arbitration Act 2017 (Act No. 44 of 2017)[102]	Section 23 – Power of arbitral tribunal to order interim measures (1) Unless otherwise agreed by the parties, the arbitral tribunal may, at the request of a party, grant interim measures. (2) An interim measure is any temporary measure, whether in the form of an award or in another form, by which, at any time prior to the issuance of the award by which the dispute is finally decided, the arbitral tribunal orders a party to- (a) maintain or restore the status quo pending determination of the dispute; (b) take action that would prevent, or refrain from taking action that is likely to cause, current or imminent harm or prejudice to the arbitral process itself; (c) provide a means of preserving assets out of which a subsequent award may be satisfied; or

98. https://www.uv.es/medarb/observatorio/leyes-arbitraje/europa-resto/chipre-international-commercial-arbitration-law.pdf
99. https://voldgiftsinstituttet.dk/wp-content/uploads/2015/01/danish_arbitration_act_2005.pdf
100. https://www.wipo.int/edocs/lexdocs/laws/en/eg/eg020en.pdf
101. https://www.flsenate.gov/Laws/Statutes/2020/Chapter684/All
102. https://www.fiji.gov.fj/getattachment/d9502667-6491-4592-85b2-eff97f245fed/Act-44---International-Arbitration-Act.aspx

Sr. No.	Country	Provision
		(d) preserve evidence that may be relevant and material to the resolution of the dispute. (3) If an arbitral tribunal has granted an interim measure, the arbitral tribunal may, on the application of any party, make an award to the same effect as the interim measure.
20.	France - Book IV - Arbitration of the Code of Civil procedure Decree no. 2011-48[103]	Article 1468 The arbitral tribunal may order upon the parties any conservatory or provisional measures that it deems appropriate, set conditions for such measures and, if necessary, attach penalties to such order. However, only courts may order conservatory attachments and judicial security.
21.	Georgia - Chapter 9 Arbitration, Title 9 Civil Procedure, Georgia Code[104]	Article 17 - Use of interim measures 1. Unless otherwise provided for by the arbitration agreement, any party, before commencement of arbitration proceedings or at any time during such proceedings but before an arbitration award is made, may request the arbitral tribunal to grant interim measures. 2. Based on an allegation made by a party within a reasonable time, the arbitral tribunal is authorised, by a written award, to order a party to: a) maintain or restore the status quo before rendering the final award; b) take measures that would prevent causing damage to the other party or to the arbitral proceeding; c) provide a means of preserving assets out of which a subsequent award may be satisfied; d) preserve and maintain evidence that may be relevant to the dispute and its resolution.
22.	Germany - Tenth Book of the Code of Civil Procedure, Arbitration Procedure[105]	Section 1041 Interim measures of protection (1) Unless otherwise agreed by the parties, the arbitral tribunal may, at the request of a party, order such interim measures of protection as the arbitral tribunal may consider necessary in respect of the subject-matter of the dispute.
23.	Greece - Code of Civil Procedure, Book VII, Book VIII[106]	No equivalent provision as Article 17 of the UNCITRAL Model Law 2006
24.	Hong Kong - Cap. 609 Arbitration Ordinance[107]	Section 35 - Article 17 of UNCITRAL Model Law (Power of arbitral tribunal to order interim measures) (1) Article 17 of the UNCITRAL Model Law, the text of which is set out below, has effect—

103. http://www.iaiparis.com/pdf/FRENCH_LAW_ON_INTERNATIONAL_ARBITRATION.pdf
104. https://matsne.gov.ge/ru/document/download/89284/5/en/pdf
105. https://sccinstitute.com/media/29988/german-arbitration-act.pdf
106. https://www.uv.es/medarb/observatorio/leyes-arbitraje/europa-resto/grecia-ccp-domestic-arbitration.pdf
107. https://www.elegislation.gov.hk/hk/cap609

Sr. No.	Country	Provision
		"Article 17. Power of arbitral tribunal to order interim measures (1) Unless otherwise agreed by the parties, the arbitral tribunal may, at the request of a party, grant interim measures. (2) An interim measure is any temporary measure, whether in the form of an award or in another form, by which, at any time prior to the issuance of the award by which the dispute is finally decided, the arbitral tribunal orders a party to- (a) maintain or restore the status quo pending determination of the dispute; (b) take action that would prevent, or refrain from taking action that is likely to cause, current or imminent harm or prejudice to the arbitral process itself; (c) provide a means of preserving assets out of which a subsequent award may be satisfied; or (d) preserve evidence that may be relevant and material to the resolution of the dispute. (2) An interim measure referred to in article 17 of the UNCITRAL Model Law, given effect to by subsection (1), is to be construed as including an injunction but not including an order under section 56. (3) If an arbitral tribunal has granted an interim measure, the tribunal may, on the application of any party, make an award to the same effect as the interim measure.
25.	Hungary - Act LX of 2017 on Arbitration[108]	Same as Article 17 of the UNCITRAL Model Law 2006 Section 18 of the Act LX of 2017 on Arbitration
26.	Ireland - Arbitration Act 2010 Number 1 of 2010[109]	Section 6 - Adoption of Model Law Subject to this Act, the Model Law shall have the force of law in the State and shall apply to arbitrations under arbitration agreements concerning— (a) international commercial arbitrations, or (b) arbitrations which are not international commercial arbitrations. Same as Article 17 of the UNCITRAL Model Law 2006 Article 17 under Schedule 1 - TEXT OF UNCITRAL MODEL LAW ON INTERNATIONAL COMMERCIAL ARBITRATION
27.	Italy - Code of Civil Procedure, Book IV, Title VIII Arbitration[110]	Article 1, paragraph 15 of the Delegation Act The power to issue interim measures in the event of express will of the parties, manifested in the arbitration agreement or in a subsequent written act, unless otherwise provided by the law.

108. https://www.ilo.org/dyn/natlex/docs/ELECTRONIC/106843/131257/F-266585574/J2017T0060P_20180102_FIN.pdf
109. http://www.irishstatutebook.ie/eli/2010/act/1/enacted/en/pdf
110. https://www.gazzettaufficiale.it/atto/serie_generale/caricaDettaglioAtto/originario?atto.dataP ubblicazioneGazzetta=2021-12-09&atto.codiceRedazionale=21G00229&elenco30giorni=false

Sr. No.	Country	Provision
28.	Jamaica - The Arbitration Act, 2017 (Act 13 of 2017)[111]	Same as Article 17 of the UNCITRAL Model Law 2006 Section 20 - Interim Measures and Preliminary Orders of the Arbitration Act, 2017
29.	Japan - Arbitration Law (Law No. 138 of 2003)[112]	Article 24. (Interim Measures of Protection) (1) Unless otherwise agreed by the parties, the arbitral tribunal may, at the request of a party, order any party to take such interim measure of protection as the arbitral tribunal may consider necessary in respect of the subject matter of the dispute.
30.	Jordan - Law No. 31 of 2001 (Jordan) Arbitration Law[113]	Article 23: a. Subject to article (13) of this law, the two arbitrating parties may agree that the arbitral tribunal is empowered to order either of them, whether by its own initiative or upon request of either party, to take whatever interim or conservative measures it find necessary in respect of the subject-matter of the dispute, and it may require (either party)(1) to provide sufficient security to cover the expenses of such measures. b. If the party to whom the order has been addressed fails to execute it, the arbitral tribunal may, upon request of the other party, authorize the latter to take the procedures necessary for such execution including the right to apply 10 to the competent court for issuing an order of enforcement.
31.	Kenya - Chapter 49 Arbitration Act (The Arbitration Act, 1995)[114]	Section 18 - Power of arbitral tribunal (1) Unless the parties otherwise agree, an arbitral tribunal may, on the application of a party (a) order any party to take such interim measure of protection as the arbitral tribunal may consider necessary in respect of the subject matter of the dispute, with or without an ancillary order requiring the provision of appropriate security in connection with such a measure; or (b) order any party to provide security in respect of any claim or any amount in dispute; or (c) order a claimant to provide security for costs.
32.	Liechtenstein - Liechtenstein Arbitration Law (Code of Civil procedure)[115]	Section 610 Power to Order Interim or Protective Measures 1) Unless otherwise agreed by the parties, the arbitral tribunal may, at the request of a party, order any party, after hearing such party, to take such interim or protective measures as the arbitral tribunal may consider necessary in respect of the subject matter of the dispute, as otherwise the enforcement of the claim would be frustrated or considerably impeded or there is a danger of irreparable harm. The arbitral tribunal may require any party to provide appropriate security in connection with such measures.

111. http://extwprlegs1.fao.org/docs/pdf/jam172060.pdf
112. https://japan.kantei.go.jp/policy/sihou/arbitrationlaw.pdf
113. https://www.ilo.org/dyn/natlex/docs/ELECTRONIC/63091/95325/F1864661120/JOR63091.pdf
114. https://ncia.or.ke/wp-content/uploads/2021/02/ArbitrationAct4of1995_2.pdf

Sr. No.	Country	Provision
33.	Lithuania - The Republic of Lithuania Law on Commercial Arbitration, 2012[116]	Article 20. Interim Measures 1. Unless otherwise agreed by the parties, an arbitral tribunal may, at the request of any party and with a notice to other parties, order to take interim measures of protection aimed at securing settlement of the party's claims and preservation of evidence. 2. Interim measures may include the following: 1) prohibition of engagement by the party in certain transactions or taking of certain actions; 2) obligation of the party to keep safe assets related to arbitral proceedings, provide a monetary deposit or a bank or insurance guarantee; 3) obligation of the party to preserve evidence that may be significant in arbitral proceedings.
34.	Louisiana - RS 9 Title 9. Civil Code - Ancillaries[117]	§4257. Power of arbitral tribunal to order interim measures Unless otherwise agreed by the parties, the arbitral tribunal may, at the request of a party, order any party to take interim measures of protection as the arbitral tribunal may consider necessary in respect of the subject matter of the dispute. The arbitral tribunal may require any party to provide appropriate security in connection with the measure.
35.	Macedonia - Law on International Commercial Arbitration of the Republic of Macedonia[118]	Article 17 Power of arbitral tribunal to order interim measures Unless otherwise agreed by the parties, the arbitral tribunal may, at the request of a party, order any party to take such interim measure of protection as the arbitral tribunal may consider necessary in respect of the subject-matter of the dispute.
36.	Malaysia - Arbitration Act 2005, Act 646[119]	Section 19 Power of arbitral tribunal to order interim measures (1) Unless otherwise agreed by the parties, a party may apply to the arbitral tribunal for any of the following orders: (a) security for costs; (b) discovery of documents and interrogatories; (c) giving of evidence by affidavit; (d) the preservation, interim custody or sale of any property which is the subject-matter of the dispute. (2) The arbitral tribunal may require any party to provide appropriate security in connection with such measure as ordered under subsection (1). (3) Unless otherwise agreed by the parties, sections 38 and 39 shall apply to orders made by an arbitral tribunal under this section as if a reference in those sections to an award were a reference to such an order.

115. https://www.newyorkconvention.org/11165/web/files/document/2/1/21372.pdf
116. https://e-seimas.lrs.lt/portal/legalAct/lt/TAD/35954312dcb311e6be918a531b2126ab?jfwid=-wd7z7zum0
117. http://legis.la.gov/legis/Law.aspx?d=408482
118. https://www.international-arbitration-attorney.com/wp-content/uploads/2013/07/Macedonia-Arbitration-Law.pdf
119. http://www.newyorkconvention.org/11165/web/files/document/1/6/16298.pdf

Sr. No.	Country	Provision
37.	Maldives - Act No: 10/2013, Arbitration Act[120]	Section 33 - Power of Arbitral Tribunal to Order Interim Measures (a) Unless otherwise agreed by the parties to a dispute submitted for arbitration, the arbitral tribunal may, at the request of a party, grant interim measures. (b) An interim measure mentioned in (a) above is any temporary measure by which, at any time prior to the issuance of the award by which the dispute is finally decided, the arbitral tribunal orders a party to: Maintain or restore the status quo pending determination of the dispute; OR Take action that would prevent any event that is likely to cause harm or prejudice to the arbitral process itself; OR Provide a means of preserving assets out of which a subsequent award may be satisfied; OR Preserve evidence that may be relevant and material to the resolution of the dispute. (c) Unless otherwise provided in this Act, the Arbitral Tribunal shall issue a order for an interim measure mentioned in (a) only after notifying the parties to the dispute and providing such parties with the opportunity to respond to the matter if they so wish.
38.	Malta - CAP. 387 Arbitration Act[121]	Section 38(6) Interim Measures and Precautional Acts (1) Unless otherwise agreed by the parties, the arbitral tribunal may, at the request of a party, order any party to take such interim measures of protection as the tribunal may consider necessary in respect of the subject matter in dispute. The arbitral tribunal may require any party to provide adequate security in connection with such measures.
39.	Mauritius - The International Arbitration Act, 2008 (Act 37 of 2008)[122]	Section 17. Interim measures by Tribunal (1) Unless otherwise agreed by the parties, the arbitral tribunal may, at the request of a party, grant interim measures, in the form of an award or in another form, by which, at any time before making the award by which the dispute is finally decided, the arbitral tribunal orders a party to - (a) maintain or restore the status quo pending determination of the dispute; (b) take action that would prevent, or refrain from taking action that is likely to cause current or imminent harm or prejudice to the arbitral process itself; (c) provide a means of preserving assets out of which a subsequent award may be satisfied;

120. https://miac.gov.mv/media/documents/Arbitration%20Act.pdf
121. http://justiceservices.gov.mt/DownloadDocument.aspx?app=lom&itemid=8854&l=1
122. https://www.wipo.int/edocs/lexdocs/laws/en/mu/mu020en.pdf

Sr. No.	Country	Provision
		(d) preserve evidence that may be relevant and material to the resolution of the dispute; or (e) provide security for costs. Third Schedule Part IV – Interim Measures by Tribunal Section 21 (Interim measures by tribunal) Articles 17 to 17G
40.	Montenegro – Decree on the Promulgation of the Law on Arbitration, 2015[123]	Article 21 - Power of arbitral tribunal to order interim measures Unless otherwise agreed by the parties, the arbitral tribunal may, at the request of a party, order an interim measure. An interim measure shall be ordered in the form of an award or in another form. By interim measure, at any time prior to the issuance of a final arbitral award, the arbitral tribunal orders a party to: 1) Maintain or restore the status quo pending determination of the dispute; 2) Take action that would prevent, or refrain from taking action that is likely to cause, current or future harm or prejudice to the arbitral process itself; 3) Preserve assets out of which the obligations imposed in the arbitral award may subsequently be enforced; or 4) Preserve evidence that may be relevant to the resolution of the dispute.
41.	Myanmar – Arbitration Law The Pyidaungsu Hluttaw Law No. 5/2016[124]	Section 19 - Power of arbitral tribunal to order interim orders (a) Unless otherwise agreed by the parties, an arbitral tribunal shall have powers to make decision, order and instructions to any party for: (1) security for costs; (2) discovery of documents and interrogatories; (3) giving of evidence by affidavit; (4) the preservation, interim custody or sale of any property which is part of the subject-matter of the dispute; (5) samples to be taken from, or any observation to be made of or experiment conducted upon, any property which is or forms part of the subject-matter of the dispute; (6) the preservation and interim custody of any evidence for the purposes of the proceedings; (7) securing the amount in dispute; (8) an interim injunction or any other interim measure. (b) An arbitral tribunal may have power to administer oaths to the parties and witnesses. (c) An arbitral tribunal may have the power to adopt inquisitorial procedures as its consider appropriate.

123. https://www.privrednakomora.me/sites/pkcg.org/files/multimedia/main_pages/files/2012/09/final_eng_zakon_o_arbitrazi_final_0.pdf
124. http://www.newyorkconvention.org/11165/web/files/document/2/1/21098.pdf

Sr. No.	Country	Provision
		(d) The power of the arbitral tribunal to order a claimant to provide security for costs as referred to in subsection (a)(1) shall not be exercised solely because the claimant is: (1) an individual ordinarily residing outside the Republic of the Union of Myanmar; (2) a corporation or an association incorporated or formed under the law of the other country. (e) All decisions, orders or instruction made by an arbitral tribunal in the course of an arbitration may apply to the court for the enforcement in accordance with the section 31.
42.	New South Wales - Commercial Arbitration Act 2010 No 61[125]	Section 17 Power of arbitral tribunal to order interim measures (cf Model Law Art 17) (1) Unless otherwise agreed by the parties, the arbitral tribunal may, at the request of a party, grant interim measures. (2) An interim measure is any temporary measure, whether in the form of an award or in another form, by which, at any time prior to the issuance of the award by which the dispute is finally decided, the arbitral tribunal orders a party to: (a) maintain or restore the status quo pending determination of the dispute, or (b) take action that would prevent, or refrain from taking action that is likely to cause, current or imminent harm or prejudice to the arbitral process itself, or (c) provide a means of preserving assets out of which a subsequent award may be satisfied, or (d) preserve evidence that may be relevant and material to the resolution of the dispute. (3) Without limiting subsection (2), the arbitral tribunal may make orders with respect to any of the following: (a) security for costs, (b) discovery of documents and interrogatories, (c) giving of evidence by affidavit, (d) the inspection of any property which is or forms part of the subject-matter of the dispute, (e) the taking of photographs of any property which is or forms part of the subject-matter of the dispute, (f) samples to be taken from, or any observation to be made of or experiment conducted on, any property which is or forms part of the subject-matter of the dispute, (g) dividing, recording and strictly enforcing the time allocated for a hearing between the parties (a stop clock arbitration). Note. Subsections (1) and (2) are substantially the same as Art 17 of the Model Law. There is no equivalent subsection (3) in the Model Law.

125. https://legislation.nsw.gov.au/view/html/inforce/current/act-2010-061#sec.17

Sr. No.	Country	Provision
43.	New Zealand – The Arbitration Act, 1996 no 99[126]	Schedule I - Rules applying to arbitration agreement Article 17A Power of arbitral tribunal to grant interim measure Unless otherwise agreed by the parties, the arbitral tribunal may, at the request of a party, grant an interim measure.
44.	Nigeria - Arbitration and Conciliation Act, Chapter 19 Laws of the Federation of Nigeria 1990[127]	Part I Arbitration Section 13 - Power of arbitral tribunal to order interim measure of protection Unless otherwise agreed by the parties, the arbitral tribunal may before or during an arbitral proceedings- (a) at the request of a party, order any party to take such interim measure of protection as the arbitral tribunal may consider necessary in respect of the subject matter of the dispute; and (b) require any party to provide appropriate security in connection with any measure taken under paragraph (a) of this section. First Schedule, Arbitration Rules Article 26 INTERIM MEASURES OF PROTECTION 1. At the request of either party, the arbitral tribunal may take any interim measures it deems necessary in respect of the subject-matter of the dispute, including measures for the conservation of the goods forming the subject-matter in dispute, such as ordering their deposit with a third person or the sale of perishable goods. 2. Such interim measures may be established in the form of an interim award. The arbitral tribunal shall be entitled to require security for the cost of such measures. 3. A request for interim measures addressed by any party to court shall not be deemed incompatible with the agreement to arbitrate, or as a waiver of the agreement.
45.	Northern Territory of Australia – Commercial Arbitration (National Uniform Legislation) Act 2011[128]	Section 17 Power of arbitral tribunal to order interim measures (Model Law Art 17) (1) Unless otherwise agreed by the parties, the arbitral tribunal may, at the request of a party, grant interim measures. (2) An interim measure is any temporary measure, whether in the form of an award or in another form, by which, at any time prior to the issuance of the award by which the dispute is finally decided, the arbitral tribunal orders a party to: (a) maintain or restore the status quo pending determination of the dispute; or (b) take action that would prevent, or refrain from taking action that is likely to cause, current or imminent harm or prejudice to the arbitral process itself; or (c) provide a means of preserving assets out of which a subsequent award may be satisfied; or

126. http://www.legislation.govt.nz/act/public/1996/0099/latest/whole.html#DLM403277
127. http://niqs.org.ng/wp-content/uploads/2018/12/Arbitration-and-Conciliation-Act.pdf
128. https://legislation.nt.gov.au/api/sitecore/Act/PDF?id=11692

Sr. No.	Country	Provision
		(d) preserve evidence that may be relevant and material to the resolution of the dispute. (3) Without limiting subsection (2), the arbitral tribunal may make orders with respect to any of the following: (a) security for costs; (b) discovery of documents and interrogatories; (c) giving of evidence by affidavit; (d) the inspection of any property which is or forms part of the subject matter of the dispute; (e) the taking of photographs of any property which is or forms part of the subject matter of the dispute; (f) samples to be taken from, or any observation to be made of or experiment conducted on, any property which is or forms part of the subject matter of the dispute; (g) dividing, recording and strictly enforcing the time allocated for a hearing between the parties (a stop clock arbitration). Note for section 17 Subsections (1) and (2) are substantially the same as Art 17 of the Model Law. There is no equivalent of subsection (3) in the Model Law.
46.	Norway - Act of 14 May 2004 No. 25 relating to Arbitration (The Arbitration Act)[129]	Section 19 - The scope of the arbitral tribunal for deciding interim measures The arbitral tribunal may, at the request of a party, order any party to take such interim measures as the arbitral tribunal shall consider necessary based on the subject matter of the dispute. The arbitral tribunal may order, by way of a condition for effecting and implementing the measure, whoever has requested such measure to provide, within a specified time limit, security respecting any consequences thereof. The arbitral tribunal may reduce or reverse an interim measure. If it turns out that the claim which the interim measure was to secure, did not exist at the time of such measure being decided, then whoever requested the implementation thereof shall indemnify other parties for the loss suffered by them as a result of the measure. The arbitral tribunal shall decide the claim for indemnification if requested to do so by a party. The provisions of this Section may be derogated by agreement.
47.	Oman - The Omani Law of Arbitration in Civil and Commercial Disputes – Royal Decree 47/97[130]	Article 24 1. Both parties to the arbitration may have an agreement to the effect that the arbitration board, on the basis of a request made by one of them, may issue orders to any of them to take suitable temporary or precautionary measures necessitated by the nature of the dispute and that, the board may order submission of an adequate security/guarantee for covering the expenses relating to the measures to be taken as per its directives.

129. https://www.chamber.no/wp-content/uploads/2014/02/Norwegian_Arbitration_Act.pdf
130. http://www.newyorkconvention.org/11165/web/files/document/2/1/21103.pdf

Sr. No.	Country	Provision
48.	Ontario - International Commercial Arbitration Act, 2017, S.O. 2017, c. 2, Sched. 5[131]	Section 5 - Application of Model Law (1) Subject to this Act, the Model Law on International Commercial Arbitration, adopted by the United Nations Commission on International Trade Law on 21 June 1985, as amended by the United Nations Commission on International Trade Law on 7 July 2006, set out in Schedule 2, has force of law in Ontario. Same (2) With respect to article 7 of the Model Law, option I applies in Ontario; option II does not. Same (3) The Model Law applies to international commercial arbitration agreements and awards made in international commercial arbitrations, whether made before or after the coming into force of this Act. Schedule 2 to this Act Article 17
49.	Oregon – Oregon International Commercial Arbitration and Conciliation Act[132]	36.486 Interim measures of protection ordered by arbitral tribunal; security. Unless otherwise agreed by the parties, at the request of a party, the arbitral tribunal may order any party to take such interim measure of protection as the arbitral tribunal may consider necessary in respect to the subject matter of the dispute. The arbitral tribunal may require any party to provide appropriate security in connection with such measure. [1991 c.405 §20]
50.	Pakistan - The Arbitration Act, 1940 Act No. X of 1940[133]	No equivalent provision as Article 17 of the UNCITRAL Model Law 2006
51.	Philippines - Alternative Dispute Resolution Act of 2004 Republic Act No. 9285[134]	Section 29. Further Authority for Arbitrator to Grant Interim Measure of Protection. Unless otherwise agreed by the parties, the arbitral tribunal may, at the request of a party, order any party to take such interim measures of protection as the arbitral tribunal may consider necessary in respect of the subject matter of the dispute following the rules in Section 28, paragraph 2. Such interim measures may include but shall not be limited to preliminary injunction directed against a party, appointment of receivers or detention, preservation, inspection of property that is the subject of the dispute in arbitration. Either party may apply with the Court for assistance in implementing or enforcing an interim measures ordered by an arbitral tribunal.

131. https://www.ontario.ca/laws/statute/17i02b#BK16
132. https://www.oregonlegislature.gov/bills_laws/ors/ors036.html
133. https://www.wipo.int/edocs/lexdocs/laws/en/pk/pk066en.pdf
134. http://www.newyorkconvention.org/11165/web/files/document/2/1/21107.pdf

Sr. No.	Country	Provision
52.	Poland - Polish Act of 17 November 1964 - Code of Civil Procedure, Part Five Arbitration[135]	Art. 1181 §1 Unless otherwise agreed by the parties, the arbitral tribunal may, at the request of a party which lent credence to its claim, order such interim measures as the arbitral tribunal considers necessary in respect of the subject-matter of the dispute. By ordering such measures the arbitral tribunal may require a party to provide appropriate security in order for the measure to be effective. §2 At the request of the party the arbitral tribunal may change or overrule the decision taken pursuant to paragraph §1. §3 The ruling of the arbitral tribunal ordering interim measures is enforceable after attachment of an enforceability clause. Art. 1214 §2 and §3 and Art. 1215 apply accordingly.
53.	Qatar - Law No. 2 of 2017 Promulgating the Civil and Commercial Arbitration Law-The Law of Arbitration in Civil and Commercial Matters[136]	Article (17) 1. Unless the Parties agree otherwise, the Arbitral Tribunal may on the application of either Party, issue provisional measures or interim awards that are dictated by the nature of the dispute, or for the purpose of preventing irreparable harm, including any of the following measures: a. Maintaining or restoring the status quo pending determination of the dispute; b. Adopting a measure to prevent the occurrence of current or imminent damage, or that would prejudice the Arbitration process itself, or to prevent the adoption of procedures that may possibly result in such damage or prejudice; c. Providing a means of preserving the assets by means of which later awards may be executed; and d. Preserving evidence that could be important or material to the determination of the dispute. The Arbitral Tribunal may require the Party requesting such procedures to submit sufficient security for costs for the provisional measure it orders or the interim award it issues.
54.	Queensland - Commercial Arbitration Act 2013 No. 8[137]	Section 17 Power of arbitral tribunal to order interim measures (cf Model Law Art 17) (1) Unless otherwise agreed by the parties, the arbitral tribunal may, at the request of a party, grant interim measures. (2) An interim measure is any temporary measure, whether in the form of an award or in another form, by which, at any time prior to the issuance of the award by which the dispute is finally decided, the arbitral tribunal orders a party to— (a) maintain or restore the status quo pending determination of the dispute; or

135. https://www.uv.es/medarb/observatorio/leyes-arbitraje/europa-resto/polonia-ccp-arbitration.pdf
136. https://www.qicdrc.gov.qa/sites/default/files/inline-files/law_no._02_2017_promulgating_the_civil_and_commercial_arbitration_law.pdf
137. https://www.legislation.qld.gov.au/view/pdf/inforce/2013-05-17/act-2013-008

Sr. No.	Country	Provision
		(b) take action that would prevent, or refrain from taking action that is likely to cause, current or imminent harm or prejudice to the arbitral process itself; or (c) provide a means of preserving assets out of which a subsequent award may be satisfied; or (d) preserve evidence that may be relevant and material to the resolution of the dispute. (3) Without limiting subsection (2), the arbitral tribunal may make orders with respect to any of the following— (a) security for costs; (b) discovery of documents and interrogatories; (c) giving of evidence by affidavit; (d) the inspection of any property which is or forms part of the subject-matter of the dispute; (e) the taking of photographs of any property which is or forms part of the subject-matter of the dispute; (f) samples to be taken from, or any observation to be made of or experiment conducted on, any property which is or forms part of the subject-matter of the dispute; (g) dividing, recording and strictly enforcing the time allocated for a hearing between the parties (a stop clock arbitration). Note— Subsections (1) and (2) are substantially the same as Art 17 of the Model Law. There is no equivalent subsection (3) in the Model Law.
55.	Republic of Costa Rica - Costa Rican Law for International Arbitration: 9285[138]	Article 17. Power of arbitral tribunal to order interim measures (1) Unless otherwise agreed by the parties, the arbitral tribunal may, at the request of a party, grant interim measures. (2) An interim measure is understood to be any temporary measure, stating the reasons, by which, at any time prior to the issuance of the award by which the dispute is finally decided, the arbitral tribunal orders a party to: (a) Maintain or restore the status quo pending determination of the dispute; (b) Take action that would prevent, or refrain from taking action that is likely to cause, current or imminent harm or prejudice to the arbitral process itself; (c) Provide a means of preserving assets out of which a subsequent award may be satisfied; or (d) Preserve evidence that may be relevant and material to the resolution of the dispute.
56.	Republic of Korea – Arbitration Act[139]	Article 18 Interim Measures (1) Unless otherwise agreed by the parties, the arbitral tribunal may, at the request of a party, grant interim measures as considered necessary.

138. https://arbitratlaw.com/wp-content/uploads/2017/01/Costa-Rican-Intl-Arbitration-Law.pdf
139. https://elaw.klri.re.kr/eng_service/lawView.do?hseq=38889&lang=ENG

Sr. No.	Country	Provision
		(2) An interim measure under paragraph (1) is any temporary measure, by which, at any time prior to the issuance of the award by which the dispute is finally decided, the arbitral tribunal orders a party to perform any of the following subparagraphs: 1. Maintain or restore the status quo pending determination of the dispute; 2. Take action that would prevent current or imminent harm or prejudice to the arbitral proceeding itself, or prohibiting action that may cause such harm or prejudice; 3. Provide a means of preserving assets subject to the execution of an arbitral award; or, 4. Preserve evidence that may be relevant and material to the resolution of the dispute.
57.	Russia - Russian Federation Law on International Commercial Arbitration[140]	Article 17. Power of arbitral tribunal to order interim measures 1. Unless otherwise agreed by the parties, the arbitral tribunal may, upon an application, order any party to take such interim measure of protection as the arbitral tribunal may consider necessary. The arbitral tribunal may require any party to provide appropriate security in connection with such measure. The orders and other procedural acts of the arbitral tribunal on taking of interim measures are binding on the parties. 2. By agreement of the parties, it may also be stipulated (including by reference to the arbitration rules) that before the constitution of the arbitral tribunal, a permanent arbitration institution is entitled to order that a party take such interim measures as it [institution] deems necessary. For such interim measures, clause 1 of this article should apply in full, as if said measures were ordered by the arbitral tribunal.
58.	Rwanda – Law on arbitration and conciliation in commercial matters, N° 005/2008[141]	Article 19: Competence of arbitral tribunal to issue interim measures Unless otherwise agreed by the parties, the arbitral tribunal may, at the request of one of the parties, grant interim measures. An interim measure is any measure, which may be taken as a decision of the court or in any other form, by which, at any time prior to the examination of the case, the arbitral tribunal orders a party the following: 1 maintaining or restoring the status quo pending determination of the dispute; 2 taking action to prevent or halting any action that is likely to cause any immediate or imminent loss or which may prejudice to the arbitral process itself; 3 providing means of preserving assets out of which a subsequent judge execution may be satisfied after the hearing; 4 preserving relevant and material evidence which may be useful in examining the case.

140. http://www.newyorkconvention.org/11165/web/files/document/2/2/22335.pdf
141. http://www.newyorkconvention.org/11165/web/files/document/2/1/21110.pdf

Sr. No.	Country	Provision
59.	Saudi Arabia - Law of Arbitration Royal decree No. M/34[142]	Article 23 1. The two parties to arbitration may agree that the arbitration tribunal shall, upon the request of either party, order either party to take, as it deems fit, any provisional or precautionary measures required by the nature of the dispute. The arbitration tribunal may require the party requesting such measures to provide sufficient financial guarantee for the execution of such proceeding.
60.	Serbia - Law on Arbitration No. 46/06[143]	Article 31 - Competence of the Arbitration Court to Impose Provisional Measures Unless the parties have agreed otherwise, the arbitration court may, at a proposal by one of the parties, impose a provisional measure, which it deems necessary with regard to the matter in dispute, and may simultaneously decide for the opposing side to lodge an appropriate security.
61.	Singapore - Arbitration Act (Chapter 10) (Domestic Arbitration Law)[144]	Section 28 - General powers exercisable by arbitral tribunal (1) The parties may agree on the powers which may be exercised by the arbitral tribunal for the purposes of and in relation to the arbitral proceedings. (2) Without prejudice to the powers conferred on the arbitral tribunal by the parties under subsection (1), the tribunal shall have powers to make orders or give directions to any party for — (a) security for costs; (b) discovery of documents and interrogatories; (c) giving of evidence by affidavit; (d) a party or witness to be examined on oath or affirmation, and may for that purpose administer any necessary oath or take any necessary affirmation; (e) the preservation and interim custody of any evidence for the purposes of the proceedings; (f) samples to be taken from, or any observation to be made of or experiment conducted upon, any property which is or forms part of the subject-matter of the dispute; and (g) the preservation, interim custody or sale of any property which is or forms part of the subject-matter of the dispute.
62.	Singapore - International Arbitration Act (Chapter 143A) (International Arbitration Law)[145]	Section 3 Model Law to have force of law (1) Subject to this Act, the Model Law, with the exception of Chapter VIII thereof, shall have the force of law in Singapore. (2) In the Model Law — "State" means Singapore and any country other than Singapore; "this State" means Singapore. Article 17 First Schedule. Power of arbitral tribunal to order interim measures

142. https://www.wipo.int/edocs/lexdocs/laws/en/sa/sa057en.pdf
143. https://www.wipo.int/edocs/lexdocs/laws/en/rs/rs028en.pdf
144. https://sso.agc.gov.sg/Act/AA2001
145. https://sso.agc.gov.sg/Act/IAA1994

Sr. No.	Country	Provision
		Unless otherwise agreed by the parties, the arbitral tribunal may, at the request of a party, order any party to take such interim measure of protection as the arbitral tribunal may consider necessary in respect of the subject-matter of the dispute. The arbitral tribunal may require any party to provide appropriate security in connection with such measure.
63.	Slovakia - [Slovak] Act No. 244/2002 of 3 April 2002 on Arbitration[146]	Section 22 Interim Measures (1) Unless otherwise agreed by the parties to arbitration, the arbitral tribunal may upon a motion of a party grant an interim measure if: it is necessary to temporarily regulate relationships between the parties, there is a risk that the enforcement of an arbitral award might be prejudiced, or there is a risk that evidence might in the future be no longer available or only available under complicated circumstances. If the parties to the arbitration have not agreed otherwise, the permanent court of arbitration may order an interim measure even before the appointment of an arbitrator (arbitrators). (2) Unless this Act states otherwise, the arbitral tribunal may order an interim measure only if the request for such measure was served upon the other party to arbitration and such party was provided with a sufficient time period for reply. (3) By an interim measure the arbitral tribunal may, in particular, order a party to arbitration to: a) pay a deposit or place an asset into the court's custody, b) refrain from taking an action in relation to certain assets or rights, c) take action, refrain from taking an action or endure some measure, d) secure evidence. (4) The arbitral tribunal may order the claimant to provide means to secure any loss that may occur as a result of the interim measure. If the claimant fails to provide means or advance on payment ordered by the arbitral tribunal within the stipulated time period, the arbitral tribunal shall dismiss the request for interim measure.
64.	Slovenia - Law on Arbitration of Slovenia[147]	Article 20 Interim Measures Ordered by Arbitral Tribunal (1) Unless otherwise agreed by the parties, the arbitral tribunal may, at the request of a party, at any time before the issuance of the final award, grant against the other party an interim measure it considers appropriate having regard to the subject matter of the dispute, after giving that other party an opportunity to present its case with respect to the request ... (2) Exceptionally, the arbitral tribunal may, if it considers it urgent, grant an interim measure before giving the other party the opportunity to present its case with respect to the request. Such a measure shall be binding on the parties, but shall not be subject to enforcement by a court.

146. https://www.international-arbitration-attorney.com/wp-content/uploads/2013/07/Slovakia-Arbitration-Law-1.pdf

147. http://www.sloarbitration.eu/Portals/0/Arbitrazno-pravo/Law%20on%20Arbitration%20of%20Slovenia.pdf

Sr. No.	Country	Provision
65.	South Africa - The Arbitration Act, 1965[148]	Section 26 - Interim award Unless the arbitration agreement provides otherwise, an arbitration tribunal may make an interim award at any time within the period allowed for making an award.
66.	South Australia - South Australia Commercial Arbitration Act 2011[149]	Section 17—Power of arbitral tribunal to order interim measures (1) Unless otherwise agreed by the parties, the arbitral tribunal may, at the request of a party, grant interim measures. (2) An interim measure is any temporary measure, whether in the form of an award or in another form, by which, at any time prior to the issuance of the award by which the dispute is finally decided, the arbitral tribunal orders a party to— (a) maintain or restore the status quo pending determination of the dispute; or (b) take action that would prevent, or refrain from taking action that is likely to cause, current or imminent harm or prejudice to the arbitral process itself; or (c) provide a means of preserving assets out of which a subsequent award may be satisfied; or (d) preserve evidence that may be relevant and material to the resolution of the dispute. (3) Without limiting subsection (2), the arbitral tribunal may make orders with respect to any of the following: (a) security for costs; (b) discovery of documents and interrogatories; (c) giving of evidence by affidavit; (d) the inspection of any property which is or forms part of the subject matter of the dispute; (e) the taking of photographs of any property which is or forms part of the subject matter of the dispute; (f) samples to be taken from, or any observation to be made of or experiment conducted on, any property which is or forms part of the subject matter of the dispute; (g) dividing, recording and strictly enforcing the time allocated for a hearing between the parties (a stop clock arbitration). Note— Subsections (1) and (2) are substantially the same as Art 17 of the Model Law. There is no equivalent subsection (3) in the Model Law.
67.	Spain - Act 60/2003 of 23 December on Arbitration[150]	Article 23. *Arbitrators' power to order interim measures* 1. Subject to any contrary agreement by the parties, the arbitrators may, at the request of a party, grant any interim measures deemed necessary in connection with the object of the dispute. The arbitrators may require the claimant to furnish sufficient security. 2. Irrespective of the form adopted by arbitral decisions on interim measures, the rules on setting aside and enforcement of awards will apply thereto.

148. https://www.gov.za/sites/default/files/gcis_document/201505/act-42-1965.pdf
149. https://www.legislation.sa.gov.au/LZ/C/A/COMMERCIAL%20ARBITRATION%20ACT%20 2011/CURRENT/2011.32.UN.PDF

Sr. No.	Country	Provision
68.	Sri Lanka - Arbitration Act. No. 11 of 1995[151]	Section 13 – Interim measures of protection (1) An arbitral tribunal may, at the request of a party, order any other party to take such Interim measures as it may consider necessary to protect or secure the claim which forms the subject matter of the dispute. The arbitral tribunal may also order the party making such request to provide the party ordered to take such interim measures, with security for any expense, loss or damage that may be caused in taking such interim measures: Provided however that, other than in exceptional cases no such order shall be made except after hearing the other parties.
69.	Sweden – The Swedish Arbitration Act (SFS 1999:116)[152]	Section 25 ... Unless the parties have agreed otherwise, the arbitrators may, at the request of a party, decide that, during the proceedings, the opposing party must undertake a certain interim measure to secure the claim which is to be adjudicated by the arbitrators. The arbitrators may prescribe that the party requesting the interim measure must provide reasonable security for the damage which may be incurred by the opposing party as a result of the interim measure.
70.	Switzerland – Private International Law Act 1987, Chapter 12: International Arbitration[153]	Article 183 Provisional and conservatory measures 1) Unless the parties have otherwise agreed, the arbitral tribunal may, on motion of one party, order provisional or conservatory measures. 2) If the party concerned does not voluntarily comply with these measures, the arbitral tribunal may request the assistance of the state judge; the judge shall apply his own law. 3) The arbitral tribunal or the state judge may make the granting of provisional or conservatory measures subject to appropriate sureties.
71.	Tasmania – Commercial Arbitration Act, 2011, Act 13 of 2011[154]	Section 17. Power of arbitral tribunal to order interim measures (cf Model Law Art 17) (1) Unless otherwise agreed by the parties, the arbitral tribunal may, at the request of a party, grant interim measures. (2) An "interim measure" is any temporary measure, whether in the form of an award or in another form, by which, at any time prior to the issuance of the award by which the dispute is finally decided, the arbitral tribunal orders a party to – (a) maintain or restore the status quo pending determination of the dispute; or (b) take action that would prevent, or refrain from taking action that is likely to cause, current or imminent harm or prejudice to the arbitral process itself; or

150. https://www.mjusticia.gob.es/cs/Satellite/Portal/1292426982249?blobheader=application%2Fpdf&blobheadername1=Content-Disposition&blobheadervalue1=attachment%3B+filename%3DAct_on_arbitration_%28Ley_60_2003__de_arbitraje%29.PDF
151. http://www.slnarbcentre.com/pdf/ARBITRATION-ACT.pdf
152. https://sccinstitute.com/media/37089/the-swedish-arbitration-act.pdf
153. https://www.swissarbitration.org/wp-content/uploads/2021/05/20210129-Chapter-12-PILA_Translation_English.pdf

Sr. No.	Country	Provision
		(c) provide a means of preserving assets out of which a subsequent award may be satisfied; or (d) preserve evidence that may be relevant and material to the resolution of the dispute. (3) Without limiting subsection (2), the arbitral tribunal may make orders with respect to any of the following: (a) security for costs; (b) discovery of documents and interrogatories; (c) giving of evidence by affidavit; (d) the inspection of any property which is or forms part of the subject matter of the dispute; (e) the taking of photographs of any property which is or forms part of the subject matter of the dispute; (f) samples to be taken from, or any observation to be made of or experiment conducted on, any property which is or forms part of the subject matter of the dispute; (g) dividing, recording and strictly enforcing the time allocated for a hearing between the parties (a "stop clock" arbitration). Note. Subsections (1) and (2) are substantially the same as Art 17 of the Model Law. There is no equivalent subsection (3) in the Model Law.
72.	Texas - Chapter 172. Arbitration and Conciliation of International Commercial Disputes, Civil Practice and Remedies Code[155]	Sec. 172.083. INTERIM MEASURES ORDERED BY ARBITRATION TRIBUNAL. (a) Except as agreed by the parties, the arbitration tribunal, at the request of a party, may order a party to take an interim measure of protection that the tribunal considers necessary concerning the subject matter of the dispute.
73.	Thailand - Arbitration Act B.E. 2545[156]	No equivalent provision as Article 17 of the UNCITRAL Model Law 2006
74.	Tunisia – Law n° 93-42 issued on April 26, related to the promulgation of the Arbitration Code[157]	Article 62 Unless otherwise agreed by the parties, the arbitral tribunal may, at the request of a party, order an interim or conservatory measure of protection if deemed necessary in accordance with the circumstances of the dispute.
75.	Turkey - Turkish International Arbitration Law, Law no. 4686, 2001[158]	Article 6 Interim measures of protection and interim attachments It is not incompatible with an arbitration agreement for a party to request, before or during arbitral proceedings, from a court an interim measure of protection or an interim attachment and for a court to grant such measure or attachment.

155. https://statutes.capitol.texas.gov/Docs/CP/htm/CP.172.htm
156. https://www.newyorkconvention.org/11165/web/files/document/2/1/21117.pdf
157. https://arbitrationlaw.com/sites/default/files/free_pdfs/Tunisia%20Arbitration%20Code.pdf

Sr. No.	Country	Provision
76.	Uganda - Chapter 4 The Arbitration and Conciliation Act[159]	Section 17. Power of arbitral tribunal. (1) Unless the parties agree, the appointing authority may, at the request of a party, order any party to take such interim measure of protection as the arbitral tribunal may consider necessary in respect of the subject matter of the dispute, and the arbitral tribunal may require any party to provide appropriate security in connection with such measure. (2) The appointing authority or a party with the approval of the appointing authority may seek assistance from the centre in the exercise of any power conferred on the appointing authority under subsection (1). (3) If a request is made under subsection (2), the court shall have, for the purposes of the arbitral proceedings, the same power to make an order for the doing of anything which the arbitral tribunal is empowered to order under subsection (1) as it would have in civil proceedings before that court, but the arbitral proceedings shall continue notwithstanding that a request has been made and is being considered by the court.
77.	Ukraine - The Law of Ukraine on International Commercial Arbitration[160]	Article 17. Power of Arbitral Tribunal to Order Interim Measures Unless otherwise agreed by the parties, the arbitral tribunal may, at the request of a party, order any party to take such interim measures of protection as the arbitral tribunal may consider necessary in respect of the subject-matter of the dispute. The arbitral tribunal may require any party to provide appropriate security in connection with such measures.
78.	United Arab Emirates - Federal Law No. (6) of 2018 on Arbitration[161]	Article (21) Interim or Conservatory Measures 1. Subject to the provisions of Article 18 of this Law, and unless otherwise agreed by the Parties, the Arbitral Tribunal may, at the request of a party or on its own motion, order any party to take such interim or conservatory measure as the Arbitral Tribunal may consider necessary given the nature of the dispute, including, in particular: a) An order to preserve evidence that may be relevant and material to the resolution of the dispute. b) Taking necessary measures to preserve goods which constitute part of the subject-matter of the dispute such as an order to deposit goods with a third party or to sell goods which are susceptible to damage. c) Preserving assets and funds out of which a subsequent award may be satisfied.

158. http://www.camera-arbitrale.it/Documenti/tial_turkey.pdf
159. https://ulii.org/akn/ug/act/2000/7/eng@2008-06-27
160. http://arbitrations.ru/userfiles/file/Law/Arbitration%20acts/ukraininan%20law%20on%20arbitration.pdf
161. https://www.tamimi.com/crm-media-uploader/fileupload/server/php/files/UAE%20Arbitration%20Law%20-%20Federal%20Law%20No%20%206%20of%202018.pdf

Sr. No.	Country	Provision
		d) Maintaining or restoring the status quo pending determination of the dispute. e) An order to take action that would prevent, or refrain from taking action that is likely to cause, current or imminent harm or prejudice to the arbitration process itself.
79.	Uruguay - Law 19,636 Approve Rules for International Commercial Arbitration[162]	Article 17 (Power of the arbitral tribunal to order provisional precautionary measures) .- 1) Unless otherwise agreed by the parties, the arbitral tribunal may, at the request of one of them, order the adoption of measures precautionary measures that it deems necessary with respect to the object of the litigation. The arbitral tribunal may require the applicant for a measure precautionary, which provides an adequate guarantee regarding the measure. 2) Any precautionary measure ordered by an arbitral tribunal is will recognize as binding, and unless the arbitral tribunal provide otherwise, if the party concerned does not submit voluntarily or if its effectiveness requires it, it will be executed, when such execution is requested, by the competent court in accordance with the provisions of article 6. 3) Precautionary measure means any temporary measure, granted in the form or not of an award, by which, at any time prior to the issuance of the award by which the controversy, the court orders one of the parties to: a) maintain or restore the status quo pending settle the controversy; b) take measures to prevent any current or imminent damage or impairment of arbitration proceedings, or refrain of carrying out certain acts that probably would cause such damage or impairment to the procedure arbitral; c) provide some means to preserve assets that allow execute the award or awards that may be issued; d) preserve evidence that may be relevant and relevant to resolve the dispute.
80.	Venezuela – Venezuelan Commercial Arbitration Act[163]	Article 26. – Unless otherwise agreed by the parties, the arbitral tribunal may order any interim measures of protection it may consider necessary with respect to subject matter of the dispute. The arbitral tribunal may require the requesting party to provide appropriate securities.
81.	Victoria - Commercial Arbitration Act 2011 No. 50 of 2011[164]	Section 17 Power of arbitral tribunal to order interim measures (cf Model Law Art 17) (1) Unless otherwise agreed by the parties, the arbitral tribunal may, at the request of a party, grant interim measures.

162. http://www.impo.com.uy/bases/leyes-originales/19636-2018
163. https://arbitrationlaw.com/sites/default/files/free_pdfs/Venezula%20Commercial%20Arbitration%20Act.pdf
164. http://arbitration.site/wp-content/uploads/2019/06/CAA-Vic-.pdf

Sr. No.	Country	Provision
		(2) An interim measure is any temporary measure, whether in the form of an award or in another form, by which, at any time prior to the issuance of the award by which the dispute is finally decided, the arbitral tribunal orders a party to— (a) maintain or restore the status quo pending determination of the dispute; or (b) take action that would prevent, or refrain from taking action that is likely to cause, current or imminent harm or prejudice to the arbitral process itself; or (c) provide a means of preserving assets out of which a subsequent award may be satisfied; or (d) preserve evidence that may be relevant and material to the resolution of the dispute. (3) Without limiting subsection (2), the arbitral tribunal may make orders with respect to any of the following— (a) security for costs; (b) discovery of documents and interrogatories; (c) giving of evidence by affidavit; (d) the inspection of any property which is or forms part of the subject-matter of the dispute; (e) the taking of photographs of any property which is or forms part of the subject-matter of the dispute; (f) samples to be taken from, or any observation to be made of or experiment conducted on, any property which is or forms part of the subject-matter of the dispute; (g) dividing, recording and strictly enforcing the time allocated for a hearing between the parties (a stop clock arbitration). Note Subsections (1) and (2) are substantially the same as Art 17 of the Model Law. There is no equivalent subsection (3) in the Model Law.
82.	Western Australia - Commercial Arbitration Act 2012, 023 of 2012[165]	Section 17. Power of arbitral tribunal to order interim measures (cf. Model Law Art 17) (1) Unless otherwise agreed by the parties, the arbitral tribunal may, at the request of a party, grant interim measures. (2) An interim measure is any temporary measure, whether in the form of an award or in another form, by which, at any time prior to the issuance of the award by which the dispute is finally decided, the arbitral tribunal orders a party to — (a) maintain or restore the status quo pending determination of the dispute; or (b) take action that would prevent, or refrain from taking action that is likely to cause, current or imminent harm or prejudice to the arbitral process itself; or

165. https://www.legislation.wa.gov.au/legislation/prod/filestore.nsf/FileURL/mrdoc_25084.pdf/$FILE/Commercial%20Arbitration%20Act%202012%20-%20%5B00-b0-06%5D.pdf?OpenElement

Sr. No.	Country	Provision
		(c) provide a means of preserving assets out of which a subsequent award may be satisfied; or (d) preserve evidence that may be relevant and material to the resolution of the dispute. (3) Without limiting subsection (2), the arbitral tribunal may make orders with respect to any of the following — (a) security for costs; (b) discovery of documents and interrogatories; (c) giving of evidence by affidavit; (d) the inspection of any property which is or forms part of the subject matter of the dispute; (e) the taking of photographs of any property which is or forms part of the subject matter of the dispute; (f) samples to be taken from, or any observation to be made of or experiment conducted on, any property which is or forms part of the subject matter of the dispute; (g) dividing, recording and strictly enforcing the time allocated for a hearing between the parties (a stop clock arbitration). Note for this section: Subsections (1) and (2) are substantially the same as Art 17 of the Model Law. There is no equivalent to subsection (3) in the Model Law
83.	Zambia - The Arbitration Act, 2000 No. 19 of 2000[166]	Section 14 - Power of arbitral tribunal to order interim and other measures (1) Unless otherwise agreed by the parties, the arbitral tribunal may, at the request of a party, order any party to take such interim measure of protection as the arbitral tribunal may consider necessary in respect of the subject-matter of the dispute and the arbitral tribunal may require any party to provide appropriate security in connection with any such measure. (2) Unless otherwise agreed by the parties, an arbitral tribunal shall have power— (a) to grant an interim injunction or other interim order; (b) to order the parties to make a deposit in respect of the fees, costs and expenses of the arbitration. (3) For the purposes of articles 17 of the First Schedule, the arbitral tribunal shall also have power— (a) to make any order it considers appropriate to compel the attendance of a witness before it to give evidence or produce documents; (b) to order any witness to submit to examination on oath or affirmation before the arbitral tribunal, or before an officer of the tribunal or any other person in order to produce information or evidence for use by the arbitral tribunal; (c) to order the discovery of documents and interrogatories;

166. http://www.newyorkconvention.org/11165/web/files/document/2/1/21396.pdf

Sr. No.	Country	Provision
		(d) to issue a commission or request for the taking of evidence out of jurisdiction; (e) to detain, preserve, or inspect any property or thing in the custody, possession or control of a party which is in issue in the arbitral proceedings and to authorise for any of the those purposes any person to enter upon any land or any building in the possession of a party, or to authorise any sample to be taken or any observation to be made or experiment to be carried out which may be necessary or expedient for the purpose of obtaining full information or evidence. (4) The arbitral tribunal or a party with the approval of the arbitral tribunal may request from the court executory assistance in the exercise of any power conferred upon the arbitral tribunal under this section.
84.	Zimbabwe - Chapter 7:15 Arbitration Act[167]	SCHEDULE (Section 2) ARTICLE 17 Power of arbitral tribunal to order interim measures (1) Unless otherwise agreed by the parties, the arbitral tribunal may, at the request of a party, order any party to take such interim measure of protection as the arbitral tribunal may consider necessary in respect of the subject matter of the dispute. The arbitral tribunal may require any party to provide appropriate security in connection with any such measure. (2) Unless otherwise agreed by the parties, an arbitral tribunal shall have power— (a) to grant an interdict or other interim order; (b) to order the parties to make a deposit in respect of the fees and costs of the arbitration.

167. https://zimlii.org/akn/zw/act/1996/6/eng@2016-12-31

Appendix C (Article 17A)

Sr. No.	Country	Provision
1.	Australia - International Arbitration Act 1974[168]	Same as UNCITRAL Model Law 2006 Sec 16 Model Law to have force of law (1) Subject to this Part, the Model Law has the force of law in Australia. (2) In the Model Law: Arbitration agreement has the meaning given in Option 1 of Article 7 of the Model Law. State means Australia (including the external Territories) and any foreign country. This State means Australia (including the external Territories). Model Law under Part V, Schedule 2 of the Arbitration Act, 1974
2.	Australian Capital Territory - Commercial Arbitration Act, 2017 A2017-7[169]	SECT 17A Conditions for granting interim measures (Model Law art 17A) (1) The party requesting an interim measure under section 17 (2) (a), (b) or (c) must satisfy the arbitral tribunal that— (a) harm not adequately reparable by an award of damages is likely to result if the measure is not ordered, and that harm substantially outweighs the harm that is likely to result to the party against whom the measure is directed if the measure is granted; and (b) there is a reasonable possibility that the requesting party will succeed on the merits of the claim. (2) The determination on the possibility referred to in subsection (1) (b) does not affect the discretion of the arbitral tribunal in making any subsequent determination. (3) With regard to a request for an interim measure under section 17 (2) (d), the requirements in subsection (1) (a) and (b) and subsection (2) apply only to the extent the arbitral tribunal considers appropriate.

168. https://www.legislation.gov.au/Details/C2011C00342
169. http://classic.austlii.edu.au/au/legis/act/consol_act/caa2017219/s17a.html

Sr. No.	Country	Provision
3.	Austria - Austrian Arbitration Act, 2013[170]	No equivalent provision as Article 17A of the UNCITRAL Model Law 2006
4.	Bahrain - Bahrain Arbitration Law No. 9/2015[171]	Same as UNCITRAL Model Law 2006 Article 1 Taking into account the provisions of international conventions in force in the Kingdom of Bahrain 1. The provisions of the " UNCITRAL " Model Law on International Commercial Arbitration Act attached to this law shall apply to all arbitration whatever the nature of the legal relationship of the dispute herewith, if this arbitration takes place in the Kingdom of Bahrain or abroad and that two parties agreed to comply with the provisions of the attached law. 2. The provisions of the attached law shall apply to all arbitration which begins after its entry into force even if based on an arbitration agreement concluded before the entry into force of this law.
5.	Bangladesh - The Arbitration Act, 2001[172]	No equivalent provision as Article 17A of the UNCITRAL Model Law 2006
6.	Belgium - Belgian Judicial Code Provisions[173]	No equivalent provision as Article 17A of the UNCITRAL Model Law 2006
7.	Bhutan - Alternative Dispute Resolution Act of Bhutan 2013[174]	Conditions for granting interim measures Section 115 The party, which request an interim measure shall satisfy the arbitral tribunal that: (1) Harm not adequately reparable by an award of damages is likely to result if the measure is not granted and such harm substantially outweighs the harm that is likely to result to the party against whom the measure is directed if the measure is granted; and (2) There is a reasonable possibility that the requesting party will succeed on the merits of the claim. Section 116 The determination on the possibility under section 115 (2) of this Act shall not affect the discretion of the arbitral tribunal in making any subsequent determination. Section 117 With regard to a request for an interim measure under section 114 (4) of this Act, the requirements in sections 115 and 116 of this Act shall apply only to the extent the arbitral tribunal considers appropriate.

170. https://www.viac.eu/images/law/ZPO_Schiedsrecht_2014_en_im_VIAC_Layout.pdf
171. https://pernetmartial.eu/sites/default/files/lois/Bahrain-Loi-d-arbitrage-arbitration-act-ley-de-arbitraje.pdf
172. http://www.mccibd.org/images/uploadimg/act_and_policy/corporate_governance/The-Arbitration-Act-2001.pdf
173. http://www.arbiter.com.sg/pdf/laws/Belgian%20Judicial%20Code%20Provisions%20(2013).pdf

Sr. No.	Country	Provision
8.	British Columbia - International Commercial Arbitration Act [RSBC 1996] Chapter 233[175]	Section 17.01 Conditions for granting interim measures (1) The party requesting an interim measure referred to in section 17 (2) (a), (c) or (e) must satisfy the arbitral tribunal that (a) harm not adequately reparable by an award of damages or other monetary award is likely to result if the measure is not ordered, (b) the harm referred to in paragraph (a) substantially outweighs the harm that is likely to result to the party against whom the measure is directed if the measure is granted, and (c) there is a reasonable possibility that the requesting party will succeed on the merits of the claim. (2) A determination of an arbitral tribunal under subsection (1) (c) does not affect the discretion of the arbitral tribunal in making any subsequent determination. (3) The requirements in subsection (1) apply, only to the extent the arbitral tribunal considers appropriate, to a request for an interim measure referred to in section 17 (2) (b) or (d).
9.	British Virgin Islands - Virgin Islands Arbitration Act, 2013[176]	UNCITRAL Model Law to have effect in the Virgin Islands. Section 4. The provisions of the UNCITRAL Model Law have the force of law in the Virgin Islands, subject to the modifications and supplements expressly provided in this Act. Application of article 17A of the UNCITRAL Model Law Section 34. Article 17A of the UNCITRAL Model Law
10.	Bulgaria - Law on International Commercial Arbitration State Gazette (SG) No. 60 of 05.08.1988[177]	No equivalent provision as Article 17A of the UNCITRAL Model Law 2006
11.	Cambodia - The Commercial Arbitration Law of the Kingdom of Cambodia 2006[178]	No equivalent provision as Article 17A of the UNCITRAL Model Law 2006
12.	Canada - Commercial Arbitration Act R.S.C., 1985, c. 17 (2nd Supp.)[179]	No equivalent provision as Article 17A of the UNCITRAL Model Law 2006 Adopted UNCITRAL Model Law 1985

174. https://www.nationalcouncil.bt/assets/uploads/docs/acts/2014/Alternative_Dispute_Resolution_Act_of_Bhutan_2013_engl0th.pdf
175. http://www.bclaws.ca/civix/document/id/complete/statreg/96233_01
176. http://www.bviiac.org/Portals/0/Files/Arbitration%20Documents/ArbitrationAct2013.pdf
177. http://www.newyorkconvention.org/11165/web/files/document/1/6/16200.pdf
178. https://www.cambodiaip.gov.kh/DocResources/372a361b-7a97-44b3-9810-79e5e6ea85f4_c786a043-b88d-4f64-9429-60a330efdc5f-en.pdf

Sr. No.	Country	Provision
13.	Connecticut - Chapter 909 Arbitration Proceedings[180]	No equivalent provision as Article 17A of the UNCITRAL Model Law 2006
14.	Croatia - Law on Arbitration Official Gazette no. 88/2001[181]	No equivalent provision as Article 17A of the UNCITRAL Model Law 2006
15.	Cyprus - The International Commercial Arbitration Law, 1987[182]	No equivalent provision as Article 17A of the UNCITRAL Model Law 2006
16.	Denmark - Danish Arbitration Act 2005[183]	No equivalent provision as Article 17A of the UNCITRAL Model Law 2006
17.	Egypt - Law No. 27/1994 Promulgating the Law Concerning Arbitration in Civil and Commercial Matters[184]	No equivalent provision as Article 17A of the UNCITRAL Model Law 2006
18.	Florida Chapter 684 - International Commercial Arbitration, Title XXXIX Commercial Relations, 2020 Florida Statutes[185]	Same as Article 17A of the UNCITRAL Model Law 2006 Article 684.0019 Conditions for granting interim measures.
19.	Fiji - International Arbitration Act 2017 (Act No. 44 of 2017)[186]	Section 24 - Conditions for granting interim measures (1) The party requesting an interim measure under section 23(2)(a), (b) and (c) shall satisfy the arbitral tribunal that—

179. https://laws-lois.justice.gc.ca/eng/acts/C-34.6/index.html
180. https://www.cga.ct.gov/current/pub/chap_909.htm
181. http://www.vsrh.hr/CustomPages/Static/HRV/Files/Legislation__Law-Arbitration-RC.pdf
182. https://www.uv.es/medarb/observatorio/leyes-arbitraje/europa-resto/chipre-international-commercial-arbitration-law.pdf
183. https://voldgiftsinstituttet.dk/wp-content/uploads/2015/01/danish_arbitration_act_2005.pdf
184. https://www.wipo.int/edocs/lexdocs/laws/en/eg/eg020en.pdf
185. https://www.flsenate.gov/Laws/Statutes/2020/Chapter684/All
186. https://www.fiji.gov.fj/getattachment/d9502667-6491-4592-85b2-eff97f245fed/Act-44---International-Arbitration-Act.aspx

Sr. No.	Country	Provision
		(a) harm not adequately reparable by an award of damages is likely to result if the measure is not ordered, and such harm substantially outweighs the harm that is likely to result to the party against whom the measure is directed if the measure is granted; and (b) there is a reasonable possibility that the requesting party will succeed on the merits of the claim. The determination on this possibility shall not affect the discretion of the arbitral tribunal in making any subsequent determination. (2) With regard to a request for an interim measure under section 23(2)(d), the requirements in subsection (1)(a) and (b) shall apply only to the extent the arbitral tribunal considers appropriate.
20.	France - Book IV - Arbitration of the Code of Civil Procedure Decree No. 2011-48[187]	No equivalent provision as Article 17A of the UNCITRAL Model Law 2006
21.	Georgia - Chapter 9 Arbitration, Title 9 Civil Practice, Georgia Code[188]	Article 18 - Conditions for granting interim measures 1. The party requesting an interim measure provided for by article 17(2)(a-c) must prove the existence of the following circumstances: a) If the interim measure is not ordered, irreparable harm not adequately compensated by an award of damages is likely to result. b) Harm caused by not ordering an interim measure substantially outweighs the harm that is likely to result to the party against whom the interim measure is directed if the measure is granted. c) There are reasonable grounds to believe that the requesting party will prevail. The determination of this belief shall not affect the discretion of the arbitral tribunal in making any subsequent award. 2. With regard to a request for an interim measure provided for by article 17(2)(d), the requirements provided for by paragraph 1 (a-c), of this article shall apply only to the extent that the arbitral tribunal considers reasonable. 3. The arbitral tribunal is entitled to require the party requesting an interim measure to provide appropriate security with relation to the interim measures. 4. If the arbitral tribunal decides that, under the given circumstances, respective interim measures should not have been granted, the party requesting an interim measure shall be liable for any costs and damages caused by such interim measures. The arbitral tribunal may award to the arbitration party against whom the interim measures were taken, such costs and damages at any stage of the arbitration proceedings.

187. http://www.iaiparis.com/pdf/FRENCH_LAW_ON_INTERNATIONAL_ARBITRATION.pdf
188. https://matsne.gov.ge/ru/document/download/89284/5/en/pdf

Sr. No.	Country	Provision
22.	Germany - Tenth Book of the Code of Civil Procedure, Arbitration Procedure[189]	No equivalent provision as Article 17A of the UNCITRAL Model Law 2006
23.	Greece - Code of Civil Procedure, Book VII, Book VIII[190]	No equivalent provision as Article 17A of the UNCITRAL Model Law 2006
24.	Hong Kong - Cap. 609 Arbitration Ordinance[191]	Same as Article 17A of the UNCITRAL Model Law 2006 Section 36 - Article 17A of UNCITRAL Model Law (Conditions for granting interim measures)
25.	Hungary - Act LX of 2017 on Arbitration[192]	Section 19 In cases under section 18 (2) a), b) and c), the party requesting the interim measure shall satisfy the arbitral tribunal that a) harm not reparable by an award of damages is likely to result if the measure is not ordered, and such harm outweighs the harm that is likely to result to the party against whom the measure is directed if the measure is granted, and b) the requesting party will succeed on the merits of the claim. The determination on this possibility shall not affect the discretion of the arbitral tribunal in making any subsequent determination.
26.	Ireland - Arbitration Act 2010 Number 1 of 2010[193]	Section 6 - Adoption of Model Law Subject to this Act, the Model Law shall have the force of law in the State and shall apply to arbitrations under arbitration agreements concerning— (a) international commercial arbitrations, or (b) arbitrations which are not international commercial arbitrations. Same as Article 17A of the UNCITRAL Model Law 2006 Article 17A under Schedule 1 - TEXT OF UNCITRAL MODEL LAW ON INTERNATIONAL COMMERCIAL ARBITRATION
27.	Jamaica - The Arbitration Act, 2017 (Act 13 of 2017)[194]	Section 21 - Conditions for granting interim measures (1) The party requesting an interim measure under section 20 (2)(a), (b) or (c) shall satisfy the arbitral tribunal that-

189. https://sccinstitute.com/media/29988/german-arbitration-act.pdf
190. https://www.uv.es/medarb/observatorio/leyes-arbitraje/europa-resto/grecia-ccp-domestic-arbitration.pdf
191. https://www.elegislation.gov.hk/hk/cap609
192. https://www.ilo.org/dyn/natlex/docs/ELECTRONIC/106843/131257/F-266585574/J2017T0060P_20180102_FIN.pdf
193. http://www.irishstatutebook.ie/eli/2010/act/1/enacted/en/pdf
194. http://extwprlegs1.fao.org/docs/pdf/jam172060.pdf

Sr. No.	Country	Provision
		(a) harm not adequately reparable by an award of damages is likely to result if the measure, is not ordered, and such harm substantially outweighs the harm that is likely to result to the party against whom the measure is directed if the measure is granted; and (b) there is a reasonable possibility that the requesting party will succeed on the merits of the claim; and the determination on this possibility shall not affect the discretion of the arbitral tribunal in making any subsequent determination. (2) With regard to a request for an interim measure under section 20(2)(d), the requirements in subsection (1)(a) and (b) shall apply only to the extent the arbitral tribunal considers appropriate.
28.	Japan - Arbitration Law (Law No. 138 of 2003)[195]	No equivalent provision as Article 17A of the UNCITRAL Model Law 2006
29.	Jordan - Law No. 31 of 2001 (Jordan) Arbitration Law[196]	No equivalent provision as Article 17A of the UNCITRAL Model Law 2006
30.	Kenya - Chapter 49 Arbitration Act (The Arbitration Act, 1995)[197]	No equivalent provision as Article 17A of the UNCITRAL Model Law 2006
31.	Liechtenstein - Liechtenstein Arbitration Law (Code of Civil Procedure)[198]	No equivalent provision as Article 17A of the UNCITRAL Model Law 2006
32.	Lithuania - The Republic of Lithuania Law on Commercial Arbitration, 2012[199]	Article 20. Interim Measures 3. A party requesting an arbitral tribunal to take interim measures referred to in points 1 and 2 of paragraph 2 of this Article must prove that: 1) his claims are likely to be founded; the determination of such likelihood shall not affect the power of the arbitral tribunal to subsequently give a different arbitral award or order in arbitral proceedings; 2) failure to take the measures can substantially preclude the enforcement of the arbitral award or render it impossible;

195. https://japan.kantei.go.jp/policy/sihou/arbitrationlaw.pdf
196. https://www.ilo.org/dyn/natlex/docs/ELECTRONIC/63091/95325/F1864661120/JOR63091.pdf
197. https://ncia.or.ke/wp-content/uploads/2021/02/ArbitrationAct4of1995_2.pdf
198. https://www.newyorkconvention.org/11165/web/files/document/2/1/21372.pdf
199. https://e-seimas.lrs.lt/portal/legalAct/lt/TAD/35954312dcb311e6be918a531b2126ab?jfwid=-wd7z7zum0

Sr. No.	Country	Provision
		3) interim measures are cost-effective and proportionate to the goal sought. 4. A party requesting an arbitral tribunal to take interim measures referred to in point 3 of paragraph 2 of this Article must prove that: 1) evidence requested to be preserved may be significant to the case; 2) there is a real risk that the failure to take interim measures will result in the destruction by the other party of evidence requested to be preserved or its damage rendering it incapable of being used in arbitral proceedings.
33.	Louisiana – RS 9 Title 9. Civil Code-Ancillaries[200]	No equivalent provision as Article 17A of the UNCITRAL Model Law 2006
34.	Macedonia - Law on International Commercial Arbitration of the Republic of Macedonia[201]	No equivalent provision as Article 17A of the UNCITRAL Model Law 2006
35.	Malaysia – Arbitration Act 2005, Act 646[202]	No equivalent provision as Article 17A of the UNCITRAL Model Law 2006
36.	Maldives – Act No: 10/2013, Arbitration Act[203]	Section 35 - Conditions to be Satisfied for Interim Order to be Granted (a) A party asking for an order for interim measure under Section 33 or 34 of this Act must satisfy the Arbitral Tribunal of the following: 1. The party may be deprived of the reasonable benefits from an arbitral award if the order is not issued at the time. 2. The balance of convenience lies with the party requesting the order rather than the party against whom the preliminary order is requested. 3. There is a prima facie case in favor of the party seeking the order. (b) A decision by the Arbitral Tribunal to issue preliminary order based on point 3 of (a) above is not proof that the final decision in the matter would be in favor of the party seeking the order. (c) In relation to a request for a preliminary order made in accordance with (a) above, the satisfaction of the Arbitral Tribunal of matters mentioned in points 1-3 of (a) will depend upon the standards set down by the Arbitral Tribunal itself.
37.	Malta – CAP. 387 Arbitration Act[204]	No equivalent provision as Article 17A of the UNCITRAL Model Law 2006

200. http://legis.la.gov/legis/Laws_Toc.aspx?folder=83&title=9
201. https://www.international-arbitration-attorney.com/wp-content/uploads/2013/07/Macedonia-Arbitration-Law.pdf
202. http://www.newyorkconvention.org/11165/web/files/document/1/6/16298.pdf
203. https://miac.gov.mv/media/documents/Arbitration%20Act.pdf
204. http://justiceservices.gov.mt/DownloadDocument.aspx?app=lom&itemid=8854&l=1

Sr. No.	Country	Provision
38.	Mauritius - The International Arbitration Act, 2008 (Act 37 of 2008)[205]	Section 17. Interim Measures by Tribunal (2) The party requesting an interim measure under subsection (1) (a), (b) or (c) shall satisfy the arbitral tribunal that - (a) harm not adequately reparable by an award of damages is likely to result if the measure is not ordered, and such harm substantially outweighs the harm that is likely to result to the party against whom the measure is directed if the measure is granted; and (b) there is a reasonable possibility that the requesting party will succeed on the merits of the claim. (3) With regard to a request for an interim measure under subsection (1)(d) or (e), the requirements in subsection (2) shall apply only to the extent the arbitral tribunal considers appropriate.
39.	Montenegro - Decree on the Promulgation of the Law on Arbitration, 2015[206]	Article 22 - Conditions for granting interim measures The party requesting an interim measure under Article 21 paragraph 2 items 1, 2 and 3 hereof, shall satisfy the arbitral tribunal that: 1) Harm not adequately reparable is likely to result if an interim measure is not ordered, and such harm substantially outweighs the harm to result to the party against whom the interim measure is ordered; and 2) There is a possibility that the party requesting an interim measure will succeed on the merits of the claim, where such possibility shall not affect the discretion of the arbitral tribunal in making any subsequent determination. With regard to a request for an interim measure under Article 21 paragraph 2 item 4 hereof, the requirements in paragraph 1 of this Article shall apply only to the extent the arbitral tribunal considers appropriate.
40.	Myanmar - Arbitration Law The Pyidaungsu Hluttaw Law No. 5/2016[207]	No equivalent provision as Article 17A of the UNCITRAL Model Law 2006
41.	New South Wales - Commercial Arbitration Act 2010 No 61[208]	Section 17A Conditions for granting interim measures (cf Model Law Art 17A) (1) The party requesting an interim measure under section 17 (2) (a), (b) or (c) must satisfy the arbitral tribunal that: (a) harm not adequately reparable by an award of damages is likely to result if the measure is not ordered, and that harm substantially outweighs the harm that is likely to result to the party against whom the measure is directed if the measure is granted, and

205. https://www.wipo.int/edocs/lexdocs/laws/en/mu/mu020en.pdf
206. https://www.privrednakomora.me/sites/pkcg.org/files/multimedia/main_pages/files/2012/09/final_eng_zakon_o_arbitrazi_final_0.pdf
207. http://www.newyorkconvention.org/11165/web/files/document/2/1/21098.pdf
208. https://legislation.nsw.gov.au/view/html/inforce/current/act-2010-061#sec.17A

Sr. No.	Country	Provision
		(b) there is a reasonable possibility that the requesting party will succeed on the merits of the claim. (2) The determination on the possibility referred to in subsection (1) (b) does not affect the discretion of the arbitral tribunal in making any subsequent determination. (3) With regard to a request for an interim measure under section 17 (2) (d), the requirements in subsection (1) (a) and (b) and subsection (2) apply only to the extent the arbitral tribunal considers appropriate.
42.	New Zealand – The Arbitration Act, 1996 No 99[209]	Schedule I- Rules applying to arbitration agreement Article 17B Conditions for granting interim measure (1) If an interim measure of a kind described in subparagraph (a), (b), or (c) of the definition of that term in article 17 is requested, the applicant must satisfy the arbitral tribunal that— (a) harm not adequately reparable by an award of damages is likely to result if the measure is not granted; and (b) the harm substantially outweighs the harm that is likely to result to the respondent if the measure is granted; and (c) there is a reasonable possibility that the applicant will succeed on the merits of the claim. (2) If an interim measure of a kind described in subparagraph (d) of the definition of that term in article 17 is requested, the applicant must satisfy the arbitral tribunal of the matters specified in paragraph (1)(a) to (c), but only to the extent that the arbitral tribunal considers appropriate. (3) If an interim measure of a kind described in subparagraph (e) of the definition of that term in article 17 is requested, the applicant must satisfy the arbitral tribunal that the applicant will be able to pay the costs of the respondent if the applicant is unsuccessful on the merits of the claim. (4) A determination by the arbitral tribunal on the matter specified in paragraph (1)(c) does not affect its discretion to make any subsequent determination.
43.	Nigeria - Arbitration and Conciliation Act Chapter 19 Laws of the Federation of Nigeria 1990[210]	No equivalent provision as Article 17A of the UNCITRAL Model Law 2006

209. http://www.legislation.govt.nz/act/public/1996/0099/latest/whole.html#DLM403277
210. http://niqs.org.ng/wp-content/uploads/2018/12/Arbitration-and-Conciliation-Act.pdf

Sr. No.	Country	Provision
44.	Northern Territory of Australia - Commercial Arbitration (National Uniform Legislation) Act 2011[211]	Section 17A Conditions for granting interim measures (Model Law Art 17A) (1) The party requesting an interim measure under section 17(2)(a), (b) or (c) must satisfy the arbitral tribunal that: (a) harm not adequately reparable by an award of damages is likely to result if the measure is not ordered, and that harm substantially outweighs the harm that is likely to result to the party against whom the measure is directed if the measure is granted; and (b) there is a reasonable possibility that the requesting party will succeed on the merits of the claim. (2) The determination on the possibility referred to in subsection (1)(b) does not affect the discretion of the arbitral tribunal in making any subsequent determination. (3) With regard to a request for an interim measure under section 17(2)(d), the requirements in subsection (1)(a) and (b) and subsection (2) apply only to the extent the arbitral tribunal considers appropriate.
45.	Norway - Act of 14 May 2004 No. 25 relating to Arbitration (The Arbitration Act)[212]	No equivalent provision as Article 17A of the UNCITRAL Model Law 2006
46.	Oman - The Omani Law of Arbitration in Civil and Commercial Disputes – Royal Decree 47/97[213]	No equivalent provision as Article 17A of the UNCITRAL Model Law 2006
47.	Ontario – International Commercial Arbitration Act, 2017, S.O. 2017, c. 2, Sched. 5[214]	Section 5 - Application of Model Law (1) Subject to this Act, the Model Law on International Commercial Arbitration, adopted by the United Nations Commission on International Trade Law on 21 June 1985, as amended by the United Nations Commission on International Trade Law on 7 July 2006, set out in Schedule 2, has force of law in Ontario. Same (2) With respect to article 7 of the Model Law, option I applies in Ontario; option II does not. Same (3) The Model Law applies to international commercial arbitration agreements and awards made in international commercial arbitrations, whether made before or after the coming into force of this Act. Schedule 2 to this Act Article 17A

211. https://legislation.nt.gov.au/api/sitecore/Act/PDF?id = 11692
212. https://www.chamber.no/wp-content/uploads/2014/02/Norwegian_Arbitration_Act.pdf
213. http://www.newyorkconvention.org/11165/web/files/document/2/1/21103.pdf
214. https://www.ontario.ca/laws/statute/17i02b#BK16

Sr. No.	Country	Provision
48.	Oregon – Oregon International Commercial Arbitration and Conciliation Act[215]	No equivalent provision as Article 17A of the UNCITRAL Model Law 2006
49.	Pakistan - The Arbitration Act, 1940 Act No. X of 1940[216]	No equivalent provision as Article 17A of the UNCITRAL Model Law 2006
50.	Philippines - Alternative Dispute Resolution Act of 2004 Republic Act No. 9285[217]	No equivalent provision as Article 17A of the UNCITRAL Model Law 2006
51.	Poland – Polish Act of 17 November 1964 - Code of Civil Procedure, Part Five Arbitration[218]	No equivalent provision as Article 17A of the UNCITRAL Model Law 2006
52.	Qatar - Law No. 2 of 2017 Promulgating the Civil and Commercial Arbitration Law-The Law of Arbitration in Civil and Commercial Matters[219]	No equivalent provision as Article 17A of the UNCITRAL Model Law 2006
53.	Queensland - Commercial Arbitration Act 2013 No. 8[220]	Section 17A Conditions for granting interim measures (cf Model Law Art 17A) (1) The party requesting an interim measure under section 17(2)(a), (b) or (c) must satisfy the arbitral tribunal that—

215. https://www.oregonlegislature.gov/bills_laws/ors/ors036.html
216. https://www.wipo.int/edocs/lexdocs/laws/en/pk/pk066en.pdf
217. http://www.newyorkconvention.org/11165/web/files/document/2/1/21107.pdf
218. https://www.uv.es/medarb/observatorio/leyes-arbitraje/europa-resto/polonia-ccp-arbitration.pdf
219. https://www.qicdrc.gov.qa/sites/default/files/inline-files/law_no._02_2017_promulgating_the_civil_and_commercial_arbitration_law.pdf
220. https://www.legislation.qld.gov.au/view/pdf/inforce/2013-05-17/act-2013-008

Sr. No.	Country	Provision
		(a) harm not adequately reparable by an award of damages is likely to result if the measure is not ordered, and that harm substantially outweighs the harm that is likely to result to the party against whom the measure is directed if the measure is granted; and (b) there is a reasonable possibility that the requesting party will succeed on the merits of the claim. (2) The determination on the possibility referred to in subsection (1)(b) does not affect the discretion of the arbitral tribunal in making any subsequent determination. (3) With regard to a request for an interim measure under section 17(2)(d), the requirements in subsection (1)(a) and (b) and subsection (2) apply only to the extent the arbitral tribunal considers appropriate.
54.	Republic of Costa Rica - Costa Rican Law for International Arbitration Law Number: 8937[221]	Same as Article 17A of UNCITRAL Model Law 2006
55.	Republic of Korea - Arbitration Act[222]	Article 18-2 (Conditions for Granting Interim Measures) (1) The party requesting an interim measure under Article 18 (2) 1 through 3 shall satisfy all of conditions in the following subparagraphs: 1. If the applicant fails to have the interim measure taken, the applicant will possibly sustain damage that cannot be redressed by an arbitral award for compensating for damage, and such damage will considerably exceed the damage that the other party is expected to sustain as a consequence of the interim measure; 2. There is a reasonable possibility that the requesting party will succeed on the merits of the claim: Provided, That the determination on this possibility shall not affect the discretion of the arbitral tribunal in making any subsequent determination. (2) With regard to a request for an interim measure under Article 18 (2) 4, the requirements in paragraph (1) shall apply only to the extent the arbitral tribunal considers appropriate.
56.	Russia - Russian Federation Law on International Commercial Arbitration[223]	No equivalent provision as Article 17A of the UNCITRAL Model Law 2006

221. https://arbitratlaw.com/wp-content/uploads/2017/01/Costa-Rican-Intl-Arbitration-Law.pdf
222. https://elaw.klri.re.kr/eng_service/lawView.do?hseq=38889&lang=ENG
223. http://www.newyorkconvention.org/11165/web/files/document/2/2/22335.pdf

Sr. No.	Country	Provision
57.	Rwanda – Law on arbitration and conciliation in commercial matters, N° 005/2008[224]	Article 20: Conditions for granting interim measures The party requesting for an interim measure in accordance with Article 19, paragraph 2 littera 1°, 2° and 3° of this Law shall satisfy the arbitral tribunal that: 1° a loss not adequately reparable by an award of damages is likely to result if the measure is not ordered, and such a loss substantially outweighs the loss that is likely to result to the party against whom the measure is directed if the measure is granted; 2° there is a reasonable possibility that the requesting party will succeed on the merits of the claim, provided that any determination on this possibility shall not affect the discretion of the arbitral tribunal in making any subsequent determination. With regard to a request for an interim measure under Article 19, littera 4 of this Law, the requirements in paragraph 1 in littera 1° and 2° of that Article shall apply only to the extent the arbitral tribunal considers appropriate.
58.	Saudi Arabia – Law of Arbitration Royal Decree No. M/34[225]	No equivalent provision as Article 17A of the UNCITRAL Model Law 2006
59.	Serbia – Law on Arbitration No. 46/06[226]	No equivalent provision as Article 17A of the UNCITRAL Model Law 2006
60.	Singapore - Arbitration Act (Chapter 10) (Domestic Arbitration Law)[227]	No equivalent provision as Article 17A of the UNCITRAL Model Law 2006
61.	Singapore - International Arbitration Act (Chapter 143A) (International Arbitration Law)[228]	No equivalent provision as Article 17A of the UNCITRAL Model Law 2006
62.	Slovakia – [Slovak] Act No. 244/2002 of 3 April 2002 on Arbitration[229]	No equivalent provision as Article 17A of the UNCITRAL Model Law 2006

224. http://www.newyorkconvention.org/11165/web/files/document/2/1/21110.pdf
225. https://www.wipo.int/edocs/lexdocs/laws/en/sa/sa057en.pdf
226. https://www.wipo.int/edocs/lexdocs/laws/en/rs/rs028en.pdf
227. https://sso.agc.gov.sg/Act/AA2001
228. https://sso.agc.gov.sg/Act/IAA1994
229. https://www.international-arbitration-attorney.com/wp-content/uploads/2013/07/Slovakia-Arbitration-Law-1.pdf

Sr. No.	Country	Provision
63.	Slovenia - Law on Arbitration of Slovenia[230]	No equivalent provision as Article 17A of the UNCITRAL Model Law 2006
64.	South Africa – The Arbitration Act, 1965[231]	No equivalent provision as Article 17A of the UNCITRAL Model Law 2006
65.	South Australia - South Australia Commercial Arbitration Act 2011[232]	Section 17A Conditions for granting interim measures (1) The party requesting an interim measure under section 17(2)(a), (b) or (c) must satisfy the arbitral tribunal that— (a) harm not adequately reparable by an award of damages is likely to result if the measure is not ordered, and that harm substantially outweighs the harm that is likely to result to the party against whom the measure is directed if the measure is granted; and (b) there is a reasonable possibility that the requesting party will succeed on the merits of the claim. (2) The determination on the possibility referred to in subsection (1)(b) does not affect the discretion of the arbitral tribunal in making any subsequent determination. (3) With regard to a request for an interim measure under section 17(2)(d), the requirements in subsections (1)(a) and (b) and subsection (2) apply only to the extent the arbitral tribunal considers appropriate.
66.	Spain - Act 60/2003 of 23 December on Arbitration[233]	No equivalent provision as Article 17A of the UNCITRAL Model Law 2006
67.	Sri Lanka - Arbitration Act. No. 11 of 1995[234]	No equivalent provision as Article 17A of the UNCITRAL Model Law 2006
68.	Sweden – The Swedish Arbitration Act (SFS 1999:116)[235]	No equivalent provision as Article 17A of the UNCITRAL Model Law 2006

230. http://www.sloarbitration.eu/Portals/0/Arbitrazno-pravo/Law%20on%20Arbitration%20of%20Slovenia.pdf
231. https://www.gov.za/sites/default/files/gcis_document/201505/act-42-1965.pdf
232. https://www.legislation.sa.gov.au/LZ/C/A/COMMERCIAL%20ARBITRATION%20ACT%202011/CURRENT/2011.32.UN.PDF
233. https://www.mjusticia.gob.es/cs/Satellite/Portal/1292426982249?blobheader=application%2Fpdf&blobheadername1=Content-Disposition&blobheadervalue1=attachment%3B+filename%3DAct_on_arbitration_%28Ley_60_2003__de_arbitraje%29.PDF
234. http://www.slnarbcentre.com/pdf/ARBITRATION-ACT.pdf
235. https://sccinstitute.com/media/37089/the-swedish-arbitration-act.pdf

Sr. No.	Country	Provision
69.	Switzerland – Private International Law Act 1987, Chapter 12: International Arbitration[236]	No equivalent provision as Article 17A of the UNCITRAL Model Law 2006
70.	Tasmania – Commercial Arbitration Act, 2011, Act 13 of 2011[237]	Section 17A. Conditions for granting interim measures (cf Model Law Art 17A) (1) The party requesting an interim measure under section 17(2)(a), (b) or (c) must satisfy the arbitral tribunal that – (a) harm not adequately reparable by an award of damages is likely to result if the measure is not ordered, and that harm substantially outweighs the harm that is likely to result to the party against whom the measure is directed if the measure is granted; and (b) there is a reasonable possibility that the requesting party will succeed on the merits of the claim. (2) The determination on the possibility referred to in subsection (1)(b) does not affect the discretion of the arbitral tribunal in making any subsequent determination. (3) With regard to a request for an interim measure under section 17(2)(d), the requirements in subsection (1)(a) and (b) and subsection (2) apply only to the extent the arbitral tribunal considers appropriate.
71.	Texas – Chapter 172. Arbitration and Conciliation of International Commercial Disputes, Civil Practice and Remedies Code[238]	No equivalent provision as Article 17A of the UNCITRAL Model Law 2006
72.	Thailand – Arbitration Act B.E. 2545[239]	No equivalent provision as Article 17A of the UNCITRAL Model Law 2006
73.	Tunisia – Law n° 93-42 issued on April 26, related to the promulgation of the Arbitration Code[240]	No equivalent provision as Article 17A of the UNCITRAL Model Law 2006

236. https://www.swissarbitration.org/wp-content/uploads/2021/05/20210129-Chapter-12-PILA_Translation_English.pdf
237. https://www.legislation.tas.gov.au/view/html/inforce/current/act-2011-013
238. https://statutes.capitol.texas.gov/Docs/CP/htm/CP.172.htm
239. https://tai.coj.go.th/th/file/get/file/20190328ecac5333356ffad0331bd601151db9f4142557.pdf

Sr. No.	Country	Provision
74.	Turkey - Turkish International Arbitration Law, Law no. 4686, 2001[241]	No equivalent provision as Article 17A of the UNCITRAL Model Law 2006
75.	Uganda – Chapter 4 The Arbitration and Conciliation Act[242]	No equivalent provision as Article 17A of the UNCITRAL Model Law 2006
76.	Ukraine - The Law of Ukraine on International Commercial Arbitration[243]	No equivalent provision as Article 17A of the UNCITRAL Model Law 2006
77.	United Arab Emirates - Federal Law No. (6) of 2018 on Arbitration[244]	No equivalent provision as Article 17A of the UNCITRAL Model Law 2006
78.	Uruguay - Law 19,636 Approve Rules for International Commercial Arbitration[245]	Article 17 (Power of the arbitral tribunal to order provisional precautionary measures).- 4) The precautionary measure will be granted by the arbitral tribunal when consider that it is necessary for the protection of a right and whenever there is danger of injury or frustration of the the duration of the process. This estimate will not prejudge the subsequent decision to which the arbitral tribunal may arrive.
79.	Venezuela – Venezuelan Commercial Arbitration Act[246]	No equivalent provision as Article 17A of the UNCITRAL Model Law 2006

240. https://arbitrationlaw.com/sites/default/files/free_pdfs/Tunisia%20Arbitration%20Code.pdf
241. http://www.camera-arbitrale.it/Documenti/tial_turkey.pdf
242. https://ulii.org/akn/ug/act/2000/7/eng@2008-06-27
243. http://arbitrations.ru/userfiles/file/Law/Arbitration%20acts/ukraininan%20law%20on%20arbitration.pdf
244. https://www.tamimi.com/crm-media-uploader/fileupload/server/php/files/UAE%20Arbitration%20Law%20-%20Federal%20Law%20No%20%206%20of%202018.pdf
245. http://www.impo.com.uy/bases/leyes-originales/19636-2018
246. https://arbitrationlaw.com/sites/default/files/free_pdfs/Venezula%20Commercial%20Arbitration%20Act.pdf

Sr. No.	Country	Provision
80.	Victoria - Commercial Arbitration Act 2011 No. 50 of 2011[247]	Section 17A Conditions for granting interim measures (cf Model Law Art 17A) (1) The party requesting an interim measure under section 17(2)(a), (b) or (c) must satisfy the arbitral tribunal that— (a) harm not adequately reparable by an award of damages is likely to result if the measure is not ordered, and that harm substantially outweighs the harm that is likely to result to the party against whom the measure is directed if the measure is granted; and (b) there is a reasonable possibility that the requesting party will succeed on the merits of the claim. (2) The determination on the possibility referred to in subsection (1)(b) does not affect the discretion of the arbitral tribunal in making any subsequent determination. (3) With regard to a request for an interim measure under section 17(2)(d)', the requirements in subsection (1)(a) and (b) and subsection (2) apply only to the extent the arbitral tribunal considers appropriate.
81.	Western Australia - Commercial Arbitration Act 2012, 023 of 2012[248]	Section 17A. Conditions for granting interim measures (cf. Model Law Art 17A) (1) The party requesting an interim measure under section 17(2)(a), (b) or (c) must satisfy the arbitral tribunal that — (a) harm not adequately reparable by an award of damages is likely to result if the measure is not ordered, and that harm substantially outweighs the harm that is likely to result to the party against whom the measure is directed if the measure is granted; and (b) there is a reasonable possibility that the requesting party will succeed on the merits of the claim. (2) The determination on the possibility referred to in subsection (1)(b) does not affect the discretion of the arbitral tribunal in making any subsequent determination. (3) With regard to a request for an interim measure under section 17(2)(d), the requirements in subsection (1)(a) and (b) and subsection (2) apply only to the extent the arbitral tribunal considers appropriate.
82.	Zambia - The Arbitration Act, 2000 No. 19 of 2000[249]	No equivalent provision as Article 17A of the UNCITRAL Model Law 2006

247. http://arbitration.site/wp-content/uploads/2019/06/CAA-Vic-.pdf
248. https://www.legislation.wa.gov.au/legislation/prod/filestore.nsf/FileURL/mrdoc_25084.pdf/$FILE/Commercial%20Arbitration%20Act%202012%20-%20%5B00-b0-06%5D.pdf?OpenElement
249. http://www.newyorkconvention.org/11165/web/files/document/2/1/21396.pdf

Sr. No.	Country	Provision
83.	Zimbabwe – Chapter 7:15 Arbitration Act[250]	No equivalent provision as Article 17A of the UNCITRAL Model Law 2006

250. https://zimlii.org/akn/zw/act/1996/6/eng@2016-12-31

Appendix D (Article 17B)

Sr. No.	Country	Provision
1.	Australia - International Arbitration Act 1974[251]	Same as UNCITRAL Model Law 2006 Sec 16 Model Law to have force of law (1) Subject to this Part, the Model Law has the force of law in Australia. (2) In the Model Law: Arbitration agreement has the meaning given in Option 1 of Article 7 of the Model Law. State means Australia (including the external Territories) and any foreign country. This State means Australia (including the external Territories). Model Law under Part V, Schedule 2 of the Arbitration Act, 1974
2.	Australian Capital Territory - Commercial Arbitration Act, 2017 A2017-7[252]	SECT 17B Applications for preliminary orders and conditions for granting preliminary orders (Model Law art 17B) [omitted] Note The Model Law, art 17B, which provides for ex parte requests for interim measures together with applications for preliminary orders directing parties not to frustrate the interim measures, has been omitted.
3.	Austria - Austrian Arbitration Act, 2013[253]	No equivalent provision as Article 17B of the UNCITRAL Model Law 2006

251. https://www.legislation.gov.au/Details/C2011C00342
252. http://classic.austlii.edu.au/au/legis/act/consol_act/caa2017219/s17b.html
253. https://www.viac.eu/images/law/ZPO_Schiedsrecht_2014_en_im_VIAC_Layout.pdf

Sr. No.	Country	Provision
4.	Bahrain - Bahrain Arbitration Law No. 9/2015[254]	Same as UNCITRAL Model Law 2006 Article 1 Taking into account the provisions of international conventions in force in the Kingdom of Bahrain 1. The provisions of the " UNCITRAL " Model Law on International Commercial Arbitration Act attached to this law shall apply to all arbitration whatever the nature of the legal relationship of the dispute herewith, if this arbitration takes place in the Kingdom of Bahrain or abroad and that two parties agreed to comply with the provisions of the attached law. 2. The provisions of the attached law shall apply to all arbitration which begins after its entry into force even if based on an arbitration agreement concluded before the entry into force of this law.
5.	Bangladesh – The Arbitration Act, 2001[255]	No equivalent provision as Article 17B of the UNCITRAL Model Law 2006
6.	Belgium – Belgian Judicial Code Provisions[256]	No equivalent provision as Article 17B of the UNCITRAL Model Law 2006
7.	Bhutan - Alternative Dispute Resolution Act of Bhutan 2013[257]	No equivalent provision as Article 17B of the UNCITRAL Model Law 2006
8.	British Columbia - International Commercial Arbitration Act [RSBC 1996] Chapter 233[258]	Section 17.02 Applications for preliminary orders and conditions for granting preliminary orders (1) Unless otherwise agreed by the parties, a party may, without notice to any other party, make a request for an interim measure together with an application for a preliminary order directing a party not to frustrate the purpose of the interim measure requested. (2) Subject to subsection (3), the arbitral tribunal may grant a preliminary order if the arbitral tribunal considers that prior disclosure of the request for the interim measure to the party against whom it is directed risks frustrating the purpose of the interim measure. (3) Section 17.01 applies to an application for a preliminary order and, for that purpose, the harm to be assessed under section 17.01 (1) (a) and (b) is the harm likely to result from the order being granted or not.

254. https://pernetmartial.eu/sites/default/files/lois/Bahrain-Loi-d-arbitrage-arbitration-act-ley-de-arbitraje.pdf
255. http://www.mccibd.org/images/uploadimg/act_and_policy/corporate_governance/The-Arbitration-Act-2001.pdf
256. http://www.arbiter.com.sg/pdf/laws/Belgian%20Judicial%20Code%20Provisions%20(2013).pdf
257. https://www.nationalcouncil.bt/assets/uploads/docs/acts/2014/Alternative_Dispute_Resolution_Act_of_Bhutan_2013_eng10th.pdf
258. http://www.bclaws.ca/civix/document/id/complete/statreg/96233_01

Sr. No.	Country	Provision
9.	British Virgin Islands - Virgin Islands Arbitration Act, 2013[259]	UNCITRAL Model Law to have effect in the Virgin Islands. Section 4. The provisions of the UNCITRAL Model Law have the force of law in the Virgin Islands, subject to the modifications and supplements expressly provided in this Act. Section 35. Application of article 17B of the UNCITRAL Model Law
10.	Bulgaria - Law on International Commercial Arbitration State Gazette (SG) No. 60 of 05.08.1988[260]	No equivalent provision as Article 17B of the UNCITRAL Model Law 2006
11.	Cambodia - The Commercial Arbitration Law of the Kingdom of Cambodia 2006[261]	No equivalent provision as Article 17B of the UNCITRAL Model Law 2006
12.	Canada - Commercial Arbitration Act R.S.C., 1985, c. 17 (2nd Supp.)[262]	No equivalent provision as Article 17B of the UNCITRAL Model Law 2006 Adopted UNCITRAL Model Law 1985
13.	Connecticut - Chapter 909 Arbitration Proceedings[263]	No equivalent provision as Article 17B of the UNCITRAL Model Law 2006
14.	Croatia - Law on Arbitration Official Gazette no. 88/2001[264]	No equivalent provision as Article 17B of the UNCITRAL Model Law 2006
15.	Cyprus - The International Commercial Arbitration Law, 1987[265]	No equivalent provision as Article 17B of the UNCITRAL Model Law 2006

259. http://www.bviiac.org/Portals/0/Files/Arbitration%20Documents/ArbitrationAct2013.pdf
260. http://www.newyorkconvention.org/11165/web/files/document/1/6/16200.pdf
261. https://www.cambodiaip.gov.kh/DocResources/372a361b-7a97-44b3-9810-79e5e6ea85f4_c786a043-b88d-4f64-9429-60a330efdc5f-en.pdf
262. https://laws-lois.justice.gc.ca/eng/acts/C-34.6/index.html
263. https://www.cga.ct.gov/current/pub/chap_909.htm
264. http://www.vsrh.hr/CustomPages/Static/HRV/Files/Legislation__Law-Arbitration-RC.pdf
265. https://www.uv.es/medarb/observatorio/leyes-arbitraje/europa-resto/chipre-international-commercial-arbitration-law.pdf

Sr. No.	Country	Provision
16.	Denmark – Danish Arbitration Act 2005[266]	No equivalent provision as Article 17B of the UNCITRAL Model Law 2006
17.	Egypt - Law No. 27/1994 Promulgating the Law Concerning Arbitration in Civil and Commercial Matters[267]	No equivalent provision as Article 17B of the UNCITRAL Model Law 2006
18.	Florida Chapter 684 – International Commercial Arbitration, Title XXXIX Commercial Relations, 2020 Florida Statutes[268]	Same as Article 17B of the UNCITRAL Model Law 2006 Article 684.002 Applications for preliminary orders and conditions for granting preliminary orders.
19.	Fiji – International Arbitration Act 2017 (Act No. 44 of 2017)[269]	Section 25 - Applications for preliminary orders and conditions for granting preliminary orders (1) Unless otherwise agreed by the parties, a party may, without notice to any other party, make a request for an interim measure together with an application for a preliminary order directing a party not to frustrate the purpose of the interim measure requested. (2) The arbitral tribunal may grant a preliminary order provided it considers that prior disclosure of the request for the interim measure to the party against whom it is directed risks frustrating the purpose of the measure. (3) The conditions defined under section 24 apply to any preliminary order, provided that the harm to be assessed under section 24(1)(a), is the harm likely to result from the order being granted or not.
20.	France – Book IV - Arbitration of the Code of Civil Procedure Decree No. 2011-48[270]	No equivalent provision as Article 17B of the UNCITRAL Model Law 2006

266. https://voldgiftsinstituttet.dk/wp-content/uploads/2015/01/danish_arbitration_act_2005.pdf
267. https://www.wipo.int/edocs/lexdocs/laws/en/eg/eg020en.pdf
268. https://www.flsenate.gov/Laws/Statutes/2020/Chapter684/All
269. https://www.fiji.gov.fj/getattachment/d9502667-6491-4592-85b2-eff97f245fed/Act-44---International-Arbitration-Act.aspx
270. http://www.iaiparis.com/pdf/FRENCH_LAW_ON_INTERNATIONAL_ARBITRATION.pdf

Sr. No.	Country	Provision
21.	Georgia - Chapter 9 Arbitration, Title 9 Civil Practice, Georgia Code[271]	No equivalent provision as Article 17B of the UNCITRAL Model Law 2006
22.	Germany - Tenth Book of the Code of Civil Procedure, Arbitration Procedure[272]	No equivalent provision as Article 17B of the UNCITRAL Model Law 2006
23.	Greece - Code of Civil Procedure, Book VII, Book VIII[273]	No equivalent provision as Article 17B of the UNCITRAL Model Law 2006
24.	Hong Kong - Cap. 609 Arbitration Ordinance[274]	Same as Article 17B of the UNCITRAL Model Law 2006 Section 37 - Article 17B of UNCITRAL Model Law (Applications for preliminary orders and conditions for granting preliminary orders)
25.	Hungary - Act LX of 2017 on Arbitration[275]	Section 20 (1) Unless otherwise agreed by the parties, the party may make a request for an interim measure together with an application for a preliminary order directing a party not to frustrate the purpose of the interim measure requested. (2) The arbitral tribunal may grant a preliminary order provided it considers that prior disclosure of the request for interim measure to the party against whom it is directed would risk frustrating the purpose of the measure.
26.	Ireland - Arbitration Act 2010 Number 1 of 2010[276]	Section 6 - Adoption of Model Law Subject to this Act, the Model Law shall have the force of law in the State and shall apply to arbitrations under arbitration agreements concerning— (a) international commercial arbitrations, or (b) arbitrations which are not international commercial arbitrations. Same as Article 17B of the UNCITRAL Model Law Article 17B under Schedule 1 - TEXT OF UNCITRAL MODEL LAW ON INTERNATIONAL COMMERCIAL ARBITRATION

271. https://matsne.gov.ge/ru/document/download/89284/5/en/pdf
272. https://sccinstitute.com/media/29988/german-arbitration-act.pdf
273. https://www.uv.es/medarb/observatorio/leyes-arbitraje/europa-resto/grecia-ccp-domestic-arbitration.pdf
274. https://www.elegislation.gov.hk/hk/cap609
275. https://www.ilo.org/dyn/natlex/docs/ELECTRONIC/106843/131257/F-266585574/J2017T0060P_20180102_FIN.pdf
276. http://www.irishstatutebook.ie/eli/2010/act/1/enacted/en/pdf

Sr. No.	Country	Provision
27.	Jamaica – The Arbitration Act, 2017 (Act 13 of 2017)[277]	Section 22 - Applications for preliminary orders and conditions for granting preliminary orders. (1) Unless otherwise agreed by the parties, a party may, without notice to any other party, make a request for an interim measure together with an application for a preliminary order directing a party not to frustrate the purpose of the interim measure requested. (2) The arbitral tribunal may grant a preliminary order provided it considers that prior disclosure of the request for the interim measure to the party against whom it is directed risks frustrating the purpose of the measure. (3) The conditions set out in section 21 apply to any preliminary order, provided that the harm to be assessed under section 21 (1)(a), is the harm likely to result from the order being granted or not.
28.	Japan – Arbitration Law (Law No.138 of 2003)[278]	No equivalent provision as Article 17B of the UNCITRAL Model Law 2006
29.	Jordan – Law No. 31 of 2001 (Jordan) Arbitration Law[279]	No equivalent provision as Article 17B of the UNCITRAL Model Law 2006
30.	Kenya – Chapter 49 Arbitration Act (The Arbitration Act, 1995)[280]	No equivalent provision as Article 17B of the UNCITRAL Model Law 2006
31.	Liechtenstein - Liechtenstein Arbitration Law (Code of Civil Procedure)[281]	No equivalent provision as Article 17B of the UNCITRAL Model Law 2006
32.	Lithuania – The Republic of Lithuania Law on Commercial Arbitration, 2012[282]	Article 21. Preliminary Orders 1. Unless otherwise agreed by the parties, a party may apply to an arbitral tribunal for interim measures without a notice to the other party by submitting an application for a preliminary order obliging the respective party, in the course of handling of the application for interim measures, not to take any actions that may affect the application of interim measures.

277. http://extwprlegs1.fao.org/docs/pdf/jam172060.pdf
278. https://japan.kantei.go.jp/policy/sihou/arbitrationlaw.pdf
279. https://www.ilo.org/dyn/natlex/docs/ELECTRONIC/63091/95325/F1864661120/JOR63091.pdf
280. https://ncia.or.ke/wp-content/uploads/2021/02/ArbitrationAct4of1995_2.pdf
281. https://www.newyorkconvention.org/11165/web/files/document/2/1/21372.pdf
282. https://e-seimas.lrs.lt/portal/legalAct/lt/TAD/35954312dcb311e6be918a531b2126ab?jfwid=-wd7z7zum0

Sr. No.	Country	Provision
		2. A party requesting an arbitral tribunal to give a preliminary order must prove that: 1) a notice to the other party of the application for interim measures may be substantially detrimental with regard to the purposes of those measures; 2) there are grounds indicated in Article 20(3)(1) and (3) of this Law. 3. A party requesting an arbitral tribunal to give a preliminary order must inform the arbitral tribunal of all circumstances that may be significant for the consideration of the application. This obligation of the party shall be valid over the period of validity of the preliminary order.
33.	Louisiana - RS 9 Title 9.Civil Code-Ancillaries[283]	No equivalent provision as Article 17B of the UNCITRAL Model Law 2006
34.	Macedonia - Law on International Commercial Arbitration of the Republic of Macedonia[284]	No equivalent provision as Article 17B of the UNCITRAL Model Law 2006
35.	Malaysia - Arbitration Act 2005, Act 646[285]	No equivalent provision as Article 17B of the UNCITRAL Model Law 2006
36.	Maldives - Act No: 10/2013, Arbitration Act[286]	Section 34 - Granting an Ex Parte Order for Interim Measures (a) Notwithstanding the provisions in Section 33 I, the Arbitral Tribunal has the power to grant an order for interim measures upon the application of one party to the dispute without notifying the other. Nevertheless, such an order may only be issued by the Arbitral Tribunal if it is satisfied that the prior disclosure of the order to the other parties to the dispute may risk frustrating the purpose of the measure.
37.	Malta - CAP. 387 Arbitration Act[287]	No equivalent provision as Article 17B of the UNCITRAL Model Law 2006
38.	Mauritius - The International Arbitration Act, 2008 (Act 37 of 2008)[288]	Same as Article 17C of the UNCITRAL Model Law 2006 Third Schedule Part IV - Interim Measures by Tribunal Section 21 (Interim measures by tribunal) Articles 17 to 17G

283. http://legis.la.gov/legis/Laws_Toc.aspx?folder=83&title=9
284. https://www.international-arbitration-attorney.com/wp-content/uploads/2013/07/Macedonia-Arbitration-Law.pdf
285. http://www.newyorkconvention.org/11165/web/files/document/1/6/16298.pdf
286. https://miac.gov.mv/media/documents/Arbitration%20Act.pdf
287. http://justiceservices.gov.mt/DownloadDocument.aspx?app=lom&itemid=8854&l=1
288. https://www.wipo.int/edocs/lexdocs/laws/en/mu/mu020en.pdf

Sr. No.	Country	Provision
39.	Montenegro – Decree on the Promulgation of the Law on Arbitration, 2015[289]	No equivalent provision as Article 17B of the UNCITRAL Model Law 2006
40.	Myanmar – Arbitration Law The Pyidaungsu Hluttaw Law No. 5/2016[290]	No equivalent provision as Article 17B of the UNCITRAL Model Law 2006
41.	New South Wales - Commercial Arbitration Act 2010 No 61[291]	Section 17B Note. Art 17B of the Model Law, which provides for ex parte requests for interim measures together with applications for preliminary orders directing parties not to frustrate the interim measures, has been omitted.
42.	New Zealand – The Arbitration Act, 1996 No 99[292]	Schedule I- Rules applying to arbitration agreement Article 17C Power of arbitral tribunal to issue preliminary order Unless otherwise agreed by the parties, a party may, without notice to any other party, apply for a preliminary order when making a request for an interim measure to be granted under article 17A. Article17D Conditions for issuing preliminary order (1) The arbitral tribunal may issue a preliminary order if it considers that prior disclosure of the request for the interim measure to the respondent risks frustrating the purpose of the measure. (2) An applicant for a preliminary order must satisfy the arbitral tribunal of the matters specified in article 17B. That article applies to a preliminary order subject to- (a) the modification that the harm to be assessed under article 17B(1)(a) is the harm likely to result from the order being issued or not; and (b) all other necessary modifications.
43.	Nigeria - Arbitration and Conciliation Act Chapter 19 Laws of the Federation of Nigeria 1990[293]	No equivalent provision as Article 17B of the UNCITRAL Model Law 2006

289. https://www.privrednakomora.me/sites/pkcg.org/files/multimedia/main_pages/files/2012/09/final_eng_zakon_o_arbitrazi_final_0.pdf
290. http://www.newyorkconvention.org/11165/web/files/document/2/1/21098.pdf
291. https://legislation.nsw.gov.au/view/html/inforce/current/act-2010-061#sec.17B
292. http://www.legislation.govt.nz/act/public/1996/0099/latest/whole.html#DLM403277
293. http://niqs.org.ng/wp-content/uploads/2018/12/Arbitration-and-Conciliation-Act.pdf

Sr. No.	Country	Provision
44.	Northern Territory of Australia - Commercial Arbitration (National Uniform Legislation) Act 2011[294]	Section 17B (not used) Note for section 17B Art 17B of the Model Law, which provides for ex parte requests for interim measures together with applications for preliminary orders directing parties not to frustrate the interim measures, has been omitted.
45.	Norway - Act of 14 May 2004 No. 25 relating to Arbitration (The Arbitration Act)[295]	No equivalent provision as Article 17B of the UNCITRAL Model Law 2006
46.	Oman - The Omani Law of Arbitration in Civil and Commercial Disputes – Royal Decree 47/97[296]	No equivalent provision as Article 17B of the UNCITRAL Model Law 2006
47.	Ontario - International Commercial Arbitration Act, 2017, S.O. 2017, c. 2, Sched. 5[297]	Section 5 - Application of Model Law (1) Subject to this Act, the Model Law on International Commercial Arbitration, adopted by the United Nations Commission on International Trade Law on 21 June 1985, as amended by the United Nations Commission on International Trade Law on 7 July 2006, set out in Schedule 2, has force of law in Ontario. Same (2) With respect to article 7 of the Model Law, option I applies in Ontario; option II does not. Same (3) The Model Law applies to international commercial arbitration agreements and awards made in international commercial arbitrations, whether made before or after the coming into force of this Act. Schedule 2 to this Act Article 17B
48.	Oregon – Oregon International Commercial Arbitration and Conciliation Act[298]	No equivalent provision as Article 17B of the UNCITRAL Model Law 2006

294. https://legislation.nt.gov.au/api/sitecore/Act/PDF?id = 11692
295. https://www.chamber.no/wp-content/uploads/2014/02/Norwegian_Arbitration_Act.pdf
296. http://www.newyorkconvention.org/11165/web/files/document/2/1/21103.pdf
297. https://www.ontario.ca/laws/statute/17i02b#BK16
298. https://www.oregonlegislature.gov/bills_laws/ors/ors036.html

Sr. No.	Country	Provision
49.	Pakistan - The Arbitration Act, 1940 Act No. X of 1940[299]	No equivalent provision as Article 17B of the UNCITRAL Model Law 2006
50.	Philippines - Alternative Dispute Resolution Act of 2004 Republic Act No. 9285[300]	No equivalent provision as Article 17B of the UNCITRAL Model Law 2006
51.	Poland – Polish Act of 17 November 1964 - Code of Civil Procedure, Part Five Arbitration[301]	No equivalent provision as Article 17B of the UNCITRAL Model Law 2006
52.	Qatar - Law No. 2 of 2017 Promulgating the Civil and Commercial Arbitration Law-The Law of Arbitration in Civil and Commercial Matters[302]	No equivalent provision as Article 17B of the UNCITRAL Model Law 2006
53.	Queensland - Commercial Arbitration Act 2013 No. 8[303]	Section 17B Applications for preliminary orders and conditions for granting preliminary orders (cf Model Law Art 17B) [omitted] Note— Art 17B of the Model Law, which provides for ex parte requests for interim measures together with applications for preliminary orders directing parties not to frustrate the interim measures, has been omitted.
54.	Republic of Costa Rica - Costa Rican Law for International Arbitration Law Number: 8937[304]	Same as Article 17B UNCITRAL Model Law 2006

299. https://www.wipo.int/edocs/lexdocs/laws/en/pk/pk066en.pdf
300. http://www.newyorkconvention.org/11165/web/files/document/2/1/21107.pdf
301. https://www.uv.es/medarb/observatorio/leyes-arbitraje/europa-resto/polonia-ccp-arbitration.pdf
302. https://www.qicdrc.gov.qa/sites/default/files/inline-files/law_no._02_2017_promulgating_the_civil_and_commercial_arbitration_law.pdf
303. https://www.legislation.qld.gov.au/view/pdf/inforce/2013-05-17/act-2013-008

Sr. No.	Country	Provision
55.	Republic of Korea - Arbitration Act[305]	No equivalent provision as Article 17B of the UNCITRAL Model Law 2006
56.	Russia - Russian Federation Law on International Commercial Arbitration[306]	No equivalent provision as Article 17B of the UNCITRAL Model Law 2006
57.	Rwanda - Law on arbitration and conciliation in commercial matters, N° 005/2008[307]	Article 24: Applications for preliminary Orders and conditions for granting them. Unless otherwise agreed by the parties, one of them may, not necessarily after consulting another party, request for an interim measure together with an application for a preliminary Order directing a party not to frustrate the purpose of the interim measure requested. The arbitral tribunal may grant a preliminary Order if it considers that prior disclosure of the request for the interim measure to the party against whom it is directed risks frustrating the purpose of the measure. The conditions defined under Article 20 apply to any preliminary Order, if the loss is assessed in accordance with Article 20, Paragraph 1, littera 1°, is the one likely to result from the Order being granted or not.
58.	Saudi Arabia - Law of Arbitration Royal Decree No. M/34[308]	No equivalent provision as Article 17B of the UNCITRAL Model Law 2006
59.	Serbia - Law on Arbitration No. 46/06[309]	No equivalent provision as Article 17B of the UNCITRAL Model Law 2006
60.	Singapore - Arbitration Act (Chapter 10) (Domestic Arbitration Law)[310]	No equivalent provision as Article 17B of the UNCITRAL Model Law 2006

304. https://arbitratlaw.com/wp-content/uploads/2017/01/Costa-Rican-Intl-Arbitration-Law.pdf
305. https://elaw.klri.re.kr/eng_service/lawView.do?hseq=38889&lang=ENG
306. http://www.newyorkconvention.org/11165/web/files/document/2/2/22335.pdf
307. http://www.newyorkconvention.org/11165/web/files/document/2/1/21110.pdf
308. https://www.wipo.int/edocs/lexdocs/laws/en/sa/sa057en.pdf
309. https://www.wipo.int/edocs/lexdocs/laws/en/rs/rs028en.pdf
310. https://sso.agc.gov.sg/Act/AA2001

Sr. No.	Country	Provision
61.	Singapore - International Arbitration Act (Chapter 143A) (International Arbitration Law)[311]	No equivalent provision as Article 17B of the UNCITRAL Model Law 2006
62.	Slovakia – [Slovak] Act No. 244/2002 of 3 April 2002 on Arbitration[312]	No equivalent provision as Article 17B of the UNCITRAL Model Law 2006
63.	Slovenia - Law on Arbitration of Slovenia[313]	No equivalent provision as Article 17B of the UNCITRAL Model Law 2006
64.	South Africa – The Arbitration Act, 1965[314]	No equivalent provision as Article 17B of the UNCITRAL Model Law 2006
65.	South Australia - South Australia Commercial Arbitration Act 2011[315]	Section 17B Note— Art 17B of the Model Law, which provides for ex parte requests for interim measures together with applications for preliminary orders directing parties not to frustrate the interim measures, has been omitted.
66.	Spain - Act 60/2003 of 23 December on Arbitration[316]	No equivalent provision as Article 17B of the UNCITRAL Model Law 2006
67.	Sri Lanka - Arbitration Act. No. 11 of 1995[317]	No equivalent provision as Article 17B of the UNCITRAL Model Law 2006
68.	Sweden – The Swedish Arbitration Act (SFS 1996:116)[318]	No equivalent provision as Article 17B of the UNCITRAL Model Law 2006

311. https://sso.agc.gov.sg/Act/IAA1994
312. https://www.international-arbitration-attorney.com/wp-content/uploads/2013/07/Slovakia-Arbitration-Law-1.pdf
313. http://www.sloarbitration.eu/Portals/0/Arbitrazno-pravo/Law%20on%20Arbitration%20of%20Slovenia.pdf
314. https://www.gov.za/sites/default/files/gcis_document/201505/act-42-1965.pdf
315. https://www.legislation.sa.gov.au/LZ/C/A/COMMERCIAL%20ARBITRATION%20ACT%202011/CURRENT/2011.32.UN.PDF
316. https://www.mjusticia.gob.es/cs/Satellite/Portal/1292426982249?blobheader=application%2Fpdf&blobheadername1=Content-Disposition&blobheadervalue1=attachment%3B+filename%3DAct_on_arbitration_%28Ley_60_2003__de_arbitraje%29.PDF
317. http://www.slnarbcentre.com/pdf/ARBITRATION-ACT.pdf
318. https://sccinstitute.com/media/37089/the-swedish-arbitration-act.pdf

Sr. No.	Country	Provision
69.	Switzerland - Private International Law Act 1987, Chapter 12: International Arbitration[319]	No equivalent provision as Article 17B of the UNCITRAL Model Law 2006
70.	Tasmania - Commercial Arbitration Act, 2011, Act 13 of 2011[320]	Section 17B. .... . Note. Art 17B of the Model Law, which provides for ex parte requests for interim measures together with applications for preliminary orders directing parties not to frustrate the interim measures, has been omitted.
71.	Texas - Chapter 172. Arbitration and Conciliation of International Commercial Disputes, Civil Practice and Remedies Code[321]	No equivalent provision as Article 17B of the UNCITRAL Model Law 2006
72.	Thailand - Arbitration Act B.E. 2545[322]	No equivalent provision as Article 17B of the UNCITRAL Model Law 2006
73.	Tunisia - Law n° 93-42 issued on April 26, related to the promulgation of the Arbitration Code[323]	No equivalent provision as Article 17B of the UNCITRAL Model Law 2006
74.	Turkey - Turkish International Arbitration Law, Law no. 4686, 2001[324]	No equivalent provision as Article 17B of the UNCITRAL Model Law 2006
75.	Uganda - Chapter 4 The Arbitration and Conciliation Act[325]	No equivalent provision as Article 17B of the UNCITRAL Model Law 2006

319. https://www.swissarbitration.org/wp-content/uploads/2021/05/20210129-Chapter-12-PILA_Translation_English.pdf
320. https://www.legislation.tas.gov.au/view/html/inforce/current/act-2011-013
321. https://statutes.capitol.texas.gov/Docs/CP/htm/CP.172.htm
322. https://tai.coj.go.th/th/file/get/file/20190328ecac5333356ffad0331bd601151db9f4142557.pdf
323. https://arbitrationlaw.com/sites/default/files/free_pdfs/Tunisia%20Arbitration%20Code.pdf
324. http://www.camera-arbitrale.it/Documenti/tial_turkey.pdf

Sr. No.	Country	Provision
76.	Ukraine - The Law of Ukraine on International Commercial Arbitration[326]	No equivalent provision as Article 17B of the UNCITRAL Model Law 2006
77.	United Arab Emirates - Federal Law No. (6) of 2018 on Arbitration[327]	No equivalent provision as Article 17B of the UNCITRAL Model Law 2006
78.	Uruguay - Law 19,636 Approve Rules for International Commercial Arbitration[328]	No equivalent provision as Article 17B of the UNCITRAL Model Law 2006
79.	Venezuela – Venezuelan Commercial Arbitration Act[329]	No equivalent provision as Article 17B of the UNCITRAL Model Law 2006
80.	Victoria - Commercial Arbitration Act 2011 No. 50 of 2011[330]	Section 17B [omitted] Note Art 17B of the Model Law, which provides for ex parte requests for interim measures together with applications for preliminary orders directing parties not to frustrate the interim measures, has been omitted.
81.	Western Australia - Commercial Arbitration Act 2012, 023 of 2012[331]	Section 17B. (Not used) Note for this section: Art 17B of the Model Law, which provides for ex parte requests for interim measures together with applications for preliminary orders directing parties not to frustrate the interim measures, has been omitted.

325. https://ulii.org/akn/ug/act/2000/7/eng@2008-06-27
326. http://arbitrations.ru/userfiles/file/Law/Arbitration%20acts/ukraininan%20law%20on%20arbitration.pdf
327. https://www.tamimi.com/crm-media-uploader/fileupload/server/php/files/UAE%20Arbitration%20Law%20-%20Federal%20Law%20No%20%206%20of%202018.pdf
328. http://www.impo.com.uy/bases/leyes-originales/19636-2018
329. https://arbitrationlaw.com/sites/default/files/free_pdfs/Venezula%20Commercial%20Arbitration%20Act.pdf
330. http://arbitration.site/wp-content/uploads/2019/06/CAA-Vic-.pdf
331. https://www.legislation.wa.gov.au/legislation/prod/filestore.nsf/FileURL/mrdoc_25084.pdf/$FILE/Commercial%20Arbitration%20Act%202012%20-%20%5B00-b0-06%5D.pdf?OpenElement

Sr. No.	Country	Provision
82.	Zambia – The Arbitration Act, 2000 No. 19 of 2000[332]	No equivalent provision as Article 17B of the UNCITRAL Model Law 2006
83.	Zimbabwe – Chapter 7:15 Arbitration Act[333]	No equivalent provision as Article 17B of the UNCITRAL Model Law 2006

332. http://www.newyorkconvention.org/11165/web/files/document/2/1/21396.pdf
333. https://zimlii.org/akn/zw/act/1996/6/eng@2016-12-31

Appendix E (Article 17C)

Sr. No.	Country	Provision
1.	Australia - International Arbitration Act 1974[334]	Same as UNCITRAL Model Law 2006 Sec 16 Model Law to have force of law (1) Subject to this Part, the Model Law has the force of law in Australia. (2) In the Model Law: Arbitration agreement has the meaning given in Option 1 of Article 7 of the Model Law. State means Australia (including the external Territories) and any foreign country. This State means Australia (including the external Territories). Model Law under Part V, Schedule 2 of the Arbitration Act, 1974
2.	Australian Capital Territory – Commercial Arbitration Act, 2017 A2017-7[335]	SECT 17C Specific regime for preliminary orders (Model Law art 17C) [omitted] Note The Model Law, art 17C, which contains safeguards for the party against whom a preliminary order is directed under art 17B, is omitted as a consequence of the omission of art 17B.
3.	Austria – Austrian Arbitration Act, 2013[336]	No equivalent provision as Article 17C of the UNCITRAL Model Law 2006
4.	Bahrain - Bahrain Arbitration Law No. 9/2015[337]	Same as UNCITRAL Model Law 2006 Article 1 Taking into account the provisions of international conventions in force in the Kingdom of Bahrain

334. https://www.legislation.gov.au/Details/C2011C00342
335. http://classic.austlii.edu.au/au/legis/act/consol_act/caa2017219/s17c.html
336. https://www.viac.eu/images/law/ZPO_Schiedsrecht_2014_en_im_VIAC_Layout.pdf
337. https://pernetmartial.eu/sites/default/files/lois/Bahrain-Loi-d-arbitrage-arbitration-act-ley-de-arbitraje.pdf

Sr. No.	Country	Provision
		1. The provisions of the " UNCITRAL " Model Law on International Commercial Arbitration Act attached to this law shall apply to all arbitration whatever the nature of the legal relationship of the dispute herewith, if this arbitration takes place in the Kingdom of Bahrain or abroad and that two parties agreed to comply with the provisions of the attached law. 2. The provisions of the attached law shall apply to all arbitration which begins after its entry into force even if based on an arbitration agreement concluded before the entry into force of this law.
5.	Bangladesh - The Arbitration Act, 2001[338]	Section 21. Powers of the arbitration tribunal to make interim orders.- (3) No order under this section shall be passed without giving a notice to the other parties: Provided that the arbitral tribunal may, where it appears that the object of taking interim measure under this section would be defeated by the delay, dispense with such notice.
6.	Belgium - Belgian Judicial Code Provisions[339]	No equivalent provision as Article 17C of the UNCITRAL Model Law 2006
7.	Bhutan - Alternative Dispute Resolution Act of Bhutan 2013[340]	No equivalent provision as Article 17C of the UNCITRAL Model Law 2006
8.	British Columbia - International Commercial Arbitration Act [RSBC 1996] Chapter 233[341]	Section 17.03 Specific regime for preliminary orders (1) Immediately after the arbitral tribunal makes a determination in respect of an application for a preliminary order, the arbitral tribunal must give notice to all the parties of the following: (a) the request for the interim measure; (b) the application for the preliminary order; (c) the preliminary order, if any; (d) all other communications, including by indicating the content of any oral communication, between any party and the arbitral tribunal in relation to a matter referred to in paragraph (a), (b) or (c). (2) At the same time, the arbitral tribunal must give an opportunity to any party against whom a preliminary order is directed to present the party's case at the earliest practicable time.

338. http://www.mccibd.org/images/uploadimg/act_and_policy/corporate_governance/The-Arbitration-Act-2001.pdf
339. http://www.arbiter.com.sg/pdf/laws/Belgian%20Judicial%20Code%20Provisions%20(2013).pdf
340. https://www.nationalcouncil.bt/assets/uploads/docs/acts/2014/Alternative_Dispute_Resolution_Act_of_Bhutan_2013_eng10th.pdf
341. http://www.bclaws.ca/civix/document/id/complete/statreg/96233_01

Sr. No.	Country	Provision
		(3) The arbitral tribunal must decide promptly on any objection to a preliminary order. (4) A preliminary order expires 20 days after the date on which it was issued by the arbitral tribunal. (5) After the party against whom a preliminary order is directed has been given notice and an opportunity to present its case, the arbitral tribunal may issue an interim measure adopting or modifying the preliminary order. (6) A preliminary order (a) is binding on the parties but is not subject to enforcement by a court, and (b) is not an arbitral award.
9.	British Virgin Islands - Virgin Islands Arbitration Act, 2013[342]	UNCITRAL Model Law to have effect in the Virgin Islands. Section 4. The provisions of the UNCITRAL Model Law have the force of law in the Virgin Islands, subject to the modifications and supplements expressly provided in this Act. Section 36. Application of article 17C of the UNCITRAL Model Law
10.	Bulgaria - Law on International Commercial Arbitration State Gazette (SG) No. 60 of 05.08.1988[343]	No equivalent provision as Article 17C of the UNCITRAL Model Law 2006
11.	Cambodia - The Commercial Arbitration Law of the Kingdom of Cambodia 2006[344]	No equivalent provision as Article 17C of the UNCITRAL Model Law 2006
12.	Canada – Commercial Arbitration Act R.S.C., 1985, c. 17 (2nd Supp.)[345]	No equivalent provision as Article 17C of the UNCITRAL Model Law 2006
13.	Connecticut - Chapter 909 Arbitration Proceedings[346]	No equivalent provision as Article 17C of the UNCITRAL Model Law 2006

342. http://www.bviiac.org/Portals/0/Files/Arbitration%20Documents/ArbitrationAct2013.pdf
343. http://www.newyorkconvention.org/11165/web/files/document/1/6/16200.pdf
344. https://www.cambodiaip.gov.kh/DocResources/372a361b-7a97-44b3-9810-79e5e6ea85f4_c786a043-b88d-4f64-9429-60a330efdc5f-en.pdf
345. https://laws-lois.justice.gc.ca/eng/acts/C-34.6/index.html
346. https://www.cga.ct.gov/current/pub/chap_909.htm

Sr. No.	Country	Provision
14.	Croatia – Law on Arbitration Official Gazette no. 88/2001[347]	No equivalent provision as Article 17C of the UNCITRAL Model Law 2006
15.	Cyprus – The International Commercial Arbitration Law, 1987[348]	No equivalent provision as Article 17C of the UNCITRAL Model Law 2006
16.	Denmark – Danish Arbitration Act 2005[349]	No equivalent provision as Article 17C of the UNCITRAL Model Law 2006
17.	Egypt - Law No. 27/1994 Promulgating the Law Concerning Arbitration in Civil and Commercial Matters[350]	No equivalent provision as Article 17C of the UNCITRAL Model Law 2006
18.	Florida Chapter 684 – International Commercial Arbitration, Title XXXIX Commercial Relations, 2020 Florida Statutes[351]	Same as Article 17C of the UNCITRAL Model Law 2006 Article 684.0021 Specific Regime for Preliminary Orders
19.	Fiji – International Arbitration Act 2017 (Act No. 44 of 2017)[352]	Section 26 Specific regime for preliminary orders (1) Immediately after the arbitral tribunal has made a determination in respect of an application for a preliminary order, the arbitral tribunal shall give notice to all parties of the request for the interim measure, the application for the preliminary order, the preliminary order, if any, and all other communications, including by indicating the content of any oral communication, between any party and the arbitral tribunal in relation thereto. (2) At the same time, the arbitral tribunal shall give an opportunity to any party against whom a preliminary order is directed to present its case at the earliest practicable time.

347. http://www.vsrh.hr/CustomPages/Static/HRV/Files/Legislation__Law-Arbitration-RC.pdf
348. https://www.uv.es/medarb/observatorio/leyes-arbitraje/europa-resto/chipre-international-commercial-arbitration-law.pdf
349. https://voldgiftsinstituttet.dk/wp-content/uploads/2015/01/danish_arbitration_act_2005.pdf
350. https://www.wipo.int/edocs/lexdocs/laws/en/eg/eg020en.pdf
351. https://www.flsenate.gov/Laws/Statutes/2020/Chapter684/All
352. https://www.fiji.gov.fj/getattachment/d9502667-6491-4592-85b2-eff97f245fed/Act-44---International-Arbitration-Act.aspx

Sr. No.	Country	Provision
		(3) The arbitral tribunal shall decide promptly on any objection to the preliminary order. (4) A preliminary order shall expire after 20 days from the date on which it was issued by the arbitral tribunal. However, the arbitral tribunal may issue an interim measure adopting or modifying the preliminary order, after the party against whom the preliminary order is directed has been given notice and an opportunity to present its case. (5) A preliminary order shall be binding on the parties but shall not be subject to enforcement by a court. Such a preliminary order does not constitute an award.
20.	France - Book IV - Arbitration of the Code of Civil Procedure Decree No. 2011-48[353]	No equivalent provision as Article 17C of the UNCITRAL Model Law 2006
21.	Georgia - Chapter 9 Arbitration, Title 9 Civil Practice, Georgia Code[354]	No equivalent provision as Article 17C of the UNCITRAL Model Law 2006
22.	Germany - Tenth Book of the Code of Civil Procedure, Arbitration Procedure[355]	No equivalent provision as Article 17C of the UNCITRAL Model Law 2006
23.	Greece - Code of Civil Procedure, Book VII, Book VIII[356]	No equivalent provision as Article 17C of the UNCITRAL Model Law 2006
24.	Hong Kong - Cap. 609 Arbitration Ordinance[357]	Same as Article 17C of the UNCITRAL Model Law 2006 Section 38 - Article 17C of UNCITRAL Model Law (Specific regime for preliminary orders)
25.	Hungary - Act LX of 2017 on Arbitration[358]	Section 21 (1) The arbitral tribunal shall give notice to all parties of the determination made in respect of an application for a preliminary order, and, at the same time, it shall provide information about the content of any oral communication between the parties and the arbitral tribunal in relation thereto.

353. http://www.iaiparis.com/pdf/FRENCH_LAW_ON_INTERNATIONAL_ARBITRATION.pdf
354. https://matsne.gov.ge/ru/document/download/89284/5/en/pdf
355. https://sccinstitute.com/media/29988/german-arbitration-act.pdf
356. https://www.uv.es/medarb/observatorio/leyes-arbitraje/europa-resto/grecia-ccp-domestic-arbitration.pdf
357. https://www.elegislation.gov.hk/hk/cap609
358. https://www.ilo.org/dyn/natlex/docs/ELECTRONIC/106843/131257/F-266585574/J2017T0060P_20180102_FIN.pdf

Sr. No.	Country	Provision
		(2) After having made a determination in respect of an application for a preliminary order, the arbitral tribunal shall give an opportunity to the party against whom a preliminary order is directed to present his case at the earliest practicable time. (3) The arbitral tribunal shall decide promptly on any objection to the preliminary order. (4) A preliminary order shall expire after twenty days from the date on which it was issued. (5) The arbitral tribunal may issue an interim measure adopting or modifying the preliminary order, after the party against whom the preliminary order is directed has been given notice and an opportunity to present its case. (6) A preliminary order shall be binding on the parties; however, it shall not be the subject of judicial enforcement.
26.	Ireland - Arbitration Act 2010 Number 1 of 2010[359]	Section 6 - Adoption of Model Law Subject to this Act, the Model Law shall have the force of law in the State and shall apply to arbitrations under arbitration agreements concerning— (a) international commercial arbitrations, or (b) arbitrations which are not international commercial arbitrations. Same as Article 17C of the UNCITRAL Model Law Article 17C under Schedule 1 - TEXT OF UNCITRAL MODEL LAW ON INTERNATIONAL COMMERCIAL ARBITRATION
27.	Jamaica - The Arbitration Act, 2017 (Act 13 of 2017)[360]	Section 23. Specific regime for Preliminary orders. (1) Immediately after the arbitral tribunal has made a determination in respect of an application for a preliminary order, the arbitral tribunal shall give notice to all parties of the request for the interim measure, the application for the preliminary order, the preliminary order, if any, and all other communications, including by indicating the content of any oral communication, between any party and the arbitral tribunal in relation thereto. (2) The arbitral tribunal shall give an opportunity to any party against whom a preliminary order is directed to present its case at the earliest practicable time. (3) The arbitral tribunal shall decide promptly on any objection to the preliminary order. (4) A preliminary order shall expire after twenty days from the date on which it was issued by the arbitral tribunal, however, the arbitral tribunal may issue an interim measure adopting or modifying the preliminary order, after the party against whom the preliminary order is directed has been given notice and an opportunity to present its case.

359. http://www.irishstatutebook.ie/eli/2010/act/1/enacted/en/pdf
360. http://extwprlegs1.fao.org/docs/pdf/jam172060.pdf

Sr. No.	Country	Provision
		(5) A preliminary order- (a) shall be binding on the parties but shall not be subject to enforcement by a court; and (b) does not constitute an award.
28.	Japan - Arbitration Law (Law No.138 of 2003)[361]	No equivalent provision as Article 17C of the UNCITRAL Model Law 2006
29.	Jordan - Law No. 31 of 2001 (Jordan) Arbitration Law[362]	No equivalent provision as Article 17C of the UNCITRAL Model Law 2006
30.	Kenya - Chapter 49 Arbitration Act (The Arbitration Act, 1995)[363]	No equivalent provision as Article 17C of the UNCITRAL Model Law 2006
31.	Liechtenstein - Liechtenstein Arbitration Law (Code of Civil Procedure)[364]	No equivalent provision as Article 17C of the UNCITRAL Model Law 2006
32.	Lithuania - The Republic of Lithuania Law on Commercial Arbitration, 2012[365]	Article 21 Preliminary Orders 1. Unless the parties have agreed otherwise, a party may request the arbitral tribunal to apply interim measures without notice to the other party by submitting an application for a preliminary ruling obligating the respective party not to take any actions that may impede the applying of interim measures during the examination of the application for interim measures. 2. The party requesting the arbitral tribunal to make a preliminary ruling shall prove that: 1) the notice to the other party on the application for interim measures may significantly prevent the goals of such measures from being achieved; 2) the grounds indicated in items 1 and 3 of Article 20.3 of this Law are present. 3. The party requesting the arbitral tribunal to make a preliminary ruling shall reveal to the arbitral tribunal all the circumstances that may be relevant in examining this request. The party shall have this duty throughout the term of the preliminary ruling.

361. https://japan.kantei.go.jp/policy/sihou/arbitrationlaw.pdf
362. https://www.ilo.org/dyn/natlex/docs/ELECTRONIC/63091/95325/F1864661120/JOR63091.pdf
363. https://ncia.or.ke/wp-content/uploads/2021/02/ArbitrationAct4of1995_2.pdf
364. https://www.newyorkconvention.org/11165/web/files/document/2/1/21372.pdf
365. https://e-seimas.lrs.lt/portal/legalAct/lt/TAD/35954312dcb311e6be918a531b2126ab?jfwid=-wd7z7zum0

Sr. No.	Country	Provision
		4. Upon issuing a preliminary order, an arbitral tribunal must, in accordance with the procedure established by Article 6 of this Law and with the immediate effect, provide each party with the application for interim measures, the application for a preliminary order, the preliminary order and, if any, correspondence between the requesting party and the arbitral tribunal, including information about the consideration of the application for the preliminary order by an oral procedure, if any. 5. An arbitral tribunal must, as effectively as possible, provide an opportunity to a party in respect of which a preliminary order has been issued, to be heard and consider objections of this party with regard to the issue of the preliminary order. 6. A preliminary order shall be valid for 20 days of its issue. In this period, after having heard a party, in respect of which the preliminary oder has been issued, and considered the objections of this party, if any, the arbitral tribunal may use respective interim measures. 7. A preliminary order shall be binding to the parties, but shall not be deemed as an enforceable document.
33.	Louisiana – RS 9 Title 9.Civil Code-Ancillaries[366]	No equivalent provision as Article 17C of the UNCITRAL Model Law 2006
34.	Macedonia - Law on International Commercial Arbitration of the Republic of Macedonia[367]	No equivalent provision as Article 17C of the UNCITRAL Model Law 2006
35.	Malaysia – Arbitration Act 2005, Act 646[368]	No equivalent provision as Article 17C of the UNCITRAL Model Law 2006
36.	Maldives – Act No: 10/2013, Arbitration Act[369]	Section 34 - Granting an Ex Parte Order for Interim Measures (b) Immediately after the Arbitral Tribunal issues an order in accordance with (a) above, the Arbitral Tribunal must without delay provide all parties to the dispute with all information related to the order. (c) When providing information mentioned in (a) above, the arbitral tribal shall provide the all parties with the application preliminary order, the preliminary order, if any, and all other communications, including any oral communication between any party and the arbitral tribunal in relation thereto.

366. http://legis.la.gov/legis/Laws_Toc.aspx?folder=83&title=9
367. https://www.international-arbitration-attorney.com/wp-content/uploads/2013/07/Macedonia-Arbitration-Law.pdf
368. http://www.newyorkconvention.org/11165/web/files/document/1/6/16298.pdf
369. https://miac.gov.mv/media/documents/Arbitration%20Act.pdf

Sr. No.	Country	Provision
		(d) In the event that the arbitral tribunal issues an order mentioned in (a) above the arbitral tribunal shall give an opportunity to any party against whom the preliminary order is directed to present its case at the earliest practicable time. The arbitral tribunal shall decide promptly on any objection to the preliminary order and inform all parties of its decision on such an objection without delay.
37.	Malta - CAP. 387 Arbitration Act[370]	No equivalent provision as Article 17C of the UNCITRAL Model Law 2006
38.	Mauritius - The International Arbitration Act, 2008 (Act 37 of 2008)[371]	Same as Article 17C of the UNCITRAL Model Law 2006 Third Schedule Part IV - Interim Measures by Tribunal Section 21 (Interim measures by tribunal) Articles 17 to 17G
39.	Montenegro - Decree on the Promulgation of the Law on Arbitration, 2015[372]	No equivalent provision as Article 17C of the UNCITRAL Model Law 2006
40.	Myanmar - Arbitration Law The Pyidaungsu Hluttaw Law No. 5/2016[373]	No equivalent provision as Article 17C of the UNCITRAL Model Law 2006
41.	New South Wales - Commercial Arbitration Act 2010 No 61[374]	Section 17C Note. Art 17C of the Model Law, which contains safeguards for the party against whom a preliminary order is directed under Art 17B, is omitted as a consequence of the omission of Art 17B.
42.	New Zealand - The Arbitration Act, 1996 No 99[375]	Schedule I - Rules applying to arbitration agreement Article 17E Procedure for preliminary order (1) Immediately after the arbitral tribunal makes a determination in respect of an application for a preliminary order, it must— (a) give notice to all the parties of— (i) the request for the interim measure; and (ii) the application for the preliminary order; and (iii) the preliminary order issued by the arbitral tribunal (if any); and

370. http://justiceservices.gov.mt/DownloadDocument.aspx?app=lom&itemid=8854&l=1
371. https://www.wipo.int/edocs/lexdocs/laws/en/mu/mu020en.pdf
372. https://www.privrednakomora.me/sites/pkcg.org/files/multimedia/main_pages/files/2012/09/final_eng_zakon_o_arbitrazi_final_0.pdf
373. http://www.newyorkconvention.org/11165/web/files/document/2/1/21098.pdf
374. https://legislation.nsw.gov.au/view/html/inforce/current/act-2010-061#sec.17C
375. http://www.legislation.govt.nz/act/public/1996/0099/latest/whole.html#DLM403277

Sr. No.	Country	Provision
		(iv) all other communications (whether oral or written) between a party and the arbitral tribunal in relation to the matters specified in subparagraph (a)(i) to (iii); and (b) give an opportunity to each respondent to present the respondent's case at the earliest practicable time. (2) The arbitral tribunal must decide promptly on any objection to the preliminary order. Article 17F Duration of preliminary order (1) A preliminary order expires 20 days after the date on which it was issued by the arbitral tribunal. (2) However, the arbitral tribunal may grant an interim measure adopting or modifying the preliminary order, after each respondent has been given— (a) notice under article 17E(1); and (b) an opportunity to present the respondent's case. Article 17G Effect of preliminary order (1) A preliminary order is binding on the parties but is not enforceable by a court. (2) A preliminary order does not constitute an award.
43.	Nigeria - Arbitration and Conciliation Act Chapter 19 Laws of the Federation of Nigeria 1990[376]	No equivalent provision as Article 17C of the UNCITRAL Model Law 2006
44.	Northern Territory of Australia - Commercial Arbitration (National Uniform Legislation) Act 2011[377]	Section 17C (not used) Note for section 17C Art 17C of the Model Law, which contains safeguards for the party against whom a preliminary order is directed under Art 17B, is omitted as a consequence of the omission of Art 17B.
45.	Norway - Act of 14 May 2004 No. 25 relating to Arbitration (The Arbitration Act)[378]	No equivalent provision as Article 17C of the UNCITRAL Model Law 2006
46.	Oman - The Omani Law of Arbitration in Civil and Commercial Disputes – Royal Decree 47/97[379]	No equivalent provision as Article 17C of the UNCITRAL Model Law 2006

376. http://niqs.org.ng/wp-content/uploads/2018/12/Arbitration-and-Conciliation-Act.pdf
377. https://legislation.nt.gov.au/api/sitecore/Act/PDF?id=11692
378. https://www.chamber.no/wp-content/uploads/2014/02/Norwegian_Arbitration_Act.pdf

Sr. No.	Country	Provision
47.	Ontario – International Commercial Arbitration Act, 2017, S.O. 2017, c. 2, Sched. 5[380]	Section 5 - Application of Model Law (1) Subject to this Act, the Model Law on International Commercial Arbitration, adopted by the United Nations Commission on International Trade Law on 21 June 1985, as amended by the United Nations Commission on International Trade Law on 7 July 2006, set out in Schedule 2, has force of law in Ontario. Same (2) With respect to article 7 of the Model Law, option I applies in Ontario; option II does not. Same (3) The Model Law applies to international commercial arbitration agreements and awards made in international commercial arbitrations, whether made before or after the coming into force of this Act. Schedule 2 to this Act Article 17C
48.	Oregon – Oregon International Commercial Arbitration and Conciliation Act[381]	No equivalent provision as Article 17C of the UNCITRAL Model Law 2006
49.	Pakistan - The Arbitration Act, 1940 Act No. X of 1940[382]	No equivalent provision as Article 17C of the UNCITRAL Model Law 2006
50.	Philippines - Alternative Dispute Resolution Act of 2004 Republic Act No. 9285[383]	No equivalent provision as Article 17C of the UNCITRAL Model Law 2006
51.	Poland – Polish Act of 17 November 1964 - Code of Civil Procedure, Part Five Arbitration[384]	No equivalent provision as Article 17C of the UNCITRAL Model Law 2006

379. http://www.newyorkconvention.org/11165/web/files/document/2/1/21103.pdf
380. https://www.ontario.ca/laws/statute/17i02b#BK16
381. https://www.oregonlegislature.gov/bills_laws/ors/ors036.html
382. https://www.wipo.int/edocs/lexdocs/laws/en/pk/pk066en.pdf
383. http://www.newyorkconvention.org/11165/web/files/document/2/1/21107.pdf
384. https://www.uv.es/medarb/observatorio/leyes-arbitraje/europa-resto/polonia-ccp-arbitration.pdf

Sr. No.	Country	Provision
52.	Qatar - Law No. 2 of 2017 Promulgating the Civil and Commercial Arbitration Law-The Law of Arbitration in Civil and Commercial Matters[385]	No equivalent provision as Article 17C of the UNCITRAL Model Law 2006
53.	Queensland - Commercial Arbitration Act 2013 No. 8[386]	Section 17C Specific regime for preliminary orders (cf Model Law Art 17) [omitted] Note— Art 17C of the Model Law, which contains safeguards for the party against whom a preliminary order is directed under Art 17B, is omitted as a consequence of the omission of Art 17B.
54.	Republic of Costa Rica - Costa Rican Law for International Arbitration Law Number: 8937[387]	Same as Article 17C UNCITRAL Model Law 2006
55.	Republic of Korea – Arbitration Act[388]	No equivalent provision as Article 17C of the UNCITRAL Model Law 2006
56.	Russia - Russian Federation Law on International Commercial Arbitration[389]	No equivalent provision as Article 17C of the UNCITRAL Model Law 2006
57.	Rwanda – Law on arbitration and conciliation in commercial matters, N° 005/2008[390]	Article 25: Specific regime for preliminary orders Immediately after the arbitral tribunal has made a determination in respect of an application for a preliminary Order, it shall give notice to the parties of the request for the interim measure, the application for the preliminary Order, and all other related communications between any party and the arbitral tribunal and including the indication of the content of any oral communication.

385. https://www.qicdrc.gov.qa/sites/default/files/inline-files/law_no._02_2017_promulgating_the_civil_and_commercial_arbitration_law.pdf
386. https://www.legislation.qld.gov.au/view/pdf/inforce/2013-05-17/act-2013-008
387. https://arbitratlaw.com/wp-content/uploads/2017/01/Costa-Rican-Intl-Arbitration-Law.pdf
388. https://elaw.klri.re.kr/eng_service/lawView.do?hseq=38889&lang=ENG
389. http://www.newyorkconvention.org/11165/web/files/document/2/2/22335.pdf
390. http://www.newyorkconvention.org/11165/web/files/document/2/1/21110.pdf

Sr. No.	Country	Provision
		At the same time, the arbitral tribunal shall give an opportunity to any party against whom a preliminary Order is directed to present his or her defence at the earliest possible time. The arbitral tribunal shall immediately take decision disputes relating to the preliminary order. A preliminary Order shall expire after fifteen (15) days from the date on which it was issued by the arbitral tribunal. However, the arbitral tribunal may issue an interim measure adopting or modifying the preliminary order, after informing the party concerned with the Order and giving the party an opportunity to present defence. A preliminary Order shall be binding on the parties as well as being enforced by an ordinary court. Such a preliminary order shall not be considered as judgement of the case.
58.	Saudi Arabia - Law of Arbitration Royal Decree No. M/34[391]	No equivalent provision as Article 17C of the UNCITRAL Model Law 2006
59.	Serbia - Law on Arbitration No. 46/06[392]	No equivalent provision as Article 17C of the UNCITRAL Model Law 2006
60.	Singapore - Arbitration Act (Chapter 10) (Domestic Arbitration Law)[393]	No equivalent provision as Article 17C of the UNCITRAL Model Law 2006
61.	Singapore - International Arbitration Act (Chapter 143A) (International Arbitration Law)[394]	No equivalent provision as Article 17C of the UNCITRAL Model Law 2006
62.	Slovakia - [Slovak] Act No. 244/2002 of 3 April 2002 on Arbitration[395]	No equivalent provision as Article 17C of the UNCITRAL Model Law 2006

391. https://www.wipo.int/edocs/lexdocs/laws/en/sa/sa057en.pdf
392. https://www.wipo.int/edocs/lexdocs/laws/en/rs/rs028en.pdf
393. https://sso.agc.gov.sg/Act/AA2001
394. https://sso.agc.gov.sg/Act/IAA1994
395. https://www.international-arbitration-attorney.com/wp-content/uploads/2013/07/Slovakia-Arbitration-Law-1.pdf

Sr. No.	Country	Provision
63.	Slovenia - Law on Arbitration of Slovenia[396]	No equivalent provision as Article 17C of the UNCITRAL Model Law 2006
64.	South Africa – The Arbitration Act, 1965[397]	No equivalent provision as Article 17C of the UNCITRAL Model Law 2006
65.	South Australia - South Australia Commercial Arbitration Act 2011[398]	Section 17C Note— Art 17C of the Model Law, which contains safeguards for the party against whom a preliminary order is directed under Art 17B, is omitted as a consequence of the omission of Art 17B.
66.	Spain - Act 60/2003 of 23 December on Arbitration[399]	No equivalent provision as Article 17C of the UNCITRAL Model Law 2006
67.	Sri Lanka - Arbitration Act. No. 11 of 1995[400]	No equivalent provision as Article 17C of the UNCITRAL Model Law 2006
68.	Sweden – The Swedish Arbitration Act (SFS 1999:116)[401]	No equivalent provision as Article 17C of the UNCITRAL Model Law 2006
69.	Switzerland – Private International Law Act 1987, Chapter 12: International Arbitration[402]	No equivalent provision as Article 17C of the UNCITRAL Model Law 2006

396. http://www.sloarbitration.eu/Portals/0/Arbitrazno-pravo/Law%20on%20Arbitration%20of%20Slovenia.pdf
397. https://www.gov.za/sites/default/files/gcis_document/201505/act-42-1965.pdf
398. https://www.legislation.sa.gov.au/LZ/C/A/COMMERCIAL%20ARBITRATION%20ACT%202011/CURRENT/2011.32.UN.PDF
399. https://www.mjusticia.gob.es/cs/Satellite/Portal/1292426982249?blobheader=application%2Fpdf&blobheadername1=Content-Disposition&blobheadervalue1=attachment%3B+filename%3DAct_on_arbitration_%28Ley_60_2003__de_arbitraje%29.PDF
400. http://www.slnarbcentre.com/pdf/ARBITRATION-ACT.pdf
401. https://sccinstitute.com/media/37089/the-swedish-arbitration-act.pdf
402. https://www.swissarbitration.org/wp-content/uploads/2021/05/20210129-Chapter-12-PILA_Translation_English.pdf

Sr. No.	Country	Provision
70.	Tasmania – Commercial Arbitration Act, 2011, Act 13 of 2011[403]	Section 17C. ... Note. Art 17C of the Model Law, which contains safeguards for the party against whom a preliminary order is directed under Art 17B, is omitted as a consequence of the omission of Art 17B.
71.	Texas - Chapter 172. Arbitration and Conciliation of International Commercial Disputes, Civil Practice and Remedies Code[404]	No equivalent provision as Article 17C of the UNCITRAL Model Law 2006
72.	Thailand - Arbitration Act B.E. 2545[405]	No equivalent provision as Article 17C of the UNCITRAL Model Law 2006
73.	Tunisia – Law n° 93-42 issued on April 26, related to the promulgation of the Arbitration Code[406]	No equivalent provision as Article 17C of the UNCITRAL Model Law 2006
74.	Turkey - Turkish International Arbitration Law, Law no. 4686, 2001[407]	No equivalent provision as Article 17C of the UNCITRAL Model Law 2006
75.	Uganda – Chapter 4 The Arbitration and Conciliation Act[408]	No equivalent provision as Article 17C of the UNCITRAL Model Law 2006
76.	Ukraine - The Law of Ukraine on International Commercial Arbitration[409]	No equivalent provision as Article 17C of the UNCITRAL Model Law 2006

403. https://www.legislation.tas.gov.au/view/html/inforce/current/act-2011-013
404. https://statutes.capitol.texas.gov/Docs/CP/htm/CP.172.htm
405. https://tai.coj.go.th/th/file/get/file/20190328ecac5333356ffad0331bd601151db9f4142557.pdf
406. https://arbitrationlaw.com/sites/default/files/free_pdfs/Tunisia%20Arbitration%20Code.pdf
407. http://www.camera-arbitrale.it/Documenti/tial_turkey.pdf
408. https://ulii.org/akn/ug/act/2000/7/eng@2008-06-27
409. http://arbitrations.ru/userfiles/file/Law/Arbitration%20acts/ukraininan%20law%20on%20arbitration.pdf

Sr. No.	Country	Provision
77.	United Arab Emirates - Federal Law No. (6) of 2018 on Arbitration[410]	No equivalent provision as Article 17C of the UNCITRAL Model Law 2006
78.	Uruguay - Law 19,636 Approve Rules for International Commercial Arbitration[411]	No equivalent provision as Article 17C of the UNCITRAL Model Law 2006
79.	Venezuela – Venezuelan Commercial Arbitration Act[412]	No equivalent provision as Article 17C of the UNCITRAL Model Law 2006
80.	Victoria - Commercial Arbitration Act 2011 No. 50 of 2011[413]	Section 17C [omitted] Note Art 17C of the Model Law, which contains safeguards for the party against whom a preliminary order is directed under Art 17B, is omitted as a consequence of the omission of Art 17B.
81.	Western Australia - Commercial Arbitration Act 2012, 023 of 2012[414]	Section 17C. (Not used) Note for this section: Art 17C of the Model Law, which contains safeguards for the party against whom a preliminary order is directed under Art 17B, is omitted as a consequence of the omission of Art 17B.
82.	Zambia – The Arbitration Act, 2000 No. 19 of 2000[415]	No equivalent provision as Article 17C of the UNCITRAL Model Law 2006
83.	Zimbabwe – Chapter 7:15 Arbitration Act[416]	No equivalent provision as Article 17C of the UNCITRAL Model Law 2006

410. https://www.tamimi.com/crm-media-uploader/fileupload/server/php/files/UAE%20Arbitration%20Law%20-%20Federal%20Law%20No%20%206%20of%202018.pdf
411. http://www.impo.com.uy/bases/leyes-originales/19636-2018
412. https://arbitrationlaw.com/sites/default/files/free_pdfs/Venezula%20Commercial%20Arbitration%20Act.pdf
413. http://arbitration.site/wp-content/uploads/2019/06/CAA-Vic-.pdf
414. https://www.legislation.wa.gov.au/legislation/prod/filestore.nsf/FileURL/mrdoc_25084.pdf/$FILE/Commercial%20Arbitration%20Act%202012%20-%20%5B00-b0-06%5D.pdf?OpenElement
415. http://www.newyorkconvention.org/11165/web/files/document/2/1/21396.pdf
416. https://zimlii.org/akn/zw/act/1996/6/eng@2016-12-31

Appendix F (Article 17D)

Sr. No.	Country	Provision
1.	Australia - International Arbitration Act 1974[417]	Same as Article 17D of UNCITRAL Model Law 2006 Sec 16 Model Law to have force of law (1) Subject to this Part, the Model Law has the force of law in Australia. (2) In the Model Law: Arbitration agreement has the meaning given in Option 1 of Article 7 of the Model Law. State means Australia (including the external Territories) and any foreign country. This State means Australia (including the external Territories). Model Law under Part V, Schedule 2 of the Arbitration Act, 1974
2.	Australian Capital Territory - Commercial Arbitration Act, 2017 A2017-7[418]	SECT 17D Modification, suspension, termination (Model Law art 17D) The arbitral tribunal may modify, suspend or terminate an interim measure it has granted, on application of any party or, in exceptional circumstances and on prior notice to the parties, on the arbitral tribunal's own initiative. Note This section is substantially the same as the Model Law, art 17D but contains no reference to preliminary orders as a consequence of this Act not including an equivalent of the Model Law, art 17B and art 17C.
3.	Austria - Austrian Arbitration Act, 2013[419]	No equivalent provision as Article 17D of the UNCITRAL Model Law 2006

417. https://www.legislation.gov.au/Details/C2011C00342
418. http://classic.austlii.edu.au/au/legis/act/consol_act/caa2017219/s17d.html
419. https://www.viac.eu/images/law/ZPO_Schiedsrecht_2014_en_im_VIAC_Layout.pdf

Sr. No.	Country	Provision
4.	Bahrain - Bahrain Arbitration Law No. 9/2015[420]	Same as UNCITRAL Model Law 2006 Article 1 Taking into account the provisions of international conventions in force in the Kingdom of Bahrain 1. The provisions of the " UNCITRAL " Model Law on International Commercial Arbitration Act attached to this law shall apply to all arbitration whatever the nature of the legal relationship of the dispute herewith, if this arbitration takes place in the Kingdom of Bahrain or abroad and that two parties agreed to comply with the provisions of the attached law. 2. The provisions of the attached law shall apply to all arbitration which begins after its entry into force even if based on an arbitration agreement concluded before the entry into force of this law.
5.	Bangladesh - The Arbitration Act, 2001[421]	No equivalent provision as Article 17D of the UNCITRAL Model Law 2006
6.	Belgium - Belgian Judicial Code Provisions[422]	Art. 1692 At the request of one of the parties, the arbitral tribunal may amend, suspend or terminate an interim or conservatory measure.
7.	Bhutan - Alternative Dispute Resolution Act of Bhutan 2013[423]	Section 118. Modification, suspension, and cancellation The arbitral tribunal may modify, suspend, or cancel the interim measure on: (1) The application of a party; or (2) Its own initiative, but only in exceptional circumstances after giving prior notice to the parties.
8.	British Columbia - International Commercial Arbitration Act [RSBC 1996] Chapter 233[424]	Section 17.04 Modification, suspension or termination of interim measures and preliminary orders On application of any party or, in exceptional circumstances and with prior notice to the parties, on the arbitral tribunal's own initiative, an arbitral tribunal may modify, suspend or terminate an interim measure or a preliminary order it has granted.
9.	British Virgin Islands - Virgin Islands Arbitration Act, 2013[425]	UNCITRAL Model Law to have effect in the Virgin Islands. Section 4. The provisions of the UNCITRAL Model Law have the force of law in the Virgin Islands, subject to the modifications and supplements expressly provided in this Act. Section 37. Application of article 17D of the UNCITRAL Model Law

420. https://pernetmartial.eu/sites/default/files/lois/Bahrain-Loi-d-arbitrage-arbitration-act-ley-de-arbitraje.pdf
421. http://www.mccibd.org/images/uploadimg/act_and_policy/corporate_governance/The-Arbitration-Act-2001.pdf
422. http://www.arbiter.com.sg/pdf/laws/Belgian%20Judicial%20Code%20Provisions%20(2013).pdf
423. https://www.nationalcouncil.bt/assets/uploads/docs/acts/2014/Alternative_Dispute_Resolution_Act_of_Bhutan_2013_eng10th.pdf
424. http://www.bclaws.ca/civix/document/id/complete/statreg/96233_01

Sr. No.	Country	Provision
10.	Bulgaria - Law on International Commercial Arbitration State Gazette (SG) No. 60 of 05.08.1988[426]	No equivalent provision as Article 17D of the UNCITRAL Model Law 2006
11.	Cambodia - The Commercial Arbitration Law of the Kingdom of Cambodia 2006[427]	No equivalent provision as Article 17D of the UNCITRAL Model Law 2006
12.	Canada - Commercial Arbitration Act R.S.C., 1985, c. 17 (2nd Supp.)[428]	No equivalent provision as Article 17D of the UNCITRAL Model Law 2006
13.	Connecticut - Chapter 909 Arbitration Proceedings[429]	No equivalent provision as Article 17D of the UNCITRAL Model Law 2006
14.	Croatia - Law on Arbitration Official Gazette no. 88/2001[430]	No equivalent provision as Article 17D of the UNCITRAL Model Law 2006
15.	Cyprus - The International Commercial Arbitration Law, 1987[431]	No equivalent provision as Article 17D of the UNCITRAL Model Law 2006
16.	Denmark - Danish Arbitration Act 2005[432]	No equivalent provision as Article 17D of the UNCITRAL Model Law 2006

425. http://www.bviiac.org/Portals/0/Files/Arbitration%20Documents/ArbitrationAct2013.pdf
426. http://www.newyorkconvention.org/11165/web/files/document/1/6/16200.pdf
427. https://www.cambodiaip.gov.kh/DocResources/372a361b-7a97-44b3-9810-79e5e6ea85f4_c786a043-b88d-4f64-9429-60a330efdc5f-en.pdf
428. https://laws-lois.justice.gc.ca/eng/acts/C-34.6/index.html
429. https://www.cga.ct.gov/current/pub/chap_909.htm
430. http://www.vsrh.hr/CustomPages/Static/HRV/Files/Legislation__Law-Arbitration-RC.pdf
431. https://www.uv.es/medarb/observatorio/leyes-arbitraje/europa-resto/chipre-international-commercial-arbitration-law.pdf
432. https://voldgiftsinstituttet.dk/wp-content/uploads/2015/01/danish_arbitration_act_2005.pdf

Sr. No.	Country	Provision
17.	Egypt - Law No. 27/1994 Promulgating the Law Concerning Arbitration in Civil and Commercial Matters[433]	No equivalent provision as Article 17D of the UNCITRAL Model Law 2006
18.	Florida Chapter 684 – International Commercial Arbitration, Title XXXIX Commercial Relations, 2020 Florida Statutes[434]	Same as Article 17D of the UNCITRAL Model Law 2006. Article 684.0022 Modification, suspension, or termination; interim measure or preliminary orders
19.	Fiji – International Arbitration Act 2017 (Act No. 44 Of 2017)[435]	Same as Article 17D of UNCITRAL Model Law 2006 Section 27 Modification, suspension and termination
20.	France – Book IV - Arbitration of the Code of Civil Procedure Decree No. 2011-48[436]	Article 1468 The arbitral tribunal has the power to amend or add to any provisional or conservatory measure that it has granted.
21.	Georgia – Chapter 9 Arbitration, Title 9 Civil Practice, Georgia Code[437]	Article 19 - Modification, suspension an termination of interim measures The arbitral tribunal, if it considers necessary, is entitled to modify, suspend or terminate an already granted interim measure, upon the request of any party, or in exceptional circumstances, upon prior notice sent to the parties, based on arbitral tribunal's own initiative.
22.	Germany – Tenth Book of the Code of Civil Procedure, Arbitration Procedure[438]	No equivalent provision as Article 17D of the UNCITRAL Model Law 2006

433. https://www.wipo.int/edocs/lexdocs/laws/en/eg/eg020en.pdf
434. https://www.flsenate.gov/Laws/Statutes/2020/Chapter684/All
435. https://www.fiji.gov.fj/getattachment/d9502667-6491-4592-85b2-eff97f245fed/Act-44---International-Arbitration-Act.aspx
436. http://www.iaiparis.com/pdf/FRENCH_LAW_ON_INTERNATIONAL_ARBITRATION.pdf
437. https://matsne.gov.ge/ru/document/download/89284/5/en/pdf
438. https://sccinstitute.com/media/29988/german-arbitration-act.pdf

Sr. No.	Country	Provision
23.	Greece - Code Of Civil Procedure, Book Vii, Book Viii[439]	No equivalent provision as Article 17D of the UNCITRAL Model Law 2006
24.	Hong Kong - Cap. 609 Arbitration Ordinance[440]	Same as Article 17D of the UNCITRAL Model Law 2006 Section 39 - Article 17D of UNCITRAL Model Law (Modification, suspension, termination)
25.	Hungary - Act LX of 2017 on Arbitration[441]	Section 22 At the request of any party or, in exceptional circumstances, in the absence of a request and without prior notice to the parties, the arbitral tribunal may modify, suspend or terminate an interim measure or a preliminary order it has granted.
26.	Ireland - Arbitration Act 2010 Number 1 of 2010[442]	Section 6 - Adoption of Model Law Subject to this Act, the Model Law shall have the force of law in the State and shall apply to arbitrations under arbitration agreements concerning— (a) international commercial arbitrations, or (b) arbitrations which are not international commercial arbitrations. Same as Article 17D of UNCITRAL Model Law 2006 Article 17D under Schedule 1 - TEXT OF UNCITRAL MODEL LAW ON INTERNATIONAL COMMERCIAL ARBITRATION
27.	Jamaica - The Arbitration Act, 2017 (Act 13 of 2017)[443]	Same as Article 17D of UNCITRAL Model Law 2006 Section 24 Modification, suspension, termination
28.	Japan - Arbitration Law (Law No.138 of 2003)[444]	No equivalent provision as Article 17D of the UNCITRAL Model Law 2006
29.	Jordan - Law No. 31 of 2001 (Jordan) Arbitration Law[445]	No equivalent provision as Article 17D of the UNCITRAL Model Law 2006
30.	Kenya - Chapter 49 Arbitration Act (The Arbitration Act, 1995)[446]	No equivalent provision as Article 17D of the UNCITRAL Model Law 2006

439. https://www.uv.es/medarb/observatorio/leyes-arbitraje/europa-resto/grecia-ccp-domestic-arbitration.pdf
440. https://www.elegislation.gov.hk/hk/cap609
441. https://www.ilo.org/dyn/natlex/docs/ELECTRONIC/106843/131257/F-266585574/J2017T0060P_20180102_FIN.pdf
442. http://www.irishstatutebook.ie/eli/2010/act/1/enacted/en/pdf
443. http://extwprlegs1.fao.org/docs/pdf/jam172060.pdf
444. https://japan.kantei.go.jp/policy/sihou/arbitrationlaw.pdf
445. https://www.ilo.org/dyn/natlex/docs/ELECTRONIC/63091/95325/F1864661120/JOR63091.pdf

Sr. No.	Country	Provision
31.	Liechtenstein - Liechtenstein Arbitration Law (Code of Civil Procedure)[447]	No equivalent provision as Article 17D of the UNCITRAL Model Law 2006
32.	Lithuania - The Republic of Lithuania Law on Commercial Arbitration, 2012[448]	Article 22. Amendment and Settlement Aside of Orders Regarding Interim Measures and Setting Aside of Preliminary Orders At the request of a party or, in exceptional cases, on its own initiative with a notice to each party, an arbitral tribunal may amend or annul an order concerning interim measures or annul a preliminary orer.
33.	Louisiana – RS 9 Title 9.Civil Code-Ancillaries[449]	No equivalent provision as Article 17D of the UNCITRAL Model Law 2006
34.	Macedonia - Law on International Commercial Arbitration of the Republic of Macedonia[450]	No equivalent provision as Article 17D of the UNCITRAL Model Law 2006
35.	Malaysia – Arbitration Act 2005, Act 646[451]	No equivalent provision as Article 17D of the UNCITRAL Model Law 2006
36.	Maldives – Act No: 10/2013, Arbitration Act[452]	Section 36 Modification, Suspension and Termination of Preliminary Order (a) The Arbitral Tribunal shall have the power to modify, suspend or terminate an interim measure or preliminary order it has granted in accordance with this Act. (b) The Arbitral Tribunal may make a decision to modify, suspend or terminate an interim measure or preliminary order as mentioned in (a) above upon application of any party once I Arbitral Tribunal is satisfied that it would be suitable to make such a decision in favor of the applicant. Or such a decision may be made on the Arbitral Tribunal's own initiative if its finds that exceptional circumstances demand such a decision.
37.	Malta – CAP. 387 Arbitration Act[453]	No equivalent provision as Article 17D of the UNCITRAL Model Law 2006

446. https://ncia.or.ke/wp-content/uploads/2021/02/ArbitrationAct4of1995_2.pdf
447. https://www.newyorkconvention.org/11165/web/files/document/2/1/21372.pdf
448. https://e-seimas.lrs.lt/portal/legalAct/lt/TAD/35954312dcb311e6be918a531b2126ab?jfwid=-wd7z7zum0
449. http://legis.la.gov/legis/Laws_Toc.aspx?folder=83&title=9
450. https://www.international-arbitration-attorney.com/wp-content/uploads/2013/07/Macedonia-Arbitration-Law.pdf
451. http://www.newyorkconvention.org/11165/web/files/document/1/6/16298.pdf
452. https://miac.gov.mv/media/documents/Arbitration%20Act.pdf

Sr. No.	Country	Provision
38.	Mauritius - The International Arbitration Act, 2008 (Act 37 of 2008)[454]	Section 17. Interim measures by Tribunal (5) The arbitral tribunal may modify, suspend or terminate an interim measure it has granted on application of any party or, in exceptional circumstances and on prior notice to the parties, on the arbitral tribunal's own initiative.
39.	Montenegro - Decree on the Promulgation of the Law on Arbitration, 2015[455]	Article 23 - Modification, suspension and termination of interim measure The arbitral tribunal may modify, suspend or decide to terminate an interim measure, upon application of any party. The arbitral tribunal may modify, suspend or decide to terminate an interim measure, in exceptional circumstances and upon prior notice to the parties, on the arbitral tribunal's own initiative.
40.	Myanmar - Arbitration Law The Pyidaungsu Hluttaw Law No. 5/2016[456]	No equivalent provision as Article 17D of the UNCITRAL Model Law 2006
41.	New South Wales - Commercial Arbitration Act 2010 No 61[457]	Section 17D Modification, suspension, termination (cf Model Law Art 17D) The arbitral tribunal may modify, suspend or terminate an interim measure it has granted, on application of any party or, in exceptional circumstances and on prior notice to the parties, on the arbitral tribunal's own initiative. Note. This section is substantially the same as Art 17D of the Model Law but contains no reference to preliminary orders as a consequence of this Act not including an equivalent of Arts 17B and 17C of the Model Law.
42.	New Zealand - The Arbitration Act, 1996 No 99[458]	Schedule I - Rules applying to arbitration agreement Article 17H Modification, suspension, and cancellation If the arbitral tribunal grants or issues an interim measure or a preliminary order, it may modify, suspend, or cancel the measure or order— (a) on the application of a party; or (b) on its own initiative, but only in exceptional circumstances and after giving prior notice to the parties.

453. http://justiceservices.gov.mt/DownloadDocument.aspx?app=lom&itemid=8854&l=1
454. https://www.wipo.int/edocs/lexdocs/laws/en/mu/mu020en.pdf
455. https://www.privrednakomora.me/sites/pkcg.org/files/multimedia/main_pages/files/2012/09/final_eng_zakon_o_arbitrazi_final_0.pdf
456. http://www.newyorkconvention.org/11165/web/files/document/2/1/21098.pdf
457. https://legislation.nsw.gov.au/view/html/inforce/current/act-2010-061#sec.17D
458. http://www.legislation.govt.nz/act/public/1996/0099/latest/whole.html#DLM403277

Sr. No.	Country	Provision
43.	Nigeria - Arbitration and Conciliation Act Chapter 19 Laws of the Federation of Nigeria 1990[459]	No equivalent provision as Article 17D of the UNCITRAL Model Law 2006
44.	Northern Territory of Australia - Commercial Arbitration (National Uniform Legislation) Act 2011[460]	Section 17D Modification, suspension, termination (Model Law Art 17D) The arbitral tribunal may modify, suspend or terminate an interim measure it has granted, on application of any party or, in exceptional circumstances and on prior notice to the parties, on the arbitral tribunal's own initiative. Note for section 17D This section is substantially the same as Art 17D of the Model Law but contains no reference to preliminary orders as a consequence of this Act not including an equivalent of Arts 17B and 17C of the Model Law.
45.	Norway - Act of 14 May 2004 No. 25 relating to Arbitration (The Arbitration Act)[461]	Section 19 The scope of the arbitral tribunal for deciding interim measures ... The arbitral tribunal may reduce or reverse an interim measure.
46.	Oman - The Omani Law of Arbitration in Civil and Commercial Disputes – Royal Decree 47/97[462]	No equivalent provision as Article 17D of the UNCITRAL Model Law 2006
47.	Ontario - International Commercial Arbitration Act, 2017, S.O. 2017, c. 2, Sched. 5[463]	Section 5 - Application of Model Law (1) Subject to this Act, the Model Law on International Commercial Arbitration, adopted by the United Nations Commission on International Trade Law on 21 June 1985, as amended by the United Nations Commission on International Trade Law on 7 July 2006, set out in Schedule 2, has force of law in Ontario. Same (2) With respect to article 7 of the Model Law, option I applies in Ontario; option II does not. Same (3) The Model Law applies to international commercial arbitration agreements and awards made in international commercial arbitrations, whether made before or after the coming into force of this Act. Schedule 2 to this Act Article 17D

459. http://niqs.org.ng/wp-content/uploads/2018/12/Arbitration-and-Conciliation-Act.pdf
460. https://legislation.nt.gov.au/api/sitecore/Act/PDF?id = 11692
461. https://www.chamber.no/wp-content/uploads/2014/02/Norwegian_Arbitration_Act.pdf
462. http://www.newyorkconvention.org/11165/web/files/document/2/1/21103.pdf
463. https://www.ontario.ca/laws/statute/17i02b#BK16

Sr. No.	Country	Provision
48.	Oregon – Oregon International Commercial Arbitration and Conciliation Act[464]	No equivalent provision as Article 17D of the UNCITRAL Model Law 2006
49.	Pakistan - The Arbitration Act, 1940 Act No. X of 1940[465]	No equivalent provision as Article 17D of the UNCITRAL Model Law 2006
50.	Philippines - Alternative Dispute Resolution Act of 2004 Republic Act No. 9285[466]	Section 28. Grant of Interim Measure of Protection. - (a) ... After constitution of the arbitral tribunal and during arbitral proceedings, a request for an interim measure of protection or modification thereof, may be made with the arbitral tribunal or to the extent that the arbitral tribunal has no power to act or is unable to act effectively, the request may be made with the Court.
51.	Poland – Polish Act of 17 November 1964 - Code of Civil Procedure, Part Five Arbitration[467]	Art. 1181 §2 At the request of the party the arbitral tribunal may change or overrule the decision taken pursuant to paragraph §1.
52.	Qatar - Law No. 2 of 2017 Promulgating the Civil and Commercial Arbitration Law-The Law of Arbitration in Civil and Commercial Matters[468]	Article 17 2. The Arbitral Tribunal may amend, stay, or cancel any provisional measure it has ordered or an interim award it has issued, either on the application of one of the Parties or on its own motion when necessary, provided that it shall notify the rest of the Parties.
53.	Queensland - Commercial Arbitration Act 2013 No. 8[469]	Section 17D Modification, suspension, termination (cf Model Law Art 17D) The arbitral tribunal may modify, suspend or terminate an interim measure it has granted, on application of any party or, in exceptional circumstances and on prior notice to the parties, on the arbitral tribunal's own initiative.

464. https://www.oregonlegislature.gov/bills_laws/ors/ors036.html
465. https://www.wipo.int/edocs/lexdocs/laws/en/pk/pk066en.pdf
466. http://www.newyorkconvention.org/11165/web/files/document/2/1/21107.pdf
467. https://www.uv.es/medarb/observatorio/leyes-arbitraje/europa-resto/polonia-ccp-arbitration.pdf
468. https://www.qicdrc.gov.qa/sites/default/files/inline-files/law_no._02_2017_promulgating_the_civil_and_commercial_arbitration_law.pdf
469. https://www.legislation.qld.gov.au/view/pdf/inforce/2013-05-17/act-2013-008

Sr. No.	Country	Provision
		Note— This section is substantially the same as Art 17D of the Model Law but contains no reference to preliminary orders as a consequence of this Act not including an equivalent of Arts 17B and 17C of the Model Law.
54.	Republic of Costa Rica - Costa Rican Law for International Arbitration Law Number: 8937[470]	Same as Article 17D of UNCITRAL Model Law 2006
55.	Republic of Korea - Arbitration Act[471]	Article 18-3 (Modification, Suspension, Termination of Interim Measures) The arbitral tribunal may modify, suspend or terminate an interim measure it has already granted, upon application of any party or, in exceptional circumstances and upon prior notice to the parties, on the arbitral tribunal's own initiative. In such case, the arbitral tribunal shall examine the parties before the modifying, suspending or terminating the interim measure.
56.	Russia - Russian Federation Law On International Commercial Arbitration[472]	No equivalent provision as Article 17D of the UNCITRAL Model Law 2006
57.	Rwanda – Law on arbitration and conciliation in commercial matters, N° 005/2008[473]	Article 26: Modification, suspension and termination of interim measures or preliminary Orders The arbitral tribunal may modify, suspend or terminate an interim measure or a preliminary Order it has granted, upon application by any party or in exceptional circumstances after notifying to the parties, on the arbitral tribunal's own initiative.
58.	Saudi Arabia – Law of Arbitration Royal Decree No. M/34[474]	No equivalent provision as Article 17D of the UNCITRAL Model Law 2006
59.	Serbia – Law on Arbitration No. 46/06[475]	No equivalent provision as Article 17D of the UNCITRAL Model Law 2006

470. https://arbitratlaw.com/wp-content/uploads/2017/01/Costa-Rican-Intl-Arbitration-Law.pdf
471. https://elaw.klri.re.kr/eng_service/lawView.do?hseq=38889&lang=ENG
472. http://www.newyorkconvention.org/11165/web/files/document/2/2/22335.pdf
473. http://www.newyorkconvention.org/11165/web/files/document/2/1/21110.pdf
474. https://www.wipo.int/edocs/lexdocs/laws/en/sa/sa057en.pdf
475. https://www.wipo.int/edocs/lexdocs/laws/en/rs/rs028en.pdf

Sr. No.	Country	Provision
60.	Singapore - Arbitration Act (Chapter 10) (Domestic Arbitration Law)[476]	No equivalent provision as Article 17D of the UNCITRAL Model Law 2006
61.	Singapore - International Arbitration Act (Chapter 143A) (International Arbitration Law)[477]	No equivalent provision as Article 17D of the UNCITRAL Model Law 2006
62.	Slovakia – [Slovak] Act No. 244/2002 of 3 April 2002 on Arbitration[478]	Section 22a (1) If the parties to arbitration agree to that end, the arbitral tribunal may, upon the request from a party, order an interim measure without granting the other party the opportunity to submit its reply to such request. The request for the interim measure shall only be served upon the other party with the delivery of the decision on such a request. (4) The arbitral tribunal shall within 30 days from the submission of the objections decide to set aside, modify or affirm the interim measure issued under Subsection 1. If the interim measure was granted by a permanent court of arbitration before the appointment of an arbitrator (arbitrators), the arbitrator (arbitrators) shall, within 30 days from the appointment, decide on the objections. The decision affirming or modifying the interim measure issued under Subsection 1 is considered a decision granting an interim measure under Section 22.
63.	Slovenia - Law on Arbitration of Slovenia[479]	Same as Article 17D of UNCITRAL Model Law 2006 Article 20 (3)
64.	South Africa – The Arbitration Act, 1965[480]	No equivalent provision as Article 17D of the UNCITRAL Model Law 2006
65.	South Australia - South Australia Commercial Arbitration Act 2011[481]	Section 17D—Modification, suspension, termination The arbitral tribunal may modify, suspend or terminate an interim measure it has granted, on application of any party or, in exceptional circumstances and on prior notice to the parties, on the arbitral tribunal's own initiative.

476. https://sso.agc.gov.sg/Act/AA2001
477. https://sso.agc.gov.sg/Act/IAA1994
478. https://www.international-arbitration-attorney.com/wp-content/uploads/2013/07/Slovakia-Arbitration-Law-1.pdf
479. http://www.sloarbitration.eu/Portals/0/Arbitrazno-pravo/Law%20on%20Arbitration%20of%20Slovenia.pdf
480. https://www.gov.za/sites/default/files/gcis_document/201505/act-42-1965.pdf
481. https://www.legislation.sa.gov.au/LZ/C/A/COMMERCIAL%20ARBITRATION%20ACT%202011/CURRENT/2011.32.UN.PDF

Sr. No.	Country	Provision
		Note— This section is substantially the same as Art 17D of the Model Law but contains no reference to preliminary orders as a consequence of this Act not including an equivalent of Arts 17B and 17C of the Model Law.
66.	Spain - Act 60/2003 of 23 December on Arbitration[482]	No equivalent provision as Article 17D of the UNCITRAL Model Law 2006
67.	Sri Lanka - Arbitration Act. No. 11 of 1995[483]	No equivalent provision as Article 17D of the UNCITRAL Model Law 2006
68.	Sweden – The Swedish Arbitration Act (SFS 1999:116)[484]	No equivalent provision as Article 17D of the UNCITRAL Model Law 2006
69.	Switzerland – Private International Law Act 1987, Chapter 12: International Arbitration[485]	No equivalent provision as Article 17D of the UNCITRAL Model Law 2006
70.	Tasmania – Commercial Arbitration Act, 2011, Act 13 of 2011[486]	Section 17D. Modification, suspension, termination (cf Model Law Art 17D) The arbitral tribunal may modify, suspend or terminate an interim measure it has granted, on application of any party or, in exceptional circumstances and on prior notice to the parties, on the arbitral tribunal's own initiative. Note. This section is substantially the same as Art 17D of the Model Law but contains no reference to preliminary orders as a consequence of this Act not including an equivalent of Arts 17B and 17C of the Model Law.

482. https://www.mjusticia.gob.es/cs/Satellite/Portal/1292426982249?blobheader=application%2Fpdf&blobheadername1=Content-Disposition&blobheadervalue1=attachment%3B+filename%3DAct_on_arbitration_%28Ley_60_2003__de_arbitraje%29.PDF
483. http://www.slnarbcentre.com/pdf/ARBITRATION-ACT.pdf
484. https://sccinstitute.com/media/37089/the-swedish-arbitration-act.pdf
485. https://www.swissarbitration.org/wp-content/uploads/2021/05/20210129-Chapter-12-PILA_Translation_English.pdf
486. https://www.legislation.tas.gov.au/view/html/inforce/current/act-2011-013

Sr. No.	Country	Provision
71.	Texas - Chapter 172. Arbitration and Conciliation of International Commercial Disputes, Civil Practice and Remedies Code[487]	No equivalent provision as Article 17D of the UNCITRAL Model Law 2006
72.	Thailand – Arbitration Act B.E. 2545[488]	No equivalent provision as Article 17D of the UNCITRAL Model Law 2006
73.	Tunisia – Law n° 93-42 issued on April 26, related to the promulgation of the Arbitration Code[489]	No equivalent provision as Article 17D of the UNCITRAL Model Law 2006
74.	Turkey - Turkish International Arbitration Law, Law no. 4686, 2001[490]	No equivalent provision as Article 17D of the UNCITRAL Model Law 2006
75.	Uganda – Chapter 4 The Arbitration and Conciliation Act[491]	No equivalent provision as Article 17D of the UNCITRAL Model Law 2006
76.	Ukraine - The Law of Ukraine on International Commercial Arbitration[492]	No equivalent provision as Article 17D of the UNCITRAL Model Law 2006
77.	United Arab Emirates - Federal Law No. (6) of 2018 on Arbitration[493]	Article 21 Interim or Conservatory Measures 3. The Arbitral Tribunal may, at the request of any party or on its own motion, amend, suspend, or cancel an interim measure it has ordered, in exceptional circumstances, by prior notice to be given to the Parties.

487. https://statutes.capitol.texas.gov/Docs/CP/htm/CP.172.htm
488. https://tai.coj.go.th/th/file/get/file/20190328ecac5333356ffad0331bd601151db9f4142557.pdf
489. https://arbitrationlaw.com/sites/default/files/free_pdfs/Tunisia%20Arbitration%20Code.pdf
490. http://www.camera-arbitrale.it/Documenti/tial_turkey.pdf
491. https://ulii.org/akn/ug/act/2000/7/eng@2008-06-27
492. http://arbitrations.ru/userfiles/file/Law/Arbitration%20acts/ukraininan%20law%20on%20arbitration.pdf

Sr. No.	Country	Provision
78.	Uruguay - Law 19,636 Approve Rules for International Commercial Arbitration[494]	No equivalent provision as Article 17D of the UNCITRAL Model Law 2006
79.	Venezuela – Venezuelan Commercial Arbitration Act[495]	No equivalent provision as Article 17D of the UNCITRAL Model Law 2006
80.	Victoria - Commercial Arbitration Act 2011 No. 50 of 2011[496]	Section 17D Modification, suspension, termination (cf Model Law Art 17D) The arbitral tribunal may modify, suspend or terminate an interim measure it has granted, on application of any party or, in exceptional circumstances and on prior notice to the parties, on the arbitral tribunal's own initiative. Note This section is substantially the same as Art 17D of the Model Law but contains no reference to preliminary orders as a consequence of this Act not including equivalents to Arts 17B and 17C of the Model Law
81.	Western Australia - Commercial Arbitration Act 2012, 023 of 2012[497]	Section 17D. Modification, suspension, termination (cf. Model Law Art 17D) The arbitral tribunal may modify, suspend or terminate an interim measure it has granted, on application of any party or, in exceptional circumstances and on prior notice to the parties, on the arbitral tribunal's own initiative. Note for this section: This section is substantially the same as Art 17D of the Model Law but contains no reference to preliminary orders as a consequence of this Act not including an equivalent of Arts 17B and 17C of the Model Law.
82.	Zambia – The Arbitration Act, 2000 No. 19 of 2000[498]	No equivalent provision as Article 17D of the UNCITRAL Model Law 2006

493. https://www.tamimi.com/crm-media-uploader/fileupload/server/php/files/UAE%20 Arbitration%20Law%20-%20Federal%20Law%20No%20%206%20of%202018.pdf
494. http://www.impo.com.uy/bases/leyes-originales/19636-2018
495. https://arbitrationlaw.com/sites/default/files/free_pdfs/Venezula%20Commercial%20 Arbitration%20Act.pdf
496. http://arbitration.site/wp-content/uploads/2019/06/CAA-Vic-.pdf
497. https://www.legislation.wa.gov.au/legislation/prod/filestore.nsf/FileURL/mrdoc_25084.pdf /$FILE/Commercial%20Arbitration%20Act%202012%20-%20%5B00-b0-06%5D.pdf? OpenElement
498. http://www.newyorkconvention.org/11165/web/files/document/2/1/21396.pdf

Sr. No.	Country	Provision
83.	Zimbabwe – Chapter 7:15 Arbitration Act[499]	No equivalent provision as Article 17D of the UNCITRAL Model Law 2006

499. https://zimlii.org/akn/zw/act/1996/6/eng@2016-12-31

Appendix G (Article 17E)

Sr. No.	Country	Provision
1.	Australia - International Arbitration Act 1974[500]	Same as Article 17E of UNCITRAL Model Law 2006 Sec 16 Model Law to have force of law (1) Subject to this Part, the Model Law has the force of law in Australia. (2) In the Model Law: Arbitration agreement has the meaning given in Option 1 of Article 7 of the Model Law. State means Australia (including the external Territories) and any foreign country. This State means Australia (including the external Territories). Model Law under Part V, Schedule 2 of the Arbitration Act, 1974
2.	Australian Capital Territory - Commercial Arbitration Act, 2017 A2017-7[501]	SECT 17E Provision of security (Model Law art 17E) (1) The arbitral tribunal may require the party requesting an interim measure to provide appropriate security in connection with the measure. (2) [omitted] Note Subsection (1) is the same as the Model Law, art 17E (1). Art 17E (2) is omitted as a consequence of this Act not including equivalents to the Model Law, art 17B and art 17C.
3.	Austria - Austrian Arbitration Act, 2013[502]	Section 593 - Ordering of Interim or Protective Measures (1) ...The arbitral tribunal may request any party to provide appropriate security in connection with such measure.

500. https://www.legislation.gov.au/Details/C2011C00342
501. http://classic.austlii.edu.au/au/legis/act/consol_act/caa2017219/s17e.html
502. https://www.viac.eu/images/law/ZPO_Schiedsrecht_2014_en_im_VIAC_Layout.pdf

Sr. No.	Country	Provision
4.	Bahrain - Bahrain Arbitration Law No. 9/2015[503]	Same as UNCITRAL Model Law 2006 Article 1 Taking into account the provisions of international conventions in force in the Kingdom of Bahrain 1. The provisions of the "UNCITRAL" Model Law on International Commercial Arbitration Act attached to this law shall apply to all arbitration whatever the nature of the legal relationship of the dispute herewith, if this arbitration takes place in the Kingdom of Bahrain or abroad and that two parties agreed to comply with the provisions of the attached law. 2. The provisions of the attached law shall apply to all arbitration which begins after its entry into force even if based on an arbitration agreement concluded before the entry into force of this law.
5.	Bangladesh – The Arbitration Act, 2001[504]	Section 21 Powers of the arbitration tribunal to make interim orders.- (2) The arbitral tribunal may require a party to provide appropriate security in connection with a measure ordered under sub-section (1).
6.	Belgium – Belgian Judicial Code Provisions[505]	Art. 1693 The arbitral tribunal may require the party requesting an interim or conservatory order to provide appropriate security.
7.	Bhutan - Alternative Dispute Resolution Act of Bhutan 2013[506]	Section 119. The arbitral tribunal may require the party requesting an interim measure to provide appropriate security in connection with the measure.
8.	British Columbia - International Commercial Arbitration Act [RSBC 1996] Chapter 233[507]	Same as Article 17E of UNCITRAL Model Law 2006 Section 17.05 Provision of Security
9.	British Virgin Islands - Virgin Islands Arbitration Act, 2013[508]	UNCITRAL Model Law to have effect in the Virgin Islands. Section 4. The provisions of the UNCITRAL Model Law have the force of law in the Virgin Islands, subject to the modifications and supplements expressly provided in this Act. Section 38. Application of article 17E of the UNCITRAL Model Law

503. https://pernetmartial.eu/sites/default/files/lois/Bahrain-Loi-d-arbitrage-arbitration-act-ley-de-arbitraje.pdf
504. http://www.mccibd.org/images/uploadimg/act_and_policy/corporate_governance/The-Arbitration-Act-2001.pdf
505. http://www.arbiter.com.sg/pdf/laws/Belgian%20Judicial%20Code%20Provisions%20(2013).pdf
506. https://www.nationalcouncil.bt/assets/uploads/docs/acts/2014/Alternative_Dispute_Resolution_Act_of_Bhutan_2013_eng10th.pdf
507. http://www.bclaws.ca/civix/document/id/complete/statreg/96233_01
508. http://www.bviiac.org/Portals/0/Files/Arbitration%20Documents/ArbitrationAct2013.pdf

Sr. No.	Country	Provision
10.	Bulgaria - Law on International Commercial Arbitration State Gazette (SG) No. 60 of 05.08.1988[509]	Art. 21 ... If such measures are admitted the Arbitral Tribunal may determine a guaranty which the petitioner shall produce.
11.	Cambodia - The Commercial Arbitration Law of the Kingdom of Cambodia 2006[510]	Article 25: Power of Arbitral Panel to Order Interim Measures ... The arbitral panel may require any party to provide appropriate security in connection with such measure.
12.	Canada - Commercial Arbitration Act R.S.C., 1985, c. 17 (2nd Supp.)[511]	Article 17 Power of Arbitral Tribunal to Order Interim Measures ... The arbitral tribunal may require any party to provide appropriate security in connection with such measure.
13.	Connecticut - Chapter 909 Arbitration Proceedings[512]	No equivalent provision as Article 17E of the UNCITRAL Model Law 2006
14.	Croatia - Law on Arbitration Official Gazette no. 88/2001[513]	Article 16 Interim measures in arbitral proceedings (1) ... The arbitral tribunal may require any party to provide appropriate security in connection with such measure.
15.	Cyprus - The International Commercial Arbitration Law, 1987[514]	Section 17 Power of arbitral tribunal to order interim measures. ... The arbitral tribunal may require any party to provide appropriate security in connection with such measure.
16.	Denmark - Danish Arbitration Act 2005[515]	Section 17 ... The arbitral tribunal may require any party to provide appropriate security in connection with such measure.

509. http://www.newyorkconvention.org/11165/web/files/document/1/6/16200.pdf
510. https://www.cambodiaip.gov.kh/DocResources/372a361b-7a97-44b3-9810-79e5e6ea85f4_c786a043-b88d-4f64-9429-60a330efdc5f-en.pdf
511. https://laws-lois.justice.gc.ca/eng/acts/C-34.6/index.html
512. https://www.cga.ct.gov/current/pub/chap_909.htm
513. http://www.vsrh.hr/CustomPages/Static/HRV/Files/Legislation__Law-Arbitration-RC.pdf
514. https://www.uv.es/medarb/observatorio/leyes-arbitraje/europa-resto/chipre-international-commercial-arbitration-law.pdf
515. https://voldgiftsinstituttet.dk/wp-content/uploads/2015/01/danish_arbitration_act_2005.pdf

Sr. No.	Country	Provision
17.	Egypt - Law No. 27/1994 Promulgating the Law Concerning Arbitration in Civil and Commercial Matters[516]	Article 24 (1) … and to require any party to provide appropriate security to cover the costs of the ordered measure.
18.	Florida – Chapter 684 – International Commercial Arbitration, Title XXXIX Commercial Relations, 2020 Florida Statutes[517]	Same as Article 17E of the UNCITRAL Model Law 2006. Article 684.0023 Provision of Security
19.	Fiji – International Arbitration Act 2017 (Act No. 44 of 2017)[518]	Same as Article 17E of UNCITRAL Model Law 2006 Section 28 Provision of security
20.	France – Book IV - Arbitration of the Code of Civil Procedure Decree No. 2011-48[519]	No equivalent provision as Article 17E of the UNCITRAL Model Law 2006
21.	Georgia – Chapter 9 Arbitration, Title 9 Civil Practice, Georgia Code[520]	Article 18 - Conditions for granting interim measures 3. The arbitral tribunal is entitled to require the party requesting an interim measure to provide appropriate security with relation to the interim measures.
22.	Germany – Tenth Book of the Code of Civil Procedure, Arbitration Procedure[521]	Section 1041 Interim measures of protection 1. … The arbitral tribunal may require any party to provide appropriate security in connection with such measure.
23.	Greece – Code of Civil Procedure, Book VII, Book VIII[522]	No equivalent provision as Article 17E of the UNCITRAL Model Law 2006

516. https://www.wipo.int/edocs/lexdocs/laws/en/eg/eg020en.pdf
517. https://www.flsenate.gov/Laws/Statutes/2020/Chapter684/All
518. https://www.fiji.gov.fj/getattachment/d9502667-6491-4592-85b2-eff97f245fed/Act-44---International-Arbitration-Act.aspx
519. http://www.iaiparis.com/pdf/FRENCH_LAW_ON_INTERNATIONAL_ARBITRATION.pdf
520. https://matsne.gov.ge/ru/document/download/89284/5/en/pdf
521. https://sccinstitute.com/media/29988/german-arbitration-act.pdf
522. https://www.uv.es/medarb/observatorio/leyes-arbitraje/europa-resto/grecia-ccp-domestic-arbitration.pdf

Sr. No.	Country	Provision
24.	Hong Kong - Cap. 609 Arbitration Ordinance[523]	Same as Article 17E of the UNCITRAL Model Law 2006 Section 40 - Article 17E of UNCITRAL Model Law (Provision of Security)
25.	Hungary - Act LX of 2017 on Arbitration[524]	Section 23 (1) The arbitral tribunal may require the party requesting an interim measure to provide appropriate security in connection with the measure. (2) The arbitral tribunal shall require the party applying for a preliminary order to provide appropriate security in connection with the order unless the arbitral tribunal considers it unnecessary to do so.
26.	Ireland - Arbitration Act 2010 Number 1 of 2010[525]	Section 6 - Adoption of Model Law Subject to this Act, the Model Law shall have the force of law in the State and shall apply to arbitrations under arbitration agreements concerning— (a) international commercial arbitrations, or (b) arbitrations which are not international commercial arbitrations. Same as Article 17E of UNCITRAL Model Law 2006 Article 17E under Schedule 1 - TEXT OF UNCITRAL MODEL LAW ON INTERNATIONAL COMMERCIAL ARBITRATION
27.	Jamaica - The Arbitration Act, 2017 (Act 13 of 2017)[526]	Same as Article 17E of UNCITRAL Model Law 2006 Section 25 Provision for security
28.	Japan - Arbitration Law (Law No.138 of 2003)[527]	Article 24. (Interim Measures of Protection) (2) The arbitral tribunal may order any party to provide appropriate security in connection with such measure as prescribed in the preceding paragraph.
29.	Jordan - Law No. 31 of 2001 (Jordan) Arbitration Law[528]	Article 23 a. Subject to article (13) of this law, the two arbitrating parties may agree that the arbitral tribunal is empowered to order either of them, whether by its own initiative or upon request of either party, to take whatever interim or conservative measures it find necessary in respect of the subject-matter of the dispute, and it may require (either party)(1) to provide sufficient security to cover the expenses of such measures.

523. https://www.elegislation.gov.hk/hk/cap609
524. https://www.ilo.org/dyn/natlex/docs/ELECTRONIC/106843/131257/F-266585574/J2017T0060P_20180102_FIN.pdf
525. http://www.irishstatutebook.ie/eli/2010/act/1/enacted/en/pdf
526. http://extwprlegs1.fao.org/docs/pdf/jam172060.pdf
527. https://japan.kantei.go.jp/policy/sihou/arbitrationlaw.pdf
528. https://www.ilo.org/dyn/natlex/docs/ELECTRONIC/63091/95325/F1864661120/JOR63091.pdf

Sr. No.	Country	Provision
30.	Kenya – Chapter 49 Arbitration Act (The Arbitration Act, 1995)[529]	Section 18 - Power of arbitral tribunal (1) … (b) order any party to provide security in respect of any claim or any amount in dispute; or
31.	Liechtenstein - Liechtenstein Arbitration Law (Code of Civil Procedure)[530]	Section 610 Power to Order Interim or Protective Measures 1. … The arbitral tribunal may require any party to provide appropriate security in connection with such measures.
32.	Lithuania – The Republic of Lithuania Law on Commercial Arbitration, 2012[531]	Article 23. Security for Compensation for Losses Likely to Result from Taking of Interim Measures or the Issue of a Preliminary Order 1. An arbitral tribunal may oblige a party to apply for interim measures to provide a security for compensation for losses of the other party likely to result from taking of interim measures. 2. An arbitral tribunal shall oblige a party requesting the issue of a preliminary order to provide a security for compensation for losses of the other party likely to result from the issue of the preliminary order, unless the arbitral tribunal considers it inappropriate or unnecessary to do so.
33.	Louisiana – RS 9 Title 9.Civil Code-Ancillaries[532]	§4257. Power of arbitral tribunal to order interim measures … The arbitral tribunal may require any party to provide appropriate security in connection with the measure.
34.	Macedonia - Law on International Commercial Arbitration of the Republic of Macedonia[533]	Article 17 Power of arbitral tribunal to order interim measures … The arbitral tribunal may require any party to provide appropriate security in connection with such measure.
35.	Malaysia – Arbitration Act 2005, Act 646[534]	Section 19 Power of arbitral tribunal to order interim measures (2) The arbitral tribunal may require any party to provide appropriate security in connection with such measure as ordered under subsection (1).
36.	Maldives – Act No: 10/2013, Arbitration Act[535]	Section 37 Provision of Security (a) The Arbitral Tribunal may require the party requesting an interim measure under this Act to provide appropriate security in connection with the measure. A preliminary order may be granted without

529. https://ncia.or.ke/wp-content/uploads/2021/02/ArbitrationAct4of1995_2.pdf
530. https://www.newyorkconvention.org/11165/web/files/document/2/1/21372.pdf
531. https://e-seimas.lrs.lt/portal/legalAct/lt/TAD/35954312dcb311e6be918a531b2126ab?jfwid=-wd7z7zum0
532. http://legis.la.gov/legis/Laws_Toc.aspx?folder=83&title=9
533. https://www.international-arbitration-attorney.com/wp-content/uploads/2013/07/Macedonia-Arbitration-Law.pdf
534. http://www.newyorkconvention.org/11165/web/files/document/1/6/16298.pdf
535. https://miac.gov.mv/media/documents/Arbitration%20Act.pdf

Sr. No.	Country	Provision
		demanding appropriate security only if the tribunal considers it inappropriate or unnecessary to do so in the circumstances. (b) "Provision of security" mentioned in (a) above refers to ordering the party requesting an interim measure to deposit an amount or guarantee of payment at the Arbitral Tribunal that would be appropriate for the payment of reparation in the event that the Arbitral Tribunal decides to award damages to the party against whom the preliminary order is made if such party suffers damages or is required to bear costs due to the performance of the interim measure contained in such a preliminary order.
37.	Malta - CAP. 387 Arbitration Act[536]	Article 17. Power of arbitral tribunal to order interim measures The arbitral tribunal may require any party to provide appropriate security in connection with such measure.
38.	Mauritius - The International Arbitration Act, 2008 (Act 37 of 2008)[537]	Section 17. Interim measures by Tribunal (6) The arbitral tribunal may require the party requesting an interim measure to provide appropriate security in connection with the measure.
39.	Montenegro - Decree on the Promulgation of the Law on Arbitration, 2015[538]	Article 24 Provision of security The arbitral tribunal may, by a decision, impose an obligation on the party requesting an interim measure to provide appropriate security.
40.	Myanmar - Arbitration Law The Pyidaungsu Hluttaw Law No. 5/2016[539]	Section 19 Power of arbitral tribunal to order interim orders (d) The power of the arbitral tribunal to order a claimant to provide security for costs as referred to in subsection (a)(1) shall not be exercised solely because the claimant is: (1) an individual ordinarily residing outside the Republic of the Union of Myanmar; (2) a corporation or an association incorporated or formed under the law of the other country.
41.	New South Wales - Commercial Arbitration Act 2010 No 61[540]	Section 17E Provision of security (cf Model Law Art 17E) (1) The arbitral tribunal may require the party requesting an interim measure to provide appropriate security in connection with the measure. (2) Note. Subsection (1) is the same as Art 17E (1) of the Model Law. Art 17E (2) is omitted as a consequence of this Act not including equivalents to Arts 17B and 17C of the Model Law.

536. http://justiceservices.gov.mt/DownloadDocument.aspx?app=lom&itemid=8854&l=1
537. https://www.wipo.int/edocs/lexdocs/laws/en/mu/mu020en.pdf
538. https://www.privrednakomora.me/sites/pkcg.org/files/multimedia/main_pages/files/2012/09/final_eng_zakon_o_arbitrazi_final_0.pdf
539. http://www.newyorkconvention.org/11165/web/files/document/2/1/21098.pdf
540. https://legislation.nsw.gov.au/view/html/inforce/current/act-2010-061#sec.17E

Sr. No.	Country	Provision
42.	New Zealand – The Arbitration Act, 1996 No 99[541]	Schedule I - Rules applying to arbitration agreement Article 17I Provision of security (1) The arbitral tribunal may require the applicant for an interim measure to provide appropriate security in connection with the measure. (2) The arbitral tribunal must require the applicant for a preliminary order to provide appropriate security in connection with the order unless it considers it inappropriate or unnecessary to do so.
43.	Nigeria - Arbitration and Conciliation Act Chapter 19 Laws of the Federation of Nigeria 1990[542]	Part I Arbitration Section 13 - Power of arbitral tribunal to order interim measure of protection (b) require any party to provide appropriate security in connection with any measure taken under paragraph (a) of this section. First Schedule, Arbitration Rules Article 26 INTERIM MEASURES OF PROTECTION (2) Such interim measures may be established in the form of an interim award. The arbitral tribunal shall be entitled to require security for the cost of such measures.
44.	Northern Territory of Australia - Commercial Arbitration (National Uniform Legislation) Act 2011[543]	Section 17E Provision of security (Model Law Art 17E) (1) The arbitral tribunal may require the party requesting an interim measure to provide appropriate security in connection with the measure. (2) (not used) Note for section 17E Subsection (1) is the same as Art 17E(1) of the Model Law. Art 17E(2) is omitted as a consequence of this Act not including equivalents to Arts 17B and 17C of the Model Law.
45.	Norway - Act of 14 May 2004 No. 25 relating to Arbitration (The Arbitration Act)[544]	Section 19 - The scope of the arbitral tribunal for deciding interim measures ... The arbitral tribunal may order, by way of a condition for effecting and implementing the measure, whoever has requested such measure to provide, within a specified time limit, security respecting any consequences thereof. ...
46.	Oman - The Omani Law of Arbitration in Civil and Commercial Disputes – Royal Decree 47/97[545]	Article 24 1. ... and that, the board may order submission of an adequate security/guarantee for covering the expenses relating to the measures to be taken as per its directives.

541. http://www.legislation.govt.nz/act/public/1996/0099/latest/whole.html#DLM403277
542. http://niqs.org.ng/wp-content/uploads/2018/12/Arbitration-and-Conciliation-Act.pdf
543. https://legislation.nt.gov.au/api/sitecore/Act/PDF?id=11692
544. https://www.chamber.no/wp-content/uploads/2014/02/Norwegian_Arbitration_Act.pdf
545. http://www.newyorkconvention.org/11165/web/files/document/2/1/21103.pdf

Sr. No.	Country	Provision
47.	Ontario - International Commercial Arbitration Act, 2017, S.O. 2017, c. 2, Sched. 5[546]	Section 5 - Application of Model Law (1) Subject to this Act, the Model Law on International Commercial Arbitration, adopted by the United Nations Commission on International Trade Law on 21 June 1985, as amended by the United Nations Commission on International Trade Law on 7 July 2006, set out in Schedule 2, has force of law in Ontario. Same (2) With respect to article 7 of the Model Law, option I applies in Ontario; option II does not. Same (3) The Model Law applies to international commercial arbitration agreements and awards made in international commercial arbitrations, whether made before or after the coming into force of this Act. Schedule 2 to this Act Article 17E
48.	Oregon – Oregon International Commercial Arbitration and Conciliation Act[547]	36.486 Interim measures of protection ordered by arbitral tribunal; security. ... The arbitral tribunal may require any party to provide appropriate security in connection with such measure.
49.	Pakistan - The Arbitration Act, 1940 Act No. X of 1940[548]	No equivalent provision as Article 17E of the UNCITRAL Model Law 2006
50.	Philippines - Alternative Dispute Resolution Act of 2004 Republic Act No. 9285[549]	Section 28. Grant of Interim Measure of Protection. – (3) The order granting provisional relief may be conditioned upon the provision of security or any act or omission specified in the order.
51.	Poland – Polish Act of 17 November 1964 - Code of Civil Procedure, Part Five Arbitration[550]	Art. 1181 §1 ... By ordering such measures the arbitral tribunal may require a party to provide appropriate security in order for the measure to be effective.

546. https://www.ontario.ca/laws/statute/17i02b#BK16
547. https://www.oregonlegislature.gov/bills_laws/ors/ors036.html
548. https://www.wipo.int/edocs/lexdocs/laws/en/pk/pk066en.pdf
549. http://www.newyorkconvention.org/11165/web/files/document/2/1/21107.pdf
550. https://www.uv.es/medarb/observatorio/leyes-arbitraje/europa-resto/polonia-ccp-arbitration.pdf

Sr. No.	Country	Provision
52.	Qatar - Law No. 2 of 2017 Promulgating the Civil and Commercial Arbitration Law-The Law of Arbitration in Civil and Commercial Matters[551]	Article (17) (1) (d) … The Arbitral Tribunal may require the Party requesting such procedures to submit sufficient security for costs for the provisional measure it orders or the interim award it issues.
53.	Queensland - Commercial Arbitration Act 2013 No. 8[552]	Section 17E Provision of security (cf Model Law Art 17E) (1) The arbitral tribunal may require the party requesting an interim measure to provide appropriate security in connection with the measure. (2) [omitted] Note— Subsection (1) is the same as Art 17E(1) of the Model Law. Art 17E(2) is omitted as a consequence of this Act not including equivalents to Arts 17B and 17C of the Model Law.
54.	Republic of Costa Rica - Costa Rican Law for International Arbitration Law Number: 8937[553]	Same as Article 17E of UNCITRAL Model Law 2006
55.	Republic of Korea – Arbitration Act[554]	Article 18-4 (Provision of Security) The arbitral tribunal may require the party requesting an interim measure to provide appropriate security.
56.	Russia - Russian Federation Law on International Commercial Arbitration[555]	Article 17. Power of arbitral tribunal to order interim measures 1. … The arbitral tribunal may require any party to provide appropriate security in connection with such measure. …

551. https://www.qicdrc.gov.qa/sites/default/files/inline-files/law_no._02_2017_promulgating_the_civil_and_commercial_arbitration_law.pdf
552. https://www.legislation.qld.gov.au/view/pdf/inforce/2013-05-17/act-2013-008
553. https://arbitratlaw.com/wp-content/uploads/2017/01/Costa-Rican-Intl-Arbitration-Law.pdf
554. https://elaw.klri.re.kr/eng_service/lawView.do?hseq=38889&lang=ENG
555. http://www.newyorkconvention.org/11165/web/files/document/2/2/22335.pdf

Sr. No.	Country	Provision
57.	Rwanda - Law on Arbitration and Conciliation in Commercial Matters, N° 005/2008[556]	Article 27: Provision of security The arbitral tribunal may require the party requesting an interim measure to provide appropriate security in connection with the measure being applied for. The arbitral tribunal shall request one of the parties applying for a preliminary Order to provide security in connection with the order unless the arbitral tribunal considers it inappropriate or unnecessary to do so.
58.	Saudi Arabia - Law of Arbitration Royal Decree No. M/34[557]	Article 23 1. ... The arbitration tribunal may require the party requesting such measures to provide sufficient financial guarantee for the execution of such proceeding.
59.	Serbia - Law on Arbitration No. 46/06[558]	Article 31 - Competence of the Arbitration Court to Impose Provisional Measures Unless the parties have agreed otherwise, the arbitration court may, at a proposal by one of the parties, impose a provisional measure, which it deems necessary with regard to the matter in dispute, and may simultaneously decide for the opposing side to lodge an appropriate security.
60.	Singapore - Arbitration Act (Chapter 10) (Domestic Arbitration Law)[559]	No equivalent provision as Article 17E of the UNCITRAL Model Law 2006
61.	Singapore - International Arbitration Act (Chapter 143A) (International Arbitration Law)[560]	Section 3 Model Law to have force of law (1) Subject to this Act, the Model Law, with the exception of Chapter VIII thereof, shall have the force of law in Singapore. (2) In the Model Law — "State" means Singapore and any country other than Singapore; "this State" means Singapore. Article 17. Power of arbitral tribunal to order interim measures ... The arbitral tribunal may require any party to provide appropriate security in connection with such measure.
62.	Slovakia - [Slovak] Act No. 244/2002 of 3 April 2002 on Arbitration[561]	Section 22 - Interim Measures (3) By an interim measure the arbitral tribunal may, in particular, order a party to arbitration to: a) pay a deposit or place an asset into the court's custody, (4) The arbitral tribunal may order the claimant to provide means to secure any loss that may occur as a result of the interim measure. If the claimant fails to provide means or advance on payment ordered by the arbitral tribunal within the stipulated time period, the arbitral tribunal shall dismiss the request for interim measure.

556. http://www.newyorkconvention.org/11165/web/files/document/2/1/21110.pdf
557. https://www.wipo.int/edocs/lexdocs/laws/en/sa/sa057en.pdf
558. https://www.wipo.int/edocs/lexdocs/laws/en/rs/rs028en.pdf
559. https://sso.agc.gov.sg/Act/AA2001
560. https://sso.agc.gov.sg/Act/IAA1994

Sr. No.	Country	Provision
63.	Slovenia - Law on Arbitration of Slovenia[562]	Article 20 Interim Measures Ordered by Arbitral Tribunal (1) ... The arbitral tribunal may require any party to provide appropriate security in connection with the measure.
64.	South Africa - The Arbitration Act, 1965[563]	No equivalent provision as Article 17E of the UNCITRAL Model Law 2006
65.	South Australia - South Australia Commercial Arbitration Act 2011[564]	Section 17E—Provision of security (1) The arbitral tribunal may require the party requesting an interim measure to provide appropriate security in connection with the measure. Note— Subsection (1) is the same as Art 17E(1) of the Model Law. Art 17E(2) is omitted as a consequence of this Act not including equivalents to Arts 17B and 17C of the Model Law.
66.	Spain - Act 60/2003 of 23 December on Arbitration[565]	Article 23. Arbitrators' power to order interim measures 1. ... The arbitrators may require the claimant to furnish sufficient security.
67.	Sri Lanka - Arbitration Act. No. 11 of 1995[566]	Section 13 - Interim measures of protection (1) The arbitral tribunal may also order the party making such request to provide the party ordered to take such interim measures, with security for any expense, loss or damage that may be caused in taking such interim measures : Provided however that, other than in exceptional cases no such order shall be made except after hearing the other parties.
68.	Sweden - The Swedish Arbitration Act (SFS 1999:116)[567]	Section 25 ... The arbitrators may prescribe that the party requesting the interim measure must provide reasonable security for the damage which may be incurred by the opposing party as a result of the interim measure.
69.	Switzerland - Private International Law Act 1987, Chapter 12: International Arbitration[568]	Article 183 2. Provisional and conservatory measures 3 The arbitral tribunal or the state judge may make the granting of provisional or conservatory measures subject to appropriate sureties.

561. https://www.international-arbitration-attorney.com/wp-content/uploads/2013/07/Slovakia-Arbitration-Law-1.pdf
562. http://www.sloarbitration.eu/Portals/0/Arbitrazno-pravo/Law%20on%20Arbitration%20of%20Slovenia.pdf
563. https://www.gov.za/sites/default/files/gcis_document/201505/act-42-1965.pdf
564. https://www.legislation.sa.gov.au/LZ/C/A/COMMERCIAL%20ARBITRATION%20ACT%202011/CURRENT/2011.32.UN.PDF
565. https://www.mjusticia.gob.es/cs/Satellite/Portal/1292426982249?blobheader=application%2Fpdf&blobheadername1=Content-Disposition&blobheadervalue1=attachment%3B+filename%3DAct_on_arbitration_%28Ley_60_2003__de_arbitraje%29.PDF
566. http://www.slnarbcentre.com/pdf/ARBITRATION-ACT.pdf
567. https://sccinstitute.com/media/37089/the-swedish-arbitration-act.pdf

Sr. No.	Country	Provision
70.	Tasmania - Commercial Arbitration Act, 2011, Act 13 of 2011[569]	Section 17E. Provision of security (cf Model Law Art 17E) (1) The arbitral tribunal may require the party requesting an interim measure to provide appropriate security in connection with the measure. (2) ... Note. Subsection (1) is the same as Art 17E(1) of the Model Law. Art 17E(2) is omitted as a consequence of this Act not including equivalents to Arts 17B and 17C of the Model Law.
71.	Texas - Chapter 172. Arbitration and Conciliation of International Commercial Disputes, Civil Practice and Remedies Code[570]	Sec. 172.083. INTERIM MEASURES ORDERED BY ARBITRATION TRIBUNAL. (b) The arbitration tribunal may require a party to provide appropriate security in connection with the interim measure ordered.
72.	Thailand - Arbitration Act B.E. 2545[571]	No equivalent provision as Article 17E of the UNCITRAL Model Law 2006
73.	Tunisia - Law n° 93-42 issued on April 26, related to the promulgation of the Arbitration Code[572]	Article 62 ... In both cases, the arbitral tribunal or the judge may require any party to provide appropriate security to cover the costs of the interim measures ordered.
74.	Turkey - Turkish International Arbitration Law, Law no. 4686, 2001[573]	Article 6 Interim measures of protection and interim attachments ... The arbitral tribunal may require any party to provide appropriate security in connection with such measure or attachment. ...
75.	Uganda - Chapter 4 The Arbitration and Conciliation Act[574]	Section 17. Power of arbitral tribunal. 1. ... and the arbitral tribunal may require any party to provide appropriate security in connection with such measure.

568. https://www.swissarbitration.org/wp-content/uploads/2021/05/20210129-Chapter-12-PILA_Translation_English.pdf
569. https://www.legislation.tas.gov.au/view/html/inforce/current/act-2011-013
570. https://statutes.capitol.texas.gov/Docs/CP/htm/CP.172.htm
571. https://tai.coj.go.th/th/file/get/file/20190328ecac5333356ffad0331bd601151db9f4142557.pdf
572. https://arbitrationlaw.com/sites/default/files/free_pdfs/Tunisia%20Arbitration%20Code.pdf
573. http://www.camera-arbitrale.it/Documenti/tial_turkey.pdf
574. https://ulii.org/akn/ug/act/2000/7/eng@2008-06-27

Sr. No.	Country	Provision
76.	Ukraine - The Law of Ukraine on International Commercial Arbitration[575]	Article 17. Power of Arbitral Tribunal to Order Interim Measures ... The arbitral tribunal may require any party to provide appropriate security in connection with such measures.
77.	United Arab Emirates - Federal Law No. (6) of 2018 on Arbitration[576]	Article (21) Interim or Conservatory Measures 2. The Arbitral Tribunal may require the party requesting the order for interim or conservatory measures to provide appropriate security to cover the costs of such measures and may further require that party to bear all damages arising in connection with the enforcement of such measures should the Arbitral Tribunal thereafter decide that the party is not entitled to secure them.
78.	Uruguay - Law 19,636 Approve Rules for International Commercial Arbitration[577]	Article 17 (Power of the arbitral tribunal to order provisional precautionary measures) .- 1. The arbitral tribunal may require the applicant for a measure precautionary, which provides an adequate guarantee regarding the measure.
79.	Venezuela - Venezuelan Commercial Arbitration Act[578]	Article 26. - ... The arbitral tribunal may require the requesting party to provide appropriate securities.
80.	Victoria - Commercial Arbitration Act 2011 No. 50 of 2011[579]	Section 17E Provision of security (cf Model Law Art 17E) (1) The arbitral tribunal may require the party requesting an interim measure to provide appropriate security in connection with the measure. (2) [omitted] Note Subsection (1) is the same as Art 17E(1) of the Model Law. Art 17E(2) is omitted as a consequence of this Act not including equivalents to Arts 17B and 17C of the Model Law
81.	Western Australia - Commercial Arbitration Act 2012, 023 of 2012[580]	Section 17E. Provision of security (cf. Model Law Art 17E) (1) The arbitral tribunal may require the party requesting an interim measure to provide appropriate security in connection with the measure. (2) ...

575. http://arbitrations.ru/userfiles/file/Law/Arbitration%20acts/ukraininan%20law%20on%20arbitration.pdf
576. https://www.tamimi.com/crm-media-uploader/fileupload/server/php/files/UAE%20Arbitration%20Law%20-%20Federal%20Law%20No%20%206%20of%202018.pdf
577. http://www.impo.com.uy/bases/leyes-originales/19636-2018
578. https://arbitrationlaw.com/sites/default/files/free_pdfs/Venezula%20Commercial%20Arbitration%20Act.pdf
579. http://arbitration.site/wp-content/uploads/2019/06/CAA-Vic-.pdf
580. https://www.legislation.wa.gov.au/legislation/prod/filestore.nsf/FileURL/mrdoc_25084.pdf/$FILE/Commercial%20Arbitration%20Act%202012%20-%20%5B00-b0-06%5D.pdf?OpenElement

Sr. No.	Country	Provision
		Note for this section: Subsection (1) is the same as Art 17E(1) of the Model Law. Art 17E(2) is omitted as a consequence of this Act not including equivalents to Arts 17B and 17C of the Model Law.
82.	Zambia - The Arbitration Act, 2000 No. 19 of 2000[581]	Section 14 - Power of arbitral tribunal to order interim and other measures 1. ... and the arbitral tribunal may require any party to provide appropriate security in connection with any such measure.
83.	Zimbabwe - Chapter 7:15 Arbitration Act[582]	ARTICLE 17 Power of arbitral tribunal to order interim measures 1. ... The arbitral tribunal may require any party to provide appropriate security in connection with any such measure.

581. http://www.newyorkconvention.org/11165/web/files/document/2/1/21396.pdf
582. https://zimlii.org/akn/zw/act/1996/6/eng@2016-12-31

Appendix H (Article 17F)

Sr. No.	Country	Provision
1.	Australia - International Arbitration Act 1974[583]	Same as Article 17F of UNCITRAL Model Law 2006 Sec 16 Model Law to have force of law (1) Subject to this Part, the Model Law has the force of law in Australia. (2) In the Model Law: Arbitration agreement has the meaning given in Option 1 of Article 7 of the Model Law. State means Australia (including the external Territories) and any foreign country. This State means Australia (including the external Territories). Model Law under Part V, Schedule 2 of the Arbitration Act, 1974
2.	Australian Capital Territory - Commercial Arbitration Act, 2017 A2017-7[584]	SECT 17F Disclosure (Model Law art 17F) (1) The arbitral tribunal may require any party promptly to disclose any material change in the circumstances on the basis of which the measure was requested or granted. (2) [omitted] Note Subsection (1) is the same as the Model Law, art 17F (1). Art 17F (2) is omitted as a consequence of this Act not including equivalents to the Model Law, art 17B and art 17C.
3.	Austria - Austrian Arbitration Act, 2013[585]	No equivalent provision as Article 17F of the UNCITRAL Model Law 2006

583. https://www.legislation.gov.au/Details/C2011C00342
584. http://classic.austlii.edu.au/au/legis/act/consol_act/caa2017219/s17f.html
585. https://www.viac.eu/images/law/ZPO_Schiedsrecht_2014_en_im_VIAC_Layout.pdf

Sr. No.	Country	Provision
4.	Bahrain - Bahrain Arbitration Law No. 9/2015[586]	Same as UNCITRAL Model Law 2006 Article 1 Taking into account the provisions of international conventions in force in the Kingdom of Bahrain 1. The provisions of the " UNCITRAL " Model Law on International Commercial Arbitration Act attached to this law shall apply to all arbitration whatever the nature of the legal relationship of the dispute herewith, if this arbitration takes place in the Kingdom of Bahrain or abroad and that two parties agreed to comply with the provisions of the attached law. 2. The provisions of the attached law shall apply to all arbitration which begins after its entry into force even if based on an arbitration agreement concluded before the entry into force of this law.
5.	Bangladesh – The Arbitration Act, 2001[587]	No equivalent provision as Article 17F of the UNCITRAL Model Law 2006
6.	Belgium – Belgian Judicial Code Provisions[588]	Art. 1694 The arbitral tribunal may require any party promptly to disclose any material change in the circumstances on the basis of which the measure was requested or granted.
7.	Bhutan - Aternative Dispute Resolution Act of Bhutan 2013[589]	Section 120. Disclosure of material circumstances The arbitral tribunal may require a party to promptly disclose a material change in the circumstances upon which an interim measure was requested or granted.
8.	British Columbia - International Commercial Arbitration Act [RSBC 1996] Chapter 233[590]	Section 17.06 Disclosure (1) The arbitral tribunal may require any party promptly to disclose any material change in the circumstances on the basis of which an interim measure was requested or granted. (2) The party applying for a preliminary order must disclose to the arbitral tribunal all circumstances that are likely to be relevant to the arbitral tribunal's determination whether to grant or maintain the order. (3) The disclosure obligation under subsection (2) continues until the party against whom the preliminary order has been requested has had an opportunity to present its case. (4) After the party against whom a preliminary order has been requested has had an opportunity to present its case, the arbitral tribunal may require any party promptly to disclose any material change in the circumstances on the basis of which the preliminary order was requested or granted.

586. https://pernetmartial.eu/sites/default/files/lois/Bahrain-Loi-d-arbitrage-arbitration-act-ley-de-arbitraje.pdf
587. http://www.mccibd.org/images/uploadimg/act_and_policy/corporate_governance/The-Arbitration-Act-2001.pdf
588. http://www.arbiter.com.sg/pdf/laws/Belgian%20Judicial%20Code%20Provisions%20(2013).pdf
589. https://www.nationalcouncil.bt/assets/uploads/docs/acts/2014/Alternative_Dispute_Resolution_Act_of_Bhutan_2013_eng10th.pdf
590. http://www.bclaws.ca/civix/document/id/complete/statreg/96233_01

Sr. No.	Country	Provision
9.	British Virgin Islands - Virgin Islands Arbitration Act, 2013[591]	UNCITRAL Model Law to have effect in the Virgin Islands. Section 4. The provisions of the UNCITRAL Model Law have the force of law in the Virgin Islands, subject to the modifications and supplements expressly provided in this Act. Section 39. Application of article 17F of the UNCITRAL Model Law
10.	Bulgaria - Law on International Commercial Arbitration State Gazette (SG) No. 60 of 05.08.1988[592]	No equivalent provision as Article 17F of the UNCITRAL Model Law 2006
11.	Cambodia - The Commercial Arbitration Law of the Kingdom of Cambodia 2006[593]	No equivalent provision as Article 17F of the UNCITRAL Model Law 2006
12.	Canada – Commercial Arbitration Act R.S.C., 1985, c. 17 (2nd Supp.)[594]	No equivalent provision as Article 17F of the UNCITRAL Model Law 2006
13.	Connecticut - Chapter 909 Arbitration Proceedings[595]	No equivalent provision as Article 17F of the UNCITRAL Model Law 2006
14.	Croatia – Law on Arbitration Official Gazette no. 88/2001[596]	No equivalent provision as Article 17F of the UNCITRAL Model Law 2006
15.	Cyprus – The International Commercial Arbitration Law, 1987[597]	No equivalent provision as Article 17F of the UNCITRAL Model Law 2006

591. http://www.bviiac.org/Portals/0/Files/Arbitration%20Documents/ArbitrationAct2013.pdf
592. http://www.newyorkconvention.org/11165/web/files/document/1/6/16200.pdf
593. https://www.cambodiaip.gov.kh/DocResources/372a361b-7a97-44b3-9810-79e5e6ea85f4_c786a043-b88d-4f64-9429-60a330efdc5f-en.pdf
594. https://laws-lois.justice.gc.ca/eng/acts/C-34.6/index.html
595. https://www.cga.ct.gov/current/pub/chap_909.htm
596. http://www.vsrh.hr/CustomPages/Static/HRV/Files/Legislation__Law-Arbitration-RC.pdf
597. https://www.uv.es/medarb/observatorio/leyes-arbitraje/europa-resto/chipre-international-commercial-arbitration-law.pdf

Sr. No.	Country	Provision
16.	Denmark – Danish Arbitration Act 2005[598]	No equivalent provision as Article 17F of the UNCITRAL Model Law 2006
17.	Egypt - Law No. 27/1994 Promulgating the Law Concerning Arbitration in Civil and Commercial Matters[599]	No equivalent provision as Article 17F of the UNCITRAL Model Law 2006
18.	Florida – Chapter 684 – International Commercial Arbitration, Title XXXIX Commercial Relations, 2020 Florida Statutes[600]	Same as Article 17F of the UNCITRAL Model Law 2006. Article 684.0024 Disclosure
19.	Fiji – International Arbitration Act 2017 (Act No. 44 of 2017)[601]	Same as Article 17F of UNCITRAL Model Law 2006 Section 29 Disclosure
20.	France – Book IV - Arbitration of the Code of Civil Procedure Decree No. 2011-48[602]	No equivalent provision as Article 17F of the UNCITRAL Model Law 2006
21.	Georgia – Chapter 9 Arbitration, Title 9 Civil Practice, Georgia Code[603]	Article 20 - Duty of disclosure The arbitral tribunal may require any party to promptly disclose information related to material changes in the circumstances, on the basis of which the interim measure was requested or granted.
22.	Germany – Tenth Book of the Code of Civil Procedure, Arbitration Procedure[604]	No equivalent provision as Article 17F of the UNCITRAL Model Law 2006

598. https://voldgiftsinstituttet.dk/wp-content/uploads/2015/01/danish_arbitration_act_2005.pdf
599. https://www.wipo.int/edocs/lexdocs/laws/en/eg/eg020en.pdf
600. https://www.flsenate.gov/Laws/Statutes/2020/Chapter684/All
601. https://www.fiji.gov.fj/getattachment/d9502667-6491-4592-85b2-eff97f245fed/Act-44---International-Arbitration-Act.aspx
602. http://www.iaiparis.com/pdf/FRENCH_LAW_ON_INTERNATIONAL_ARBITRATION.pdf
603. https://matsne.gov.ge/ru/document/download/89284/5/en/pdf
604. https://sccinstitute.com/media/29988/german-arbitration-act.pdf

Sr. No.	Country	Provision
23.	Greece - Code Of Civil Procedure, Book VII, Book VIII[605]	No equivalent provision as Article 17F of the UNCITRAL Model Law 2006
24.	Hong Kong - Cap. 609 Arbitration Ordinance[606]	Same as Article 17F of the UNCITRAL Model Law 2006 Section 41 - Article 17F of UNCITRAL Model Law (Disclosure)
25.	Hungary - Act LX of 2017 on Arbitration[607]	Section 24 (1) The arbitral tribunal may require any party to immediately disclose any substantial change in the circumstances on the basis of which the measure was requested or granted. (2) The party applying for a preliminary order shall disclose to the arbitral tribunal all circumstances that are likely to be relevant to the arbitral tribunal's determination whether to grant or maintain the order, and such obligation shall continue until the party against whom the preliminary order has been requested has had an opportunity to present his case. Thereafter, the provisions of paragraph (1) shall apply.
26.	Ireland - Arbitration Act 2010 Number 1 of 2010[608]	Section 6 – Adoption of Model Law Subject to this Act, the Model Law shall have the force of law in the State and shall apply to arbitrations under arbitration agreements concerning— (a) international commercial arbitrations, or (b) arbitrations which are not international commercial arbitrations. Same as Article 17F of UNCITRAL Model Law 2006 Article 17F under Schedule 1 - TEXT OF UNCITRAL MODEL LAW ON INTERNATIONAL COMMERCIAL ARBITRATION
27.	Jamaica - The Arbitration Act, 2017 (Act 13 of 2017)[609]	Same as Article 17F of UNCITRAL Model Law 2006 Section 26 Disclosure
28.	Japan - Arbitration Law (Law No.138 of 2003)[610]	No equivalent provision as Article 17F of the UNCITRAL Model Law 2006
29.	Jordan - Law No. 31 of 2001 (Jordan) Arbitration Law[611]	No equivalent provision as Article 17F of the UNCITRAL Model Law 2006

605. https://www.uv.es/medarb/observatorio/leyes-arbitraje/europa-resto/grecia-ccp-domestic-arbitration.pdf
606. https://www.elegislation.gov.hk/hk/cap609
607. https://www.ilo.org/dyn/natlex/docs/ELECTRONIC/106843/131257/F-266585574/J2017T0060P_20180102_FIN.pdf
608. http://www.irishstatutebook.ie/eli/2010/act/1/enacted/en/pdf
609. http://extwprlegs1.fao.org/docs/pdf/jam172060.pdf
610. https://japan.kantei.go.jp/policy/sihou/arbitrationlaw.pdf

Sr. No.	Country	Provision
30.	Kenya – Chapter 49 Arbitration Act (The Arbitration Act, 1995)[612]	No equivalent provision as Article 17F of the UNCITRAL Model Law 2006
31.	Liechtenstein - Liechtenstein Arbitration Law (Code of Civil Procedure)[613]	No equivalent provision as Article 17F of the UNCITRAL Model Law 2006
32.	Lithuania – The Republic of Lithuania Law on Commercial Arbitration, 2012[614]	Article 20 Interim Measures 5. An arbitral tribunal may oblige a party to give a prompt notice of a substantial change of circumstances in relation to which the issue of taking interim measures has been resolved. Article 21. Preliminary Orders 3. A party requesting an arbitral tribunal to give a preliminary order must inform the arbitral tribunal of all circumstances that may be significant for the consideration of the application. This obligation of the party shall be valid over the period of validity of the preliminary order.
33.	Louisiana – RS 9 Title 9.Civil Code-Ancillaries[615]	No equivalent provision as Article 17F of the UNCITRAL Model Law 2006
34.	Macedonia - Law on International Commercial Arbitration of the Republic of Macedonia[616]	No equivalent provision as Article 17F of the UNCITRAL Model Law 2006
35.	Malaysia – Arbitration Act 2005, Act 646[617]	No equivalent provision as Article 17F of the UNCITRAL Model Law 2006
36.	Maldives – Act No: 10/2013, Arbitration Act[618]	Section 38 Disclosure (a) The Arbitral Tribunal may require any party promptly to disclose any material change in the circumstances on the basis of which the order for an interim measure was requested or granted.

611. https://www.ilo.org/dyn/natlex/docs/ELECTRONIC/63091/95325/F1864661120/JOR63091.pdf
612. https://ncia.or.ke/wp-content/uploads/2021/02/ArbitrationAct4of1995_2.pdf
613. https://www.newyorkconvention.org/11165/web/files/document/2/1/21372.pdf
614. https://e-seimas.lrs.lt/portal/legalAct/lt/TAD/35954312dcb311e6be918a531b2126ab?jfwid=-wd7z7zum0
615. http://legis.la.gov/legis/Laws_Toc.aspx?folder=83&title=9
616. https://www.international-arbitration-attorney.com/wp-content/uploads/2013/07/Macedonia-Arbitration-Law.pdf
617. http://www.newyorkconvention.org/11165/web/files/document/1/6/16298.pdf
618. https://miac.gov.mv/media/documents/Arbitration%20Act.pdf

Sr. No.	Country	Provision
37.	Malta - CAP. 387 Arbitration Act[619]	No equivalent provision as Article 17F of the UNCITRAL Model Law 2006
38.	Mauritius - The International Arbitration Act, 2008 (Act 37 of 2008)[620]	Section 17. Interim measures by Tribunal (7) The arbitral tribunal may require any party promptly to disclose any material change in the circumstances on the basis of which the measure was requested or granted.
39.	Montenegro - Decree on the Promulgation of the Law on Arbitration, 2015[621]	Article 25 Disclosure The arbitral tribunal may require the parties promptly to disclose any change in the facts on the basis of which the interim measure was requested or ordered.
40.	Myanmar - Arbitration Law The Pyidaungsu Hluttaw Law No. 5/2016[622]	No equivalent provision as Article 17F of the UNCITRAL Model Law 2006
41.	New South Wales - Commercial Arbitration Act 2010 No 61[623]	Section 17F Disclosure (cf Model Law Art 17F) (1) The arbitral tribunal may require any party promptly to disclose any material change in the circumstances on the basis of which the measure was requested or granted. (2) Note. Subsection (1) is the same as Art 17F (1) of the Model Law. Art 17F (2) is omitted as a consequence of this Act not including equivalents to Arts 17B and 17C of the Model Law.
42.	New Zealand - The Arbitration Act, 1996 No 99[624]	Schedule I - Rules applying to arbitration agreement Article 17J Disclosure of material circumstances (1) The arbitral tribunal may require a party to promptly disclose to the arbitral tribunal a material change in the circumstances upon which an interim measure was requested or granted. (2) The applicant for a preliminary order must disclose to the arbitral tribunal all circumstances that are likely to be relevant to the arbitral tribunal's determination as to whether to issue or extend the order. (3) The obligation in paragraph (2) continues until each respondent has had an opportunity to present the respondent's case, after which paragraph (1) applies.

619. http://justiceservices.gov.mt/DownloadDocument.aspx?app=lom&itemid=8854&l=1
620. https://www.wipo.int/edocs/lexdocs/laws/en/mu/mu020en.pdf
621. https://www.privrednakomora.me/sites/pkcg.org/files/multimedia/main_pages/files/2012/09/final_eng_zakon_o_arbitrazi_final_0.pdf
622. http://www.newyorkconvention.org/11165/web/files/document/2/1/21098.pdf
623. https://legislation.nsw.gov.au/view/html/inforce/current/act-2010-061#sec.17F
624. http://www.legislation.govt.nz/act/public/1996/0099/latest/whole.html#DLM403277

Sr. No.	Country	Provision
43.	Nigeria - Arbitration and Conciliation Act Chapter 19 Laws of the Federation of Nigeria 1990[625]	No equivalent provision as Article 17F of the UNCITRAL Model Law 2006
44.	Northern Territory of Australia - Commercial Arbitration (National Uniform Legislation) Act 2011[626]	Section 17F Disclosure (Model Law Art 17F) (1) The arbitral tribunal may require any party promptly to disclose any material change in the circumstances on the basis of which the measure was requested or granted. (2) (not used) Note for section 17F Subsection (1) is the same as Art 17F(1) of the Model Law. Art 17F(2) is omitted as a consequence of this Act not including equivalents to Arts 17B and 17C of the Model Law.
45.	Norway - Act of 14 May 2004 No. 25 relating to Arbitration (The Arbitration Act)[627]	No equivalent provision as Article 17F of the UNCITRAL Model Law 2006
46.	Oman - The Omani Law of Arbitration in Civil and Commercial Disputes – Royal Decree 47/97[628]	No equivalent provision as Article 17F of the UNCITRAL Model Law 2006
47.	Ontario - International Commercial Arbitration Act, 2017, S.O. 2017, c. 2, Sched. 5[629]	Section 5 - Application of Model Law (1) Subject to this Act, the Model Law on International Commercial Arbitration, adopted by the United Nations Commission on International Trade Law on 21 June 1985, as amended by the United Nations Commission on International Trade Law on 7 July 2006, set out in Schedule 2, has force of law in Ontario. Same (2) With respect to article 7 of the Model Law, option I applies in Ontario; option II does not. Same (3) The Model Law applies to international commercial arbitration agreements and awards made in international commercial arbitrations, whether made before or after the coming into force of this Act. Schedule 2 to this Act Article 17F

625. http://niqs.org.ng/wp-content/uploads/2018/12/Arbitration-and-Conciliation-Act.pdf
626. https://legislation.nt.gov.au/api/sitecore/Act/PDF?id = 11692
627. https://www.chamber.no/wp-content/uploads/2014/02/Norwegian_Arbitration_Act.pdf
628. http://www.newyorkconvention.org/11165/web/files/document/2/1/21103.pdf
629. https://www.ontario.ca/laws/statute/17i02b#BK16

Sr. No.	Country	Provision
48.	Oregon – Oregon International Commercial Arbitration and Conciliation Act[630]	No equivalent provision as Article 17F of the UNCITRAL Model Law 2006
49.	Pakistan - The Arbitration Act, 1940 Act No. X of 1940[631]	No equivalent provision as Article 17F of the UNCITRAL Model Law 2006
50.	Philippines - Alternative Dispute Resolution Act of 2004 Republic Act No. 9285[632]	No equivalent provision as Article 17F of the UNCITRAL Model Law 2006
51.	Poland – Polish Act of 17 November 1964 - Code of Civil Procedure, Part Five Arbitration[633]	No equivalent provision as Article 17F of the UNCITRAL Model Law 2006
52.	Qatar - Law No. 2 of 2017 Promulgating the Civil and Commercial Arbitration Law-The Law of Arbitration in Civil and Commercial Matters[634]	No equivalent provision as Article 17F of the UNCITRAL Model Law 2006
53.	Queensland - Commercial Arbitration Act 2013 No. 8[635]	Section 17F Disclosure (cf Model Law Art 17F) (1) The arbitral tribunal may require any party promptly to disclose any material change in the circumstances on the basis of which the measure was requested or granted. (2) [omitted] Note— Subsection (1) is the same as Art 17F(1) of the Model Law. Art 17F(2) is omitted as a consequence of this Act not including equivalents to Arts 17B and 17C of the Model Law.

630. https://www.oregonlegislature.gov/bills_laws/ors/ors036.html
631. https://www.wipo.int/edocs/lexdocs/laws/en/pk/pk066en.pdf
632. http://www.newyorkconvention.org/11165/web/files/document/2/1/21107.pdf
633. https://www.uv.es/medarb/observatorio/leyes-arbitraje/europa-resto/polonia-ccp-arbitration.pdf
634. https://www.qicdrc.gov.qa/sites/default/files/inline-files/law_no._02_2017_promulgating_the_civil_and_commercial_arbitration_law.pdf

Sr. No.	Country	Provision
54.	Republic of Costa Rica - Costa Rican Law for International Arbitration Law Number: 8937[636]	Same as Article 17F of UNCITRAL Model Law 2006
55.	Republic of Korea - Arbitration Act[637]	Article 18-5 (Disclosure) The arbitral tribunal may require any party to promptly disclose any material change in the circumstances of the interim measure or on the basis of which the measure was requested.
56.	Russia - Russian Federation Law on International Commercial Arbitration[638]	No equivalent provision as Article 17F of the UNCITRAL Model Law 2006
57.	Rwanda – Law on Arbitration and Conciliation in Commercial Matters, N° 005/2008[639]	Article 28: Disclosure of changes The party requesting for an interim measure shall immediately, with undue delay, disclose any material change in the circumstances on the basis of which the measure was requested or granted. The party applying for a preliminary Order shall disclose to the arbitral tribunal all circumstances that are likely to be relevant to the arbitral tribunal's determination whether to grant or maintain the Order, and such obligation shall continue until the party against whom the order has been requested has had an opportunity to present its case. Thereafter, the applying party shall also have to know immediately the material change with respect to the preliminary Order that a requesting party has with respect to an interim measure under Paragraph 1 of this Article.
58.	Saudi Arabia – Law of Arbitration Royal Decree No. M/34[640]	No equivalent provision as Article 17F of the UNCITRAL Model Law 2006
59.	Serbia – Law on Arbitration No. 46/06[641]	No equivalent provision as Article 17F of the UNCITRAL Model Law 2006

635. https://www.legislation.qld.gov.au/view/pdf/inforce/2013-05-17/act-2013-008
636. https://arbitratlaw.com/wp-content/uploads/2017/01/Costa-Rican-Intl-Arbitration-Law.pdf
637. https://elaw.klri.re.kr/eng_service/lawView.do?hseq=38889&lang=ENG
638. http://www.newyorkconvention.org/11165/web/files/document/2/2/22335.pdf
639. http://www.newyorkconvention.org/11165/web/files/document/2/1/21110.pdf
640. https://www.wipo.int/edocs/lexdocs/laws/en/sa/sa057en.pdf
641. https://www.wipo.int/edocs/lexdocs/laws/en/rs/rs028en.pdf

Sr. No.	Country	Provision
60.	Singapore - Arbitration Act (Chapter 10) (Domestic Arbitration Law)[642]	No equivalent provision as Article 17F of the UNCITRAL Model Law 2006
61.	Singapore - International Arbitration Act (Chapter 143A) (International Arbitration Law)[643]	No equivalent provision as Article 17F of the UNCITRAL Model Law 2006
62.	Slovakia – [Slovak] Act No. 244/2002 of 3 April 2002 on Arbitration[644]	No equivalent provision as Article 17F of the UNCITRAL Model Law 2006
63.	Slovenia - Law on Arbitration of Slovenia[645]	No equivalent provision as Article 17F of the UNCITRAL Model Law 2006
64.	South Africa – The Arbitration Act, 1965[646]	No equivalent provision as Article 17F of the UNCITRAL Model Law 2006
65.	South Australia - South Australia Commercial Arbitration Act 2011[647]	Section 17F—Disclosure (1) The arbitral tribunal may require any party promptly to disclose any material change in the circumstances on the basis of which the measure was requested or granted. Note— Subsection (1) is the same as Art 17F(1) of the Model Law. Art 17F(2) is omitted as a consequence of this Act not including equivalents to Arts 17B and 17C of the Model Law.
66.	Spain - Act 60/2003 of 23 December on Arbitration[648]	No equivalent provision as Article 17F of the UNCITRAL Model Law 2006

642. https://sso.agc.gov.sg/Act/AA2001
643. https://sso.agc.gov.sg/Act/IAA1994
644. https://www.international-arbitration-attorney.com/wp-content/uploads/2013/07/Slovakia-Arbitration-Law-1.pdf
645. http://www.sloarbitration.eu/Portals/0/Arbitrazno-pravo/Law%20on%20Arbitration%20of%20Slovenia.pdf
646. https://www.gov.za/sites/default/files/gcis_document/201505/act-42-1965.pdf
647. https://www.legislation.sa.gov.au/LZ/C/A/COMMERCIAL%20ARBITRATION%20ACT%202011/CURRENT/2011.32.UN.PDF
648. https://www.mjusticia.gob.es/cs/Satellite/Portal/1292426982249?blobheader=application%2Fpdf&blobheadername1=Content-Disposition&blobheadervalue1=attachment%3B+filename%3DAct_on_arbitration_%28Ley_60_2003__de_arbitraje%29.PDF

Sr. No.	Country	Provision
67.	Sri Lanka - Arbitration Act. No. 11 of 1995[649]	No equivalent provision as Article 17F of the UNCITRAL Model Law 2006
68.	Sweden – The Swedish Arbitration Act (SFS 1999:116)[650]	No equivalent provision as Article 17F of the UNCITRAL Model Law 2006
69.	Switzerland – Private International Law Act 1987, Chapter 12: International Arbitration[651]	No equivalent provision as Article 17F of the UNCITRAL Model Law 2006
70.	Tasmania – Commercial Arbitration Act, 2011, Act 13 of 2011[652]	Section 17F. Disclosure (cf Model Law Art 17F) (1) The arbitral tribunal may require any party promptly to disclose any material change in the circumstances on the basis of which the measure was requested or granted. (2) … Note. Subsection (1) is the same as Art 17F(1) of the Model Law. Art 17F(2) is omitted as a consequence of this Act not including equivalents to Arts 17B and 17C of the Model Law.
71.	Texas - Chapter 172. Arbitration and Conciliation of International Commercial Disputes, Civil Practice and Remedies Code[653]	No equivalent provision as Article 17F of the UNCITRAL Model Law 2006
72.	Thailand – Arbitration Act B.E. 2545[654]	No equivalent provision as Article 17F of the UNCITRAL Model Law 2006
73.	Tunisia – Law n° 93-42 issued on April 26, related to the promulgation of the Arbitration Code[655]	No equivalent provision as Article 17F of the UNCITRAL Model Law 2006

649. http://www.slnarbcentre.com/pdf/ARBITRATION-ACT.pdf
650. https://sccinstitute.com/media/37089/the-swedish-arbitration-act.pdf
651. https://www.swissarbitration.org/wp-content/uploads/2021/05/20210129-Chapter-12-PILA_Translation_English.pdf
652. https://www.legislation.tas.gov.au/view/html/inforce/current/act-2011-013
653. https://statutes.capitol.texas.gov/Docs/CP/htm/CP.172.htm
654. https://tai.coj.go.th/th/file/get/file/20190328ecac5333356ffad0331bd601151db9f4142557.pdf

Sr. No.	Country	Provision
74.	Turkey - Turkish International Arbitration Law, Law no. 4686, 2001[656]	No equivalent provision as Article 17F of the UNCITRAL Model Law 2006
75.	Uganda – Chapter 4 The Arbitration and Conciliation Act[657]	No equivalent provision as Article 17F of the UNCITRAL Model Law 2006
76.	Ukraine - The Law of Ukraine on International Commercial Arbitration[658]	No equivalent provision as Article 17F of the UNCITRAL Model Law 2006
77.	United Arab Emirates - Federal Law No. (6) of 2018 on Arbitration[659]	No equivalent provision as Article 17F of the UNCITRAL Model Law 2006
78.	Uruguay - Law 19,636 Approve Rules for International Commercial Arbitration[660]	No equivalent provision as Article 17F of the UNCITRAL Model Law 2006
79.	Venezuela – Venezuelan Commercial Arbitration Act[661]	No equivalent provision as Article 17F of the UNCITRAL Model Law 2006
80.	Victoria - Commercial Arbitration Act 2011 No. 50 of 2011[662]	Section 17F Disclosure (cf Model Law Art 17F) (1) The arbitral tribunal may require any party promptly to disclose any material change in the circumstances on the basis of which the measure was requested or granted. (2) [omitted]

655. https://arbitrationlaw.com/sites/default/files/free_pdfs/Tunisia%20Arbitration%20Code.pdf
656. http://www.camera-arbitrale.it/Documenti/tial_turkey.pdf
657. https://ulii.org/akn/ug/act/2000/7/eng@2008-06-27
658. http://arbitrations.ru/userfiles/file/Law/Arbitration%20acts/ukraininan%20law%20on%20arbitration.pdf
659. https://www.tamimi.com/crm-media-uploader/fileupload/server/php/files/UAE%20Arbitration%20Law%20-%20Federal%20Law%20No%20%206%20of%202018.pdf
660. http://www.impo.com.uy/bases/leyes-originales/19636-2018
661. https://arbitrationlaw.com/sites/default/files/free_pdfs/Venezula%20Commercial%20Arbitration%20Act.pdf
662. http://arbitration.site/wp-content/uploads/2019/06/CAA-Vic-.pdf

Sr. No.	Country	Provision
		Note Subsection (1) is the same as Art 17F(1) of the Model Law. Art 17F(2) is omitted as a consequence of this Act not including equivalents to Arts 17B and 17C of the Model Law.
81.	Western Australia - Commercial Arbitration Act 2012, 023 of 2012[663]	Section 17F. Disclosure (cf. Model Law Art 17F) (1) The arbitral tribunal may require any party promptly to disclose any material change in the circumstances on the basis of which the measure was requested or granted. (2) ... Note for this section: Subsection (1) is the same as Art 17F(1) of the Model Law. Art 17F(2) is omitted as a consequence of this Act not including equivalents to Arts 17B and 17C of the Model Law.
82.	Zambia - The Arbitration Act, 2000 No. 19 of 2000[664]	No equivalent provision as Article 17F of the UNCITRAL Model Law 2006
83.	Zimbabwe - Chapter 7:15 Arbitration Act[665]	No equivalent provision as Article 17F of the UNCITRAL Model Law 2006

663. https://www.legislation.wa.gov.au/legislation/prod/filestore.nsf/FileURL/mrdoc_25084.pdf/$FILE/Commercial%20Arbitration%20Act%202012%20-%20%5B00-b0-06%5D.pdf?OpenElement
664. http://www.newyorkconvention.org/11165/web/files/document/2/1/21396.pdf
665. https://zimlii.org/akn/zw/act/1996/6/eng@2016-12-31

Appendix I (Article 17G)

Sr. No.	Country	Provision
1.	Australia - International Arbitration Act 1974[666]	Same as Article 17G of UNCITRAL Model Law 2006 Sec 16 Model Law to have force of law (1) Subject to this Part, the Model Law has the force of law in Australia. (2) In the Model Law: Arbitration agreement has the meaning given in Option 1 of Article 7 of the Model Law. State means Australia (including the external Territories) and any foreign country. This State means Australia (including the external Territories). Model Law under Part V, Schedule 2 of the Arbitration Act, 1974
2.	Australian Capital Territory – Commercial Arbitration Act, 2017 A2017-7[667]	SECT 17G Costs and damages (Model Law art 17G) (1) The party requesting an interim measure is liable for any costs and damages caused by the measure to any party if the arbitral tribunal later determines that, in the circumstances, the measure should not have been granted. (2) The arbitral tribunal may award such costs and damages at any point during the proceedings. Note This section is substantially the same as the Model Law, art 17G but the reference to applications for preliminary orders is omitted as a consequence of this Act not including equivalents to the Model Law, art 17B and art 17C.
3.	Austria – Austrian Arbitration Act, 2013[668]	No equivalent provision as Article 17G of the UNCITRAL Model Law 2006

666. https://www.legislation.gov.au/Details/C2011C00342
667. http://classic.austlii.edu.au/au/legis/act/consol_act/caa2017219/s17g.html
668. https://www.viac.eu/images/law/ZPO_Schiedsrecht_2014_en_im_VIAC_Layout.pdf

Sr. No.	Country	Provision
4.	Bahrain - Bahrain Arbitration Law No. 9/2015[669]	Same as UNCITRAL Model Law 2006 Article 1 Taking into account the provisions of international conventions in force in the Kingdom of Bahrain 1. The provisions of the " UNCITRAL " Model Law on International Commercial Arbitration Act attached to this law shall apply to all arbitration whatever the nature of the legal relationship of the dispute herewith, if this arbitration takes place in the Kingdom of Bahrain or abroad and that two parties agreed to comply with the provisions of the attached law. 2. The provisions of the attached law shall apply to all arbitration which begins after its entry into force even if based on an arbitration agreement concluded before the entry into force of this law.
5.	Bangladesh – The Arbitration Act, 2001[670]	No equivalent provision as Article 17G of the UNCITRAL Model Law 2006
6.	Belgium – Belgian Judicial Code Provisions[671]	Art. 1695 The party requesting an interim or conservatory measure shall be liable for any costs and damages caused by the measure to another party if the arbitral tribunal later determines that, in the circumstances, the measure should not have been granted. The arbitral tribunal may award such costs and damages at any point during the proceedings.
7.	Bhutan - Alternative Dispute Resolution Act of Bhutan 2013[672]	Cost and damages Section 121. An applicant for an interim measure is liable for any costs and damages caused to any party by the measure if the arbitral tribunal later determines that, in the circumstances, the measure should not have been granted or issued. Section 122. The arbitral tribunal may award costs and damages at any time during the arbitral proceedings.
8.	British Columbia - International Commercial Arbitration Act [RSBC 1996] Chapter 233[673]	Same as Article 17G of UNCITRAL Model Law 2006 Section 17.07 Costs and damages

669. https://pernetmartial.eu/sites/default/files/lois/Bahrain-Loi-d-arbitrage-arbitration-act-ley-de-arbitraje.pdf
670. http://www.mccibd.org/images/uploadimg/act_and_policy/corporate_governance/The-Arbitration-Act-2001.pdf
671. http://www.arbiter.com.sg/pdf/laws/Belgian%20Judicial%20Code%20Provisions%20(2013).pdf
672. https://www.nationalcouncil.bt/assets/uploads/docs/acts/2014/Alternative_Dispute_Resolution_Act_of_Bhutan_2013_eng10th.pdf
673. http://www.bclaws.ca/civix/document/id/complete/statreg/96233_01

Sr. No.	Country	Provision
9.	British Virgin Islands - Virgin Islands Arbitration Act, 2013[674]	UNCITRAL Model Law to have effect in the Virgin Islands. Section 4. The provisions of the UNCITRAL Model Law have the force of law in the Virgin Islands, subject to the modifications and supplements expressly provided in this Act. Section 40. Application of article 17G of the UNCITRAL Model Law
10.	Bulgaria - Law on International Commercial Arbitration State Gazette (SG) No. 60 of 05.08.1988[675]	No equivalent provision as Article 17G of the UNCITRAL Model Law 2006
11.	Cambodia - The Commercial Arbitration Law of the Kingdom of Cambodia 2006[676]	No equivalent provision as Article 17G of the UNCITRAL Model Law 2006
12.	Canada – Commercial Arbitration Act R.S.C., 1985, c. 17 (2nd Supp.)[677]	No equivalent provision as Article 17G of the UNCITRAL Model Law 2006
13.	Connecticut - Chapter 909 Arbitration Proceedings[678]	No equivalent provision as Article 17G of the UNCITRAL Model Law 2006
14.	Croatia – Law on Arbitration Official Gazette no. 88/2001[679]	No equivalent provision as Article 17G of the UNCITRAL Model Law 2006
15.	Cyprus – The International Commercial Arbitration Law, 1987[680]	No equivalent provision as Article 17G of the UNCITRAL Model Law 2006
16.	Denmark – Danish Arbitration Act 2005[681]	No equivalent provision as Article 17G of the UNCITRAL Model Law 2006

674. http://www.bviiac.org/Portals/0/Files/Arbitration%20Documents/ArbitrationAct2013.pdf
675. http://www.newyorkconvention.org/11165/web/files/document/1/6/16200.pdf
676. https://www.cambodiaip.gov.kh/DocResources/372a361b-7a97-44b3-9810-79e5e6ea85f4_c786a043-b88d-4f64-9429-60a330efdc5f-en.pdf
677. https://laws-lois.justice.gc.ca/eng/acts/C-34.6/index.html
678. https://www.cga.ct.gov/current/pub/chap_909.htm
679. http://www.vsrh.hr/CustomPages/Static/HRV/Files/Legislation__Law-Arbitration-RC.pdf
680. https://www.uv.es/medarb/observatorio/leyes-arbitraje/europa-resto/chipre-international-commercial-arbitration-law.pdf

Sr. No.	Country	Provision
17.	Egypt - Law No. 27/1994 Promulgating the Law Concerning Arbitration in Civil and Commercial Matters[682]	No equivalent provision as Article 17G of the UNCITRAL Model Law 2006
18.	Florida – Chapter 684 – International Commercial Arbitration, Title XXXIX Commercial Relations, 2020 Florida Statutes[683]	Same as Article 17G of the UNCITRAL Model Law 2006. Article 684.0025 Costs and damages
19.	Fiji – International Arbitration Act 2017 (Act No. 44 of 2017)[684]	Same as Article 17G of UNCITRAL Model Law 2006 Section 30 Costs and damages
20.	France – Book IV - Arbitration of the Code of Civil Procedure Decree No. 2011-48[685]	No equivalent provision as Article 17G of the UNCITRAL Model Law 2006
21.	Georgia – Chapter 9 Arbitration, Title 9 Civil Practice, Georgia Code[686]	Article 18 - Conditions for granting interim measures 4. If the arbitral tribunal decides that, under the given circumstances, respective interim measures should not have been granted, the party requesting an interim measure shall be liable for any costs and damages caused by such interim measures. The arbitral tribunal may award to the arbitration party against whom the interim measures were taken, such costs and damages at any stage of the arbitration proceedings.
22.	Germany – Tenth Book of the Code of Civil Procedure, Arbitration Procedure[687]	Section 1041 Interim measures of protection (4) If a measure ordered under subsection 1 proves to have been unjustified from the outset, the party who obtained its enforcement is obliged to compensate the other party for damage resulting from the enforcement of such measure or from his providing security in order to avoid enforcement. This claim may be put forward in the pending arbitral proceedings.

681. https://voldgiftsinstituttet.dk/wp-content/uploads/2015/01/danish_arbitration_act_2005.pdf
682. https://www.wipo.int/edocs/lexdocs/laws/en/eg/eg020en.pdf
683. https://www.flsenate.gov/Laws/Statutes/2020/Chapter684/All
684. https://www.fiji.gov.fj/getattachment/d9502667-6491-4592-85b2-eff97f245fed/Act-44---International-Arbitration-Act.aspx
685. http://www.iaiparis.com/pdf/FRENCH_LAW_ON_INTERNATIONAL_ARBITRATION.pdf
686. https://matsne.gov.ge/ru/document/download/89284/5/en/pdf
687. https://sccinstitute.com/media/29988/german-arbitration-act.pdf

Sr. No.	Country	Provision
23.	Greece - Code Of Civil Procedure, Book VII, Book VIII[688]	No equivalent provision as Article 17G of the UNCITRAL Model Law 2006
24.	Hong Kong - Cap. 609 Arbitration Ordinance[689]	Same as Article 17G of the UNCITRAL Model Law 2006 Section 42 - Article 17G of UNCITRAL Model Law (Costs and damages)
25.	Hungary - Act LX of 2017 on Arbitration[690]	Section 25 The party requesting an interim measure or applying for a preliminary order shall be liable for any costs and damages caused by the measure or the order if the arbitral tribunal later determines that, in the circumstances, the measure or the order should not have been granted. The arbitral tribunal may award such costs and damages at any point during the proceedings.
26.	Ireland - Arbitration Act 2010 Number 1 of 2010[691]	Section 6 - Adoption of Model Law Subject to this Act, the Model Law shall have the force of law in the State and shall apply to arbitrations under arbitration agreements concerning— (a) international commercial arbitrations, or (b) arbitrations which are not international commercial arbitrations. Same as Article 17G of UNCITRAL Model Law 2006 Article 17G under Schedule 1 - TEXT OF UNCITRAL MODEL LAW ON INTERNATIONAL COMMERCIAL ARBITRATION
27.	Jamaica - The Arbitration Act, 2017 (Act 13 of 2017)[692]	Section 27 Costs and damages (1) The party requesting an interim measure or applying for a preliminary order shall be liable for any costs and damages caused by the measure or the order to any party if the arbitral tribunal later determines that, in the circumstances, the measure or the order should not have been granted. (2) The arbitral tribunal may award such costs and damages at any point during the proceedings.
28.	Japan - Arbitration Law (Law No.138 of 2003)[693]	No equivalent provision as Article 17G of the UNCITRAL Model Law 2006
29.	Jordan - Law No. 31 of 2001 (Jordan) Arbitration Law[694]	No equivalent provision as Article 17G of the UNCITRAL Model Law 2006

688. https://www.uv.es/medarb/observatorio/leyes-arbitraje/europa-resto/grecia-ccp-domestic-arbitration.pdf
689. https://www.elegislation.gov.hk/hk/cap609
690. https://www.ilo.org/dyn/natlex/docs/ELECTRONIC/106843/131257/F-266585574/J2017T0060P_20180102_FIN.pdf
691. http://www.irishstatutebook.ie/eli/2010/act/1/enacted/en/pdf
692. http://extwprlegs1.fao.org/docs/pdf/jam172060.pdf
693. https://japan.kantei.go.jp/policy/sihou/arbitrationlaw.pdf

Sr. No.	Country	Provision
30.	Kenya – Chapter 49 Arbitration Act (The Arbitration Act, 1995)[695]	No equivalent provision as Article 17G of the UNCITRAL Model Law 2006
31.	Liechtenstein - Liechtenstein Arbitration Law (Code of Civil Procedure)[696]	No equivalent provision as Article 17G of the UNCITRAL Model Law 2006
32.	Lithuania - The Republic of Lithuania Law on Commercial Arbitration, 2012[697]	Article 23. Security for Compensation for Losses Likely to Result from Taking of Interim Measures or the Issue of a Preliminary Order 1. An arbitral tribunal may oblige a party applying for interim measures to provide a security for compensation for losses of the other party likely to result from taking of interim measures. 2. An arbitral tribunal shall oblige a party requesting the issue of a preliminary order to provide a security for compensation for losses of the other party likely to result from the issue of the preliminary order, unless the arbitral tribunal considers it inappropriate or unnecessary to do so. Article 24. Compensation for Losses Likely to Result from Taking of Interim Measures or the Issue of a Preliminary Order 1. A party that has applied for interim measures or a preliminary order shall be liable for losses resulting from taking of such measures or the issue of the preliminary order provided that, in the process of arbitral proceedings, it is established that the interim measures or the preliminary order is unfounded. 2. At the request of a party, an arbitral tribunal may, by a final arbitral award, oblige a party at the request of which interim measures have been taken to cover losses resulting from taking of such interim measures.
33.	Louisiana – RS 9 Title 9.Civil Code-Ancillaries[698]	No equivalent provision as Article 17G of the UNCITRAL Model Law 2006
34.	Macedonia - Law on International Commercial Arbitration of the Republic of Macedonia[699]	No equivalent provision as Article 17G of the UNCITRAL Model Law 2006

694. https://www.ilo.org/dyn/natlex/docs/ELECTRONIC/63091/95325/F1864661120/JOR63091.pdf
695. https://ncia.or.ke/wp-content/uploads/2021/02/ArbitrationAct4of1995_2.pdf
696. https://www.newyorkconvention.org/11165/web/files/document/2/1/21372.pdf
697. https://e-seimas.lrs.lt/portal/legalAct/lt/TAD/35954312dcb311e6be918a531b2126ab?jfwid=-wd7z7zum0
698. http://legis.la.gov/legis/Laws_Toc.aspx?folder=83&title=9

Sr. No.	Country	Provision
35.	Malaysia – Arbitration Act 2005, Act 646[700]	No equivalent provision as Article 17G of the UNCITRAL Model Law 2006
36.	Maldives - Act No: 10/2013, Arbitration Act[701]	Section 39 Costs and Damages (a) The party requesting an interim shall be liable for any costs and damages caused by the measure or the order to any party if the arbitral tribunal later determines that, in the circumstances, the measure or the order should not have been granted. (b) The arbitral tribunal may award such costs and damages as mentioned in (a) above at any point during the proceedings.
37.	Malta - CAP. 387 Arbitration Act[702]	No equivalent provision as Article 17G of the UNCITRAL Model Law 2006
38.	Mauritius - The International Arbitration Act, 2008 (Act 37 of 2008)[703]	Section 17. Interim measures by Tribunal (8) The arbitral tribunal may, at any time in the arbitral proceedings, order the party who requested the interim measure to pay damages and costs to another party where the arbitral tribunal determines that, in the circumstances, the measure requested should not have been granted.
39.	Montenegro – Decree on the Promulgation of the Law on Arbitration, 2015[704]	Article 26 Costs and damages The party requesting an interim measure shall be liable for any costs and damages caused by the measure to the other party if the arbitral tribunal later determines that, in the circumstances, the measure should not have been granted. The arbitral tribunal may award the costs and damages referred to in paragraph 1 of this Article at any point during the proceedings.
40.	Myanmar - Arbitration Law The Pyidaungsu Hluttaw Law No. 5/2016[705]	No equivalent provision as Article 17G of the UNCITRAL Model Law 2006
41.	New South Wales - Commercial Arbitration Act 2010 No 61[706]	Section 17G Costs and damages (cf Model Law Art 17G) (1) The party requesting an interim measure is liable for any costs and damages caused by the measure to any party if the arbitral tribunal later determines that, in the circumstances, the measure should not have been granted.

699. https://www.international-arbitration-attorney.com/wp-content/uploads/2013/07/Macedonia-Arbitration-Law.pdf
700. http://www.newyorkconvention.org/11165/web/files/document/1/6/16298.pdf
701. https://miac.gov.mv/media/documents/Arbitration%20Act.pdf
702. http://justiceservices.gov.mt/DownloadDocument.aspx?app=lom&itemid=8854&l=1
703. https://www.wipo.int/edocs/lexdocs/laws/en/mu/mu020en.pdf
704. https://www.privrednakomora.me/sites/pkcg.org/files/multimedia/main_pages/files/2012/09/final_eng_zakon_o_arbitrazi_final_0.pdf
705. http://www.newyorkconvention.org/11165/web/files/document/2/1/21098.pdf
706. https://legislation.nsw.gov.au/view/html/inforce/current/act-2010-061#sec.17G

Sr. No.	Country	Provision
		(2) The arbitral tribunal may award such costs and damages at any point during the proceedings. Note. This section is substantially the same as Art 17G of the Model Law but the reference to applications for preliminary orders is omitted as a consequence of this Act not including equivalents to Arts 17B and 17C of the Model Law.
42.	New Zealand – The Arbitration Act, 1996 No 99[707]	Schedule I - Rules applying to arbitration agreement Article 17K Costs and damages (1) An applicant for an interim measure or a preliminary order is liable for any costs and damages caused to any party by the measure or order if the arbitral tribunal later determines that, in the circumstances, the measure or order should not have been granted or issued. (2) The arbitral tribunal may award those costs and damages at any time during the arbitral proceedings.
43.	Nigeria - Arbitration and Conciliation Act Chapter 19 Laws of the Federation of Nigeria 1990[708]	No equivalent provision as Article 17G of the UNCITRAL Model Law 2006
44.	Northern Territory of Australia - Commercial Arbitration (National Uniform Legislation) Act 2011[709]	Section 17G Costs and damages (Model Law Art 17G) (1) The party requesting an interim measure is liable for any costs and damages caused by the measure to any party if the arbitral tribunal later determines that, in the circumstances, the measure should not have been granted. (2) The arbitral tribunal may award such costs and damages at any point during the proceedings. Note for section 17G This section is substantially the same as Art 17G of the Model Law but the reference to applications for preliminary orders is omitted as a consequence of this Act not including equivalents to Arts 17B and 17C of the Model Law.
45.	Norway - Act of 14 May 2004 No. 25 relating to Arbitration (The Arbitration Act)[710]	Section 19 The scope of the arbitral tribunal for deciding interim measures ... If it turns out that the claim which the interim measure was to secure, did not exist at the time of such measure being decided, then whoever requested the implementation thereof shall indemnify other parties for the loss suffered by them as a result of the measure. The arbitral tribunal shall decide the claim for indemnification if requested to do so by a party. ...

707. http://www.legislation.govt.nz/act/public/1996/0099/latest/whole.html#DLM403277
708. http://niqs.org.ng/wp-content/uploads/2018/12/Arbitration-and-Conciliation-Act.pdf
709. https://legislation.nt.gov.au/api/sitecore/Act/PDF?id=11692
710. https://www.chamber.no/wp-content/uploads/2014/02/Norwegian_Arbitration_Act.pdf

Sr. No.	Country	Provision
46.	Oman - The Omani Law of Arbitration in Civil and Commercial Disputes - Royal Decree 47/97[711]	No equivalent provision as Article 17G of the UNCITRAL Model Law 2006
47.	Ontario - International Commercial Arbitration Act, 2017, S.O. 2017, c. 2, Sched. 5[712]	Section 5 - Application of Model Law (1) Subject to this Act, the Model Law on International Commercial Arbitration, adopted by the United Nations Commission on International Trade Law on 21 June 1985, as amended by the United Nations Commission on International Trade Law on 7 July 2006, set out in Schedule 2, has force of law in Ontario. Same (2) With respect to article 7 of the Model Law, option I applies in Ontario; option II does not. Same (3) The Model Law applies to international commercial arbitration agreements and awards made in international commercial arbitrations, whether made before or after the coming into force of this Act. Schedule 2 to this Act Article 17G
48.	Oregon – Oregon International Commercial Arbitration and Conciliation Act[713]	No equivalent provision as Article 17G of the UNCITRAL Model Law 2006
49.	Pakistan - The Arbitration Act, 1940 Act No. X of 1940[714]	No equivalent provision as Article 17G of the UNCITRAL Model Law 2006
50.	Philippines - Alternative Dispute Resolution Act of 2004 Republic Act No. 9285[715]	Section 28. Grant of Interim Measure of Protection. - (7) A party who does not comply with the order shall be liable for all damages resulting from noncompliance, including all expenses, and reasonable attorney's fees, paid in obtaining the order's judicial enforcement.
51.	Poland – Polish Act of 17 November 1964 - Code of Civil Procedure, Part Five Arbitration[716]	Art. 1182 If an order for interim measures by the arbitral tribunal was obviously unjustified, the party for the benefit of which such measure was ordered is liable for damages caused thereby. The claim for damages may be pursued in the pending proceedings before the arbitral tribunal.

711. http://www.newyorkconvention.org/11165/web/files/document/2/1/21103.pdf
712. https://www.ontario.ca/laws/statute/17i02b#BK16
713. https://www.oregonlegislature.gov/bills_laws/ors/ors036.html
714. https://www.wipo.int/edocs/lexdocs/laws/en/pk/pk066en.pdf
715. http://www.newyorkconvention.org/11165/web/files/document/2/1/21107.pdf

Sr. No.	Country	Provision
52.	Qatar - Law No. 2 of 2017 Promulgating the Civil and Commercial Arbitration Law-The Law of Arbitration in Civil and Commercial Matters[717]	Article (17) 4. The Party who requests an interim measure or award shall be liable for any costs and compensation for any damages caused by such measure or award to any Party, if the Arbitral Tribunal subsequently decides that the measure or the award was not warranted by the circumstances. The Arbitral Tribunal may require the said Party to pay costs and compensation at any time during the proceedings.
53.	Queensland - Commercial Arbitration Act 2013 No. 8[718]	Section 17G Costs and damages (cf Model Law Art 17G) (1) The party requesting an interim measure is liable for any costs and damages caused by the measure to any party if the arbitral tribunal later determines that, in the circumstances, the measure should not have been granted. (2) The arbitral tribunal may award such costs and damages at any point during the proceedings. Note— This section is substantially the same as Art 17G of the Model Law but the reference to applications for preliminary orders is omitted as a consequence of this Act not including equivalents to Arts 17B and 17C of the Model Law.
54.	Republic of Costa Rica - Costa Rican Law for International Arbitration Law Number: 8937[719]	Same as Article 17G of UNCITRAL Model Law 2006
55.	Republic of Korea - Arbitration Act[720]	Article 18-6 (Costs and Damages) (1) The party requesting an interim measure shall be liable to pay or compensate for the costs and damages caused by the interim measure to the other party if the arbitral tribunal later determines that, in the circumstances, the interim measure was unjustified. (2) The arbitral tribunal may issue an order, in the form of an arbitral award, for the payment of costs or the compensation for damage under paragraph (1) at any time during the arbitral proceeding.

716. https://www.uv.es/medarb/observatorio/leyes-arbitraje/europa-resto/polonia-ccp-arbitration.pdf
717. https://www.qicdrc.gov.qa/sites/default/files/inline-files/law_no._02_2017_promulgating_the_civil_and_commercial_arbitration_law.pdf
718. https://www.legislation.qld.gov.au/view/pdf/inforce/2013-05-17/act-2013-008
719. https://arbitratlaw.com/wp-content/uploads/2017/01/Costa-Rican-Intl-Arbitration-Law.pdf
720. https://elaw.klri.re.kr/eng_service/lawView.do?hseq=38889&lang=ENG

Sr. No.	Country	Provision
56.	Russia - Russian Federation Law On International Commercial Arbitration[721]	No equivalent provision as Article 17G of the UNCITRAL Model Law 2006
57.	Rwanda - Law on Arbitration and Conciliation in Commercial Matters, N° 005/2008[722]	Article 29: Costs and damages The party requesting for an interim measure or applying for a preliminary order shall be liable for any costs and damages caused by the measure or the order to any party if the arbitral tribunal later determines that, in the circumstances, the measure or the order should not have been granted. The arbitral tribunal may award such costs and damages at any time the arbitration is not concluded.
58.	Saudi Arabia - Law of Arbitration Royal Decree No. M/34[723]	No equivalent provision as Article 17G of the UNCITRAL Model Law 2006
59.	Serbia - Law on Arbitration No. 46/06[724]	No equivalent provision as Article 17G of the UNCITRAL Model Law 2006
60.	Singapore - Arbitration Act (Chapter 10) (Domestic Arbitration Law)[725]	No equivalent provision as Article 17G of the UNCITRAL Model Law 2006
61.	Singapore - International Arbitration Act (Chapter 143A) (International Arbitration Law)[726]	No equivalent provision as Article 17G of the UNCITRAL Model Law 2006
62.	Slovakia - [Slovak] Act No. 244/2002 of 3 April 2002 on Arbitration[727]	Section 22 Interim Measures (4) The arbitral tribunal may order the claimant to provide means to secure any loss that may occur as a result of the interim measure. If the claimant fails to provide means or advance on payment ordered by the arbitral tribunal within the stipulated time period, the arbitral tribunal shall dismiss the request for interim measure.

721. http://www.newyorkconvention.org/11165/web/files/document/2/2/22335.pdf
722. http://www.newyorkconvention.org/11165/web/files/document/2/1/21110.pdf
723. https://www.wipo.int/edocs/lexdocs/laws/en/sa/sa057en.pdf
724. https://www.wipo.int/edocs/lexdocs/laws/en/rs/rs028en.pdf
725. https://sso.agc.gov.sg/Act/AA2001
726. https://sso.agc.gov.sg/Act/IAA1994
727. https://www.international-arbitration-attorney.com/wp-content/uploads/2013/07/Slovakia-Arbitration-Law-1.pdf

Sr. No.	Country	Provision
63.	Slovenia - Law on Arbitration of Slovenia[728]	No equivalent provision as Article 17G of the UNCITRAL Model Law 2006
64.	South Africa - The Arbitration Act, 1965[729]	No equivalent provision as Article 17G of the UNCITRAL Model Law 2006
65.	South Australia - South Australia Commercial Arbitration Act 2011[730]	Section 17G—Costs and damages (1) The party requesting an interim measure is liable for any costs and damages caused by the measure to any party if the arbitral tribunal later determines that, in the circumstances, the measure should not have been granted. (2) The arbitral tribunal may award such costs and damages at any point during the proceedings. Note— This section is substantially the same as Art 17G of the Model Law but the reference to applications for preliminary orders is omitted as a consequence of this Act not including equivalents to Arts 17B and 17C of the Model Law.
66.	Spain - Act 60/2003 of 23 December on Arbitration[731]	No equivalent provision as Article 17G of the UNCITRAL Model Law 2006
67.	Sri Lanka - Arbitration Act. No. 11 of 1995[732]	Section 13 Interim Measures of Protection The arbitral tribunal may also order the party making such request to provide the party ordered to take such interim measures, with security for any expense, loss or damage that may be caused in taking such interim measures: Provided however that, other than in exceptional cases no such order shall be made except after hearing the other parties.
68.	Sweden - The Swedish Arbitration Act (SFS 1999:116)[733]	Section 25 ... The arbitrators may prescribe that the party requesting the interim measure must provide reasonable security for the damage which may be incurred by the opposing party as a result of the interim measure.

728. http://www.sloarbitration.eu/Portals/0/Arbitrazno-pravo/Law%20on%20Arbitration%20of%20Slovenia.pdf
729. https://www.gov.za/sites/default/files/gcis_document/201505/act-42-1965.pdf
730. https://www.legislation.sa.gov.au/LZ/C/A/COMMERCIAL%20ARBITRATION%20ACT%202011/CURRENT/2011.32.UN.PDF
731. https://www.mjusticia.gob.es/cs/Satellite/Portal/1292426982249?blobheader=application%2Fpdf&blobheadername1=Content-Disposition&blobheadervalue1=attachment%3B+filename%3DAct_on_arbitration_%28Ley_60_2003__de_arbitraje%29.PDF
732. http://www.slnarbcentre.com/pdf/ARBITRATION-ACT.pdf
733. https://sccinstitute.com/media/37089/the-swedish-arbitration-act.pdf

Sr. No.	Country	Provision
69.	Switzerland - Private International Law Act 1987, Chapter 12: International Arbitration[734]	No equivalent provision as Article 17G of the UNCITRAL Model Law 2006
70.	Tasmania - Commercial Arbitration Act, 2011, Act 13 of 2011[735]	Section 17G. Costs and damages (cf Model Law Art 17G) (1) The party requesting an interim measure is liable for any costs and damages caused by the measure to any party if the arbitral tribunal later determines that, in the circumstances, the measure should not have been granted. (2) The arbitral tribunal may award such costs and damages at any point during the proceedings. Note. This section is substantially the same as Art 17G of the Model Law but the reference to applications for preliminary orders is omitted as a consequence of this Act not including equivalents to Arts 17B and 17C of the Model Law.
71.	Texas - Chapter 172. Arbitration and Conciliation of International Commercial Disputes, Civil Practice and Remedies Code[736]	No equivalent provision as Article 17G of the UNCITRAL Model Law 2006
72.	Thailand - Arbitration Act B.E. 2545[737]	No equivalent provision as Article 17G of the UNCITRAL Model Law 2006
73.	Tunisia - Law n° 93-42 issued on April 26, related to the promulgation of the Arbitration Code[738]	No equivalent provision as Article 17G of the UNCITRAL Model Law 2006

734. https://www.swissarbitration.org/wp-content/uploads/2021/05/20210129-Chapter-12-PILA_Translation_English.pdf
735. https://www.legislation.tas.gov.au/view/html/inforce/current/act-2011-013
736. https://statutes.capitol.texas.gov/Docs/CP/htm/CP.172.htm
737. https://tai.coj.go.th/th/file/get/file/20190328ecac5333356ffad0331bd601151db9f4142557.pdf
738. https://arbitrationlaw.com/sites/default/files/free_pdfs/Tunisia%20Arbitration%20Code.pdf

Sr. No.	Country	Provision
74.	Turkey - Turkish International Arbitration Law, Law no. 4686, 2001[739]	No equivalent provision as Article 17G of the UNCITRAL Model Law 2006
75.	Uganda – Chapter 4 The Arbitration and Conciliation Act[740]	No equivalent provision as Article 17G of the UNCITRAL Model Law 2006
76.	Ukraine - The Law of Ukraine on International Commercial Arbitration[741]	No equivalent provision as Article 17G of the UNCITRAL Model Law 2006
77.	United Arab Emirates - Federal Law No. (6) of 2018 on Arbitration[742]	Article (21) Interim or Conservatory Measures 2. The Arbitral Tribunal may require the party requesting the order for interim or conservatory measures to provide appropriate security to cover the costs of such measures and may further require that party to bear all damages arising in connection with the enforcement of such measures should the Arbitral Tribunal thereafter decide that the party is not entitled to secure them.
78.	Uruguay - Law 19,636 Approve Rules for International Commercial Arbitration[743]	Article 17 (Power of the arbitral tribunal to order provisional precautionary measures) .- 6) The applicant for a precautionary measure will be responsible for the costs and damages that such measure causes to either party, provided that the arbitral tribunal determines subsequently that, in the circumstances of the case, it should not have requested the measure. The arbitral tribunal may condemn him at any time during the proceedings to pay the costs and damages.
79.	Venezuela – Venezuelan Commercial Arbitration Act[744]	No equivalent provision as Article 17G of the UNCITRAL Model Law 2006

739. http://www.camera-arbitrale.it/Documenti/tial_turkey.pdf
740. https://ulii.org/akn/ug/act/2000/7/eng@2008-06-27
741. http://arbitrations.ru/userfiles/file/Law/Arbitration%20acts/ukraininan%20law%20on%20arbitration.pdf
742. https://www.tamimi.com/crm-media-uploader/fileupload/server/php/files/UAE%20Arbitration%20Law%20-%20Federal%20Law%20No%20%206%20of%202018.pdf
743. http://www.impo.com.uy/bases/leyes-originales/19636-2018
744. https://arbitrationlaw.com/sites/default/files/free_pdfs/Venezula%20Commercial%20Arbitration%20Act.pdf

Sr. No.	Country	Provision
80.	Victoria - Commercial Arbitration Act 2011 No. 50 of 2011[745]	Section 17G Costs and damages (cf Model Law Art 17G) (1) The party requesting an interim measure is liable for any costs and damages caused by the measure to any party if the arbitral tribunal later determines that, in the circumstances, the measure should not have been granted. (2) The arbitral tribunal may award such costs and damages at any point during the proceedings. Note This section is substantially the same as Art 17G of the Model Law but the reference to applications for preliminary orders is omitted as a consequence of this Act not including equivalents to Arts 17B and 17C of the Model Law.
81.	Western Australia - Commercial Arbitration Act 2012, 023 of 2012[746]	Section 17G. Costs and damages (cf. Model Law Art 17G) (1) The party requesting an interim measure is liable for any costs and damages caused by the measure to any party if the arbitral tribunal later determines that, in the circumstances, the measure should not have been granted. (2) The arbitral tribunal may award such costs and damages at any point during the proceedings. Note for this section: This section is substantially the same as Art 17G of the Model Law but the reference to applications for preliminary orders is omitted as a consequence of this Act not including equivalents to Arts 17B and 17C of the Model Law.
82.	Zambia - The Arbitration Act, 2000 No. 19 of 2000[747]	No equivalent provision as Article 17G of the UNCITRAL Model Law 2006
83.	Zimbabwe - Chapter 7:15 Arbitration Act[748]	No equivalent provision as Article 17G of the UNCITRAL Model Law 2006

745. http://arbitration.site/wp-content/uploads/2019/06/CAA-Vic-.pdf
746. https://www.legislation.wa.gov.au/legislation/prod/filestore.nsf/FileURL/mrdoc_25084.pdf/$FILE/Commercial%20Arbitration%20Act%202012%20-%20%5B00-b0-06%5D.pdf?OpenElement
747. http://www.newyorkconvention.org/11165/web/files/document/2/1/21396.pdf
748. https://zimlii.org/akn/zw/act/1996/6/eng@2016-12-31

Appendix J (Article 17H)

Sr. No.	Country	Provision
1.	Australia - International Arbitration Act 1974[749]	Same as Article 17H of UNCITRAL Model Law 2006 Sec 16 Model Law to have force of law (1) Subject to this Part, the Model Law has the force of law in Australia. (2) In the Model Law: Arbitration agreement has the meaning given in Option 1 of Article 7 of the Model Law. State means Australia (including the external Territories) and any foreign country. This State means Australia (including the external Territories). Model Law under Part V, Schedule 2 of the Arbitration Act, 1974
2.	Australian Capital Territory – Commercial Arbitration Act, 2017 A2017-7[750]	SECT 17H Recognition and enforcement (Model Law art 17H) (1) An interim measure issued by an arbitral tribunal under the law of the Territory is to be recognised as binding and, unless otherwise provided by the arbitral tribunal, enforced on application to the court, subject to the provisions of section 17I. (2) An interim measure issued by an arbitral tribunal under the law of a State or another Territory is to be recognised as binding in the ACT and, unless otherwise provided by the arbitral tribunal, enforced on application to the court, irrespective of the State or other Territory in which it was issued, subject to the provisions of section 17I. (3) The party who is seeking or has obtained recognition or enforcement of an interim measure must promptly inform the court of any termination, suspension or modification of that interim measure.

749. https://www.legislation.gov.au/Details/C2011C00342
750. http://classic.austlii.edu.au/au/legis/act/consol_act/caa2017219/s17h.html

Sr. No.	Country	Provision
		(4) The court may, if it considers it proper, order the requesting party to provide appropriate security if the arbitral tribunal has not already made a determination with respect to security or where such a decision is necessary to protect the rights of third parties. Note This section differs from the Model Law, art 17H to the extent necessary to apply art 17H as incorporated in this Act in the context of domestic commercial arbitrations.
3.	Austria - Austrian Arbitration Act, 2013[751]	Section 593 - Ordering of Interim or Protective Measures (3) Upon request of a party the District Court ("Bezirksgericht") in whose district the opponent of the party at risk has its seat, domicile or habitual residence within Austria at the time of the first filing of the request, otherwise the District Court ("Bezirksgericht") in whose district the enforcement of the interim or protective measure shall be carried out, shall enforce such measure. Where the measure provides for a means of protection unknown to Austrian law, the court may, upon request and after hearing the other party, enforce such measure of protection under Austrian law which comes closest to the measure ordered by the arbitral tribunal. In this case the court may also, upon request, reformulate the measure ordered by the arbitral tribunal in order to safeguard the realization of its purpose. (5) The court may hear the other party prior to ruling on the enforcement of the measure under paragraph (1). If the other party has not been heard prior to the ruling, it may file an objection against the granting of the enforcement ("Widerspruch") within the meaning of section 397 Enforcement Act ("Exekutionsordnung"). In both cases the other party may only rely on grounds for refusing the enforcement as set out in paragraph (4). In these proceedings the court has no jurisdiction to rule on claims for damages pursuant to section 394 Enforcement Act ("Exekutionsordnung").
4.	Bahrain - Bahrain Arbitration Law No. 9/2015[752]	Same as UNCITRAL Model Law 2006 Article 1 Taking into account the provisions of international conventions in force in the Kingdom of Bahrain 1. The provisions of the " UNCITRAL " Model Law on International Commercial Arbitration Act attached to this law shall apply to all arbitration whatever the nature of the legal relationship of the dispute herewith, if this arbitration takes place in the Kingdom of Bahrain or abroad and that two parties agreed to comply with the provisions of the attached law. 2. The provisions of the attached law shall apply to all arbitration which begins after its entry into force even if based on an arbitration agreement concluded before the entry into force of this law.

751. https://www.viac.eu/images/law/ZPO_Schiedsrecht_2014_en_im_VIAC_Layout.pdf
752. https://pernetmartial.eu/sites/default/files/lois/Bahrain-Loi-d-arbitrage-arbitration-act-ley-de-arbitraje.pdf

Sr. No.	Country	Provision
5.	Bangladesh - The Arbitration Act, 2001[753]	Section 21 Powers of the arbitration tribunal to make interim orders.- (4) An order of an arbitral tribunal requiring the taking of interim measures may be enforced by the court, on an application made therefor, by the party requesting the taking of such interim measures.
6.	Belgium - Belgian Judicial Code Provisions[754]	Art. 1696 § 1. An interim or protective measure issued by an arbitral tribunal shall be recognised as binding and, unless otherwise provided by the arbitral tribunal, enforced by the Court of First Instance, irrespective of the country in which it was issued, subject to the provisions of article 1697. § 2. The party who is seeking or has obtained recognition or enforcement of an interim or conservatory measure shall promptly inform the sole arbitrator or the chairman of the arbitral tribunal of any termination, suspension or modification of that measure. § 3. The Court of First Instance where recognition or enforcement is sought may, if it considers it proper, order the requesting party to provide appropriate security if the arbitral tribunal has not already made a determination with respect to security or where such a decision is necessary to protect the rights of the respondent and of third parties.
7.	Bhutan - Alternative Dispute Resolution Act of Bhutan 2013[755]	Recognition and enforcement of interim measures Section 123. Unless otherwise provided by the arbitral tribunal, an interim measure granted by an arbitral tribunal shall be recognized as binding and enforced upon application to the competent court, irrespective of the country in which it was granted subject to the provisions of section 125 of this Act. Section 124. The party who seeks or has obtained recognition or enforcement of an interim measure shall promptly inform the court of any termination, suspension or modification of that interim measure.
8.	British Columbia - International Commercial Arbitration Act [RSBC 1996] Chapter 233[756]	Same as Article 17H of UNCITRAL Model Law 2006 Section 17.08 Recognition and Enforcement

753. http://www.mccibd.org/images/uploadimg/act_and_policy/corporate_governance/The-Arbitration-Act-2001.pdf
754. http://www.arbiter.com.sg/pdf/laws/Belgian%20Judicial%20Code%20Provisions%20(2013).pdf
755. https://www.nationalcouncil.bt/assets/uploads/docs/acts/2014/Alternative_Dispute_Resolution_Act_of_Bhutan_2013_eng10th.pdf
756. http://www.bclaws.ca/civix/document/id/complete/statreg/96233_01

Sr. No.	Country	Provision
9.	British Virgin Islands - Virgin Islands Arbitration Act, 2013[757]	Section 41. Substitution of article 17H of the UNCITRAL Model Law Section 59 has effect in substitution for article 17H of the UNCITRAL Model Law in relation to the recognition and enforcement of interim measures. Section 59 Enforcement of orders and directions of arbitral tribunals (1) An order or direction made, whether in or outside the Virgin Islands, in relation to arbitral proceedings by an arbitral tribunal is enforceable in the same manner as an order or direction of the Court that has the same effect, but only with the leave of the Court. (2) Leave to enforce an order or direction made outside the Virgin Islands is not to be granted, unless the party seeking to enforce the order or direction can demonstrate that it belongs to a type or description of order or direction that may be made in the Virgin Islands in relation to arbitral proceedings by an arbitral tribunal. (3) If leave is granted under subsection (1), the Court may enter judgment in terms of the order or direction. (4) A decision made by the Court to grant or refuse to grant leave under subsection (1) is not subject to appeal. (5) An order or direction referred to in this section includes an interim measure.
10.	Bulgaria - Law on International Commercial Arbitration State Gazette (SG) No. 60 of 05.08.1988[758]	No equivalent provision as Article 17H of the UNCITRAL Model Law 2006
11.	Cambodia - The Commercial Arbitration Law of the Kingdom of Cambodia 2006[759]	No equivalent provision as Article 17H of the UNCITRAL Model Law 2006
12.	Canada – Commercial Arbitration Act R.S.C., 1985, c. 17 (2nd Supp.)[760]	No equivalent provision as Article 17H of the UNCITRAL Model Law 2006
13.	Connecticut - Chapter 909 Arbitration Proceedings[761]	No equivalent provision as Article 17H of the UNCITRAL Model Law 2006

757. http://www.bviiac.org/Portals/0/Files/Arbitration%20Documents/ArbitrationAct2013.pdf
758. http://www.newyorkconvention.org/11165/web/files/document/1/6/16200.pdf
759. https://www.cambodiaip.gov.kh/DocResources/372a361b-7a97-44b3-9810-79e5e6ea85f4_c786a043-b88d-4f64-9429-60a330efdc5f-en.pdf
760. https://laws-lois.justice.gc.ca/eng/acts/C-34.6/index.html
761. https://www.cga.ct.gov/current/pub/chap_909.htm

Sr. No.	Country	Provision
14.	Croatia - Law on Arbitration Official Gazette no. 88/2001[762]	Article 16 Interim measures in arbitral proceedings (2) If a party to which interim measures relate does not agree to undertake them voluntarily, the party that made the motion for such measures may request their enforcement before the competent court.
15.	Cyprus - The International Commercial Arbitration Law, 1987[763]	No equivalent provision as Article 17H of the UNCITRAL Model Law 2006
16.	Denmark - Danish Arbitration Act 2005[764]	No equivalent provision as Article 17H of the UNCITRAL Model Law 2006
17.	Egypt - Law No. 27/1994 Promulgating the Law Concerning Arbitration in Civil and Commercial Matters[765]	Article 24 2. If the party against whom the order was issued fails to execute it, the arbitral tribunal, upon the request of the other party, may authorize the latter to undertake the procedures necessary for the execution of the order, without prejudice to the right of said party to apply to the president of the court specified in Article 9 of this Law for rendering an execution order.
18.	Florida - Chapter 684 - International Commercial Arbitration, Title XXXIX Commercial Relations, 2020 Florida Statutes[766]	Same as Article 17H of the UNCITRAL Model Law 2006 Article 684.0026 Recognition and enforcement
19.	Fiji - International Arbitration Act 2017 (Act No. 44 of 2017)[767]	Same as Article 17H of UNCITRAL Model Law 2006 Section 31 Recognition and enforcement
20.	France - Book IV - Arbitration of the Code of Civil Procedure Decree No. 2011-48[768]	No equivalent provision as Article 17H of the UNCITRAL Model Law 2006

762. http://www.vsrh.hr/CustomPages/Static/HRV/Files/Legislation__Law-Arbitration-RC.pdf
763. https://www.uv.es/medarb/observatorio/leyes-arbitraje/europa-resto/chipre-international-commercial-arbitration-law.pdf
764. https://voldgiftsinstituttet.dk/wp-content/uploads/2015/01/danish_arbitration_act_2005.pdf
765. https://www.wipo.int/edocs/lexdocs/laws/en/eg/eg020en.pdf
766. https://www.flsenate.gov/Laws/Statutes/2020/Chapter684/All
767. https://www.fiji.gov.fj/getattachment/d9502667-6491-4592-85b2-eff97f245fed/Act-44---International-Arbitration-Act.aspx
768. http://www.iaiparis.com/pdf/FRENCH_LAW_ON_INTERNATIONAL_ARBITRATION.pdf

Sr. No.	Country	Provision
21.	Georgia – Chapter 9 Arbitration, Title 9 Civil Practice, Georgia Code[769]	Article 21 - Recognition and enforcement of interim measures 1. An interim measure issued by an arbitral tribunal is binding and must be enforced by filing an application to a court, regardless of the country in which the arbitration award on interim measure was rendered, as provided for by article 22 of this law. If the enforcement of the interim measures does not require the filing of an application to a court in accordance with Georgian legislation, the arbitral tribunal is authorized to set different rules for their enforcement. 2. The party who files a motion to a court for recognition and enforcement of an interim measure, or whose motion has been granted, is obliged to promptly inform the court of any termination, suspension or modification of that interim measure granted by the arbitral tribunal. 3. The court may order the party moving for the recognition and enforcement of interim measures to provide appropriate security as provided for by article 18 (3) of this Law. 4. An arbitration award provided for by article 17 (2), of this Law shall be submitted to the court for the recognition and enforcement in accordance with the rules established by article 44 (2) of this Law.
22.	Germany – Tenth Book of the Code of Civil Procedure, Arbitration Procedure[770]	Section 1041 Interim measures of protection (2) The court may, at the request of a party, permit enforcement of a measure referred to in subsection 1, unless application for a corresponding interim measure has already been made to a court. It may recast such an order if necessary for the purpose of enforcing the measure.
23.	Greece – Code Of Civil Procedure, Book VII, Book VIII[771]	No equivalent provision as Article 17H of the UNCITRAL Model Law 2006
24.	Hong Kong – Cap. 609 Arbitration Ordinance[772]	Section 43. Article 17H of UNCITRAL Model Law (Recognition and enforcement) Section 61 has effect in substitution for article 17H of the UNCITRAL Model Law. Section 61. Enforcement of orders and directions of arbitral tribunal (1) An order or direction made, whether in or outside Hong Kong, in relation to arbitral proceedings by an arbitral tribunal is enforceable in the same manner as an order or direction of the Court that has the same effect, but only with the leave of the Court. (2) Leave to enforce an order or direction made outside Hong Kong is not to be granted, unless the party seeking to enforce it can demonstrate that it belongs to a type or description of order or direction that may be made in Hong Kong in relation to arbitral proceedings by an arbitral tribunal.

769. https://matsne.gov.ge/ru/document/download/89284/5/en/pdf
770. https://sccinstitute.com/media/29988/german-arbitration-act.pdf
771. https://www.uv.es/medarb/observatorio/leyes-arbitraje/europa-resto/grecia-ccp-domestic-arbitration.pdf
772. https://www.elegislation.gov.hk/hk/cap609

Sr. No.	Country	Provision
		(3) If leave is granted under subsection (1), the Court may enter judgment in terms of the order or direction. (4) A decision of the Court to grant or refuse to grant leave under subsection (1) is not subject to appeal. (5) An order or direction referred to in this section includes an interim measure.
25.	Hungary - Act LX of 2017 on Arbitration[773]	Section 26 Enforcement of interim measures (1) An interim measure issued by an arbitral tribunal shall be enforced in accordance with the rules on judicial enforcement, subject to the provisions of section 27 on refusal. (2) The party who is seeking or has obtained enforcement of an interim measure shall immediately notify the court of the termination, suspension or modification of that interim measure.
26.	Ireland - Arbitration Act 2010 Number 1 of 2010[774]	Section 6 - Adoption of Model Law Subject to this Act, the Model Law shall have the force of law in the State and shall apply to arbitrations under arbitration agreements concerning— (a) international commercial arbitrations, or (b) arbitrations which are not international commercial arbitrations. Same as Article 17H of UNCITRAL Model Law 2006 Article 17H under Schedule 1 - TEXT OF UNCITRAL MODEL LAW ON INTERNATIONAL COMMERCIAL ARBITRATION
27.	Jamaica - The Arbitration Act, 2017 (Act 13 of 2017)[775]	Same as Article 17H of UNCITRAL Model Law 2006 Section 28 Recognition and enforcement
28.	Japan - Arbitration Law (Law No.138 of 2003)[776]	No equivalent provision as Article 17H of the UNCITRAL Model Law 2006
29.	Jordan - Law No. 31 of 2001 (Jordan) Arbitration Law[777]	Article 23: b. If the party to whom the order has been addressed fails to execute it, the arbitral tribunal may, upon request of the other party, authorize the latter to take the procedures necessary for such execution including the right to apply to the competent court for issuing an order of enforcement.
30.	Kenya - Chapter 49 Arbitration Act (The Arbitration Act, 1995)[778]	No equivalent provision as Article 17H of the UNCITRAL Model Law 2006

773. https://www.ilo.org/dyn/natlex/docs/ELECTRONIC/106843/131257/F-266585574/J2017T0060P_20180102_FIN.pdf
774. http://www.irishstatutebook.ie/eli/2010/act/1/enacted/en/pdf
775. http://extwprlegs1.fao.org/docs/pdf/jam172060.pdf
776. https://japan.kantei.go.jp/policy/sihou/arbitrationlaw.pdf
777. https://www.ilo.org/dyn/natlex/docs/ELECTRONIC/63091/95325/F1864661120/JOR63091.pdf

Sr. No.	Country	Provision
31.	Liechtenstein - Liechtenstein Arbitration Law (Code of Civil Procedure)[779]	Section 610 Power to Order Interim or Protective Measures 3) Upon application of a party the Court shall enforce such a measure. Where the measure provides for a measure of protection unknown to Liechtenstein law, the court can upon request and after having heard the opposing party, execute such measure of protection under Liechtenstein law that comes closest to the measure of the arbitral tribunal. In this case, the court can also upon request amend the measure of the arbitral tribunal in order to safeguard the realization of its purpose.
32.	Lithuania – The Republic of Lithuania Law on Commercial Arbitration, 2012[780]	Article 25. Enforcement of Orders on Interim Measures and Grounds for a Refusal to Issue A Writ of Execution 1. An order of an arbitral tribunal on application of interim measures shall be an enforceable document. 2. Where an order of an arbitral tribunal on application of interim measures is not enforced, Vilnius Regional Court shall, at the request of a party, issue a writ of execution according to the procedure established by the Code of Civil Procedure of the Republic of Lithuania (hereinafter: 'the Code of Civil Procedure'). An application for the issue of the writ of execution shall be considered at a court hearing with a notice to the parties to the arbitral proceedings. The failure of the parties to appear in court shall not prevent the Court from resolving the matter of the issue of the writ of execution. 3. A party at the request of which Vilnius Regional Court has issued a writ of execution to enforce an order on application of interim measures must give the Court a prompt notice of the replacement or cancellation of interim measures. An application for the amendment or setting aside of the writ of execution shall be considered at a court hearing with a notice to the parties to the arbitral proceedings. The failure of the parties to appear in court shall not prevent the Court from resolving the matter of the amendment or setting aside of the writ of execution. Article 26. Recognition or Enforcement of Foreign Arbitral Awards or Orders on Interim Measures and Grounds for the Refusal to Recognise or Enforce a Foreign Arbitral Award or Order 1. An arbitral award or order on application of interim measures given in any other state may be recognised and enforced on the territory of the Republic of Lithuania. 2. An application of a party for the recognition and permission to enforce an arbitral award or order of an arbitral tribunal on application of interim measures shall be filed with the Court of Appeal of Lithuania. The provisions of Article 51(2) of this Law shall mutatis mutandis apply to the content of this application.

778. https://ncia.or.ke/wp-content/uploads/2021/02/ArbitrationAct4of1995_2.pdf
779. https://www.newyorkconvention.org/11165/web/files/document/2/1/21372.pdf
780. https://e-seimas.lrs.lt/portal/legalAct/lt/TAD/35954312dcb311e6be918a531b2126ab?jfwid=-wd7z7zum0

Sr. No.	Country	Provision
33.	Louisiana – RS 9 Title 9.Civil Code-Ancillaries[781]	No equivalent provision as Article 17H of the UNCITRAL Model Law 2006
34.	Macedonia - Law on International Commercial Arbitration of the Republic of Macedonia[782]	Article 17 Power of arbitral tribunal to order interim measures If a party to which interim measure relates does not agree to undertake it voluntarily, the party that made the motion for such measures may request its enforcement before the competent court.
35.	Malaysia – Arbitration Act 2005, Act 646[783]	No equivalent provision as Article 17H of the UNCITRAL Model Law 2006
36.	Maldives – Act No: 10/2013, Arbitration Act[784]	Section 40 Recognition and Enforcement by the Courts (a) An interim measure issued by an arbitral tribunal shall be recognized as binding and, unless otherwise provided by the arbitral tribunal, enforced upon application to the competent court. (b) A preliminary order issued under this Act may be recognized in accordance with (a) above, and a subsequent order for the enforcement of it may be issued, by the competent court, only after the court makes proper deliberations upon the application to the court by the party seeking recognition and enforcement. Section 41 Notifying the court of Changes to the Interim Measure The party who has applied for recognition or enforcement by the courts under Section 40, (a) of this Act, of an interim measure awarded under the same, shall promptly inform the court of any termination, suspension or modification of that interim measure by the Arbitral Tribunal. Section 42 Demanding Security from the Party Seeking the Order The court where recognition or enforcement of a preliminary order for an interim measure issued under this Act is sought may, if it considers proper, order the requesting party to provide appropriate security even if the arbitral tribunal has not already made a determination with respect to security.
37.	Malta – CAP. 387 Arbitration Act[785]	No equivalent provision as Article 17H of the UNCITRAL Model Law 2006

781. http://legis.la.gov/legis/Laws_Toc.aspx?folder=83&title=9
782. https://www.international-arbitration-attorney.com/wp-content/uploads/2013/07/Macedonia-Arbitration-Law.pdf
783. http://www.newyorkconvention.org/11165/web/files/document/1/6/16298.pdf
784. https://miac.gov.mv/media/documents/Arbitration%20Act.pdf
785. http://justiceservices.gov.mt/DownloadDocument.aspx?app=lom&itemid=8854&l=1

Sr. No.	Country	Provision
38.	Mauritius - The International Arbitration Act, 2008 (Act 37 of 2008)[786]	Section 18. Recognition and enforcement of interim measures (1) An interim measure granted by an arbitral tribunal shall, subject to this section, be recognised as binding and, unless otherwise provided by the arbitral tribunal, enforced on application to the Supreme Court, irrespective of the country in which it was issued. (2) The party who is seeking or has obtained recognition or enforcement of an interim measure shall promptly inform the Supreme Court of any termination, suspension or modification of that measure. (3) The Supreme Court may, on an application for recognition or enforcement of an interim measure and if it considers it proper, order the requesting party to provide appropriate security if the arbitral tribunal has not already made a determination with respect to security or where such a decision is necessary to protect the rights of third parties.
39.	Montenegro - Decree on the Promulgation of the Law on Arbitration, 2015[787]	Article 27 Recognition and enforcement of interim measures An interim measure ordered by an arbitral tribunal, irrespective of the country in which it was ordered, shall be recognized as binding and enforced on the basis of the decision of the court referred to in Article 6 paragraph 1 hereof, upon application of the parties, except in the case referred to in Article 28 hereof. An interim measure referred to in paragraph 1 of this Article shall not be enforced if the arbitral tribunal decides to modify, suspend or terminate the interim measure. The party who is seeking or has obtained recognition or enforcement of an interim measure shall promptly inform the court of any modification, suspension or termination of that interim measure. The court before which recognition or enforcement of an interim measure is sought may, if it considers it necessary, order the requesting party to provide appropriate security if the arbitral tribunal has not already made a determination with respect to security or where necessary to protect the rights of third parties.
40.	Myanmar - Arbitration Law The Pyidaungsu Hluttaw Law No. 5/2016[788]	Section 19 Power of arbitral tribunal to order interim orders (e) All decisions, orders or instruction made by an arbitral tribunal in the course of an arbitration may apply to the court for the enforcement in accordance with the section 31.
41.	New South Wales - Commercial Arbitration Act 2010 No 61[789]	Section 17H Recognition and enforcement (cf Model Law Art 17H) (1) An interim measure issued by an arbitral tribunal under the law of this State is to be recognised as binding and, unless otherwise provided by the arbitral tribunal, enforced on application to the Court, subject to the provisions of section 17I.

786. https://www.wipo.int/edocs/lexdocs/laws/en/mu/mu020en.pdf
787. https://www.privrednakomora.me/sites/pkcg.org/files/multimedia/main_pages/files/2012/09/final_eng_zakon_o_arbitrazi_final_0.pdf
788. http://www.newyorkconvention.org/11165/web/files/document/2/1/21098.pdf
789. https://legislation.nsw.gov.au/view/html/inforce/current/act-2010-061#sec.17H

Sr. No.	Country	Provision
		(2) An interim measure issued by an arbitral tribunal under the law of another State or Territory is to be recognised as binding in this State and, unless otherwise provided by the arbitral tribunal, enforced on application to the Court, irrespective of the State or Territory in which it was issued, subject to the provisions of section 17I. (3) The party who is seeking or has obtained recognition or enforcement of an interim measure must promptly inform the Court of any termination, suspension or modification of that interim measure. (4) The Court may, if it considers it proper, order the requesting party to provide appropriate security if the arbitral tribunal has not already made a determination with respect to security or where such a decision is necessary to protect the rights of third parties. Note. This section differs from Art 17H of the Model Law to the extent necessary to apply Art 17H as incorporated in this Act in the context of domestic commercial arbitrations.
42.	New Zealand - The Arbitration Act, 1996 No 99[790]	Schedule I - Rules applying to arbitration agreement Article 17L Recognition and enforcement (1) An interim measure granted by an arbitral tribunal must be recognised as binding and, unless otherwise provided by the arbitral tribunal, enforced upon application to the competent court, irrespective of the country in which it was granted. (2) Paragraph (1) is subject to article 17M. (3) The applicant for recognition or enforcement of an interim measure under article 35 must promptly inform the court of any modification, suspension, or cancellation of that interim measure. (4) The court may, if it considers it proper, order the applicant to provide appropriate security if— (a) the arbitral tribunal has not already made a decision with respect to the provision of security; or (b) the decision with respect to the provision of security is necessary to protect the rights of third parties.
43.	Nigeria - Arbitration and Conciliation Act Chapter 19 Laws of the Federation of Nigeria 1990[791]	No equivalent provision as Article 17H of the UNCITRAL Model Law 2006
44.	Northern Territory of Australia - Commercial Arbitration (National Uniform Legislation) Act 2011[792]	Section 17H Recognition and enforcement (Model Law Art 17H) (1) An interim measure issued by an arbitral tribunal under the law of the Territory is to be recognised as binding and, unless otherwise provided by the arbitral tribunal, enforced on application to the Court, subject to the provisions of section 17I.

790. http://www.legislation.govt.nz/act/public/1996/0099/latest/whole.html#DLM403277
791. http://niqs.org.ng/wp-content/uploads/2018/12/Arbitration-and-Conciliation-Act.pdf
792. https://legislation.nt.gov.au/api/sitecore/Act/PDF?id = 11692

Sr. No.	Country	Provision
		(2) An interim measure issued by an arbitral tribunal under the law of a State or another Territory is to be recognised as binding in the Territory and, unless otherwise provided by the arbitral tribunal, enforced on application to the Court, irrespective of the State or Territory in which it was issued, subject to the provisions of section 17I. (3) The party who is seeking or has obtained recognition or enforcement of an interim measure must promptly inform the Court of any termination, suspension or modification of that interim measure. (4) The Court may, if it considers it proper, order the requesting party to provide appropriate security if the arbitral tribunal has not already made a determination with respect to security or where such a decision is necessary to protect the rights of third parties. Note for section 17H This section differs from Art 17H of the Model Law to the extent necessary to apply Art 17H as incorporated in this Act in the context of domestic commercial arbitrations.
45.	Norway - Act of 14 May 2004 No. 25 relating to Arbitration (The Arbitration Act)[793]	No equivalent provision as Article 17H of the UNCITRAL Model Law 2006
46.	Oman - The Omani Law of Arbitration in Civil and Commercial Disputes – Royal Decree 47/97[794]	Article 24 2. In case, the party who is issued with such an order fails to execute the same, the arbitration board, on the basis of a request made by the other party, may grant permission to such other party to take necessary steps for the execution of the order. This shall be without prejudice to the right held by this party to make a request to the President of the Commercial court for issue of an order and for its execution.
47.	Ontario - International Commercial Arbitration Act, 2017, S.O. 2017, c. 2, Sched. 5[795]	Section 5 - Application of Model Law (1) Subject to this Act, the Model Law on International Commercial Arbitration, adopted by the United Nations Commission on International Trade Law on 21 June 1985, as amended by the United Nations Commission on International Trade Law on 7 July 2006, set out in Schedule 2, has force of law in Ontario. Same (2) With respect to article 7 of the Model Law, option I applies in Ontario; option II does not. Same (3) The Model Law applies to international commercial arbitration agreements and awards made in international commercial arbitrations, whether made before or after the coming into force of this Act. Schedule 2 to this Act Article 17H

793. https://www.chamber.no/wp-content/uploads/2014/02/Norwegian_Arbitration_Act.pdf
794. http://www.newyorkconvention.org/11165/web/files/document/2/1/21103.pdf

Sr. No.	Country	Provision
48.	Oregon – Oregon International Commercial Arbitration and Conciliation Act[796]	No equivalent provision as Article 17H of the UNCITRAL Model Law 2006
49.	Pakistan - The Arbitration Act, 1940 Act No. X of 1940[797]	No equivalent provision as Article 17H of the UNCITRAL Model Law 2006
50.	Philippines - Alternative Dispute Resolution Act of 2004 Republic Act No. 9285[798]	Section 28. Grant of Interim Measure of Protection. - (5) The order shall be binding upon the parties. (6) Either party may apply with the Court for assistance in Implementing or enforcing an interim measure ordered by an arbitral tribunal. SEC. 29. Further Authority for Arbitrator to Grant Interim Measure of Protection. – ... Either party may apply with the Court for assistance in implementing or enforcing an interim measures ordered by an arbitral tribunal.
51.	Poland – Polish Act of 17 November 1964 - Code of Civil Procedure, Part Five Arbitration[799]	Art. 1181 §3 The ruling of the arbitral tribunal ordering interim measures is enforceable after attachment of an enforceability clause. Art. 1214 §2 and §3 and Art. 1215 apply accordingly. Art. 1214 § 2 The court shall decide on enforcement of arbitral awards or settlement reached before the arbitral tribunal which are capable of being enforced by attaching an enforcement clause. § 3 Recognition or enforcement of an arbitral award or the settlement shall be refused by the court if: 1) the dispute was not capable of submission to arbitration under the law; 2) the recognition or enforcement of the arbitral award or settlement reached before the arbitral tribunal would be contrary to fundamental public policy rules of the Republic of Poland (the public order clause). Art. 1215 § 1 The court shall decide on recognition or enforcement of a foreign arbitral award or settlement after the hearing.

795. https://www.ontario.ca/laws/statute/17i02b#BK16
796. https://www.oregonlegislature.gov/bills_laws/ors/ors036.html
797. https://www.wipo.int/edocs/lexdocs/laws/en/pk/pk066en.pdf
798. http://www.newyorkconvention.org/11165/web/files/document/2/1/21107.pdf
799. https://www.uv.es/medarb/observatorio/leyes-arbitraje/europa-resto/polonia-ccp-arbitration.pdf

Sr. No.	Country	Provision
		§ 2 Regardless of the grounds referred to in Art. 1214, the court, on request of a party, shall refuse recognition or enforcement of the foreign arbitral award or settlement reached before the arbitral tribunal, if a party furnishes proof that: 1) there was no arbitration agreement, the agreement is not valid, ineffective or has expired under the law applicable to it, 2) it was not given proper notice of the appointment of an arbitrator, of the arbitral proceedings or was otherwise unable to present its case before the arbitral tribunal, 3) the award deals with a dispute not contemplated by or falling beyond the scope of the arbitration agreement, provided that, if the decisions on matters submitted to arbitration can be separated from those not so submitted or falling beyond the scope of such submission, the court may refuse recognition and enforcement only of those parts of the award which contains decisions on matters not contemplated by or falling beyond the scope of the arbitration agreement. 4) composition of the arbitral tribunal or the arbitral procedure was not in accordance with the agreement of the parties or the law of the country in which the arbitration took place; 5) the award has not yet become binding on the parties or has been set aside or suspended by a court of the country in which, or under the law of which, that award was made.
52.	Qatar - Law No. 2 of 2017 Promulgating the Civil and Commercial Arbitration Law-The Law of Arbitration in Civil and Commercial Matters[800]	Article (17) 3. The Party in whose favour the order for provisional measures or an interim award is issued may, after it obtains written permission from the Arbitral Tribunal, request the Competent Judge to order the enforcement of the order or award issued by the Arbitral Tribunal, or any part of it. Copies of any request for permission or enforcement shall be sent, pursuant to this Article, to the rest of the Parties. The Competent Judge shall order the enforcement of the mentioned order or award, unless such order or award contradicts the law or public policy.

800. https://www.qicdrc.gov.qa/sites/default/files/inline-files/law_no._02_2017_promulgating_the_civil_and_commercial_arbitration_law.pdf

Sr. No.	Country	Provision
53.	Queensland - Commercial Arbitration Act 2013 No.8[801]	Section 17H Recognition and enforcement (cf Model Law Art 17H) (1) An interim measure issued by an arbitral tribunal under the law of this State is to be recognised as binding and, unless otherwise provided by the arbitral tribunal, enforced on application to the Court, subject to the provisions of section 17I. (2) An interim measure issued by an arbitral tribunal under the law of another State or Territory is to be recognised as binding in this State and, unless otherwise provided by the arbitral tribunal, enforced on application to the Court, irrespective of the State or Territory in which it was issued, subject to the provisions of section 17I. (3) The party who is seeking or has obtained recognition or enforcement of an interim measure must promptly inform the Court of any termination, suspension or modification of that interim measure. (4) The Court may, if it considers it proper, order the requesting party to provide appropriate security if the arbitral tribunal has not already made a determination with respect to security or where such a decision is necessary to protect the rights of third parties. Note— This section differs from Art 17H of the Model Law to the extent necessary to apply Art 17H as incorporated in this Act in the context of domestic commercial arbitrations.
54.	Republic of Costa Rica - Costa Rican Law for International Arbitration Law Number: 8937[802]	Same as Article 17H of UNCITRAL Model Law 2006
55.	Republic of Korea - Arbitration Act[803]	Article 18-7 (Recognition and Enforcement of Interim Measures) (1) The party who wishes to obtain recognition of an interim measure issued by an arbitral tribunal may file a petition with a court to seek a decision to approve the measure, and the party who intends to seek compulsory execution on the basis of the interim measure may file a petition with a court to seek a decision that authorizes the execution. (2) The party who is seeking or has obtained recognition or enforcement of an interim measure shall promptly inform the court of any termination, suspension or modification of that interim measure. (3) The court where recognition or enforcement of an interim measure is sought may, if it considers it necessary, order the requesting party to provide appropriate security if the arbitral tribunal has yet to make such an order with respect to the interim measure or where such a decision is necessary to protect the rights of third parties. (4) The provisions concerning preservative measures in the Civil Execution Act shall apply mutatis mutandis to the execution of interim measures.

801. https://www.legislation.qld.gov.au/view/pdf/inforce/2013-05-17/act-2013-008
802. https://arbitratlaw.com/wp-content/uploads/2017/01/Costa-Rican-Intl-Arbitration-Law.pdf
803. https://elaw.klri.re.kr/eng_service/lawView.do?hseq=38889&lang=ENG

Sr. No.	Country	Provision
56.	Russia - Russian Federation Law On International Commercial Arbitration[804]	Article 17. Power of arbitral tribunal to order interim measures 1. ... The orders and other procedural acts of the arbitral tribunal on taking of interim measures are binding on the parties.
57.	Rwanda – Law on Arbitration and Conciliation in Commercial Matters, N° 005/2008[805]	No equivalent provision as Article 17H of the UNCITRAL Model Law 2006
58.	Saudi Arabia – Law of Arbitration Royal Decree No. M/34[806]	Article 23 2. If the party against whom the order has been issued fails to execute such an order, the arbitration tribunal may, upon the request of the other party, authorize said party to take necessary measures for its execution, without prejudice to the right of the arbitration tribunal or the other party to request the competent agency to enforce such order.
59.	Serbia – Law on Arbitration No. 46/06[807]	No equivalent provision as Article 17H of the UNCITRAL Model Law 2006
60.	Singapore - Arbitration Act (Chapter 10) (Domestic Arbitration Law)[808]	No equivalent provision as Article 17H of the UNCITRAL Model Law 2006
61.	Singapore - International Arbitration Act (Chapter 143A) (International Arbitration Law)[809]	Section 3 Model Law to have force of law (1) Subject to this Act, the Model Law, with the exception of Chapter VIII thereof, shall have the force of law in Singapore. (2) In the Model Law — “State” means Singapore and any country other than Singapore; “this State” means Singapore. Section 12 Powers of arbitral tribunal (6) All orders or directions made or given by an arbitral tribunal in the course of an arbitration shall, by leave of the High Court or a Judge thereof, be enforceable in the same manner as if they were orders made by a court and, where leave is so given, judgment may be entered in terms of the order or direction.

804. http://www.newyorkconvention.org/11165/web/files/document/2/2/22335.pdf
805. http://www.newyorkconvention.org/11165/web/files/document/2/1/21110.pdf
806. https://www.wipo.int/edocs/lexdocs/laws/en/sa/sa057en.pdf
807. https://www.wipo.int/edocs/lexdocs/laws/en/rs/rs028en.pdf
808. https://sso.agc.gov.sg/Act/AA2001
809. https://sso.agc.gov.sg/Act/IAA1994

Sr. No.	Country	Provision
62.	Slovakia - [Slovak] Act No. 244/2002 of 3 April 2002 on Arbitration[810]	Section 22c (1) The interim measure issued by the arbitral tribunal shall, with the exception of an interim measure issued under Section 22a, constitute an enforcement order, execution of which shall be effected by separate legislation8b. (2) An objection to enforcement, where the enforceable decision is an interim measure granted by an arbitral tribunal, shall also be upheld by the court if the obliged party satisfies the court that: a) the conditions for an interim measure by an arbitral tribunal under this Act or in accordance with the parties' agreement were not satisfied; b) the party that requested the grant of an interim measure failed to comply with the arbitral tribunal's order to provide security, c) the interim measure was set aside or modified. (3) The relevant court for enforcement or execution of the award shall, even without motion, refuse to enforce an arbitral tribunal's interim measure if it finds that it is against the public order of the Slovak Republic.
63.	Slovenia - Law on Arbitration of Slovenia[811]	Article 20 Interim Measures Ordered by Arbitral Tribunal (4) If the party fails to comply with the interim order issued by the arbitral tribunal, the court shall permit, at the request of the other party, the enforcement of the measure in accordance with article 43 of this Law, unless a request for the issuance of such an interim measure has already been made before the court.
64.	South Africa - The Arbitration Act, 1965[812]	No equivalent provision as Article 17H of the UNCITRAL Model Law 2006
65.	South Australia - South Australia Commercial Arbitration Act 2011[813]	Section 17H—Recognition and enforcement (1) An interim measure issued by an arbitral tribunal under the law of this State is to be recognised as binding and, unless otherwise provided by the arbitral tribunal, enforced on application to the Court, subject to the provisions of section 17I. (2) An interim measure issued by an arbitral tribunal under the law of another State or Territory is to be recognised as binding in this State and, unless otherwise provided by the arbitral tribunal, enforced on application to the Court, irrespective of the State or Territory in which it was issued, subject to the provisions of section 17I. (3) The party who is seeking or has obtained recognition or enforcement of an interim measure must promptly inform the Court of any termination, suspension or modification of that interim measure.

810. https://www.international-arbitration-attorney.com/wp-content/uploads/2013/07/Slovakia-Arbitration-Law-1.pdf
811. http://www.sloarbitration.eu/Portals/0/Arbitrazno-pravo/Law%20on%20Arbitration%20of%20Slovenia.pdf
812. https://www.gov.za/sites/default/files/gcis_document/201505/act-42-1965.pdf
813. https://www.legislation.sa.gov.au/LZ/C/A/COMMERCIAL%20ARBITRATION%20ACT%202011/CURRENT/2011.32.UN.PDF

Sr. No.	Country	Provision
		(4) The Court may, if it considers it proper, order the requesting party to provide appropriate security if the arbitral tribunal has not already made a determination with respect to security or if such a decision is necessary to protect the rights of third parties. Note— This section differs from Art 17H of the Model Law to the extent necessary to apply Art 17H as incorporated in this Act in the context of domestic commercial arbitrations.
66.	Spain - Act 60/2003 of 23 December on Arbitration[814]	Article 23. Arbitrators' power to order interim measures 2. Irrespective of the form adopted by arbitral decisions on interim measures, the rules on setting aside and enforcement of awards will apply thereto.
67.	Sri Lanka - Arbitration Act. No. 11 of 1995[815]	Section 13 Interim Measures of Protection (2) An order of an arbitral tribunal requiring the taking of interim measures may be enforced by the High Court, on an application made therefore, by the party requesting the taking of such interim measures. (3) An application to the High Court, under subsection (2), for the enforcement of interim measures, shall be deemed not to be incompatible with section 5 or the arbitration agreement or a waiver of the agreement.
68.	Sweden – The Swedish Arbitration Act (SFS 1999:116)[816]	No equivalent provision as Article 17H of the UNCITRAL Model Law 2006
69.	Switzerland – Private International Law Act 1987, Chapter 12: International Arbitration[817]	No equivalent provision as Article 17H of the UNCITRAL Model Law 2006
70.	Tasmania – Commercial Arbitration Act, 2011, Act 13 of 2011[818]	Section 17H. Recognition and enforcement (cf Model Law Art 17H) (1) An interim measure issued by an arbitral tribunal under the law of this State is to be recognised as binding and, unless otherwise provided by the arbitral tribunal, enforced on application to the Court, subject to the provisions of section 17I . (2) An interim measure issued by an arbitral tribunal under the law of another State or a Territory is to be recognised as binding in this State and, unless otherwise provided by the arbitral tribunal, enforced on application to the Court, irrespective of the State or Territory in which it was issued, subject to the provisions of section 17I .

814. https://www.mjusticia.gob.es/cs/Satellite/Portal/1292426982249?blobheader=application%2Fpdf&blobheadername1=Content-Disposition&blobheadervalue1=attachment%3B+filename%3DAct_on_arbitration_%28Ley_60_2003__de_arbitraje%29.PDF
815. http://www.slnarbcentre.com/pdf/ARBITRATION-ACT.pdf
816. https://sccinstitute.com/media/37089/the-swedish-arbitration-act.pdf
817. https://www.swissarbitration.org/wp-content/uploads/2021/05/20210129-Chapter-12-PILA_Translation_English.pdf

Sr. No.	Country	Provision
		(3) The party who is seeking or has obtained recognition or enforcement of an interim measure must promptly inform the Court of any termination, suspension or modification of that interim measure. (4) The Court may, if it considers it proper, order the requesting party to provide appropriate security if the arbitral tribunal has not already made a determination with respect to security or where such a decision is necessary to protect the rights of third parties. Note. This section differs from Art 17H of the Model Law to the extent necessary to apply Art 17H as incorporated in this Act in the context of domestic commercial arbitrations.
71.	Texas - Chapter 172. Arbitration and Conciliation of International Commercial Disputes, Civil Practice and Remedies Code[819]	No equivalent provision as Article 17H of the UNCITRAL Model Law 2006
72.	Thailand - Arbitration Act B.E. 2545[820]	No equivalent provision as Article 17H of the UNCITRAL Model Law 2006
73.	Tunisia - Law n° 93-42 issued on April 26, related to the promulgation of the Arbitration Code[821]	Article 62 ... If the party against whom the order was issued refuses to comply, the arbitral tribunal may seek the assistance of the President of the Tunis Court of Appeals.
74.	Turkey - Turkish International Arbitration Law, Law no. 4686, 2001[822]	Article 6 Interim measures of protection and interim attachments ... The arbitral tribunal shall not grant interim measures or interim attachments [a] that are required to be enforced through execution offices or to be executed through other official authorities or [b] that bind third parties. If a party does not comply with the interim measure or attachment, the other party may request the assistance of the competent court for taking an interim measure of protection or an interim attachment. The competent court, if necessary, may hear [the case in question] through a substitute court.

818. https://www.legislation.tas.gov.au/view/html/inforce/current/act-2011-013
819. https://statutes.capitol.texas.gov/Docs/CP/htm/CP.172.htm
820. https://tai.coj.go.th/th/file/get/file/20190328ecac5333356ffad0331bd601151db9f4142557.pdf
821. https://arbitrationlaw.com/sites/default/files/free_pdfs/Tunisia%20Arbitration%20Code.pdf
822. http://www.camera-arbitrale.it/Documenti/tial_turkey.pdf

Sr. No.	Country	Provision
75.	Uganda – Chapter 4 The Arbitration and Conciliation Act[823]	No equivalent provision as Article 17H of the UNCITRAL Model Law 2006
76.	Ukraine - The Law of Ukraine on International Commercial Arbitration[824]	No equivalent provision as Article 17H of the UNCITRAL Model Law 2006
77.	United Arab Emirates - Federal Law No. (6) of 2018 on Arbitration[825]	Article (21) Interim or Conservatory Measures 4. A party for whom an interim measure has been ordered may, after obtaining written permission from the Arbitral Tribunal, request the competent court to order the enforcement of the order of the Arbitral Tribunal or any part thereof within fifteen days of receipt of the request. Copies of any request for permission or enforcement hereunder shall be sent simultaneously to all the other Parties.
78.	Uruguay - Law 19,636 Approve Rules for International Commercial Arbitration[826]	Article 17 (Power of the arbitral tribunal to order provisional precautionary measures) .- 2) Any precautionary measure ordered by an arbitral tribunal is will recognize as binding, and unless the arbitral tribunal provide otherwise, if the party concerned does not submit voluntarily or if its effectiveness requires it, it will be executed, when such execution is requested, by the competent court in accordance with the provisions of article 6.
79.	Venezuela – Venezuelan Commercial Arbitration Act[827]	Article 28. The arbitral tribunal or a party with the approval of the arbitral tribunal may request assistance of a competent Court of First Instance in taking necessary evidence and in order to enforce the requested interim measures of protection. The First Instance Court shall respond to such a request within the scope of its jurisdiction and in conformity with applicable norms.
80.	Victoria - Commercial Arbitration Act 2011 No. 50 of 2011[828]	Section 17H Recognition and enforcement (cf Model Law Art 17H) (1) An interim measure issued by an arbitral tribunal under the law of this State is to be recognised as binding and, unless otherwise provided by the arbitral tribunal, enforced on application to the Court, subject to the provisions of section 17I.

823. https://ulii.org/akn/ug/act/2000/7/eng@2008-06-27
824. http://arbitrations.ru/userfiles/file/Law/Arbitration%20acts/ukraininan%20law%20on%20arbitration.pdf
825. https://www.tamimi.com/crm-media-uploader/fileupload/server/php/files/UAE%20Arbitration%20Law%20-%20Federal%20Law%20No%20%206%20of%202018.pdf
826. http://www.impo.com.uy/bases/leyes-originales/19636-2018
827. https://arbitrationlaw.com/sites/default/files/free_pdfs/Venezula%20Commercial%20Arbitration%20Act.pdf
828. http://arbitration.site/wp-content/uploads/2019/06/CAA-Vic-.pdf

Sr. No.	Country	Provision
		(2) An interim measure issued by an arbitral tribunal under the law of another State or Territory is to be recognised as binding in this State and, unless otherwise provided by the arbitral tribunal, enforced on application to the Court, irrespective of the State or Territory in which it was issued, subject to the provisions of section 17I. (3) The party who is seeking or has obtained recognition or enforcement of an interim measure must promptly inform the Court of any termination, suspension or modification of that interim measure. (4) The Court may, if it considers it proper, order the requesting party to provide appropriate security if the arbitral tribunal has not already made a determination with respect to security or where such a decision is necessary to protect the rights of third parties. Note This section differs from Art 17H of the Model Law to the extent necessary to apply Art 17H as incorporated in this Act in the context of domestic commercial arbitrations.
81.	Western Australia - Commercial Arbitration Act 2012, 023 of 2012[829]	Section 17H. Recognition and enforcement (cf. Model Law Art 17H) (1) An interim measure issued by an arbitral tribunal under the law of this State is to be recognised as binding and, unless otherwise provided by the arbitral tribunal, enforced on application to the Court, subject to the provisions of section 17I. (2) An interim measure issued by an arbitral tribunal under the law of another State or Territory is to be recognised as binding in this State and, unless otherwise provided by the arbitral tribunal, enforced on application to the Court, irrespective of the State or Territory in which it was issued, subject to the provisions of section 17I. (3) The party who is seeking or has obtained recognition or enforcement of an interim measure must promptly inform the Court of any termination, suspension or modification of that interim measure. (4) The Court may, if it considers it proper, order the requesting party to provide appropriate security if the arbitral tribunal has not already made a determination with respect to security or where such a decision is necessary to protect the rights of third parties. Note for this section: This section differs from Art 17H of the Model Law to the extent necessary to apply Art 17H as incorporated in this Act in the context of domestic commercial arbitrations.
82.	Zambia - The Arbitration Act, 2000 No. 19 of 2000[830]	No equivalent provision as Article 17H of the UNCITRAL Model Law 2006

829. https://www.legislation.wa.gov.au/legislation/prod/filestore.nsf/FileURL/mrdoc_25084.pdf/$FILE/Commercial%20Arbitration%20Act%202012%20-%20%5B00-b0-06%5D.pdf?OpenElement
830. http://www.newyorkconvention.org/11165/web/files/document/2/1/21396.pdf

Sr. No.	Country	Provision
83.	Zimbabwe – Chapter 7:15 Arbitration Act[831]	ARTICLE 17 Power of arbitral tribunal to order interim measures (3) The arbitral tribunal or a party with the approval of the arbitral tribunal may request from the High Court executory assistance in the exercise of any power conferred upon the arbitral tribunal under paragraphs (1) and (2) of this article. (4) If a request is made under paragraph (3) of this article, the High Court shall have, for the purpose of giving effect to the request, the same powers it would have in civil proceedings before it.

831. https://zimlii.org/akn/zw/act/1996/6/eng@2016-12-31

Appendix K (Article 17I)

Sr. No.	Country	Provision
1.	Australia - International Arbitration Act 1974[832]	Same as Article 17I of UNCITRAL Model Law 2006 Sec 16 Model Law to have force of law (1) Subject to this Part, the Model Law has the force of law in Australia. (2) In the Model Law: Arbitration agreement has the meaning given in Option 1 of Article 7 of the Model Law. State means Australia (including the external Territories) and any foreign country. This State means Australia (including the external Territories). Model Law under Part V, Schedule 2 of the Arbitration Act, 1974
2.	Australian Capital Territory - Commercial Arbitration Act, 2017 A2017-7[833]	SECT 17I Grounds for refusing recognition or enforcement (Model Law art 17I) (1) Recognition or enforcement of an interim measure may be refused only - (a) at the request of the party against whom it is invoked if the court is satisfied that— (i) such a refusal is warranted on the grounds set out in section 36 (1) (a) (i) to (iv); or (ii) the arbitral tribunal's decision with respect to the provision of security in connection with the interim measure issued by the arbitral tribunal has not been complied with; or (iii) the interim measure has been terminated or suspended by the arbitral tribunal or, where so empowered, by the court of the State or other Territory in which the arbitration takes place or under the law of which that interim measure was granted; or

832. https://www.legislation.gov.au/Details/C2011C00342
833. http://classic.austlii.edu.au/au/legis/act/consol_act/caa2017219/s17i.html

Sr. No.	Country	Provision
		(b) if the court finds that— (i) the interim measure is incompatible with the powers conferred on the court unless the court decides to reformulate the interim measure to the extent necessary to adapt it to its own powers and procedures for the purposes of enforcing that interim measure and without modifying its substance; or (ii) any of the grounds set out in section 36 (1) (b) (i) or (ii) apply to the recognition and enforcement of the interim measure. (2) Any determination made by the court on any ground in subsection (1) is effective only for the purposes of the application to recognise and enforce the interim measure. (3) The court must not, in making a determination with respect to the recognition or enforcement sought, undertake a review of the substance of the interim measure. Note This section is substantially the same as the Model Law, art 17I but has been modified to the extent necessary to apply art 17I as incorporated in this Act in the context of domestic commercial arbitrations.
3.	Austria – Austrian Arbitration Act, 2013[834]	Section 593 – Ordering of Interim or Protective Measures (4) The court shall refuse to enforce a measure under paragraph (1) if 1. the seat of the arbitral tribunal is within Austria and the measure suffers from a defect which would constitute grounds for setting aside an arbitral award made in Austria pursuant to sections 611 paragraph (2), 617 paragraphs (6) and (7) or section 618; 2. the seat of the arbitral tribunal is not within Austria and the measure suffers from a defect which would constitute grounds for refusal of recognition or enforcement of a foreign arbitral award; 3. the enforcement of the measure would be incompatible with an Austrian court measure which was either requested or issued previously, or with a foreign court measure which was issued previously and must be recognized; 4. the measure provides for a means of protection unknown to Austrian law and no appropriate means of protection as provided by Austrian law has been requested. (6) The court shall, upon request, set aside the enforcement if 1. the term of the measure as set by the arbitral tribunal has expired; 2. the arbitral tribunal has limited the scope of or set aside the measure; 3. one of the cases set out in section 399 paragraph (1) numbers 1 to 4 Enforcement Act ("Exekutionsordnung") exists, unless such a circumstance was unsuccessfully raised with the arbitral tribunal and no obstacles to recognizing (paragraph 4) the decision of the arbitral tribunal exist in this regard; 4. security pursuant to paragraph (1) has been provided that the enforcement is superfluous.

834. https://www.viac.eu/images/law/ZPO_Schiedsrecht_2014_en_im_VIAC_Layout.pdf

Sr. No.	Country	Provision
4.	Bahrain - Bahrain Arbitration Law No. 9/2015[835]	Same as UNCITRAL Model Law 2006 Article 1 Taking into account the provisions of international conventions in force in the Kingdom of Bahrain 1. The provisions of the " UNCITRAL " Model Law on International Commercial Arbitration Act attached to this law shall apply to all arbitration whatever the nature of the legal relationship of the dispute herewith, if this arbitration takes place in the Kingdom of Bahrain or abroad and that two parties agreed to comply with the provisions of the attached law. 2. The provisions of the attached law shall apply to all arbitration which begins after its entry into force even if based on an arbitration agreement concluded before the entry into force of this law.
5.	Bangladesh – The Arbitration Act, 2001[836]	Section 21 Powers of the arbitration tribunal to make interim orders.- (5) The application filed before the Court for the enforcement of the interim measures under sub-section (4) shall be deemed not to be incompatible with section 7 or with arbitration agreement or a waiver of the agreement.
6.	Belgium – Belgian Judicial Code Provisions[837]	Art. 1697 §1. Recognition or enforcement of an interim or conservatory measure may be refused only: a) At the request of the party against whom it is invoked: i) If such refusal is warranted on the grounds set forth in article 1721, §1(a), i., ii., iii., iv. or v.; or ii) if the arbitral tribunal's decision with respect to the provision of security has not been complied with; or iii) if the interim or conservatory measure has been terminated or suspended by the arbitral tribunal or, where so empowered, by the court of the State in which the arbitration takes place or under the law of which that interim measure was granted; or b) if the Court of First Instance finds that any of the grounds set forth in article 1721, §1(b) apply to the recognition and enforcement of the interim or conservatory measure. § 2. Any determination made by the Court of First Instance on any ground in § 1 shall be effective only for the purposes of the application to recognise and enforce the interim or conservatory measure. The Court of First Instance where recognition or enforcement is sought shall not, in making that determination, undertake a review of the substance of the interim or conservatory measure.

835. https://pernetmartial.eu/sites/default/files/lois/Bahrain-Loi-d-arbitrage-arbitration-act-ley-de-arbitraje.pdf
836. http://www.mccibd.org/images/uploadimg/act_and_policy/corporate_governance/The-Arbitration-Act-2001.pdf
837. http://www.arbiter.com.sg/pdf/laws/Belgian%20Judicial%20Code%20Provisions%20(2013).pdf

Sr. No.	Country	Provision
7.	Bhutan - Alternative Dispute Resolution Act of Bhutan 2013[838]	Section 125. Grounds for refusing recognition or enforcement The recognition or enforcement of an interim measure may be refused at the request of the respondent if the court is satisfied that: (1) The refusal is warranted on the grounds set out in section 150 of this Act; or (2) The interim measure has been suspended or cancelled by the arbitral tribunal or, if so empowered, by the competent court of the country in which the arbitration took place or under the law of which that interim measure was granted.
8.	British Columbia - International Commercial Arbitration Act [RSBC 1996] Chapter 233[839]	Section 17.09 Grounds for refusing recognition or enforcement (1) Recognition or enforcement of an interim measure may be refused only (a) at the request of the party against whom the interim measure is directed if the court is satisfied that (i) such refusal is warranted on the grounds referred to in section 36 (1) (a) (i), (ii), (iii) or (iv), (ii) a decision of the arbitral tribunal with respect to the provision of security in connection with the interim measure has not been complied with, or (iii) the interim measure has been suspended or terminated by the arbitral tribunal or, where so empowered, by a court of the state in which the arbitration takes place or under the law of which that interim measure was granted, or (b) if the court finds that (i) the interim measure is incompatible with the powers conferred upon the court, unless the court decides to reformulate the interim measure to the extent necessary to adapt the interim measure to its own powers and procedures for the purposes of enforcing that interim measure and without modifying its substance, or (ii) any of the grounds referred to in section 36 (1) (b) (i) or (ii) apply to the recognition or enforcement of the interim measure. (2) A determination made by the court on a ground referred to in subsection (1) is effective only for the purposes of the application to recognize or enforce the interim measure. (3) The court where recognition or enforcement is sought may not, in making a determination on a ground referred to in subsection (1), undertake a review of the substance of the interim measure.
9.	British Virgin Islands - Virgin Islands Arbitration Act, 2013[840]	Section 42 Article 17I of the UNCITRAL Model Law does not have effect.

838. https://www.nationalcouncil.bt/assets/uploads/docs/acts/2014/Alternative_Dispute_Resolution_Act_of_Bhutan_2013_engl0th.pdf
839. http://www.bclaws.ca/civix/document/id/complete/statreg/96233_01

Sr. No.	Country	Provision
10.	Bulgaria - Law on International Commercial Arbitration State Gazette (SG) No. 60 of 05.08.1988[841]	No equivalent provision as Article 17I of the UNCITRAL Model Law 2006
11.	Cambodia - The Commercial Arbitration Law of the Kingdom of Cambodia 2006[842]	No equivalent provision as Article 17I of the UNCITRAL Model Law 2006
12.	Canada - Commercial Arbitration Act R.S.C., 1985, c. 17 (2nd Supp.)[843]	No equivalent provision as Article 17I of the UNCITRAL Model Law 2006
13.	Connecticut - Chapter 909 Arbitration Proceedings[844]	No equivalent provision as Article 17I of the UNCITRAL Model Law 2006
14.	Croatia - Law on Arbitration Official Gazette no. 88/2001[845]	No equivalent provision as Article 17I of the UNCITRAL Model Law 2006
15.	Cyprus - The International Commercial Arbitration Law, 1987[846]	No equivalent provision as Article 17I of the UNCITRAL Model Law 2006
16.	Denmark - Danish Arbitration Act 2005[847]	No equivalent provision as Article 17I of the UNCITRAL Model Law 2006

840. http://www.bviiac.org/Portals/0/Files/Arbitration%20Documents/ArbitrationAct2013.pdf
841. http://www.newyorkconvention.org/11165/web/files/document/1/6/16200.pdf
842. https://www.cambodiaip.gov.kh/DocResources/372a361b-7a97-44b3-9810-79e5e6ea85f4_c786a043-b88d-4f64-9429-60a330efdc5f-en.pdf
843. https://laws-lois.justice.gc.ca/eng/acts/C-34.6/index.html
844. https://www.cga.ct.gov/current/pub/chap_909.htm
845. http://www.vsrh.hr/CustomPages/Static/HRV/Files/Legislation__Law-Arbitration-RC.pdf
846. https://www.uv.es/medarb/observatorio/leyes-arbitraje/europa-resto/chipre-international-commercial-arbitration-law.pdf
847. https://voldgiftsinstituttet.dk/wp-content/uploads/2015/01/danish_arbitration_act_2005.pdf

Sr. No.	Country	Provision
17.	Egypt - Law No. 27/1994 Promulgating the Law Concerning Arbitration in Civil and Commercial Matters[848]	No equivalent provision as Article 17I of the UNCITRAL Model Law 2006
18.	Florida – Chapter 684 – International Commercial Arbitration, Title XXXIX Commercial Relations, 2020 Florida Statutes[849]	Same as Article 17I of the UNCITRAL Model Law 2006. Article 684.0027 Grounds for refusing recognition or enforcement.
19.	Fiji – International Arbitration Act 2017 (Act No. 44 of 2017)[850]	Same as Article 17I of UNCITRAL Model Law 2006 Section 32 Grounds for refusing recognition or enforcement
20.	France – Book IV - Arbitration of the Code of Civil Procedure Decree No. 2011-48[851]	No equivalent provision as Article 17I of the UNCITRAL Model Law 2006
21.	Georgia – Chapter 9 Arbitration, Title 9 Civil Practice, Georgia Code[852]	Article 22 - Grounds for refusing recognition or enforcement 1. A motion for recognition or enforcement of an interim measure may be refused and not granted only, if: a) a party against whom the motion is brought applies to a court and proves that: a.a) refusal of recognition and enforcement of interim measures is grounded on circumstances set forth in article 45 (1); a.b) the arbitral tribunal's decision to provide appropriate security with regard to the interim measures has not been enforced; a.c) the interim measures have been terminated or suspended by the arbitral tribunal or, by a court of a state in which the arbitration takes place or under the law of which the interim measures were granted;

848. https://www.wipo.int/edocs/lexdocs/laws/en/eg/eg020en.pdf
849. https://www.flsenate.gov/Laws/Statutes/2020/Chapter684/All
850. https://www.fiji.gov.fj/getattachment/d9502667-6491-4592-85b2-eff97f245fed/Act-44---International-Arbitration-Act.aspx
851. http://www.iaiparis.com/pdf/FRENCH_LAW_ON_INTERNATIONAL_ARBITRATION.pdf
852. https://matsne.gov.ge/ru/document/download/89284/5/en/pdf

Sr. No.	Country	Provision
		b) the court finds that: b.a) the enforcement of interim measure exceeds the power of the court, unless the court decides to reformulate the interim measure without modification of its substance to the extent necessary for the enforcement of the interim measure in accordance with the rules established by the legislation. b.b) The grounds provided for by article 45 (b)(b.a) and (b)(b.b), are applicable to the recognition and enforcement of an interim measure. 2. A decision rendered by a court, on any grounds provided for by paragraph 1 of this article, is effective only for the purposes of the motion to recognize and enforce an interim measure. 3. The court in which recognition and enforcement is sought, in the process of making its decision, does not undertake a review of the substance of the interim measure.
22.	Germany - Tenth Book of the Code of Civil Procedure, Arbitration Procedure[853]	No equivalent provision as Article 17I of the UNCITRAL Model Law 2006
23.	Greece - Code Of Civil Procedure, Book VII, Book VIII[854]	No equivalent provision as Article 17I of the UNCITRAL Model Law 2006
24.	Hong Kong - Cap. 609 Arbitration Ordinance[855]	Section 44. Article 17I of UNCITRAL Model Law (Grounds for refusing recognition or enforcement) Article 17I of the UNCITRAL Model Law does not have effect.
25.	Hungary - Act LX of 2017 on Arbitration[856]	Section 27 Grounds for refusing enforcement Enforcement of an interim measure may be refused only a) at the request of the party against whom it is invoked if the court is satisfied that: aa) any of the grounds set forth in section 47 (2) a) exists; or ab) the decision of the arbitral tribunal requiring the provision of security with respect to the interim measure has not been complied with; or ac) the arbitral tribunal terminated or suspended the interim measure; or b) if the court finds that ba) the interim measure is incompatible with the powers of the court; or bb) with respect to the interim measure, any of the grounds set forth in section 47 (2) b) exists.

853. https://sccinstitute.com/media/29988/german-arbitration-act.pdf
854. https://www.uv.es/medarb/observatorio/leyes-arbitraje/europa-resto/grecia-ccp-domestic-arbitration.pdf
855. https://www.elegislation.gov.hk/hk/cap609

Sr. No.	Country	Provision
26.	Ireland – Arbitration Act 2010 Number 1 of 2010[857]	Section 6 – Adoption of Model Law Subject to this Act, the Model Law shall have the force of law in the State and shall apply to arbitrations under arbitration agreements concerning— (a) international commercial arbitrations, or (b) arbitrations which are not international commercial arbitrations. Same as Article 17I of UNCITRAL Model Law 2006 Article 17I under Schedule 1 - TEXT OF UNCITRAL MODEL LAW ON INTERNATIONAL COMMERCIAL ARBITRATION
27.	Jamaica – The Arbitration Act, 2017 (Act 13 of 2017)[858]	Section 29 Grounds for refusing recognition or enforcement. (1) Recognition or enforcement of an interim measure may be refused only- (a) at the request of the party against whom it is invoked if the court is satisfied that- (i) the refusal is warranted on the grounds set out in section 57(1)(a)(i), (ii), (iii) or (iv); or (ii) the arbitral tribunal's decision with respect to the provision of security in connection with the interim measure issued by the arbitral tribunal has not been complied with; or (iii) the interim measure has been terminated or suspended by the arbitral tribunal or, where so empowered, by the court of the State in which the arbitration takes place or under the Act of which that interim measure was granted; or (b) if the court finds that- (i) the interim measure is incompatible with the powers conferred upon the court unless the court decides to reformulate the interim measure to the extent necessary to adapt it to its own powers and procedures for the purposes of enforcing that interim measure and without modifying its substance; or (ii) any of the grounds set out in section 57(1)(b)(i) or (ii), apply to the recognition and enforcement of the interim measure. (2) Any determination made by the court on any ground specified in subsection (1) shall be effective only for the purposes of the application to recognize and enforce the interim measure. (3) The court, where recognition or enforcement is sought, shall not, in making that determination, undertake a review of the substance of the interim measure.
28.	Japan – Arbitration Law (Law No.138 of 2003)[859]	No equivalent provision as Article 17I of the UNCITRAL Model Law 2006

856. https://www.ilo.org/dyn/natlex/docs/ELECTRONIC/106843/131257/F-266585574/J2017T0060P_20180102_FIN.pdf
857. http://www.irishstatutebook.ie/eli/2010/act/1/enacted/en/pdf
858. http://extwprlegs1.fao.org/docs/pdf/jam172060.pdf

Sr. No.	Country	Provision
29.	Jordan - Law No. 31 of 2001 (Jordan) Arbitration Law[860]	No equivalent provision as Article 17I of the UNCITRAL Model Law 2006
30.	Kenya - Chapter 49 Arbitration Act (The Arbitration Act, 1995)[861]	No equivalent provision as Article 17I of the UNCITRAL Model Law 2006
31.	Liechtenstein - Liechtenstein Arbitration Law (Code of Civil Procedure)[862]	Section 610 Power to Order Interim or Protective Measures 4) The court shall refuse to enforce a measure under paragraph 1) of this Article, if 1. the place of arbitration is in this state and the measure suffers from a defect which would constitute a reason for setting aside an arbitral award of this state under §§ 628 paragraph 2), 634 paragraph 6) and 7) or 635 of this Law; 2. the place of arbitration is not in this state and the measure suffers from a defect which would constitute cause for refusal of recognition or enforcement of a foreign arbitral award; 3. the enforcement of the measure would be incompatible with a court measure of this state which was either applied for or made earlier, or would be incompatible with a foreign court measure which was made earlier and which is to be recognized; 4. the measure provides for a measure of protection unknown to Liechtenstein law and no appropriate measure of protection as provided by Liechtenstein law was applied for. 6) The court shall set aside the enforcement if: 1. the term of the measure as set by the arbitral tribunal has expired; 2. the arbitral tribunal has limited the scope of or set aside the measure; 3. a case as referred to in Article 291 paragraph 1) lit. a to e of the Liechtenstein Enforcement Act (Exekutionsordnung) is considered; unless such case was already unsuccessfully argued before the arbitral tribunal and no obstacles against recognition (paragraph 4) exist with regard to the decision of the arbitral tribunal; 4. security as referred to in paragraph 1) of this Article has been provided which renders the enforcement of the measure unnecessary.

859. https://japan.kantei.go.jp/policy/sihou/arbitrationlaw.pdf
860. https://www.ilo.org/dyn/natlex/docs/ELECTRONIC/63091/95325/F1864661120/JOR63091.pdf
861. https://ncia.or.ke/wp-content/uploads/2021/02/ArbitrationAct4of1995_2.pdf
862. https://www.newyorkconvention.org/11165/web/files/document/2/1/21372.pdf

Sr. No.	Country	Provision
32.	Lithuania – The Republic of Lithuania Law on Commercial Arbitration, 2012[863]	Article 25. Enforcement of Orders on Interim Measures and Grounds for a Refusal to Issue A Writ of Execution 4. Vilnius Regional Court may refuse to issue a writ of execution only in the case where: 1) data provided to determine the obligatory content of the writ of execution are insufficient and this cannot be rectified during the consideration of the application for the issue of the writ of execution; 2) a party in respect of which the writ of execution is requested provides evidence that an arbitral tribunal failed to inform him, in an appropriate manner, of the consideration of the matter of taking of interim measures and thus prevented him from providing his explanations in this relation; 3) an arbitral tribunal has evidently exceeded its competence in issuing the order concerning taking of interim measures; 4) an order of the arbitral tribunal on security for compensation for losses likely to result from application of interim measures has not been executed; 5) the arbitral tribunal has amended or annulled the order on application of interim measures. 5. A separate appeal may be filed against the order of Vilnius Regional Court refusing the issue of a writ of execution. Article 26. Recognition or Enforcement of Foreign Arbitral Awards or Orders on Interim Measures and Grounds for the Refusal to Recognise or Enforce a Foreign Arbitral Award or Order 3. By its order, the Court of Appeal of Lithuania may refuse to recognise or enforce a foreign arbitral award or order on application of interim measures, where: 1) such an award or order is not enforceable on the territory of the Republic of Lithuania; 2) there are grounds indicated in Article 25(4)(2), (3), (4) and (5) of this Law. 4. The provisions of Article 51(3) of this Law shall mutatis mutandis apply to appeals against orders of the Court of Appeal of Lithuania, as defined in this Article.
33.	Louisiana – RS 9 Title 9.Civil Code-Ancillaries[864]	No equivalent provision as Article 17I of the UNCITRAL Model Law 2006
34.	Macedonia - Law on International Commercial Arbitration of the Republic of Macedonia[865]	No equivalent provision as Article 17I of the UNCITRAL Model Law 2006

863. https://e-seimas.lrs.lt/portal/legalAct/lt/TAD/35954312dcb311e6be918a531b2126ab?jfwid=-wd7z7zum0
864. http://legis.la.gov/legis/Laws_Toc.aspx?folder=83&title=9

Sr. No.	Country	Provision
35.	Malaysia - Arbitration Act 2005, Act 646[866]	No equivalent provision as Article 17I of the UNCITRAL Model Law 2006
36.	Maldives - Act No: 10/2013, Arbitration Act[867]	Section 43 Grounds for Refusing Recognition or Enforcement (a) Recognition or enforcement by the courts of an order for interim measure issued by an Arbitral Tribunal under this Act may be refused only at the request of the party against whom such order is invoked if the court is satisfied that the following grounds exist: 1. The enforcement of such an order for an interim measure would not be warranted on the grounds that one of the circumstances spelled out in Section 74, (a), 1, has arisen; OR 2. The Arbitral Tribunal's decision with respect to the provision of security in connection with the interim measure issued by the arbitral tribunal has not been complied with; OR 3. The interim measure has been terminated or suspended by the arbitral tribunal or, where so empowered, terminated by the court. (b) Even if the party against whom a preliminary order is issued under this Act is unable to satisfy the court of any of the grounds spelled out in (a) above, the court may on its own initiative refuse to recognize or enforce such order in the following instances: 1. The court finds that the interim measure is incompatible with the powers conferred upon the court; OR 2. The court does not wish to reformulate the interim measure to the extent necessary to adapt to its own powers and procedures for the purposes of enforcing the interim measure; OR 3. The court finds that any of the grounds set forth in Section 74, (a), 2, of this Act apply to the recognition and enforcement of the interim measure. Section 44 Determination Made by Court In Relation with Request (a) Any determination made by the court for the recognition and enforcement of a preliminary order for an interim measure issued under this Act shall be effective only for the purposes of the application to recognize and enforce the interim measure. (b) The court where recognition or enforcement is sought does not, in making that determination, undertake a review of the substance of the interim measure.
37.	Malta - CAP. 387 Arbitration Act[868]	No equivalent provision as Article 17I of the UNCITRAL Model Law 2006

865. https://www.international-arbitration-attorney.com/wp-content/uploads/2013/07/Macedonia-Arbitration-Law.pdf
866. http://www.newyorkconvention.org/11165/web/files/document/1/6/16298.pdf
867. https://miac.gov.mv/media/documents/Arbitration%20Act.pdf
868. http://justiceservices.gov.mt/DownloadDocument.aspx?app=lom&itemid=8854&l=1

Sr. No.	Country	Provision
38.	Mauritius - The International Arbitration Act, 2008 (Act 37 of 2008)[869]	Section 18. Recognition and enforcement of interim measures (4) Recognition or enforcement of an interim measure may be refused only - (a) at the request of the party against whom it is invoked where the Court is satisfied that - (i) the refusal is warranted on a ground set out in section 39(2)(a); (ii) the arbitral tribunal's decision with respect to the provision of security in connection with the measure issued by the arbitral tribunal has not been complied with; or (iii) the interim measure has been terminated or suspended by the arbitral tribunal or, where so empowered, by the Court of the State in which the arbitration takes place or under the law of which that interim measure was granted; or (b) where the Court finds that - (i) the measure is incompatible with the powers conferred on the Court unless the Court decides to reformulate the measure to the extent necessary to adapt it to its own power and procedures for the purposes of enforcing that measure and without modifying its substance; or (ii) any of the grounds set out in section 39(2)(b) apply to the recognition and enforcement of the measure. (5) Any determination made by the Court on any ground in subsection (4) shall be effective only for the purposes of the application to recognise and enforce the interim measure. The Court where recognition or enforcement is sought shall not, in making that determination, undertake a review of the substance of the interim measure.
39.	Montenegro - Decree on the Promulgation of the Law on Arbitration, 2015[870]	Article 28 Grounds for refusing recognition and enforcement of an interim measure Recognition and enforcement of an interim measure may be refused at the request of the party against whom it has been ordered if the court is satisfied that: 1) Such refusal is warranted on the grounds set forth in Article 52 paragraph 1 items 1 to 4 hereof; 2) The arbitral tribunal's decision referred to in Article 24 hereof has not been complied with; or 3) The interim measure has terminated or has been suspended by the arbitral tribunal or by the court of the State in which the arbitration takes place, where the court is so empowered, or of the State under the law of which that interim measure was ordered.

869. https://www.wipo.int/edocs/lexdocs/laws/en/mu/mu020en.pdf
870. https://www.privrednakomora.me/sites/pkcg.org/files/multimedia/main_pages/files/2012/09/final_eng_zakon_o_arbitrazi_final_0.pdf

Sr. No.	Country	Provision
		Recognition and enforcement of an interim measure may also be refused if the court finds that: 1) The interim measure is incompatible with the powers conferred upon the court in accordance with the legislation of Montenegro, unless the court decides, for the purposes of enforcing the interim measure, to modify that interim measure, in accordance with the legislation, without modifying its substance; or 2) There is any of the grounds set forth in Article 52 paragraph 2 items 1 or 2 hereof. Determination made by the court on any ground in paragraphs 1 and 2 of this Article shall be effective only for the purposes of the application to recognize and enforce the interim measure. The court where recognition and enforcement of an interim measure is sought shall not, in making that determination, undertake a review of the substance of the interim measure.
40.	Myanmar - Arbitration Law The Pyidaungsu Hluttaw Law No. 5/2016[871]	No equivalent provision as Article 17I of the UNCITRAL Model Law 2006
41.	New South Wales - Commercial Arbitration Act 2010 No 61[872]	Section 17I Grounds for refusing recognition or enforcement (cf Model Law Art 17I) (1) Recognition or enforcement of an interim measure may be refused only: (a) at the request of the party against whom it is invoked if the Court is satisfied that: (i) such a refusal is warranted on the grounds set out in section 36 (1) (a) (i), (ii), (iii) or (iv), or (ii) the arbitral tribunal's decision with respect to the provision of security in connection with the interim measure issued by the arbitral tribunal has not been complied with, or (iii) the interim measure has been terminated or suspended by the arbitral tribunal or, where so empowered, by the court of the State or Territory in which the arbitration takes place or under the law of which that interim measure was granted, or (b) if the Court finds that: (i) the interim measure is incompatible with the powers conferred on the Court unless the Court decides to reformulate the interim measure to the extent necessary to adapt it to its own powers and procedures for the purposes of enforcing that interim measure and without modifying its substance, or (ii) any of the grounds set out in section 36 (1) (b) (i) or (ii) apply to the recognition and enforcement of the interim measure.

871. http://www.newyorkconvention.org/11165/web/files/document/2/1/21098.pdf

Sr. No.	Country	Provision
		(2) Any determination made by the Court on any ground in subsection (1) is effective only for the purposes of the application to recognise and enforce the interim measure. (3) The Court must not, in making a determination with respect to the recognition or enforcement sought, undertake a review of the substance of the interim measure. Note. This section is substantially the same as Art 17I of the Model Law but has been modified to the extent necessary to apply Art 17I as incorporated in this Act in the context of domestic commercial arbitrations.
42.	New Zealand - The Arbitration Act, 1996 No 99[873]	Schedule I - Rules applying to arbitration agreement Article 17M Grounds for refusing recognition or enforcement (1) Recognition or enforcement of an interim measure may be refused only— (a) at the request of the respondent if the court is satisfied that— (i) the refusal is warranted on the grounds set out in article 36(1)(a)(i), (ii), or (iv); or (ii) the arbitral tribunal's decision with respect to the provision of security in connection with the interim measure granted by it has not been complied with; or (iii) the interim measure has been suspended or cancelled by the arbitral tribunal or, if so empowered, by the court of the country in which the arbitration took place or under the law of which that interim measure was granted; or (b) if the court finds that— (i) the interim measure is incompatible with the powers conferred on the court, unless the court decides to reformulate the interim measure to the extent necessary to adapt it to its own powers and procedures for the purposes of enforcing that interim measure and without modifying its substance; or (ii) any of the grounds set out in article 36(1)(b) apply to the recognition and enforcement of the interim measure. (2) A determination made by the court on any ground in paragraph (1) is effective only for the purposes of the application to recognise and enforce the interim measure. (3) The court must not, in making that determination, undertake a review of the substance of the interim measure.
43.	Nigeria - Arbitration and Conciliation Act Chapter 19 Laws of the Federation of Nigeria 1990[874]	No equivalent provision as Article 17I of the UNCITRAL Model Law 2006

873. http://www.legislation.govt.nz/act/public/1996/0099/latest/whole.html#DLM403277
874. http://niqs.org.ng/wp-content/uploads/2018/12/Arbitration-and-Conciliation-Act.pdf

<table>
<tr><th>Sr. No.</th><th>Country</th><th>Provision</th></tr>
<tr><td>44.</td><td>Northern Territory of Australia - Commercial Arbitration (National Uniform Legislation) Act 2011[875]</td><td>Section 17I Grounds for refusing recognition or enforcement (Model Law Art 17I)
(1) Recognition or enforcement of an interim measure may be refused only:
(a) at the request of the party against whom it is invoked if the Court is satisfied that:
(i) such a refusal is warranted on the grounds set out in section 36(1)(a)(i), (ii), (iii) or (iv); or
(ii) the arbitral tribunal's decision with respect to the provision of security in connection with the interim measure issued by the arbitral tribunal has not been complied with; or
(iii) the interim measure has been terminated or suspended by the arbitral tribunal or, where so empowered, by the court of the State or Territory in which the arbitration takes place or under the law of which that interim measure was granted; or
(b) if the Court finds that:
(i) the interim measure is incompatible with the powers conferred on the Court unless the Court decides to reformulate the interim measure to the extent necessary to adapt it to its own powers and procedures for the purposes of enforcing that interim measure and without modifying its substance; or
(ii) any of the grounds set out in section 36(1)(b)(i) or (ii) apply to the recognition and enforcement of the interim measure.
(2) Any determination made by the Court on any ground in subsection (1) is effective only for the purposes of the application to recognise and enforce the interim measure.
(3) The Court must not, in making a determination with respect to the recognition or enforcement sought, undertake a review of the substance of the interim measure.
Note for section 17I
This section is substantially the same as Art 17I of the Model Law but has been modified to the extent necessary to apply Art 17I as incorporated in this Act in the context of domestic commercial arbitrations.</td></tr>
<tr><td>45.</td><td>Norway - Act of 14 May 2004 No. 25 relating to Arbitration (The Arbitration Act)[876]</td><td>No equivalent provision as Article 17I of the UNCITRAL Model Law 2006</td></tr>
</table>

875. https://legislation.nt.gov.au/api/sitecore/Act/PDF?id=11692
876. https://www.chamber.no/wp-content/uploads/2014/02/Norwegian_Arbitration_Act.pdf

Sr. No.	Country	Provision
46.	Oman - The Omani Law of Arbitration in Civil and Commercial Disputes – Royal Decree 47/97[877]	No equivalent provision as Article 17I of the UNCITRAL Model Law 2006
47.	Ontario - International Commercial Arbitration Act, 2017, S.O. 2017, c. 2, Sched. 5[878]	Section 5 - Application of Model Law (1) Subject to this Act, the Model Law on International Commercial Arbitration, adopted by the United Nations Commission on International Trade Law on 21 June 1985, as amended by the United Nations Commission on International Trade Law on 7 July 2006, set out in Schedule 2, has force of law in Ontario. Same (2) With respect to article 7 of the Model Law, option I applies in Ontario; option II does not. Same (3) The Model Law applies to international commercial arbitration agreements and awards made in international commercial arbitrations, whether made before or after the coming into force of this Act. Schedule 2 to this Act Article 17I
48.	Oregon – Oregon International Commercial Arbitration and Conciliation Act[879]	No equivalent provision as Article 17I of the UNCITRAL Model Law 2006
49.	Pakistan - The Arbitration Act, 1940 Act No. X of 1940[880]	No equivalent provision as Article 17I of the UNCITRAL Model Law 2006
50.	Philippines - Alternative Dispute Resolution Act of 2004 Republic Act No. 9285[881]	No equivalent provision as Article 17I of the UNCITRAL Model Law 2006
51.	Poland – Polish Act of 17 November 1964 - Code of Civil Procedure, Part Five Arbitration[882]	No equivalent provision as Article 17I of the UNCITRAL Model Law 2006

877. http://www.newyorkconvention.org/11165/web/files/document/2/1/21103.pdf
878. https://www.ontario.ca/laws/statute/17i02b#BK16
879. https://www.oregonlegislature.gov/bills_laws/ors/ors036.html
880. https://www.wipo.int/edocs/lexdocs/laws/en/pk/pk066en.pdf
881. http://www.newyorkconvention.org/11165/web/files/document/2/1/21107.pdf

Sr. No.	Country	Provision
52.	Qatar - Law No. 2 of 2017 Promulgating the Civil and Commercial Arbitration Law-The Law of Arbitration in Civil and Commercial Matters[883]	No equivalent provision as Article 17I of the UNCITRAL Model Law 2006
53.	Queensland - Commercial Arbitration Act 2013 No. 8[884]	Section 17I Grounds for refusing recognition or enforcement (cf Model Law Art 17I) (1) Recognition or enforcement of an interim measure may be refused only— (a) at the request of the party against whom it is invoked if the Court is satisfied that— (i) such a refusal is warranted on the grounds set out in section 36(1)(a)(i), (ii), (iii) or (iv); or (ii) the arbitral tribunal's decision with respect to the provision of security in connection with the interim measure issued by the arbitral tribunal has not been complied with; or (iii) the interim measure has been terminated or suspended by the arbitral tribunal or, where so empowered, by the court of the State or Territory in which the arbitration takes place or under the law of which that interim measure was granted; or (b) if the Court finds that— (i) the interim measure is incompatible with the powers conferred on the Court unless the Court decides to reformulate the interim measure to the extent necessary to adapt it to its own powers and procedures for the purposes of enforcing that interim measure and without modifying its substance; or (ii) any of the grounds set out in section 36(1)(b)(i) or (ii) apply to the recognition and enforcement of the interim measure. (2) Any determination made by the Court on any ground in subsection (1) is effective only for the purposes of the application to recognise and enforce the interim measure. (3) The Court must not, in making a determination with respect to the recognition or enforcement sought, undertake a review of the substance of the interim measure.

882. https://www.uv.es/medarb/observatorio/leyes-arbitraje/europa-resto/polonia-ccp-arbitration.pdf
883. https://www.qicdrc.gov.qa/sites/default/files/inline-files/law_no._02_2017_promulgating_the_civil_and_commercial_arbitration_law.pdf
884. https://www.legislation.qld.gov.au/view/pdf/inforce/2013-05-17/act-2013-008

Sr. No.	Country	Provision
		Note— This section is substantially the same as Art 17I of the Model Law but has been modified to the extent necessary to apply Art 17I as incorporated in this Act in the context of domestic commercial arbitrations.
54.	Republic of Costa Rica - Costa Rican Law for International Arbitration Law Number: 8937[885]	Same as Article 17I of UNCITRAL Model Law 2006
55.	Republic of Korea - Arbitration Act[886]	Article 18-8 (Grounds for Refusing Recognition or Enforcement) (1) Recognition or enforcement of an interim measure may be refused only if it falls under one of the following subparagraphs: 1. At the request of the party against whom the interim measure is invoked if the court is satisfied that: (a) The other party to the interim measure proves any of the following facts: (i) A fact under Article 36 (2) 1 (a) or (d); (ii) The fact that the other party to the interim measure was not able to present his or her case because the party was not given proper notice of the appointment of an arbitrator or of the arbitral proceeding or due to any other cause or event; (iii) The fact that the dispute subject to the interim measure is not eligible for an arbitration agreement or that the interim measure is beyond the scope of the arbitration agreement: Provided, That the recognition or execution of the interim measure only for the part not eligible for an arbitration agreement may be denied, if the part eligible for the arbitration agreement is separable from the part ineligible for the arbitration agreement; (b) Where an asset has not been provided as security for the interim measure according to an order issued by the court or the arbitral tribunal; (c) Where the interim measure has been terminated or suspended by the arbitral tribunal. 2. Where the court, ex officio, finds that either of the following grounds exists: (a) Where the court has no authority to execute the interim measure: Provided, That the foregoing shall not apply where the court makes a decision to alter the interim measure to the necessary extent, without altering the substance of the interim measure, in order to execute the interim measure;

885. https://arbitratlaw.com/wp-content/uploads/2017/01/Costa-Rican-Intl-Arbitration-Law.pdf
886. https://elaw.klri.re.kr/eng_service/lawView.do?hseq=38889&lang=ENG

Sr. No.	Country	Provision
		(b) Where any of the grounds set forth in Article 36 (2) 2 (a) or (b) exists. (2) No court shall examine the substance of an interim measure when it makes a decision on a petition filed to seek the recognition or execution of the interim measure under Article 18-7. (3) The judgment of a court based on any of the grounds referred to in paragraph (1) shall be valid only for the decision on the recognition and execution of the relevant interim measure.
56.	Russia - Russian Federation Law on International Commercial Arbitration[887]	No equivalent provision as Article 17I of the UNCITRAL Model Law 2006
57.	Rwanda – Law on Arbitration and Conciliation in Commercial Matters, N° 005/2008[888]	No equivalent provision as Article 17I of the UNCITRAL Model Law 2006
58.	Saudi Arabia – Law of Arbitration Royal Decree No. M/34[889]	No equivalent provision as Article 17I of the UNCITRAL Model Law 2006
59.	Serbia – Law on Arbitration No. 46/06[890]	No equivalent provision as Article 17I of the UNCITRAL Model Law 2006
60.	Singapore - Arbitration Act (Chapter 10) (Domestic Arbitration Law)[891]	No equivalent provision as Article 17I of the UNCITRAL Model Law 2006
61.	Singapore - International Arbitration Act (Chapter 143A) (International Arbitration Law)[892]	No equivalent provision as Article 17I of the UNCITRAL Model Law 2006

887. http://www.newyorkconvention.org/11165/web/files/document/2/2/22335.pdf
888. http://www.newyorkconvention.org/11165/web/files/document/2/1/21110.pdf
889. https://www.wipo.int/edocs/lexdocs/laws/en/sa/sa057en.pdf
890. https://www.wipo.int/edocs/lexdocs/laws/en/rs/rs028en.pdf
891. https://sso.agc.gov.sg/Act/AA2001
892. https://sso.agc.gov.sg/Act/IAA1994

Sr. No.	Country	Provision
62.	Slovakia - [Slovak] Act No. 244/2002 of 3 April 2002 on Arbitration[893]	Section 22d (1) A party to arbitration may request the relevant court to set aside an interim measure if conditions for issuance of such measure under this Act or under the parties' agreement were not satisfied. The setting aside of an interim measure granted under Section 22a can be requested by a party if its objections under Section 22a(3) were unsuccessful. Sections 40(2) and 41 and 42 shall apply mutatis mutandis. The decision of a court dismissing an interim measure may be appealed. A binding and enforceable decision of a court dismissing an interim measure is binding on the arbitral tribunal. (2) The court shall decide on a challenge to an interim measure without undue delay, but in any case within 30 days
63.	Slovenia - Law on Arbitration of Slovenia[894]	No equivalent provision as Article 17I of the UNCITRAL Model Law 2006
64.	South Africa - The Arbitration Act, 1965[895]	No equivalent provision as Article 17I of the UNCITRAL Model Law 2006
65.	South Australia - South Australia Commercial Arbitration Act 2011[896]	Section 17I—Grounds for refusing recognition or enforcement (1) Recognition or enforcement of an interim measure may be refused only— (a) at the request of the party against whom it is invoked if the Court is satisfied that— (i) such a refusal is warranted on the grounds set out in section 36(1)(a)(i), (ii), (iii) or (iv); or (ii) the arbitral tribunal's decision with respect to the provision of security in connection with the interim measure issued by the arbitral tribunal has not been complied with; or (iii) the interim measure has been terminated or suspended by the arbitral tribunal or, if so empowered, by the court of the State or Territory in which the arbitration takes place or under the law of which that interim measure was granted; or (b) if the Court finds that— (i) the interim measure is incompatible with the powers conferred on the Court unless the Court decides to reformulate the interim measure to the extent necessary to adapt it to its own powers and procedures for the purposes of enforcing that interim measure and without modifying its substance; or

893. https://www.international-arbitration-attorney.com/wp-content/uploads/2013/07/Slovakia-Arbitration-Law-1.pdf
894. http://www.sloarbitration.eu/Portals/0/Arbitrazno-pravo/Law%20on%20Arbitration%20of%20Slovenia.pdf
895. https://www.gov.za/sites/default/files/gcis_document/201505/act-42-1965.pdf
896. https://www.legislation.sa.gov.au/LZ/C/A/COMMERCIAL%20ARBITRATION%20ACT%202011/CURRENT/2011.32.UN.PDF

Sr. No.	Country	Provision
		(ii) any of the grounds set out in section 36(1)(b)(i) or (ii) apply to the recognition and enforcement of the interim measure. (2) Any determination made by the Court on any ground in subsection (1) is effective only for the purposes of the application to recognise and enforce the interim measure. (3) The Court must not, in making a determination with respect to the recognition or enforcement sought, undertake a review of the substance of the interim measure. Note— This section is substantially the same as Art 17I of the Model Law but has been modified to the extent necessary to apply Art 17I as incorporated in this Act in the context of domestic commercial arbitrations.
66.	Spain - Act 60/2003 of 23 December on Arbitration[897]	No equivalent provision as Article 17I of the UNCITRAL Model Law 2006
67.	Sri Lanka - Arbitration Act. No. 11 of 1995[898]	No equivalent provision as Article 17I of the UNCITRAL Model Law 2006
68.	Sweden - The Swedish Arbitration Act (SFS 1999:116)[899]	No equivalent provision as Article 17I of the UNCITRAL Model Law 2006
69.	Switzerland - Private International Law Act 1987, Chapter 12: International Arbitration[900]	No equivalent provision as Article 17I of the UNCITRAL Model Law 2006
70.	Tasmania - Commercial Arbitration Act, 2011, Act 13 of 2011[901]	Section 17I. Grounds for refusing recognition or enforcement (cf Model Law Art 17I) (1) Recognition or enforcement of an interim measure may be refused only - (a) at the request of the party against whom it is invoked if the Court is satisfied that -

897. https://www.mjusticia.gob.es/cs/Satellite/Portal/1292426982249?blobheader=application%2Fpdf&blobheadername1=Content-Disposition&blobheadervalue1=attachment%3B+filename%3DAct_on_arbitration_%28Ley_60_2003__de_arbitraje%29.PDF
898. http://www.slnarbcentre.com/pdf/ARBITRATION-ACT.pdf
899. https://sccinstitute.com/media/37089/the-swedish-arbitration-act.pdf
900. https://www.swissarbitration.org/wp-content/uploads/2021/05/20210129-Chapter-12-PILA_Translation_English.pdf
901. https://www.legislation.tas.gov.au/view/html/inforce/current/act-2011-013

Sr. No.	Country	Provision
		(i) such a refusal is warranted on the grounds set out in section 36(1)(a)(i), (ii), (iii) or (iv); or (ii) the arbitral tribunal's decision with respect to the provision of security in connection with the interim measure issued by the arbitral tribunal has not been complied with; or (iii) the interim measure has been terminated or suspended by the arbitral tribunal or, where so empowered, by the court of the State or Territory in which the arbitration takes place or under the law of which that interim measure was granted; or (b) if the Court finds that – (i) the interim measure is incompatible with the powers conferred on the Court unless the Court decides to reformulate the interim measure to the extent necessary to adapt it to its own powers and procedures for the purposes of enforcing that interim measure and without modifying its substance; or (ii) any of the grounds set out in section 36(1)(b)(i) or (ii) apply to the recognition and enforcement of the interim measure. (2) Any determination made by the Court on any ground in subsection (1) is effective only for the purposes of the application to recognise and enforce the interim measure. (3) The court must not, in making a determination with respect to the recognition or enforcement sought, undertake a review of the substance of the interim measure. Note. This section is substantially the same as Art 17I of the Model Law but has been modified to the extent necessary to apply Art 17I as incorporated in this Act in the context of domestic commercial arbitrations.
71.	Texas - Chapter 172. Arbitration and Conciliation of International Commercial Disputes, Civil Practice and Remedies Code[902]	No equivalent provision as Article 17I of the UNCITRAL Model Law 2006
72.	Thailand – Arbitration Act B.E. 2545[903]	No equivalent provision as Article 17I of the UNCITRAL Model Law 2006

902. https://statutes.capitol.texas.gov/Docs/CP/htm/CP.172.htm
903. https://tai.coj.go.th/th/file/get/file/20190328ecac5333356ffad0331bd601151db9f4142557.pdf

Sr. No.	Country	Provision
73.	Tunisia – Law n° 93-42 issued on April 26, related to the promulgation of the Arbitration Code[904]	No equivalent provision as Article 17I of the UNCITRAL Model Law 2006
74.	Turkey - Turkish International Arbitration Law, Law no. 4686, 2001[905]	No equivalent provision as Article 17I of the UNCITRAL Model Law 2006
75.	Uganda – Chapter 4 The Arbitration and Conciliation Act[906]	No equivalent provision as Article 17I of the UNCITRAL Model Law 2006
76.	Ukraine - The Law of Ukraine on International Commercial Arbitration[907]	No equivalent provision as Article 17I of the UNCITRAL Model Law 2006
77.	United Arab Emirates - Federal Law No. (6) of 2018 on Arbitration[908]	No equivalent provision as Article 17I of the UNCITRAL Model Law 2006
78.	Uruguay - Law 19,636 Approve Rules for International Commercial Arbitration[909]	No equivalent provision as Article 17I of the UNCITRAL Model Law 2006
79.	Venezuela – Venezuelan Commercial Arbitration Act[910]	No equivalent provision as Article 17I of the UNCITRAL Model Law 2006

904. https://arbitrationlaw.com/sites/default/files/free_pdfs/Tunisia%20Arbitration%20Code.pdf
905. http://www.camera-arbitrale.it/Documenti/tial_turkey.pdf
906. https://ulii.org/akn/ug/act/2000/7/eng@2008-06-27
907. http://arbitrations.ru/userfiles/file/Law/Arbitration%20acts/ukraininan%20law%20on%20arbitration.pdf
908. https://www.tamimi.com/crm-media-uploader/fileupload/server/php/files/UAE%20Arbitration%20Law%20-%20Federal%20Law%20No%20%206%20of%202018.pdf
909. http://www.impo.com.uy/bases/leyes-originales/19636-2018
910. https://arbitrationlaw.com/sites/default/files/free_pdfs/Venezula%20Commercial%20Arbitration%20Act.pdf

Sr. No.	Country	Provision
80.	Victoria - Commercial Arbitration Act 2011 No. 50 of 2011[911]	Section 17I Grounds for refusing recognition or enforcement (cf Model Law Art 17I) (1) Recognition or enforcement of an interim measure may be refused only— (a) at the request of the party against whom it is invoked if the Court is satisfied that— (i) such a refusal is warranted on the grounds set out in section 36(1)(a)(i),(ii), (iii) or (iv); or (ii) the arbitral tribunal's decision with respect to the provision of security in connection with the interim measure issued by the arbitral tribunal has not been complied with; or (iii) the interim measure has been terminated or suspended by the arbitral tribunal or, where so empowered, by the court of the State or Territory in which the arbitration takes place or under the law of which that interim measure was granted; or (b) if the Court finds that— (i) the interim measure is incompatible with the powers conferred on the Court unless the Court decides to reformulate the interim measure to the extent necessary to adapt it to its own powers and procedures for the purposes of enforcing that interim measure and without modifying its substance; or (ii) any of the grounds set out in section 36(1)(b)(i) or (ii) apply to the recognition and enforcement of the interim measure. (2) Any determination made by the Court on any ground in subsection (1) is effective only for the purposes of the application to recognise and enforce the interim measure. (3) The Court must not, in making a determination with respect to the recognition or enforcement sought, undertake a review of the substance of the interim measure. Note This section is substantially the same as Art 17I of the Model Law but has been modified to the extent necessary to apply Art 17I as incorporated in this Act in the context of domestic commercial arbitrations.
81.	Western Australia - Commercial Arbitration Act 2012, 023 of 2012[912]	Section 17I. Grounds for refusing recognition or enforcement (cf. Model Law Art 17I) (1) Recognition or enforcement of an interim measure may be refused only— (a) at the request of the party against whom it is invoked if the Court is satisfied that —

911. http://arbitration.site/wp-content/uploads/2019/06/CAA-Vic-.pdf
912. https://www.legislation.wa.gov.au/legislation/prod/filestore.nsf/FileURL/mrdoc_25084.pdf/$FILE/Commercial%20Arbitration%20Act%202012%20-%20%5B00-b0-06%5D.pdf?OpenElement

Sr. No.	Country	Provision
		(i) such a refusal is warranted on the grounds set out in section 36(1)(a)(i), (ii), (iii) or (iv); or (ii) the arbitral tribunal's decision with respect to the provision of security in connection with the interim measure issued by the arbitral tribunal has not been complied with; or (iii) the interim measure has been terminated or suspended by the arbitral tribunal or, where so empowered, by the court of the State or Territory in which the arbitration takes place or under the law of which that interim measure was granted; or (b) if the Court finds that — (i) the interim measure is incompatible with the powers conferred on the Court unless the Court decides to reformulate the interim measure to the extent necessary to adapt it to its own powers and procedures for the purposes of enforcing that interim measure and without modifying its substance; or (ii) any of the grounds set out in section 36(1)(b)(i) or (ii) apply to the recognition and enforcement of the interim measure. (2) Any determination made by the Court on any ground in subsection (1) is effective only for the purposes of the application to recognise and enforce the interim measure. (3) The Court must not, in making a determination with respect to the recognition or enforcement sought, undertake a review of the substance of the interim measure. Note for this section: This section is substantially the same as Art 17I of the Model Law but has been modified to the extent necessary to apply Art 17I as incorporated in this Act in the context of domestic commercial arbitrations.
82.	Zambia - The Arbitration Act, 2000 No. 19 of 2000[913]	No equivalent provision as Article 17I of the UNCITRAL Model Law 2006
83.	Zimbabwe - Chapter 7:15 Arbitration Act[914]	No equivalent provision as Article 17I of the UNCITRAL Model Law 2006

913. http://www.newyorkconvention.org/11165/web/files/document/2/1/21396.pdf
914. https://zimlii.org/akn/zw/act/1996/6/eng@2016-12-31

Appendix L (Article 17J)

Sr. No.	Country	Provision
1.	Australia - International Arbitration Act 1974[915]	Same as Article 17J of UNCITRAL Model Law 2006 Sec 16 Model Law to have force of law (1) Subject to this Part, the Model Law has the force of law in Australia. (2) In the Model Law: Arbitration agreement has the meaning given in Option 1 of Article 7 of the Model Law. State means Australia (including the external Territories) and any foreign country. This State means Australia (including the external Territories). Model Law under Part V, Schedule 2 of the Arbitration Act, 1974
2.	Australian Capital Territory - Commercial Arbitration Act, 2017 A2017-7[916]	SECT 17J Court-ordered interim measures (Model Law art 17J) (1) The court has the same power of issuing an interim measure in relation to arbitration proceedings as it has in relation to proceedings in courts. (2) The court is to exercise the power in accordance with its own procedures taking into account the specific features of a domestic commercial arbitration. Note This section is substantially the same as the Model Law, art 17J but has been modified to the extent necessary to apply art 17J as incorporated in this Act in the context of domestic commercial arbitrations.
3.	Austria - Austrian Arbitration Act, 2013[917]	No equivalent provision as Article 17J of the UNCITRAL Model Law 2006

915. https://www.legislation.gov.au/Details/C2011C00342
916. http://classic.austlii.edu.au/au/legis/act/consol_act/caa2017219/s17j.html
917. https://www.viac.eu/images/law/ZPO_Schiedsrecht_2014_en_im_VIAC_Layout.pdf

Sr. No.	Country	Provision
4.	Bahrain - Bahrain Arbitration Law No. 9/2015[918]	Same as UNCITRAL Model Law 2006 Article 1 Taking into account the provisions of international conventions in force in the Kingdom of Bahrain 1. The provisions of the " UNCITRAL " Model Law on International Commercial Arbitration Act attached to this law shall apply to all arbitration whatever the nature of the legal relationship of the dispute herewith, if this arbitration takes place in the Kingdom of Bahrain or abroad and that two parties agreed to comply with the provisions of the attached law. 2. The provisions of the attached law shall apply to all arbitration which begins after its entry into force even if based on an arbitration agreement concluded before the entry into force of this law.
5.	Bangladesh - The Arbitration Act, 2001[919]	No equivalent provision as Article 17J of the UNCITRAL Model Law 2006
6.	Belgium - Belgian Judicial Code Provisions[920]	Art. 1698 The Court ruling in summary proceedings shall have the same power of issuing an interim or conservatory measure in relation to arbitration proceedings, irrespective of whether they take place on Belgian territory, as it has in relation to court proceedings. The Court shall exercise such power in accordance with its own procedures taking into account the specific features of arbitration.
7.	Bhutan - Alternative Dispute Resolution Act of Bhutan 2013[921]	No equivalent provision as Article 17J of the UNCITRAL Model Law 2006
8.	British Columbia - International Commercial Arbitration Act [RSBC 1996] Chapter 233[922]	Section 17.10 Court-ordered interim measures (1) A court has the same powers to issue an interim measure in relation to arbitral proceedings, irrespective of whether the place of those proceedings is in British Columbia, as that court has in relation to court proceedings. (2) The court must exercise the powers referred to in subsection (1) in accordance with its own procedures in consideration of the specific features of international arbitration. (3) When requested to grant an interim measure, the court may, if it considers it proper, refer the request to an arbitral tribunal.

918. https://pernetmartial.eu/sites/default/files/lois/Bahrain-Loi-d-arbitrage-arbitration-act-ley-de-arbitraje.pdf
919. http://www.mccibd.org/images/uploadimg/act_and_policy/corporate_governance/The-Arbitration-Act-2001.pdf
920. http://www.arbiter.com.sg/pdf/laws/Belgian%20Judicial%20Code%20Provisions%20(2013).pdf
921. https://www.nationalcouncil.bt/assets/uploads/docs/acts/2014/Alternative_Dispute_Resolution_Act_of_Bhutan_2013_eng10th.pdf
922. http://www.bclaws.ca/civix/document/id/complete/statreg/96233_01

Sr. No.	Country	Provision
9.	British Virgin Islands - Virgin Islands Arbitration Act, 2013[923]	Section 43. Court-ordered interim measures (1) Article 17J of the UNCITRAL Model Law is substituted by this section. (2) On the application of a party, the Court may, in relation to any arbitral proceedings which have been or are to be commenced in or outside the Virgin Islands, grant an interim measure. (3) The powers conferred by this section may be exercised by the Court irrespective of whether or not similar powers may be exercised by an arbitral tribunal under section 33 in relation to the same dispute. (4) The Court may decline to grant an interim measure under subsection (2) on the ground that (a) the interim measure being sought is currently the subject of arbitral proceedings; and (b) the Court considers it more appropriate for the interim measure sought to be dealt with by the arbitral tribunal. (5) In relation to arbitral proceedings which have been or are to be commenced outside the Virgin Islands, the Court may grant an interim measure under subsection (2) only if (a) the arbitral proceedings are capable of giving rise to an arbitral award, whether interim or final, that may be enforced in the Virgin Islands under this Act or any other enactment; and (b) the interim measure sought belongs to a type or description of interim measure that may be granted in the Virgin Islands by the Court in relation to arbitral proceedings. (6) Subsection (5) applies even if (a) the subject matter of the arbitral proceedings would not, apart from that subsection, give rise to a cause of action over which the Court would have jurisdiction; or (b) the order sought is not ancillary or incidental to any arbitral proceedings in the Virgin Islands. (7) In exercising the power conferred under subsection (2) in relation to arbitral proceedings outside the Virgin Islands, the Court shall have regard to the fact that the power is (a) ancillary to the arbitral proceedings outside the Virgin Islands; and (b) for the purposes of facilitating the process of a court or arbitral tribunal outside the Virgin Islands that has primary jurisdiction over the arbitral proceedings. (8) The Court has the same power to make any incidental order or direction for the purposes of ensuring the effectiveness of an interim measure granted in relation to arbitral proceedings outside the Virgin Islands as if the interim measure were granted in relation to arbitral proceedings in the Virgin Islands.

923. http://www.bviiac.org/Portals/0/Files/Arbitration%20Documents/ArbitrationAct2013.pdf

Sr. No.	Country	Provision
		(9) An interim measure referred to in subsection (2) means an interim measure referred to in article 17 (2) of the UNCITRAL Model Law, as provided in section 33 (1), as if the reference (a) to arbitral tribunal in that article were a reference to the Court, and (b) to arbitral proceedings in that article were a reference to court proceedings, and is to be construed as including an injunction but not including an order under section 58. (10) A decision, order or direction made or issued by the Court under this section is not subject to appeal.
10.	Bulgaria - Law on International Commercial Arbitration State Gazette (SG) No. 60 of 05.08.1988[924]	No equivalent provision as Article 17J of the UNCITRAL Model Law 2006
11.	Cambodia - The Commercial Arbitration Law of the Kingdom of Cambodia 2006[925]	No equivalent provision as Article 17J of the UNCITRAL Model Law 2006
12.	Canada – Commercial Arbitration Act R.S.C., 1985, c. 17 (2nd Supp.)[926]	No equivalent provision as Article 17J of the UNCITRAL Model Law 2006
13.	Connecticut - Chapter 909 Arbitration Proceedings[927]	No equivalent provision as Article 17J of the UNCITRAL Model Law 2006
14.	Croatia – Law on Arbitration Official Gazette no. 88/2001[928]	No equivalent provision as Article 17J of the UNCITRAL Model Law 2006
15.	Cyprus – The International Commercial Arbitration Law, 1987[929]	No equivalent provision as Article 17J of the UNCITRAL Model Law 2006

924. http://www.newyorkconvention.org/11165/web/files/document/1/6/16200.pdf
925. https://www.cambodiaip.gov.kh/DocResources/372a361b-7a97-44b3-9810-79e5e6ea85f4_c786a043-b88d-4f64-9429-60a330efdc5f-en.pdf
926. https://laws-lois.justice.gc.ca/eng/acts/C-34.6/index.html
927. https://www.cga.ct.gov/current/pub/chap_909.htm
928. http://www.vsrh.hr/CustomPages/Static/HRV/Files/Legislation__Law-Arbitration-RC.pdf

Sr. No.	Country	Provision
16.	Denmark - Danish Arbitration Act 2005[930]	No equivalent provision as Article 17J of the UNCITRAL Model Law 2006
17.	Egypt - Law No. 27/1994 Promulgating the Law Concerning Arbitration in Civil and Commercial Matters[931]	No equivalent provision as Article 17J of the UNCITRAL Model Law 2006
18.	Florida - Chapter 684 - International Commercial Arbitration, Title XXXIX Commercial Relations, 2020 Florida Statutes[932]	Same as Article 17J of the UNCITRAL Model Law 2006 Article 684.0028 Court-ordered interim measures
19.	Fiji - International Arbitration Act 2017 (Act No. 44 of 2017)[933]	Same as Article 17J of UNCITRAL Model Law 2006 Section 33 Court-ordered interim measures
20.	France - Book IV - Arbitration of the Code of Civil Procedure Decree No. 2011-48[934]	No equivalent provision as Article 17J of the UNCITRAL Model Law 2006
21.	Georgia - Chapter 9 Arbitration, Title 9 Civil Practice, Georgia Code[935]	Article 23 - Court-ordered interim measures 1. An arbitration party may apply to a court requesting granting interim measures. 2. A court has the same power of issuing an interim measure with relation to arbitration proceedings, regardless of the place of arbitration, as it has power regarding proceedings in the courts. 3. The court shall exercise such powers in accordance with the procedures provided for by the Civil Procedure Code of Georgia, Chapter XXIII, except article 198 (2)(f) and (i), considering the requirements for arbitration proceedings.

929. https://www.uv.es/medarb/observatorio/leyes-arbitraje/europa-resto/chipre-international-commercial-arbitration-law.pdf
930. https://voldgiftsinstituttet.dk/wp-content/uploads/2015/01/danish_arbitration_act_2005.pdf
931. https://www.wipo.int/edocs/lexdocs/laws/en/eg/eg020en.pdf
932. https://www.flsenate.gov/Laws/Statutes/2020/Chapter684/All
933. https://www.fiji.gov.fj/getattachment/d9502667-6491-4592-85b2-eff97f245fed/Act-44---International-Arbitration-Act.aspx
934. http://www.iaiparis.com/pdf/FRENCH_LAW_ON_INTERNATIONAL_ARBITRATION.pdf
935. https://matsne.gov.ge/ru/document/download/89284/5/en/pdf

Sr. No.	Country	Provision
22.	Germany – Tenth Book of the Code of Civil Procedure, Arbitration Procedure[936]	No equivalent provision as Article 17J of the UNCITRAL Model Law 2006
23.	Greece – Code Of Civil Procedure, Book VII, Book VIII[937]	No equivalent provision as Article 17J of the UNCITRAL Model Law 2006
24.	Hong Kong – Cap. 609 Arbitration Ordinance[938]	Section 45. Article 17J of UNCITRAL Model Law (Court-ordered interim measures) (1) Article 17J of the UNCITRAL Model Law does not have effect. (2) On the application of any party, the Court may, in relation to any arbitral proceedings which have been or are to be commenced in or outside Hong Kong, grant an interim measure. (3) The powers conferred by this section may be exercised by the Court irrespective of whether or not similar powers may be exercised by an arbitral tribunal under section 35 in relation to the same dispute. (4) The Court may decline to grant an interim measure under subsection (2) on the ground that— (a) the interim measure sought is currently the subject of arbitral proceedings; and (b) the Court considers it more appropriate for the interim measure sought to be dealt with by the arbitral tribunal. (5) In relation to arbitral proceedings which have been or are to be commenced outside Hong Kong, the Court may grant an interim measure under subsection (2) only if— (a) the arbitral proceedings are capable of giving rise to an arbitral award (whether interim or final) that may be enforced in Hong Kong under this Ordinance or any other Ordinance; and (b) the interim measure sought belongs to a type or description of interim measure that may be granted in Hong Kong in relation to arbitral proceedings by the Court. (6) Subsection (5) applies even if— (a) the subject matter of the arbitral proceedings would not, apart from that subsection, give rise to a cause of action over which the Court would have jurisdiction; or (b) the order sought is not ancillary or incidental to any arbitral proceedings in Hong Kong.

936. https://sccinstitute.com/media/29988/german-arbitration-act.pdf
937. https://www.uv.es/medarb/observatorio/leyes-arbitraje/europa-resto/grecia-ccp-domestic-arbitration.pdf
938. https://www.elegislation.gov.hk/hk/cap609

Sr. No.	Country	Provision
		(7) In exercising the power under subsection (2) in relation to arbitral proceedings outside Hong Kong, the Court must have regard to the fact that the power is— (a) ancillary to the arbitral proceedings outside Hong Kong; and (b) for the purposes of facilitating the process of a court or arbitral tribunal outside Hong Kong that has primary jurisdiction over the arbitral proceedings. (8) The Court has the same power to make any incidental order or direction for the purposes of ensuring the effectiveness of an interim measure granted in relation to arbitral proceedings outside Hong Kong as if the interim measure were granted in relation to arbitral proceedings in Hong Kong. (9) An interim measure referred to in subsection (2) means an interim measure referred to in article 17(2) of the UNCITRAL Model Law, given effect to by section 35(1), as if— (a) a reference to the arbitral tribunal in that article were the court; and (b) a reference to arbitral proceedings in that article were court proceedings, and is to be construed as including an injunction but not including an order under section 60. (10) A decision, order or direction of the Court under this section is not subject to appeal.
25.	Hungary - Act LX of 2017 on Arbitration[939]	Section 28 PROCEEDINGS OF THE COURT In relation to arbitration proceedings, irrespective of their place, the Hungarian court shall have the same material jurisdiction to order a preliminary taking of evidence (Chapter XXIV of Pp.), a provisional measure (Chapter VIII of Pp.), and a security measure (Chapter X of Vht.), as well as to insert an enforcement clause into a deed [sections 23/B (1) a) and 23/C of Vht.], and to require the provision of a security in a separate claim in accordance with the rules on litigation proceedings (section 6:523 of Ptk.) as it has in relation to proceedings in courts. In the course of this, the court having material and territorial jurisdiction shall proceed with due consideration of the characteristics of arbitration.
26.	Ireland - Arbitration Act 2010 Number 1 of 2010[940]	Section 6 - Adoption of Model Law Subject to this Act, the Model Law shall have the force of law in the State and shall apply to arbitrations under arbitration agreements concerning— (a) international commercial arbitrations, or (b) arbitrations which are not international commercial arbitrations. Same as Article 17J of UNCITRAL Model Law 2006 Article 17J under Schedule 1 - TEXT OF UNCITRAL MODEL LAW ON INTERNATIONAL COMMERCIAL ARBITRATION

939. https://www.ilo.org/dyn/natlex/docs/ELECTRONIC/106843/131257/F-266585574/J2017T0060P_20180102_FIN.pdf
940. http://www.irishstatutebook.ie/eli/2010/act/1/enacted/en/pdf

Sr. No.	Country	Provision
27.	Jamaica – The Arbitration Act, 2017 (Act 13 of 2017)[941]	Section 30. Court-Ordered Interim Measures A court shall- (a) have the same power of issuing an interim measure in relation to arbitration proceedings, irrespective of whether their place is in Jamaica, as it has in relation to proceedings in courts; and (b) exercise such power in accordance with its own procedures in consideration of the specific features of international arbitration.
28.	Japan – Arbitration Law (Law No.138 of 2003)[942]	No equivalent provision as Article 17J of the UNCITRAL Model Law 2006
29.	Jordan – Law No. 31 of 2001 (Jordan) Arbitration Law[943]	No equivalent provision as Article 17J of the UNCITRAL Model Law 2006
30.	Kenya – Chapter 49 Arbitration Act (The Arbitration Act, 1995)[944]	No equivalent provision as Article 17J of the UNCITRAL Model Law 2006
31.	Liechtenstein - Liechtenstein Arbitration Law (Code of Civil Procedure)[945]	No equivalent provision as Article 17J of the UNCITRAL Model Law 2006
32.	Lithuania – The Republic of Lithuania Law on Commercial Arbitration, 2012[946]	No equivalent provision as Article 17J of the UNCITRAL Model Law 2006
33.	Louisiana – RS 9 Title 9.Civil Code-Ancillaries[947]	No equivalent provision as Article 17J of the UNCITRAL Model Law 2006

941. http://extwprlegs1.fao.org/docs/pdf/jam172060.pdf
942. https://japan.kantei.go.jp/policy/sihou/arbitrationlaw.pdf
943. https://www.ilo.org/dyn/natlex/docs/ELECTRONIC/63091/95325/F1864661120/JOR63091.pdf
944. https://ncia.or.ke/wp-content/uploads/2021/02/ArbitrationAct4of1995_2.pdf
945. https://www.newyorkconvention.org/11165/web/files/document/2/1/21372.pdf
946. https://e-seimas.lrs.lt/portal/legalAct/lt/TAD/35954312dcb311e6be918a531b2126ab?jfwid=-wd7z7zum0
947. http://legis.la.gov/legis/Laws_Toc.aspx?folder=83&title=9

Sr. No.	Country	Provision
34.	Macedonia - Law on International Commercial Arbitration of the Republic of Macedonia[948]	No equivalent provision as Article 17J of the UNCITRAL Model Law 2006
35.	Malaysia - Arbitration Act 2005, Act 646[949]	No equivalent provision as Article 17J of the UNCITRAL Model Law 2006
36.	Maldives - Act No: 10/2013, Arbitration Act[950]	Section 45 Court-Ordered Interim Measures (a) A court shall have the same power as the Arbitral Tribunal has in the course of arbitral proceedings, with regards to issuing an interim measure on its own initiative, in relation to arbitral proceedings, irrespective of whether the place of such proceedings is in the territory of the Maldives. (b) The court shall exercise its power to issue an interim measure in relation to an arbitration proceeding in accordance with its own procedures as well as the specific features of international arbitration.
37.	Malta - CAP. 387 Arbitration Act[951]	No equivalent provision as Article 17J of the UNCITRAL Model Law 2006
38.	Mauritius - The International Arbitration Act, 2008 (Act 37 of 2008)[952]	Section 19. Powers of Supreme Court to issue interim measures (1) The Supreme Court shall have the same power of issuing an interim measure in relation to arbitration proceedings, irrespective of whether their juridical seat is Mauritius, as a Judge in Chambers has in relation to Court proceedings in Mauritius, and it shall exercise that power in accordance with the applicable Court procedure in consideration of the specific features of international arbitration. (2) Unless the parties otherwise agree, the power to issue interim measures under subsection (1) shall be exercised in accordance with subsections (3) to (6). (3) Where the case is one of urgency, the Court may, on the ex parte application of a party or proposed party to the arbitral proceedings, make such order as it thinks necessary. (4) Where the case is not one of urgency, the Court shall act only on the application of a party to the arbitral proceedings made - (a) on notice to the other parties and to the arbitral tribunal; and (b) with the permission of the arbitral tribunal or the agreement in writing of the other parties.

948. https://www.international-arbitration-attorney.com/wp-content/uploads/2013/07/Macedonia-Arbitration-Law.pdf
949. http://www.newyorkconvention.org/11165/web/files/document/1/6/16298.pdf
950. https://miac.gov.mv/media/documents/Arbitration%20Act.pdf
951. http://justiceservices.gov.mt/DownloadDocument.aspx?app=lom&itemid=8854&l=1
952. https://www.wipo.int/edocs/lexdocs/laws/en/mu/mu020en.pdf

Sr. No.	Country	Provision
		(5) The Court shall act only if or to the extent that the arbitral tribunal, and any arbitral or other institution or person vested by the parties with power in that regard, has no power or is unable for the time being to act effectively. (6) Where the Court so orders, an order made by it under this section shall cease to have effect on the order of the arbitral tribunal or of any such arbitral or other institution or person having power to act in relation to the subject matter of the order.
39.	Montenegro – Decree on the Promulgation of the Law on Arbitration, 2015[953]	Article 29 Court-ordered interim measures When ordering an interim measure in arbitration proceedings, the court shall act in accordance with the rules of procedure of enforcement and security, irrespective of whether the seat of an arbitral tribunal is in the territory of Montenegro, while taking into consideration the specific features of international arbitration.
40.	Myanmar - Arbitration Law The Pyidaungsu Hluttaw Law No. 5/2016[954]	No equivalent provision as Article 17J of the UNCITRAL Model Law 2006
41.	New South Wales - Commercial Arbitration Act 2010 No 61[955]	Section 17J Court-ordered interim measures (cf Model Law Art 17J) (1) The Court has the same power of issuing an interim measure in relation to arbitration proceedings as it has in relation to proceedings in courts. (2) The Court is to exercise the power in accordance with its own procedures taking into account the specific features of a domestic commercial arbitration. Note. This section is substantially the same as Art 17J of the Model Law but has been modified to the extent necessary to apply Art 17J as incorporated in this Act in the context of domestic commercial arbitrations.
42.	New Zealand – The Arbitration Act, 1996 No 99[956]	No equivalent provision as Article 17J of the UNCITRAL Model Law 2006
43.	Nigeria - Arbitration and Conciliation Act Chapter 19 Laws of the Federation of Nigeria 1990[957]	No equivalent provision as Article 17J of the UNCITRAL Model Law 2006

953. https://www.privrednakomora.me/sites/pkcg.org/files/multimedia/main_pages/files/2012/09/final_eng_zakon_o_arbitrazi_final_0.pdf
954. http://www.newyorkconvention.org/11165/web/files/document/2/1/21098.pdf
955. https://legislation.nsw.gov.au/view/html/inforce/current/act-2010-061#sec.17J
956. http://www.legislation.govt.nz/act/public/1996/0099/latest/whole.html#DLM403277
957. http://niqs.org.ng/wp-content/uploads/2018/12/Arbitration-and-Conciliation-Act.pdf

Sr. No.	Country	Provision
44.	Northern Territory of Australia - Commercial Arbitration (National Uniform Legislation) Act 2011[958]	Section 17J Court-ordered interim measures (Model Law Art 17J) (1) The Court has the same power of issuing an interim measure in relation to arbitration proceedings as it has in relation to proceedings in courts. (2) The Court is to exercise the power in accordance with its own procedures taking into account the specific features of a domestic commercial arbitration. Note for section 17J This section is substantially the same as Art 17J of the Model Law but has been modified to the extent necessary to apply Art 17J as incorporated in this Act in the context of domestic commercial arbitrations.
45.	Norway - Act of 14 May 2004 No. 25 relating to Arbitration (The Arbitration Act)[959]	No equivalent provision as Article 17J of the UNCITRAL Model Law 2006
46.	Oman - The Omani Law of Arbitration in Civil and Commercial Disputes - Royal Decree 47/97[960]	No equivalent provision as Article 17J of the UNCITRAL Model Law 2006
47.	Ontario - International Commercial Arbitration Act, 2017, S.O. 2017, c. 2, Sched. 5[961]	Section 5 - Application of Model Law (1) Subject to this Act, the Model Law on International Commercial Arbitration, adopted by the United Nations Commission on International Trade Law on 21 June 1985, as amended by the United Nations Commission on International Trade Law on 7 July 2006, set out in Schedule 2, has force of law in Ontario. Same (2) With respect to article 7 of the Model Law, option I applies in Ontario; option II does not. Same (3) The Model Law applies to international commercial arbitration agreements and awards made in international commercial arbitrations, whether made before or after the coming into force of this Act. Schedule 2 to this Act Article 17J
48.	Oregon - Oregon International Commercial Arbitration and Conciliation Act[962]	No equivalent provision as Article 17J of the UNCITRAL Model Law 2006

958. https://legislation.nt.gov.au/api/sitecore/Act/PDF?id = 11692
959. https://www.chamber.no/wp-content/uploads/2014/02/Norwegian_Arbitration_Act.pdf
960. http://www.newyorkconvention.org/11165/web/files/document/2/1/21103.pdf
961. https://www.ontario.ca/laws/statute/17i02b#BK16

Sr. No.	Country	Provision
49.	Pakistan - The Arbitration Act, 1940 Act No. X of 1940[963]	No equivalent provision as Article 17J of the UNCITRAL Model Law 2006
50.	Philippines - Alternative Dispute Resolution Act of 2004 Republic Act No. 9285[964]	No equivalent provision as Article 17J of the UNCITRAL Model Law 2006
51.	Poland – Polish Act of 17 November 1964 - Code of Civil Procedure, Part Five Arbitration[965]	No equivalent provision as Article 17J of the UNCITRAL Model Law 2006
52.	Qatar - Law No. 2 of 2017 Promulgating the Civil and Commercial Arbitration Law-The Law of Arbitration in Civil and Commercial Matters[966]	No equivalent provision as Article 17J of the UNCITRAL Model Law 2006
53.	Queensland - Commercial Arbitration Act 2013 No. 8[967]	Section 17J Court-ordered interim measures (cf Model Law Art 17J) (1) The Court has the same power of issuing an interim measure in relation to arbitration proceedings as it has in relation to proceedings in courts. (2) The Court is to exercise the power in accordance with its own procedures taking into account the specific features of a domestic commercial arbitration. Note— This section is substantially the same as Art 17J of the Model Law but has been modified to the extent necessary to apply Art 17J as incorporated in this Act in the context of domestic commercial arbitrations.

962. https://www.oregonlegislature.gov/bills_laws/ors/ors036.html
963. https://www.wipo.int/edocs/lexdocs/laws/en/pk/pk066en.pdf
964. http://www.newyorkconvention.org/11165/web/files/document/2/1/21107.pdf
965. https://www.uv.es/medarb/observatorio/leyes-arbitraje/europa-resto/polonia-ccp-arbitration.pdf
966. https://www.qicdrc.gov.qa/sites/default/files/inline-files/law_no._02_2017_promulgating_the_civil_and_commercial_arbitration_law.pdf
967. https://www.legislation.qld.gov.au/view/pdf/inforce/2013-05-17/act-2013-008

Sr. No.	Country	Provision
54.	Republic of Costa Rica - Costa Rican Law for International Arbitration Law Number: 8937[968]	Same as Article 17J of UNCITRAL Model Law 2006
55.	Republic of Korea - Arbitration Act[969]	No equivalent provision as Article 17J of the UNCITRAL Model Law 2006
56.	Russia - Russian Federation Law On International Commercial Arbitration[970]	No equivalent provision as Article 17J of the UNCITRAL Model Law 2006
57.	Rwanda - Law on Arbitration and Conciliation in Commercial Matters, N° 005/2008[971]	No equivalent provision as Article 17J of the UNCITRAL Model Law 2006
58.	Saudi Arabia - Law of Arbitration Royal Decree No. M/34[972]	No equivalent provision as Article 17J of the UNCITRAL Model Law 2006
59.	Serbia - Law on Arbitration No. 46/06[973]	No equivalent provision as Article 17J of the UNCITRAL Model Law 2006
60.	Singapore - Arbitration Act (Chapter 10) (Domestic Arbitration Law)[974]	No equivalent provision as Article 17J of the UNCITRAL Model Law 2006
61.	Singapore - International Arbitration Act (Chapter 143A) (International Arbitration Law)[975]	Section 3 Model Law to have force of law (1) Subject to this Act, the Model Law, with the exception of Chapter VIII thereof, shall have the force of law in Singapore. (2) In the Model Law — "State" means Singapore and any country other than Singapore; "this State" means Singapore.

968. https://arbitratlaw.com/wp-content/uploads/2017/01/Costa-Rican-Intl-Arbitration-Law.pdf
969. https://elaw.klri.re.kr/eng_service/lawView.do?hseq=38889&lang=ENG
970. http://www.newyorkconvention.org/11165/web/files/document/2/2/22335.pdf
971. http://www.newyorkconvention.org/11165/web/files/document/2/1/21110.pdf
972. https://www.wipo.int/edocs/lexdocs/laws/en/sa/sa057en.pdf
973. https://www.wipo.int/edocs/lexdocs/laws/en/rs/rs028en.pdf
974. https://sso.agc.gov.sg/Act/AA2001
975. https://sso.agc.gov.sg/Act/IAA1994

Sr. No.	Country	Provision
		Section 12A Court-ordered interim measures (1) This section shall apply in relation to an arbitration — (a) to which this Part applies; and (b) irrespective of whether the place of arbitration is in the territory of Singapore. (2) Subject to subsections (3) to (6), for the purpose of and in relation to an arbitration referred to in subsection (1), the High Court or a Judge thereof shall have the same power of making an order in respect of any of the matters set out in section 12(1)(c) to (i) as it has for the purpose of and in relation to an action or a matter in the court. (3) The High Court or a Judge thereof may refuse to make an order under subsection (2) if, in the opinion of the High Court or Judge, the fact that the place of arbitration is outside Singapore or likely to be outside Singapore when it is designated or determined makes it inappropriate to make such order. (4) If the case is one of urgency, the High Court or a Judge thereof may, on the application of a party or proposed party to the arbitral proceedings, make such orders under subsection (2) as the High Court or Judge thinks necessary for the purpose of preserving evidence or assets. (5) If the case is not one of urgency, the High Court or a Judge thereof shall make an order under subsection (2) only on the application of a party to the arbitral proceedings (upon notice to the other parties and to the arbitral tribunal) made with the permission of the arbitral tribunal or the agreement in writing of the other parties. (6) In every case, the High Court or a Judge thereof shall make an order under subsection (2) only if or to the extent that the arbitral tribunal, and any arbitral or other institution or person vested by the parties with power in that regard, has no power or is unable for the time being to act effectively. (7) An order made by the High Court or a Judge thereof under subsection (2) shall cease to have effect in whole or in part (as the case may be) if the arbitral tribunal, or any such arbitral or other institution or person having power to act in relation to the subject-matter of the order, makes an order which expressly relates to the whole or part of the order under subsection (2).
62.	Slovakia - [Slovak] Act No. 244/2002 of 3 April 2002 on Arbitration[976]	No equivalent provision as Article 17J of the UNCITRAL Model Law 2006
63.	Slovenia - Law on Arbitration of Slovenia[977]	No equivalent provision as Article 17J of the UNCITRAL Model Law 2006

976. https://www.international-arbitration-attorney.com/wp-content/uploads/2013/07/Slovakia-Arbitration-Law-1.pdf
977. http://www.sloarbitration.eu/Portals/0/Arbitrazno-pravo/Law%20on%20Arbitration%20of%20Slovenia.pdf

Sr. No.	Country	Provision
64.	South Africa - The Arbitration Act, 1965[978]	No equivalent provision as Article 17J of the UNCITRAL Model Law 2006
65.	South Australia - South Australia Commercial Arbitration Act 2011[979]	Section 17J—Court-ordered interim measures (1) The Court has the same power of issuing an interim measure in relation to arbitration proceedings as it has in relation to proceedings in courts. (2) The Court is to exercise the power in accordance with its own procedures taking into account the specific features of a domestic commercial arbitration. Note— This section is substantially the same as Art 17J of the Model Law but has been modified to the extent necessary to apply Art 17J as incorporated in this Act in the context of domestic commercial arbitrations.
66.	Spain - Act 60/2003 of 23 December on Arbitration[980]	No equivalent provision as Article 17J of the UNCITRAL Model Law 2006
67.	Sri Lanka - Arbitration Act. No. 11 of 1995[981]	No equivalent provision as Article 17J of the UNCITRAL Model Law 2006
68.	Sweden - The Swedish Arbitration Act (SFS 1999:116)[982]	No equivalent provision as Article 17J of the UNCITRAL Model Law 2006
69.	Switzerland - Private International Law Act 1987, Chapter 12: International Arbitration[983]	No equivalent provision as Article 17J of the UNCITRAL Model Law 2006

978. https://www.gov.za/sites/default/files/gcis_document/201505/act-42-1965.pdf
979. https://www.legislation.sa.gov.au/LZ/C/A/COMMERCIAL%20ARBITRATION%20ACT%20 2011/CURRENT/2011.32.UN.PDF
980. https://www.mjusticia.gob.es/cs/Satellite/Portal/1292426982249?blobheader=application %2Fpdf&blobheadername1=Content-Disposition&blobheadervalue1=attachment%3 B+filename%3DAct_on_arbitration_%28Ley_60_2003__de_arbitraje%29.PDF
981. http://www.slnarbcentre.com/pdf/ARBITRATION-ACT.pdf
982. https://sccinstitute.com/media/37089/the-swedish-arbitration-act.pdf
983. https://www.swissarbitration.org/wp-content/uploads/2021/05/20210129-Chapter-12-PILA _Translation_English.pdf

Sr. No.	Country	Provision
70.	Tasmania – Commercial Arbitration Act, 2011, Act 13 of 2011[984]	Section 17J. Court-ordered interim measures (cf Model Law Art 17J) (1) The Court has the same power of issuing an interim measure in relation to arbitration proceedings as it has in relation to proceedings in courts. (2) The Court is to exercise the power in accordance with its own procedures taking into account the specific features of a domestic commercial arbitration. Note. This section is substantially the same as Art 17J of the Model Law but has been modified to the extent necessary to apply Art 17J as incorporated in this Act in the context of domestic commercial arbitrations.
71.	Texas - Chapter 172. Arbitration and Conciliation of International Commercial Disputes, Civil Practice and Remedies Code[985]	No equivalent provision as Article 17J of the UNCITRAL Model Law 2006
72.	Thailand – Arbitration Act B.E. 2545[986]	No equivalent provision as Article 17J of the UNCITRAL Model Law 2006
73.	Tunisia – Law n° 93-42 issued on April 26, related to the promulgation of the Arbitration Code[987]	No equivalent provision as Article 17J of the UNCITRAL Model Law 2006
74.	Turkey - Turkish International Arbitration Law, Law no. 4686, 2001[988]	No equivalent provision as Article 17J of the UNCITRAL Model Law 2006
75.	Uganda – Chapter 4 The Arbitration and Conciliation Act[989]	No equivalent provision as Article 17J of the UNCITRAL Model Law 2006

984. https://www.legislation.tas.gov.au/view/html/inforce/current/act-2011-013
985. https://statutes.capitol.texas.gov/Docs/CP/htm/CP.172.htm
986. https://tai.coj.go.th/th/file/get/file/20190328ecac5333356ffad0331bd601151db9f4142557.pdf
987. https://arbitrationlaw.com/sites/default/files/free_pdfs/Tunisia%20Arbitration%20Code.pdf
988. http://www.camera-arbitrale.it/Documenti/tial_turkey.pdf
989. https://ulii.org/akn/ug/act/2000/7/eng@2008-06-27

Sr. No.	Country	Provision
76.	Ukraine - The Law of Ukraine on International Commercial Arbitration[990]	No equivalent provision as Article 17J of the UNCITRAL Model Law 2006
77.	United Arab Emirates - Federal Law No. (6) of 2018 on Arbitration[991]	No equivalent provision as Article 17J of the UNCITRAL Model Law 2006
78.	Uruguay - Law 19,636 Approve Rules for International Commercial Arbitration[992]	Article 17 (Power of the arbitral tribunal to order provisional precautionary measures) .- 7) The court will enjoy the same competence to dictate measures injunctions at the service of arbitration proceedings, with regardless of whether they are substantiated in the Republic or not. The court shall exercise said jurisdiction in accordance with its own procedures and taking into account the traits hallmarks of international arbitration.
79.	Venezuela - Venezuelan Commercial Arbitration Act[993]	No equivalent provision as Article 17J of the UNCITRAL Model Law 2006
80.	Victoria - Commercial Arbitration Act 2011 No. 50 of 2011[994]	Section 17J Court-ordered interim measures (cf Model Law Art 17J) (1) The Court has the same power of issuing an interim measure in relation to arbitration proceedings as it has in relation to proceedings in courts. (2) The Court is to exercise the power in accordance with its own procedures taking into account the specific features of a domestic commercial arbitration. Note This section is substantially the same as Art 17J of the Model Law but has been modified to the extent necessary to apply Art 17J as incorporated in this Act in the context of domestic commercial arbitrations.

990. http://arbitrations.ru/userfiles/file/Law/Arbitration%20acts/ukraininan%20law%20on%20arbitration.pdf
991. https://www.tamimi.com/crm-media-uploader/fileupload/server/php/files/UAE%20Arbitration%20Law%20-%20Federal%20Law%20No%20%206%20of%202018.pdf
992. http://www.impo.com.uy/bases/leyes-originales/19636-2018
993. https://arbitrationlaw.com/sites/default/files/free_pdfs/Venezula%20Commercial%20Arbitration%20Act.pdf
994. http://arbitration.site/wp-content/uploads/2019/06/CAA-Vic-.pdf

Sr. No.	Country	Provision
81.	Western Australia - Commercial Arbitration Act 2012, 023 of 2012[995]	Section 17J. Court-ordered interim measures (cf. Model Law Art 17J) (1) The Court has the same power of issuing an interim measure in relation to arbitration proceedings as it has in relation to proceedings in courts. (2) The Court is to exercise the power in accordance with its own procedures taking into account the specific features of a domestic commercial arbitration. Note for this section: This section is substantially the same as Art 17J of the Model Law but has been modified to the extent necessary to apply Art 17J as incorporated in this Act in the context of domestic commercial arbitrations.
82.	Zambia - The Arbitration Act, 2000 No. 19 of 2000[996]	No equivalent provision as Article 17J of the UNCITRAL Model Law 2006
83.	Zimbabwe - Chapter 7:15 Arbitration Act[997]	No equivalent provision as Article 17J of the UNCITRAL Model Law 2006

995. https://www.legislation.wa.gov.au/legislation/prod/filestore.nsf/FileURL/mrdoc_25084.pdf/$FILE/Commercial%20Arbitration%20Act%202012%20-%20%5B00-b0-06%5D.pdf?OpenElement
996. http://www.newyorkconvention.org/11165/web/files/document/2/1/21396.pdf
997. https://zimlii.org/akn/zw/act/1996/6/eng@2016-12-31

Appendix M (Institutional Rules)

Sr. No.	Arbitration Institutes	Rules
1.	American Arbitration Association Commercial Arbitration Rules[998]	R-37. Interim Measures (a) The arbitrator may take whatever interim measures he or she deems necessary, including injunctive relief and measures for the protection or conservation of property and disposition of perishable goods. (b) Such interim measures may take the form of an interim award, and the arbitrator may require security for the costs of such measures. (c) A request for interim measures addressed by a party to a judicial authority shall not be deemed incompatible with the agreement to arbitrate or a waiver of the right to arbitrate.
2.	Asian International Arbitration Centre, Arbitration Rules, 2018[999]	Rule 8 Interim Measures 1. The arbitral tribunal may, at the request of a Party, grant interim measures pursuant to Article 26. 2. A Party in need of urgent interim measures prior to the constitution of the arbitral tribunal may submit a request to appoint an emergency arbitrator to the Director pursuant to Schedule 3.
3.	Bangalore International Mediation Arbitration & Conciliation Centre (BIMACC)[1000]	No provision

998. https://www.adr.org/sites/default/files/Commercial%20Rules.pdf
999. https://www.aiac.world/wp-content/arbitration/Arbitration-Rules-2018.pdf
1000. http://www.bimacc.org/download/BIMACC-Arbitration-Rules.pdf

Sr. No.	Arbitration Institutes	Rules
4.	Center for Arbitration and Mediation of the Chamber of Commerce Brazil-Canada (CAM-CCBC) Arbitration Rules, 2012[1001]	ARTICLE 8 - PROVISIONAL MEASURES 8.1. Unless the parties have otherwise agreed, the Arbitral Tribunal can grant provisional measures, both injunctive and anticipatory, that can, at the discretion of the Arbitral Tribunal, be subject to the provision of guarantees by the requesting party. 8.2. If there is an urgent matter and the Arbitral Tribunal has not yet been constituted, the parties can seek provisional or injunctive measures from the competent judicial authority, if another manner has not been expressly agreed by them. In this case, the parties must inform the CAM-CCBC of the decisions. 8.2.1 As soon as the Arbitral Tribunal is constituted, it will have the authority to uphold, amend or revoke the previously granted measures. 8.2.2. A request made by one of the parties to a judicial authority to obtain these measures, or the enforcement of similar measures granted by an Arbitral Tribunal, will not be considered a violation of, or waiver to, the arbitration agreement and will not interfere with the jurisdiction of the Arbitral Tribunal.
5.	Chamber of Arbitration of Milan, Arbitration Rules, 2010[1002]	ART. 22 – POWERS OF THE ARBITRAL TRIBUNAL 2. The Arbitral Tribunal may issue all urgent and provisional measures of protection, also of anticipatory nature, that are not barred by mandatory provisions applicable to the proceedings.
6.	Chamber of Arbitration of Milan, Arbitration Rules, 2019[1003]	ART. 26 – INTERIM OR PROVISIONAL MEASURES 1. At request of a party, the Arbitral Tribunal may issue all urgent and provisional measures of protection, also of anticipatory nature, that are not barred by mandatory provisions applicable to the proceedings. 2. In any case, unless otherwise agreed by the parties, the Arbitral Tribunal, at request of a party, has the power to adopt any determination of provisional nature with binding contractual effect upon the parties. 3. The Arbitral Tribunal may order the party requesting an interim measure to provide appropriate security for costs as a condition to issue the measure. 4. Any request for interim measures made by a party to a judicial authority does not imply any waiver of the effects of the arbitration agreement or of the request for arbitration, if any.

1001. http://www.arbiter.com.sg/pdf/rules/CAM%20CCBC%20Arbitration%20Rules%202012.pdf
1002. http://www.camera-arbitrale.it/upload/documenti/arbitrato/REG%20Arbitrale_ENG_FRA_ITA_2010%20con%20indicazione%20nuovo%20indirizzo%20e%20uff%20roma.pdf
1003. http://www.camera-arbitrale.it/upload/documenti/arbitrato/2019-cam-arbitration-rules.pdf

Sr. No.	Arbitration Institutes	Rules
7.	Chinese European Arbitration Centre, Arbitration Rules, 2012[1004]	ARTICLE 26 Interim measures 1. The arbitral tribunal may, at the request of a party, grant interim measures. 2. An interim measure is any temporary measure by which, at any time prior to the issuance of the award by which the dispute is finally decided, the arbitral tribunal orders a party, for example and without limitation, to: (a) Maintain or restore the status quo pending determination of the dispute; (b) Take action that would prevent, or refrain from taking action that is likely to cause, (i) current or imminent harm or (ii) prejudice to the arbitral process itself; (c) Provide a means of preserving assets out of which a subsequent award may be satisfied; or (d) Preserve evidence that may be relevant and material to the resolution of the dispute. 3. The party requesting an interim measure under paragraphs 2 (a) to (c) shall satisfy the arbitral tribunal that: (a) Harm not adequately reparable by an award of damages is likely to result if the measure is not ordered, and such harm substantially outweighs the harm that is likely to result to the party against whom the measure is directed if the measure is granted; and (b) There is a reasonable possibility that the requesting party will succeed on the merits of the claim. The determination on this possibility shall not affect the discretion of the arbitral tribunal in making any subsequent determination. 4. With regard to a request for an interim measure under paragraph 2 (d), the requirements in paragraphs 3 (a) and (b) shall apply only to the extent the arbitral tribunal considers appropriate. 5. The arbitral tribunal may modify, suspend or terminate an interim measure it has granted, upon application of any party or, in exceptional circumstances and upon prior notice to the parties, on the arbitral tribunal's own initiative. 6. The arbitral tribunal may require the party requesting an interim measure to provide appropriate security in connection with the measure. 7. The arbitral tribunal may require any party promptly to disclose any material change in the circumstances on the basis of which the interim measure was requested or granted. 8. The party requesting an interim measure may be liable for any costs and damages caused by the measure to any party if the arbitral tribunal later determines that, in the circumstances then prevailing, the measure should not have been granted. The arbitral tribunal may award such costs and damages at any point during the proceedings. 9. A request for interim measures addressed by any party to a judicial authority shall not be deemed incompatible with the agreement to arbitrate, or as a waiver of that agreement.

Sr. No.	Arbitration Institutes	Rules
8.	Delhi International Arbitration Centre (DAC) (Arbitration Proceedings) Rules old[1005]	Rule 19. Interim measures ordered by Arbitral Tribunal – (1) The Arbitral Tribunal may, at the request of a party, order a party to take any interim measure of protection in respect of the subject-matter of the dispute, as it may consider necessary. (2) The Arbitral Tribunal may require a party to provide appropriate security in connection with a measure ordered under sub-rule (1). (3) The party requesting for Interim Measures under sub rule (1) shall satisfy the Arbitral Tribunal that there is a reasonable possibility that it is likely to succeed on the merits of its claim and that it may suffer irreparable damage, i.e. while granting interim measure the Arbitral Tribunal is satisfied that the party seeking interim measure has a prima facie case, the balance of convenience is in its favour and that non granting of interim measure will result in irreparable loss or damages, which cannot be compensated in terms of money. The determination of Arbitral Tribunal in respect of such request shall not affect the discretion of the Arbitral Tribunal in making subsequent determination. (4) The Arbitral Tribunal may modify, suspend or terminate an interim measure granted by it, upon an application by a party if the circumstances so warrant.
9.	Delhi International Arbitration Centre (DIAC) (Arbitration Proceedings) Rules, 2018[1006]	Rule 15. Interim Relief – 15.1 A party may, during the arbitral proceedings apply to the Arbitral Tribunal for an interim measure of protection in respect of the subject matter of the dispute as it may consider necessary, including – (i) for the appointment of a guardian for a minor or person of unsound mind for the purposes of arbitral proceedings; or (ii) for an interim measure of protection in respect of any of the following matters namely: - (a) the preservation, interim custody or sale of any goods which are the subject matter of the arbitration agreement; (b) securing the amount in dispute in the arbitration; (c) the detention, preservation or inspection of any property or thing which is the subject-matter of the dispute in arbitration, or as to which any question may arise therein and authorizing for any of the aforesaid purposes any person to enter upon any land or building in the possession of any party or authorizing any samples to be taken, or any observation to be made, or experiment to be tried, which may be necessary or expedient for the purpose of obtaining full information or evidence;

1004. https://www.ceac-arbitration.com/fileadmin/documents/rules/ceac-rules-2012-en.pdf
1005. http://www.dacdelhi.org/topics.aspx?mid=55
1006. http://www.dacdelhi.org/topics.aspx?mid=74

Sr. No.	Arbitration Institutes	Rules
		(d) interim injunction or the appointment of a receiver; (e) such other interim measures of protection as may appear to the arbitral tribunal to be just and convenient and the arbitral tribunal shall have the same power for making orders, as the Court has for the purpose of, and in relation to, any proceedings before it. 15.2 The Arbitral Tribunal may modify, suspend or terminate an interim measure granted by it, upon an application by a party if the circumstances so warrant.
10.	DIFC - LCIA Arbitration Centre, Arbitration Rules 2021[1007]	Article 25 Interim and Conservatory Measures 25.1 The Arbitral Tribunal shall have the power upon the application of any party, after giving all other parties a reasonable opportunity to respond to such application and upon such terms as the Arbitral Tribunal considers appropriate in the circumstances: (i) to order any respondent party to a claim, counterclaim or cross-claim to provide security for all or part of the amount in dispute, by way of deposit or bank guarantee or in any other manner; (ii) to order the preservation, storage, sale or other disposal of any monies, documents, goods, samples, property, site or thing under the control of any party and relating to the subject-matter of the arbitration; and (iii) to order on a provisional basis, subject to a final decision in an award, any relief which the Arbitral Tribunal would have power to grant in an award, including the payment of money or the disposition of property as between any parties. Such terms may include the provision by the applicant party of a cross-indemnity, secured in such manner as the Arbitral Tribunal considers appropriate, for any costs or losses incurred by the respondent party in complying with the Arbitral Tribunal's order. Any amount payable under such cross-indemnity and any consequential relief may be decided by the Arbitral Tribunal by one or more awards in the arbitration. 25.2 The Arbitral Tribunal shall have the power upon the application of a party, after giving all other parties a reasonable opportunity to respond to such application, to order any claiming, counterclaiming or cross-claiming party to provide or procure security for Legal Costs and Arbitration Costs by way of deposit or bank guarantee or in any other manner and upon such terms as the Arbitral Tribunal considers appropriate in the circumstances. Such terms may include the provision by the applicant of a cross-indemnity, itself secured in such manner as the Arbitral Tribunal considers appropriate, for any costs and losses incurred by such claimant, counterclaimant or cross-claimant in complying with the Arbitral Tribunal's order. Any amount payable under such cross-indemnity and any consequential

1007. http://www.difc-lcia.org/arbitration-rules-2021.aspx

Sr. No.	Arbitration Institutes	Rules
		relief may be decided by the Arbitral Tribunal by one or more awards in the arbitration. In the event that a claiming, counterclaiming or cross-claiming party does not comply with any order to provide security, the Arbitral Tribunal may stay that party's claims, counter-claims or cross- claims or dismiss them by an award. 25.3 A party may apply to a competent state court or other legal authority for interim or conservatory measures that the Arbitral Tribunal would have power to order under Article 25.1: (i) before the formation of the Arbitral Tribunal; and (ii) after the formation of the Arbitral Tribunal, in exceptional cases and with the Arbitral Tribunal's authorisation, until the final award. After the Commencement Date, any application and any order for such measures before the formation of the Arbitral Tribunal shall be communicated promptly in writing by the applicant party to the Registrar; after its formation, also to the Arbitral Tribunal; and in both cases also to all other parties. 25.4 By agreeing to arbitration under the Arbitration Agreement, the parties shall be taken to have agreed not to apply to any state court or other legal authority for any order for security for Legal Costs or Arbitration Costs.
11.	Dubai International Arbitration Centre, Arbitration and Conciliation Rules, 1994[1008]	No provision
12.	Dubai International Arbitration Centre, Arbitration Rules, 2007[1009]	Article (31) Interim and Conservatory Measures of Protection 31.1 Subject to any mandatory rules of the applicable law, at the request of a party, the Tribunal may issue any provisional orders or take other interim or conservatory measures it deems necessary, including injunctions and measures for the conservation of goods which form part of the subject matter in dispute, such as an order for their deposit with a third person or for the sale of perishable goods. The Tribunal may make the granting of such measures subject to appropriate security being furnished by the requesting party. 31.2 Measures and orders contemplated under this Article may take the form of an interim or provisional award. 31.3 A request addressed by a party to a competent judicial authority for interim or conservatory measures, or for security for the claim or counter-claim, or for the implementation of any such measures or orders granted by the Tribunal, shall not be deemed incompatible with, or a waiver of, the Arbitration Agreement. 31.4 Any such request and any measures taken by the competent judicial authority must be notified without delay to the Centre by the party making such a request or seeking such measures. The Centre shall inform the Tribunal thereof.

1008. http://www.diac.ae/idias/rules/1994/chapter6/

Sr. No.	Arbitration Institutes	Rules
13.	German Arbitration Institute (DIS) Arbitration Rules, 1998[1010]	Section 20 Interim measures of protection 20.1: Unless otherwise agreed by the parties, the arbitral tribunal may, at the request of a party, order any interim measure of protection as the arbitral tribunal may consider necessary in respect of the subject-matter of the dispute. The arbitral tribunal may require any party to provide appropriate security in connection with such measure. 20.2: It is not incompatible with an arbitration agreement for a party to request an interim measure of protection in respect of the subject-matter of the dispute from a court before or during arbitral proceedings.
14.	German Arbitration Institute (DIS) Arbitration Rules, 2018[1011]	Article 25 Interim Relief 25.1 Unless the parties have agreed otherwise, the arbitral tribunal may, at the request of a party, order interim or conservatory measures, and may amend, suspend or revoke any such measure. The arbitral tribunal shall transmit the request to the other party for comments. The arbitral tribunal may request any party to provide appropriate security in connection with such measures. 25.2 In exceptional circumstances, the arbitral tribunal may rule on a request pursuant to Article 25.1 without giving prior notice to or receiving comments from the other party, if otherwise it would risk frustrating the purpose of the measure. In such case, the arbitral tribunal shall notify the other party of the request, at the latest, when ordering the measure. The arbitral tribunal shall promptly grant the other party a right to be heard. Thereafter, the arbitral tribunal shall confirm, amend, suspend, or revoke the measure. 25.3 The parties may request interim or conservatory measures from any competent court at any time.
15.	Hong Kong International Arbitration Centre (HKIAC) Administered Arbitration Rules, 2008[1012]	Article 24 - Interim Measures of Protection 24.1 At the request of either party, the arbitral tribunal may order any interim measures it deems necessary or appropriate. 24.2 Such interim measures may be established in the form of an interim award. The arbitral tribunal shall be entitled to order the provision of appropriate security by a party seeking an interim measure. 24.3 A request for interim measures addressed by any party to a court of competent jurisdiction shall not be deemed incompatible with the agreement to arbitrate, or as a waiver of that agreement. 24.4 The arbitral tribunal shall have discretion to apportion the costs relating to a request for interim measures in an order, an interim award or in the final award.

1009. http://www.diac.ae/idias/rules/
1010. http://www.disarb.org/en/16/rules/dis-arbitration-rules-98-id10
1011. http://www.disarb.org/upload/rules/2018-DIS-Arbitration-Rules.pdf
1012. https://www.hkiac.org/sites/default/files/ck_filebrowser/PDF/arbitration/HKIAC_AAR_EC.pdf

Sr. No.	Arbitration Institutes	Rules
16.	Hong Kong International Arbitration Centre (HKIAC) Administered Arbitration Rules, 2013[1013]	Article 23 – Interim Measures of Protection and Emergency Relief 23.1 A party may apply for urgent interim or conservatory relief (the "Emergency Relief") prior to the constitution of the arbitral tribunal pursuant to the procedures set out in Schedule 4 (the "Emergency Arbitrator Procedures"). 23.2 At the request of either party, the arbitral tribunal may order any interim measures it deems necessary or appropriate. 23.3 An interim measure, whether in the form of an order or award or in another form, is any temporary measure ordered by the arbitral tribunal at any time prior to the issuance of the award by which the dispute is finally decided, that a party, for example and without limitation: (a) maintain or restore the status quo pending determination of the dispute; (b) take action that would prevent, or refrain from taking action that is likely to cause, current or imminent harm or prejudice to the arbitral process itself; (c) provide a means of preserving assets out of which a subsequent award may be satisfied; or (d) preserve evidence that may be relevant and material to the resolution of the dispute. 23.4 When deciding a party's request for an interim measure under Article 23.2, the arbitral tribunal shall take into account the circumstances of the case. Relevant factors may include, but are not limited to: (a) harm not adequately reparable by an award of damages is likely to result if the measure is not ordered, and such harm substantially outweighs the harm that is likely to result to the party against whom the measure is directed if the measure is granted; and (b) there is a reasonable possibility that the requesting party will succeed on the merits of the claim. The determination on this possibility shall not affect the discretion of the arbitral tribunal in making any subsequent determination. 23.5 The arbitral tribunal may modify, suspend or terminate an interim measure it has granted, upon application of any party or, in exceptional circumstances and upon prior notice to the parties, on the arbitral tribunal's own initiative. 23.6 The arbitral tribunal may require the party requesting an interim measure to provide appropriate security in connection with the measure. 23.7 The arbitral tribunal may require any party promptly to disclose any material change in the circumstances on the basis of which an interim measure was requested or granted.

1013. https://www.hkiac.org/sites/default/files/ck_filebrowser/PDF/arbitration/2013_hkiac_rules.pdf

Sr. No.	Arbitration Institutes	Rules
		23.8 The party requesting an interim measure may be liable for any costs and damages caused by the measure to any party if the arbitral tribunal later determines that, in the circumstances then prevailing, the measure should not have been granted. The arbitral tribunal may award such costs and damages at any point during the arbitration. 23.9 A request for interim measures addressed by any party to a competent judicial authority shall not be deemed incompatible with the arbitration agreement(s), or as a waiver thereof.
17.	Hong Kong International Arbitration Centre (HKIAC) Administered Arbitration Rules, 2018[1014]	Article 23 – Interim Measures of Protection and Emergency Relief 23.1 A party may apply for urgent interim or conservatory relief ("Emergency Relief") prior to the constitution of the arbitral tribunal pursuant to Schedule 4. 23.2 At the request of either party, the arbitral tribunal may order any interim measures it deems necessary or appropriate. 23.3 An interim measure, whether in the form of an order or award or in another form, is any temporary measure ordered by the arbitral tribunal at any time before it issues the award by which the dispute is finally decided, that a party, for example and without limitation: (a) maintain or restore the status quo pending determination of the dispute; or (b) take action that would prevent, or refrain from taking action that is likely to cause, current or imminent harm or prejudice to the arbitral process itself; or (c) provide a means of preserving assets out of which a subsequent award may be satisfied; or (d) preserve evidence that may be relevant and material to the resolution of the dispute. 23.4 When deciding a party's request for an interim measure under Article 23.2, the arbitral tribunal shall take into account the circumstances of the case. Relevant factors may include, but are not limited to: (a) harm not adequately reparable by an award of damages is likely to result if the measure is not ordered, and such harm substantially outweighs the harm that is likely to result to the party against whom the measure is directed if the measure is granted; and (b) there is a reasonable possibility that the requesting party will succeed on the merits of the claim. The determination on this possibility shall not affect the discretion of the arbitral tribunal in making any subsequent determination. 23.5 The arbitral tribunal may modify, suspend or terminate an interim measure it has granted, upon application of any party or, in exceptional circumstances and upon prior notice to the parties, on the arbitral tribunal's own initiative.

1014. https://www.hkiac.org/sites/default/files/ck_filebrowser/PDF/arbitration/2018_hkiac_rules.pdf

Sr. No.	Arbitration Institutes	Rules
		23.6 The arbitral tribunal may require the party requesting an interim measure to provide appropriate security in connection with the measure. 23.7 The arbitral tribunal may require any party promptly to disclose any material change in the circumstances on the basis of which an interim measure was requested or granted. 23.8 The party requesting an interim measure may be liable for any costs and damages caused by the measure to any party if the arbitral tribunal later determines that, in the circumstances then prevailing, the measure should not have been granted. The arbitral tribunal may award such costs and damages at any point during the arbitration. 23.9 A request for interim measures addressed by any party to a competent authority shall not be deemed incompatible with the arbitration agreement, or as a waiver thereof.
18.	Indian Institute of Arbitration and Mediation (IIAM) Arbitration Rules, 2017[1015]	Rule 8 Interim Relief The arbitral tribunal may, at the request of a party, grant interim measures pursuant to Article 26. Article 26 Interim Measures of UNCITRAL ARBITRATION RULES (As revised in 2010) 1. The arbitral tribunal may, at the request of a party, grant interim measures. 2. An interim measure is any temporary measure by which, at any time prior to the issuance of the award by which the dispute is finally decided, the arbitral tribunal orders a party, for example and without limitation, to: a. Maintain or restore the status quo pending determination of the dispute; b. Take action that would prevent, or refrain from taking action that is likely to cause, (i) current or imminent harm or (ii) prejudice to the arbitral process itself; c. Provide a means of preserving assets out of which a subsequent award may be satisfied; or d. Preserve evidence that may be relevant and material to the resolution of the dispute. 3. The party requesting an interim measure under paragraphs 2 (a) to (c) shall satisfy the arbitral tribunal that: a. Harm not adequately reparable by an award of damages is likely to result if the measure is not ordered, and such harm substantially outweighs the harm that is likely to result to the party against whom the measure is directed if the measure is granted; and b. There is a reasonable possibility that the requesting party will succeed on the merits of the claim. The determination on this possibility shall not affect the discretion of the arbitral tribunal in making any subsequent determination. 4. With regard to a request for an interim measure under paragraph 2 (d), the requirements in paragraphs 3 (a) and (b) shall apply only to the extent the arbitral tribunal considers appropriate.

1015. https://www.arbitrationindia.com/pdf/rules_arbitration.pdf

Sr. No.	Arbitration Institutes	Rules
		5. The arbitral tribunal may modify, suspend or terminate an interim measure it has granted, upon application of any party or, in exceptional circumstances and upon prior notice to the parties, on the arbitral tribunal's own initiative. 6. The arbitral tribunal may require the party requesting an interim measure to provide appropriate security in connection with the measure. 7. The arbitral tribunal may require any party promptly to disclose any material change in the circumstances on the basis of which the interim measure was requested or granted. 8. The party requesting an interim measure may be liable for any costs and damages caused by the measure to any party if the arbitral tribunal later determines that, in the circumstances then prevailing, the measure should not have been granted. The arbitral tribunal may award such costs and damages at any point during the proceedings. 9. A request for interim measures addressed by any party to a judicial authority shall not be deemed incompatible with the agreement to arbitrate, or as a waiver of that agreement.
19.	International Centre for Alternative Dispute Resolution (ICADR) Arbitration Rules, 1996[1016]	Rule 13. Interim measures ordered by arbitral tribunal.— (1) The arbitral tribunal may, on an application made by a party to the dispute, make an order granting any interim measure of protection listed in subsection (1) of section 17 of the Arbitration Act. (2) The arbitral tribunal shall have the same power for making orders, as the Court has for the purpose of, and in relation to, any proceedings before it. (3) An order made by the arbitral tribunal under this rule shall be enforceable under the Code of Civil Procedure, 1908 (5 of 1908) in the same manner as if it were an order of the Court.
20.	International Chamber of Commerce (ICC) Arbitration Rules, 2017[1017]	ARTICLE 28 Conservatory and Interim Measures 1 Unless the parties have otherwise agreed, as soon as the file has been transmitted to it, the arbitral tribunal may, at the request of a party, order any interim or conservatory measure it deems appropriate. The arbitral tribunal may make the granting of any such measure subject to appropriate security being furnished by the requesting party. Any such measure shall take the form of an order, giving reasons, or of an award, as the arbitral tribunal considers appropriate. 2 Before the file is transmitted to the arbitral tribunal, and in appropriate circumstances even thereafter, the parties may apply to any competent judicial authority for interim or conservatory measures. The application of a party to a judicial authority for such measures or for the implementation of any such measures ordered by an arbitral tribunal shall not be deemed to be an infringement or a waiver of the arbitration agreement and shall not affect the relevant powers reserved to the arbitral tribunal. Any such application and any measures taken by the judicial authority must be notified without delay to the Secretariat. The Secretariat shall inform the arbitral tribunal thereof.

1016. http://icadr.nic.in/file.php?123?12:1473159419

Sr. No.	Arbitration Institutes	Rules
21.	Korean Commercial Arbitration Board (KCAB), International Arbitration Rules, 2007[1018]	Article 28 Conservatory and Interim Measures 1. Unless the parties have otherwise agreed, as soon as the file has been transmitted to it, the Arbitral Tribunal may at the request of a party order any interim or conservatory measure it deems appropriate. The Arbitral Tribunal may make the granting of any such measure subject to appropriate security being furnished by the requesting party. Any such measure shall take the form of an order, giving reasons, or of an Award, as the Arbitral Tribunal considers appropriate. 2. Before the file is transmitted to the Arbitral Tribunal, and in appropriate circumstances even thereafter, the parties may apply to any competent judicial authority for interim or conservatory measures. The application of a party to a judicial authority for such measures or for the implementation of any such measures ordered by an Arbitral Tribunal shall not be deemed to be an infringement or a waiver of the arbitration agreement and shall not affect the relevant powers reserved to the Arbitral Tribunal. Any such application and any measures taken by the judicial authority must be notified without delay to the Secretariat. The Secretariat shall inform the Arbitral Tribunal thereof.
22.	Korean Commercial Arbitration Board (KCAB), International Arbitration Rules, 2011[1019]	Article 28. Conservatory and Interim Measures 1. Unless the parties have agreed otherwise, as soon as the file has been transmitted to it, the Arbitral Tribunal may at the request of a party order any interim or conservatory measure it deems appropriate. The Arbitral Tribunal may make the granting of any such measure subject to appropriate security being furnished by the requesting party. Any such measure shall take the form of an order, giving reasons, or of an Award, as the Arbitral Tribunal considers appropriate. 2. Before the file is transmitted to the Arbitral Tribunal, and in appropriate circumstances even thereafter, the parties may apply to any competent judicial authority for interim or conservatory measures. The application of a party to a judicial authority for such measures or for the implementation of any such measures ordered by an Arbitral Tribunal shall not be deemed to be an infringement or a waiver of the arbitration agreement and shall not affect the relevant powers reserved to the Arbitral Tribunal. Any such application and any measures taken by the judicial authority must be notified without delay to the Secretariat. The Secretariat shall inform the Arbitral Tribunal thereof.

1017. https://iccwbo.org/content/uploads/sites/3/2017/01/ICC-2017-Arbitration-and-2014-Mediation-Rules-english-version.pdf.pdf
1018. http://www.kcabinternational.or.kr/common/index.do?jpath=/contents/sub020102&CURRENT_MENU_CODE=MENU0008&TOP_MENU_CODE=MENU0007
1019. http://www.arbiter.com.sg/pdf/rules/KCAB%20International%20Arbitration%20Rules%20(2011).pdf

Sr. No.	Arbitration Institutes	Rules
23.	Korean Commercial Arbitration Board (KCAB), International Arbitration Rules, 2016[1020]	Article 32. Conservatory and Interim Measures 1. Unless the parties have agreed otherwise, as soon as the file has been transmitted to it, the Arbitral Tribunal may order any of the following conservatory and interim measures it deems appropriate at the request of a party: (a) To maintain or restore the status quo pending determination of the dispute; (b) To take action that would prevent, or refrain from taking action that is likely to cause, current or imminent harm or prejudice to the arbitration proceedings themselves; (c) To provide a means of preserving assets out of which a subsequent award may be satisfied; or (d) To preserve evidence that may be relevant and material to the resolution of the dispute. 2. The Arbitral Tribunal may grant a measure in Paragraph 1 subject to appropriate security being furnished by the requesting party. Any such measure shall take the form of an order with reasons or of an Award, as the Arbitral Tribunal considers appropriate. 3. Before the file is transmitted to the Arbitral Tribunal, and in appropriate circumstances even thereafter, the parties may apply to any competent judicial authority for conservatory and interim measures. The application of a party to a judicial authority for such measure or for the implementation of any such measure ordered by the Arbitral Tribunal shall not be deemed to be an infringement or a waiver of the arbitration agreement and shall not affect the relevant powers reserved to the Arbitral Tribunal. Any such application and any measures taken by the judicial authority must be notified without delay to the Secretariat and the Secretariat shall inform the Arbitral Tribunal thereof. 4. In arbitrations in which an arbitration agreement was entered into after the effective date of the Rules, a party in need of urgent conservatory and interim measures prior to the constitution of the Arbitral Tribunal may apply for such measure pursuant to the procedures set forth in Appendix 3.
24.	London Court of International Arbitration (LCIA) Rules, 1998[1021]	Article 25 Interim and Conservatory Measures 25.1 The Arbitral Tribunal shall have the power, unless otherwise agreed by the parties in writing, on the application of any party: (a) to order any respondent party to a claim or counterclaim to provide security for all or part of the amount in dispute, by way of deposit or bank guarantee or in any other manner and upon such terms as the Arbitral Tribunal considers appropriate. Such terms may include the provision by the claiming or counterclaiming party of a cross-indemnity, itself secured in such manner as the Arbitral Tribunal considers appropriate,

1020. http://www.kcabinternational.or.kr/common/index.do?jpath=/contents/sub020101
1021. https://www.lcia.org/Dispute_Resolution_Services/LCIA_Arbitration_Rules.aspx

Sr. No.	Arbitration Institutes	Rules
		for any costs or losses incurred by such respondent in providing security. The amount of any costs and losses payable under such cross-indemnity may be determined by the Arbitral Tribunal in one or more awards; (b) to order the preservation, storage, sale or other disposal of any property or thing under the control of any party and relating to the subject matter of the arbitration; and (c) to order on a provisional basis, subject to final determination in an award, any relief which the Arbitral Tribunal would have power to grant in an award, including a provisional order for the payment of money or the disposition of property as between any parties. 25.2 The Arbitral Tribunal shall have the power, upon the application of a party, to order any claiming or counterclaiming party to provide security for the legal or other costs of any other party by way of deposit or bank guarantee or in any other manner and upon such terms as the Arbitral Tribunal considers appropriate. Such terms may include the provision by that other party of a cross-indemnity, itself secured in such manner as the Arbitral Tribunal considers appropriate, for any costs and losses incurred by such claimant or counterclaimant in providing security. The amount of any costs and losses payable under such cross-indemnity may be determined by the Arbitral Tribunal in one or more awards. In the event that a claiming or counterclaiming party does not comply with any order to provide security, the Arbitral Tribunal may stay that party's claims or counterclaims or dismiss them in an award. 25.3 The power of the Arbitral Tribunal under Article 25.1 shall not prejudice howsoever any party's right to apply to any state court or other judicial authority for interim or conservatory measures before the formation of the Arbitral Tribunal and, in exceptional cases, thereafter. Any application and any order for such measures after the formation of the Arbitral Tribunal shall be promptly communicated by the applicant to the Arbitral Tribunal and all other parties. However, by agreeing to arbitration under these Rules, the parties shall be taken to have agreed not to apply to any state court or other judicial authority for any order for security for its legal or other costs available from the Arbitral Tribunal under Article 25.2.
25.	London Court of International Arbitration (LCIA) Rules, 2014[1022]	Article 25 Interim and Conservatory Measures 25.1 The Arbitral Tribunal shall have the power upon the application of any party, after giving all other parties a reasonable opportunity to respond to such application and upon such terms as the Arbitral Tribunal considers appropriate in the circumstances:

1022. https://www.lcia.org/Dispute_Resolution_Services/lcia-arbitration-rules-2014.aspx

Sr. No.	Arbitration Institutes	Rules
		(i) to order any respondent party to a claim or cross-claim to provide security for all or part of the amount in dispute, by way of deposit or bank guarantee or in any other manner; (ii) to order the preservation, storage, sale or other disposal of any documents, goods, samples, property, site or thing under the control of any party and relating to the subject-matter of the arbitration; and (iii) to order on a provisional basis, subject to a final decision in an award, any relief which the Arbitral Tribunal would have power to grant in an award, including the payment of money or the disposition of property as between any parties. Such terms may include the provision by the applicant party of a cross-indemnity, secured in such manner as the Arbitral Tribunal considers appropriate, for any costs or losses incurred by the respondent party in complying with the Arbitral Tribunal's order. Any amount payable under such cross-indemnity and any consequential relief may be decided by the Arbitral Tribunal by one or more awards in the arbitration. 25.2 The Arbitral Tribunal shall have the power upon the application of a party, after giving all other parties a reasonable opportunity to respond to such application, to order any claiming or cross-claiming party to provide or procure security for Legal Costs and Arbitration Costs by way of deposit or bank guarantee or in any other manner and upon such terms as the Arbitral Tribunal considers appropriate in the circumstances. Such terms may include the provision by that other party of a cross-indemnity, itself secured in such manner as the Arbitral Tribunal considers appropriate, for any costs and losses incurred by such claimant or cross-claimant in complying with the Arbitral Tribunal's order. Any amount payable under such cross-indemnity and any consequential relief may be decided by the Arbitral Tribunal by one or more awards in the arbitration. In the event that a claiming or cross-claiming party does not comply with any order to provide security, the Arbitral Tribunal may stay that party's claims or cross-claims or dismiss them by an award. 25.3 The power of the Arbitral Tribunal under Article 25.1 shall not prejudice any party's right to apply to a state court or other legal authority for interim or conservatory measures to similar effect: (i) before the formation of the Arbitral Tribunal; and (ii) after the formation of the Arbitral Tribunal, in exceptional cases and with the Arbitral Tribunal's authorisation, until the final award. After the Commencement Date, any application and any order for such measures before the formation of the Arbitral Tribunal shall be communicated promptly in writing by the applicant party to the Registrar; after its formation, also to the Arbitral Tribunal; and in both cases also to all other parties. 25.4 By agreeing to arbitration under the Arbitration Agreement, the parties shall be taken to have agreed not to apply to any state court or other legal authority for any order for security for Legal Costs or Arbitration Costs.

Sr. No.	Arbitration Institutes	Rules
26.	Mumbai Centre for International Arbitration (MCIA) Rules, 2016[1023]	Rule 15.Interim Relief 15.1 The Tribunal may, at the request of a party, issue an order granting an injunction or any other interim relief it deems appropriate. The Tribunal may order the party requesting interim relief to provide appropriate security in connection with the relief sought. 15.2 Where permitted under applicable law, a party may apply to any court or other judicial authority for interim or conservatory relief. Any such application is permissible solely to the extent that the Tribunal has no power or is unable for the time being to act effectively. Any application and any order for such measures after the formation of the Tribunal shall be promptly communicated by the applicant to the Tribunal and to all other parties.
27.	Nani Palkhivala Arbitration Centre Rules[1024]	Rule 33 : Powers of Tribunal while adjudicating disputes ... The Arbitral Tribunal may:- ... (b) Make any interim order, in accordance with the provisions of the Arbitration and Conciliation Act, 1996; ...
28.	Rules of the Court of Arbitration of the Hamburg Chamber of Commerce, 2000[1025]	Article 18 (Interim measures) Unless otherwise agreed by the parties, the Court of Arbitration may, at the request of a party, grant any provisional or protective measures it may consider necessary with respect to the subject-matter of the dispute. The Court of Arbitration may require any party to provide appropriate security in connection with such measure.
29.	Russian Arbitration Center, Arbitration Rules, 2019[1026]	Article 46. Interim Measures 1. Unless the Parties agreed otherwise, the Arbitral Tribunal, or, prior to the constitution of the Arbitral Tribunal, the person specified in Paragraphs 1 or 3 of Article 49 of the Arbitration Rules, may, upon the application of any Party, issue an order ordering one of the Parties to undertake urgent provisional measures aimed at securing the claim or property interests, as well as at preserving the evidence that may be relevant for the arbitration and essential for resolving the dispute (hereinafter, the "interim measures") it deems appropriate. 2. Interim measures shall be introduced if the failure to introduce them may obstruct or frustrate performance of the award, as well as for the purpose of preventing significant harm to any of the Parties. 3. Interim measures shall correspond to the value of the claim. Article 47. Application for Interim Measures 1. The application for interim measures may be filed together with the Request or the Claim, or separately therefrom at any stage of the proceedings prior to the issuance of the arbitral award.

1023. https://mcia.org.in/mcia-rules/english-pdf/
1024. http://www.nparbitration.com/Documents/pdf/NPAC-Rules-Book.pdf
1025. https://www.hk24.de/en/fairplay/arbitration-mediation-conciliation/arbitration/court-arbitration-rules-1168690
1026. https://centerarbitr.ru/wp-content/uploads/2019/11/Rules-RAC-eng-2019.pdf

Sr. No.	Arbitration Institutes	Rules
		2. If interim measures need to be introduced prior to the constitution of the Arbitral Tribunal, this shall be specifically stated in the application for interim measures. In this case, the application for interim measures shall also specify why the issue of introduction of interim measures cannot be postponed until the constitution of the Arbitral Tribunal. Article 48. Procedure for Introducing, Amending and Cancelling Interim Measures 1. The application for interim measures shall be considered by the Arbitral Tribunal no later than on the day following the date of receipt hereof by the RIMA, without notifying the Parties and without the Parties' participation, except where the Arbitral Tribunal finds the information and documents submitted by the respective Party insufficient to decide the issue of introduction of interim measures. In that case, the Arbitral Tribunal may request that the Parties submit additional information and documents, as well as hold oral hearings to decide on the issue of introduction of interim measures. 2. The Arbitral Tribunal (or the person specified in Paragraphs 1 or 3 of Article 49 of the Arbitration Rules) may request, in its order to introduce interim measures, that any of the Parties provide appropriate security in view of the interim measures introduced. 3. The Arbitral Tribunal may upon the application of any Party amend or annul the order to introduce interim measures, including the order to introduce interim measures issued in accordance with Article 49 of the Arbitration Rules, if there are sufficient grounds for doing so. The Arbitral Tribunal may hold oral hearings to decide the issue of annulment of the interim measures introduced. 4. Copies of the order introducing, refusing to introduce, amending or annulling the interim measures shall be sent to the Parties no later than on the day following the date of its issuance. Article 49. Procedure for Introducing Interim Measures Prior to the Constitution of the Arbitral Tribunal 1. The order to introduce interim measures prior to the constitution of the Arbitral Tribunal may be issued by the President of the Board. Such interim measures shall be subject to the rules of this Chapter regulating interim measures introduced by the Arbitral Tribunal, subject to special rules provided in this Article. 2. When deciding the issue of introduction of interim measures, the President of the Board shall proceed from the provisions of Article 7 of the Internal Rules on the prohibition of the conflict of interests. 3. In case of a conflict of interest or in any other case where the resolution of the issue of introduction of interim measures by the President of the Board appears to be impossible, he/she shall immediately report this to the Executive Administrator and the Parties and remand the application for interim measures to the RIMA together with any and all documents received for resolving the issue of introduction of interim measures. In this case, the Executive Administrator shall, upon agreement with the members of the Board, file

Sr. No.	Arbitration Institutes	Rules
		such an application and documents with one of the members of the Board for resolving the issue of introduction of interim measures. 4. When resolving the issue of introduction of interim measures in accordance with Paragraph 3 of this Article, the Executive Administrator may prolong the term set forth in Paragraph 1 of Article 48 of the Arbitration Rules, but for no longer than until the end of the business day following the submission of the application and documents to the member of the Board for resolving the issue of introduction of interim measures. 5. The Arbitral Tribunal shall not be bound by the conclusions of the President of the Board (or the person resolving the issue of introduction of the interim measures in accordance with Paragraph 3 of this Article) contained in the order to introduce or refuse to introduce interim measures issued by him/her. 6. The Party filing the application for interim measures prior to the constitution of the Arbitral Tribunal shall pay a special administrative fee defined in Article 1 of the Rules on Arbitration Fees and Arbitration Costs. Article 50. Enforcement of the Arbitral Tribunal's Order Granting Interim Measures 1. The Arbitral Tribunal's order to introduce interim measures shall be performed by the Parties immediately after their receipt of the same. 2. If the claims are satisfied, the interim measures shall remain effective until the arbitral award has been de facto enforced. 3. If the claims are not satisfied or arbitration is ceased, or if the Arbitral Tribunal issues an order annulling the interim measures, the interim measures shall terminate from the moment the respective decision or order is issued. 4. The damages inflicted to a Party as a result of the breach of the interim measures, adopted in accordance with Article 46-49 of the Arbitration Rules, may be recovered from the breaching Party. The Arbitral Tribunal considers the recovery of such damages upon rendering of an arbitral award. Article 51. Interim Measures Granted by State Courts with Respect to Arbitration 1. Any Party is entitled to file with a competent court an application for interim measures intended to secure the claims in the arbitration administered by the RIMA under the procedure prescribed by the procedural laws. 2. The Party shall file an application for interim measures intended to secure the claims in the arbitration administered by the RIMA with a competent court at the seat of arbitration or at the Respondent's address or at the location of the Respondent's property, which could be subject to the interim measures. 3. The application for interim measures filed with a competent court shall be accompanied, inter alia, by the following exhibits:

Sr. No.	Arbitration Institutes	Rules
		1) a copy of the Request admitted for hearing or a copy of the Claim, in each case authenticated by the Executive Administrator, or a copy of the Request or the Claim certified by a notary; 2) a duly certified copy of the Arbitration Agreement. 4. The application for interim measures intended to secure the claims in the arbitration administered by the RIMA shall be considered by a competent court in accordance with the applicable procedural laws. The decision granting security of the claims or refusing to grant such security shall be rendered by the competent court in accordance with the applicable procedural laws. 5. The Arbitral Tribunal's decision refusing to satisfy the claims shall serve as a sufficient ground for termination of the security of such interim measures granted by a competent court.
30.	Singapore International Arbitration Centre (SIAC) Rules, 2007[1027]	Rule 24: Additional Powers of the Tribunal 24.1 In addition and not in derogation of the powers conferred by any applicable law of the arbitration, the Tribunal shall have the power to: ... j. order an interim injunction or any other interim measure;
31.	Singapore International Arbitration Centre (SIAC) Rules, 2010[1028]	Rule 26: Interim and Emergency Relief 26.1 The Tribunal may, at the request of a party, issue an order or an award granting an injunction or any other interim relief it deems appropriate. The Tribunal may order the party requesting interim relief to provide appropriate security in connection with the relief sought. 26.2 A party in need of emergency interim relief prior to the constitution of the Tribunal may apply for such relief pursuant to the procedures set forth in Schedule 1. 26.3 A request for interim relief made by a party to a judicial authority prior to the constitution of the Tribunal, or in exceptional circumstances thereafter, is not incompatible with these Rules.
32.	Singapore International Arbitration Centre (SIAC) Rules, 2013[1029]	Rule 26: Interim and Emergency Relief 26.1 The Tribunal may, at the request of a party, issue an order or an award granting an injunction or any other interim relief it deems appropriate. The Tribunal may order the party requesting interim relief to provide appropriate security in connection with the relief sought. 26.2 A party in need of emergency interim relief prior to the constitution of the Tribunal may apply for such relief pursuant to the procedures set forth in Schedule 1. 26.3 A request for interim relief made by a party to a judicial authority prior to the constitution of the Tribunal, or in exceptional circumstances thereafter, is not incompatible with these Rules.

1027. https://www.siac.org.sg/our-rules/rules/siac-rules-2007
1028. https://www.siac.org.sg/our-rules/rules/siac-rules-2010
1029. https://www.siac.org.sg/our-rules/rules/siac-rules-2013

Sr. No.	Arbitration Institutes	Rules
33.	Singapore International Arbitration Centre (SIAC) Rules, 2016[1030]	Rule 30: Interim and Emergency Relief 30.1 The Tribunal may, at the request of a party, issue an order or an Award granting an injunction or any other interim relief it deems appropriate. The Tribunal may order the party requesting interim relief to provide appropriate security in connection with the relief sought. 30.2 A party that wishes to seek emergency interim relief prior to the constitution of the Tribunal may apply for such relief pursuant to the procedures set forth in Schedule 1. 30.3 A request for interim relief made by a party to a judicial authority prior to the constitution of the Tribunal, or in exceptional circumstances thereafter, is not incompatible with these Rules.
34.	Stockholm Chamber of Commerce (SCC) Rules, 1999[1031]	Article 31 Interim Measures (1) Unless the parties have agreed otherwise, the Arbitral Tribunal may, during the course of the proceedings and at the request of a party, order a specific performance by the opposing party for the purpose of securing the claim which is to be tried by the Arbitral Tribunal. The Arbitral Tribunal may order the requesting party to provide reasonable security for damage which may be inflicted on the opposing party as a result of the specific performance in question. (2) A request addressed by a party to a judicial authority for interim measures shall not be deemed to be incompatible with the arbitration agreement or these Rules.
35.	Stockholm Chamber of Commerce (SCC) Rules, 2007[1032]	Article 32 Interim measures (1) The Arbitral Tribunal may, at the request of a party, grant any interim measures it deems appropriate. (2) The Arbitral Tribunal may order the party requesting an interim measure to provide appropriate security in connection with the measure. (3) An interim measure may take the form of an order or an award. (4) A request for interim measures made by a party to a judicial authority is not incompatible with the arbitration agreement or with these Rules.
36.	Stockholm Chamber of Commerce (SCC) Rules, 2017[1033]	Article 37 Interim measures (1) The Arbitral Tribunal may, at the request of a party, grant any interim measures it deems appropriate. (2) The Arbitral Tribunal may order the party requesting an interim measure to provide appropriate security in connection with the measure. (3) An interim measure shall take the form of an order or an award.

1030. https://www.siac.org.sg/our-rules/rules/siac-rules-2016
1031. https://sccinstitute.com/media/56035/1999_web_a4_vanliga_2004_eng_rev_2005.pdf
1032. https://sccinstitute.com/media/56030/2007_arbitration_rules_eng.pdf
1033. https://sccinstitute.com/media/293614/arbitration_rules_eng_17_web.pdf

Sr. No.	Arbitration Institutes	Rules
		(4) Provisions with respect to interim measures requested before arbitration has commenced, or before a case has been referred to an Arbitral Tribunal, are set out in Appendix II. (5) A request for interim measures made by a party to a judicial authority is not incompatible with the arbitration agreement or with these Rules.
37.	UNCITRAL Arbitration Rules, 1976[1034]	Article 26 INTERIM MEASURES OF PROTECTION 1. At the request of either party, the arbitral tribunal may take any interim measures it deems necessary in respect of the subject-matter of the dispute, including measures for the conservation of the goods forming the subject-matter in dispute, such as ordering their deposit with a third person or the sale of perishable goods. 2. Such interim measures may be established in the form of an interim award. The arbitral tribunal shall be entitled to require security for the costs of such measures. 3. A request for interim measures addressed by any party to a judicial authority shall not be deemed incompatible with the agreement to arbitrate, or as a waiver of that agreement.
38.	UNCITRAL Arbitration Rules, 2010[1035]	Article 26 Interim measures 1. The arbitral tribunal may, at the request of a party, grant interim measures. 2. An interim measure is any temporary measure by which, at any time prior to the issuance of the award by which the dispute is finally decided, the arbitral tribunal orders a party, for example and without limitation, to: (a) Maintain or restore the status quo pending determination of the dispute; (b) Take action that would prevent, or refrain from taking action that is likely to cause, (i) current or imminent harm or (ii) prejudice to the arbitral process itself; (c) Provide a means of preserving assets out of which a subsequent award may be satisfied; or (d) Preserve evidence that may be relevant and material to the resolution of the dispute. 3. The party requesting an interim measure under paragraphs 2 (a) to (c) shall satisfy the arbitral tribunal that: (a) Harm not adequately reparable by an award of damages is likely to result if the measure is not ordered, and such harm substantially outweighs the harm that is likely to result to the party against whom the measure is directed if the measure is granted; and (b) There is a reasonable possibility that the requesting party will succeed on the merits of the claim. The determination on this possibility shall not affect the discretion of the arbitral tribunal in making any subsequent determination.

1034. https://www.uncitral.org/pdf/english/texts/arbitration/arb-rules/arb-rules.pdf
1035. https://uncitral.un.org/sites/uncitral.un.org/files/media-documents/uncitral/en/arb-rules-revised-2010-e.pdf

Sr. No.	Arbitration Institutes	Rules
		4. With regard to a request for an interim measure under paragraph 2 (d), the requirements in paragraphs 3 (a) and (b) shall apply only to the extent the arbitral tribunal considers appropriate. 5. The arbitral tribunal may modify, suspend or terminate an interim measure it has granted, upon application of any party or, in exceptional circumstances and upon prior notice to the parties, on the arbitral tribunal's own initiative. 6. The arbitral tribunal may require the party requesting an interim measure to provide appropriate security in connection with the measure. 7. The arbitral tribunal may require any party promptly to disclose any material change in the circumstances on the basis of which the interim measure was requested or granted. 8. The party requesting an interim measure may be liable for any costs and damages caused by the measure to any party if the arbitral tribunal later determines that, in the circumstances then prevailing, the measure should not have been granted. The arbitral tribunal may award such costs and damages at any point during the proceedings. 9. A request for interim measures addressed by any party to a judicial authority shall not be deemed incompatible with the agreement to arbitrate, or as a waiver of that agreement.
39.	Vienna International Arbitral Centre (VIAC) Rules of Arbitration, 2006[1036]	Article 22 Interim Measures of Protection 1 Unless otherwise agreed by the parties, the sole arbitrator (arbitral tribunal) may, at the request of a party order any party, after hearing such party, to take such interim measure of protection as the sole arbitrator (arbitral tribunal) may consider necessary in respect of the subject matter of the dispute, as otherwise the enforcement of the claim would be frustrated or considerably impeded or there is a danger of irreparable harm. The sole arbitrator (arbitral tribunal) may require any party to provide appropriate security in connection with such measure. The parties are obliged to comply with such orders, whether or not they are enforceable by State courts. 2 Measures referred to in paragraph (1) are to be ordered in writing and a signed copy is to be served on each party. In arbitral proceedings with more than one arbitrator the signature of the presiding arbitrator or, if he is prevented, the signature of another arbitrator shall suffice, provided that the presiding arbitrator or another arbitrator records on the order the reason preventing the signature. 3 Unless the parties have agreed otherwise, the measures are to be substantiated. The measure must include the date on when it was ordered and the place of arbitration. The measure shall be deemed to have been ordered on that date and at that place.

1036. https://www.viac.eu/images/documents/vienna_rules/VIAC_Arbitration_Rules_2006_1.pdf

Sr. No.	Arbitration Institutes	Rules
		4 The measures and the records on the serving are joint documents of the parties and the sole arbitrator (arbitral tribunal). The sole arbitrator (arbitral tribunal) shall discuss with the parties the possibility of depositing the measure and the records on the serving. 5 The sole arbitrator (the presiding arbitrator) or, if he is prevented, another arbitrator, shall upon the motion of a party, confirm the unappealability and enforceability of the measure on a copy of the measure. 6 This provision does not prevent the parties from applying to any competent State organ for interim measures of protection. Such an application to a State organ for ordering such measures or for the enforcement of measures ordered by the sole arbitrator (arbitral tribunal) shall not constitute an infringement or waiver of the arbitration agreement and shall not affect the powers of the sole arbitrator (arbitral tribunal). The Secretariat and the sole arbitrator (arbitral tribunal) must be immediately informed of any such application as well as of all measures ordered by the State organ.
40.	Vienna International Arbitral Centre (VIAC) Rules of Arbitration, 2013[1037]	Article 33 INTERIM AND CONSERVATORY MEASURES (1) Unless the parties have agreed otherwise, as soon as the file has been transmitted to the arbitral tribunal (Article 11), the arbitral tribunal may at the request of a party grant interim or conservatory measures against another party as well as amend, suspend or revoke any such measures. The other parties shall be heard before the arbitral tribunal renders any decision on interim or conservatory measures. The arbitral tribunal may require any party to provide appropriate security in connection with such a measure. The parties shall comply with such orders, irrespective of whether they are enforceable before State courts. (2) Any orders for interim or conservatory measures pursuant to this Article shall be in writing. In an arbitration with more than one arbitrator the signature of the chairman shall suffice. If the chairman is hindered from acting, the signature of another arbitrator shall suffice, provided the arbitrator signing the order records the grounds for why the chairman's signature is missing. (3) Unless the parties have agreed otherwise, orders for interim or conservatory measures shall state the reasons upon which they are based. The order shall identify the date on which it was issued and the place of arbitration. (4) Orders for measures shall be preserved for the record in the same manner as awards (Article 36 paragraph 5). (5) The provisions of paragraphs 1 to 4 of this Article do not prevent the parties from applying to any competent State authority for interim or conservatory measures. A request to a State authority to order such measures or to enforce such measures already ordered by the arbitral

1037. https://www.viac.eu/images/documents/vienna_rules/Wiener_Regeln_Brosch%C3%BCre_en_Onlinefassung_inkl_Mediationsregeln_20151217.pdf

Sr. No.	Arbitration Institutes	Rules
		tribunal shall not constitute an infringement or waiver of the arbitration agreement and shall not affect the powers of the arbitral tribunal. The parties shall immediately inform the Secretariat and the arbitral tribunal of any such request as well as of all measures ordered by the State authority.
41.	Vienna International Arbitral Centre (VIAC) Rules of Arbitration, 2018[1038]	Article 33 INTERIM AND CONSERVATORY MEASURES / SECURITY FOR COSTS (1) Unless the parties have agreed otherwise, as soon as the file has been transmitted to the arbitral tribunal (Article 11), the arbitral tribunal may, at the request of a party, grant interim or conservatory measures against another party as well as amend, suspend or revoke any such measures. The other parties shall be heard before the arbitral tribunal renders any decision on interim or conservatory measures. The arbitral tribunal may require any party to provide appropriate security in connection with such a measure. The parties shall comply with such orders, irrespective of whether they are enforceable before national courts. (2) Any orders for interim or conservatory measures pursuant to this Article shall be in writing. In an arbitration with more than one arbitrator, the signature of the chairperson shall suffice. If the chairperson is hindered from acting, the signature of another arbitrator shall suffice, provided the arbitrator signing the order records the reasons for the absence of the chairperson's signature. (3) Unless the parties have agreed otherwise, orders for interim or conservatory measures shall state the reasons upon which they are based. The order shall identify the date on which it was issued and the place of arbitration. (4) Orders for interim and conservatory measures shall be retained in the same manner as awards (Article 36 paragraph 5). (5) The provisions of paragraphs 1 to 4 of this Article do not prevent the parties from applying to any competent national authority for interim or conservatory measures. A request to a national authority to order such measures or to enforce such measures already ordered by the arbitral tribunal shall not constitute an infringement or waiver of the arbitration agreement and shall not affect the powers of the arbitral tribunal. The parties shall immediately inform the Secretariat and the arbitral tribunal of any such request as well as of all measures ordered by the national authority. (6) The arbitral tribunal may, at the request of the respondent, order the claimant to provide security for costs, if the respondent shows cause that the recoverability of a potential claim for costs is, with a sufficient degree of probability, at risk. When deciding on a request for security for costs, the arbitral tribunal shall give all parties the opportunity to present their views.

1038. https://www.viac.eu/images/documents/vienna_rules/Wiener_Regeln_2018_Brosch%C3%BCre_en_Onlinefassung_Einzelseiten_2._Auflage_20200401.pdf

Sr. No.	Arbitration Institutes	Rules
		(7) If a party fails to comply with an order by the arbitral tribunal for security for costs, the arbitral tribunal may, upon request, suspend in whole or in part, or terminate, the proceedings (Article 34 paragraph 2.4).

Bibliography

Books

Alan Redfern, Interim Measures, in Newman & Hill (eds), The Leading Arbitrators' Guide to International Arbitration, (2nd edn. New York Juris Publishing Inc. 2008).

Alexis Mourre, Judicial Penalties and Specific Performance in International Arbitration, in De Ly & Levy (eds), Interest, Auxiliary and Alternative Remedies in International Arbitration, 5 Dossiers of the ICC Institute of World Business Law (Kluwer Law International 2008).

Ali Yesilirmak, Provisional Measure in International Commercial Arbitration, 12 International Arbitration Law Library, (London, London University 2005).

Amir Ali & Sir John Woodroffe, Law on Execution of Decree and Orders (New Delhi, Delhi Law House 2017).

André Abbud & Daniel de Andrade Levy, et al., The Brazilian Arbitration Act: A Case Law Guide, (Kluwer Law International 2019).

Andreas A. Frischknecht & Yasmine Lahlou, et al., Enforcement of Foreign Arbitral Awards and Judgments in New York, (Kluwer Law International 2018).

Anirudh Wadhwa & Anirudh Krishnan, Justice R S Bachawat Law of Arbitration and Conciliation (Lexis Nexis 2017).

Anurag K. Agarwal, Contracts and Arbitration for Managers (Sage Publications Pvt. Ltd. 2016).

Arne Fuchs & Lisa Richman, Chapter II: The Arbitration Agreement and Arbitrability, Third-Party Funding in International Arbitration: A Comparative Analysis, in Christian Klausegger & Peter Klein, et al. (eds), Austrian Yearbook on International Arbitration 2020, (2020).

Atul Setalvad, Conflict of Laws, (Lexis Nexis 2007).

Audley William Sheppard, English Arbitration Act (Chapter 23), Part I, Power of Court in Relation to Arbitral Proceedings, Section 44 [Court powers exercisable in support of arbitral proceedings], in Loukas A. Mistelis (ed.), Concise International Arbitration (Kluwer Law International 2015).

Avtar Singh, Law of Arbitration and Conciliation (Eastern Book Company 2019).

B M Prasad & Manish Mohan, The MLJ Manual of the Civil Procedure (Lexis Nexis 2015).

Beechey & Kenny, How to Control the Impact of Time Running Between the Occurrence of the Damage and Its Full Compensation: Compensatory and Alternative Remedies in Interim Relief Proceedings, in L. Levy & F. De Ly (eds), Interest, Auxiliary and Alternative Remedies in International Arbitration (Kluwer Law International 2008).

Bernhard Berger & Franz Kellerhals, International and Domestic Arbitration in Switzerland, (Hart Publishing 2015).

Berthold Goldman, Arbitrage Commercial International, Jurisclasseur Droit International, Fascicule 586|5|2, No. 77 as translated by Schwartz, Provisional Measures, in ICC (ed.), Conservatory Measures.

Black's Law Dictionary (2004).

Bommel van der Bend & Marnix A. Leijten, et al. (eds), A Guide to the NAI Arbitration Rules: Including a Commentary on Dutch Arbitration Law (Kluwer Law International 2009).

Bruce Harris, Rowan Planterose & Jonathan Tecks, The Arbitration Act 1996, A Commentary, (Blackwell Publications 2007).

Bucher & P. Tschanz, International Arbitration in Switzerland, (Basel Helbing & Lichtenhahn 1988).

Chunilal Karsandas Takawani, Civil Procedure with Limitation Act, 1963 and Chapter on Commercial Courts, (Eastern Book Company 2017).

Carlos González-Bueno (ed.), The Spanish Arbitration Act: A Commentary, (Madrid, Dykinson S.L. 2016).

Casey and Mills, Arbitration Law of Canada: Practice and Procedure, (Juris Net LLC 2005).

Cedric Ryngaert, Jurisdiction in International Law, (OUP 2008).

Chandra Bhushan Upadhyay, Digest, Cases and Materials, on Civil Procedure Code, 1970-1989 (1990).

Cheshire, & Geoffrey Chevalier, Cheshire & North's Private International Law, (Butterworths 1987).

Christoph H. Schreuer et al., The ICSID Convention: A Commentary, (2nd ed. Cambridge University Press 2009).

Christopher Boog, The Laws Governing Interim Measures in International Arbitration, in Franco Ferrari and Stefan Kröll (eds), Conflict of Laws in International Arbitration, (Munich, Sellier European Law Publishers 2010).

Clyde Croft, Christopher Kee & Jeffrey Waincymer, A Guide to the UNCITRAL Arbitration Rules, (Cambridge University Press 2013).

Crina Baltag, Chapter 15: Anti-Suit Injunctions and Other Means of Indirect Enforcement of an Arbitration Agreement, in Stavaros L. Brekoulakis & Julian D.M. Lew, et al. (eds), The Evolution and Future of International Arbitration, International Arbitration Law Library, (Kluwer Law International 2016).

Alan Redfern and Martin Hunter, Law and Practice of International Commercial Arbitration, (Sweet and Maxwell 2004).

D. P. Mittal, Law of Arbitration ADR and Contract, (Taxmann 2001).

David Shenton & Wolfgang Kühn, Interim Court Remedies in Support of Arbitration, (International Bar Association 1987).

David D Caron, Stephan W Schill, Abby Cohen Smutny & Epaminontas E Triantafilou (eds), Practising Virtue: An Introduction, (OUP 2015).

David D. Caron & Lee M. Caplan, The UNCITRAL Arbitration Rules: A Commentary (OUP 2013).

Donald Francis Donovan, The Scope and Enforceability of Provisional Measures in International Commercial Arbitration a Survey of Jurisdictions, the Work of UNCITRAL and Proposals for Moving Forward, in Albert Jan Van den Berg (ed.), International Commercial Arbitration: Important Contemporary Questions, 11 ICCA Congress Series (Kluwer Law International 2003).

David Joseph Q.C, Jurisdiction and Arbitration Agreements and Their Enforcement (Sweet & Maxwell 2010).

David M. Lindsey & Yasmine Lahlou, The Law Applicable to International Arbitration in New York, in Carter & Fellas (eds), International Commercial Arbitration in New York (OUP 2010).

David St. John Sutton & Judith Gill, et al., Russell on Arbitration (Sweet & Maxwell 2018).

De Ly & Lévy (eds), Interest, Auxiliary and Alternative Remedies in International Arbitration (Kluwer Law International 2008).

Dinshaw Fardunji Mulla, et al., Mulla the Code of Civil Procedure (Lexis Nexis 2017).

David W. Rivkin & Donald F. Donovan, Arbitration World: Jurisdictional Comparisons, United States, Evidence Gathering (London: The European Lawyer, 2006).

Eric A. Schwartz, Security for Costs and Third-Party Funding, a Bridge Too Far, Liber Amicorum William Laurence Craig, (Lexis Nexis 2016).

Eric A Schwartz, The Practice & Experience of ICC Courts, in Conservatory & Provisional Measures in International Arbitration, ICC International Court of Arbitration (Paris ICC 1993).

Eduardo Zuleta Jaramillo, The Relationship Between Interim and Final Award: Res Judicata Concerns, in Albert Jan van den Berg (ed.), Arbitration Advocacy in Changing Times, 15 ICCA Congress Series, 233 (Kluwer Law International, 2011).

Edward Dumbauld, Interim Measures of Protection in International Controversies (Springer Dordrecht 1932).

Emilia Onyema, International Commercial Arbitration and the Arbitrators Contract (Routledge 2010).

Emmanuel Gaillard, Reflections on the Use of Anti-Suit Injunction in International Arbitration, in Loukas Mistelis & Julian Lew (eds), Pervasive Problems in International Arbitration (Kluwer Law International 2006).

Emmanuel Gaillard, Anti-suit Injunctions Issued by Arbitrators, in Albert Jan van den Berg (ed.), International Arbitration 2006: Back to Basics? 13 ICCA Congress Series, (The Hague: Kluwer Law International, 2007).

Emmanuel Gaillard & John Savage, Fouchard Gaillard Goldman on International Commercial Arbitration (Kluwer Law International 1999).

Eric Schwartz, The Practices and Experience of the ICC Court, in ICC (ed.), Conservatory and Provisional Measures in International Arbitration, (1993).

Fredrick Pollock & Dinshaw Fardunji Mulla, Pollock & Mulla's Indian Contract and Specific Relief Acts (Lexis Nexis 2010).

Franco Ferrari & Stefan Kröll (eds), Conflict of Laws in International Arbitration (Munich Sellier European Law Publishers 2010).

Francisco Gonsalez De Cossio, Interim Measure in Arbitration: Towards a Better Injury Standard, in Albert Jan Van den Berg (ed.), Legitimacy: Myths, Realities, Challenges, 18 ICCA Congress Series (Kluwer Law International 2015).

Frank Vischer, Article 183, in Girsberger, A. Heini, M. Keller, J. Kren. Kostkiewicz, K. Siehr, F. Vischer & P. Volken, Zurich Commentary on the Swiss PILA, (2004).

Frank-Bernd Weigand & Antje Baumann, Practitioner's Handbook on International Commercial Arbitration (OUP 2009).

Frédéric Bachand, The UNCITRAL Model Law's Take on Anti-Suit Injunctions, in Emmanuel Galliard (ed.), Anti-Suit Injunctions in International Arbitration (Juris Publishing Inc. 2005).

G. K. Kwatra, The Arbitration and Conciliation Law of India: With Case Law of UNCITRAL Model Law on Arbitration (New Delhi Indian Council of Arbitration 2010).

Georg Von Segesser & Christoph Kurth, Interim Measures, in Gabrielle Kaufmann-Kohler & Blaise Stucki, International Arbitration in Switzerland: A Handbook for Practitioners (The Hague Kluwer Law International 2004).

Gabrielle Kaufmann-Kohler & Antonio Rigozzi, Arbitrage International, (OUP 2010).

Gabrielle Kaufmann-Kohler & Antonio Rigozzi, International Arbitration: Law and Practice in Switzerland (Oxford University Press 2015).

Gary B. Born, International Commercial Arbitration (Kluwer Law International 2021).

Geoffrey C. Hazard, Jr. et al., Cases and Materials on Pleading and Procedure State and Federal (Foundation Pr.1994).

Georgios Petrochilos, Procedural Law in International Arbitration (OUP 2004).

Gerhard Walter, Wolfgang Bosch & Brönnimann, Internationale Schiedsgerichtsbarkeit in der Schweiz (Stampfli Verlag1991).

Giuditta Cordero-Moss, International Commercial Arbitration Different Forms and Their Features (Cambridge University Press 2013).

Gustav Flecke-Giammarco & Christopher Boog, et al. (eds), The DIS Arbitration Rules: An Article-by-Article Commentary, (Kluwer Law International 2020).

Horacio A. Grigera-Naon, Latin America: Overcoming Traditional Hostility Towards Arbitration, in International Commercial Arbitration: Recent Developments, PLI Com. Law & Practice Course Handbook Series No. 477, (1988).

Howard Holtzmann, A Task for the 21st Century: Creating a New International Court for Resolving Disputes on the Enforceability of Arbitral Awards, in Martin Hunter & Arthur Marriott, et al. (eds), The Internationalization of International Arbitration, (London Graham & Trotman 1995).

Howard M. Holtzmann & Joseph Neuhaus, et al., A Guide to the 2006 Amendments to the UNCITRAL Model Law on International Commercial Arbitration: Legislative History and Commentary (Kluwer Law International, 2015).

John George Woodroffe, The Law Relating to Injunctions in British India (Calcutta Thacker, Spink & Co. 1900).

Jacob C. Jorgensen (ed.), Finding, Freezing and Attaching Assets: A Multi-Jurisdictional Handbook, (Wolters Kluwer 2016).

Jakob Ragnwaldh & Fredrik Andersson, et al., A Guide to the SCC Arbitration Rules, (Kluwer Law International 2019).

Jan Paulson, Interference by National Courts in Lawrence, in W. Newman & Richard D. Hill (eds), The Leading Arbitrators Guide to International Arbitration (New York Juris Net LLC 2004).

Jan Paulson, The Idea of Arbitration (OUP 2013).

Jan Paulson, The Revised UNCITRAL Rules (2013).

Jean-François Poudret & Sébastien Besson, Droit comparé de l'arbitrage international, (Bruylant 2002).

Jean-Francois Poudret & Sabastian Besson, Comparative Law of International Arbitration (London Sweet and Maxwell 2007).Jean Rouche & Gerald H. Pointon, et al., French Arbitration Law and Practice: A Dynamic Civil Law Approach to International Arbitration (Kluwer Law International 2009).

Jean-Jacques Arnaldez, Yves derains & Dominique Hascher, Collection of Arbitral Awards 2001-2007/Recueil des sentences arbitrales de la CCI 2001-2007 (2009).

Jeffrey Waincymer, International Arbitration: The Process of an Arbitration (Wolters Kluwer 2012).

Jerome B. Elkind, Interim Protection: A Functional Approach (Brill Academic Pub. 1981).

J.-J. Arnaldez, Y. Derains & D. Hascher (eds), Collection of ICC Arbitral Awards 1991-1995 (Kluwer Law International 1997).

Joaquim T. de Paiva Muniz & Ana Tereza Palhares Basílio, Arbitration Law of Brazil: Practice and Procedure (Juris Publishing Inc. 2006).

John Savage & Emmanuel Gaillard, Fouchard Gaillard and Goldman on International Commercial Arbitration (Kluwer Law International 1999).

Jonas von Goeler, Third-Party Funding in International Arbitration and Its Impact on Procedure, International Arbitration Law Library (Kluwer law International 2016).

Jonathan R. C. Atkins & David Joseph, Jurisdiction and Arbitration Agreements and Their Enforcement (Sweet and Maxwell 2005).

Jose Maria Abascal Zamora, The Art of Interim Measures, in Albert van den Berg (ed.), International Arbitration 2006: Back to the Basics? (13 ICCA Congress Series, Kluwer Law International 2007).

Julian D Lew, The Case for the Publication of Arbitration Award, in Jan C. Schultz & Albert J. van den Berg (eds), The Art of Interim Measures (1982).

Julian D M Lew, Control of Jurisdiction by Injunctions Issued by National Courts, in Albert Jan van den Berg (ed.), International Arbitration 2006: Back to Basics?, 13 ICCA Congress Series (Kluwer Law International 2007).

Julian D.M. Lew, Anti-suit Injunctions Issued by National Courts: To Prevent Arbitration Proceedings, in Emmanuel Galliard (ed.), Anti-suit Injunctions in International Arbitration, 2 IAI Series on International Arbitration (Juris Net LLC 2005).

Julian D.M. Lew, Loukas A. Mistelis & Stefan Kröll, Comparative International Commercial Arbitration (Kluwer Law International 2003).

Julian D.M. Lew & Harris Bor, et al. (eds), Arbitration in England, with Chapters on Scotland and Ireland, (Kluwer Law international 2013).

Justice M.L. Singhal et al., Cases and Materials on Code of Civil Procedure (Lexis Nexis 2011).

K P Berger, International Economic Arbitration (Kluwer Law International 1993).

K.P. Berger, The New German Arbitration Law in International Perspective (The Hague Kluwer Law International 2000).

Kaj Hober, Interim Measures by Arbitrators, in Albert Jan van den Berg (ed.), International Arbitration 2006: Back to Basics? 13 ICCA Congress Series, 739 (Kluwer Law International 2007).

Kieron O'Callaghan & Jerome Finnis, Chapter 20: Support and Supervision by the Courts, in Julian David Mathew Lew & Harris Bor, et al. (eds), Arbitration in England, with Chapters on Scotland and Ireland (Kluwer Law International 2013).

L. Collins, Essays in International Litigation and the Conflict of Laws (OUP 1994).

Laurence Craig, William W. Park & Jan Paulsson, Annotated Guide to the 1998 ICC Arbitration Rules (Oceana Publications Inc. 1998).

Laurence Craig, William W. Park & Jan Paulsson, International Chamber of Commerce Arbitration (Oceana Publications Inc. 2000).

Laurence Shore & Tai-Heng Cheng, et al., Introduction, in Laurence Shore & Tai-Heng Cheng, et al. (eds), International Arbitration in the United States, (Kluwer Law International 2017).

Laurent Lévy, Anti-suit Injunctions Issued by Arbitrators, in Emmanuel Gaillard (ed.), Anti-suit Injunctions in International Arbitration, IAI International Arbitration Series No. 2, (Huntington: Jurisnet LLC, 2005).

Laurent Levy & Filip De Ly, Interests, Auxiliary and Alternative Remedies in International Arbitration (Kluwer Law international 2008).

Lawrence Collins, Dicey and Morris on Conflict of Laws, (Sweet & Maxwell 1993).

Lawrence W. Newman & Colin Ong, Interim Measures in International Arbitration 246 (JurisNet LLC 2014).

Lira Goswami, Interim Reliefs: The Role of the Courts, in Albert Jan van den Berg (ed.), International Arbitration and National Courts: The Never Ending Story, ICCA Congress Series Volume 10 (2001).

Lisa Bench Nieuwveld & Victoria Shannon Sahani, Third-Party Funding in International Arbitration (Kluwer Law International 2017).

Loukas Mistelis & Julian Lew (eds), Pervasive Problems in International Arbitration (Kluwer Law International 2006).

Lucy Reed, Jan Paulsson & Nigel Blackaby, Guide to ICSID Arbitration (Kluwer Law International 2011).

Luis Enrique Graham, Interim Measures: Ongoing Regulations and Practices (A View from the UNCITRAL Arbitration Regime), in Albert Jan Van den Berg (ed.), 50 years of the New York Convention: ICCA International Arbitration Conference, 14 ICCA Congress Series (2009).

Luke Notage & Richard Garnett (eds), International Arbitration in Australia (Annandale N.S.W. The Federation Press 2010).

M. Gusy, J. Hosking & F. Schwarz, A Guide to the ICDR International Arbitration Rules, (OUP 2011).

Madhusudan Saharay, Textbook on Arbitration & Conciliation with Alternative Dispute Resolution. (Universal Law Publishing 2017).

Mads Andenas & Duncan Fairgrieve, Tom Bingham and the Transformation of the Law: A Liber Amicorum (OUP 2009).

Malcolm Holmes and Chester Brown, The International Arbitration Act 1974: A Commentary (Lexis Nexis Butterworths 2011).

Manuel Arroyo (ed.), Arbitration in Switzerland: The Practitioner's Guide (Kluwer Law International 2018).

Marco Stacher &Michael Feit, Chapter 18, Part VII: Parallel Proceedings and Lis Pendens, in Manuel Arroyo (ed.), Arbitration in Switzerland: The Practitioner's Guide (2nd ed. Kluwer Law International 2018).

Margaret L. Moses, The Principles and Practice of International Commercial Arbitration (Cambridge University Press 2008).

Marianne Roth, UNCITRAL Model Law on International Commercial Arbitration, in Practitioner's Handbook on International Commercial Arbitration (OUP 2010).

Marike R. P. Paulsson, The 1958 New York Convention in Action, (Kluwer Law International 2016).

Matthew Gearing, Sheila Ahuja & Arun Mal, Ashwani Minda v. U-Shin The Delhi High Court's Recent Observations on Emergency Arbitrator Relief and the Availability of Court-Ordered Interim Measures (27 May 2020), (Allen & Overy).

Mauro Rubino-Sammartano, International Arbitration Law and Practice, (Kluwer Academic Pub. 2001).

Mauro Rubino-Sammartano, International Arbitration Law and Practice, (3d ed. JurisNet LLC 2014).

Maxi Scherer & Lisa Richman, et al., Arbitrating under the 2014 LCIA Rules: A User's Guide, (Kluwer Law International 2015).

Meg Kinnear & Geraldine R. Fischer, et al. (eds), Building International Investment Law: The First 50 Years of ICSID (Wolters Kluwer 2015).

Melissa Magliana, Chapter 3, Part II: Commentary on the Swiss Rules, Article 26 [Interim Measures of Protection], in Manuel Arroyo (ed.), Arbitration in Switzerland: The Practitioner's Guide (2nd edn. Kluwer Law International 2018).

Merkin, Robert, Louis Flannery & Great Britain, et al., Arbitration Act 1996, Anonymous Translator (2014).

Micha Bühler & Marco Stacher, Chapter 18, Part IV: Costs in International Arbitration, in Manuel Arroyo (ed.), Arbitration in Switzerland: The Practitioner's Guide 2578 (2nd edn. Kluwer Law International 2018).

Michael J Mustill & Stewart C Boyd, The Law and Practice of Commercial Arbitration in England (Butterworths 1989).

Nadja Erk-Kubat, Chapter 3: Jurisdictional Pleas and Actions with Parallel Proceedings before an Arbitral Tribunal and a National Court, in Parallel Proceedings in International Arbitration: A Comparative European Perspective, 30 International Arbitration Law Library (Kluwer Law International 2014).

Nael G. Bunni, Interim Measures in International Commercial Arbitration: A Commentary on the Report of Luis Enrique Graham, Interim Measures: Ongoing Regulations and Practices (A View from the UNCITRAL Arbitration Regime), in Albert Jan Van den Berg (ed.), 50 Years of the New York Convention: ICCA International Arbitration Conference, 14 ICCA Congress Series, (2009).

Naresh Markanda & P. C. Markanda, Law Relating to Arbitration & Conciliation. (Lexis Nexis 2016).

Neil Kaplan, Hong Kong in Paulsson (gen ed.), International Handbook (1999).

Neil Kaplan QC, Interim Measures a Practical Experience, in International Arbitration 2006: Back to Basics?, in Albert Jan van den Berg (ed.), ICCA Congress Series No. 13 (The Hague: Kluwer Law International, 2007).

Nigel Blackaby & J. Martin Hunter et al., Redfern and Hunter on International Arbitration (OUP 2015).

Nilima Bhadbhade, Specific Performance of Contracts: The Tests of Inadequacy and Effective Enforcement (Lexis Nexis 2014).

Niuscha Bassiri, Commentary on Part VI of the Belgian Judicial Code, Chapter IV: Article 1696, in Niuscha Bassiri & Maarten Draye (eds), Arbitration in Belgium, (Kluwer Law International 2016).

Niuscha Bassiri & Maarten Draye (eds), Arbitration in Belgium (Kluwer Law International 2016).

Om Prakash Malhotra & Indu Malhotra, The Law and Practice of Arbitration and Conciliation: The Arbitration and Conciliation Act, 1996 (Lexis Nexis 2006).

PA Karrer, Interim Measurers Issued by Arbitral Tribunals and the Courts: Less Theory, Please, in Albert Jan van Der Berg (ed.), in International Arbitration and National Courts: The Never Ending Story, (Kluwer Law International, 2001).

P C Markanda, Rajesh Markanda & Naresh Markanda, Arbitration: Step by Step (2nd edn. Lexis Nexis 2017).

Patricia Nacimiento & Stefan Michael Kroll, et al. (eds), Arbitration in Germany: The Model Law in Practice (2nd edn. Wolters Kluwer Law 2015).

Paul Friedland & Kate Brown, A Claim for Monetary Relief for Breach of Agreement to Arbitrate as a Supplement or Substitute to an Anti-suit Injunction, in Albert Jan Van Den Berg (ed.), International Arbitration 2006: Back to Basics?, 13 ICCA Congress Series, (The Hague: Kluwer Law International, 2007).

Pete Turner and Reza Mohtashami, A Guide to the LCIA Arbitration Rules (OUP 2009).

Peter Binder, Article 17H (2006 Version): Recognition and Enforcement in Peter Binder, International Commercial Arbitration and Mediation in UNCITRAL Model Law Jurisdictions (4th edn. Kluwer Law international 2019).

Piero Bernardini, The Italian Law on Arbitration: Text and Notes (Kluwer Law international 1998).

Pierre A. Karrer, Anti-Arbitration Injunctions: Theory and Practice, in Albert Jan Van den Berg (ed.), International Arbitration 2006: Back to Basics?, 13 ICCA Congress Series (2007).

Pierre A. Karrer, Interim Measures Issued by Arbitral Tribunals and the Courts: Less Theory, Please, in Albert Jan van den Berg (ed.), International Arbitration and National Courts: The Never Ending Story, 10 ICCA Congress Series, (2001).

Pyoung-Keun Kang, The Relationship Between International Arbitration and National Courts with Specific Reference to Provisional Measures (1996).

R. Merkin, The Arbitration Act 1996: An Annotated Guide, (LLP Professional Publishing London 2000).

Richard Garnett & Michael Pryles, Enforcement of Foreign Awards in Australia and New Zealand, in Luke Notage & Richard Garnett (eds), International Arbitration in Australia (The Federation Press 2010).

RS Jindal, Aruneshwar Gupta & C S P Sastri, Supreme Court on Arbitration and Contracts: An Exhaustive Topical Referencer of Supreme Court Judgments on Arbitration and Contract (2nd edn. Universal Law Publishing 2017).

S.C. Sarkar & P.C. Sarkar, Sarkar Code of Civil Procedure (12th edn. Lexis Nexis 2017).

Shabtai Rosenne, Provisional Measures in International Law: The International Court of Justice and the International Tribunal for the Law of the Sea (OUP 2005).

Sigvard Jarvin, Comment on, 1986, in Sigvard Jarvin, Yves Derains & Jan-Jacques Arnaldez (eds), Collection of ICC Awards 1986-1990 517 (Deventer 1994).

Sigvard Jarvin, Aspects of the Arbitral Proceedings, in ICC (ed.), The New 1998 ICC Rules of Arbitration, (ICC Publication No. 586) (Paris: ICC Publishing 1997).

Sigvard Jarvin & Yves Derains (eds), Collection of ICC Arbitral Awards 1974-1985 (Kluwer 1990).

Sigvard Jarvin, To What Extent Are Procedural Decisions of Arbitrators Subject to Court Review? ('Procedural Decisions'), in Albert Jan van den Berg (ed.), Improving the Efficiency of Arbitration Agreements and Awards: 40 Years of Application of the New York Convention, 9 ICCA Congress Series No. (1999).

Starvos L. Berkoulakis & Julian D.M. Lew, et al. (eds), The Evolution and Future of International Arbitration, International Arbitration Law Library 252 (Kluwer Law International 2016).

Stavros L. Brekoulakis & Jonas von Goeler, Chapter I: The Arbitration Agreement and Arbitrability, It's all about the Money: The Impact of Third-Party Funding on Costs Awards and Security for Costs in International Arbitration, in Christian Klausegger & Peter Klein, et al. (eds), Austrian Yearbook on International Arbitration 2017, Austrian Yearbook on International Arbitration, (Manz'sche Verlags- und Universitätsbuchhandlung 2017).

Stephan Balthasar, International Commercial Arbitration: A Handbook (Hart Publishing 2016).

Stephen M. Schwebel, Anti-Suit Injunctions in International Arbitration: An Overview, in Emmanuel Galliard (ed.), Anti-Suit Injunctions in International Arbitration 5 (Juris Pub. 2005).

Stephen R. Bond, The Nature of Conservatory and Provisional Measures, in ICC (ed.), Conservatory and Provisional Measures in International Arbitration (Paris 1993).

Steven Gee & Lord Bingham, Anti-Suit Injunctions and Arbitration, in Mads Andenas & Duncan Fairgrieve (eds), TOM Bingham and the Transformation of the Law: A Liber Amicorum 638 (Oxford Scholarship Online, 2009).

Stone Sweet Alec, The Evolution of International Arbitration (OUP 2017).

Stuart Abercrombie & Mark David Davis, The UNCITRAL Arbitration Rules in Practice: The Experience of the Iran-United States Claims Tribunal, (Deventer: Kluwer International Law 1992).

Sudipto Sarkar & VR Manohar, Sarkar's The Law of Civil Procedure (10th edn. Lexis Nexis 2002).

Sukumar Ray & M.R. Mallick, Ganguly's Civil Court Practice and Procedure (14th edn. Eastern Law House 2016).

Sukumar Ray, Mitra's Civil Reference (5th edn. Eastern Law House 2019).

Thayananthan Baskaran, Arbitration in Malaysia: A Commentary on the Malaysian Arbitration Act, (Kluwer Law International 2019).

Thomas E. Carbonneau, Toward a New Federal Law on Arbitration (OUP 2014).

Thomas Rüede & Reimer Hadenfeldt, Schweizerische Schiedsgerichtsbarkeit nach Konkordat und iprg, 253 (2nd edn. Zurich Schulthess 1993).

Tushar Kumar Biswas, Introduction to Arbitration in India: The Role of the Judiciary (Kluwer Law International 2013).

Seetharam R. Avadhani, Civil Adjudication Law, Practice and Procedure (2nd edn. ALD Publications 2017).

Van Vechten Veeder, The Need for Cross-border Enforcement of Interim Measures Ordered by a State Court in Support of the International Arbitral Process, in Albert Jan van den Berg (ed.), New Horizons in International Commercial Arbitration and Beyond, 12 ICCA Congress Series, (ICCA & Kluwer Law International 2005).

William Laurence Craig & William W. Park, et al., International Chamber of Commerce Arbitration 471 (3rd edn. Oceana Publishing Inc. 2000).

William Laurence Craig, William. W. Park & Jan Paulsson, Craig, Park and Paulson's Annotated Guide to the 1988 ICC Arbitration Rules with Commentary (Oceana Publishing Inc. 1998).

William Michael Reisman et al., International Commercial Arbitration Cases and Materials and Notes on the Resolution of International Business Disputes (The Foundation Press 1997).

William W. Park, The Arbitrator's Jurisdiction to Determine Jurisdiction, I. Introduction: The Limits of Language, in Albert Jan Van den Berg (ed.), International Arbitration 2006: Back to Basics?, 13 ICCA Congress Series, (ICCA & Kluwer Law International 2007).

Y.P. Bhagat, Code of Civil Procedure (with Exhaustive Case Law) (Universal Law Publishing 2017).

Yearbook Commercial Arbitration, 1224 XXXIII (Kluwer law International 2008).

Yves Derains & Eric Schwartz, A Guide to the ICC Rules of Arbitration (2nd edn. Kluwer Law International 2005).

Zheng Sophia Tang, Jurisdiction and Arbitration Agreements (Routledge 2014).

Zhivko Stalev, Interim Measures of Protection in the Context of Arbitration, in Albert Jan van den Berg (ed.), International Arbitration in a Challenging World, 6 ICCA Congress Series, (1994).

Zhivko Stalev, Interim Measures of Protection in the Context of Arbitration, in Albert Jan van den Berg (ed.), International Arbitration in Changing World, 6 ICCA Congress Series (1994).

Zia Mody and Thiruvallore T. Arvind, Redeeming Sisyphus: The Need to Invigorate Interim Relief in International Commercial Arbitration, in Albert Jan van den Berg (ed.), International Arbitration and National Courts: The Never-Ending Story (The Hague Kluwer Law International 2001).

Articles

Aditya Swarup, The Prima Facie Standard for Interim Injunctions in India, 4 NLU Delhi Students Law Journal (2017).

Ajar Rab, Arbitration & Conciliation Amendment Act, 2015: Enforcing Interim Orders, Where Is the Relief? 4 NLU-D Student Law Journal (2017).

Ajar Rab, Comparing Specific Performance under the Specific Relief (Amendment) Act 2018 with the CISG and the UNIDROIT Principles: The Problems of the 'Un-Common Law' in India, 7 NLS Business Law Review (2021).

Ajar Rab, Defining the Contours of The Public Policy Exception: A New Test For Arbitrability in India, 7 (2) Indian Journal of Arbitration Law (2019).

Alan Redfern & Sam O'Leary, Why It Is Time for International Arbitration to Embrace Security for Costs, 32 Arbitration International (2016).

Alan Scott Rau, Provisional Relief in Arbitration: How Things Stand in the United States, 22 Journal of International Arbitration (2005).

Alastair Henderson, Security for Costs in Arbitration in Singapore, 7 (1) Asian International Arbitration Journal (2011).

Albert Jan Van Den Berg, The New York Convention, 1958: An Overview, published on the website of ICCA, available at, www.arbitration-icca.org/media/0/12125884 227980/newyorkconventionof1958overview.pdf.

Ali Yesilirmak, Interim and Conservatory Measures in ICC Arbitral Practice, 11 (1) ICC International Ct. Arbitration Bulletin, (2000).

Ali Yesilirmak, Interim and Conservatory measures in ICC Arbitral Practice 1999-2008, ICC Bulletin, Special Supplement, (2011).

Andreas Reiner, Les mesures provisoires et conservatoires et L'Arbitrage international, notamment l'Arbitrage CCI, 125 Journal du droit international, (1998).

Andrew Bell, Forum Shopping and Venue in Transnational Litigation 172 (2003) as cited in Daniel Tan, Anti-Suit Injunctions and the Vexing Problem of Comity, 45 (3) Virginia Journal of International Law (2005).

Andrew Chan & Renita Sophia Crasta, Interim Measures in Aid of Foreign Arbitration: A Re-Think, 20 Singapore Academy Law Journal (2008).

Andrew de Lotbinière McDougall & Dipen Sabharwal, et al., Mandatory Time Limit for Rendering Awards under Indian Law: How Good Intentions Can Lead to Bad Outcomes, 5(2) Indian Journal of Arbitration Law (2017).

Andrew E Costa, Between Arbitration and Litigation: Interim Measures and Freezing Orders in International Commercial Arbitration, 20 (3) Alternative Resolutions (2011).

Anne Hermann, Drawing a Contrast: Interim Measure of Protection in International Arbitral Proceedings: the United States v Germany, 9 Vindobana Journal of International Arbitration (2005).

Akash Srivastava, Emergency Arbitration and India: A Long Overdue Friendship, 10 (1) Indian Journal of Arbitration Law (2021).

Aren Goldsmith & Lorenzo Melchionda, Everything You Ever Wanted to Know (But Were Afraid to Ask) Part Two, International Business Law Journal (2012).

Ava Boroso, Overview of U.S. Court Treatment of Interim Measures in Support of International Arbitration, Young Arbitration Review (2018).

Badri Srinivasan, Arbitration and the Supreme Court: A Tale of Discordance Between the Text and Judicial Determination, 4 NUJS Law Review (2011).

Ben H. Sheppard Jr. & John M. Townsend, Holding the Fort until the Arbitrators Are Appointed: The New ICDR International Emergency Rule, Dispute Resolution Journal (2006).

Benjamin Andoh, the Freezing Injunction Today, 31 (2) Business Law Review, (2010).

Benoit Le Bars & Tejas Shiroor, Provisional Measures in Investment Arbitration: Wading Through the Murky Waters of Enforcement, VI (1) Indian Journal of Arbitration Law (2017).

Berger Bernhard, Arbitration Practice: Security for Costs: Trends and Developments in Swiss Arbitral Case Law, 28 (1) ASA Bulletin, (Kluwer Law International 2010).

Berk Demirkol, Ordering Cessation of Court Proceedings to Protect the Integrity of Arbitration Agreements under the Brussels Regime, 65 International and Comparative Quarterly (2016).

Bernardo Cremades Sanz Pastor, Is Exclusion of Concurrent Courts Jurisdiction over Conservatory Measures to Be Introduced Through a Revision of the Convention, 6 (3) Journal of International Arbitration, (Kluwer Law International 1989).

Bernardo M. Cremades, The Need for Conservatory and Preliminary Measures, 27 (5) International Business Law, (1999).

Bernhard Berger, Arbitration Practice: Security for Costs: Trends and Developments in Swiss Arbitral Case Law, 28 (1) ASA Bulletin (2010).

C Chatterjee & Anna Lefcovitch, Guidelines for Enforcement of Worldwide Freezing Orders: An Analysis, 8 (3) Journal of Banking Regulation (2007).

Christian H. Hausmaninger, The ICC Rules for a Pre-arbitral Referee Procedure: A Step Towards Solving the Problem of Provisional Relief in International Commercial Arbitration, 7 ICSID Review for Investment Law Journal, (1992).

C.P. Ojiegbe, From West Tankers to Gazprom: Anti-suit Injunctions, Arbitral Anti-suit Orders and the Brussels I Recast, 11 (2) Journal of Private International Law, (2015).

Caline Mouawad & Elizabeth Silbert, A Guide to Interim Measure in Investor-State Arbitration, 29 (3) Arbitration International, (2013).

Charles N. Brower & W. Micheal Tupman, Court-Ordered Provisional Measures under the New York Convention, 80 American Journal of International Law (1986).

Chetan Phull, U.S. Anti-Suit Injunctions in Support of International Arbitration: Five Questions American Courts Ask, 31 (1) Journal of International Arbitration 31 (Kluwer Law International 2011).

Chiann Bao, International Arbitration in Asia on the Rise: Cause & Effect, 4 (1) The Arbitration Brief (2014).

Choong Lyong Ha, Interim Measures in the United States' Arbitration 19 (3) Journal of Arbitration Studies (2009).

Christer Söderlund, Lis Pendens, Res Judicata and the Issue of Parallel Judicial Proceedings, 22 (4), Journal of International Arbitration (2005).

Christian Hausmaninger, The ICC Rules for a Pre-arbitral Referee Procedure: A Step Towards Solving the Problem of Provisional Relief in International Commercial Arbitration?, 7 ICSID Law Review Foreign Investment Law Journal (1992).

Christopher Huntley, The Scope of Article 17: Interim Measures under the UNCITRAL Model Law, 9 Vindobona Journal of International Commercial Law and Arbitration, (2005).

Chukwudi Paschal Ojiegbe, From West Tankers to Gazprom: Anti-Suit Injunctions, Arbitral Anti-Suit Orders and the Brussels I Recast, 11 (2) Journal of Private International Law (2015).

Critical Analysis of Granting Interim Measures in Arbitration in the Context of Jordan Arbitration Law No. 16. 2018, 10 (4) Beijing Law Review (2019).

Clyde & Co, Arbitration Committee Newsletter, Vol. 22 No. 1 (June 2017).

Alan Redfern, Arbitration and the Courts: Interim Measures of Protection - Is the Tide about to Turn, 30 Texas International Law Journal (1995).

Julian D.M. Lew, Commentary on Interim and Conservatory Measures in ICC Arbitration Cases, 11(1) ICC Ct. Bulletin (2000).

Daniel J. Dorward, The Forum Non Conveniens Doctrine and the Judicial Protection of Multilateral Corporations from Forum Shopping Plaintiffs, 19 (1) University of Pennsylvania Journal of International Economic Law, (1998).

David A.R. Williams, Defining the Role of the Court in Modern International Commercial Arbitration, Asian International Arbitration Journal (Singapore International Arbitration Centre in cooperation with Kluwer Law International 2014).

David Caron, Interim Measures of Protection: Theory and Practice in Light of the Israel-United States Claims Tribunal, 46 The Rabel Journal of Comparative and International Private Law (1986).

David E. Wagoner, Interim Relief in International Arbitration: Enforcement Is a Substantial Problem, 51 (4) Dispute Resolution Journal (1996).

David Howell, Interim Measures of Protection in International Arbitration Proceedings: Towards a New Paradigm, 8 (1) Asian Dispute Review (2006).

David W. Raack, A History of Injunctions in England Before 1700, 61 Indiana Law Journal, 539 (1986).

Decision in Arbitration No. 22 of 1972, 12 ASA Bulletin (1994).

Decision of Geneva Chamber of Commerce of 25 September 1997, 19 ASA Bulletin (2001).

Delphine Constantin, Indian Case Law Review: Anti-Arbitration Injunctions, 2015 International Business Law Journal, (2015).

Denis Gareth Brock and Laura Feldman, Recent Trends in the Conduct of Arbitrations', 30 (2) Journal of International Arbitration, (Kluwer Law International 2013).

Dmytro Galagan & Patricia Živković, If They Finance Your Claim, Will They Pay Me If I Win: Implications of Third Party Funding on Adverse Costs Awards in International Arbitration, European Scientific Journal (April 2015).

Doak Bishop, Combating Arbitral Terrorism: Anti-Arbitration Injunctions Increasingly Threaten to Frustrate the International Arbitral System.

Donald Francis Donovan, Powers of the Arbitrators to Issue Procedural Orders, Including Interim Measures of Protection, and the Obligation of Parties to Abide by Such Orders, 10 (1) ICC Dispute Resolution Bulletin, (1999).

Douglas Laycock, Death of the Irreparable Injury Rule, 103 Harvard Law Review, (1990).

Dr Francis Gurry, The Need for Speed, WIPO Arbitration and Mediation Center Biennial IFCAI Conference, (24 October 1997).

Dunning et al., Using Article 37 of the ICDR International Arbitration Rules: Obtaining Emergency Relief, 62 Dispute Resolution Journal (2007).

Eric A. Schwartz, Interim and Emergency Relief in Arbitration Proceedings, 63 Dispute Resolution Law Journal, (2008).

Emmanuel Gaillard & Philippe Pinsolle, The ICC Pre-arbitral Referee: First Practical Experience, 20 Arbitration International, (2004).

Emmanuel Gaillard, Anti-Suit Injunctions in International Arbitration 1 (IAI Series on International Arbitration No. 2, Juris Publishing Inc. 2005).

Extract from a Procedural Order in ICC Arbitration No. 21 (1989), 12 ASA Bulletin, (1994).

F.A. Mann, The Consequences of an International Wrong in International and National Law, 48 British Yearbook of International Law, (1976-1977).

Fali S. Nariman, India and International Arbitration, 41 George Washington International Law Review, (2009).

Flavia Foz Mange, Anti-Suit Injunctions in International Arbitration: Protecting the Procedure or Pushing the Settlement, 4 (2) Dispute Resolution International Law (2010).

Friedrich K. Juenger, Forum Shopping, Domestic and International, 63 (3) Tulane Law Review (1989).

Gary Soo, Securing Costs in Hong Kong Arbitration, International Arbitration Law Review, Issue 1 (2000).

Geoffrey C. Hazard, Jr. et al., Cases and Materials on Pleading and Procedure, State and Federal (1994).

Geoffrey Fisher & Steven R. Swanson, Anti-Suit Injunctions in Support of International Arbitration, 81 (2) Tulane Law Review (2006).

George A. Bermann, The Use of Anti-Suit Injunctions in International Litigation, 28 Columbia Journal Transnational Law (1990).

Grace Gunah Kim, After the ECJ'S West Tankers: The Clash of Civilizations on the Issue of an Anti-suit Injunction, 12 (2) Cardozo Journal of Conflict Resolution (2011).

Hakeem Seriki, Anti-arbitration Injunctions and the English Courts: Judicial Interference or Judicial Protection? International Arbitration Law Review (2013).

Hans Van Houtte, Ten Reasons Against a Proposal for Ex Parte Interim Measures of Protection in Arbitration, 20 (1) Arbitration International, (2004).

Henry Bernard Eder, The Key Role of State Courts Before the Commencement of Arbitral Proceedings: Referral to Arbitration and Provisional and Conservatory

Measures, 18 Asian Dispute Review, (Hong Kong International Arbitration Centre 2016).

Ibrahim F.I. Shihata & Antonio R. Parra, The Experience of the International Centre for Settlement of Investment Disputes, 14 ICSID Review for Investment Law Journal, (1999).

Jean E. Kalicki, Security for Costs in International Arbitration, 3 Transnational Dispute Management (2006).

James E. Castello, Arbitral Ex Parte Interim Relief, 58 (3) Dispute Resolution Journal, (2003).

James J Spigelman AC, Freezing Orders in International Commercial Litigation, 22 Singapore Academy Law Journal (2010).

Jamie Maples & Tim Goldfarb, Anti-Suit Injunctions: Expanding Protection for Arbitration under English Law, 7 (2) Dispute Resolution International, (2013).

Jan Paulsson, A Better Mousetrap: 1990 ICC Rules for a Pre-Arbitral Referee Procedure, 18 International Business Law Review, (1990).

Jan Schaefer, New English, German and Hong Kong Law Compared, 2.2 Elec. J. Comp. L. (1998).

Jarrod Wong, The Issuance of Interim Measures in International Disputes: A Proposal Requiring a Reasonable Possibility of Success on the Underlying Merits, 33(3), Georgia Journal of International and Comparative Law, (2005).

Jean Kalicki, Security for Costs in International Arbitration, 1 Transnational Dispute Management (2006).

Jean-Paul Beraudo, Recognition and Enforcement of Interim Measures of Protection Ordered by Arbitral Tribunals, 22 (3) Journal of International Arbitration (2005).

Jennifer L. Gorskie, US Courts and the Anti-Arbitration Injunction, 28 (2) Arbitration International, (2012).

Joanna Simoes, Interim Measures Issued by National Courts in Aid of International Arbitration: A Brazilian Perspective, Warwick Student Law Review (2011).

John Fellas, Anti-Suit Injunctions: Litigating Across Borders, 3 Transnational Dispute Management, (2006).

John G. Merrills, Interim Measures of Protection in the Recent Jurisprudence of the International Court of Justice, 44 International and Comparative Law Quarterly (1995).

John Gaffney, Non-Party Autonomy: Displacing the Negative Effect of the Principle of 'Competence-Competence' in England?, 29 (1) Journal of International Arbitration, (2012).

Jonas von Goeler, Third-Party Funding in International Arbitration and Its Impact on Procedure, 35 International Arbitration Law Library, (Kluwer Law International 2016).

Joseph Lee, Court-Subsidiarity and Interim Measures in Commercial Arbitration: A Comparative Study of UK, 6 (2) Singapore and Taiwan, Contemporary Asia Arbitration Journal (2013).

Julian D.M. Lew, Commentary on Interim and Conservatory Measures in ICC Arbitration Cases, 11(1) ICC Ct. Bulletin (2000).

Julian D. M. Lew, Commentary on Interim Measures in ICC Arbitration Cases, 11(1) ICC Int'l Ct Arbitration Bulletin 28 (2000).

Julian DM Lew, Does National Court Involvement Undermine the International Arbitration Process?, 24 (3) American University International Law Review (2009).

K Puharic, Developments in Slovenian Arbitration Law, 16 Croatian Arbitration Yearbook 244 (2009).

K.P. Berger, International Economic Arbitration, 9 Studies in Transnational Economic Law, (Kluwer Law and Taxation Publishers 1993).

K.R. Avinash, A Comparative Analysis of the Law Relating to the Anti-Arbitration Injunction, Bharti Law Review (2014).

Kartikey Mahajan, Making the Case for Post-award Interim Relief for Award: Debtor, 3 (2) Indian Journal of Arbitration Law (2014).

Katherine Lynch, Security for Costs in Domestic and International Arbitration in England and Hong Kong, 12 (2) Journal of International Arbitration, (Kluwer Law International 1995).

Kathryn E. Vertigan, Foreign Anti-Suit Injunctions: Taking a Lesson from the Act of State Doctrine, 76 George Washington Law Review (2007).

Kern Alexander, The Mareva Injunction and Anton Piller Order: The Nuclear Weapons of English Commercial Litigation, 11 (3) Florida Journal of International Law (1997).

L.K. Cheong, et al., Interim Measures in Aid of Foreign Arbitrations, Time for the Deus ex Machina?, 21 Singapore Academy Law Journal (2009).

Las Laycock, The Death of the Irreparable Injury Rule, 103 Harvard Law Review (1990).

Lemenez & Quigley, The ICDR's Emergency Arbitrator Procedure in Action, Part I: A Look at the Empirical Data, 63 Dispute Resolution Law Journal, (2008).

Locknie Hsu, Orders for Security for Costs and International Arbitration in Singapore, 3 (4) International Arbitration Law Review, (2000).

Lord Justice Mustill, A New Arbitration Act for the United Kingdom?: The Response of the Departmental Advisory Committee to the UNCITRAL Model Law, 6 (1) Arbitration, (1990).

Lye Kah Cheong & Yeo Chuan Tat, et al., Interim Measures in Aid of Foreign Arbitrations, Time for the Deus ex Machina?, 21 Singapore Academy Law Journal, (2009).

Markus Wirth, Interim or Preventive Measures in Support of International Arbitration in Switzerland, ASA Bulletin (2000).

M. I. M. Aboul-Enein, Issuing Interim Relief Measures in International Arbitration in the Arab States, 3 Journal of World Investment (2002).

Michael A. Calvo, The New ICC Rules of Arbitration: Substantial and Procedural Changes, 14(4) Journal of International Arbitration (1997).

Mahadev Mohan & Eu-Yen Tay, The New International Arbitration (Amendment) Bill: A Broader Framework for Interim Relief or Just a Tune-Up, 22 Singapore Academy Law Journal, (2010).

Marc Blessing, State Arbitrations: Predictably Unpredictable Solutions? 22 (6) Journal of International Arbitration, (Kluwer Law International 2005).

Marco Stacher, You Don't Want to Go There: Anti-Suit Injunctions in International Commercial Arbitration, 23 ASA Bulletin, (Kluwer Law International 2005).

Marinanne Roth, Interim Measures, 2012 (2) Journal of Dispute Resolution (2012).

Markus Wirth, Interim or Preventive Measures in Support of International Arbitration in Switzerland, 18 ASA Bulletin, (2000).

Michael F. Hoellering, Interim Measures and Arbitration: The Situation in the United States, 46 (2) Arbitration Journal, (1991).

Michael F. Hoellering, Interim Relief in Aid of International Commercial Arbitration, 1 Wisconsin International Law Journal 2 (1984) reprinted in Arbitration & the Law (1984).

Michael Kerr, Concord and Conflict in International Arbitration, 13 Arbitration International (1997).

Michael Pryles, Interlocutory Orders and Convention Awards: The Case of Resort Condominiums v. Bolwell, 10 Arbitration International, (1994).

Michael Reisman & Heide Iravani, The Changing Relation of National Courts and International Commercial Arbitration, 21 American Review of International Arbitration (2010).

Mika Savola, Interim Measures and Emergency Arbitrators Proceedings, 23 Croatian Arbitration Yearbook 86 (2016).

Milica Arsic, Anti-Suit Injunctions in International Arbitration, Harmonious Journal of Legal and Social Studies in South East Europe (2016).

Nadia Darwazeh & Adrien Leleu, Disclosure and Security for Costs or How to Address Imbalances Created by Third-Party Funding, 33 (2) Journal of International Arbitration (2016).

Nakul Dewan, Interim Measures in Arbitration: A Comparative Analysis of Indian and English Arbitration Act, International Business Law Journal (2003).

Nathalie Voser, Interim Relief in International Arbitration: The Tendency Towards a More Business-Oriented Approach, 1 (2) Dispute Resolution International (2007).

Neil Kaplan, Arbitration in Asia: Developments and Crises, Part 2, 19 Journal of International Arbitration (2002).

Nelson Goh, Court-Ordered Interim Relief Against States in Aid of Arbitration: Sovereign Immunity, Waiver and Comity, in Maxi Scherer (ed.), 34 (4) Journal of International Arbitration, (Kluwer Law International 2017).

Nicholas Poon, The Use and Abuse of Anti-Arbitration Injunctions: A Way Forward for Singapore, 25 Singapore Academy of Law Journal (2013).

Noah Rubins, In God We Trust, All Others Pay Cash: Security for Costs in International Commercial Arbitration, 11 American Review of International Arbitration (2000).

Nudrat B. Majeed, Commentary on the Hubco Judgment, 16 Arbitration International, (2000).

Olga Vishnevskaya, Anti-Suit Injunctions from Arbitral Tribunals in International Commercial Arbitration: A Necessary Evil? 32 (2) Journal of International Arbitration (Kluwer Law International 2015).

Otto Sandrock, The Cautio Judicatum Solvi in Arbitration Proceedings or the Duty of an Alien Claimant to Provide Security for the Costs of the Defendant, 14 Journal of International Arbitration, (Kluwer Law International 1997).

Patricia Shaughnessy, Pre-arbitral Urgent Relief: The New SCC Emergency Arbitrator Rules, 27 Journal of International Arbitration (2010).

Paul F. Kirgis, Judicial Review and the Limits of Arbitral Authority: Lessons from the Law of Contract, 81 St. Johns Law Review 99 (2007).

Paul Michell, Interim Measure in Canadian Commercial Arbitration, 32 Advoc. Quarterly, (2007).

Peter Fitzpatrick, Security for Costs under the Arbitration Act, 1996, International Arbitration Law Review, (1998).

Philip Jeyaretnam, The Granting of Mareva Injunction in Support of Foreign Court Proceedings, 28 Singapore Academy Law Journal (2016).

Philippe Pinsolle, Third Party Funding and Security for Costs, Journal for International Arbitration, (2013).

Pratibha M. Singh & Devashish Krishnan, The Indian 1996 Arbitration Act: Solutions for a Current Dilemma, 18 Journal of International Arbitration (2001).

Pratyush Panjwan & Harshad Pathak, Assimilating the Negative Effect of Kompetenz-Kompetenz in India: Need to Revisit the Question of Judicial Intervention?, 2 (2), Indian Journal of Arbitration Law (2014).

R. A. Schutze, The Precedential Effect of Arbitration Decisions, 11 (3) Journal of International Arbitration (1994).

Rahim Moloo, Arbitrators Granting Anti-suit Orders: When Should They and on What Authority?, 26 Journal of International Arbitration, (2009).

Rajendra Barot & Sonali Mathur, Laying Old ghosts to Rest, or Not?: The 'Section 9' Enigma Continues ..., 5 (1), Indian Journal of Arbitration Law, (2016).

Richard W. Naimark & Stephanie E. Keer, Analysis of UNCITRAL Questionnaires on Interim Relief, 16 (3) Mealey's IAR, (2001).

Robert Briner, Interim Awards, 25 (4) International Business Lawyer (1997).

Rolf Trittmann, When Should Arbitrators Issue Interim or Partial Awards and or Procedural Orders?, 20 (3) Journal for International Arbitration, (Kluwer Law International, 2003).

Ronald J. Bettauer, India and International Arbitration: The Dabhol Experience, 381 George Washington International Law Review 41 (2009).

Ronald Wong, Interim Relief in Aid of International Commercial Arbitration: A Critique on the International Arbitration Act, 24 Singapore Academy of Law Journal (2012).

Rukmini Das & Anisha Keyal, Judicial Intervention in International Arbitration, 2 NUJS Law Review (2009).

Stacie I. Strong, Anti-Arbitration Injunctions in Cases Involving Investor-State Arbitration: British Caribbean Bank Ltd. v. the Government of Belize, 15 (1-2) Journal of World Investment Trade (2014).

S. I. Strong, Anti-Suit Injunctions in Judicial and Arbitral Procedures in the United States, 66 American Society of Comparative Law 172-173 (Oxford University Press 2018).

S.M. Ferguson, Interim Measures of Protection in International Commercial Arbitration: Problems, Proposed Solutions, and Anticipated Results, 12 International Trade Law Journal (2003).

S.R. Subramanian, Anti-Arbitration Injunctions and Their Relief Compatibility with the New York Convention and the Indian Law of Arbitration: Future Directions for Indian Law And Policy, Arbitration International, (Oxford University Press 2018).

Saarthak Jain & Kashish Makkar, The Dilution of Interim Anti-Arbitration Injunctions in Devi Resources: Pro-enforcement Approach Gone too Far?, 36(2) Arbitration International (2020).

Sarthak Malhotra & Sujoy Sur, Standards Applicable to Interim Reliefs in India: A Comprehensive Analytical Investigation, 5 (1) Indian Journal of Arbitration Law (2016).

Sharad Bansal & Divyanshu Agarwal, Are Anti-Arbitration Injunctions A Malaise? An Analysis in the Context of Indian Law, 31 Arbitration International (2015).

Sigvard Jarvin, Choosing the Place of Arbitration: Where Do We Stand?, 16 International Business Law (1988).

Steven R. Swanson, Anti-Suit Injunctions in Support of International Arbitration, 81 Tulane Law Review (2006).

Steven R. Swanson, The Vexatiousness of a Vexation Rule: International Comity and Anti-Suit Injunctions, 30 (1) George Washington. Journal of International Law & Economics (1996).

Sumeet Kachwaha, The Arbitration Law of India a Critical Analysis, Asian International Arbitration Journal 105-126 (2005).

Sumit Rai, Proposed Amendments to the Indian Arbitration Act: A Fraction of the Whole?, 3 Journal of International Dispute Settlement (2011).

Sundaresh Menon & Elaine Chao, Reforming the Model Law Provisions on Interim Measures of Protection, 2 (1) Asian International Arbitration Journal, (Kluwer Law International 2006).

Thomas E Carbonneau, 'Arbitracide': The Story of Anti-Arbitration Sentiment in the US Congress, 18 American Review of International Arbitration (2007).

Tomas Kennedy-Grant, Interim Measures under the UNCITRAL Model Law on International Commercial Arbitration: The Impact of the 2006 Amendments, 10 (1) Asian International Arbitration Journal, (2014).

Tijana Kojovic, Court Enforcement of Arbitral Decisions on Provisional Relief-How Is Provisional?, 18(5) Journal of International Arbitration, (2001).

Trevor Hartley, Comity and the Use of Anti-Suit Injunctions in International Litigation, 35 American Journal of Comparative Law (1987).

UK Departmental Advisory Committee. Lord Justice Mustill, A New Arbitration Act for the United Kingdom?: The Response of the Departmental Advisory Committee to the UNCITRAL Model Law, 6 (1) Arbitration International, (1990).

Niranjan Venkatesan & Shantanu Narvane, Bhatia International Rightly Overruled: The Consequences of Three Errors in BALCO, 9 Supreme Court Cases Journal (2012).

V.V. Veeder, The Need for Cross-border Enforcement of Interim Measures Ordered by a State Court In Support of the International Arbitral Process, in Albert Jan Van den Berg (ed.), New Horizons in International Commercial Arbitration and Beyond.

Vidhu Gupta, Stretching the Limits of Statutory Interpretation: Critical Review of Bhatia International v. Bulk Trading, 5 NALSAR Student Law Review (2010).

Von Segesser, Vorsorgliche Massnahmen im Internationalen Schiedsprozess, 25 ASA Bulletin (2007).

Weixia Gu, Security for Costs in International Commercial Arbitration, 22 (3) Journal of International Arbitration (2005).

Wiliam Laurence Craig, William Park & John Paulson, International Chamber of Commerce Arbitration (3rd ed. Oceana Publications, Inc 1998).

William Kirtley & Koralie Wietrzykowski, Should an Arbitral Tribunal Order Security for Costs When an Impecunious Claimant Is Relying upon Third-Party Funding, 30 (1) Journal of International Arbitration, (Kluwer Law International 2013).

William W. Park, The Arbitrator's Jurisdiction to Determine Jurisdiction, I. Introduction: The Limits of Language, in Albert Jan Van den Berg (ed.), International Arbitration 2006: Back to Basics?, 13 ICCA Congress Series.

Yu Prytyka, Interim Measures in International Commercial Arbitration, 2011 (2) Law of Ukraine Legal Journal (2011).

Yves Derains, Arbitral Ex Parte Interim Relief: The View Against, 58 OCT Dispute Resolution Journal, (2003).

Yves Derains, The View Against Arbitral Ex Parte Interim Relief: Confirmation that the Best May Be the Enemy of the Good, 58 (3) Dispute Resolution Journal, (2003).

Working Group Reports

Explanatory Note by the UNCITRAL Secretariat on the 1985 Model Law on International Commercial Arbitration as amended in 2006 (20 September 2007), available at: https://www.uncitral.org/pdf/english/texts/arbitration/ml-arb/MLARB-explanatoryNote20-9-07.pdf

Note by the Secretariat in UNCITRAL Working Group of its Forty-Third Session, 2005, A/CN.9/WG.II/WP.138, available at: https://undocs.org/en/A/CN.9/WG.II/WP.138.

Report of Secretary General on Analytical Commentary on Draft Text of A Model Law on International Commercial Arbitration, in its Eighteenth Session, (1985), UN Doc A/CN.9/264, available at: https://undocs.org/en/A/CN.9/264.

Report of the Secretary General for Settlement of Commercial Disputes, in its Thirty Second Report, 2000, A/CN.9/WG.II/WP.108, available at: https://undocs.org/en/A/CN.9/WG.II/WP.108.

Report of the Secretary General for Settlement of Commercial Disputes, in its Thirty-Fifth Session, 2000, A/CN.9/WG.II/WP.110, available at: https://undocs.org/en/A/CN.9/WG.II/WP.110.

Report of UNCITRAL Working Group on the work of its Fortieth Session, 2004, A/CN.9/547, available at: https://undocs.org/en/A/CN.9/547.

Report of UNCITRAL Working Group on the work of its Forty-First Session, 2004, A/CN.9/569, available at: https://undocs.org/en/A/CN.9/569.

Report of UNCITRAL Working Group on the work of its Forty Second Session, 2005, A/CN.9/573, available at: https://undocs.org/en/A/CN.9/573.

Report of UNCITRAL Working Group on the work of its Forty-Seventh Session, 2007, A/CN.9/641, available at: https://undocs.org/en/A/CN.9/641.

Report of UNCITRAL Working Group on the work of its Forty-Third Session, 2005, A/CN.9/589, available at: https://undocs.org/en/A/CN.9/589.

Report of UNCITRAL Working Group on the work of its Sixth Session, 1983, A/CN.9/245, available at: https://undocs.org/en/A/CN.9/245.

Report of UNCITRAL Working Group on the work of its Thirty-Ninth Session, 2003, A/CN.9/545, available at: https://undocs.org/en/A/CN.9/545.

Report of UNCITRAL Working Group on the work of its Thirty Second Session, June 2000, A/CN.9/468, available at: https://undocs.org/en/A/CN.9/468.

Report of UNCITRAL Working Group on the work of its Thirty-Seventh Session, 2002, A/CN.9/23, available at: https://undocs.org/en/A/CN.9/523.

Report of UNCITRAL Working Group on the work of its Thirty-Sixth Session, 2002, A/CN.9/508, available at: https://undocs.org/en/A/CN.9/508.

Report of UNCITRAL Working Group on the work of its Thirty-Eighth session, 2003, A/CN.9/524, available at: https://undocs.org/en/A/CN.9/524.

Report of UNCITRAL Working Group on the work of its Thirty-Fourth Session, 2001, A/CN.9/487, available at: https://undocs.org/en/A/CN.9/487.

Reports

Government of India, Ministry of Law & Justice, Cabinet Approves the Arbitration and Conciliation (Amendment) Bill, 2018, available at: http://pib.nic.in/newsite/PrintRelease.aspx?relid=177128.

Government of India, Ministry of Law and Justice: Proposed Amendments to the Arbitration & Conciliation Act, 1996: A Consultation Paper, available at: https://www.legallyindia.com/images/stories/docs/Arbitration-Act-LawMin-ConsultationPaper-on-Arb-Act-April2010-1.pdf.

Justice B. N. Srikrishna, Report of the High-Level Committee to Review the Institutionalisation of Arbitration Mechanism in India, (30 July 2017), 68, available at: http://legalaffairs.gov.in/sites/default/files/Report-HLC.pdf.

Justice Saraf Committee Report on Arbitration, 29 January 2005.

Krishna Sarma, Momota Oinam & Angshuman Kaushik, *Development and Practice of Arbitration in India: Has It Evolved as an Effective Legal Institution*, CDDRL Working Papers, Number 103 (October 2009), http://docplayer.net/51441019-Cddrl-working-papers-development-and-practice-of-arbitration-in-india-has-it-evolved-as-an-effective-legal-institution-number-103-october-2009.html.

Law Commission of India, 246th Report of the Commission on Amendment to the Arbitration and Conciliation Act, 1996, available at: http://lawcommissionofindia.nic.in/reports/report246.pdf.

Law Commission of India, Report No. 176th – Arbitration and Conciliation (Amendment) Bill, 2001, (12 September 2001), available at: http://lawcommissionofindia.nic.in/arb.pdf.

Law Commission of India, Report No. 194 – Verification of Stamp Duties and Registration of Arbitral Awards, (7 June 2005) available at: https://lawcommissionofindia.nic.in/reports/report194.pdf.

Law Commission of India, Report No. 76 – Arbitration Act, 1940, (9 November 1978), available at: http://lawcommissionofindia.nic.in/51-100/Report76.pdf.

Queen Mary University of London and White and Case, 2012 International Arbitration Survey: Current and Preferred Practices in the Arbitral Process, available at: http://www.arbitration.qmul.ac.uk/media/arbitration/docs/2012_International_Arbitration_Survey.pdf.

Report of Secretary General on Analytical Commentary on Draft Text of A Model Law on International Commercial Arbitration, in its Eighteenth Session, (1985), UN Doc A/CN.9/264, available at: https://undocs.org/en/A/CN.9/264.

Report of the Expert Committee on Specific Relief Act, 1963, Government of India, May 2016, 11.3.1, available at http://practicalacademic.blogspot.com/2018/05/download-expert-committee-report-on.html.

Report of the ICCA-Queen Mary Task Force on Third-Party Funding in International Arbitration, 172 (April 2018), available at, https://www.arbitration-icca.org/media/10/40280243154551/icca_reports_4_tpf_final_for_print_5_april.pdf.

Report of the Secretary General for Settlement of Commercial Disputes, in its Thirty Second Report, 2000, A/CN.9/WG.II/WP.108, available at: https://undocs.org/en/A/CN.9/WG.II/WP.108.

Resolution adopted on the report of the third committee (18 November 1995), U.N. Doc A/RES/40/17, available at: https://undocs.org/en/A/RES/40/17.

Resolution adopted by General Assembly in its Sixty-First Session (18 December 2006), G.A. Res. 61/33, pmbl., U.N. Doc. A/RES/61/33, available at: https://research.un.org/en/docs/ga/quick/regular/61.

Resolution adopted on the report of the third committee (18 November 1995), U.N. Doc A/RES/40/17, available at: https://undocs.org/en/A/RES/40/17.

Singapore Parliamentary Debates, Official Report (31 October 1994) Vol. 63 at cols 625-626 (Associate Professor Ho Peng Kee, Parliamentary Secretary to the Minister for Law).

Blogs/Online Resources

Ajar Rab & Ankit Singh, *BGS V. NHPC: Implications Beyond the 'Seat' & 'Venue' Debate*, (5 March 2020), available at:http://rsrr.in/2020/03/05/bgs-v-nhpc-implications-beyond-the-seat-venue-debate/.

Ajar Rab, *Contract Law and Specific Relief: The 'Un-common' Indian Law*, (25 November 2019), available at: https://ijiel.in/blog/f/contract-law-and-specific-relief-the-%E2%80%98un-common%E2%80%99-indian-law?blogcategory=International+Commercial+Law.

Albert Jan Van Den Berg, *The New York Convention, 1958: An Overview*, available at:https://cdn.arbitration-icca.org/s3fs-public/document/media_document/media012125884227980new_york_convention_of_1958_overview.pdf.

Alessandro Villani & Manuela Caccialanza, *Interim Relief Through Emergency Arbitration: An Upcoming Goal or Still an Illusion?*, (14 July 2017), available at:

http://arbitrationblog.kluwerarbitration.com/2017/07/14/interim-relief-emergency-arbitration-upcoming-goal-still-illusion/.

Alexis Mourre, *French Courts Firmly Reject Anti-Arbitration Injunctions*, (6 May 2010), available at: http://arbitrationblog.kluwerarbitration.com/2010/05/06/french-courts-firmly-reject-anti-arbitration-injunctions/?doing_wp_cron = 1591465914.9855411052703857421875.

Andre de A Cavalcanti Abbud & Gustavo Santos Kulesza, *Interim Measures and Anti-Arbitration Injunctions in Brazil*, (4 August 2014), available at: http://kluwerarbitrationblog.com/2014/08/04/interim-measures-and-anti-arbitration-injunctions-in-brazil/.

Andrew Cannon, *An Anti-Suit Injunction to Protect a Non-existent Arbitration*, (30 June 2011), available at: http://arbitrationblog.kluwerarbitration.com/2011/06/30/anti-suit-injunction/.

Ankit Singh, *Seat and Venue: Why Brahmani River Is Good Law?*, (3 October 2019), available at: https://indiacorplaw.in/2019/10/seat-venue-brahmani-river-good-law.html.

Badri Srinivasan, *Scope of Jurisdiction to Award Interim Measures vis-à-vis Third Parties (Part VIII)*, (15 November 2010), available at: http://practicalacademic.blogspot.com/2010/11/scope-of-jurisdiction-to-award-interim_15.html.

Ben Giaretta, Akshay Kishore & Ashurst Singapore, *Anti-arbitration Injunctions: Mixed Signals from India*, (1 January 2015), available at: https://www.ashurst.com/en/news-and-insights/legal-updates/anti-arbitration-injunctions-mixed-signals-fromindia/.

Benson Lim & Adriana Uson, *Relooking at Consent in Arbitration*, (12 February 2019), available at: http://arbitrationblog.kluwerarbitration.com/2019/02/12/relooking-at-consent-in-arbitration/?doing_wp_cron = 1591432623.898384094238281250000#: ~ :text = International%20treaties%20and%20national%20laws,is%20an%20agreement%20to%20arbitrate.

Bhavana Sunder, Ashish Kabra & Vyapak Desai, *Contract Enforcement Finally Sees Relief*, (27 July 2018), available at: http://www.nishithdesai.com/information/research-and-articles/nda-hotline/nda-hotline-single-view/article/contract-enforcement-finally-sees-relief-amendments-to-the-specific-relief-act.html?no_cache = 1&cHash = 8dafbcfeca599325b1443cdbec7acd25.

Chrysanthi Markaki, *Anti-suit v. Anti-arbitration Injunctions in International Commercial Arbitration: Which One Prevails in European Union, UK and Greece? Choosing the Most 'Proper' One* 14, (2018), available at: https://repository.ihu.edu.grxmlui/bitstream/handle/11544/29126/c.markaki_llm_16-02-2018.pdf?sequence = 2.

Damian Honey & Martina Kelly, *English Court Support for Arbitration: Recent Development*, (February 2018), available at: https://www.hfw.com/English-Court-Support-for-Arbitration-Recent-Developments-February-2018.

David Wilson, *Emergency Arbitrator Rules among Four Major Arbitral Institutions: Both Alike and Different*, available at: https://www.expertguides.com/articles/emergency-arbitrator-rules-among-four-major-arbitral-institutions-both-alike-and-different/aralfynx.

Doak Bishop, *Combating Arbitral Terrorism: Anti-Arbitration Injunctions Increasingly Threaten to Frustrate the International Arbitral System*, available at: https://www.kslaw.com/library/pdf/bishop7.pdf.

Duncan Bagshaw, *Stay No More: English Commercial Court Reviews Section 9 Test (Again)*, (10 August 2018), available at: https://www.shlegal.com/insights/stay-no-more-english-commercial-court-reviews-section-9-test-(again).

Economic Law Practice, *Arbitration in India: Curated View*, (2019), available at: https://elplaw.in/wp-content/uploads/2019/05/Arbitration-in-India-curated-views.pdf.

Elizabeth Kantor, *Emergency Arbitration of Construction Disputes: Choose Wisely or End Up Spoilt for Choice*, (15 February 2017), available at:http://arbitrationblog.kluwerarbitration.com/2017/02/15/emergency-arbitration-construction-disputes-choose-wisely-end-spoilt-choice.

Emmanuel Kaufman, *An Argentine Court Orders a Corporation Not to Initiate Arbitration Before ICSID: Should Investors Be Worried?*, (5 June 2019), available at:http://arbitrationblog.kluwerarbitration.com/2019/06/05/an-argentine-court-orders-a-corporation-not-to-initiate-arbitration-before-icsid-should-investors-be-worried/?doing_wp_cron=1589866347.6500990390777587890625.

Gary Born, *Interpreting Section 9(1) of the Arbitration Act 1996: Lombard v GATX*, (24 May 2012), available at: http://arbitrationblog.kluwerarbitration.com/2012/05/24/interpreting-section-91-of-the-arbitration-act-1996-lombard-v-gatx/?doing_wp_cron=1590838778.7553598880767822265625.

Gary Born, *Irish High Court on Full Versus Prima Facie Judicial Consideration of Whether an Arbitration Agreement Exists*, (13 December 2010), available at: http://arbitrationblog.kluwerarbitration.com/2010/12/13/irish-high-court-on-full-versus-prima-facie-judicial-consideration-of-whether-an-arbitration-agreement-exists/?doing_wp_cron=1590838569.4271209239959716796875 .

Georgios Martsekis, *Everyone Should Do His Own or Everyone Should Have His Own? An Analysis on the Requirements of Conferral of the Arbitral Tribunal's Jurisdiction*, (30 May 2020), available at: http://arbitrationblog.kluwerarbitration.com/2020/05/30/everyone-should-do-his-own-or-everyone-should-have-his-own-an-analysis-on-the-requirements-of-conferral-of-the-arbitral-tribunals-jurisdiction/?doing_wp_cron=1591467627.8653640747070312500000.

Gracious Timothy, *Recognition and Enforcement of Interim Measures under the Indian Arbitration Amendment Act of 2015*, available at: https://papers.ssrn.com/sol3/papers.cfm?abstract_id=3045678.

It would Take Delhi HC 466 Yrs to Clear Backlog: CJ, (13 February 2009), available at: http://archive.indianexpress.com/news/it-would-take-delhi-hc-466-yrs-to-clear-backlog-cj/423127/2.

Justin Williams, Hamish Lal & Richard Hornshaw, *Arbitration Procedures and Practice in the UK (England and Wales): Overview*, available at: https://uk.practicallaw.thomsonreuters.com/4-502-1378?transitionType=Default&contextData=(sc.Default)&firstPage=true&bhcp=1.

Leon Chung, Elizabeth Macknay & Elizabeth Poulos, *Arbitration Procedures and Practice in Australia: Overview*, available at: https://uk.practicallaw. thomsonreuters.com/1-618-2164?transitionType = Default&contextData = (sc.Default)&firstPage = true&bhcp = 1.

Lomesh K Nidumuri, *Critical Analysis of the Arbitration and Conciliation (Amendment) Act, 2015*, (25 May 2016), available at: https://www.mondaq.com/india/arbitration-dispute-resolution/494184/critical-analysis-of-the-arbitration-and-conciliation-amendment-act-2015.

Margaret Moses, *Barring the Courthouse Door? Anti-Suit Injunctions in International Arbitration*, (14 November 2011), available at: http://arbitrationblog.kluwerarbitration.com/2011/11/14/barring-the-courthouse-door-anti-suit-injunctions-in-international-arbitration/.

Marike Paulsson, *Chapter 2: The New York Convention as an Instrument*, available at: https://www.arbitration-icca.org/media/9/87217006027030/paulsson_chapter_2.pdf

Martin Valasek & Jenna Anne de Jong, *Enforceability of Interim Measures and Emergency Arbitrator Decisions*, (5 July 2018), available at: https://www.lexology.com/library/detail.aspx?g = 15f02d64-cc66-445c-9b0c-65f9440c0c4a.

Maxi Scherer, Dharshini Prasad & Dina Prokic, *The Principle of Equal Treatment in International Arbitration*, (3 September 2018), available at:https://papers.ssrn.com/sol3/papers.cfm?abstract_id = 3377237.

Michael McIlwrath, *Anti-Arbitration: An International Pledge to Arbitrate Commercial Disputes?*, (29 March 2011), available at: http://arbitrationblog.kluwerarbitration.com/2011/03/29/anti-arbitration-an-international-pledge-to-arbitrate-commercial-disputes/?doing_wp_cron = 1590838546.9601058959960937500000.

Michelle Grando, *The Coming of Age of Interim Relief in International Arbitration: A Report from the 28th Annual ITA Workshop*, (20 July 2016), available at: http://arbitrationblog.kluwerarbitration.com/2016/07/20/the-coming-of-age-of-interim-relief-in international-arbitration-a-report-from-the-28th-annual-ita-workshop/.

Mihir Naniwadekar, *On 'Prima Facie' Cases and 'Originality': Part I*, (8 November 2008), available at: https://spicyip.com/2008/11/on-prima-facie-cases-and-originality.html.

Mikal Brondmo & Jhonny Johansen, et al., *Norway: International Arbitration 2019*, (8 August 2019), available at: https://practiceguides.chambers.com/practice-guides/international-arbitration-2019/norway

Mohit Mahla, *Indian Arbitration Cart: Moving Forward or Backward*, (6 June 2015), available at: http://arbitrationblog.kluwerarbitration.com/2015/06/06/indian-arbitration-cart-moving-forward-or-backward/.

Mostafa A Hagras, *The Egyptian Arbitration Law and Anti-Arbitration Injunctions due to Expiry the Time Limit for the Final Award: Case Study*, available at: https://youngicca-blog.com/the-egyptian-arbitration-law-and-anti-arbitration-injunctions-due-to-expiry-the-time-limit-for-the-final-award-case-study/.

Nick Peacock, Donny Surtani & Kritika Venugopal, *The Dispute Resolution and Arbitration Landscape in India*, (May 2017), available at:https://www. herbe rtsmithfreehills.com/latest-thinking/arbitration-in-india-dispute-resolution-in-the-worlds-largest-democracy.

Nilima Bhadbhade, *Specific Performance of Contracts: The Tests of Inadequacy and Effective Enforcement* (2014), c.f. Report of the Expert Committee on Specific Relief Act, 1963, Government of India, (26 May 2016), available at: http://practicalacademic.blogspot.com/2018/05/download-expert-committee-report-on.html.

Paata Simsive, *Indirect Enforceability of Emergency Arbitrator's Orders*, (15 April 2015), available at: http://arbitrationblog.kluwerarbitration.com/2015/04/15/indirect-enforceability-of-emergency-arbitrators-orders/.

Purvi Kaya, *The Seat vs Venue Conundrum in Cases of Unclear Arbitration Clauses: Hardy and Antrix Bad in Law?*, (14 January 2020), available at: https://indiacorplaw.in/2020/01/seat-vs-venue-conundrum-cases-unclear-arbitration-clauses-hardy-antrix-bad-law.html.

Rachel Thomas, *How Closely Linked Are the UNCITRAL Model Law on International Commercial Arbitration and Indian Arbitration Regulations?*, available at: https://viamediationcentre.org/readnews/NDY = /How-closely-linked-are-the-UNCITRAL-Model-Law-on-International-Commercial-Arbitration-and-Indian-Arbitration-Regulations.

Rishab Gupta & Anokan Ghosh, *Choice Between Interim Relief from Indian Courts and Emergency Arbitrator* (10 May 2017), available at: http://arbitrationblog.kluwerarbitration.com/2017/05/10/choice-between-interim-relief-from-indian-courts-and-emergency-arbitrator/.

Rohan Deshpande, *Habitual Residence under the Indian Arbitration Regime*, (11 June 2020), available at: https://indiacorplaw.in/2020/06/habitual-residence-under-the-indian-arbitration-regime.html.

Saber Habibi Savadkouhi, *International Commercial Arbitration: A Legal Analysis with Special Reference to the Contemporary Issues under Indian Law*, (2014), available at: https://shodhganga.inflibnet.ac.in/bitstream/10603/110130/11/11_chapter%201.pdf.

Sadaff Habib, *2018 In Review: A Tug of War for International Arbitration in Africa*, (17 January 2019), available at: http://arbitrationblog.kluwerarbitration.com/2019/01/17/2018-in-review-a-tug-of-war-for-international-arbitration-in-africa/.

Sean Hardy, Pinsent Masons MPillay & Raman Kaur, *Anti-Suit Injunctions in Favour of Arbitration: a Permanent Fixture in Singapore?*, available at: https://siarb.org.sg/resources/120-articles/283-anti-suit-injunctions-in-favour-of-arbitration-a-permanent-fixture-in-singapore.

Sharad Bansal, *The Standard of Review of Interim Orders of an Arbitral Tribunal Seated in India: A Significant Step Towards Certainty*, (21 November 2018), available at: http://arbitrationblog.kluwerarbitration.com/2018/11/21/the-standard-of-review-of-interim-orders-of-an-arbitral-tribunal-seated-in-india-a-significant-step-towards-certainty/.

Shivam Jasra, *Power of Courts and Arbitral Tribunals to Issue Interim Measures in India: A Critical Analysis of 2015 Amendment*, (15 December 2019), available at:https://www.latestlaws.com/articles/power-of-courts-and-arbitral-tribunals-to-issue-interim-measures-in-india-a-critical-analysis-of-2015-amendment-by-shivam-jasra/.

Singhania and Partners, *India: Emergency Arbitration in India: Concept and Beginning*, available at: https://www.mondaq.com/advicecentre/content/3958/Emergency-Arbitration-In-India-Concept-And-Beginning.

The London Court of International Arbitration, Facts and Figures, Costs and Duration: 2013-2016, available at: http://www.lcia.org/media/download.aspx?MediaId=596.

Vivek Krishnani, *Determination of Supervisory Jurisdiction by the Indian Supreme Court: Venue in the Driver's 'Seat'?*, (14 October 2019), available at:https://indiacorplaw.in/2019/10/determination-supervisory-jurisdiction-indian-supreme-court-venue-drivers-seat.html.

Yaroslav Petrov, *JKX vs. Ukraine: An Update on the Enforcement of Emergency Arbitrator's Award*, (12 August 2016), available at: http://arbitrationblog.kluwerarbitration.com/2016/08/12/jkx-vs-ukraine-an-update-on-the-enforcement-of-emergency-arbitrators-award/.

Table of Cases

A

C

D

F

G

J

K

N

O

Q

S

T

Z

Table of Institutional Rules

Table of Statutes

www.ingramcontent.com/pod-product-compliance
Lightning Source LLC
LaVergne TN
LVHW020004031026
849161LV00023B/870